DELUXE EDITION

HALLEY'S

BIBLE HANDBOOK

with the
**NEW INTERNATIONAL
VERSION**

"The Bible is the most priceless possession of the human race."

HENRY H. HALLEY

DELUXE EDITION

HALLEY'S
BIBLE HANDBOOK

with the
**NEW INTERNATIONAL
VERSION**

ZONDERVAN

ZONDERVAN.com/
AUTHORTRACKER
follow your favorite authors

ZONDERVAN

Halley's Bible Handbook with the New International Version
Completely revised and expanded 25th edition of *Halley's Bible Handbook*

This title is also available as a Zondervan ebook product.
Visit www.zondervan.com/ebooks for more information.

Requests for information should be addressed to:

Zondervan, *Grand Rapids, Michigan 49530*

Library of Congress Cataloging-in-Publication Data

Halley, Henry Hampton, 1874–1965.
     Halley's Bible handbook with the New International Version / by Henry H. Halley.
                p. cm.
     Includes bibliographical references and index.
     ISBN 978-0-310-25994-7
     1. Bible — Commentaries. I. Title.
BS491.2.H355 2000
220.7'7 — dc 021

99-059615

Maps by International Mapping
Revising editor/writer: Ed M. van der Maas
Archaeology and geography: Carl G. Rasmussen
Church history and Jewish history: Ruth F. van der Maas
Supervising editor: James E. Ruark and David Frees
Interior design: Tracey Walker and Ben Fetterley

Printed in China

---

09 10 11 12 13 14 15 16 • 31 30 29 28 27 26 25 24 23 22 21 20 19 18 17 16 15 14 13 12 11 10 9 8 7 6 5 4 3

Contents

Foreword

The 25th edition of *Halley's Bible Handbook* represents a continuation of my great-grandfather's ministry. Henry H. Halley dedicated his life to the spreading of God's Word. His desire was for everyone to read, know, and love the Bible and to believe and accept its God-inspired message.

It is my heartfelt desire that this 25th edition of *Halley's Bible Handbook,* now with Bible study tips, updated archaeological information, and new maps and pictures, continues to be a blessing to every reader.

I would like to express my deep love and appreciation for my grandmother, Julia Berry, who nurtured and supported *Halley's Bible Handbook* for many years after the death of her father, Henry Halley. Her early work on this 25th edition provided us insight into her father's ministry and became our guide as we completed the revisions.

Many thanks to all those who have supported and helped with this 25th edition, especially my mother, Julie Schneeberger; my husband, Gary Wicker; Dr. Stan Gundry, Ed and Ruth van der Maas, and Carl Rasmussen. We have seen many awesome examples of how the Lord has clearly worked through this team of people and others to complete this new edition of *Halley's Bible Handbook.*

As always, this Handbook is, in the words of my great-grandfather, "dedicated to the proposition that Every Christian should be a Constant and Devoted Reader of the Bible; and that the primary business of the Church and Ministry is to lead, foster, and encourage their people in that habit."

— Patricia Wicker

Sunrise on granite mountains.

Sources

The following sources and resources are cited in this book. Permission has been granted as appropriate by the publishers for material used in or adapted for this book. Page numbers indicate where this material is found in *Halley's Bible Handbook*.

Books and Bibles

Cairns, Earle E. *Christianity Through the Centuries.* 3d ed. Grand Rapids: Zondervan, 1996.

Douglas, J. D. *The NIV Compact Dictionary of the Bible.* Grand Rapids: Zondervan, 1989.

Douglas, J. D., and Merrill C. Tenney. *The New International Dictionary of the Bible.* Grand Rapids: Zondervan, 1987.

Expositor's Bible Commentary. Frank E. Gaebelein, gen. ed. 12 vols. Grand Rapids: Zondervan, 1976–92.

Fee, Gordon D., and Douglas Stuart. *How to Read the Bible for All Its Worth.* 2d ed. Grand Rapids: Zondervan, 1993.

Josephus, Flavius. *The Jewish War* and *Antiquities of the Jews.*

Kohlenberger III, John R. *Your Guide to Bible Reference Books and Software.* Grand Rapids: Zondervan, 1998. (Pages 965ff.)

Kohlenberger III, John R., and Edward W. Goodrick. *The NIV Exhaustive Concordance.* Grand Rapids: Zondervan, 1990.

Kuhatschek, Jack. *Applying the Bible.* Grand Rapids: Zondervan, 1995.

The Methodist Hymnal. The Official Hymnal of the Methodist Church. Nashville: Methodist Publishing House, 1939.

The New Strong's Exhaustive Concordance. Nashville: Thomas Nelson, 1997.

NIV Application Commentary. 19 vols. Grand Rapids: Zondervan, 1995– .

NIV Life Application Study Bible. Grand Rapids: Zondervan, 1998.

The NIV Matthew Henry Commentary in One Volume. Grand Rapids: Zondervan, 1992.

The NIV Study Bible. Grand Rapids: Zondervan, 1995. (Pages 150, 157, 170–71.)

Pritchard, James B. *Ancient Near Eastern Texts: Relating to the Old Testament.* 3d ed. Princeton, NJ: Princeton University Press, 1969.

Rasmussen, Carl G. *The Zondervan NIV Atlas of the Bible.* Grand Rapids: Zondervan, 1989. (Page 1016.)

Stott, John R. W. *Understanding the Bible.* Expanded ed. Grand Rapids: Zondervan, 1999.

Tenney, Merrill C. *The Zondervan Pictorial Encyclopedia of the Bible.* 5 vols. Grand Rapids: Zondervan, 1975.

Thiele, Edwin R. *The Mysterious Numbers of the Hebrew Kings.* Rev. ed. Grand Rapids: Zondervan, 1982. (Page 226.)

Walton, John H. *Chronological and Background Charts of the Old Testament.* Rev. and expanded ed. Grand Rapids: Zondervan, 1994. (Pages 136, 337, 1021.)

Word Biblical Commentary. 52 vols. Nashville: Word Books, 1982– .

Photographs and Illustrations and Other Materials

Distance charts on pages 1022–23: Copyright © Carl Rasmussen.

Illustration on pages 482–83: Copyright © Dr. Leen Ritmeyer, Ritmeyer Archaeological Design, Harrogate, England.

Photographs on page 148: Kiene, Paul F. *The Tabernacle of God in the Wilderness.* Grand Rapids: Zondervan, 1977.

Bierling, Neal, and Joel Bierling. *Zondervan Image Archives CD-ROM.* Grand Rapids: Zondervan, 1999.

Outline of the harmony of the Gospels on pages 520–21: Taken from *The NIV Harmony of the Gospels* (New York: HarperCollins, 1988). Used by permission of Robert L. Thomas and Stanley N. Gundry. All rights reserved.

Maps by International Mapping.

The Amman Archaeological Museum. Amman, Jordan.

The British Museum. London, England.

The Cairo Museum. Cairo, Egypt.

Direct Design.

The House of Anchors. Kibbutz Ein Gev. Sea of Galilee, Israel.

The Egyptian Ministry of Antiquities.

The Ephesus Archaeological Museum. Selchok, Turkey.

The Eretz Israel Museum. Tel Aviv, Israel.

The Yigal Allon Center. Kibbutz Ginosar, on the western shore of the Sea of Galilee, Israel.

COLLECTION OF THE ISRAEL MUSEUM, JERUSALEM and COURTESY OF THE ISRAEL ANTIQUITIES AUTHORITY, EXHIBITED AT THE ISRAEL MUSEUM, JERUSALEM.

COLLECTION OF THE ISRAEL MUSEUM, JERUSALEM and COURTESY OF THE ISRAEL ANTIQUITIES AUTHORITY, EXHIBITED AT THE SHRINE OF THE BOOK, THE ISRAEL MUSEUM, JERUSALEM.

The Isma-iliya Museum. Isma-ilia, Egypt.

The Istanbul Archaeological Museum. Istanbul, Turkey.

Dr. James C. Martin.

The Jordanian Ministry of Antiquities. Amman, Jordan.

"Reproduction of the City of Jerusalem at the time of the Second Temple – located on the grounds of the Holyland Hotel, Jerusalem." Photographed by permission.

Musée du Louvre, Autorisation de photographer et de filmer – Louvre. Paris, France.

The Church of Annunciation Museum. Nazareth, Israel.

Preserving Bible Times, Inc.

COLLECTION OF THE ISRAEL MUSEUM, JERUSALEM and COURTESY OF THE ISRAEL ANTIQUITIES AUTHORITY, EXHIBITED AT THE ROCKEFELLER MUSEUM, JERUSALEM.

On license Ministero per I Beni e le Attivita Culturali – Soprintendenza Archaeologica di Roma. Rome, Italy.

Sola Scriptura. The Van Kampen Collection on display at the Holy Land Experience in Orlando, Florida.

The Turkish Ministry of Antiquities. Ankara, Turkey.

The Heart of
the Bible

NOTE TO THE READER

The following pages are the heart and soul of *Halley's Bible Handbook*.

Dr. Halley's goal was not to write a book that would help people *know* more *about* the Bible. Dr. Halley's passion was to get people and churches to *read* the Bible in order that they might meet and listen to the God of the Bible and come to love His Son, Jesus Christ.

The rest of this book is of little lasting value if Dr. Halley's central convictions, stated so passionately and forcefully in this section, are ignored.

We urge you to take the time to read—and periodically reread—this section.

THE HEART OF THE BIBLE

This book is built on two central convictions:

1. The Bible is God's Word.
2. Christ is the center and heart of the Bible.

I. The Bible Is God's Word

Apart from any theory of inspiration, or any theory of how the Bible books came to their present form, or how much the text may have suffered in transmission at the hands of editors and copyists; apart from the question of how much is to be interpreted literally and how much figuratively, or what is historical and what may be poetical—if we simply assume that the Bible is just what it appears to be and study its 66 books to know their contents, we will find a unity of thought that indicates that one Mind inspired the writing and compilation of the whole collection of books. We will find that it bears the stamp of its Author and that it is in a unique and distinctive sense the Word of God.

Many people hold the view that the Bible is a collection of ancient stories about people's efforts to find God, a record of human experiences in their reaching for God that led to a gradually improving idea of God by building on the experiences of preceding generations. This means, of course, that the many, many passages in the Bible in which it is said that God spoke are merely using a figure of speech and that God did not really speak. Rather, people put their ideas into religious language that *claimed* to be the language of God, and in reality it was only what they themselves *imagined* God might say. This viewpoint reduces the Bible to the level of other books. It is made into a human book pretending to be divine, rather than a divine book.

We reject this view utterly, and with abhorrence! We believe that the Bible is not an account of human efforts to find God, but rather an account of God's effort to reveal Himself to humanity. It is God's own record of His dealings with people in His unfolding revelation of Himself to the human race. The Bible is the revealed will of the Creator of all of humanity, given to His creatures by the Creator Himself, for instruction and guidance along life's paths.

There can be no question that the books of the Bible were composed by human authors; we don't even know who some of these authors were. Nor do we know just *how* God directed these authors to write. But we believe and know that God *did* direct them and that these books therefore must be exactly what God wanted them to be.

There is a difference between the Bible and all other books. Authors may pray for God's help and guidance, and God does help and guide them. There are many good books in the world that leave the unmistakable impression that God helped the authors to write them. But even the most saintly authors would hardly presume to claim for their books that *God* wrote them.

Yet that is what the Bible claims for itself and what the people of God through the millennia have learned and understood and claimed. God Himself superintended and directed the writing of the Bible books in such a way that what was written was the writing of God. The Bible is God's Word in a sense in which no other book in the world is God's Word.

Many statements in the Bible are expressed in ancient thought forms and ancient language forms. Today we would express these same ideas in a different form and in modern language rather than in the language of ancient times. But even so, the Bible contains precisely the things God wants mankind to know, in exactly the form in which He wants us to know them. And to the end of time, the "dear old Book" will remain the one and only answer to humanity's quest for God.

- Everyone should love the Bible.
- Everyone should be a regular reader of the Bible.
- Everyone should strive to live by the Bible's teachings.
- The Bible should have the central place in the life and work of every church and every pulpit.
- *The pulpit's one business is the simple teaching of God's Word,* expressing in the language of today the truths that are expressed in ancient thought and language forms in the Bible.

2. Christ Is the Center and Heart of the Bible

The Bible consists of two parts: the Old Testament and the New Testament.

- The Old Testament is an account of a nation: Israel.
- The New Testament is an account of a man: Jesus, God's Son.

The nation was founded and nurtured by God to bring the Man into the world. In Jesus, God Himself became a man to provide the means for the redemption of mankind. Jesus also gives humanity a concrete, definite, tangible idea of what kind of person to think of when we think of God: God is like Jesus. Jesus was God incarnate, God in human form.

His appearance on the earth is the central event of all history: the Old Testament sets the stage for it; the New Testament describes it.

Jesus the Christ (the Messiah) lived the most memorable, beautiful life ever known. He was born of a virgin and led a sinless life. As a man, Jesus was the kindest, tenderest, gentlest, most patient, most sympathetic man who ever lived. He loved people. He hated to see people in trouble. He loved to forgive. He loved to help. He did marvelous miracles to feed hungry people. For relief of the suffering He forgot to take food for Himself. Multitudes, weary, pain-ridden, and heartsick, came to Him and found healing and relief. It is said of Him, and of no other, that if all the deeds of kindness that He did were written down, the world could not contain the books.

That is the kind of man Jesus was.

That is the kind of person God is.

Then Jesus died on the cross to take away the sin of the world, to become the Redeemer and Savior of humanity.

He rose from the dead and is alive now—not merely a historical character but a living Person. This is the most important fact of history and the most vital force in the world today.

The whole Bible is built around this beautiful story of Christ and around His promise of life eternal to those who accept Him. The Bible was written only that people might believe, and understand, and know, and love, and follow Christ.

Christ, the center and heart of the Bible, the center and heart of history, is also the center and heart of our lives. Our eternal destiny is in His hand. Our acceptance or rejection of Him as our Lord and Savior determines for each of us eternal glory or eternal ruin—heaven or hell, one or the other.

The most important decision anyone is ever called on to make is to settle in one's heart, once for all, the matter of one's attitude toward Christ.

On that depends everything.

It is a glorious thing to be a Christian, the most exalted privilege of mankind. The Creator of all things wants to have a personal relationship with each and every one of us! To accept Christ as Savior, Lord, and Master, and to strive sincerely and devotedly to follow in the way of life He taught, is certainly and by far the most reasonable and most satisfactory way to live. It means peace, peace of mind, contentment of heart, forgiveness, happiness, hope, life abundant, life that shall never end.

How can anyone be so blind, or so dumb, as to go through life and face death without the Christian hope? Apart from Christ, what is there, what can there be, either for this world or the next, to make life worthwhile? We all have to die. Why try to laugh it off or try to deny it? It seems as if every human being would want to welcome Christ with open arms and consider it the proudest privilege of his or her life to wear the Christian name.

In the final analysis, the most marvelous thing in life is the consciousness, in the inner depths of our soul, that we live for Christ. And though our efforts be ever so feeble, we toil at our daily tasks in hope of being able to have done something to lay as an offering at His feet, in humble gratitude and adoration, when we meet Him face to face.

THE HABIT OF BIBLE READING

Everybody should love the Bible. Everybody should read the Bible.

Everybody.

It is God's Word. It holds the solution of life. It tells about the best Friend humanity ever had, the noblest, kindest, truest Man who ever walked on this earth.

It is the most beautiful story ever told. It is the best guide to human conduct ever known. It gives a meaning, a glow, a joy, a victory, a destiny, and a glory to life elsewhere unknown.

There is nothing in history, or in literature, that in any way compares with the simple record of the Man of Galilee, who spent His days and nights ministering to the suffering, teaching human kindness, dying for human sin, rising to life that shall never end, and promising eternal security and eternal happiness to all who will come to Him.

Most people, in their serious moods, must have some question in their minds as to how things are going to stack up when the end comes. Laugh it off and toss it aside as we may, that day will come. And then what?

Well, it is the Bible that has the answer. And an unmistakable answer it is. There is a God. There is a heaven. There is a hell. There is a Savior. There will be a day of judgment. Happy is the person who in this life makes his or her peace with the Christ of the Bible and gets ready for the final takeoff.

How can any thoughtful person keep his or her heart from warming up to Christ and to the book that tells about Him? Everybody ought to love the Bible. Everybody. Everybody.

Yet the widespread neglect of the Bible by churches and by church people is simply appalling. Oh, we talk about the Bible, and defend the Bible, and praise the Bible, and exalt the Bible. Yes indeed! But many church members seldom ever even look into a Bible—indeed, would be ashamed to be seen reading the Bible. And an alarming percentage of church leadership generally seems to be making no serious effort to get people to be Bible readers.

We are intelligent about everything else in the world. Why not be intelligent about our religion? We read newspapers, magazines, novels, and all kinds of books, and listen to the radio and watch television by the hour. Yet most of us do not even know the names of the Bible books. Shame on us! Worse still, the pulpit, which could easily remedy the situation, seems often not to care and generally does not emphasize personal Bible reading.

Individual, direct contact with God's Word is the principal means of Christian growth. All the leaders in Christian history who displayed any kind of spiritual power have been devoted readers of the Bible.

The Bible is the book we live by. Bible reading is the means by which we learn, and keep fresh in our minds, the ideas that mold our lives. Our lives are the product of our thoughts. To live right, we need to think right. We must read the Bible frequently and regularly so that God's thoughts may be frequently and regularly in our minds; so that His thoughts may become our thoughts; so that our ideas may become conformed to God's ideas; so that we may be transformed into God's own image and be made fit for eternal companionship with our Creator.

We may, indeed, absorb Christian truth, in some measure, by attending religious services, listening to sermons, Bible lessons, and testimonies, and by reading Christian literature.

But however good and helpful these things may be, they give us God's truth secondhand, diluted through human channels and, to quite an extent, obscured by human ideas and traditions.

Such things cannot possibly take the place of reading for ourselves the Bible itself, and grounding our faith and hope and life directly in God's Word, rather than in what people say about God's Word.

God's Word is the weapon of the Spirit of God for the redemption and perfection of the human soul. It is not enough to listen to others talk and teach and preach about the Bible. We need to keep ourselves, every one of us, in direct touch with God's Word. It is the power of God in our hearts.

Bible reading is a basic Christian habit.

We do not mean that we should worship the Bible as a fetish. But we do worship the God and the Savior the Bible tells us about. And because we love our God and our Savior, we love dearly and devotedly the book that is from Him and about Him.

Nor do we mean that the habit of Bible reading is in itself a virtue, for it is possible to read the Bible without applying its teachings to one's own life. And there are those who read the Bible and yet are mean and crooked and un-Christian. But they are the exception.

As a rule, Bible reading, if done in the right spirit, is a habit out of which all Christian virtues grow—the most effective character-forming power known to mankind.

Bible reading is an act of religious devotion. Our attitude toward the Bible is a pretty sure indication of our attitude toward Christ. If we love a person, we love to read about him or her, do we not? If we could only bring ourselves to think of our Bible reading as an act of devotion to Christ, we might be inclined to treat the matter less lightly.

It is a glorious thing to be a Christian. The most exalted privilege any mortal can have is to walk through life hand in hand with Christ as Savior and Guide. Or, to put it more correctly, to toddle along at His side and, though always stumbling, never letting go of His hand.

This personal relationship of each of us with Christ is one of the intimate things of life, and we do not talk much about it, probably because we often believe that we are so pitifully unworthy to wear His name. Why would the Creator of all things care about *me?* But deep down in our hearts, in our serious moods, we know that because of our weakness, our worldliness, our frivolity, our selfishness, and our sins, we need Him more than we love anything else in this world. He is our Father. And in our saner moments we know that we should not willingly offend or hurt Him for anything. Why would we intentionally hurt the One who loves us and whom we love? We are thoughtless.

The Bible is the book that tells about Christ and His immeasurable love for us. Is it possible to love Christ and at the same time be complacently indifferent to His Word? Is it possible? Each one of us has to make daily choices—to serve Him and not the world. The Bible teaches us how!

The Bible is also the best devotional book. Booklets and books of daily devotions, now published in such abundance, may have their place. But they are no substitute for the Bible. The Bible is God's own word, and no other book can take its place. Every Christian, young and old, should be a faithful reader of the Bible.

George Mueller, who, in his orphanages in Bristol, England, did by prayer and trust one of the most remarkable things in Christian history, attributed his success, on the human side, to his love for the Bible. He said:

I believe that the one chief reason that I have been kept in happy useful service is that I have been a lover of Holy Scripture. It has been my habit to read the Bible through four times a year; in a prayerful spirit, to apply it to my heart, and practice what I find there. I have been for sixty-nine years a happy man.

Helps to Bible Study

The Bible is a big book, in reality a library of books from the far distant past. And we need all the help we can get in trying to understand it. But even so, it is surprising how largely the Bible is self-interpretive when we know what is in it. There are difficulties aplenty in the Bible, even beyond the comprehension of the most erudite. But, for all that, the main teachings of the Bible are unmistakable, so plain that a child can understand the heart of the Bible. (At the end of this book you will find suggestions for books that are helpful in studying the Bible [see p. 965]. But they should *never* take the place of the simple reading of the Bible with an open heart and mind.)

Accept the Bible just as it is, for exactly what it claims to be. Don't worry about the theories of the critics. The ingenious efforts of modern criticism to undermine the historical reliability of the Bible will pass; the Bible itself will still stand as the light of the human race to the end of time. Pin your faith to the Bible. It is God's Word. It will never let you down. For us human beings, it is the rock of ages. Trust its teachings, and be happy forever.

Read the Bible with an open mind. Don't try to straitjacket all its passages into the mold of a few pet doctrines. And don't read into its passages ideas that are not there. But try to search out fairly and honestly the main teachings and lessons of each passage. Thus we will come to believe what we ought to believe; for the Bible is abundantly able to take care of itself if given a chance.

Read the Bible thoughtfully. In Bible reading, we need to watch ourselves very closely, lest our thoughts wander and our reading become perfunctory and meaningless. We must determine resolutely to keep our minds on what we are reading, to do our best to understand what we can and not to worry too much about what we don't understand, and to be on the lookout for lessons for ourselves.

Keep a pencil at hand. It is a good thing, as we read, to mark passages we like and to go now and then through the pages and reread passages we have marked. In time a well-marked Bible will become very dear to us, as the day draws near for us to meet the Author.

Habitual, systematic reading of the Bible is what counts. Occasional or spasmodic reading does not mean much. Unless we have some sort of system to follow, and hold to it with resolute determination, the chances are that we will not read the Bible very much at all. Our inner life, like our body, needs its daily food.

A certain time each day, whatever reading plan we follow, should be set aside for it. Otherwise we are likely to neglect or forget to read the Bible. First thing in the morning is good if our work routine permits it. Or in the evening, at the close of the day's work, we might find ourselves freer from the strain of hurry. Or perhaps both morning and evening. For some, a period in the middle of the day may be more suitable.

The particular time of day does not greatly matter. The important thing is that we choose a time that best fits in with our daily round of work, and that we try to stick with it and not be discouraged if now and then our routine is broken by things beyond our control.

On Sundays we might do a good part of our Bible reading, since it is the Lord's day, set aside for the Lord's work.

Memorize the names of the Bible books. Do this first. The Bible is composed of 66 books. Each of these books is about something. The starting point for any sort of intelligent conception of the Bible is, first of all, to know what those books are, the order in which they are arranged, and, in a general way, what each one is about. (See p. 43.)

Memorize favorite verses. Thoroughly memorize them and repeat them often to yourself—sometimes when you are alone, or in the night to help put yourself to sleep on the everlasting arms. These are the verses that we live on.

To run God's thoughts through our mind often will make our mind grow to become more like God's mind; and as our mind grows more like God's mind, our whole life will be transformed into His image. It is one of the very best spiritual helps we can have.

Plans of Bible Reading

There are many different plans for Bible reading. Several plans are suggested later in this book (see p. 956). One plan will appeal to one person, another plan to another person. The same person may, at different times, like different plans. The particular plan does not greatly matter. The essential thing is that we read the Bible with some degree of regularity.

Our plan of reading should cover the whole Bible with reasonable frequency. It is all God's Word, all one story, a literary structure of profound and marvelous unity, centered around Christ. Christ is the heart and climax of the Bible. The whole Bible may very properly be called the story of Christ. The Old Testament paves the way for His coming. The four Gospels tell the story of His earthly life. The New Testament letters explain His teachings. And Revelation shows us His triumph.

A well-balanced plan of Bible reading, we think, might be something like this: for every time we read the Bible through, let us read the New Testament an extra time or two, with frequent rereading of favorite chapters in both Testaments.

Later in this book you will find several Bible reading plans (see p. 956) as well as a section that explains the kinds of Bible study tools available to help you understand what you read, such as concordances, study Bibles, Bible dictionaries, and commentaries, and what each is used for (see p. 965).

GOING TO CHURCH AS
AN ACT OF WORSHIP

"All Christian people ought to go to church each and every week, unless hindered by sickness, or *necessary* work, or some other necessity."

In a consumer society such as ours, the first reaction is, Why? What do I get out of church?

That question misses the point.

We are not the purpose of the church—*God* is. Going to church should be an act of worship. Every Sunday belongs to Christ. If all Christians were to attend church every Sunday, our churches would overflow. It would mean power for the church. It would be a witness to the community—people who worship their Savior as a matter of love rather than convenience. The purpose of the church is to hold Christ before the people. The church was founded by Christ. Christ is the heart of the church, and its Lord. The church exists to bear witness to Christ. Christ Himself, not the church, is the transforming power in people's lives. The mission of the church is to exalt Christ, so that He Himself may do His own blessed work in the hearts of people.

That method will never change. The invention of printing, which made Bibles and Christian literature cheap and abundant so that people may read for themselves about Christ, and the coming of radio and television, which allow us to sit at home and listen to or watch sermons and church services—these will never do away with the need for the church. It is God's plan that His people, in every community, throughout the whole world, at this appointed time, meet together, in this public way, to thus publicly honor Christ.

However, all too often individuals use the church as a spiritual filling station. We run on empty all week and then expect the church to make up for what we do not do—*spend time during the week reading and reflecting on God's Word.*

If we neglect the habit of reading the Bible, we go to church spiritually starved. We will look to the church to fill our empty souls. And we will be disappointed, because the church cannot, in one or two hours on Sunday morning, fill the void that we create by neglecting the Word of God.

Come to church prepared. Read your Bible beforehand. You will be blessed, and Christ will be exalted!

NOTABLE SAYINGS ABOUT THE BIBLE

Billy Graham: We have in our generation people who question if the Bible is the Word of God. From beginning to end, the Bible is God's Word, inspired by the Holy Spirit. When I turn to the Bible, I know that I am reading truth. And I turn to it every day.*

George Mueller of Bristol: The vigor of our spiritual life will be in exact proportion to the place held by the Bible in our life and thoughts. I solemnly state this from the experience of fifty-four years. . . . I have read the Bible through one hundred times, and always with increasing delight. Each time it seems like a new book to me. Great has been the blessing from consecutive, diligent, daily study. I look upon it as a lost day when I have not had a good time over the Word of God.

D. L. Moody: I prayed for faith, and thought that some day faith would come down and strike me like lightning. But faith did not seem to come. One day I read in the tenth chapter of Romans, "Now faith cometh by hearing, and hearing by the Word of God." I had closed my Bible, and prayed for faith. I now opened my Bible, and began to study, and faith has been growing ever since.

Abraham Lincoln: I believe the Bible is the best gift God has ever given to man. All the good from the Savior of the world is communicated to us through this book.

W. E. Gladstone: I have known ninety-five of the world's great men in my time, and of these eighty-seven were followers of the Bible. The Bible is stamped with a specialty of origin, and an immeasurable distance separates it from all competitors.

George Washington: It is impossible to rightly govern the world without God and the Bible.

Daniel Webster: If there is anything in my thoughts or style to commend, the credit is due to my parents for instilling in me an early love of the Scriptures. If we abide by the principles taught in the Bible, our country will go on prospering and to prosper; but if we and our posterity neglect its instructions and authority, no man can tell how sudden a catastrophe may overwhelm us and bury all our glory in profound obscurity.

Thomas Carlyle: The Bible is the truest utterance that ever came by alphabetic letters from the soul of man, through which, as through a window divinely opened, all men can look into the stillness of eternity, and discern in glimpses their far-distant, long-forgotten home.

John Ruskin: Whatever merit there is in anything that I have written is simply due to the fact that when I was a child my mother daily read me a part of the Bible and daily made me learn a part of it by heart.

Charles A. Dana: The grand old Book still stands; and this old earth, the more its leaves are turned and pondered, the more it will sustain and illustrate the pages of the Sacred Word.

Thomas Huxley: The Bible has been the Magna Charta of the poor and oppressed. The human race is not in a position to dispense with it.

Patrick Henry: The Bible is worth all other books which have ever been printed.

---

*Taken from Billy Graham's sermon, "Jesus Christ Is Truth," © 1991 Billy Graham Evangelistic Association. Used by permission.

U. S. Grant: The Bible is the anchor of our liberties.

Horace Greeley: It is impossible to enslave mentally or socially a Bible-reading people. The principles of the Bible are the groundwork of human freedom.

Andrew Jackson: That book, sir, is the rock on which our republic rests.

Robert E. Lee: In all my perplexities and distresses, the Bible has never failed to give me light and strength.

Lord Tennyson: Bible reading is an education in itself.

John Quincy Adams: So great is my veneration for the Bible that the earlier my children begin to read it the more confident will be my hope that they will prove useful citizens of their country and respectable members of society. I have for many years made it a practice to read through the Bible once every year.

Immanuel Kant: The existence of the Bible, as a book for the people, is the greatest benefit which the human race has ever experienced. Every attempt to belittle it is a crime against humanity.

Charles Dickens: The New Testament is the very best book that ever was or ever will be known in the world.

Sir William Herschel: All human discoveries seem to be made only for the purpose of confirming more and more strongly the truths contained in the Sacred Scriptures.

Sir Isaac Newton: There are more sure marks of authenticity in the Bible than in any profane history.

Goethe: Let mental culture go on advancing, let the natural sciences progress in ever greater extent and depth, and the human mind widen itself as much as it desires; beyond the elevation and moral culture of Christianity, as it shines forth in the gospels, it will not go.

Bible Backgrounds

Oasis in desert near mountain.

What the Bible Is

The Bible is a collection of 66 "books" that were written over a period of more than 1,500 years. In a typical printed Bible, the longest book (Psalms) takes up more than 100 pages, the shortest (2 John) less than a page.

More than 40 different people wrote the various books of the Bible. Some of them were rich, some were poor. Among them were kings, poets, prophets, musicians, philosophers, farmers, teachers, a priest, a statesman, a sheepherder, a tax collector, a physician, and a couple of fishermen. They wrote in palaces and in prisons, in great cities and in the wilderness, in times of terrible war and in times of peace and prosperity. They wrote stories, poems, histories, letters, proverbs, and prophecies.

The Bible is not a textbook or a book of abstract theology, to be analyzed, discussed, and understood only by highly educated theologians and experts. It is a book about real people and about the God who is real.

The Bible is the inspired Word of God. Theologians and scholars have argued endlessly about the question how a book written by so many authors over so many centuries can possibly be inspired by God. But it is like sitting down at dinner and arguing about the recipe instead of tasting the food, enjoying it, and being nourished by it.

As "the proof of the pudding is in the eating," so is the proof of the Bible in the reading—with open mind and open heart. Such a reading will show that the Bible is a divinely inspired, interwoven message from God (compare John 7:17).

Because it was written so long ago, there are things that we, in the 21st century, may find difficult to understand. But our heart and spirit can grasp what God's heart and His Spirit tell us: that we are beloved by Him, now and forever.

Palm tree with dates.

How the Bible
Is Organized

At first glance, the Bible is a collection of longer and shorter writings without any apparent organization except for the main division into two parts, the **Old Testament** and the **New Testament**.

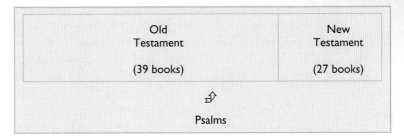

	Old Testament (39 books)	New Testament (27 books)

Psalms

The Old Testament takes up about three-fourths of the Bible, the New Testament about one-fourth. The book of Psalms is approximately in the middle of the Bible.

The Two Testaments

The Old Testament was written *before* the time of Christ. It was written mostly in Hebrew, the language of the Jewish people, and the Old Testament continues to be the Bible of the Jewish people. In the very early days of the church, during the first decades after Jesus' death and resurrection, the Hebrew Bible was the only Bible Christians had. It was not until later, when the New Testament came into existence, that the Hebrew Bible was called "Old Testament." The word "testament" here means "covenant" (a solemn agreement or contract that establishes a formal relationship with mutual obligations). The Hebrew Bible speaks of the covenant God made with Abraham, the patriarch of the Jewish people. The New Testament is about the new covenant that God made with all people through Jesus Christ.

Thus, the **Old Testament** looks forward to the coming of Jesus, the Messiah (or Christ), who will save us from our sins and establish God's kingdom, founded on justice and mercy. The **New Testament** tells the story of Jesus and contains writings by His early followers.

Three Groups of Books in Each Testament

Each Testament

- Begins with a group of **historical books** and
- Ends with **prophetic books** (the New Testament has only one predominantly prophetic book, Revelation)

Between the historical and prophetic books are

- **Poetic** books (Old Testament) and
- **Letters** or epistles (New Testament)

The Old Testament Books

1. The Historical Books

The Old Testament has 17 historical books, arranged in chronological order. The Jewish people called (and call) the first five historical books the Torah (Hebrew for "law," since these books contain the laws God gave to Moses). These five books are also called the Pentateuch (Greek for "five books"). The history covered in these books can be divided into six periods (see also the next section, "What the Bible Is About").

2. The Poetic Books

Between the historical books and the prophetic books of the Old Testament are five poetic books that contain some of the most beautiful poetry ever written. Especially the book of Psalms, which expresses the full range of

OLD TESTAMENT		
Historical Books	*Poetic Books*	*Prophetic Books*
Genesis	Job	Isaiah
Exodus	Psalms	Jeremiah
Leviticus	Proverbs	Lamentations
Numbers	Ecclesiastes	Ezekiel
Deuteronomy	Song of Songs	Daniel
Joshua		Hosea
Judges		Joel
Ruth		Amos
I Samuel		Obadiah
2 Samuel		Jonah
I Kings		Micah
2 Kings		Nahum
I Chronicles		Habakkuk
2 Chronicles		Zephaniah
Ezra		Haggai
Nehemiah		Zechariah
Esther		Malachi

human emotions from depression to jubilant trust in God, has been a source of comfort and inspiration for Jews and Christians for three millennia.

3. The Prophetic Books

The Old Testament contains 17 prophetic books. The first five of these books are called the Major Prophets because they are much longer than the other 12, which are called the Minor Prophets. (Lamentations is a short book that is included with the Major Prophets because it was written by the prophet Jeremiah, who also wrote the book of Jeremiah, the second book of the Major Prophets.)

The New Testament Books

1. The Historical Books

Between the end of the Old Testament and the beginning of the New Testament is a period of about 400 years. We know quite a bit about those "silent years" from other books that are not part of the Old Testament or New Testament (see pages 471–490).

The New Testament contains five historical books: the four Gospels, which describe the life of Christ, and the book of Acts, which tells the story of the early church, mostly through the work of the apostle Paul.

NEW TESTAMENT		
Historical Books	**Letters**	**Prophetic Books**
Matthew	Romans	Revelation
Mark	I Corinthians	
Luke	2 Corinthians	
John	Galatians	
Acts	Ephesians	
	Philippians	
	Colossians	
	I Thessalonians	
	2 Thessalonians	
	I Timothy	
	2 Timothy	
	Titus	
	Philemon	
	Hebrews	
	James	
	I Peter	
	2 Peter	
	I John	
	2 John	
	3 John	
	Jude	

2. The Letters, or Epistles

The New Testament contains 21 letters, or epistles. The first 13 of these were written by the apostle Paul; they are arranged by length, from the longest (Romans) to the shortest (Philemon). Others were written by the apostle John (three letters), Peter (two letters), and James and Jude (one letter each); there is uncertainty as to who wrote the letter to the Hebrews.

All the letters were written during the early decades of the church.

3. The Prophetic Book

The New Testament has only one prophetic book: Revelation. (The Greek word for revelation is *apokalupsis,* meaning an unveiling or uncovering. For this reason, the book of Revelation is also called the Apocalypse.)

What the Bible Is About

| The Story | The Story Behind the Story |

THE OLD TESTAMENT

① In the Beginning

Creation, Adam and Eve, Fall, Cain and Abel,
Noah and the Flood, Babel

"In the beginning God created the heavens and the earth." The first two chapters of the Bible describe how God created all things. The last thing He created was mankind, whom God created "male and female"—***Adam and Eve***. Creation was good and harmonious.

But in the third chapter this harmony is destroyed. Adam and Eve are deceived by the serpent (Satan) and choose to disobey God. They do the one thing He had told them not to do: they eat from a forbidden tree because they want to be like God. It is a small act—with cosmic consequences.

Their disobedience ***("the Fall")*** brings disharmony and death into the world and the universe. Humanity is now separated, not only from one another and from creation, but from God. All history, and each life, now ends in death.

The Fall is followed by a number of disastrous things:

• Adam and Eve are expelled from the ***Garden of Eden***.

• ***Cain and Abel:*** The sons of Adam and Eve. Cain kills Abel.

• ***Noah and the Flood:*** Things get so bad that God decides to destroy the human race in a flood. Only Noah and his family and representative pairs of the animals survive in the ark.

The first three chapters of Genesis set the stage for all that happens in the rest of the Bible. Adam and Eve's sin separated humanity from God. As a result we also lost our God-given harmony within ourselves, with each other, and with the rest of creation. But God, who loves the human beings He created, promises that He will undo what Adam and Eve did in disobedience. He will restore harmony between humanity and Himself, between people, and in all of creation. God promises that a descendant of Adam and Eve will be the key—He will bring salvation, He will set things right between God and his creation.

Throughout the rest of the Bible, this is the story behind the story: ***God is at work setting things right***. (In the New Testament we see that ***He has already accomplished this through Jesus***.) "Regular" history—the kind found in history books—may seem chaotic, but the story behind the story tells us that all of history is moving to the point where God's plan of salvation and redemption for the universe will be complete, when, as the last book in the Bible says,

The Story	The Story Behind the Story
• **The Tower of Babel:** The people of the world want to build a city with a "tower that reaches to the heavens." Like Adam and Eve, they want to be like God. But God intervenes and confuses the language of the world. From there, the Lord scatters them over the face of the whole earth. Ever since, people have spoken different languages.	*The dwelling of God is with men, and he will live with them. They will be his people, and God himself will be with them and be their God. He will wipe every tear from their eyes. There will be no more death or mourning or crying or pain, for the old order of things has passed away (Revelation 21:3−4).*

② The Time of the Patriarchs

Abraham, Isaac, Jacob, Joseph

God tells **Abraham** to go from Ur of the Chaldeans to Canaan. There they have a son, **Isaac,** even though Sarah, Abraham's wife, is well beyond child-bearing age. Isaac, his son **Jacob,** and Jacob's 12 sons are known as the **patriarchs** of Israel, since the whole nation—the 12 tribes—descended from them. ("Israel" is the name God gave Jacob.) One of Jacob's sons, **Joseph,** ends up in Egypt, where he becomes second-in-command to the Pharaoh and saves the country from famine. Joseph's whole family then comes down to Egypt, where they live for some 400 years.	With God's choice of Abraham begins the preparation of a nation through which the promised Redeemer will come. God promises Abraham that he will have innumerable descendants, who will possess the land of Canaan (Palestine) and through whom God will bless the entire world. These promises are part of the covenant (solemn agreement) that God makes with Abraham. These promises are fulfilled slowly but surely—even though Abraham sees very little of this fulfillment himself. Through Abraham's great-grandson Joseph, God takes Abraham's descendants to Egypt. There they end up suffering oppression and slavery. But their relative isolation also allows the nation to grow without the danger of being absorbed into the various Canaanite nations—which would undoubtedly have happened had they stayed in Canaan.

③ The Exodus from Egypt

Moses, Aaron, Red Sea, Mount Sinai

After 400 years, the Israelites have become so numerous that the Pharaoh gets worried that they may take over the country. He puts them to slave labor on his building projects. **Moses** is an Israelite who was raised at the court by Pharaoh's daughter. God calls him to deliver the Israelites from their slavery and to take them	God prepares Moses to lead the Israelites out of Egypt by using the Egyptian court to give Moses the education he would need for the enormous task ahead. As God had done with Abraham, He now makes a **covenant with the people of Israel at Mount Sinai.** As part of this covenant God gives this

The Story	The Story Behind the Story
back to Canaan, the land God had promised to their forefather Abraham. **Aaron,** Moses' brother, goes with him to Pharaoh. Pharaoh refuses to let the people go. God encourages him to change his mind by sending 10 horrible plagues. The last of the plagues allows the angel of death to kill all firstborn children, but God protects the Israelites by instructing them to put some lamb's blood on their doorposts so the angel of death will pass over them. (This is the beginning of the **Passover.**) After this, Pharaoh agrees to let the people go. He later changes his mind and pursues the Israelites, but his entire army drowns in the **Red Sea,** after God creates a path and allows only the Israelites to cross. At **Mount Sinai,** God gives Israel His laws. Because they have no faith that God will help them conquer the land, the Israelites end up spending 40 years in the wilderness.	group of slaves who had never learned to function as a nation a body of laws to govern their daily lives once they settle in the Promised Land. Part of this covenant is the warning that disobedience will bring disaster, while obedience to the covenant by keeping God's laws will bring blessing. Their survival and success depend entirely on whether or not they obey God. They learn the truth of this the hard way when their disobedience and lack of faith in the wilderness lead to a 40-year period of wandering before they finally are allowed to enter the Promised Land.

④ The Conquest and Settlement of Canaan

Joshua, the Judges (Deborah, Gideon, Samson)

Moses dies and **Joshua** takes over. He leads the Israelites into the Promised Land across the Jordan near **Jericho.** They conquer part of the land, and each of the 12 tribes is given a piece of it. But there is no central authority, and for several centuries the various tribes disobey and leave God. God then allows a foreign army to punish them, but when they cry out to God, He sends them a leader (called a **Judge**) to defeat the enemy. But soon the whole cycle starts over again. Among the Judges are **Gideon** and **Samson**.	God's promise that Abraham's descendants will possess the land now begins to be fulfilled. At Ai they again receive a demonstration of the abject failure that is the result of ignoring God and His instructions. As the land is conquered and settled, the seeds for future problems are sown. The Israelites fail to take all of the land, as God had commanded, and the remaining Canaanites will be a constant source of seduction away from God. This becomes very clear in the period of the Judges, when the various tribes are again and again in danger of completely forgetting the God who brought them out of Egypt.

⑤ The Monarchy and the Divided Kingdom

Samuel, Saul, David, Solomon, two kingdoms: Israel and Judah

Finally the Israelites ask for a king. **Samuel**, the last Judge, first makes **Saul** king. Saul starts out well, but ends up committing suicide in battle.

Then **David** becomes king and unites all the tribes into the kingdom of Israel, with Jerusalem as its capital. (This is around 1000 B.C.)

David's son **Solomon** succeeds him. He builds the **temple** in Jerusalem and is spectacularly wealthy.

But after Solomon's death, the northern 10 tribes secede and establish their own kingdom. This **northern kingdom** is now called **"Israel";** the **southern kingdom** (with only two tribes, Judah and Benjamin) is called **"Judah."** Jerusalem and the temple are in Judah.

The northern kingdom has a series of bad kings. It is finally destroyed in 722 B.C. by the **Assyrians.** The people are taken away and disappear forever in history.

The southern kingdom has some good kings and some bad kings. It is finally captured by the **Babylonians,** who destroy Jerusalem and the temple in 586 B.C. The people are taken to Babylonia.

The worship of God should have united the 12 tribes. Instead, the Israelites decide that they want a king so that they, too, can become a nation like the others around them. David establishes the kingdom that unites all the tribes. God now makes a **covenant with David** that from his dynasty will come the Great King who will personify God's ideal king. This King will rule forever with justice and mercy. This covenant with David is the next step in the unfolding of God's plan.

Sadly, the kingdom ends in failure. First it is divided into two smaller kingdoms. The northern kingdom rejected God from the very beginning and was overrun, and its people were deported after a couple of centuries. The southern kingdom—in spite of the fact that Jerusalem and the temple of God were there, and in spite of a number of God-fearing kings—also ended up rejecting God, which led to their deportation by the Babylonians.

But the family lineage of David continued, and God would keep the promise He made to David.

⑥ The Babylonian Exile and the Return from Exile

Ezra, Nehemiah, Esther

While the Jews (the people from Judah) are in Babylonia, the Babylonians are defeated by the **Persians.** The Persians allow the Jews to return to Jerusalem. The temple and the walls are rebuilt under **Ezra** and **Nehemiah.** (The return takes place in stages over a period of about a century.)

The story of Esther is a vignette from this period; Esther's courage may have influenced the Persian king to support the return of the Jews to Jerusalem.

The Babylonian exile brought profound changes in the way the Jewish people saw themselves and their relationship with God. No longer could they blithely claim that God would never allow His temple to be destroyed or His people to be conquered by other nations. Much soul-searching took place: Had God deserted His people? Had God canceled His covenant with Abraham, with His people, and with David because they had not fulfilled their obligations under the covenant?

The Story	The Story Behind the Story
[The five books of **poetry and wisdom** (Job through Song of Songs) and the 17 books of the **prophets** (Isaiah through Malachi) were written largely during the periods of the kingdom and of the exile and return (periods ⑤ and ⑥).]	Yet the prophets had not only predicted the judgment of God on His people and the fall of Jerusalem—they had also said that, in spite of appearances, God had *not* abandoned His people. The terrible experience of the Exile brought about a focus on the promise that God would yet accomplish the ultimate fulfillment of all His promises by sending the Messiah.

The 400 Years Between the Testaments

Between the end of the Old Testament and the beginning of the New Testament there is a span of about 400 years. During this time many changes take place. • The **Romans** rather than the Persians are now the great world power. • In the Babylonian exile, the **synagogue** becomes very important as the place where people come together for worship and the study of the Hebrew Bible (our Old Testament). • For about 100 of the 400 years between the testaments, the Jews are independent again under the **Maccabees.** • Two groups that begin during this 400-year period are the **Sadducees** and the **Pharisees.** The teachings of Jesus are closest to those of the Pharisees, but the Pharisees end up being His staunchest opponents. • The group that is in charge of everyday matters in Palestine, including religious matters, is the **Sanhedrin,** which consists of Pharisees, Sadducees, teachers of the Law, and the high priest. • The central section of Palestine is Samaria. The **Samaritans** are partially related to the Jews and worship God, but on Mount Gerizim rather than in Jerusalem. The Jews avoid them at all costs.	After the Babylonian exile, the Jews return to Jerusalem. Through four centuries of conflict, God prepares the world around Israel for the coming of the promised Redeemer. The Greek empires give the then-known world a common language, Greek, while later the Roman Empire provides a stable government and worldwide peace (the *Pax Romana*) as well as a remarkable road system. All of this allows the rapid spread of the Good News of Jesus—of God come to earth to reconcile the world with Himself.

THE NEW TESTAMENT

⑦ The Life of Jesus

Jesus, John the Baptist, Crucifixion, Resurrection

The Old Testament, from Abraham to Malachi, covers about 2000 years of history—the New Testament only about 70 (and the first 25–30 of those only very briefly).

The *four Gospels* (Matthew, Mark, Luke, and John) all tell the story of Jesus' life, but each with a somewhat different emphasis.

Jesus' virgin **birth** to Mary (ca. 4 B.C.—see p. 495) is told mostly in Luke. Only one story is recorded about His youth—His visit to the temple in Jerusalem when He was 12. We also know that He took up the trade of His earthly father, Joseph; He became a carpenter.

Then, when Jesus is about 30, a prophet appears in the wilderness near the Jordan River, **John the Baptist,** who tells the people to repent and to show their repentance by being baptized. He also announces that someone greater than he will come who will "baptize with the Holy Spirit and with fire." Jesus insists on also being baptized by John.

After this, Jesus begins His own ministry of preaching that the **kingdom of God** is near. He heals many people and preaches in the synagogues. And He claims to be the fulfillment of what the prophets, including John the Baptist, had promised for centuries: the "anointed one" of God (**Messiah** in Hebrew, **Christ** in Greek), who would establish God's kingdom on earth.

The problem is that the leaders of the people (the Pharisees, Sadducees, and the teachers of the Law) see the miracles Jesus performs but cannot believe that Jesus really is who He claims He is: the Son of God. They think Jesus' claim is blasphemy, and therefore, they say, He must be able to do miracles because He is in league with the devil. But many people believe in Jesus.

Jesus is the fulfillment of God's promises to Abraham and David. His death and resurrection will reunite God with His people. He is the one through whom the whole world will be blessed. He is the King from David's house. But His **kingdom** is not based on external, worldly power. Rather, it is based on justice, mercy, humility, and the irresistible power of love. Jesus shows what God is like. He does not force submission, but asks for a response freely given: faith and trust in Him.

But the people of Israel cannot accept this radical revision of their expectations—they prefer a king who would restore Israel to political power. Jesus is crucified on the charge of blasphemy. But His **death** is a victory, the victory of love over the destructive power of sin. It is a victory because God raises Jesus from the dead. His **resurrection** shows that death is no longer the end, but rather a new beginning. Because of the Resurrection, we know that the truth we seek, and the healing of our guilt, our loneliness, and our isolation from God and one another, are found in Jesus.

Jesus voluntarily gave up His life. His shed blood paid the price for our sins and thus opened the way for *a new covenant*—not only with Abraham, Israel, or David, but with all people everywhere who want to be God's people. This new covenant does not require the keeping of laws and is not based on works, but is based on God's grace alone. Eternal salvation is freely given by Him to those who believe and have accepted Jesus as their Lord and Savior. God made His plan of redemption very simple and available to everyone!

The Story	The Story Behind the Story
Jesus chooses *12 disciples* (who will later be called apostles) to travel with Him and to be taught by Him. Peter (also called Simon Peter) is the leader among the Twelve. Peter, John, and James, John's brother, form the inner circle among the disciples.	This was the ultimate purpose behind the earlier covenants—to establish a new covenant through the blood of Jesus.
Jesus keeps teaching and doing miracles, but as it becomes clear that He is not going to establish God's kingdom by throwing the Romans out of the country, many people quit following Him. They do not understand (and even the disciples don't understand) that Jesus' mission is not political but to set things right between God and humanity—that God's kingdom must first be established in the hearts of those who follow Jesus.	
In the end, the leaders decide to kill Jesus, but they want to do it in a way that will not upset the people and that also gives the appearance of being legal. (The events of the last week of Jesus' life are described in detail in all four Gospels.) One of the disciples, *Judas,* betrays Jesus to the leaders. After trying in vain to find witnesses who can provide grounds for a death sentence, the leaders finally condemn Jesus to death because He claims to be God's Son—which He had been saying all along. He is then *crucified* by the Romans.	
But after three days the grave is empty—Jesus has *risen from the dead!* He appears to His disciples for a period of 40 days and then ascends to heaven.	

⑧ The Early Church

Pentecost, Peter, Paul

The story of the early church begins soon after the Ascension, with the coming of the Holy Spirit on Jesus' disciples on the day of *Pentecost.* This gives them courage to preach and teach about Jesus even though the Jewish leaders are opposed to them and throw some of them into jail.	Jesus came first for the descendants of Abraham, the Israelites. But the Gospel of Jesus is for the whole world—it is the blessing promised 3000 years ago to Abraham. We see in the early church how God makes sure that the Good Good News of Jesus will be spread all over the world. God's people are no longer merely an ethnic or political group.
One of the fiercest opponents of the followers of Jesus is *Saul* of Tarsus.	

The Story	The Story Behind the Story
He belongs to the party of the Pharisees and genuinely believes that he is doing God's work when he tries to wipe out the church. Then, on the road to Damascus, he meets the resurrected Jesus and turns from a fierce opponent to an equally fierce follower of Jesus. He is henceforth known by his Roman name, **Paul,** and most of Acts is about Paul's travels around the eastern part of the Roman Empire (known as his three **"missionary journeys"**) and his trip to Rome, where he is imprisoned. A problem for the early church is getting used to the idea that the Gospel of Jesus is not just for the Jews but for *all* people. The apostle **Peter** has to be shown by God that it is okay to baptize non-Jews—even Romans (Acts 10). It takes a special meeting of the apostles in Jerusalem to decide that non-Jewish Christians do not have to become Jews (by physical circumcision) before they become Christians (Acts 15). The door to God's kingdom is wide open—God is an equal-opportunity God! The rest of the New Testament is mostly taken up with **letters** written by Paul (the first 13, Romans through Philemon) and others (Hebrews through Jude). The final book is **Revelation,** which is a book of God's final judgment on nonbelievers and the fulfillment of God's promise to the church. In spite of outward appearances and Satan's threats, God will win in the end, and His church—those who trust Him—will be with Him forever!	God's people are all those who, regardless of race, gender, or talents, respond in faith to God's proclamation that we are reconciled to Him through Jesus.

The next two pages give a quick overview of where each period of biblical history is found in the Bible.

A. THE OLD TESTAMENT

① **In the Beginning**

Creation, Adam and Eve, Cain and Abel, Noah and the Flood, Babel

② **The Time of the Patriarchs**

Abraham, Isaac, Jacob, Joseph

③ **The Exodus from Egypt**

Moses, Aaron, Red Sea, Mount Sinai

④ **The Conquest and Settlement of Canaan**

Joshua, the Judges (Deborah, Gideon, Samson)

⑤ **The Monarchy and the Divided Kingdom**

Samuel, Saul, David, Solomon, two Kingdoms: Israel and Judah

⑥ **The Babylonian Exile and the Return from Exile**

Ezra, Nehemiah, Esther

> *Books that were written during the last two periods above (Kingdom, Exile and Return):*
>
> Poetry and Proverbs—*Job, Psalms, Proverbs*
>
> The Prophets—*Isaiah, Jeremiah, Daniel, Jonah*

B. THE 400 YEARS BETWEEN THE TESTAMENTS

C. THE NEW TESTAMENT

⑦ **The Life of Jesus**

Jesus, John the Baptist, Crucifixion, Resurrection

⑧ **The Early Church**

Pentecost, Peter, Paul

> *Books that were written during the last period above (the Early Church)*
>
> The Letters—*Paul, Peter, John, Jude, James*
>
> The Prophecy *(Revelation)*

OLD TESTAMENT		
Historical Books	**Poetic Books**	**Prophetic Books**
① ‖ Genesis 1–11		
② ‖ Genesis 12–50		
③ ‖ Exodus Leviticus Numbers Deuteronomy		
④ ‖ Joshua Judges Ruth		

⑤ ‖ 1 Samuel
2 Samuel
1 Kings
2 Kings
1 Chronicles
2 Chronicles
	Job
	Psalms
	Proverbs
	Ecclesiastes
	Song of Songs
		Isaiah Hosea
		Jeremiah Joel
		Lamentations Amos
		Ezekiel Obadiah
		Daniel Jonah
		    Micah
		    Nahum
		    Habakkuk
		    Zephaniah

⑥ ‖ Ezra Nehemiah Esther		Haggai Zechariah Malachi

NEW TESTAMENT		
Historical Books	**Letters**	**Prophetic Books**
⑦ ‖ Matthew Mark Luke John		
⑧ ‖ Acts	Romans *Through* Jude	Revelation

The Main Thought of Each Bible Book

(Some of the books have a principal thought; others are about a number of things.)

Genesis	Founding of the Hebrew Nation
Exodus	The Covenant with the Hebrew Nation
Leviticus	Laws of the Hebrew Nation
Numbers	Journey to the Promised Land
Deuteronomy	Laws of the Hebrew Nation
Joshua	The Conquest of Canaan
Judges	First 300 Years in the Land
Ruth	Beginning of the Messianic Family of David
1 Samuel	Organization of the Kingdom
2 Samuel	Reign of David
1 Kings	Division of the Kingdom
2 Kings	History of the Divided Kingdom
1 Chronicles	Reign of David
2 Chronicles	History of the Southern Kingdom
Ezra	Return from Captivity
Nehemiah	Rebuilding Jerusalem
Esther	Escape of Israel from Extermination
Job	Problem of Suffering
Psalms	National Hymnbook of Israel
Proverbs	Wisdom of Solomon
Ecclesiastes	Vanity of Earthly Life
Song of Songs	Glorification of Wedded Love
Isaiah	The Messianic Prophet
Jeremiah	A Last Effort to Save Jerusalem
Lamentations	A Dirge over the Desolation of Jerusalem
Ezekiel	"They Shall Know That I Am God"
Daniel	The Prophet at Babylon
Hosea	Apostasy of Israel
Joel	Prediction of the Holy Spirit Age
Amos	Ultimate Universal Rule of David
Obadiah	Destruction of Edom
Jonah	An Errand of Mercy to Nineveh

Micah	Bethlehem to Be Birthplace of the Messiah
Nahum	Destruction of Nineveh
Habakkuk	"The Just Shall Live by Faith"
Zephaniah	Coming of a "Pure Language"
Haggai	Rebuilding the Temple
Zechariah	Rebuilding the Temple
Malachi	Final Message to a Disobedient People
Matthew	Jesus the Messiah
Mark	Jesus the Wonderful
Luke	Jesus the Son of Man
John	Jesus the Son of God
Acts	Formation of the Church
Romans	Nature of Christ's Work
1 Corinthians	Various Church Disorders
2 Corinthians	Paul's Vindication of His Apostleship
Galatians	By Grace, Not by Law
Ephesians	Unity of the Church
Philippians	A Missionary Epistle
Colossians	Deity of Jesus
1 Thessalonians	The Lord's Second Coming
2 Thessalonians	The Lord's Second Coming
1 Timothy	The Care of the Church in Ephesus
2 Timothy	Paul's Final Word
Titus	The Churches of Crete
Philemon	Conversion of a Runaway Slave
Hebrews	Christ the Mediator of a New Covenant
James	Good Works
1 Peter	To a Persecuted Church
2 Peter	Prediction of Apostasy
1 John	Love
2 John	Caution Against False Teachers
3 John	Rejection of John's Helpers
Jude	Imminent Apostasy
Revelation	Ultimate Triumph of Christ

The Setting of the Bible

1. Why the Setting Is Important

The Bible is full of people, places, and events—it tells of God's concrete dealings with humanity and humanity's relationship with God in the day-to-day situations and problems of real life.

While an understanding of the message of the Bible—the Gospel of God's eternal love for His people—does not depend on our knowledge of the historical, geographical, and cultural background or setting of the Bible, such knowledge will often add a concrete dimension to our reading of the Scriptures that can help put the biblical message in sharper focus.

For example, in Genesis 23, Abraham's wife Sarah has died, and Abraham needs a place to bury her. God had promised that the land of Canaan would belong to Abraham and his descendants, but at this point he doesn't own even a square inch of it; he is still a nomad. Abraham approaches Ephron the Hittite, who owns the cave in which he wants to bury Sarah. The story reflects an established pattern of negotiating. Ephron seems to be very generous, but in reality he ends up selling the cave to Abraham for an exorbitant price. This was the only part of Canaan Abraham owned when he died, and he paid many times what this little piece of it was worth—yet Abraham continued to have faith in God's promise that one day his descendants would own all of the land (see Hebrews 11:8–10).

Herod the Great built the monumental structure of the Machpelah over the traditional location of the cave purchased by Abraham for Sarah's burial.

Similarly, geography often plays a role in the Bible. When God called Abraham to go from Ur of the Chaldeans to Canaan, almost due west of Ur, Abraham ended up in Haran, almost as far north of Canaan as Ur was east of it (Genesis 12). The problem was not that Abraham had a poor sense of direction. Rather, it was impossible for Abraham to travel due west to Canaan, since between Ur and Canaan there was only desert. Abraham had to follow the River Euphrates, the one reliable source of water on a journey of some 600 miles as the crow flies, before heading south to Canaan. (See page 49 for more on roads and travel during biblical times.)

2. The Ancient Near East

The setting of the Bible is what is today called the **Middle East:** modern Egypt, Turkey, Israel, Lebanon, Syria, Jordan, Saudi Arabia, Iraq, and Iran. This same region is referred to as the **Ancient Near East** when we look at its history.

It is an area smaller than the United States, much of it desert. The earliest great civilizations prospered around the rivers in this region—the Egyptian Empire along the Nile River, the Sumerian, Assyrian, Babylonian, and Persian Empires around the Euphrates and Tigris Rivers, in what is now Iraq.

We sometimes have the mistaken notion that Abraham, with whom the story of God's people begins, lived in rather primitive times. Nothing could be further from the truth—unless we assume that technology and urban sprawl are the hallmark of civilization. When God called Abraham (ca. 2000 B.C.),

- Egypt had already had a flourishing civilization for more than a millennium; the pyramids had been standing for almost five centuries.

Relief of the Assyrian army besieging their enemies. It was the Assyrian army that destroyed the northern tribes of Israel in 722 B.C.

- On the island of Crete, the great Minoan civilization had already prospered for more than five centuries.
- The region around the Euphrates and Tigris Rivers (also called Mesopotamia = "Between the Rivers") was the scene of the great Sumerian civilization. Ur of the Chaldeans, where Abraham came from, was a thriving city on the Euphrates River.
- Great civilizations also flourished farther east, in the Indus Valley and in China.

It was not until after the end of the Old Testament (ca. 400 B.C.) that the center of power moved westward, away from the Ancient Near East, first to Greece and then to Rome.

3. The World Powers of Biblical Times

There were six great empires during biblical times. (The exact boundaries fluctuated, and some of the boundaries were never clearly defined.) The first three empires were east and southeast of the Mediterranean Sea; the last three show a gradual shift toward the west, until with the Roman Empire the focus of power shifted from northern Africa and the Near East to Europe.

- **Egyptian Empire.** Became the home of Israel when the Patriarchs moved to Egypt at the end of Genesis; the Israelites left Egypt in the Exodus, 400 years later.
- **Assyrian Empire.** Destroyed the northern kingdom, Israel, in 722 B.C. and deported its people. Its capital was Nineveh (which was spared after Jonah preached there).
- **Babylonian Empire.** Destroyed Jerusalem and the southern kingdom, Judah, in 586 B.C. and deported its people to Babylonia. Its capital was Babylon (where the prophet Daniel rose to prominence).
- **Persian Empire.** Destroyed the Babylonian Empire in 539 B.C. Its capitals were Persepolis and Susa (the latter providing the setting for the book of Esther). The first Persian ruler, Darius, allowed the Jews to go back to Jerusalem.
- **Greek Empire.** Founded by Alexander the Great around 330 B.C. After Alexander's death, the empire was divided into four empires (see pp. 472–74). The legacy of the Greek Empire was not political but cultural: Hellenism (see p. 481).
- **Roman Empire.** The empire that was in its glory days during the time of Christ and the early church (see pp. 645–53; for the Roman Empire after the time of Christ, see pp. 895–901).

4. Roads and Travel in Biblical Times

Our understanding of both the Old and the New Testament accounts can be enhanced by understanding the influence that roads and weather played in the course of biblical events.

In ancient times, the location of roads was determined to a large extent by the natural features of the landscape. Most roads through the rugged hill country of Judah generally followed the mountain ridges, since a more direct route would mean climbing in and out of many valleys and ravines.

Water—either too much or too little—was also a problem. Roads in valleys and low-lying areas could flood during the rainy season or become too muddy for use. Travel during the dry summer season was much easier than traveling on muddy, rain-soaked roads in the winter months. The spring and summer seasons were "the time when kings go off to war" (2-Samuel 11:1) because the roads were dry and the newly harvested grain was available to feed their troops.

Too little water, on the other hand, was an even more serious problem. When Abraham traveled from Ur to Canaan (see map on p. 109), he could not simply go west, which would have saved him hundreds of miles, since there were no sources of water in the Arabian Desert. Instead, he had to follow one of the major international trade routes that connected Mesopotamia with Egypt, Turkey, and Arabia. From Ur, these routes followed the great rivers, the Euphrates and the Tigris, and both went through Haran, almost 400 miles to the north of Canaan.

The Major International Routes

The "major international routes" were not unlike the transcontinental trails in the early American West, such as the Oregon Trail. Basic "road-building" operations included the removal of stones from the path, the clearing of trees and bushes, the maintaining of shallow fords in the river beds, and possibly the construction of trails along steep slopes. But these major routes generally followed relatively easy terrain and were never far from water sources.

These roads had to be recleared and releveled periodically, especially when an important personage such as a king was to travel on them. Thus

The international highway used both by merchants and soldiers ran through the Jezreel Valley.

it is not just poetic language, but rather a statement about actual road maintenance when we read, "Prepare the way for the Lord, make straight paths for him. Every valley shall be filled in, every mountain and hill made low" (Luke 3:5) — that is, ruts or eroded low spots must be filled in, and bumps must be removed.

Living near an international highway brought economic benefits. These roads served as thoroughfares for itinerant tradesmen and merchants, for the conveyance of governmental and commercial messages, and for the transportation of scarce supplies, such as copper, iron, tin, gold, silver, incense, dyes, and pottery. (Bulkier items such as timber and stones were usually shipped on boats and rafts.) Those who controlled the roads — whether brigands or a more permanent central government — could derive considerable income from the traffic on these highways. The central government could collect tolls from passing caravans, sell food and lodging, and offer the services of military escorts that could be hired by the caravans to ensure their safe passage through "dangerous" territory.

On the other hand, these same roads were also used for military expeditions, which brought no economic benefit but only enormous risk in the case of hostile armies.

Those living along the international routes were also exposed to new intellectual, cultural, linguistic, and religious influences, and this inevitably led to a degree of assimilation. For example, the ease of travel in and out of Samaria helps to explain the openness of that area to non-Israelite religious and cultural influences.

The remoteness of the Hill Country of Judah and the relatively difficult access to Jerusalem made the southern kingdom less susceptible to foreign influences. This difference helps explain why the deportation of the northern kingdom happened some 130 years earlier than the deportation of the southern kingdom, Judah (see pp. 199–201).

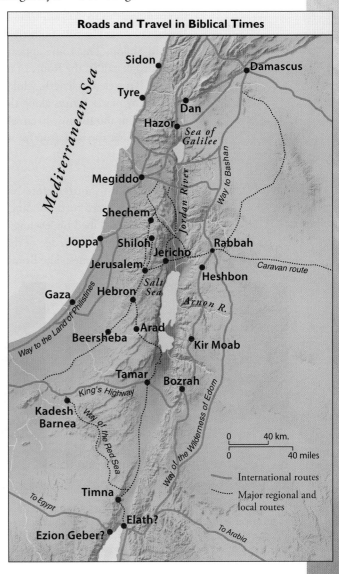

Roads and Travel in Biblical Times

Roads in Canaan

By the time Abraham arrived in the land of Canaan (ca. 2000 B.C.), the lines of communication within the country were already well established. Two international highways ran through the country, one along the coast (sometimes referred to as "the Way of the Sea"), the other east of the Jordan River (the Transjordanian highway). The western international highway probably played a role in the story of Joseph, who found his brothers near Dothan, was thrown into a cistern, and then was sold to Midianite merchants, who took him to Egypt (Genesis 37:12–28). Dothan was less than 15 miles from the western highway, and the cistern may have been even closer.

The map on page 49 shows many of the regional and local routes in Canaan. One of these is especially important for biblical studies: the interregional route that ran from Beersheba in the south to Shechem in the north — via Hebron, Bethlehem, Jerusalem, Gibeah, Ramah, Bethel/Ai, and Shiloh. This route appears again and again in the biblical text. Some people call it "the Route of the Patriarchs" because Abraham, Isaac, and Jacob traveled its length, while others refer to it as "the Ridge Route," for in many places it runs along the ridge of the watershed of the Judean and Ephraim mountains. Even when it is not specifically mentioned, it often furnishes the backdrop for many events recorded in the Bible.

Roman Roads

It was not until shortly before New Testament times that the Romans developed advanced road-building techniques, which included the preparation of the roadbed by leveling the ground and cutting rocks, the use of curbing to mark the edge of the roads, attention to drainage, and the laying of paving stones. The Roman Empire developed a system of roads

These streets in Pompeii are exactly as they were in A.D. 79, when an eruption of Mount Vesuvius buried them under volcanic ash. These urban streets had sidewalks and pedestrian crossings: the large stones in the road are stepping stones, since the roads were also designed to carry off rainwater. The ruts show that the width of Roman carts had to be standardized to be able to pass between the stones.

that ultimately would stretch from Scotland to the Euphrates—some 53,000 miles in all. (The U.S. Interstate Highway System, by way of comparison, consists of approximately 30,000 miles of road.) It is probable that the construction of a rather well-developed road system had already begun in Syria and Judah in New Testament times.

Travel

Besides walking, early modes of transportation included donkeys, solid-wheeled carts, and chariots. Camels eventually began to be used to carry heavy loads, especially in caravans. Horses were used in the second and first millennia B.C. to draw chariots and to serve in cavalry units; during the Persian period (538–332 B.C.) and later, their use for everyday travel became more common. In New Testament times all these means of transportation were used, and the improvement of the road system increased the use of carts and chariots.

The Israelites never were a seafaring nation. The sea often is used as a symbolic representation of chaos and of the nations in opposition to God. Thus Jonah's running away from God to the sea is more than just going west instead of east—it involves symbolically moving toward all that is in opposition to God. Yet God controls the sea and its inhabitants. And in Revelation 21:1, the statement "the sea is no more" may also mean that at last the rebellious nations no longer can trouble God's creation.

5. The Promised Land: Israel

Much of biblical history took place in and around the land of Israel. Understanding the geography of this area provides valuable insight as one studies the biblical events that took place here. Israel is a country that is about the size of the state of New Jersey, with a total of 8,019 square miles of land.

The Four Major Zones

The city of Jerusalem, which is the capital of Israel and the center stage of biblical history, lies halfway between the **Mediterranean Sea** and the **Arabian** or **Eastern Desert**. Squeezed between the sea and the desert—which are only 70 miles apart at the latitude of Jerusalem—are four "zones" that run north-south:

1. The **coastal plain**, which at the latitude of Jerusalem is less than 12 miles wide.
2. The **central mountain range**, on which Jerusalem is situated at an elevation of approximately 2,500 feet, is about 36 miles wide.
3. The **Rift Valley**, through which the Jordan River runs. It is part of the Rift Valley system that extends for 3,700 miles from Africa to southern Turkey.

4. The **Transjordanian mountains,** which rise steeply on the eastern side of the Rift Valley and then slope gradually toward the Arabian Desert.

The Arabian or Eastern Desert stretches eastward some 450 miles, from the Transjordanian mountains to the Euphrates River.

The Seasons

In biblical times, Israel was primarily an agrarian country. It is sometimes difficult for people living in urban areas to realize how utterly dependent on the weather the Israelites were—not just the farmers, but the nation as a whole. When crops failed, famine followed. In desperation, Jacob sent his sons to Egypt for grain (see Genesis 42:1–3). And Elijah's prayer that it would not rain (1 Kings 17:1; 18:41–46; 5:17–18) was more than a request for a few unpleasantly dry summers—it potentially meant famine and disaster.

The average amount of rainfall varies considerably in different parts of the country (Amos 4:6–8). In some years, parts of the country can go without rain for four or five consecutive weeks during the months of January and February, usually the rainiest months of the year. In those regions where the total annual average is only 12 to 16 inches, the growth of grain crops is by no means assured, for a variation of only 4 to 6 inches can spell disaster. In areas where average rainfall is high, farmers can sow and "reap a hundredfold" (Genesis 26:12) in "normal" years, but even there a series of drought years can be devastating and, in the past, could drive people from the land (Genesis 12:10).

The Israelites knew that it was Yahweh, the Lord, who had His eyes on the land continually, from the beginning of the year to its end, and that their obedience to His commandments would bring blessing, while disobedience would bring drought and disaster (Deuteronomy 11:8–17). But given the uncertainties about the amount and distribution of the

Looking south along the shoreline toward Caesarea Maritima which lies on the coastal plain just south of Mt. Carmel.

rainfall, it is no wonder that some Israelites were drawn to participate in the worship of Baal, the Canaanite storm god, who was believed to bring fertility to the land.

Israel's year is divided into two main seasons: the rainy season (mid-October through April) and the dry season (mid-June through mid-September), separated by transitional months.

The Dry Season—Summer (Mid-June to Mid-September)

In contrast to the ever-changing weather conditions in many parts of North America, conditions in Israel during the summer months are relatively stable. Warm days and cooler nights are the rule, and it almost never rains. In Jerusalem, for example, the average August daytime high temperature is 86º F (30º C), the nighttime average low is 64º F (18º C).

Summer days are relatively cloudless; in fact, Israel is one of the sunniest countries in the world. On a typical summer day, temperatures begin to climb immediately after sunrise. Within a short time a cooling sea breeze begins to blow in from the west. After passing through the coastal plain, it reaches Jerusalem in the mountains at about noon, and its cooling effect prevents the temperature from rising significantly during the afternoon hours. But the breeze usually does not reach Transjordan until mid-to-late afternoon, so temperatures there continue to climb through most of the day.

The summer months see grapes, figs, pomegranates, olives, melons, and other crops ripening. The summer dew and deep root systems bring needed moisture to these crops. Most of the fruits are harvested in August and September. During the summer, shepherds move their flocks of sheep and goats westward, allowing them to feed on the stubble of the wheat and barley fields that were harvested in the spring. Because the soil is dry during the summer months, travel is fairly easy. In biblical times, caravans and armies moved easily through most parts of the country, the armies helping themselves to plentiful supplies of grain at the expense of the local population.

The First Transitional Season— (Mid-September to Mid-October)

The first transitional season, from mid-September to mid-October, marks the end of the stable, dry, summer conditions. It is the time of the fruit harvest, and farmers begin to look anxiously for the onset of the rainy season. In the fall, travel on the Mediterranean becomes dangerous (Acts 27:9) and remains so throughout the winter months.

The Rainy Season—Winter (Mid-October to April)

The rainy season, from mid-October through April, is characterized by occasional rain storms that roll in off the Mediterranean Sea, normally bringing three days of rain followed by several days of dry weather (although deviations from this norm are frequent). During January the mean daily temperature in Jerusalem is 50º F (10º C). Jerusalem receives

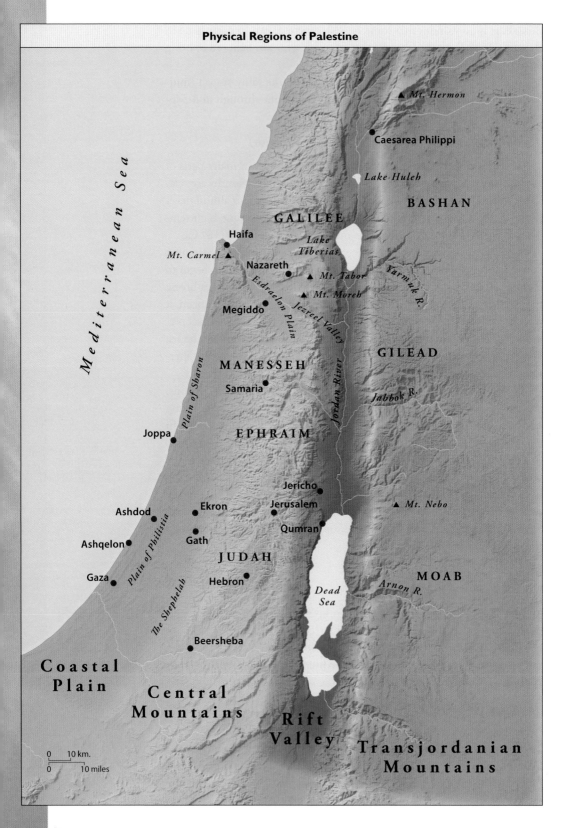

Physical Regions of Palestine

Mediterranean Sea

▲ *Mt. Hermon*

● Caesarea Philippi

Lake Huleh

BASHAN

GALILEE

Haifa ●

Lake Tiberias

Mt. Carmel ▲

Nazareth ●

▲ *Mt. Tabor*

Yarmuk R.

Esdraelon Plain

▲ *Mt. Moreh*

Megiddo ●

Jezreel Valley

GILEAD

MANESSEH

Samaria ●

Jordan River

Jabbok R.

Plain of Sharon

EPHRAIM

Joppa ●

Jericho ●

▲ *Mt. Nebo*

Ashdod ●

Ekron ●

Jerusalem ●

Ashqelon ●

Gath ●

Qumran ●

Plain of Philistia

JUDAH

Gaza ●

Hebron ●

Dead Sea

MOAB

Arnon R.

The Shephelah

Beersheba ●

Coastal Plain

Central Mountains

Rift Valley

Transjordanian Mountains

0   10 km.
0   10 miles

snow only once or twice each year, but it rarely remains on the ground more than a day.

However, cold temperatures, combined with wind and rain, can make life uncomfortable in the hilly regions—a discomfort the people gladly bear because of the life-giving power of the rains. During a typical year a farmer plows his field and plants his grain crops after the "autumn rains" of October through December have softened the hard, sun-baked soil. The grain crops grow from December through February, when 75 percent of the rain falls, and continue to ripen during March and April as the rains begin to taper off. These "spring rains" are important for producing bumper crops.

Rain is so important that Hebrew has several words for it, each referring to a different part of the rainy season. Deuteronomy 11:14 reads, "Then I will send rain [Heb. *matar;* Dec.–Feb.] on your land in its season, both autumn [Heb. *yoreh;* Oct.–Dec.] and spring rains [Heb. *malqosh;* March–April], so that you may gather in your grain, new wine and oil" (see also Jeremiah 5:24; Hosea 6:3).

The Second Transitional Season—(May to Mid-June)

The second transitional season lasts from early May through mid-June. The temperatures gradually rise, and the season is punctuated by a series of hot, dry, dusty days during which the winds blow in from the eastern and southern deserts. On these days, which are called by the names of the winds *hamsin, sirocco,* or *sharav,* the temperature often rises 25° F (14° C) above normal, and the relative humidity can drop by as much as 40 percent. The *hamsin* wind conditions can be very debilitating to both humans and beasts, and they completely dry up the beautiful flowers and grasses that covered the landscape during the winter months (Isaiah 40:7–8). The positive effect of these winds, however, is that the hot, dry weather aids the ripening of the grains by "setting" them before the harvest. It is during this season that first the barley and then the wheat harvest takes place.

6. The Holy City: Jerusalem

Jerusalem holds a special place in the hearts and thoughts of Jews, Christians, and Moslems. It is mentioned some 800 times in the Bible, from Genesis 14:18 ("Salem") to Revelation 21:10 (the New Jerusalem). Although today Jerusalem boasts a population of nearly half a million people, its origins were humble.

Location

The importance of Jerusalem is a bit surprising, given its location. It is not near one of the two major international highways (see p. 47), and the only road that passed by it was the north-south Ridge Route, and even that ran about a half mile west of the ancient core of the city.

Jerusalem lies in the Hill Country of Judea, at an elevation of 2,500 feet, which gave it the benefit of many natural defenses. The Dead Sea, the Rift Valley cliffs, the Wilderness of Judea, and the rugged hill country provided protection on the east, west, and south. It was somewhat easier to approach the city from the north or south, along the Ridge Route, but access to the Ridge Route from either the coast or the Rift Valley was difficult. Because of the easier approaches from the north and the northwest, invading armies have often assaulted Jerusalem from a northerly direction.

Thus, besides being removed from the main routes of commerce (and of military expeditions), Jerusalem enjoyed the security of its natural defenses. If Jerusalem was not a natural center of commerce because of its location, neither was it situated in the heart of an extraordinarily rich agricultural region. In fact, Jerusalem was perched right on the boundary between the desert and "the sown" (areas suitable for agriculture). Jerusalem itself receives ample supplies of winter rain (approximately 25 inches per year), as do the hills to the west, so that they are able to produce a variety of crops, but just over the Mount of Olives, to the east of Jerusalem, lies the barren Judean Desert.

Difficult as it is to imagine this today, during early periods the hills in and around the city were covered with trees. Beginning some 5000 years ago, large trees were cut down to provide timber for buildings and ships, while both larger and smaller trees were used to fuel the fires in lime and pottery kilns and to heat houses in the winter months. Areas that had been cleared could be used for agricultural purposes, and on the more level terrain — for example, the Valley of Rephaim to the southwest of Jerusalem — grain crops were planted (Isaiah 17:5).

Topography

Jerusalem is surrounded by hills that are higher than the hills on which the core of the ancient city was built. Roughly speaking, the ancient city can be visualized as sitting on a rise in the bottom of a large bowl, where the rim of the bowl is higher than the rise within it. "As the mountains surround Jerusalem, so the LORD surrounds his people both now and forevermore" (Psalm 125:2).

Biblical Jerusalem was built on two parallel north-south ridges. The western ridge, which is the higher and broader of the two, is bounded on the west by the Hinnom Valley, which curves around and also runs along the south edge of the hill.

The narrower and lower eastern ridge is bounded on the east by the Kidron Valley. Both the Hinnom and the Kidron are mentioned in the Bible, but the valley between the eastern and western ridges is not. For lack of a better name, geographers often call it the Central Valley, or — following the lead of the Jewish historian Josephus — the Tyropoeon ("Cheesemakers") Valley (*War* 5.4.1).

In many ways the western ridge is the more natural one to settle on, both because it has a relatively large surface area and thus can support more people, and because it is higher and seems to have better natural defenses (higher, steeper slopes) than the eastern ridge. In spite of this, it was the lower, cigar-shaped, southern portion of the eastern ridge that was settled first. The reason why the ancient core of Jerusalem developed on this insignificant, down-in-a-basin hill was that the only good-sized spring in the whole area — the Gihon Spring — was located alongside the eastern ridge in the Kidron Valley.

David Captures the City

The city was on the border between the territories of the tribes of Benjamin and Judah, although it was technically inside Benjamin. During the period of the Judges, the city belonged to the Jebusites and was called Jebus (Judges 19:11 – 12). It was finally captured by King David, who attacked the city at its weakest point — its water supply. Since the spring of Gihon was outside the city, a tunnel or shaft had apparently been dug to the spring or a nearby pool to ensure a water supply in times of siege. Whether David's commander, Joab, entered the city by climbing up the

Looking north to the City of David and the Temple Mount. David captured ancient Jerusalem from the Jebusites who lived on the small ridge south of the Temple Mount nestled between the Kidron Valley (to the east [right]) and Tyropean Valley (to the west [left]).

water shaft or by cutting off the water supply to the city isn't clear—but Jebus surrendered (2 Samuel 5:6–8).

With the capture of Jerusalem, David accomplished several strategic goals. First, he removed a foreign enclave from a border area and thus removed a potential threat to the Israelite tribes.

Second, because of Jerusalem's neutral location—neither in the heartland of Judah, like Hebron, David's former capital, nor in the northern part of Israel—it was a capital acceptable to both David's own tribe of Judah and to the tribes of the north who had recently acknowledged him as king.

Besides, by capturing Jerusalem himself, it became the personal property of David and his descendants that could not be claimed by his own or any other tribe—it became the royal seat of the Davidic dynasty. In addition, David brought the ark of the covenant from Kiriath Jearim to Jerusalem, thus establishing it as the major center of worship for all the Israelite tribes (2 Samuel 6:1–23; 1 Chronicles 13:1–14).

The city that David captured was small—approximately 15 acres (6 hectares) in size, with a population of 2000 to 2400. He evidently took up residence in the old Jebusite fortress called Zion, and from that point on, the fortress as well as the city as a whole could be called the "City of David" (e.g., 2 Samuel 5:7).

Jerusalem Under Solomon

Toward the end of his reign, David purchased the threshing floor of Araunah the Jebusite, a site to the north of (and higher than) the ancient city core; this is the place where Solomon eventually built the temple (2 Samuel 24:18–25; 1 Chronicles 21:18–26). Soon after Solomon became king, David died and was buried in the City of David (1 Kings 2:10). Evidently a royal cemetery was established where many of his descendants, up through Hezekiah (d. 686 B.C.), were buried, but it has not been found.

In the fourth year of his reign (966 B.C.), Solomon began building the temple, a task that took seven years. The exact location of the temple is not known, although an old tradition and modern research places it in the immediate vicinity of the Moslem shrine called the Dome of the Rock, which now occupies the highest point of the temple area.

Under Solomon the city more than doubled in size, from about 15 acres to about 37 acres, with a population of about 4500 to 5000 people. Among the increased population were at least some of the foreign wives whom Solomon married. It was for them that Solomon built a number of pagan shrines "on a hill east of Jerusalem" (1 Kings 11:7–8)—probably on the southern portion of the Mount of Olives. The location of these shrines was such that they towered over both the City of David and the temple of the true and living God.

Jerusalem from Solomon to Its Destruction

With the secession of the north from the south after Solomon's death (930 B.C.), Solomon's successors ruled over a much smaller territory consisting of Judah and a portion of Benjamin. Jerusalem remained the seat of the government for the Davidic dynasty, and the Solomonic temple continued to be the focal point for the worship of the God of Israel.

During the period of the Divided Monarchy (930–722 B.C.), Jerusalem was attacked a number of times: by the Egyptian pharaoh Shishak during the reign of Rehoboam (925 B.C.; 1 Kings 14:22–28; 2-Chronicles 12:2–4), and by Hazael of Aram Damascus during the reign of Joash (ca. 813 B.C.; 2 Kings 12:17–18; 2 Chronicles 24:17–24). In each case, lavish gifts, taken from the temple treasury, bought off the aggressors.

But in the days of Amaziah of Judah, King Joash of Israel attacked the city and "broke down the wall of Jerusalem from the Ephraim Gate to the Corner Gate—a section about six hundred feet long" (ca. 790 B.C.; 2 Chronicles 25:23).

We are also told that during the 8th century B.C., "Uzziah built towers in Jerusalem at the Corner Gate, at the Valley Gate and at the angle of the wall . . ." (2 Chronicles 26:9) as he strengthened the defenses of the city—perhaps in response to the growing Assyrian threat in the person of Tiglath-Pileser III. It seems very probable that during Uzziah's reign (792–740 B.C.) and during the reign of his successors, Jerusalem expanded westward so as to include the southern portion of the western ridge. The large increase in the size of Jerusalem at this time was probably due to the fact that settlers from the northern kingdom moved south so as to avoid the Assyrian onslaught; they may have thought that Jerusalem would never be taken by a foreign power because the temple of the Lord was there, and that the Lord would never allow such an indignity to be perpetrated (Psalm 132:13–18).

Soon after the fall of the northern kingdom in 722 B.C., Hezekiah revolted against his Assyrian overlords (see pp. 260–63) and needed to strengthen Jerusalem's defenses. Evidently it was during his reign that the suburb that had developed on the southern portion of the western ridge was enclosed by a new wall (Isaiah 22:10). The total area of the walled city had swelled to 150 acres (61 ha.) and boasted a population of about 25,000.

Since the major water supply of the city, the Gihon Spring, was at some distance from the newly enclosed suburb and thus was exposed to enemy attack, Hezekiah devised a plan to divert the water to a spot inside the city walls, closer to the western hill. He did this by digging an underground tunnel that followed a serpentine path to a point in the Central Valley, which, although it was outside of the old city wall of the City of David, was inside the newly constructed city wall on the western hill. This diversion of the spring water is mentioned not only in the Bible (2 Kings 20:20; 2 Chronicles 32:30), but also in a Hebrew inscription that was discovered at the southern end of the 1,750-foot tunnel (see p. 262).

In 701 B.C. Sennacherib of Assyria attacked. Although he sent some of his army and commanders to Jerusalem to demand its surrender— Sennacherib boasted that he had shut Hezekiah up in Jerusalem like a bird in a cage—he had to retreat when, according to the biblical text, a large portion of his army was destroyed through divine intervention (2 Kings 19:35).

During the 8th and 7th centuries B.C., there were both good and bad rulers in Jerusalem. On the negative side were Ahaz and Manasseh, both of whom sacrificed children in the Valley of Ben Hinnom (2 Chronicles 28:3; 33:6; cf. 2 Kings 23:10). It was during Ahaz's reign that at least a portion of the temple area was remodeled and a new altar, based on a pagan pattern from Damascus, was built to replace the old one (2 Kings 16:10–18).

During this same period there were also two godly kings, Hezekiah and Josiah, who worked to undo the evil their predecessors had perpetrated by taking steps to cleanse and refurbish the temple. It was during such a rebuilding, in the days of Josiah (ca. 622 B.C.), that the Book of the Law was discovered, and in obedience to its commands, additional reforms were instituted (2 Kings 22; 2 Chronicles 34). But because of the continuing sins of the people and their leaders, God's judgment finally fell on Jerusalem. In 586 B.C., when the Babylonian king Nebuchadnezzar destroyed both the city and the temple, most of the people were deported to Babylonia.

The Rebuilding of Jerusalem

Fifty years later, the first group of Jews—some 50,000—was allowed to return to Jerusalem. They rebuilt the sacrificial altar, but it was not until some 20 years later that the temple was rebuilt under Zerubbabel and completed in 516 B.C. (Ezra 6). This second temple was a much more modest structure than Solomon's temple had been. A second return was led by Ezra in 458 B.C., but the city walls were not rebuilt until 445 B.C., under Nehemiah, almost a century after the first Jews returned from Babylon.

From the time of Nehemiah (445 B.C.) until the beginning of the 2nd century B.C., not too much is known about Jerusalem. The city remained under Persian control until 332 B.C., when Alexander the Great conquered the Middle East. After his death in 323 B.C. the Ptolemies of Egypt gained control of Palestine and Judah, and it is generally assumed that under their benign rule a priestly aristocracy governed from Jerusalem.

But early in the 2nd century B.C., the Seleucid king Antiochus III defeated the Ptolemies (198 B.C.), and the change in rule was welcomed by most of the Jewish population. With his support, repairs were made to the temple and a large pool—possibly the Pool of Bethesda—was constructed (Ecclesiasticus 50:1–3).

Antiochus IV (175–164 B.C.), however, tried to stamp out the Jewish religion. The temple in Jerusalem was desecrated, and a statute of the chief Greek god, Olympian Zeus, was set up in its precincts (168 B.C.). It addition, other Greek structures were erected in Jerusalem, including a gymnasium and a citadel. The citadel, called the Akra in Greek, was built on the eastern ridge just south of the temple area and was so tall that it towered over the temple area. Although Judas Maccabaeus's forces were able to retake Jerusalem, to purify the temple (164 B.C.), and to reestablish sacrificial worship, the Seleucid garrison in the Akra remained a thorn in the side of the Jews until Judas's brother Simon (142–135 B.C.) captured and demolished it—even leveling the hill upon which it had stood (Josephus, *Antiq.* 13.6.7 [215]).

At the end of the Hellenistic period the Hasmonean brothers Aristobulus II and Hyrcanus II vied with each other for the office of high priest and control of the country. In the end, the Roman general Pompey intervened and marched on Jerusalem. After he set up camps to the southwest and northwest of the city, the city on the western ridge was handed over to him by the followers of Hyrcanus. However, the supporters of Aristobulus put up a defense on the eastern ridge. In response, Pompey erected a siege dike around the ridge and, after building assault ramps, attacked the temple area from the west, across the ruins of the bridge that had spanned the Central Valley, and also from the north.

The arrival of Pompey marked the beginning of the long period of control over Jerusalem by Rome and its Byzantine successor, which would last until the time of the Persian and Arab conquests (A.D. 614 and 639), save for brief periods during the first and second Jewish revolts.

Jerusalem Under Herod the Great

At the beginning of the period of Roman rule, Jerusalem experienced great expansion, construction, and beautification under the leadership of the Roman client-king Herod the Great (37–4 B.C.). One of his great achievements was the refurbishing of the temple and the Temple Mount. Although he was limited in what he could do to the temple building itself—the divine word and tradition dictated its basic dimensions—he spent more than a year and a half beautifying and refurbishing the structure.

He did not face similar restrictions when it came to the courts that surrounded the temple, and so he spent great sums on expanding these. He is said to have doubled the size of the platform area so that it reached its present size—which is almost twice the size of the city of Jerusalem captured by David some 1000 years earlier. Although no remnants of Herod's temple have been found that can be identified as such with certainty, the huge platform on which its courts were built has survived. The area is now

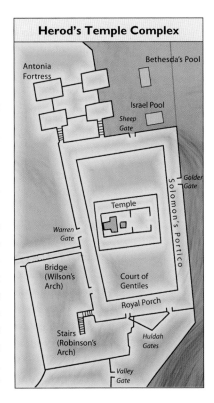

Herod's Temple Complex

occupied by Moslem structures and is called the Haram esh-Sharif—the Noble Sanctuary.

In constructing this large platform, Herod made use of some existing walls, especially on the east, but he expanded the platform to the north, west, and south. Indeed, the western expansion was such that part of the Central Valley was filled in and covered over. Today some 26 courses of Herodian stones, founded on bedrock, are still standing. These stones are cut so precisely that no mortar was used in the construction of the wall. A typical stone weighs two to 10 tons, while the largest of the known stones measures 46 x 10 x 10 feet and weighs 415 tons! A portion of this is known as the "Western Wall" or "Wailing Wall."

Along the upper perimeter of the huge temple platform Herod built or refurbished a number of covered colonnades. The most famous of these was the southern one, the "Royal Colonnade." It consisted of 162 columns arranged in four rows, forming a long basilica-shaped building. The columns themselves were 27 feet (8 m.) high and 4.6 feet (1.4 m.) in diameter and were crowned with Corinthian capitals. Although nothing of the colonnade remains today, the appearance of its outer wall can be surmised from the pilaster-recessed design that is evident in the Herodian structure that encloses the Tomb of the Patriarchs in Hebron as well as from architectural fragments found in recent excavations (see photo on p. 117).

To the south of the Temple Mount, large portions of the formal staircase that led up to the Huldah Gates have been discovered. The foundations of the gates are still visible in the southern wall of the Haram enclosure (the so-called double and triple gates). Although they are now closed, the underground passages that lead up to the top of the mount inside the wall are still preserved. In excavations along the southern portion of the western enclosure wall, portions of the north-south street, a city drain, and most interestingly, the piers that supported a platform and staircase that led south, from a gate in the southern section of the western wall of the Temple Mount into the Central Valley, have been found. A large, dressed stone has also been found, inscribed in Hebrew with the words "For the place of the trumpet blowing." Evidently, this stone had fallen from its position on the southwest pinnacle of the Temple Mount, where it had marked the spot where the priest stood to blow the trumpet to announce to the citizens of Jerusalem the beginning of the Sabbath, New Moon, New Year, and other special days.

It took Herod almost 10 years to complete the major construction on the Temple Mount, but crews were still working on the project long after Herod's death in 4 B.C., during Jesus' lifetime (John 2:20; ca. A.D. 28), and even as late as A.D. 64 — only six years before it was destroyed by the Romans in A.D. 70.

To the northwest of the temple Herod rebuilt the fortress that had

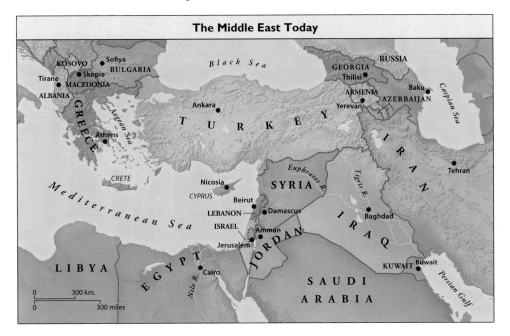

The Middle East Today

stood there and named it the Antonia, after his friend Mark Antony. This fortress, situated on a rocky scarp, towered over the temple area and housed a garrison whose duty it was to monitor and control the crowds that gathered in the temple precincts. It is traditionally assumed that it was here that Jesus stood before Pilate on the day of His crucifixion, but it is more likely that Pilate was staying at the palace of Herod Antipas, and that that was where Jesus was interrogated, humiliated, and condemned. What is certain is that the apostle Paul was taken to the Antonia Fortress ("the barracks") after being rescued from an angry mob by Roman soldiers (Acts 21:34).

(For the history of Jerusalem from the time of the New Testament until the present, see pp. 937–54.)

Ruins of library at Ephesus.

Writing, Books, and the Bible

Until about the 18th century, knowledge of the past was limited. Where facts were missing, the imagination took over and filled the gaps.

Thus, in 1572 the Dutch artist Maerten van Heemskerck made a drawing of the ancient city of Babylon. It looked like a European city of his day, with a few exotic elements thrown in, such as the spiral steeple on the tower and the citizens' lack of clothing. And he was not alone. Rembrandt's paintings of biblical scenes show oddly Dutch interiors, while the great Italian painters of the Renaissance often use the Italian countryside as the backdrop for biblical paintings.

The Industrial Revolution brought with it the need to move large quantities of soil for the building of factory foundations, railways, and so forth. In the process, artifacts came to light that were clearly ancient, and people began to think about the past in more concrete terms.

A 16th-century view of the past: Van Heemskerck's city of Babylon.

Egypt

In 1798, Napoleon staged an expedition to Egypt. He took with him a number of scholars to survey the antiquities of Egypt and to bring some of them to France. (The most visible reminder of this is the great obelisk on the Place de la Concorde in Paris, erected by Rameses II in 1250 B.C. in Luxor and moved to Paris in 1831.) The scholars with Napoleon saw the pyramids, the Great Sphinx, and the many temples and statues that were partially buried in the sand. They also saw the hieroglyphics that covered many of these monuments and realized that they were a written language, but no one had any idea what they meant. Thus these monuments were mute witnesses to ancient grandeur—and Egyptian history remained by and large a closed book.

A relatively modest discovery provided the clue. In Rosetta, a town at the western edge of the Nile Delta, a piece of black granite was found, about 4 x 2½ feet—somewhat smaller than a fully opened newspaper—that contained three inscriptions, one above the other. The bottom one was Greek, which was known and could be translated, but the top one was in Egyptian hieroglyphics and the middle one in Demotic, a simplified Egyptian script. The Greek text indicated that the stone contained a decree of Ptolemy V and was made around 200 B.C.

Assuming that all three languages on the Rosetta Stone meant the same thing, one of the problems was that no one knew whether the hieroglyphs were ideographic (each sign representing an idea) or phonetic (each sign representing a sound). The breakthrough came with the realization that

Until the hieroglyphics of Egypt were deciphered, monuments such as this obelisk of Rameses II at Luxor were mute.

the name of Ptolemy V in the hieroglyphic text was surrounded by a cartouche, or frame (see photo below). In 1822, the French scholar Jean-François Champollion finally succeeded in deciphering the hieroglyphic inscriptions (it turned out that the hieroglyphics were partly ideographic, partly phonetic). His achievement was due in part to the fact that he had also studied Coptic, a language derived from Egyptian that is still in use today as the liturgical language of the Coptic church.

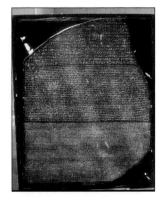

The Rosetta Stone contained Greek, Demotic, and Egyptian Hieroglyphic inscriptions which became the key to deciphering Egyptian Hieroglyphs.

Mesopotamia

Interest in the antiquities of Mesopotamia, where the Sumerian, Assyrian, and Babylonian empires had flourished, began at about the same time. In 1811, Claude James Rich, an agent of the British East India Company who lived in Baghdad, 50 miles northeast of the site of ancient Babylon, became curious after seeing some inscribed bricks brought in by a fellow agent. Rich visited the site of Babylon. He stayed for 10 days, during which he located and charted the vast collection of mounds that had once been Babylon. With the help of inhabitants of the region he dug into the mounds and found a few tablets, which he carried back to Baghdad.

In 1820 he visited Mosul and spent four months sketching a plan of the mounds just across the river, which he suspected were the ruins of Nineveh. Here also he collected tablets and inscriptions that neither he nor anyone else could read.

The key to deciphering the Babylonian language turned out to be, as had been the case with Egyptian hieroglyphs, the discovery of an inscription in three languages. This time it was a massive inscription, chiseled some 400 feet above the ground into a vertical rock wall, 200 miles northeast of Babylon. The inscription had been made by order of King Darius Hyspastes of Persia in 516 B.C. (This was the same Darius under whom the temple in Jerusalem was rebuilt, as told in Ezra, and the Behistun inscription was made in the same year the temple was completed.) The inscription gave a long account, in Persian, Elamite, and Babylonian, of the conquests of Darius.

Sir Henry Rawlinson, the British consul-general in Baghdad, had some knowledge of Persian. With amazing perseverance he began copying the inscriptions in 1835. It involved a great deal of physical risk, but he continued his self-appointed

A cartouche with the name of Rameses II, who some believe to have been the Pharaoh of the Exodus.

Most cuneiform tablets contain only text. This tablet shows text above an Assyrian map and dates perhaps to the 9th century B.C.

task off and on until, in 1847, he finished his copying, with the help of ladders from below and swings from above—and especially the assistance of "a wild Kurdish boy," whose name remains unknown. His efforts paid off: soon Rawlinson was able to decipher the Babylonian language.

Ancient Libraries

The key to the ancient Babylonian language had been found just in time for the vast treasures of ancient Babylonian literature that were discovered during that period. In 1842, Paul Emil Botta, the French consul at Mosul, began digging in the mounds near Mosul that had intrigued Rich so much, and in the following 10 years he laid bare the magnificent palace of Sargon at Khorsabad.

Sir Austen Henry Layard, an Englishman who is called the "father of Assyriology," discovered in 1845–51, at Nineveh and Calah, ruins of the palaces of five Assyrian kings who are named in the Bible, and the great library of Ashur-banipal, which is estimated to have contained 100,000 volumes.

Thus it turned out that, contrary to what had been thought before, the ancient Near East was highly literate. Large libraries had been brought together that might contain royal archives, dictionaries, and

Niches used to hold scrolls found in the subterranean remains of perhaps the world's greatest ancient library established at Alexandria, Egypt.

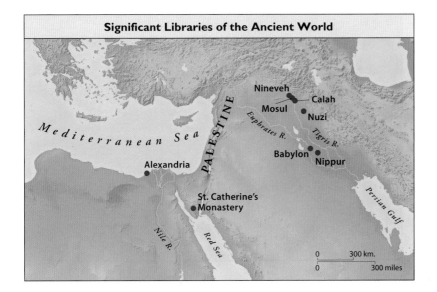

Significant Libraries of the Ancient World

other reference works, as well as books on law, religion, science, and literature.

Another one of the great collections of tablets that has been found is the library of Sargon (722–705 B.C.), which consists of 25,000 tablets, and the royal library of Ashurbanipal (662–626 B.C.), with 20,000 tablets. (Both of these libraries are now in the British Museum.) Other major finds were made at Nuzi (20,000 tablets from the 2nd millennium B.C.), at Nippur, 50 miles southeast of Babylon (some 50,000 tablets from the 4th and 5th centuries B.C.), and elsewhere.

Perhaps the greatest library of all antiquity was that of Alexandria, Egypt. Alexandria and its library were founded by Alexander the Great a little before 300 B.C. The library collected books dealing with all areas of learning. It truly became a repository for all the knowledge of the ancient world. The books in the library were not clay tablets, but scrolls of papyrus or parchment.

The Septuagint (the Greek translation of the Old Testament) was made in Alexandria in the middle of the 3rd century B.C., probably in this library.

Sadly, the magnificent collection of books was destroyed when the Arabs, under Caliph Omar, conquered Egypt in 642 A.D. According to legend, Omar's rationale for burning the library was quite simple: if the books agreed with the Koran, they were superfluous; if they disagreed, they were evil. (It may well be, however, that after three centuries of Christian control of Alexandria, not much was left of the collection, given the antagonism toward pagan learning in the early centuries of the church.)

Monasteries were also places where books were collected and preserved. Manuscripts of the Bible and other writings were copied in monasteries during the Middle Ages.

Hittite pictographs. Examples of the earliest writings reveal scribes wrote using pictures to communicate.

We will never know how many priceless manuscripts were lost or destroyed over the years—even in monasteries. One of the two earliest, most valuable, and most complete manuscripts of the Bible was discovered by accident in St. Catherine's Monastery, in the shadow of Mount Sinai (hence the name of the manuscript, Codex Sinaiticus; see pp. 994–95). It was waiting, with other manuscripts, to be used for fuel in a fireplace.

The Development of Writing

It was not until some of the major ancient languages had been deciphered that it became possible to piece together when and how writing developed. This was not merely an academic issue. In the 19th century the view held (based on "scientific evidence") that writing did not develop until after the

A portion of a relief of Sennacherib's attack on Lachish (2 Chronicles 32). Without an understanding of the cuneiform inscriptions, it would have been virtually impossible to identify this relief as representing a biblical event. (See also on p. 283.)

time of Moses, so that the first five books of the Bible could not possibly have been written by Moses and that, in fact, the early portions of Scripture were essentially frauds.

But careful study of the evidence has shown that writing developed around 3150 B.C. — more than a millennium before Abraham and more than a millennium and a half before Moses!

Writing

The invention of writing was without question one of the most significant inventions in human history. It was the watershed between what we call prehistory and history — between the past we can know only from physical remains (monuments, implements, human remains, etc.) and the past we can also know to some extent through written texts. Without written texts to help us reconstruct the past, we are limited to conjecture and guesswork. (An indication of this is the frequency with which objects from preliterate societies are identified as "religious objects" — which often means that we don't have a clue as to their significance.)

Writing was invented to meet the practical needs of an increasingly complex society. As trade grew, it became obvious that it was unsatisfactory to keep track of shipments, goods, and payments by means of counting-stones with symbols for objects or animals scratched in them. Thus, around 3100 B.C. the Sumerians in Mesopotamia came up with a system of hundreds of somewhat simplified pictograms (pictures that represent specific things) as well as signs for measures and numbers. These were pressed into clay tablets, which made it possible to maintain more or less permanent records.

Once writing was in use, the relatively complex symbols became increasingly simplified (streamlining is not a modern invention) and ultimately became simple, abstract, and geometric forms. But the symbols still were cumbersome in that each word or each syllable required a separate symbol. (In English we use a few symbols for whole words — for example, @, #, $, %, &.)

The idea that it was possible to capture language by means of writing soon traveled along the trade routes to the east and west. The Elamites

Phoenician script. Alphabetic writing derived from the Phoenician alphabet.

Hieroglyphics were an integral part of Egyptian art. These scenes show the soul of the deceased hovering over the body (top); the mummy being prepared (middle); the funeral procession (bottom).

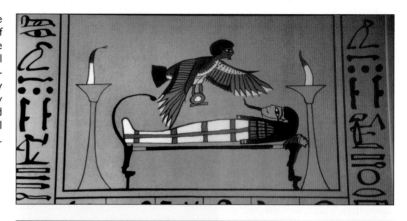

to the east adopted the new writing, and from there it traveled to India and then to China.

When the Egyptians learned of the art of writing, they — unlike the Assyrians and Babylonians, who adapted the earliest writing symbols — created their own symbols, the hieroglyphics.

The Alphabet

Next to the invention of writing itself, the most important development was the invention of *phonetic* symbols — the alphabet. No longer did each word or syllable require a separate symbol. *Any* word now could be expressed with somewhere between 20 and 30 symbols. The invention of alphabetic writing is usually credited to the Phoenicians, who lived north of Canaan, although we do not in fact know exactly where and when the oldest alphabet came into existence. But it was sometime around 1500 B.C. What is known is that all later alphabets were either derived from the Phoenician alphabet or created under the influence of its derivatives.

The Phoenicians initially had no symbols for vowels (a, e, i, o, u), only for consonants. The Hebrew alphabet, which, like all alphabets, derives from the Phoenician, also only has signs for consonants. Later, when Hebrew ceased to be a living language, there was a need for vowels to be added to make sure that the text was read correctly. This was done in the period A.D. 500–1000 by Jewish scholars known as the Masoretes, who indicated vowels by means of small lines and dots placed in, under, and above the consonants. (Today Hebrew, once again a living language, is again written without vowels.)

In the beginning God created

Hebrew text without vowel points

בראשית ברא אלהים

Hebrew text with vowel points

בְּרֵאשִׁית בָּרָא אֱלֹהִים

The Hebrew text of the first words of Genesis, both without vowels and with the vowel "pointings" that were added during the Middle Ages.

(The downside of the alphabet is that any written text can only be understood by those who speak the specific language. The use of symbols for words or ideas makes it possible for a language such as Chinese to be read and understood by people who speak different dialects and cannot understand one another when they speak.)

The third major development, after writing and the alphabet, was the invention of printing, which revolutionized the world.

Writing, Books, and the Bible

It is difficult for us, inundated as we are with written words, to imagine what it must have been like to encounter writing for the first time. A person's words could travel without that person—or even anyone who had heard him or her speak—being present. Magic indeed! It is not surprising that in mythology, writing is viewed as a gift from the gods. At first, writing was available only to an elite group in which priests figured prominently, since writing was a means of guarding and transmitting sacred

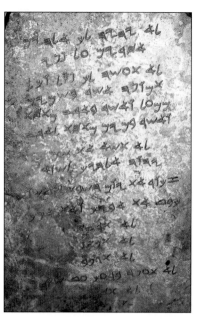

The Ten Commandments in Hebrew script. Alphabetic writing was used by the Lord to record the Laws given to Moses on Mt. Sinai.

knowledge. (Writing was also a way to preserve the knowledge of a ruler's exploits and through selectivity a highly effective means of propaganda, since only victories were memorialized, while defeats were ignored or somehow cast in a positive light.)

There are numerous references in the Bible to the writing of books and to the places where they were deposited. As early as Exodus 17:14, after Israel's defeat of Amalek, Moses was told, "Write this on a scroll as something to be remembered." There is no indication where the scroll was deposited, but it is noteworthy that the next statement is that "Moses built an altar" (this took place before the building of the Tabernacle).

Similarly, soon after he received the Ten Commandments, "Moses . . . wrote down everything the LORD had said," and again, his next act was the building of an altar (Exodus 24:4).

From the very beginning, the Israelites were a people of the Book. The words of God and the narrative of His actions on behalf of His people are preserved *and read* to the people: "[Moses] took the Book of the Covenant and read it to the people" (Exodus 24:7).

Qumran Cave 4. Dead Sea Scrolls were discovered in the Caves near Qumran.

The priests and Levites were the acknowledged keepers of these sacred volumes. At the end of the Ten Commandments we read, "After Moses finished writing in a book the words of this law from beginning to end, he gave this command to the Levites who carried the ark of the covenant of the LORD: 'Take this Book of the Law and place it beside the ark of the covenant of the LORD your God'" (Deuteronomy 31:24–26).

In Deuteronomy we also read that when in the future Israel gets a king, and the king "takes the throne of his kingdom, he is

Three columns of the Isaiah Scroll. The book of Isaiah was among the ancient scrolls discovered near Qumran.

to write for himself on a scroll a copy of this law, *taken from that of the priests, who are Levites.* It is to be with him, and he is to read it all the days of his life so that he may learn to revere the LORD his God and follow carefully all the words of this law and these decrees" (Deuteronomy 17:18).

When Israel got its first king, Saul, "Samuel explained to the people the regulations of the kingship. He wrote them down on a scroll and deposited it before the LORD" (1 Samuel 10:25). This writing down and depositing it in the tabernacle was not simply a matter of keeping record but rather a solemn ceremony that put Saul under an obligation to God and the people. The scroll would serve as a witness against him before God if he failed to fulfill his royal office.

An Egyptian scribe. In ancient cultures, scribes (who specialized in reading and writing) were held in high esteem.

The first books of the Bible are variously referred to as the Book of the Covenant or the Book of the Law. During a period when Judah, the southern kingdom, ignored the Lord, the Book of the Law was actually lost for a period of time and then rediscovered by Hilkiah in the temple (2 Kings 18:18ff.; 23:2, 21; 2 Chronicles 34:14–15). And Jehoshaphat (872–848 B.C.) sent Levites out to teach in Judah: "They taught throughout Judah, taking with them the Book of the

The caves at Qumran where the Dead sea Scrolls were found. The jar and the scroll pictured here are replicas. The actual scrolls had to be unrolled with special methods, and most ended up in fragments that had to be pieced together.

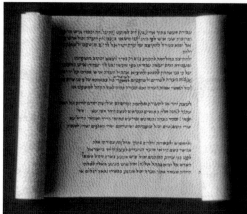

Law of the LORD; they went around to all the towns of Judah and taught the people" (2 Chronicles 17:9).

Thus, the writings commanded by God were in some way identified with the ark of the covenant, the tabernacle, the priests, and the Levites. This would seem to imply that there was a library in the temple in Jerusalem, but there is no direct statement in the Bible to support this. However, it is clear that there were collections of books in Israel. In addition to the Book of the Law there are references to other books: the Book of the Wars of the Lord (Numbers 21:14), the Book of Jasher (Joshua 10:12–13), the Book of Nathan the Prophet and the Book of Gad the Seer (1 Chronicles 29:29), and the Chronicles of the Seers (2 Chronicles 33:19). These books, now all lost, must have been in existence and accessible, since they are referred to in the same way we would use "For further information, see. . . ."

In addition to these sources mentioned directly, there must have been collections of treaties, genealogies, business transactions, and the like. The first 11 chapters of 1 Chronicles, for example, required an extensive collection of genealogical records. Ecclesiastes 12:12 also indirectly supports the idea of collections of books: "Of making many books there is no end."

The oldest library that has been preserved is the library at Qumran, about a mile west of the northwest corner of the Dead Sea, which contained the famous Dead Sea Scrolls. This collection of scrolls—some complete, some only fragmentary—consisted of several hundred manuscripts, about 100 of them biblical manuscripts. They were discovered by accident by a Bedouin in 1947. The library was put there by a Jewish sect with a monastery in the vicinity. The manuscripts date from the last century B.C. and the first century A.D. One of the manuscripts contained the book of Isaiah. It was about 1000 years older than the oldest copy that was known before 1947, and the two turned out to be virtually identical!

How We Got the Bible

For more information on how we got the Bible and how it was transmitted over the centuries, see pages 987–1007.

Arabah Desert, south of the Dead Sea.

The Old Testament

IN THE BEGINNING

Genesis 1 – 11

In the beginning God created the heavens and the earth." In quiet grandeur and simplicity it is stated, without argument, without explanation.

The first 11 chapters of Genesis are part of a much larger work: the Pentateuch—the first five books of the Bible, which according to tradition were written by Moses. He wrote these books *for the people of Israel* on their way to Canaan, the Promised Land.

Genesis 1 – 11 sets the stage and holds the key to our understanding of the entire Bible, both Old and New Testaments. Within these few chapters, God reveals Himself to us—He is the Creator, our loving Father, the provider, and a just judge. God creates man in His own image, with a free will. Satan, the great deceiver, introduces sin into God's perfect creation. God cannot tolerate sin. Because God is a just judge, there is consequence for sin. God has a plan to redeem man to Himself and put an end to Satan's power forever.

God's redemptive plan, which is introduced in Genesis 1 – 11, provides for us the backdrop of why God chose Noah and why He chooses Abraham. This is also why He will make Abraham a blessing to the world—God's plan for the redemption of the world runs through Abraham and through the nation of Israel and leads us ultimately to Jesus Christ, our Savior.

Genesis 1 – 11

**Creation; Adam and Eve
Cain and Abel; Noah and the Flood
Tower of Babel**

God saw all that he had made, and it was very good. —GENESIS 1:31

"I have set my rainbow in the clouds, and it will be the sign of the covenant between me and the earth. . . . Never again will the waters become a flood to destroy all life." —GENESIS 9:13–15

Who Wrote Genesis?

Ancient Hebrew and Christian traditions say that Moses, guided by God, composed Genesis from ancient documents that were already in existence in his day. The book of Genesis ends about 300 years before Moses. Moses could have received this information only by direct revelation from God, or through such historical records as had been handed down from his forefathers.

How Genesis Is Organized

The book begins with the "Creation Hymn," followed by 10 "accounts" (KJV, generations), which constitute the framework of Genesis. It seems that they were incorporated bodily by Moses, with such additions and explanations as he may have been guided by God to make. These 11 documents are as follows:

1. Creation Hymn (1:1–2:3).
2. The account of "the heavens and the earth when they were created" (2:4–4:26).
3. The account of Adam's line (5:1–6:8).
4. The account of Noah (6:9–9:28).
5. The account of "Shem, Ham and Japheth, Noah's sons" (10:1–11:9).
6. The account of Shem (11:10–26).
7. The account of Terah (11:27–25:11).
8. The account of "Abraham's son Ishmael, whom Sarah's maidservant, Hagar the Egyptian, bore to Abraham" (25:12–18).
9. The account of "Abraham's son Isaac" (25:19–35:29).
10. The account of "Esau (that is, Edom)" (36:1–43).
11. The account of Jacob (37:2–50:26).

These 11 documents form the book of Genesis.

- The first six accounts cover the period from creation until about 2000 B.C. (Genesis 1–11).
- The last five accounts cover the life of Abraham and the three generations after him, from about 2000 B.C. until about 1800 B.C.

The book begins with the creation and the first humans in the Garden of Eden. It ends with Abraham's descendants in Egypt.

Between the end of Genesis and the beginning of the next book, Exodus, is a gap of about 400 years.

1. The "Creation Hymn," Genesis 1:1 to 2:3

A poetic description, in measured, majestic movement, of the successive steps of creation, cast in the mold of the oft-recurring biblical number seven. In all literature, scientific or otherwise, there is no more sublime account of the origin of things.

Who wrote the "Creation Hymn"? Used by Moses, but written, no doubt, long before. Writing was in common use long before the days of Moses. Furthermore, some of God's "commands, decrees, and laws" were in existence in the days of Abraham, 600 years before Moses (Genesis 26:5).

How did the writer know what happened before man appeared? No doubt God revealed the remote past, as later the distant future was made known to the prophets.

Who knows, perhaps God Himself may have taught this hymn to Adam? And it may have been recited by word of mouth, around the family circle, or sung as a ritual in primitive worship (hymns constituted a large part of the very earliest forms of literature), generation after generation, until writing was invented; God Himself then guarded its transmission until finally it found its intended place as the opening statement in the divine Book of the Ages.

Who Made God?

Every child asks this question—and no one can answer it. There are some things beyond us. We cannot conceive of the beginning of time, nor the end of time, nor the boundaries of space. The world has been in existence always, or it was made out of nothing—one or the other. Yet we can conceive of neither.

This we do know: the highest of all things within reach of our thinking is personality, mind, intelligence. Where did it come from? Could the inanimate create intelligence? In faith we accept, as the ultimate in our thinking, a power higher than ourselves—God—in hope that someday, in the beyond, we shall understand the mysteries of existence.

> *So God created man in his own image, in the image of God he created him; male and female he created them. God blessed them and said to them, "Be fruitful and increase in number; fill the earth and subdue it."*
> —Genesis 1:27–28

If the Bible is God's Word, as we believe it is, and if God knew from the beginning that He was going to use the Bible as a main instrument in the redemption of humanity, why should it be difficult to believe that God Himself gave the germ and nucleus of that Word?

Gen. 1:1 | THE CREATION OF THE UNIVERSE

"In the beginning" God created the universe. What follows, in the "seven days," is a description of the forming of substance already created in preparation for the creation of Adam.

Whether the seven days were days of 24 hours, or long, successive periods, we do not know. The word "day" has variable meanings. In 1:5 it is used as a term for light. In 1:8 and 1:13 it seems to mean a day of 24 hours. In 1:14 and 1:16 it seems to refer to a 12-hour day. In 2:4 it seems to cover the whole period of creation. In passages such as Joel 3:18, Acts 2:20, and John 16:23, "that day" seems to mean the whole Christian era. In passages such as 2 Timothy 1:12 the expression seems to refer to the era beyond the Lord's Second Coming. And in Psalm 90:4 and 2 Peter 3:8, "With the Lord a day is like a thousand years, and a thousand years are like one day."

Note that the six days form three pairs (days 1 and 4; 2 and 5; 3 and 6). In the first of each pair the realm is created that is later populated by the objects or beings that are created in the second.

Day 1:	Light and dark	Day 4:	Lights of day and night
Day 2:	Sea and sky	Day 5:	Creatures of water and air
Day 3:	Fertile earth	Day 6:	Creatures of the land; land animals; humans' provision of food

THE STRUCTURE OF THE ACCOUNT OF EACH OF THE SIX DAYS	
in Genesis 1:2–2:3	
1. Announcement	"and God said"
2. Command	"let there be," "let [them] be gathered," etc.
3. Report	"and it was so"
	—a descriptive phrase telling what God did
	—a word of naming or blessing
4. Evaluation	"it was good"
5. Temporal statement	"there was evening, and there was morning—the ___ day"

First Day: Light, 1:2–5

The heavens and the earth were created by God in the beginning—sometime in the dateless past. All was dark, empty, and formless until God said, "Let there be light," and there was light. We see that God's creative power is manifested by simply speaking. His first creative word called forth light in the midst of darkness.

In John 1:1–2 we learn that the "Word" (Jesus) was in the beginning, and that the "Word" was with God and was God. John further tells us that "through him [the Word] all things were made; without him nothing was made that has been made" (1:3).

God did not just make a physical universe: "God saw all that he had made, *and it was very good*" (Genesis 1:31). Whatever God makes is very good indeed, because the Word through which He created all things is the very essence of goodness, beauty, and light: "In him [Jesus] was life, and that life was the light of men. The light shines in the darkness" (John 1:4), now as it did at the very beginning of creation.

Second Day: The Expanse, 1:6–8

The expanse (KJV, firmament), called "sky," is the atmosphere, or layer of air between the water-covered earth and the clouds above, made possible by the cooling of the earth's waters.

Third Day: Land and Vegetation, 1:9–13

Up to this point, the earth's surface seems to have been entirely covered with water. God commanded the water to gather in one place that He called "seas." We envision that the earth's crust, as it became cooler and thicker, began to buckle, and islands and continents began to appear. There was as yet no rain, but dense mists watered the newly formed land, which was still warm by its own heat. A tropical climate was everywhere, and vegetation must have grown rapidly and in gigantic proportions.

Fourth Day: Sun, Moon, and Stars, 1:14–19

On the fourth day, God created the sun, moon, and stars. It is likely that seasons came when the earth's surface ceased to receive heat primarily from within and became dependent on the sun's heat.

In v. 16 we learn that the "greater light" rules the day and the "lesser light" rules the night. These sources of light have three primary functions (vv. 17–18): they give light to the earth, they govern the day and night, and they separate light from darkness.

These passages are beautiful examples of how God has manifested His image, His divine characteristics, in all of His creation.

Fifth Day: Sea Animals and Birds, 1:20–25

By God's blessing and with His command, "be fruitful and increase in number," the sea creatures and birds filled the waters and increased on the earth.

Note the progression: inanimate things on the first and second days, plant life on the third day, and animal life on the fifth day.

Sixth Day: Land Animals and Man, 1:24–31

The earth was at last ready for animals and, ultimately, man. God reveals that each living creature on the land is created "according to their kind."

Tarawtula Nebula. "The heavens declare the glory of God." (Psalm 19:1)

This refutes the notion that all species of animals evolved from a single, common, primeval organism. It supports the scientific evidence that living creatures have adapted over time to their environment, while there is no convincing evidence that one species of animal has evolved into another.

God created Adam and Eve in His own image. God's divine blessing and benediction for male and female together was to flourish and multiply so as to fill the earth and exercise rulership (stewardship) over all creation. God's universal reign is reflected in the rulership that He commissions humanity to carry out over all earthly creation. In a sense, God has created the earth as man's training camp, where He is preparing us for our eternal destiny where we will rule and reign with Christ over all the universe (2 Timothy 2:12; Revelation 3:21).

God saw everything that He had made, and it was "good" (1:4, 10, 12, 18, 21, 25, 31). But soon the picture darkened. God must have known beforehand that it would, and He must have regarded his whole work of the creation of humanity as but a step toward the glorious world that will yet emerge from it, as is told in the closing chapters of the book of Revelation.

It is interesting to note that God declared all that he had made on the sixth day "*very* good" perhaps to stress the relative significance of this day in comparison to the prior days.

What Is the "Image of God"?

Passages such as Genesis 9:6 and James 3:9 show that the image of God in humans was not lost at the time of the Fall and that even those who are not part of the people of God possess it. The phrase "image of God" is not used frequently in Scripture, and its exact meaning is difficult to determine.

- Some have suggested that it may refer to some spiritual, mental, and/or psychological quality in humans, such as the ability to think, to feel emotions, or to choose (= free will).
- Others stress the context of Genesis 1:26–27, where the emphasis is on humans "ruling" over God's creation. From the context it is possible to suggest that as God created, so those who are bestowed with His image are also to be "creators"; for example, the first humans were commanded to name the animals and to "be fruitful and multiply."
- Finally, some stress the "relational" quality of the Triune Godhead that is hinted at in the phrases "let *us*" and "*our* image." They suggest that just as there are relationships within the Godhead, so too humans have the ability to enter into relationship with God and with other humans, and that this is what the image is. (However, this characteristic of the Godhead is not fully revealed until much later—e.g., John 1:1–5.)

It may be that a correct understanding of the concept actually includes aspects of more than one of the above interpretations. A major point to be remembered is that we, as humans created in God's image, are related to God in a special way that is not shared by other animal life. And as humans we need to remember that we *all* are bearers of that image—which, of course, should influence how we treat each other.

Seventh Day: God Rested, 2:1–3

God did not rest in an absolute sense (John 5:17), but from this particular creative work. This was the basis of the Sabbath (Exodus 20:11). The "Sabbath rest" is also an image of heaven (Hebrews 4:4, 9).

ARCHAEOLOGICAL NOTE: Babylonian Creation Stories. Various epics of creation have been found in the ruins of Babylon, Nineveh, Nippur, and Ashur which are strikingly similar to the "Creation Hymn" of Genesis. These epics were written on clay tablets from before the time of Abraham.

These Babylonian and Assyrian (as well as the Egyptian) creation stories are all grossly polytheistic. They usually argue for the preeminence of one of the gods and often reflect conflict or war among the gods. The creation account in Genesis stands in stark contrast to these stories by its simplicity and clarity: "In the beginning God created...."

There are points of similarity between the Babylonian and Assyrian creation stories and the Genesis account—for example, the sequence of the creative acts: expanse (firmament), dry land, celestial lights, humans. But the similarities do not prove dependence, although the simplicity of the Genesis account could argue for the Babylonian and Assyrian stories' being corrupted traditions based on the simple, divine original.

2. The Account of the Heavens and Earth, Genesis 2:4 to 4:26

This is sometimes called the "second creation story." It starts with a reference to the desolate condition of the earth (2:5–6), which corresponds to the early part of the third day in the first account (1:9–10), and then gives some details omitted from the first account. From there it proceeds with the story of the Fall. It is supplemental to, not in contradiction with, the first account.

Who was the original author of this document? It carries the story down to the sixth generation of Cain's descendants (4:17–22) and closes while Adam was still alive. (He lived to the eighth generation of Seth's descendants, 5:4–25.) So everything in this account happened in Adam's lifetime. If writing was not invented while Adam was yet alive, may it not be that Adam told these things over and over in his family circle, so that at least their substance took a sort of fixed form until writing was invented?

> The man said, "This is now bone of my bones and flesh of my flesh; she shall be called 'woman,' for she was taken out of man." For this reason a man will leave his father and mother and be united to his wife and they will become one flesh."
> —Genesis 2:23–24

Gen. 2:4–17 | THE GARDEN OF EDEN

In chapter 1 the Creator is called "God" (Elohim), the "generic" name of the Supreme Being. Here it is "the LORD God" (Yahweh Elohim), His personal name. It is the first step in God's revelation of Himself.

No rain, but "streams" (vv. 5–6). The translation "mist" (KJV, NASB) would seem preferable. It would mean that for a while, the earth was watered by heavy fogs, because the earth's surface was so warm, and consequent vapors so dense, that cooling raindrops on the far outer fringes of the clouds would turn to vapor again before they reached the earth.

The tree of life (v. 9; 3:23) indicates that immortality is dependent on something outside ourselves. This tree will again be accessible to those who belong to Christ at the end (Revelation 2:7; 22:2, 14).

The tree of the knowledge of good and evil" (vv. 9, 17) was "good for food," "pleasing to the eye," and "desirable for gaining wisdom" (3:6). Whatever the exact nature of this tree—literal, figurative, or symbolic—the essence of Adam and Eve's sin was this: they wanted to transfer control of their lives from God to themselves. God had, in substance, told them they could do anything they wanted to, *except* for that one thing. As long as they were in right relationship with God—in other words, as long as they recognized God as their creator and master—they experienced life as God had intended it to be, and they were truly the crown of God's creation. They were completely satisfied with this life until Satan, in the form of a serpent, deceived them into thinking that if they were like God and knew what He knows, life would be even better. Once this seed of deception had been planted, they became dissatisfied. They wanted to "be like God." They wanted to be their own master and sole master of God's creation. Is that not the essence of human sin? From the beginning, God designed humans to live forever; the one condition was obedience to God. Adam and Eve allowed themselves to be deceived by the enemy and in turn disobeyed God. Then began the long, slow process of redemption, by a Savior through whom we may regain our lost estate.

Gen. 2:18–25 | THE CREATION OF WOMAN

It was already stated in 1:27 that man was created "male and female." Here the way in which woman was created is more fully told. And here, at the start of the human race, is also found the divine origin and sanctity of marriage: one man, one woman, one flesh (v. 24).

Scripture represents marriage as an earthly counterpart to the relationship between Christ and the church (Ephesians 5:25–32; Revelation 19:7; 21:2, 9). The church is called the "bride" of Christ. Adam's bride was made from his side, while he was asleep (vv. 21–22). This may be a primeval picture of the church, the bride of Christ, who receives its life from Him.

Naked but without shame (v. 25). It may be that they were "clothed" in the ethereal light of God, as Jesus was when He was transfigured

The Location of the Garden of Eden

The Garden of Eden was on the Euphrates and Tigris rivers, at their junction with the Pishon and Gihon (2:10–14). The Pishon and Gihon have not been identified. The Euphrates and Tigris originate in the Caucasus mountain region of southwest Asia, flow southeastward, and empty into the Persian Gulf (see map). Two possible locations have been suggested, one near the headwaters of the Tigris and Euphrates, the other near the mouth of the Euphrates in ancient Babylonia (see map on p. 92).

(Mark 9:3), and that that light vanished when sin entered—but it will one day again clothe the redeemed (Revelation 3:4; 21:23). Of all God's creatures, as far as we know, humanity alone wears clothing, a badge of our sinful nature and a symbol of our need for God's redemptive covering.

Gen. 3 | THE FALL OF MAN

It was effected through the subtlety of the serpent. The serpent is represented as speaking itself. But later Scripture indicates that it was Satan speaking through the serpent (2 Corinthians 11:3, 14; Revelation 12:9; 20:2). He managed to get Adam and Eve to disobey their Creator. The dreadful work was done. And the pall of sin and pain and death fell on a world that God had made beautiful and had pronounced good.

Why Did God Make Humans So That They Could Sin?

Is there any other way He could have made them? Could there be a moral creature without the power to choose? Freedom is God's gift to humanity: freedom to think, freedom of conscience—even freedom to disobey God.

In a train wreck, the engineer, who could have saved his life by jumping, stuck to his post and thereby saved the passengers, but lost his own life. They erected a monument, not to the train—it did only what its machinery forced it to do—but to the engineer, who, of his own volition, chose to give his life to save the passengers.

What virtue is there in obeying God if in our nature there is no inclination to do otherwise? But if, of our own choice, and against the steady urge of our nature, we obey God, we find our true humanity.

Artistic motif of the Garden of Eden in the Church of Annunciation at Nazareth. "The Fall" refers to Adam and Eve's mutiny against their Creator recorded in Genesis 3.

But Did Not God Foreknow That Man Would Sin?

Yes—and He foreknew the fearful consequences. He also foreknew the ultimate outcome. We suffer, and we wonder why God has made such a world. But one day, after all has come to its final destination, our suffering will be over, and our questions will cease, and with the redeemed of all ages we will join in never-ending hallelujahs of praise to God for creating us as He did, and for leading us on to life, joy, and glory in the endless ages of eternity (Revelation 19:1–8).

The Effect of Sin on Nature

Here, in the opening pages of the Bible, we have a primeval explanation of nature as it is today: on a mundane level, a common hatred of snakes (3:14–15); pain in childbirth (v. 15); and the earth's spontaneous production of useless weeds, while food-bearing vegetation has to be cultivated (vv. 17–19). But there are also foreshadowings of Christ in the offspring of the woman (v. 15) and in sacrifice and atonement (4:4).

The offspring of the woman (v. 15). Here, immediately after the fall of man, is God's prophecy that His creation of human beings would yet prove to be successful, through the "offspring of the woman." This is the Bible's first hint of a coming redeemer. The use of "he" (v. 15) shows that one person is meant. There has been only one descendant of Eve who was born of woman without the involvement of a man. Here, right at the start of the Bible story, is this first foreshadowing of Christ. And as the Bible story unfolds, there are other hints, pictures, and plain

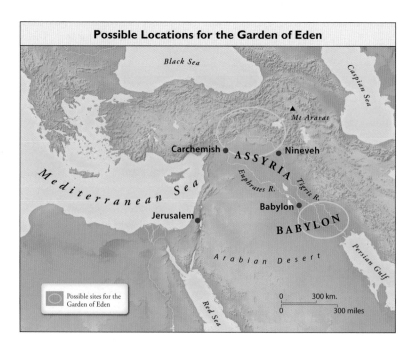

Possible Locations for the Garden of Eden

Black Sea

Caspian Sea

Mt Ararat

Carchemish • **ASSYRIA** • Nineveh

Mediterranean Sea

Euphrates R.

Tigris R.

Babylon •

BABYLON

Jerusalem •

Arabian Desert

Persian Gulf

Possible sites for the Garden of Eden

0   300 km.
0   300 miles

Red Sea

statements that become clearer and more abundant, so that, as we come to the end of the Old Testament, a fairly complete picture of Christ has been drawn. (See pp. 453–68, "The Messiah in the Old Testament.")

The mother of all the living (v. 20). The atonement of Christ is based on the unity of the race in Adam. One man's sin brought death. One man's death brought redemption (Romans 5:12–19).

Gen. 4 | CAIN AND ABEL

Assuming that Adam and Eve were created full-grown, Cain, when he killed Abel, must have been about 129 years old; for Seth was born soon after (v. 25), at which time Adam was 130 (5:3).

Abel's sacrifice (v. 4) was acceptable because his actions were righteous (1 John 3:12) and because it was offered in faith (Hebrews 11:4). It seems that God had instituted such sacrifice when sin came into the world. It is a sort of primeval picture of the atoning death of Christ.

Cain's wife (v. 17) must have been his sister, for Eve was the "mother of all living" (3:20). Adam had unnamed sons and daughters (5:4); tradition says that he had 33 sons and 27 daughters.

Who was there for Cain to be afraid of? (v. 14). In the 130 years from Adam's creation to Abel's murder, a good many generations had been born, and the total population could have increased to many thousands.

The mark on Cain (v. 15). Whatever it was, the people must have understood what it meant.

Cain's city (v. 17), somewhere east of Eden, was probably only a village of rude huts, with a wall for defense, to serve as a sort of headquarters for his outcast offspring.

In Cain's family, polygamy soon followed murder (v. 19). God had ordained in the beginning that one man and one woman live together in marriage (2:24). But man soon managed otherwise.

3. The Account of Adam, Genesis 5:1 to 6:8

This is the third document of the book of Genesis (see p. 83). It carries the story to the 500th year of Noah's life (5:32).

| Gen. 5 | **THE GENEALOGY FROM ADAM TO NOAH** |

The ages in this genealogy are extraordinarily long; for example: Adam, 930 years; Seth, 912 years; Methuselah, 969 years (the oldest person in the Bible); Noah, 950 years. The great age to which they lived is ordinarily explained on the theory that sin had only begun to have its malign influence on the human race.

When the numbers in this chapter are added together, there would appear to have been 1,656 years between the creation of Adam and the Flood. Some think that, because this genealogy and the one in chapter 11 each has 10 generations, they may be abbreviated (as is the case in the genealogy of Jesus in Matthew 1).

Enoch, vv. 21–24

Enoch was the best of the first generations. In a society of unspeakable wickedness, he "walked with God." Born 622 years after the creation of Adam, he was contemporary with Adam for 308 years. "God took him" when he was only 365 years old, 69 years before the birth of Noah.

The only other person to be taken up by God without having to die was Elijah (2 Kings 2). Enoch and Elijah may have been intended by God to be a kind of foreshadowing of the happy fate of the saints who will also be taken up alive when the Lord returns (1 Thessalonians 4:17).

Methuselah, vv. 25–27

At 969 years, he was the oldest of the 10 men listed in chapter 5. He was the son of Enoch. His life overlapped that of Adam by 243 years and that of Shem by 98 years, thus forming a connecting link between the Garden of Eden and the post-Flood world. He died the year of the Flood.

| Gen. 6:1–8 | **PRE-FLOOD WICKEDNESS** |

The "sons of God" (v. 2) are thought to have been either fallen angels, to which there may be reference in 2 Peter 2:4 and Jude 6, or leaders in Sethite families who intermarried with godless descendants of Cain. These abnormal marriages, whatever they were, filled the earth with corruption and violence.

Jesus regarded the Flood as a historical fact, and He likened the time of His coming again to the days of Noah (Matthew 24:37–39). What is going on in the world today makes us wonder if those days may be returning.

The 120 years in v. 3 may refer to the time left before the Flood or a reduced life span after the longevity of those mentioned in chapter 5.

4. The Account of Noah, Genesis 6:9 to 9:28

This is the fourth document in the book of Genesis (see p. 83). It contains the story of the Flood, as told, and perhaps recorded, by Noah, and handed on by Shem to Abraham.

Gen. 6:9–18 | NOAH AND THE ARK

The ark was about 450 feet long, 75 feet wide, 45 feet high. It had three decks, divided into compartments, with a row of windows around the top. It must have been very similar in size and proportion to ocean ships of today. With man being situated on the banks of a great river, boat building was one of his earliest accomplishments. Cuneiform tablets indicate that at the dawn of history the inhabitants of Babylonia engaged in transport by river. If this is true, then boat building and river traffic may have been familiar to Noah from childhood.

According to the dimensions given in Genesis, the ark was for at least five millennia the largest ship ever built—until 1858, when the 669-foot-long *Great Eastern* was built.

Gen. 6:19–7:5 | THE ANIMALS

In 6:19–21 and 7:2 it is explained that seven pairs of clean animals, but only one pair of each of the others, were to be taken into the ark. Some have calculated that there was room in the ark for 7000 species of animals.

Other Flood Traditions

Traditions of a catastrophic flood are found in many ancient cultures:

- Egyptian tradition: The gods at one time purified the earth by a great flood, from which only a few shepherds escaped.
- Greek tradition: Deucalion warned that the gods were going to bring a flood upon the earth because of its great wickedness; he built an ark, which came to rest on Mount Parnassus. A dove was sent out twice.
- Hindu tradition: Manu, warned, built a ship in which he alone escaped from a deluge that destroyed all creatures.
- Chinese tradition: Fa-He, founder of Chinese civilization, is represented as having escaped from a flood—sent because man had rebelled against heaven—with his wife, three sons, and three daughters.
- English tradition: The Druids had a legend that the world had been re-peopled by a righteous patriarch who had been saved in a strong ship from a flood sent to destroy man for his wickedness.
- Polynesian tradition: Stories of a Flood from which eight escaped.
- Mexican tradition: One man and his wife and children were saved in a ship from a flood which overwhelmed the earth.
- Peruvian tradition: One man and one woman were saved in a box that floated on the flood waters.
- Native American tradition: Various legends, in which one, three, or eight persons were saved in a boat above the waters on a high mountain.
- Greenland tradition: The earth once tilted over, and all men were drowned, except one man and one woman, who re-peopled the earth.

It was a gigantic task to build the ark, gather the animals, and store the necessary food. Noah and his three sons could not have done it alone. Being the grandson of Methuselah and great grandson of Enoch, Noah may, as the Babylonian tradition says, have been a city-king and may have employed thousands of men in the work. It was undoubtedly the subject of constant ridicule, but Noah persisted in faith (2 Peter 2:5; Hebrews 11:7).

Perhaps the ark is also a symbol of our salvation in Jesus. Noah, his family, and the animals all passed through the door of the ark (7:13). The door is a common symbol of Christ (Matthew 7:7; 2 Corinthians 2:12). Verse 16 states that "the LORD shut him in"—Noah and his family could not have saved themselves. We, like Noah, are saved by God's grace. We merely must pass through the door.

Gen. 7:6–8:19 | THE FLOOD

"On that day all the springs of the great deep burst forth, and the flood-gates of the heavens were opened" (7:11). The Euphrates Valley might almost be called the Isthmus of the Eastern Hemisphere, where the Mediterranean Sea and Indian Ocean approach each other (as the Atlantic and Pacific Oceans come close together at the Isthmus of Panama). The Armenian mountain country is almost like an island system, with the Caspian and Black seas on the north, the Mediterranean on the west, and the Persian Gulf and Indian Ocean on the south. A cataclysmic subsidence of the region would cause the waters to pour in from these seas, as rain poured down from above.

Gen. 8:20–9:17 | THE RAINBOW

It may be that the Flood produced a clarified air that made the Rainbow clearly visible. And God designated it as the sign of His covenant with mankind that there would never be another Flood (9:8–17). The earth's next destruction will be by fire (2 Peter 3:7).

Gen. 9:18–28 | NOAH'S PROPHECY

Noah curses Ham and blesses Shem and Japheth. This "curse on Ham" has often been used against people of non-white races, especially black people. It has been used to support the supposed superiority of the white race as well as a justification for slavery and all kinds of discrimination.

But Noah speaks about *Canaan* (another name for Ham). For the Israelites, who received this book from Moses as they were on their way to the Promised Land—that is, Canaan—Noah's prophecy was an encouragement: God, through Noah, had placed a curse on the Canaanites. The Israelites could therefore advance without fear, since God would give the Canaanites into their hands. This is underscored by the blessings on Shem and Japheth: "Blessed be the LORD, the God of Shem!" and "May God extend . . ." (vv. 26–27). The Israelites, as descendants of Shem, could rely on God's presence.

How Much Time Did Noah Spend in the Ark?

- Noah went into the ark seven days before it began to rain (7:4, 10).
- It began to rain on the 17th day of the 2nd month of Noah's 600th year (7:11). It rained for 40 days (7:12).
- The waters flooded the earth for 150 days (7:24; 8:3).
- The ark came to rest on the 17th day of the 7th month (8:4).
- Noah removed the ark's covering on the 1st day of the 1st month of Noah's 601st year (8:13).
- Noah and his family went out of the ark on the 27th day of the 2nd month (8:14–19).
- This means that they were in the ark for 1 year and 17 days (5 months floating, 7 months on the mountain).

It is difficult to define the "Canaanites" as a specific racial group. Their language, like Hebrew, was Semitic, but their origins appear to have been diverse. They were unified by what can be spoken of as a Canaanite culture.

5. The Account of the Sons of Noah, Genesis 10:1 to 11:9

The fifth document of Genesis (see p. 83), prepared, probably, by Shem and handed on to Abraham; Shem lived from 98 years before the Flood until 150 years after the birth of Abraham (11:10).

Gen. 10 | THE NATIONS DESCENDED FROM NOAH

Noah's family disembarked from the ark on Mount Ararat, near the headwaters of the Euphrates. Then, it seems, they migrated back, 500 miles, to Babylonia, their pre-Flood home. Then, 100 years later (v. 25), they were scattered by the confusion of languages.

The descendants of Japheth (vv. 2–5) went northward, settled in regions around the Black and Caspian seas; and became progenitors of the Caucasian races of Europe and Asia.

Has Noah's Ark Been Found?

In recent years, several reports have been published claiming that the remains of Noah's ark have been found, high up in the Ararat mountains. While it is tempting to accept these reports as supporting the historical truthfulness of the Bible, to date none of the reports has provided any concrete evidence (other than photographs that would not lead anyone to suspect that they showed the ark unless one were specifically looking for it). On the contrary: one thing these reports seem to have in common is that for one reason or another, any concrete evidence—such as a piece of wood from the ark—has regrettably disappeared or been lost. Until an incontrovertible case with evidence has been made that Noah's ark has indeed been found, it remains lost.

The credibility of the Word of God is not helped by questionable "proofs" that lack factual integrity. The Word of God in its full integrity is its own best defense!

Mt. Ararat. Noah's ark came to rest on a mountain in the Ararat region.

The descendants of Ham (vv. 6 – 20) went southward. The names given seem to indicate south and central Arabia, Egypt, the eastern shore of the Mediterranean, and the east coast of Africa. Canaan, son of Ham, and his descendants settled, and gave their name to, the land which later became the homeland of the Jews.

The descendants of Shem (vv. 21 – 31; Shemites or Semites) included Jews, Assyrians, Syrians, and Elamites in the northern Euphrates Valley and its borders.

Nimrod (vv. 8 – 12) was the most outstanding leader in the 400 years between the Flood and Abraham. Grandson of Ham (v. 8) and born soon after the Flood, he may have lived through the whole period (judging from the ages mentioned in 11:10 – 16). He was a very enterprising man.

His fame as a "mighty hunter" (v. 9) meant that he was protector of the people at a time when wild animals were a continual menace. Early Babylonian seals represented a king in combat with a lion; this may be a tradition of Nimrod.

In his ambition to control the rapidly multiplying and spreading race, he seems to have been leader in the building of the Tower of Babel (v. 10; 11:9). And after the confusion of languages and the dispersion of the people, Nimrod seems later to have resumed work on Babylon. Then he built three nearby cities—Erech, Akkad, and Calneh—and consolidated them into one kingdom under his own rule. Babylonia was long known as "the Land of Nimrod."

Still ambitious to control the ever-spreading race, Nimrod went 300 miles farther north and founded Nineveh (though one version says it was Asshur) and three nearby cities: Rehoboth Ir, Calah, and Resen. This constituted Nimrod's northern kingdom. For many centuries afterward, these two cities, Babylon and Nineveh, founded by Nimrod, were the leading cities of the world.

Gen. 11:1–9 | THE TOWER OF BABEL

The confusion of languages occurred in the fourth generation after the Flood, about the time of the birth of Peleg (10:25), which was 101 years after the Flood and 326 years before the call of Abraham (10:26). It was God's method of dispersing the race so that the kingdom man was creating would never exclude God's kingdom.

For many years it was believed that the Tower of Babel looked like a Babylonian ziggurat, a type of stepped tower. But the ziggurats evolved from simpler religious structures, and the final form of the ziggurat did not appear in Mesopotamia until well into the third millennium B.C.—when there were already many different languages.

Whatever the exact historical event may have been like, the purpose behind the Tower of Babel was similar to that of Adam and Eve in

As God scattered the people "over the face of the whole earth" after Babel, cultures developed and travel and commerce grew. One can imagine that the generations from Shem to Abram used caravanserai such as this one: an inn near an oasis in one of the desert areas of the Middle East. There is no roof for protection from the sparse rainfall, but there are walls to keep out wild animals and marauders.

Genesis 3. The people wanted to build a *migdal,* a fortified city, with "a tower that reaches the heavens" (vv. 3–4)—that is, they wanted to be autonomous and grab divine power. They wanted to transcend their human limitations.

The significance of the Tower of Babel becomes clear when we look at it in contrast to the Day of Pentecost (Acts 2), which is its counterpoint:

Genesis 11	Acts 2
Babel, the city built by people	Jerusalem, the city of God
The people reach for heaven	God the Spirit descends from heaven
Languages are confused; people no longer can understand each other	A single language is understood by all those present
The people are scattered	The people come from all over

6. The Account of Shem, Genesis 11:10–26

The sixth document in the book of Genesis (see p. 83). In 10:21–31, Shem's descendants are named. Here the line is carried straight from Shem to Abraham, covering 10 generations (427 years). Shem himself may have recorded this entire genealogy, for his life spanned the entire period it covers.

According to these figures:

- It was 1,656 years from Adam to the Flood; 427 years from the Flood to Abraham.
- Adam's life overlapped Methuselah's by 243 years.
- Methuselah's life overlapped Noah's by 600 years, Shem's by 98 years.

	Age at son's birth	Total age		Age at son's birth	Total age
Adam	130	930	Arpachshad,		
Seth	105	912	born after Flood	2	
Enosh	90	905	Arpachshad	35	438
Kenan	70	910	Shelah	30	433
Mahalalel	65	895	Eber	34	464
Jared	162	962	Peleg	30	239
Enoch	65	365	Reu	32	239
Methuselah	187	969	Serug	30	230
Lamech	182	777	Nahor	29	148
Noah, at Flood	600	950	Terah	130	205
TOTAL	1,656		Abraham		
			entered Canaan	75	
			TOTAL	427	

- There were 126 years between the death of Adam and the birth of Noah.
- Noah lived 350 years after the Flood; he died two years before birth of Abraham.
- Shem lived from 98 years before the Flood until 502 years after the Flood.
- Shem lived until 75 years after Abraham entered Canaan.
- Noah lived to see the 9th generation of his own descendants.
- In the righthand column, all but Peleg and Nahor were alive at the birth of Abraham.

In a period of such longevity, the population increased very rapidly, although the ages became gradually shorter after the Flood.

Hebron. Tomb of the Patriarchs.

THE TIME OF THE PATRIARCHS

GENESIS 12–50

The stories of God's dealings with Abraham, Isaac, Jacob, and Joseph (the ancestors of the Israelite people who are also called the patriarchs of Israel) are recorded in Genesis 12–50. A major focus of these narratives is the multifaceted promise that God gave them and reiterated to them. This promise provides a significant framework for God's continuing dealings with humanity (see pp. 107–8).

According to the plain reading of passages such as 1 Kings 6:1, Exodus 12:40, and others, Abraham would have entered the land of Canaan in 2091 B.C. at age 75—about midway through the archaeological period known as Middle Bronze I (2200–2000 B.C.). The thriving commercial center of Ur, located in southern Mesopotamia, that Abraham had left earlier is quite well-known due to the excavations of the site and to the thousands of cuneiform tablets that have been found at Ur and in its vicinity.

The land of Canaan that Abram entered with Sarah and his nephew Lot was not nearly as progressive. During this period people lived in tents in very small, unwalled settlements (most less than three acres in size). There is, in fact, in the archaeological record of Palestine a complete absence of walled cities during this time. Archaeologically, this period seems to be characterized by people living in tents and burying their dead in shaft-type tombs, in tumuli (artificial mounds), or under dolmens (two or more stones placed upright with a stone put horizontally on top). This fits well with the biblical portrayal of the Patriarchs as living in tents (mentioned 24 times in Genesis 12–50) and making a living by herding (sheep and goats are mentioned 24 times) and farming (sowing and reaping in 26:12).

At the time of Abraham's death in 1991 B.C., the land of Canaan was moving into the Middle Bronze II period (2000–1550 B.C.). During this period large fortified cities were again built, although it is probable that the majority of the population continued to live in the countryside as herders and farmers. The Egyptian story of Sinuhe (which can be found in *Ancient Near Eastern Texts* 18–23) dates from about 1962 B.C. (during the days of Isaac); it describes Canaan as a land filled with figs, grapes, wine, honey, olives, fruit, barley, wheat, and cattle (compare Deuteronomy 8:8).

At the time of Jacob's move to Egypt (1876 B.C.), that country was experiencing a time of stability during the 12th Dynasty. At a minimum it maintained commercial contacts with peoples in the eastern Mediterranean region as well as those to its south, in Nubia. Unfortunately, no extrabiblical records have been found as yet that refer to any of the people mentioned in this section of Scripture.

Bedouin life. The Patriarchs were nomadic and lived in tents.

Mesopotamia, too, was experiencing a period of prosperity at this time (called the Old Babylonian period). It was during this time that the famous Hammurabi ruled, who is known especially for his laws, known as the Code of Hammurabi. In addition to written documents found in southern Mesopotamia, a huge cuneiform archive was discovered at Mari, located farther north on the Euphrates. The Mari tablets actually mention several of the more prominent city-states in Canaan: Hazor (175 acres in size) and Leshem (later known as Dan; Joshua 19:47; Judges 18:29). In addition, some of the personal names (though not the people themselves) found in the Mari tablets parallel names mentioned in the biblical text, and the political alliances, tribal activities, and cultural background reflected in the tablets do help illustrate the general lifestyle of the people during this period.

A dolmen, used for burial, in the Golan Heights. Dolmens similar to this (standing stones capped by a horizontal stone) have also been found in Europe, especially in Britain and France.

BIBLICAL DATES	
2091 B.C.	Abram entered Canaan
2066 B.C.	Isaac born
2006 B.C.	Jacob born
1991 B.C.	Abraham died
1886 B.C.	Isaac died
1876 B.C.	Jacob moved to Egypt
DATES FOR PALESTINE	
(Periods in Palestinian history are named after materials used.)	
2200–2000 B.C.	*(Middle Bronze I)* People lived mostly in tents. There were no significant cities. The dead were placed in tombs, on dolmens (two or more vertical slabs of rock with a horizontal rock on top; see photo on p. 104), or in tumuli (artificial mounds).
2000–1550 B.C.	*(Middle Bronze II)* Larger cities were established. Well-preserved city gates from this period have been found at Dan and Ashkelon. Palestine had international contacts with both Mesopotamia and Egypt.
EGYPTIAN DATES	
(Periods in Egyptian history are defined largely by the pharaonic dynasties.)	
2160–2010 B.C.	*(First Intermediate Period: Dynasties IX and X)* A time of instability in Egypt. Abraham visited Egypt during this period (Genesis 12:10–20).
2106–1786 B.C.	*(Middle Kingdom: Dynasties XI and especially XII. The periods overlap, since for a period of time Egypt was a divided country)* A time of stability and prosperity in Egypt. Joseph and then Jacob and children moved to Egypt.
1786–1550 B.C.	*(Second Intermediate Period: Dynasties XIV–XVII)* The oppression of Israel probably began during dynasties XV and XVI (the Hyksos dynasties; Exodus 1:8–9).

Genesis 12–50

The Beginning of the Story of Redemption
Abraham, Isaac, Jacob, Joseph

The LORD had said to Abram, "Leave your country, your people and your father's household and go to the land I will show you. I will make you into a great nation and I will bless you; I will make your name great, and you will be a blessing. I will bless those who bless you, and whoever curses you I will curse; and all peoples on earth will be blessed through you." —GENESIS 12:1–3

After this, the word of the Lord came to Abram in a vision: "Do not be afraid, Abram. I am your shield, your very great reward. . . . Look up at the heavens and count the stars—if indeed you can count them." Then he said to him, "So shall your offspring be." Abram believed the Lord, and he credited it to him as righteousness. —GENESIS 15:1, 5–6

7. The Account of Terah, Genesis 11:27 to 25:11

The story of Abraham, recorded, probably, by Abraham and Isaac. The last verses of chapter 11 provide the genealogical link between Terah and Abraham, while the actual story of Abraham begins in chapter 12.

Gen. 12:1–3 | THE CALL OF ABRAHAM

Here begins the story of redemption. It had been hinted at in the Garden of Eden (Genesis 3:15). Now, 400 years after the Flood, God calls Abraham to be the founder of a nation through which He would make the reclamation and redemption of mankind a reality.

God promised Abraham, a righteous man who believed in God, not in the idols of those around him, that his descendants would

1. Inherit the land of Canaan
2. Become a great nation
3. Be a blessing to all nations

This promise (12:2–3; 22:18) is the foundation for the rest of the Bible. God first called Abraham in Ur (Genesis 11:31; Acts 7:2–4), and again in Haran (12:1–4), Shechem (12:7), Bethel (13:14–17), and twice in Hebron (15:5, 18; 17:1–8). The promise was repeated to his son Isaac (26:3–4) and to his grandson Jacob (28:13–14; 35:11–12; 46:3–4). These same promises are also found later in God's covenant with David (see on 2 Samuel 7).

It seems, from 11:26, 32; 12:4; and Acts 7:2–4, that Abraham was born when his father was 130 years old, and that he was not the first-born, as may be inferred from 11:6. He was 75 when he entered Canaan, about 80 when he rescued Lot and met Melchizedek, 86 when Ishmael was born, 99 when Sodom was destroyed, 100 when Isaac was born, 137 when Sarah died, and 160 when Jacob was born. He died at 175, which was 115 years before Jacob's migration to Egypt.

GOD'S PROMISES TO ABRAHAM	
"I will make you into a great nation" (you will have numerous descendants)	Genesis 12:2; 13:16; 15:18; et al.
"I will bless you"	Genesis 12:2
"I will make your name great"	Genesis 12:2
"You will be a blessing"	Genesis 12:2
"I will bless those who bless you"	Genesis 12:2
"Whoever curses you I will curse"	Genesis 12:3
Divine blessing for Jews as well as Gentiles	Genesis 12:3; 22:18; 26:4 (see Galatians 3:16)
Your descendants will occupy Canaan	Genesis 15:18; 17:8
The promise is eternal	Genesis 13:15; 17:7–8, 13, 19; 48:4
Kings will descend from you	Genesis 17:6, 8
God will be Israel's God forever	Genesis 17:7–8

Gen. 12:4–9 | ABRAHAM'S ENTRANCE INTO CANAAN

Haran, about 600 miles northwest of Ur and 400 miles northeast of Canaan, was Abraham's first stopping place. He had set out from Ur in search of a land where he could build a nation free from idolatry, not knowing where he would end up (Hebrews 11:8). But Haran was already a well-settled region, with roads to Babylon, Assyria, Syria, Asia Minor, and Egypt, along which caravans and armies constantly marched. So, after the death of his father, Terah, Abraham, under the call of God, moved on in search of a more sparsely settled land.

Shechem, Abraham's first stopping place in Canaan, in the center of the land, was in a beautiful valley between Mount Ebal and Mount Gerizim. Here Abraham built an altar to God, but soon he moved on south in further exploration of the land.

Bethel, 20 miles south of Shechem and 10 miles north of Jerusalem, was Abraham's next stopping place. It was one of the highest points in Canaan, with a magnificent view in every direction. Abraham was following the ridge of the mountain range, probably because the Jordan Valley on the east and the Coastal Plain on the west were already pretty well settled. In Bethel, too, he built an altar, as he did later at Hebron, and as he had done at Shechem, not only as an acknowledgement to God, but also as a statement of his faith to the people among whom he had come to live. He must have liked Bethel; for that is where he settled when he returned from Egypt, until he and Lot separated (chap. 13).

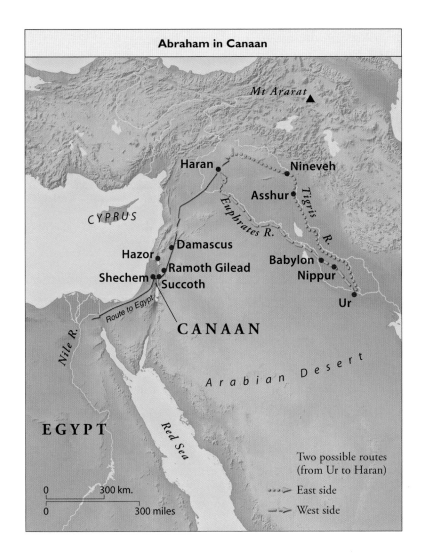

Abraham in Canaan

Mt Ararat

Haran

Nineveh

Asshur

CYPRUS

Euphrates R.

Tigris R.

Hazor

Damascus

Shechem

Ramoth Gilead

Succoth

Babylon

Nippur

Ur

Route to Egypt

CANAAN

Nile R.

Arabian Desert

EGYPT

Red Sea

0   300 km.

0   300 miles

Two possible routes
(from Ur to Haran)

••••➤ East side

—➤ West side

Gen. 12:10–20 | ABRAHAM IN EGYPT

As he traveled on south from Bethel, Abraham must have passed close to
Jerusalem. Because of a famine, he went to Egypt, to stay there until the
famine was over. He managed to get himself into trouble in Egypt. His wife,
Sarah, was beautiful, and powerful rulers had a practice of confiscating beau-

tiful women for
themselves and
killing their hus-
bands. His cau-
tious subterfuge
of calling Sarah
his "sister" was
not exactly a
lie. She was his

Beni Hasan tomb
painting. Semitic
connection to Egypt
during the period
of the Patriarchs
is evidenced in the
tombs paintings at
Beni Hasan.

When Abraham went to Egypt, the pyramids, including the famous pyramids at Gizah (bottom), were already almost half a millennium old.

Not all early attempts at pyramid building in the 26th century B.C. were successful. The earliest pyramid is the so-called step pyramid of Pharaoh Djoser (top), which was a stable structure. But the pyramid at Maidum, which was probably completed by Pharaoh Snofru of the 3rd Dynasty, was a different matter. The core was a large, eight-step pyramid. Around this core, fill was added to create a true pyramid, with an outer casing. Through a combination of design and construction problems, the outer part of the pyramid collapsed at some point, leaving the core surrounded by a mound of rubble.

half-sister (20:12). Marriage between near relatives was common in early ages until the growth of families offered wider selection.

Gen. 13 | ABRAHAM AND LOT SEPARATE

Lot was Abraham's nephew. They had been together since they had left Ur many years before. But now their flocks and herds had become so extensive, and their herdsmen so quarrelsome over pasture lands, that

The "bent" pyramid at Dashur is the result of a design change after part of the pyramid had been built, perhaps occasioned by the collapse of the Maidum pyramid. The sides in the original design were apparently too steep.

Abraham's Visit to Egypt

It is well known from Egyptian inscriptions and artwork that throughout Egypt's history, "Asiatics" from Canaan entered Egypt for various reasons. From the days of the Patriarchs, dating from perhaps just a few years before Joseph entered Egypt (ca. 1891 B.C.), we have the painting on the wall of the tomb of Khum-hotep III that depicts 37 Asiatics entering Egypt for trading purposes. The colorful dress of both men and women are well represented. However, it is not necessary to draw the conclusion from this that the Patriarchs were merchant/traders, for Asiatics entered Egypt for many reasons, including getting food and water for their families and flocks.

it seemed best to separate. Abraham magnanimously gave Lot his choice of all the land. Lot foolishly chose the Plain of Sodom. Abraham chose Hebron, which was his home from then on.

Gen. 14 | ABRAHAM DEFEATS BABYLONIAN KINGS

Abraham wanted to rescue Lot and must have been something of a military genius. With 318 men of his own and some help from

A modern Bedouin tent, probably not unlike the tents Abraham lived in. The tent was (and in parts of the Near East still is) the most convenient and logical home for a nonsedentary people. It does not necessarily reflect a primitive lifestyle nor poverty and absence of luxury: Abraham was a wealthy man.

Under the protective roof is what remains of the gate of the city of Dan of Abraham's day. Abraham pursued the kings who had taken his nephew Lot captive "as far as Dan." Little did Abraham know that some of his descendants (the northern kingdom) would later go "as far as Dan" to worship a golden calf there, rather than the true God. (1 Kings 12:30)

his neighbors, he sent these four kings running by means of a midnight surprise attack. Armies then were small, and "kings" were in effect tribal princes. Abraham was a sort of king, perhaps the head of a sizable clan.

The kings mentioned in Genesis 14 are known only from the biblical text. (The attempted equation of biblical Amraphel with the Babylonian king Hammurabi is not very plausible.) It is known, from cuneiform documents found at Mari and elsewhere, that during the patriarchal period, various kings often made alliances in fighting against other kings — a situation that is reflected in Genesis 14.

Melchizedek, 14:18–20

The priest-king of Salem (Jerusalem). Hebrew tradition says that he was Shem, the son of Noah and survivor of the Flood, who was still alive — earth's oldest living man. He was a priest, in the patriarchal age, of the whole race. If so, it is a hint that God had already chosen, right after the Flood, Jerusalem to be the scene of human redemption. Whoever he was, as both a priest and king, Melchizedek was a picture and "type" of Christ (Psalm 110; Hebrews 5–7). We do know that he conferred a blessing on Abraham and that Abraham's response was to give him tithes, which was a tenth part of everything he possessed. Many Christians today follow Abraham's example by offering their tithes to God through their churches and other ministries. Surely they, too, receive God's blessings.

Gen. 15–17 | GOD'S PROMISES TO ABRAHAM RENEWED

God renewed His covenant with Abraham graphically through the ancient custom of passing between the pieces of sacrificed animals. This solemn action signified an oath between the parties of covenant that "May it be so done to me if I do not keep my oath and pledge."

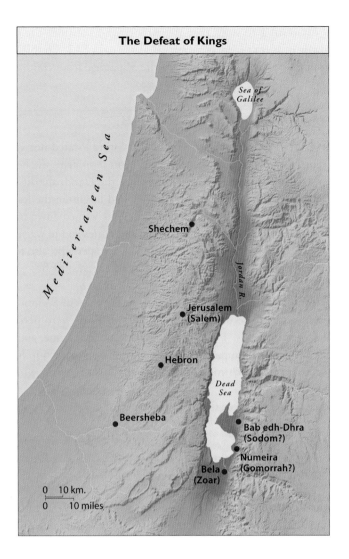

The Defeat of Kings

The promises include the prediction that before his descendants would actually live in Canaan, they would spend 400 years in a foreign land (15:13), meaning Egypt. In addition, when Abraham was 100 and Sarah 90, Isaac was promised. Their impatience with regard to God's fulfillment of this promise prompted them to ask the assistance of their maidservant, Hagar. This was the custom of the day, to ensure the birth of a male heir. Thirteen years later, God reminded Abraham that he needed to keep his part of the covenant. Ultimately, God's will and promise was manifested in the birth of Isaac. The name "Isaac" means "he laughs"—a name given by God quite possibly in response to Abraham and Sarah's initial disbelief (17:17; 18:12).

God also instituted circumcision as the symbol of the covenant with Abraham and his descendants, a physical marking of Abraham's male descendants as belonging to God's nation.

It is interesting to note that the Arabs, who consider themselves descendants of Ishmael, are circumcised at the age of 13. To this people and to others, circumcision serves as a rite of passage from childhood to manhood.

Gen. 18–19 | SODOM AND GOMORRAH

These two cities were cesspools of evil. They were located not very far from Hebron, the home of Abraham, and from Jerusalem, the home of Melchizedek. It had been only 400 years since the Flood, almost within the memory of people then living. Yet they had forgotten the lesson of that cataclysmic destruction of the race. And God "rained down burning sulfur" on these two cities, to refresh men's memories and to warn of the wrath of God that is in store for the wicked—and, perhaps, also to serve as a foreshadowing of earth's final doom in a holocaust of fire (2 Peter 2:5–6; 3:7, 10; and Revelation 8:5, 7; 9:17–18; 16:8).

Jesus compared the time of His return to the days of Sodom (Luke 17:26–32) and to the days before the Flood. Both were periods of unspeakable wickedness. Today, with greed, brutality, crime, and racial and religious conflict rampant on a scale never before known in history, it does not require much imagination to see the end toward which we are heading, however much good men and statesmen may try to avert it. Unless there comes a worldwide movement of repentance, the day of doom may not be far off.

The sons born to Lot's daughters (vv. 37–38) began the lineage of the Moabites and Ammonites, who became bitter enemies of Abraham's descendants (1 Samuel 14:47; 2 Chronicles 20:1).

ARCHAEOLOGICAL NOTE: Sodom and Gomorrah. The exact locations of Sodom and Gomorrah, Admah, Zeboiim, and Zoar (see Genesis 14) are not known. Scholars have usually looked for sites near the southern end of the Dead Sea, where the name "Zoar" was preserved into the Byzantine Period (4th–6th century A.D.). The Dead Sea lies at 1,300 feet below sea level—the lowest spot on earth. The surrounding area is a desolate landscape with numerous salt formations. In addition, black masses of bitumen float to the surface, and some have suggested that these factors, along with seismic activity, may have led to the destruction of Sodom and Gomorrah.

Although serious searches have been made, no certain identification has been confirmed. There do not appear to be any remains under the southern end of the Dead Sea—the level of which has been dropping in recent years—contrary to what some biblical students have suggested. Along the southeastern end of the Dead Sea there are five large antiquity sites which date to the Early Bronze Age (3150–2200 B.C.): Bab edh–Dhra, Numeira, Zoar, Feifa, and Khanazir. Several of these sites had massive fortifications, and Early Bronze burials in the region are said to number over 500,000 persons! On the surface of several of the sites is a spongy, black, charcoal-like substance that some have tried to relate to the destruction of Sodom and Gomorrah. At the present time, although there are five sites, just as there are five cities mentioned in Genesis 14, it is difficult to maintain that these are the five "cities of the plain" mentioned in Genesis, since archaeologically they must be dated prior to the age of the Patriarchs on almost any dating scheme used.

This statuette of a ram caught in a thicket dating about 2,600 B.C. was discovered in the Great Death-Pit at Ur and is a reminder of the ram Abraham sacrificed as a substitute for Isaac.

| Gen. 20 | **SARAH AND ABIMELECH** |

Although Hebron was his main home, Abraham from time to time moved from place to place in search of pasture for his herds. In Gerar, a Philistine city some 40 miles west of Hebron near the seacoast, he had another experience like the one he had had with Pharaoh (12:10–20). Sarah must have been extremely beautiful to attract the attention of kings, especially considering her age. Isaac and Rebekah had a similar experience in Gerar with a later Philistine king also named Abimelech (chap. 26).

| Gen. 21 | **THE BIRTH OF ISAAC** |

Ishmael, at the time, was about 15 years old (vv. 5, 8; 16:16). The apostle Paul used the story of these two children as an allegory of the Mosaic and Christian covenants (the old and new covenants, Galatians 4:21–31).

Beersheba (vv. 30–31), where Abraham, Isaac, and Jacob lived much of the time, was at the southernmost border of Canaan, some 20 miles southwest of Hebron and about 150 miles from Egypt. It was a place of "seven wells." Wells in a semi-desert country like that were priceless possessions.

Gen. 22 | ABRAHAM OFFERS ISAAC

It was a test of Abraham's faith. Note that God did not "tempt" him. God does not tempt (James 1:13), but rather tests us to confirm our faith (Exodus 20:20) or prove our commitment to Him (Deuteronomy 8:2). Satan, on the other hand, tempts us (1 Corinthians 7:5) in an attempt to make us fall and to pull us away from the will of God in our lives.

God had promised that Isaac would be the father of nations (17:16). Yet, here God commands that Isaac be killed before he had any children. Abraham had faith that God would provide an alternate sacrifice or bring Isaac back to life (Hebrews 11:19). We do not know how God made the command known to Abraham, but that it was the voice of God Abraham could not have doubted, for he certainly would not have set out to perform a task so cruel and revolting without being certain that God had commanded it. The idea originated with God, not with Abraham.

The offering of Isaac was a foreshadowing of the death of Christ. A father offering his only son (Isaac was the "only son" of the promise, 21:12). The son dead for three days (in Abraham's mind, v. 4). A substitution. An actual sacrifice. And this took place on Mount Moriah, the very same place where 2000 years later God's own Son was offered. Thus it was a foreshadowing, here at the birth of the Hebrew nation, of the grand event the nation was born to bring about.

Moriah

Although the exact location of Abraham's attempt to sacrifice Isaac is not known, v. 2 says it was in "the region of Moriah." The writer of Chronicles (2 Chronicles 3:1) indicates that it was at, or near, that same site where Solomon later built the first temple. Today a Moslem shrine, the Dome of the Rock, erected in A.D. 691, stands over the highest piece of bedrock in the area. It preserves the above traditions as well as the Moslem tradition that this is the spot from which Muhammed made his night journey to heaven.

Gen. 23 | SARAH'S DEATH

At Hebron, in the city gate, Abraham purchased the cave of Machpelah to bury his wife, Sarah. Today, in the older part of Hebron, is a large structure called the Cave of Machpelah, a place sacred to Jews, Christians, and Moslems and currently inaccessible to all. The exterior of the structure is composed of large Herodian stones (37–4 B.C.), and inside that enclosure are the remains of a Byzantine/Crusader church, a mosque, and a synagogue. There are three pairs of cenotaphs (above-ground monuments): a pair for Abraham and Sarah; a pair for Isaac and Rebecca; and a pair for Jacob and Leah. The underground chambers have not been

The exterior of the Tomb of the Patriarchs in Hebron. According to tradition, it is built on the location of the Cave of Machpelah. The massive outside walls date back to Herod the Great and give us a clue as to how the outside walls of the temple area may originally have looked.

completely investigated, or reported on, but the visible stone work there also seems to be Herodian.

| Gen. 24 | **BETROTHAL OF ISAAC AND REBEKAH**

Rebekah was Isaac's second cousin. Abraham's purpose in sending his chief servant (probably Eliezer of Damascus; see 15:2) back to his own people for a wife for Isaac was to keep his descendants free from idolatry. If Isaac had married a Canaanite girl, how different the whole history of Israel might have been. What a lesson for young people in the matter of choosing a mate!

| Gen. 25:1–11 | **ABRAHAM'S DEATH**

Sarah had died at the age of 127, at which time Abraham was 137. He lived for 38 years after that, in which time he married Keturah. She bore him six sons, of whom came the Midianites. Five hundred years later, Moses would marry a Midianite woman (Exodus 2:16–21). On the whole, Abraham was the "greatest, purest, and most venerable of the patriarchs, revered by Jews, Mohammedans, and Christians," friend of God, father of the faithful. Generous, unselfish, yet fully human. A man of great character, with unbounded trust in God.

8. The Account of Ishmael, Genesis 25:12–18

The eighth document of Genesis (see p. 83). Ishmael was Abraham's son by Hagar, Sarah's Egyptian servant (chap. 16). The Ishmaelites made Arabia their home and became known generally as Arabians. Thus Abraham was the father of the present Arab world. Rivalry between Isaac and Ishmael has persisted through the centuries in the antagonism between Jews and Arabs.

9. The Account of Isaac, Genesis 25:19 to 35:29

The ninth document of Genesis (see p. 83). It contains the story of Isaac and Jacob, handed down by Jacob to his sons.

| Gen. 25:19–34 | BIRTH OF JACOB AND ESAU |

Esau, the firstborn, was Isaac's natural heir, who would inherit the promises God had made to Abraham. But God, knowing before they were born the qualities of the two men, chose Jacob to be transmitter of the precious heritage; He hinted at this to their mother (v. 23), and it was the background of Jacob's deal with Esau (v. 31).

Jacob's deal with Esau secured him the birthright that God all along intended him to have. Esau's transfer of his birthright for a meal demonstrated that he was "godless" (Hebrews 12:16), since at the heart of the birthright were the covenant promises that Isaac had inherited from Abraham. The owner of the birthright, generally the firstborn, also received at least a double portion of the father's wealth at the time the father's death.

In the line of covenant promise, all Abraham's sons were eliminated except Isaac. Of Isaac's sons, Esau was eliminated and Jacob alone chosen. With Jacob the process of elimination stopped, and all Jacob's descendants were included in the Chosen Nation.

| Gen. 26 | ISAAC AMONG THE PHILISTINES |

Not much is told of Isaac's life beyond this incident of Abimelech and Rebekah and the argument over wells. Isaac had inherited the bulk of his father's extensive flocks and herds; he was prosperous and peaceable, and his life was uneventful.

Note that the Patriarchs not only had sheep, goats, camels, and donkeys, but also lived a somewhat sedentary lifestyle, for "Isaac planted crops in that land and the same year reaped a hundredfold, because the LORD blessed him" (v. 12).

Isaac was born when Abraham was 100 and Sarah 90. He was 37 when his mother died, 40 when he married, 60 when Jacob was born, 75 when Abraham died, 137(?) when Jacob

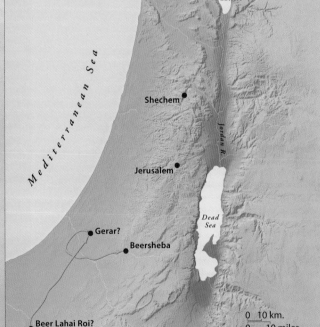

Isaac's Wanderings

fled, 157(?) when Jacob returned, and 167 when Joseph was sold. He died at 180, in the year Joseph became ruler of Egypt. Abraham lived 175 years; Isaac, 180; Jacob, 147; Joseph, 110.

The statement about God's "requirements, commands, decrees, and laws" (v. 5) would seem to indicate that the beginnings of God's written Word were already in existence in Abraham's day.

Gen. 27 JACOB GETS HIS FATHER'S BLESSING

Jacob had already bought the birthright from Esau (25:31–34). It was now necessary to get his father to validate the transfer by receiving the corresponding blessing. This he accomplished by deception. In evaluating the moral quality of Jacob's act, a number of things need to be considered: (1) his mother put him up to it; (2) he wanted the birthright because it was the channel of God's promise of blessing to the whole world; (3) with only his human understanding, he thought there was no other way to obtain it; (4) Esau cared nothing for it; (5) Jacob paid dearly for his fraud (see under chap. 29); (6) God Himself, laying the foundation of His plans for the world (Romans 9:10–13), made the choice before the boys were born (25:23).

Isaac's predictions (vv. 29, 40). God must have put these words into Isaac's mouth, for they did come true. Jacob's descendants did gain a dominant position among the nations and in time produced Christ. Esau's descendants, the Edomites, were subservient to Israel; in time they did throw off Israel's yoke (2 Kings 8:20–22); and they have disappeared from history.

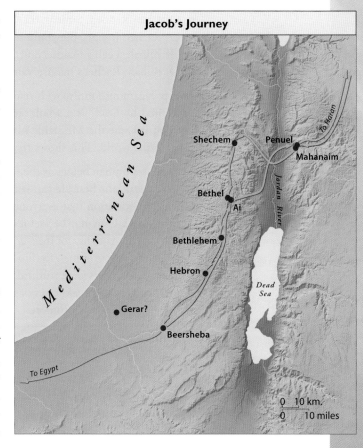

Jacob's Journey

Gen. 28 JACOB'S VISION AT BETHEL

The transfer of the birthright from Esau to Jacob had been validated by Isaac. It is now validated in heaven. God Himself assures Jacob that from now on he is to be the recognized bearer of the promises. The ladder is a hint that the promises will culminate in something that would bridge heaven and earth. Jesus said that He was that Ladder (John 1:51) and the only Mediator between God and men (1 Timothy 2:5).

Jacob is thought to have been 77 years old at this time. He was 15 when Abraham died, 84 when he married, 90 when Joseph was born, 98 when he returned to Canaan, 120 when Isaac died, 130 when he went to Egypt, and 147 when he died.

His first 77 years were spent in Canaan, the next 20 in Haran, then 33 in Canaan, and the last 17 in Egypt.

| Gen. 29–30 | JACOB'S SOJOURN IN HARAN |

Haran was 400 miles northeast of Canaan. It was the place where Jacob's mother, Rebekah, had been raised, and from which his grandfather Abraham had migrated many years before. Laban was Jacob's uncle. Jacob was there 20 years. They were years of hardship and suffering. A wife whom he did not want was forced on him by deceit, just as he had gotten his father's blessing by deceit. He had begun to reap what he had sown.

Jacob's Family

Jacob had two wives and two concubines whom, except for one, he did not want but who were forced on him. Of these, 12 sons were born:

- Of Leah: Reuben, Simeon, Levi, Judah, Issachar, Zebulun
- Of Rachel: Joseph, Benjamin
- Of Zilpah, Leah's maidservant: Gad, Asher
- Of Bilhah, Rachel's maidservant: Dan, Naphtali

This polygamous family, with many shameful things to its discredit, was accepted by God, as a whole, to be the beginning of the Twelve Tribes that became the Messianic Nation, chosen by God to bring the Savior into the world. This shows that

- God uses human beings as they are to serve His purposes; He does, so to speak, the best He can with the material He has.
- It is no indication that everyone whom God thus uses will be eternally saved. One may be useful in serving God's plans in this world and yet fail to qualify for the eternal world in the day when God shall judge the secrets of men for final disposition (Romans 2:12–16).
- The Bible writers were truthful. No other book narrates with such utter candor the weaknesses of its heroes and things so contrary to the ideals it aims to promote.

| Gen. 31–33 | JACOB'S RETURN TO CANAAN |

Jacob had left Canaan 20 years before, alone and empty-handed. (At this point, Isaac was still living; Abraham had been dead for about 100 years.) Now, he was returning, a tribal prince, rich in flocks, herds, and servants. God had kept His promise to Jacob (28:15). Laban's parting words to

Jacob (31:49) contain the beautiful Mizpah benediction, "The LORD watch between me and thee, when we are absent one from another" (KJV).

Angels, on Jacob's departure from Canaan, had wished him Godspeed (28:12). Now, on his return, angels welcome him home (32:1). Jacob was now entering his inheritance in the Promised Land of Canaan. God had been with him thus far. Jacob remembered that Esau had vowed to kill him (27:41), and he prayed for God's continued protection.

Jacob sent a peace party ahead to his brother Esau with many gifts. The men returned with news that Esau was coming to meet Jacob. Jacob was still afraid. He felt he needed God more than ever (32:24–30).

That night God appeared to Jacob in the form of a man. Jacob had the upper hand in wrestling with "the man" all night, but God showed Jacob that He was more powerful by disabling Jacob's hip socket with His touch. Jacob refused to stop wrestling until "the man" blessed him. In this way Jacob finally acknowledged that he needed God's blessing. As Jacob acknowledged God, so God acknowledged Jacob by changing his name to "Israel," meaning "He struggles with God."

After Jacob's encounter with God, he saw Esau coming with his men. He soon realized that Esau came to him in peace. Their meeting was one of reconciliation. They separated again in peace, and Jacob entered Canaan.

Gen. 34 | DINAH AVENGED BY SIMEON AND LEVI

On his return, Shechem was Jacob's first stopping place in Canaan. There he bought a parcel of ground and erected an altar to God, as if planning to make it his home, temporarily at least. But the bloody act of Simeon and Levi made him odious to his neighbors, and he soon moved on to Bethel.

Gen. 35 | GOD RENEWS THE COVENANT AT BETHEL

Bethel was the place where, 20 years before, in his flight from Canaan, Jacob had seen the heavenly ladder and God had made him heir to the Abrahamic promises. Now God reassures him that those promises shall be fulfilled. Jacob set up a stone pillar in recognition of the place where God had talked to him. Later, on their way to Ephrath (Bethlehem), Rachel gave birth to Benjamin. She unfortunately died in childbirth. Jacob buried her and created a tomb.

Then Jacob moved on to Hebron, the home of Abraham and Isaac. Sometime after his arrival, Isaac died at the age of 180. Together Jacob and Esau buried their father in the family tomb.

10. The Account of Esau, Genesis 36:1–43

The 10th document composing Genesis (see p. 83). It contains a brief account of the origin of the Edomites.

Goats grazing near Bethel. It was at Bethel that God reassured Jacob of the promises He had made to Abraham.

Esau, in personal character, was profane and irreligious; he "despised" his birthright. Compared with Esau, Jacob was more fit to be the father of God's Messianic Nation.

(On the Edomites and the land of Edom, see pp. 421–22.)

The Amalekites (v. 12) were a branch of Esau's descendants. They were a wandering tribe, centering mainly around Kadesh, in the northern part of the Sinai Peninsula, but roaming in wide circles, even into Judah and far to the east. They were the first to attack Israel upon their departure from Egypt, and they oppressed Israel during the period of the Judges.

Jobab (v. 34) is thought by some to have been the Job of the book of Job. Eliphaz and Teman (vv. 10–11) are named in the book of Job. This chapter may supply the setting for the book of Job.

11. The Account of Jacob, Genesis 37:2 to 50:26

The 11th and final document composing Genesis contains the story of Joseph and Israel's migration to Egypt. Joseph, probably more than any of the Patriarchs, was a type or symbol of the people of Israel, who struggled with God and men and yet, with God's blessing, overcame all circumstances. Joseph was a source of blessing to all the nations (12:2–3). Through Joseph, Abraham's family became a great nation in Egypt. This became the backdrop for the great exodus described in the next book of the Bible.

Gen. 37 | JOSEPH SOLD INTO EGYPT

The **richly ornamented robe** (v. 3; KJV, coat of many colors) was a badge of favoritism, possibly indicating Jacob's intention to make Joseph heir to the birthright.

Reuben, Jacob's firstborn, was natural heir to the birthright; but he was disqualified because of his illicit relationship with one of his father's concubines (35:22; 49:3–4; 1 Chronicles 5:1–2). **Simeon and Levi,** second and third in line of succession (29:31–35), were passed over because of their crime at Shechem (34:25–30; 49:5–7). **Judah,** the fourth son, was next in line, and the family may have expected that the birthright would go to him.

But Joseph, though Jacob's 11th son, was Rachel's firstborn. Rachel was Jacob's best-loved wife, and Joseph was his favorite son (v. 3). So the robe looked suspicious. And Joseph's dreams of his own ascendancy (vv. 5–10) aggravated the situation.

Thus Judah and Joseph appear to have been rivals for the birthright. This may explain Judah's active part in selling Joseph into slavery (vv. 26–27). The rivalry between Judah and Joseph passed to their descendants. The tribes of Judah and Ephraim (Joseph's son) were contenders for supremacy. Judah took the lead under David and Solomon. Then, under the leadership of Ephraim, the Ten Tribes seceded (1 Kings 12).

> "Don't be afraid. Am I in the place of God? You intended to harm me, but God intended it for good to accomplish what is now being done, the saving of many lives. So then, don't be afraid. I will provide for you and your children."
> —Genesis 50:20–21

Gen. 38 | JUDAH'S CHILDREN

This chapter is probably inserted because Judah was progenitor of the Messiah, and it was in accord with the Old Testament purpose to preserve family registers all along the line of succession, even though they contained some things not very praiseworthy.

Gen. 39 | JOSEPH IMPRISONED

Joseph was of unblemished character, unusually handsome, with an exceptional gift for leadership and an ability to make the best of every unpleasant situation. He was born in Haran, 75 years after the death of Abraham, 30 years before the death of Isaac (when his father was about 90), and eight years before they returned to Canaan. At 17 he was sold into Egypt and spent 13 years in Potiphar's house and in prison. At age 30 he became ruler of Egypt. He died at age 110.

Joseph gained the attention of Pharaoh by interpreting his dreams as an agent of God. Joseph made it clear that interpretations belong to God (40:8).

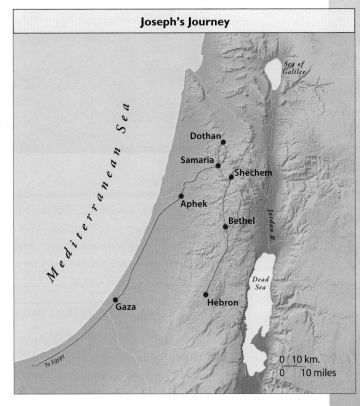

Joseph's Journey

Sea of Galilee

Mediterranean Sea

Dothan

Samaria

Shechem

Aphek

Bethel

Jordan R.

Dead Sea

Gaza

Hebron

To Egypt

0   10 km.
0   10 miles

These images from the Pharaonic Village in Cairo show the kind of life Joseph and his descendants may have lived in Goshen during the good years before a new pharaoh put the Israelites to forced labor on his building projects.

Joseph's interpretation was that God was going to bring to Egypt seven years of great abundance followed by seven years of famine. Through the dream, God gave Pharaoh, who did not know God, a warning and provided a plan of provision that would support the people through this time. Pharaoh recognized God's favor on Joseph and put him in charge of the whole land of Egypt.

Gen. 40–41 | JOSEPH MADE RULER OF EGYPT

Joseph married a daughter of the priest of On. But although he had a heathen wife and ruled a heathen kingdom, he maintained his childhood faith in the God of his fathers, Abraham, Isaac, and Jacob.

Gen. 42–45 | JOSEPH MAKES HIMSELF KNOWN

This has been called one of the most beautiful stories in all literature. The most touching incident in the story is when Judah, who many years before had been the ringleader in selling Joseph into slavery (37:26), now offers to become hostage for Benjamin (44:18–34).

Gen. 46–47 | JACOB AND HIS FAMILY SETTLE IN EGYPT

God had planned that Israel should be nurtured for a while in Egypt, which was the most advanced civilization of that day. As Jacob left Canaan, God gave him assurance that his descendants would return (46:3–4).

Gen. 48–49 | JACOB'S BLESSING AND PROPHECY

Jacob seems to have split the birthright, designating Judah as the channel of the messianic promise (49:10), yet pronouncing national prestige on Joseph's son Ephraim (48:19–22; 49:22–26; 1 Chronicles 5:1–2).

Jacob's prophecy about the Twelve Tribes parallels to a remarkable degree the subsequent history of the tribes. "Shiloh" (v. 10) is commonly taken to be a name for the Messiah. The tribe of Judah produced David, and David's family produced Christ.

Gen. 50 | THE DEATHS OF JACOB AND JOSEPH

Jacob's body was taken back to Hebron for burial. And Joseph exacted an oath of his brothers that when Israel returned to Canaan, they would carry his bones. This belief that Canaan would be their homeland was not forgotten; and 400 years later, when they set out for Canaan, the Israelites took Joseph's bones along (Exodus 13:19).

THE EXODUS FROM EGYPT
Exodus – Deuteronomy

Egypt

Modern Egypt covers almost 400,000 square miles (just over a million square kilometers). But 96 percent of this area is desert, and 99 percent of the population lives on the 4 percent of the land that is usable, which stretches along the Nile River in a valley 2 to 20 miles wide, with an average width of about 10 miles, and 750 miles long. Only there where the Nile enters the Mediterranean Sea does this valley widen into a broad delta through which a number of branches from the Nile flow. The Delta, a triangle, is about 100 miles north and south, and about 150 miles east and west, from Port Said to Alexandria. It is the most fertile part of Egypt. The land of Goshen, where the Israelites lived, was the eastern part of the Delta.

The floor of the valley is covered with a black alluvial deposit of rich soil of unparalleled fertility, replenished each year by the overflow of the Nile, which rises an average of 25 feet once a year.

Surrounded and protected by the desert, one of the first great civilizations in history developed in this narrow Nile Valley, and nowhere else have the remains of an ancient civilization been so well preserved. The dry desert climate has preserved, for thousands of years, materials that would have perished long since in other climates, such as papyrus and leather.

The population of modern Egypt is about 50 million; in Old Testament times it was between 1½ and 5 million.

When Was the Exodus?

There are two major views regarding the date of the Exodus from Egypt. The first, called the **Early Date Theory** is based on a literal reading of 1 Kings 6:1: "In the four hundred and eightieth year after the Israelites had come out of Egypt, in the fourth year of Solomon's reign over Israel, in the month of Ziv, the second month, he began to build the temple of the LORD."

Since Solomon began to rule in 970 B.C., the fourth year of his reign would be 966 B.C. The text says that the Exodus from Egypt took place 480 years before this; that gives 1446 B.C. as the approximate date of the Exodus. In this view, Moses would have grown up and lived for 40 years at the court of three very powerful kings of the 18th Dynasty, Thutmose I, II, and III. (For more details on the Egyptian kings and pharaohs, see next section.) It is then possible — though not at all certain — that Hatshepsut was the Egyptian princess, mentioned in Exodus 2, who adopted Moses.

The internal chronology of the biblical text when set against Egyptian chronology would thus indicate that Moses fled Egypt during the long reign of the very powerful Thutmose III and returned—after tending Jethro's sheep for 40 years—to the court of Amenhotep II, during whose reign he led Israel out of Egypt (ca. 1446 B.C.).

Those who hold to a **Late Date Theory** of the Exodus (around 1290 B.C.) point to Exodus 1:11: "So they put slave masters over them to oppress them with forced labor, and they built Pithom and Rameses as store cities for Pharaoh." They argue that the Rameses mentioned here must be named for one of the Rameses pharaohs of the 19th Dynasty—usually Rameses II.

Arguments and counterarguments are put forth by all sides, based on additional factors of biblical and Egyptian chronology as well as on the results of archaeological excavations in Israel and Jordan relating to the conquest of the land by the Israelites—ca. 1400 B.C. (early date) or ca. 1250 B.C. (late date). Sites such as Jericho, Ai, and Hazor figure prominently in the discussion, for they are said to have been burned and destroyed by the invading Israelites (see the book of Joshua).

All, however, are agreed that Israel was in the land by Merneptah's fifth year (ca. 1231 B.C.): Israel is actually mentioned on a stela of Merneptah as already living in the land of Canaan.

The early date—though not without problems—fits the biblical as well as the extrabiblical data the best.

Who Was the Pharaoh of the Exodus?

According to the biblical data, Jacob and his family entered Egypt around 1876 B.C., which would have been during the reign of King Sesostris III of the 12th Dynasty. The kings of the 15th and 16th Dynasties were Hyksos, a Semitic line of conquerors from Asia, possibly kin to the Israelites, who had pressed in from Syria.

Thutmose III (1500-1450 B.C.) kneeling in worship with offerings of two wine jars. Although the Pharaoh of the Exodus is not mentioned in the Bible and thus much debated, it was Thutmose III, who built Egypt into a dominant nation, setting the stage for the Hebrews' exodus out of Egypt.

It is possible that the "new king, who did not know about Joseph" (Exodus 1:8), during whose rule the oppression began, was one of the kings of these Hyksos dynasties. As a member of a small ruling elite, the Hyksos king would have been afraid that his more numerous subjects would revolt ("the Israelites have become much too numerous for us," Exodus 1:9). The Hyksos were driven out by King Ahmose of the 18th Dynasty, around 1570 B.C. It is possible that after the Hyksos were driven out, the oppression of the Israelites actually increased, since the Hyksos, like the Israelites, were Semites and their expulsion resulted in a general anti-Semitic reaction. Ahmose also made Palestine and Syria tributaries to Egypt.

Amenhotep I (1545 B.C.).

Thutmose I (1529 B.C.). Boasted that he ruled from the third cataract of the Nile to the Euphrates River about 700 miles to the northeast of Egypt. First royal rock-cut tomb.

Thutmose II (1517 B.C.). Hatshepsut, his half-sister and wife, was the real ruler.

Hatshepsut (1504 B.C.). Daughter of Thutmose I. Regent for Thutmose II and Thutmose III. The first great queen in history. A most remarkable woman, and one of Egypt's greatest and most vigorous rulers. She had many of her statues represent her as a man. She extended the empire and built many monuments, such as the two great obelisks at Karnak and the great temple at Deir el Bahri, furnished with many statues of herself. Thutmose III hated her, and when she died, one of his first acts was to take her name off all monuments and destroy all her statues. Those at Bahri were broken to pieces, flung into a quarry, and covered by drifting sands.

Thutmose III (1504 B.C.). Queen Hatshepsut, his half-sister, was regent during the early years of his reign, and though he despised her, she completely dominated him. His sole rule began in 1482 B.C., in which year he made the first of 17 campaigns into the Levant (the region east of the Mediterranean Sea between Greece and Egypt), taking control of the area. After her death, he ruled alone for 30 years. He was the greatest conqueror in Egyptian history. He subdued Ethiopia and ruled to the Euphrates, creating a great empire. He raided Palestine and Syria 17 times. He accumulated great wealth, engaged in vast building enterprises, and recorded his achievements in detail on walls and monuments. He is thought to have been one of the oppressors of Israel. If so, then the famous Queen Hatshepsut may have been the pharaoh's daughter who rescued and brought up Moses.

Amenhotep II (1453 B.C.). Many scholars think he was the pharaoh of the Exodus. He maintained the empire founded by Thutmose III. Interestingly, he is not known for military campaigns late in his reign — perhaps because of the loss of his chariots and troops at the Red Sea?

Thutmose IV (1426 B.C.). The chariot in which he rode has been found. His mummy is now at Cairo.

Amenhotep III (1416 B.C.). Under him, the empire experienced its era of greatest splendor. He raided Canaan during the early years of his reign. He built vast temples. During his years, and those of his successor, Akhenaten, the cuneiform documents found at el–Amarna were written. His mummy is in Cairo.

Akhenaten (1380 B.C.). Under him, Egypt lost its Asiatic Empire. He attempted to establish monotheistic sun worship.

Tutankhamen (1377 B.C.). Son-in-law of Akhenaten. He restored the old religion. He was one of the lesser rulers of Egypt, at the close of the most brilliant period of Egyptian history. He is famous now for the amazing riches and magnificence of his tomb, which was discovered by Howard Carter in 1922—the first tomb of a pharaoh to be discovered that had not been robbed. The inner coffin, which contains his mummy, is made of solid gold.

Rameses II (1304 B.C.). After several lesser rulers, Rameses II was one of the greatest of the pharaohs, though inferior to Thutmose III and Amenhotep III. He ruled for 67 years and was a great builder, a great self-promoter, and something of a plagiarist, claiming credit in some cases for accomplishments of his predecessors. He reestablished the empire from Ethiopia to the Euphrates and raided and pillaged Palestine repeatedly. He completed the great hall at Karnak and other vast works, including fortifications, canals, and temples, which were built by slaves taken in war or captives from the far south, along with the native working class, toiling in gangs in the quarry or brick fields, or dragging great stone blocks over soft earth. Some scholars consider him to be the pharaoh of the Exodus (the so-called Late Date Exodus; see preceding section).

Merneptah (1236 B.C.). On his stela he mentions having defeated Israel—"Israel is laid waste, his seed is not"—indicating that Israel was already in the land of Canaan.

What Route Did the Israelites Follow After the Exodus?

The books of Exodus and Numbers contain a considerable amount of geographical information in the narrative of the Exodus and the journey to the land of Canaan. But many of the places and regions mentioned remain unknown. The major reason for this is that the population of the desert-wilderness regions of the Sinai Peninsula, the Negev, and parts of southern Transjordan was nomadic. Without a continuity of a sedentary population, the preservation of ancient place names is almost impossible.

The other difficulty is that archaeologists have not discovered any remains that can be attributed to the Israelites in those regions through which they traveled. This, however, could be expected, for a nomadic people, living in tents and using animal skins instead of pottery for containers, would leave few permanent remains behind.

Thus scholars are divided on the location even of major landmarks such as the Red Sea and Mount Sinai. It has been noted that nine different proposals have been made for the location of the Red Sea or Reed Sea—including three lakes near the Mediterranean Sea, four lakes along the line of the present-day Suez Canal, and the Gulf of Suez and the Gulf of Elath. There are also 12 different candidates for Mount Sinai:

five in the southern part of the Sinai Peninsula, four in the north, one in the center, one in Midian (Saudi Arabia), and one in Edom (southern Transjordan).

In spite of these uncertainties, a few suggestions can be made:

1. After leaving Rameses (Tell el-Dab'a), the Israelites journeyed to Succoth (possibly Tell el-Maskhuta in the Wadi Tumilat). For fear of their becoming discouraged because of war, "God did not lead them by the way of the land of the Philistines" (Exodus 13:17 NASB). "God did not lead them on the road through the Philistine country, though that was shorter" (Exodus 13:17 NIV). This well-known route from Sile to Gaza, across the northern Sinai Peninsula, was the one pharaohs Thutmose III and Amenhotep II had used so effectively on their frequent campaigns to Canaan, and it must have been well fortified by Egyptian troops. Thus a northern route for the Exodus seems excluded.

2. Since the Israelites were led "around by the desert road toward the Red Sea" (Exodus 13:18), it appears that they were heading southeast toward modern Suez. The location of Etham ("fort" in Egyptian), Migdol ("fort" in Semitic), Baal Zephon, and Pi Hahiroth are problematic. The suggestion that Hahiroth refers to the low ground between Jebel Geneife and the Bitter Lakes is plausible but not certain. Etham and Migdol could be any of a number of Egyptian forts located near the present-day Suez Canal.

3. On the next stage of their journey the Israelites crossed the Red Sea. Since the Hebrew text literally means "Reed Sea," many scholars look for a location in the lake/marsh that used to exist in the region through which the Suez Canal now passes. The suggestion for a location near the junction of the Great and Little Bitter lakes is as plausible as any. According to 19th-century travelers, the water at that spot was not very deep, and they even mention that at times the depth of the water decreased when the wind shifted. According to the text, the "Lord drove the sea back with a strong east wind" (Exodus 14:21).

4. The identification of Mount Sinai (Horeb) with Jebel Musa ("Mount Moses") is based on Christian tradition dating back to the 4th century A.D., about 1,750 years after the event. There, during the Byzantine period (A.D. 324–640), the desert monastery of St. Catherine was established. Although the Greek Orthodox monks today like to point out the very site of the giving of the Law, the place where the golden calf was erected, the plain where the Israelites camped, the site of the burning bush, and so on, the suggested identification of Mount Sinai with Jebel Sin Bisher deserves careful attention. Its location agrees with some of the biblical data. For example, it is located approximately three days'

journey from Egypt (Exodus 3:18; 5:3; 8:27), at a desert junction where there are fair supplies of water; possibly the Amalekites fought with Israel for control of this junction and the water sources (Exodus 17). It is close to Egypt on the road that led directly from Midian to Egypt, and thus it would make a plausible location for the burning bush incident. Moses could have been bringing Jethro's sheep along this road in order to use the water and pasture land found on the eastern edge of the Nile delta when the Lord appeared to him in the burning bush. This is said to have taken place near the mountain where he would later worship him (Exodus 3:1). Since it is reasonable to assume that Moses used the way of the wilderness on his return to Egypt, the meeting of Moses and Aaron at the "mountain of God" could well have been at this spot (Exodus 4:27).

5. The location of Marah, where the water was bitter (Exodus 15:23), and of Elim, where there were 12 springs and 70 palm trees (v. 27), depends on where one locates Mount Sinai. If Jebel Sin Bisher is accepted as Mount Sinai, then the identifications of Marah and Elim with Bir Mara ("bitter well" in Arabic) and Ayun Musa ("the spring of Moses") are plausible. If the more traditional site of Sinai at Jebel Musa is maintained, then identifications of Marah and Elim with Ein Hawwara and Gharandal are also possible.

Exodus

The 400 Years in Egypt
The Exodus from Egypt
The Ten Commandments
The Tabernacle

By day the LORD went ahead of them in a pillar of cloud to guide them on their way and by night in a pillar of fire to give them light, so that they could travel by day or night. Neither the pillar of cloud by day nor the pillar of fire by night left its place in front of the people. —EXODUS 13:21–22

Moses answered the people, "Do not be afraid. Stand firm and you will see the deliverance the LORD will bring you today. The Egyptians you see today you will never see again. The LORD will fight for you; you need only to be still."

Then the LORD said to Moses, "Why are you crying out to me? Tell the Israelites to move on." —EXODUS 14:13–15

The title of this book comes from the Septuagint, the ancient Greek translation of the Old Testament. The word means "exit" or "departure." Exodus is book two of the Pentateuch (see pp. 81, 988). The traditional view held by most Bible scholars is that Moses wrote the bulk of the Pentateuch after Israel's exodus from Egypt and during their 40 years of wandering in the desert.

Exodus gives us insight into God's nature, and it also provides a foundational theology as to who God is, how He is to be worshiped, His laws, His covenant with Israel, and His overall plan of redemption. Through the Exodus, His Ten Commandments, and the laws given in the Book of the Covenant, we see God's loving and just character and we obtain a greater understanding of the depth of His holiness.

Ex. 1 ISRAEL IN EGYPT

A total of 430 years elapsed between Jacob's migration to Egypt and the Exodus (12:40–41). Genesis ended with the death of Joseph, and Exodus begins 300 years later with the birth of Moses. During these centuries the Israelites had become very numerous (v. 7). At the time of the Exodus there were 600,000 men above age 20, besides women and children (Numbers 1:46), which would total about 3 million Israelites. For 70 persons to grow to this number in 430 years, they would have had to double about every 25 years, which is entirely possible. (The growth of the population in the United States in 400 years, from relatively few to more than a quarter billion, makes the statement about the growth of the Israelites credible — even allowing for the fact that the U.S. population grew in part because of immigration.)

Making sun-dried mudbricks. These bricks deteriorated over time. Baked mudbricks required more labor than other kinds, but lasted longer and were sometimes used for exterior walls.

After the death of Joseph, a change of dynasty made the Israelites a race of slaves. But the family records of Abraham, Isaac, and Jacob, no doubt, had been carried to Egypt, and through the long years of slavery the promise that Canaan would one day be their national home, and that they would be free, was steadfastly cherished.

Ex. 2 MOSES

Exodus begins the story of Moses. His life and work are the subject matter of not only the book of Exodus, but also of Leviticus, Numbers, and Deuteronomy. Moses stands out as one of the greatest—perhaps *the* greatest—man of the pre-Christian world. He took a race of slaves and, under inconceivably trying circumstances, molded them into a powerful nation that has altered the whole course of history.

Moses was a Levite—he was of the tribe of Levi (v. 1). The sister who engineered his rescue was Miriam (15:20). His father may have been Amram, his mother Jochebed (6:20), although they may have been more distant ancestors. And what a mother! She so thoroughly instilled the traditions of his people in him in childhood that all the splendor and temptations of the heathen palace never eradicated those early impressions. He had the finest education Egypt could offer, but it did not turn his head or cause him to lose his childhood faith.

His 40 Years in the Palace

Moses, as he grew to manhood, is thought to have been appointed to high office in the government of Egypt. Josephus says he commanded an army in the south. He must have attained considerable power, reputation, and skill; otherwise it is not likely that he would have undertaken so gigantic a task as the deliverance of Israel, which (according to Acts 7:25) he had in mind when he intervened in the Egyptian's beating of a Hebrew slave (vv. 11–15). But though conscious of his power, he failed, because the people were not ready for his leadership—and neither was Moses himself.

His 40 Years in the Desert

These 40 years, in God's providence, were part of Moses' training. The loneliness and roughness of the wilderness developed sturdy qualities he could hardly have acquired in the softness of the palace. It familiarized him with the region in which he later led Israel for 40 years.

The center of Midian (v. 15), the country where Moses went, was on the eastern shore of the Gulf of Akaba, although the Midianites controlled the regions west of the gulf and to the north as well. In Moses' day they controlled the rich pasturelands around Sinai.

Moses married a Midianite woman, Zipporah (v. 21), a daughter of Jethro (who is also called Reuel; 2:18; 3:1). Jethro, as priest of Midian, must have been a ruler. The Midianites were also descendants of Abraham, through Keturah (Genesis 25:2), and must have had traditions of Abraham's God. Moses had two sons, Gershom and Eliezer (18:3–4).

Ex. 3–4 | THE BURNING BUSH

After a life of brooding over the sufferings of his people and the age-old promises of God, the call to deliver Israel came at last, directly from God, when Moses was 80 years old. But Moses was no longer self-confident, as he had been in his younger years. He was reluctant to go and made all kinds of excuses. But in the end he went, assured of divine help and armed with the power to work miracles.

Ex. 5 | MOSES' FIRST DEMAND

Pharaoh was insolent. He ordered the supervisors to lay even heavier burdens on the Israelites; they were to make the same number of bricks as before, but now they also had to find their own straw (2:10–19). Moses soon lost favor with the Israelites, who were quick to blame him for the increased level of oppression. God continued to press Moses to again approach Pharaoh for their release and to tell the Israelites that He had not forgotten His covenant with them.

Ex. 6 | THE GENEALOGY OF MOSES

This is considered an abbreviated genealogy that mentions only the more prominent ancestors. According to this genealogy, Moses was the grandson of Kohath, yet in his day there were 8,600 Kohathites (Numbers 3:28). Thus there is uncertainty as to the exact translation of v. 20.

Ex. 7 | THE FIRST OF THE 10 PLAGUES

The waters of the Nile turned to blood. Pharaoh's magicians (Jannes and Jambres, 2 Timothy 3:8) imitated the miracle on a small scale. Whatever the nature of the miracle, the fish died and people could not drink the water.

The Nile was a god to the Egyptians. Without the Nile, Egypt would be a lifeless desert.

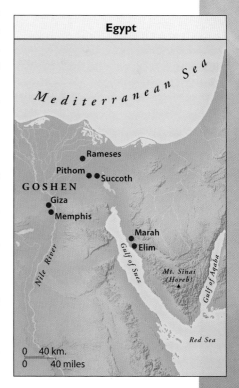

Egypt

Mediterranean Sea

Rameses
Pithom • • Succoth
GOSHEN
Giza
Memphis
Marah
Elim
Gulf of Suez
Nile River
Mt. Sinai (Horeb)
Gulf of Akaba
Red Sea

0   40 km.
0   40 miles

The 10 Plagues and the Gods of Egypt

The 10 plagues were aimed at the gods of Egypt and were designed to give proof of the power of the God of Israel over the gods of Egypt. Over and over it is repeated that by these miracles both Israel and Egyptians would come to "know that the LORD is God" (6:7; 7:5, 17; 8:22; 10:2; 14:4, 18). Later, in the desert, the manna and the quail were intended to show the same thing (16:6, 12).

Pharaoh's heart was hardened on his own accord during the first five plagues. God hardened his heart during the other five. Without them, Israel never would have been delivered, and there would have been no Hebrew nation.

Plague		God(s)
1. Nile turned to blood	7:14–25	**Khnum**, the guardian of the Nile **Hopi**, the spirit of the Nile **Osiris**, the giver of life, whose bloodstream was the Nile
2. Frogs	8:1–15	**Heqt**, the god of resurrection, who also assisted women in childbirth and whose form was a frog
3. Gnats (mosquitoes)	8:16–19	
4. Flies	8:20–32	
5. Plague on cattle	9:1–7	**Hathor**, the mother goddess, whose form was a cow **Apis**, the bull god, who was the living personification of **Ptah** (the creator god) and the symbol of fertility
6. Boils	9:8–12	**Imhotep**, the god of medicine
7. Hail	9:13–35	**Nut**, the sky goddess **Isis**, the goddess of life **Seth**, the protector of crops
8. Locusts	10:1–20	**Isis**, the goddess of life **Seth**, the protector of crops
9. Darkness	10:21–29	**Re, Aten, Atum, Horus**, all of whom were sun gods of sorts
10. Death of firstborn	11:1–12:36	**Pharaoh**, considered a god **Osiris**, the giver of life

—Adapted from John H. Walton, *Chronological and Background Charts of the Old Testament*

Ex. 8 PLAGUES OF FROGS, GNATS, AND FLIES

The frog represented Heqt, the Egyptian god of resurrection. At Moses' command, frogs swarmed out of the Nile and filled houses. The magicians again imitated the miracle, but this time Pharaoh was convinced and promised to let Israel go. But he quickly changed his mind.

The third plague was gnats. Moses hit the dust, and it became gnats (mosquitoes) on both man and beast. The magicians tried to imitate this miracle, but failed—in fact, they were convinced that it was of God. They ceased their efforts to oppose Moses and advised Pharaoh to give in.

The fourth plague consisted of swarms of flies that covered the people and filled the houses of the Egyptians. But there were no flies on the Israelites.

Still Pharaoh hardened his heart (vv. 15, 32). God's purpose was to make Pharaoh repent. But when a man sets himself against God, even God's mercies result in further hardening.

Ex. 9 PLAGUE ON LIVESTOCK; BOILS; HAIL

The plague on Egypt's livestock was a terrible blow at Egyptian gods. The bull was a chief god. Again there is a distinction between Egyptians and Israelites: the Egyptians' livestock died in vast numbers, but not one of those belonging to Israelites. "All" in v. 6 refers to the livestock of the Egyptians that were left in the fields. Moses gave them until the next day (v. 5) so that God-fearing Egyptians had time to move their livestock out of danger. Verses 19–21 refer to livestock that survived.

The boils, the sixth plague, came on both man and beast, and even on the magicians, from ashes which Moses sprinkled into the air.

Before the seventh plague came and hail fell, a merciful warning was again extended to God-fearing Egyptians to drive their cattle to cover. Again there is a distinction between Egyptians and Israelites: no hail fell in Goshen.

By this time the people of Egypt had become convinced (10:7). The sudden appearance and disappearance of the plagues, at the word of Moses, on such a vast scale, were accepted as evident miracles from God. But Pharaoh hesitated because of the immense economic impact the loss of his slave labor would have—Israelite labor had contributed greatly to Egypt's rise to power.

It is not known how long a period the 10 plagues covered. Pharaoh, no doubt, would have killed Moses had he dared. But with each new plague, Moses' prestige went up and up (11:3).

Ex. 10 PLAGUES OF LOCUSTS, DARKNESS

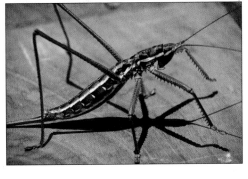

Locusts were one of the worst of the plagues. They came in vast clouds and would eat every green thing. At night they would cover the ground in layers to a depth of four or five inches. When mashed, the smell would be unbearable. The mere threat of a locust plague caused Pharaoh's officials to beg him to yield (v. 7).

The plague of darkness was a direct blow at Ra, or Re, Egypt's sun god. There was midnight darkness over Egypt for three days, but light where Israelites dwelt. Pharaoh yielded—but again changed his mind.

"[The locusts] covered all the ground until it was black. They devoured all that was left after the hail — everything growing in the fields and the fruit on the trees. Nothing green remained on tree or plant in all the land of Egypt." This description in Exodus 10:5 is not an exaggeration. A swarm of locusts can indeed darken the sun and strip an entire area of anything green in a very short time.

The Lord instructed the Israelites to put blood on the doorpost during the first Passover. The memory of this event is still observed by Egyptian villagers in the Nile Delta who put blood on their doors to prevent sickness, disease, and death from entering their homes.

Ex. 11–12 DEATH OF EGYPT'S FIRSTBORN

At last, the final and most devastating blow fell. Pharaoh yielded and Israel departed.

The Israelites "borrowed" jewelry and clothes from the Egyptians (12:35 KJV). The fact is that they "asked" (NASB, NIV) — these were not loans, but outright gifts in payment of debts for accumulated generations of slave labor. God Himself had commanded the people to ask for these gifts (3:21–22; 11:2–3), and the Egyptians were only too glad to comply, for they feared the God of Moses (12:33) and what He could do to them. A large part of Egypt's wealth was thus transferred to Israel. Some of it was used in the construction of the tabernacle.

The Beginning of Passover

The lamb, the blood on the doorposts, the death of the firstborn, deliverance out of a hostile country, and the celebration of the Feast of Passover throughout Israel's history — all were intended by God to be a grand historical picture of Christ the Passover Lamb and our deliverance, by His blood, from a hostile world and from the slavery of sin. Other Scriptures refer to Jesus as our sacrificial lamb:

- "A lamb without blemish or defect" (1 Peter 1:19)
- "Look, the Lamb of God, who takes away the sins of the world!" (John 1:29)
- "When he saw Jesus passing by, he said 'Look, the Lamb of God!'" (John 1:36)
- "For Christ, our Passover lamb, has been sacrificed" (1 Corinthians 5:7)
- "Then I saw a Lamb, looking as if it had been slain . . ." (Revelation 5:16)

Unleavened bread was to be eaten during the Passover Feast as a perpetual reminder of the haste with which the people left Egypt (12:34).

Ex. 13 THE CONSECRATION OF THE FIRSTBORN

The Israelites' firstborn were to be consecrated to God perpetually, as a reminder of the Israelites' redemption by the death of Egypt's firstborn.

Jesus was consecrated to God in accordance with this law, since he was Mary's firstborn son (Luke 2:7, 22–30).

The route to Canaan which the Israelites followed (v. 17) was not the direct route along the coast of the Mediterranean Sea, since there were garrisons of Egyptian soldiers stationed along this route, which also went through the country of the Philistines. The most feasible route was the longer but safer way through the wilderness of the Sinai Peninsula (see pp. 130–32).

The pillar of cloud by day and pillar of fire by night (vv. 21–22). As they left Egypt and had to travel through hostile territory, God took them under His own care, with this visible sign of His guidance and protection. It never left them until they reached the Promised Land, 40 years later (14:19, 24; 33:9, 10; 40:34–38; Numbers 9:15, 23; 10:11).

Ex. 14 CROSSING THE RED SEA

The place where they crossed may have been near the location of the Bitter Lakes, now part of the Suez Canal. God used a "strong east wind" to dry up the sea (v. 21). The waters parted and formed a "wall of water" on either side (15:8; 14:22). This, as well as the timing of the waters' return so that the Israelites were saved and the Egyptians destroyed, could have been done only by a direct miraculous act of God. It alarmed the neighboring nations (15:14–16).

Ex. 15 THE SONG OF MOSES

This song seems to prefigure the mightier works for which the redeemed will sing praises to God through endless ages of eternity. The deliverance out of Egypt under Moses was so similar to what the deliverance of the church out of the world at the time of the end will be, that one of the triumphant songs of the redeemed in the book of Revelation is called "the Song of Moses and the Lamb" (Revelation 15:3).

Crossing the Sea

The "tongue" of the Gulf of Suez may have reached farther north in Moses' day than it does today. The sea then would have flowed north into the depressions known today as the Bitter Lakes. If a steady wind (v. 21) pushed the shallow water north into the Bitter Lakes, it would have lowered the level of the water so that a land bridge would appear, which is not an uncommon phenomenon. The waters on the north and the south then were a "wall" or "defense." There is no need to assume perpendicular heaps of water defying gravity—although there is no question that God could have done exactly that. The Egyptian pursuit implies that the enemy saw no more than a strange, but not completely unnatural phenomenon. They could not attack from either flank. They followed through the exposed sea mud and were caught and tangled by the returning tide (v. 25) following the relaxed pressure of the wind.

Ex. 16 MANNA AND QUAIL

After one month of traveling, the hardships of desert life began to affect the Israelites' dispositions. They began to complain, thinking about what they had in Egypt, rather than about what God would give them in the Promised Land (vv. 2–3).

Manna was a small round flake used for making bread. It tasted, it is said, like wafers made with honey (v. 31). It was either a direct creation or a natural product miraculously multiplied. It fell with the dew each night and looked like coriander seed. The manna was ground in mills or beat in mortars, then boiled in pots, and cakes were made of it. Each person was allowed an omer (about two quarts or two liters) daily. On the sixth day there was always enough to last over the Sabbath. The manna began one month after they left Egypt and was given daily throughout the 40 years in the wilderness until they crossed the Jordan. Then it ceased as suddenly as it began (Numbers 11:6–9; Joshua 5:12). Jesus regarded manna as a foreshadowing of Himself (John 6:31–58).

Quail (v. 13) are mentioned only twice: here and a year later, after Israel had left Mount Sinai (Numbers 11:31–34). The people had great herds of cattle (Exodus 12:38), which they could use only sparingly as food. In Egypt the Israelites had eaten mostly fish instead of red meat.

Ex. 17 WATER FROM THE ROCK

Shortly before this, Moses had made the waters of Marah sweet (15:25). Here, in Rephidim, he produces water out of a rock. Later he performs a

---

Mount Sinai

Also called Horeb. The Peninsula of Sinai is triangular in shape, situated between two arms of the Red Sea. The west shore is about 180 miles long; the east shore about 130; and the north border line about 150. The northern part of the peninsula is desert; the southern part is a "great cluster of rugged chaotic mountains."

The region was probably named for Sin, the Babylonian moon god. It was early known for its mines of copper, iron, ochre, and precious stones. Long before the days of Abraham, the kings of the East had made a road around the north and west fringes of the Arabian Desert to the Sinai region.

There is some debate as to which mountain in the Sinai Peninsula is Mount Sinai. The two most likely possibilities are Ras es-Safsafeh and Jebel Musa, both of which are located on a granite ridge of about three miles. Ras es-Safsafeh (6,643 ft.) is on the northern edge, Jebel Musa (7,497 ft.) on the southern edge. Tradition and most modern scholars accept Jebel Musa as Mount Sinai; others prefer Ras es-Safsafeh because there is a considerable plain at the foot of the mountain where the Israelites could have camped (see Exodus 20:18). Another possible (though less likely) candidate is Jebel Sin Bisher, about 50 miles north-northwest of Jebel Musa (see pp. 131–32).

At the foot of Jebel Musa is St. Catherine's monastery, where Friedrich Tischendorf discovered the famous 4th-century manuscript of the Greek Bible known as the Codex Sinaiticus (see pp. 994–95).

For a people who had never known anything but the flat country of Goshen and the Nile delta, Mount Sinai itself must have been imposing indeed. And it is little wonder that the people were terrified when the Lord appeared: "On the morning of the third day there was thunder and lightning, with a thick cloud over the mountain, and a very loud trumpet blast. Everyone in the camp trembled. Then Moses led the people out of the camp to meet with God, and they stood at the foot of the mountain. Mount Sinai was covered with smoke, because the LORD descended on it in fire. The smoke billowed up from it like smoke from a furnace, the whole mountain trembled violently, and the sound of the trumpet grew louder and louder. Then Moses spoke and the voice of God answered him" (Exodus 19:16–19).

similar miracle at Meribah (Numbers 20:1–13); however, he performs it in a way not pleasing to God. God rebukes Moses and Aaron and states that they will never enter the Promised Land. The battle with Amalek (vv. 8–15) is the first attempt, outside of Egypt, to interfere with Israel's march to Canaan. As a result, God commanded that the Amalekites be exterminated (v. 14; Deuteronomy 25:17–19).

Ex. 18 JETHRO'S ADVICE

Moses was inspired in a degree given to few men, yet it was through the counsel of this friendly Midianite prince, his father-in-law, that he came to a more efficient organization of the people. God uses human advice to help even the great!

Ex. 19 GOD'S VOICE ON MOUNT SINAI

They were at Mount Sinai about 11 months (v. 1; Numbers 10:11). In a terrific thunderstorm, accompanied by earthquakes and supernatural trumpet blasts, and the mountain capped with terrifying flames, God spoke the Ten Commandments and gave the Law.

Five hundred years later, at this same mountain, the prophet Elijah was given a hint that God's work would be accomplished, not by means of fire and earthquake, but by the still, small voice, the "gentle whisper" of God's message (1 Kings 19:11–12).

Sinai mountains. There are several traditional locations for Horeb in the mountains of southern Sinai.

Ex. 20 THE TEN COMMANDMENTS

"I am the LORD your God....
You shall have no other gods before me.
You shall not make for yourself an idol...
You shall not misuse the name of the LORD your God....
Remember the Sabbath day by keeping it holy....
Honor your father and your mother....
You shall not murder.
You shall not commit adultery.
You shall not steal.
You shall not give false testimony against your neighbor.
You shall not covet .... anything that belongs to your neighbor."
—Exodus 20:2–17

These Commandments were afterward engraved on both sides of two tablets of stone, "inscribed by the finger of God." "The tablets were the work of God; the writing was the writing of God, engraved on the tablets" (31:18; 32:15–16). They were kept for centuries in the ark of the covenant (see pp. 147–48). It is thought that they may have been destroyed in the destruction of Jerusalem by the Babylonians (see pp. 244–47).

The Ten Commandments were the basis of Hebrew law. Four of them have to do with our attitude toward God; six, with our attitude toward fellow human beings. Jesus condensed them into two: "Love the Lord your God with all your heart and with all your soul and with all your mind" and "Love your neighbor as yourself" (Matthew 22:37–39; see Deuteronomy 6:5 and Leviticus 19:18).

Reverence for God is the basis of the Ten Commandments. Jesus indicated that He considered it the most basic and essential quality in man's approach to God and made it the first petition in the Lord's Prayer: "Hallowed be your name." It is surprising how many people, in their ordinary conversation, continually blaspheme the name of God and use it in such a light and trivial way. It is even more surprising how many preachers and Christians use God's name with a facile familiarity that lacks any reverence or awe, as if they were God's equals.

Ex. 21–24 THE BOOK OF THE COVENANT

After the Ten Commandments, this was the first installment of the Law for the Hebrew nation. These laws were written in a book. Then the covenant that pledged to obey the Law was sealed with blood (24:4, 7–8).

The laws cover every aspect of daily life, from kindness toward widows and orphans to the death penalty for murder to hospitality toward strangers. Although many of the specific, individual laws no longer apply to us, the principles behind them most certainly do. Fairness, justice, and mercy are the foundation of Israel's Law—which becomes very clear when we compare them with the laws of the nations around Israel.

Do not cook a young goat in its mother's milk (23:19): A number of explanations have been suggested for this unusual command; it may be a warning against adopting a pagan, Canaanite ritual.

Ex. 25–31 DIRECTIONS FOR THE TABERNACLE

God Himself gave the pattern in great detail (25:9). It is recorded twice: first in these chapters, where God explains how it is to be made; then in chapters 35–40, where the details are repeated to indicate that this is exactly how it had been built—according to God's instructions. This repetition strikes us as redundant, but to the Hebrew ear it reflected the importance and solemnity of the building process. (See also Numbers 7, where the same list of gifts is repeated 12 times!)

The tabernacle was a "likeness" of something, a "copy and shadow" of heavenly things (Hebrews 8:5). It had special meaning to the Hebrew nation; yet it was a "pattern of things to come" (see Hebrews 9–10).

The tabernacle and, later, the temple, which was built by King Solomon based on the pattern of the tabernacle, were the center of Jewish national life. Of direct divine origin, the tabernacle was an immensely important representation of certain ideas God wished to impress on mankind, foreshadowing many teachings of the Christian faith.

(For a more detailed description of the tabernacle, see below under chapters 35–40.)

Ex. 32–33 THE GOLDEN CALF

The bull, the principal god of Egypt called Apis, later also would become the god of the Ten Tribes (1 Kings 12:28). This pitiful apostasy, so soon

The Tabernacle

The tabernacle itself consisted of two rooms. The first room, the Holy Place, was 15 feet high and wide and 30 feet long. The second room, the Most Holy Place, was exactly half as large: it was a cube measuring 15 x 15 x 15 feet.

Sinai Tabernacle reconstruction. The Lord provided Moses with the instructions for the design of the Tabernacle and its components.

A tent covered the tabernacle, consisting of three layers of coverings. The first was made of goat's hair cloth. Over it was a covering of red leather made of ram's skins. The final covering was badger skin (or possibly seal or porpoise skin).

There was a clear progression in the arrangement of the courtyard and the tabernacle. Israelites could bring their sacrifices to the altar in the courtyard, but beyond the altar only the priests could go and enter the Holy Place (after washing their hands and feet). But no one could enter the Most Holy Place, the place of God's Presence, except the high priest and only once a year, on the Great Day of Atonement (see pp. 152–53).

The Holy Place

The first thing that must have struck the priests entering the Holy Place was how different it smelled. The acrid smells from the altar of burnt offering were left behind, and the sweet smell of incense filled this room.

The incense altar. The incense altar was small, only 3 feet high and 18 inches square. Incense was burned on the altar, morning and evening (30:8). Its smoke rising into the sky symbolized prayer—daily, regular prayer (see also Revelation 8:3–5).

The lampstand. There were no windows in the tabernacle, but the coverings may have let in some light, since the lampstand was to be lit at twilight and to be kept burning from evening until morning (27:21;

30:7 – 8). Made of pure gold, it was 5 feet high and 3½ feet across the top. The shape of the lampstand, with its seven lamps, is still a common symbol in Judaism today: the menorah.

The lighted lamp symbolizes God's Word (Psalms 105; 119; 2 Peter 1:19) or God's guidance (2 Samuel 22:29; Psalm 18:28).

The lampstands of Solomon's temple were patterned after this lampstand (which may actually have been used in the temple). They were no doubt among the treasures taken to Babylon and afterward returned (Ezekiel 1:7).

The lampstand in Herod's temple, in Jesus' day, may have been one of these lampstands. It was taken to Rome when the temple was destroyed in A.D. 70 and is represented on the Arch of Titus (see photo p. 940). Tradition says that the lampstand was later "respectfully deposited in the Christian church at Jerusalem" in A.D. 533, but nothing further is known of it.

The table. Finally, there was a table, 27 inches high, 18 inches wide, and 3 feet long. On this table 12 loaves of bread were placed, one for each of the 12 tribes of Israel. The loaves were replaced every week. They represented Israel's gratitude for God's provisions.

The Most Holy Place

The Most Holy Place was the place of the presence of God. It was separated from the Holy Place by what must have been a superbly beautiful **curtain**, in blue, purple, and scarlet, embroidered with cherubim.

Solomon's temple, and later Herod's temple, were patterned after the tabernacle, and the Holy Place and the Most Holy Place were still separated by a curtain, even though the structure itself was made of stone and wood. The curtain of the temple was torn from top to bottom when Christ died (Matthew 27:51), signifying that, at that moment, the door to God's presence was open to all.

Only one item stood in the Most Holy Place: **the ark of the covenant.** It was a chest made of acacia wood and overlaid with pure gold. It measured 45 x 27 x 27 inches. The lid of the ark, made of solid gold, was called the "atonement cover" (KJV, mercy seat). At each end of the cover stood a cherub, made of one piece with the atonement cover. The cherubim faced each other, their wings spread out, and looked down toward the atonement cover. We can only speculate exactly how they may have looked.

Inside the ark were four items: the two stone tablets on which Moses had received the Ten Commandments, a pot of manna, and Aaron' staff (Numbers 17:1 – 11). These were a continual reminder of what was most important: God's covenant with His people (the two tablets), His gracious material provisions (the manna), and His provision of a way to Him through the priesthood, and specifically through the high priest (the staff; see also Hebrews 8).

The ark of the covenant was probably lost in the Babylonian captivity. In Revelation 11:19, John saw the ark "in the temple." But that was in a vision, certainly not meaning that the actual, material ark was there; for in heaven there will be "no temple" (Revelation 21:22).

This overview of the tabernacle shows the tent of meeting inside the court-yard. The smoke of the sacrificial fire rose, and the cloud of the glory of God descended and filled the dwelling. In this way the presence of the Lord Most High was revealed to His people.

Constructed in accordance with the plans of God, the front part (the Holy Place) of this gold-covered structure was twice as long as the back part (the Holy of Holies).

Leviticus

**Laws Concerning Sacrifices,
the Priesthood, and Sacred Feasts
Various Laws**

"I am the LORD who brought you up out of Egypt to be your God; therefore be holy, because I am holy."

—LEVITICUS 11:45

"Do not seek revenge or bear a grudge against one of your people, but love your neighbor as yourself. I am the LORD."

—LEVITICUS 19:18

The title of this book comes from the Septuagint, the ancient Greek translation of the Old Testament. The word *Leviticus* means "about, or relating to, the Levites."

The Levites are all those who belong to the tribe of Levi, one of the 12 tribes of Israel. Because God spared the firstborn of Israel in the last plague that came over Egypt (Exodus 11:4 – 12:13), all firstborn sons and firstborn animals belonged to God. The animals were sacrificed while the men were redeemed. To be redeemed, the family paid a price to the priest instead of giving their firstborn over to the service of the temple. God appointed the Levites to take the place of the firstborn to serve God. One clan or family of the Levites, the family of Aaron, was set apart to be priests. The rest of the Levites were to be assistants to the priests. Their duties were the care of the tabernacle, and later the care of the temple; and to be teachers, scribes, musicians, officers, and judges. (See on 1 Chronicles 23.)

The tribe of Levi was the only tribe that did not get its own land after the Israelites conquered Canaan; instead, they received 48 cities, scattered throughout the country (Numbers 35:7; Joshua 21:19). Since they did not receive land, they could not support themselves; they were supported by the tithes of the rest of Israel.

The book of Leviticus contains the bulk of the system of laws under which the Hebrew nation lived, laws that were administered by the Levitical priesthood. These laws were given mostly at Mount Sinai, with additions, repetitions, and explanations throughout the desert wanderings.

Old Testament Sacrifices

Sacrifice	OT References	Elements	Purpose
Burnt offering	Lev 1; 6:8–13; 8:18–21; 16:24	Bull, ram, or male bird (dove or young pigeon for the poor); wholly consumed; no defect	Voluntary act of worship; atonement for unintentional sin in general; expression of devotion, commitment and complete surrender to God
Grain offering	Lev 2; 6:14–23	Grain, fine flour, olive oil, incense, baked bread (cakes or wafers), salt; no yeast or honey; accompanied burnt offering and fellowship offering (along with drink offering)	Voluntary act of worship; recognition of God's goodness and provisions; devotion to God
Fellowship offering	Lev 3; 7:11–34	Any animal without defect from herd or flock; variety of breads	Voluntary act of worship; thanksgiving and fellowship (included a communal meal)
Sin offering	Lev 4:1–5:13; 6:24–30; 8:14–17; 16:3–22	1. Young bull: for high priest and congregation 2. Male goat: for leader 3. Female goat or lamb: for common person 4. Dove or pigeon: for the poor 5. Tenth of an ephah of fine flour: for the very poor	Mandatory atonement for specific unintentional sin; confession of sin; forgiveness of sin; cleansing from defilement
Guilt offering	Lev 5:14–6:7; 7:1–6	Ram or lamb	Mandatory atonement for unintentional sin requiring restitution; cleansing from defilement; make restitution; pay 20% fine

From *The NIV Study Bible*. Used by permission.

Lev. 8–9 THE CONSECRATION OF AARON

Before the time of Moses, sacrifices were offered by heads of families. But now that the nation is organized, a place is set apart for sacrifice, a ritual is prescribed, and a hereditary priesthood is created in a solemn ceremony. Aaron was to be high priest, and he was to be succeeded by his firstborn son. The priesthood was maintained by tithes (one-tenth of a family's income, whether money, livestock, or produce) and parts of some sacrifices. They received 13 cities (Joshua 21:13–19).

The high priest's garments. Every detail had been specified by God (Exodus 28). A robe of blue, with bells at the bottom.

The ephod, which was a sort of cape or sleeveless vestment, consisting of two pieces joined on the shoulders, that hung one at the front and one on the back of the high priest, with an onyx stone on each shoulder, each bearing six names of the tribes: made of gold, blue, purple, scarlet, and fine linen.

The breastplate, about 10 inches square, of gold, blue, purple, scarlet, and fine linen, double, open at the top, fastened with gold chains to the Ephod, adorned with 12 precious stones, each stone bearing the name of a tribe. The breastplate contained the Urim and Thummim, which were used to learn the will of God; we don't know exactly what they were, but they were used to cast lots.

The Divine Origin of the Sacrificial System

God placed the system of sacrifices at the very center and heart of Jewish national life. Whatever its immediate applications and implications may have been to the Jews, the unceasing sacrifice of animals and the never-ending glow of altar fires were without doubt designed by God to burn into the consciousness of the people of Israel a sense of their deep sinfulness. They were also, for more than a millennium, a picture that pointed forward to the coming sacrifice of Christ on the cross. The Levitical priesthood was divinely ordained to be the mediator between God and the Hebrew nation through the bringing of animal sacrifices. But those sacrifices were fulfilled in Christ. Animal sacrifices are no longer necessary. Christ Himself is our Great High Priest, the only Mediator between God and humanity, as Hebrews 8–10 makes very clear. Thus Christ is both our Sacrifice and our High Priest, our Mediator.

Lev. 10 NADAB AND ABIHU

The swift and terrible punishment on Nadab and Abihu was a warning against highhanded treatment of God's ordinances. It is also a warning to us and to church leaders not to distort the Gospel of Christ with all kinds of human additions and traditions.

Lev. 11 CLEAN AND UNCLEAN ANIMALS

Before the Flood there was a distinction between clean and unclean animals (Genesis 7:2). Through Moses this distinction acquired the force of divine law. It was based partly on the wholesomeness of a particular kind of animal as food, and partly on religious considerations, designed to serve as one of the marks of separation of Israel from other nations. Jesus abrogated the distinction (Mark 7:19), making all meats clean (see also Acts 10:9–16).

Lev. 12 PURIFICATION OF MOTHERS AFTER CHILDBIRTH

The uncleanness of mothers did not result from the birth but from the bleeding. There is no clear reason why the period of separation was 40 days if the baby was a boy, 80 days if it was a girl.

Lev. 13–14 THE TEST FOR SKIN DISEASES

These regulations were for the purpose of controlling the spread of infectious skin diseases, of which the most loathsome and dreaded was leprosy. The word translated "leprosy" in the KJV has a range of meanings, including leprosy, skin disease, and even mildew. Primitive as this approach may seem to us, these simple measures undoubtedly saved many lives.

Lev. 15 CEREMONIAL UNCLEANNESS

The elaborate system of specifications as to how a person could become ceremonially unclean and what had to be done about it was, it seems, designed to promote personal physical cleanliness (and thus help prevent illness) as well as a continual recognition of God's involvement in all areas of life.

"Love Your Neighbor as Yourself"

This injunction (19:18) is one of the highlights of the Mosaic Law. It is the second great commandment Jesus quoted (Matthew 22:39; the first great commandment—Love the LORD your God with all your heart and with all your soul and with all your mind—is found in Deuteronomy 6:5). The law instructed the people to show great consideration to the poor. Wages were to be paid day by day. No interest was to be charged ("usury" in the KJV refers to interest of any kind). Loans and gifts were to be made to the needy. A portion of the harvest was to be left in the fields for the poor. All through the Old Testament, unceasing emphasis is placed on kindness to widows, orphans, and strangers. The weak and the poor are everyone's responsibility.

Lev. 16 THE ANNUAL DAY OF ATONEMENT

The annual Day of Atonement (still celebrated in Judaism today in modified form and known by its Hebrew name, Yom Kippur) fell on the 10th day of the seventh month (the month Tishri, see p. 1025). It was the

Reconstruction of the ark of the covenant. The high priest entered the Holy of Holies only on the Day of Atonement and sprinkled blood on the ark of the covenant.

most solemn day of the year. Each time, the removal of sin was only for one year (Hebrews 10:3), but it pointed forward to its eternal removal (Zechariah 3:4, 8–9; 13:1; Hebrews 10:14).

After the sacrificial goat had been offered, the high priest laid his hands on the head of the scapegoat, confessing over him the sins of the people. The goat was then sent away into the wilderness, bearing away with it the sins of the people. This ceremony was one of God's historical foreshadowings of the coming atonement for human sin by the death of Christ.

Lev. 17 | THE MANNER OF SACRIFICE

The Law required the presentation of animals for sacrifice at the door of the tabernacle. The eating of blood was strictly forbidden (3:17; 7:26–27; 17:10–16; Genesis 9:4; Deuteronomy 12:16, 23–25), and still is (Acts 15:29). One reason is that blood is a symbol of life and as such must be treated with respect. To this day, in orthodox Judaism, any animal destined for human consumption must be slaughtered according to very strict regulations and under rabbinic supervision to ensure that all the blood has drained out of the meat. Only then can the meat be sold as kosher.

Lev. 18 | CANAANITE ABOMINATIONS

The reason that some of these things, such as incest, sodomy, and sexual relations with animals, are even mentioned is that they were common practice among Israel's neighbors.

Lev. 19–20 | MISCELLANEOUS LAWS

These chapters contain a number of miscellaneous laws, ranging from the Sabbath, to sorcery, to kindness to strangers. The diversity of these laws shows that God is interested in *all* aspects of life. He did not give laws only to keep Israel from doing what was wrong, but also to tell Israel what it meant to live as the nation chosen by God and as people who loved God.

Concubinage, polygamy, divorce, and slavery were allowed but greatly restricted (19:20; Exodus 21:2–11; Deuteronomy 21:15; 24:1–4). Moses' law lifted marriage to a far higher level than existed in surrounding nations. Slavery was tempered by humane considerations; it never existed on a large scale among the Jews, nor with such cruelties as were prevalent in Egypt, Assyria, Greece, Rome, and other nations. An Israelite could not be a slave forever (see on Leviticus 25).

Lev. 21–22 | PRIESTS AND SACRIFICES

These chapters are an elaboration on the provisions of chapters 1–9. Priests must be without physical defect and may marry only a virgin. Sacrificial animals must also be without defect and at least eight days old.

Lev. 23–24 FEASTS, LAWS CONCERNING THE TABERNACLE, BLASPHEMY

For a description of the feasts of Israel, see comments on Deuteronomy 16.

The lamp in the tabernacle was to burn perpetually. The bread placed before the Lord (KJV, showbread) was to be changed each Sabbath. Blasphemy was to be punished with death.

An eye for an eye (24:19–21). This legislation was not intended to give permission for revenge, but rather the opposite: it severely *limited* revenge or retaliation to what was just, instead of allowing a cycle of retaliation and counter-retaliation to spin out of control (see on Matthew 5:38 and Luke 6:27).

Lev. 25 THE SABBATH YEAR AND THE YEAR OF JUBILEE

Every seventh year was a Sabbath year. The land was to lie fallow. No sowing, no reaping, no pruning of vineyards. Spontaneous produce was to be left for the poor and the temporary resident (KJV, sojourner). God promised enough in the sixth year to meet the needs of the seventh year. Debts of fellow Jews were to be canceled.

Every 50th year was a Year of Jubilee. It followed the seventh Sabbath Year, so that two years of rest would come together. It began on the Day of Atonement. All debts were canceled, slaves of Israelite origin were set free, and lands that had been sold were returned. (This was intended to ensure that a family's land would remain in the family in perpetuity.) Jesus seemed to regard the Year of Jubilee as a sort of picture of the rest He came to proclaim for God's people (Leviticus 25:10; Luke 4:19).

Lev. 26 OBEDIENCE OR DISOBEDIENCE

This chapter of magnificent promises and frightful warnings is, like Deuteronomy 28, one of the great chapters of the Bible.

Lev. 27 VOWS AND TITHES

Vows were a voluntary promise to God to perform some service or do something pleasing to Him in return for some hoped benefits. A vow had to be spoken to be binding (Deuteronomy 23:23). Israelites made special vows by promising or dedicating persons, animals, houses, family land, or land they had purchased to the service of the temple. In most cases, however, an equivalent value or price was paid to the priest for the person or thing being dedicated. When the price had been paid, the person or thing was said to have been redeemed.

This idea of redemption is carried forward into the New Testament in Galatians 3:13, where Christ is said to have redeemed us "from the curse of the law by becoming a curse for us." In 1 Corinthians 6:19 – 20, Paul teaches the early Christians, "You are not your own; your were bought at a price."

One-tenth of the produce of the land and of the increase of flocks and herds was to be given to God; this is called the tithe (Genesis 14:20; 28:22; Leviticus 27:30 – 32; Numbers 18:21 – 28; Deuteronomy 12:5 – 6, 11, 17 – 18; 14:23, 28 – 29; 26:12; the word *tithe* is derived from the Old English word for *tenth*).

Three tithes are mentioned in the Old Testament: the Levitical tithe, the festival tithe, and every third year the tithe for the poor. Some think there was only one tithe that was used partly for festivals and every third year partly for the poor. Others think that the festival tithe was taken out of the nine-tenths left after the Levitical tithe had been paid.

The tithe was in use long before the days of Moses. Abraham and Jacob paid tithes. Among the Jews the tithe was for the support of the Levites, who functioned both as civil officials and in religious service (see on 1 Chronicles 23).

God claimed as His own not only the tithes, but also the firstborn sons of all families (in place of whom He accepted the tribe of Levi), the firstborn of all flocks and herds, and firstfruits of the field. The firstfruits of the harvest were to be offered at Passover, and no part of the new crop could be used until this had been done (Leviticus 23:14). The first crop of a young orchard (the fourth year) was to be given to God in its entirety, and no fruit of the orchard could be used until this was done. The clear lesson is: Put God first in life.

The Number Seven in the Law of Moses

The number 7 played a significant symbolic role in the Mosaic Law.

- Every 7th day was a Sabbath.
- Every 7th year was a Sabbath year.
- Every 7th Sabbath year (7 x 7) was followed by a Year of Jubilee.
- Every 7th month was especially holy, with three feasts.
- There were 7 weeks between Passover and Pentecost.
- The Passover Feast lasted 7 days.
- The Feast of Tabernacles lasted 7 days.
- At the Passover, 14 lambs (twice 7) were offered daily.
- At the Feast of Tabernacles, 14 lambs (twice 7), and 70 bullocks were offered daily.
- At Pentecost, 7 lambs were offered.

(See also pp. 830 – 31.)

Numbers

The 40 Years in the Desert
Israel's Journey to the Promised Land

"The LORD bless you and keep you; the LORD make his face shine upon you and be gracious to you; the LORD turn his face toward you and give you peace."
—NUMBERS 6:24–26

The Lord's anger burned against Israel and he made them wander in the desert forty years, until the whole generation of those who had done evil in his sight was gone.
—NUMBERS 32:13

Numbers begins with the Lord organizing Israel into an army en route to establish God's kingdom in the Promised Land. Throughout the journey we see the Israelites' rebellion as well as God's anger against their disobedience. But despite God's judgment, He is faithful in bringing Israel into the land of promise. We see God's grace renewed time and time again.

Num. 1 | THE CENSUS

This census, taken at Mount Sinai, showed 603,550 males above the age of 20, not including Levites (vv. 45–47). Another census, taken 38 years later, showed 601,730 males above 20 (see on chapter 26).

Num. 2–4 | THE ORGANIZATION OF THE CAMP

Every detail was assigned with military precision. This was necessary in handling so vast a crowd of people. The tribes were arranged in specific locations around the tabernacle when they camped, and they also had a specific marching order when they traveled. The arrangement (see diagram on next page) allowed for an orderly transition from camping to traveling.

Judah and the eastern tribes led the march. The tabernacle was protected by the southern and western tribes to the south and north respectively, while the northern tribes brought up the rear.

Num. 5–6 | MISCELLANEOUS LAWS

What stands out in these chapters is the beautiful priestly blessing (6:24–26). The Hebrew word *shalom* does not mean quite the same as our word "peace." It is not merely absence of war or conflict (although it includes that) or a peaceful feeling. Rather, it means wholeness, well-being, harmony.

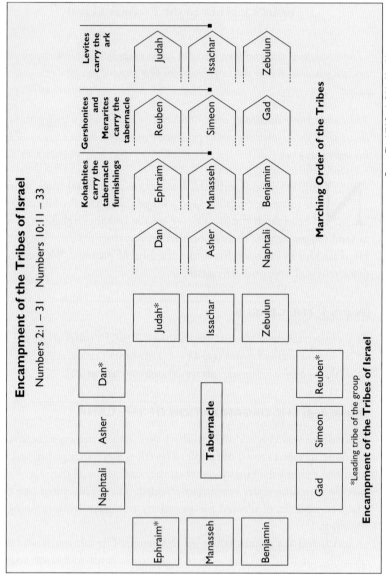

Encampment of the Tribes of Israel

Numbers 2:1 – 31   Numbers 10:11 – 33

Marching Order of the Tribes

Levites carry the ark

Judah
Issachar
Zebulun

Gershonites and Merarites carry the tabernacle

Reuben
Simeon
Gad

Kohathites carry the tabernacle furnishings

Ephraim
Manasseh
Benjamin

Dan
Asher
Naphtali

Naphtali
Asher
Dan*

Judah*
Issachar
Zebulun

Tabernacle

Gad
Simeon
Reuben*

Ephraim*
Manasseh
Benjamin

*Leading tribe of the group

Encampment of the Tribes of Israel

— From The NIV Study Bible. Used by permission.

Num. 7–9 | PREPARATION FOR THE JOURNEY

The offerings of the leaders of the 12 tribes (chap. 7) are all exactly the same. To us, repeating the same list 12 times seems redundant and boring, but to the Hebrew mind it emphasizes the solemnity and seriousness of the event. Also, each tribe, regardless of its size, gave the same gifts, so no tribe can later claim precedence.

For the presence of God in the cloud (9:15–25), see on Exodus 13:21.

Num. 10–11 | THEY SET FORWARD TO THE PROMISED LAND

The people stayed at Mount Sinai for one year. Then the cloud lifted. The silver trumpets sounded. Judah led the march. And they were on their way.

Within three days, at Taberah, they began to complain (10:33; 11:1–3). That was their specialty—they knew how to complain. God sent them quail, but He also sent a plague (see on Exodus 16).

Num. 12 | MIRIAM AND AARON OPPOSE MOSES

Before it was all over, poor Miriam wished she had never started the thing. Moses was "very humble" (v. 3). The KJV says he was "very meek." What an admirable trait in one of the greatest men of the ages! Jesus, quoting Psalm 37:11, said, "Blessed are the meek, for they will inherit the earth" (Matthew 5:5; see 11:29).

Num. 13–14 | THE 12 SPIES SENT TO CANAAN

Moses planned to go directly from Mount Sinai to Canaan. He went straight to Kadesh, 150 miles north of Sinai and 50 miles south of Beersheba, the southern gateway to Canaan, intending to enter at once.

But the spies brought a discouraging report, and the people refused to go forward. In fact, they would have stoned Moses if it had not been for God's miraculous intervention. This was the crucial point of the journey. Within sight of the Promised Land, they turned back. For them the opportunity never returned—God could no longer turn away from their continuous rebellion. Because of their disobedience to undertake the conquest of Canaan, this group forfeited their entrance into the Promised Land. They were condemned to live out their lives wandering in the desert. Only their children would experience the joy previously planned for them. Caleb and Joshua, the two spies who wanted to go forward, were the only ones of the 600,000 men over 20 who lived to enter Canaan.

Num. 15–19 | VARIOUS LAWS; KORAH

Korah, jealous of Moses, sought to usurp his leadership. Moses went straight to God, and God settled the matter in no time. The earth opened, and the rebels went down.

Moses' Troubles

Moses surely had a lot of troubles. No sooner was he out of Egypt than trouble began. The Amalekites attacked immediately, and a year later, at Kadesh, the Edomites, Moabites, Ammonites, Amorites, and Midianites all joined hands to block Israel's path to Canaan.

And his own people, who had been delivered out of Egypt and sustained by marvelous miracles, grumbled and grumbled, and complained and complained, and rebelled and rebelled. They began complaining while still in Egypt. Then at the Red Sea. Then at Marah. Then in the Desert of Zin (KJV, Wilderness of Sin). Then again at Rephidim, at Taberah, at Hazeroth, and at Meribah. Now, at Kadesh, in sight of the Promised Land, they flatly refused to go farther, which must have almost broken Moses' heart.

Besides all this, Moses had no end of trouble with his own trusted leaders. Aaron made the golden calf at Sinai. Miriam and Aaron tried to usurp his authority (chap. 12). Ten of the 12 spies led the people in their refusal to enter Canaan. The people were ready to stone Moses (14:10; Exodus 17:4).

And, last of all, Moses was not permitted to enter the Promised Land himself — the lifetime dream of his heart.

Except for the miraculous grace of God, we do not see how he could have borne up under it all. But when, on the banks of the Jordan River, God took him to see the "land that I promised on oath to Abraham, Isaac and Jacob" (32:11), Moses understood.

The Wilderness of Zin. The leadership of Moses was tested by the harsh conditions of the wilderness of Zin.

Num. 20 | FINAL START FOR CANAAN

There seems to be a gap of 38 years between chapters 19 and 20, covering the period between the first arrival at Kadesh (13:26) and the final departure from Kadesh for Canaan. In chapter 33 there is a list of encampments, 40 in all, from Egypt to the Plains of Moab. Of these, 18 were between Rithmah and Kadesh. We judge, from the expression "in Kadesh many days" (Deuteronomy 1:46) and the mention of these 18 encampments between the first and second arrivals

An oasis in the Sinai Desert. These small patches of green in the vast expanses of sand and rock indicate the presence of water — but not necessarily enough water for a large nation. When God gave the Israelites water from the rock, it was not merely a display of His power — it was a matter of survival for His people.

at Kadesh, that Kadesh may have been a sort of general headquarters or home base, with the people traveling to these other encampments as God directed. They would remain for some time at one spot, with their flocks and herds on the surrounding hills and valleys, and then move on.

Moses' sin, which cost him his entry into the Promised Land, appears to have been his failure to give God credit for the miracle of water out of the rock (10:12). It may also have been due to his failure to believe that a word alone could bring forth water. His striking of the rock twice with his staff showed a lack of trust in God and disrespect toward His holiness.

Miriam, Aaron, and Moses all died in the same year. Miriam died at Kadesh (20:1), Aaron at Mount Hor (20:28), and Moses on Mount Nebo (Deuteronomy 32:50; 34:1, 5). Miriam was about 130 years old; Aaron, 123; and Moses, the youngest of the siblings, a mere 120.

Num. 21 | FROM KADESH TO THE JORDAN

Perhaps the coalition of Amalekites and Canaanites just to the north of Kadesh seemed too strong for Israel to attempt the direct route to Hebron. At any rate, God had other plans. They started eastward, to go up along the eastern shore of the Dead Sea, through the territory of Edom. But the Edomites (the descendants of Jacob's brother Esau, Genesis 25:30) refused permission.

Moses then turned south, down the Arabah, the desolate valley that extends from the Dead Sea south to the Red Sea, "a vast and dreadful desert," for the long, circuitous, and hazardous route around Edom and Moab, and then north, along the borders of Arabia, to the Plains of Moab, opposite Jericho, just east of the north end of the Dead Sea. God commanded Moses not to do the Edomites, Moabites, or Ammonites harm, even though they tried to stop Israel.

The bronze snake (21:6–9) is a foreshadowing of the Gospel. As those who were bitten by the poisonous snakes looked to the bronze

Bronze snakes discovered at ancient Pithom. When the Israelites looked up at the bronze snake that Moses lifted up in the wilderness, their lives were spared.

snake and were healed, so we, who have been wounded by sin, if we look to Jesus, will live (John 3:14).

The bronze snake was preserved, but at some point the Israelites turned it into an idol, called it Nehushtan, and began burning incense to it. It was destroyed by King Hezekiah 700 years after Moses made it (2 Kings 18:4).

The conquest of Gilead and Bashan (21:21–35). The Amorites, who had crossed to the east of the Jordan, attacked Israel. Moses had refrained from attacking any of the nations through whose country they marched. But now that the Amorites attacked, the Israelites fought back and took their country. Then Bashan attacked and was defeated as well. The region east of the Jordan now belonged to the Israelites.

ARCHAEOLOGICAL NOTE: Kadesh Barnea. Kadesh Barnea is located on the southwestern border of the land of Canaan. From there the Israelites sent spies into the land of Canaan, and after having been forbidden to enter the land because of disbelief, they evidently spent a good portion of the 38 years of their "wanderings" camped in the vicinity. Kadesh (Barnea) is usually identified with a series of good-sized springs located in the region of Ain Qudeirat and Ain Qudeis. This area is located about 50 miles southwest of Beersheba. Archaeological excavations have revealed the remains of a series of small fortresses from the 10th to 6th centuries B.C., but no actual physical remains from the time of the Israelite encampment there.

How Could the Desert Support 2¹/₂ Million People for 40 Years?

Only by the direct miraculous help of God. The miracles were so continuous and so stupendous that the clear intent of the record is to show that it could not have been done except by the hand of God. To those who find it difficult to believe these things, we answer that it is easier to believe them, exactly as they are recorded, than to believe the strange and fanciful theories invented to discredit them. The events in the wilderness are in accord with the entire Bible story. The numbers recorded may be a misreading of the text. Perhaps the "thousands" were "clan groups." If so, it might be possible to drastically reduce the totals without doing injustice to the text.

The purpose of the wilderness miracles may have been

- To preserve the nation; in God's plan the nation had been established to pave the way for a coming Messiah.
- To teach the nation, which had been nurtured in Egyptian idolatry, faith in the one, true God; and to give them concrete proof, which would be a reminder for all time to come that God can be trusted in all the circumstances of life.
- To impress the surrounding nations, particularly the Canaanites, with the fact that the movement of Israel toward Canaan was of God, and that it would be with God, rather than merely a group of people without much fighting experience, that they would have to reckon.

Aside from various accompanying miracles, the transplanting of a whole nation from one land to another, meanwhile maintaining it for 40 years in a desert, was in itself one of the most stupendous miracles of the ages.

Wilderness Wanderings

Num. 22–25 | BALAAM

Balaam's prophecies were a remarkable prediction of Israel's influential place in history through a "Star" that would arise out of Jacob (24:17). Though God used him to speak true prophecy, Balaam, for money, was the instigator of Israel's shameful sin with Moabite and Midianite women, for which Balaam was slain and 24,000 Israelites perished (31:8, 16; 25:9). And Balaam's name became a synonym for false teachers (2 Peter 2:15; Jude 11; Revelation 2:14).

Num. 26 | THE SECOND CENSUS

Wilderness life must have been hard. Of the more than 600,000 males above the age of 20 that were included in the first census (chap. 1), only two survived. The younger generation, hardened by the desert, were a different class of men from what their fathers had been as slaves freshly freed from a hard but predictable life, from the "flesh pots" (KJV; NIV "pots of meat," Exodus 16:3) of Egypt.

Num. 27–36 | VARIOUS REGULATIONS AND EVENTS

For the feasts and offerings (chaps. 28–29), see pp. 150, 169–70.

For the settling of 2½ tribes east of the Jordan (chap. 32) and directions for the division of the land (chap. 34), see on Joshua 13.

For the Levitical cities (chap. 35), see on Joshua 21.

For the Jewish calendar, see p. 1025.

The Miracles of Moses

While miracles are a conspicuous feature of the Bible, they are not abundant in all parts of the Bible. Miracles (not including prophecies and their fulfillment), are particularly noticeable in four periods, centuries apart:

- The period of the Exodus and the conquest of Canaan (Moses and Joshua)
- The period of struggle against idolatry (Elijah and Elisha)
- The period of the Babylonian captivity (Daniel)
- The period of Jesus and the Apostles

Aside from Jesus, it has never been given to any man to be the mediator of so many stupendous manifestations of divine power: the 10 plagues on Egypt, the crossing of the Red Sea, the water that was made sweet at Marah, the provision of quail in the Desert of Zin and at Taberah, the manna that was supplied daily for 40 years, the Ten Commandments written on a stone with God's finger, God's talking face-to-face with Moses so that Moses' face shone, to name but a few.

Moses could not have delivered Israel out of Egypt and sustained them in the wilderness for 40 years without the direct miraculous help of God. But this high privilege, as in the case of the apostle Paul, was accompanied by almost unbelievable suffering.

Deuteronomy

**Moses' Farewell Address:
A Treaty Between God and Israel**

*Love the Lord your God with all your heart and with all your soul and
with all your strength.* —DEUTERONOMY 6:5

*The eternal God is your refuge,
and underneath are the everlasting arms.*

—DEUTERONOMY 33:27

The title of this book, Deuteronomy, comes from the Septuagint, the Greek translation of the Bible, and means "second law," or "repetition of the law." In Exodus, Leviticus, and Numbers, many laws had been given to the Israelites. Now, at the border of Canaan, with the people ready to enter the land at last, these laws are rehearsed and expounded, in anticipation of—and with applications to—settled life in Canaan. The form is that of a formal treaty between God and His people (see p. 166).

Many parts of Deuteronomy can be read not only for their content, but also for the sheer eloquence and beauty of their language.

Deut. 1–3 FROM SINAI TO THE JORDAN

A retrospective summary of Numbers 1–33. After one of the noblest and most heroic accomplishments of the ages, Moses' final appeal to God to let him go over the Jordan was denied (3:23–28)—because God had something better for him, in a better world (see Hebrews 11:28–34, 39–40).

Deut. 4–5 CLING TO GOD'S WORD

Earnest exhortations to observe God's commandments, to teach them diligently to their children, and to shun idolatry—with the ever-recurring reminder that their safety and prosperity would depend on their loyalty and obedience to God.

The Ten Commandments (chap. 5) are also found in Exodus 20.

Deut. 6 THE GREAT COMMANDMENT

Hear, O Israel: The Lord our God, the Lord is one (v. 4): This is the beginning of the Jewish confession of faith (vv. 6–9), the *Shema* (Hebrew for "hear").

Deuteronomy: A Treaty Between God and Israel

The book of Deuteronomy is more than simply a restatement of the Law. It is, in fact, a formal treaty between God and the people of Israel.

The discovery in 1906–07 of some 10,000 tablets in the ancient Hittite capital Khattusa (Boghaz-koy in modern Turkey) provided examples of Hittite treaties that show that Deuteronomy has all the elements contained in Hittite treaties from the 2nd millennium B.C., largely in the same sequence, as the chart below shows.

Joshua 24 also follows the treaty format.

Order of Sections in Hittite Treaties	Description	Deut.	Joshua 24
Introduction of Speaker	Identifies the author and his right to proclaim the treaty	1:1–5	vv. 1–2
Historical Prologue	Survey of past relationship between parties	1:6–3:29	vv. 2–13
Stipulations	Listing of obligations	chaps. 4–26	vv. 14–25
Statement Concerning Document	Storage and instructions for public reading	27:2–3	v. 26
Witnesses	Usually identifies the gods who are called on to witness the oath	chaps. 31–32	vv. 22, 27
Curses and Blessings	How the deity will respond to adherence or violation of the treaty	chap. 28	v. 20

"Love the LORD your God with all your heart and with all your soul and with all your strength" (v. 5). This is repeated over and over (10:12; 11:1, 13, 22) and was reemphasized by Jesus (Matthew 22:37) and given first place in His teaching.

The Israelites were not to rely only on public instruction to keep God's ideas and the knowledge of Him alive among His people; they were to teach them diligently at home (6:6–9). Because books were few and scattered, the people were to write certain important parts of the Law on their doorposts, bind them on their arms and foreheads, and talk of them constantly. Although this command may have been intended as a figure of speech, it later gave rise to mezusas (small boxes with a piece of Scripture in them, attached to doorposts) and phylacteries (small containers with a piece of Scripture that are strapped to the arm and the forehead) that are worn to this day on certain occasions in orthodox Jewish circles.

> *Man does not live on bread alone but on every word that comes from the mouth of the LORD.*
> — Deuteronomy 8:3

Deut. 7 | CANAANITES AND IDOLS MUST BE DESTROYED

The Israelites were to destroy the Canaanites and all their idols. They should not make any agreements or covenants with them, nor should they intermarry with them. This sharp division was necessary in order to save Israel from idolatry and its abominations.

Behind these very strict commands stands God's love for Israel, stated in some of the most beautiful verses in Scripture (7:6–11). It was not because Israel was better or more important than other nations—it was that God had chosen Israel simply because He loved them.

The Moabite idol, Chemosh (ca. 850 B.C.). The Lord instructed the Israelites to destroy all idolatry that they encountered.

Deut. 8 | WONDERS OF THE WILDERNESS RECALLED

For 40 years God had humbled and tested them—and fed them with manna, while their clothes did not wear out and their feet did not swell (v. 4)—that they might learn to trust God and live by His Word (2–5).

Deut. 9–10 | ISRAEL'S PERSISTENT REBELLION

Three times over, Israel is reminded that God's wondrous dealings with them were not because they were so righteous (9:4–6)—they had been a rebellious and stubborn people all the way.

Deut. 11 | BLESSINGS OF OBEDIENCE

This great chapter, like chapters 6 and 28, is an appeal for devotion to God's Word and obedience to His commandments as the basis for national prosperity, with wonderful promises and ominous warnings.

Deut. 12–15 | VARIOUS ORDINANCES

All idols *must* be destroyed. Moses, reared in the hotbed of Egyptian idolatry and surrounded all his life by idol-worshiping peoples, never made any compromise with idolatry. And his repeated warnings came true: idolatry did turn out to be the ruin of the nation.

"Rejoice" is a favorite word in the Psalms and in the New Testament Epistles; note how often the word is used in Deuteronomy (12:7, 12, 18; 14:26; 16:11; 26:11; 32:43; 33:18).

Clean and unclean animals (14:1–21), see on Leviticus 11.
Tithes (14:22–29), see on Leviticus 27.
Sabbath year (15:1–11), see on Leviticus 25.
Slavery (15:12–18), see on Leviticus 19.
Firstfruits (15:19–23), see on Leviticus 27.

Deut. 16 | FEASTS

Three times a year all male Israelites were required to appear before God: at the feasts of Passover, Pentecost, and Tabernacles. Besides these three there were other feasts, chief among them the Day of Atonement (Yom Kippur). This was the only day of the year the high priest was allowed to enter the Most Holy Place (KJV, Holy of Holies); see Leviticus 16.

Feasts in Israel

- The **Passover** and the Feast of **Unleavened Bread** were kept in the spring and lasted seven days. They commemorated Israel's deliverance in the Exodus from Egypt. Passover was celebrated at the beginning of the religious year.
- **Pentecost**, also called the Feast of Weeks, of Harvest, or of Firstfruits, was kept on the 50th day after the Passover and lasted one day.
- **Tabernacles**, also called the Feast of Ingathering, was kept five days after the Day of Atonement and lasted seven days.
- The Feast of **Trumpets** (later called **Rosh Hashanah** or New Year's Day), on the 1st day of the 7th month, ushered in the civil year (see on Numbers 28).
- The **Day of Atonement**, see on Leviticus 16.

Israel's feasts were designed to keep God in the thought of the people and, on a practical level, to promote national unity. Later, when the northern ten tribes seceded and formed the northern kingdom (Israel), Jeroboam I realized that if his people continued to worship the God of Abraham, Isaac, and Jacob, they would have to go to Jerusalem in the southern kingdom (Judah) three times a year. Making a clean break with the southern kingdom was politically essential, which is why Jeroboam instituted a "new" national religion and set up pagan altars at Bethel and Dan in the south and north of his kingdom.

Deut. 17 | THE PREDICTION OF A KING

God here foretold that Israel would have a king, adding some instructions and some warnings (17:14–20). The monarchy would not come until several centuries later (see on 1 Samuel 8).

When in the days of Samuel the people asked for a king, Samuel told them that, in asking for a king, the people were rejecting God. This is not a contradiction. The fact that God foreknew does not mean that He approved—only that He foreknew what they would want and that He wanted to be consulted in their choice. In rejecting the form of government that God had given them—a theocracy (literally, "rule of God"; compare with democracy, "rule of the people")—they were rejecting God. Note that the kings were to be lifelong readers of God's Word (vv. 18–20). What a suggestion to present-day rulers! Note also that the kings began to do right away what God had said they should not do: multiply to themselves wives and horses and gold (16–17; 1 Kings 10:14–29; 11:1–13).

Deut. 18 | THE PROPHET LIKE MOSES

This prediction (18:15–19) may have a secondary reference to the prophetic order as a whole, that is, to the succession of prophets, such as
Isaiah and Joel, whom God would raise up for emergencies in Israel's
history. But the language of this prediction unmistakably points to one
specific individual: the Messiah. It is one of the most specific predictions
of Christ in all of the Old Testament. Jesus Himself so understood it
(John 5:46), as did Peter (Acts 3:22).

The Hebrew nation was founded by God as the medium through which
one day all nations would be blessed. Here is an explicit statement that
the system on which the Hebrew nation was now being organized—the
one given through Moses, the Law—would not be the system by which
Israel would bless all nations; the Law would be superseded by another
system, given by another prophet, which would contain God's message to
all nations. Judaism was to be fulfilled in and superseded by the Gospel.

Deut. 19 | CITIES OF REFUGE

These cities provided sanctuary for those who had caused accidental
death—they were safe from prosecution or revenge here. Moses had
already set aside three such cities east of the Jordan: Bezer, Ramoth, and
Golan (Deuteronomy 4:41–43). Later Joshua set aside three cities of
refuge west of the Jordan: Kedesh, Shechem, and Hebron. All six cities of
refuge were Levitical cities and are included in the total of 48 cities given
to the Levites (Numbers 35:6).

Deut. 20 | RULES OF WARFARE

Those who had built a new house, or had planted a new vineyard, or were
engaged to be married, or were afraid or fainthearted were to be excused

A nawami, or burial
place, in the Sinai
Desert. These struc-
tures date back to
3400–3150 B.C. and
thus were already
almost 2000 years
old when the Israel-
ites traveled through
the region.

Old Testament Feasts and Other Sacred Days

Name	OT References	OT Time	Modern Equivalent
Sabbath	Ex 20:8–11; 31:12–17; Lev 23:3; Dt 5:12–15	7th day	Same
Sabbath Year	Ex 23:10–11; Lev 25:1-7	7th year	Same
Year of Jubilee	Lev 25:8–55; 27:17–24; Nu 36:4	50th year after 7 × 7 years	Same
Passover	Ex 12:1–14; Lev 23:5; Nu 9:1–14; 28:16; Dt 16:1–3a, 4b–7	1st month (Abib) 14	Mar.–Apr.
Unleavened Bread	Ex 12:15–20; 13:3–10; 23:15; 34:18; Lev 23:6–8; Nu 28:17–25; Dt 16:3b, 4a, 8	1st month (Abib) 15–21	Mar.–Apr.
Firstfruits	Lev 23:9–14	1st month (Abib) 16	Mar.–Apr.
Weeks (Pentecost) (Harvest)	Ex 23:16a; 34:22a; Lev 23:15–21; Nu 28:26–31; Dt 16:9–12	3rd month (Sivan) 6	May–June
Trumpets (Later: Rosh Hasha-nah—New Year's Day)	Lev 23:23–25; Nu 29:1–6	7th month (Tishri) 1	Sept.–Oct.
Day of Atone-ment (Yom Kippur)	Lev 16; 23:26–32; Nu 29:7–11	7th month (Tishri) 10	Sept.–Oct.
Tabernacles (Booths) (Ingathering)	Ex 23:16b; 34:22b; Lev 23:33–36a, 39–43; Num 29:12–34; Dt 16:13–15; Zec 14:16–19	7th month (Tishri) 15–21	Sept.–Oct.
Sacred Assembly	Lev 23:36b; Nu 29:35–38	7th month (Tishri) 22	Sept.–Oct.
Purim	Est 9:18–32	12th month (Adar) 14–15	Feb.–Mar.

On Kislev 25 (mid-Dec.) Hanukkah, the Feast of Dedication, or Festival of Lights, commemorated the purification of the temple and altar in the Maccabean period (165/4 B.C.).

Description	Purpose	NT References
Day of rest; no work	Rest for people and animals	Mt 12:1–14; 28:1; Lk 4:16; Jn 5:9; Ac 13:42; Col 2:16; Heb 4:1–11
Year of rest; fallow fields	Rest for land	
Canceled debts; liberation of slaves and indentured servants; land returned to original family owners	Help for poor; stabilize society	
Slaying and eating a lamb, together with bitter herbs and bread made without yeast, in every household	Remember Israel's deliverance from Egypt	Mt 26:17; Mk 14:12–26; Jn 2:13; 11:55; 1 Co 5:7; Heb 11:28
Eating bread made without yeast; holding several assemblies; making designated offerings	Remember how the Lord brought the Israelites out of Egypt in haste	Mk 14:1; Ac 12:3; 1 Co 5:6–8
Presenting a sheaf of the first of the barley harvest as a wave offering; making a burnt offering and a grain offering	Recongnize the Lord's bounty in the Land	Ro 8:23; 1 Co 15:20–23
A festival of joy; mandatory and voluntary offerings, including the firstfruits of the wheat harvest	Show joy and thankfulness for the Lord's blessing of harvest	Ac 2:1–4, 20:16; 1 Co 16:8
An assembly on a day of rest commemorated with trumpet blasts and sacrifices	Present Israel before the Lord for His favor	
A day of rest, fasting, and sacrifices of atonement for priests and people and atonement for the tabernacle and altar	Cleanse priests and people from their sins and purify the Holy Place	Ro 3:24–26; Heb 9:7 10:3, 19–22
A week of celebration for the harvest; living in booths and offering sacrifices	Memorialize the journey from Egypt to Canaan; give thanks for the productivity of Canaan	Jn 7:2, 37
A day of convocation, rest, and offering sacrifices	Commemorate the closing of the cycle of feasts	
A day of joy and feasting and giving presents	Remind the Israelites of their national deliverance in the time of Esther	

This feast is mentioned in Jn 10:22. In addition, new moons were often special feast days (Nu 10:10; 1 Ch 23:31; Ezr 3:5; Ne 10:33; Ps 81:3; Isa 1:13–14; 66:23; Hos 5:7; Am 8:5; Col 2:16).

From *The NIV Study Bible.* Used by permission.

from military service. The Canaanites were to be destroyed—but food-bearing trees should be spared.

Deut. 21–26 | VARIOUS LAWS

These laws range from matters such as public atonement in the case of an unsolved murder (21:1–9), to a rebellious son (if he does not accept discipline he must be put to death, 21:18–21), to the requirement of building a parapet or rail around the flat roof of a house (22:8).

The variety of these laws and the large and small issues they cover show God's concern for His people as well as His concern for social justice and the protection of the weak—even a bird sitting on eggs is protected by God (22:6–7).

We may well wonder whether the practical holiness reflected in God's laws has been improved upon by our "enlightened" laws, more than three millennia later.

Deut. 27 | THE LAW TO BE RECORDED ON MOUNT EBAL

The law was to be recorded on large stones once Israel had crossed the Jordan. Joshua, who had been one of the two spies who wanted to enter Canaan 40 years before and who became Moses' successor, did this (Joshua 8:30–32). In an age when books were scarce, it was a custom to record laws on stones and set them up in various cities, so the people could know them. This was done in Egypt and in Babylonia, for example, with the Code of Hammurabi (see p. 104). Moses commanded Israel to make this the very first thing they did on arrival in Canaan. The stones were to be covered with plaster on which the laws were to be written "very clearly" (v. 28).

Deut. 28 | THE GREAT PROPHECY ABOUT THE JEWS

Chapter 28 is the "curses and blessings" section of the treaty between God and Israel (see introductory note to Deuteronomy). Here the consequences of both obedience and disobedience to the "stipulations" of the covenant are presented. This chapter is the foundation for the message of the prophets, who would again and again remind Israel of their obligations to God (which as a nation they had willingly accepted) and the consequences of their disobedience. From this chapter flow both the prophecies of impending doom that permeate most of the prophetic writings, as well as the promise of restoration: if God's people turn back to Him, God will honor His covenant and bless them. Verses 58–68 are a grim reflection of the realities of the last centuries: the dispersion of the Jews (the Diaspora), their wanderings, unceasing persecutions, their trembling of heart and pining of soul, even until the present time.

Deut. 29–30 | THE COVENANT AND FINAL WARNINGS

Moses' last words, as he envisions the fearful consequences of disobedience and apostasy, are, "See, I set before you today life and prosperity, death and destruction" (30:15). Serving God is the way of life; serving idols leads to certain death.

Deut. 31 | JOSHUA TO SUCCEED MOSES; MOSES WRITES THE LAW IN A BOOK

Forty years earlier, Moses had written God's words in a book (Exodus 17:14; 24:4, 7). He had also kept a diary of his journeys (Numbers 33:2). Now his book was completed, and he handed it over to the priests and Levites, with instructions that it must be read periodically to the people.

The constant teaching of God's written Word to the people is the safest and most effective way to guard against the corruption of their religion. When Israel gave heed to God's Word, they prospered. When they neglected it, they suffered adversity.

Reading of God's book brought about the great reformation under Josiah (2 Kings 23) and the renewal under Ezra (Nehemiah 8)—and the Reformation that began with Luther's reading of the Word of God. The New Testament books were written to be read in the churches (Colossians 4:16; 1 Thessalonians 5:27). God's Word is the power of God in the human heart. Oh, that the present-day pulpit would somehow learn to keep itself in the background while putting God's Word in the foreground!

Mount Nebo

Mount Nebo is the highest peak of Mount Pisgah, eight miles east of the mouth of the Jordan. From its summit the hill countries of Judah, Ephraim, and Manasseh could be seen. Later, somewhere in the vicinity, possibly on the plain or in the valleys below, the angels came down and took Elijah away to join Moses in glory (2 Kings 2:11).

Looking West from Mt. Nebo at sunset across the Jordan Valley toward the Dead Sea into the Promised Land.

The magnificent statue of Moses by Michelangelo, in St. Peter's in Vincoli in Rome. In medieval and Renaissance art, Moses was often represented with horns on his head, due to a mistake in the Vulgate (Latin) translation of Exodus 34:29 (*horns* instead of *was radiant*).

Deut. 32 | THE SONG OF MOSES

After Moses had finished "writing the book," he composed a song for the people to sing. He had celebrated their deliverance from Egypt with a song (Exodus 15), and he had written another one, which is known to us as the 90th Psalm. Popular songs are among the best means of writing ideas on people's hearts — for good or for evil! Deborah and David poured out their souls to God in song (Judges 5; 2 Samuel 22). The church, from its inception until now, has used this same means to perpetuate and spread the truths for which it stands.

Deut. 33 | THE BLESSINGS OF MOSES

This chapter records the blessing Moses bestowed on each of the tribes, with predictions about each. This is similar to Jacob's blessing his sons shortly before his death (Genesis 49).

Deut. 34 | DEATH OF MOSES

At age 120, his eye not weak nor his strength gone (v. 7), the old man climbed Mount Pisgah and, as he viewed the Promised Land, into which he longed to go, God gently lifted him into the better land. In a moment his soul had passed within the veil, and he was at home with God. God buried his body, no one knows where. His remains were removed beyond the reach of idolatry.

Here ends the first part of the Old Testament. These five books, which occupy one-fourth of the Old Testament and are almost as large as the entire New Testament, were all written by one man, Moses. What a man Moses must have been! How intimate with God! What a work he did! What a benefactor to mankind! Forty years in the palace of Pharaoh; 40 years a refugee in Midian; 40 years the leader of Israel in the desert. He delivered a nation of some 2½ million people from servitude, transplanted them from one country to another, and organized for them a system of jurisprudence that has had a lasting impact on much of the world's civilization.

As thy days, so shall thy strength be.
— Deuteronomy 33:25 KJV

The Conquest and Settlement of Canaan

The conquest of the land of Canaan, under the leadership of Joshua, began around 1406 B.C. and probably lasted for some 10 to 15 years. These events are described in Joshua 1–12. Soon after the conquest, or even while it was still under way, territory was allotted to each of the Israelite tribes. This was the beginning of Israel's settlement of the land of Canaan, the land that the Lord had promised to Abraham (and his descendants) some 500 years earlier (Genesis 12:1–3, etc.). The Lord was bringing them into the "mountain of your inheritance—the place . . . made for your dwelling, the sanctuary . . . your hands established" (Exodus 15:17). Here the Israelites would have a chance to live their lives in obedience to, and worship of, the true and living God. It was here that the Levites, who were to teach God's Law to the people, were allotted 48 cities scattered throughout the land (Joshua 20; 1 Chronicles 6:39–66) so that their godly influence could permeate the people of God.

But the writers of the books of Joshua and Judges were well aware that not all of the Promised Land was under Israelite control (Joshua 13:1–6; Judges 3:1–3). As the tribes attempted to settle in their allotted territories, they encountered the opposition of peoples such as the Canaanites, Moabites, Ammonites, and Philistines. But what was more serious was that in some instances Israel began to adopt the pagan religious practices of these peoples!

At times, the worship of Baal and Asherah became common among God's people as they failed to respond with gratitude to God's gracious dealings with them. In response to Israel's sinful disobedience, God used the pagan nations to oppress His people—as instruments of His judgment. Israel would eventually respond in repentance, and then God sent them a deliverer, a "Judge" (there are 12 of them mentioned in Scripture), to deliver them. After each deliverance, Israel typically enjoyed a period of "rest"—freedom from oppression—but unfortunately, Israel (or portions of it) would relapse into sin and the cycle would begin again.

During the period of the Judges (ca. 1390–1050 B.C.), there was no king in Israel. Ideally, Israel was to be a "theocracy," that is, a nation whose ruler was the Lord (Joshua 8:23). It appears that for much of the period of the Judges the tribes gathered for worship at Shiloh, some 20 miles north of Jerusalem, for there the tabernacle and the ark of the covenant were located.

In the period just before the Israelites' conquest of Canaan, strong Egyptian kings such as Thutmose III and Amenhotep II had been active in Canaan. But the 400 cuneiform tablets found at El Amarna indicate that the time of the conquest and immediately thereafter (ca. 1400–1350 B.C.) was a period of more limited Egyptian influence in Canaan. Indeed, during the period of the Judges, groups of people from the Aegean area, known as the "Sea Peoples," percolated into the regions along the eastern shores of the Mediterranean Sea, including the land of Canaan. Among them were the Philistines, who settled in southwest Canaan in the cities of Gaza, Ashkelon, Ashdod, Ekron, and Gath. The military conflicts between the Philistines and Israel (under Samson and Samuel) would eventually push the Israelites toward kingship.

During the middle of the period of the Judges, Egyptian rulers such as Seti I, Rameses II, and others passed through Canaan on their way north, to do battle with the kingdoms of Mitanni and the Hittites. But since the Israelites did not interfere with these troop movements, and since the movements were generally in territory controlled by Canaanites and others — that is, not by the Israelites — no record of any battles between Egypt and Israel is found in the book of Judges. However, the Egyptian ruler Merneptah does say in one of his texts that "Israel is laid waste [and] his seed is not" (*Ancient Near Eastern Texts,* p. 378) as a result of a campaign in his fifth year (ca. 1231 B.C.).

Archaeologically, the era of the Judges (1390–1050 B.C.) is known as the Late Bronze II (1400–1200 B.C.) and Iron I (1200–1000 B.C.) ages. Generally, this seems to have been a time when the strong Canaanite city-states were declining in size and influence, while newcomers — such as the Israelites — were gaining a foothold in the hill country, establishing small farmsteads and settlements there. Throughout, and especially at the end of, this period, Israel's near neighbors (especially the Ammonites to the east and the Philistines to the southwest) continued to grow stronger, so that the physical existence of God's people hung in the balance. It would take personalities such as Saul, but especially David, to complete the conquest of the land that had begun under Joshua 400 years earlier.

Joshua

The Conquest and Settlement of Canaan

"Do not let this Book of the Law depart from your mouth; meditate on it day and night, so that you may be careful to do everything written in it. Then you will be prosperous and successful."

—JOSHUA 1:8

"Choose for yourselves this day whom you will serve. . . . But as for me and my household, we will serve the LORD."

—JOSHUA 24:15

The Man Joshua

Joshua was of the tribe of Ephraim (Numbers 13:8). He had been a personal assistant of Moses throughout the 40 years of wilderness wandering. He went with Moses on Mount Sinai (Exodus 24:13). He was one of the 12 spies, and one of the two who wanted to go ahead and conquer the land in God's strength (Numbers 13:8, 16). Josephus says that Joshua was 85 when he succeeded Moses. It is thought that it took about six years to subdue the Canaanites, and Joshua spent the rest of his life settling and governing the 12 tribes. Joshua was in charge of Israel for about 25 years. He died at age 110 and was buried in Timnath Serah, in Ephraim.

> *"As I was with Moses, so I will be with you; I will never leave you nor forsake you."*
>
> —Joshua 1:5

Joshua was a great warrior who disciplined his forces and sent out spies—but he also prayed and trusted in God. He led his people into the Promised Land, and he may have been a prototype of his greater Successor, Jesus (the Greek form of Joshua), who is leading His own into the Promised Land of heaven.

Josh. 1 | THE BOOK

This is a grand chapter. Israel had a Book. It was only a fraction of what we now have in God's Word, but oh how important! God's solemn warning to Joshua, standing at the threshold of a gigantic task, was to be very careful to keep close to the words of that Book. Joshua listened and obeyed, and God honored him with phenomenal success. What a lesson for church leaders!

Rahab's House on the Wall (2:15)

Archaeologists have found that in Jericho, houses were indeed built between the inner and outer walls of the city (see note on p. 180).

Josh. 2 | THE TWO SPIES AND RAHAB

Rahab had heard of the miracles God had done on behalf of Israel, and she had become convinced that Israel's God was the true God (2:10–11). And when she met the spies she decided, at the risk of her life, to cast her lot with Israel and the God of Israel. Rahab and her household were spared during the Israelite attack on Jericho. A scarlet cord tied in the window of her house indicated that the household was not to be harmed. The function of this red marker was similar to the purpose of the blood of the Passover lamb on the doorposts in Egypt when the firstborn of Egypt died but the firstborn of the Israelites were spared (Exodus 12:13, 22–23). She may not have been as bad as the word "prostitute" now implies. She lived among people without morals. Some priestesses of the Canaanite religion were temple prostitutes. Her profession was considered honorable by the people among whom she lived, and not disgraceful, as it now is among us.

Rahab married an Israelite named Salmon (Matthew 1:5). Caleb had a son named Salmon (1 Chronicles 2:51). It may have been the same Salmon. If so, then she married into a leading family of Israel. She became an ancestress of Boaz (Ruth 2–4), of David, and of Christ. She is named among the heroes of faith (Hebrews 11:31).

Looking southeast on the Old Testament site of Jericho. While staying at the home of Rahab, the Israelite spies learned the city of Jericho was disabled by fear.

Josh. 3 | CROSSING THE JORDAN

When the ark of the Lord, the most sacred of the tabernacle furnishings signifying the Lord's throne, stood at the water's edge, the river "piled up in a great heap," at Adam (3:16), 22 miles to the north. Below that, the water drained off and left the pebbly river bottom dry enough to walk on.

The Levites then carried the ark into the passage ahead of the people of Israel. God was leading His people into the Promised Land!

At Adam, the Jordan flows through clay banks 40 feet high, which are subject to landslides. In 1927 an earthquake caused these banks to collapse, so that no water flowed past them for 21 hours. God may have used some such means to make the waters "stand" for Joshua. At any rate, it was a mighty miracle and terrified the already frightened Canaanites (5:1).

Jesus, 1,400 years later, was baptized in the same Jordan that Joshua and the Israelites crossed.

Josh. 4 | THE MEMORIAL STONES

There were two piles of memorial stones: one where the ark stood on the east bank of the river (4:9), the other on the west side, at Gilgal, where they stayed. The stones were placed there so that generations to come would not forget the enormous miracle that had happened there.

Josh. 5 | THE FIRST PASSOVER IN THE PROMISED LAND

At long last the Israelites were in the Promised Land, although they still had to capture it. On the fourth day after they crossed the Jordan, their first act was to keep the Passover (4:19; 5:10). The next day the manna ceased (5:12), ending 40 years of God's special provision. They were now to receive provisions directly from the Promised Land. Then God sent the commander of His invisible army to encourage Joshua for the task ahead (5:13–15).

Jericho owes its existence to a perennial spring and an oasis; in Deuteronomy 34:3 it is called the "City of Palms." It bills itself today, with some justification, as the "World's Oldest City." The oldest town on the site dates back to the 8th millennium B.C. It had a revetment wall with at least one tower with a built-in stairway.

Josh. 6 | THE FALL OF JERICHO

Jericho was taken by direct intervention of God, to inspire the Israelites with confidence at the beginning of their conquest of peoples more powerful than they. Led by the ark of the Lord, with trumpets blowing, they walked around the city seven days. Hovering above were the invisible hosts of the Lord (5:14), waiting for the appointed hour. And on the seventh day, at the blast of the trumpets, the walls fell.

In an amazing prophecy, a curse was pronounced on anyone who would attempt to rebuild the city (6:26; see on 1 Kings 16:34).

Jericho was roughly six miles from the Jordan; Gilgal, Joshua's headquarters, was probably about halfway between. The wall of Jericho enclosed about 10 acres. It was a place where the people from the heavily populated surroundings could find refuge in case of an attack.

New Testament Jericho was about a mile south of the ruins of Old Testament Jericho. The modern village of Jericho is about a mile to the southeast.

ARCHAEOLOGICAL NOTE: Jericho. Jericho has been much excavated in the 20th century: by Warren, by Sellin and Watzinger, by Garstang, by Kenyon, and by an Italian team. What John Garstang thought were the walls destroyed by Joshua turned out to actually be the walls of a city that existed about 1000 years before Joshua. However, Kathleen Kenyon's negativism about the correlation of the biblical and archaeological data is also not warranted. Bryant Wood, in his analysis of all of the data, has reasonably suggested the following. What the archaeologists call City IV was destroyed about 1400 B.C. This date agrees well with the internal chronology of the Bible, which would place the conquest of Joshua at about 1406 B.C. City IV was surrounded by an inner and an outer city wall. The outer wall was supported by a massive sloping stone structure (revetment wall). Between the two walls, houses from City IV have been found (note the position of Rahab's house on the city wall; Joshua 2:15).

It seems that City IV was first destroyed by an earthquake and then by fire — burnt debris, in some places three or more feet thick, has been found at various locations on the tell. Among the debris were pottery, household utensils, and even carbonized grain — indicating that the destruction had taken place in the spring of the year, just after the harvest (2:6; 3:15; and note that Israel celebrated the Passover just before the conquest of Jericho, 5:10 and cf. 3:15). It also indicated that there had not been a long siege (large quantities of grain were found; the biblical texts say the city was taken within seven days, 6:15), and that the inhabitants did not have time to flee with their belongings before the destruction. In addition, carbon-14 (C_{14}) tests on the organic material place the destruction at about 1400 B.C. Even Egyptian scarabs (seals) found in tombs there do not name pharaohs who ruled after 1400 B.C.

Josh. 7–8 | THE FALL OF AI AND BETHEL

Right after the miraculous crossing of the Jordan and the miraculous fall of Jericho, Israel met with a dreadful defeat at Ai — because of one man's disobedience. It was a terrible shock to Israel. It was a disciplinary lesson. God was with them, but He meant them to understand that He expected obedience.

THE OLD TESTAMENT — The Conquest and Settlement of Canaan

ARCHAEOLOGICAL NOTE: Bethel and Ai. Archaeological evidence can be found to correlate the conquest of Jericho and Hazor with the biblical data of Joshua's conquests. However, the conquest of Ai, described in Joshua 7–8, has not yet been illuminated by archaeological finds.

Biblical Ai is usually associated with et-Tell, because the topographical setting of et-Tell is close to that of Ai described in Scripture (east of Bethel, valleys and hills in the proper locations, etc.). However, extensive archaeological excavations at et-Tell have shown that it was not inhabited between about 2300 B.C. and 1100 B.C. This of course means that it could not have been conquered by Joshua around 1400 B.C.—for no one was living there then.

Attempts have been made to identify other tells in the area east of **Bethel** (which is usually identified with the village of Beitin) with biblical Ai, but to date a definitive identification has not yet been made. Recently a two-acre site called Khirbet el-Maqatir has been suggested as meeting the textual, geographical, and especially the archaeological requirements for Ai—it is east of Bethel, has a hill and valley to the north, etc., and it apparently has the remains of a small fortress from about 1400 B.C., the very time of Joshua's conquest. But certainty about this suggested identification is not possible until the archaeological profile of the site has been completely substantiated.

Related to the question of the proper identification of Ai is the identification of its twin city—Bethel. The almost universally accepted identification of Bethel with the antiquity site in the Arab village of Beitin is based on topographical, historical, and limited archaeological evidence, but especially on the fact that the biblical name Bethel seems to be preserved

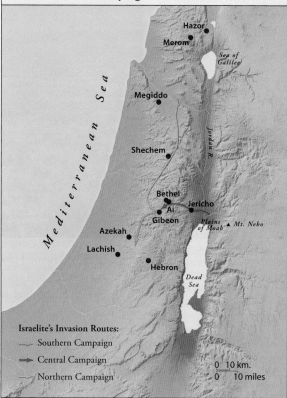

The Israelite Campaigns in the Promised Land

Israelite's Invasion Routes:
— Southern Campaign
➔ Central Campaign
— Northern Campaign

0   10 km.
0   10 miles

The Canaanites and Amorites

"Canaan" was one of the ancient names for the land of Israel (see Numbers 34:1–12 for its specific boundaries), and its inhabitants were often called "Canaanites" during the second millennium B.C. In a more restricted sense the Bible places the Canaanites on the coastlands, in the valleys, and in the Jordan Valley. "Amorite" is also a term which can be used to refer to the ancient inhabitants of Israel, but in a more special sense it can refer to a group of people who live in the Hill Country—on either side of the Rift Valley. Sihon, who lived in Heshbon, east of the Dead Sea, is called the "king of the Amorites" (Numbers 21:26).

The distant hill covered with trees marks the general location of where Joshua read the Law on Mt. Ebal and archaeologists discovered remains of an altar. Abraham set up his first altar in the Promised Land in the valley below at Shechem.

in the name Beitin. However, a small minority of researchers have suggested that Bethel should really be identified with a large, archaeologically rich site called Ras et–Tahuneh, located in the Arab city of el–Birah, just east of Ramallah. Both et–Tell and Khirbet el–Makatir, the sites proposed for Ai, are east of a north-south line drawn through either Beitin or Ras et-Tahuneh — thus fulfilling the textual requirements of being east of Bethel — but only Khirbet el–Makatir has the archaeological remains dating to the days of Joshua.

Since time and again archaeological discoveries have demonstrated the trustworthiness of the biblical text, it seems best to await further discoveries to help answer the puzzling question as to the proper identification of biblical Ai.

Josh. 8:30–35 | THE LAW RECORDED AT MOUNT EBAL

Moses had commanded that this be done (see on Deuteronomy 27). Shechem, in the center of the land, was between Mount Ebal and Mount Gerizim, in a valley of surpassing beauty. Here, 600 years before, Abraham had erected his first altar in the land. And here Joshua, in solemn ceremony, read the Book of the Law to the people.

Josh. 9–10 | THE BATTLE IN WHICH THE SUN STOOD STILL

Gibeon, about six miles northwest of Jerusalem, was one of the land's greatest cities (10:2). The Gibeonites, frightened after the fall of Jericho and Ai, made haste to enslave themselves to Israel. This enraged the kings of Jerusalem, Hebron, Jarmuth, Lachish, and Eglon, and the five of them marched against Gibeon. Then Joshua, honoring his ill-advised commitment to the people of Gibeon, came to their rescue. This led to the famous battle of Gibeon, Beth Horon, and westward, where the sun stood still for a whole day. Exactly what happened or how, we do not know. Some people claim to have calculated that the calendar lost a day around that time. At any rate, in some way or other, daylight was miraculously prolonged so that Joshua's victory might be complete.

ARCHAEOLOGICAL NOTE: Lachish and Debir. Lachish and Debir are named among cities whose inhabitants were defeated by Joshua (10:32, 39).

Lachish. Archaeological excavations at Tell ed-Duweir have suggested that at the time of the conquest, Lachish was an important but unfortified Canaanite city. Its lack of a defensive wall may have led to its speedy conquest. The Bible does not actually describe its conquest and destruction in the same terms as it does that of Jericho, Ai, and Hazor.

Debir (Kiriath Sepher). The older identification of Debir with Tell Beit Mirsim is no longer accepted, for according to Joshua 15:49, Debir is to be located in the Hill Country of Judah, not in the lowlands. Consequently, Debir is now identified with Khirbet Rabud (8½ miles south-southwest of Hebron — in the Hill Country of Judah), which has produced evidence of being inhabited and conquered at the time of Israel's entrance into Canaan (ca. 1400 B.C.).

Josh. 11	**THE KINGS OF THE NORTH DEFEATED**

In the battle of Beth Horon, where the sun stood still, Joshua had broken the power of the kings of the South. Now his victory over the kings of the North, at Merom, gave him control of the whole land. Joshua's strategy was to separate the north from the south of Canaan by capturing the center first, after which he could more easily subdue both parts.

The Israelites fought hard, yet it was God who gave them the land by means of three stupendous miracles: the crossing of the Jordan, the fall of Jericho, and the standing still of the sun.

This view from the mound of what once was Hazor, with Israeli soldiers approaching, could be the same perspective from which the king of Hazor watched Joshua and the Israelites approach.

ARCHAEOLOGICAL NOTE: Hazor. Joshua "burned up Hazor itself" (11:11). Archaeological excavations have found the ashes of this fire, with pottery evidence that it had occurred about 1400 B.C.

Also: an Amarna Tablet, written to Pharaoh, 1380 B.C., by the Egyptian envoy in north Palestine, says, "Let my lord the king recall what Hazor and its king have already had to endure." The only ruler in Canaan who is called a "king" in the nearly 400 Amarna Tablets, is the ruler of Hazor. Note also that in the Bible Hazor was called "the head of all these kingdoms" (Joshua 11:10).

Thus, Joshua's conquest of Palestine is attested by great layers of ashes, bearing marks of Joshua's time, in Jericho, Debir, and Hazor, exactly confirming biblical statements.

Josh. 12 | LIST OF DESTROYED KINGS

At Shechem, Joshua and the Israelites renewed their commitment to God's covenant with Israel. Joshua set up a great stone as a witness. This stone, at the site of ancient Shechem, is like the one Joshua erected, although it is most likely not the original one.

Thirty-one kings are named. Generally speaking, the whole land was conquered (10:40; 11:23; 21:43). However, small groups of Canaanites remained (13:2–7; 15:63; 23:4; Judges 1:2, 21, 27, 29, 30, 31, 33, 35) who, after Joshua's death, made trouble for Israel. Also, the land of the Philistines, Sidon, and the Lebanon region were still unconquered.

Josh. 13–22 | THE DIVISION OF THE LAND

The map on page 184 shows the approximate location of the land that was assigned to each of the 12 tribes of Israel. There were six cities of refuge (chap. 20; see on Deuteronomy 19), and 48 cities for the Levites, including 13 for the priests (21:19, 14). The altar by the Jordan (chap. 22) was intended as a token of national unity for a nation divided by a great river.

Josh. 23–24 | JOSHUA'S FAREWELL ADDRESS

Joshua had received from Moses the written Law of God (1:8). He now added his own book to it (24:26). Joshua made good use of written documents, or "books," as Moses had done (see on Deuteronomy 31). He had the land surveyed with "a book" (18:9). He read to the people the "book" of Moses (8:34). And at Mount Ebal he "wrote on stones" a copy of the Law (8:32).

The main burden of Joshua's final speech was against idolatry. Canaanite idolatry was such an aesthetic combination of religion and free indulgence of carnal desires that only persons of exceptional strength of character could withstand its allurements.

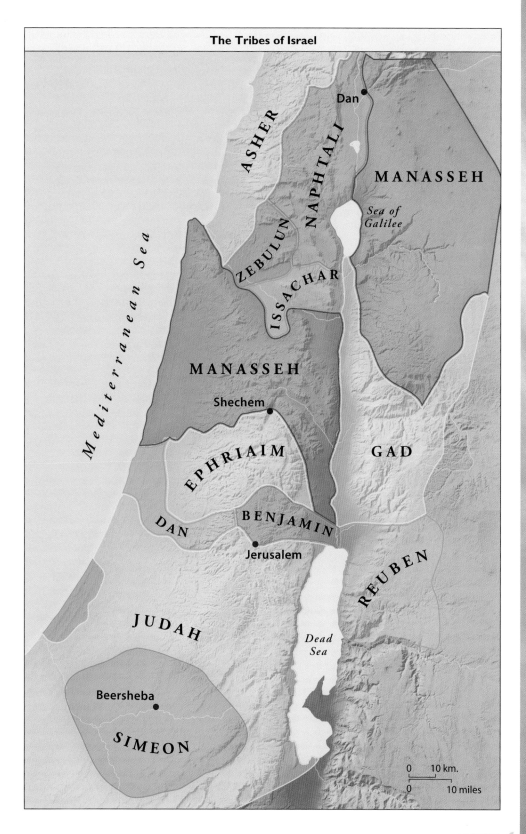

The Tribes of Israel

ASHER

NAPHTALI

Dan

MANASSEH

Sea of Galilee

Mediterranean Sea

ZEBULUN

ISSACHAR

MANASSEH

Shechem

EPHRIAIM

GAD

DAN

BENJAMIN

Jerusalem

REUBEN

JUDAH

Dead Sea

Beersheba

SIMEON

0   10 km.

0   10 miles

Judges

300 Years of Oppression
and Deliverance

"But you have forsaken me and served other gods, so I will no longer save you. Go and cry out to the gods you have chosen. Let them save you when you are in trouble!"

But the Israelites said to the Lord, "We have sinned. Do with us whatever you think best, but please rescue us now." Then they got rid of the foreign gods among them and served the LORD. And he could bear Israel's misery no longer. —JUDGES 10:13–16

The Period of the Judges

The Hebrew nation, after the death of Joshua, had no strong central government. They were a confederacy of 12 independent tribes, with no unifying element except their God. The form of government in the days of the Judges is spoken of as a "theocracy," that is, God Himself was supposed to be the direct ruler of the nation. But the people did not take their God very seriously—they were continually falling into idolatry. Being more or less in a state of anarchy, harassed at times by civil war among themselves, and surrounded by enemies who made attempt after attempt to exterminate them, the Hebrew nation was very slow in its national development. The Israelites did not become a great nation until they were organized into a kingdom in the days of Samuel and David.

The exact duration of the period of the Judges is uncertain. When we add all the years of the oppressions, of the individual Judges, and of the periods of rest, they add up to 410 years (see chart p. 188). But some of these figures may overlap. Jephthah, who lived near the end of the period, spoke of it as 300 years (11:26). It is thought to have been, in round numbers, about 300 years, roughly from about 1400 until 1100 B.C. The entire period from the Exodus to King Solomon, which includes also the 40-year period of travel through the wilderness as well as the eras of Eli, Samuel, Saul, and David, is given as 480 years in 1 Kings 6:1.

There were also oppressions by Sidonians and Maonites (10:12).

Judg. 1 | CANAANITES THAT WERE LEFT IN THE LAND

Joshua had destroyed the Canaanites in some sections of the land and had kept others in subjection (Joshua 10:40, 43; 11:23; 13:2–7; 21:43–45; 23:4; 24:18). After his death, there remained considerable numbers of Canaanites (Judges 1:28, 29, 30, 32, 33, 35).

Oppressor(s)	Years of Oppression	Judge	Years of Rest
Mesopotamians	8	Othniel, of Debir in Judah	40
Moabites Ammonites Amalekites	18	Ehud, of Benjamin	80
Philistines		Shamgar	
Canaanites	20	Deborah, of Ephraim; Barak, of Naphtali	40
Midianites Amalekites	7	Gideon, of Manasseh	40
		Abimelech (usurper), of Manasseh	3
		Tola, of Issachar	23
		Jair, of Gilead, in E Manasseh	22
Ammonites	18	Jephthah, of Gilead, in E Manasseh	6
		Ibzan, of Bethlehem, in Judah(?)	7
		Elon, of Zebulun	10
		Abdon, of Ephraim	8
Philistines	40	Samson, of Dan	20
TOTAL	111		299

God had commanded Israel to utterly destroy or drive out the Canaanites (Deuteronomy 7:2–4). Had Israel fully obeyed this command, they would have saved themselves a lot of trouble.

Looking west toward the elongated mound once occupied by the Philistine city of Gath, hometown of Goliath. During the time of the Judges the Israelites were to drive out cultures like the Philistines who lived in such cities.

ARCHAEOLOGICAL NOTE: Iron in Palestine. The Bible states that the reason Israel could not drive out the Canaanites and Philistines is that they had iron, while Israel did not (1:19; 4:3; Joshua 17:16–18; 1 Samuel 13:19–22). Only after Saul and David broke the power of the Philistines did iron come into use in Israel (2 Samuel 12:31; 1 Chronicles 22:3; 29:7).

Although iron objects begin to appear in Palestine at about the time of the arrival of the Philistines, it wasn't until the 11th century that they became more common. Broken spears, hoes, etc., were not discarded, but were typically melted down and the metal recast.

Judg. 2 | APOSTASY AFTER THE DEATH OF JOSHUA

As the hardy, wilderness-bred generation, who under the powerful leadership of Joshua had conquered the land, died off, the new generation found itself settled in a land of plenty and soon lapsed into the easy-going ways of their idolatrous neighbors.

The Refrain Running Through the Book

The refrain of the book is, "Every man did that which was right in his own eyes" (KJV), or as the NIV puts it, "Everyone did as he saw fit" (17:6; 21:25). They were again and again falling away from God into the worship of idols. When they did this, God delivered Israel into the hands of foreign oppressors. Then, when Israel in their suffering and distress turned back and cried to God, God had pity on Israel and raised up Judges, who saved Israel from their enemies. As long as the Judge lived, the people served God. But soon after the Judge died, the people would leave God and go back to their old ways.

Invariably, when they served God, they prospered, but when they served idols, they suffered. Israel's troubles were due directly to their

Gezer was one of the cities the Israelites failed to take in their conquest of Canaan. This is the "high place" of Gezer, where idols were worshiped. The city was finally captured in Solomon's time by the pharaoh of Egypt, who set it on fire, killed its inhabitants, and gave it as a wedding gift to Solomon, who rebuilt Gezer (1 Kings 9:16–17).

disobedience. They did not keep themselves from worshiping idols. They did not exterminate the inhabitants of the land as they had been commanded. And thus, from time to time, the struggle for mastery was renewed.

Judg. 3 | OTHNIEL, EHUD, SHAMGAR

Othniel, of Debir, south of Hebron, saved Israel from the Mesopotamians, who invaded from the northeast.

Ehud saved Israel from Moabites, Ammonites, and Amalekites. The story of how he used his left-handedness to kill Eglon, king of Moab, is told in graphic detail.

The *Moabites* were descendants of Lot. They occupied the tableland east of the Dead Sea. Their god, Chemosh, was worshiped by human sacrifice. They had repeated wars with Israel.

The *Ammonites* were also descendants of Lot. Their territory was next to Moab, beginning about 30 miles east of the Jordan. Their god, called Molech, was worshiped by the burning of little children.

Moab and Ammon, the ancestors of these two nations, were the product of an incestuous relationship (Genesis 19:30–38).

The *Amalekites* were descendants of Esau. They were a nomadic tribe, centered mainly in the northern part of the Sinai peninsula but roaming in wide circles, even into Judah and far to the east. They were the first to attack Israel after their departure from Egypt. Moses authorized their extinction (Exodus 17:8–16). They have disappeared from history.

Shamgar, of whom little is told, saved Israel from the Philistines.

The *Philistines* were descendants of Ham. They occupied the Coastal Plain between modern Tel Aviv and Gaza, and they again oppressed Israel in Samson's day.

Judg. 4–5 | DEBORAH AND BARAK

Deborah and Barak saved Israel from the Canaanites, who had been subdued by Joshua but had become powerful again. With their chariots made of iron they had a major advantage over Israel. Deborah is the only female Judge. Her faith and courage put Barak's to shame.

ARCHAEOLOGICAL NOTE: Kings of Hazor. Again, the king of Hazor led the northern Canaanite rulers into battle against the Israelites. Jabin seems to have been a "dynastic name" used by some of the rulers of Hazor, for not only are there at least two Jabins of Hazor in the Bible, but the name has also been found on a cuneiform tablet discovered at Hazor itself. There is archaeological evidence that Hazor was destroyed about 1200 B.C., which chronologically fits well with the story of Deborah and Barak.

Judg. 6–8 | GIDEON

For seven years, Midianites, Amalekites, and Arabians (6:3; 8:24) had swarmed into the land, in such numbers that the Israelites sought refuge in caves and made hidden pits for their grain (6:2–4, 11). Gideon, with the direct help of God and an army of 300 men armed with torches hidden in pitchers, gave them such a terrific beating that they came no more.

This was the second time the Amalekites invaded Israel (see under chapter 3).

The *Midianites* were nomadic descendants of Abraham and Keturah (Genesis 25:1–6). Their main center was in Arabia, just east of the Red Sea, but they roamed far and wide. Moses had lived among them for 40 years and married one of them (Exodus 2:15–21). Gradually they were absorbed into the Arabians.

The *Arabians* were descendants of Ishmael (Genesis 16). Arabia was the great peninsula (1,500 miles north and south, 800 east and west) that is today Saudi Arabia and Yemen.

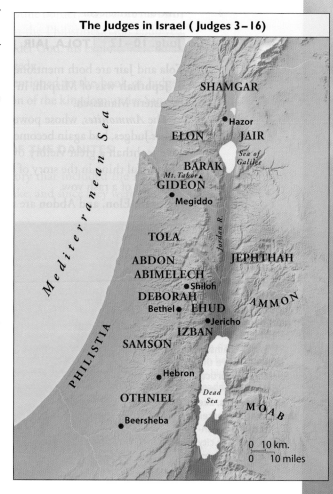

The Judges in Israel (Judges 3–16)

SHAMGAR
Hazor
ELON   JAIR
Sea of Galilee
BARAK
Mt. Tabor ▲
GIDEON
● Megiddo
Mediterranean Sea
Jordan R.
TOLA
ABDON   JEPHTHAH
ABIMELECH
● Shiloh
DEBORAH   AMMON
Bethel ● ● EHUD
● Jericho
IZBAN
SAMSON
PHILISTIA
● Hebron
Dead Sea
OTHNIEL   MOAB
● Beersheba

0   10 km.
0   10 miles

Picking grain in the fields near Bethlehem. Ruth went to glean grain from the fields of Boaz in this same area.

landowner's widow, Naomi, and her widowed daughter-in-law, Ruth. Boaz, the next eligible kinsman-redeemer, then purchases the land and also acquires Ruth for marriage. Boaz declares this redemption in the midst of 10 witnesses so that there is no question regarding the integrity of his actions.

The genealogy in 4:17–22 may actually be the main reason why the book of Ruth was written. It shows that Ruth and Boaz had a son, Obed, whose son was Jesse, whose son was David.

In ancient cities, the gate served the same purpose as the forum did later in Roman cities and public squares did in European cities. Here people met, the king held audience, and business was transacted. It was a more leisurely time: Boaz waited until the person he needed to deal with showed up. In later times, when cities were fortified, the gate also became a key part of the city's defense. This gate at Megiddo shows rooms on both sides where defenders could hide.

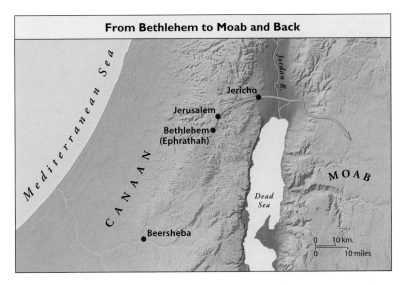

From Bethlehem to Moab and Back

Boaz was a descendant of Rahab, the prostitute from Jericho (Joshua 2:1; Matthew 1:5; see on Joshua 2). Thus David's great-grandmother, Ruth, was a Moabitess, and his great-grandfather, Boaz, was part Canaanite. The chosen family within the Chosen Nation thus has Canaanite and Moabite blood in its veins.

It is fitting that from *this* bloodline would come the Messiah for all nations. Rahab and Ruth became part of God's promises and His plan, not by birth but by their faith in, and their practical commitment to, God and His people — the same way in which people from all nations still can share in God's eternal promises.

It was in a field near Bethlehem that Ruth gleaned. Hundreds of years later, also in a field near Bethlehem, angels announced the birth of Ruth's descendant, Jesus, to startled shepherds.

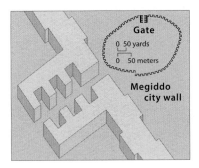

Gate

0   50 yards

0   50 meters

Megiddo
city wall

City of David (Jerusalem) today.

THE MONARCHY: DAVID, SOLOMON, AND THE DIVIDED KINGDOM
1 Samuel – 2 Chronicles

The term *monarchy* refers to the time when God's people were ruled by earthly kings (and in one instance a queen, Athaliah). The *united monarchy* designates the time when both the northern and southern groupings of tribes were united under one king. The term usually refers to the days of David and Solomon but sometimes is used to include Saul's kingship, which was just prior to David's. At the death of Solomon (930 B.C.) the kingdom split into two parts: the southern (including Judah, Benjamin, and Simeon) and the northern (the remaining tribes). This period is known as the *divided monarchy*.

The transition from the period of the Judges (during which God raised up and empowered specific persons for specific purposes) to that of a "theocratic monarchy" (in which a king was to reign over Israel as God's representative) is described in 1 Samuel. The identities of the inspired authors of the books of Samuel and Kings are unknown, and although early, perhaps partial, editions of these books no doubt existed, both books seem to be dealing with questions that Jews may have been asking during the Babylonian exile (586–538 B.C.). These exiles had recently witnessed and experienced the downfall of the Davidic monarchy (586 B.C.); the capture and burning of Jerusalem and the temple; the ravaging of their families, friends, and neighbors; and their own deportation from the land. The totality of these recent experiences stood in stark contrast to the glorious (eternal!) promises that God had made to their ancestors (for example, Genesis 12:1–4; 2-Samuel 7; Psalm 132).

BIBLICAL SOURCES FOR THE PERIOD OF THE UNITED AND DIVIDED MONARCHIES		
Period	**Date**	**Major Biblical Passages**
Saul	1050–1010 B.C.	I Samuel 9–31; I Chronicles 8 and 10
David	1010–970 B.C.	I Samuel 16–2 Samuel–I Kings 2; I Chronicles 11–29
Solomon	970–931 B.C.	I Kings 1–11; 2 Chronicles 1–9
Divided kingdom	931–722 B.C.	I Kings 12–2 Kings 17; 2 Chronicles 10–28. Israel taken into captivity by the Assyrians in 722 B.C.
Judah alone	722–586 B.C.	2 Kings 18–25; 2 Chronicles 29–36 Judah taken into captivity by the Babylonians in 586 B.C.

First Samuel seems to be answering the exiles' question, How did we get a dynastic kingship in the first place? In it, the author describes Samuel's role in anointing Saul and eventually David, tracing the latter's rise to power in contrast to Saul's tragic end.

Second Samuel seems to deal with the question, Who was this David, the first king in his dynasty, and what was so special about him? In other words, why should we be so concerned about the fate of *his* dynasty? The answer, of course, is that God, through His prophets Samuel and Nathan, had selected David and his successors to be the ones through whom He would rule His people (2 Samuel 7) — they would be "theocratic monarchs." Connected to this choice/promise were the related promises that God would "dwell" in Jerusalem, specifically in the temple, and that from there He would rule over, protect, bless, communicate with, forgive, and provide for His people.

The exiles' question was, Why did this disaster happen to us? The answer given in the books of Samuel and Kings is: you, your ancestors, and your rulers, in spite of God's call to repentance and reform, have chosen, in general, the path of disloyalty to God and of disobedience to the stipulations of the "Torah" (= teaching) of the Living God. This disloyalty was evident even as the kingship was being established, it was evident even in the life of the so-called ideal ruler David, and it continued to be evident in the lives of David's successors and the people they governed. Because of disloyalty and disobedience, the covenant curses (see Leviticus 26 and Deuteronomy 28) had fallen upon God's people.

The books of **1 and 2 Chronicles** cover much the same period of Israel's history, although they trace Israel's beginnings back to Adam. Even though the "chronicler" makes use of material from Samuel and Kings, the perspective in these books is a bit different. Most importantly, the message of Chronicles was *addressed to people who were living in the post-exilic period* (that is, some time after the first return, under the leadership of Sheshbazzar and Zerubbabel, had taken place in 538 B.C.; see pp. 267–68). Even though many of the people receiving this message were living in the Promised Land, even in Jerusalem, and were worshiping God at the rebuilt temple, they were well aware that this was not the glorious restoration that previously had been promised by their prophets. Indeed, they were living under the dominating rule of a foreign power (the Persians), there was no reigning Davidic king, the "glory of God" had not returned to the rebuilt temple, and life in the land was not the sought-for "rest" that had been promised. Their question seems to have been, Is there any future for us, for God's people?

The chronicler's answer is *yes*. He emphasizes that the chief legacy of the Davidic dynasty was actually the temple and its service (via the Levitical priesthood). In the chronicler's presentation of Israel's history, emphasis is placed on David as the one making preparations for building

FAST FACTS ON THE DIVIDED KINGDOM		
	North (Israel)	**South (Judah)**
Capitals	Shechem Penuel Tirzah Samaria	Jerusalem
Number of Kings	19	19 and one queen
Dynasties	9	1 (Davidic)
Rulers assassinated or suicide	8	4 (plus 2 killed by non-Judeans)
Worship centers	Bethel Dan Samaria (plus others)	Jerusalem (plus others)
Destruction of the kingdoms	722 B.C. by the Assyrians	586 B.C. by the Babylonians
Major enemies at various times	Southern (Judean) kingdom Philistia Arameans (Damascus) Edomites Assyrians	Northern (Israelite) kingdom Egypt (including Ethiopia) Philistia Ammonites Arameans (Damascus) Edomites Moabites Assyrians Egyptians Babylonians

the temple, on Solomon as the temple builder, and on God-fearing rulers such as Jehoshaphat, Hezekiah, and Josiah who instigated and led religious reforms.

So, in spite of the fact that conditions were not yet all that had been promised, the small and struggling Judean community had a great history and heritage, and they were being encouraged to follow in the more positive footsteps of previous godly rulers and generations as they awaited God's fuller restoration of the land, the temple, and the ideal Davidic ruler—the Anointed One, the Messiah.

Thus historical books such as Samuel, Kings, and Chronicles should be read, not as mere political, economic, military, or ethnic history, but as a "re-presentation" of Israel's history (almost like an extended sermon) that addressed, in the first instance, the readers/hearers of the exilic and postexilic periods.

If you read only one chapter in the books of Samuel, Kings, or Chronicles, be sure to read 2 Samuel 9!

1 Samuel

Samuel, the Last Judge
Saul, the First King; David, God's King
(approx. 1100–1050 B.C.)

*"As for me, far be it from me that I should sin against the L*ORD *by failing to pray for you.
And I will teach you the way that is good and right."*   —I SAMUEL 12:23

*"The L*ORD *does not look at the things man looks at. Man looks at the outward appearance,
but the L*ORD *looks at the heart."*   —I SAMUEL 16:7

In the Hebrew Old Testament, 1 and 2 Samuel are one book called
Samuel. The translators of the Septuagint divided this writing into
two books called the "First and Second Books of the Kingdoms."

First Samuel begins with the background and birth of Samuel. He
began his preparation for ministry and leadership as a small boy serving Eli. Eventually Samuel's influence as a prophet, priest, and Judge
extended throughout the nation. Samuel anointed both Saul and David
as kings, marking the transition from the period of the Judges to the
monarchy.

Author

The author of the book of Samuel is unknown. While Samuel is the
subject of the book, it is unlikely that he actually wrote this book, since
his death is recorded in 1 Samuel 25:1. Whoever wrote these books used
the Book of Jashar as a source (2 Samuel 1:18) and may also have had
access to other sources from this period, such as the Annals of King
David (1 Chronicles 27:24) and the records of Samuel, Nathan, and Gad
(1 Chronicles 29:29).

Samuel, Kings, and Chronicles

The entire history of the kingdom of Israel is told in the two books of Samuel
and the two books of Kings. The books of Chronicles tell the same story.

In broad outline,

- 1–2 Samuel = 1 Chronicles
- 1–2 Kings = 2 Chronicles (both 1 Kings and 2 Chronicles begin
  with Solomon)

The main differences are that

- 1 Chronicles begins with a lengthy genealogy—beginning with Adam—
  but it omits the stories of Samuel and Saul (except for Saul's suicide);
- 2 Chronicles omits entirely the history of the northern kingdom.

The Scene of Samuel's Ministry

The Four Towns of Samuel's Judicial and Priestly Circuit

- **Ramah,** about five miles north of Jerusalem, was his birthplace, judicial residence, and place of burial (1:19; 7:17; 25:1).
- **Bethel,** about seven miles north of Ramah, was Samuel's northern office. It was one of the four highest points in the land (the others are Mount Ebal, Hebron, and Mizpah). The view over the land from Bethel is magnificent. Here, 800 years before, Jacob had seen the heavenly ladder (Genesis 28:10–20).
- **Mizpah,** 2½ miles northwest of Ramah, was an important gathering place for the tribes of Israel during the days of Samuel (1 Samuel 7:5–7; 10:17).
- **Gilgal,** about 10 miles east of Ramah, near Jericho, was the place where the Israelites camped after crossing the Jordan under Joshua and where Joshua had placed a memorial (Joshua 4:19–24). It continued as a worship center during the days of Samuel and Saul.

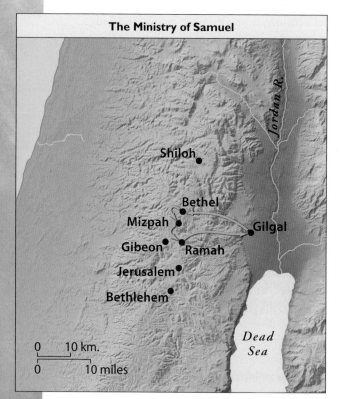

The Ministry of Samuel

Other Towns

- **Gibeah** (Tell-el-Ful), about two miles south of Ramah, was Saul's capital.
- **Gibeon,** 2½ miles west of Ramah, was where Saul grew up, and the "High Place of Gibeon" (1 Samuel 13:3) was located only one mile southwest of Gibeon, at Nebi Samwil. This was an important worship site for the tribes of Israel; later the tabernacle was placed here (2 Chronicles 1:5).
- **Bethlehem,** David's birthplace and later the birthplace of Jesus, was 11 miles south of Ramah.
- **Shiloh,** about 15 miles north of Ramah, was where the tabernacle stood from the time of Joshua to Samuel and where Samuel ministered as a child at the tabernacle.
- **Kiriath Jearim,** where the ark of the covenant was kept after its return from the Philistines, was about nine miles southwest of Ramah.

Tell Shiloh.
Samuel served in the
Tabernacle that was
set up at Shiloh.

- **Jerusalem,** about five miles south of Ramah, was still in the hands of the Jebusites in Samuel's day. It was later captured by David.

| I Sam. 1:1–2:11 | BIRTH OF SAMUEL |

Samuel was of the tribe of Levi (1 Chronicles 6:33–38). His mother, Hannah, was a marvelous example of motherhood; her son turned out to be one of the noblest and purest characters in history.

Shiloh (1:3).

- Joshua set up the tabernacle in Shiloh (Joshua 18:1). Every year Israel went to Shiloh to bring sacrifices (1 Samuel 1:3).
- David brought the ark of the covenant to Jerusalem (2 Samuel 6:15) about 1000 B.C.
- Jeremiah (7:12–15), about 600 B.C., refers to Shiloh as being in ruins. The implication of these passages is that Shiloh was an important city during the period from Joshua to Samuel, and that sometime before 600 B.C. it was destroyed, deserted, and ceased to exist.

ARCHAEOLOGICAL NOTE: Shiloh. Danish, and later Israeli, excavations at Shiloh have found that it was a worship center from 1650 B.C. During the Canaanite occupation it was surrounded by a massive wall, which in places is preserved to a height of 25 feet. Excavations demonstrate that it was a worship center when occupied by the Israelites as well. Some have speculated that the tabernacle was set up on several rock-cut terraces on the north side of the tell. The site was destroyed in 1050 B.C., probably by the Philistines.

Ruins of Shiloh. Immediately after the conquest of Canaan under Joshua, the tabernacle was set up in Shiloh (Joshua 18:1). It apparently remained there until the days of Samuel. The tabernacle itself may have been replaced by a more permanent structure during that time (I Samuel 3:3, "temple"; I Samuel 3:15, "doors").

I Sam. 2:12–36

CHANGE IN THE PRIESTHOOD ANNOUNCED

Hannah's prophetic prayers in 2:31–35 seem to have application to Samuel, who succeeded Eli as Judge and also as acting priest (7:9; 9:11–14); but they also have reference to a priesthood that shall last forever (2:35).

They were fulfilled when Solomon displaced Abiathar of Eli's family with Zadok of another line (1 Kings 2:27; 1 Chronicles 24:3, 6). But their ultimate fulfillment is in the eternal priesthood of Christ. In chapters 8–10, we are told how Samuel initiated a change in the form of government, from government by Judges to a kingdom. Under the kingdom, the offices of king and priest were kept separate.

Here in verse 35 an eternal priesthood is promised, and in 2 Samuel 7:16 David is promised an eternal throne. The eternal priesthood and the eternal throne looked forward to the Messiah, in whom they merged—Christ became man's eternal Priest and eternal King. The temporary merging of the offices of Judge and priest in the person of Samuel, during the period of transition from Judges to kingdom, seems to have been a sort of historical foreshadowing of the final fusing of the two offices in Christ. In addition, Samuel was recognized as a prophet (1 Samuel 3:20), which is the third office that Christ combined in Himself (see Deuteronomy 18:15, "a prophet like me"): King (Judge), Priest, and Prophet.

I Sam. 3 **SAMUEL'S PROPHETIC CALL**

Samuel was a prophet (3:20). He served as a priest, offering sacrifices (7:9). And he judged Israel (7:15–17). His circuit included Bethel, Gilgal, and Mizpah, with his main office at Ramah. He was the last Judge, the first prophet, and the founder of the monarchy. His main mission was the organization of the kingdom.

The form of government under the Judges had been a failure (see introductory note to the book of Judges). So God raised up Samuel to unify the nation under a king. (See below on chapters 8–10.)

| I Sam. 4–7 | THE ARK IS CAPTURED BY THE PHILISTINES |

The ark, after its capture by the Philistines, was never taken back to Shiloh, and Shiloh ceased to be a place of importance. The ark remained in Philistine cities for seven months, during which time the Philistines suffered great plagues. So great were the plagues that the Philistines pleaded to Israel to take back the ark—which they gleefully did! It was taken to Beth Shemesh and then to Kiriath Jearim, where it remained for 20 years (7:2). Later it was taken to Jerusalem by David, who built a tent for it (2 Samuel 6:12; 2 Chronicles 1:4). It stayed in that tent until Solomon built the temple. Nothing is known of the history of the ark after the destruction of Jerusalem by the Babylonians some 450 years later.

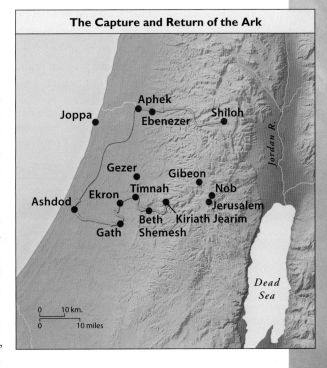

The Capture and Return of the Ark

The tabernacle, after the ark was gone from Shiloh, was apparently moved to Nob (21:1; Mark 2:26) and then to Gibeon (1 Chronicles 21:29) until Solomon put it in the temple (1 Kings 8:4).

After the return of the ark from the Philistines, Samuel, with the aid of God, administered a terrific defeat to the Philistines at the place where they had captured the ark (4:1; 7:12).

I Sam. 8–10 | ORGANIZATION OF THE KINGDOM

Up to this time the form of government had been the theocracy (see p. 187). In a predatory world that only recognized the law of the jungle, a nation needed to be fairly strong in order to survive. So God, accommodating Himself to human ways, permitted His nation to unify, as other nations did, under a king. The first king, Saul, was a failure. But the second king, David, was a magnificent success.

ARCHAEOLOGICAL NOTE: Saul's House in Gibeah. "Saul also went to his home in Gibeah" (10:26). William F. Albright (1922–23) found in Gibeah, in the stratum of 1050 B.C., the ruins of the small fortress Saul had built.

I Sam. 11–15 | SAUL AS KING

Saul was of the tribe of Benjamin, which had almost been annihilated in the days of the Judges, and of the city of Gibeah, where the horrible story had started (see Judges 19–21).

Tall, handsome, and humble, Saul began his reign with a brilliant victory over the Ammonites. Any misgivings about the new kingdom disappeared.

Then followed Samuel's warning, to nation and king, not to forget God, a warning confirmed by a miraculous thunderstorm (chap. 12).

Saul's first mistake (chap. 13). His successes rapidly went to his head. Humility gave place to pride. He offered sacrifices, which was the exclusive function of priests. This was the first sign of Saul's growing sense of self-importance.

Saul ruled the kingdom of Israel from Gibeah.

Saul's second mistake (chap. 14). His silly order for the army to abstain from food, and his senseless death sentence for Jonathan, showed the people what a fool they had for a king.

Saul's third mistake (chap. 15). This time Saul deliberately disobeyed God. For this he heard Samuel's ominous pronouncement, "Because you have rejected God, God has rejected you from being king."

I Sam. 16 | **DAVID SECRETLY ANOINTED TO BE KING**

The anointing could not have been done openly, for then Saul would have killed David. Its purpose was to give David a chance to train himself for the office. God took David under His care (v. 13).

David was short of stature, of fair complexion and hand-some, of immense physical strength and great personal attractive-ness, a man of war, prudent in speech, very brave, musical, and religious.

His fame as a musician brought him to the notice of King Saul, who did not at the time know that David had been anointed to be his successor. David became Saul's armor-bearer. This brought David into close association with the king and his counselors, so that unknow-ingly Saul helped train David for his future responsibilities as king.

I Sam. 17 | **DAVID AND GOLIATH**

It seems that David's first residence at the court was only temporary and that he returned to Bethlehem. Some years passed, and the boy David had so changed in appearance that Saul did not recognize him (vv. 55–58).

Socoh, where Goliath was encamped, was some 14 miles west of Bethlehem. Goliath was about nine feet tall. His armor weighed about 120 pounds, and his spearhead alone about 15 pounds. David's offer to take on Goliath with only a staff and a sling was an act of unheard-of bravery and amazing trust in God. His victory thrilled the nation. He became the king's son-in-law, commander of the armies, and the nation's popular hero.

I Sam. 18–20 | **SAUL'S JEALOUSY OF DAVID**

David's popularity turned Saul against him. Saul tried to kill him, but David fled and for years was a fugitive in the mountains and in the wilderness.

Jonathan's friendship for David (chap. 20). Jonathan was heir to the throne. His brilliant victory over the Philistines (chap. 14) and his nobility of character were good evidence that he would have made a worthy king. But he had found out that God had ordained David to be king, and his graceful self-effacement in giving up his succession to the throne and his unselfish devotion to David, whom he could have hated as a rival, form one of the noblest stories of friendship in history.

Jonathan initiated a covenant with David, symbolized by the giving of robe, tunic, sword, bow, and belt. This act reflected Jonathan's recognition that David would take Jonathan's place as Saul's successor.

I Sam. 21–27 | DAVID A FUGITIVE FROM SAUL

David escaped to the Philistines, feigning insanity. Sensing danger, he fled first to the cave of Adullam in west Judah, then to Moab, then back to south Judah, where he stayed in Keilah, Ziph, and Maon. He had accumulated 600 followers. Saul was in hot pursuit, but David always escaped. A number of the Psalms were composed by David during this period (Psalms 18, 52, 54, 57, 59).

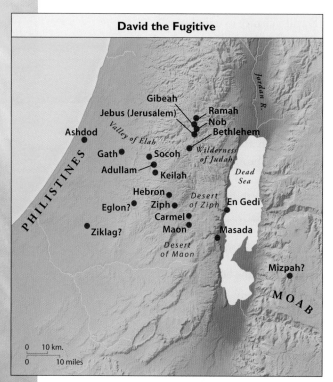

David the Fugitive

At En-gedi, Saul was trapped. But David refused to come to the throne by murder, no matter how justified it might seem, and spared Saul's life. Again, at Ziph, Saul acknowledged being a fool — but kept on being one.

Samuel died, and all Israel came together and mourned him. He was buried in Ramah (1 Samuel 25:1).

At Maon, David met Abigail, a woman whom God provided as a pattern of good behavior in an unfortunate marriage. She eventually became David's wife. David finally found refuge among the Philistines again and stayed there until the death of Saul.

I Sam. 28–31 | THE DEATH OF SAUL

The Philistines invaded the land and encamped at Mount Gilboa. One of the Philistine princes had wanted David and his men to go along with them. But the other princes did not trust David. So David remained behind and with his 600 men guarded the south against the Amalekites.

In the meantime, Saul was thoroughly frightened and sought, through a witch at Endor, an interview with the spirit of Samuel. The straightforward simplicity of the narrative seems to imply that the spirit of Samuel did actually appear. However, there is difference of opinion as to whether the apparition was real or fraudulent. At any rate, Saul committed suicide in the battle. He had reigned 40 years (Acts 13:21).

ARCHAEOLOGICAL NOTE: The Fate of Saul's Head and Armor. It is stated in 31:10 that "they put [Saul's] armor in the temple of the Ashtoreths" in Beth Shan, and in 1 Chronicles 10:10 it is said that they "hung up his head in the temple of Dagon."

Beth Shan (Beisan) is just east of Mount Gilboa, at the junction of the Jezreel and Jordan valleys. The University Museum of Pennsylvania (1921–33) uncovered, in an 11th-century B.C. stratum at Beth Shan, the ruins of twin temples, which may have been the very buildings in which Saul's armor and head were fastened; at least, it is proof that there were such temples in Beth Shan in Saul's day.

2 Samuel

The Reign of David
(approx. 1010–970 B.C.)

"When your days are over and you rest with your fathers, I will raise up your offspring to succeed you, who will come from your own body, and I will establish his kingdom. . . . "Your house and your kingdom will endure forever before me; your throne will be established forever."

—2 SAMUEL 7:12, 16

The second book of Samuel continues the history of God's establishment of the kingdom of Israel. It begins with David becoming king over Judah and eventually over all of Israel. It tells of David's 40-year reign, including his wars; his capture of Jerusalem and the bringing of the ark to Jerusalem; God's promise of an everlasting kingdom; his sin with Bathsheba; and the loss of his sons. The book ends with David reflecting on his life in what is perhaps his last poetic testimony.

| 2 Sam. 1–6 | **DAVID BECOMES KING OVER ALL OF ISRAEL** |

It is helpful to read 2 Samuel 1–6 and 1 Chronicles 11–16 together, since this clearly shows the difference in focus between, on the one hand, the books of Samuel and Kings, and on the other, the books of Chronicles. (For a description of these differences, see p. 228.)

Both 2 Samuel 1–6 and 1 Chronicles 11–13 cover the period from the death of Saul up to God's promise to David. But 2 Samuel 1–6 describes at some length the war between the house of Saul and the house of David and the intrigues it involved, while 1 Chronicles 11–16 skips the war with the house of Saul and goes into detail about David's mighty

---

Samuel, Kings, and Chronicles

The entire history of the kingdom of Israel is told in the two books of Samuel and the two books of Kings. The books of Chronicles tell the same story.

In broad outline,

- 1–2 Samuel = 1 Chronicles
- 1–2 Kings = 2 Chronicles (both 1 Kings and 2 Chronicles begin with Solomon)

The main differences are that

- 1 Chronicles begins with a lengthy genealogy—beginning with Adam— but it omits the stories of Samuel and Saul (except for Saul's suicide);
- 2 Chronicles omits entirely the history of the northern kingdom.

men and warriors. Chronicles also pays more attention to the ark of the covenant: it describes the return of the ark from the Philistines who had captured it (chap. 13), an event that is ignored in 2 Samuel, and it devotes two chapters (15–16) to the bringing of the ark to Jerusalem, which is covered in a single chapter (6) in 2 Samuel.

Jerusalem

ARCHAEOLOGICAL NOTE: Gihon Spring and Ancient Water System. The one natural water source for the city of Jerusalem is the Gihon Spring, situated down in the Kidron Valley. The ancient core of Jerusalem developed just to the west of this spring, on a defensible hill. It is because of this spring that the city of Jerusalem was built here.

The tunnels, shafts, and towers close to this spring have been carefully studied by scholars since the 19th century. It appears that the pre-Israelite population built massive towers to guard the water sources, and they also enlarged natural tunnels and shafts that led from inside the city to the spring. In this way they were able to draw water from the spring during times of siege without ever having to go outside of the city walls. It is probable that Joab led David's troops through this tunnel system and thus captured the city from the Jebusites: "Anyone who conquers the Jebusites will have to use the water shaft to reach those 'lame and blind' who are David's enemies" (2 Samuel 5:8; compare also 1 Chronicles 11:4–9).

ARCHAEOLOGICAL NOTE: Millo. In her excavations of the old ancient core of the City of David, Kathleen Kenyon and, after her, Yigal Shiloh discovered that Jerusalem had been built on a series of ascending terraces. These terraces were constructed by building a retaining wall, and filling (Heb. *millo*) in behind it. Then houses and other structures were

Gihon spring. The Gihon spring provided a consistent water source for ancient Jerusalem.

built on the fill (*millo*). One of the duties of a good king, from the time of David onward, was to build up "the area around it [i.e., the City of David], from the supporting terraces [Heb. *millo*] inward" (2 Samuel 5:9).

2 Sam. 7 | GOD PROMISES DAVID AN ETERNAL THRONE

The Old Testament is the story of God's dealings with the Hebrew nation for the purpose of one day blessing all nations.

As the story unfolds, it is explained that the way the Hebrew nation would bless all nations is through the family of David. It is further explained that the family of David would bless the world through a great King who would one day be born into the family, a King who would live forever and establish a kingdom of endless duration.

This water shaft at Gibeon goes down some 33 feet and leads to a tunnel 40 feet long. At the end is a water chamber that may be the pool of Gibeon referred to in 2 Samuel 2:12. After the fall of Jericho, the Gibeonites tricked Joshua into making a treaty with them (Joshua 9–10). It was when Joshua defended Gibeon from the Amorites that the sun stood still over the city.

ARCHAEOLOGICAL NOTE: The David Inscription at Dan. Until recently, no mention of "David" had been found in any extrabiblical text dating to the Old Testament period. Now fragments of a carved stone victory stele have been found at Dan—one of the northernmost towns in Israel. Beautifully inscribed, the stele describes in Aramaic the victory of the king of Aram (Damascus) over the kings of Israel and Judah. Among the lines is a mentioning of "the house of David"—a clear reference to the Davidic dynasty, some 150 to 200 years after David had died.

2 Sam. 8–10 | DAVID'S VICTORIES

After Saul's death, David had been made king over Judah. Seven years later he was made king over all of Israel. He was 30 when he became king. He reigned over Judah alone for 7½ years, and over all of Israel for 33 years, a total of 40 years (5:3–5). He died at age 70.

Soon after becoming king over all Israel, David made Jerusalem his capital. Situated in an impregnable position, with valleys on three sides, and with the tradition of Melchizedek, the priest of God Most High (Genesis 14:18; Salem is thought to be the ancient name for Jerusalem—compare Psalm 76:2), David decided to make it his nation's capital.

> ### The Promises
>
> Thus the promise of an eternal king who was to come from David's family was repeated over and over—to David himself, to Solomon, and again and again in the Psalms and by the prophets Amos, Isaiah, Micah, Jeremiah, and Zechariah, over a period of some 500 years.
>
> When the time came, the angel Gabriel was sent to Nazareth, to Mary, who was of the family of David, and he said:
>
> "Do not be afraid, Mary, you have found favor with God. You will be with child and give birth to a son, and you are to give him the name Jesus. He will be great and will be called the Son of the Most High. The Lord God will give him the throne of his father David, and he will reign over the house of Jacob forever; his kingdom will never end" (Luke 1:30–33).
>
> In this Child the promises to and about David found their fulfillment.

He took it, brought in the ark of God, and planned the temple (chaps. 5–7), which his son Solomon would build.

David was very successful in his wars. He completely subdued the Philistines, Moabites, Syrians, Edomites, Ammonites, Amalekites, and all neighboring nations. "The LORD gave David victory wherever he went" (8:6).

David took an insignificant nation and in a few years built it into a mighty kingdom. In the southwest, the Egyptian world empire had declined. In the east, in Mesopotamia, the Assyrian and Babylonian world empires had not yet arisen. And here, on the highway between Egypt and Mesopotamia, the kingdom of Israel under David became almost overnight, not a world empire, but perhaps the single most powerful kingdom on earth at the time.

| 2 Sam. 11–12 | **DAVID AND BATHSHEBA** |

This was the blackest spot in David's life: adultery and instigation to murder to cover up the adultery. His remorse made him a broken man. God forgave him but pronounced a fearful sentence: "The sword will never depart from your house" (12:10)—and it never did. David reaped exactly what he had sown, and even more—a long, hard, and bitter harvest. His daughter Tamar was raped by her brother Amnon, who in turn was murdered by their brother Absalom. Absalom led a rebellion against his father, David, and was killed in the struggle. David's wives were violated in public, as he had secretly violated the wife of Uriah. Thus David's glorious reign was clouded by unceasing troubles. What a lesson for those who think they can sin, and sin, and sin, and get away with it!

And yet—this was the man after God's own heart (1 Samuel 13:14; Acts 13:22). David's reactions showed him to be just that. Some of the Psalms (for example, 32 and 51) were born of this bitter experience.

2 Sam. 13–21 | DAVID'S TROUBLES

Absalom probably knew that Solomon was to be David's successor as king, hence this effort to steal the throne from his father, David. Judging by the space given to the account of Absalom, it must have been one of the most troublesome things in David's reign. It involved the defection of some of David's advisers and utterly broke his heart. But Absalom was finally killed, and David was restored to his throne. (For a note on the gateway mentioned in 18:33, see p. 196.)

Then followed Sheba's rebellion (chap. 20). Absalom's attempted usurpation probably weakened David's hold on the people. So Sheba tried his hand at it, but soon was crushed. Then the Philistines grew bold again (chap. 21), but again David was victorious.

2 Sam. 22 | DAVID'S SONG OF PRAISE

Here, as in many psalms, David exhibits his unfailing trust in God and his unbounded gratitude to God for His constant care.

2 Sam. 23 | DAVID'S LAST WORDS

This is David's last psalm. It shows what David's mind was focused on at the close of his glorious but troubled life: the justice of his reign as king, his creation of the Psalms, his devotion to God's Word, and God's covenant with him that promised an eternal dynasty.

2 Sam. 24 | THE PEOPLE NUMBERED

It is difficult to see just why the taking of a national census was a sin. God Himself had ordered such a census both at the beginning and at the end of the 40 years of wilderness wanderings (Numbers 1:2; 26:2). In this

The Dome of the Rock now sits on the area of the ancient Temple mount. The plague of death that resulted from David numbering the people ceased after he made a sacrifice to the Lord on the threshing floor at the location where the Temple was later built by Solomon.

case, David's decision to count the people may indicate that he who had so consistently, all his life, relied implicitly on God was beginning to rely on the greatness of his kingdom. The census was Satan's idea (1 Chronicles 21:1). Satan may have considered it an opportunity to move David away from his trust in God to trust in himself. At any rate, God regarded the act as a sin to be punished.

The census showed a population of about a million and a half fighting men, exclusive of Levi and Benjamin (1 Chronicles 21:5), which would mean a total population of probably about 6 to 8 million.

In punishment, God sent the plague. The Angel of the Lord, who brought the plague, was stopped by God at a place near Jerusalem, the threshing floor of Araunah the Jebusite. David bought the threshing floor from Araunah, so that it became the royal property of the House of David. David built an altar on it (v. 25) and later Solomon built the temple there (2 Chronicles 3:1).

David

All in all, David was a grand character. He did some things that were very wrong, but he was a most remarkable man, especially when viewed in the light of his time and in comparison with other oriental rulers. He was, heart and soul, devoted to God and the ways of God. In a world of idolatry and in a nation that was continually falling away into idolatry, David stood like a rock for God. In every circumstance of life he went directly to God, in prayer, in thanks, in repentance, or in praise. His two great accomplishments were the kingdom and the Psalms.

1 Kings

**The Reign of Solomon
The Division and Decay of the
Kingdom; Elijah**

*Elijah went before the people and said, "How long will you waver between two opinions? If
the LORD is God, follow him; but if Baal is God, follow him."* —1 KINGS 18:21

P arallel stories should be read in both 1 Kings and in 2 Chronicles,
since they often include different details and even events.

In the Hebrew Old Testament, 1 and 2 Kings are one book.
The translators of the Septuagint divided it into two books. First Kings
opens with the Hebrew nation in its glory. Second Kings closes with
the nation in ruin. Together they cover a period of about 400 years,
approximately 970–586 B.C. Except for a few high spots, the story that
begins full of promise with the golden age of Hebrew history soon turns
into a sad story of division and decay and ends with the destruction of
Jerusalem and the deportation of the citizens of what was left of David
and Solomon's once mighty kingdom.

Author

The author of the books of Kings is not known. A Jewish tradition says
that it was Jeremiah. Whoever the author was, he makes frequent reference to state annals and other historical records that existed in his day,
such as the Book of the Acts of Solomon, the Book of the Chronicles of
the Kings of Judah, and the Book of the Chronicles of the Kings of Israel
(1 Kings 11:41; 14:19, 29; 15:7, 23, 31; 16:5, 14, 27, etc.). It appears
that there was an abundance of written records to which the author had
access, guided, of course, by the Spirit of God.

Samuel, Kings, and Chronicles

The entire history of the kingdom of Israel is told in the two books of Samuel
and the two books of Kings. The books of Chronicles tell the same story.

In broad outline,

- 1–2 Samuel = 1 Chronicles
- 1–2 Kings   = 2 Chronicles (both 1 Kings and 2 Chronicles begin
                  with Solomon)

The main differences are that

- 1 Chronicles begins with a lengthy genealogy—beginning with Adam—
  but it omits the stories of Samuel and Saul (except for Saul's suicide);
- 2 Chronicles omits entirely the history of the northern kingdom.

King David was buried in the City of David (the ancient core of Jerusalem just south of the temple), as were all kings of Judah through Ahaz. The largest opening may be the tomb of David. Not much can be seen, since the site was quarried extensively during the Roman period.

1 Kings 1–2 | SOLOMON BECOMES KING

Solomon was the son of David and Bathsheba, the wife of Uriah (2 Samuel 11:1–12:24). Though not in line for the succession, he was chosen by David, and approved by God, to be David's successor (1:30; 1 Chronicles 22:9–10).

Adonijah, David's fourth son, it seems, was heir expectant to the throne (2:15, 22; 2 Samuel 3:3–4), for the three eldest sons (Amnon, Absalom, and probably Chiliab) were dead. So while David was on his deathbed, and before Solomon was formally anointed king, Adonijah plotted to seize the kingdom. But the plot was thwarted by Nathan the prophet. Solomon was generous in his treatment of Adonijah. But Adonijah persisted in his effort to steal the throne, and it was not long until he also was executed (1 Kings 1:1–2:25).

1 Kings 3 | SOLOMON CHOOSES WISDOM

"So give your servant a discerning heart to govern your people and to distinguish between right and wrong. For who is able to govern this great people of yours?"
—1 Kings 3:9

This event took place at Gibeon (3:4), where at the time the tabernacle and the bronze altar were located (1 Chronicles 21:29), about six miles northwest of Jerusalem. The ark had been brought to Jerusalem by David (3:15; 2 Samuel 6:1–16). God told Solomon to ask whatever he wanted. Solomon asked for wisdom to govern his people. That pleased God, and God richly rewarded him (vv. 10–12)—a marvelous picture of true greatness and youthful piety!

1 Kings 4 | SOLOMON'S POWER, WEALTH, AND WISDOM

Solomon had inherited the throne of the most powerful kingdom then in existence. It was an era of peace and prosperity. Solomon had vast business enterprises and was famous for his literary attainments.

He wrote 3000 proverbs, more than 1000 songs, and scientific works on botany and zoology (vv. 32–33). He wrote Ecclesiastes and the Song of Songs (also called the Song of Solomon), as well as most of the book of Proverbs.

I Kings 5–8 SOLOMON BUILDS THE TEMPLE

Solomon began building the temple in the fourth year of his reign. He built it according to specific design instructions that God had given to his father, David. The temple was finished in roughly seven years.

(See on 2 Chronicles 2–7.)

I Kings 9–10 THE SPLENDOR OF SOLOMON'S KINGDOM

These two chapters are an expansion of chapter 4. Solomon devoted himself to commerce and gigantic public works. He made a deal with the king of Tyre that allowed him to use his navy on the Mediterranean. He had a navy at Ezion Geber, on the Gulf of Aqaba, and controlled the trade route south through Edom to the coasts of Arabia, India, and Africa. He built his empire by peaceful commerce.

The era of David and Solomon was the golden age of Hebrew history. David was a warrior; Solomon was a builder. David made the kingdom; Solomon built the temple. In the world outside Israel, this was the age of Homer, the beginning of Greek history. Egypt, Assyria, and Babylon were weak. Israel was the most powerful kingdom in all the Ancient Near East, Jerusalem one of the most magnificent cities, and the temple one of the most splendid buildings. People came from the ends of the earth to hear Solomon's wisdom and see his glory. The famous Queen of Sheba exclaimed, "Not even half was told me" (10:7).

Solomon's annual income and his supply of gold were enormous: he made large shields of gold and small shields of gold, all the vessels of his palace were made of gold, his throne was ivory overlaid with gold. Gold was as common in Jerusalem as stones (10:10–22; 2 Chronicles 1:15). Within five years after Solomon's death, Shishak, king of Egypt, came and took all this gold away (14:25–26; 2 Chronicles 12:2, 9–11).

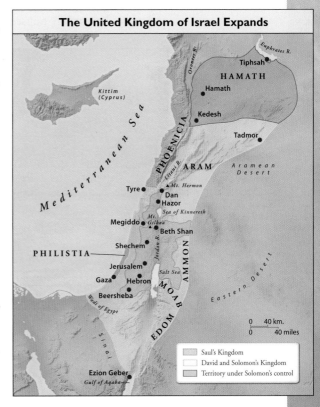

The United Kingdom of Israel Expands

Euphrates R.
Tiphsah
HAMATH
Hamath
Kittim (Cyprus)
Kedesh
Tadmor
Mediterranean Sea
PHOENICIA
ARAM
Aramean Desert
Tyre
Mt. Hermon
Dan
Hazor
Sea of Kinnereth
Megiddo
Mt. Gilboa
Beth Shan
Shechem
PHILISTIA
Jordan R.
Jerusalem
Salt Sea
AMMON
Gaza
Hebron
MOAB
Beersheba
Wadi of Egypt
EDOM
Eastern Desert
Sinai
Ezion Geber
Gulf of Aqaba

0   40 km.
0   40 miles

Saul's Kingdom
David and Solomon's Kingdom
Territory under Solomon's control

ARCHAEOLOGICAL NOTE: The Water System at Megiddo. Although not mentioned frequently in Scripture, this city sat astride one of the great trade routes of antiquity. When the Egyptian king Thutmose III conquered the city (ca. 1482 B.C.), he said that the "capture of Megiddo, was like the capture of a thousand towns"—so great was its importance. At Megiddo, a gate, wall, palaces, and storerooms from the time of Solomon have been discovered. During the days of wicked Ahab, a vertical shaft, 120 feet deep, was cut on the west side of the mound, and a 215-foot horizontal tunnel was then cut in order to bring water from outside the city to inside its walls, in order to provide its residents with water during times of siege. Throughout history the armies of the world have attempted to control this strategic spot, and so it has become the symbol for the great final battle (Revelation 16:16), the "Battle of Armageddon" (Heb. *Har* [mount] *Megiddo*).

ARCHAEOLOGICAL NOTE: The Fate of Solomon's Gold. Records show that Shishak and his son Osorkon gave over 383 tons of precious metal to the Egyptian deities. Perhaps some of this was the very same gold Shishak had taken from Solomon's son Rehoboam.

ARCHAEOLOGICAL NOTE: Solomon's Stables. The author speaks of Solomon's horses and chariots in 10:26, 28. Megiddo, along with Gezer and Hazor, is named as one of the cities Solomon fortified and where he possibly housed his chariots and horses (9:15, 19).

The remains of the city of Megiddo. (Note the partial tell that has not yet been excavated.) Solomon had the walls of the city built with forced labor. Later, King Josiah battled Pharaoh Neco of Egypt in the plain of Megiddo and was killed (2 Chronicles 35:22). Here in the plain of Megiddo the great battle of the End, the battle of Armageddon (Har Megiddo) will be fought (Revelation 16:16).

The Oriental Institute uncovered structures at Megiddo that may be Solomon's stables (although some archaeologists believe that the structures may have been used as storerooms; and some would actually date them to the time of Ahab rather than Solomon). (See also p. 228.)

The high place at Dan, where King Jeroboam placed one of the golden calves. (The other one was near the southern border, close to Jerusalem, in Bethel.)

ARCHAEOLOGICAL NOTE: Solomon's Navy at Ezion Geber. Solomon built a navy in Ezion Geber (9:26). This was for his trade with Arabia, India, and the east coast of Africa. Ezion Geber was located at the north end of the Gulf of Akaba, on the Red Sea, although its exact location is not certain. Some have suggested Tell el–Kheleifeh (excavated by Nelson Glueck), while others suggest identifying it with the island anchorage called Jezirat Faraun, nine miles southwest of the northern tip of the Red Sea.

I Kings 11 | SOLOMON'S WIVES AND APOSTASY

Solomon's glorious reign was clouded by a grand mistake: his marriage to women from other nations, who brought their idols with them. He had 700 wives and 300 concubines (11:3), which would seem to make this wise man of the ages, in this respect at least, just a plain, common fool. Many of these women were daughters of gentile princes, whom he married for the sake of political alliance. For them, he who had built God's temple built heathen altars alongside it. Thus idolatry, which David had been so zealous to suppress, was reestablished in the palace. This brought to a close the glorious era ushered in by David and started the nation on its road to ruin. The besotted apostasy of Solomon's old age is one of the most pitiful spectacles in the Bible. Perhaps the account of it was intended by God to be an example of what luxury and ceaseless rounds of pleasure will do to even the best of men.

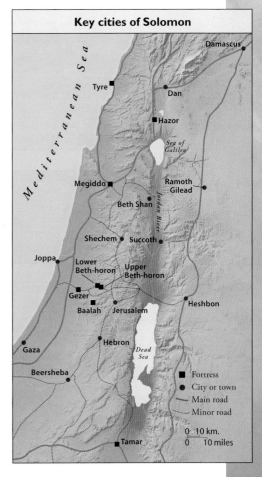

Key cities of Solomon

Mediterranean Sea
Damascus
Tyre
Dan
Hazor
Sea of Galilee
Megiddo
Ramoth Gilead
Beth Shan
Jordan River
Shechem
Succoth
Joppa
Lower Beth-horon
Upper Beth-horon
Gezer
Heshbon
Baalah
Jerusalem
Gaza
Hebron
Dead Sea
Beersheba
Tamar

■ Fortress
● City or town
— Main road
--- Minor road

0 10 km.
0 10 miles

The Two Kingdoms—930–722 B.C.

Sidon

Dan

ARAM

PHOENICIA

Mediterranean Sea

Sea of Galilee

Kishon R.

Yarmuk R.

Jordan R.

Samaria

I S R A E L

Shechem

Jabbok R.

Bethel

Rabbah

Jerusalem

Bethlehem

Dead Sea

Arnon R.

Gaza

PHILISTIA

Besor Br.

Beersheba

M O A B

J U D A H

Zered R.

E D O M

0 10 km.
0   10 miles

I Kings 12 | THE DIVISION OF THE KINGDOM

The kingdom had lasted 120 years: 40 years under Saul (Acts 13:21), 40 years under David (2 Samuel 5:4), and 40 years under Solomon (1 Kings 11:42). After Solomon's death the kingdom was divided. Ten tribes formed the northern kingdom and took the name "Israel" with them. The two remaining tribes, Judah and Benjamin, formed the southern kingdom, called "Judah."

The northern kingdom lasted a little over 200 years. It was destroyed by Assyria in 722 B.C. The 10 tribes were deported and disappeared from history. The southern kingdom lasted a little over 300 years. It was destroyed by Babylon shortly after about 586 B.C.

The secession of the 10 tribes was of God (11:11, 31; 12:15), both as punishment for apostasy of Solomon and as a lesson to Judah.

I Kings 13–14 | JEROBOAM, KING OF ISRAEL (931–910 B.C.)

Jeroboam, encouraged by the prophet Ahijah and promised the throne of the Ten

Jeroboam instituted calf worship and built a high place at Bethel and Dan.

Tribes and a lasting dynasty if only he would walk in God's ways, led a revolt against Solomon. Solomon tried to kill him, so he fled to the court of Shishak, the king of Egypt.

After Solomon's death, Jeroboam returned and established the Ten Tribes as an independent kingdom. But he disregarded Ahijah's warning and instituted calf worship. God sent Ahijah to Jeroboam again, this time to tell him that Israel would be rooted up out of the land and scattered in the country beyond the Euphrates (14:10, 15). This amazing prophecy, which called Josiah by name 300 years before he was born (13:2), was fulfilled (2 Kings 23:15–18).

After the division of the kingdom, there was long, continued war between Israel and Judah.

I Kings 14:21–31 | REHOBOAM, KING OF JUDAH
(931–913 B.C.) *(See on 2 Chronicles 10.)*

I Kings 15:1–8 | ABIJAH, KING OF JUDAH (931–911 B.C.)
(See on 2 Chronicles 13.)

The Religion of the Northern Kingdom

Jeroboam, the founder of the northern kingdom, in order to keep the two kingdoms separate, adopted calf worship as the state religion of his newly formed kingdom. The worship of God had become identified with Judah, Jerusalem, and the family of David. The calf came to stand as a symbol of Israel's independence of Judah. Jeroboam established calf worship so firmly in the northern kingdom that it was not swept away until the fall of the kingdom. His two main religious centers were Bethel in the south and Dan in the northern part of the kingdom.

There was always a tendency for the Israelites to join in the worship of the Canaanite deity Baal. His worship was actively promoted by Jezebel, but actively opposed by the prophets Elijah and Elisha and by King Jehu. Baal and other pagan deities were also intermittently worshiped by the Judeans.

Every one of the 19 kings of the northern kingdom followed the worship of the golden calf. Some of them also served Baal. But not one ever attempted to bring the people back to God.

The Religion of the Southern Kingdom

Judah in principle worshiped God, although most of the kings of Judah served idols and walked in the evil ways of the kings of Israel. Some of Judah's kings served God, and at times there were great reformations in Judah. But on the whole, in spite of repeated warnings, Judah sank lower and lower in the horrible practices of Baal worship and other Canaanite religions, until it was too late and Judah was overrun by the Babylonians.

I Kings 15:9–24 | ASA, KING OF JUDAH (911–870 B.C.)
(See on 2 Chronicles 14.)

THE KINGS OF ISRAEL AND JUDAH — A CHRONOLOGY			
Kings of Israel		*Kings of Judah*	
Jeroboam	933–911	Rehoboam	933–916
Nadab	911–910	Abijah	915–913
Baasha	910–887	Asa	912–872
Elah	887–886		
Zimri	886		
Omri	886–875		
Ahab	875–854	Jehoshaphat	874–850
Ahaziah	855–854	Jehoram	850–843
Joram	854–843	Ahaziah	843
Jehu	843–816	Athaliah (queen)	843–837
Jehoahaz	820–804	Joash	843–803
Joash	806–790	Amaziah	803–775
Jeroboam II	790–749	Uzziah	787–735
Zechariah	748	Jotham	749–734
Shallum	748		
Menahem	748–738		
Pekahiah	738–736	Ahaz	741–726
Pekah	748–730		
Hoshea	730–721	Hezekiah	726–697
		Manasseh	697–642
		Amon	641–640
		Josiah	639–608
		Jehoahaz	608
		Jehoiakim	608–597
		Jehoiachin	597
		Zedekiah	597–586

—From E. R. Thiele, *The Mysterious Numbers of the Hebrews Kings*, rev. ed.

I Kings 15:25–32 | NADAB, KING OF ISRAEL (910–909 B.C.)

Nadab was the son of Jeroboam. He walked in the sins of his father, and he reigned for only two years before he was assassinated by Baasha, who killed Jeroboam's entire family.

I Kings 15:33–16:7 | BAASHA, KING OF ISRAEL (909–886 B.C.)

After capturing the throne by violence, Baasha reigned 24 years. He walked in the sins of Jeroboam. He warred with Judah, which made an appeal to Assyria to attack him.

THE TWO KINGDOMS — AN OVERVIEW		
The Northern Kingdom, Israel, 933–721 B.C.		
First	50 years:	Harassed by Judah and Syria
Next	40 years:	Quite prosperous under Omri's dynasty
Next	40 years:	Brought very low under Jehu and Jehoahaz
Next	50 years:	Reached its greatest extent under Jeroboam II
Last	30 years:	Anarchy, ruin, and captivity
The Southern Kingdom, Judah, 931–586 B.C.		
First	80 years:	Quite prosperous, growing in power
Next	70 years:	Considerable disaster; introduction of Baalism
Next	50 years:	Reached its greatest extent under Uzziah
Next	15 years:	Began to pay tribute to Assyria under Ahaz
Next	30 years:	Regained independence under Hezekiah
Last	100 years:	Mostly a vassal of Assyria
Relations Between the Northern and Southern Kingdoms		
Next	80 years:	Continuous war between them
Second	80 years:	Peace between them
Last	50 years:	Intermittent war, to the end

I Kings 16:8–14 | ELAH, KING OF ISRAEL (886–885 B.C.)

Elah, the son of Baasha, reigned two years. Given to debauchery, he was assassinated while he was drunk, by Zimri, who killed his entire family.

I Kings 16:15–20 | ZIMRI, KING OF ISRAEL (885 B.C.)

Zimri reigned all of seven days. He was a military officer whose only accomplishment was the extermination of the short-lived Baasha dynasty. He committed suicide by setting his palace on fire.

I Kings 16:21–28 | OMRI, KING OF ISRAEL (885–874 B.C.)

Omri was chosen king by acclamation and reigned 12 years. He was more evil than all the kings of Israel before him. Yet he gained such prominence that for a long time after his death, Israel was still known as the land of Omri. He made Samaria his capital (Tirzah, some 10 miles east of Samaria, had been the northern capital until then; 14:17; 15:33).

 ARCHAEOLOGICAL NOTE: Omri.

- The Moabite Stone (850 B.C.) mentions Omri, king of Israel.
- An inscription of Adad-nirari III (810–782 B.C.) mentions the land of Israel as "Omri."
- The Black Obelisk of Shalmaneser III (858–824 B.C.) speaks of tribute from Jehu, successor to Omri.

The destruction of Samaria by the Assyrians in 722 B.C. is still visible in the remains of the palace of Omri and Ahab in Samaria.

- In 16:24 it is said that Omri built Samaria. A Harvard University expedition found in the ruins of Samaria the foundations of Omri's palace, evidence that he established a new capital there.

I Kings 16:29–22:40   **AHAB, KING OF ISRAEL (874–853 B.C.)**

Ahab reigned for 22 years. He was the most wicked of all the kings of Israel. He married Jezebel, a princess from Sidon, who was an imperious, unscrupulous, vindictive, determined, devilish woman—a demon incarnate. She built a temple for Baal in Samaria, maintained 850 prophets of Baal and Ashtoreth, killed God's prophets, and abolished the worship of the Lord (18:13, 19). Her name is later used for prophetesses who sought to seduce the church to commit spiritual adultery (Revelation 2:20).

ARCHAEOLOGICAL NOTE: Ahab. Although the biblical writers were not fond of the wicked Ahab, archaeologists have found extensive remains (palaces, storerooms, fortresses, etc.) at sites such as Dan, Hazor, Megiddo, Jezreel, Samaria, and elsewhere. Indeed, he was so powerful that in a battle against the powerful Assyrian monarch Shalmaneser III at Qarqar (853 B.C.), he supplied more chariots (2000) than any of the other allied forces.

Elijah, I Kings 17 to 2 Kings 2

Six chapters are given to Ahab's reign, while most of the kings of Israel are covered in only part of one chapter. The reason is that the story of Ahab is largely the story of Elijah. Elijah was God's answer to Ahab and Jezebel. God sent Elijah to eradicate Baalism, a cruel religion.

Elijah's rare, sudden, and brief appearances, his undaunted courage and fiery zeal, the brilliance of his triumphs, the pathos of his despondency, the glory of his departure, and the calm beauty of his reappearance with Jesus on the Mount of Transfiguration (Matthew 17:3–4; Mark 9:4; Luke 9:30–33) make him one of the grandest characters Israel ever produced.

I Kings 17–18 | THE DROUGHT

God gave Elijah power to shut the heavens for 3½ years so it did not rain. During this time Elijah was fed by ravens in the Kerith Ravine and by the widow of Sarepta, whose jar of flour and jug of oil did not run out.

Elijah's venture of faith on Mount Carmel was magnificent. God must have revealed to Elijah, some way or other, that he would send the fire and rain. But it all made no impression on Jezebel.

📜 **ARCHAEOLOGICAL NOTE: Baal Worship.** The Canaanites, and eventually many Israelites and Judeans, worshiped the storm god Baal—the one who brought fertility to the land. In addition, they worshiped the sex goddess Asherah. Numerous fertility figurines have been found in archaeological excavations in Israel. From some of the texts found at Ugarit (a city in Syria) we know that Canaanite worship could include ritual dancing and the cutting and slashing of one's body—which is exactly what the 450 prophets of Baal and the 400 prophets of Asherah did on Mount Carmel (1 Kings 18:25–29).

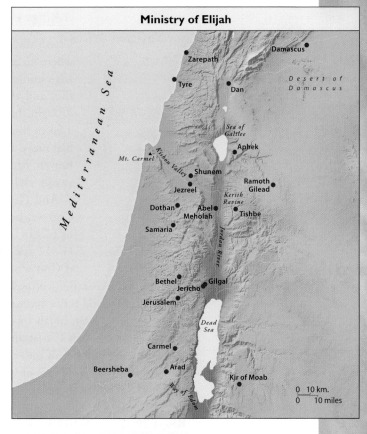

Ministry of Elijah

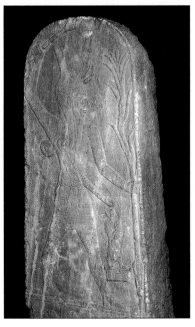

Stele of Baal holding a lightning rod. The Lord used a drought to show His displeasure with Baal worship in Israel.

> The Lord said, "Go out and stand on the mountain in the presence of the Lord, for the Lord is about to pass by." Then a great and powerful wind tore the mountains apart and shattered the rocks before the Lord, but the Lord was not in the wind. After the wind there was an earthquake, but the Lord was not in the earthquake. After the earthquake came a fire, but the Lord was not in the fire. And after the fire came a gentle whisper.
>
> — 1 Kings 19:11–12

1 Kings 19 | THE STILL SMALL VOICE

Utterly discouraged, Elijah fled to Mount Horeb, where he asked God to let him die (19:4). Elijah's ministry had been a ministry of miracles, fire, and the sword. He had caused a severe drought, had been sustained by ravens and by a jar of flour and jug of oil that never ran out, had raised the dead, had called down fire from heaven, had slain the prophets of Baal with the sword, and had brought rain to the land.

And God taught him a wonderful lesson: God was not in the wind, or in the earthquake, or in the fire, but in "a still small voice" (vv. 11–12 KJV; NIV, "a gentle whisper"). It seems as if God was telling Elijah that while force and spectacular demonstrations of power are sometimes necessary, God's real work in the world is not accomplished by such methods.

Many centuries later, Elijah appeared again, on the Mount of Transfiguration, talking with Christ and Moses about the work that now at last was being introduced into the world, namely, the transforming of human lives into the image of God by the gentle whisper of Christ speaking in the hearts of men.

1 Kings 20–22 | AHAB'S DEATH

Ahab closed his reign with a brutal crime against Naboth. He was slain in war with Syria — the end of a contemptible character.

ARCHAEOLOGICAL NOTE: Shalmaneser and Ahab. An inscription of Shalmaneser III (858–824 B.C.) mentions Ahab: "I destroyed . . . 2000 chariots and 10,000 men of Ahab king of Israel."

ARCHAEOLOGICAL NOTE: Ahab's "Ivory House." "The palace he built and inlaid with ivory" (22:39). The Harvard University Expedition to Samaria found remains of Ahab's palace. Scattered about on the floors and in the courtyards were hundreds of exquisitely carved ivory fragments. Many contained Phoenician and/or Egyptian motifs. They probably had been used as inlays in the palace furniture of the Israelite kings — compare the "beds inlaid with ivory" in Amos 6:4.

1 Kings 22:41–50 | JEHOSHAPHAT, KING OF JUDAH
(872–848 B.C.) *(See on 2 Chronicles 17.)*

1 Kings 22:51–53 | AHAZIAH, KING OF ISRAEL
(853–852 B.C.) *(See on 2 Kings 1.)*

2 Kings

The Divided Kingdom
Elisha
The End of Both Kingdoms

"This is what the LORD, the God of your father David, says: I have heard your prayer and seen your tears; I will heal you."

—2 KINGS 20:5

Parallel stories should be read in both 2 Kings and in 2 Chronicles, since they often include different details and even events.

The books 1 and 2 Kings were originally one book. First Kings tells the story of the kingdom, beginning with Solomon, through the division of the kingdom after Solomon's death, and the first 80 years after the division of the kingdom. Second Kings continues the parallel accounts of the two kingdoms, Judah and Israel.

The story of the northern kingdom, Israel, continues for another 130 years or so, until the Assyrians come, destroy the kingdom, and deport the people of Israel, who, as an identifiable group, disappear forever into the mists of history.

The story of the southern kingdom, Judah, continues for another 130 years after the fall of Israel, until the kingdom of Judah is overrun by the Babylonians, Jerusalem is destroyed, and the people of Judah are taken to Babylonia in what is known as the Babylonian captivity, from which some would return about 50 years later to rebuild Jerusalem (Ezra, Nehemiah).

The second book of Kings covers the last 12 kings of the northern kingdom and the last 16 kings of the southern kingdom (see under 1 Kings 12)—a period of about 250 years, approximately 850–586 B.C.

Elijah and Elisha were prophets sent by God in an effort to save the northern kingdom. Their combined ministry lasted about 75 years in the

---

Samuel, Kings, and Chronicles

The entire history of the kingdom of Israel is told in the two books of Samuel and the two books of Kings. The books of Chronicles tell the same story.

In broad outline,

- 1–2 Samuel   =   1 Chronicles
- 1–2 Kings   =   2 Chronicles (both 1 Kings and 2 Chronicles begin with Solomon)

The main differences are that

- 1 Chronicles begins with a lengthy genealogy—beginning with Adam—but it omits the stories of Samuel and Saul (except for Saul's suicide);
- 2 Chronicles omits entirely the history of the northern kingdom.

middle period of the northern kingdom, about 875–800 B.C., through the reigns of six kings: Ahab, Ahaziah, Joram, Jehu, Jehoahaz, and Joash.

2 Kings 1 | AHAZIAH, KING OF ISRAEL (853–852 B.C.)

The account of his reign starts back in 1 Kings 22:51. He was coregent with his father, Ahab, and wicked like him. He reigned for two years. We have here another of Elijah's fire miracles (vv. 9–14).

2 Kings 2 | ELIJAH TAKEN UP IN A CHARIOT OF FIRE

Elijah was a native of Gilead, in the land of Jephthah. A child of the wild loneliness of mountain ravines, he wore a mantel of sheep skin or coarse camel hair, with his own thick, long hair hanging down his back. His mission was to drive Baalism out of Israel. His ministry may have lasted about 25 years, through the reigns of the wicked Ahab and Ahaziah. He had some hard and rough and very disagreeable work to do.

He thought he had failed. And though intimate with God in a measure that has been given to few people, he was utterly human, like us: he asked God to take his life. But God did not think he had failed. When his work was done, God sent a deputation of angelic chariots to take Elijah away in triumph to heaven.

Elijah had recently been on Mount Horeb, where Moses had given the Law. Now, conscious that the time of his departure had come, he headed straight for the land of Moses' burial, Mount Nebo (Deuteronomy 34:1), as if he wanted to be with Moses in death.

Elijah had been a prophet of fire. He had called down fire from heaven on Mount Carmel, and he had called down fire to destroy the officers of Ahaziah. Now he is borne away to heaven in a chariot of fire. Only one other, Enoch, was taken to God without having to pass through the experience of death (Genesis 5:24). Possibly the experience of these two men may have been intended by God to be a sort of dim foreshadowing of the Rapture of the church, in that glad day when angel chariots shall sweep in and swing low to gather us up to welcome the returning Savior.

"Don't be afraid," the prophet answered. "Those who are with us are more than those who are with them."
And Elisha prayed, "O Lord, open his eyes so he may see." Then the Lord opened the servant's eyes, and he looked and saw the hills full of horses and chariots of fire all around Elisha.
—2 Kings 6:16–17

Elisha, 2 Kings 2 to 13

Elijah, instructed by God, had anointed Elisha to be his successor (1 Kings 19:16–21) and had taken him on as his apprentice. As Elijah went away to heaven, his mantle fell on Elisha, and Elisha began immediately to work miracles, as Elijah had done.

The waters of the Jordan were divided for Elisha, as just before they had divided for Elijah (2:8, 14). The spring at Jericho was healed (2:21). Forty-two boys at Bethel were torn by bears (2:24). God, not Elisha, sent the bears. Bethel was a seat of Baal worship. The boys apparently were taunting Elisha's God.

The village of Shunem is situated in the valley near the base of Mt. Moreh with modern city of Afula on the ridge to the left (N). The Lord used Elisha in the village of Shunem to raise a widow's son from the dead.

God had hinted to Elijah that fire and sword were not the methods by which God's real work would be accomplished (1 Kings 19:12). Nevertheless, fire and sword continued to be used—Baalism could understand no other language. Elisha anointed Jehu to exterminate official Baalism (1 Kings 19:16–17; 2 Kings 9:1–10). And Jehu did so, with a vengeance (chaps. 9–10).

2 Kings 3–9 | JEHORAM (JORAM), KING OF ISRAEL (852–841 B.C.)

Jehoram reigned 12 years and was killed by Jehu (9:24). During his reign, the king of Moab, who had paid tribute to Ahab, rebelled (3:4–6).

ARCHAEOLOGICAL NOTE: The Moabite Stone. Chapter 3 is an account of Jehoram's effort to subdue Moab again. Mesha, king of Moab (2 Kings 3:4), made his own record of this rebellion. It was found in 1868 at Dibon, in Moab, 20 miles east of the Dead Sea, by F. A. Klein, a German missionary. It is a black basalt stone, 3 feet high, 2 feet wide, 14 inches thick, with an inscription of Mesha. It is known as the Moabite Stone. While the Berlin Museum was negotiating for it, the Clermont-Ganneau of Jerusalem tried to make a paper squeeze (a papier-mâché impression) of it—and was partially successful.

The next year Arabs, by lighting a fire around it and pouring cold water over it, broke it in pieces to spite the Ottoman governor. Later the French secured the pieces, and by putting them together—along with pieces of the paper squeeze—saved the inscription. It is now in the Louvre Museum.

This is part of the text written on the Moabite Stone (Chemosh is the god of Moab):

> I [am] Mesha, son of Chemosh, king of Moab . . . my father had reigned over Moab thirty years and I reigned after my father. . . .

As for Omri, king of Israel, he humbled Moab many years, for Chemosh was angry at his land [Moab]. And his [Omri's] son followed him and he also said, "I will humble Moab." In my time he spoke [thus], but I have triumphed over him and over his house, while Israel has perished forever.

He then describes the capture of the cities of Medeba, Ataroth, Nebo, and Jahaz. This is what he says about the fall of Nebo:

And Chemosh said to me, "Go, take Nebo from Israel!" So I went by night and fought against it from the break of dawn until noon, taking it and slaying all, seven thousand men, boys, women, girls, and maid-servants, for I had devoted them to destruction for [the god] Ashtar-Chemosh.

---

2 Kings 4–7 | ELISHA'S MIRACLES

Elisha had begun his ministry with miracles, as told in chapter 2. Miracle upon miracle follows. A widow's oil supply is increased. The Shunammite's son is raised from the dead. A poisonous stew is made edible. Loaves of bread are multiplied. Naaman's leprosy is healed. An ax head is made to float. Samaria is delivered by Elisha's invisible chariots. The Syrians are routed by horses and chariots of God (7:6). Nearly all that is recorded of Elisha is about his miracles. Most of Elisha's miracles were acts of kindness and mercy.

Jesus understood Elisha's healing of Naaman as prefiguring that He Himself would also be sent to other nations (Luke 4:25–27).

---

2 Kings 8:1–15 | ELISHA ANOINTS HAZAEL

Elisha anointed Hazael to succeed Ben-Hadad as king of Syria—a prophet of Israel anointed a foreign king to punish the prophet's own nation. God had instructed that this be done (1 Kings 19:15) as punishment on Israel for their frightful sins (10:32–33).

ARCHAEOLOGICAL NOTE: Ben-Hadad and Hazael. How Hazael became king of Syria is told in 2 Kings 8:7–15. An account is also found in an inscription of Shalmaneser III, king of Assyria, who says: "I defeated Hadadezer [i.e., Ben-Hadad] of Damascus. I stretched upon the ground 20,000 of his strong warriors . . . the remnants of his troops I pushed into the Orontes river; Hadadezer (himself) perished. Hazael, a commoner [lit., son of nobody] seized the throne."

Elisha's Ministry

Elisha began his ministry in the reign of Jehoram (3:1, 11), probably about 850 B.C., and continued through the reigns of Jehu and Jehoahaz. He died in the reign of Joash (13:14–20), about 800 B.C.

He was a farm boy, of Abel Meholah in the upper Jordan valley (1 Kings 9:16, 19). He received his prophetic training from Elijah (1 Kings 19:21; 2 Kings 3:11). He and Elijah were very different. Elijah was like the tempest and earthquake; Elisha, like the "still small voice," the "gentle whisper." Elijah was flint-like; Elisha, gentle, gracious, diplomatic. Elijah was a man of the wilderness, with a cloak of camel's hair; Elisha lived in cities and dressed like other people. Yet Elijah's mantle fell on Elisha (1 Kings 19:19; 2 Kings 2:13).

Ministry of Elisha

Elisha's Miracles

Elisha's miracles are recorded in chapters 2 and 4–7. Among them was one of the Bible's seven recorded resurrections.

Elisha's Seminary Work

Samuel, it seems from 1 Samuel 19:20, had started a school of prophets at Ramah. Elisha had such schools at Bethel, Jericho, Gilgal, and other places (2 Kings 2:3, 5; 4:38; 6:1). Beside these, he appears to have resided at Carmel, Shunem, Dothan, and Samaria (2 Kings 2:25; 4:10, 25; 6:13, 32). He must have been a sort of pastor-prophet-teacher, as well as an adviser to the king. His advice was always acted on. He did not approve of all that the kings did, but in times of crisis he came to their rescue.

This relief from the stele of Shalmaneser III (also known as the Black Obelisk) shows Jehu bowing down. The winged disk above Jehu represents the god Assur; the star represents the goddess Ishtar.

Elisha, in the northern kingdom, may have been contemporary with the prophet Joel in the southern kingdom. He may have been a teacher of Jonah and Amos, who were boys at the time.

Elijah and Elisha, in their personal lives and public work, seem to have been a prototype-in-action of John the Baptist and Jesus. John is called Elijah (Matthew 11:14), and Jesus' ministry of kindness was an extensive expansion of Elisha's ministry of the same nature. They illustrate the fact that men of utterly different personality may work together for the same ends.

2 Kings 8:16–24 | JORAM, KING OF JUDAH *(See on 2 Chronicles 21.)*

2 Kings 8:25–29 | AHAZIAH, KING OF JUDAH
(See on 2 Chronicles 22.)

2 Kings 9–10 | JEHU, KING OF ISRAEL (841–814 B.C.)

Jehu reigned for 28 years. He was an officer of Ahab's bodyguard and was anointed by a prophet to be king, to eliminate the house of Ahab, and to eradicate Baalism. He proceeded immediately and furiously to do the bloody work for which Jehu was well fitted. He was intrepid, relentless, pitiless. Perhaps no one else could have done it. He killed Joram, the king of Israel; Jezebel; Ahaziah, the king of Judah (who was Ahab's son-in-law); Ahab's 70 sons; the brothers of Ahaziah; all the friends and partisans of Ahab's house; all the priests of Baal, and all the worshipers of Baal; and he destroyed the temple and pillars of Baal. Sadly, even though Jehu eradicated Baal worship, he made no effort to keep the Law of God but did what King Jeroboam had done—practiced calf worship (see p. 225).

If we wonder at God's use of an agent like Jehu, we must remember that Baalism was unspeakably vile. God sometimes uses people and nations who are far from what they ought to be to execute His judgments on the wicked.

While Jehu was occupied with his bloody revolution in Israel, Hazael, the king of Syria (who had been anointed by Elisha; 8:1–15) took away Gilead and Bashan, Israel's territory east of the Jordan (10:32–33). Jehu also had his troubles with Assyria, whose power was rising with ominous rapidity.

ARCHAEOLOGICAL NOTE: Jehu and Shalmaneser's Black Obelisk. At Calah, near Nineveh, Sir Austen Henry Layard found in 1846 a block of black stone in the ruins of the palace of Shalmaneser, seven feet high, covered with reliefs and inscriptions that depicted his exploits. It is called the Black Obelisk and is now in the British Museum (see photo page 236).

In the second line from the top is a figure kneeling at the feet of the king, and above it this inscription: "The tribute of Jehu, son [successor] of Omri. I received from him silver, gold, a golden *saplu*-bowl, a golden vase with pointed bottom, golden tumblers, golden buckets, tin, a staff for a king. . . ."

ARCHAEOLOGICAL NOTE: Jezebel. Jezebel "painted her eyes, arranged her hair and looked out of a window" (9:30). At archaeological excavations throughout Israel, small boxes, vials, and containers—made of ivory, stone, pottery, and glass—have been found. Some of these were used for the preparation of cosmetics. Substances such as kohl were used for black; turquoise for green; and ochre for red.

ARCHAEOLOGICAL NOTE: Megiddo. In the extensive excavations at Megiddo, several palaces, storerooms (or stables), a city gate, city wall, and a large underground water system from the days of Ahab have been found.

Megiddo gave its name to the area where the armies opposing God's people will assemble and the great and final battle of the ages will be waged: Armageddon (*Har Megiddo*, Mountain of Megiddo; Revelation 16:16). Megiddo was situated on the south side of the Jezreel Valley, 10 miles southwest of Nazareth, at the entrance to a pass across the Carmel mountain range, on the main highway between Asia and Africa. It thus held a key position between the Euphrates and the Nile and was the meeting place of armies from the East and from the West. Thutmose III, who made Egypt a world empire, said, "Megiddo is worth a thousand cities."

It was at Megiddo in World War I that General Edmund Henry Allenby (1918) broke the power of the Turkish army. It is said that more blood has been shed around this hill than any other spot on earth.

2 Kings 11 | ATHALIAH, QUEEN OF JUDAH
(See on 2 Chronicles 22.)

2 Kings 12 | JEHOASH, KING OF JUDAH

(See on 2 Chronicles 24.)

2 Kings 13:1–9 | JEHOAHAZ, KING OF ISRAEL (814–798 B.C.)

Jehoahaz reigned for 17 years. Under him Israel was brought very low by the Syrians.

2 Kings 13:10–25 | JEHOASH (JOASH), KING OF ISRAEL (798–782 B.C.)

Jehoash reigned for 16 years. He warred with Syria and retook the cities his father had lost. He also warred with Judah and plundered Jerusalem.

The water tunnel at Megiddo, which dates probably from the time of King Ahab (9th century B.C.). The shaft is located inside the city walls, ensuring access in case of a siege; it goes down some 115 feet and then extends for another 175 feet.

2 Kings 14:1–22 | AMAZIAH, KING OF JUDAH

(See on 2 Chronicles 25.)

2 Kings 14:23–29 | JEROBOAM II, KING OF ISRAEL (793–753 B.C.)

Jeroboam II, who reigned for 41 years, continued the wars of his father Joash against Syria and, with the help of the prophet Jonah (v. 25), brought the northern kingdom to its greatest extent. The idolatry and abominable social conditions of Jeroboam's reign were challenged by the ministry of the prophets Amos and Hosea.

ARCHAEOLOGICAL NOTE: A Seal of Jeroboam's Servant. In 1904, in the layer of ruins belonging to Jeroboam's time, a beautiful jasper seal was found at Megiddo, bearing the inscription "Belonging to Shema, Servant [i.e., official] of Jeroboam." It was later lost in Istanbul.

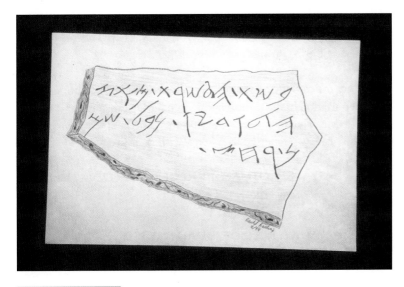

This piece of pottery (called an *ostracon*) is probably a receipt from the days of Jeroboam II. It reads, "In the 10th year, from Azzah [a town] to Gaddiyau [a person], a jar of fine oil." Pottery shards were used to record transactions and as "note paper." In Greece, ostraca were used in voting. If a person was voted out of the community, he was "ostracized."

| 2 Kings 15:1–7 | AZARIAH, KING OF JUDAH |

(*See on 2 Chronicles 26.*)

| 2 Kings 15:8–12 | ZECHARIAH, KING OF ISRAEL (753–752 B.C.) |

Zechariah reigned for only six months before he was assassinated.

| 2 Kings 15:13–15 | SHALLUM, KING OF ISRAEL (752 B.C.) |

Shallum, who had assassinated Zechariah, was himself assassinated by Menahem after a reign of one month.

| 2 Kings 15:16–22 | MENAHEM, KING OF ISRAEL (752–742 B.C.) |

Menahem reigned for 10 years, a cold-blooded and brutal king.

ARCHAEOLOGICAL NOTE: Menahem. Menahem paid tribute to Pul (= Tiglath-pileser III), king of Assyria (vv. 19–20). One of Pul's inscriptions says, "I received tribute from . . . of Menahem of Samaria." Pul's inscriptions also mention Pekah and Hoshea of Israel (see below).

| 2 Kings 15:23–26 | PEKAHIAH, KING OF ISRAEL (742–740 B.C.) |

Pekiah reigned for two years before he, like Zechariah and Shallum, was assassinated.

| 2 Kings 15:27–31 | PEKAH, KING OF ISRAEL (752–732 B.C.) |

Pekah reigned for 20 years. A powerful military officer, who may have been coregent with Menahem and Pekahiah, Pekah attacked Judah in alliance with Syria. Judah appealed to Assyria for help. The king of Assyria came and conquered both Israel and Syria, taking away the inhabitants of north and east Israel. This was the so-called Galilee captivity (734 B.C.). Of the northern kingdom, only Samaria was left. This story is told in more detail in 2 Chronicles and Isaiah 7.

ARCHAEOLOGICAL NOTE: The Deportation. The beginning of the deportation of the northern kingdom by Tiglath-pileser III (v. 29) is recorded in Tiglath-pileser's inscription: "The people of the land of Omri [i.e., Israel] I deported to Assyria, with their property."

2 Kings 15:32–38 | JOTHAM, KING OF JUDAH (750–732 B.C.)
(See on 2 Chronicles 27.)

2 Kings 16 | AHAZ, KING OF JUDAH (735–716 B.C.)
(See on 2 Chronicles 28.)

2 Kings 17 | HOSHEA, THE LAST KING OF ISRAEL (730–722 B.C.)

Hoshea reigned for nine years. He paid tribute to the king of Assyria, but made a secret alliance with the king of Egypt. Then came the Assyrians and administered the final death-blow to the northern kingdom. Samaria fell, and its people followed the rest of Israel into captivity. The prophets at that time were Hosea, Isaiah, and Micah. The northern kingdom had lasted about 200 years. Every one of its 19 kings had walked in the sins of Jeroboam, its founder. God had sent prophet after prophet and judgment after judgment in an effort to turn the nation back from its sins. But in vain. Israel insisted on worshiping its idols. There was no remedy, and God removed Israel from the land.

Deportation of Israel by Assyria, 722 B.C.

ARCHAEOLOGICAL NOTE: Hoshea. Hoshea killed Pekah and reigned in his stead (15:30). Hoshea brought tribute to the king of Assyria (17:3).

An inscription of Tiglath-pileser III says, "Israel [lit., Omri-land] . . . all its inhabitants [and] their possessions I led to Assyria. They overthrew their king Pekah and I placed Hoshea as king over them. I received from them 10 talents of gold and 1000 talents of silver as their tribute and brought them to Assyria."

ARCHAEOLOGICAL NOTE: The Captivity of Israel. Second Kings says, "The king of Assyria . . . marched against Samaria and laid siege to it for three years. . . . [He] captured Samaria and deported the Israelites. . . . The king of Assyria brought people from Babylon . . . and settled them in the towns of Samaria" (17:5–6, 24).

Assyrian relief of a battle scene from the palace of Nineveh. The Assyrian army defeated the Israelites leading to their exile from the land.

An inscription of Sargon (see pp. 244, 346) says, "In my first year I captured Samaria. I took captive 27,290 people. People of other lands, who never paid tribute, I settled in Samaria."

Assyria

The Assyrian Empire destroyed the kingdom of Israel. In recent years, annals of Assyrian kings have been found in which they recorded their exploits. In these annals, the names of 10 Hebrew kings occur: Omri, Ahab, Jehu, Menahem, Pekah, Hoshea, Uzziah, Ahaz, Hezekiah, and

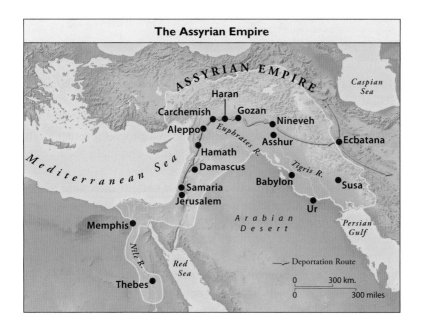

The Assyrian Empire

Manasseh. Many statements are found in these records that illuminate biblical statements.

The capital of Assyria was the great city of Nineveh (see pp. 431–32).

It was Assyria's policy to deport conquered peoples to other lands, which would destroy their sense of nationalism and make them easier to control.

The Assyrians were great warriors. Most nations then were robber nations, and the Assyrians seem to have been about the worst of them all. They built their empire on the loot of other peoples. They practiced incredible cruelty.

Assyria was founded before 2000 B.C. by colonists from Babylon, and for many centuries was subject to, or in conflict with, Babylon. Around 1300 B.C. Shalmaneser I threw off the yoke of Babylon and ruled the whole Euphrates valley. Then Assyria declined. Tiglath-pileser I

Ashurbanipal calmly confronting a wounded lion, emphasizing his power and courage (top left). Assyrian archers carrying the heads of their enemies in triumph (bottom left). Assyrian archers presenting the heads of their enemies (perhaps along with other gifts). They took "head count" very literally (top). A magnificent image of a mortally wounded lion (bottom).

(1115–1076) made Assyria again a great kingdom, but another period of decline followed—until the brilliant epoch of 300 years in which Assyria was a world empire, under the following kings, many of whom play a role in the Bible (names in bold):

- Assur-nasir-pal II (884–858 B.C.). He was warlike and cruel. Welded Assyria into the best fighting machine of the ancient world.
- **Shalmaneser III** (858–824). First Assyrian king to come in conflict with Israel. Ahab fought him. Jehu paid him tribute.
- Period of decline under Shamsi-adad V (824–810), Adad-nirari III (810–782), Shalmaneser IV (782–773), Assur-dan III (773–754), Assur-nirari V (754–745).
- **Tiglath-pileser III** (745–727). Pul was his personal name. He carried northern Israel into captivity (734 B.C.) (See under Isaiah 7.)

- **Shalmaneser V** (727–722). He besieged Samaria and died in the siege.
- **Sargon II** (721–705). He completed the destruction of Samaria and the deportation of Israel. (Sargon I was a Babylonian king who lived 2000 years earlier.)
- **Sennacherib** (704–681). Most famous of the Assyrian kings. He was defeated by an angel of the Lord. He burned Babylon. (See under 2 Chronicles 32.)
- **Esarhaddon** (681–669). He rebuilt Babylon and conquered Egypt. One of the greatest of the Assyrian kings.
- **Assur-banipal** (669–633), (or Osnapper, Ezra 4:10 KJV). Destroyed Thebes (in Egypt). Collected a great library. Powerful, cruel, literary.
- The end of the Assyrian Empire under Assur-etil-ilani, Sin-sar-iskun, and Ashur-uballit (633–608). Beset by Scythians, Medes, and Babylonians, the brutal empire fell.

---

2 Kings 18–25 | THE LAST EIGHT KINGS OF JUDAH, HEZEKIAH TO ZEDEKIAH (716–586 B.C.)

For notes on these kings, see on 2 Chronicles 29–36.

Deportation of Judah by Babylon, 605 B.C.

---

2 Kings 25 | ZEDEKIAH (597–586 B.C.), Last King of Judah

The captivity of Judah was accomplished in four phases.

- In **605 B.C.** Nebuchadnezzar, king of Babylon, defeated Jehoiakim and took temple treasures as well as the sons of prominent families, including Daniel, to Babylon (2 Chronicles 36:6–7; Daniel 1:1–3).
- In **597 B.C.** Nebuchadnezzar came again and took the rest of the treasures, as well as King Jehoiachin and 10,000 of the princes, officers, and prominent citizens, to Babylon (2 Kings 24:14–16). Among those taken captive was the prophet Ezekiel.
- In **586 B.C.** the Babylonians came again. They burned Jerusalem, tore down its walls, put out the eyes of King Zedekiah, and carried him in chains to Babylon, with 832 captives. All that was left in the land was a remnant of the poorest class of people (2 Kings 25:8–12; Jeremiah 52:28–30).

    It took the Babylonians a year and a half to subdue Jerusalem. They besieged it in the tenth month of the ninth year of Zedekiah, and the city fell in the fourth month of the eleventh year of his reign. A month later the city was burned.

    Thus Nebuchadnezzar was 20 years in the process of destroying Jerusalem. He could have done it at first, had he wanted to. But he only wanted tribute. Daniel, whom he took to Babylon at the

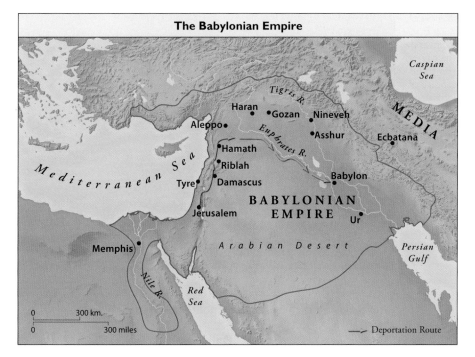

The Babylonian Empire

beginning of the 20 years, soon became Nebuchadnezzar's friend and adviser and may have had a restraining influence on him. In the end, it was Judah's persistence in making an alliance with Egypt that forced Nebuchadnezzar to wipe Jerusalem off the map.

- In **581 B.C.**, five years after the burning of Jerusalem, the Babylonians came again and took 745 more captives (Jeremiah 52:30), even after a considerable group, including Jeremiah, had fled to Egypt (Jeremiah 43). The fall of Jerusalem was accompanied by the ministry of three great prophets, Jeremiah, Ezekiel, and Daniel.

The captivity of Judah by Babylon had been predicted 100 years before by Isaiah and Micah (Isaiah 39:6; Micah 4:10). Now that it was accomplished, Jeremiah predicted that it would last 70 years (Jeremiah 25:11–12).

This was the end of David's earthly kingdom. It had lasted 400 years. It revived, in a spiritual sense, with the arrival of Christ, and will be consummated in glory at His return.

ARCHAEOLOGICAL NOTE: Nebuchadnezzar. Nebuchadnezzar burned the cities of Lachish and Jerusalem (25:9; Jeremiah 34:7); massive destruction levels have been found at both cities. At Lachish a broken piece of pottery with writing on it speaks of the cities of Lachish and Azekah—just as Jeremiah 34:7 does. In Jerusalem, massive destruction by the Babylonians has been found by Shiloh's excavations in the

Aerial view of Lachish looking East. Nebuchadnezzar besieged the city of Lachish prior to his final capture of Jerusalem.

old City of David and by Nahum Avigad (a defensive tower, ash, and arrowheads) in the Jewish Quarter of the Old City.

Babylon

- Assyria took Israel away in captivity (734–722 B.C.).
- Babylon took Judah away in captivity (605–586 B.C.).
- Assyria occupied the northern part of the Euphrates-Tigris valley.
- Babylon occupied the southern part of the Euphrates-Tigris valley.
- Nineveh was the capital of the Assyrian Empire.
- Babylon was the capital of the Babylonian Empire.
- Nineveh and Babylon were 300 miles apart (see map on p. 241).

The Old Babylonian Empire (2000–1600 B.C.)

- Around 2000 B.C. Babylon became the dominating power of the world.
- This was the era of the great lawgiver Hammurabi (ca. 1800 B.C.; see p. 104).
- Then followed 1000 years of intermittent struggle, followed by 250 years of Assyrian supremacy (884–605 B.C.; see pp. 241–44).

The New Babylonian Empire (625–539 B.C.)

The New Babylonian, or Neo-Babylonian Empire, broke the power of Assyria and, in its westward sweep, destroyed Judah and conquered Egypt. Its kings were as follows:

- **Nabopolassar** (625–605 B.C.) threw off the yoke of Assyria in 625 B.C. and established the independence of Babylon. With the aid of Cyaxares the Mede, he conquered and destroyed Nineveh

(612 B.C.). Nabopolassar's son Nebuchadnezzar became commander of his father's armies, and in 605 B.C. became coregent with his father.

- **Nebuchadnezzar** (605–562 B.C.), the greatest of all Babylonian kings, was one of the mightiest monarchs of all time. He reigned for 45 years. The Babylonian Empire was largely his achievement. He extended the power of Babylon over most of the then-known world and beautified the city of Babylon almost beyond imagination (see p. 396).

  He was the one who carried the Jews into captivity, including Daniel and Ezekiel. He took a great liking to Daniel and made him one of his chief advisers. And Daniel's influence, no doubt, must have eased the lot of Jewish captives. (See further about Nebuchadnezzar and Babylon, pp. 398–99.)

- Under Nebuchadnezzar's successors the Babylonian Empire began to decline: Evil-Merodach (562–560 B.C.), Neriglissar (559–556 B.C.), Labashi-Marduk (556 B.C.), and Nabonidus (556–539 B.C.).

- **Nabonidus**'s son, Belshazzar, was coregent with him during the last few years of his reign and thus the second-most powerful person in Babylon. This is why he could only offer Daniel the third-highest position as a reward for interpreting the handwriting on the wall (Daniel 5:7; for the story of the handwriting on the wall and the fall of Babylon, see p. 400).

- The city of Babylon, and with it the Babylonian Empire, fell to the Medes and Persians. Supremacy passed to Persia in 539 B.C. and would last until Persia was in turn conquered by Alexander the Great in 331 B.C.

The Babylonian Empire lasted 70 years. The 70 years of Judah's exile coincided exactly with the 70 years during which Babylon ruled the world. The year in which Cyrus, king of Persia, conquered Babylon (539 B.C.) was the same year in which he authorized the return of the Jews to their own land.

Babylon, oppressor of God's Old Testament people, appears again in the book of Revelation as the embodiment of the forces of evil that oppose God (Revelation 17).

Chronicles as rather dry reading, they contain the story of God's dealings with His people. And in reading them we may find some of the finest jewels of Scripture.

I Chron. 1–9 | THE GENEALOGIES

The immediate purpose of these genealogies seems to be the resettling of the land in accordance with the public records. Those who had returned from the Babylonian captivity were entitled to the lands formerly held by their own families. In the Old Testament land had been apportioned to families and could not be sold in perpetuity out of the family (see on Leviticus 25).

In the same way, the priesthood was hereditary. A priest was to be succeeded by his son. This was the law of the land.

This is also true of the royal line of David. The most important and precious of all promises was that the world's Savior would come from David's family. The central interest of these genealogies is their tracing of David's family line. (See further pp. 199–201.)

Most of the genealogies are incomplete, with many breaks in the lists. But the main line is there. They were probably compiled from many records that had been written on tablets, papyrus, or vellum and partly copied from preceding Old Testament books.

These nine chapters of genealogies represent the generation-to-generation flow of all preceding biblical history. They need not be read for devotional purposes as often as some other parts of Scripture. But these and similar genealogies are the skeleton framework of the Old Testament, the thing that binds the whole Bible together and gives it unity, and that takes it out of the realm of legend and into the pages of real history.

> "Then you will have success if you are careful to observe the decrees and laws that the LORD gave Moses for Israel. Be strong and courageous. Do not be afraid or discouraged."
>
> — I Chronicles 22:13

Sources for the Books of Chronicles

Frequent reference is made to other histories, annals, and official archives:

- The annals of King David (1 Chronicles 27:24)
- The records of Samuel the seer, the records of Nathan the prophet, and the records of Gad the seer (1 Chronicles 29:29)
- The records of Nathan the prophet, the prophecy of Ahijah the Shilonite, and the visions of Iddo the seer (2 Chronicles 9:29)
- The records of Shemaiah the prophet and of Iddo the seer (2 Chronicles 12:15)
- The annotations of the prophet Iddo (2 Chronicles 13:22)
- The annals of Jehu the son of Hanani, which are recorded in the book of the kings of Israel (2 Chronicles 20:34)
- The annotations on the book of the kings (2 Chronicles 24:27)
- The other events of Uzziah's reign are recorded by Isaiah (2 Chronicles 26:22)
- The vision of the prophet Isaiah (2 Chronicles 32:32)
- The book of the kings of Judah and Israel (2 Chronicles 32:32)
- The records of the seers (2 Chronicles 33:19)

This stepped stone structure was discovered in the administrative area of the City of David.

| 1 Chron. 10–12 | **DAVID MADE KING (1010–970 b.c.)**

The book of 2 Samuel and the book of 1 Chronicles, except for the genealogies, are both devoted entirely to the reign of David. But 1 Chronicles pays special attention to the organization of the temple services. Written after the return from captivity, 1 Chronicles, we might say, is a sort of historical sermon, based on 2 Samuel and designed to encourage the returned exiles in the work of restoring temple worship to its proper place in their national life.

In 2 Samuel 2–4 we are told how David was made king over Judah after the death of Saul and reigned for 7½ years from his capital at Hebron. During this time there was war with Saul's son Ish-bosheth. After Ish-bosheth's death, David was made king over all Israel.

David's first act as king over all Israel was to capture Jerusalem and make it the capital of the nation, as is told more fully in 2 Samuel 5. Jerusalem was more centrally located and virtually impregnable, on a mountain with valleys on the east, west, and south sides. During the 400 years from Joshua to David, Israel had been unable to take it, so the Jebusites were still there (Joshua 15:63; 2 Samuel 5:6–10; 1 Chronicles 11:4–5). Jerusalem became the City of David in a very literal sense: it was his personal property.

ARCHAEOLOGICAL NOTE: The Watercourse. This watercourse (Heb. *sinnor;* 2 Samuel 5:8), by which Joab and David's men gained entrance to Jerusalem, was discovered in 1998 by Ronny Reich and Eli Shukron. It consists of a large pool, which collected water from the Gihon Spring and was guarded by two massive towers. An underground secret passageway led from inside the city to a point where water could be drawn from the pool—so that the residents of the city did not have to go outside the city wall to draw water.

🏛️ **ARCHAEOLOGICAL NOTE: David's Jerusalem.** In the 1980s, a rounded "stepped–stone" structure, five stories high, was discovered. It apparently supported an old Jebusite citadel (maybe called "Zion") which was captured by David. David's city made use of the massive city wall that the Canaanites had built about 1800 B.C. The city captured by David was about 15 acres in size and housed about 2000 people.

I Chron. 13–16 | THE ARK BROUGHT TO JERUSALEM

The ark had been captured by the Philistines (1 Samuel 4:11). It remained with them for seven months (1 Samuel 6:1) before it was sent back by the Philistines to Israel in order to stop the plagues that had accompanied its capture and possession. It then stayed at Kiriath Jearim, some 8½ miles northwest of Jerusalem, for 20 years (1 Samuel 7:2). David, after establishing Jerusalem as the national capital, called all Israel together to bring the ark to Jerusalem in a grand ceremonial procession.

But the unfortunate Uzzah incident interrupted the procession (13:10). Uzzah's death for his impulsive gesture to save the ark (13:9) seems severe to us. However, only Levites were to carry the ark (15:2, 13), and Uzzah's act was in direct violation of the Law (Numbers 4:15). His death was a warning to be careful.

After three months at the house of Obed-Edom (13:14), who was a Levite (15:17–18, 21, 24), the ark was brought into Jerusalem amid great rejoicing and placed in a tent that David had made for it (15:1). The original tabernacle was at Gibeon, six miles northwest of Jerusalem (21:29).

David's polygamy (14:3) was against the law of God. But it was the custom of ancient kings, one of the signs of prestige and royalty, which the people seemed to expect of their rulers—a custom toward which, in Old Testament times, God seemed lenient. However, David reaped a harvest of family troubles (see on 2 Samuel 13).

I Chron. 17 | DAVID'S PLAN TO BUILD THE TEMPLE

Building the temple was David's idea. God was satisfied with a tent (vv. 4–6), but God gave in, although He would not allow David to build the temple because he had been a man of war and had shed much blood (22:8; 28:3). The task of building the temple was assigned to David's son and successor, Solomon (17:11–14; 28:6).

I Chron. 18–20 | DAVID'S VICTORIES *(See on 2 Samuel 8.)*

I Chron. 21 | THE PEOPLE NUMBERED *(See on 2 Samuel 24.)*

I Chron. 22 | DAVID'S PREPARATIONS FOR THE TEMPLE

Though forbidden to actually build the temple, David laid the plans for it and devoted a large part of his reign to collecting vast amounts of gold and silver and all kinds of building material, estimated to have amounted not to millions but to several billion dollars in today's market. It was to be "of great magnificence and fame and splendor in the sight of all the nations" (22:5). It was to be the crowning glory of the kingdom. David's charge to Solomon and the leaders of Israel is expanded in chapter 28.

I Chron. 23 | DUTIES OF THE LEVITES

Now that the temple was to be permanently located in Jerusalem, there would be no more need to carry the tabernacle (v. 26), so the work of the Levites was restructured. Some of them were to oversee the work of the temple (v. 4); some were to be doorkeepers (v. 5); others, musicians (v. 5; 15:16); and there was to be a choir of 4000 Levites. Some Levites were to be officers and judges over Israel, away from the temple, while others handled the affairs of the king (23:4; 26:29, 32). Thus it certainly looks as if the Levites' duties involved the service of God as well as a significant role in the civil government.

I Chron. 24–25 | THE ORGANIZATION OF THE PRIESTS AND LEVITES

The priests were divided into 24 divisions for service in the sanctuary. They were the officials of the sanctuary and officials of God (v. 5) and were in charge of the sacrifices. Their business in reality ceased with the coming of Christ. Ironically, it was Levite priests who engineered the crucifixion of Christ (Matthew 27:1, 6, 20, 41).

The Levites were further organized, some to serve as gatekeepers in the temple, others to take charge of the temple treasury, and some especially as musicians, whose business did not cease with the coming of Christ but rather took on new meaning. David was a great musician. With all his soul, he delighted in making the heavens ring with songs of praise to God (15:27–28; 16:41–42). The musicians included some of the sons of Asaph; the headings of Psalm 50 and 73–83 indicate that they are psalms of Asaph.

> David also said to Solomon his son, "Be strong and courageous, and do the work. Do not be afraid or discouraged, for the LORD God, my God, is with you. He will not fail you or forsake you until all the work for the service of the temple of the LORD is finished."
> — I Chronicles 28:20

I Chron. 27 | MILITARY, CIVIL, AND COURT LEADERS

David also arranged for the appointment of army commanders, tribal officers, and overseers of the royal household. The latter was, in oriental fashion, very extensive, with orchards, vineyards, herds, workers—everything to ensure that the king's needs were well supplied.

David's final words and his last prayer concern the temple. That is what his heart was on, as his soul took its flight to the house not made with hands. The man after God's own heart had served his generation nobly. And what a joy it must have been when he met Him who later bore the name "Son of David"!

2 Chronicles

The Reign of Solomon
The History of Judah

*"If my people, who are called by my name, will humble themselves and pray and seek my face
and turn from their wicked ways, then will I hear from heaven and will forgive their sin and
will heal their land."* — 2 Chronicles 7:14

arallel stories should be read in both 2 Chronicles and in 1–2
Kings, since they often include different details and even events.

---

2 Chron. 1–9 | THE TEMPLE AND THE GLORY OF SOLOMON'S REIGN (970–931 B.C.)

(See also on 1 Kings 1–11.) For 400 years, Israel had only had a tent,
the tabernacle, as the house of God among them, and God, it seems, had
been satisfied (2 Samuel 7:5–7). Yet, when it appeared expedient that
they have a temple, God wanted to have a say as to the kind of building it
should be. He gave David plans for it in his own handwriting (1 Chronicles 28:19; Exodus 25:9); it would be magnificent, and it would be
famous throughout the world (1 Chronicles 22:5).

David had wanted to build the temple, but he was not allowed to
because he was a man of war (1 Chronicles 22:8). God helped David in
his wars, but He did not think that a man of war should build His house.
Otherwise, conquered nations might feel bitter toward Israel's God, and
God's purpose was to win, through His nation, other nations to Himself.

The temple was built of great stones, cedar beams, and boards, overlaid
inside with gold (1 Kings 6:14–22; 7:9–12). The gold and silver and other
materials used in building the temple (1 Chronicles 22:14–16; 29:2–9)

Samuel, Kings, and Chronicles

The entire history of the kingdom of Israel is told in the two books of Samuel
and the two books of Kings. The books of Chronicles tell the same story,
often with diffrent details.

In broad outline,

- 1–2 Samuel = 1 Chronicles
- 1–2 Kings = 2 Chronicles (both 1 Kings and 2 Chronicles begin
  with Solomon)

The main differences are that

- 1 Chronicles begins with a lengthy genealogy—beginning with Adam—
  but it omits the stories of Samuel and Saul (except for Saul's suicide);
- 2 Chronicles omits entirely the history of the northern kingdom.

Asherah figurines. Under the reform of king Asa, "Asherah" figurines were destroyed.

2 Chron. 17–20 | JEHOSHAPHAT, KING OF JUDAH (872–848 B.C.)

(Told also in 1 Kings 22:41–50.) He reigned 25 years. He followed in the footsteps of his father and sought the Lord in all things. He inaugurated a system of public instruction by sending priests and Levites with the Book of the Law on regular circuits, to teach the people. He established courts of justice throughout the land. He maintained a vast army and became so powerful that he intimidated his neighbors, including the Philistines. Even when he made an unwise alliance with King Ahab of Israel, God still protected him (18:30–32).

2 Chron. 21 | JEHORAM (JORAM), KING OF JUDAH (853–841 B.C.)

(Told also in 2 Kings 8:16–24.) Jehoram reigned eight years. Son of a good father and grandfather, he was ruined by his marriage to a wicked woman, Athaliah, a daughter of the infamous Jezebel (1 Kings 18:4, 13; 19:1–2; 21; 2 Kings 9). Under his reign Jerusalem was plundered by Arabs and the Philistines. He died, unmourned, of a horrible intestinal disease, perhaps an extreme form of dysentery, and was not even buried with royal honor: "He passed away, to no one's regret, and was buried in the City of David, but not in the tombs of the kings" (21:20).

2 Chron. 22:1–9 | AHAZIAH (JEHOAHAZ), KING OF JUDAH (841 B.C.)

(Told also in 2 Kings 8:25–29.) Ahaziah reigned only one year. He was the son of Athaliah and the grandson of Jezebel. He was very wicked and was killed by Jehu (2 Kings 9:14–29).

2 Chron. 22:10–23:21 | ATHALIAH, QUEEN OF JUDAH
(841–835 B.C.)

(Told also in 2 Kings 11.) Athaliah reigned six years. She was a daughter of the infamous Jezebel, and devilish like her mother. She had married Jehoram, the king of Judah, and ruined him. She was the mother of Judah's next king, Ahaziah, who was as evil as she. Thus, she was queen for eight years and queen mother for one year, in addition to the six years she ruled in her own right — 15 years in all. Fanatically devoted to Baalism, she massacred her own grandchildren.

2 Chron. 24 | JOASH (JEHOASH), KING OF JUDAH
(835–796 B.C.)

(Told also in 2 Kings 12.) Joash reigned 40 years (which probably include Athaliah's six years). Joash was a grandson of Athaliah. While Athaliah was murdering the royal house, Joash, the son of Ahaziah, was taken away as a baby and hidden in the temple for six years. When Joash was seven years old, his uncle, Jehoiada the high priest, engineered the removal of Athaliah and placed Joash on the throne. Jehoiada was the real ruler as long as he lived. Under his tutorship, Joash cleared the land of Baalism, repaired the temple, which Athaliah had broken into and desecrated, and restored the worship of God.

Joash did what was right as long as Jehoiada was alive. But after Jehoiada's death, the prominent leaders of Judah, who had known the licentious worship of Ashtoreth, convinced him to set up the idols again. Joash even ordered Zechariah, the son of Jehoiada who had placed him on the throne, to be stoned to death. Within a year after Zechariah's death, the Syrians came, plundered Jerusalem, and killed the leaders who had persuaded Joash. Joash himself was assassinated in his bed as revenge for the execution of Zechariah. He was buried without royal honor.

2 Chron. 25 | AMAZIAH, KING OF JUDAH (796–767 B.C.)

(Told also in 2 Kings 14:1–22.) Amaziah reigned 29 years. Amaziah did right, yet ended up worshiping the gods of the Edomites. He lost a war with Israel, and Jerusalem was plundered by Israel's king. He was assassinated.

2 Chron. 26 | UZZIAH (AZARIAH), KING OF JUDAH
(792–740 B.C.)

(Told also in 2 Kings 15:1–7.) Uzziah reigned 52 years, part of which may have been as coregent with his father, Amaziah. He did what was right and set himself to seek God. As long as he sought God, God made him to prosper. He had a huge army, with remarkably sophisticated equipment (vv. 13–15). He was victorious over the Philistines, Arabs, and Ammonites. Under Uzziah, the kingdom of Judah reached its greatest extent since the secession of the Ten Tribes in 931 B.C. But he became arrogant, and God afflicted him with leprosy.

 ARCHAEOLOGICAL NOTE: Uzziah. Because Uzziah was a leper, he was not buried in the tombs of the kings of Judah but "in a field for burial that belonged to the kings" (2 Chronicles 26:23). Evidently his bones were eventually reburied, for E. L. Sukenik discovered, in 1931, in a Russian monastery on the Mount of Olives, a limestone plaque, 14 by 13 inches, from the Second Temple Period, written in Hebrew script, which says, "Hither were brought the bones of Uzziah, king of Judah. Not to be opened!" But the actual remains of the king were not discovered.

| 2 Chron. 27 | JOTHAM, KING OF JUDAH (750–732 B.C.) |

(Told also in 2 Kings 15:32–38.) Jotham reigned 16 years, mostly as coregent with his father. He became mighty because he did what was right in the eyes of the Lord, as his father Uzziah had done. Uzziah's leprosy undoubtedly served as a warning to Jotham.

ARCHAEOLOGICAL NOTE: Jotham. A seal has been found in the excavations at Tell el-Kheleifeh inscribed: "Belonging to Jotham."

| 2 Chron. 28 | AHAZ, KING OF JUDAH (735–716 B.C.) |

(Told also in 2 Kings 16.) Ahaz reigned 16 years. Part of this time he seems to have been coregent with his father—but he was utterly different: a wicked young king who set himself against the policies of his forefathers. He reintroduced Baal worship and revived Molech worship—he even burnt his own sons in the fire. But it helped him not. Syria and Israel attacked him from the north, the Edomites from the east, and the Philistines from the west. Judah paid a very high price for Ahaz's sins.

| 2 Chron. 29–32 | HEZEKIAH, KING OF JUDAH (716–687 B.C.) |

(Told also in 2 Kings 18–20.) Hezekiah reigned 29 years. He inherited a disorganized realm and a heavy burden of tribute to Assyria, but he began his reign with a great reformation. He destroyed the idols Ahaz had set up, reopened and cleansed the temple, and restored the worship of God. He trusted in God, and God was with him. He prospered and gained independence from Assyria. The prophet Isaiah was his trusted adviser.

In Hezekiah's 14th year, Sennacherib invaded Judah. He sent a taunting message to Hezekiah—not in Aramaic, the language of commerce and diplomacy, but in Hebrew, so that all the people could understand it (2 Kings 18:17–37). Hezekiah paid him tribute.

During a visit of envoys from Babylon, Hezekiah foolishly showed them the wealth of Jerusalem and the temple (2 Kings 20:12–15), perhaps in hopes of establishing an alliance with the Babylonians against the Assyrians.

Sennacherib again invaded Judah (701 B.C.). Hezekiah strengthened the wall of Jerusalem, built the water tunnel, and made great military preparations. Then followed the great deliverance by the Angel of the Lord (2 Kings 19:35). This victory brought Hezekiah great prestige and power.

ARCHAEOLOGICAL NOTE: Ivory Pomegranate. A tiny ivory pomegranate from the days of the Judean king Hezekiah (late 8th century B.C.) surfaced in the antiquities market. It was probably once the head on the

This portion of Sennacherib's relief shows his attack on Lachish. The defenders are throwing burning torches down on the siege towers and the ladders used to scale the walls. The rest of the relief shows the attackers pouring water on the leather covers of the siege towers to keep them from catching fire.

The six-sided prism of baked clay on which Senncherib details his exploits. The prism is only 15 inches tall.

top of a scepter used by Israelite priests in the First Temple in Jerusalem. It is inscribed in ancient Hebrew characters and reads: "Holy to the priests, belonging to the T[emple of Yahwe]h" (the words in brackets are restored).

ARCHAEOLOGICAL NOTE: Hezekiah's Wall. Hezekiah repaired and built the walls of Jerusalem (32:5; Isaiah 22:10). Professor Nahum Avigad found over 200 feet of a wall dating to the 8th century B.C. (Hezekiah's century), which was 23 feet thick and in places was preserved to a height of over 10 feet. (See also on Isaiah 22:10.)

ARCHAEOLOGICAL NOTE: Hezekiah's Tunnel and the Siloam Inscription. The tunnel by which Hezekiah brought water into the city (32:3–4; 2 Kings 20:20) has been found. The Gihon Spring was situated at the east foot of Ophel Hill (see map below), just outside the wall. Hezekiah's workmen cut a tunnel through solid rock, under the hill, that runs 1,700 feet southwest from the spring to the Pool of Siloam inside the wall, thus diverting the water of the spring from its natural flow into the Brook Kidron. The tunnel is an average height of about six feet and an average width of 2½ feet. Its drop is seven feet. At its southern exit the Siloam Inscription was found.

The Siloam Inscription was discovered in 1880 by some schoolboys at the south end of the tunnel. This five-line inscription, written in Hebrew, was carelessly cut from the rock, sent to Istanbul, and now resides in a museum. This inscription describes the construction of the tunnel:

"The tunnel was driven through. And this was the way in which it was cut through: While [the stonecutters were lifting up their pick], each man toward his fellow (i.e., from opposite ends), and while there were still three cubits to be cut through, [there was heard] the voice of a man calling to his fellow. . . . And when the tunnel was driven through, the stonecutters hewed the rock, each man toward his fellow, axe against axe. And the water flowed from the spring toward the reservoir for 1,200 cubits, and the height of the rock above the heads of the stonecutters was 100 cubits."

ARCHAEOLOGICAL NOTE: Sennacherib's Invasion of Judah. In his invasion of Judah (32:1), Sennacherib took fortified cities of Judah (2 Kings 18:13), laid siege to Jerusalem (2 Kings 18:17), but returned without taking Jerusalem (2 Kings 19:35–36). Sennacherib's own account of this invasion has been found on a clay prism he himself had made. One copy of it is now in the Oriental Institute Museum in Chicago. Sennacherib says in part:

"As to Hezekiah, the Jew, he did not submit to my yoke. I laid siege to 46 of his strong cities, walled forts, and to the countless small villages in their vicinity, and conquered [them]. . . . I drove out of them 200,150 people, young and old, male and female, horses, mules, donkeys, camels, big and small cattle beyond counting and

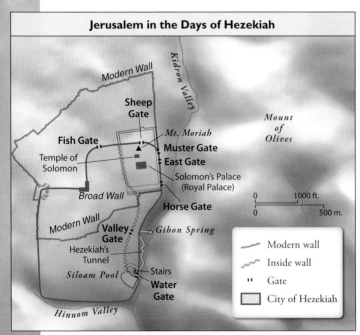

Jerusalem in the Days of Hezekiah

Modern Wall
Kidron Valley
Sheep Gate
Mt. Moriah
Mount of Olives
Fish Gate
Muster Gate
Temple of Solomon
East Gate
Solomon's Palace (Royal Palace)
Broad Wall
Horse Gate
Modern Wall
Valley Gate
Gihon Spring
Hezekiah's Tunnel
Siloam Pool
Stairs
Water Gate
Hinnom Valley

0   1000 ft.
0   500 m.

〰 Modern wall
〰 Inside wall
" Gate
▭ City of Hezekiah

Assyrian relief. The fierce battle over Lachish in the Sennacherib relief discovered at Nineveh depicts Assyrian soldiers flaying their Judean prisoners alive.

considered [them] booty. Hezekiah himself I made prisoner in Jerusalem, his royal residence, like a bird in a cage. I surrounded him with earthwork in order to molest those who were leaving his city's gate. . . . Thus I reduced his country, but I still increased his tribute."

While no Assyrian king would ever record a defeat such as Sennacherib's army suffered before the walls of Jerusalem (2 Kings 19:35 – 36), it is significant that he did not claim to have taken Jerusalem. It is indeed a most remarkable confirmation of biblical history.

ARCHAEOLOGICAL NOTE: The Tribute Hezekiah Sent to Sennacherib. The inscription of Sennacherib relates to the account in 2 Kings 18:14 – 16 and says: "Hezekiah himself, whom the terror-inspiring splendor of my lordship had overwhelmed and whose . . . troops had deserted him, did send to me, later, to Nineveh, my lordly city, together with 30 talents of gold, 800 talents of silver, precious stones, . . . In order to deliver the tribute and to do obeisance as a slave he sent his [personal] messenger."

ARCHAEOLOGICAL NOTE: Lachish. Lachish is among the cities named which suffered at the hands of Sennacherib (32:9). At Lachish there is a huge burn level dated to the destruction of Sennacherib in 701 B.C. On the walls of Sennacherib's palace at Nineveh, uncovered by Sir Austen Henry Layard, a long sculptured relief of his encampment at Lachish bore this inscription: "Sennacherib, king of the world, king of Assyria, sat upon [his] throne and passed in review the booty taken from Lachish."

ARCHAEOLOGICAL NOTE: Sennacherib's Assassination. Concerning Sennacherib's assassination (32:21; 2 Kings 19:36 – 37), an Assyrian inscription says: "On the 20th day of Tebet, Sennacherib was killed by his sons in revolt. On the 18th day of Sivan, Esarhaddon, his son, ascended the throne."

2 Chron. 33:1–20 | MANASSEH, KING OF JUDAH (697–642 B.C.)

(Told also in 2 Kings 21:1–18.) Manasseh was the wickedest of all of Judah's kings and had the longest reign — 55 years. He rebuilt the idols his father Hezekiah had destroyed and reestablished Baal worship. He burnt his own children in the fire. He filled Jerusalem with blood. Tradition says that he had the prophet Isaiah sawn in half.

ARCHAEOLOGICAL NOTE: Manasseh. An inscription of King Esarhaddon of Assyria (681–668 B.C.) says, "During my march [to Egypt] 22 kings from the seashore, the islands, and the mainland, servants who belong to me, brought heavy gifts to me and kissed my feet." A related inscription lists these 22 kings, among whom is Manasseh, king of Judah.

2 Chron. 33:21–25 | AMON, KING OF JUDAH (643–641 B.C.)

(Told also in 2 Kings 21:19–25.) Amon reigned for two years and was wicked.

2 Chron. 34–35 | JOSIAH, KING OF JUDAH (641–609 B.C.)

(Told also in 2 Kings 22–23.) Josiah became king when he was eight years old and reigned for 31 years. When he was 16, he began to seek after the God of David, and he began his reforms when he was 20. The finding of the Book of the Law, when Josiah was 26, gave great impetus to his reforms — the most thoroughgoing reformation Judah had known yet. But the people were at heart idolaters; the long and wicked reign of Manasseh had just about obliterated God from their thinking. Josiah's reforms delayed, but could not avert, the fast approaching doom of Judah.

Pharaoh's march against Carchemish (35:20–24) gave a final blow to the sinking Assyrian Empire. Josiah, as a vassal of Assyria, considered it his duty to attack the Pharaoh. He did so at Megiddo and was killed.

2 Chron. 36:1–4 | JEHOAHAZ (JOAHAZ), KING OF JUDAH (609 B.C.)

(Told also in 2 Kings 23:30–34.) After reigning all of three months, Jehoahaz was deposed by Pharaoh and taken to Egypt, where he died.

2 Chron. 36:5–8 | JEHOIAKIM, KING OF JUDAH (609–598 B.C.)

(Told also in 2 Kings 23:34–24:7.) Jehoiakim was placed on the throne by Pharaoh and reigned 11 years. After three years he was subdued by

Babylon (Daniel 1:1) and served the king of Babylon for three years. Then he revolted. The king of Babylon came and bound him in chains to carry him to Babylon (2 Chronicles 36:6). But he died, or was killed, before he could leave the city, and he received "the burial of a donkey—dragged away and thrown outside the gates of Jerusalem" (Jeremiah 22:19; 36:30). He was conceited, hard-hearted, and wicked, the exact opposite of his father Josiah. He repeatedly tried to kill the prophet Jeremiah (Jeremiah 26:21; 36:26).

2 Chron. 36:8–10 — JEHOIACHIN (JECONIAH), KING OF JUDAH (598–597 B.C.)

(Told also in 2 Kings 24:6–17.) Jehoiachin reigned for three months before he was taken to Babylon, where he lived at least 37 years (2 Kings 24:15; 25:27).

ARCHAEOLOGICAL NOTE: Jehoiachin. A number of storage jar handles bearing the seal impression "Belonging to Eliakim, steward of Jehoiachin" have been found in excavations at Tell Beit Mirsim, Beth Shemesh, and Ramat Rahel.

Jehoiachin was released from prison in Babylon and given a regular allowance of rations by the king of Babylon (2 Kings 25:27–30). Cuneiform ration tablets found at Babylon also indicate that Jehoiachin and his relatives received rations from the Babylonian monarch.

2 Chron. 36 — ZEDEKIAH, KING OF JUDAH (597–586 B.C.)

(Told also in 2 Kings 24–25). Zedekiah was placed on the throne by King Nebuchadnezzar of Babylon and reigned for 11 years. He was a weak king. In his fourth year he visited Babylon, but later rebelled against it. Then Nebuchadnezzar came, destroyed Jerusalem, took Zedekiah, put out his eyes, and carried him in chains to Babylon, where he died in prison (Jeremiah 52:11).

The people of Judah were taken to Babylonia, in what is known as the Babylonian captivity or the Babylonian exile.

This was the apparent end of David's kingdom. (See further under 2 Kings 25.) After the kingdom of Judah came to an end, Gedaliah was made governor of the region (2 Kings 25:22; see on Jeremiah 40).

Some of the people who were left behind when most of Judah was deported to Babylon fled to Egypt, along with the prophet Jeremiah (2 Kings 25:26; see on Jeremiah 42).

Unlike the northern kingdom, which was deported to Assyria and disappeared from the scene, Judah survived its Babylonian captivity. The proclamation of Cyrus almost 50 years later would initiate the rebuilding of Jerusalem and the temple (v. 22; see on Ezra 1).

Ishtar Gate at Babylon.

THE BABYLONIAN EXILE AND THE RETURN FROM EXILE
Ezra–Esther

Ezra, Nehemiah, Esther

The three books of Ezra, Nehemiah, and Esther, which cover about 100 years (538–432 B.C.), form the closing section of Old Testament history. They tell the story of the Jews' return from Babylon, of the rebuilding of the temple and Jerusalem, and of the reestablishment of the Jews' national life in their homeland.

The last three of the Old Testament prophets—Haggai, Zechariah, and Malachi—lived and worked during this same period of return and restoration.

The Exile (586–538 B.C.)

With the fall of Jerusalem to the Babylonians in 586 B.C., the people of God entered a new phase of their history. The period from 586 to 538 B.C. is called the "Exilic period," or the "Babylonian exile," or the "Babylonian captivity." By "exile" it is meant that a large number of Israelites and Judeans now were living outside of the Promised Land—in "foreign countries."

The deportations of Israelites had actually begun during the time of the Assyrian attacks on, and eventual conquest of, Israel in 733 and 722 B.C. (See pp. 240–41, 381.) After the battle of Carchemish (on the west bank of the Euphrates, on the modern border between Syria and Turkey) in 609 B.C., the Babylonians replaced the Assyrians as the world power. God used them as His instrument of judgment as they deported Judeans in 605, 597, 586, and 582 B.C. In addition, it is probable that a good number of Israelites and Judeans emigrated of their own accord to Syria, Egypt, or even Asia Minor (Turkey) in order to avoid the onslaught of the Assyrians and Babylonians—thus beginning their "exile" from the land of promise.

These deportees must have been asking themselves a number of questions. Given that God promised the land of Canaan to the descendants of Abraham *forever*—how is it that the land is now controlled by pagans, while we, God's people, have been deported from it? If God chose the Davidic dynasty to rule *forever* (2 Samuel 7)—why is there now no reigning Davidic king (Psalm 89)? How can God allow the place He Himself chose for His presence to dwell (Psalms 132, 137)—Jerusalem and God's temple—to be in ruins and under foreign control? The answer, of course, was that the continual sinning of the leaders and of the people of Israel and Judah had led to God's judgment upon them:

the covenant curses of Deuteronomy 28 (especially vv. 32–37) and Leviticus 26 (vv. 33–39) had fallen upon them. (See p. 166.)

It was during this time of questioning and exile that the book of Kings (our 1 and 2 Kings) was written to show the people how their disobedience and that of their ancestors during the past 400 years had led to the destruction of Jerusalem and of the temple and to the sorry state of the Davidic dynasty. God's people had not repented, in spite of the insistent and persistent call of God's prophets—such as Elijah and Elisha—to do so.

Returns from Exile (538, 458, and 444 B.C.)

But God had also promised that, after judgment, restoration would follow. And in 539 B.C. (after the Persians had replaced the Babylonians as the world-dominating power) the Persian king Cyrus issued a decree that any Jews who wished to do so could return to Judah and rebuild their temple.

There were actually three returns from Babylonia, as recorded in the books of Ezra and Nehemiah. After the first return, under Zerubbabel, the temple was rebuilt. After the second return, under Ezra, and the third return, under Nehemiah, the walls of Jerusalem were rebuilt. The events of the book of Esther fall between the first and second returns (between Ezra 6 and 7).

The three returns:

538 B.C.	**Zerubbabel** With 42,360 Jews, 7,337 servants, 200 singers, 736 horses, 245 mules, 435 camels, 6,720 donkeys, and 5,400 gold and silver vessels • The **temple is rebuilt** under Zerubbabel the governor and Joshua the priest (Ezra 3–6) • The prophets Haggai and Zechariah
458 B.C.	**Ezra** With 1,754 males, 100 talents of gold, 750 talents of silver. It is not stated whether women and children also went. It takes four months.
444 B.C.	**Nehemiah** Nehemiah, as governor, goes with an armed escort to rebuild and fortify Jerusalem, at government expense • The **walls of Jerusalem are rebuilt** under Nehemiah the governor and Ezra the priest (Ezra 7–10; Nehemiah) • The prophet Malachi

The "Post-exilic" Period (538–ca. 400 B.C.)

The decree of Cyrus, the return led by Sheshbazzar in 538 B.C., and the completion of the rebuilding of the temple in 516 B.C. "technically" meant that the Babylonian exile was over. Thus, the period from 538 B.C. until ca. 400 B.C., when the prophetic voice ceased with the last of

Israel's prophets, is called the "post-exilic period." The truth, of course, is that the majority of Jews living outside the Promised Land did not return to Judah, for very large Jewish communities flourished not only in Babylonia, but also in Egypt, Syria, and Asia Minor.

On the international scene, Persia ruled the area from the Indus River in the east to the western shores of Asia Minor on the Aegean Sea. During Persian rule there were many new cultural developments: coinage came into more widespread use, the legal system developed, and a postal road from Susa (near ancient Babylon) to Sardis (near the Aegean coast), about 1,700 miles in length, aided long-distance communication. The fortunes of Jews living outside of Judea varied. Usually life in "exile" (later more commonly called "diaspora") was not too bad — as evidenced by the Murashu documents, which provide details about Jewish trading — but on occasion Jews were persecuted — as recorded in the book of Esther and in the extrabiblical Aramaic documents found at Elephantine in southern Egypt.

Many Jews, both in and out of the land of Judah, adopted the Aramaic language (Ezra 4:8–6:18; 7:12–26; and Daniel 2:4–7:28 are written in Aramaic). It may have been that the institution of the synagogue has its origins in this period — for how and where do you worship God when you don't live in Judah or Jerusalem? (The Jews who lived in Elephantine had actually built a temple there during the 5th century B.C.!) It is evident that these scattered Jewish communities had their own leadership — note the elders mentioned in Ezekiel (8:1; 14:1; 20:1) — and some of them main-

---

The Persian Empire

The policy of the Assyrian and Babylonian kings had been to deport conquered peoples and scatter them in other lands. The policy of the Persian kings was exactly the opposite: they repatriated those peoples, that is, they sent them back to their own lands.

The Persian kings were more humane than either the Assyrian or the Babylonian kings. One of the first acts of the first Persian king, Cyrus, a singularly noble and just monarch, was to authorize the return of the Jews to their own land.

Five Persian kings played a role in the history of Judah:

- **Cyrus** (539–530 B.C.) conquered Babylon (539 B.C.) and made Persia a world empire. He permitted the Jews to return to their homeland, in fulfillment of Isaiah's prophecy (see pp. 356–57).
- **Cambyses** (530–522 B.C.) is thought to have been the Artaxerxes mentioned in Ezra 4:7, 11, 23, who stopped work on the temple.
- **Darius I** (522–486 B.C.) authorized completion of the temple (Ezra 6).
- **Xerxes (Ahasuerus)** (485–464 B.C.) is famous for his wars with Greece. Esther became his wife (see pp. 281–84), Mordecai his prime minister.
- **Artaxerxes I (Longimanus)** (464–423 B.C.) was very favorably disposed toward the Jews. He authorized Nehemiah, his cupbearer, to rebuild Jerusalem.

Inscribed bowl of Artaxerxes I (464-424 B.C.). (The British Museum) The inscription reads: "Artaxerxes, the great king, king of kings, king of countries, son of Xerxes the king, of Xerxes son of Darius the king, the Achaemenian, in whose house this drinking-cup saucer made of silver was made." The Persian rulers in the time of Ezra, Nehemiah, and Esther include Cyrus, Cambyses, Darius I, Xerxes, and Artaxerxes.

tained close contact with the Jewish leadership in Jerusalem: Aramaic correspondence from the 5th century B.C. has been found from Elephantine in southern Egypt, addressed to Jews in Jerusalem.

There is not much written material to help illuminate the life of those who remained in the land during the exilic period. However, a recent archaeological discovery at Ketef Hinnom in Jerusalem seems to indicate a degree of prosperity for at least *some* of those who were left behind in the land by the Babylonians. But it must be remembered that Jerusalem and the surrounding cities had been devastated by the Babylonians, and that living conditions for most of those still living in the land must have been less than ideal.

As the post-exilic period got under way and the temple and then the walls of Jerusalem were rebuilt in 516 and 444 B.C. respectively, the fragile Judean community was harassed by the Samaritans to the north, the Ammonites to the east, the Arabs to the south, and the Ashdodites to the west. It also seems reasonable to assume that at this time, when Judah was vulnerable, their age-old enemy the Edomites moved into the Hill Country of Judah, into the Hebron area.

The temple, its priesthood, and its service were certainly focal points for the reconstituted Jewish community. It was during this time that the book of Chronicles was written, emphasizing that these institutions were an important legacy bequeathed to the post-exilic community. Israel's history was retold with this in mind as the writer of Chronicles stressed the community's connection to the past—even tracing genealogies back to Abraham and Adam! The writer also emphasized the biblical principle that obedience typically leads to blessing while disobedience leads to disaster; that Israel, as God's people, was a unity; and that the activities of godly kings were divinely approved. All of this was to encourage the fledgling community to remain united and faithful to God.

It was to this community that persons such as Zerubbabel, Haggai, Zechariah, Ezra, Nehemiah, and Malachi ministered, trying to assure them that God had not abandoned them. However, they seemed to be aware of the fact that although the exile had technically "ended," God's presence had not yet returned to the temple, nor had He delivered His people as completely as He had promised (compare Isaiah 40–66 and Jeremiah 31). Even though they were aware that the actual return fell short of the return promised by the prophets, they, as God's people, were being called upon to remain faithful to Him — to await the climactic deliverance from exile that was still to come.

The End of the Persian Empire

Almost a century after the time of Artaxerxes I (the king who had allowed Nehemiah to go back to Jerusalem and rebuild its walls), the last Persian king, Darius III, was defeated by Alexander the Great of Macedonia in the famous battle of Arbela, near the site of Nineveh, in 331 B.C. The end of the Persian Empire marked the beginning of the rise of Greece. For the first time in history, the center of world power shifted from Asia to Europe. Later it would shift even farther west, to Rome and the greatest empire the world had yet seen — the Roman Empire — of which the Jews and their country were a part at the time of the New Testament. (For a summary of the fascinating 400-year history from the time of Nehemiah to the time of Christ, see pp. 471–90.)

Ezra 2 | THE REGISTER OF THOSE WHO RETURNED

According to verses 64–65, a total of 42,360 Jews returned, plus servants. However, when the numbers in the list are added together, the total falls about 11,000 short of this number. This surplus of 11,000 is thought to have been composed of exiles from tribes other than Judah. Ephraim and Manasseh are mentioned in 1 Chronicles 9:3. Israel is named in Ezra 10:25. The term "all Israel" is used of those who returned, and 12 bulls and 12 he-goats, representing the 12 tribes, were sacrificed (2:70; 6:17; 8:35). This would make it appear as if the returning exiles of Judah, in their homeward journey, gathered in some from other tribes. It helps us to understand how, in New Testament times, Jews were still spoken of as the Twelve Tribes (Luke 22:30; Acts 26:7; James 1:1).

Ezra 3 | THE FOUNDATION OF THE TEMPLE IS LAID

In the seventh month of the first year of their return the Israelites built the altar and kept the Feast of Tabernacles, in joyous thanksgiving to God. In the second month of the following year, when the foundation

The stele of King Ashurbanipal of Assyria in the British Museum.

of the temple was laid, they made the heavens ring with their shouts of praise and thanksgiving. But the older men, who had seen the first temple, wept aloud, so insignificant would the new temple be compared with Solomon's temple.

Zerubbabel (v. 2), the governor (Haggai 1:1), was a grandson of King Jehoiachin, who had been deported to Babylon (1 Chronicles 3:17–19). He was the one who would have been king, had there been a kingdom. With fine courtesy, Cyrus appointed him to be governor of Judah.

Ezra 4 | THE WORK IS STOPPED

As work on the temple and wall (v. 16) progressed, the peoples to whom the Jews' land had been given, and their neighbors, began to object, and through intimidation and intrigue they succeeded in stopping the work for 15 years, until the reign of Darius I.

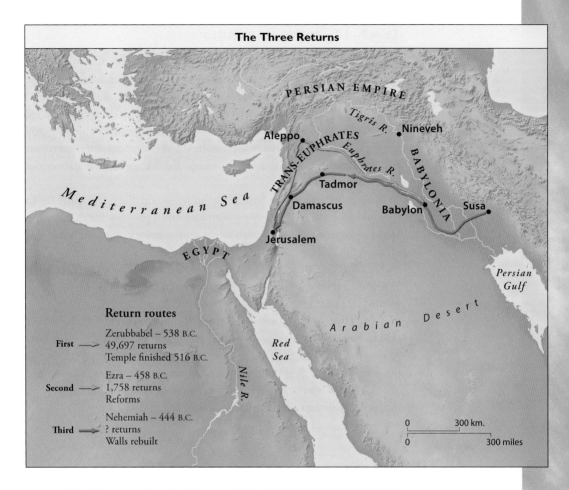

The Three Returns

PERSIAN EMPIRE

Aleppo

Tigris R.

Nineveh

TRANS-EUPHRATES

Euphrates R.

BABYLONIA

Tadmor

Damascus

Babylon

Susa

Mediterranean Sea

Jerusalem

EGYPT

Persian Gulf

Red Sea

Arabian Desert

Nile R.

Return routes

First → Zerubbabel – 538 B.C.
49,697 returns
Temple finished 516 B.C.

Second → Ezra – 458 B.C.
1,758 returns
Reforms

Third → Nehemiah – 444 B.C.
? returns
Walls rebuilt

| 0 | 300 km. |
| 0 | 300 miles |

Ezra 5–6 | THE TEMPLE COMPLETED

Darius I was friendly toward the Jews, and in his second year (520 B.C.), 16 years after the Jews had been allowed to go home, work on the temple was resumed with the encouragement of the prophets Haggai and Zechariah. Shortly thereafter came the decree from Darius for the temple to be completed, with an order to draw on the royal treasury for the needed funds. Within four years it was completed and dedicated amid great rejoicing.

The famous Behistun inscription, which supplied the key to the ancient Babylonian language (see p. 70), was made by this same Darius.

Ezra 7–8 | EZRA'S JOURNEY TO JERUSALEM

Between chapters 6 and 7 is a gap of about 60 years. The temple was completed in 515 B.C., and Ezra came to Jerusalem in 458 B.C., in the reign of Artaxerxes I, who was Queen Esther's stepson. Ezra the priest went to teach Judah the Law of God, to beautify the temple, and to restore the temple service.

Ezra 9–10 | MIXED MARRIAGES

When Ezra arrived in Jerusalem, he found a situation that made him heartsick. The people, priests, Levites, and leaders had freely intermarried with their idolatrous neighbors—a thing that God had again and again forbidden the Jews to do. In fact, it was the very thing that had led the Jews into idolatry before, which had been the cause of their captivity. God had sent prophet after prophet, and judgment after judgment, and at last had resorted to the captivity, almost wiping the nation out of existence.

Now a little remnant had come home—and they are again up to their old tricks of intermarrying with idolatrous peoples. Ezra's measures to rid them of their non-Jewish wives may seem severe to us, but it was effective.

Ezra helped in further reforms, as noted in the book of Nehemiah. Tradition makes him the originator of synagogue worship and president of the Great Synagogue.

The Great Synagogue was a council, consisting of 120 members, said to have been organized by Nehemiah in about 410 B.C., with Ezra as president. Its purpose was the rebuilding of the religious life of the returned captives. It is thought to have governed the returned Jews until about 275 B.C. and to have played an important role in gathering, grouping, and restoring the canonical books of the Old Testament.

Nehemiah

The Walls of Jerusalem Are Rebuilt

When all our enemies heard about this, all the surrounding nations were afraid and lost their self-confidence, because they realized that this work had been done with the help of our God.

—Nehemiah 6:16

"Do not grieve, for the joy of the Lord is your strength."

—Nehemiah 8:10

When Nehemiah went to Jerusalem in 444 B.C., Ezra had been there for 14 years. But Ezra was a priest, teaching religion to the people. Nehemiah came as civil governor, with authority from the king of Persia to rebuild the walls of Jerusalem and to make it once again a fortified city. By then, the Jews had been home nearly 100 years, but they had made little progress beyond rebuilding the temple—and a very insignificant temple at that—because whenever they would start work on the walls, their more powerful neighbors would either intimidate them into stopping or through intrigue get orders from the Persian court for the work to stop.

| Neh. 1–2 | NEHEMIAH'S JOURNEY TO JERUSALEM |

Parts of the book are in the first person; they are direct quotations from Nehemiah's official reports.

Nehemiah was a man of prayer, patriotism, action, courage, and perseverance. His first impulse always was to pray (1:4; 2:4; 4:4, 9; 6:9, 14). He spent four months in prayer before he made his request to the king (1:1; 2:1).

Nehemiah was cupbearer to King Artaxerxes (1:11; 2:1), a trusted and important official. Artaxerxes I was king of Persia (464–423 B.C.), son of Xerxes, and thus the stepson of Queen Esther, the Jewess.

Esther became queen of Persia about 60 years after the Jews had returned to Jerusalem. This must have given the Jews great prestige at the Persian court. Esther most probably was still alive, and an influential personage in the palace, when both Ezra and Nehemiah went to Jerusalem. Our guess is that we have Esther to thank for Artaxerxes' kindly feeling toward the Jews and his interest in having Jerusalem rebuilt.

| Neh. 3 | THE GATES REPAIRED |

ARCHAEOLOGICAL NOTE: Nehemiah's Jerusalem. Remains of the "Broad Wall" (3:8), the "Valley Gate" (3:13), the "Pool of Siloam" (3:15), and the "Water Gate" (2:14) have been found in the course of

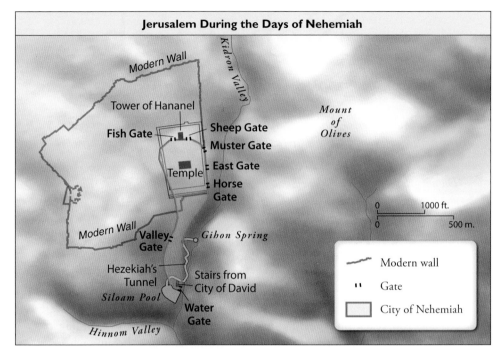

Jerusalem During the Days of Nehemiah

Kidron Valley

Modern Wall

Tower of Hananel

Fish Gate

Sheep Gate

Muster Gate

Temple

East Gate

Horse Gate

Mount of Olives

0 — 1000 ft.
0 — 500 m.

Modern Wall

Valley Gate

Gihon Spring

Hezekiah's Tunnel

Stairs from City of David

Siloam Pool

Water Gate

Hinnom Valley

Modern wall

'' Gate

☐ City of Nehemiah

archaeological excavations in Jerusalem. The city that Nehemiah fortified was actually slightly smaller than the one the Babylonians had destroyed. In fact, it was smaller than Solomon's Jerusalem—perhaps 35 acres in size. Nehemiah's Jerusalem was completely limited to portions of the eastern hill, where the original City of David had stood.

Foundations of the southern tower dated to the period of Nehemiah discovered in the City of David are evidence of the important role that Nehemiah played in reconstructing the walls of Jerusalem.

| Neh. 4–6 | **THE WALL BUILT** |

Old-time enemies of the Jews, who were now in possession of the land—Moabites, Ammonites, Ashdodites, Arabians, and the recently imported Samaritans — craftily and bitterly opposed the rebuilding of the wall of Jerusalem. They mobilized their armies and marched against Jerusalem. But Nehemiah, with faith in God, skillfully armed and arranged his men and went straight ahead with the work, day and night. And in spite of all obstacles, the wall was finished in 52 days. Almost a century and a half after its destruction in 586 B.C., Jerusalem was once again a fortified city.

Neh. 7–8 | PUBLIC READING OF THE BOOK OF LAW

After the wall was built, Nehemiah and Ezra gathered the people together to organize their national life. Chapter 7 is about the same as Ezra 2: it gives the list of those who had returned to Jerusalem with Zerubbabel nearly a century before. There were certain genealogical matters that had to be attended to.

Then, for seven days, every day from early morning till midday, Ezra and his helpers opened the Book of the Law, read from the Law of God, and provided explanations so that the people understood what they heard. This public reading and exposition of God's Book brought a great wave of repentance among the people, a great revival, and a solemn covenant to keep the Law, as recorded in chapters 9–10.

> They read from the Book of the Law of God, making it clear and giving the meaning so that the people could understand what was being read.
> —Nehemiah 8:8

It should be noted that it was the finding of the Book of the Law that brought about Josiah's great reformation (2 Kings 22). It was Martin Luther's finding of a Bible that led to the Reformation and brought religious liberty to our modern world. The weakness of many present-day churches is their neglect of the very Bible they profess to follow—the great need of today's pulpit is simple expository preaching.

Neh. 9–12 | COVENANT. DEDICATION OF THE WALL

In deep penitence and great earnestness, the people made a covenant: "In view of all this, we are making a binding agreement, putting it in writing, and our leaders, our Levites and our priests are affixing their seals to it." They bound themselves to walk in God's Law (9:38; 10:29). The wall was dedicated, and one-tenth of the population was brought into the city to live, and its government and temple services were organized.

Neh. 13 | NEHEMIAH'S FINAL REFORMS

The last recorded acts of Nehemiah involve reforms concerning tithes, the Sabbath, and marriages between Jews and non-Jews. Nehemiah was governor of Judah for at least 12 years (5:14). Josephus says that he lived to a great age and governed Judah for the rest of his life.

Esther

The Deliverance of the Jews
from Annihilation

"Go, gather together all the Jews who are in Susa, and fast for me. Do not eat or drink for three days, night or day. I and my maids will fast as you do. When this is done, I will go to the king, even though it is against the law. And if I perish, I perish."

—ESTHER 4:16

In the canon, this book comes after the book of Nehemiah, but the events it describes took place about 30 years before Nehemiah.

- The first group of Jews returned to Jerusalem in 538 B.C. Twenty years later the temple was completed (Ezra 1–6).
- The story of Esther takes place about 40 years after the temple was rebuilt. She became queen of Persia in 478 B.C. and saved the Jews from being massacred in 473 B.C.
- Fifteen years after Queen Esther saved the Jews, Ezra went to Jerusalem (458 B.C.), and 13 years after that Nehemiah rebuilt the walls of Jerusalem.

It seems that Esther made possible the work of Nehemiah. Her marriage to the king must have given Jews great prestige. It is impossible to guess what might have happened to the Hebrew nation had there been no Esther. Except for her, Jerusalem might never have been rebuilt, and there might have been a different story to tell to all future ages.

This book of Esther is not just a story with a moral. It is about a very important historical event: the Hebrew nation's deliverance from annihilation in the days following the Babylonian captivity. If the Hebrew nation had been wiped out of existence 500 years before it brought Christ into the world, it would have made all the difference in the world: no Hebrew nation, no Messiah; no Messiah, a lost world. This beautiful Jewish girl of long ago, though she herself may not have known it, yet played her part in paving the way for the coming of the world's Savior.

Est. 1 | QUEEN VASHTI DEPOSED

Ahasuerus was another name for Xerxes, who ruled Persia from 486 to 464 B.C., one of the most illustrious monarchs of the ancient world. The great feast described in this chapter, as has been learned from Persian inscriptions, was held in preparation for his famous expedition against Greece, in which he fought the battles of Thermopylae and Salamis (480 B.C.).

It seems that he deposed Vashti in 483 B.C., before he left, and married Esther in 478 B.C., after he returned from his expedition against Greece (1:3; 2:16).

ARCHAEOLOGICAL NOTE: The Palace at Susa. Shushan, or Susa, 200 miles east of Babylon, was the winter residence of Persian kings. Its site was identified by W. K. Loftus (1852), who found an inscription of Artaxerxes II (404–359 B.C.): "My ancestor Darius built this palace in former times. In the reign of my grandfather [Artaxerxes I] it was burned. I have restored it."

This palace was the residence of Darius, who authorized the rebuilding of the temple; of Xerxes, Esther's husband, and of Artaxerxes I, who authorized Nehemiah to rebuild Jerusalem. Susa was the place where Daniel had his vision (Daniel 8). The remains of Susa are scattered over 100 acres, and the site, beginning in 1851, has been excavated (except during the two World Wars) for more than 100 years! From these excavations, it is evident that the author of Esther was familiar with the city. The royal palace itself was almost 2½ acres in size, with a whole series of courtyards, audience hall, residences, and auxiliary rooms.

| Est. 2 | ESTHER BECOMES QUEEN |

Ahasuerus (Xerxes) died 13 years later. Esther, no doubt, lived far into the reign of her stepson, Artaxerxes. As queen-mother she may have been a person of influence in Persia in the days of Ezra and Nehemiah.

Capitals from the palace at Susa. Esther and Mordecai achieved positions of power at the palace in Susa where these capitals once stood.

| Est. 3–7 | HAMAN'S DECREE |

The decree was a call to kill all the Jews in all the provinces (3:12–13). This was in the king's 12th year (3:7), after Esther had been queen for five years. Her lament, "I have not been summoned to come to the king for these thirty days," may indicate that the novelty of Esther had worn off, and Esther took a great risk in inviting the king to the banquet.

But the king came, and when the king saw Esther again, his reaction shows that she still pleased him (5:3), even though she had been his wife for five years.

The outcome was that Haman was hanged, and his place was given to Mordecai, Esther's cousin.

The name of God is not mentioned in the book, perhaps because it may have been copied from Persian records. Yet God's providential care of His people is nowhere more evident.

ARCHAEOLOGICAL NOTE: Mordecai. A person named Marduka, whose name was found on a cuneiform tablet from Borsippa in southern Iraq, was evidently a minister at the Persian court in Susa and may actually have been the biblical Mordecai.

Est. 8–9 | DELIVERANCE. THE FEAST OF PURIM

Since a decree issued by a Persian king could not be changed (8:8; Daniel 6:15), the decree for the Jews' massacre could not be reversed. But Esther did persuade the king to make another decree that authorized the Jews to resist and slay all who would attack them, which they did. Thus Esther saved the Jewish race from annihilation. This was the origin of the Feast of Purim, which Jews still observe. Esther was not only beautiful, but wise. We admire her for her patriotism and bravery and tact.

This story shows us that God's favor can cause civil law to be reversed. It also shows how God uses His faithful servants to influence and direct ungodly authority. What a comfort this is in a world that has so many ungodly leaders. We must pray for the godly civil servants so that God's plan can be done through them as it was with Esther.

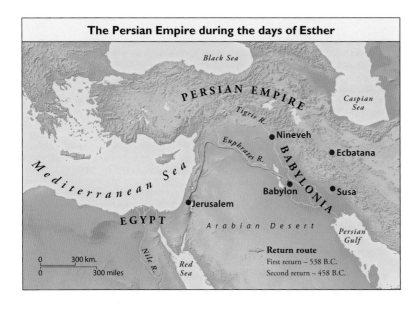

The Persian Empire during the days of Esther

Black Sea

PERSIAN EMPIRE

Caspian Sea

Tigris R.

Nineveh

Ecbatana

Euphrates R.

BABYLONIA

Mediterranean Sea

Babylon

Susa

Jerusalem

EGYPT

Arabian Desert

Persian Gulf

Return route
First return – 538 B.C.
Second return – 458 B.C.

0   300 km.
0   300 miles

Nile R.

Red Sea

Est. 10 | MORDECAI'S GREATNESS

Mordecai became more and more powerful; he was second in rank after the king of Persia (9:4; 10:3). His acts of power and his greatness were written in detail in the official records of the kings of Media and Persia. This was in the reign of Xerxes, the mighty monarch of the Persian Empire. Xerxes' prime minister was a Jew; his favorite wife was a Jewess — Mordecai and Esther, the brains and heart of the palace! This paved the way for the work of Ezra and Nehemiah. Like Joseph in Egypt and Daniel in Babylon, so here God used Mordecai and Esther in Persia.

POETRY AND WISDOM

Job – Song of Songs

Poetry and wisdom literature in the Old Testament are closely related. Wisdom literature is generally poetic in form, but the reverse is not true: not all Old Testament poetry is wisdom literature.

Five Old Testament books are clearly poetic: Job, Psalms, Proverbs, Ecclesiastes, and the Song of Songs. (In the Hebrew Bible these books are not grouped together as they were in the Septuagint and are in our Bibles.) Of these five books, four are wisdom (Job, Proverbs, Ecclesiastes, Song of Songs), while the book of Psalms is not.

1. Poetry

As much as one-third of the Old Testament may be poetry. The reason for the vagueness of this statement is that it is sometimes difficult to determine where Hebrew prose ends and Hebrew poetry begins.

A few books of the Old Testament are essentially without poetry: Leviticus, Ruth, Ezra, Nehemiah, Esther, Haggai, and Malachi—but even in these books an occasional poetic form slips in.

And some books are not poetic but contain well-defined poems, such as Genesis 49; Exodus 15; Deuteronomy 33; and Judges 5.

Characteristics of Hebrew Poetry

English poetry usually rhymes. Hebrew poetry does not. Instead, Hebrew poetry has two primary characteristics that can be easily recognized, even in an English translation: imagery and parallelism.

Figurative Language and Images

- Perhaps the best-known example is "The LORD *is* my shepherd" (Psalm 23:1; a metaphor).
- Another example is "I am *like* an olive tree flourishing in the house of God" (Psalm 52:8; a simile).
- There is exaggeration for effect: "With your help I can advance against a troop; with my God I can scale a wall" (Psalm 18:29; hyperbole).
- Hebrew poetry also often speaks of inanimate things as if they were alive: "Let the rivers clap their hands, let the mountains sing together for joy" (Psalm 98:8; personification).

Parallelism

Parallelism involves a relationship of thought between two or more lines. It can be looked at as a "rhythm of thought." For example,

- "The LORD watches over the way of the righteous, but the way of the wicked will perish" (Psalm 1:6; the second line states the opposite of the first).

- "For as high as the heavens are above the earth, so great is his love for those who fear him" (Psalm 103:11; the first line is a simile, the second line its literal meaning; emblematic parallelism).
- "Trust in the LORD and do good; dwell in the land and enjoy safe pasture" (Psalm 37:3; the second line completes the thought of the first line; synthetic or climactic parallelism).
- "LORD, who may dwell in your sanctuary? Who may live on your holy hill?" (Psalm 15:1; both lines express the same thought in different words; synonymous parallelism).

Other Characteristics

- Hebrew poetry also uses refrains, for example in Psalms 42–43, where the refrain is found three times: "Why are you downcast, O my soul? Why so disturbed within me? Put your hope in God, for I will yet praise him, my Savior and my God."
- Sometimes the same statement is made both at the beginning and at the end of a poem, for example in Psalm 118, which begins and ends with the words "Give thanks to the LORD, for he is good; his love endures forever."
- Finally, there is the use of acrostic patterns, in which the first line of a psalm or poem (for example, in the book of Lamentations) begins with the first letter of the alphabet, the second line or strophe with the second letter of the alphabet, and so on. An example is Psalm 119; in many Bibles the Hebrew letter that begins each strophe is printed (Aleph, Beth, etc.).

2. Wisdom Literature

The Hebrew word for wisdom has a much broader meaning than the English word "wisdom." It includes, for example, skill in the making of things, which is akin to our idea of craftsmanship (Exodus 31:3; Jeremiah 9:17).

Wisdom in Hebrew encompasses the willingness and ability to rightly perceive, and to be rightly related to, the created world in all its aspects. God has made the world a certain way, and wisdom means living in accordance with that basic structure of the universe.

Wisdom literature is *poetic* in form but *practical* in content. It does not try to communicate factual or abstract knowledge but rather to teach practical skill in living. Wisdom literature, therefore, is the Old Testament's "instruction manual for life."

Jeremiah 18:18 shows how important wisdom was considered to be. It is mentioned alongside the Law and the Prophets: "For the teaching of the law by the priest will not be lost, nor will counsel from the wise, nor the word from the prophets."

The books of Proverbs, Ecclesiastes, Job, the Song of Songs, and some of the psalms, such as Psalms 1 and 119, are traditionally considered wisdom literature.

- **Job** is wisdom because it deals with the central issue of faith and suffering.

- **Ecclesiastes** is wisdom because it warns against cynicism and points the reader toward simple faith in God.
- The **Song of Songs** is wisdom because it describes the intimacy of human marital love.

In the New Testament, the letter of James is reminiscent of Old Testament wisdom literature.

Kinds of Wisdom Statements

Some of the more significant types of wisdom statements are

- **Aphorisms.** This is what we usually think of as a "proverb": a short, pithy saying that has general validity, such as our "A stitch in time saves nine." Much of the book of Proverbs, beginning with chapter 10, consists of aphorisms.
- **Instruction.** These are longer, stylized discussions about wisdom, such as Proverbs 1:8–9:18.
- **"Better" sayings.** Better is A with B than C with D. For example, "Better a little with righteousness than much gain with injustice" (Proverbs 16:8).
- **Disputation** (verbal controversy). The best example is the book of Job.

Job

The Problem of Suffering

"Shall we accept good from God, and not trouble?" —JOB 2:10

"I know that my Redeemer lives,
and that in the end he will stand upon the earth.
And after my skin has been destroyed,
yet in my flesh I will see God." —JOB 19:25–26

J ob is the first of the so-called poetic or wisdom books, a group of five books that also includes Psalms, Proverbs, Ecclesiastes, and the Song of Songs. It is a magnificent book that deals with the problem of suffering: if God is good and just, why do people suffer?

The Scene of the Book

The land of Uz (1:1) is thought to have been along the border between Palestine and Arabia, extending from Edom north and east toward the Euphrates River, skirting the caravan route between Babylon and Egypt.

Job

In a postscript to the book of Job, the Septuagint, following ancient tradition, identified Job with Jobab, the second king of Edom (Genesis 36:33). Names and places mentioned in the book seem to give it a setting among the descendants of Esau (see under chapter 2). The book has the atmosphere of very primitive times and seems to have its setting among the early tribes descended from Abraham, along the northern border of Arabia, roughly contemporaneous with Israel's stay in Egypt.

Author of the Book

Nothing is known about the author of the book. Ancient Jewish tradition ascribed the book to Moses. We could speculate that while Moses was in the wilderness of Midian (Exodus 2:15), which bordered on the country of the Edomites, he could have heard the story of Job from Job's descendants. Since Job was a descendant of Abraham, Moses could naturally recognize him as being within the circle of God's revelation. Modern critics assign a much later date to the book of Job, but in the end it is the content of the book that is important, not our speculative guesses about its origins.

Nature of the Book

Job may be called a historical poem, that is, a poem based on an event that actually took place. Job was a great and well-known man in his part of the world. All at once, in a single day, he was crushed by a number of overwhelming calamities. His vast herds of camels were stolen, and those who guarded the camels were killed by a band of Chaldean robbers. At the same time, his herds of oxen were stolen, and those who took care of them were killed by a band of Sabean robbers, and his 7000 sheep and their attending servants were killed by a thunderstorm. To top it all off, his 10 children were all killed by a cyclone, and Job himself came down with a most hideous and painful disease.

Job's fate became known far and wide, and for months Job was the topic of public conversation everywhere (7:3). The book contains some of the things that Job, his friends, and God said or wrote.

Subject of the Book

The book of Job deals with the problem of human suffering. Since very early times, people have been troubled by the awful inequalities and injustices of life: how could a good God make a world like this, where there is so much suffering? The truth is that God made a good and perfect world (Genesis 1:31). He created man and woman and placed them in the Garden of Eden, where they were in perfect relationship with Him — every need was met and they were greatly blessed. Unfortunately, they listened to Satan's deceiving message: "For God knows that when you eat of it your eyes will be opened, and you will be like God, knowing good and evil." Adam and Eve's disobedience separated them and all mankind from the good and perfect world that God made for His people. Because of their sin, all people are born into a world of suffering.

Fortunately, God had a plan to reunite Himself with man and woman so that mankind may once again be free from suffering. God sent His Son, Jesus, to pay the price for our sins. Through His death and resurrection, mankind has the opportunity to regain its right relationship with God and ultimately to live an eternal life free from suffering.

Job had very little knowledge of God. Most of God's Word had not been written yet. Job, with the "help" of his friends, is trying to interpret his suffering without "knowledge" of God (38:1; 42:1–3). Spending time with his friends trying to determine the cause of this suffering does not benefit Job — rather, it prolongs his suffering. Eventually Job stops talking and listens to God. Job receives "knowledge," or revelation, of God as the omnipotent Creator. With this revelation, Job acknowledges that God can do all things (42:2). He is now able to focus on the awe-inspiring reality of God instead of on his own suffering. Job repents, and God delivers him from his suffering. God then instructs Job to pray an intercessory prayer for his friends. Job is obedient to God and prays for his friends. After Job's prayer, God restores Job to prosperity. God actually doubles Job's fortune and blesses the latter part of Job's life more than the first.

In the end, Job's battle with Satan is over and God restores Job. God does not allow us to suffer without reason. At times the cause of the suffering may be hidden from our understanding in the mystery of God's divine purpose (see Isaiah 55:8–9). But we must trust in Him and always turn to Him, even in times of suffering. What a powerful witness it is to the world for Christians to not be full of anger and resentment toward God when suffering! We know that He is a God who loves us and does only what is right.

The Structure of the Book

Apart from the introduction (chaps. 1–2) and the conclusion or epilogue (42:7–17), the book of Job consists of speeches by Job, by his friends, and finally by God Himself.

Job's three friends—Eliphaz, Bildad, and Zophar—take turns trying to explain to Job why he is suffering, and Job answers each in turn. They go for three rounds (chaps. 4–14; 15–21; 22–26). In the first two rounds, all three friends speak up; in the third round only Eliphaz and Bildad speak, while Zophar remains silent—he has given up on Job.

Job then makes a long speech in which he calls for vindication, since he feels that his suffering is unjust (chaps. 29–31). After this a fourth friend, Elihu, speaks up and cautions Job against blaming God (chaps. 32–37). Finally, God Himself addresses Job in some of the most majestic chapters of the Bible (chaps. 38–42:6). Job repents, and God blesses Job even more than before.

Job, His Friends, and the Problem of Suffering

In reading through the book of Job, we must remember that Job never knew *why* he was suffering—nor what the final outcome would be. The first two chapters of Job explain to us why it happened and make it clear that the reason for his suffering was not punishment for sin, but rather a test of Job's faith that God was confident Job would pass. But while we as readers of Job know this, Job himself did not.

Job 1–2 | PROLOGUE—JOB TESTED

The book opens with an account of Job, a desert prince—or what was in those days called a king—who had immense wealth and influence and was famous for his integrity, his piety, and his benevolence: a good man, who suffered fearful reverses that came so suddenly and overwhelmingly that it stunned all of those who heard about it.

> "Naked I came from my mother's womb,
> and naked I will depart.
> The LORD gave and the LORD has taken away;
> may the name of the LORD be praised."
> —Job 1:21

Leper colony. Part of Job's test was dealing with a deforming skin disease which may have been similar to leprosy.

Satan accused Job of having ulterior motives for being a good man—of being mercenary. Then God permitted Satan to test his accusation. Job stood the test and in the end was blessed more than ever.

Job's disease (2:7) is thought to have been a form of leprosy, perhaps complicated by elephantiasis, one of the most horrible and painful diseases known in the oriental world.

Job's Friends

Three friends come to comfort Job in his suffering. For seven days and nights they do fine: they simply sit with Job. "Then they sat on the ground with him for seven days and seven nights. No one said a word to him, because they saw how great his suffering was" (2:13).

- **Eliphaz the Temanite** (2:11) was a descendant of Esau (Genesis 36:11), an Edomite.
- **Bildad the Shuhite** was a descendant of Abraham and Keturah (Genesis 25:2).
- **Zophar the Naamathite** was of unknown origin or locality. All three were probably nomad princes.
- A fourth friend, who does not enter the picture until after the other three have quit speaking, is **Elihu the Buzite** (32:2), a descendant of Abraham's brother Nahor (Genesis 22:21).

In the conversations that follow, Job speaks nine times; Eliphaz, three times; Bildad, three times; Zophar, twice; Elihu, once; and God, in a majestic finale, once.

All three friends try to explain that there is—*has* to be—a connection between Job's present suffering and his past life. They are looking for a logical, cause-and-effect relationship. Their arguments can all be reduced to this:

    a. Job is suffering.
    b. God is just and would not allow a person to suffer without reason.
    c. Therefore, Job must have done something bad to deserve this suffering.

Before his friends come, Job refuses to blame God: "The LORD gave and the LORD has taken away; may the name of the LORD be praised" (1:21); and, "Shall we accept good from God, and not trouble?" (2:10).

But the more Job defends himself against the logic of his friends, the more he adopts their approach and builds his own argument:

    a. I am suffering.
    b. I know that I have done nothing to deserve this suffering.
    c. The logical conclusion would be that, therefore, God must be unjust.

But Job never quite draws that final conclusion; rather, it is,

    c. Therefore, God has some explaining to do.

The three friends each base their accusations on different arguments.

- Eliphaz **appeals to experience and observation:** "Consider now: Who, being innocent, has ever perished? Where were the upright ever destroyed? As I have observed, those who plow evil and those who sow trouble reap it" (4:7–8).
- Bildad **appeals to tradition:** "Ask the former generations and find out what their fathers learned, for we were born only yesterday and know nothing, and our days on earth are but a shadow. Will they not instruct you and tell you? Will they not bring forth words from their understanding?" (8:8–10).
- Zophar arrogantly speaks as if he knows exactly what God thinks—he **appeals to his own view of God:** "Oh, how I wish that God would speak, that he would open his lips against you and disclose to you the secrets of wisdom, for true wisdom has two sides. Know this: God has even forgotten some of your sin" (11:5–6). Ironically, when God finally *does* speak, it is not to condemn Job, but to condemn Zophar and his friends (42:7–9).

The final answer Job receives is not philosophical or logical. It is a majestic presentation by God Himself of who He is (38:1–42:6)—the only satisfactory answer to the problem of human suffering. It does not answer the questions our logical mind comes up with, but it will satisfy our heart: "I know that my Redeemer lives, and that in the end he will stand upon the earth. And after my skin has been destroyed, yet in my flesh I will see God" (19:25–26).

The grand lesson of the book as a whole is that Job, through his suffering, in the end comes to see God in His majesty and greatness as he had never seen Him before. That is the true reward. The fact that Job is also abundantly rewarded with greater prosperity and blessedness than he had at first is almost an afterthought (42:12–16).

Job 3 | JOB'S COMPLAINT

Job wishes he had never been born and longs for death.

Job 4–14 | THE FIRST CYCLE OF SPEECHES

Chapters 4–5. Eliphaz speaks. He advises Job to turn to God (5:8) and suggests that if Job would only repent, his troubles would disappear (5:17–27).

Chapters 6–7. Job's reply. Job is disappointed in his friends. He longs for sympathy, not stinging reproof (6:14–30). He seems dazed. He knows full well that he is not a wicked man, yet his body is "clothed with worms" (7:5). He just cannot understand: even if he has sinned, it surely was not so serious as to deserve such terrible punishment. He prays that he may die (6:9).

Chapter 8. Bildad speaks. He insists that God is just and that Job's troubles must be evidence of his wickedness—if he will only turn to God, all will be well again.

Chapters 9–10. Job's reply. Job insists that he is not guilty (10:7) and that God sends misfortune on the blameless as well as the wicked (9:22). He complains bitterly and wishes again that he had never been born (10:18–22).

Chapter 11. Zophar speaks. He brutally and arrogantly tells Job that his punishment is less than he deserves (v. 6), and he insists that if Job will put away his sin, his sufferings will pass and be forgotten, and security, prosperity, and happiness will return (13–19).

Chapters 12–14. Job's reply. He grows sarcastic at their cutting words: "Doubtless you are the people, and wisdom will die with you! But I have a mind as well as you; I am not inferior to you. Who does not know all these things?" (12:2–3). They're simply stating (and restating) conventional wisdom, but it doesn't apply here!

Job says he wants to "speak to the Almighty and to argue my case with God. You, however, smear me with lies; you are worthless physicians, all of you!" (13:3–4). He tells them in no uncertain terms that he wants them to shut up: "If only you would be altogether silent! For you, that would be wisdom" (13:5, 13).

Job asks God to speak and to tell him what it is he has done wrong (13:20–23).

> "Though he slay me, yet will I hope in him."
> —Job 13:15

Job 15–21 | THE SECOND CYCLE OF SPEECHES

Chapter 15. Eliphaz's second speech. The argument becomes heated. His sarcasm becomes bitter (vv. 2–13). Job's eyes flash (v. 12).

Chapters 16–17. Job's reply. If you were in my place, I could shake my head at you and "make fine speeches against you." The difference is that "my mouth would encourage you; comfort from my lips would bring you relief" (16:4–5). Only those who have suffered can truly enter into the suffering of others—as Christ can understand and enter into our suffering. Job is desperate: "Who can see any hope for me?" (17:15).

Chapter 18. Bildad's second speech. In a fit of anger, he cries to Job, Why do you "tear yourself to pieces in your anger?" (v. 4). And assuming Job's wickedness, he tries to frighten Job into repentance by depicting the awful doom of the wicked.

Chapter 19. Job's reply. His friends abhor him (v. 19); his wife is a stranger to him (v. 17); children despise him (v. 18); he begs for some compassion from his friends: "Have pity on me, my friends, have pity, for the hand of God has struck me. Why do you pursue me as God does? Will you never get enough of my flesh?" (v. 21).

Then, suddenly, out of the depths of despair, as the sunlight breaks through a rift in the clouds, Job bursts forth into one of the most sublime expressions of faith ever uttered: "I know that my Redeemer lives, and that in the end he will stand upon the earth. And after my skin has been destroyed, yet in my flesh I will see God; I myself will see him with my own eyes—I, and not another. How my heart yearns within me!" (vv. 25–27).

Chapter 20. Zophar's second speech. Zophar is offended by Job's words. Assuming Job's wickedness, he sets out to portray the deplorable fate in store for the wicked.

Chapter 21. Job's reply. Job agrees that the wicked suffer in the end—but in the meantime they seem to be doing rather well. They grow old and increase in power, and their homes are safe and free from fear (vv. 7–9). The prosperity of the wicked undermines the friends' argument—there seems to be no necessary connection between suffering and wickedness! (v. 34). Suffering seems to be a tool that Satan uses to deceive the righteous. The wicked are already lost souls—why would Satan waste any time on them? Their self-centered lifestyle will likely keep them in Satan's camp without any extra effort on his part.

Job 22–26 | THE THIRD CYCLE OF SPEECHES

Chapter 22. Eliphaz's third speech. He bears down harder and harder on Job's wickedness, claiming especially that Job has mistreated the poor.

Chapters 23–24. Job's reply. He again protests his blamelessness. "I have not departed from the commands of his lips; I have treasured the words of his mouth more than my daily bread" (23:12). This shows that Job does not base his claim to blamelessness on his own feelings, but rather measures himself against what God Himself has said—which makes it all the more difficult to understand why God does not give Job some kind of explanation.

Chapter 25. Bildad's third speech. It is a very short speech. They have reached a stalemate. Neither side wants to give in, and the debate simply fizzles. Zophar doesn't even bother to speak again.

Chapter 26–27. Job's reply. Job states his dilemma as bluntly as he can. On the one hand, "I will never admit you are in the right; till I die, I will not deny my integrity" (27:5). On the other hand, "the fate God allots to the wicked" (27:13) is annihilation—they will be no more, and all they possess will go to others. Job's argument and the friends' argument, side by side, without resolution.

Job 28 | AN INTERLUDE ON WISDOM

Chapter 28 interrupts not only the flow but also the tone of Job's argument. This chapter is very much like the book of Proverbs—a discussion of the question where wisdom may be found.

Job 29–31 | JOB'S CALL FOR VINDICATION

The tone of these chapters is different from that in earlier chapters. Job no longer is in the heat of the argument. He seems deflated and sounds sad rather than angry. But he continues to call for vindication.

He contrasts his past prosperity, happiness, honor, respect, kindness, and usefulness (chap. 29) with his present sufferings (chap. 30). Then he wearily asks that *if* he had done any of the things his three friends accused him of, God might tell him what it was (chap. 31). And with that more or less resigned speech, Job finally runs out of things to say—which is when he can begin to listen to God.

Job 32–37 | ELIHU'S SPEECH

Job had silenced the three friends. Elihu was angry at them because they falsely accused Job. And he was angry with Job because as the argument wore on, Job increasingly was intent on justifying himself rather than God. Now it was Elihu's turn to tell them a thing or two.

Elihu correctly points out that Job is coming very close to accusing God of being unjust. Elihu paves the way for God's speech to Job. And in the end, God is angry with the first three friends, but not with Elihu.

Job 38–41 | GOD SPEAKS

These are some of the most awe-inspiring chapters in the Bible. God speaks to Job, but not with answers to the questions Job had been hurling at Him. Rather, God turns it around: *He* does the questioning and asks Job to answer *Him*. God shows and reminds Job of His power and majesty — of who He is. And He asks Job if he is anything compared to God's greatness.

Job is speechless and admits that he has no answer (40:4–5). God continues — until in the end Job repents. Job, the man who thought he knew God, now says, "My ears had heard of you but now my eyes have seen you. Therefore I despise myself and repent in dust and ashes" (42:5–6). Through his suffering, Job goes from a limited understanding of God to a life-changing experience of the greatness, majesty, and power of God — but also an experience of God's love, since God gives Job a personal answer to a very real and difficult question. But it is an answer that comes only after Job runs out of words, so that he can listen.

Job 42:7–17 | EPILOGUE—JOB RESTORED

After Job repents, God instructs him to pray for his friends. After Job prays, God makes him prosperous again and gives him twice as much as he had before his suffering (42:10). Job had come through his trials magnificently, and God blessed his old age with generous rewards (42:12–17).

Job's obedience in praying for his friends marks a turning point in his life. His experience seems to call us to pray for those who cause us to suffer.

Bedouin with his herds. Following the test, God restored Job's prosperity.

Psalms

Why are you downcast, O my soul?
Why so disturbed within me?
Put your hope in God,
for I will yet praise him,
my Savior and my God.

—PSALM 42:11

Authorship of the Psalms

In the titles or superscriptions of the Psalms, 73 psalms are ascribed to David, 12 to Asaph, 11 to the sons of Korah, two to Solomon (72, 127), one to Moses (90), and one to Ethan (89); 50 of the psalms are anonymous.

Some of the anonymous psalms may have been written by the author of the preceding psalm so that one title applies to both psalms. David, no doubt, was author of some of the anonymous psalms.

But the titles are not a certain indication of authorship, since "of," "to," and "for" are the same preposition in Hebrew. A psalm "of" David may have been one that he himself wrote, or it may have been written "for" David or dedicated "to" David.

However, the titles are very ancient, and the most natural assumption is that they indicate authorship. Some modern critics have made a desperate effort to read David out of the picture. But there is every reason to accept, and no substantial reason to question, that the book of Psalms is largely the work of David. The New Testament recognizes it as such.

Thus we speak of the Psalms as the psalms of David, because he was the principal writer or compiler. (Similarly, we refer to the book of Proverbs as the proverbs of Solomon, even though not all of them were written by him.) It is generally accepted that a few psalms were in existence before David's time and formed the nucleus of a hymnal for worship. This was greatly enlarged by David, added onto from generation to generation, and brought to completion, it is thought, in its present form by Ezra.

David was a warrior of great bravery, a military genius, and a brilliant statesman who led his nation to its pinnacle of power. He was also a poet and a musician, and he loved God with all his heart.

David's creation of the Psalms was in reality a far grander accomplishment than his creation of the kingdom. The book of Psalms is one of the noblest monuments of the ages and has outlasted David's original kingdom by more than two millennia.

In the Psalms the real character of David is portrayed. And in the Psalms God's people generally see a pretty fair picture of themselves, of their struggles, their sins, their sorrows, their aspirations, their joys, their failures, and their victories.

David has earned the undying gratitude of millions upon millions of God's redeemed people for the Psalms.

Jesus was very fond of the Psalms. He said that many things in the Psalms referred to Him (Luke 24:44). So thoroughly did they become a part of Him that in His dying agonies on the cross He quoted from them (22:1; Matthew 27:46; 31:5; Luke 23:46).

Of the 283 quotations from the Old Testament in the New Testament, 116 (more than 40 percent) are from the Psalms.

Classification of the Psalms

From very ancient times, the Psalms have been divided into five books. This division is already found in the Hebrew Bible and the Septuagint, perhaps in imitation of the five books of the Pentateuch. Within these five books of psalms there are some further subgroups.

The Psalms Were Written to Be Sung

The Bible is full of singing—singing as an act of worship, singing as an expression of gratitude, even singing to express sorrow and lament.

- At the dawn of creation "the morning stars sang together, and all the angels of God shouted for joy" (Job 38:7).
- Moses sang and taught the people to sing (Exodus 15; Deuteronomy 32).

Musical Instruments

The Israelites had stringed instruments (harp and lyre), wind instruments (flute, pipe, horn, trumpet), and instruments to be beaten (tambourine and cymbal). David had an orchestra of 4000, for which he made the instruments (1 Chronicles 23:5).

- **Harp:** The harp seems to have been a vertical, angular instrument, larger in size, louder, and lower in pitch than the lyre.
- **Lyre:** It is generally accepted that the lyre was a ten-stringed, rectangular zither.
- **Flute:** The flute, or shepherd's pipe, was made of reeds and was used both for entertainment and for calming the sheep.
- **Pipe:** The pipe (chalil) was a double-reed instrument and is the biblical equivalent of the modern oboe.
- **Horn:** A horn, or shofar, was originally a ram's horn without a mouthpiece. It was used chiefly as a signal instrument in both religious and secular ceremonies.
- **Trumpet:** Jewish historian Josephus has described the trumpet as a straight tube, "a little less than a cubit long," its mouthpiece wide and its body expanding into a bell-like ending.
- **Tambourine:** The tambourine was a small drum made of a wooden hoop and probably two skins, without any jingling contrivance such as the modern tambourine has.
- **Cymbal:** The only permanent percussive instrument in the temple orchestra was the cymbal. In Psalm 150 two types of cymbals are mentioned. The larger clashing cymbals were played with two hands. The resounding cymbals were much smaller and were played with one hand—the cymbals being attached to the thumb and the middle finger.

THE FIVE DIVISIONS OF THE BOOK OF PSALMS

		Smaller Groups of Psalms	Notes
Book I	Psalms 1–41	[no groups]	
Book II	Psalms 42–72	Psalms of Sons of Korah, 42–49	Miktam is probably a musical or literary term
		Miktam Psalms, 56–60	
Book III	Psalms 73–89	Psalms of Asaph, 73–83	
Book IV	Psalms 90–106	[no groups]	
Book V	Psalms 107–150	Hallel Psalms, 113–118	Hallel = praise
		Songs of Degrees, 120–134	Pilgrim songs
		Psalms of Thanksgiving, 135–139	
		Psalms of Protection, 140–143	
		Hallelujah Psalms, 146–150	Hallelujah = praise the Lord

Statements in the Psalms that in the New Testament are explicitly said to refer to Christ

- "You are my Son; today I have become your Father" (2:7; Acts 13:33).
- "You put everything under his feet" (8:6; Hebrews 2:6–10).
- "Because you will not abandon me to the grave, nor will you let your Holy One see decay" (16:10; Acts 2:27).
- "My God, my God, why have you forsaken me?" (22:1; Matthew 27:46).
- "He trusts in the LORD; let the LORD rescue him" (22:8; Matthew 27:43).
- "They have pierced my hands and my feet" (22:16; John 20:25).
- "They divide my garments among them and cast lots for my clothing" (22:18; John 19:24).
- "Here I am, I have come . . . to do your will, O my God" (40:7–8; Hebrews 10:7).
- "Even my close friend, whom I trusted, he who shared my bread, has lifted up his heel against me" (41:9; John 13:18).
- "Your Throne, O God, will last for ever and ever" (45:6; Hebrews 1:8).
- "Zeal for your house consumes me" (69:9; John 2:17).
- "They put gall in my food and gave me vinegar for my thirst" (69:21; Matthew 27:34, 48).
- "May another take his place of leadership" (109:8; Acts 1:20).
- "The LORD says to my Lord: 'Sit at my right hand until I make your enemies a footstool for your feet'" (110:1; Matthew 22:44).
- "The LORD has sworn and will not change his mind: 'You are a priest forever, in the order of Melchizedek'" (110:4; Hebrews 7:17).
- "The stone the builders rejected has become the capstone" (118:22; Matthew 21:42).
- "Blessed is he who comes in the name of the LORD" (118:26; Matthew 21:9).

See further under 2 Samuel 7 and Matthew 2:22.

- Israel sang on the journey to the Promised Land (Numbers 21:17).
- Deborah and Barak sang praise to God (Judges 5).
- David sang with all his heart (Psalm 104:33).
- Hezekiah's singers sang the words of David (2 Chronicles 29:28–30).
- Two choirs sang when the walls of Jerusalem were finished (Nehemiah 12:42).
- Jesus and the disciples sang at the Last Supper (Matthew 26:30).
- Paul and Silas sang in prison (Acts 16:25).
- In heaven, 10,000 times 10,000 angels sing, and the whole redeemed creation joins in the chorus (Revelation 5:11–13). In heaven everybody will sing — and will never tire of singing.

Liturgical and Musical Notations in the Psalms

The meaning of a number of Hebrew terms used in the titles of the Psalms is not clear, for example, *miktam* (Psalms 16, 56–60) and *maskil* (Psalm 32 and others). These terms are very ancient and predate the Septuagint.

The word *selah* occurs 71 times in the Psalms; it is found at intervals in some Psalms as well as at the end. It may be a musical marker, but its meaning is not clear.

Leading Ideas in the Psalms

Trust is the foremost idea in the book, repeated over and over. Whatever the occasion, joyous or terrifying, it drove David straight to God. Whatever his weaknesses, David literally lived in God.

Praise was always on his lips. David was always asking God for something and always thanking Him with his whole soul for the answers to his prayers.

Rejoice is another favorite word. David's unceasing troubles could never dim his joy in God. Over and over he cries, "Sing," or "Shout for joy." Psalms is a book of devotion to God.

Unfailing love (KJV, mercy) occurs hundreds of times. David often spoke of the justice, righteousness, and anger of God, but God's unfailing love was what he always returned to.

Messianic Psalms

Many psalms, written 1000 years before Christ, contain statements that are wholly inapplicable to any person in history other than Christ. These are called messianic psalms. (The Greek word *Christ* is the same as the Hebrew *Messiah*.) Some references to David seem to point forward to the coming great King in David's family. Besides passages that are clearly messianic, there are many expressions that seem to be veiled foreshadowings of the Messiah.

The most clearly messianic psalms are

Psalm 2:	The deity and universal reign of the Messiah
Psalm 8:	Through the Messiah, humanity is to rule creation
Psalm 16:	His resurrection from the dead
Psalm 22:	His suffering
Psalm 45:	His royal bride (the church) and his eternal throne

Psalm 69:   His suffering
Psalm 72:   The glory and eternity of His reign
Psalm 89:   God's oath that Messiah's throne will be without end
Psalm 110:   Eternal King and Priest
Psalm 118:   His rejection by His nation's leaders
Psalm 132:   Eternal heir to David's throne

Book I: Psalms 1 to 41

Ps. 1 | DELIGHT IN GOD'S WORD

The book of Psalms opens with an exaltation of God's Word. If David so loved the few writings that then constituted God's Word, how much more should we love that same Word, which has now been brought to completion. (Other psalms of the Word are Psalm 19 and Psalm 119.)

Blessed are those who derive their understanding of life from God's Word rather than from their worldly neighbors. Happiness and prosperity are theirs; not so the wicked. Over and over the godly and the wicked are contrasted.

Note, too, that the book of Psalms begins with a blessing or beatitude, like the Sermon on the Mount (Matthew 5:3–12). Its first word is "Blessed."

Some of David's "Beatitudes" in the Psalms:

- "Blessed is the man . . . [whose] delight is in the law of the LORD" (1:1–2).
- "Blessed are all who take refuge in him" (2:12).
- "Blessed is he whose transgressions are forgiven" (32:1).
- "Blessed is the nation whose God is the LORD" (33:12).
- "Blessed is the man who takes refuge in him" (34:8).
- "Blessed is he who has regard for the weak" (41:1).
- "Blessed are those who dwell in your house" (84:4).
- "Blessed are those whose strength is in you" (84:5).
- "Blessed is the man you discipline, O LORD" (94:12).

Trees growing by the waterfall of Caesarea Philippi. "He is like a tree planted by streams of water." (Psalm 1:3)

- "Blessed is the man who fears the LORD" (112:1).
- "Blessed are they who keep his statutes and seek him with all their heart" (119:2).

Ps. 2 | A HYMN OF THE COMING MESSIAH

This is the first of the messianic psalms (see pp. 300–301). It speaks of His deity (v. 7) and His universal reign (v. 8).

Ps. 3 | DAVID'S TRUST IN GOD

Written at the time of Absalom's rebellion (2 Samuel 15). A most remarkable example of peaceful trust at a very trying time. David could sleep because "the LORD sustains me."

Ps. 4 | AN EVENING PRAYER

Another hymn of trust, as David prepared to sleep, so to speak, at the bosom of God. It speaks of trust in God (v. 5), gladness of heart (v. 7), peace of mind (v. 8), communion with God in our bedtime meditations (v. 4), confidence that God is watching (v. 8).

Ps. 5 | A MORNING PRAYER

Beset by treacherous enemies, David prays and shouts for joy, confident that God will protect him. David must have had many enemies. He refers to them again and again. Many of the most magnificent psalms came out of David's troubles.

Ps. 6 | THE CRY OF A BROKEN HEART

In time of sickness, bitter grief, tears, humiliation, shame, and reproach by enemies, perhaps on account of David's sin with Bathsheba (2 Samuel 11). This is the first of the penitential psalms (see on Psalm 32).

Ps. 7 | ANOTHER PRAYER FOR PROTECTION

In grave danger, David protests his own righteousness (see on Psalm 32). Cush, in the title, possibly may have been one of Saul's officers in pursuit of David (see on Psalm 54).

Ps. 8 | MAN THE CROWN OF CREATION

Worldwide praise will be brought about under the Messiah, in the day of His triumphant reign (Hebrews 2:6–9). Jesus quoted verse 2 as referring to an incident in His own life (Matthew 21:16).

Ps. 9 | THANKS FOR VICTORIES

Victories over enemies, national and individual. God sits as King forever. Let the nations realize that they are only human, only creatures. Praise and trust God.

This psalm, together with Psalm 10, forms an acrostic: the initial letters of successive verses follow the order of the Hebrew alphabet. It may have been used as an aid to memory. Other acrostic psalms are Psalms 25, 34, 37, 111, 112, 119, 145.

Ps. 10 | DAVID'S PRAYER FOR HELP

Prayer for help in the face of wickedness, oppression, and robbery, apparently within his own realm. Wickedness troubled David greatly, especially defiance of God. To David, as to other Bible writers, there are just two kinds of people: the righteous and the wicked—though many try to be both.

Pss. 11–13 | PREVALENCE OF WICKEDNESS

The wicked walk on every side. David is overwhelmed by his wicked enemies, almost to the point of death. But he nevertheless trusts in God and sings for joy. Psalms such as these seem to belong to the period when David was hiding from Saul (1 Samuel 18–26).

Ps. 14 | UNIVERSAL SINFULNESS

This psalm is almost the same as Psalm 53. It is quoted in Romans 3:10–12. Unbelievers are here called fools: widespread wickedness shows what fools people are. For as sure as there is a God, there will be a day of reckoning, a day of judgment for the wicked. But living among the wicked are God's people, for whom Judgment Day will be a day of joy.

Ps. 15 | TRUE CITIZENS OF ZION

The true citizens of Zion are righteous, truthful, just, and honest. Thomas Jefferson called this psalm "the picture of a true gentleman."

Ps. 16 | RESURRECTION OF THE MESSIAH

David appears to be speaking of himself, yet words about the coming Davidic King find their way into David's mouth (v. 10) and are quoted in the New Testament as a prediction of Jesus' resurrection (Acts 2:27). Verses 8 and 11 are especially magnificent.

Ps. 17 | A PRAYER FOR PROTECTION

Overwhelmed by enemies, David looks to God. He proclaims his own innocence and trusts in God. Surrounded by people who love this world, David set his heart on the world beyond (vv. 14–15).

Ps. 18 | DAVID'S HYMN OF THANKSGIVING

David wrote this psalm after years of running from Saul, when he had become king and had the kingdom firmly established. He attributed it all to God, his Strength, Rock, Fortress, Deliverer, Support, Refuge, Shield, Horn, Stronghold. One of the best psalms.

Head of nations (vv. 43–45) was only partially true of David; it looked forward beyond the time of David to the throne of David's greater descendent, Christ, the Messiah. This psalm is repeated in 2 Samuel 22.

Ps. 19 | NATURE AND THE WORD

The wonder and glory of creation, and the perfection and power of God's Word. The God of nature is made known to humanity through His written Word. These thoughts about God's Word are greatly expanded in Psalm 119. The closing prayer (vv. 13–14) is one of the best prayers in the whole Bible. God's Word is perfect, sure, true; it gives joy and is sweeter than honey.

Ps. 20 | A SONG OF TRUST

This would appear to be a battle hymn, sung while setting up the military banners, with a prayer for victory as David entered battle. His trust was not in chariots and horses (v. 7), but in the Lord.

Ps. 21 | THANKS FOR VICTORY

Victory after the battle which had been prayed for in Psalm 20. It refers to David, but it seems also to contain a messianic hint in its reference to the eternal nature of the King's reign (v. 4).

Ps. 22 | A PSALM OF THE CRUCIFIXION

This is a cry of anguish from David. But, though written 1000 years before the days of Jesus, it is so vivid a description of the crucifixion of Jesus that one would almost think that the writer was personally present at the cross: Jesus' dying words (v. 1), the sneers of His enemies (vv. 7–8), His hands and feet pierced (v. 16), His garments divided (v. 18). Some of these statements are not applicable to David, nor to any known event in history except the crucifixion of Jesus.

Ps. 23 | THE SHEPHERD PSALM

One of the best-loved chapters in the Old Testament. David may have composed this psalm while he was yet a shepherd boy, watching his father's flocks on the very same field where, 1000 years later, the angel choir announced the birth of Jesus.

Ps. 24 | THE KING'S ARRIVAL IN ZION

This psalm may have been written when the ark of the covenant was brought to Jerusalem (2 Samuel 6:12–15). Maybe we will sing it on that great day when the King of glory comes again.

Ps. 25 | PRAYER OF A SIN-OPPRESSED SOUL

David had periods of depression, brought on by his sins and troubles. There are many petitions here that we would do well to make our own. Read this psalm often.

Shepherd with his flock. "The Lord is my shepherd, I shall lack nothing." (Psalm 23:1)

Ps. 26 | DAVID PROTESTS HIS INTEGRITY

This psalm is very different from the preceding one; David speaks positively and forcefully about his own integrity. (See on Psalm 32.)

Ps. 27 | DEVOTION TO GOD'S HOUSE

God was the strength of David's life. David trusted God fearlessly. He loved to sing, and to pray, and to wait on the Lord.

Ps. 28 | A PRAYER

A prayer, with thanksgiving for its being answered. David was without hope, except for God. He depended on Him and rejoiced in Him.

Ps. 29 | THE VOICE OF GOD

The voice of God in the thunderstorm, sometimes frightening. The image is suggestive of the terrifying, cataclysmic events at the end of the world.

Ps. 30 | DEDICATION OF DAVID'S PALACE

Written after David had conquered Jerusalem and made it his capital (2 Samuel 5:11; 7:2). David had often been near death, but God brought him through. He would sing and praise God forever.

Ps. 31 | A SONG OF TRUST

David, in constant danger, trouble, grief, or humiliation, always implicitly trusted in God. Jesus quoted His dying words from this psalm (v. 5; Luke 23:46).

Ps. 32 | A PSALM OF PENITENCE

This psalm was occasioned, no doubt, by David's sin with Bathsheba (2 Samuel 11–12). He can find no words to express his shame and humiliation. Yet this is the same David who repeatedly avowed his righteousness (Psalms 7:3, 8; 17:1–5; 18:20–24; 26:1–14).

How can we reconcile these paradoxical features of David's life? (1) It is possible that the statements about his righteousness were made before David made this dreadful mistake. (2) In most things David was righteous. (3) Most important, there is a vast difference between a sin of weakness and willful, habitual sin. A good person may sin and yet be a good person. David's remorse showed that was true in his case. That is quite different from wicked people who purposely, willfully, and habitually flout all the laws of decency. (See on 2 Samuel 11.)

Augustine is said to have had this psalm written on the wall in front of his bed, where it was always in view, reading it incessantly, weeping as he read.

Other penitential psalms are Psalms 6, 25, 38, 51, 102, 130, 143.

Ps. 33 | A PSALM OF JOY AND PRAISE

David speaks of a "new song" (v. 3; the same words are found in Psalm 40:3; 96:1; 98:1; 144:9). There are old songs that will never grow old; but to God's people, as they travel along life's road, there are again and again new deliverances and new joys that put new meaning into old songs, all of which will be taken up into the great new outbursts of joy at the dawn of heaven's glories (Revelation 5:9; 14:3).

Ps. 34 | DAVID'S THANKS FOR DELIVERANCE

In every trouble David went straight to God in prayer, and after every deliverance he went instantly to God in thanks and praise. What a glorious thing to thus *live in God*. How that must please God. Someone has said, "Thank God for the starlight, and He will give you the moonlight; thank Him for the moonlight, and He will give you the sunlight; thank Him for the sunlight, and by and by He will take you where He Himself is the Light."

Ps. 35 | A CURSING PSALM

In this psalm David calls on God to act, to help him against his enemies. But God is silent and seems far away (vv. 22–23). What makes it even more difficult for David is that those who seek to kill him are his enemies without cause: they hate him without reason (v. 19). This was not an isolated experience (see Psalms 38:19; 69:4; 109:3; 119:78, 86, 161; and Lamentations 3:52). Jesus applied the same thought to Himself in John 15:25: "But this is to fulfill what is written in their Law: 'They hated me without reason.'"

Pss. 36–37 | TRUST IN GOD

Psalm 36. The wickedness of people contrasted with the mercy and faithfulness of God.

Psalm 37. This is one of the best-loved psalms. David, always puzzled by the fact that wickedness seems to prevail, here states his philosophy as to how to live among wicked people: do good, trust God, don't worry.

Ps. 38 | A PSALM OF BITTER ANGUISH

This is one of the penitential psalms (see on Psalm 32). It seems that David was suffering from a loathsome disease, caused by his sin, which led even his closest friends and nearest relatives to stay away from him. His enemies, by contrast, had multiplied and become very bold. It shows how the "man after God's own heart" sometimes went to the depths in sorrow and humiliation for his sin.

Ps. 39 | THE FRAILTY AND VANITY OF LIFE

Jeduthun (also mentioned in the titles of Psalms 62 and 77) was one of David's three music leaders; the other two were Asaph and Heman (1 Chronicles 16:37–42). He was also the king's seer, according to 2 Chronicles 35:15.

Ps. 40 | PRAISE FOR A GREAT DELIVERANCE

The Law of God was in his heart (v. 8), yet David was utterly crushed by his sins (v. 12). The last part of this psalm is the same as Psalm 70. This psalm would seem to contain a messianic reference (vv. 7–8; see Hebrews 10:5–7).

Ps. 41 | A PRAYER FOR DELIVERANCE

This psalm is thought to belong to the time when David's son Absalom tried to usurp the throne (2 Samuel 15) at a time when David's sickness (vv. 3–8) created an opportunity for the plot to mature. The close friend (v. 9) must have been Ahithophel, the Old Testament Judas (2 Samuel 15:12; John 13:18).

The Psalms of Vengeance

There are seven psalms in which the psalmist hurls God's curses on his enemies, in no uncertain terms (Psalms 6; 35; 59; 69; 83; 109; 137). For example,

May his days be few; . . .

May his children be fatherless
*   and his wife a widow.*

May his children be wandering beggars;
*   may they be driven from their ruined homes.*

May a creditor seize all he has;
*   may strangers plunder the fruits of his labor.*

May no one extend kindness to him
*   or take pity on his fatherless children.*

May his descendants be cut off,
*   their names blotted out from the next generation.*

May the iniquity of his fathers be remembered before the LORD;
*   may the sin of his mother never be blotted out.*

                                              —PSALM 109:8–14

These psalms are also called the imprecatory psalms because the psalmist showers imprecations (curses) on his enemies. Fourteen other psalms include an imprecatory prayer (for example, 3:7; 5:10; 7:14–16). The expression of hatred and the desire for vindication are also found in the prayers of Jeremiah (11:18–20; 15:15–18; 17:18; 18:19–23; 20:11–12) and Nehemiah (6:14; 13:29).

What are we to do with these psalms that seem to squarely contradict Jesus' command to love our enemies (Luke 6:27–28)? Some people simply write them off. They feel that the Old Testament preaches law and vengeance, whereas the New Testament teaches love for God and neighbor. Therefore these psalms have no place in the Christian life.

But they forget that Jesus took the two great commandments ("Love the Lord your God with all your heart and . . . soul and . . . mind . . . and . . . your neighbor as yourself," Matthew 22:37–39) directly from the Old Testament (Deuteronomy 6:5; Leviticus 19:18). And His command to love our enemies is also found in the Old Testament:

> "Do not gloat when your enemy falls; when he stumbles, do not let your heart rejoice. . . . If your enemy is hungry, give him food to eat; if he is thirsty, give him water to drink" (Proverbs 24:17; 25:21).

And "an eye for an eye and a tooth for a tooth" (Exodus 21:24) is not, as is often assumed, a legalization of vengeance. Rather, it limits those who have been wronged to the recovery of actual damages rather than punitive damages. It is a humane law, designed to prevent an ever-escalating spiral of revenge.

The Old Testament already contains the key teachings of Jesus—and the New Testament clearly does not teach only "sweetness and light." Jesus condemned Korazin and Capernaum (Matthew 11:21–24) and severely criticized the leaders and the unbelief of the Jews (Matthew 7:23 [compare with Psalm 6:8]; Mark 11:14; 12:9). The apostles also had very strong words for heretics and evildoers (1 Corinthians 5:5; Galatians 1:8–9; 5:12; 2 Timothy 4:14 [compare with Psalm 62:12]; 2 Peter 2; 2 John 7–11; Jude 3–16).

The fact is that in *both* the Old and the New Testament we find the requirement to love *as well as* the requirement to hate evil.

What bothers us about the imprecatory psalms is their *concreteness*. "God hates sin but loves the sinner" was as true in the Old Testament as it is now. But in the Old Testament, sin and evil are not viewed as abstractions; rather, they exist in their concrete manifestations—real actions by real people.

In the Old Testament, God's people, the nation of Israel, is a concrete reality. The nation lives in a specific place, the Promised Land. The temple is an actual place where God is present. And above all, the God of Israel is known through His concrete acts in history, foremost among them the Exodus from Egypt. And just as God's presence is known through His concrete acts in history, *so evil is known through its concrete manifestations.*

In the Lord's Prayer, we ask, "Deliver us from the evil one" (or, "from evil"). The psalmists make the same request, but in more concrete form: deliver us from evil by delivering us from the evil *ones*. In the New Testament, evil and sin oppose the coming of God's kingdom. In the Old Testament, evil and sin oppose the kingdom of God's people, Israel. But in both cases, sin and evil are an assault on God Himself by opposing that which is dearest to His heart.

The imprecatory psalms are a constant reminder that evil is not an abstraction but a stark, everyday reality. They remind us that God hates evil, not in the abstract, but in people's actions or failure to act—whether these are actions of unbelievers or of God's own people. (Note how often the psalmists cry out for forgiveness for their own sins!)

Book II: Psalms 42 to 72

Pss. 42–43 | THIRST FOR THE HOUSE OF GOD

These two psalms form one poem, describing the desire for God's house on the part of someone in exile in the Hermon region, east of the Jordan (42:6), among ungodly and hostile people.

The Sons of Korah, mentioned in the titles of Psalms 42–49, 84, 85, 87, and 88, were a family of Levites, organized by David into a musical guild (1 Chronicles 6:31–48; 9:19, 22, 33).

Ps. 44 | A CRY OF DESPAIR

A cry of despair in a time of national disaster, when their army, it seems, had been overwhelmingly defeated.

Ps. 45 | WEDDING SONG OF A KING

The psalmist shifts from speaking to the king to addressing God, who sits on an eternal throne. This psalm may, in part, have reference to David or Solomon. But some of its statements are wholly inapplicable to either, or to any other human sovereign. It surely seems to be a song of the Messiah, anticipating the marriage of the Lamb (Revelation 19:7).

Ps. 46 | ZION'S BATTLE SONG

This psalm is the basis for Luther's famous hymn "A Mighty Fortress Is Our God," the song of the Reformation.

Pss. 47–48 | GOD REIGNS

God is King. Zion is the city of God. This God is our God forever. God is on the throne—let the earth rejoice!

Israelite fortress of Arad. "The Lord Almighty is with us; the God of Jacob is our fortress." (Psalm 46:1)

Pss. 49–50 | THE VANITY OF RICHES

God is the owner of the earth and everything in and on it. In giving to God we merely return that which is His own. These psalms, which speak of the vanity of life, since death comes to all, are similar to Psalm 39.

Ps. 51 | PRAYER FOR MERCY

A penitential psalm (see on Psalm 32), written in the aftermath of David's sin with Bathsheba (2 Samuel 11–12). "Create in me a pure heart" (v. 10) is a prayer we all would do well to pray constantly.

Ps. 52 | DAVID'S TRUST IN GOD

David's trust in God is contrasted with the wicked boastfulness of his enemy Doeg (1 Samuel 21:7; 22:9). David is confident that he will be delivered.

Ps. 53 | UNIVERSAL SINFULNESS OF MEN

This psalm is similar to Psalm 14. It is quoted in Romans 3:10–12. The meaning of the terms *mahalath* and *maskil* in the title is not known, although they are most likely musical or literary terms.

Ps. 54 | DAVID'S CRY TO GOD

Written when the Ziphites told Saul where David was hiding (1 Samuel 26). Other psalms composed while David was on the run from Saul are Psalm 7(?), 34, 52, 54, 56, 57, 59, 63(?), and 142.

Ps. 55 | BETRAYED BY FRIENDS

Like Psalm 41, this seems to belong to the time of Absalom's rebellion and to refer specifically to Ahithophel (vv. 12–14; 2 Samuel 15:12–13). It is a preview of the betrayal of Jesus by Judas. David trusts in God.

Ps. 56 | PRAYER FOR DELIVERANCE

Like Psalm 34, a prayer for deliverance from the Philistines (1 Samuel 21:10–15). David used his own resources to the limit, even faking insanity. Yet he prayed and trusted in God for the result. Psalm 34 is his song of thanks for his escape.

Ps. 57 | DAVID'S PRAYER

David's prayer in the cave of Adullam, while hiding from Saul (1 Samuel 22:1; 24:1; 26:1). His heart was fixed on trusting God (v. 7).

Ps. 58 | DESTRUCTION OF THE WICKED

The day of retribution is sure. David complained much about the prevalence of wickedness. And he repeated over and over that evil does not pay — in the long run. It is still so.

Ps. 59 | ANOTHER OF DAVID'S PRAYERS

David's prayer when Saul sent soldiers to entrap David at home (1 Samuel 19:10–17). But again David trusted in God. Another golden poem.

Ps. 60 | A PSALM OF DISCOURAGEMENT

Written at a time when the war with the Syrians and Edomites (2 Samuel 8:3–14) was not going well. Other psalms in time of national reverses are Psalm 44, 74, 79, and 108. David's prayer was answered (2 Samuel 8:14).

Ps. 61 | A HYMN OF CONFIDENCE

Prayed while David apparently was away from home on some distant expedition (v. 2), or possibly at the time of Absalom's rebellion.

Ps. 62 | A POEM OF IMPASSIONED DEVOTION

Devotion to God and unwavering trust in Him. David had a lot of trouble but never failed to trust in God.

Ps. 63 | A HYMN OF THE WILDERNESS

David's thirst for God. It seems to belong to the period when David was in the wilderness of Engedi (1 Samuel 24), fleeing from Absalom, but confident of restoration.

Ps. 64 | PRAYER FOR PROTECTION

Prayer for protection from plots of secret enemies. David is confident that through God he will triumph.

Ps. 65 | A SONG OF THE SEA AND THE HARVEST

God crowns the year with goodness. The earth shouts for joy with its abundant crops.

Ps. 66 | A SONG OF NATIONAL THANKSGIVING

Praise God, fear God, sing, rejoice—God keeps His eye on the nations.

Ps. 67 | A MISSIONARY PSALM

In anticipation of the Good News of the Gospel encircling the earth. Let the nations sing for joy!

Ps . 68 | A BATTLE MARCH

The battle march of God's victorious armies. This psalm has been the favorite of many in times of persecution.

Ps. 69 | A PSALM OF SUFFERING

Like Psalm 22, this psalm provides glimpses of the suffering Messiah. It is quoted in the New Testament (vv. 4, 9, 21–22, 25; John 2:17; 15:25; 19:28–30; Acts 1:20; Romans 11:9; 15:3).

Ps. 70 | AN URGENT CRY FOR HELP

God never failed David. The believer's joy in God in a time of persecution. About the same as the latter part of Psalm 40.

Ps. 71 | A PSALM OF OLD AGE

A retrospective on a life of trust, beset by troubles and enemies all the way, but with his joy in God undimmed.

Ps. 72 | THE GLORY AND GRANDEUR OF MESSIAH'S REIGN

This is one of Solomon's psalms (the other one is Psalm 127). Solomon's kingdom was at the pinnacle of its glory. We may think that this psalm was, in part, a description of his own peaceful and glorious reign. But some of its statements, and its general tenor, can allude only to the kingdom of One greater than Solomon. (See further pp. 458–61.)

Book III: Psalms 73 to 89

Ps. 73 | PROSPERITY OF THE WICKED

The solution to the problem of the prosperity of wicked people is this: consider their final end. This is one of Asaph's psalms (the others are 50, 74–83). Asaph was David's song leader (1 Chronicles 15:16–20; 16:5). Hezekiah's choirs sang Asaph's psalms (2 Chronicles 29:30).

Ps. 74 | NATIONAL DISASTER

Jerusalem was in ruins (vv. 3, 6–7). This psalm may refer either to the time of Shishak's invasion (1 Kings 14:25) or to the Babylonian captivity.

Ps. 75 | GOD IS JUDGE

The certain destruction of the wicked and the certain triumph of the righteous on the day when the earth shall be dissolved.

Ps. 76 | THANKS FOR A GREAT VICTORY

This psalm seems to refer to the destruction of Sennacherib's army by the Angel of God at Jerusalem (2 Kings 19:35).

Pss. 77–78 | HISTORICAL PSALMS

A review of God's marvelous works in His dealings with Israel. The contrast between God's mighty works and Israel's habitual unfaithfulness and disobedience.

Pss. 79–80 | NATIONAL DISASTER

Like Psalm 74, these psalms belong to a time of great disaster, such as the invasion of Shishak (1 Kings 14:25), or the fall of the northern kingdom, or the Babylonian captivity.

Pss. 81–82 | ISRAEL'S WAYWARDNESS

The cause of Israel's troubles lies in their turning their back on God. If they had only listened to God, things would have been different. Unjust judges must share in the blame, since they have forgotten their responsibility to the supreme Judge.

Ps. 83 | A PRAYER FOR PROTECTION

Prayer for protection from a conspiracy of federated nations: Edomites, Arabians, Moabites, Ammonites, Amalekites, Philistines, and others.

Ps. 84 | GOD'S HOUSE

The blessedness of devotion to God's house. "Better is one day in your courts [the temple courts] than a thousand elsewhere" (v. 10). Nearness to God is what matters—also for the church.

Pss. 85–86 | THANKSGIVING AND A CRY FOR MERCY

Thanksgiving for return from captivity, and a prayer for the restoration of the land and for a better future. It is also a prayer for mercy: even though the psalmist is godly, yet he is in need of forgiveness.

Ps. 87 | ZION

God's love for Zion. What is said here of Zion more truly applies to the church. Our birth in Zion (our birth into God's people) is recorded in heaven (v. 6).

Ps. 88 | A LIFELONG SUFFERER

Prayer of a shut-in suffering from a prolonged and terrible disease. One of the saddest of the psalms.

Ps. 89 | GOD'S OATH

God's solemn promise that David's throne will be forever. A magnificent psalm. Ethan, in the title, was one of David's song leaders (1 Chronicles 15:17).

Book IV: Psalms 90 to 106

Ps. 90 | THE ETERNITY OF GOD

The eternity of God and the shortness of human life. Since this is a psalm of Moses, who lived 400 years before David, it may have been the first psalm to be written. Moses wrote other songs (Exodus 15; Deuteronomy 32). Rabbinic tradition assigns the 10 psalms that follow, 91–100, also to Moses.

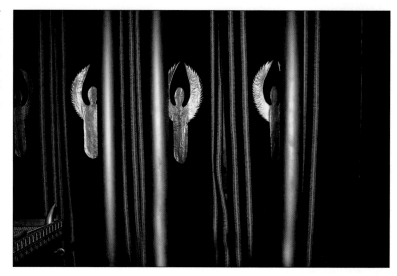

Reconstruction of the Tabernacle curtain embroidered with angels. "For He will command His angels concerning you to guard you in all your ways." (Psalm 91:11)

Ps. 91 | A HYMN OF TRUST

One of the best-loved psalms. Magnificent! Amazing promises of security to those who trust God. Read it often.

Ps. 92 | A SABBATH HYMN OF PRAISE

This hymn seems to look back to the Sabbath (the seventh day) of Creation, and forward to the age of the eternal Sabbath. The wicked will perish, the godly flourish.

Pss. 93–94 | THE MAJESTY OF GOD

God's majesty and the destruction of the wicked. The power, holiness, and eternity of God's throne. From everlasting, God reigns forevermore. Wickedness is prevalent in this world, but in the end, God's justice prevails: the doom of the wicked is certain. This is one of the most frequent themes of Scripture.

Pss. 95–97 | THE REIGN OF GOD

Continuing the idea of Psalm 93, these are called "theocratic psalms" because they relate to the sovereignty and rule of God (theocracy = "rule by God"; compare democracy, "rule by the people"), with hints of the kingly reign of the coming Messiah.

Psalm 95. Sing! Rejoice! God is King; let us kneel before Him. We are His people; let us listen to His voice. Verses 7–11 are quoted in Hebrews 3:7–11 as words of the Holy Spirit.

Psalm 96. Sing! Be joyful. Be thankful. Praise God. It will be a day of triumph for God's people when He comes to judge the world. Let the heavens be glad and the earth rejoice. The Day of Judgment is on the way.

Psalm 97. The Lord comes. The earth is moved. A coronation anthem that refers, possibly, to both the first and the second comings of Christ.

Ps. 98 | A SONG OF JUBILANT JOY

Since this is a new song (v. 1), it may be one of those sung in heaven (Revelation 5:9–14). (See also under Psalm 33.)

Pss. 99–100 | GOD REIGNS—WORSHIP HIM

Psalm 99. God reigns. God is holy, let the nations tremble. God loves justice and righteousness. He answers prayer.

Psalm 100. Praise God. His love endures forever, and His faithfulness through all generations.

Ps. 101 | A PSALM FOR RULERS

This may have been written when David ascended the throne. It states the principles on which he would base his reign.

Ps. 102 | A PRAYER OF PENITENCE

Written in a time of terrible affliction, humiliation, and reproach (see on Psalm 32). The eternity of God (vv. 25–27) is quoted in Hebrews 1:10–12 as applying to Christ.

Ps. 103 | A PSALM OF GOD'S MERCY

Thought to have been written in David's old age, this psalm summarizes God's dealings with him. One of the best-loved psalms.

Ps. 104 | A NATURE PSALM

God the Creator and caretaker of all the world. This psalm reminds us of Jesus' words, "Are not two sparrows sold for a penny? Yet not one of them will fall to the ground apart from the will of your Father" (Matthew 10:29).

Pss. 105–106 | TWO HISTORICAL PSALMS

A poetic summary of Israel's history that focuses especially on their miraculous delivery out of Egypt.

Book V: Psalms 107 to 150

Pss. 107–109 | GOD'S UNFAILING LOVE AND JUSTICE

Psalm 107. The wonders of God's love in His dealings with His people and in His management of the works of nature.

Psalm 108. This seems to be one of David's battle songs. It is almost identical with parts of Psalms 57 and 60.

Psalm 109. Vengeance on God's adversaries. One of the cursing psalms (see on Psalm 35). In the New Testament, verse 8 is applied to Judas, who betrayed Jesus.

Ps. 110 | THE ETERNAL REIGN OF THE COMING KING

This psalm cannot refer to any person in history except Christ; yet it was written 1000 years before Christ (vv. 1, 4). Quoted in the New Testament as referring to Christ (Matthew 22:44; Acts 2:34; Hebrews 1:13; 5:6).

Pss. 111–112 | SONGS OF PRAISE

Psalm 111. The majesty, honor, righteousness, unfailing love, justice, faithfulness, truth, holiness, and eternity of God.

Psalm 112. The blessedness of those who fear God and are righteous, merciful, gracious, and kind to the poor, who love the ways and Word of God, and whose heart is fixed on God. Everlasting blessedness is theirs.

Pss. 113–118 | THE HALLEL PSALMS

"Hallel" means praise. The Hallel psalms were sung in families on the night of the Passover: Psalms 113 and 114 at the beginning of the meal, Psalms 115–118 at the close of the meal. They must have been the hymns that Jesus and His disciples sang at the Last Supper (Matthew 26:30).

Psalm 113. A song of praise. Begins and ends with "Hallelujah," which means "praise God."

Psalm 114. A song of the Exodus, recalling the wonders and miracles of Israel's deliverance out of Egypt and the beginning of the Passover feast. The earth, sea, rivers, mountains, and hills trembled at God's presence.

Psalm 115. The Lord is the only God. Blessed are His people, they who trust in Him and not in the gods of the nations. Idols are no smarter than they who make them. Our God is God — where are the gods of the nations? Our God will bless us, and we will bless His name forevermore.

Psalm 116. A song of gratitude to God for deliverance from death and temptation, and for repeated answers to prayer. One of the best psalms.

Psalm 117. A summons to the nations to accept the Lord. Quoted as such in Romans 15:11. This is the middle chapter in the Bible — and the shortest. Yet it contains the essence of the Psalms.

Psalm 118. This was the farewell hymn Jesus sang with His disciples as He left the Passover on His way to Gethsemane and Calvary (Matthew 26:30). It embodied a prediction of His rejection (vv. 22, 26; Matthew 21:9, 42).

Ps. 119 | THE GLORIES OF GOD'S WORD

With 176 verses, this is the longest chapter in the Bible. Every verse mentions the Word of God under one or another of these names: law, statutes, righteous laws, decrees, commands, precepts, word, ways (KJV, also testimony, ordinances), except vv. 90, 121, 122, 132.

It is an acrostic, or alphabetic, psalm. Its has 22 stanzas, each beginning with a letter of the Hebrew alphabet, in sequence. What is more, each stanza has eight lines, and each of the eight lines in a stanza begins with the same letter (see on Psalm 9).

Also called songs of degrees, or pilgrim songs. Believed to have been designed to be sung a capella by pilgrims traveling up to the religious feasts at Jerusalem. The roads that led to Jerusalem from all directions went literally uphill (see p. 56), hence "going up to Jerusalem" and songs of "ascent." Or they may have been sung going up the 15 steps to the men's court in the temple.

Psalm 120. A prayer for protection by one who lived among deceitful and treacherous people, far away from Zion.

Psalm 121. Pilgrims may have sung this hymn as they first caught sight of the mountains surrounding Jerusalem.

Psalm 122. This may have been what the pilgrims sang as they neared the temple gate within the city walls.

Psalm 123. And this may have been sung inside the temple courts as the pilgrims lifted their eyes to God in prayer for His mercy.

Psalm 124. A hymn of thanksgiving and praise for repeated national deliverance in times of fearful danger.

Psalm 125. A hymn of trust. As the mountains are round about Jerusalem, so God is round about His people.

Psalm 126. A song of thanksgiving for return from captivity. The people felt as if they were dreaming. (See Psalm 137.)

Psalm 127. This seems like a combination of two poems, one about temple building, the other about family building. This is one of Solomon's two psalms (the other is Psalm 72).

Psalm 128. A wedding song. A continuation of the second half of Psalm 127. Godly families are the basis of national prosperity.

Psalm 129. Israel's prayer for the overthrow of her enemies, who, generation after generation, had harassed her.

Psalm 130. Keeping our eyes on God. A cry for mercy. This is one of the penitential psalms. (See on Psalm 32.)

Psalm 131. A psalm of humble, childlike trust in God. The psalmist's soul is stilled and quieted, as a child with his mother.

The snow-capped peak of Mount Hermon. Moisture in any form is a blessing in a dry climate: "It is as if the dew of Hermon were falling on Mount Zion. For there the LORD bestows his blessing, even life forevermore." (Psalm 133:3)

Psalm 132. A poetic restatement of God's unbreakable promise to David of an eternal dynasty.

Psalms 133–134. A psalm of brotherly love and of life forevermore, and a psalm about those Levites who "work the night shift" in the temple.

Pss. 135–139 | PSALMS OF THANKSGIVING

Psalm 135. A song of praise for God's wonderful works in nature and in history.

Psalm 136. This seems to be an expansion of Psalm 135, about God's mighty works of creation and His dealings with Israel, arranged for antiphonal singing. "His love endures forever" occurs in every verse. It is called a Hallel (praise) psalm, was sung at the opening of the Passover, and was a favorite temple song (1 Chronicles 16:41; 2 Chronicles 7:3; 20:21; Ezra 3:11).

Psalm 137. A psalm of the captivity, sung by exiles in a foreign land longing for home. They expect sure retribution for those who took them captive. This is not a psalm of thanksgiving, but its counterpart, Psalm 126, written after they got back from Babylon, is full of gratitude.

Psalm 138. A song of thanksgiving, apparently on the occasion of some notable answer to prayer.

Psalm 139. God's universal presence and infinite knowledge. He knows our every thought, word, and act—nothing is hidden from Him. The closing sentence is one of the most needed prayers in the whole Bible.

Pss. 140–143 | PRAYERS FOR PROTECTION

Psalm 140. David had many enemies—who drove him ever closer to God. The ultimate destruction of the wicked.

Psalm 141. Another one of David's prayers for protection against being driven to sin.

Psalm 142. One of David's prayers in early life, while hiding in a cave from Saul (1 Samuel 22:1; 24:3).

Psalm 143. David's penitent cry for help and guidance, possibly when he was being pursued by Absalom (2 Samuel 17, 18).

Pss. 144–145 | SONGS OF PRAISE

Psalm 144. One of David's battle songs. His army may have chanted hymns such as this as they moved into battle.

Psalm 145. David may have had his army sing a hymn such as this after a battle, in gratitude for victory.

Pss. 146–150 | HALLELUJAH PSALMS

These last five psalms are called Hallelujah psalms, since each begins and ends with "Hallelujah," which means "praise the Lord." The word also appears often in other psalms.

The grand outburst of Hallelujahs with which the book of Psalms comes to a climactic close is carried over to the end of the Bible itself and is echoed in the heavenly choirs of the redeemed (Revelation 19:1, 3–4, 6).

Psalm 146. God reigns. As long as I live I will praise God.

Psalm 147. Let all creation praise God. Sing unto God with thanksgiving. Let Israel and Zion praise God.

Psalm 148. Let the angels praise God. Let the sun, moon, and stars praise God. Let the heavens shout, "Hallelujah!"

Psalm 149. Let the saints praise God. Let them sing for joy. Let Zion rejoice. Hallelujah!

Psalm 150. Hallelujah! Praise God with trumpet and harp. Let everything that has breath praise God. Hallelujah!

Proverbs

Wise Sayings about the Practical Affairs of Everyday Life

Trust in the LORD *with all your heart*
and lean not on your own understanding;
in all your ways acknowledge him,
and he will make your paths straight.
Do not be wise in your own eyes;
fear the LORD *and shun evil.*

—PROVERBS 3:5−7

"The fear of the LORD *is the beginning of wisdom,*
and knowledge of the Holy One is understanding."

—PROVERBS 9:10

Like the book of Psalms and the Pentateuch, this book is divided into five parts: the way of Wisdom, by Solomon (chaps. 1–9); the main collection of the proverbs of Solomon (chaps. 10–24); Hezekiah's collection of Solomon's proverbs (chaps. 25–29); the words of Agur (chap. 30); the words of King Lemuel (chap. 31).

Thus, most of the proverbs are ascribed to Solomon. Solomon appears to be to the book of Proverbs what David is to the book of Psalms: the main author. The difference is that Psalms is a book of devotion, while Proverbs is a book of practical ethics.

Solomon

As a young man, Solomon had a consuming passion for knowledge and wisdom (1 Kings 3:9–12). He became the literary prodigy of the world of his day. His intellectual attainments were the wonder of the age. Kings came from the ends of the earth to hear him. He lectured on botany and zoology. He was a scientist, a political ruler, a businessman with vast enterprises, a poet, moralist, and preacher. (See on 1 Kings 4 and 9.)

What Is a Proverb?

A proverb is a brief, popular statement that expresses a general truth ("A stitch in time saves nine"). Most of the book consists of unconnected proverbs. But the Hebrew word for "proverb" can also include longer, connected exhortations, such as chapter 2. Most of the proverbs in the book of Proverbs express a contrast ("Many are the plans in a man's heart, but it is the LORD's purpose that prevails," 19:21) or a statement with an elaboration or consequence ("Listen to advice and accept instruction, and in the end you will be wise," 19:20). Many proverbs use figurative language ("Pleasant words are a honeycomb, sweet to the soul and healing to the bones," 16:24).

Proverbs are designed primarily for teaching, especially the young—compact, practical statements that stick in the mind. They cover a wide range of subjects: wisdom, righteousness, fear of God, knowledge, morality, chastity, diligence, self-control, trust in God, proper use of riches, consideration for the poor, control of the tongue, kindness toward enemies, choice of companions, training of children, honesty, idleness, laziness, justice, helpfulness, cheerfulness, common sense, and more.

Proverbs and Experience

This book aims to inculcate virtues that the Bible insists on throughout. Over and over and over, in all the Bible, God has supplied us with a great abundance of instruction as to how He wants us to live, so that there can be no excuse for our missing the mark.

The teachings of this book of Proverbs are not expressed with the words "This is what the LORD says," as in the Law of Moses, where the same things are taught as a direct command of God. Rather, they are given as coming out of the experience of a man who tried out and tested just about everything that people are involved in. Moses had said, "These things are the commandments of God." Solomon here says, "Experience shows that God has commanded us those things that are best for us—the essence of human wisdom lies in keeping God's commandments." Proverbs are like an owner's manual for life. An owner's manual explains what needs to be done to avoid serious problems, but it does not guarantee that nothing will ever go wrong.

God, in the long record of His revelation of Himself and His will, resorted, it seems, to every possible method to convince us—not only by commandment and by precept, but also by example—that God's commandments are worth living by.

Solomon's fame was a sounding board that carried his voice to the ends of the earth and made him an example to all the world of the wisdom of God's ideas.

This book of Proverbs has been called one of the best guidebooks to success that a young person can follow.

There is also an incidental element of humor in the book of Proverbs, especially in the images some of the proverbs evoke: "Even a fool is thought wise if he keeps silent, and discerning if he holds his tongue" (17:28). "Better to live on a corner of the roof than share a house with a quarrelsome wife" (21:9). There is also a delightful description of the effects of too much alcohol (23:31–35).

Prov. 1–9 | THE PROVERBS OF SOLOMON (BOOK I)

Chapter 1. The Object of the Book. To promote wisdom, discipline, understanding, righteousness, justice, equity, prudence, knowledge, discretion, learning, guidance (vv. 2–7). What splendid words! Wisdom (found 41 times in the book) is more than knowledge and insight; it includes skill in living a morally sound life. It can also include skill at a craft (in Exodus 31:3, for example, "skill" is the same word as "wisdom").

The starting point is the fear of God (v. 7); next, paying attention to parental instruction (vv. 8–9) and avoiding bad companions (vv. 10–19).

Wisdom cries aloud her warnings, but if these warnings are ignored, the consequences are dire indeed (vv. 20–33).

Chapter 2. Wisdom must be sought wholeheartedly. The place to find it is God's Word (v. 6). Then follows a warning against the adulteress (KJV, strange woman), a warning that is often repeated. While wisdom is personified in Proverbs as a pure and morally beautiful woman, the adulteress is the opposite of wisdom—she is folly personified.

Chapter 3. A superb and beautiful chapter: kindness, truth, long life, peace, trust in God, honoring God with our material possessions, prosperity, security, happiness, blessedness.

Chapter 4. Wisdom is "the principal thing"—it is supreme (NIV). Therefore, get wisdom! The path of the righteous grows brighter and brighter, while the path of the wicked will grow darker and darker.

Chapter 5. Marital joy and loyalty. A warning against unchaste love. Solomon had many women, but advised against it. He seemed to think the one-wife arrangement better (vv. 18–19). Chapters 5–7 speak about loose women. Judging from the space Solomon devotes to them, there must have been a good many such women then (Ecclesiastes 7:28). In the background is always the imagery of God-given wisdom that leads to moral living (personified in the wife of one's youth) and the pursuit of folly that leads to disaster (personified in the adulteress).

Chapter 6. Warnings against questionable business obligations, laziness, cunning hypocrisy, haughtiness, lying, trouble-making, disregard of parents, illegitimate love.

Chapter 7. Warning against the adulteress whose husband is away from home. Again, an indirect warning against folly and the betrayal of wisdom.

Chapters 8–9. Wisdom, personified as a woman, inviting everyone to share in the bounty of her banquet, in contrast to lustful women who call out to the simple, "Stolen water is sweet; food eaten in secret is delicious!" (9:13–18).

Prov. 10–24	THE PROVERBS OF SOLOMON (BOOK 2)

Chapter 10. Terse contrasts between wise men and fools, righteous and wicked, diligent and lazy, rich and poor.

Plowing: "From the strength of an ox comes an abundant harvest" (Proverbs 14:4), but "a sluggard does not plow in season, so at harvest he looks but finds nothing" (20:4).

Chapter 11. Dishonest business practices (KJV, a false balance; NIV, dishonest scales) are an abomination to God. A beautiful woman without discretion is like a jewel in a swine's snout. A generous person will prosper.

Chapter 12. A worthy woman is the glory of her husband. Lying lips are an abomination to God. The diligent will receive precious blessings. No harm befalls the righteous.

Chapter 13. He who guards his mouth guards his life. Hope deferred makes the heart sick. The way of the transgressor is hard. Walk with wise men, and you will be wise.

Chapter 14. He who has a short temper will do foolish things. He who is slow to anger is a person of great understanding. Fear of God is a fountain of life. Tranquility of heart gives life to the body. He who oppresses the poor shows contempt for their Maker.

Chapter 15. A soft answer turns away anger. A gentle tongue is a tree of life. The prayer of the upright is God's delight. A wise son brings joy to his father.

Chapter 16. People make plans, but God directs their steps. Pride comes before destruction. Gray hair is a crown of splendor—it is attained in a life of righteousness.

Chapter 17. To have a fool for a son brings grief. A cheerful heart is a good medicine. Even a fool, when he keeps his mouth shut, is considered wise.

Chapter 18. A fool's mouth is his destruction. Death and life are in the power of the tongue. Before honor goes humility. He who finds a wife finds a good thing.

Chapter 19. A prudent wife is from God. He who has pity on the poor lends to God—God will repay him. Many are the plans in people's hearts, but God's purpose prevails.

Chapter 20. Wine is a mocker. It is an honor for a man to avoid strife, but every fool is quick to quarrel. Lips that speak knowledge are a rare jewel. Diverse weights and dishonest scales are an abomination to God.

Chapter 21. It is better to live on a corner of the roof than share a house with a quarrelsome wife. Whoever shuts his ear to the cry of the poor will not be heard when he cries out. Whoever guards his tongue keeps his soul from trouble. The horse is prepared for battle, but the victory is of God.

Chapter 22. A good name is to be preferred over great riches. Train a child in the way he should go, and when he is old he will not turn from it. A generous man will be blessed. See a man skilled in his work? He shall serve before kings.

Chapter 23. Do not wear yourself out to get rich. Listen to your father and mother; let them rejoice in you when they are old. Do not withhold discipline from a child. Listen to your father, who gave you life, and do not despise your mother when she is old. A rather humorous description of the effects of too much drink (vv. 29–35).

Chapter 24. In a multitude of counselors is safety. I went by the field of a lazy person; it was overgrown with thorns. An honest answer is like a kiss on the lips. A little sleep, a little slumber, and poverty will come on you like a bandit.

Prov. 25–29 | **THE PROVERBS OF SOLOMON (BOOK 3)**

This group of Solomon's proverbs (chaps. 25–29) is here said to have been copied by men of King Hezekiah (25:1). Hezekiah lived more than 200 years

Coneys, one of four creatures described in Proverbs 30:24 – 28 as "small, yet . . . extremely wise."

after Solomon. Solomon's manuscript may have been worn out, and a basic item in Hezekiah's reform movement was a renewed interest in God's Word (2 Kings 18).

Chapter 25. A word fitly spoken is like apples of gold in baskets of silver. If your enemy hungers, feed him; if he thirsts, give him something to drink; and God will reward you (see Luke 6:35).

Chapter 26. See a man wise in his own conceit? There is more hope for a fool than for him. A lying tongue hates those whom it has wounded.

Chapter 27. Do not boast about tomorrow, for you know not what a day may bring forth (see Matthew 6:34). More proverbs about fools.

Chapters 28 – 29. He who hides his eyes from the poor shall have many a curse. A fool vents all his anger, but a wise man keeps it back and stills it. Further dissertations on fools.

Prov. 30 | THE WORDS OF AGUR

It is not known who Agur was—perhaps a friend of Solomon. Solomon liked his proverbs so well that he thought it worthwhile to include them in his own book.

Prov. 31 | THE SAYINGS OF KING LEMUEL

A mother's counsel to a king. Lemuel may have been another name for Solomon. If so, then Bathsheba was the mother who taught him this beautiful poem.

Few mothers have raised finer boys. As a young man, Solomon's character was as splendid as any in history. In his old age, however, he did depart from what he had been taught—contrary to his own proverb (22:6). The chapter is about mothers rather than kings.

The book of Proverbs ends with a superb acrostic poem in praise of the wife of noble character: "A wife of noble character who can find? She is worth far more than rubies."

Ecclesiastes

The Meaninglessness of Earthly Life

"Meaningless! Meaningless!"
says the Teacher.
"Utterly meaningless!
Everything is meaningless."

—Ecclesiastes 1:2

Vanity of vanities, saith the Preacher, vanity of vanities; all is vanity.

—Ecclesiastes 1:2 KJV

Solomon, the author of this book, was in his day the most famous and most powerful king in the world, noted for his wisdom, riches, and literary attainments (see on 1 Kings 4 and 9).

Meaningless! Meaningless! Everything Is Meaningless

This is the theme of the book. It also embodies an attempt to give a philosophic answer as to how best to live in a world where everything appears to be meaningless. The book contains many things of superb beauty and transcendent wisdom. But it is radically different from the Psalms: its predominant mood is one of unutterable melancholy.

David, Solomon's father, in his long and hard struggle to build the kingdom, was forever shouting, "Rejoice," "Shout for joy," "Sing," "Praise God." Solomon, sitting in peaceful security on the throne David had built, with honor, splendor, power, and living in almost fabled luxury, was the one man in all the world whom people would have thought to be happy. Yet his unceasing refrain was, "Everything is meaningless." And the book, a product of Solomon's old age, leaves us with the distinct impression that Solomon was not a happy man. The word "meaningless" occurs 37 times!

Eternity

Eternity (3:11) is a more correct translation than "world" (KJV) and may suggest the key thought of the book: "Eternity in people's hearts." In the inmost depths of our nature we have a longing for things eternal. But back then, God had not yet revealed very much about things eternal.

In various places in the Old Testament there are hints and glimpses of the future life, and Solomon seems to have had some vague ideas about it. But it was Christ who brought life and immortality to light (2 Timothy 1:10). Christ, by His resurrection from the dead, gave the world a concrete demonstration of the certainty of life beyond the grave. And Solomon, who lived almost 1000 years before Christ, could not possibly have the same feeling of sureness about the life beyond that Christ later gave the world.

But Solomon saw earthly life at its best. Not a whim but he was able to gratify it. He seems to have made it his chief business in life to see how good a time he could have. And this book, the result of Solomon's experience, has running through it a note of unspeakable pathos: All is "vanity and vexation of spirit" (KJV) or, as we would say, All is meaningless and a chasing after wind (NIV).

How Can Such a Book Be God's Word?

God stands behind the writing of this book. Not all of Solomon's ideas were God's ideas (see note on 1 Kings 11). But the general, self-evident lessons of the book are from God. God gave Solomon wisdom and unparalleled opportunity to observe and explore every avenue of earthly life. And after much research and experiment, Solomon concluded that on the whole, humanity found little solid happiness in life, and in his own heart he found an unutterable yearning for something beyond himself. Thus the book, in a way, is humanity's cry for a Savior.

With the coming of Christ, the cry was answered. The vanity of life disappeared. Life is no longer meaningless but full of joy and peace. Jesus never used the word "meaningless." But He talked much of His joy, even under the shadow of the Cross. "Joy" is one of the key words of the New Testament. In Christ, humanity found the desire of the ages: life—full, abundant, joyous, glorious life.

Eccl. 1–4 | ALL IS VANITY

In a world where everything passes away and fails to satisfy, Solomon set himself to answer the question, What is the solution to the problem of life in such a world? The world is one of unending monotony. Solomon felt the meaninglessness of life and the emptiness and uselessness of his own vast works. Even wisdom, which Solomon sought so diligently and prized so highly, was disappointing. The pursuits and pleasures of humanity in general seemed to him to be merely a chasing after wind. And it was all made worse by the wickedness and cruelties of men.

The misnamed Colossae of Memnon — they are actually statues of Pharaoh Amenophis III of Egypt — stand forlornly in the plain, guarding nothing. The temple that once stood behind them is long gone: an apt illustration of the ultimate meaninglessness of power and glory.

"Remember Him before the silver cord is severed or the golden bowl is broken." (Ecclesiastes 12:6)

Eccl. 5–10 | MISCELLANEOUS PROVERBS

Solomon's favorite form of literature was proverbs. In these chapters he intersperses proverbs with various observations relating to the general theme of the book. In 7:27–28 there may be an oblique reference to Solomon's experience with his 700 wives and 300 concubines (1 Kings 11:1–11). One would guess, from 7:26–28, that he had had some difficulty in holding the faithless women of his court in line.

Eccl. 11–12 | SOLOMON'S ANSWER

Solomon's answer to his question, What is it that we can do in a world where all is meaningless? is scattered throughout the book and is summed up at the close: eat, drink, rejoice, do good, live joyfully with your wife, do with full commitment what your hands find to do, and above all, fear God, keeping your eyes on the day of final judgment. With all his complaints about the nature of creation, Solomon had no doubt as to the existence and justice of the Creator. God is mentioned at least 40 times in this book — more frequently than vanity or meaningless/meaninglessness!

Interpretations

On the face of it, the poem is a song of praise to the joys of married life. Its essence is to be found in its tender and devoted expressions of the intimate delights of married love. Even if it is no more than that, it is worthy of a place in God's Word, for marriage was ordained of God (Genesis 2:24). And human happiness and welfare depend to a very large extent on proper mutual attitudes in the intimate relationship of married life.

However, both Jews and Christians have seen deeper meanings in this poem. Jews read it at Passover as an allegory referring to the Exodus, when God took Israel to Himself as His bride. His love for Israel then is here exemplified in the spontaneous love of a great king for a humble young woman. In the Old Testament, Israel is called God's wife (Jeremiah 3:1; Ezekiel 16, 23).

Christians have usually regarded it as a song of Christ and the church. In the New Testament the church is called the bride of Christ (Matthew 9:15; 25:1; John 3:29; 2 Corinthians 11:2; Ephesians 5:23; Revelation 19:7; 21:2; 22:17). In this view, human marriage is a counterpart to and foretaste of the relationship between Christ and His church.

How could a man with a harem of 1000 women have a love for any one of them that would be fit to be a portrayal of Christ's love for the church? A number of Old Testament saints were polygamists. Even though God's Law was against it from the beginning, as Christ so plainly stated, in Old Testament times God nevertheless seems to have accommodated Himself, in measure, to prevailing customs. Kings generally had many wives. It was one of the prerogatives and status symbols of royalty. And Solomon's devotion to this lovely girl seems to be genuine and unmistakable. Also, he was a king in the family that was to produce the Messiah. And it seems not unfitting that his marriage should, in a sense, prefigure the Messiah's eternal marriage to His bride. The joys of this song, we think, will find their zenith in the hallelujahs of the Lamb's marriage supper (Revelation 19:6–9).

An Outline of the Poem

It is not always easy to see who is speaking. The outline below is consistent with the content of the book, but other outlines are also possible. (It helps to mark in the Bible which verses belong to which of the three speakers, so that the poem can be read through in its entirety without interruptions.)

The King	The Bride (the Shulammite)	Chorus of Palace Women
Chapter 1: The bride expresses her love for the king, and the king for his bride.		
	1:2-4a	
		1:4b ("we rejoice . . . ")
	1:4c-7 ("How right . . .")	
		1:8
1:9–11		
	1:12–14	
1:15		

	1:16		
1:17			

Chapters 2–3: The bride thinks about the king both day and night.

	2:1		
2:2			
	2:3–13		
2:14–15			
	2:16–3:11		

Chapter 4: The king also cannot keep from thinking about his bride, who invites him into her garden of marital delights.

4:1–15			
	4:16		

Chapter 5: The bride remembers the delight of their union, and she is almost overwhelmed by her love for the king.

5:1a			
			5:1b
			("Eat, O friends . . .")
	5:2–8		
			5:9
	5:10–16		

Chapter 6:1–7:9a: The king's response to the bride's expression of her love; the bride's contentment.

			6:1
	6:2–3		
6:4–9			
			6:10
6:11–12			
			6:13a
6:13b–7:9a ("Why would you gaze . . .")			

Chapter 7:9b–8:14: The bride's frustration that social custom and the king's official duties limit the time she can spend with him. The final expression of love and commitment.

	7:9b–8:4 ("May the wine . . .")		
			8:5a
	8:5b–7 ("Under the tree . . .")		
	8:10–12		
8:13			
	8:14		

Mount Carmel.

The Prophets

Isaiah – Malachi

Originally, the term "prophet" was applied to individuals who provided significant military and judicial leadership — for example, Moses (Deuteronomy 18:15) and Deborah (Judges 4:4). It was also used of persons who had ecstatic experiences of contact with God (Numbers 11:24–29; 1 Samuel 19:20–24; 2 Kings 3:15) and of individuals who were protected by God in some special way (Abraham, Genesis 20:7; see also Psalm 105:15).

During the monarchy, prophets became advisers to the kings (1 Samuel 22:5; Isaiah 37:1–4; Jeremiah 37:16–17). There were at times many prophets: in the days of Ahab there were 400 (1 Kings 22:6).

The important early prophets (Samuel, Elijah, Elisha) did not leave behind any writings that have been preserved. They advised the king, and if necessary opposed him (Elijah and Ahab!), but it is the later, writing prophets who stand out most clearly as the voice of God in the face of the people's disobedience. They address not only the king but also the nation as a whole.

The prophets of Israel were individuals called by God to bring the people back to God. The office of prophet was not hereditary like that of priest or king. Prophets were chosen from many different walks of life, and the call was not an invitation but a divine appointment (see Amos 7:15).

The Prophets and the Covenant

The prophets were not merely preachers. They were the voice of the covenants God made with Abraham (Genesis 12, 15), with Israel at Mount Sinai (Exodus 24), and with David (2 Samuel 7).

These covenants were in effect treaties, with mutual obligations and with a clear statement of what would happen if the people kept the stipulations of the covenant and what would happen if they ignored them. Deuteronomy 28 outlines the curses and blessings that will result from disobedience and obedience. (Deuteronomy follows the format of Hittite treaties; see p. 166.)

Thus, when the prophets warn of the disasters that will befall Israel or Judah because of their disobedience, they are saying that the covenant warnings given hundreds of years before are about to be fulfilled. In the same way, since the covenant also specifies blessing as the reward for obedience, the prophets can promise blessing if the people turn back to God. The future is thus "contingent" upon the people's response to the message of the prophets—until a point of no return is reached.

But even then, the prophets can promise future blessing. God made the covenant because He loved Israel. That is why God will be faithful to the covenant, even if Israel is not—in fact, He will go beyond the terms of the covenant and replace it with a new covenant. This covenant will be written on people's hearts rather than on stone tablets (see the magnificent promises in Jeremiah 30–31, especially 31:31–37).

The prophets are thus the spiritual conscience of the nation. They are appointed to remind kings, priests, and people of their obligations to God and people.

There were many prophets in Israel who never wrote or whose writings have not been preserved. There also appears to have been an order of prophets, with its own schools (see p. 207). The prophets whose writings we still have (and the two great prophets about whom we read in the books of Kings and Chronicles, Elijah and Elisha) were very conscious of speaking in the name of the Lord. The constantly reiterated, solemn introduction to their message is, "This is what the Lord says" or "The word of the Lord came to me."

The false prophets, of which there were apparently many, remembered the promises of blessing in the covenant and reassured the people that God would never allow His temple and Jerusalem, His city, or Israel, His people, to be destroyed. They conveniently forgot that the covenant also spelled out the curse that disobedience would bring on the people and the land. They also forgot that, not religious rituals, but the love of God for His people and of His people for Him were the foundation of the covenant. Religious rituals were significant only if they were the expression of an inner attitude. God can get along very well without a temple and sacrifices—but in His love He greatly desires the love of His people.

When the prophets spoke up for justice and advocated concern for the poor, they did not say these things because they had come to a more enlightened vision than their contemporaries. Rather, they appealed to the ancient covenant, of which justice and social concern were an essential part: for example, concern for widows and orphans, for the poor, and for foreigners, as well as the provisions of the Year of Jubilee, which (if kept) would make it impossible for any family to descend permanently into landless poverty.

To:	Judah	Israel	Nineveh	Babylon	Captives from Judah	Edom
Early Prophets						
Samuel (1 Samuel) 1050–1000 B.C.	✓					

Prophet	Date						
Elijah (I Kings 17– 2 Kings 2)	875–848 B.C.		✓				
Elisha (I Kings 19: 2 Kings 2–13)	848–797 B.C.		✓				
Micaiah (I Kings 22)	849 B.C.		✓				
Assyrian Age							
Jonah	770 B.C.			✓			
Amos	760 B.C.		✓				
Hosea	760–730 B.C.		✓				
Isaiah	740–700 B.C.	✓					
Micah	737–690 B.C.	✓					
Babylonian Age							
Nahum	650 B.C.			✓			
Habakkuk	630 B.C.	✓					
Zephaniah	627 B.C.	✓					
Jeremiah	627–580 B.C.	✓					
Daniel	605–530 B.C.				✓		
Ezekiel	593–570 B.C.					✓	
Persian Age							
Haggai	520 B.C.	✓					
Zechariah	520–518 B.C.	✓					
Joel	500 B.C.	✓					
Obadiah	500 B.C.						✓
Malachi	443 B.C.	✓					

—Based on John H. Walton, *Chronological and Background Charts of the Old Testament*

The Prophets of Israel and Judah

The chart on pp. 336–37 shows that the early prophets and the earliest writing prophets addressed Israel (the northern kingdom), which ceased to exist in 722 B.C. when the Assyrians destroyed Samaria. Beginning with Isaiah, the prophets addressed Judah, the southern kingdom.

(Note that the dates are approximate; especially the dates of Obadiah and Joel are uncertain.)

Isaiah

The Messianic Prophet

"Holy, holy, holy is the LORD Almighty;
the whole earth is full of his glory."

—ISAIAH 6:3

You will keep in perfect peace
   him whose mind is steadfast,
   because he trusts in you.

—ISAIAH 26:3

"Arise, shine, for your light has come,
and the glory of the LORD rises upon you."

—ISAIAH 60:1

(For a summary of Isaiah's prophecies about the Messiah, see p. 359.)

Isaiah is called the messianic prophet because he was so thoroughly imbued with the idea that his nation was to be a nation through whom one day a great and wonderful blessing would come from God to all nations: the Messiah, sent from God, who would bring peace, justice, and healing to the whole world. He was continually focused on the day when that great and wonderful work would be done.

The New Testament says that Isaiah "saw the glory of Christ, and spoke of him" (John 12:41).

The Man Isaiah

Isaiah was a prophet of the southern kingdom, Judah, at the time the northern kingdom, Israel, had already been destroyed by the Assyrians.

Isaiah lived during the reigns of kings Uzziah, Jotham, Ahaz, and Hezekiah. God called him in the year of Uzziah's death, but he may have received some of his visions earlier (see on 6:1). According to Jewish tradition, Isaiah was executed by King Manasseh. We may tentatively place his active ministry at about 740–700 B.C.

Rabbinic tradition has it that Isaiah's father, Amoz (not the same as Amos the prophet), was a brother of King Amaziah. This would make Isaiah a first cousin of King Uzziah and a grandson of King Joash, and thus of royal blood, a man of the palace.

Isaiah wrote other books, which have not been preserved to us: a *Life of Uzziah* (2 Chronicles 26:22) and a *Book of the Kings of Israel and Judah* (2 Chronicles 32:32). He is quoted in the New Testament more than any other prophet. What a mind he had! In some of his rhapsodies he reaches heights unequaled even by Shakespeare, Milton, or Homer.

An unsubstantiated Jewish tradition (The Ascension of Isaiah) claims that Isaiah was sawed in half during the reign of King Manasseh of Judah. Hebrews 11:37 ("they were sawed in two") may refer to Isaiah's death.

The Assyrian Background of Isaiah's Ministry

The Assyrian Empire had been expanding for 150 years before the days of Isaiah. As early as 840 B.C., Israel, under King Jehu, had begun to pay tribute to Assyria. While Isaiah was still a young man (734 B.C.), Assyria took away the population of the northern part of Israel. Thirteen years later (721 B.C.), Samaria fell, and the rest of Israel was forced into exile. Then, a few years later, Sennacherib of Assyria came into Judah, destroyed 46 walled cities, and took 200,000 captives with him. Finally, in 701 B.C., when Isaiah was an old man, the Assyrians were stopped before the walls of Jerusalem by an angel of God (2 Chronicles 32:21). Thus Isaiah's whole life was spent under the shadow of the threat of Assyria, and he himself witnessed the ruin of his entire nation at their hands, except Jerusalem.

ARCHAEOLOGICAL NOTE: The Isaiah Scroll. All original copies of Bible books, as far as is known, have been lost. Our Bible is made from copies of copies. Until the invention of printing in A.D. 1454, these copies were made by hand.

Old Testament books were written in Hebrew (and a few sections in Aramaic). New Testament books were written in Greek. The oldest known, extant, complete Bible manuscripts date from the 4th and 5th centuries A.D. They are in Greek, containing, for the Old Testament, the Septuagint, which was a Greek translation of the Hebrew Old Testament made in the 3rd century B.C. (See pp. 489–90, 988.)

Sennacherib prism. During the days of Isaiah, the Lord delivered Jerusalem from the Assyrian siege of Jerusalem (701 B.C.) referred to not only in the Bible but also in this prism of Sennacherib.

The oldest known existing Hebrew manuscripts of Old Testament books were made about A.D. 900. These contain what is called the Masoretic Text of the Hebrew Old Testament, from which our English translations of Old Testament books have been made. The Masoretic Text comes from a comparison of all available manuscripts, copied from previous copies by many different lines of scribes. In these manuscripts there is so little variation that Hebrew scholars are in general agreement that our present Bible text is essentially the same as that in the original books themselves.

Then, in 1947, at Ain Fashkha, about seven miles south of Jericho and one mile west of the Dead Sea, some wandering Arab Bedouins, carrying goods from the Jordan Valley to Bethlehem and searching for a lost goat in a wadi (stream or river bed) that empties into the Dead Sea, came upon a partially collapsed cave, in which they found a number of crushed jars from which ends of scrolls protruded. The Bedouins pulled out the scrolls, took them along, and passed them on to St. Mark's Syrian Orthodox Convent in Jerusalem, who turned them over to the American Schools of Oriental Research. These and other scrolls that were later found in that same vicinity, Qumran, are known as the Dead Sea Scrolls.

> *The wolf will live with the lamb,*
> *the leopard will lie down with the goat,*
> *the calf and the lion and the yearling together;*
> *and a little child will lead them. . . .*
> *They will neither harm nor destroy on all my*
> *holy mountain, for the earth will be full of the*
> *knowledge of the LORD*
> *as the waters cover the sea.*
>
> *—Isaiah 11:6, 9*

One of these scrolls was identified as the book of Isaiah, written 2000 years ago—1000 years older than any known manuscript of any Hebrew Old Testament book. It is a scroll, written in ancient Hebrew script on parchment, about 24 feet long, made up of sheets of about 10 by 15 inches, sewn together. It was made in the 2nd century B.C.

This and the other scrolls had originally been carefully sealed in earthenware jars. Evidently they were part of a Jewish library that had been hidden in this isolated cave in time of danger, perhaps during the Roman conquest of Judea.

Bible scholars have concluded that the Dead Sea Scrolls of Isaiah are essentially the same as the book of Isaiah in our Bible—a voice from 2000 years ago confirming the integrity of our Bible. In all, 22 copies of the book of Isaiah have been found at Qumran, though not all are complete.

CONTEMPORARY KINGS OF JUDAH		
Uzziah	792–740 B.C.	A good king with a long and successful reign
Jotham	750–732	A good king; mostly coregent with Uzziah
Ahaz	735–716	Very wicked (see under 2 Chronicles 28)
Hezekiah	716–687	A good king (see under 2 Chronicles 29)
Manasseh	697–643	Very wicked (see under 2 Chronicles 33)
CONTEMPORARY KINGS OF ISRAEL		
Jeroboam II	793–753 B.C.	A long, prosperous, but idolatrous reign
Zechariah	753–752	Assassinated
Shallum	752	Assassinated
Menahem	752–742	Extremely brutal
Pekahiah	742–740	Assassinated by Pekah
Pekah	752–732	Under Pekah the northern part of Israel was taken into captivity (734 B.C.)
Hoshea	732–722	The last king of Israel; Samaria fell in 721 B.C.

The Grand Achievement of Isaiah's Life

Isaiah's greatest achievement was the deliverance of Jerusalem from the Assyrians. It was through his prayer, and by his advice to King Hezekiah, and by the direct miraculous intervention of God, that the dreaded Assyrian army was sent home in disarray from before the walls of Jerusalem. (See chapters 36–37.) Sennacherib, king of Assyria, lived 20 years after this, but he never again marched against Jerusalem.

Isa 1 | THE APPALLING WICKEDNESS OF JUDAH

This frightful indictment seems to belong to the middle period of Hezekiah's reign, after the fall of the northern kingdom, when the Assyrians had invaded Judah and had carried away a large part of its population, so that Jerusalem alone was left (vv. 7–9). Hezekiah's reforms had barely scratched the surface of the rotten life of the people. The dreaded Assyrian tornado was drawing ever closer and closer.

But it made no difference. The diseased nation, instead of cleansing itself, only paid more meticulous attention to the camouflage of devotion to religious services. Isaiah's scathing denunciation of their hypocritical religiosity (vv. 10–17) reminds us of Jesus' merciless condemnation of the scribes and Pharisees (Matthew 23). The point is that making a show of religiosity is of no avail for "Sodom" (v. 10). Only genuine repentance and obedience would save them (vv. 16–23). Then Isaiah turns from this sickening picture to the day of Zion's purification and redemption, when the wicked will be left to burn like a dried-up oak tree (vv. 24–31).

Isa. 2–4 | A PRE-VISION OF THE CHRISTIAN AGE

These three chapters seem to be an expansion of the closing thought of chapter 1. They deal with the future glory of Zion in contrast to God's judgment on the wicked. The allusion to idols and foreign customs (2:6–9) may locate this vision in the reign of Ahaz. The peace described may also prophesy conditions in the New Jerusalem after Christ's return, when the wicked have been judged (Revelation 21).

Zion will be the center of world civilization in an era of universal and endless peace (2:2–4). This passage of magnificent optimism was uttered at a time when Jerusalem was a veritable cesspool of filth. Whatever, whenever, wherever that happy age is to be, it will be the inheritance of God's people, with the wicked left out. (See further under 11:6–9.)

Coming judgment for idol worshipers (2:5–22). Suffering and exile lie ahead for Judah (3:1–15)—even for the fashionable ladies of Jerusalem (3:16–26). Their experience will be like that of the ladies of luxury in Samaria, described in Amos 4:1–3.

Seven women to one man (4:1), because the men will have been killed in war.

The coming "Branch" (4:2–6). This is Isaiah's first mention of the future Messiah. "The Branch" would be a new shoot coming out of the stump of the fallen family tree of David (11:1; 53:2; Jeremiah 23:5; 33:15; Zechariah 3:8; 6:12). He would be the one to purge the filth from Zion and make her a blessing to the world.

Isa. 5 | A SONG OF THE VINEYARD

A sort of funeral dirge. After centuries of most extraordinary care, God's vineyard—His nation—turns out to be fruitless and disappointing, so it is now to be abandoned. Jesus' parable of the vineyard (Matthew 21:33–45) seems to be an echo of this parable. The sins Isaiah denounces here especially are greed, injustice, and drunkenness. The vast estates of the rich, accumulated by robbery of the poor, soon would become wasteland.

A **bath** (v. 10) is six gallons (22 liters), a **homer** is six bushels, and an **ephah** is only one-tenth of a homer. The harvest does not even recover the investment in seed.

Draw sin along (v. 18) as if sin and wickedness were their most prized possessions; they scoff at the idea that God would punish them.

Distant nations (vv. 25–30): the mighty nations are like docile dogs to God—He whistles and they come—the Assyrians in Isaiah's own time; the Babylonians who, 100 years later, destroyed Jerusalem; and the Romans, who in A.D. 70 struck the death-blow to Jewish national existence.

Isa. 6 | ISAIAH'S CALL

There is difference of opinion as to whether this vision came before the visions of the first five chapters. The dates mentioned in the book are in chronological sequence (6:1; 7:1; 14:28; 20:1; 36:1). This indicates that the book follows a general chronological order, but not necessarily in all particulars. Isaiah, in later life, probably rearranged visions he had written down at various times of his long ministry, guided in part by the sequence of thoughts, so that some chapters may antedate preceding chapters.

Also, opinion varies as to whether this was Isaiah's original call or a summons to a special mission. The statement in 1:1 indicated that some of his ministry was in the days of Uzziah, while this call came in the year of Uzziah's death. This may imply that he had already done some earlier preaching and that this call was God's authorization for Isaiah's ministry in the future.

The particular task to which Isaiah was called seems, on the face of it, to have been the bringing about of the final hardening of the nation so as to ensure its destruction (vv. 9–10). But God's purpose, of course, was not to harden the nation but rather to bring it to repentance in order to save it from destruction. This is clearly illustrated in the case of Jonah, whose announcement of the destruction of Nineveh caused the city to repent. Isaiah's whole ministry—with its marvelous visions and climaxed by one of the most stupendous miracles of the ages—was, so to speak, God's frantic waving of a red flag to halt the nation in its mad sweep toward the precipice of destruction. But when a nation sets itself against God, even His wondrous mercy results only in further hardening.

For how long? (v. 11): how long shall this hardening process go on? The answer is bleak: until the land is ruined and the people are gone (vv. 11–12).

Tenth (v. 13): a remnant will be left, but it will in its turn also be destroyed. This was uttered in 735 B.C. Within a year, the northern portion of Israel was taken away by the Assyrians. Within 14 years, all the rest of the northern kingdom had fallen (721 B.C.), and Judah (roughly a "tenth") alone was left. Another 100 years, and Judah was also destroyed (586 B.C.).

Isa. 7 | THE CHILD "IMMANUEL"

The occasion of this prophecy was the invasion of Judah by the kings of Syria and Israel. They first attacked Judah separately (2 Chronicles 28:5–6), then together (2 Kings 16:5). Their object was to replace Ahaz with another king (v. 6). Ahaz appealed to the king of Assyria for help (2 Kings 16:7). The king of Assyria responded with an invasion of Syria and the northern part of Israel and took their populations with them into exile in 734 B.C. (2 Kings 15:29; 16:9).

In the early part of this Syro-Israelite attack on Jerusalem, Isaiah assured Ahaz that the attack would fail, Syria and Israel destroyed, and Judah saved. The **65 years** (v. 8) is thought to cover the period from the first deportation of Israel (734 B.C.) to the settlement of foreigners in the land by Esarhaddon around 670 B.C. (2 Kings 17:24; Ezra 4:2).

The virgin and her son Immanuel (vv. 10–16). This is spoken of as a "sign" intended to give the skeptical Ahaz assurance of speedy deliverance. A "sign" is a miracle that is performed to provide evidence for the truth. The virgin is not named, but the reference is to something very unusual that is not further explained but that would happen in the immediate future in David's family (Ahaz's own household). It is a case of blending pictures that are on the near and the far horizons, as is so frequent in the prophets.

The royal character of the child is indicated in 8:8; the context identifies him with the child called "Wonderful Counselor, Mighty God, Everlasting Father, Prince of Peace" in 9:6–7, who can be no other than the future Messiah. It is so quoted in Matthew 1:23. Thus, as Isaiah is talking to Ahaz of signs in his own family—the house of David—God projects before his mind an image of a greater sign yet to occur in David's family: the virgin birth of the greater Son of David Himself.

For to us a child is born, to us a son is given, and the government will be on his shoulders.

And he will be called Wonderful Counselor, Mighty God, Everlasting Father, Prince of Peace.

Of the increase of his government and peace there will be no end.

—Isaiah 9:6–7

Judah to be devastated by Assyria (vv. 17–25)—the same Assyria that was helping Judah against Israel and Syria. It happened within Isaiah's lifetime; Jerusalem alone remained.

Isa. 8 | "MAHER-SHALAL-HASH-BAZ"

Three children are mentioned in connection with the invasion of Judah by Syria and Israel: one in the family of David, Immanuel (7:13–14), and two in Isaiah's own family: Shear-Jashub (7:3) and Maher-Shalal-Hash-Baz (8:1–4).

Shear-Jashub means "a remnant shall return." Isaiah, foreseeing the Babylonian captivity of Judah 100 years before it came to pass, envisions a rescued remnant and gives his son this name of promise. That remnant and its glorious future are the main theme of Isaiah's book.

Maher-Shalal-Hash-Baz means "quick to the plunder, swift to the spoil"—that is, Syria and Israel will soon be destroyed. Thus naming his child for the idea of swift deliverance is Isaiah's way of emphasizing what he had already predicted in 7:4, 7, 16. And it promptly happened. Then the victorious Assyrians swept on into Judah (v. 8) and were stopped by direct intervention of God (37:36).

Thus the names of Isaiah's sons reflect the heart of his daily preaching: present deliverance, coming exile or captivity, future glory.

The distress and gloom of the exile (vv. 9–22). Isaiah is told to write his prophecy and to preserve it for reference in the day of its fulfillment (v. 16).

Isa. 9 | THE WONDERFUL CHILD

The setting for this sublime vision was the fall of Israel, which Isaiah had just predicted in chapters 7–8. Zebulun and Naphtali (v. 1), the Galilee region, was the first region to fall to the Assyrians (2 Kings 15:29). But that same region would one day have the proud honor of giving to the world the Redeemer of humanity, the King of the ages. In 2:2–4 Isaiah sees Zion's future universal reign; in 4:2–6 he sees the King Himself (John 12:41); in 7:14 His virgin birth is predicted; and here, in 9:6–7, Isaiah speaks in measured, majestic words of His deity and the eternal nature of His throne.

Samaria's persistent impenitence (9:8–10:4). Following his habit of suddenly shifting back and forth between his own time and the future, Isaiah abruptly turns his eyes toward Samaria. Many of the inhabitants of the Galilee region were carried away in 734 B.C., but Samaria held out until 721 B.C. These lines seem to belong to the 13 years in between, when the people who were left still persevered in their defiance of both God and the Assyrians. It is a poem of four stanzas, warning Samaria of what was in store for them.

Isa. 10:5–34 | THE ADVANCING ASSYRIANS

This was written after the fall of Samaria (v. 11), in defiance of the boastful Assyrians as they marched on into Judah, up to the very gates of Jerusalem. The cities named in vv. 28–32 were just north of Jerusalem. God had used the Assyrians to punish Israel, but here He cautions them against overestimating their power (v. 15) and promises them a humiliating defeat (v. 26), like the defeat of the Midianites by Gideon (Judges 7:19–25) and that of the Egyptians in the Red Sea (Exodus 14). Sargon, one year after he had destroyed Samaria, turned southward, invaded Judah (720 B.C.), took a number of Philistine cities, and defeated the Egyptian army. In 713 B.C. Sargon's army again invaded Judah, Philistia, Edom, and Moab, and in 701 B.C. a vast army of Assyrians came again into the land—at which time God made good His promise and dealt the Assyrians such a sudden and violent blow that they never marched against Jerusalem again (37:36).

Isa. 11–12 | THE "BRANCH" AND HIS KINGDOM

A new shoot growing out of the base of an olive tree. "A shoot will come up from the stump of Jesse." (Isaiah 11:1)

These chapters are an expansion of 2:2–4; 4:2–6; 7:14; 9:1–7. Here Isaiah again suddenly turns his eyes to the far future, after predicting the overthrow of the Assyrian army, and gives us one of the most glorious pictures of the world to come in all of Scripture. A world without war, ruled by a righteous and benevolent King of Davidic descent, consisting of the redeemed of all nations together with the restored remnant of Judah. Whether this will ever be in our world of flesh and blood or in an era "beyond the veil," we do not know. But that it is to be is as sure as the morning. The subject is continued again in 25:6. Chapter 12 is a song of praise for the day of triumph, which God put in Isaiah's mouth, one of the songs in the hymnbook of heaven, which we will all sing when we get there, when all discordant elements shall have disappeared.

Isa. 13:1–14:27 | THE FALL OF BABYLON

In Isaiah's time, Assyria was the dominant power of the world, while Babylon was under the control of Assyria. Babylon rose to become the dominant world power in 605 B.C. and fell to the Medes and Persians in 539 B.C. Thus Isaiah sang of the fall of Babylon 100 years before its rise. Modern critics, therefore, claim that these cannot be the words of Isaiah but must be those of some later prophet, spoken after the fact. However, it is specifically stated that they are Isaiah's words (13:1).

The splendor to which Babylon rose 100 years after Isaiah's day, to become the Queen City of the pre-Christian world, "the glory of kingdoms" (13:19), "the city of gold" (14:4), is here as clearly envisioned as if Isaiah had been there. But the burden of the prophecy is the fall of Babylon, pictured in such detail that it awes us into profound wonderment. The Medes, who in Isaiah's day were an almost unknown people, are named as the destroyers of Babylon (13:17–19).

The gist of the prophecy is this: Babylon shall supersede Assyria (14:25), and Media shall supersede Babylon (13:17), and Babylon shall pass away forever (13:19–22; 14:22–23). (For fulfillment of this astonishing prediction, see under 2 Kings 25.)

The point of special interest was that the fall of Babylon would mean the release of the captives or exiles (14:1–4). Within one year after the fall of Babylon, Cyrus, the Medo-Persian king, issued a decree that allowed the Jews to return to their homeland (Ezra 1:1).

A hundred years after Isaiah, when Babylon had risen to power and was demolishing Jerusalem, Jeremiah would take up Isaiah's cry for vengeance (see Jeremiah 50–51).

Babylon, as oppressor of the Jews, was the counterpart and pattern of a New Testament power that will enslave the people of the earth (Revelation 17–19).

Isa. 14:28–32 | PHILISTIA

The **snake** (v. 29) probably means Tiglath-pileser, who had taken certain Philistine cities and who had died just a year ahead of Ahaz (v. 28). The more poisonous viper and the "darting, venomous serpent" were Sargon and Sennacherib, who completed the desolation of Philistia. **Envoys** (v. 32) probably were Philistine ambassadors asking Jerusalem for help against the Assyrians. (Other denunciations of the Philistines are found in Jeremiah 47; Amos 1:6–8; Zephaniah 2:4–7; Zechariah 9:5–7.)

Isa. 15–16 | MOAB

Moab was a rolling plateau of rich pasturelands lying east of the Dead Sea. The Moabites were descendants of Lot (Genesis 19:37), and thus a nation related to the Jews. This was one of Isaiah's earlier predictions, now reiterated with a time limit of three years (16:14). The cities named were pillaged by Tiglath-pileser III in 732 B.C., by Sargon II in 713 B.C., and by Sennacherib in 701 B.C. It is not indicated to which of these three Isaiah refers. But Isaiah advises the Moabites that it would be to their advantage to renew their allegiance to the house of David (16:1–5); at the mention of the house of David an image of the future Messiah comes into his vision (v. 5). In the family tree of David there was a Moabitess: Ruth (Ruth 4:17–22). (For other prophecies about Moab, see Jeremiah 48; Amos 2:1–3; Zephaniah 2:8–11.)

Isa. 17 | DAMASCUS

A continuation of the thought of chapter 7, probably written at about the same time, during the Syro-Israelite attack on Judah (734 B.C.), and fulfilled shortly thereafter in the invasions of Tiglath-pileser and Sargon. It is directed also against Israel (vv. 3–4) because they were in alliance with Damascus.

Look to their Maker (v. 7): the remnant left in the northern kingdom returned to Jehovah, as indicated in 2 Chronicles 34:9. Isaiah closes with

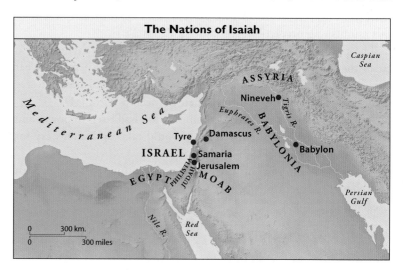

The Nations of Isaiah

a vision of the overthrow of the Assyrians, following their victory over Syria and Israel (vv. 12–14; especially v. 14, which seems a definite reference to 37:36).

Isa. 18 | CUSH

Cush (KJV, Ethiopia) was southern Egypt, whose powerful king at that time ruled over all of Egypt. This is not a prophecy of doom, but seems rather to refer to the excitement and call to arms among the Cushites at the advance of Sennacherib's army into Judah, whose fall would leave open the gateway for the Assyrian march on into Egypt (vv. 1–3). The miraculous deliverance of Jerusalem (vv. 4–6; 37:36) is the cause for Cush's message of gratitude for the destruction of the Assyrian army (v. 7; see 2 Chronicles 32:23).

Isa. 19 | EGYPT

A period of anarchy and internal conflict (vv. 1–4). This actually began at about the time of Isaiah's death. The **cruel master** (v. 4) is the Assyrian king Esarhaddon, who shortly after Isaiah's death subdued Egypt (670 B.C.).

The decline and disintegration of Egypt is predicted (vv. 5–17). This all came to pass (see Jeremiah 46; Ezekiel 29).

Egypt and Assyria will accept the religion of Judah (vv. 18–25). After the Babylonian exile, many Jews remained in the Euphrates valley, and great numbers of them settled in Egypt. Alexandria, the second-leading city of the world in Jesus' day, had a significant Jewish population. The Septuagint translation of the Old Testament was made there. "City of Destruction" is probably a reference to Heliopolis, the city of the sun god (the Hebrew words for "sun" and "destruction" are almost identical). It was destroyed by Nebuchadnezzar (see Jeremiah 43:12–13).

Isa. 20 | EGYPT AND CUSH

Isaiah's warning of their defeat and captivity is intended to discourage Judah from looking to Egypt for aid against Assyria. This was 711 B.C. The prediction was fulfilled 11 years later. Sennacherib's annals for 701 B.C. say: "I fought with the kings of Egypt, accomplished their overthrow, and captured alive charioteers and sons of the king." Esarhaddon further ruined Egypt (see under 19:1–4).

Sargon (v. 1): this was the only known mention of Sargon's name until archaeological excavations of the 19th century revealed him as one of the greatest of the Assyrian kings.

Isa. 21 | BABYLON, EDOM, ARABIA

Babylon (vv. 1–10), surrounded by a vast system of dikes and canals, was like a city in the sea. This is a graphic announcement of its fall. The mention of Elam and Media (v. 2) point to Babylon's capture by Cyrus (539 B.C.; see further under chapters 13–14).

Dumah (vv. 11–12) was the name of a district south of Edom; here the name is used for Edom, of which Seir was the central district.

Arabia (vv. 13–17) refers to the desert between Edom and Babylon. Dedan, Tema, and Kedar were places where leading Arabian tribes lived. This is a prediction that they will experience a terrific blow within a year—and indeed, Sargon invaded Arabia in 715 B.C.

Isa. 22 | JERUSALEM

Jerusalem is referred to as the Valley of Vision because the hill on which it was situated was surrounded by valleys, with higher hills beyond, and was the place where God revealed Himself. Jerusalem is rebuked for giving itself to reckless indulgence while besieged by the Assyrian army. Their defense (vv. 9–11; 2 Chronicles 32:3–5) included everything except turning to God.

The demotion of Shebna, the palace steward (vv. 15–25), may have been because he, an officer of the house of David, was the leader in the city's frivolous conduct in the face of grave danger. The elevation of Eliakim ("God raises up") to the office of steward may have messianic implications (vv. 22–25).

ARCHAEOLOGICAL NOTE: Hezekiah's Wall. In the Jewish Quarter of Jerusalem, Professor Nahum Avigad discovered the remains of a huge wall (the preserved portion is over 200 feet long, 21 feet thick, and 10 feet high). This wall was built on top of houses that had been destroyed—as 22:10 says of Hezekiah: "You counted the buildings in Jerusalem and tore down houses to strengthen the wall."

ARCHAEOLOGICAL NOTE: Shebna's Tomb. The tomb of Shebna, mentioned in vv. 15–25, may have been found east of the old ancient core of Jerusalem by Charles Clermont-Ganneau in 1870. The inscription on this tomb, situated in the village of Silwan, as translated by Professor Avigad reads (partially restored): "This is [the tomb of Shebna]—yahu who is over the house. . . . Cursed be the man who will open this." The same title "who is over the house" is used of Shebna in Isaiah 22:15.

Isa. 23 | TYRE

Tyre had for centuries been the maritime center of the world's commerce. It had planted colonies all around the Mediterranean. The grain of Egypt was one of the principal commodities in which it traded. It suffered terribly at the hands of the Assyrians, who had recently extended their sway over Babylon (v. 13). Tyre's overthrow, its status as a forgotten city for 70 years, and its restoration are here predicted (vv. 14–18). This is thought to refer to its subjugation by Nebuchadnezzar. (See further under Ezekiel 26–28.)

Isa. 24 | WORLD CONVULSIONS

This vision seems to relate to the same period that Jesus spoke of in Matthew 24. It delineates the fearful calamities under which the earth, with all its castes, occupations, and social distinctions, shall pass away. As Jeremiah said of Babylon that it would "sink to rise no more" (Jeremiah 51:64), so Isaiah here says of the earth (v. 20). He seems to be predicting the destruction of the earth as further described in 2 Peter 3:7, 10–13 and Revelation 20. Later he looks beyond to "new heavens and a new earth" (65:17–66:24; Revelation 21:1).

Isa. 25 | THE ABOLITION OF DEATH

Here Isaiah has transported himself beyond the crash of worlds into the age of the new heavens and new earth, and he puts into the mouth of the redeemed a song of praise to God for His wonderful works. He also describes a feast of rich food for all the peoples (v. 6) and the most wonderful of events—the destruction of death and the wiping away of all tears (v. 8). Some interpret these verses as referring to Jesus' death and resurrection. However, it seems more likely that they describe the great marriage supper of the Lamb yet to come (Revelation 19:7–9; Matthew

22:4). The feast, further described in Revelation 19, is followed by the casting of the beast and the false prophet into the lake of fire. This is called the "second death" (Revelation 20:14).

As further evidence that Isaiah is speaking of an event yet to occur, we note that he is describing an event that "wipes away the tears from all faces." We know that Isaiah is not referring to Jesus' death and resurrection because today we still experience suffering and tears on earth. The event that Isaiah is describing has clearly not taken place yet. John tells us in Revelation 20 that after the second death we will live with Christ in the New Jerusalem and that "God shall wipe away all tears from their eyes; and there shall be no more death, neither sorrow, nor crying neither shall there be any more pain: for the former things are passed away" (Revelation 21:4 KJV).

The mention of Moab (v. 10) illustrates Isaiah's mental habit of abrupt transition back and forth between future glory and present local circumstance. The fate of Moab, constant rival and recurrent enemy of Judah, may be used here as typical of the fate of Zion's enemies generally.

Isa. 26 | A SONG OF TRUST AND TRIUMPH

A continuation of the song of the preceding chapter. The "strong city" (v. 1), with God's salvation as its protection, stands in contrast to the "lofty city" (v. 5), the stronghold of the wicked. The grandest verse in the chapter is verse 19: the resurrection of God's people. "The earth will disclose the blood shed upon her" (v. 21) in the day of judgment, when man's long reign of wickedness shall be ended.

Isa. 27 | REVIVAL OF GOD'S VINEYARD

In 5:1–7 Isaiah sang the funeral dirge for God's vineyard. Here it is a joy-song of the vineyard coming to life again. Israel will blossom again

Grapevines grew on the ground in ancient Israel. Isaiah prophesied about the day of restoration of God's people when he spoke about the revival of the vineyard. (Isaiah 27)

Isa. 33 | JUST BEFORE THE BATTLE

Chapters 28–33 belong to the terrifying days of the Assyrian siege of Jerusalem, as told in chapters 36–37. Sennacherib's army was pillaging cities and ravaging the countryside (vv. 8–9). The people were panic-stricken (vv. 13–14). Through it all, Isaiah goes calmly about, assuring the people that God will smite the enemy with terror and that they shall flee, leaving behind their plunder, or loot (vv. 3–4). God Himself protects Jerusalem like an encircling stream in which the enemy's disintegrating ships will sink (vv. 21–23; see chapters 36–37).

Isa. 34 | GOD'S WRATH ON THE NATIONS

Like chapter 24, this chapter seems to be a vision of the end time. Edom is used as a typical example of God's wrath. Once populous and fertile, it is now one of the most desolate regions on earth, inhabited mainly by wild beasts, birds, and reptiles (vv. 10–15; see under Obadiah 16–17). Isaiah challenges future ages to note his words about Edom.

Isa. 35 | THE JOY OF THE REDEEMED

One of the greatest chapters in the Bible. A poem of rare and superb beauty. It presents a picture of the last times, when the redeemed, after long suffering, finally shine forth in all the radiance of their heavenly glory. Returning exiles traveling along the highway (vv. 8–10) offer a marvelous image of the redeemed traveling home to God.

Isa. 36–37 | THE ASSYRIAN ARMY OVERTHROWN

The defeat of the Assyrian army is recorded three times: here, in 2 Kings 18–19, and in 2 Chronicles 32. It is one of the most astounding miracles of the Old Testament. In one night the Assyrian army is destroyed by direct divine intervention (37:36). This is the grand climax of which Isaiah had given repeated assurance: 10:24–34; 17:12–14; 29:5–8, 14; 30:27–33; 31:4–9; 33:3–4, 21–23; 38:6.

Sennacherib invaded Judah in 701 B.C. He boasts of capturing 46 strong, walled cities at that time and of having shut Hezekiah up in Jerusalem "like a bird in a cage." However, Sennacherib's texts do not speak of the capture of Jerusalem, and indeed, it appears that God answered Hezekiah's prayer, for after 185,000 of his troops were killed, Sennacherib returned to Assyria, and Jerusalem was thus delivered. Revelation 16:14; 19:19; and 20:8 describe another time when all the world's mightiest armies will be gathered together to battle God. Once again, God will destroy them in an instant just as He destroyed the Assyrian army.

HEZEKIAH'S SICKNESS. BABYLON'S HERALDS

Hezekiah's sickness occurred around 703 B.C., 15 years before his death (38:5). The deliverance from Assyria was still in the future (38:6). Hezekiah's miraculous recovery had created interest in Babylon (2 Chronicles 32:31; Isaiah 38:7–8). The visit of the Babylonian envoys to Jerusalem must have looked suspicious to Sennacherib and may have hastened his invasion.

Magnificent Rhapsodies of the Future, Isaiah 40 to 66

Isaiah spent his life under the threatening shadow of the Assyrian Empire. The Assyrians had destroyed the northern portion of Israel in 733 B.C. and the rest of the northern kingdom, including Samaria, in 722 B.C. They had invaded Judah in 712 B.C. and by 701 B.C. had taken all of Judah except Jerusalem. Throughout these years Isaiah

---

Two Isaiahs?

Nowhere in the book itself, or in the Bible, or in Jewish or Christian tradition is there any mention, or even a hint, of two authors. A "second Isaiah" is the creation of modern biblical criticism. The book of Isaiah in our Bible, and in Jesus' day, is *one* book, not two. It is not a patchwork, but from beginning to end is characterised by unity of thought, set forth in sublime language that makes it one of the grandest works ever written. There was just one Isaiah, and notwithstanding the critics, this is his book.

---

had steadfastly predicted that Jerusalem would stand. It did stand. This was the grand achievement of Isaiah's life. God had saved his city when doom seemed certain. But now, with the Assyrian crisis past, Isaiah, who had already prophesied that Jerusalem would later fall to Babylon (39:6–7), assumes that the Babylonian exile is an accomplished fact and in his mind's eye takes his stand with the exiles. So clear were some of his visions that in them he speaks of the future as if it were already past.

VOICES OF COMFORT

Some of the sentences seem to be utterances of angels, who cry to Isaiah, or to each other, in exultation over the wondrous things in store for God's people when the long night of suffering is past. The advent of Christ is the subject of vv. 1–11. Verses 3–5 are quoted in all four Gospels as referring to His arrival on earth (Matthew 3:3; Mark 1:3; Luke 3:4–6; John 1:23). Mention, in this connection, of God's Word as eternally impregnable (vv. 6–8) means that God's prophetic promises cannot fail — Christ and heaven are sure. The infinite power of God, and the eternal

He tends his flock like a shepherd:
He gathers the lambs in his arms and carries them close to his heart;
he gently leads those that have young.
—Isaiah 40:11

youth of those who trust Him, form the subject matter of vv. 12–31. It is a grand chapter.

Isa. 41 | THE RISE OF CYRUS

Cyrus is not named here, but he is named later, in 44:28 and 45:1, and unmistakably is the "one from the east" (v. 2) and the "one from the north" (v. 25; armies from the east always entered Palestine from the north, since they had to follow the Euphrates River). Isaiah died 150 years before the days of Cyrus, yet here is a vision of Cyrus's rapid conquest of the world, which is ascribed to the providence of God (v. 4). God promises protection for Israel (vv. 8–20) and then challenges the gods of the nations to show their ability to predict the future (vv. 21–29; see under chapter 44).

Isa. 42 | THE SERVANT OF THE LORD

Another vision of the coming Messiah and His work (vv. 1–17); it is quoted as such in Matthew 12:17–21. But in vv. 18–25, the Lord's servant is the nation Israel, who had to be corrected over and over for its failure to follow God.

Isa. 43 | GOD'S CARE OF ISRAEL

God had formed the nation for Himself. The nation had been consistently disobedient. Still, they were God's nation, and through all their sins and sufferings God would work to demonstrate to all the world that He, and He alone, is God.

Isa. 44–45 | CYRUS

These two chapters are a prediction of Israel's return from exile under Cyrus, with special emphasis on God's unique power to predict the future. Cyrus, king of Persia, reigned 539–530 B.C. He permitted the Jews to return to Jerusalem and issued a decree authorizing the rebuilding of the temple (2 Chronicles 36:22–23; Ezra 1:1–4). Isaiah prophesied in 745–695 B.C., more than 150 years before the days of Cyrus. Yet he calls him by name and predicts that he will rebuild the temple, which in Isaiah's day had not even been destroyed yet.

The main point of these two chapters is that God's superiority over idols is proven by His ability to foretell the future, an idea that recurs throughout chapters 40–48 (41:21–24; 42:8–9; 43:9–13; 44:6–8; 45:20–21; 46:9–11; 48:3–7). The calling of Cyrus by name long before he was born is given as an example of God's power to know (and direct) the future (45:4–6). If this is not a prediction, it does not even make sense in the connection in which it is used. Critics who assign these chapters to post-exilic authorship have strange ideas of contextual unity.

One of Isaiah's foremost theses was that predictive prophecy is an evidence of deity. He was very fond of ridiculing idols and idol-wor-

This inscription proclaims Cyrus as the king of the world who made the land dwell in peace. It was this Cyrus who liberated the Israelites as prophesied by Isaiah.

shipers—these gods that the nations worship cannot even do what human beings can do: they cannot see, nor speak, nor hear. But, says Isaiah, our God, whom we worship in our Hebrew nation, not only can do what human beings can do, He can do some things that they cannot do: He can foretell things to come. Then Isaiah invites a conference of nations, where they can all compare their gods, and asks if any nation has in its literature ancient predictions of things that happened later. We have, he says, in our national literature, going back way into the past, a continuous stream of predictions of things that afterward came true.

Isa. 46–48 | THE FALL OF BABYLON

God declares, "I am God, and there is no other.... I make known the end from the beginning, from ancient times, what is still to come" (46:9–10). From the earliest chapters of Genesis, God's Word unveils the entire story. Beyond the heartbreaking tragedy of the fall of man in the Garden of Eden, God can see the joyous celebration of Revelation 21 and 22. And in Revelation 22:13, God declares, "I am the Alpha and Omega, the First and the Last, the Beginning and the End."

A continuation of chapters 13–14. Babylon's many idols, sorcerers, and astrologers would be of no avail against the armies of Cyrus (47:12–15). Instead, the golden images of her vaunted gods, helpless to save not only their city but even themselves, would be hauled away as loot on beasts and in wagons (46:1–2). Isaiah reiterates again God's exclusive and unique power to predict and control the course of history. It is a solemn restatement of the prediction of the fall of Babylon at the hands of Cyrus, and of the deliverance of the Jews.

The Lord's chosen ally (48:14), that is, Cyrus, who was a singularly noble and just monarch.

THE SERVANT OF JEHOVAH

In the preceding chapters (40–48), a leading idea was that God's predictions of the future are evidence of His deity.

In chapters 49–55, the thoughts revolve around the Servant of God. In some passages the servant seems to be the nation Israel, and in other passages the Messiah, the One in whom Israel would be personified. The passages are pretty well blended so that the context must indicate which is meant.

It is a resumption of thoughts that have been accumulating (41:8; 42:1, 19; 43:10; 44:1–2, 21; 49:3–6; 52:13; 53:11).

These chapters seem to be a sort of soliloquy of the Servant, with interspersed replies from God, having to do mainly with the Servant's work of bringing all nations to God.

Isa. 51–52 **ZION'S REDEMPTION AND RESTORATION**

Israel's release from the sufferings of the exile is as certain as God's wondrous works of the past. It is a part of God's eternal plan, to build from one pair, Abraham and Sarah (51:2), a redeemed world of endless glory (51:6). Chapter 52 is a song of the day of Zion's triumph.

A Summary of Isaiah's Predictions

Fulfilled in His Own Lifetime

- Judah will be delivered from Syria and Israel (7:4–7, 16)
- Syria and Israel will be destroyed by Assyria (8:4; 17:1–14)
- Assyria will invade Judah (8:7–8)
- Philistines will be subjugated (14:28–32)
- Moab will be plundered (15 and 16)
- Egypt and Ethiopia will be conquered by Assyria (20:4)
- Arabia will be pillaged (21:13–17)
- Tyre will be subdued (23:1–12)
- Jerusalem will be delivered from Assyria (see under 36)
- Hezekiah's life will be extended 15 years (38:5)

Fulfilled After Isaiah's Time

- Babylonian captivity (39:5–7)
- Babylon will be overthrown by Cyrus (46:11)
- And the Medes and Elamites (13:17; 21:2; 48:14)
- Babylon's perpetual desolation (13:20–22)
- Cyrus called by name (44:28; 45:1, 4)
- Cyrus's conquest of the world (41:2–3)
- Cyrus will liberate the captives (45:13)
- Cyrus will rebuild Jerusalem (44:28; 45:13)
- Israel will be restored (27:12–13; 48:20; 51:14)
- Israel's religion will permeate Egypt and Assyria (19:18–25)
- Israel's religion will spread over the whole world (27:2–6)
- Tyre's captivity and restoration (23:13–18)
- Edom's perpetual desolation (34:5–17)

(Chart continues on following page)

THE OLD TESTAMENT — The Prophets

- His advent (40:3–5)
- His virgin birth (7:14)
- Galilee will be the scene of His ministry (9:1–2)
- His deity and the eternity of His throne (9:6–7)
- His sufferings (53)
- He will die with the wicked (53:9)
- He will be buried with the rich (53:9)
- The might and gentleness of His reign (40:10–11)
- The righteousness and blessings of His reign (32:1–8; 61:1–3)
- His justice and kindness (42:3–4, 7)
- His rule over Gentiles (2:2–3; 42:1, 6; 49:6; 55:4–5; 56:6; 60:3–5)
- His vast influence (49:7, 23)
- Idols will disappear (2:18)
- A warless world will be brought into being (2:4; 65:25)
- The earth will be destroyed (24; 26:21; 34:1–4)
- Death will be destroyed (25:8; 26:19)
- God's people will be called by a new name (62:2; 65:15)
- A new heaven and a new earth will be created (65:17; 66:22)
- The righteous and the wicked will be eternally separated (66:15, 22–24)

Isa. 53 | JEHOVAH'S SERVANT A MAN OF SORROWS

One of the best-loved chapters in all the Bible. It is a picture of the suffering Savior. It begins at 52:13 and is so vivid in detail that one would almost think of Isaiah as standing at the foot of the cross. It is so clear in his mind that he speaks of it in the past tense, as if it had already happened. Yet it was written seven centuries before Jesus' death on Calvary. It cannot possibly fit any person in history other than Christ.

Isa. 54–55 | ZION'S VAST EXPANSION

The Servant of God, by virtue of His suffering, would rejuvenate Zion and lead Zion onward and upward to heights of endless glory. Chapter 55 is the Servant's invitation to all the world to enter His kingdom and share His blessings.

Isa. 56–59 | SINS OF ISAIAH'S DAY

The sins of Isaiah's day—the profaning of the Sabbath, the gluttony of Israel's leaders, the widespread idolatry with its vile practices, the punctilious fasting while practicing flagrant injustice—are all surely to be avenged.

Isa. 60–62 | ZION'S REDEEMER

A song of the Messianic Age, beginning at 59:20, picturing an era of world evangelization, blending into the eternal glory of heaven. Chapter 60 is one of the grandest chapters of the Bible. It speaks of how the Gentiles will bless Zion. Jesus quoted 61:1–3 as referring to Himself (Luke 4:18).

Zion will receive a **new name** (62:2), and God's servants will be called by **another name** (65:15). Until the coming of Christ, God's people were known as Jews, or Hebrews. After that they were called Christians. But "another name" may also refer to a new identity or nature, rather than to merely a new label. In Revelation 21:2, John describes one of the high points of his vision: "I saw the Holy City, the new Jerusalem, coming down out of heaven from God, prepared as a bride beautifully dressed for her husband." This same wedding imagery is used by Isaiah (62:5).

A **crown of splendor** (62:3) is what the redeemed are to God. Although the visible church has been corrupted at the hands of people and has often been anything but a "crown of splendor," yet it is true of the body of God's faithful saints. Throughout eternity they will be God's delight and joy (vv. 3–5).

Isa. 63–64 THE EXILES' PRAYER

It is a bit puzzling to see Edom mentioned here (63:1–6). These two chapters, except for the first six verses, are in the nature of a prayer to God to liberate exiled Israel. The Edomites, age-old enemies of Judah, had allied themselves with the Babylonians in destroying Jerusalem (see under Obadiah), and may here be meant to symbolize all the enemies of God's people. The bloodstained warrior, trampling Edom in his wrath, "mighty to save" Zion (63:1), is identical with Zion's Redeemer of the preceding three chapters. The language seems to be the basis for the imagery of the Lord's coming in Revelation 14 and 19:11–16.

Isa. 65–66 THE NEW HEAVENS AND NEW EARTH

These two chapters are God's answer to the exiles' prayer of the previous two chapters. The prayer shall be answered. The faithful remnant shall be restored (65:8–10). New nations shall be brought into the fold (65:1; 66:8). All shall be called by a new name (65:15). They shall inherit new heavens and a new earth (65:17; 66:22). The faithful and the disobedient shall be forever separated, with eternal blessedness for the righteous ones, eternal punishment for the others (66:22–24). Jesus Himself endorsed these words (Mark 9:48). Peter's closing message to Christians was to keep their eyes on the new heavens and the new earth (2 Peter 3:10–14). The Bible reaches its final climax in a magnificent vision of the new heavens and the new earth in Revelation 21–22, which is an expansion of the vision of Isaiah 66. No temple or sacrifice, it seems, will be needed in the new order (66:1–4), because "now the dwelling of God is with men, and he will live with them" (Revelation 21:3).

Jeremiah

God's Final Effort to Save Jerusalem

Is there no balm in Gilead?
  Is there no physician there?
Why then is there no healing
  for the wound of my people?

—JEREMIAH 8:22

The heart is deceitful above all things
  and beyond cure.
Who can understand it?

—JEREMIAH 17:9

(For the last kings of Judah, see pp. 264–65.)

Jeremiah lived about 100 years after the prophet Isaiah. Isaiah had saved Jerusalem from Assyria. Jeremiah tried to save Jerusalem from Babylon, but failed.

Jeremiah lived through 40 terrible years. He was called to be a prophet in 626 B.C. Twenty years later, in 605 B.C., Jerusalem was partly destroyed. It was further ruined in 597 B.C., and finally burned to the ground in 586 B.C. Jeremiah experienced the end of the monarchy, the final agony of the nation of Judah. He was a pathetic, lonely figure, who was God's final appeal to the Holy City, which had become hopelessly and fanatically attached to idols. Jeremiah cried out that if only they would repent, God would save them from Babylon.

As Assyria had been the background of Isaiah's ministry 150 years earlier, so Babylonia was the backdrop of Jeremiah's ministry.

The Internal Situation

The northern kingdom, Israel, had fallen, as had much of Judah, the southern kingdom, which had suffered reverse after reverse, until Jerusalem was all that was left of the once great kingdom of David and Solomon. But still the people of Jerusalem ignored the continued warnings of the prophets and grew more and more hardened in their idolatry and wickedness. The hour of doom was about to strike.

> "The time is coming," declares the LORD,
>   "when I will make a new covenant
> with the house of Israel
>   and with the house of Judah. . . .
> I will put my law in their minds
>   and write it on their hearts.
> I will be their God,
>   and they will be my people. . . .
> I will forgive their wickedness
>   and will remember their sins no more."
>
> —Jeremiah 31:31, 33–34

Barrel cylinder of Nebuchadnezzar II (605-562 B.C.) describing some of his accomplishments. It was king Nebuchadnezzar that "set fire to the temple of the Lord, the royal palace and all the houses of Jerusalem." (2 Kings 25:8–10)

The International Situation

A three-cornered contest for world supremacy was going on between Assyria, Babylonia, and Egypt. For 300 years Assyria, in the northern Euphrates valley, with Nineveh as its capital, had ruled the world; but now it was growing weak. Babylonia, in the southern Euphrates valley, was becoming powerful. Egypt, in the Nile valley, which 1000 years before had been a world power, was again becoming ambitious. At about the midpoint of Jeremiah's ministry, Babylonia won the contest. It broke the power of Assyria (610 B.C.) and a few years later crushed Egypt in the battle of Carchemish (605 B.C.). For 70 years Babylonia ruled the world—the same 70 years as those of the exile (or Babylonian captivity) of the Jewish people.

Jeremiah's Message

From the beginning of his ministry, 20 years before the issue was settled, Jeremiah insisted that Babylonia would be the victor. All through his incessant and bitter complaints over Judah's wickedness, the following ideas recur again and again:

1. Judah is going to be destroyed by victorious Babylonia.
2. If Judah will turn from her wickedness, somehow God will save her from destruction at the hands of Babylon.
3. Later, when there no longer seemed to be any hope of Judah's repentance, came a message of renewed hope: if Judah, as a matter of political expediency, will submit to Babylon, she shall be spared.

Contemporary Prophets

- **Jeremiah** was the leader among the brilliant constellation of prophets clustered around the destruction of Jerusalem.
- **Ezekiel**, a fellow priest, somewhat younger than Jeremiah, preached in Babylonia among the captives the same things that Jeremiah was preaching in Jerusalem.
- **Daniel**, a man of royal blood, held the line in the palace of Nebuchadnezzar.
- **Habakkuk** and **Zephaniah** helped Jeremiah in Jerusalem.
- **Nahum**, at the same time, was predicting the fall of Nineveh.
- **Obadiah**, at the same time, predicted the ruin of Edom.

4. Judah will be destroyed, but she shall recover and yet dominate the world.
5. Babylon, the destroyer of Judah, shall herself be destroyed, never to rise again.

Jeremiah's Boldness

Jeremiah unceasingly advised Jerusalem to surrender to the king of Babylon, so much so that his enemies accused him of being a traitor. Nebuchadnezzar rewarded him for giving this advice to his people: he not only spared his life but also offered him any honor he would accept, even a place of honor in the court at Babylon (39:12). But Jeremiah cried aloud, over and over, that the king of Babylon was committing a heinous crime in destroying the Lord's people, and because of this crime Babylon itself would be destroyed and abandoned forever (see chapters 50–51).

The Chronology of Jeremiah's Book

Some of Jeremiah's messages are dated. Dates are found in the following verses:

- In Josiah's reign: 1:2; 3:6.
- In Jehoiakim's reign: 22:18; 25:1; 26:1; 35:1; 36:1; 45:1.
- In Zedekiah's reign: 21:1; 24:1, 8; 27:3, 12; 28:1; 29:3; 32:1; 34:2; 37:1; 38:5; 39:1; 49:34; 51:59.
- In Egypt: 43:7, 8; 44:1.

THE CONTEMPORARY KINGS OF JUDAH		
Manasseh	(698–644 B.C.)	Reigned 55 years. Very wicked (see under 2 Chronicles 33). Jeremiah was born during his reign.
Amon	(643–640 B.C.)	Reigned 2 years. The long and wicked reign of his father Manasseh had sealed the doom of Judah.
Josiah	(640–609 B.C.)	Reigned 31 years. A good king, under whom a great reformation took place. Jeremiah began his ministry in Josiah's 13th year. But the reformation had only outward effect; at heart the people were still idolaters.
Jehoahaz	(609 B.C.)	Reigned 3 months. Was taken to Egypt.
Jehoiakim	(609–598 B.C.)	Reigned 11 years. Openly supported idol worship. Boldly defiant of God and a bitter enemy of Jeremiah.
Jehoiachin	(598–597 B.C.)	Reigned 3 months. Was taken to Babylon.
Zedekiah	(597–586 B.C.)	Reigned 11 years. Rather friendly toward Jeremiah, but a weak king; a tool in the hands of his wicked officials.

This quickly shows that the book is not arranged in chronological order. Some late messages come early in the book, and some early messages come late in the book. These messages were delivered orally, and perhaps repeatedly, for years, possibly before Jeremiah began to write them. The writing of such a book was a long and laborious task. Parchment, made of sheep or goat skins, was scarce and expensive. It was made into a long roll and wound around a stick. This may, in part, account for the lack of order in Jeremiah's book. After writing an incident or discourse, some other utterance delivered previously would be suggested, and he would write it down, in some cases without dating it, thus filling up the parchment as he unrolled it.

Jer. 1 | THE CALL OF JEREMIAH

Jeremiah was called to a hard and thankless task. Like Moses (Exodus 3:11; 4:10), he was reluctant to accept the responsibility. The call came when he was "only a child," probably about 20.

Anathoth (v. 1), his home, was about 2½ miles northeast of Jerusalem; it is now called Anata.

The **boiling pot** (v. 13; KJV, caldron) is the Babylonian army. The first message Jeremiah has to deliver is that Jerusalem will be destroyed by Babylonia (v. 14).

Jer. 2 | ISRAEL'S APOSTASY

In an impassioned rebuke for their shameless idolatry, Israel is compared to a wife who has left her husband for other men, turning herself into a common prostitute.

Jer. 3 | JUDAH WORSE THAN ISRAEL

In chapter 2, "Israel" means the whole nation. In this chapter it means the northern kingdom, which 300 years before had split off from Judah and

THE CHRONOLOGY OF JEREMIAH'S TIMES	
628 B.C.	Josiah begins his reforms (see on 2 Chronicles 34).
626 B.C.	Jeremiah is called by God.
622 B.C.	The Book of the Law is found. Josiah's great reformation (2 Kings 22–23).
609 B.C.	Josiah is slain at Megiddo by Pharaoh.
612 B.C.	Nineveh is destroyed by Babylonia.
605 B.C.	Judah is subdued by Babylonia. The first captivity.
605 B.C.	Battle of Carchemish: Babylon crushes Egypt.
597 B.C.	Jehoiachin is taken prisoner.
593 B.C.(?)	Zedekiah visits Babylon.
586 B.C.	Jerusalem is burned. The temporary end of David's kingdom.

which had been taken away by the Assyrians a century ago. Judah, blind to the significance of Israel's fall, not only did not repent, but under the wicked reign of Manasseh sunk to lower and lower depths of depravity. The reunion of Judah and Israel is predicted (vv. 17–18; also 50:4–5; Hosea 1:11). Again the metaphor of an adulterous wife (v. 20).

Jer. 4 | THE APPROACHING DESOLATION OF JUDAH

This chapter describes the advance of the Babylonian armies that destroyed Jerusalem (605–586 B.C.). For some time it was thought that Judah suffered a Scythian invasion shortly before that of the Babylonians. But the passages in Jeremiah on the enemy "from the north" fit much better what is known of the Babylonians than of the wild Scythians from the Caucus region: the reference to "an ancient and enduring nation" (5:15); the use of "chariots" (4:13); the army's capture of "cities of Judah" (4:16; 6:6); their battle array in regular ranks (6:23); their love of Jerusalem (4:30). The Babylonians did indeed come to Judah from the north (see map on p. 275).

Jer. 5 | UNIVERSAL DEPRAVITY OF JUDAH

Had there been one righteous man, God would have spared the city (v. 1). They indulge in promiscuous sex like animals (vv. 7–8). They scoff at the prophet's warnings (v. 12). Their lifestyle is one of deceit, oppression, and robbery (vv. 26–28). The people actually love the religious and political rottenness in which they live (vv. 30–31; for a note on false prophets [v. 30], see under chapter 23).

Jer. 6 | DESTRUCTION FROM THE NORTH

A vivid prophetic description of the destruction of Jerusalem at the hands of the Babylonian invaders (vv. 22–26), which became a horrible reality in Jeremiah's own lifetime. Over and over (vv. 16–19) he warns, with pathetic insistence, that repentance is their last possible chance to escape ruin.

Jer. 7 | REPENTANCE THEIR ONLY HOPE

This is one of Jeremiah's heartrending appeals for repentance, based on God's amazing promise that if only the people would listen to their God, Jerusalem would never fall (vv. 5–7). With all their abominable practices (vv. 9, 31), and even though they had put idols in the temple (v. 30), they still had a superstitious regard for the temple and its services. They seemed to think that, come what may, God would not let Jerusalem be destroyed because His temple was there (vv. 4, 10).

The **Queen of Heaven** (v. 18) is Ashtoreth, the principal female Canaanite deity, whose worship was accompanied by the most degrading forms of immorality.

The **Valley of Ben Hinnom** (vv. 31–32) is the valley on the south side of Jerusalem. It was used as a trash dump and also as the place where children were burnt as sacrifices to the god Molech. (From the name Valley of Hinnom, *ge'hinnom*, was later derived from the Greek name used for hell in the New Testament, *gehenna*.)

Jer. 8 | "THE HARVEST IS PAST"

Fully conscious of the futility of his appeals and rebukes, Jeremiah speaks of the impending desolation of Judah as if it were already accomplished (v. 20). The insistence of the false prophets (vv. 10–11) that Jerusalem was in no danger constituted one of Jeremiah's most difficult problems (see under chapter 23).

Jer. 9 | THE BROKENHEARTED PROPHET

Jeremiah, a man of sorrows, in the midst of a people abandoned to everything vile (8:6; 9:2–9), wept day and night at the thought of the frightful, impending retribution. He moved among them, begging, pleading, persuading, threatening, entreating, imploring that they turn from their wickedness. But in vain.

Jer. 10 | JEHOVAH THE TRUE GOD

It seems that the threat of Babylonian invasion spurred the people of Judah to great activity in the manufacture of idols—as if idols could save them. This gave Jeremiah occasion to remind them that what they were doing, rather than helping them, was in fact a further aggravation of their already appalling sin against God.

Jer. 11 | THE BROKEN COVENANT

This chapter seems to belong to the period of reaction, after Josiah's great reformation (told in 2 Kings 23), when the people had restored their idols. Their response to Jeremiah's rebuke was to plot his death (9:21).

Jer. 12 | JEREMIAH'S COMPLAINT

Contrasting his own sufferings with the apparent prosperity of those against whom he was preaching, and who were ridiculing his threats (v. 4), Jeremiah complains of the ways of God. But there is no security in prosperity—Jeremiah's opponents will be uprooted (v. 14). Then God gives the promise of future restoration (vv. 15–17).

Jer. 13 | THE RUINED BELT

Jeremiah made considerable use of symbols in his preaching (see on 19:1). The linen belt (KJV, girdle) was probably richly decorated, a conspicuous part of Jeremiah's dress as he walked about the streets of Jerusalem. Later, rotted, ragged, and dirty, it served again to attract attention—of a different kind. As curious crowds gathered around the prophet, it gave him occasion to explain that Judah, with whom Jehovah had clothed Himself to walk among people, once beautiful and glorious, would, like his belt, be ruined and be good for nothing but to be thrown away.

Jer. 14–15 JEREMIAH'S INTERCESSION

A prolonged drought had stripped the land of food. Jeremiah's heart ached at seeing the people suffer, even though they hated, ridiculed, and mocked him. His intercession before God is as near an approach to the spirit of Christ as is to be found anywhere in the Old Testament.

Jer. 16 JEREMIAH FORBIDDEN TO MARRY

In some cases, the domestic life of the prophets was used to reinforce the message they preached. Isaiah and Hosea were married and gave their children names that expressed their main messages. Jeremiah was commanded to remain single, as a kind of symbolic backdrop to his persistent predictions of impending bloody slaughter: what is the use of raising a family just to be butchered in the frightful carnage about to be loosed upon the inhabitants of Judah? Again, God promises restoration (vv. 14–15).

Jer. 17 JUDAH'S SIN INDELIBLE

Judah's downfall is inevitable. Yet the promise is held before them again and again that if only they turn to God, Jerusalem will remain forever (vv. 24–25).

Jer. 18 THE POTTER'S CLAY

A very apt illustration of God's power to alter the destiny of a nation. Jeremiah used it as the basis for another appeal to the wicked nation to amend its ways. But again, it was in vain.

Jer. 19 THE CLAY JAR

It may have been a jar or vase of exquisite workmanship. Being shattered in the presence of Jerusalem's leaders was an impressive way of reannouncing the impending ruin of the city.

Some other symbols Jeremiah used to gain attention to his preaching were the ruined belt (chap. 13), abstinence

Late Iron Age pottery (7th century B.C.) discovered near Bethlehem. Jeremiah shattered a clay jar to illustrate the coming destruction of Jerusalem. (Jeremiah 19)

hour, Jeremiah was commanded of God to buy a field, in public ceremony, and put away the deed for safekeeping, to emphasize his prediction that the captives would return and the land would once again be cultivated.

Jer. 33 | "THE BRANCH"

Most of the 20 Davidic kings who reigned over Judah during the 400 years between David and the Babylonian exile were very bad. Only a few were worthy of the name of David. In chapters 22–23 Jeremiah bitterly indicts this royal dynasty to whom God had given the promise of an eternal throne. Here in chapter 33 he repeats with a fuller explanation the prophecy of one great King, "the Branch," in whom the promise would be fulfilled.

Jer. 34 | ZEDEKIAH'S PROCLAMATION OF LIBERTY

During the siege of Jerusalem, King Zedekiah proclaimed freedom to all slaves, evidently to gain God's favor; but he failed to enforce his own proclamation.

ARCHAEOLOGICAL NOTE: The "Lachish Letters." In Jeremiah 34:7, Lachish and Azekah are mentioned as being besieged by the king of Babylonia. Fragments of 21 letters, written during this siege, from an outpost of Lachish to the captain of the guard who was defending Lachish, were found in 1935.

These letters were written just before Nebuchadnezzar launched his final attack by kindling fires against the city walls. They were found in a deposit of ash and charcoal on the floor of the guardroom.

In one of the letters, the outpost says that he was "watching for signals from Lachish," and that "he could see no signals from Azekah" (perhaps it had already fallen).

Evidently the letter indicates that someone in the Hill Country was looking for signal fires from either Lachish or Azekah to indicate the progress of the Babylonian advance. Such a lookout point exists a few miles east of Lachish, at the western edge of the hill country.

Jer. 35 | THE EXAMPLE OF THE RECABITES

The Recabites were a tribe, descended from Recab, who are mentioned during the time of Moses (1 Chronicles 2:55; Numbers 10:29–32; Judges 1:16). They had adhered to their ancestor's command to drink no wine (2 Kings 10:15, 23) and were held up by Jeremiah in stinging contrast to the disobedient citizens of Jerusalem.

Jer. 36 | THE KING BURNS JEREMIAH'S BOOK

At this time Jeremiah had been prophesying for 23 years, from the 13th year of Josiah to the 4th year of Jehoiakim. He is now commanded to gather these prophecies into a book so that they can be read to the people, because Jeremiah himself is not free to speak to the people (v. 5). It took a year or so to write the book (vv. 1, 9). The reading of the book made a profound impression on some of the officials, but the king brazenly and defiantly burned the book. Jeremiah then wrote it all over again.

Jer. 37–38 | JEREMIAH'S IMPRISONMENT

During the siege, when the Babylonians had temporarily withdrawn, Jeremiah attempted to leave the city to go to his home in Anathoth, probably because of the scarcity of food in Jerusalem. Because of his persistent advice to surrender to the king of Babylon, this looked to his enemies as if it might be an effort to join the Babylonians. Thus he was imprisoned on suspicion of being a traitor who worked in the interest of the Babylonians. Zedekiah was friendly to Jeremiah, but he was a weak king.

Jer. 39 | JERUSALEM BURNED

This event is told also in chapter 52, in 2 Kings 25 (see note there), and in 2 Chronicles 36. Nebuchadnezzar, knowing of Jeremiah's life-long admonishing Jerusalem to submit to him, now offered to confer on Jeremiah any honor that he would accept, even a place at the Babylonian court (11–14; 40:1–6).

Jer. 40–41 | GEDALIAH MADE GOVERNOR

Gedaliah, whom Nebuchadnezzar appointed governor over Judah, was the son of Ahikam, Jeremiah's friend (40:5; 26:24). But within three months he was assassinated (39:2; 41:1).

ARCHAEOLOGICAL NOTE: Gedaliah's Seal. In 1935, in the layer of ashes left by Nebuchadnezzar's fire when he burned Lachish, a seal was found among the "Lachish Letters" bearing this inscription, "Belonging to Gedaliah, the one who is over the house."

ARCHAEOLOGICAL NOTE: Jaazaniah's (Jezaniah's) Seal. Mentioned in Jeremiah 40:8 and 2 Kings 25:23, Jaazaniah was one of Gedaliah's army captains. In 1932, in the ruins of Mizpah, the seat of Gedaliah's government (Jeremiah 40:6), an exquisite agate seal was found with the representation of a fighting cock inscribed, "Belonging to Jaazaniah, servant of the king."

Jer. 42–43 | DEPARTURE FOR EGYPT

The remnant, fearing reprisal by Nebuchadnezzar for the slaying of Gedaliah, fled to Egypt, though explicitly warned of God that it would mean extinction. They took Jeremiah along.

📜 **ARCHAEOLOGICAL NOTE: Tahpanhes.** The site of Tahpanhes (43:8–13) has been identified about 10 miles west of the Suez Canal. It was a fortress city on the northern border of Lower Egypt that guarded the road to Syria. In 1886 Sir Flinders Petrie uncovered the ruins of a large castle, in front of which was a "great open platform of brick work," which may have been the very place where Jeremiah hid the stones (43:8).

Nebuchadnezzar's annals state that he did invade Egypt in 568 B.C., which was 18 years after Jeremiah uttered the prophecy that he would (43:10).

Thus, Abraham's descendants returned to Egypt as a defeated and hopeless remnant nearly 900 years after they had been liberated from Egypt by God's mighty hand in the Exodus.

Jer. 44 | JEREMIAH'S FINAL APPEAL

This last effort to induce the people to abandon their idolatry failed. They were defiant.

Queen of Heaven (v. 17) was a Babylonian title for Ishtar, whose worship involved acts of immorality; the women hid themselves behind their husbands' consent, which was required for the women's religious vows to have validity (vv. 15, 19).

The place and manner of Jeremiah's death are not known. One tradition is that he was stoned to death in Egypt. Another is that he was taken from Egypt to Babylon by Nebuchadnezzar, along with Baruch, his secretary, and died there.

Jer. 45 | BARUCH

Baruch, Jeremiah's secretary (scribe), was a man of prominence, with high ambitions (v. 5). He was recognized as having great influence with Jeremiah (43:3). He is reminded that earthly recognition provides only an illusion of self-worth—it dies with the people who bestow it.

Jer. 46 | EGYPT

A description of the defeat of the Egyptian army at Carchemish (605 B.C.), in the middle period of Jeremiah's life (vv. 1–12); and a later prophecy that Nebuchadnezzar will invade Egypt (vv. 13–26; see under 43:8–13, of which these verses are an expansion). More than a century before, Isaiah had prophesied the Assyrian invasions of Egypt (see under Isaiah 18–20). Ezekiel also prophesied about Egypt (Ezekiel 19–32).

Jer. 47 | THE PHILISTINES

This prophecy, foretelling the desolation of Philistia by Babylon, was fulfilled 20 years later when Nebuchadnezzar took Judah. Other prophets who spoke about and against the Philistines were Isaiah (14:28–32), Amos (1:6–8), Ezekiel (25:15–17), Zephaniah (2:4–7), and Zechariah (9:1–7).

Residential area of the Philistine site at Tel Qasile.

Jeremiah's prophecy concerning Memphis (46:16) came true. About all that remains of the once-great city of Memphis in Egypt are an alabaster sphinx and a rather shabby-looking, giant statue of Pharaoh Rameses II.

Jer. 48 | MOAB

A picture of the impending desolation of Moab. Moab helped Nebuchadnezzar against Judah, but later was devastated by him (582 B.C.). For centuries the land has lain desolate and sparsely inhabited, the ruins of its many cities testifying to its population in ancient times. Its restoration (v. 47) and that of Ammon (49:6) may have been fulfilled in their absorption into the general Arab race, some of whom were present at Pentecost when the Gospel was first proclaimed to the world (Acts 2:11). Or it may mean that the land will yet again be prosperous. Other prophecies about Moab are Isaiah 15–16; Ezekiel 25:8–11; Amos 2:1–3; and Zephaniah 2:8–11.

Jer. 49 | AMMON, EDOM, SYRIA, HAZOR, ELAM

A prediction that Nebuchadnezzar will conquer these nations, which he did. Ammon, see under Ezekiel 25:1–11. Edom, see under Obadiah.

Jer. 50–51 | PREDICTION OF THE FALL OF BABYLON

The fall and permanent destruction of Babylon are here predicted, as Isaiah had done earlier (Isaiah 13:17–22), in language matching the grandeur of the theme (51:37–43). The Medes, at the head of a league of nations, are named as the conquerors (50:9; 51:11, 27–28).

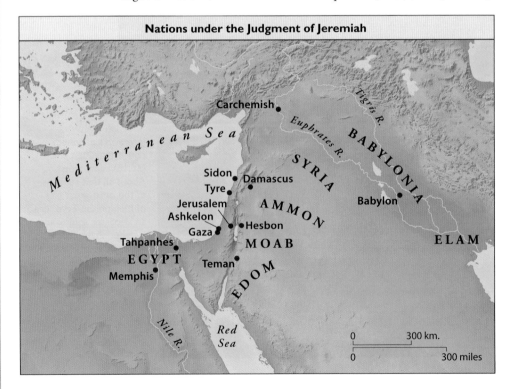

Nations under the Judgment of Jeremiah

These two chapters, pronouncing the doom of Babylonia, were copied in a separate book and sent to Babylon in a deputation headed by King Zedekiah, seven years before Nebuchadnezzar burned Jerusalem (51:59–64). The book was to be read publicly and then, in solemn ceremony, sunk in the Euphrates, with the words, "So will Babylon sink to rise no more."

Jer. 52 | CAPTIVITY OF JUDAH *(SEE ON 2 KINGS 24–25.)*

ARCHAEOLOGICAL NOTE: Personal Seals and Bullae. A seal was a device in which a design or name is engraved, so that when it is pressed into a soft substance such as clay or wax, it will leave a permanent impression when the substance hardens. The impression made by a seal is called a *bulla* (plural *bullae*). Some seals were flat; others were cylindrical and were rolled into the wax or clay.

Seals were used as a mark of authenticity on letters and official documents (1 Kings 21:8; Esther 3:12); as a means to keep a book, document, or room from being tampered with (similar to our "sealing" court documents or a crime scene; Jeremiah 32:14); as a proof of delegated authority (Esther 3:10; 8:2); and as an official mark of ownership, for example, on jar handles and jar stoppers.

"Seal" is also used figuratively — for example, in Deuteronomy 32:34; Romans 4:11; 15:28; 1 Corinthians 9:2; Ephesians 1:13; 4:30; Revelation 5:1; 7:2–4; 10:4.

Numerous seals and bullae have been found that date back to the Old Testament era; a number of these actually belonged to people mentioned in the Old Testament.

- The seal of **Seriah** son of Neriah, who was commanded by Jeremiah to take a scroll of Jeremiah's prophecies concerning Babylon to Babylon (Jeremiah 51:59–64), is known to exist in a private collection. It reads: "Belonging to Seriah [son of] Neriyahu."
- An impression has been found of the seal that actually belonged to Jeremiah's scribe, **Baruch**. The inscription on the bulla contains a longer form ("Berechiah") of the name Baruch. It reads: "Belonging to Berechiah son of Neriah the scribe." See Jeremiah 32:12; 34:1–7; and chapters 36 and 45.
- An impression of the seal of the very person commanded to arrest Baruch and Jeremiah has been found. It reads: "Belonging to Jerahmeel the king's son" — see Jeremiah 36:26: "Instead, the king commanded Jerahmeel, a son of the king . . . to arrest Baruch the scribe and Jeremiah the prophet. But the Lord had hidden them."
- An impression of the seal of "**Gemariah** son of Shaphan the secretary" (Jeremiah 36:10), the one in whose room Baruch read the words of Jeremiah from the scroll to the people, was found by Yigal

Shiloh in his excavations in the City of David. It reads: "Belonging to Gemaryahu, son of Shaphan."

- A seal impression was found at Tell el-Umeiri in Jordan, east of the Dead Sea, from the early 6th century B.C. It reads: "Belonging to Milkom'ur, servant of Baalyasha." This Baalyasha is probably to be identified with "Baalis the king of the sons of Ammon," mentioned in Jeremiah 40:14.
- Recently the actual seal of "Ba'alis, king of the sons of Ammon" has come to light — the very king who plotted the murder of Gedaliah (Jeremiah 40:13 – 41:2).

Lamentations

A Lament over the Desolation of Jerusalem

Because of the LORD's great love we are not consumed,
*   for his compassions never fail.*
They are new every morning;
*   great is your faithfulness.*
The LORD is good to those whose hope is in him,
*   to the one who seeks him;*
it is good to wait quietly
*   for the salvation of the LORD.*

—LAMENTATIONS 3:22–23, 25–26

This short book is Jeremiah's lament over the city he had done his best to save. Yet, in his sorrow he also expresses his faith that Jerusalem will rise again from its ruins (3:21, 31–32). Jerusalem did indeed rise and gave its name to the capital of a redeemed world of eternal glory, the New Jerusalem (Hebrews 12:22; Revelation 21:2).

An Appendix to Jeremiah

The last chapter of Jeremiah should be read as an introduction to this book. The Septuagint adds the introduction, "And it came to pass, after Israel was led into captivity and Jerusalem was laid waste, that Jeremiah sat weeping, and lamented this lamentation over Jerusalem, and said. . . ."

But unlike our Bible, the Hebrew Old Testament does not put Lamentations immediately after Jeremiah, but rather in a group of books called the Ketubim or Writings, to which belong the Song of Songs, Ruth, Lamentations, Ecclesiastes, and Esther. These were on separate rolls because they were read at different feasts. To this day, the book of Lamentations is read in synagogues throughout the world, wherever there are Jews, on the ninth day of the fourth month, the day of fasting that commemorates the fall of the temple (Jeremiah 52:6).

An Acrostic

The book consists of five poems, four of which are acrostics—that is, each verse begins with a different letter of the Hebrew alphabet, in alphabetic sequence. This was a favorite form of Hebrew poetry, adopted in part as an aid to memory. In chapters 1, 2, and 4 there is one verse for each letter, or 22 verses per chapter, since the Hebrew alphabet has 22 letters. Chapter 3 has three verses per letter, and thus 66 verses in all. Chapter 5 has 22 verses, but not in alphabetic order. (See also "Poetry and Wisdom," p. 285.)

Its Immediate Use

The book must have been composed in the three months between the burning of Jerusalem and the departure of the remnant to Egypt (Jeremiah 39:2; 41:1, 18; 43:7). During this time the seat of government was at Mizpah (Jeremiah 40:8). Probably a number of copies were made; some were taken to Egypt, others sent to Babylon for the exiles to memorize and sing.

Lam. 1 | ZION DESOLATE

It is not easy to define the subject of each chapter. The same ideas, in different wording, run through all the chapters: the horrors of the siege and the desolate ruins, all due to Zion's sins. Jeremiah, stunned, dazed, and heartbroken, weeps with inconsolable grief. The emphasis in this chapter is that the people brought the catastrophe upon themselves by their sins (5, 8–9, 14, 18, 20, 22).

Lam. 2 | GOD'S ANGER

The devastation of Jerusalem is attributed to the anger of God (1–4, 6, 21–22). Jerusalem, situated on a mountain and surrounded by yet higher mountains, was because of its location the most beautiful city then known, "the perfection of beauty" (v. 15), even when compared with Babylon, Nineveh, Thebes, and Memphis, which were built on river plains. Moreover, it was the city of God's special care, chosen by Him for a unique mission — to be the main channel for God's dealings with people. It was the most favored and highly privileged city in all the world, beloved of God in an exceptional way and under His special protection. Moreover, it was so well fortified that it was generally believed to be impregnable (4:12). But this City of God had become worse than Sodom (4:6). That the God of love is also a God of wrath is a teaching that is stated and illustrated again and again throughout the Bible.

Lam. 3 | JEREMIAH'S GRIEF

In this chapter Jeremiah seems to be complaining that God has ignored him and his prayers (v. 8): "You have covered yourself with a cloud so that no prayer can get through" (v. 44). Though complaining, he justifies God, acknowledging that they deserved worse (v. 22). The high point of the book is verses 21–39.

Lam. 4–5 | SUFFERINGS OF THE SIEGE

Jeremiah could not keep his mind off the horrors of the siege, the cries of starving children (2:11–12, 19; 4:4), women who boiled their babies for food (2:20; 4:10).

The city of Jerusalem. The book of Lamentations is a song of grieving over the pending destruction of Jerusalem by the Babylonians.

But in spite of its horrible sufferings, Jerusalem failed to learn its lesson. After the exile it was rebuilt, and in Jesus' day it had again become a great and beautiful city. Yet they crucified the Son of God, after which followed its eradication by the armies of Rome in A.D. 70. (See under Hebrews 13.)

Ezekiel

**The Fall of Jerusalem
Judgments on Surrounding Nations
The Restoration of Israel**

"When I say to a wicked man, 'You will surely die,' and you do not warn him or speak out to dissuade him from his evil ways in order to save his life, that wicked man will die for his sin, and I will hold you accountable for his blood. But if you do warn the wicked man and he does not turn from his wickedness or from his evil ways, he will die for his sin; but you will have saved yourself." ——EZEKIEL 3:18–19

Ezekiel was a prophet of the Babylonian captivity (or exile). He was taken to Babylon in 597 B.C., 11 years before Jerusalem was destroyed and the southern kingdom, Judah, ceased to exist.

The northern kingdom, Israel, had been taken into exile by the Assyrians 120 years earlier. This had happened in three stages, of which especially the last one should have been a warning to Judah:

734 B.C.	Galilee and northern and eastern Israel are overrun by Tiglath-pileser.
722 B.C.	Samaria and the rest of Israel are captured by Sargon.
701 B.C.	200,000 of the inhabitants of Judah are taken into exile by Sennacherib.

The Babylonian exile of Judah also took place in three stages:

605 B.C.	Some captives are taken to Babylon, including Daniel.
597 B.C.	More captives are taken to Babylon, including Ezekiel.
586 B.C.	Jerusalem is burned.

The Babylonian exile lasted 70 years, from 605 to 535 B.C. Ezekiel was in Babylon from 597 until at least 570 B.C.

Ezekiel and Daniel

Daniel had been in Babylon for nine years and had already attained great fame when Ezekiel arrived (14:14, 20). Daniel lived and worked in the palace, Ezekiel in the country.

Ezekiel and Jeremiah

Jeremiah was the older of the two. Ezekiel may have been his pupil. Ezekiel preached the same things among the exiles that Jeremiah was preaching in Jerusalem: the certainty of Judah's punishment for her sins.

Ezekiel and the Book of Revelation

Some of Ezekiel's visions reappear in the book of Revelation:

- The cherubim (Ezekiel 1; Revelation 4)
- Gog and Magog (Ezekiel 38; Revelation 20)
- Eating the book (Ezekiel 3; Revelation 10)
- The New Jerusalem (Ezekiel 40–48; Revelation 21)
- The river of the water of life (Ezekiel 47; Revelation 22)

"They Will Know That I Am the Lord"

This expression is a dominant note of the book. It occurs 62 times, in 27 of the 48 chapters (**6:**7, 10, 13, 14; **7:**4, 9, 27; **11:**10, 12; **12:**15, 16, 20; **13:**9, 14, 21; **14:**8; **15:**7; **16:**62; **17:**21, 24; **20:**12, 20, 28, 38, 42, 44; **21:**5; **22:**16, 22; **23:**49; **24:**24, 27; **25:**5, 7, 11, 17; **26:**6; **28:**22, 23, 24, 26; **29:**6, 9, 16, 21; **30:**8, 19, 25, 26; **32:**15; **33:**29; **34:**27, 30; **35:**4, 9, 12, 15; **36:**11, 23, 36, 38; **37:**6, 13, 14, 28; **38:**16, 23; **39:**6, 7, 22, 23, 28).

Ezekiel's mission appears to have been to explain why God caused or permitted Judah's captivity. It was because of the unspeakable abominations of which they had been guilty—abominations for which other nations had been wiped out. But for Judah, it was punishment for the sake of correction: through their punishment they would come to know that God is God. They did. The Babylonian captivity cured the Jews of their idolatry.

The Chronology of Ezekiel's Book

The pivot around which the book revolves is the destruction of Jerusalem, which occurred in 586 B.C. Ezekiel's prophecies began six years before that and continued for 16 years thereafter, covering a period of 22 years. Until the fall of Jerusalem, Ezekiel was constantly predicting the certainty of its fall (chaps. 1–24). After that, his prophecies deal with the overthrow of surrounding nations (chaps. 25–32) and the reestablishment and glorious future of Israel (chaps. 33–48).

His visions, with minor exceptions, are presented in chronological sequence. The years are dated from King Jehoiachin's captivity, which was 597 B.C.

The **thirtieth year** (1:1), which was the equivalent of the **fifth year** of the exile of King Jehoiachin (1:2), is thought to have been the 30th year of Ezekiel's life—the age at which Levites began their service (Numbers 4:3; Jesus and John the Baptist both began their work at age 30). Or, it may have been the 30th year in the Babylonian calendar, which began with the year in which Nebopolasar won Babylonia's independence from Assyria (625 B.C.).

The dates of Ezekiel's visions are as follows:

Chapter 1:2	5th year	4th month	5th day	July 31, 593 B.C.	First vision
Chapter 8:1	6th year	6th month	5th day	Sept. 17, 592 B.C.	Transport to Jerusalem
Chapter 20:1	7th year	5th month	10th day	Aug. 14, 591 B.C.	Israel's history
Chapter 24:1	9th year	10th month	10th day	Jan 15, 588 B.C.	The siege begins (2 Kings 25:1)

The siege of Jerusalem began in the 9th year, in the 10th month, on the 10th day.

Chapter 26:1	11th year		1st day	Apr. 23, 587– Apr. 13, 586 B.C.	Against Tyre
Chapter 29:1	10th year	10th month	12th day	Jan. 7, 587 B.C.	Against Egypt
Chapter 29:17	27th year	1st month	1st day	Apr. 26, 571 B.C.	Egypt in exchange for Tyre
Chapter 30:20	11th year	1st month	7th day	Apr. 29, 587 B.C.	Against Pharaoh
Chapter 31:1	12th year	12th month	1st day	June 21, 585 B.C.	Against Pharaoh

Jerusalem fell in the 11th year, in the 4th month, on the 9th day.

Chapter 32:1	12th year	12th month	1st day	March. 3, 585 B.C.	Lament over Pharaoh
Chapter 32:17	12th year		15th day	Apr. 13, 586– Apr. 1, 585 B.C.	Egypt is dead
Chapter 33:21	12th year	10th month	5th day	585 B.C.	The first fugitive arrives
Chapter 40:1	25th year	1st(?) month	10th day	573 B.C.	Vision of the future

Since Ezekiel was so meticulous in dating his visions, down to the exact day, it is assumed that all that comes after a given date belongs to that date until the next date is mentioned.

Ezek. 1:1–3 | EZEKIEL'S HOME AND DATE

Ezekiel was taken captive with King Jehoiachin (597 B.C.) and speaks of "our exile" (33:21; 40:1). He had a wife (24:15–18) and a home (8:1). He lived by the River Kebar, the great ship canal that branched off from the Euphrates north of Babylon and ran through Nippur back to the Euphrates. Nippur, about 50 miles southeast of Babylon, was Calneh, one of the cities Nimrod had built (Genesis 10:10). Tel Abib seems to have been Ezekiel's hometown (3:15, 24), and it is thought to have been near Nippur.

The conditions of the Jews in the Babylonian exile were relatively mild. They were placed in a specific location—Tel Aviv or Tel Abib—but they appear to have been allowed to travel freely in the country and to engage in commerce. They were regarded more as colonists than as slaves.

Son of Man is how Ezekiel is addressed 90 times. In Daniel 7:13 this title is used of the Messiah. It was the title by which Jesus commonly spoke of Himself (see under John 1:14).

Visions and symbolic actions are characteristic of Ezekiel's book. Some of his symbolic actions were accompanied by painful personal sufferings. He had to remain silent for a long period (3:26; 24:27; 33:22). He had to lie on his side in one position for over a year (4:5–6). He had to eat food cooked over cow manure (4:15). And his wife, whom he dearly loved ("the delight of your eyes") was suddenly taken from him, but he was not allowed to mourn (24:16–18).

Ezek. 1:4–28 | EZEKIEL'S VISION OF GOD

The "living creatures" are identified as cherubim (10:20). They stood, one in the middle of each side of a square, their outspread wings touching at the corners of the square. Each cherub had four faces: the face of a man, looking outward from the square; on his right, the face of a lion; on his left, the face of an ox; in the rear, looking toward the center of the square, the face of an eagle. There were four immense whirling wheels (10:6), one beside each cherub. The wheels "sparkled like chrysolite," and their rims were full of eyes. This fourfold living creature moved like flashes of lightning from place to place, with noise like the roar of the ocean.

Above the living creatures was a crystal platform, and on the platform, a throne of blue sapphire. The whole vision was set within a vast storm cloud, with whirling flashes of fire. This was the form in which God appeared to Ezekiel. It signified His glory, power, omniscience, omnipresence, omnipotence, sovereignty, majesty, and holiness.

Cherubim guarded the entrance to the tree of life (Genesis 3:24). Likenesses of cherubim were placed on the ark of the covenant (Exodus 25:18–20) and embroidered on the curtain of the tabernacle (Exodus 26:31). They were reproduced in olive wood in the temple (1 Kings 6:23, 29; 2 Chronicles 3:14). They are interwoven in biblical thought from the beginning as angelic attendants of God. In Revelation (4:6–7; 5:6; 6:1, 6; 7:11; 14:3; 15:7; 19:4), they are intimately connected with the unfolding of the last things.

Ezek. 2–3 | EZEKIEL'S COMMISSION

Ezekiel is warned at the outset that he is being called to a life of hardship and persecution. His message is delivered to him from God in the form of

14th-century Hebrew scroll. The Lord gave Ezekiel an unrolled scroll with a message of mourning and woe. (Ezekiel 2:9–10)

a book, which he is commanded to eat (this also happened to the apostle John in Revelation 10:9). In his mouth the book was "sweet," which seems to mean that he found joy in being God's messenger, though the message was a message of woe. Eating the book, whether literally or only in a vision, signified thoroughly digesting its contents so that its message would become a part of himself. In 3:17–21 God seemed to lay upon Ezekiel the responsibility for the doom of his nation, which he could escape only by a faithful declaration of God's message. He was also warned that God would, at times, impose silence upon him (3:26; 24:27; 33:22); this was a caution to Ezekiel to speak not his own ideas, but only what God commanded.

| Ezek. 4–7 | THE SYMBOLIC SIEGE OF JERUSALEM |

Ezekiel's opening message to the exiles, who were hoping for a speedy return to Jerusalem, was this graphic warning that Jerusalem was about to be destroyed, that they would soon be joined by other exiles, and that their exile would last at least 40 years. The number 40 may be meant as a round number denoting a generation. At this time (592 B.C.) some of the captives had already been there 13 years. In six more years, Jerusalem was burned. From that point on, the captivity lasted 50 years, 586–536 B.C.

Although the basic meaning of this section is clear, the numbers have given rise to many explanations. Certain things are plain: each day represented a year, and the years signified a period during which God's people would receive discipline. Some understand the numbers as referring to Israel's stay in Egypt (390 years) and the wilderness wanderings (40 years); these numbers, then, are symbolic rather than actual and warn of a time of captivity *similar to* that in Egypt, though not necessarily of the same length.

Normally the numbers would be taken as periods of time separated into two distinct and successive intervals. Ezekiel's reference point for chronological purposes was King Jehoiachin's deportation in 597 B.C. This would therefore appear to be the natural starting point for measuring the time periods in these verses. The 430 years would denote the punishment inflicted by conquering foreign powers on the children of Israel and Judah from the deportation of Jehoiachin, their recognized king, to the inception of the Maccabean rebellion in 167 B.C. During the Maccabean period the Jews once again were in charge in Judah. Though this is a possible solution, we must avoid being dogmatic about these numbers.

As a sign of famine, Ezekiel lived on bread baked on excrement. Throughout the siege he lay on one side, either continuously or for the greater part of each day, which, combined with the famine rations he was allowed to eat each day, meant great discomfort.

Chapter 5. When the siege is finished, he is commanded, as a further symbol of the fate of Jerusalem's inhabitants, to shave off his hair, burn part of it, and scatter the rest to the winds.

Chapters 6–7. A sort of dirge over the destruction and desolation of the land of Israel; the main point is that the Jews would, by this terrible punishment, come to know that God is God.

Ezek. 8–11 | EZEKIEL'S VISION-JOURNEY TO JERUSALEM

In September of 592 B.C., a year and two months after his call, Ezekiel was transported in a vision to Jerusalem, where God showed him the abhorrent idolatries that were being practiced in the temple. The "idol that provokes jealousy" (8:3) probably was Asherah, a Canaanite fertility goddess. Secret animal worship (8:10) was probably an Egyptian cult. It was led by Jaazaniah II, whose father Shaphan had been a leader in Josiah's reformation (2 Kings 22:8) and whose brothers Ahikam and Gemariah were Jeremiah's close friends (Jeremiah 26:24; 36:10, 25), even while Jeremiah himself was crying out in horror at the sacrilege.

This is the only biblical reference to the Babylonian fertility god **Tammuz**. It is possible that the women of Jerusalem were bewailing his dying, which they felt caused the annual wilting of vegetation. The date of this vision was in the months of August/September. This month later became known in the Hebrew calendar as the month of Tammuz (see p. 1025).

Thus, in spite of warning after warning and punishment after punishment, the once powerful kingdom of Judah, reduced now almost to the point of extinction, was still sinking lower and lower into the depths of idolatrous infamy—a stench no longer to be endured by God.

Chapter 9. A vision of the slaughter of Jerusalem's idolaters, except for the faithful who bore the mark of the angel-scribe (vv. 3–4; similar to Revelation 14:1, where the 144,000 have their Father's name written on their foreheads).

Chapter 10. Reappearance of the cherubim of chapter 1, now to oversee the destruction and slaughter of Jerusalem.

Chapter 11. A vision of the future restoration of the exiles, humbled, purified, and cured of idolatry (vv. 10, 12).

His mission completed, Ezekiel is taken back to his home in exile to tell the exiles everything he had seen (8:1; 11:25).

Ezek. 12 | EZEKIEL MOVES HIS HOUSEHOLD GOODS

Another symbolic action to emphasize Jerusalem's impending exile. Here is an amazingly detailed prophecy of Zedekiah's fate: his secret flight, his capture, and his removal to Babylon without seeing it (vv. 10, 12–13). Five years later, it happened: Zedekiah attempted a secret escape, was captured, had his eyes put out, and was taken to Babylon (Jeremiah 52:7–11).

Ezek. 13 | FALSE PROPHETS

There were many false prophets, both in Jerusalem and among the exiles. The charms (v. 18) and veils (vv. 18, 21) must have been used in some sort of magical rite. The Bible avoids explicit descriptions of the occult.

Ezek. 14 | HYPOCRITICAL INQUIRERS

To a delegation of idol lovers, God's answer is not words but the swift and terrible destruction of idolatrous Israel. It may be that for Daniel's sake Nebuchadnezzar had spared Jerusalem thus far (v. 14), but it is now to be spared no longer.

Ezek. 15 | THE PARABLE OF THE USELESS VINE

A vine that does not produce fruit is utterly useless, since its wood cannot be used for anything except as fuel. In the same way, Jerusalem was no longer fit for anything but burning.

Ezek. 16 | THE ALLEGORY OF THE UNFAITHFUL WIFE

This chapter is a very graphic and vivid portrayal of Israel's idolatry under the image of a bride, loved by her husband, who made her a queen and lavished upon her silks and sealskins and every beautiful thing, but who then made herself a prostitute to every man that passed by, outdoing even Sodom and Samaria in wickedness. (See Jeremiah 1–2.)

Ezek. 17 | THE PARABLE OF THE TWO EAGLES

The first eagle (v. 3) was the king of Babylon. The "topmost shoot" (v. 4) was Jehoiachin, who was taken to Babylon (2 Kings 24:11–16) six years before this parable was uttered. The "seed of the land" (vv. 5, 13) was Zedekiah (2 Kings 24:17).

The other eagle (v. 7) was the king of Egypt, toward whom Zedekiah looked for help. For his treachery, Zedekiah will be taken to Babylon, to be punished and to die there (v. 13–21; this is a repetition of what Ezekiel had previously prophesied, 12:10–16). This happened five years later (2 Kings 25:6–7). The "tender sprig" (vv. 22–24), which God would later plant in the restored royal family of David, had its fulfillment in the Messiah.

Ezek. 18 | "THE SOUL WHO SINS IS THE ONE WHO WILL DIE"

Much is said in the Prophets about the fact that Israel's exile was the result of the cumulative sins of earlier generations. The generation of the exile, overlooking the fact that they were "worse than their fathers," was now trying to lay *all* the blame on their fathers. The burden of this chapter is that God judges every individual on the basis of his or her own individual and personal conduct. It is an impassioned appeal to the wicked to repent (vv. 30–32).

Ezek. 19 | A DIRGE OVER THE FALL OF DAVID'S THRONE

Under the imagery of a lioness, David's family, once great and powerful, is now overthrown. The first cub (v. 3) was Jehoahaz (Shallum), who was taken to Egypt (2 Kings 23:31–34). The second cub (v. 5) was either Jehoiachin or Zedekiah, both of whom were taken to Babylon (1 Kings 24:8–25:7).

Ezek. 20 | A REVIEW OF ISRAEL'S IDOLATRIES

Generation after generation Israel had wallowed in the filth of idol worship. But note the prophecy of restoration (see also chapter 37).

Ezek. 21 | THE SWORD OF BABYLON

The sword is about to be drawn against Jerusalem and Ammon.

The south (20:46) is the land of Judah.

Until he comes to whom it rightfully belongs (21:27): "it" is the overturning of Zedekiah's throne (vv. 25–27). This will be the end of David's kingdom until the coming of the Messiah (34:23–24; 37:24; Jeremiah 23:5–6).

Ezek. 22 | THE SINS OF JERUSALEM

Over and over Ezekiel names the sins of Jerusalem: she defiles herself with idols, sheds blood, profanes the Sabbath, practices robbery, commits promiscuous adultery; and the princes, priests, and prophets are greedy for dishonest gain.

Ezek. 23 | OHOLAH AND OHOLIBAH

Two sisters, insatiable in their lewdness, are a parable of Israel's idolatry. Oholah is Samaria; Oholibah, Jerusalem. Both have grown old in their adulteries. Again and again the relationship between husband and wife is used to represent the relationship between God and his people (see under chapter 16). Promiscuous adultery must have been very widespread (16:32; 18:6, 11, 15; 22:11; 23:43; Jeremiah 5:7–8; 7:9; 9:2; 23:10, 14; 29:23).

Ezek. 24 | THE COOKING POT

The cooking pot is symbolic of the destruction of Jerusalem, which is very near. The rust on the pot represents the bloodshed and immorality of the city.

The death of Ezekiel's wife (vv. 15–24) occurred on the day the siege of Jerusalem began (vv. 1, 18; 2 Kings 25:1). It is a heartrending sign to the exiles that their beloved Jerusalem was now to be taken from them. Silence was imposed on Ezekiel until news came, three years later, that the city had fallen (v. 27; 33:21–22).

Ezek. 25 | AMMON, MOAB, EDOM, PHILISTIA

These four nations were Judah's closest neighbors, who rejoiced at Judah's destruction by Babylon. Ezekiel here predicts for them the same fate, as did Jeremiah (Jeremiah 27:1–7). Nebuchadnezzar subdued the Philistines when he took Judah, and four years later he invaded Ammon, Moab, and Edom.

Ezek. 26-28 | TYRE. VISIONS OF 586 B.C.

These visions of the doom of Tyre were given to Ezekiel in the same year that Jerusalem fell, that is, the 11th year (26:1).

Chapter 26. A prophecy of Nebuchadnezzar's siege and Tyre's permanent desolation. The following year, in 585 B.C., Nebuchadnezzar laid siege to Tyre. It took him 13 years to conquer the city.

Tyre, located 12 miles north of the Israeli-Lebanese border, was a double city; part of it was built on an island, part on the mainland, in a fertile and well-watered plain at the western foot of the Lebanon mountain range. It was the great maritime power of the ancient world and reached its zenith from the 12th to the 6th centuries B.C., with colonies on the north and west coasts of Africa, in Spain, and in Britain. Tyre controlled the commerce of the Mediterranean — the wares of all nations passed through its port. It was a city renowned for its splendor and fabulous wealth.

With Nebuchadnezzar's conquest, Tyre ceased to be an independent power. It was later subdued by the Persians, and again by Alexander the Great (332 B.C.). It never recovered its former glory and has for centuries

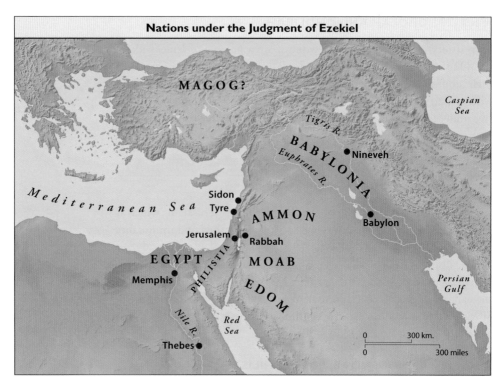

Nations under the Judgment of Ezekiel

MAGOG?

Caspian Sea

Tigris R.

BABYLONIA

•Nineveh

Euphrates R.

Mediterranean Sea

Sidon•
Tyre•

AMMON

•Babylon

Jerusalem•
•Rabbah

EGYPT

MOAB

Persian Gulf

Memphis•

PHILISTIA

EDOM

Nile R.

Red Sea

0 ___ 300 km.
0 ___ 300 miles

Thebes•

been a "bare rock" where fishermen "spread fishnets" (26:4–5, 14), an amazing fulfillment of Ezekiel's prophecy that it "will never be rebuilt" (26:14, 21; 27:36; 28:19).

Chapter 27. Tyre, mistress of the Mediterranean, is pictured under the image of a majestic ship of incomparable beauty, bearing the wares and treasures of the nations, but about to be sunk.

Chapter 28:1–19. The overthrow of Tyre's proud king, who, on his inaccessible and impregnable island throne, took any threat to his security lightly.

Inscription describing Nebuchadnezzar's battle at Carchemish, victory over the Egyptian forces, and ultimate capture of Jerusalem. In six visions, Ezekiel prophesied Nebuchadnezzar's defeat of Egypt.

Chapter 28:20–24. The overthrow of Sidon, 20 miles north of Tyre. It was taken by Nebuchadnezzar when he took Tyre.

Chapter 28:25–26. The restoration of Israel, after the hostile neighbor nations shall have disappeared.

| Ezek. 29-32 | EGYPT. SIX VISIONS |

Six visions that predict Nebuchadnezzar's invasion of Egypt and Egypt's permanent reduction to a place of minor importance. Nebuchadnezzar invaded and plundered Egypt in 568 B.C. Egypt never quite recovered its former glory (29:15).

First Vision (29:1–16). January 587 B.C., 18 months before the fall of Jerusalem. As Tyre was pictured as a ship in chapter 27, in this vision Egypt is pictured as a crocodile, monarch of the Nile, and one of the gods of Egypt.

The 40 years of Egypt's captivity and desolation (vv. 11–12): it was nearly 40 years from Nebuchadnezzar's conquest of Egypt to the rise of Persia (536 B.C.), under whose rule all captive peoples were allowed to return to their native lands.

Second Vision (29:17–30:19). April 571 B.C., 16 years after the fall of Jerusalem. This vision, given many years after the other five visions, on the eve of Nebuchadnezzar's march into Egypt, is inserted here for unity of subject. He and his army obtained no material reward from their campaign against Tyre (29:18); Nebuchadnezzar, God's servant in punishing the nations, had besieged Tyre for 13 years (ending in 573 B.C.). Considering the length of the siege, the booty had been disappointing because so many inhabitants had fled with their wealth. But now he will make up for it in Egypt (v. 20). "No longer will there be a prince" (30:13), that is, a native ruler of importance.

Third Vision (30:20–26). April 587 B.C., 15 months before Jerusalem fell. "Have broken" (v. 21) probably refers to the defeat of Pharaoh's army (Jeremiah 37:5–9).

Fourth Vision (chap. 31). June 587 B.C., 13 months before Jerusalem fell. Egypt is warned to remember the fate of Assyria, which was more powerful than Egypt yet had fallen to Babylon.

Fifth Vision (32:1–16). March 585 B.C., eight months after Jerusalem fell. A lamentation over Egypt, to be crushed at the hands of Babylon.

Sixth Vision (32:17–32). March 585 B.C., eight months after Jerusalem fell. A picture of Egypt and her companions in the realm of the dead.

Ezek. 33	NEWS OF THE FALL OF JERUSALEM

This happens a year and a half after the city had fallen (see chronology on p. 381). Ezekiel had been silent since the day the siege had begun, a period of three years (24:1, 26–27; 32:22). The visions against Tyre and Egypt of chapters 26–31, most of which came during those three years, must have been written, not spoken.

Ezekiel's first statement after receiving news of the fall was that the wicked left in Judah would be exterminated (vv. 23–29). Five years later Nebuchadnezzar took 745 more captives (Jeremiah 52:30).

Then follows a note about Ezekiel's popularity with the exiles (vv. 30–33), who were charmed by his speech but continued to be unrepentant.

Ezek. 34	AN INDICTMENT OF THE SHEPHERDS OF ISRAEL

Responsibility for the captivity of Israel is here laid directly at the door of the greedy and cruel kings and priests who had exploited the people and led them astray. Against this background Ezekiel sees a vision of the future Shepherd of God's people in the coming Messiah (vv. 15, 23–24), under whom they shall never again suffer — "there will be showers of blessing" (v. 26).

Ezek. 35 | THE DOOM OF EDOM

Now that the inhabitants of Judah had been taken away, Edom saw an opportunity to take possession of their land (v. 10; 36:2, 5). But three years later the same fate befell Edom. (See under Obadiah.)

Ezek. 36 | THE LAND OF ISRAEL TO BE REINHABITED

Now desolate, it will one day become like the Garden of Eden (v. 35), populated by a penitent Judah and Israel (vv. 10, 31). This will be for the glory of God's own name (vv. 22, 32).

Ezek. 37 | THE VISION OF THE DRY BONES

This vision is a prediction of the national resurrection of scattered Israel, their return to their own land, and the reunion of Judah and Israel under the reign of an everlasting king called "David" (vv. 24–26). It is a plain forecast of the conversion of the Jews to Christ, as Paul also foretold in Romans 11:15, 25–26.

The vision encompasses the "whole house of Israel" (v. 11), both Judah and Israel, the southern kingdom and the northern kingdom. The return of Judah is told in Ezra and Nehemiah, where there is no mention of returned exiles of Israel. Yet those returned are called "Israel" (Ezra 9:1; 10:5; Nehemiah 9:2; 11:3).

There is difference of opinion as to how much of this is to be interpreted literally as referring to the Jews and what may be a foreshadowing of the new covenant in its universal aspect (vv. 26–28). It is not always easy to draw a clear line between what is to be taken literally and what figuratively. For instance, it would seem that the great battle of Gog and Magog of chapters 38–39, which is still future, could not be fought with literal bows and arrows, war clubs, and spears (39:9).

David (37:24) is not literal David, but the Messiah. The term "Israel" in the New Testament, while usually used of Jews, is sometimes applied to Christians (Galatians 6:16), and it is indicated that Gentiles were included in the meaning (Romans 2:28–29; 4:13–16; Galatians 3:7–9, 29; Philippians 3:3). So this vision of a reinhabited land and a revived and glorified nation, making all due allowance for its evident literal meaning, may also be a symbolic image of a regenerated earth, as the book of Revelation depicts heaven under the image of a magnificent earthly city (Revelation 21). Biblical prophecies of the future were often pictured in terms of what was then present. We think that in such passages as this there may be both a literal and a figurative meaning, just as in Matthew 24 some of Jesus' words seem to refer both to the destruction of Jerusalem and to the end of the world, the one typical of the other.

The Messiah is central in Ezekiel's visions of Israel's future. He calls Him "the Prince" (34:23–24; 37:24–25; 44:3; 45:7; 46:16–18; 48:21).

Ezek. 38–39 | GOG AND MAGOG

Much has been written (and speculated) about the prophetic meaning of Gog and Magog. **Gog** is apparently a leader or king whose name appears only here and in Revelation 20:8. Attempts have been made to identify Gog with historical rulers, such as Gyges, king of Lydia (ca. 660 B.C.). Possibly the name is purposely vague, standing for an as yet undisclosed enemy of God's people. In the book of Revelation, Gog and Magog are used to represent all nations in Satan's final, furious attack on the people of God (Revelation 20:7–10).

In Ezekiel 39:16, **Magog** appears to be the name of a people. But since the Hebrew prefix *ma* can mean "place of," Magog may here simply mean "land of Gog." From the time they entered Canaan, the Israelites had experienced hostilities from other Semitic peoples. The coalition Ezekiel envisions will include and be led by nations descended from Japheth.

The "chief prince" is evidently a military commander-in-chief. (An alternative meaning is "prince of Rosh"; if this is correct, Rosh would be the name of an unknown people or place. There is no evidence from the Ancient Near East that a country named Rosh ever existed. Rosh is sometimes thought to refer to Russia because of the similar sound; however, the word "Russia" dates from the late 11th century A.D. — more than 1,500 years after Ezekiel's day.)

Magog, a descendant of Japheth (Genesis 10:2), is identified by Josephus (*Antiq.* 1.123) as the land of the Scythians, a mountainous region around the Black and Caspian seas. This position is generally accepted.

Meshech and **Tubal** were sons of Japheth (see Genesis 10:2; 1 Chronicles 1:5) and are probably to be located in eastern Asia Minor (cf. 27:13; 32:26). They are peoples and territories to the north of Israel (cf. vv. 6, 15; 39:2). Thus, Gog is a person from the region of Magog who is the chief ruler, or prince, over the geographical areas Meshech and Tubal. These areas, or countries, seem to be located generally south of the Black and Caspian seas in what are now the countries of Russia, Turkey, and Iran.

As in the days of the Assyrians and Babylonians, the major attack will again come from the north in confederation with peoples from the east. With the help of God, those attacking will be so overwhelmingly defeated that their weapons will supply fuel for seven years (39:9) and it will take seven months to bury their dead (39:12).

Ezek. 40–48 | THE REBUILT TEMPLE

In April 572 B.C., at the time of the Passover, 14 years after the destruction of Jerusalem, Ezekiel makes his second journey in a vision to Jerusalem; the first had been 19 years earlier (8:1, 3), on a mission of doom for the city.

This second vision-journey is to give specifications for Jerusalem's reconstruction and deals largely with details concerning the new temple.

This vision was not fulfilled in the return from Babylon. It is clearly a prediction of the Messianic Age.

Some interpret it literally as meaning that the 12 tribes will one day again inhabit the land and be distributed as here indicated, that the temple will be rebuilt literally in all particulars as here specified, and that there will be literal animal sacrifices. They call it "the millennial temple."

Others interpret it figuratively and take the vision to be a metaphorical preview of the whole Christian era under the image of a revived, restored, and glorified nation.

This temple of Ezekiel's vision, with its courts, arrangements, and furnishings, follows roughly, though with many variations, the general plan of Solomon's temple.

God was to live in this temple "forever" (43:7). This can hardly be said of a literal, material temple. It must be a figurative representation of something, since Jesus, in John 4:21–24, abrogated temple worship and there will be no temple in heaven (Revelation 21:22).

Offerings and sacrifices (45:9–46:24). One wonders why there should be sacrifices under the reign of "the prince." The epistle to the Hebrews explicitly states that sacrifices were fulfilled and done away in the death of Christ, "once for all." Those who think that this temple is a literal "millennial temple" consider that these animal sacrifices are to be offered by the Jewish nation while it is still unconverted, or that the sacrifices are commemorative of the death of Christ.

The life-giving stream (47:1–12). This is one of Ezekiel's grandest passages. Joel and Zechariah also spoke of this stream (Joel 3:18; Zechariah 14:8). It seems to be a picture of heaven's "river of the water of life" (Revelation 22:1–2). Whatever specific or literal application these waters may have, certainly, without any straining whatever, they can be understood as a beautiful picture of the benign influences of Christ, coming out of Jerusalem and flowing forth, in an ever-widening, ever-deepening stream, to the whole wide world, blessing the nations with their life-giving qualities, on into the eternities of heaven.

The east gate of the temple is to be closed, except to "the prince" (44:1–3).

The sacred area for the city, temple, priests, and Levites was to be in the approximate center of the land, with the lands of "the prince" on either side (45:1–8).

Boundaries of the land and the location of the tribes (47:13–48:29). The land was not quite as large as the domain of David. Roughly, it was the southern half of the eastern shore of the Mediterranean, about 400 miles north-south and averaging about 100 miles east-west. The tribes are not in their original arrangement, but as here indicated.

The city (48:30–35) is 7½ miles square. The pattern is, in part, that of the New Jerusalem (Revelation 21). The city is the home of God (v. 35).

Daniel

The Hebrew Statesman-Prophet at Babylon

"If we are thrown into the blazing furnace, the God we serve is able to save us from it, and he will rescue us from your hand, O king. But even if he does not, we want you to know, O king, that we will not serve your gods or worship the image of gold you have set up." —DANIEL 3:17–18

When Daniel was lifted from the den, no wound was found on him, because he had trusted in his God. —DANIEL 6:23

While still a mere youth, Daniel was carried to Babylon, where he lived during the whole period of the Babylonian exile, at times occupying high office in the Babylonian and Persian empires.

The Book of Daniel

The book itself presents Daniel as its author (7:1, 28; 8:2; 9:2; 10:1–2; 12:4–5). Its genuineness was sanctioned by Christ (Matthew 24:15) and accepted by the Jews and early Christians. The traditional view, that the book is a true historical document dating from the days of Daniel himself, persisted unanimously among Christian and Jewish scholars until the rise of modern criticism. The critics, in the name of modern scholarship, assume it to be a settled fact that the book was written by an unknown author who lived 400 years after Daniel, who assumed Daniel's name and palmed off his own writing as the genuine work of a hero long dead. But how can we think that God could be a party to the deception? We suspect that the real crux of the attempt to discredit the book of Daniel is an unwillingness to accept the marvelous miracles and amazing prophecies recorded in the book.

The book of Daniel, like the rest of the Old Testament, is written in Hebrew—except for the section from 2:4 to 7:28, which is in Aramaic (what used to be called Chaldee). Aramaic was the commercial and diplomatic language of the time. This is what might be expected in a book written for Jews living among Babylonians, containing copies of official Babylonian documents in their original Babylonian language. (See pp. 67–68.)

This book is considered by many to be generally historical in nature in chapters 1–6 and apocalyptic (revelatory) or prophetic in chapters 7–12. There are similarities between events and visions described in Daniel with those presented in the book of Revelation.

Dan. 1	DANIEL

Daniel was in the first group of captives taken from Jerusalem to Babylon (605 B.C.). He was of royal or noble blood (v. 3). Josephus says that

Remains of the Hanging Gardens of Babylon. The Hanging Gardens were considered a magnificent feature of the palatial estates of Babylon.

Daniel and his three friends were related to King Zedekiah, which gave them easier entree to the palace of Babylon. Handsome, brilliant young men, who were under the special care of God and trained by Him to bear witness to His name at the heathen court that then ruled the world. The royal food and wine (v. 8), which they refused to eat, may have been foods that had been offered in sacrifice to Babylonian idols or foods that were not allowed under the dietary laws of Moses.

Daniel's meteoric rise to worldwide fame is indicated in Ezekiel 14:14, 20; 28:3, written only 15 years later, while Daniel was still a very young man. What a remarkable man! Unswerving in his own religious convictions, yet so loyal to his idolatrous king that he was trusted with the affairs of the empire.

Dan. 2 | THE STATUE IN NEBUCHADNEZZAR'S DREAM

This event occurred in the second year of Nebuchadnezzar's reign as sole ruler, which means that Daniel was still a young man, having been in Babylon only three years.

The four world empires here predicted as part of Nebuchadnezzar's dream are generally understood to have been the Babylonian (head of pure gold), Persian (breast and arms of silver), Greek (belly and thighs of brass), and Roman empires (legs of iron and feet and toes of partly iron and partly baked clay). From the days of Daniel to the coming of Christ, the world was ruled by these four empires, exactly as Daniel had predicted. In the days of the Roman Empire, Christ appeared and set up a kingdom that started as a grain of mustard seed, passed through many adversities, and will become a universal and everlasting kingdom, blossoming into full glory at the Lord's return.

Critics who assign a Maccabean date to the book of Daniel, in order to explain it as referring to past events rather than being a prediction of the future, find it necessary to place all four empires before the date of composition, that is, before the Maccabean revolt. They then consider the Persian empire to be two empires, the Median and Persian, in order to make the Greek empire the fourth. But after the fall of Babylon there were not both a Median empire and a Persian empire. To make it appear so is only an effort to distort the facts of history in order to substantiate a theory. Medes and Persians constituted one empire under the rule of Persian kings. Darius the Mede was only a sub-king, who ruled for a little while under Cyrus the Persian until Cyrus arrived in Babylon.

It is far more likely that the divided kingdom refers to the Roman Empire, which came after the Greek Empire. The Roman Empire was

---

The City of Babylon

Babylon, the scene of Daniel's ministry, was perhaps the most magnificent city of the ancient world. Situated in the cradle of the human race, it had been built around the Tower of Babel (Genesis 11:9) and was a favorite residence of Babylonian, Assyrian, and Persian kings, and even of Alexander the Great, who had plans to further beautify it that came to naught because of his early death.

A commanding city through the whole pre-Christian era, Babylon was brought to the zenith of its power and glory in the days of the prophet Daniel, by King Nebuchadnezzar, who, during his 45-year reign, never wearied of building and beautifying its palaces and temples.

It was captured by the Medes and Persians (Daniel 5) but remained an important city through the Persian period. After Alexander the Great it declined, and by the time of Christ its political and commercial supremacy had gone, and soon the greater part of the once-mighty city was in ruins. Its bricks have been used in building Baghdad and repairing canals. For centuries it has been a desolate heap of mounds, a place for the beasts of the desert; a remarkable fulfillment of prophecy; still uninhabited except for a little village at the southwest corner.

The ruins of Babylon are an eerie reflection of Isaiah's prophecy: "She will never be inhabited or lived in through all generations; no Arab will pitch his tent there, no shepherd will rest his flocks there. But desert creatures will lie there, jackals will fill her houses; there the owls will dwell, and there the wild goats will leap about. Hyenas will howl in her strongholds, jackals in her luxurious palace" (Isaiah 13:20 – 22; see Jeremiah 51:37 – 43).

The Hanging Gardens

The most spectacular construction in Babylon was the Hanging Gardens, which were considered one of the Seven Wonders of the Ancient World. Nebuchadnezzar had the gardens built inside the walls of his palace to ease the homesickness of his wife, Amytis, from Media, which was a wild, mountainous country, very unlike the flat plains surrounding Babylon.

The lowest level of the garden stood on arches 80 feet tall. On top of that a 10-foot-high, recessed level was built, and another one on top of that, recessed further. There may have been six levels in all, creating a gigantic staircase some 140 feet tall. The terraces were waterproofed with lead, bitumen, and reeds and then filled with rich soil. On the terraces Nebuchadnezzar planted trees, shrubs, and flowers, so that the whole looked like a beautiful mountainside.

The terraces were irrigated from the Euphrates. A series of pipes ran from the river to an underground cistern. Next to the cistern a slim tower that reached the top terrace contained an endless chain of water buckets that were kept moving night and day by slaves on a treadmill. The Hanging Gardens were still in existence two centuries after Nebuchadnezzar, when Alexander the Great captured the city.

divided into a western empire and an eastern empire (Byzantium) in the 4th century A.D. and was never conquered, but fell due to internal disintegration and corruption.

Moreover, nothing happened in the Maccabean period that answers to the rock that "was cut out . . . , but not by human hands" (2:44–45). These verses allude to a fifth kingdom—an eternal kingdom of God that will never be destroyed, that will not be left to another people, that will bring an end to all other kingdoms.

This prophecy of the four kingdoms is further expanded under different images in chapter 7 (the four beasts), chapter 8 (the ram and the goat), chapter 9 (the 70 weeks), and chapter 11 (the struggles between the kings of the North and kings of the South). See pages 47–48 for an overview of these four kingdoms.

Dan. 3 | **THE FIERY FURNACE**

According to the Septuagint, this incident occurred in the 18th year of Nebuchadnezzar's reign, after Daniel and his three friends had been in Babylon for about 20 years. That was 586 B.C., the same year Nebuchadnezzar burned Jerusalem.

Just as many years earlier God had revealed the dream of Nebuchadnezzar and its interpretation to Daniel, so He now puts into the hearts of these three men the firm determination to be true to Him—and then He goes with them into the fire, not only to honor their faith but to demonstrate before the assembled dignitaries of the far-flung empire the power of the God of Jerusalem over the vaunted gods of Babylon. Thus God manifested Himself a second time in the palace of the mighty empire, and a second time the mighty Nebuchadnezzar bowed before God and proclaimed Him to be the true God to the utmost bounds of his empire.

Dan. 4 | **NEBUCHADNEZZAR'S INSANITY AND RECOVERY**

This is the story of another dream of Nebuchadnezzar's that Daniel interpreted, and that came true. Nebuchadnezzar was smitten with a mental disease in which he fancied himself a beast and tried to act like one, roaming among the animals in the parks of the palace grounds. A third time, Nebuchadnezzar bowed before God and proclaimed His power to all the world.

Dan. 5 | **BELSHAZZAR'S FEAST**

The feast took place on the night of the fall of Babylon. Daniel had been in Babylon for 70 years and was now a very old man. He apparently no longer had a prominent position at the court, since the queen had to bring Daniel to Belshazzar's attention (vv. 10–12).

The handwriting on the wall (vv. 25–28). This is how the ancient historians Xenophon, Herodotus, and Berosus relate the fall of Babylon:

"Cyrus diverted the Euphrates into a new channel, and, guided by two deserters, marched through the dry bed into the city, while the Babylonians were carousing at a feast of their gods."

Inscriptions state that the Persian army, under Gobryas, took Babylon without a battle, that he killed the son of the king, and that Cyrus entered later.

Dan. 6 | DANIEL IN THE LIONS' DEN

Daniel had been a high official of the Babylonian Empire under Nebuchadnezzar, and though Daniel was by now a very old man,

---

The Babylonian Empire

The Babylonian Empire ruled the ancient Near East during two periods, almost a millennium apart.

The Old Babylonian Empire (2000–1600 B.C.)
- Around 2000 B.C. Babylon became the dominating power of the world
- This was the era of the great lawgiver Hammurabi (ca. 1800 B.C.).
- Then followed 1000 years of intermittent struggle, followed by 250 years of Assyrian supremacy (884–605 B.C.).

The New Babylonian Empire (625–539 B.C.)

The New Babylonian or Neo-Babylonian Empire broke the power of Assyria and, in its westward sweep, destroyed Judah and conquered Egypt. Its kings were

- **Nabopolassar** (625–605 B.C.), who threw off the yoke of Assyria in 625 B.C. and established the independence of Babylon. With the aid of Cyaxares the Mede he conquered and destroyed Nineveh (612 B.C.). His son Nebuchadnezzar became commander of his father's armies and in 605 B.C. became coregent with his father.
- **Nebuchadnezzar** (605–562 B.C.), the greatest of all Babylonian kings, was one of the mightiest monarchs of all time. (See p. 399).
- Under Nebuchadnezzar's successors the Babylonian Empire began to decline: Evil-Merodach (562–560), Neriglissar (559–556), Labashi-Marduk (556), and Nabonidus (556–539 B.C.).
- **Nabonidus's** son, Belshazzar, was coregent with him during the last few years of his reign, and thus the second-most powerful person in Babylon. This is why he could only offer Daniel the third-highest position as a reward for interpreting the handwriting on the wall (Daniel 5:7; for the story of the handwriting on the wall and the fall of Babylon, see p. 400).
- The city of Babylon, and with it the Babylonian Empire, fell to the Medes and Persians. Supremacy passed to Persia in 539 B.C. and would last until Persia was in turn conquered by Alexander the Great in 331 B.C.

The Babylonian Empire lasted 70 years. The 70 years of Judah's exile coincided exactly with the 70 years during which Babylon ruled the world. The year in which Cyrus, king of Persia, conquered Babylon (539 B.C.) was the same year in which he authorized the return of the Jews to their own land.

Babylon, oppressor of God's Old Testament people, appears again in the book of Revelation as the embodiment of the forces of evil that oppose God (Revelation 17).

Basalt statue of a lion near the palace of Nebuchadnezzar in Babylon. God sent His angels to close the mouths of the lions. (Daniel 6)

probably over 90, Darius, the conqueror of Babylon, immediately put him in charge of the Babylonian government. This probably was because Daniel had just foretold the victory of the Medes (5:28). What a compliment to his wisdom, integrity, and fairness! Yet he was unswerving in his personal devotion to his own God (v. 10). What faith and courage!

Dan. 7 | THE FOUR BEASTS

This is a continuation of the prophecy of chapter 2, which was spoken 60 years earlier: four world empires, and then the kingdom of God. In chapter 2 these are represented by a statue with a head of gold, chest and arms of silver, belly and thighs of brass, and feet of iron and clay, broken in pieces by a stone. In this chapter these same four world empires are represented as a lion, a bear, a leopard, and a terrifying beast. The fourth beast may also correspond to the imagery of the seven-headed, 10-horned beast of Revelation 13.

The image in chapter 2 might be from man's perspective—the kingdoms are seen as a mighty warrior—while the images given to Daniel in

Nebuchadnezzar

Daniel was adviser to King Nebuchadnezzar, the genius and real builder of the New Babylonian Empire. Of its 70 years' existence, he ruled 44 years.

Nabopolassar, the father of Nebuchadnezzar and viceroy of Babylon, threw off the Assyrian yoke in 626 B.C. and ruled the city from 626 until 605 B.C.

In 605 B.C. Nebuchadnezzar was placed at the head of his father's armies. Invading the western countries, he wrested control of Palestine from Egypt (605 B.C.) and took some Jewish captives to Babylon, among them Daniel.

That same year he became coregent with his father; he became sole ruler a year later. He proved to be one of the mightiest monarchs of all time.

In 605 B.C., he broke the power of Egypt in the famous battle of Carchemish. In that same year Nebuchadnezzar took Jerusalem and deported a number of persons of high rank, among them young Daniel and Hananiah, Mishael, and Azariah (1:1, 6).

In 597 B.C. he crushed a rebellion in Palestine and took King Jehoiachin and many captives to Babylon, among them the prophet Ezekiel.

In 586 B.C. he burned Jerusalem and took more captives. For 13 years his army besieged the city of Tyre (585–573 B.C.).

In ca. 582 B.C. he invaded and plundered Moab, Ammon, Edom, and Lebanon; and in 581 he again took captives from Judah. In 572 he invaded and plundered Egypt. He died 562 B.C.

Daniel exerted a powerful influence over him; and three times Nebuchadnezzar called the God of Daniel "God" (2:47; 3:29; 4:34).

chapter 8 may be from God's perspective: the kingdoms, which in the end will all be conquered, are seen as voracious beasts.

These four world empires are commonly taken to be Babylonia, Persia, Greece, and Rome (see under chap. 2), representing the period from Daniel to the end of the church age (Christ's second coming . . .).

The "ten horns" of the fourth beast (v. 24), which may correspond to the 10 toes of 2:41–42, are taken to be the 10 kings or kingdoms into which the Roman Empire was divided or that were established and given power by the Roman Empire. Prophetically, the 10 horns may refer to a powerful 10-nation confederacy that will form in the last days. Some believe that this confederacy may arise in the geographic area that was once the old Roman Empire (which, unlike the three kingdoms before it, was never conquered and destroyed but fell through internal corruption).

The "other horn" (vv. 8, 20, 24–25), which came up among the 10 horns, may be a world power that was not one of the 10 original powers and may refer to the Antichrist (Revelation 13). The image of three horns uprooted by the "little horn" (7:8) seems to foretell a world leader who will overpower three of the 10 kings, after which great oppression follows. This world leader is ultimately judged, slain, and thrown into "the blazing fire" (v. 11).

Note that the beast described in Daniel 7 matches the beast of Revelation 13 but that the characteristics are listed in reverse order (lion, bear, leopard). This could be explained by the fact that Daniel was looking forward to the end of times in his dream and John has been transported into the future and had the opportunity to witness the end-time events and look back through history at the events leading up to the end times.

In v. 13, Daniel describes "the son of man." This is the first reference to Christ the Messiah as the "son of man"—a title that Jesus used of Himself. The "son of man" will be given authority, glory, and sovereign power. All the nations and people of every language will worship Him, and His dominion will never end. This account parallels the description of "the Lamb" in Revelation 14.

Dan. 8 | THE RAM AND THE GOAT

This chapter contains further predictions about the second and third world empires spoken of in chapters 2 and 7, that is, the Persian and Greek empires.

The Persian Empire, represented in 7:5 as a devouring bear, is here presented as a two-horned ram (vv. 3–4), since the empire was a coalition of Medes and Persians.

The Greek Empire was pictured in 7:6 as a four-headed leopard; here it is portrayed as a swift goat with one great horn, bounding furiously from the west; the great horn is broken and replaced with four horns.

The Miracles in the Book of Daniel

Wonderful things are told in this book. To those who find it difficult to believe these things, we say: let us remember that for 1000 years God had been nurturing the Hebrew nation for the purpose of establishing, through that nation, in a world of idol-worshiping nations, the idea that God is God. Now God's nation had been destroyed by a nation that worshiped idols. That was plain evidence to all the world that the gods of Babylon were more powerful than the God of the Jews. It was a crisis in God's struggle with idolatry. If ever there was a time when God needed to do something to show who God is, it was during the Babylonian exile. Strange indeed it would have been if nothing unusual had happened. Hard as it may be to believe these miracles, it would be harder to believe the rest of the story without them.

At least the Jews, who from the very beginning had always been falling into idolatry, were now at last, in the Babylonian exile, convinced that their own God was the true God. These miracles also had a powerful influence on both Nebuchadnezzar and Darius (3:29; 6:26).

Time Periods in the Book of Daniel

"A time, times, and half a time"

- Denotes the duration of the other horn of the fourth beast (7:25).
- Denotes the period from Daniel to the time of the end (12:6–7).
- Is used in Revelation 12:14 as identical to 42 months and to 1,260 days (Revelation 11:2–3; 12:6, 14; 13:5), the period of time the Holy City was trampled, the two witnesses prophesied, the woman was in the wilderness, and the revived beast was on the throne.

The word "time," in the phrase "a time, times, and half a time" is generally taken to mean year; the phrase thus means 3½ years, which is 42 months, or 1,260 days.

By some, this is taken to refer to a literal 3½ years. Others, on the year-day interpretation (Numbers 14:34; Ezekiel 4:6), take it to be a period of 1,260 years. Still others look upon the figures, not as defining time limits or periods, but as being symbolic: 7 is the symbol of completeness, while 3½, which is half of 7, represents incompleteness—that is, the reign of evil will be only temporary.

2,300 evenings and mornings (8:14) is the time the sanctuary was trampled by the little horn of the third beast. It means either 2,300 days or 2,300 half-days, that is, 1,150 days; The former is almost double 3½ years; the latter is slightly less than 3½ years.

1,290 days (12:11) is the duration of "the abomination that causes desolation," from its beginning to the time of the end.

1,335 days (12:12) apparently is an extension of 45 days beyond the 1,290-day period, culminating in final blessedness.

70 weeks (9:24) is the period from the decree to rebuild Jerusalem to the coming of the Messiah. It includes "seven weeks" of times of trouble (9:25) and one week in which the Anointed One was to be cut off (9:26–27).

These time periods are used in close connection with the phrase "abomination that causes desolation" set up by the little horn of the third beast (8:13; 11:31); this "abomination" also follows the cutting off of the Messiah (9:27) and is the point from which the 1,290 days run (12:11). Jesus quotes this expression, "abomination that causes desolation," as referring to the impending destruction of Jerusalem by the Roman army (Matthew 24:15), in a discourse that blends "short-term" prophecies with prophecies involving the end of the world.

Time of trouble (9:25, 27) refers to the seven weeks at the beginning and one week at the end of the 70-week period. A **time of distress such as has not happened from the beginning of the nations** (12:1) is predicted for the "time of the end" (12:4, 9, 13); Jesus quotes the expression as referring to both the destruction of Jerusalem and the end of the world (Matthew 24:21).

The desecration of the temple by Antiochus (see pp. 473–74) lasted 3½ years (168–165 B.C.). The Roman war against Jerusalem lasted 3½ years (A.D. 67–70).

We think that no one interpretation can exhaust the meaning of these time marks of Daniel. Possibly they may be taken literally as well as in some sense figuratively and symbolically. Possibly they may have their primary fulfillment in an event of history, a secondary fulfillment in another event, and their ultimate fulfillment at the time of the end. The desecration of the temple by Antiochus and the destruction of Jerusalem by Titus may be forerunners and symbols of the Great Tribulation in the days of Antichrist.

We should not be too disappointed if we fail to feel sure that we understand, for Daniel himself felt that it was beyond understanding (8:27).

The great horn was Alexander the Great, who broke the Persian Empire in 331 B.C. This prophecy was written in 539 B.C., 200 years before its fulfillment. It is a most remarkable prediction of the outcome of a clash between two world-empires, neither of which had, at the time of the prediction, yet arisen.

Four horns (vv. 8, 21–22) and four heads (7:6) are the four kingdoms into which Alexander's empire was divided (see on chap. 11).

The little horn (v. 9), which arose out of the four, is generally agreed to mean Antiochus Epiphanes (175–163 B.C.), of the Syrian branch of the Greek Empire, who made a determined effort to stamp out the Jewish religion (see under 11:21–35). Yet the repeated phrase "time of the end" (vv. 17, 19) may mean that along with the near view of Antiochus there may have been in the distant background of the vision the ominous outline of a far more terrible destroyer (v. 26) who would darken the closing days of history and of whom Antiochus was a symbolic forerunner.

Dan. 9 | THE 70 WEEKS, OR 70 "SEVENS"

The Babylonian captivity, which was then drawing to a close, had lasted 70 years. Daniel is here told by the angel that it would still be "70 sevens" until the coming of the Messiah (v. 24). The word translated "seven" is generally understood to mean "week" here.

The 70 weeks are generally understood to mean 70 weeks of years, that is, 70 times 7 years, or 490 years. The Exile had been 70 years; the period between the Exile and the coming of the Messiah would be seven times that long.

The number seven, and cycles of seven, sometimes have symbolic meanings, yet the actual facts of this prophecy are most amazing:

The date from which the 70 weeks was to be counted was the decree to rebuild Jerusalem (v. 25). There were three decrees issued by Persian kings for this purpose (539 B.C., 458 B.C., 444 B.C.; see under Ezra). The main one of these was the one in 458 B.C.

The 70 weeks are subdivided into 7 weeks, 62 weeks, and 1 week (vv. 25, 27). It is difficult to see the application of the 7 weeks, but the 69 weeks (62 + 7) equal 483 days, which, according to the commonly accepted year-day theory (Ezekiel 4:6), means 483 years.

This 483 years is the period between the decree to rebuild Jerusalem and the coming of the Anointed One (v. 25). The decree to rebuild Jerusalem was issued in 458 B.C. Adding 483 years to 457 B.C. brings us to A.D. 26, the very year in which Jesus was baptized and began His public ministry. A most remarkable fulfillment of Daniel's prophecy, even to the year.

Further, within 3½ years Jesus was crucified, that is, "in the middle of the 'seven'" (in the middle of the week) "the Anointed One" was "cut off"; He atoned for wickedness and brought in everlasting righteousness

(vv. 24, 26–27). Thus Daniel foretold not only the time at which the Messiah would appear, but also the duration of His public ministry and His atoning death for human sin.

Some think that the remaining half of the 70th week was completed in the few years after Christ's death and resurrection. Others believe that the fulfillment of the 70th week was suspended at the death and resurrection of Christ and will remain suspended as long as Israel is scattered; the last half of the "one week" then belongs to the time of the end.

Yet another viewpoint is that there is an indeterminate interval between the 69th and 70th weeks. Some believe that the 70th week will begin at Christ's second coming and the rapture of the church. This, then, marks the beginning of the seven years referred to as the Great Tribulation period. It is thought that during this time the "little horn" of chapter 8 will rise to power and enter into a seven-year covenant with the Jews (Israel). This covenant is then broken after 3½ years and the remaining 3½ years represent a time of great war and destruction, leading up to the great and final battle of Armageddon. (See Revelation 7:14 regarding the tribulation period.)

Dan. 10 ANGELS OF THE NATIONS

This last vision (chaps. 10–12) was given two years after the Jews had returned to Palestine (534 B.C.). God lifted the veil and showed Daniel some realities of the unseen world—conflicts going on between superhuman intelligences, good and bad, in their effort to control the movements of nations. Some of them sought to protect God's people. Michael was the guardian angel of Israel (13:21). An unnamed angel talked with Daniel. Greece had its angel (v. 20), and so did Persia (vv. 13, 20).

It seems that God was showing Daniel some of his secret agencies in operation to bring about the return of Israel. One of them helped Darius (11:1). In this chapter they are represented as being interested in the destiny of Israel; in Revelation, angels are concerned with the destiny of the church. In Revelation 12:7–9, Michael and his angels are at war with Satan and his angels. According to Ephesians 6:12, the powers of the unseen world are the chief enemies against which Christians have to fight. There was great angelic activity when Jesus was born. Jesus Himself believed in angels (see under Matthew 4:11).

Dan. 11 KINGS OF THE NORTH AND KINGS OF THE SOUTH

Chapters 2, 7, 8, 9, and 11 contain predictions about four empires and events from the time of Daniel until the end of the church age. Some hold that these predictions refer to later world powers and events, from the rapture of the church to the end, which culminate with the battle at Armageddon (Revelation 16:13–16).

Here is a general outline of the world history covered in Daniel's prophecies:

- Babylonian Empire (605–539 B.C.)
- Persian Empire (539–332 B.C.)
- Greek Empire, with its four divisions (331–146 B.C.)
- Wars of Syrian and Egyptian Greek kings (323–146 B.C.)
- Antiochus Epiphanes, desecration of Jerusalem (175–163 B.C.)
- Roman Empire (146 B.C.–A.D. 400)
- Public ministry of Christ (A.D. 26–30)
- Destruction of Jerusalem by Roman army (A.D. 70)
- World troubles and the resurrection at "time of the end"

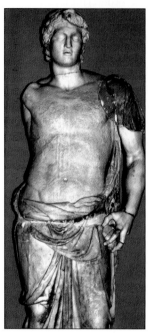

Statue of Alexander the Great. Some believe that Daniel's prophesy of the "mighty king who will rule with great power and do as he pleases" mentioned in Daniel 11:3 is a reference to Alexander the Great.

These predictions are progressive in their explanations of details. In chapter 2 we have a general statement that from the days of Daniel to the days of the Messiah there would be four world empires. Chapter 7 gives details about the fourth empire. In chapter 8 we find details about the second and third empires, and in chapter 11 still more details about the third empire.

Following the death of Alexander the Great in 331 B.C., the Greek Empire—the third empire—was divided among his generals into four regions: Greece, Asia Minor, Syria, Egypt. In this chapter the kings of Syria are called "kings of the North." The kings of Egypt are called "kings of the South." Daniel's predictions of the movements of these kings were uttered 200 years before there was a Greek Empire and

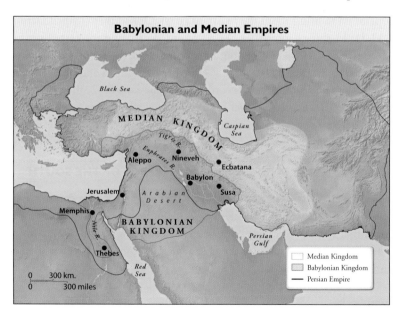

Babylonian and Median Empires

Black Sea

MEDIAN KINGDOM

Caspian Sea

Tigris R.

Euphrates R.

Aleppo

Nineveh

Ecbatana

Babylon

Jerusalem

Arabian Desert

Susa

Memphis

BABYLONIAN KINGDOM

Nile R.

Persian Gulf

Thebes

Red Sea

0   300 km.
0   300 miles

☐ Median Kingdom
☐ Babylonian Kingdom
— Persian Empire

nearly 400 years before these kings existed. His minute description of their movements is a most extraordinary parallel between prediction and subsequent history. Chapter 11 is the prewritten history of the period between the two Testaments. Here is an outline of events answering to the verses in which they were predicted (for a general overview of this period between the Old and New Testaments, see pp. 471–90).

Three kings in Persia (v. 2): Cambyses, Gaumata, and Darius I. The fourth was Xerxes, the richest and most powerful of the Persian kings; he invaded Greece, but was defeated at Salamis (480 B.C.).

A mighty king (vv. 3–4): Alexander the Great and the fourfold division of his kingdom into Greece, Asia Minor, Syria, and Egypt.

King of the South (v. 5): Ptolemy I Soter of Egypt; **one of his commanders**, Seleucus I Nicator, originally an officer under Ptolemy I, became king of Syria and the most powerful of Alexander's successors.

Daughter (v. 6): Berenice, daughter of Ptolemy II, was given in marriage to Antiochus II and was murdered.

One of her family line (v. 7): Ptolemy III, a brother of Berenice, invaded Syria in retaliation and won a great victory (8).

Two sons (v. 10): Seleucus III and Antiochus III.

Verses 11–19: Ptolemy IV defeated Antiochus III with great loss in the battle of Raphia, near Egypt in 217 B.C. Antiochus III, after 14 years, returned with a great army against Egypt (v. 13). The Jews helped Antiochus (v. 14). Antiochus defeated the forces of Egypt (v. 15). Antiochus conquered Palestine (v. 16). Antiochus gave his daughter Cleopatra in treacherous marriage alliance to Ptolemy V, hoping through her to get control of Egypt; but she stood with her husband (v. 17). Antiochus then invaded Asia Minor and Greece and was defeated by the Roman army at Magnesia in 190 B.C. (vv. 18–19). He returned to his own country and was assassinated.

A contemptible person (vv. 21–35): Antiochus IV Epiphanes. Not the rightful heir, he got the throne by treachery (v. 21). He made himself master of Egypt, partly by force and partly by cunning deceit (vv. 22–25). Ptolemy VI, son of Cleopatra and nephew of Antiochus, was defeated by the treachery of his subjects (v. 26). Under the guise of friendship, Antiochus and Ptolemy vied with each other in treachery (v. 27). Returning from Egypt, Antiochus attacked Jerusalem, killed 80,000, took 40,000, and sold 40,000 Jews into slavery (v. 28). Antiochus again invaded Egypt. But the Roman fleet compelled him to withdraw (v. 29). He vented his anger on Jerusalem and desecrated the temple (vv. 30–31). He was helped by apostate Jews (v. 32). Verses 36–45 may refer to both Antiochus Epiphanes and the Antichrist.

Dan. 12 | **THE TIME OF THE END**

Daniel closes his prophecies concerning the epochs and events of world history with a sweep forward to the end (vv. 4, 9, 13), when there shall be distress as never before (v. 1), followed by the resurrection of the dead and the everlasting glory of the saints (vv. 2–3).

A time of distress such as has not happened from the beginning of nations (v. 1) is not inapplicable to our own generation: torture, suffering, and death of entire populations—genocide—by demon dictators, no more intense perhaps than the atrocities perpetrated by Antiochus, Titus, and the Roman emperors, but on a scale unparalleled in all previous history.

Many will go here and there to increase knowledge (v. 4) is to be a characteristic of the time of the end. This, too, applies to our own generation as it has to no other: modes of travel and means of communication on a scale never before dreamed of.

The nuclear bomb, biological warfare, terrorism—it makes us wonder if we may be living in the period Jesus spoke of as the setting for His return: "On the earth, nations will be in anguish and perplexity at the roaring and tossing of the sea. People will faint from terror, apprehensive of what is coming on the world" (Luke 21:25–26).

Summary of Daniel's Prophecies

- The statue: four kingdoms, and then God's everlasting kingdom (chap. 2)
- Nebuchadnezzar's insanity and recovery (chap. 4)
- The fall of Babylon and the rise of the Persian Empire (chap. 5)
- The "fourth" empire, its "ten horns," and "other horn" (chap. 7)
- The Greek Empire and its "four horns" (chap. 8)
- The 70 weeks: the time from Daniel to the Messiah (chap. 9)
- The troubles of the Holy Land during the period between the Testaments (chap. 11)
- Signs of the time of the end (chap. 12)

Hosea

Israel's Idolatry, Wickedness, Captivity, and Restoration

"Yet the Israelites will be like the sand on the seashore, which cannot be measured or counted. In the place where it was said to them, 'You are not my people,' they will be called 'sons of the living God.'"
—HOSEA 1:10

"They sow the wind
and reap the whirlwind.
The stalk has no head;
it will prod uce no flour.
Were it to yield grain,
foreigners would swallow it up."
—HOSEA 8:7

Hosea was the only one of the writing prophets to come from the northern kingdom, Israel; he speaks of its king as "our" king (7:5). The name Hosea means "salvation." His message was primarily aimed at the northern kingdom, with occasional reference to the southern kingdom, Judah.

Date

Judging from the kings mentioned in 1:1, Hosea must have prophesied for at least 38 years, though almost nothing is known about him except what we read in this book. But since his prophetic activity is dated by reference to a number of kings of Judah, the book was probably written in Judah after the fall of the northern capital, Samaria (722–721 B.C.)—an idea suggested by references to Judah throughout the book.

Hosea began his ministry when Israel, under Jeroboam II (793–753), was at the zenith of its power. Hosea then witnessed the rapid disintegration and fall of the northern kingdom, going from its peak to its end in less than 30 years:

- Jeroboam II (793–753). A reign of great prosperity
- Zechariah (753–752). Reigned six months; assassinated by Shallum
- Shallum (752). Reigned one month; assassinated by Menahem
- Menahem (752–742). Unspeakably cruel; a puppet of Assyria
- Pekahiah (742–740). Assassinated by Pekah
- Pekah (752–732). Assassinated by Hoshea
- Hoshea (732–722). Fall of Samaria (721). End of northern kingdom

The kings of the southern kingdom during whose reigns he prophesied (1:1) were

- Uzziah (792–740), a good king
- Jotham (750–732), a good king
- Ahaz (735–716), a very wicked king

- Hezekiah (716–687), a good king, during whose reign Samaria fell

Hosea was a younger contemporary of the prophet Amos and an older contemporary of the prophets Isaiah and Micah.

The Situation

Some 200 years before Hosea's time, the Ten Tribes had seceded and set up an independent kingdom, with the golden calf as its official national god. During those two centuries God had sent the prophets Elijah, Elisha, Jonah, and Amos. Now God sent Hosea.

Hosea faced as horrendous a mess as is found anywhere in the Bible. The degradation of the people was unbelievable. Yet Hosea labored unceasingly to make them see that God still loved them.

Hos. 1–3 | HOSEA'S WIFE AND CHILDREN

Israel, God's "bride" (Ezekiel 16:8–15), had forsaken God and had given herself to the worship of other gods, which was spiritual adultery. Now Hosea is commanded by God to take an adulterous wife (1:2). The simple, natural implication of the language is that it was an actual experience in Hosea's life, and a generally accepted interpretation is that Hosea, a prophet of God, was actually commanded by God to marry an unchaste woman, as a symbol of God's love for wayward Israel. (Or perhaps she was a woman who, if she was chaste at first, afterward proved unfaithful, left him, and became the paramour of a man who could better satisfy her fondness for luxury; 2:5.) The idolatrous worship of the land was so universally accompanied by immoral practices (4:11–14) that it was hard for a woman to be chaste, and adultery (the KJV uses the forceful term "whoredom") was rampant.

Some of the language applies to Hosea's family literally, some to the nation figuratively, some to both, with the literal and figurative alternating. "His sentences fall like the throbs of a broken heart."

Hosea's reconciliation with his wife (3:1–5). Hosea still loved his wife and bought her back (3:1–2), but he required her to remain for a time without conjugal privilege, as a prophetic image of Israel remaining "many days without king and without sacrifice" before their eventual return to their God and David their king (3:3–4).

Hosea's children. Not only was Hosea's marriage an illustration of the

Hosea's message was directed to the Northern Kingdom

Damascus
Mediterranean Sea
PHOENICIA
Dan
A R A M
Mt. Carmel
Sea of Galilee
Jezreel
Jordan R.
I S R A E L
Samaria
Bethel
Jerusalem
J U D A H
Dead Sea
0 10 km.
0 10 miles

thing he was preaching, but the names of his children proclaim the main messages of his life.

Jezreel (1:4–5), his firstborn, was named after the city of Jehu's bloody brutality (2 Kings 10:1–14). The valley of Jezreel was the age-old battlefield on which the kingdom was about to collapse. By naming his child Jezreel, Hosea was saying to the king and to the nation, "The hour of retribution and punishment has come."

Lo-Ruhamah (1:6), the name of the second child, meant "not loved." God's mercy had come to an end for Israel, though there would be a respite for Judah (v. 7).

Lo-Ammi (1:9), the name of the third child, meant "Not my people."

Hosea then repeats the two names without the "Lo" prefix—Ammi and Ruhamah—"My people" and "My loved one" (2:1), looking forward to the time when Israel would again be God's people. And in a play on the words, he predicts the day when other nations will be called the people of God (1:10), a verse Paul quotes to support his message that the Gospel will also be extended to include Gentiles (Romans 9:25).

Hos. 4 | THE CHARGE AGAINST ISRAEL

Idolatry is the source of their horrible crimes (vv. 1–3). Priests feed on the sins of the people (vv. 4–10). The young women are harlots, married women entertain other men, men visit prostitutes (vv. 11–14). Judah (v. 15) had not sunk into idolatry as deeply as Israel and was spared for about 100 years after Israel was destroyed. Ephraim (v. 17), the largest and most central of the northern tribes, is used as a name for the whole northern kingdom.

Beth Aven (v. 15) is another name for Bethel, the main center of idolatry in the northern kingdom.

Hos. 5 | THE JUDGMENT AGAINST ISRAEL

Priests, king, and people are "rebels" against God (vv. 1–3). Steeped in sin and proud of it; "their deeds do not permit them to return to their God"—a terrible statement about the possibility of irreversible rejection of God (vv. 4–5).

Illegitimate children (v. 7), that is, by men other than their husbands.

Intent on pursuing idols (v. 11), the result of King Jeroboam I's decision to create, for political reasons, a form of idolatry that would compete with the worship of God in Jerusalem (1 Kings 12:26–33) when he first established the northern kingdom.

Hos. 6–7 | ISRAEL IS UNREPENTANT

On the third day (6:2) probably means that after a short period Israel would be restored; it is generally understood to be an intimation of Jesus the Messiah's resurrection on the third day. Gilead (6:8) and Shechem

(6:9) were two of the main cities of the northern kingdom and were particularly horrible as centers of vice and violence.

Hot as an oven; they devour their rulers (7:7; v. 4) probably refers to the period of passionate indulgence and violence in which four of their kings were assassinated in quick succession, even while Hosea was speaking.

A flat cake not turned (7:8) is burnt on one side and raw on the other and therefore unfit for use.

Hair . . . sprinkled with gray (7:9) is a symptom of the approaching end.

Hos. 8 | "THEY SOW THE WIND AND REAP THE WHIRLWIND"

Set up kings without my consent (v. 4): God had appointed David's family to rule his people. The Ten Tribes had rebelled and set up a different line of kings for themselves.

Sold herself to lovers (v. 9): Israel flirted with Assyria by paying tribute.

Hos. 9–10 | ISRAEL'S PUNISHMENT

Return to Egypt (9:3): not literally, but to Egypt-like bondage in Assyria, although after the captivity many Jews did settle in Egypt.

Bull figurine discovered in Samaria. Hosea announced that the calf-idols would be broken in pieces.

The prophet is considered a fool (9:7) is either Hosea's opinion of false prophets or, more probably, the people's opinion of Hosea.

They have sunk deep into corruption (9:9), as in the days of Gibeah, where one woman was raped all night long by a group of men (Judges 19:24–26).

Wanderers among the nations (9:17): the wandering began in Hosea's lifetime and has continued with relentless persistence through the centuries, for the Jews as for no other nation.

The **calf-idol of Beth Aven** [Bethel] (10:5) shall be broken in pieces (8:6), and thorns and thistles shall grow over their altars (10:8).

Shalman (10:14) is probably Shalmaneser V.

Hos. 11:1–11   GOD'S LOVE FOR ISRAEL

Out of Egypt (v. 1): this is quoted in Matthew 2:15 as referring to the flight of Jesus' parents to Egypt. Even as the messianic nation was called out of Egypt in its childhood, so the Messiah Himself in His childhood was called out of Egypt.

My people are determined to turn from me (v. 7), but God's heart is still yearning for them with compassion (8–11).

Hos. 11:12–12:14   ISRAEL'S SIN

Assyria and Egypt (v. 2): Israel's lying diplomacy, making secret agreements with both Assyria and Egypt to play them against each other, would bring disaster.

Bethel (v. 4), the center of their abominable idolatry, was the very spot where their father Jacob had dedicated his life to God (Genesis 28:13–15).

Hos. 13   THE LORD'S ANGER AGAINST ISRAEL

Guilty of Baal worship (v. 1): the addition of Baal worship to Jeroboam I's calf worship, under Ahab (1 Kings 16:30–33), brought national death.

Hos.14   ISRAEL WILL RETURN TO GOD

The Lord's wayward bride shall return to her husband and once again respond to His love, as in the days of her youth (2:14–20).

have known each other, although we have no indication that they in fact did.

We can speculate that as a boy, Amos could have known Jonah and heard him tell of his visit to Nineveh. He could also have known Elisha and heard him tell of his association with Elijah. Jonah and Elisha were passing off the stage as Amos was coming on. Joel also may have been Amos's contemporary or a near predecessor. It may have been Joel's plague of locusts to which Amos refers (4:9). Hosea may have been in Bethel at the time of Amos's visit. Hosea was the younger and continued his work after Amos was gone, and Isaiah and Micah were also beginning their prophetic ministry as Amos was ending his.

Amos 1–2 DOOM OF ISRAEL AND NEIGHBOR NATIONS

Farmer from Tekoa. The prophet Amos, like this farmer, lived in the village of Tekoa and worked in his nearby orchards.

Amos starts with a general impeachment of the whole region: Syria, Philistia, Phoenicia, Edom, Ammon, Moab, Judah, and Israel —eight nations in all. He arraigns each under the same formula, **for three sins, even for four,** and specifies their particular sins. He then centers his attention on Israel.

Exile (KJV, captivity) is one of the key words of the book (1:5, 15; 5:5, 27; 6:7; 7:9, 17). Within 30 years these predictions were fulfilled, and Israel went from the zenith of its power to destruction and exile.

Tekoa (1:1), the home of Amos, was 10 miles southwest of Jerusalem, five miles from Bethlehem, at an elevation of 2,700 feet, at the edge of the pasturelands overlooking the bleak wilderness of Judea. Amos would today be called a layman, for he was neither a priest nor a professional prophet, but a shepherd who also took care of sycamore trees (7:14). The sycamore was a species of fig of poor quality, a cross between fig and mulberry.

The **earthquake** (1:1) must have been very severe, for it was remembered for 200 years (Zechariah 14:5) and was ominously compared to God's Day of Judgment (Revelation 16:18).

Amos 3 THE LUXURIOUS PALACES OF SAMARIA

Samaria, the capital of the northern kingdom, was situated on a hill 300 feet high, in a valley of surpassing beauty, surrounded on three sides by mountains. It was as impregnable as it was beautiful. Its palatial residences had been built on the backs of the poor (2:6–7; 3:10; 5:11; 8:4–7), with a heartlessness that would shock even the heathen Egyptians and Philistines (3:9–10).

Bethel (v. 14), where Amos was speaking (7:13), was one of the religious centers of the northern kingdom, 12 miles north of Jerusalem. Jeroboam I had set up a golden calf here to be worshiped (1 Kings 12:25–33; the other golden calf was set up at Dan in the north), which was still there (Hosea 13:2). To this degenerate center of idolatry came Amos with God's final warning.

Cities and Nations Mentioned by Amos

Amos 4 | "PREPARE TO MEET YOUR GOD"

The pampered ladies of Samaria (vv. 1–3) were living in sumptuous indulgence on gains squeezed out of the poor.

Cows of Bashan (v. 1) were fatted animals, pampered until taken away for slaughter. Within a few years these women would be taken away with **hooks** (v. 2). Assyrians literally led their captives by ropes attached to hooks through the lip.

Ironically, the Israelites were pitiless in their cruelty, yet intensely religious (vv. 4–5). What a satire on religion!

God's repeated efforts to save them had been in vain. The time had come for the nation to meet its God (vv. 6–13).

Amos 5 | THE DAY OF GOD

A lament over the fall of Israel (vv. 1–3), another appeal to turn to God (vv. 4–9), and another denunciation of their evil ways (vv. 10–27). Verses 18–26 seem to indicate that they were willing to turn and offer sacrifices to God instead of to the calf. However, what Amos wanted was not sacrifices but a reformation of the heart, a radical change in the way they lived.

Amos 6 | THE CAPTIVITY

Over and over Amos contrasts the voluptuous ease, palatial luxury, and feeling of security of the leaders and the rich with the intolerable sufferings that are about to befall them.

Amos 7 | THREE VISIONS OF DESTRUCTION

The **locusts** symbolize the destruction of the land. Amos interceded, and God relented (vv. 1–3).

The **fire** is another symbol of the coming destruction. Again Amos interceded, and again God relented (vv. 4–6).

The **plumb line** indicates that the city is being measured for destruction. Twice God had relented—but no more. He had punished and punished, and forgiven and forgiven. Their case was hopeless (vv. 7–9).

How long Amos was at Bethel is not known. But his repeated denunciations and warnings had a great impact on the land (v. 10). **Amaziah, the priest at Bethel,** reported to Jeroboam II that Amos was "raising a conspiracy" (vv. 10–17). But Amos grew bolder and bolder, telling Amaziah that the priest himself would be a captive.

Amos 8 | THE BASKET OF RIPE FRUIT

This is another symbol that the sinful kingdom was ripe for ruin. And Amos reiterates the causes: greed, dishonesty, and merciless brutality toward the poor. Over and over, through many images, the Bible makes it plain that there is no possible way to escape the consequences of persistent sin.

Amos 9 | THE FUTURE GLORY OF DAVID'S KINGDOM

Further prediction of exile (vv. 1–8). Within 30 years it came to pass, and the apostate kingdom ceased to exist.

The restored throne of David (vv. 8–15). An ever-recurrent prophetic vision of radiant days beyond the gloom. Amos lived near Bethlehem, the city of David. He took it to heart that the Ten Tribes had renounced the Davidic throne, which God had ordained for His people, and that for 200 years they had obstinately declined to return to its fold.

God's final word is this: in days to come, David's kingdom, which they had despised, will recover and rule, not over one nation only, but over a world of nations, in eternal glory.

Obadiah

The Doom of Edom

The kingdom will be the LORD's. —OBADIAH 21

The Edomites

Edom was in a rocky range of mountains south of the Dead Sea, stretching about 100 miles north and south and about 20 miles east and west. It was well watered, with abundant pasturage. Its capital was Sela (es-Sela; now better known as Petra), which was carved high in a perpendicular cliff far back in the mountain canyons, overlooking a valley of marvelous beauty. The Edomites would go out on raiding expeditions and then retreat to their impregnable strongholds high up in the rocky gorges.

The Edomites were descendants of Esau, but they were always bitter enemies of the Jews, perpetuating the conflict between Esau and Jacob (Genesis 25:23; 27:41). They refused passage to Moses (Numbers 20:14–21) and were always ready to aid an attacking army.

Date

Obadiah's prophecy was occasioned by a plundering of Jerusalem in which the Edomites participated. There were four such plunderings:

1. In the reign of Jehoram, 853–841 B.C. (2 Chronicles 21:8, 16–17; Amos 1:6)
2. In the reign of Amaziah, 806–767 B.C. (2 Chronicles 25:11–12, 23–24)
3. In the reign of Ahaz, 735–716 B.C. (2 Chronicles 28:16–21)
4. In the reign of Zedekiah, 597–586 B.C. (2 Chronicles 36:11–21; Psalm 137:7)

There are various opinions as to which of these four raids was the reason for Obadiah's prophecy. Inasmuch as the destruction of Judah is mentioned (vv. 11–12), the prophecy is generally assigned to the reign of Zedekiah, when Jerusalem was burnt by the Babylonians (586 B.C.).

Other Scriptures that foretell Edom's doom are Isaiah 34:5–15; Jeremiah 19:7–22; Ezekiel 25:12–14; 35:1–15; Amos 1:11–12.

Fulfillment of the Prophecy

Obadiah predicted that the Edomites would be destroyed forever and be as if they had never been (vv. 10, 16, 18), and that a remnant of Judah would be saved—the kingdom of Judah's God would yet prevail (vv. 17, 19, 21).

Edomite cultic shrine at biblical Tamar. A reminder of Obadiah's pronouncement of the coming destruction of Edom.

The end of the Edomite kingdom may have come as a result of the campaigns of the Neo-Babylonian ruler Nabonidus, sometime after 552 B.C. The Nabateans took over Edom's territory. The few Edomites that were left were confined to a region in south Judea, where for four centuries they continued to exist as active enemies of the Jews. In 126 B.C. they were subdued by John Hyrcanus, one of the Maccabean rulers (see p. 475), and were absorbed into the Jewish state. When Palestine was conquered by the Romans in 63 B.C., the Herods, an Edomite (Idumean) family, were placed in charge of Judah. This was the last hurrah of the Edomites. With the destruction of Jerusalem in A.D. 70, they disappeared from history.

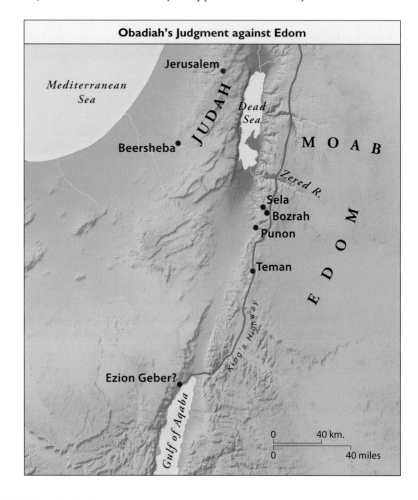

Obadiah's Judgment against Edom

Jonah

An Errand of Mercy to Nineveh

On the first day, Jonah started into the city. He proclaimed: "Forty more days and Nineveh will be overturned.". . . The Ninevites believed God. . . . When God saw what they did and how they turned from their evil ways, he had compassion and did not bring upon them the destruction he had threatened. . . . But Jonah was greatly displeased and became angry.

— JONAH 3:4 – 5, 10; 4:1

God said, "Nineveh has more than a hundred and twenty thousand people who cannot tell their right hand from their left, and many cattle as well. Should I not be concerned about that great city?"

— JONAH 4:11

Nineveh was the capital of the Assyrian Empire, which dominated the Ancient Near East for about 300 years (900 – 605 B.C.). It began its rise to world power about the time of the division of the Hebrew kingdom, at the close of Solomon's reign. It gradually absorbed and destroyed the northern kingdom of Israel.

Thus Jonah, whose name means "dove," was called by God to be a messenger. His message would prolong the life of the enemy nation that was already in the process of exterminating the northern kingdom of Israel, his own nation. No wonder he fled in the opposite direction — he was in patriotic dread of the brutal and relentless military machine that was closing in on God's people.

Jonah was a native of Gath Hepher. He lived in the reign of Jeroboam II (793 – 753 B.C.) and helped recover some of Israel's lost territory (2 Kings 14:25). Thus, Jonah was a statesman as well as a prophet. His mission to Nineveh might even have been considered treasonous by some.

Is the Book Historical?

Because of the fish story, unbelieving minds rebel at accepting the book as factual. They call it fiction, or an allegory, or a parable, or a prose poem. Jesus unmistakably regarded it as historical fact (Matthew 12:39 – 41). It takes considerable straining to make anything else out of Jesus' language. He called it a "sign" of His own resurrection. He put the fish, the repentance of the Ninevites, His resurrection, and the Judgment Day in the same category. He surely was talking of reality when He spoke of His resurrection and the Judgment Day. Thus Jesus accepted the Jonah story, and for us that settles it. We believe that it actually occurred just as recorded; that Jonah himself, under the direction of God's Spirit, wrote the book, with no attempt to excuse his own unworthy behavior; and that the book, under the direction of God's Spirit, was placed among the sacred writings in the temple as a part of God's unfolding revelation of Himself.

The fish. The word means "great fish" or "sea monster," rather than "whale." Many "sea monsters" have been found large enough to swallow a man. However, the point of the story is that it was a miracle, a divine attestation of Jonah's mission to Nineveh. Except for some such astounding miracle, the Ninevites would have paid little attention to Jonah (Luke 11:30).

God's Purpose in Sending Jonah to Nineveh

- Mainly, it seems to have been intended by God as a hint to His own nation that He was also interested in other gentile nations. Israel was jealous of its favored relationship with God and was unwilling to share the Lord's compassion with the Gentiles.
- It may have postponed the destruction of Israel, for "violence" was one of the things the Ninevites repented of (3:8).
- Jonah's home was Gath Hepher (2 Kings 14:25), near Nazareth, the home of Jesus, of whom Jonah was a "sign."
- Jesus quoted Jonah's rescue as a prophetic picture of His own resurrection on the "third" day (Matthew 12:40).
- Joppa, where Jonah embarked to avoid preaching to another nation, was the very place God chose, 800 years later, to tell Peter to receive people from other nations (Acts 10).

So, all in all, the story of Jonah is a grand historical picture of the Messiah's resurrection and mission to all nations. (The other prophet who spoke against Nineveh was Nahum; see pp. 431–32.)

Jonah 1 | JONAH'S FLIGHT

Tarshish (v. 3) is thought to have been Tartessus, a Phoenician mining colony in southwestern Spain, near Gibraltar. Jonah was heading for the farthest end of the then-known world.

Jonah 2 | JONAH'S PRAYER

He must have been used to praying in the words of the Psalms, so like this beautiful prayer. His return landing may have been near Joppa and may have been witnessed by many.

Assyrian Kings Who Were Involved with Israel

- Shalmaneser III (858–824 B.C.). Began to "cut off Israel" (2 Kings 17:3–4)
- Adad-Nirari III (810–782). Took tribute from Israel. Jonah's visit
- Tiglath-pileser III (745–727). Deported most of the northern part of the northern kingdom, Israel
- Shalmaneser V (727–722). Besieged Samaria
- Sargon II (721–705). Deported the rest of Israel (See Isaiah)
- Sennacherib (704–681). Invaded Judah (See Isaiah)
- Esar-Haddon (681–669). Very powerful
- Ashurbanipal (668–626). Most powerful and brutal (See Nahum?)

Two weak kings followed (626–607), and the giant empire fell in 605 B.C.

Joppa is the only natural harbor between the Bay of Acco (near modern Haifa) and the Egyptian frontier. Today it takes a great deal of imagination to think of Joppa as the place where Jonah left on a risky sea voyage, disobedient to God because he refused to help his nation's enemies.

Jonah 3:5–9 | NINEVEH'S REPENTANCE

Jonah, in his preaching, no doubt told of his experience with the fish, with witnesses accompanying him to verify his story. Speaking in the name of the God of the nation the Ninevites had begun to plunder, they took him seriously and became terrified.

Jonah 3:10–4:4 | JONAH'S DISAPPOINTMENT

He had come, not to seek the Ninevites' repentance, but to announce their doom. But God was pleased at their repentance and deferred punishment, much to Jonah's chagrin. (See further under Nahum.)

Jonah 4:5–11 | GOD'S LOVE FOR ALL OF HIS CREATION

Jonah was angry with God for showing compassion on Nineveh, an enemy of Israel. God wanted Jonah to understand His compassion for the Gentiles so He set up a situation that would help Jonah see God's

This marble sarcophagus depicts scenes from the life of Jonah and dates to around A.D. 300.

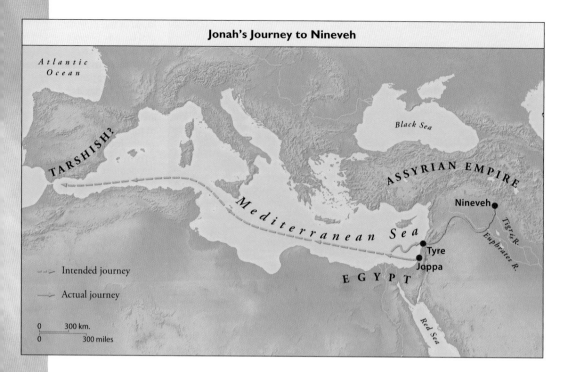

Jonah's Journey to Nineveh

Atlantic Ocean

Black Sea

TARSHISH?

ASSYRIAN EMPIRE

Nineveh

Mediterranean Sea

Tigris R.

Euphrates R.

Tyre

Joppa

EGYPT

Red Sea

--·-- Intended journey

--·-- Actual journey

| 0 | 300 km. |
| 0 | 300 miles |

love for His creation. God made a vine grow up over the place where Jonah sat. Jonah appreciated the protection from the sun that the vine provided. The next day, God removed the vine and Jonah grieved for the loss of the vine. God pointed out to Jonah how he was mourning the loss of a simple vine in which he had invested nothing. God used this situation to illustrate to Jonah how much more God grieves for this creation, including the people and animals of Nineveh.

Micah

The Impending Fall of Israel and Judah
The Messiah Will Be Born at Bethlehem

"But you, Bethlehem Ephrathah,
  though you are small among the clans of Judah,
out of you will come for me
  one who will be ruler over Israel,
whose origins are from of old,
  from ancient times."

—Micah 5:2

Micah prophesied in Judah, the southern kingdom, during the reigns of Jotham, Ahaz, and Hezekiah. Jotham and Hezekiah were good kings; Ahaz was extremely wicked. Thus Micah witnessed the apostasy of the government as well as its recovery. His home was Moresheth, on the Philistine border, near Gath, about 30 miles southwest of Jerusalem. He was a contemporary of the prophets Isaiah and Hosea.

Micah's message was to both Israel and Judah and was addressed primarily to their capitals, Samaria and Jerusalem. The three main ideas in Micah's message are the sins of Samaria and Jerusalem, their destruction, and their restoration. These three ideas are intermingled in the book, with abrupt transitions between present desolation and future glory.

Mic. 1 | SAMARIA DOOMED

Samaria was the capital of the northern kingdom, whose rulers were directly responsible for the pervasive national corruption (v. 5). Since their apostasy from God 200 years before (1 Kings 12), they had adopted calf worship and Baal worship and had adopted other Canaanite, Syrian, and Assyrian idols and idolatrous practices. God had sent Elijah, Elisha, and Amos (1 Kings 7 – 2 Kings 2; 2 Kings 3 – 13) to turn them back from idols. But in vain. They were about ripe for the death blow. Micah lived to see his words come true (v. 6). In 734 B.C. the Assyrians deported all of the northern part of Israel, and in 722 Samaria itself became a "heap of rubble."

The places named in vv. 10 – 15 were in the western foothills of Judah, Micah's home territory. They were eventually devastated by Sennacherib of Assyria in his campaign of 701 B.C., during which he claims to have destroyed 46 strong-walled cities of Judah — probably including those mentioned by Micah.

Mic. 2–3 | THE BRUTALITY OF THE RULERS

In addition to their idolatry (1:5–7), the ruling classes were merciless in their treatment of the poor, seizing their fields, even their clothes, and ejecting women with small children from their homes. On top of all this, their priests were fortune-tellers who condoned their unjust and cruel practices and used the Lord as a talisman: "Is not the Lord among us? No disaster will come upon us" (3:11). Micah, having mentioned the captivity (1:16), now abruptly pictures their restoration, with God marching at their head (2:12–13).

Mic. 3 | JERUSALEM ALSO INDICTED

Micah continues to rebuke the leaders of Israel for the wanton and inhuman cruelty of the ruling classes. But Jerusalem is as bad as Samaria (v. 10), in particular the religious leaders (vv. 5–7, 11). Then Micah pronounces the doom of Jerusalem (v. 12), as he had earlier predicted the fall of Samaria (1:6).

Mic. 4 | ZION'S UNIVERSAL REIGN

Micah now shifts abruptly to a vision of a warless, happy, prosperous, God-fearing world, with Zion at its head. What a contrast! Micah 4:1–3 is the same as Isaiah 2:2–4—sublime, grand words that are worthy of repetition.

Suddenly, in the midst of this rhapsody of the future, the prophet reverts to his own troubled times and the doom of Jerusalem, which he had just mentioned (3:12), announcing that the people will be carried away captive to Babylon (4:10). It is an amazing prophecy. At the time Micah prophesied, Assyria was sweeping everything before it. This was 100 years before the rise of the Babylonian Empire. Yet Jerusalem survived the Assyrian onslaught and outlived Assyria, which was overthrown by Babylonia—which would destroy Jerusalem in 586 B.C. and deport its people to Babylonia.

Mic. 5 | ZION'S COMING KING

A ruler from Bethlehem shall be at the head of Zion. In 4:1–8, Micah describes the glorious future; in 4:9–10, he goes back to the Exile; in 4:11–12, he goes further back, to his own time, to describe the siege of Jerusalem by the Assyrians. In 4:13, there is again a forward sweep to the future.

Then, in 5:1, Micah returns to the siege of Jerusalem. This is the setting for the appearance of the deliverer from Bethlehem (vv. 2–5). In Micah's own day it referred to the deliverance from Assyria (5–6). But beyond the horizon, in the dim distance, loomed the majestic figure of the coming Messianic King, who made His advent from eternity ("from of old, from ancient times," v. 2) by way of Bethlehem. Zion's deliverance from Assyria by the Angel of God (2 Kings 19:35; 2 Chronicles 32:21; Isaiah 37:35) was, in some respects, a foreshadowing of a coming greater deliverance by the Savior of all humanity. Many Old Testament predictions of Christ were blurred because they were viewed through the historic situations of the prophet's own times, yet too clear to be mistaken. Unques-

Key Locations in Micah's Message

Mediterranean Sea
Sea of Galilee
Samaria
ISRAEL
Jordan R.
Jerusalem
Bethlehem
Gath
Moresheth Gath
Lachish
JUDAH
Dead Sea

0   10 km.
0   10 miles

tionably the eternal Ruler from Bethlehem (v. 2) is to be identified with the wonderful Child of Isaiah 9:6–7. This is the only place in the Old Testament where it is specifically stated that the Christ would be born in Bethlehem (see under Matthew 2:22).

Sheep grazing outside the village of Bethlehem, birthplace of the Messiah. "But you, Bethlehem Ephrathah, though you are small among the clans of Judah, out of you will come for me one who will be ruler over Israel." (Micah 5:2)

Mic. 6 | JEHOVAH'S CONTROVERSY WITH HIS PEOPLE

Again, the sins of Micah's times: ingratitude toward God, religious pretense, dishonesty, idolatry—and certain punishment.

Mic. 7 | ZION'S FINAL TRIUMPH

Micah laments the prevailing treachery, violence, and bloodthirstiness. He promises punishment, yet closes with a vision of the future when God, with His people, shall rule and the promises to Abraham will be completely fulfilled at last.

Nahum

The Doom of Nineveh

Who can withstand his indignation?
Who can endure his fierce anger?
His wrath is poured out like fire;
the rocks are shattered before him.

—NAHUM 1:6

The Lord is good,
a refuge in times of trouble.
He cares for those who trust in him.

—NAHUM 1:7

Two of the so-called Minor Prophets spoke exclusively to and about Nineveh, the capital of the Assyrian Empire:

- **Jonah,** in about 770 B.C., delivered a message of mercy to the great city.
- **Nahum,** 120 years later (650 B.C.) spoke a message of doom.
- **Zephaniah,** a contemporary of Nahum, also predicted Nineveh's destruction.
- In addition, **Isaiah,** who ministered midway between Jonah and Nahum, predicted the fall of the Assyrians (Isaiah 10).

Together they illustrate God's way of dealing with nations: prolonging the day of grace, in the end sending punishment for sins.

The Prophet Nahum

Little is known of Nahum, whose name means "comfort." He is identified as "the Elkoshite." Since the 16th century, an Arab tradition has identified Elkosh with Al Ovosh, a village near modern Mosul in Iraq. Byzantine writers—including Eusebius and Jerome—however, understood the prophet's home to be somewhere in Galilee. Many have speculated that the New Testament Capernaum ("Town of Nahum") was home to him, but there is no proof of this, nor are there any remains there from the 7th century B.C.

Nahum's Date

The book itself indicates the time frame within which it belongs. Thebes (Hebrew name: No-Amon) had fallen (3:8–10; 663 B.C.). The fall of Nineveh, which took place in 612 B.C., is still in the future. Thus Nahum wrote between 663 and 612 B.C.

Nahum pictures Nineveh in the full swing of its glory. Its troubles began with the Scythian invasion (626 B.C.), and it may be a good guess to place this prophecy shortly before the Scythian invasion (between 630 and 624 B.C.)—which would make Nahum a contemporary of Zephaniah, who also predicted the ruin of Nineveh in language of amazing vividness (Zephaniah 2:13–15). (See also Jonah, pp. 423–26.)

Nahum 1–3 | NINEVEH'S UTTER RUIN

Throughout these three chapters, in language spoken partly *about* Nineveh and partly *to* Nineveh, the city's destruction is foretold in astonishing and graphic detail.

God's "slowness to anger" (1:3) may have been mentioned as a reminder of Jonah's visit to Nineveh years before. God's wrath (1:2–8), throughout the Bible, is the opposite of His mercy.

The fall of "the city of blood" (3:1) would be news of immense joy to the world it had so pitilessly crushed, especially Judah.

The great number of protecting canals along the edges of the walls gave Nineveh an appearance "like a pool [of] water" (2:8).

Zephaniah predicted the fall of Nineveh in these words: "This is the carefree city that lived in safety. She said to herself, 'I am, and there is none besides me.' What a ruin she has become, a lair for wild beasts! All who pass by her scoff and shake their fists" (Zephaniah 2:15).

The tell of Kuyunjik at ancient Nineveh. Nahum foretells the destruction of Nineveh in graphic detail.

Habakkuk

The Invasion of Judah and the Doom of the Chaldeans

"The righteous will live by his faith."

—HABAKKUK 2:4

*"For the earth will be filled with the knowledge
of the glory of the LORD,
as the waters cover the sea."*

—HABAKKUK 2:14

This prophecy belongs to the period between 625 and 606 B.C. It probably dates to about 607 B.C., early in Jehoiakim's reign. The Chaldeans (Babylonians) were sweeping westward (1:6), but had not yet reached Judah (3:16).

The chronology of the period:

641–601 B.C.	King Josiah's great reformation; the prophet Zephaniah.
625 B.C.	Babylon declares its independence from Assyria.
612 B.C.	The Babylonians destroy Nineveh.
609 B.C.	Jehoahaz reigns three months and is taken to Egypt.
609–598 B.C.	Jehoiakim, a very wicked king; the prophet Habakkuk(?)
605 B.C.	The Babylonians invade Judah and take captives.
597 B.C.	Jehoiachin reigns three months and is taken to Babylon.
597–586 B.C.	Zedekiah, a weak, wicked king; he is taken to Babylon.
586 B.C.	Jerusalem is burned; the land is desolated.

Hab. 1:1–11 | HABAKKUK'S COMPLAINT

The prophecy is a complaint to God that He allows His own nation to be destroyed for its wickedness by a nation that is even more wicked. Habakkuk could not see the justice in this. God's answer is that He does have a purpose in the terrorizing conquests of the Chaldean armies.

Hab. 1:12–2:20 | HABAKKUK'S SECOND COMPLAINT

Acknowledging that Judah deserves correction and punishment for her sins, Habakkuk asks for further enlightenment. God's answer is that the Babylonians, drunk with the blood of nations, shall themselves be destroyed—and God's people shall yet fill the earth.

Hab. 3 | HABAKKUK'S PRAYER

A cry to God to again perform His miracles, as He had done in the past. Yet Habakkuk speaks with sublime resignation and confidence in the eternal security of God's people (16–19). The lesson of the book is, "The righteous will live by his faith" (2:4). Faith is the ability to feel so sure of God that, no matter how dark the day, there is no doubt as to the outcome. For God's people there is a glorious future. It may be a long way off, but it is absolutely sure. Thus, in the midst of his gloom and despair, Habakkuk could be an optimist of the first magnitude.

The East India House Inscription which describes the status and pride of the Babylonian ruler, Nebuchadnezzar, helps expose the reason for Habakkuk's complaint about the success of the Babylonian military.

Zephaniah

The Great Day of God Is at Hand

Sing, O Daughter of Zion;
shout aloud, O Israel!
Be glad and rejoice with all your heart,
O Daughter of Jerusalem!
The LORD has taken away your punishment,
he has turned back your enemy.
The LORD, the King of Israel, is with you;
never again will you fear any harm.

—ZEPHANIAH 3:14–15

Z ephaniah, who prophesied in the days of King Josiah (1:1), was a great-great-grandson of King Hezekiah (1:1), which made him a relative of King Josiah (641–609 B.C.). Josiah, who came to the throne after the 55-year-long wicked reign of Manasseh, brought about a great reformation (see under 2 Chronicles 34), in which the prophet Zephaniah was a prime mover.

This prophecy was thus uttered not many years before Judah's day of doom struck: in 586 B.C. the Babylonians destroyed Jerusalem and took the people of Judah to Babylonia.

Zeph. 1:1–2:3 AN IMPENDING DAY OF WRATH FOR JUDAH

The Day of Judgment—called the Day of the Lord, the great day of the Lord, the day of the Lord's wrath—is mentioned over and over (1:7, 8, 9, 10, 14, 15, 16, 18; 2:2, 3; 3:8). It will be a day of terror and is about to come upon Judah and the surrounding nations. This is an unmistakable reference to the Babylonian invasion and to Judah's captivity, which followed 20 years after this prophecy. Finally, it may also be a sort of symbolic depiction of the catastrophes that will happen at the time of the end, pictured more fully in the book of Revelation.

Zeph. 2:4–3:8 A DAY OF WRATH FOR THE NATIONS

Gaza, Ashkelon, Ashdod, Ekron (v. 4) were cities of the Philistines. "Kerethite people" (2:5) is another name for Philistines. **Cushites** (2:12):

Molech (or Moloch)

Molech (1:5) is the god especially of the Ammonites. To please some of his wives, Solomon introduced Molech worship in Israel (1 Kings 11:7). The worship of Molech involved child sacrifices. During and after the time of King Manasseh, the main place for the worship of Molech was the Valley of Ben Hinnom (2 Chronicles 33:6), whose Hebrew name (*ge-hinnom*) later was used as a Greek name for hell (*gehenna*) because of the evil committed there.

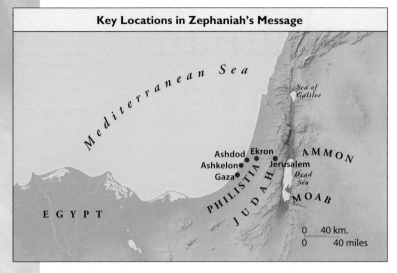

Key Locations in Zephaniah's Message

Mediterranean Sea

Sea of Galilee

Jordan R.

Ashdod • Ekron •
Ashkelon •
Gaza • PHILISTIA
JUDAH
Jerusalem
Dead Sea
AMMON
MOAB

EGYPT

0   40 km.
0   40 miles

Cush was south of Egypt and north of Ethiopia; at the time of Zephaniah, a Cushite dynasty ruled Egypt.

Within 20 years all these lands — Philistia, Moab, Ammon, Cush, and Assyria, the terror of the world, with its proud capital Nineveh — would lay desolate under the heel of Babylon.

The assembly of the nations and the pouring out of God's wrath on them (3:8) may also be a foreshadowing of God's judgment poured out of the seven bowls of God's wrath on the earth in Revelation 16:1. In v. 8 God declares that the whole world will be consumed by fire. This may be a prediction of the lake of fire (Revelation 20:14) into which all evil will be thrown, leaving the earth purified as described in Revelation 20 – 21.

| Zeph. 3:9 – 20 | **THE COMING OF A "PURE LANGUAGE"** |

The calm after the storm. Three times the prophet speaks of a remnant being saved (2:3, 7; 3:12 – 13), and twice he mentions their return from captivity (2:7; 3:20). Then the Lord will "purify the lips of the peoples" so that they may all, near and far, worship God. Pure lips are lips that speak truth and worship in truth. This is the prediction of a complete and perfect revelation of God. As a result of this revelation, converts from among all nations will be brought to God, joyful with glad songs of redemption, so that all the earth will resound with the praise of God's people.

The elongated mound of Ekron (Tel Mikne). Zephaniah announced a day of judgment on proud cities such as the Philistine city of Ekron.

These passages seem to predict the millennial reign of Christ (Revelation 20:4 – 6) on earth that will follow the tribulation. God's final judgment of Satan and the inhabitants of the earth follows this period of peace. Then God's grand finale presents us with a new heaven and a new earth that is pure and where God lives with His people (Revelation 21 – 22).

Haggai

Make Rebuilding the Temple Your Priority

"'The glory of this present house will be greater than the glory of the former house,' says the LORD Almighty. 'And in this place I will grant peace,' declares the LORD Almighty." —HAGGAI 2:9

Haggai, Zechariah, Malachi

These three prophets belong to the period after the return from the Babylonian captivity or exile (which is why they are also called the post-exilic prophets). The story of this period is told in the books of Ezra, Nehemiah, and Esther. (See under Ezra.)

Haggai and Zechariah urged the people to finish rebuilding the temple, which had been begun but not finished (520–516 B.C.). Malachi is thought to have been associated with Nehemiah, nearly 100 years later, in the rebuilding of the walls of Jerusalem.

The dates of Zechariah's recorded messages are best correlated with those of Haggai and with other historical events as shown on the table on page 438.

Haggai and His Book

Haggai may have been an old man who had seen the first temple (2:3). His book consists of four brief discourses: 1:1–11 (followed by a response of Zerubbabel and the people, 1:12–15); 2:1–9; 2:10–19; 2:20–23.

The Situation

Judah had been conquered, Jerusalem burned, the temple demolished, and the people carried away to Babylon (605–586 B.C., as told in 2 Kings 24–25). After 70 years' captivity, about 50,000 Jews had returned to their own land, by edict of King Cyrus (538 B.C.), and had begun to rebuild the temple. But soon after they laid the foundation, the work was stopped by their enemy neighbors.

Nothing further was done for 15 years. In the meantime, a new king, Darius, had ascended the Persian throne. He was kindly disposed toward the Jews. And under the preaching of Haggai and Zechariah, work was resumed, and the temple was completed in four years (520–516 B.C.). But Jerusalem was still a city without a wall: the wall of Jerusalem was not built until about 70 years later, under Nehemiah.

Hag. 1 | WORK ON THE TEMPLE BEGINS

Fifteen years earlier, the foundation of the temple had been laid (Ezra 3:10), but nothing more had been done since then. The people had lost interest.

538 B.C		50,000 Jews, under Zerubbabel, return to Jerusalem.
536 B.C		In the 7th month they build the altar and offer sacrifices.
535 B.C		In the 2nd month work on the temple begins and is stopped.
	August 29	Haggai's 1st message (Haggai 1:1–11; Ezra 5:1).
	September 21	Resumption of the building of the temple (Haggai 1:12–15; Ezra 5:2). The rebuilding seems to have been hindered from 536 to about 530 (Ezra 4:1–5), and the work ceased altogether from about 530 to 520 (Ezra 4:24).
	October 17	Haggai's 2nd message (Haggai 2:1–9).
	October/ November	Beginning of Zechariah's preaching (Zechariah 1:1–6).
	December 18	Haggai's 3rd message (Haggai 2:10–19).
	December 18	Haggai's 4th message (Haggai 2:20–23).
519–518 B.C		Tattenai's letter to Darius concerning the rebuilding of the temple (Ezra 5:3–6:14). There must have been a lapse of time between the resumption of the building and Tattenai's appearance.
519 B.C	February 15	Zechariah's eight night visions (Zechariah 1:7–6:8).
	February 16(?)	Joshua's crowning (Zechariah 6:9–15).
518 B.C	December 7	Urging of repentance, promise of blessings (Zechariah 7–8).
516 B.C	March 12	Dedication of the temple (Ezra 6:15–18).
After 480(?) B.C		Zechariah's final prophecy (Zechariah 9–14).
458 B.C		Ezra comes to Jerusalem and makes certain reforms.
444 B.C		Nehemiah rebuilds the wall. Period of Malachi.

God, speaking through Haggai, informs them that this was the reason for their poor crops. One of the most insistent Old Testament teachings is that national adversity is due to national disobedience to God.

Haggai's message had an immediate effect. People accepted it as God's word, and in less than a month, work on the temple was underway.

Wheat field full of tares, thistles and thorns. Haggai informs the people that their crop is poor due to their negative attitude in rebuilding the temple.

Hag. 2 | THE FUTURE GLORY OF GOD'S HOUSE

Within another month, the old foundations had been cleared sufficiently to reveal the outline of the building. Then Haggai came forward with his vision of the temple's future, beside whose glory Solomon's temple itself would pale into insignificance.

This is distinctly a messianic vision. Haggai's mind was on the temple he was helping Zerubbabel build. But his words were God's words, and God's mind, in a sense deeper perhaps than even Haggai himself realized, was on another temple, yet to come, of which Solomon's temple and Zerubbabel's temple were but dim pictures. This temple would be the church, built not of stones, but of the souls of the redeemed (1 Corinthians 3:16–17; 2 Corinthians 6:16; Ephesians 2:21). This is the temple of which Haggai speaks.

Shake the heavens and the earth (vv. 6–7). Though this may have had immediate reference to political upheavals, it is quoted in Hebrews 12:26 as referring to the judgment of the nations at the second coming of Christ.

The desired of all nations (v. 7) may refer to the Messiah. Or it may refer to people ("the highly esteemed, the leaders") or articles of value, such as King Darius's gift to the temple (Ezra 6:8).

It was midwinter (v. 10). The earth had not yet had time to bear its crops. But the people had stirred themselves and had put their hands to the task of building God's house. And God promises that henceforth their crops would be sure. Since we know that God's promises are good for all ages, there is practical application in these verses. If we build only our own houses (live a self-centered life), our harvest in life will be limited. But if we make building God's house (build the church, Christ's body) our priority, then all the rest will be given to us and our harvest will be great.

Haggai closes with a vision of the crowning of Zerubbabel, who represented David's family (see under Zechariah 4).

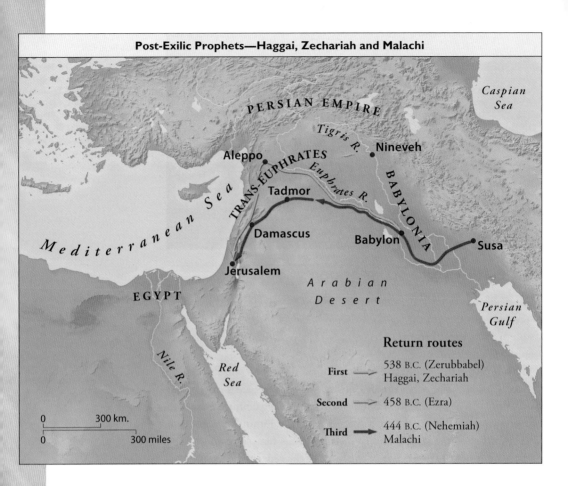

Post-Exilic Prophets—Haggai, Zechariah and Malachi

Caspian Sea

PERSIAN EMPIRE

Tigris R.

Nineveh

Aleppo

TRANS-EUPHRATES

Euphrates R.

BABYLONIA

Tadmor

Damascus

Babylon

Susa

Mediterranean Sea

Jerusalem

Arabian Desert

Persian Gulf

EGYPT

Red Sea

Nile R.

0   300 km.
0   300 miles

Return routes

First —— 538 B.C. (Zerubbabel)
Haggai, Zechariah

Second —— 458 B.C. (Ezra)

Third —— 444 B.C. (Nehemiah)
Malachi

Zechariah

Rebuilding the Temple
Visions of the Coming Messiah and His Universal Kingdom

"This is what the LORD Almighty says: 'Administer true justice; show mercy and compassion to one another. Do not oppress the widow or the fatherless, the alien or the poor. In your hearts do not think evil of each other.'" —ZECHARIAH 7:9–10

Rejoice greatly, O Daughter of Zion!
Shout, Daughter of Jerusalem!
See, your king comes to you,
righteous and having salvation,
gentle and riding on a donkey,
on a colt, the foal of a donkey.

—ZECHARIAH 9:9

Zechariah was a contemporary of Haggai. Both ministered during the time immediately after the first return from the Babylonian exile, when the temple in Jerusalem was being rebuilt (see p. 268). While Haggai seems to have been an old man, it seems that Zechariah was a young man, for he was a grandson of Iddo, who had returned to Jerusalem 16 years before (Nehemiah 12:4, 16).

Haggai had been preaching for two months, and the work on the temple had already started, when Zechariah began his ministry. Haggai's total recorded ministry lasted a little less than four months, Zechariah's about two years. But they were no doubt on hand during the entire four-year period during which the temple was rebuilt, exhorting and helping.

The book of Zechariah is considerably larger than that of Haggai. It teems with messianic flashes, mentioning many details of the life and work of Christ.

Zech. 1:1–6 | THE CAPTIVITY DUE TO DISOBEDIENCE

This opening message of Zechariah came between Haggai's second and third messages (between vv. 9 and 10 of Haggai 2), when work on the temple was a little over a month along and its unimposing appearance and lack of splendor were disheartening to the people. Some people were old enough to remember Solomon's temple, which had been destroyed more than 50 years earlier. Those who were born in Babylonia had heard their parents tell about the temple and its beauty, and they may well have formed a mental image of the old temple that was even grander than the temple really had been.

Zechariah warns against their evident rising tendency to return to the ways of their disobedient fathers, which had brought them to their present pitiful condition in the first place. He then proceeds to encourage them with visions God had given him of the magnificent future.

Zech. 1:7–17 THE VISION OF THE HORSES

The only indication in the first six chapters as to the time of the visions is in 1:7, when work on the temple was about five months along. So we assume that the visions came one after the other and were written down at the time.

God's messages through the prophets generally came by the direct moving of God's Spirit on a prophet's mind. But here they are given through an angel, who talks back and forth with the prophet.

This vision of the horses means that the whole world was at rest under the iron hand of the Persian Empire, whose king, Darius, was favorably disposed toward the Jews and had decreed that the temple should be built. This vision concludes with the proclamation that Jerusalem shall once again be a great and prosperous city (see below, under chapter 2).

Zech. 1:18–21 THE VISION OF FOUR HORNS AND FOUR CRAFTSMEN

The four horns represent the nations that had destroyed Judah and Israel. The four craftsmen (KJV, carpenters) represent God's destroyers of those nations. It was a figurative way of saying that the prevailing world powers would be broken and that Judah would again be exalted. God is on the throne, even when His people are temporarily vanquished. These verses provide insight into the interpretation of Revelation 13:1 and 17:12, where "horns" are also used to symbolize nations.

Zech. 2 THE VISION OF THE MEASURING LINE

This grand chapter is a forecast of a Jerusalem so populous and prosperous and secure that it will overflow its walls, since God Himself is its protection. Work on the temple, five months along, progressed nicely, and the people no doubt were making plans to rebuild the wall of Jerusalem, which, as it turned out, was not built until 75 years later. But their plans to rebuild are the setting for this vision of the day when "many nations" shall come to the God of the Jews and will be His people.

Zech. 3 THE VISION OF JOSHUA THE HIGH PRIEST

A pre-vision of the atonement of Christ. Joshua the high priest is clothed in filthy garments, symbolizing the sinfulness of the people. Joshua's filthy garments are removed, meaning that the people's sins are forgiven and they are accepted by God. It is a picture of the time when the sins of humanity will be removed "in one day" (v. 9), as the coming "Branch" in David's house (the Messiah; v. 8 and 6:12) is "pierced" (12:10), and "a fountain will be opened to cleanse them from sin" (13:1; see further under 13:1–9).

Zech. 4 | THE LAMPSTAND AND TWO OLIVE TREES

What is said here is meant directly for Zerubbabel and the temple he was building. But there is an unmistakable reference to a later, more glorious house, to be built by a descendant of Zerubbabel, called the Branch. It is an exhortation to take courage, in the day of small beginnings, by keeping our eyes

The lampstand (menorah) represents the light-bearing qualities of God's house.

on the grandeur of the end. The candlestick is a symbolic representation of God's house, or the light-bearing qualities of God's house. The lampstand was in the tabernacle and in the temple. In Revelation 1:20 the lampstand represents the church. The two olive trees seem to represent Joshua and Zerubbabel. In chapter 3 the vision was specially for Joshua; here it is specially for Zerubbabel. The imagery here is carried over into the vision of the "two witnesses" in Revelation 11. Some people believe that the witnesses represent Moses and Elijah.

Zech. 5:1–4 | THE FLYING SCROLL

A sheet, like an unrolled wall map, 30 feet long and 15 feet wide, inscribed with curses against stealing and swearing, soars over the land; it removes sin by destroying the sinners.

Zech. 5:5–10 | THE FLYING BASKET

Another representation of the removal of sin. A basket, looking like a small bushel basket (the basket holds one ephah, or three-fifths bushel) and containing a woman, is taken away, out of the land, by two other women. While sin is here represented by a woman, it is also by women that she is removed (v. 9). Might this possibly be a prophetic hint that the coming Branch, the Messiah who would remove people's sin in one day (3:8–9), would be brought into the world by a woman without the agency of man? The imagery here is somewhat similar to that of the scapegoat of Leviticus 16, on whose head the sins of the people were placed and borne away into the wilderness.

Zech. 6:1–8 | THE FOUR CHARIOTS

The chariots are messengers of God's judgments, patrolling the earth, executing the decrees of God on Israel's enemies. This is an expansion of the thought in the vision of the horns and the craftsmen (1:18–21).

Zech. 6:9–15 | THE CORONATION OF JOSHUA

This is a prophetically symbolic act, expanding on the vision of the Branch (3:8–9) and the vision about Zerubbabel (4:6–9).

The Branch (v. 12) is the name of the coming Messiah in David's family (Isaiah 4:2; 11:1, 10; Jeremiah 23:5–6; 33:15–17; Revelation 5:5; 22:16).

Zerubbabel, the governor, was a grandson of King Jehoiachin, who had been carried to Babylon, and thus was heir to David's throne. What is said of Zerubbabel refers in part to himself personally and in part to his family—that is, David's family—and more particularly to the one great representative of David's family, the coming Messiah.

To David's family God had, among other things, assigned the task of building God's house. To David himself God gave, in His own handwriting, the plans and specifications of the temple (1 Chronicles 28:11, 19), and according to those specifications David's son Solomon built the temple (2 Chronicles 2–7), the most magnificent building in all the world at that time. Zerubbabel, a descendant of David, was now (520–516 B.C.) engaged in rebuilding the temple. He was assured that he would bring it to completion (4:6–9), with mystic hints of yet another temple to be built by the Branch, with help from "those who are far away" (6:12–15).

The Branch was to be of Zerubbabel's (David's) family, the kingly line (from the tribe of Judah). But here Joshua the priest (from the tribe of Levi) is crowned and is represented as the Branch, sitting on the throne of David (6:12–13). This would appear to represent a symbolic merging of the two offices of king and priest in the coming Messiah.

Zech. 7–8 | QUESTIONS ABOUT FASTING

For 70 years the people had been fasting in the fourth, fifth, seventh, and tenth months (8:19) to mourn the destruction of the temple. Now that it looked as if they were soon to have a temple again, the question arose as to whether these fasts should be continued. In reply, Zechariah reminds them that there had been good reason for their fasts: penitence for past disobedience and the resulting suffering. But now their fasts had become a mere outward pretense, a way to exhibit their own holiness, and their religious feasts were for their own pleasure.

Then, following prophetic custom of alternating scenes of present distress and future glory, Zechariah draws a picture of the age when fasts shall be joyful feasts (8:19).

The Jews—once a mighty nation with ancient traditions that said they had been designed by their God to be the leading people of all the world—were now an insignificant and despised remnant who existed in their own land only by permission of Persian kings. Zechariah tried hard to encourage the people by repeating over and over that it would not be forever thus: soon the mighty empire that then ruled would be broken, and God's people would yet come into their own.

Zechariah's picture of a prosperous and peaceful Zion, its streets full of happy boys and girls and old men and old women (8:3–5), of a Zion that is the center of the world's civilization, where all the nations of the earth come to learn of the God of the Jews (8:22–23), is also found in other passages (1:17; 2:4, 11; 14:8, 16).

Zech. 9–11 GOD'S JUDGMENTS ON NEIGHBORING NATIONS

Chapters 9–14 contain things that have evident reference to the conquest by Alexander the Great and its aftermath, which came 200 years after Zechariah.

Chapter 9 seems to be a forecast of Judah's struggle with Greece. Alexander the Great, when he invaded Palestine in 332 b.c., devastated the cities named in vv. 1–7, in the order in which they are named, and yet spared Jerusalem (v. 8). Verses 13–17 seem to refer to the continuation of Judah's struggle against the Greek Ptolemies and Seleucids into the Maccabean period (see pp. 473–75). Throughout history and even today Judah (Israel) continues to struggle with its neighbors.

A picture of Zion's coming King (9:9–10) is here set amid scenes of Judah's fierce struggle with Greece. Verse 9 is quoted in the New Testament as referring to the Triumphal Entry of Christ into Jerusalem (Matthew 21:5; John 12:15). In the same breath (v. 10), the prophet sweeps forward to the day of final triumph — from a glimpse at the beginning of Messiah's kingdom to a glimpse at the end.

Chapter 10 is a forecast of the full restoration of God's scattered people. In Zechariah's day only a small remnant had returned.

Chapter 11 is a parable of shepherds. God's flock had been scattered and slaughtered because their shepherds had been false. In the arraignment of the false shepherds is a picture of their rejection of the Good Shepherd (vv. 12–13). We might not, from the context, connect this passage with the betrayal of Christ by Judas Iscariot, except that it is so quoted in the New Testament (Matthew 26:15; 27:9–10). The fact that it is so quoted is a key to God's meaning in the passage. The rejection of their true Shepherd was accompanied by the breaking of the two staffs called Favor and Union — that is, the covenant of God's protecting care and the postponement of their reunion in the land. When we stray from our relationship with God, we withdraw from God's protective care and fall short of our own land of promise and blessing.

Then they are delivered into the hands of the worthless shepherd (vv. 15–17). This is thought to refer to the destruction of Jerusalem by the Romans, shortly after the death of Christ, and the consequent scattering of the Jews (the Diaspora); or it may be the personification of the whole list of those who persecute the Jews, from the Maccabean period to the time of the beast of Revelation 13.

Chapters 9–11 are called an "oracle" (a message coming from God) concerning neighboring nations (9:1); chapters 12–14 are called an "oracle" concerning Israel (12:1). The two sections are quite similar. Both are an expansion and continuation of ideas in the visions of the first eight chapters, the same ideas recurring again and again in different dress.

Judah's coming struggle with all nations (12:1–6). The description of this struggle is continued in 14:1–8. Some consider the language to be a figurative representation of God's struggle with the nations through the whole Christian era. Others apply it more literally to the time of the end.

Mourning in the house of David (12:7–13:9). The thoughts here are evidently centered around the house of David. Though the language is difficult, yet it clearly depicts a tragedy of some kind or other that takes place in the family of David, an occasion for great sorrow, when some leading member of the family would be killed (13:7), his hands would be pierced (12:10; 13:6), and a fountain for sin would be opened (13:1). It was to happen in the day when "the house of David will be like God" (12:8). Only one member of David's family was God: that one was Jesus. This identifies the person here referred to as the "Branch" of 3:8, who would "remove the sin of this land in a single day" (3:9) and who would "build the temple of the Lord" (6:12) and rule from sea to sea. (See also under 6:9–15.) It is an amazingly detailed forecast of Jesus' death that is not applicable in any way to any other known person. Thus the death of the Branch in David's family would be the source of God's power against the nations (12:2–4), and its effectiveness would be shown in the eventual removal of idols and false prophets from the earth (13:2–5).

Judah's struggle with the nations (14:1–2). (See on 12:1–6.)

God's victory and universal reign (14:3–21). This speaks of the grand consummation of the prophetic dreams, the day of the Lord's return, and the inauguration of His everlasting kingdom. Some biblical scholars think that verses 4–8 mean that Jesus, when He returns, will literally

---

Summary of Zechariah's Prophecies Concerning Christ

- His atoning death for the removal of sin (3:8–9; 13:1)
- As builder of the house of God (6:12)
- His universal reign as King and Priest (6:13; 9:10)
- Triumphal Entry (9:9, quoted in Matthew 21:5; John 12:15)
- Betrayal for 30 pieces of silver (11:12, quoted in Matthew 27:9–10)
- His deity (12:8)
- His hands pierced (12:10; 13:6, quoted in John 19:37)
- A stricken Shepherd (13:7, quoted in Matthew 26:31; Mark 14:27)

Here are plain statements that not only forecast, in specific language, the great doctrines of the coming Messiah's atoning death for human sin, His deity, and His universal kingdom, but also mention detailed incidents in His life, such as His entry into Jerusalem riding on a colt and His betrayal for 30 pieces of silver.

make His throne on the Mount of Olives, that the mountain will literally be cleft, that waters literally will flow eastward and westward from Jerusalem, and that Jerusalem will literally be the center of pilgrimages from nations outlined in verses 10–21. Others take the language to be a figurative representation of the new heavens and the new earth, under the imagery of a benign, prosperous, and all-powerful earthly kingdom, the way Revelation 21 describes heaven under the imagery of a magnificent earthly city.

Malachi admonishes Israel for their use of blemished and diseased animals for sacrifice.

insulted by His own nation will be honored by all the other nations of the world (v. 11).

Mal. 2 | MARRIAGES WITH GENTILE NEIGHBORS

Priests, who had been ordained by God to lead the people in righteousness (vv. 5–7), were responsible for this deplorable situation. They had become so debased, mercenary, and corrupt that the name "priest" had become a word of contempt among the people.

Loose marriage morals (vv. 10–16). Jews were divorcing their wives to marry non-Jewish women. This was a double sin, with disastrous effects on the proper rearing of children.

Skepticism was at the root of their religious indifference and their low morals. Noticing that wicked nations were more prosperous, the people were asking, "What's the use of serving God?" (See under 3:13–18.)

Mal. 3:1–6 | THE COMING DAY OF THE LORD

Malachi's reply to their skepticism is that the coming Day of Judgment will answer their taunts and will show whether it pays to serve God (v. 5; see further under 3:13–18).

Tithing

There is much debate in the church today whether tithing is a requirement for the New Testament Christian. Some classify the tithe as an Old Testament law that was superceded by the Gospel and is therefore no longer a requirement for the New Testament church. But the New Testament makes it clear that Jesus is a priest "in the order of Melchizedek" (Psalm 110:4; Hebrews 5:6–10; 6:20–7:28). God tells us very little about Melchizedek except that he was a righteous priest and king who blessed Abram in the name of the most high God and received tithes from Abram (Genesis 14:18–20). It is commonly accepted by Christians that Melchizedek is a type of Jesus. The New Testament church would be well advised to consider tithing, for God's promised blessing is great!

Mal. 3:7–12 | TITHES

Another abrupt change of subject. Withholding tithes is called "robbing God." According to the Mosaic Law, one-tenth of all income was God's property, to which the donor had no more right than he had to another man's property. Note God's promise of prosperity to faithful tithers and the challenge to test the validity of His promise.

Mal. 3:13–18 | NATIONAL SKEPTICISM AGAIN

The Jews did not believe God's promise about tithes. They considered that money and effort offered to God were wasted. Malachi's answer is, Wait and see—the end will show whether it was indeed so (vv. 16–17). This beautiful passage pictures the faithful few, in a time of general apostasy, and God recording their names for recognition in "that day."

Mal. 4 | THE COMING DAY OF THE LORD

Four times Malachi sweeps forward to "the Day of the Lord" (1:11; 3:1–6, 16–18; 4:1–6). He calls it "The Day" (3:2, 17; 4:1, 3, 5). It seems to refer to the whole Christian era, with special application to the time of the end.

The Closing Words of the Old Testament

- **The final exhortation:** Remember the Law of Moses, which I gave him! (v. 4).
- **The final prediction:** Elijah will usher in "the Day of the Lord" (v. 5). He did, 400 years later, in the person of John the Baptist (Matthew 3:1–12; 11:14). This passage may also be predictive of Christ's second coming in the day of final judgment. Might this also foretell Elijah as one of the two witnesses in Revelation 11?
- **The final promise:** Love between parents and children (v. 6; quoted in Luke 1:17), a symbolic reference to the promise of God's love for His people.
- **The final word:** "Curse" (in both the Hebrew and the English text), meaning that the plight of mankind would be hopeless should the Lord fail to come.
- Thus closes the Old Testament. Four hundred years later, the New Testament begins with the words, "A record of the genealogy of Jesus Christ [the Messiah]" (Matthew 1:1).

Judean Desert, east of Jerusalem.

THE MESSIAH IN THE OLD TESTAMENT
Foreshadowings and Predictions
of the Coming Messiah

"Messiah" is the Hebrew word for "Anointed One" (the Greek word is Christ). Anointing was common in the Ancient Near East; it involved the applying of oil to a person (or on occasion, a thing). There were three kinds of anointing in the Old Testament: ordinary, medical, and sacred.

- **Ordinary anointing** with scented oils was common (Ruth 3:3; Psalm 104:15; Proverbs 27:9); it was discontinued during a time of mourning (2 Samuel 14:2; Daniel 10:3; Matthew 6:17). Guests were anointed as a mark of respect (Psalm 23:5; Luke 7:46). The dead were prepared for burial by anointing (Mark 14:8; 16:1).
- **Medical anointing**—not necessarily with oil—was customary for the sick and wounded (Isaiah 1:6; Luke 10:34). Jesus' disciples anointed with oil (Mark 6:13; James 5:14).
- The purpose of **sacred anointing** was to dedicate the thing or person to God. Thus the stone Jacob used for a pillow at Bethel (Genesis 28:18) and the tabernacle and its furniture (Exodus 30:22–29) were anointed.

More important here is the anointing of **prophets** (1 Kings 19:16; 1 Chronicles 16:22), **priests** (Exodus 28:41; 29:7; Leviticus 8:12, 30), and **kings** (1-Samuel 9:16; 10:1; 16:1, 12–13; 2 Samuel 2:7; 1 Kings 1:34; 19:16). The oil symbolized the Holy Spirit, empowering them for a particular work in the service of God. Thus "the Lord's anointed" was the common term for a king (1 Samuel 12:3; Lamentations 4:20).

The Old Testament points toward a coming Redeemer who is called Anointed One (Messiah) twice (Psalm 2:2; Daniel 9:25–26). The expectation of a coming Messiah became widespread by the time of Jesus.

The New Testament shows that Jesus is the expected Messiah. He was anointed with the Holy Spirit at His baptism (John 1:32–33), showing that He was indeed the Messiah (Luke 4:18, 21; Acts 9:22; 17:2–3; 18:5, 28). That is why Jesus is given the title "Christ," which is the Greek word for Anointed One. Jesus the Messiah—Jesus Christ—is anointed to be prophet, priest, and king all at once (Moses, Melchizedek, and David; see below, Genesis 14:18–20; Deuteronomy 18:15–19; 2 Samuel 7:16).

The following are some of the most remarkable foreshadowings and predictions of Jesus found throughout the Old Testament.

The Pentateuch (Genesis–Deuteronomy)

Genesis 3:15. The Seed of the Woman

"I will put enmity between you and the woman, and between your offspring and hers; he will crush your head, and you will strike his heel."

This seems to say that God is determined, in spite of Adam and Eve's sin, to bring His creation of mankind to a successful end. As the Fall was set in motion through Eve, so will redemption come through woman. It will be the "seed of the woman," that is, born of woman without the agency of man. It seems like a primeval hint of the virgin birth of Christ, for there has been only one descendant of Eve who was born of woman without being begotten by man.

Genesis 4:3–5. Abel's Offering

In the course of time Cain brought some of the fruits of the soil as an offering to the LORD. But Abel brought fat portions from some of the first-born of his flock. The LORD looked with favor on Abel and his offering, but on Cain and his offering he did not look with favor.

This would seem to indicate the institution of blood sacrifice, right at the start, as the condition for humanity's acceptance by God. It is a hint that stands at the beginning of a long line of pictures and predictions of Christ's atoning death for human sin.

Genesis 12:3; 18:18; 22:18. The Call of Abraham

"Through your offspring all nations on earth will be blessed."

Here is a clear, definite statement to Abraham, repeated three times, that in him God was founding a nation for the express purpose of blessing all nations through it. This was the nation through whom the Messiah would come.

Genesis 14:18–20. Melchizedek

Then Melchizedek king of Salem brought out bread and wine. He was priest of God Most High, and he blessed Abram, saying, "Blessed be Abram by God Most High, Creator of heaven and earth. And blessed be God Most High, who delivered your enemies into your hand." Then Abram gave him a tenth of everything."

In Psalm 110:4 it is said of the coming Messiah, "You are a priest forever, in the order of Melchizedek." In Hebrews 7, Melchizedek, as a king-priest, is called a "type" (a foreshadowing) of Jesus.

Thus Melchizedek is a foreshadowing of the coming Person who was the purpose behind the formation of Abraham's nation—the Messiah, the Savior of mankind. Little is known about Melchizedek other than that he was a king-priest who gave blessings and received tithes. Melchizedek lived in Salem (Jerusalem), the same city where Jesus was crucified. And the bread and wine are a marvelous primeval picture of the Lord's Supper and all that it means!

Genesis 22:1–19. Abraham Offers Isaac

We see a father offering his son, who was, for three days, as good as dead in his father's mind (22:4); a substitutionary sacrifice (22:13); on Mount Moriah (22:2), the same place where Abraham had paid tithes to Melchizedek (14:18; Salem is on Mount Moriah), the same place where Jesus was crucified.

As Melchizedek was a foreshadowing of the *Person* Abraham's nation would bring into the world, so this sacrifice seems to be a foreshadowing of the *event* in that Person's life by which He would do His work. What an apt picture of the death and resurrection of Christ!

Genesis 26:4; 28:14. The Promise Repeated

"All peoples on earth will be blessed through you and your offspring."

The same promise that was made three times to Abraham is here repeated to Isaac and then to Jacob.

Genesis 49:10–11. "He to Whom the Scepter Belongs" (KJV, Shiloh)

"The scepter will not depart from Judah, nor the ruler's staff from between his feet, until he comes to whom it belongs and the obedience of the nations is his. . . . He will wash his garments in wine, his robes in the blood of grapes."

Senusert I of Egypt holding the scepter that represented his political authority. "The scepter will not depart from Judah, nor the ruler's staff from between his feet, until he comes to whom it belongs." (Genesis 49:10)

Here is the first clear, definite prediction that one Person would arise in Abraham's nation to rule all nations (Heb. *Shiloh*, He whose right it is). He must be the One of whom Melchizedek was a shadow. He would appear in the tribe of Judah. His garments washed in the blood of grapes may be an image of His crucifixion.

Exodus 12. Institution of the Passover

Israel's deliverance out of Egypt through the death of Egypt's firstborn. The Lord spared the firstborn in the houses of the Israelites that were marked with the blood of a lamb. This feast was to be kept annually throughout all generations. It became Israel's principal feast, observed in memory of their deliverance.

The Passover was celebrated for 1,400 years, the central feast of the Hebrew nation. It was unmistakably designed by God to foreshadow the basic event of human redemption, the death of Christ, the Lamb of God. He died on the cross at a Passover feast, bringing eternal deliverance from sin for those marked with His blood, even as the first Passover brought deliverance from Egypt for Israel. It shows how much God's mind was on the coming of Christ long before He came.

Leviticus 16. The Day of Atonement

The Day of Atonement took place once a year. It involved two goats. One was killed as a sin-offering. The high priest laid hands on the head of the other, called the scapegoat, confessing the people's sin. Then the scapegoat was led away and let go in the wilderness.

This, and the whole system of Levitical sacrifices that were so much a part of Hebrew life, are clear, historical foreshadowings of the atoning death of the coming Messiah.

Numbers 21:6–9. The Bronze Snake

Then the LORD sent venomous snakes among them; they bit the people and many Israelites died. The people came to Moses and said, "We sinned when we spoke against the LORD and against you. Pray that the LORD will take the snakes away from us." So Moses prayed for the people.

The LORD said to Moses, "Make a snake and put it up on a pole; anyone who is bitten can look at it and live." So Moses made a bronze snake and put it up on a pole. Then when anyone was bitten by a snake and looked at the bronze snake, he lived.

This happened in the wilderness, after the Exodus, on the way to the Promised Land. Jesus understood this to be a picture of Himself being lifted up on the cross (John 3:14). Mankind, bitten by sin in the Garden of Eden, may look to Him and live.

Numbers 24:17, 19. The Star

"A star will come out of Jacob; a scepter will rise out of Israel. . . . A ruler will come out of Jacob and destroy the survivors of the city."

Here is another definite prediction of a person, a brilliant ruler: evidently meaning the same person as "He to whom the scepter belongs" (KJV, Shiloh) of Genesis 49:10, who is to rule the nations.

Deuteronomy 18:15–19. A Prophet Like Moses

The LORD your God will raise up for you a prophet like me from among your own brothers. You must listen to him. For this is what you asked of the LORD your God at Horeb on the day of the assembly when you said, "Let us not hear the voice of the LORD our God nor see this great fire anymore, or we will die."

The LORD said to me: "What they say is good. I will raise up for them a prophet like you from among their brothers; I will put my words in his mouth, and he will tell them everything I command him. If anyone does not listen to my words that the prophet speaks in my name, I myself will call him to account."

God would raise up a prophet like Moses, through whom God would speak to mankind.

Thus, in the first five books of the Old Testament there is a specific prediction, repeated five times, that the Hebrew nation was established for the one express purpose of blessing all nations.

These books also contain specific predictions that there would be one Person through whom the nation would fulfill its mission. And there are various hints about the nature of this Person's work, especially His sacrificial death. Thus some leading characteristics of Christ's life were drawn, in fairly distinct lines, some 1,400 years before Christ came.

The Other Historical Books (Joshua–Esther)

Joshua

This book seems to have no direct prediction of the Messiah, though Joshua himself is thought, in a sense, to have been a type (foreshadowing) of Jesus. The names are the same: "Jesus" is the Greek form of the Hebrew "Joshua." As Joshua led Israel into the Promised Land, so Jesus will lead His people into heaven.

Ruth

And they named him Obed. He was the father of Jesse, the father of David (4:17).

Ruth was the great-grandmother of David. Boaz was of Bethlehem and was a kinsman-redeemer who acquired Ruth as his wife. Boaz is a type (foreshadowing) of Christ, who was born 1,100 years later in Bethlehem. Christ was also a kinsman-redeemer, as He paid a price, with His blood, to acquire the church (often referred to as the bride of Christ).

1 Samuel 16. David

David is anointed king over Israel. From here on, David is the central figure of Old Testament history. The most specific and most abundant of all messianic prophecies cluster around his name. Abraham was the founder of the messianic nation, and David the founder of the messianic family within the nation.

2 Samuel 7:16. David Is Promised an Eternal Throne

"Your throne will be established forever."

Here begins a long line of promises that David's family will reign forever over God's people.

This promise is repeated over and over throughout the rest of the Old Testament, with an ever-increasing mass of detail and specific explanations: the promise will find its ultimate fulfillment in one great King, who will Himself live forever and establish a kingdom of endless duration.

This eternal King evidently is the same person previously spoken of as a priest after the order of Melchizedek, "He to whom the scepter belongs" (KJV, Shiloh), the Star, and the Prophet like Moses.

1 Kings 9:5. The Promise Repeated to Solomon

"I will establish your royal throne over Israel forever."

The promise is repeated over and over to David and Solomon.

However, the books of Kings and Chronicles relate the story of the fall of David's kingdom and the exile of the Hebrew nation, apparently bringing to naught God's promise to David's family of an eternal throne.

But in the period covered by these books, many prophets cried out that the promise would yet be fulfilled.

The books of Ezra, Nehemiah, and Esther relate the story of the return of the fallen and scattered Hebrew nation, without direct messianic predictions. However, the reestablishment of the nation in its own land was a necessary antecedent to the fulfillment of promises about David's throne.

Poetic Books (Job–Song of Songs)

Job 19:25–27. "My Redeemer Lives"

The book of Job is a discussion of the problem of suffering, without much direct bearing, as far as we can see, on the messianic mission of the Hebrew nation — except in Job's exultant outburst of faith, "I know that my Redeemer lives, and that in the end he will stand upon the earth."

Psalms

The book of Psalms, written mostly by David himself, is full of predictions and foreshadowings of the eternal King who would come out of

David's family. Some of them, in a limited and secondary sense, may refer to David himself. But on the whole they are inapplicable to any person in history other than Christ—written 1000 years before Christ came.

Psalm 2. The Lord's Anointed

The kings of the earth take their stand and the rulers gather together against the LORD and against his Anointed One (v. 2). . . . "I have installed my King on Zion, my holy hill" (v. 6). . . . "You are my Son" (v. 7). . . . "I will make the nations your inheritance" (v. 8). . . . Kiss the Son. . . . Blessed are all who take refuge in him (v. 12).

Evidently meaning that the eternal King is to arise in David's family. A very positive statement as to His deity, His universal reign, and the blessedness of those who trust Him.

Psalm 16:10. His Resurrection

You will not abandon me to the grave, nor will you let your Holy One see decay.

This is quoted in Acts 2:27, 31 as referring to the resurrection of Christ. There had been many hints of the coming Messiah's death. Here is a clear-cut prediction of His victory over death and of life forevermore.

Psalm 22. A Fore-Picture of the Crucifixion

"My God, my God, why have you forsaken me?" (v. 1).

Even His dying words are foretold (Matthew 27:46).

"All who see me mock me; they hurl insults, shaking their heads: 'He trusts in the LORD; let the LORD rescue him. Let him deliver him, since he delights in him'" (vv. 7–8).

Sneers of His enemies, in their exact words (Matthew 27:43).

"They have pierced my hands and my feet" (v. 16).

This indicates crucifixion as the manner of His death (John 20:20, 25).

"They divide my garments among them and cast lots for my clothing" (v. 18).

Even this detail is forecast (Matthew 27:35).

What can all this refer to except the crucifixion of Jesus? Yet it was written 1000 years before it happened.

Psalm 41:9. To Be Betrayed by a Friend

My close friend, whom I trusted, he who shared my bread, has lifted up his heel against me.

Apparently David is referring to his own friend, Ahithophel (2 Samuel 15:12). But Jesus quoted it as a foreshadowing of His betrayal by Judas (John 13:18–27; Luke 22:47–48).

Psalm 45. The Reign of God's Anointed

God, your God, has set you above your companions by anointing you with the oil of joy (v. 7).

Your throne, O God, will last for ever and ever (v. 6).

In your majesty ride forth victoriously (v. 4).

I will perpetuate your memory through all generations; therefore the nations will praise you for ever and ever (v. 17).

Here is depicted the glorious reign of a king, bearing the name of God, seated on an eternal throne. It can refer to no other than the eternal King who would come from David's family. It is a wedding song of Christ and His bride, the church.

Psalm 69:21. Gall and Vinegar

They put gall in my food and gave me vinegar for my thirst.

Another incident in the coming Messiah's sufferings (Matthew 27:34, 48).

Psalm 72. His Glorious Reign

In his days the righteous will flourish (v. 7).

He will rule from sea to sea and from the River to the ends of the earth (v. 8).

All Kings will bow down to him and all nations will serve him (v. 11).

Praise be to his glorious name forever; may the whole earth be filled with his glory (v. 19).

This psalm seems, in part, to have been a description of the reign of Solomon. But some of its statements, and its general tenor, surely refer to One who will be greater than Solomon.

Psalm 78:2. To Speak in Parables

I will open my mouth in parables.

Another detail of the Messiah's life: His method of teaching in parables. This verse is quoted in Matthew 13:34–35.

Psalm 89. The Endlessness of David's Throne

"I have made a covenant with my chosen one, I have sworn to David" (v. 3).

"I will establish your line forever and make your throne firm through all generations" (v. 4).

"I will also appoint him my firstborn, the most exalted of the kings of the earth" (v. 27).

"My covenant with him will never fail" (v. 28).

"I have sworn by my holiness—and I will not lie to David. . . . his throne . . . will be established forever" (vv. 35–37).

God's oath, repeated over and over, that David's throne will be forever, under God's firstborn.

Reconstruction of throne discovered at tel Dan. "I will establish your line forever and make your throne firm through all generations." (Psalm 89:4)

Psalm 110. Messiah to Be King and Priest

The LORD says to my Lord: "Sit at my right hand until I make your enemies a footstool for your feet" (v. 1).

"You are a priest forever, in the order of Melchizedek" (v. 4).

The eternal dominion and eternal priesthood of the coming King. Jesus quoted this as referring to Himself in Matthew 2:42–44.

Psalm 118:22. Messiah to Be Rejected by Rulers

The stone the builders rejected has become the capstone.

Jesus quoted this as referring to Himself in Matthew 21:42–44.

The Prophets (Isaiah–Malachi)

Isaiah 2:2–4. A Magnificent Vision of the Messianic Age

In the last days, the mountain of the LORD's temple will be established as chief among the mountains; . . . all nations will stream to it. Many peoples will come and say, "Come, let us go up to . . . the house of the God of Jacob. He will teach us his ways, so that we may walk in his paths." The law will go out from Zion, the word of the LORD from Jerusalem. He will judge between the nations and will settle disputes for many peoples. They will beat their swords into plowshares and their spears into pruning hooks. Nation will not take up sword against nation, nor will they train for war anymore.

Isaiah is the preeminent book of messianic prophecy in the Old Testament. His language is unsurpassed in all literature as he goes into ecstasy over the glories of the reign of the coming Messiah.

Isaiah 4:2, 5–6. The Branch of the Lord

In that day the Branch of the LORD will be beautiful and glorious. . . . Then the LORD will create over all of Mount Zion and over those who assemble there a cloud of smoke by day and a glow of flaming fire by night; over all the glory will be a canopy. It will be a shelter and shade from the heat of the day, and a refuge and hiding place from the storm and rain.

The Messiah is here represented as a branch that grows up out of the stump of the family tree of David, becoming a guide and refuge for His people. (See comments on Isaiah 11:1–10.)

Isaiah 7:13–14. Immanuel

"Hear now, you house of David! . . . The virgin will be with child and will give birth to a son, and will call him Immanuel."

This seems to say that someone who will be called Immanuel will be born in David's family, of a virgin. This evidently refers to the same person as the branch of 4:2 and 11:1, and the wonderful child of 9:6. The deity of the child is implied in the name Immanuel, which means "God with us." Thus the virgin birth and the deity of the Messiah are here foretold. It is quoted in Matthew 1:23 as referring to Jesus.

Isaiah 9:1–2, 6–7. The Wonderful Child

In . . . Galilee . . . the people walking in darkness have seen a great light;. . . For to us a child is born, to us a son is given: and the government will be on his shoulders. And he will be called Wonderful Counselor, Mighty God, Everlasting Father, Prince of Peace. Of the increase of his government and peace there will be no end. He will reign on David's throne and over his kingdom, establishing and upholding it with justice and righteousness from that time on and forever.

This child, unmistakably, is the eternal King promised to David's family (2 Samuel 7:16). It is the same person spoken of centuries earlier as "He to whom the scepter belongs" (KJV, Shiloh), the Star, and the Prophet like Moses. His deity is here emphasized. His ministry will be in Galilee. Altogether a very accurate forecast of Jesus.

Isaiah 11:1–10. The Reign of the Branch

A shoot will come up from the stump of Jesse; from his roots a Branch will bear fruit (v. 1).

That is, a shoot out of the stump of David's family tree—the Messiah.

The Spirit of the LORD will rest on him—the Spirit of wisdom and of understanding (v. 2).

The Root of Jesse will stand as a banner for the peoples; the nations will rally to him (v. 10).

He will strike the earth with the rod of his mouth (v. 4).

The wolf will live with the lamb, the leopard will lie down with the goat, the calf and the lion and the yearling together; and a little child will lead them. The cow will feed with the bear, their young will lie down together, and the lion will eat straw like the ox (vv. 6–7).

They will neither harm nor destroy on all my holy mountain, for the earth will be full of the knowledge of the LORD as the waters cover the sea (v. 9).

A magnificent description of universal peace in the world-to-be under the reign of the coming Messiah.

Isaiah 25:6–9; 26:1, 19. The Resurrection of the Dead

On this mountain the LORD . . . will swallow up death forever. The Sovereign LORD will wipe away the tears from all faces (25:6, 8).

In that day . . . your dead will live; their bodies will rise. . . . The earth will give birth to her dead (26:1, 19).

A forecast of both the resurrection of Jesus on Mount Zion and a general resurrection.

Isaiah 35:5–6. Messiah's Miracles

Then will the eyes of the blind be opened and the ears of the deaf unstopped. Then will the lame leap like a deer, and the mute tongue shout for joy.

An exact description of Jesus' ministry of miracles.

Isaiah 35:8–10. Messiah's Highway

A highway will be there . . . called the way of holiness.

"The ransomed of the LORD will return. They will enter Zion with singing; everlasting joy will crown their heads. Gladness and joy will overtake them, and sorrow and sighing will flee away."

Holiness, happiness, singing, joy—there will be no more sorrow or tears, ever, for the people of the coming Messiah.

Isaiah 40:5, 10–11. Messiah's Tenderness

"The glory of the LORD will be revealed, and all mankind together will see it." . . . See, the Sovereign LORD comes with power, and his arm rules for him. . . . He tends his flock like a shepherd: He gathers the lambs in his arms and carries them close to his heart; he gently leads those that have young.

Another preview of the glory of Jesus, His power, and His gentleness toward the weak of His flock.

Isaiah 42:1–11. Gentiles

"Here is my servant" (v. 1). . . . "I will keep you and will make you to be a covenant for the people and a light for the Gentiles" (v. 6). . . . "In his law the islands will put their hope" (v. 4). . . . Sing to the LORD a new song, his praise from the ends of the earth (v. 10).

Israel's coming King will rule over Gentiles also, and they will cover the whole earth with songs of praise and joy.

Isaiah 53. The Messiah's Sufferings

Who has believed our message and to whom has the arm of the LORD been revealed? . . . He was despised and rejected by men, a man of sorrows, and familiar with suffering. . . . Surely he took up our infirmities and carried our sorrows. . . . But he was pierced for our transgressions, he was crushed for our iniquities; the punishment that brought us peace was upon him, and by his wounds we are healed. We all, like sheep, have gone astray, each of us has turned to his own way; and the LORD has laid on him the iniquity of us all. He was oppressed and afflicted, yet he did not open his mouth; he was led like a lamb to the slaughter. . . . Yet it was the LORD's will to crush him and cause him to suffer. . . . By his knowledge my righteous servant will justify many, and he will bear their iniquities . . . because he poured out his life unto death.

The most conspicuous feature in the prophecies about the coming King is that He would suffer. It was hinted at in Abel's sacrifice and in Abraham's offering of Isaac. It was vividly foreshadowed in the institution of the Passover feast and in the annual Day of Atonement. Some of the details of His suffering are described in Psalm 22. And here in Isaiah 53, detail upon detail is added, making the picture more complete.

In chapters 54, 55, 60, and 61, the suffering King fills the earth with songs of joy.

Isaiah 60. To Be Light of the World

"See, darkness covers the earth" (v. 2).

"Arise, shine, for your light has come, and the glory of the LORD rises upon you" (v. 1).

"The LORD will be your everlasting light, and your days of sorrow will end" (v. 20).

In the New Testament, Jesus is repeatedly called the Light of the World.

Isaiah 62:2; 65:15. A New Name

You will be called by a new name (62:2).

"But to his servants he will give another name" (65:15).

In Old Testament times, God's people were called Israelites. Since the days of Christ, they have been called Christians.

Jeremiah 23:5–6. The Branch

"The days are coming," declares the Lord, "when I will raise up to David a righteous Branch, a King. . . . This is the name by which he will be called: The Lord Our Righteousness."

Isaiah 4 and 11 speak of the coming King as a branch out of the family of David. Here Jeremiah repeats that name and asserts His deity.

Ezekiel 37:24–25. The Prince of the House of David

"My servant David will be king over them, and they will all have one shepherd. They will follow my laws and be careful to keep my decrees. They will live in the land I gave to my servant Jacob, the land where your fathers lived. They and their children and their children's children will live there forever, and David my servant will be their prince forever."

A glorious vision of the ultimate fulfillment of God's promise to David. Not only will the Messiah, David's descendant, be a good shepherd to His people, but also the people will live by God's laws in a kingdom of peace.

Ezekiel 47:1–12. The Life-giving Stream

I saw water coming out from under the threshold of the temple toward the east. . . . As the man went eastward with a measuring line in his hand, he measured off a thousand cubits and then led me through water that was ankle-deep. He measured off another thousand cubits and led me through water that was knee-deep. He measured off another thousand and led me through water that was up to the waist. He measured off another thousand, but now it was a river that I could not cross, because the water had risen and was deep enough to swim in—a river that no one could cross. . . . He said to me, "This water flows toward . . . the Sea. When it empties into the Sea, the water there becomes fresh. Swarms of living creatures will live wherever the river flows. . . . Fruit trees of all kinds will grow on both banks of the river. Their leaves will not wither, nor will their fruit fail. . . . Their fruit will serve for food and their leaves for healing."

In describing the reign of the Prince, Ezekiel presents a transcendently beautiful picture of the life-giving impact of God's presence under the image of a stream flowing from the temple out to the whole world.

Daniel 2. The Four Kingdoms

"In the time of those kings, the God of heaven will set up a kingdom that will never be destroyed, nor will it be left to another people. It will

crush all those kingdoms and bring them to an end, but it will itself endure forever" (v. 44).

In the nearly 600 years from Daniel to Christ there were four world empires: Babylon, Persia, Greece, and Rome. They are exactly described in the imagery of this second chapter of Daniel. In Daniel 7 the same four empires are described more fully. It was in the days of the Roman Empire that Christ appeared.

Hosea 1:10. The Gentiles Will Be Included

"In the place where it was said to them, 'You are not my people,' they will be called 'sons of the living God.'"

Here Hosea repeats what has already been said time and again, that the Messiah's kingdom will include all nations.

Hosea 11:1. Out of Egypt

"Out of Egypt I called my son."

A way of saying that part of the Messiah's childhood would be spent in Egypt (Matthew 2:15).

Joel 2:28, 32; 3:13–14. The Gospel Era

"I will pour out my Spirit on all people. . . . And everyone who calls on the name of the Lord will be saved. . . . Swing the sickle, for the harvest is ripe." . . . Multitudes, multitudes in the valley of decision!

The Messiah will institute an era of world evangelization under the leadership of the Holy Spirit (Acts 2:16–21).

Amos 9:11 – 14. David's Fallen Throne to Rise

"I will bring back my exiled people Israel; they will rebuild the ruined cities and live in them" (v. 14).

"In that day I will restore David's fallen tent . . . so that they may possess the remnant of Edom and all the nations that bear my name" (vv. 11 – 12).

Israel will be restored, as will the dynasty of David, in the person of the Messiah (Christ). But the Messiah's rule will not be limited to Israel alone—it will include the Gentiles as well (see Acts 15:12 – 21).

Jonah 1:17. A Sign to Nineveh

Jonah was inside the fish three days and three nights.

Jesus took this to be a foreshadowing of His own death and resurrection—a sign to the world (Matthew 12:40).

Micah 5:2 – 5. Bethlehem to Be Messiah's Birthplace

"You, Bethlehem, . . . out of you will come for me one who will be ruler over Israel, whose origins are . . . from ancient times. . . . For then his greatness will reach to the ends of the earth. And he will be their peace."

Micah evidently refers to the King so often mentioned before.

Zephaniah 3:9. A New Language

"Then will I purify the lips of the peoples, that all of them may call on the name of the LORD and serve him shoulder to shoulder."

That is, the people will know and serve God, purified by the Gospel of Christ.

Haggai 2:6 – 7. The Desire of All Nations

"A little while . . . and the desired of all nations will come, and . . . fill this house with glory."

That will be the crowning day for David's Son, here typified in Zerubbabel (2:23).

Zechariah

"I am going to bring my servant, the Branch" (3:8).

"Shout, Daughter of Jerusalem! See, your king comes to you, . . . gentle and riding on a donkey" (9:9).

"On that day . . . the house of David will be like God" (12:8).

"I will remove the sin of this land in a single day" (3:9).

So they paid me thirty pieces of silver. . . . So I . . . threw them into the house of the Lord to the potter (11:12 – 13).

"They will look on me, the one they have pierced" (12:10).

"On that day a fountain will be opened . . . to cleanse them from sin and impurity" (13:1).

It is doubtful that Zechariah himself understood the exact meaning of all these prophecies, some of which refer to very specific events in the life of Jesus (see 1 Peter 1:10–12). But looking back, we can see how these prophecies have been fulfilled in Jesus.

Malachi 3:1; 4:5. A Forecast of John the Baptist

"See, I will send my messenger . . . the prophet Elijah before that great and dreadful day of the Lord comes . . . who will prepare the way before me."

In Matthew 11:7–14, Jesus, speaking of John the Baptist, quotes this passage from Malachi and expressly states that it refers to John the Baptist.

The 400 Years
Between the
Testaments

Modin, the Maccabean burial site.

The 400 Years Between the Testaments

The world of the New Testament is very different from that of the Old Testament. The changes that took place over four centuries affected every area of life. Many of these changes are interrelated.

Political and Cultural Changes

- The *Romans,* instead of the Persians, now control Palestine.
- Greek thought and culture *(Hellenism),* rather than the gods of the Canaanites such as Baal and Molech, now threaten to derail God's people.

Geographical Changes

- Palestine is divided into *Judea, Galilee, Samaria*; on the east side of the Jordan River are *Perea* and the *Decapolis.* Furthermore, there are now (sometimes sizable) Jewish communities in most major cities of the Roman Empire, each with its own synagogue. This is referred to as the *Diaspora,* or dispersion.

Religious Changes

- **Religious parties:** The parties of the *Pharisees* and *Sadducees* (as well as the political parties of the *Zealots* and *Herodians*) did not exist in the Old Testament.
- **Religious functionaries:** *Teachers of the Law* ("scribes") and *rabbis* (teachers) play a prominent role. The *chief priests* as a group with its own identity is not found in the Old Testament.
- **Religious institutions:** The *temple* and the temple area have been transformed from the modest structure built by the post-exilic Jews into a magnificent complex. In addition, each town now has a *synagogue*, a place for worship and study of the Word of God.

Language and Writings

- The common language in Palestine is no longer *Hebrew* but *Aramaic*. The language of commerce and communications throughout the Roman Empire is *Greek*.
- These changes in language necessitated translations of the Hebrew Bible (our Old Testament): the *Septuagint,* a Greek translation, and the *Targums,* Aramaic paraphrases.

We will look at each of these in more detail.

A. Four Centuries of Political Change

1. The Persian Period, 430–332 B.C.

The story of the Old Testament ends around 430 B.C. with the prophet Malachi. The Babylonians, who had destroyed Jerusalem in 586 B.C., had been conquered by the Medes and Persians. The Persian king Cyrus allowed the Jews to go back to Jerusalem in 536 B.C. Under Ezra and Nehemiah, the temple and the city walls were rebuilt. Thus, at the close of the Old Testament, Judah was a Persian province.

Not much is known of Jewish history during this period, except that Persian rule was, for the most part, mild and tolerant. (For Persian kings of this period, see p. 269.)

2. The Greek Period, 331–167 B.C.

Up to this time, the great powers of the world had been in Asia and Africa. But looming ominously on the western horizon was the rising power of Greece.

The beginnings of Greek history are veiled in myth. It is thought to have begun about the 12th century B.C., the time of the biblical book of Judges. The Trojan War, immortalized in Homer's *Iliad* and *Odyssey,* took place around 1000 B.C. — the age of David and Solomon.

The beginning of authentic Greek history has usually been reckoned from the first Olympiad in 776 B.C. (which is within a few years of the founding of the city of Rome, which according to tradition took place in 753 B.C.). Greek culture and art were spectacularly original and creative (unlike later Roman art, which was much more severe and imitative). Greek culture reached its zenith in the city of Athens in the 5th century B.C., the Golden Age of Greece. This was the era of the great statesmen, philosophers, and dramatists (see p. 676).

This Golden Age of Greece was approximately the same period during which the temple and walls of Jerusalem were rebuilt under Zerubbabel, Ezra, and Nehemiah after the Babylonian exile.

Alexander the Great was the son of King Philip of Macedonia, north of Greece. In 336 B.C., at the age of 20, he assumed command of the Greek army and swept eastward over the lands that had been under the rule of Egypt, Assyria, Babylon, and Persia. By 331 B.C. the whole world lay at his feet.

When Alexander invaded Palestine in 332 B.C., he showed great consideration toward the Jews, spared Jerusalem, and offered the Jews inducements to settle in Alexandria, Egypt. He established Greek cities all over his conquered domains, with the intent of spreading Greek culture and the Greek language throughout the world. After a brief reign, he died in 323 B.C. at the age of 33. His empire did not last, but his dream did: Greek language and culture (Hellenism) would dominate the world for many centuries (see p. 481).

Under Egyptian Rule (The Ptolemies)

After Alexander's death, his empire was divided among four of his generals. Palestine lay between the two eastern sections of the empire, Syria and Egypt. Syria went to Seleucus (who was the first of the Seleucid dynasty), Egypt to Ptolemy (the first of the Ptolemies). Palestine went first to Syria, but shortly thereafter passed to Egypt (301 B.C.) and remained under Egyptian control until 198 B.C.

Under the Ptolemies the condition of the Jews was mainly peaceful. During this period, Alexandria in Egypt became an influential center of Judaism.

Under Syrian Rule (The Seleucids)

King Antiochus the Great of Syria recaptured Palestine in 198 B.C., which thus passed back to the kings of Syria, the Seleucids. Initially the Seleucids were tolerant toward the Jews, but that soon changed.

Antiochus IV Epiphanes (175 – 164 B.C.) was frustrated by the Jews' refusal to give up their religion and identity. He turned violently bitter against them and made a furious and determined effort to exterminate them and their religion. He devastated Jerusalem (168 B.C.) and desecrated the temple by offering a pig (a ceremonially unclean animal according to the Law of Moses) on its altar. He then put an altar to Zeus — the main Greek god, called Jupiter

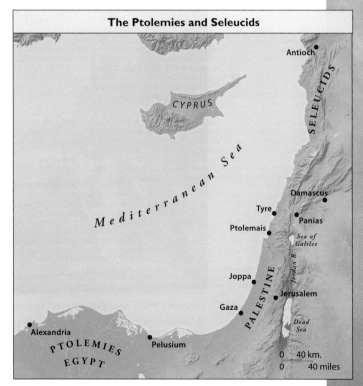

The Ptolemies and Seleucids

Antioch

SELEUCIDS

CYPRUS

Mediterranean Sea

Damascus

Tyre

Panias

Ptolemais

Sea of Galilee

Joppa

PALESTINE

Jerusalem

Gaza

Dead Sea

Alexandria

PTOLEMIES
EGYPT

Pelusium

Jordan R.

0   40 km.

0   40 miles

The menorah is used during the Feast of Hanukkah (Feast of Lights) that recalls the liberation of Jerusalem around 165 B.C.

by the Romans — in the temple, prohibited temple worship, forbade circumcision on pain of death, sold thousands of Jewish families into slavery, destroyed all copies of Scripture that could be found, slaughtered everyone discovered in possession of such copies, and resorted to every conceivable torture to force Jews to renounce their religion. This led to one of the most heroic feats in history — the Maccabean revolt.

3. A Century of Independence (The Maccabean Period, 167–63 B.C.)

This period is called the Maccabean, Hasmonean, or Asmonean period. Mattathias, a priest of intense patriotism and unbounded courage, was infuriated by the attempt of Antiochus Epiphanes to destroy the Jews and their religion. He gathered a group of loyal Jews and raised the standard of revolt. He had five heroic and warlike sons: Judas, Jonathan, Simon, John, and Eleazar.

Solomon's Pools near Bethlehem. This is one of three pools built at different levels. an aqueduct carried the water from the pools to Jerusalem, 45 miles away. It is a remarkable feat of engineering, since there is a 300-foot drop between the pools and Jerusalem. These probably date from the Hasmonean (Maccabean) period (2nd century B.C.), although tradition says they were built by Solomon.

Mattathias died in 166 B.C. His mantle fell upon his son Judas, who was a warrior of amazing military genius. He won battle after battle against unbelievable and impossible odds. He captured Jerusalem in 165 B.C. and purified and rededicated the temple. This was the origin of the Feast of Hanukkah, which means Feast of Dedication (also called the Feast of Lights). Judas united the priestly and civil authority in himself and thus established the line of Hasmonean priest-rulers who for the next 100 years governed an independent Judea. They were Mattathias (167–166 B.C.); Judas, his son (166–161); Jonathan, Judas's brother (161–144); Simon, Jonathan's brother (144–135); John Hyrcanus (135–106), son of Jonathan; and Aristobulus and his sons (106–63), who were unworthy of the Maccabean name.

4. The Roman Period
(63 B.C.–A.D. 636)

Two rivals for the office of high priest both appealed to Rome for help. The Roman general Pompey came in 63 B.C. and decided to resolve the dispute by making Palestine part of the Roman Empire. Antipater, an Idumean (Edomite, descendant of Esau), was appointed ruler of Judea. He was succeeded by his son, Herod the Great, who was king of Judea 37–4 B.C. Herod was a shrewd politician who managed to get himself in the good graces of the Jews. One of the means was rebuilding and expanding the temple in spectacularly beautiful fashion. But he was a brutal, cruel man.

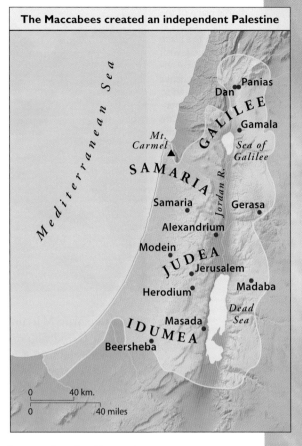

The Maccabees created an independent Palestine

The spectacular building projects of Herod the Great are illustrated by the theater, stadium, and palace at Caesarea Maritima.

Burial place of the Maccabeans at Modin, the place where the Jewish revolt against Antiochus Epiphanes began that led to the last independent Jewish state (166–63 B.C.) until the establishment of the state of Israel in 1948.

He had his wife Mariamne I killed, and later also three of his sons. This is the Herod who ruled Judah when Jesus was born, and it was he who had the children of Bethlehem killed (see p. 533; for the Herodian family, see p. 1019).

B. Geographical Changes

1. Palestine

At the close of the Old Testament, Palestine was a Persian province. In the time of Christ, the land of Palestine was divided into three regions or provinces: Galilee in the north, Samaria in the center, and Judea in the south. East of the Jordan River were Perea and the Decapolis.

History played a major role in how the people in these regions viewed each other.

Galilee is an area of about 50 by 30 miles. It was a fertile area, crossed by major trade routes. When the kingdom of David and Solomon was divided, the northern kingdom that seceded consisted more or less of what in the New Testament would be called Galilee and Samaria. When the northern kingdom fell to the Assyrians in 722 B.C., the population was deported to Assyria, and in its place pagan immigrants were brought in to settle the area. This is why the area is referred to as "Galilee of the Gentiles" (Isaiah 9:1; Matthew 4:15).

The non-Jewish element may have had a negative impact on Jewish worship and religious practices among the Galileans, who were readily identifiable by their accent and dialect (Matthew 26:73). The people from Judea looked down on Galileans, as Nathanael's question shows: "Nazareth! Can anything good come from there?" (John 1:46), as does the sentiment that no prophet could come out of Galilee (John 7:52). Yet this is where Jesus spent most of his ministry.

Samaria was slightly smaller than Galilee. The city of Samaria was destroyed by the Assyrians in 722 B.C., and its inhabitants were deported. In Jesus' day, the population of Samaria, like that of Galilee, consisted of a mixture of Israelites who had managed somehow to escape deportation and new immigrants of non-Israelite origin. The Samaritans developed their own type of Yahweh worship, based on the five books of Moses alone, and built a temple on Mount Gerizim. (There are still Samaritans today who celebrate the Passover on Mount Gerizim, near the ruins of their temple.)

When the Jews returned under Ezra and Nehemiah, the Samaritans wanted to take part in the rebuilding of the temple, but were rebuffed. Around that time a group of Jewish dissidents left Jerusalem and went to live in Samaria. All this led to a permanent religious and political rift between Jews and Samaritans. Jews avoided traveling through Samaria if at all possible, and it is easy to underestimate how remarkable Jesus' trip through Samaria was (John 4:1–42) and how strong the mixed emotions were that were generated by the parable of the Good Samaritan (Luke 10:30–37).

Judea was more or less the territory of the old kingdom of Judah (Judea is the Latinized form of Judah). It was approximately 55 by 55 miles, although its boundaries were never precisely fixed. After the death of Herod, his son Archelaus became ruler, but was banished by the Romans, who annexed Judea to the province of Syria. Judea was under direct Roman control until A.D. 37, when Herod Agrippa I became king of Judea.

The Decapolis (lit., "ten cities") was a group of 10 cities established by Greeks in the wake of Alexander the Great's conquest. They enjoyed essential independence under Rome. Near Gadara, one of the cities, Jesus allowed demons to enter a herd of swine (Mark 5:1–20). Jesus became popular in the Decapolis (Matthew 4:24–25; Mark 7:31–37).

Perea was the small territory east of the Jordan River, opposite Samaria and Judea. Its population was primarily Jewish. In the Gospels it is never mentioned by name but is referred to as the land "beyond the Jordan" (see Matthew 4:15, 25; 19:1; Mark 3:7–8). John baptized in Bethany (KJV, Bethabara) "on the other side of the Jordan" (John 1:28). Jesus did much of His teaching in Perea and made His final journey to Jerusalem from there (John 10:40; 11:54).

2. The Diaspora, or Dispersion

Diaspora refers to the Jews living outside Palestine while maintaining their religious faith. The two deportations—first of the northern kingdom of Israel by the Assyrians in 721 B.C., and then of the southern kingdom of Judah by the Babylonians in 586 B.C.—had dispersed the Jews. Many of those who had been taken to Babylon, and their descendants, did not return to Jerusalem under Ezra and Nehemiah but chose to stay.

Herod the Great was an almost compulsive builder. In addition to Caesarea (see pp. 475, 558) and the temple in Jerusalem, he built a number of palace-fortresses, among them Masada (see pp. 938–39), Machaerus, where John the Baptist was beheaded, and the Herodion or Herodium.

The Herodion was built within view of Jerusalem, into the top of a hill. The exacavated soil was added to the outside of the hill to give it its volcano-like appearance (top left). In the plain below, Herod built another large palace, a large pool (top right), and residences for his staff.

From the air, the plan of the palace can clearly be seen, with its four towers and double walls (bottom left). Inside (bottom right) Herod must have felt safe, since there was only one entrance with a staircase of 200 white marble steps.

the five books of Moses; they did not even accept the authority of the prophets and other Scriptures.

The Pharisees and Jesus often clashed—yet they had much in common theologically, and Jesus had many nonadversarial contacts with Pharisees (Luke 7:36ff.; 11:37; 13:31–33; 14:1; Mark 12:28–34; Matthew 23:1–2). At the same time, Jesus rejected the validity of the oral laws of the Pharisees (see "Teachers of the Law," p. 484) and also their emphasis on ritual purity that made the Pharisees refuse any contact with "sinners." Jesus came with the *invitation to all people* to enter the kingdom of God (including the Pharisees), while the Pharisees in effect *disinvited* all who did not live by the same standards as they—which was most people. It was especially this exclusivism that Jesus objected to in the Pharisees; by using only standards of external behavior to measure people's relationship with God, they failed to realize that it is what is inside a person that counts, and that they therefore needed God's grace as much as the worst sinner. And it was this external religion that made it very difficult for them to believe in Jesus (who did not do all the things the Pharisees felt a religious person should do).

The Sadducees

The party of the Sadducees consisted of wealthy priests and their friends in the aristocracy. They were religiously conservative in that they accepted the authority of the five books of Moses but not of the prophets

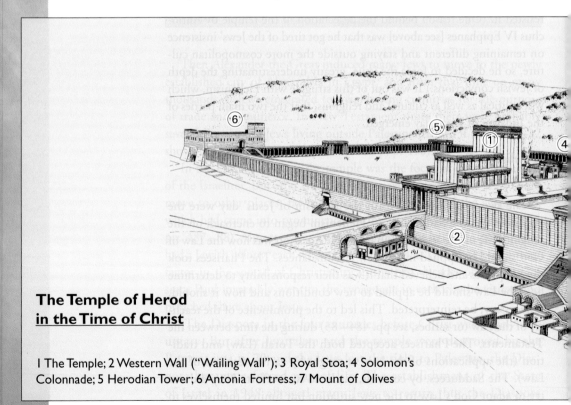

The Temple of Herod in the Time of Christ

1 The Temple; 2 Western Wall ("Wailing Wall"); 3 Royal Stoa; 4 Solomon's Colonnade; 5 Herodian Tower; 6 Antonia Fortress; 7 Mount of Olives

Tyrian coins. The Sadducees controlled the economy of the Temple and thus demanded local money be exchanged for Tyrian coins to be used in Temple transactions as these coins held the highest quantity of silver.

and other later writings. Thus, when they question Jesus about the resurrection (Matthew 22:23–33), Jesus uses a quote from Exodus 3:6, since a quote from the prophets would not have carried weight with them. At the same time, they were the group who wielded political power, which led them to endorse—for pragmatic purposes—some aspects of Hellenism. When Palestine became part of the Roman Empire, the Sadducees

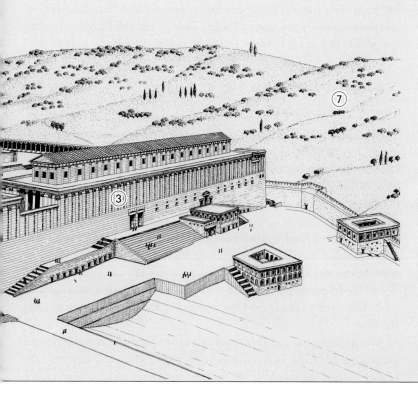

collaborated with the Romans and tried to maintain the status quo, lest they lose their position of leadership.

The Sadducees had more power than the Pharisees (although the common people sided with the Pharisees) until A.D. 70. With the destruction of the temple—the focus of their power—the Sadducees simply ceased to have any role and disappeared. The Pharisees, on the other hand, became the true leaders of the Jewish people after A.D. 70 by providing them with a religious life apart from the temple. After the failed revolution of Bar Kochba (A.D. 132–35; see pp. 940, 943) the Romans recognized the Pharisees as the governing body for Jewish life.

Other Parties

Two other parties are mentioned in the New Testament, the Zealots and the Herodians. They were more political than religious in nature.

Zealots: The Zealots were a nationalistic party that fiercely opposed the Roman occupation. It is not certain whether the Zealots were already a party by the time of Jesus' ministry or did not become a party until later. One of Jesus' disciples was Simon the Zealot (Luke 6:15); if there was already a party or group known as Zealots, Simon may have belonged to them. If not, "Zealot" may be a nickname based on his personality, similar to Jesus' calling John and James "Sons of Thunder."

Herodians: Nothing is known about the Herodians except that, judging from their name, they apparently supported the Herodian dynasty and thus indirectly the rule of Rome. They joined the Pharisees in their opposition to Jesus (Matthew 22:16; Mark 3:6; 12:13).

2. Religious Functionaries

Teachers of the Law (Scribes)

In antiquity, scribes were a special class of people who copied documents and recorded information. They were governmental secretaries and copyists who copied the Scriptures. As time went on, they became more influential and took leading roles in government.

When Judah was deported to Babylonia, the people suddenly found themselves in entirely new circumstances, and it was not always clear how the Law of God applied to specific new situations. This is when the scribes became interpreters and teachers of the Law. They did now what before the Exile the prophets had done: tell the people how to live as God's people. Ezra was a scribe as well as a priest, and he took it upon himself to teach the Law to the people who had returned from Babylon.

When during the Hellenistic period many of the priests compromised the teachings of the Law by embracing pagan ideas and customs, the scribes became the defenders of the Law and the teachers of the masses.

They acted, in fact, like nobility (see Matthew 23:5–7; Mark 12:38–39; Luke 11:43; 20:46).

The scribes, in their zeal to protect the Law, actually added to its requirements—they "built a fence around the Law" of detailed, specific commandments that would keep the people from coming even close to breaking the Law. For example, the "Sabbath journey"—a specific distance one was allowed to walk on the Sabbath—was instituted to make sure that the people would not break the commandment to rest on the Sabbath. But as Jesus pointed out, they were so anxious to keep the letter of the Law that they failed to either understand or implement its spirit. And Jesus refused to be bound by the scribal additions to the Law, which earned Him their enmity (Mark 12:40; Luke 20:47).

Priests

According to the Old Testament, all priests had to be descendants of Aaron, Moses' brother, from the tribe of Levi. The priests were divided into 24 "courses" or groups, each one of which served in the temple one week at a time, twice a year. Most priests lived outside Jerusalem (for example, Zechariah; Luke 1:8–9). The priests who lived in Jerusalem and were connected full-time to the temple were considered far more important than the ordinary priests.

High Priest

The high priest was to be a direct descendant of Aaron, the first high priest. It was a hereditary office.

During the century of independence under the Hasmoneans, the high priest was both the religious and the political leader. This led in the end to disaster, when the office became for all practical purposes secular. During the Roman period, the high priest was appointed much like other government officials. From the time of Herod the Great until the destruction of Jerusalem in A.D. 70, there were no fewer than 28 high priests!

Interestingly, it may be that the Jewish leaders themselves continued to view a former high priest as still having official standing, even though he had been deposed, since according to the Law of Moses, the high priest remained in office until his death. When Jesus was arrested, He was first sent to Annas (who had not been high priest for 15 years!) and only then to Caiaphas, who was the high priest at that time. In Acts 4:6, Annas is called the high priest, even though technically he no longer was.

Chief Priests

It is not entirely certain who the chief priests were. It is likely that they were past and present high priests, or perhaps members of the high-priestly families (see Acts 4:6). Or they may have included the priests who formed the permanent temple staff. In any event, they constituted a well-defined group.

Rabbis

"Rabbi" means "my master," "my lord." It was used as a general term of respect. John the Baptist's disciples referred to John as rabbi, and Jesus was called rabbi by His disciples. John explains the term "rabbi" as meaning teacher (John 1:38; 20:16). Jesus warns His disciples that they should not be like the professional scribes in their desire to be called rabbi (Matthew 23:2–12).

"Rabbi" did not become an official title until much later. The professional, ordained, salaried rabbi did not appear until the Middle Ages.

The Sanhedrin

During the reign of the Hellenistic kings (see p. 473), Palestine was more or less self-governing. An aristocratic council of elders was in charge, presided over by the high priest. This group later developed into the Sanhedrin, which consisted of elders, chief priests, and teachers of the law.

During the Roman period, the internal government of Palestine was largely in the hands of the Sanhedrin, and its authority was even recognized in the Diaspora (Acts 9:2; 22:5; 26:12).

It is probable that the authority of the Sanhedrin was limited to Judea after the death of Herod the Great, which was why the Sanhedrin could not touch Jesus as long as He was in Galilee. The Sanhedrin was abolished after the destruction of Jerusalem in A.D. 70.

3. Religious Institutions

The Temple

The first "house of God" the Israelites built was the tabernacle, a portable tent that could be moved around during the wanderings in the wilderness immediately after the Exodus (see pp. 145–48).

The first temple in Jerusalem was planned by King David and built by his son, King Solomon, around 950 B.C. When the Babylonians overran the southern kingdom, Judah, in 586 B.C., they destroyed Jerusalem and the temple and deported the people to Babylonia. This was the beginning of the Babylonian exile.

After King Cyrus allowed the people to return to Jerusalem under Zerubbabel and Ezra, the first thing they did was rebuild the temple. But the second temple was relatively plain and far less imposing than the first temple, which many of those who returned had never seen, since they had been born in Babylonia. Yet they had heard much about it and had perhaps developed a somewhat exaggerated idea of the first temple's splendor.

When Herod the Great became king, one of the things he did to win over the people was to expand and beautify the temple. Since the temple stood on the top of a hill, the only way to enlarge the temple area was to build massive retaining walls and fill the area inside the walls to create a great platform. Herod doubled the size of the original platform of Solomon's temple. Part of the wall Herod built is still visible and is known as the Wailing Wall; it shows how remarkable and impressive the temple must have been.

Herod died in 4 B.C., almost 70 years before the temple complex was completely finished (A.D. 64). Sadly, the finished temple stood for only six years in all its splendor. In A.D. 66, the Jews revolted against Rome, and four years later, in A.D. 70, Jerusalem and the temple were destroyed. Today the Dome of the Rock, a Muslim mosque, stands where the temple once stood.

Just outside the temple area, at its northwest corner, Herod the Great built a fortress and named it the Antonia, after Mark Anthony (best known for falling in love with Queen Cleopatra of Egypt). The tower overlooked the temple and the temple courts and was used by the Romans to keep an eye out for disturbances in the temple area and the city. The Antonia served its intended purpose when the crowd got out of hand and was ready to kill Paul (Acts 21:30ff.). There were two flights of stairs that connected the fortress (called "the barracks" in Acts 21:34) with the temple area; these are the stairs the Roman commander and his troops ran down, and from which Paul addressed the crowd.

Synagogues

In the New Testament we encounter synagogues everywhere, both in Palestine and throughout the Roman Empire. Wherever the apostle Paul went to preach, he first went to the synagogue in that city.

Remains of the synagogue at Gamla near the Sea of Galilee are some of the earliest discovered to date.

The synagogue was "invented" during the Babylonian exile. The temple in Jerusalem—the central place of worship for all Jews—had been destroyed. So wherever there was a group of Jews, they would get together and read and study the Hebrew Scriptures (our Old Testament). These meetings then were formalized in the institution of the synagogue.

Unlike the temple, where sacrifices were central, in the synagogue the focus was on teaching. Any male present could be asked to read from the Scriptures—first from the Pentateuch and then from the Prophets—and any male present could be asked to preach. This is why Jesus could preach in the synagogue (Luke 4:16–30), and later Paul also (for example, Acts 13:15ff.).

Christian worship (as well as Muslim worship) is patterned after the model of the synagogue.

D. Languages and Writings in the New Testament Era

1. Languages

Aramaic replaced Hebrew as the common language in Palestine after the Babylonian exile. It is a Semitic language related to Hebrew, yet different enough that it could not be readily understood by the average person in Old Testament times (see 2 Kings 18:26; also Genesis 31:47, where Laban uses Aramaic and Jacob uses Hebrew). Aramaic was the language of commerce and diplomacy during the centuries before Alexander the Great. This is why in the book of Ezra we find several official documents in Aramaic rather than in Hebrew (Ezra 4:8–6:18 and 7:12–26; Ezra wrote the connecting verses between the documents also in Aramaic).

No synagogues have been found that date back to the days of Jesus, although the Gospels and Acts indicate that there must have been one in every significant town. These remains are from the 3rd-century synagogue at Capernaum.

Hebrew is the language of the Old Testament. But by the time of the New Testament, Hebrew had become mainly the language of religion, since the Hebrew Bible was written in Hebrew. Many people could still read and write Hebrew, but it was no longer their everyday language.

Latin was the language of Rome, but while it was the language of imperial officialdom, it was not the language commonly spoken throughout the empire.

Greek was the common language or *lingua franca* that tied the Roman Empire together. Its role was similar to that of English in the modern world. Alexander the Great had succeeded in making the Greek language, and to a large extent Greek culture, dominant throughout his empire (see p. 481), and he succeeded so well that Greek as the common language outlasted his empire by several centuries.

It is safe to assume that Jesus could read and perhaps speak Hebrew (Luke 4:17) but that He usually spoke Aramaic. (His command when raising Jairus's daughter was *Talitha Koum,* which is Aramaic for "Little girl, I say to you, get up!") He probably also spoke at least some Greek, although there is no proof of this.

The apostles wrote in Greek, although some of their letters are clearly written by people who did not have a native command of the language. There are also "Semiticisms" in the New Testament—expressions that are Semitic (Hebrew or Aramaic) in form and would have sounded odd to a native Greek speaker. (A modern equivalent would be "I make the door closed"—a Germanism for "I close the door.")

It is thought that Matthew may have first written his Gospel in Aramaic and later translated it into Greek.

2. Writings

The Old Testament was written in Hebrew, but the people spoke mostly Aramaic or Greek. In fact, in cities such as Alexandria in Egypt there were many Jews whose families had lived there for many generations and who spoke only Greek. If Judaism was to survive, it was necessary for people to be able to read and understand the Old Testament. To this end, translations were made and used in Jesus' day: the Septuagint for Greek-speaking Jews and the Targums for Aramaic-speaking Jews.

The Septuagint

The Septuagint is a translation of the Hebrew Old Testament into Greek, made in Alexandria. According to tradition, 70 Jews, skillful linguists, were sent from Jerusalem to Egypt at the request of Ptolemy Philadelphus (285–247 B.C.) and completed the translation in 70 days.

In reality, the translation was done over a period of time. The Torah (Genesis–Deuteronomy) was translated first, and later the rest of the Old Testament books were added. It was called the Septuagint because of the 70 translators who were reputed to have begun it (*septuaginta* = Greek for 70; the common abbreviation for Septuagint is LXX, the Roman numeral for 70). The quality of the translation of the Torah (Pentateuch) is excellent, but the other books vary a great deal in quality.

The Septuagint was in common use in the days of Christ. Many of the quotations from the Old Testament in the New Testament (which was written in Greek) are from the Septuagint.

The Targums

The Targums are translations of the Hebrew Old Testament books into Aramaic. They were originally oral translations, paraphrases, and interpretations that had their origin in the Babylonian captivity, when Hebrew lost its standing as the primary language of the Jewish exiles and was replaced by Aramaic. These oral paraphrases were later written down and became increasingly necessary as the use of Aramaic became prevalent in Palestine. In the synagogue, a passage would often be read in Hebrew, followed by the Targum of that same passage.

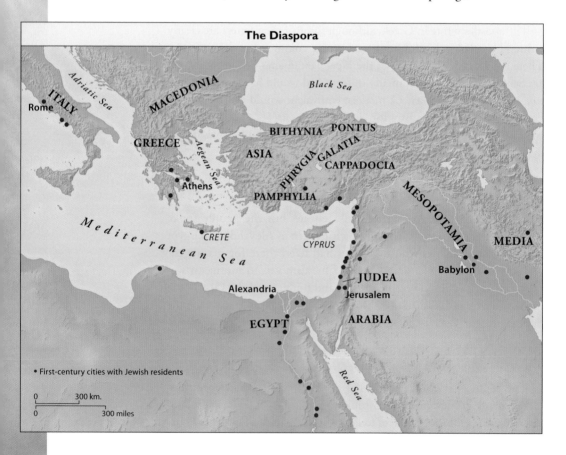

The Diaspora

• First-century cities with Jewish residents

The New Testament

The site traditionally regarded as the place where Jesus was born.

The Life of Jesus: An Overview

Matthew, Mark, Luke, and John did not simply write about what happened in the past. They wrote from the perspective of the Resurrection and the coming of the Holy Spirit at Pentecost. The did not write a story that had an ending, but a story that was a beginning—the beginning of the church and the beginning of the coming of the kingdom of God.

They arranged their material in slightly different ways because they each had a somewhat different audience and purpose (see p. 517). Sometimes the Gospel writers indicate that certain stories happened one after the other, at other times they put together a number of stories and events because they have a similar theme, without any indication that they happened in that particular sequence. Besides, during the two years or more that the disciples spent with Jesus, He must have taught and preached similar messages many times, and He must have performed similar miracles many times—many lame people were healed, many blind people could see again, and so forth.

All this means that it is not easy to fit all the materials in the Gospels neatly into a single narrative. But the broad outlines are clear.

The Eight Periods of Jesus' Life

For convenience' sake, the life of Jesus can be divided into eight periods, as follows:

		Approx. Duration	*Location(s)*
①	**Birth and Youth**	30 years	Bethlehem, Egypt, Nazareth
②	**Preparation for Ministry**		Jordan River and wilderness
③	**Early Ministry in Judea**	8 months	Judea, Samaria
④	**Ministry in Galilee**	2 years	Galilee
⑤	**Later Ministry in Judea**	1 month	Perea and Judea
⑥	**Ministry in Perea**	4 months	Perea and Judea
⑦	**The Last Week: Crucifixion and Resurrection**	7 days	Judea, Jerusalem
⑧	**Appearances after the Resurrection**	40 days	Jerusalem, Galilee

All four Gospels give more space to the last week of Jesus' life, His crucifixion, and His resurrection (Period ⑦) than to any other period. The chart below shows the difference in the Gospels in the amount of space they devote to some of the other periods.

We will look at each of the eight periods briefly. For a detailed outline ("harmony") of the Gospels, see pp. 520–28.

THE LIFE OF JESUS IN THE FOUR GOSPELS		Matthew	Mark	Luke	John
	Pre-Incarnation Existence of Jesus				1:1–3
①	**Jesus' Birth and Youth**	1–2		1–2	
②	**Preparation for Ministry**				
	John the Baptist	3:1–12	1:1–8	3:1–20	1:6–42
	Jesus' Baptism	3:13–17	1:9–11	3:21–22	
	Jesus' Temptation	4:1–11	1:12–13	4:1–13	
	Preliminary Miracle				2:1–11
③	**Early Judean Ministry** (about 8 months)				2:13–4:3
	Visit to Samaria				4:4–42
④	**Galilean Ministry** (about 2 years)	4:12–19:1	1:14–10:1	4:14–9:51	4:43–54:6
	Visit to Jerusalem				5:1–47
⑤	**Later Judean Ministry** (about 1 month)			10:1–13:21	7:2–10:39
⑥	**Perean Ministry** (about 4 months)	19:1–20:34	10:1–52	13:22–19:28	10:40–11:57
⑦	**The Last Week**	21–27	11–15	19:29–24:1	12–19
⑧	**Post-Resurrection Appearances**	28	16	24	20–21

Period ①: Jesus' Birth and Youth (About 30 Years)

- Matthew 1–2
- Luke 1–2

Mark and John say nothing about the birth, childhood, and youth of Jesus. Matthew and Luke record different incidents (see under Luke 1:5–80). To harmonize these into exact chronological sequence is not easy. Here are probable, approximate dates:

7 or 6 b.c.	Announcement to Zechariah	Luke 1:5–25
6 months later	Announcement to Mary	Luke 1:26–38
	Mary's visit to Elizabeth	Luke 1:39–56
3 months later	Mary's return to Nazareth	Luke 1:56
	Announcement to Joseph	Matthew 1:18–24
	Birth of John the Baptist	Luke 1:57–80

6 or 5 B.C.	Birth of Jesus	Matthew 1:25; Luke 2:1–7
	Announcement to shepherds	Luke 2:8–20
8 days later	Jesus' circumcision	Luke 2:21
32 days later	Jesus' presentation	Luke 2:22–38
4 B.C.	Visit of the Wise Men	Matthew 2:1–12
	Flight to Egypt	Matthew 2:13–15
	The children of Bethlehem killed	Matthew 2:16–18
3 B.C.	Return to Nazareth	Matthew 2:19–23; Luke 2:39

How Could Jesus Have Been Born Five or Six Years "Before Christ"?

Placing Jesus' birth several years B.C., "Before Christ," is not the result of critical scholarship trying to undermine the reliability of the Bible. Rather, it is the result of a mathematical error made by a monk some 1,500 years ago.

Jesus was born when the Jewish nation was part of the Roman Empire, and in the empire, years were counted from the founding of the city of Rome. But when the Roman Empire fell and Christianity became the universal religion in what had once been the Roman Empire, a monk named Dionysius Exiguus, at the request of Emperor Justinian, made a new calendar in A.D. 526. This calendar was to replace the Roman calendar, and it counted years from the birth of Christ.

The new calendar divided history into the years before Christ (B.C.) and after the birth of Christ (A.D., which stands for *Anno Domini*, "in the year of [our] Lord").

However, long after the Christian calendar had replaced the Roman calendar, it was discovered that Dionysius had made a mistake. He had placed the birth of Jesus in 753 AUC (*Ab Urbe Condita*, "From the founding of the city [of Rome]"). He should have placed it a few years earlier, in about 749 or even 747 AUC.

On What Date Was Jesus Born?

Jesus' birthday is now celebrated on December 25, but there is nothing in the Bible to support that particular date. It first appears as the date of Jesus' birthday in the 4th century, in the Western church. In the Eastern church the date is January 6, which is celebrated as Epiphany in the Western church. (On the division of the church into a Western church and an Eastern church, see page 907.)

December 25 as the date to celebrate the birth of Jesus goes back to at least the 4th century, although the reasons for the choice of this date are obscure. In some countries (such as Britain), Christmas replaced an existing, pre-Christian festival.

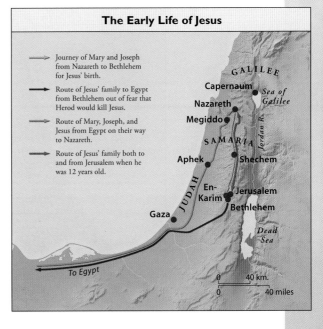

The Early Life of Jesus

- → Journey of Mary and Joseph from Nazareth to Bethlehem for Jesus' birth.
- → Route of Jesus' family to Egypt from Bethlehem out of fear that Herod would kill Jesus.
- → Route of Mary, Joseph, and Jesus from Egypt on their way to Nazareth.
- → Route of Jesus' family both to and from Jerusalem when he was 12 years old.

GALILEE
Capernaum
Sea of Galilee
Nazareth
Megiddo
SAMARIA
Jordan R.
Aphek
Shechem
JUDAH
En-Karim
Jerusalem
Gaza
Bethlehem
Dead Sea
To Egypt

0   40 km.
0   40 miles

Period ②: Preparation for Ministry

John the Baptist; Jesus' Baptism and Temptation

- Matthew 3:1–4:11
- Mark 1:1–13
- Luke 3:1–4:13
- John 1:6–42

This is a brief but important period in Jesus' life. John the Baptist was the one who prepared the way for the expected Messiah, as foretold by the prophet Isaiah. He set the stage for Jesus' ministry by preaching the need for repentance in the face of the coming of the kingdom of God. He helped focus the expectation of the nation so that when Jesus began His ministry, the people were prepared.

Jesus insisted on being baptized by John — He gave His endorsement to John's ministry, and God in turn gave Jesus His endorsement: "This is my Son, whom I love; with him I am well pleased" (Matthew 3:17).

Jesus then went into the wilderness for 40 days and was tempted by Satan three times — and each time Jesus appealed to God's Word: "It is written" (Matthew 4:4, 6, 10; Luke 4:4, 8, 10).

John's Gospel does not mention Jesus' baptism and temptation.

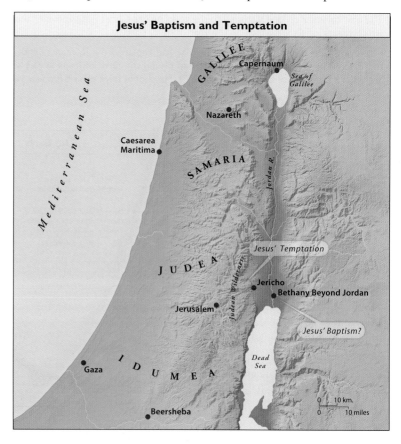

Jesus' Baptism and Temptation

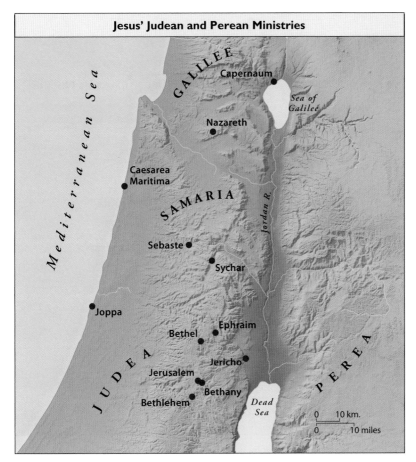

Jesus' Judean and Perean Ministries

Period ③: Jesus' Early Ministry in Judea (About 8 Months)

- John 2:1–4:42

This period, which probably lasted about eight months, is recorded only in the gospel of John (2:1–4:42). The period in Judea is preceded by a miracle in Cana, in Galilee, where Jesus turned water into wine, and it concludes with Jesus' visit with the Samaritan woman. Jesus' nighttime visit with Nicodemus, in which He explains the need to be born again, also takes place during this period.

Period ④: Jesus' Ministry in Galilee (About 2 Years)

- Matthew 4:12–19:1
- Mark 1:14–10:1
- Luke 4:14–9:51
- John 4:43–7:1

The Galilean ministry started in December, four months before the harvest (John 4:35, 43).

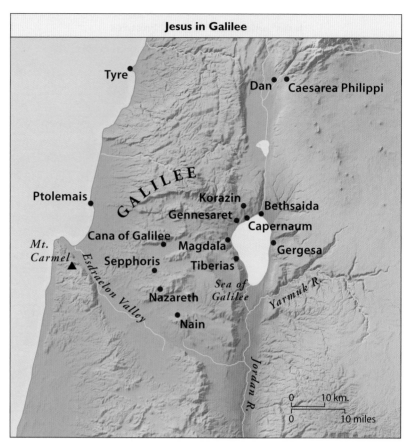

Jesus in Galilee

Matthew, Mark, and Luke (the so-called Synoptic Gospels, see p. 519) generally seem to follow a chronological order in presenting this period, though not in every detail; they differ on the order of many of the incidents. Bible scholars differ in their opinion as to which of the three is more strictly chronological. Since the gospel writers seem to have been guided by other considerations than chronology in grouping their material, and since indications of time and place are largely ignored, it is not possible to arrive at an exact chronological arrangement of all of the material that is recorded.

There are, however, some markers—events and periods in the Galilean ministry that have a clear indication of time and around which others may be grouped.

- The 5000 were fed at Passover time (John 6:4). John the Baptist was beheaded just before that (Matthew 14:12–13). At the same time, the Twelve returned from their preaching tour (Luke 9:10).
- All three writers place the Transfiguration shortly before the final departure from Galilee.
- The final departure from Galilee was either just before the Feast of Tabernacles (October) or the Feast of Dedication (December)

(Luke 9:51; John 7:1–10; 10:22) — most likely the latter, for the earlier was in secret (John 7:10), the latter public (Luke 10:1).

This makes a period of five or eight months between the feeding of the 5000 and the Transfiguration; Jesus spent part of this period in the regions north of Galilee, of which not much is told.

The main part of the story of the Galilean ministry is concerned with the 16 months preceding the feeding of the 5000, a period of intense activity and great popularity.

Period ⑤: Jesus' Later Ministry in Judea (About 1 Month)

- Luke 10:1–13:21
- John 7:2–10:39

This period is marked by opposition. The authorities try to arrest Jesus (John 7:32–52) and even excommunicate a man born blind, who was healed by Jesus and refused (in a delightful interchange!) to side with the religious authorities against Jesus (John 9:1–34).

Luke records several parables, including the parable of the Good Samaritan (Luke 10:25–27), but also a series of woes and warnings (Luke 11:37–12:59). It is clear that after the initial period of popularity, the tide has turned and the road to the Cross is becoming inevitable.

Period ⑥: Jesus' Ministry in Perea (About 4 Months)

- Matthew 19–20
- Mark 10
- Luke 13:22–19:28
- John 10:40–11:57

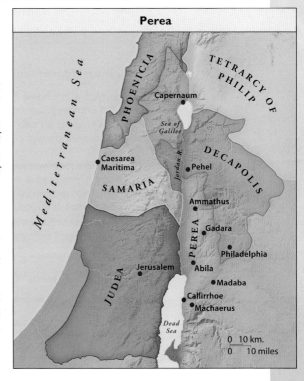

Conflict and controversy continue. But it is especially during this period that Jesus' concern and care for people — shown in His teaching, healings, and the raising of Lazarus (John 11:17–44) — stand out against the ever-darkening background of the authorities' hatred for Him.

Period ⑦: Jesus' Last Week

In all four Gospels, the last week of Jesus' life is described at length. It occupies about one-third of Matthew, one-third of Mark, one-fourth of Luke, and half of John. John devotes seven chapters, about a third of his book, to the day of the crucifixion (the Jewish day begins at sunset and ends at the following sunset).

Since the Gospels are based on eyewitness reports, the details in the four Gospels differ, and it is not always easy to get a clear picture of the sequence of events. This is especially true of the morning of the Resurrection. Below are outlines of

1. The events of the last week
2. Jesus' movements on the last night
3. The Crucifixion
4. The Resurrection

It is important to remember that these outlines must of necessity be somewhat tentative since we do not have enough information to be absolutely certain about every detail.

I. The Last Week of Jesus' Life on Earth	
Saturday:	Arrives in Bethany (John 12:1)
Sunday:	The Triumphal Entry. Jesus weeps over Jerusalem
Monday:	The fig tree cursed. Merchants thrown out of the temple
Tuesday:	Jesus' last day in the temple
	Judas's bargain with the priests (or next day?)
Wednesday:	Day of quiet at Bethany
Thursday:	*Evening:* the Last Supper (see note under Matthew 26)
	Night: the agony in Gethsemane
Friday:	Trial and crucifixion
Sunday:	Jesus rises from the dead

2. Jesus' Movements on the Last Night

- The Last Supper, held perhaps at the home of Mary, the mother of Mark. From here, at about eight or nine o'clock in the evening, Jesus went to Gethsemane, a mile distant.
- Gethsemane. Here He was in agony for two, three, or perhaps even four hours. Then He was arrested and taken to the house of the high priest, in the vicinity of which He had eaten the Last Supper.
- At the high priest's house. Here Jesus was kept from midnight to daylight. He was condemned, mocked, spit upon, denied by Peter, and at daylight officially sentenced and sent to Pilate.
- Pilate's judgment hall, in the Antonia Fortress. Pilate tried to escape responsibility and sent Jesus to Herod (Herod Antipas, the son of Herod the Great?).
- Herod's palace. Here he was mocked and then sent back to Pilate.
- Again before Pilate. He was whipped and sentenced to be crucified.

3. Jesus' Crucifixion

This is a tentative outline of the sequence of events during the Crucifixion.

- At 9 A.M. Jesus arrives at Golgotha. As they are about to drive the nails into His hands and feet, they offer Him wine mixed with gall, to stupefy Him and to deaden the sense of pain. But He refuses it.

- As they nail Him to the cross, Jesus says, "Father, forgive them, for they do not know what they are doing." It is hard for us to control our anger for His murderers, even just reading about it. But He was absolutely without resentment.
- His garments are divided among the soldiers. A sign reading "King of the Jews" is placed above His head. It is written in three languages, Hebrew, Latin, and Greek, so that all may read and understand what crime He is accused of.
- He is mocked, jeered, and scoffed at by the chief priests, elders, scribes, and soldiers—a hard-hearted, inhuman, brutal, contemptible crowd.
- After perhaps an hour or two, Jesus says to the penitent robber, "I tell you the truth, today you will be with me in paradise" (see on Luke 23:32–43).
- Jesus says to His mother, speaking about John, "Dear woman, here is your son." To John He says, "Here is your mother" (John 19:26–27). What a glorious death! He prayed for His murderers, promised paradise to the robber, and provided a home for His mother—which was His last earthly act.
- A darkness falls that lasts from noon until three o'clock. His first three hours on the cross were marked by words of mercy and kindness. Now He enters the final stage of suffering for human sin. Perhaps the darkness symbolizes God's withdrawal. What Jesus suffered in that last awful three hours we can never know in this world. (See on John 19:33–34.)
- His last four utterances come just as He is expiring.

  "My God, my God, why have you forsaken me?" Alone, in the pains of hell, to keep us from going there.

  "I am thirsty." Burning fever and excruciating thirst were the accompaniments of crucifixion. It may have meant more (see Luke 16:24). They offer Him vinegar. His sufferings over, He takes it.

  "It is finished." A cry of triumphant relief and joy. The long reign of human sin and death is broken.

  "Father, into your hands I commit my spirit."

- An earthquake, the curtain in the temple tears in half, the tombs are opened.
- The centurion believes. The crowds are grief-stricken.
- Blood and water come from Jesus' side. (See on John 19:34.)
- Joseph and Nicodemus ask for Jesus' body for burial.
- And thus night settles on the blackest, foulest crime in history.

The Order of Events on the Resurrection Morning

It is not easy to harmonize the fragmentary records of the four Gospels about the resurrection of Jesus into a connected, consecutive story. We are not told all the incidents in the precise order of their occurrence.

In a typical Roman crucifixion the nail was driven through a wooden plank placed on the outside of the heel bone to prevent the nail from pulling out.

We must remember that different groups of disciples, who were staying in various locations in and around the city, went to the tomb, and that they were not expecting Jesus to rise (see p. 642); they went to the tomb to complete the embalming of His body for permanent burial.

The first sight of the empty tomb, and the announcement of the angel that Jesus had risen, threw them into wild excitement. They ran to tell the others, hurrying back and forth in alternating joy, fear, anxiety, wonder, and bewilderment.

Many things happened that are not recorded. Of what is recorded, one writer gives in a single sentence what another describes in detail. Some, in a general statement, cover various incidents. No one gives a full account.

4. Jesus' Resurrection	
If the four accounts of the Resurrection had all been identical, we might suspect that the four Gospel writers all used a single, agreed-upon story. As it is, the four accounts bear all the marks of eyewitness accounts of an overwhelming experience. A glance at the accounts as presented in the four Gospels shows how different the perspective of each is.	
Matthew	The women visit the tomb
	Jesus appears to the women
	The guards are bribed
	Jesus appears to the Eleven in Galilee
Mark	The women visit the tomb
	Jesus appears to Mary Magdalene
	Jesus appears to two disciples on the road to Emmaus
	Jesus appears to the Eleven in Jerusalem on the first evening
	The Ascension
Luke	The women visit the tomb
	Peter runs to the tomb
	Jesus appears to the two; and to Peter
	Jesus appears to the Eleven in Jerusalem on the first evening
	Final appearance, 40 days later
	The Ascension
John	Mary Magdalene visits the tomb
	Peter and John run to the tomb
	Jesus appears to Mary Magdalene
	Jesus appears to the Eleven on the first evening; Thomas is absent
	Jesus appears to the Eleven a week later; Thomas is present
	Jesus appears to the Seven at the Sea of Galilee

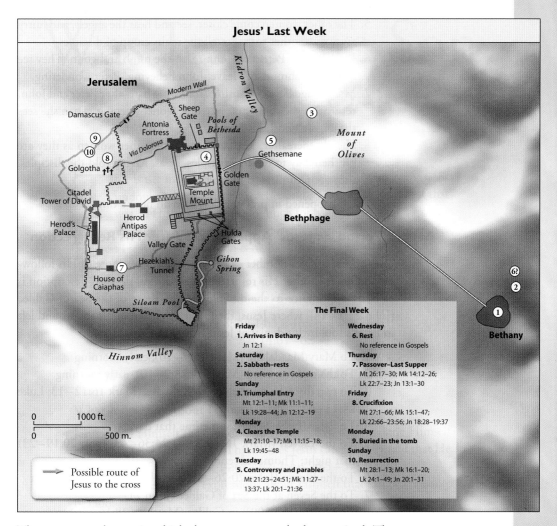

Jesus' Last Week

Jerusalem

Modern Wall

Damascus Gate

Sheep Gate

Pools of Bethesda

Antonia Fortress

⑨

⑩

Via Dolorosa

⑧

Golgotha ✝✝✝

Citadel Tower of David

Herod's Palace

Herod Antipas Palace

Valley Gate

Hezekiah's Tunnel

⑦

House of Caiaphas

Siloam Pool

Hinnom Valley

Temple Mount

Golden Gate

Hulda Gates

Gihon Spring

④

Kidron Valley

③

⑤

Gethsemane

Mount of Olives

Bethphage

⑥?

②

①

Bethany

0 ———— 1000 ft.
0 ———— 500 m.

→ Possible route of Jesus to the cross

The Final Week

Friday
1. Arrives in Bethany
   Jn 12:1
Saturday
2. Sabbath–rests
   No reference in Gospels
Sunday
3. Triumphal Entry
   Mt 21:1–11; Mk 11:1–11;
   Lk 19:28–44; Jn 12:12–19
Monday
4. Clears the Temple
   Mt 21:10–17; Mk 11:15–18;
   Lk 19:45–48
Tuesday
5. Controversy and parables
   Mt 21:23–24:51; Mk 11:27–
   13:37; Lk 20:1–21:36

Wednesday
6. Rest
   No reference in Gospels
Thursday
7. Passover–Last Supper
   Mt 26:17–30; Mk 14:12–26;
   Lk 22:7–23; Jn 13:1–30
Friday
8. Crucifixion
   Mt 27:1–66; Mk 15:1–47;
   Lk 22:66–23:56; Jn 18:28–19:37
Monday
9. Buried in the tomb
Sunday
10. Resurrection
   Mt 28:1–13; Mk 16:1–20;
   Lk 24:1–49; Jn 20:1–31

There are several ways in which the accounts may be harmonized. The following is generally, though tentatively, accepted.

1. At the first break of dawn, two or more groups of women, from the places where they were staying in Jerusalem or Bethany, probably a mile or two distant, start groping their way toward the tomb.

2. It is probably about this time that Jesus is emerging from the tomb, accompanied by angels who roll away the stone and neatly fold the shroud.

3. The guards, meantime, frightened and dazed, flee to tell the priests who had placed them there.

4. About sunrise, as the women approach the tomb, Mary Magdalene — ahead of her group, seeing the tomb empty, but not seeing the angel nor hearing his announcement that Jesus has risen (John 20:13, 15) — turns and runs to tell Peter and John.

Sheep looking through the opening of the sheepfold where the shepherd sits to function as the door.

- "Anyone who has seen me has seen the Father" (John 14:9).
- "I and the Father are one" (John 10:30).
- "All authority in heaven and on earth has been given to me" (Matthew 28:18).
- "I am with you always, to the very end of the age" (Matthew 28:20).
- Who else could have said such things about himself? Of whom else could we say them?

What Others Said About Jesus

- Mark called Jesus "the Son of God" (Mark 1:1).
- John called Jesus "the Son of God" (John 3:16, 18; 20:31).
- John the Baptist called Jesus "the Son of God" (John 1:34).
- Nathanael called Jesus "the Son of God" (John 1:49).
- Peter called Jesus "the Son of God" (Matthew 16:16).
- Martha called Jesus "the Son of God" (John 11:27).
- The disciples called Jesus "the Son of God" (Matthew 14:33).
- The angel Gabriel called Jesus "the Son of God" (Luke 1:32, 35).
- God Himself called Jesus His own "beloved Son" (Matthew 3:17 KJV; 17:5; Mark 1:11; 9:7; Luke 3:22; 9:35).
- Evil spirits called Jesus "the Son of God" (Matthew 8:29; Mark 3:11; 5:7; Luke 4:41).
- It was commonly recognized that Jesus claimed to be the Son of God:
  - "If you are the Son of God . . ." (Matthew 4:3, 6).
  - "Truly you are the Son of God" (Matthew 14:33).
  - "If thou be the Son of God, come down from the cross" (Matthew 27:40 KJV).

- "He said, 'I am the Son of God'" (Matthew 27:43).
- "Surely he was the Son of God!" (Matthew 27:54).
- "He claimed to be the Son of God" (John 19:7).
- The Rock on which Jesus said He would build His church (Matthew 16:18) was the truth that He is the Son of God.
- Jesus is Himself called God (John 1:1; 10:33; 20:28; Romans 9:5; Colossians 1:16; 2:9; 1 Timothy 1:17; Hebrews 1:8; 1 John 5:20; Jude 25).

What the Old Testament Said

- The Old Testament prophets foretold Jesus' deity:
- "He will be called . . . Mighty God, Everlasting Father" (Isaiah 9:6).
- "This is the name by which he will be called: The LORD Our Righteousness" (Jeremiah 23:6; 33:16).
- "On that day . . . the house of David will be like God" (Zechariah 12:8).

Thus, neither Jesus Himself, nor the Scriptures, leave any possible doubt as to the nature of Jesus' Person. Why not accept the record just as it is? If He was only a good man, He can do nothing for us except set us an example. If He was really God, He can be to us a Savior as well as an example.

Other Statements by Jesus

Other things Jesus said make sense if He is the Son of God—but if He is not, they strike us as the ravings of someone with delusions of grandeur.

- "I am the light of the world" (John 8:12).
- "I am the good shepherd" (John 10:11).
- "You are from below; I am from above. You are of this world; I am not of this world" (John 8:23).
- "Your father Abraham rejoiced at the thought of seeing my day; he saw it and was glad" (John 8:56).
- "Moses . . . wrote about me" (John 5:46).
- "You diligently study the Scriptures because you think that by them you possess eternal life. These are the Scriptures that testify about me" (John 5:39).
- "The Father who sent me has himself testified concerning me" (John 5:37).
- "The very work that the Father has given me to finish, and which I am doing, testifies that the Father has sent me" (John 5:36).
- "If I had not done among them what no one else did, they would not be guilty of sin" (John 15:24).

- "If you do not believe that I am the one I claim to be, you will indeed die in your sins" (John 8:24).
- "Blessed are the eyes that see what you see. For I tell you that many prophets and kings wanted to see what you see but did not see it, and to hear what you hear but did not hear it" (Luke 10:23–24).
- "The Queen of the South . . . came from the ends of the earth to listen to Solomon's wisdom, and now one greater than Solomon is here. . . . The men of Nineveh . . . repented at the preaching of Jonah, and now one greater than Jonah is here" (Matthew 12:42, 41).

Names and Titles Applied by the Scripture to Christ	
✦ The Christ	✦ Lord
✦ The Messiah	✦ Lord of All
✦ Savior	✦ Lord of Glory
✦ Redeemer	✦ Lord of Lords
✦ Wonderful Counselor	✦ Blessed and Only Potentate
✦ Faithful Witness	✦ King of Israel
✦ The Word of God	✦ King of Kings
✦ The Truth	✦ Ruler of the Kings of the Earth
✦ The Light of the World	✦ Prince of Life
✦ The Way	✦ Prince of Peace
✦ The Good Shepherd	✦ The Son of David
✦ Mediator	✦ The Branch
✦ Deliverer	✦ The Root and Offspring of David
✦ The Great High Priest	✦ The Bright and Morning Star
✦ The Author and Perfecter of Our Faith	✦ Immanuel
✦ The Captain of Our Salvation	✦ The Second Adam
✦ Our Advocate	✦ The Lamb of God
✦ The Son of God	✦ The Lion of the Tribe of Judah
✦ The Son of Man	✦ The Alpha and the Omega
✦ God	✦ The First and the Last
✦ The Holy One of God	✦ The Beginning and the End
✦ Only Begotten Son	✦ The Beginning of the Creation of God
✦ Mighty God	✦ The Firstborn of All Creation
✦ The Image of God	✦ The Amen
✦ Everlasting Father	✦ Christ

What Was Jesus Like?

As a man, Jesus lived the most memorable and beautiful life ever known. He was the kindest, tenderest, gentlest, most patient, most sympathetic man who ever lived. He loved people. He hated to see people in trouble. He loved to forgive. He loved to help. He did marvelous miracles to feed hungry people. For relief of the suffering, He forgot to take food for Himself. Multitudes, weary, pain-ridden, and heartsick, came to Him and found healing and relief. It is said of Him, and of no other, that if all the deeds of kindness that He did were written down, the world could not contain the books. That is the kind of man Jesus was.

Jesus' Love

Jesus talked a great deal about love—love often manifested in the plain, old-fashioned everyday habit of common kindness.

Judging by what He said, He would rather see that His followers have love for one another than any other character trait. Not that our love for each other will save us—if we are ever saved, it is He who saves us. But there are things in us that please or displease Him.

He hints that heaven will be inhabited exclusively by those who have learned how to love one other. This is the second great commandment: "Love your neighbor as yourself." The first and greatest commandment is "Love the Lord your God with all your heart and with all your soul and with all your mind. . . . All the Law and the Prophets hang on these two commandments" (Matthew 22:37–40; Mark 12:30–31; Luke 10:27; John 13:34). Jesus came to build a world of beings like Himself, and in the end no others will be there (Matthew 25:34–41).

He further said that there are going to be some surprises in the Day of Judgment. Some people who have been used to thinking of themselves as very religious are going to find out, after it is too late, that they have been altogether overlooking the things that really matter, the so-called little things (Matthew 25:44).

Jesus further makes the remarkable statement that not one single act of kindness, no matter how small, will ever go unrewarded in God's universe (Matthew 10:42).

Jesus' Forgiving Spirit

Jesus was not only the most loving and kindest man who ever lived but also the tenderest. He loved to forgive. He Himself was without sin. But how His heart ached in sympathy for those who were having a hard time with their sins! One of the most beautiful pictures in all the Bible is that of Jesus and His tenderness toward the sinful woman weeping at His feet (Luke 7:36–50).

The fact that He was tender and forgiving toward that outcast, sinful woman is a kind of guarantee that He will be tender and forgiving toward His church—toward us.

Even if we have not sinned the way the woman had, we have sinned. And to God, sin is sin. And it is, no doubt, just as hard—perhaps harder—for God to forgive our respectable, refined, polite, selfish, snobbish sins as it is for Him to forgive the grosser sins of the poor souls who have lost in the battle of life.

It is no small consolation to know that the One before whom we ourselves shall stand to be judged is that kind of person. He was merciful to that broken woman in the thing in which she needed His mercy. We may therefore feel that He will be merciful to us in the things in which we need His mercy.

Is this tenderness of Jesus toward the weak and wayward an encouragement to keep on sinning? No. It is the very thing that produces in us a determination to overcome.

Jesus showed His righteous indignation at the corruption of the temple leadership when He turned over their tables used for changing money located among the columns of the double-story Royal Stoa (top of photo).

And the closer our walk with Him, paradoxical as it may seem, the more we realize our sinfulness and our need of His mercy. And the more we realize our own sinfulness, the less ready we will be to judge others, and the more we will be able to be kind and forgiving ourselves.

Jesus' Appearance

There is no hint as to Jesus' personal appearance in the New Testament. Being a carpenter, He must have had considerable physical strength. Speaking so effectively to vast multitudes in the open air, we imagine He must have had a powerful voice. There are hints that He had a sense of humor. We know little about His appearance.

From His discourses, conversations, and teachings, we think of Jesus as being always under control, never in a hurry, in perfect poise, slow and majestic in all His movements. However, we know that there were rare occasions when Jesus lost His temper and expressed frustration and anger. The scene describing Jesus driving out merchants and overturning tables of moneychangers as He cleared the temple during His final days in Jerusalem, just prior to His arrest and crucifixion, helps us see Jesus' humanity with His divinity. He was an ordinary man, and it was not His appearance that drew people, but who He was and what He said—His person and His message.

Hillside considered to be the place Jesus delivered the Sermon on the Mount.

The 12 Disciples

E arly in His ministry, Jesus chose 12 men to be His disciples. It took about a year and a half to complete His choice of disciples. These 12 men traveled with Jesus and listened to Him teach for at least two years. They were ordinary people: at least four were fishermen, and one was a tax collector (see p. 529). We do not know what the others were. All were Galileans, except Judas, the betrayer. There was not a single professional religionist in the group, not one who advertised his piety by the kind of clothes he wore. In fact, the opposite was true: Jesus' disciples were attacked by the religious leaders because they did *not* obey the religious rules about fasting, about working on the Sabbath, and about ritual hand-washing.

Who Were the Twelve?

Why Jesus chose these 12 men we do not know. The four Gospels each list the 12 disciples in a somewhat different order. The only one who occupies the same place in all four lists is Peter (also called Simon and Simon Peter), who was the leader among the 12 and is listed first in all four Gospels. Three of the 12 were Jesus' "inner circle": Peter, James, and John the brother of James.

Peter. First mentioned at the time of John's baptism of Jesus (John 1:40–42). At this first recorded meeting with Jesus, Jesus renamed him, as if He had already decided to make Simon an apostle. Simon was his natural name; his new name was Peter (Greek) or Cephas (Aramaic), both meaning "rock." This was reaffirmed three years later, at Peter's confession (Matthew 16:18).

Peter was a native of Bethsaida (John 1:44) and had a home in Capernaum (Mark 1:29). Either he had two homes, or he had moved from Bethsaida to Capernaum. Peter was married (Matthew 8:14; Mark 1:30; Luke 4:38), and his wife went about with him in his work as an apostle (1 Corinthians 9:5).

Peter was a partner in the fishing business with James and John (Luke 5:10). Evidently he was a very well-to-do businessman. He was energetic, enthusiastic, impulsive, impetuous, a natural-born leader. He was generally the spokesman of the Twelve.

The name Jesus gave him, "Rock," was indicative of Peter's real character, which Jesus well understood: his strength of conviction, courage, and boldness, even though he did once deny his Master and once failed to stand up for the truth at Antioch. He was fearless under persecution. He laid the foundations of the church in Judea and led it onward with such momentum that the rulers stood aghast. (See further the introduction to 1 Peter.)

John. (See introductory note to the Gospel of John.)

Matthew. (See introductory note to the Gospel of Matthew.)

James. The older brother of John. Jesus nicknamed the two brothers Boanerges, Sons of Thunder. Does this indicate that possibly Jesus had a playful sense of humor? Not much is known of James. He was the first of the twelve to die, killed by Herod in A.D. 44. (This was Herod Agrippa I, the son of Herod Antipas, who had John the Baptist beheaded, and the grandson of Herod the Great, who had the children of Bethlehem killed.) Tradition says that most of the twelve died as martyrs.

Matthew 10:2–4	Mark 3:16–19	Luke 6:12–19	Acts 1:13
Simon	Simon	Simon	Peter [= Simon]
Andrew	James	Andrew	James
James	John	James	John
John	Andrew	John	Andrew
Philip	Philip	Philip	Philip
Bartholomew	Bartholomew	Bartholomew	Thomas
Thomas	Matthew	Matthew	Bartholomew
Matthew	Thomas	Thomas	Matthew
James, son of Alphaeus	James, son of Alphaeus	James, son of Alphaeus	James, son of Alphaeus
Thaddaeus	Thaddaeus	Simon the Zealot	Simon the Zealot
Simon the Zealot	Simon the Zealot	Judas, son of James [= Thaddaeus]	Judas, son of James [= Thaddaeus]
Judas Iscariot	Judas Iscariot	Judas Iscariot	[Matthias, who replaced Judas]

Each of the four books lists the 12 disciples in a somewhat different order.

Two families were partners in the fishing business: James and John (with their father, Zebedee) and the two brothers Simon and Andrew. They had hired servants. It must have been a fairly large business. All four became apostles. Three of them belonged to the inner-circle friends of Jesus.

Andrew. From Bethsaida. He and John were Jesus' first converts. He brought his brother Peter to Christ. Tradition says that he preached in Asia Minor, Greece, and Scythia (areas now included in the Ukraine, Russia, and Kazakhstan).

Philip. Also from Bethsaida. He was a fellow-townsman of Peter and Andrew. He brought Nathanael to Christ. He had a matter-of-fact kind of mind. According to tradition, he preached in Phrygia and in Hierapolis.

Bartholomew. Thought to be the surname of Nathanael, who came from Cana. Perhaps it was through him that Jesus came to the wedding feast. According to tradition, he preached in Parthia (part of modern-day Iran).

Ruins of Cana. Bartholomew (Nathaniel) came from Cana in Galilee, which now lies desolate.

Thomas. A twin. Cautious, thoughtful, skeptical, gloomy. Tradition has him laboring in Syria, Parthia, Persia, and India.

James. Son of Alphaeus. Called James the Lesser, probably because of his stature. Tradition says he preached in Palestine and Egypt.

Thaddaeus. Thought to be the same as Judas, son of James; he is also called Lebbaeus. Tradition says he was sent to Abgarus, king of Edessa, and to Syria, Arabia, and Mesopotamia.

Simon. Nicknamed the Zealot (Greek) or the Cananaean (Aramaic). Nothing is known of him. The Zealots were an intensely nationalistic sect, the direct opposite of the tax collectors. Jesus chose a Zealot and a tax collector, who came from bitterly rival factions.

Judas Iscariot. The betrayer. He came from Kerioth, a town of Judah. He was thus the only non-Galilean disciple. He was greedy and dishonest and expected rich rewards when his Master would be seated on the throne of David. He was disappointed when he saw his worldly dream fade. After his betrayal, he hanged himself (Matthew 27:5).

The Training of the 12 Disciples

Jesus' primary purpose in coming into the world was to die as the Lamb of God to heal humanity's broken relationship with God and to rise from the dead to bring eternal life to mankind. But His life, death, and resurrection would be useless to the world unless the world knew about it. If the men to whom He entrusted His work should fail Him, His coming to earth would have been in vain.

The first sending out of the Twelve (Matthew 10:1–42) was a part of their training and was also part of Jesus' method of advertising to the nation that the Messiah had arrived. There were no media—the only means of spreading the news was by word of mouth. (Later, 70 followers were sent out for the same purpose.) These men authenticated their message by special miracles, not only to attract attention but also to indicate to the nation the extraordinary nature of the One whom they proclaimed.

Their training was not an easy task, for they were being trained for a work utterly different from what they *thought* they were being trained for. They began to follow Jesus with no thought whatsoever of becoming preachers. They were expecting that, as the Messiah, He would establish a political world empire of which they would be the administrators. (See further under Matthew 13.)

Jesus' method of changing their minds about the work that He and they had to do was to present Himself to them in all the fullness of His divine glory, so that, no matter how differently He talked and acted from the way they expected the Messiah to talk and act, they would still believe that He was the one. That is one of the reasons He performed miracles and that He was transfigured before their eyes (John 20:30–31).

But even at the end, the Twelve did not understand some of the most important things Jesus tried to teach them. Jesus told them that He would be executed — yet when it happened, they were devastated because they had not grasped that this had to happen in God's plan. Jesus also told them that He would rise again from the dead after three days in the grave — but when it happened, they did not believe it. Ironically, the Jewish leaders who had Jesus put to death *did* remember what Jesus had said about His resurrection and put a guard in front of the grave! (Matthew 27:63–65).

Not until after His resurrection and the descent of the Holy Spirit did the Twelve finally understand that it was to be a kingdom in which Jesus would reign in the hearts of men, and that their part would be simply telling the story of Jesus. That is all. The story would do its own work. If men truly hear the story of Jesus, they will love Him, because the story of Jesus shows by word and example that God loves them.

These 12 men — later called "apostles" (emissaries) rather than "disciples" (followers) — became the founders of the Christian church. The group as a whole (with the exception of Judas) must have been men of the very highest grade, for Jesus knew and understood people. What magnificent men they must have been!

The Four Gospels

Matthew – John

The four Gospels are the most important part of the Bible—more important than all the rest of the Bible put together, more important than all the rest of the books in the whole world put together. For we could better afford to be without the knowledge of everything else than to be without the knowledge of Christ.

The Bible books that precede the Gospels (the Old Testament) anticipate, and those that follow explain, the central figure of the four Gospels, Jesus Christ.

Why Are There Four Gospels?

At one time there were many more Gospels than the four we have (Luke 1:1). Jesus lived in a period of great literary activity—the age of military memoirs (Julius Caesar), of philosophical writings (Cicero and Seneca), of great poetry (Virgil, Horace, Livy, Plutarch, and Pliny) and history (Tacitus). Within a generation, the story of Jesus had spread over the whole known world and had enlisted countless thousands of devoted followers. Naturally there was a great demand for written narratives of His life.

God Himself, we believe, took a hand in the preparation and preservation of these particular four, which contain what He wanted to be known about Christ. In the Old Testament there are some duplicate narratives from the centuries of Israel's monarchy (in the books of Samuel, Kings, and Chronicles). But here are four entire Bible books that (with the exception of four chapters out of a total of 89) cover one period of about 3½ years—the last years in the life of one person: Jesus of Nazareth. It must mean that this story is of superlative importance.

Whatever other writings there may have been that narrated the life of Jesus perished—mostly, no doubt, in the imperial persecutions of the first three centuries. The ones that survived are those which we have in the New Testament, which God, in His providence, watched over and preserved as being sufficient to convey His Word to all future generations. (See further under Mark 1, Luke 1, John 1.)

Four Authors

Matthew was a tax collector; Luke, a physician; John, a fisherman. We do not know what Mark's occupation was.

- **Matthew** and **John** were disciples of Jesus.

- **Mark** was a companion of Peter; his Gospel contains what he had heard Peter tell again and again.
- **Luke** was a companion of Paul; his Gospel contains what he had heard Paul preach from one end of the Roman Empire to the other—which he then verified by his own investigation.

They all told the same story. They traveled far and wide. They often went together. John and Peter worked together. Mark was associated with both Peter and Paul, and Luke and Mark were in Rome together between A.D. 61 and 63 (Colossians 4:10, 14).

Four Audiences

The four Gospels were ultimately intended for all mankind, but each was originally written for a more specific audience.

- Matthew's original, it is thought, may have been made for **the church in Jerusalem,** from which other churches obtained copies.
- Mark may have intended his book for **the church in Rome.** Copies, no doubt, were sent to other churches.
- Luke wrote his Gospel for an individual named **Theophilus,** who may have been a high official in the Roman government. (Luke also wrote the book of Acts for the same Theophilus.)
- John's Gospel is thought to have been intended originally for **the church in Ephesus.**

God inspired these men to write exactly what He wanted them to write for the use of all people of all generations, yet they themselves must have had in mind the background of their immediate readers, which may have influenced their choice of material.

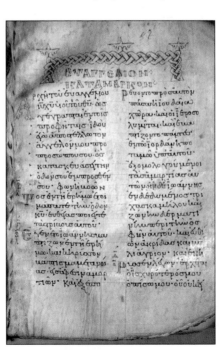

9th-century Greek Gospel of Mark. Many think that Mark's Gospel was the first of the Gospels to be written.

Four Perspectives

Not only did the four evangelists write for different readers, but each one reflected his own personality in his writing. They had the same story to tell, the story of a man, of how He lived, and what He did and said. But each told the story in his own way, mentioning that which especially appealed to him, which is what accounts for differences between the Gospels.

- Matthew, writing for Jewish Christians, presents **Jesus the Messiah**, who fulfills the Old Testament prophecies.
- Mark stresses action rather than teaching. He presents **Jesus the Wonderful,** whose rejection, suffering, and death were an essential part of His mission.
- Luke presents **Jesus the Son of Man,** who brings salvation by identifying with humanity in all its weakness. He heals the sick and seeks out those rejected by society.
- John shows **Jesus the Son of God.** He begins with Jesus' pre-existence and focuses on the unity between Jesus and God, His Father.

The Four Gospels Compared

For a comparison of the contents of the four Gospels, see p. 494, "The Life of Jesus."

The "Synoptic Problem"

Matthew, Mark, and Luke are called the Synoptic Gospels (or simply the Synoptics) because they give the same general view (synopsis) of Christ's life and record, to some extent, the same things. The similarities between the Synoptics have led scholars to wonder how the three Gospels came to be so similar in some places, yet so different in others. Did the authors borrow from one another, or did they perhaps use a common source that we no longer have? These and similar questions are commonly referred to as "the synoptic problem."

Some think that Mark's was the earliest of the Gospels, that Matthew expanded Mark's Gospel, and that Luke made use of both Matthew's and Mark's Gospels. Others think that Matthew wrote first and that Mark put together an abridged edition of Matthew's Gospel.

But it is not necessary to think that Matthew, Mark, and Luke quoted from, or in any way made use of, each other's Gospels. The events of Jesus' life and His sayings were repeated orally for years by the apostles and others and were in common circulation among Christians. They were the substance of the daily preaching of the apostles.

Also, we must not forget that in Jesus' day, people were not exposed to endless streams of words and images from the media and other forms of communication. Stories such as those about Jesus' life were much more likely to get lodged in people's memory, perhaps even down to the exact words.

At the same time, it is likely that, from the beginning, many of these things were written down, some perhaps in a mere fragmentary way, others in more complete form. And when Matthew, Mark, and Luke wrote their Gospels, they chose that which suited their purposes from the fund of knowledge, both oral and written, that was in general circulation among Christians. Besides, Matthew had been an eyewitness of most of

Jesus' ministry, Mark had heard Peter tell the stories again and again, and Luke did a great deal of careful research and must have spoken at length with eyewitnesses.

Contradictions in the Gospels?

It is surprising with what abandon the statement is made in many present-day scholarly works that the four Gospels contain contradictions. But when we see what the things are that they call contradictions, we are tempted to lose respect for some of the so-called scholarship. The fact that there are different details and slight variations in describing the same incident makes the testimony of the various writers all the more trustworthy, for it precludes the possibility of collusion among them, of telling an agreed-upon version of the facts of Jesus' life.

A HARMONY OF THE GOSPELS

—Adapted From *The NIV Study Bible,* copyright © 1995 Zondervan Publishing House. Used by permission.

	Matthew	Mark	Luke	John
A Preview of Who Jesus Is				
Luke's purpose in writing a Gospel			1:1–4	
John's prologue: Jesus Christ, the preexistent Word incarnate				1:1–18
Jesus' lineage through Joseph and Mary	1:1–17		3:23b–38	
The Early Years of John the Baptist				
John's birth foretold to Zechariah			1:5–25	
Jesus' birth foretold to Mary			1:26–38	
Mary's visit to Elizabeth; Elizabeth's song			1:39–45	
Mary's song of joy			1:46–56	
John's birth			1:57–66	
Zechariah's prophetic song			1:67–79	
John's growth and early life			1:80	
The Early Years of Jesus Christ				
Jesus' birth explained to Joseph	1:18–25			
Birth of Jesus			2:1–7	
Praise of the angels; witness of the shepherds			2:8–20	
Circumcision of Jesus			2:21	
Jesus presented in the temple; Simeon and Anna			2:22–38	
Visit of the Magi	2:1–12			
Escape to Egypt; murder of boys in Bethlehem	2:13–18			
Return to Nazareth	2:19–23		2:39	
Growth and early life of Jesus			2:40	
Jesus' first Passover in Jerusalem			2:41–50	
Jesus' growth to adulthood			2:51–52	

	Matthew	Mark	Luke	John
The Public Ministry of John the Baptist				
His ministry launched		1:1	3:1−2	
His person, proclamation, baptism	3:1−6	1:2-6	3:3−6	
His messages to the Pharisees, crowds, and others	3:7−10		3:7−14	
His description of Christ	3:11−12	1:7−8	3:15−18	
The End of John's Ministry and the Beginning of Christ's Public Ministry				
Jesus' baptism by John	3:13−17	1:9−11	3:21−23a	
Jesus' temptation in the desert	4:1−11	1:12−13	4:1−13	
John's testimony about himself to the priests and Levites				1:19−28
John's testimony to Jesus as the Son of God				1:29−34
Jesus' first followers				1:35−51
Jesus' first miracle: water becomes wine				2:1−11
Jesus' first stay in Capernaum				2:12
First cleansing of the temple at Passover				2:13−22
Early response to Jesus' miracles				2:23−25
Nicodemus's interview with Jesus				3:1−21
John superseded by Jesus				3:22−36
Jesus' departure from Judea	4:12	1:14a	3:19−20; 4:14a	4:1−4
Discussion with a Samaritan woman				4:5−26
Challenge of a spiritual harvest				4:27−38
Evangelization of Sychar				4:39−42
Arrival in Galilee				4:43−45
The Ministry of Christ in Galilee				
Opposition at Home and a New Headquarters				
Nature of the Galilean ministry	4:17	1:14b−15	4:14b−15	
Child at Capernaum healed by Jesus				4:46−54
Ministry and rejection at Nazareth			4:16−31a	
Move to Capernaum	4:13−16			
Disciples Called and Ministry Throughout Galilee				
Call of the four	4:18−22	1:16−20	5:1−11	
Teaching in synagogue of Capernaum authenticated by healing		1:21−28	4:31b−37	
Peter's mother-in-law, others healed	8:14−17	1:29−34	4:38−41	
Tour of Galilee with Simon and others	4:23−25	1:35−39	4:42−44	
Cleansing of a man with leprosy	8:2−4	1:40−45	5:12−16	
Forgiving and healing of a paralytic	9:1−8	2:1−12	5:17−26	
Call of Matthew	9:9	2:13−14	5:27−28	
Banquet at Matthew's home	9:10−13	2:15−17	5:29−32	
Jesus defends feasting instead of fasting, with three parables	9:14−17	2:18−22	5:33−39	
Sabbath Controversies and Withdrawals				
Jesus heals an invalid on the Sabbath				5:1−9
Effort to kill Jesus for breaking Sabbath and saying He was equal with God				5:10−18

	Matthew	Mark	Luke	John
Discourse demonstrating the Son's equality with the Father				5:19–47
Controversy over picking grain on Sabbath	12:1–8	2:23–28	6:1–5	
Healing of a man's hand on Sabbath	12:9–14	3:1–6	6:6–11	
Withdrawal to Sea of Galilee with large crowds	12:15–21	3:7–12		
Appointment of the Twelve and Sermon on the Mount				
Twelve apostles chosen		3:13–19	6:12–16	
Setting of the Sermon	5:1–2		6:17–19	
Blessings and woes	5:3–12		6:20–26	
Responsibility while awaiting the kingdom	5:13–16			
Law, righteousness, and the kingdom	5:17–20			
Six contrasts in interpreting the Law	5:21–48		6:27–30, 32–36	
Three hypocritical acts to be avoided	6:1–18			
Three prohibitions against avarice and more	6:19–7:6		6:37–42	
Application and conclusion	7:7–27		6:31, 43–49	
Reaction of the crowds	7:28–8:1			
Growing Fame and Emphasis on Repentance				
A centurion's faith and healing of his servant	8:5–13		7:1–10	
A widow's son raised at Nain			7:11–17	
John the Baptist's relationship to the kingdom	11:2–19		7:18–35	
Woes upon Korazin and Bethsaida	11:20–30			
Jesus' feet anointed by sinful, contrite woman			7:36–50	
First Public Rejection by Jewish Leaders				
A tour with the Twelve and other followers			8:1–3	
Blasphemous accusation by teachers of the Law and Pharisees	12:22–37	3:20–30		
Request for a sign refused	12:38–45			
Announcement of new spiritual kinship	12:46–50	3:31–35	8:19–21	
Secrets About the Kingdom Given in Parables				
To the Crowds by the Sea				
The setting of the parables	13:1–3a	4:1–2	8:4	
The parable of the soils	13:3b–23	4:3–25	8:5–18	
The parable of the seed's spontaneous growth		4:26–29		
The parable of the weeds	13:24–30			
The parable of the mustard tree	13:31–32	4:30–32		
The parable of the leavened loaf	13:33–35	4:33–34		
To the Disciples in the House				
The parable of the weeds explained	13:36–43			
The parable of the hidden treasure	13:44			
The parable of the valuable pearl	13:45–46			
The parable of the net	13:47–50			
The parable of the house owner	13:51–53			
Continuing Opposition				
Crossing the lake and calming the storm	8:18, 23–27	4:35–41	8:22–25	

	Matthew	Mark	Luke	John
Healing the Gerasene demoniacs	8:28–34	5:1–20	8:26–39	
Return to Galilee, healing of a woman, raising Jairus's daughter	9:18–26	5:21–43	8:40–56	
Three miracles of healing; another blasphemous accusation	9:27–34			
Final visit to unbelieving Nazareth	13:54–58	6:1–6a		
Final Galilean Campaign				
Shortage of workers	9:35–38	6:6b		
Commissioning of the Twelve	10:1–42	6:7–11	9:1–15	
Workers sent out	11:1	6:12–13	9:6	
Antipas's mistaken identification of Jesus	14:1–2	6:14–16	9:7–9	
Earlier imprisonment and beheading of John the Baptist	14:3–12	6:17–19		
The Ministry of Christ Around Galilee				
Lesson on the Bread of Life				
Return of the workers		6:30	9:10a	
Withdrawal from Galilee	14:13–14	6:31–34	9:10b–11	6:1–3
Feeding the 5000	14:15–21	6:35–44	9:12–17	6:4–13
Attempt to make Jesus king blocked	14:22–23	6:45–46		6:14–15
Walking on the water during a storm on the lake	14:24–33	6:47–52		6:16–21
Healings at Gennesaret	14:34–36	6:53–56		
Discourse on the true bread of life				6:22–59
Defection among the disciples				6:60–71
Lesson on the Leaven of the Pharisees, Sadducees, and Herodians				
Conflict over ceremonial uncleanness	15:1–3a, 7–9b, 3b–6, 10–20	7:1–23		7:1
Ministry to a believing Greek woman in Tyre and Sidon	15:21–28	7:24–30		
Healings in Decapolis	15:29–31	7:31–37		
Feeding the 4000 in Decapolis	15:32–38	8:1–9a		
Return to Galilee; encounter with Pharisees and Sadducees	15:39–16:4	8:9b–12		
Warning about the error of Pharisees, others	16:5–12	8:13–21		
Healing a blind man at Bethsaida		8:22–26		
Lesson of Messiahship Learned and Confirmed				
Peter's identification of Jesus as the Christ; first prophecy of the church	16:13–20	8:27–30	9:18–21	
First direct prediction of rejection, crucifixion, and resurrection	16:21–26	8:31–37	9:22–25	
Coming of the Son of Man and judgment	16:27–28	8:38–9:1	9:26–27	
Transfiguration of Jesus	17:1–8	9:2–8	9:28–36a	
Discussion of resurrection, Elijah, and John the Baptist	17:9–13	9:9–13	9:36b	
Lessons on Responsibility to Others				
Healing of demoniac boy; unbelief rebuked	17:14–20	9:14–29	9:37–43a	

	Matthew	Mark	Luke	John
Second prediction of death and resurrection	17:22–23	9:30–32	9:43b–45	
Payment of temple tax	17:24–27			
Rivalry over greatness in the kingdom	18:1–5	9:33–37	9:46–48	
Warning against causing believers to sin	18:6–14	9:38–50	9:49–50	
Treatment and forgiveness of a sinning brother	18:15–35			
Journey to Jerusalem for the Feast of Tabernacles				
Complete commitment required of followers	8:19–22		9:57–62	
Ridicule by Jesus' half-brothers				7:2–9
Journey through Samaria			9:51–56	7:10
The Later Judean Ministry of Christ				
Ministry Beginning at the Feast of Tabernacles				
Mixed reaction to Jesus' teaching and miracles				7:11–31
Frustrated attempt to arrest Jesus				7:32–52
Jesus' forgiveness of a woman caught in adultery				7:53–8:11
Conflict over Jesus' claim to be the light of the world				8:12–20
Jesus' relationship to God the Father				8:21–30
Jesus' relationship to Abraham, and attempted stoning				8:31–59
Healing of a man born blind				9:1–7
Response of the blind man's neighbors				9:8–12
Excommunication of the blind man by the Pharisees				9:13–34
Jesus' identification to the blind man				9:35–38
Spiritual blindness of the Pharisees				9:39–41
Allegory of the good shepherd and the thief				10:1–18
Further division among the Jews				10:19–21
Private Lessons on Loving Service and Prayer				
Commissioning of the Seventy-two			10:1–16	
Return of the Seventy-two			10:17–24	
Story of the Good Samaritan			10:25–37	
Jesus' visit with Mary and Martha			10:38–42	
Lesson on how to pray; parable of the bold friend			11:1–13	
Second Debate with the Teachers of the Law and the Pharisees				
Third blasphemous accusation; second debate			11:14–36	
Woes to the Pharisees and teachers of the law			11:37–54	
Warning the disciples about hypocrisy			12:1–12	
Warning about greed and trust in wealth			12:13–34	
Warning against being unprepared for the Son of Man's coming			12:35–48	
Warning about the coming division			12:49–53	
Warning against failing to discern the present time			12:54–59	
Two alternatives: repent or perish			13:1–9	
Opposition for healing a woman on the Sabbath			13:10–21	
Another attempt to stone or arrest Jesus for blasphemy				10:22–39

	Matthew	Mark	Luke	John
The Ministry of Christ in and Around Perea				
Principles of Discipleship				
From Jerusalem to Perea				10:40–42
Question about salvation and the kingdom			13:22–30	
Anticipation of Jesus' death and His sorrow over Jerusalem			13:31–35	
Healing of a man with dropsy; three parables suggested by the occasion			14:1–24	
Cost of discipleship			14:25–35	
Parables in defense of association with sinners			15:1–32	
Parable to teach the proper use of money			16:1–13	
Story to teach the danger of wealth			16:14–31	
Four lessons on discipleship			17:1–10	
Sickness and death of Lazarus				11:1–16
Lazarus raised from the dead				11:17–44
Decision of the Sanhedrin to put Jesus to death				11:45–54
Teaching While on Final Journey to Jerusalem				
Healing of 10 lepers on way through Galilee and Samaria			17:11–21	
Instructions regarding the Son of Man's coming			17:22–37	
Two parables on prayer: the persistent widow, and the Pharisee and the tax collector			18:1–14	
Conflict with Pharisaic teaching on divorce	19:1–12	10:1–12		
Example of little children and the kingdom	19:13–15	10:13–16	18:15–17	
Riches and the kingdom	19:16–30	10:17–31	18:18–30	
Parable of the landowner's sovereignty	20:1–16			
Third prediction of Jesus' death and resurrection	20:17–19	10:32–34	18:31–34	
Warning against ambitious pride	20:20–28	10:35–45		
Healing of blind Bartimaeus and his companion	20:29–34	10:46–52	18:35–43	
Salvation of Zacchaeus			19:1–10	
Parable to teach responsibility while the kingdom is delayed			19:11–28	
The Formal Presentation of Christ to Israel and the Resulting Conflict				
Triumphal Entry and the Fig Tree				
Arrival at Bethany				11:55–12:1, 9–11
Triumphal entry into Jerusalem	21:1–3, 6–7, 4–5, 8–11, 14–17	11:1–11	19:29–44	12:12–10
Cursing of the fig tree	21:18–19a	11:12–14		
Second cleansing of the temple	21:12–13	11:15–18	19:45–48	
Request of some Greeks to see Jesus				12:20–36a
Different responses of Jesus and the crowds				12:36b–50
Withered fig tree and lesson on faith	21:19b–22	11:19–25	21:37–38	
Official Challenge to Christ's Authority				
Questioning of Jesus' authority by chief priests and others	21:23–27	11:27–33	20:1–8	

	Matthew	Mark	Luke	John
Jesus' question and three parables	21:28–22:14	12:1–12	20:9–19	
Attempts to trap Jesus with question about paying taxes to Caesar	22:15–22	12:13–17	20:20–26	
Sadducees' question about the resurrection	22:23–33	12:18–27	20:27–40	
A Pharisee's legal question	22:34–40	12:28–34		
Christ' Response to His Enemies' Challenges				
Christ's relationship to David as Son and Lord	22:41–46	12:35–37	20:41–44	
Seven woes against the teachers of the law and Pharisees	23:1–36	12:38–40	20:45–47	
Jesus' sorrow over Jerusalem	23:37–39			
A poor widow's gift of all she had		12:41–44	21:1–4	

Prophecies in Preparation for the Death of Christ

The Olivet Discourse: Jesus Speaks Prophetically

	Matthew	Mark	Luke	John
Setting of the discourse	24:1–3	13:1–4	21:5–7	
Beginning of birth pains	24:4–14	13:5–13	21:8–19	
Abomination of desolation and subsequent stress	24:15–28	13:14–23	21:20–24	
Coming of the Son of Man	24:29–31	13:24–27	21:25–27	
Signs of nearness but unknown time	24:32–41	13:28–32	21:28–33	
Five parables on watchfulness and faithfulness	24:42–25:30	13:33–37	21:34–36	
Judgment at the Son of Man's coming	25:31–46			
Arrangements for Betrayal				
Plot by the Sanhedrin to arrest and kill Jesus	26:1–5	14:1–2	22:1–2	
Mary's anointing of Jesus for burial	26:6–13	14:3–9		12:2–8
Judas's agreement to betray Jesus	26:14–16	14:10–11	22:3–6	
The Last Supper				
Preparation for the Passover meal	26:17–19	14:12–16	22:7–13	
Beginning of the Passover meal; dissension over greatness	26:20	14:17	22:14–16, 24–30	
Washing the disciples' feet				13:1–20
Identification of the betrayer	26:21–25	14:18–21	22:21–23	13:21–30
Prediction of Peter's denial	26:31–35	14:27–31	22:31–38	13:31–38
The Lord's Supper instituted (1 Cor. 11:23–26)	26:26–29	14:22–25	22:17–20	
Discourse and Prayers from the Upper Room to Gethsemane				
Questions about Jesus' destination, the Father, and the Holy Spirit				14:1–31
The vine and the branches				15:1–17
Opposition from the world				15:18–16:4
The coming and ministry of the Spirit				16:5–15
Prediction of joy over Jesus' resurrection				16:16–22
Promise of answered prayer and peace				16:23–33
Jesus' prayer for the disciples and all believers				17:1–26
Jesus' agonizing prayers in Gethsemane	26:30, 36–46	14:26, 32–42	22:39–46	18:1

	Matthew	Mark	Luke	John
The Death of Christ				
Betrayal and Arrest				
Jesus betrayed, arrested, forsaken	26:47–56	14:43–52	22:47–53	18:2–12
Trial				
First Jewish phase, before Annas				18:13–14, 19–23
Second Jewish phase, before Caiaphas and the Sanhedrin	26:57, 59–68	14:53, 55–65	22:54a, 63–65	18:24
Peter's denials	26:58, 69–75	14:54, 66–72	22:54b–62	18:15–18, 25–27
Third Jewsih phase, before the Sanhedrin	27:1	15:1a	22:66–71	
Remorse and suicide of Judas Iscariot (Acts 1:18–19)	27:3–10			
First Roman phase, before Pilate	27:2, 11–14	15:1b–5	23:1–5	18:28–38
Second Roman phase, before Herod Antipas			23:6–12	
Third Roman phase, before Pilate	27:15–26	15:6–15	23:13–25	18:39–19:16a
Crucifixion				
Mockery by the Roman soldiers	27:27–30	15:16–19		
Journey to Golgotha	27:31–34	15:20–23	23:26–33a	19:16b–17
First three hours of crucifixion	27:35–44	15:24–32	23:33b–43	19:18, 23–24 19–22, 25–27
Last three hours of crucifixion	27:45–50	15:33–37	23:44–45a, 46	19:28–30
Witness of Jesus' death	27:51–56	15:38–41	23:45b, 47–49	
Burial				
Certification of Jesus' death and procurement of his body	27:57–58	15:42–45	23:50–52	19:31–38
Jesus' body placed in a tomb	27:59–60	15:46	23:53–54	19:39–42
The tomb watched by the women and guarded by the soldiers	27:61–66	15:47	23:55–56	
TheResurrection and Ascension of Christ				
The Empty Tomb				
The tomb visited by the women	28:1	16:1		
The stone rolled away	28:2–4			
The tomb found to be empty by the women	28:5–8	16:2–8	24:1–8	20:1
The tomb found to be empty by Peter and John			24:9–12	20:2–10
The Post Resurrection Appearances				
Appearance to Mary Magdalene		[16:9–11]		20:11–18
Appearance to the other women	28:9–10			
Report of the soldiers to the Jewish authorities	28:11–15			
Appearance to the two disciples traveling to Emmaus		[16:12–13]	24:13–32	
Report of the two disciples to the rest (1 Cor. 15:5a)			24:33–35	

	Matthew	Mark	Luke	John
Appearance to the ten assembled disciples		[16:14]	24:36–43	20:19–25
Appearance to the eleven assembled disciples (1 Cor. 15:5b)				20:26–31
Appearance to the seven disciples while fishing				21:1–25
Appearance to the Eleven in Galilee (1 Cor. 15:6)	28:16–20	[16:15–18]		
Appearance to James, Jesus' brother (1 Cor. 15:7)				
Appearance to the disciples in Jerusalem (Acts 1:3–8)			24:44–49	
The Ascension				
Christ's parting blessing and departure (Acts 1:9–12)		[16:19–20]	24:50–53	

Matthew

Jesus the Messiah

"You are the light of the world. . . . Let your light shine before men, that they may see your good deeds and praise your Father in heaven."
—Matthew 5:14, 16

"But seek first his kingdom and his righteousness, and all these things will be given to you as well."
—Matthew 6:33

- For a general introduction to all four Gospels, see p. 517.
- For an overview of the life of Jesus, see p. 493.

Matthew's Emphasis: Jesus Is the Promised Messiah

The special emphasis of Matthew is that Jesus is the Messiah foretold by the Old Testament prophets. He quotes from and refers to the Old Testament more often than any other New Testament author and seems to have had particularly Jewish readers in mind.

The term "kingdom" or "kingdom of heaven" occurs so often (43 times) that this Gospel is often called the Gospel of the Kingdom.

Matthew presents his material overall in chronological order, but within that order he often groups his material by subject matter. He gives Jesus' discourses quite fully, especially the Sermon on the Mount (chaps. 5–7) and Jesus' discourse about the coming end of the world (chaps. 24–25).

Customs Law (A.D. 62). Before being called as a disciple of Jesus, Matthew functioned as a tax collector under Roman law.

Matthew

This Gospel does not name its author, but it has been accepted as the work of Matthew ever since the early church fathers, beginning with Papias, who was a student of the apostle John.

We know almost nothing of Matthew, who is also called Levi. He is mentioned in the four lists of the Twelve: Matthew 10:3; Mark 3:18; Luke 6:15; Acts 1:13 (see p. 514). The only other mention is his call to follow Jesus (Matthew 9:9–13; Mark 2:14–17; Luke 5:27–32).

The only thing Matthew says about himself is that he was a tax collector for the Romans. These tax collectors had to be rather well off, since they had to prepay each year's taxes and then were allowed to recover the amount, with interest, from the people. Although the interest charges were in theory limited to a fair amount, the reality was that often the tax collectors charged more than they should. But the real problem was that the Law of Moses strictly prohibited charging fellow Jews any interest at all (Leviticus 25:36; Deuteronomy 23:19–20; the KJV uses the archaic word "usury" instead of "interest," which is misleading). Thus, the tax collectors ordinarily were viewed as people who did not care about the Law of Moses and were generally despised.

As a tax collector, Matthew was used to keeping records, and he was a personal companion of Jesus through most of Jesus' public ministry. Luke tells us that Matthew made a great feast for Jesus and gave up all to follow Him. But Matthew does not even give himself credit for that. He loses sight of himself in his efforts to tell the story of his Master. We love him for his self-effacing humility, and we marvel at the grace of God in choosing such a man to be the author of what is said to be the most widely read book in all the world, the first book in the New Testament.

Tradition says that Matthew preached in Palestine for some years and then traveled to foreign countries. It is thought that he wrote his Gospel originally in Hebrew and that some years later, probably around A.D. 60, he issued a more complete edition in Greek.

Matt. 1:1–17 | GENEALOGY OF JESUS

Matthew and Luke both give a genealogy of Jesus (Luke 3:23–38). The coming of Christ to the earth had been anticipated from the beginning. In the early days of human history God had chosen one family, that of Abraham, and later on a family within the larger Abrahamic family, that of David, to be the family through which His Son would make entrance into the world.

The genealogy in Matthew is abridged. Some names are omitted, as was frequently done in genealogies, without invalidating the line of descent.

The 42 generations, in three groups of 14 each, cover 2000 years (the first group, 1000 years; the second group, 400 years; the third group, 600 years). The third group, however, names only 13 generations, the 14th spot evidently being intended for Mary.

The genealogy as given in Luke is somewhat different. Matthew goes back to Abraham, Luke to Adam. Matthew starts at the beginning (Abraham was the father of Isaac, etc.), Luke at the end (Joseph was the son of Heli, etc.; Luke 3:23). From David to Jesus they present separate lines of descent, touching in Shealtiel and Zerubbabel.

The commonly accepted view is that Matthew gives Joseph's line, showing Jesus to be legal heir to the promises given to Abraham and David, and that Luke gives Mary's line, showing Jesus' blood descent: "who as to his human nature was a descendant of David" (Romans 1:3).

Mary's genealogy, in accordance with Jewish usage, was in her husband's name. Joseph was the son of Heli (Luke 3:23) — that is, Heli's son-in-law. Jacob was Joseph's father (Matthew 1:16).

These genealogies are given more fully in 1 Chronicles 1–9; they form the framework of Old Testament history. Carefully guarded through long centuries of change and upheaval, they contain a family line through which a promise was transmitted for 4000 years, a fact unparalleled in history.

Matt. 1:18–25	THE BIRTH OF JESUS

Only Matthew and Luke tell of the birth and childhood of Jesus, and each tells different incidents. (See on Luke 1:5–80.)

Mary, for the first three months after the visit of the heavenly messenger, was away at the home of Elizabeth (Luke 1:36). When she returned to Nazareth and Joseph learned of her condition, it must have filled him with perplexity as to what he should do. But he was a good man, and he wanted to protect Mary from what he supposed would be public disgrace or worse.

Then the angel appeared to him and explained what was happening. To avoid scandal, he still had to keep the family secret, for nobody would have believed Mary's story. Only later, when Jesus' divine nature was authenticated by His miracles and His resurrection from the dead, could Mary speak freely of her heavenly secret and the supernatural conception of her child. (For a note on the Virgin Birth, see on Luke 1:26–38.)

Joseph

Very little is told of Joseph. He went with Mary to Bethlehem and was with her when Jesus was born (Luke 2:4, 16). He was with Mary when Jesus was presented in the temple (Luke 2:33). He took them to Egypt and brought them back to Nazareth (Matthew 2:13, 19–23). He also took the 12-year-old Jesus to Jerusalem (Luke 2:43, 51). The only further reference to him is that he was a carpenter and the head of a family of at least seven children (Matthew 13:55–56).

He surely must have been a good and exemplary man to have been thus chosen of God to be the foster-father of God's own Son. He may have died before Jesus began his public ministry, though the language of Matthew 13:55 and John 6:42 may imply that he was still alive. He must have died before Jesus' crucifixion, otherwise why did Jesus commit the care of his mother to John (John 19:26–27)?

Mary

After the stories of the birth of Jesus and His visit to Jerusalem at the age of 12, very little is said of Mary. According to Matthew 13:55–56, she was the mother of at least six children besides Jesus. At her suggestion, Jesus turned water into wine at Cana, His first miracle (John 2:1–11). Later, she is mentioned as trying to get to Him in the crowd; Jesus' words on that occasion plainly indicate that her family relation to Him gave her no special spiritual advantage (Matthew 12:46; Mark 3:31; Luke 8:19). She was present at the crucifixion and was committed by Jesus to the care of John (John 19:25–27). There is no record of Jesus appearing to her after His resurrection, although the fact that there is no record does not mean that it did not happen. The last mention of Mary is in Acts 1:14, where she was with the disciples in prayer. This is all the Scripture has to say about Mary.

One can, however, envision Mary as a quiet, meditative, devoted, wise woman, one who has shared the cares common to motherhood. We admire her, honor her, and love her because she was the mother of our Savior. We can only imagine the impact on Mary's life of being chosen by God to supernaturally bring forth the Savior of the world. What a blessed woman she was!

Who were the brothers and sisters of Jesus mentioned in Matthew 13:55–56 and Mark 6:3? The plain, simple, natural meaning of these passages is that they were Mary and Joseph's own children. This is the opinion commonly held among Bible commentators.

Mary Magdalene, a follower of Jesus, is also mentioned several times in the New Testament (Matthew 27:56, 61; 28:1; Mark 15:40, 47; 16:9; Luke 8:2; 24:10; John 19:25; 20:1–18; see note on Luke 8:1–3).

(For note on Bethlehem, see p. 589.)

Matt. 2:1–12 | VISIT OF THE WISE MEN

This must have occurred in the period when Jesus was between 40 days and two years old (2:16; Luke 2:22, 39). It would have taken the Magi (or Wise Men) some time to get to Jerusalem after they first saw the star (v. 7), although probably quite a bit less than two years. And it took

The Star of the Wise Men

The star that guided the Wise Men to Bethlehem has been the subject of much speculation. Several possible explanations have been suggested:

- A supernova or new star. This involves a very distant star in which an explosion takes place so that for a time the star becomes many times brighter than usual—sometimes so bright that it can be seen during the daytime. But there is no record of a supernova around the time of Jesus' birth.
- A comet. The best-known of these is Halley's comet, which actually was visible in 12–11 B.C. But this is rather too long before the actual date of Jesus' birth in 6 or 5 B.C.
- A conjunction of planets. In 7–6 B.C., three planets appeared close together: Jupiter, Saturn, and Mars. This is a rare triple conjunction known as the *conjunctio magna,* or great conjunction. This conjunction took place in the zodiacal constellation Pisces, which was sometimes associated with the last days and with the Hebrews, while Saturn was considered the star of the Syria-Palestine region and Jupiter was associated with the world ruler.

But what matters in the end is that God, either by supernatural means or by the supernatural use of a natural event, guided the Wise Men, as representatives of the Gentiles, to worship the King of the Jews who will one day be King of all.

some time before Herod realized that the Magi weren't coming back. So Herod, in order to be sure, took the outside limit. We know that the child was no longer in the manger, as is sometimes pictured, but in the house (v. 11; see on Luke 2:6–7).

These Wise Men belonged to the learned class, those who were the advisers of the kings. They came from Babylon or the country beyond, the land where the human race had its origin, the land of Abraham, the land of the Jewish captivity (the Babylonian exile, see p. 267), where many Jews still lived. They were perhaps familiar with the Jewish Scriptures and knew of the expectation of a coming Messianic King. It was the land of Daniel, and they may have known of Daniel's prophecies.

They were men of high standing, for they had access to Herod. We usually speak of the three Wise Men or Magi, but Scripture does not say how many there were—probably more. They certainly would have traveled with an entourage of perhaps dozens, for it would not be safe for a small group to travel 1000 miles over terrain infested with bandits. Their arrival in Jerusalem was with a sufficient show of importance to stir the whole city.

The Magi symbolized the homage of the nations to the newborn King, who one day would be worshiped by all nations. One of the objects of their visit, which they themselves did not know, was to supply money for the child's flight to Egypt. The parents were poor, and if it had not been for the gold and other expensive gifts brought by the Wise Men, escape from Herod might not have been possible.

The gifts of the Magi can also be interpreted as foreshadowing Jesus' life and death. The gold, representing royalty, foretells Jesus as King. The incense, symbolic of the prayers of the high priests rising up to heaven, foretells Jesus as High Priest. The myrrh, often used as a burial oil, foretells Jesus' death. The return of the Wise Men to their home countries may have paved the way for the later preaching of the Gospel.

Matt. 2:13–15 | THE FLIGHT TO EGYPT

Even this incident did not escape God's unfailing eye in the long line of prophecies that looked forward to the Messiah (v. 15; Hosea 11:1). The angel (v. 13) who directed their flight to Egypt probably was Gabriel, to whom God had entrusted the care of the infant Child (see on Luke 2:8–20). The stay in Egypt was short, probably only a year or two, for Herod soon died and it was safe to return. (See the chronology of Jesus' childhood, p. 494.)

Matt. 2:16–18 | THE CHILDREN OF BETHLEHEM KILLED BY HEROD

It is strange that someone who believed in the coming of the Christ (2:4) could have been conceited (and stupid) enough to think that he could thwart His coming!

This, too, was directed by the angel. It seems from v. 22 that Joseph was planning to return to Bethlehem in Judea, the ancestral city of David, to make it their permanent home as the proper place in which to rear the

Old Testament Prophecies of Christ Quoted in the Gospels

Matthew uses Old Testament quotations in abundance. He wants to show that the incidents of Christ's life are fulfillments of the prophetic predictions of the Old Testament. What follows is a list of Old Testament prophecies that are quoted in the four Gospels, particularly in Matthew, as having been fulfilled in Christ. Most of them quite clearly refer to the Messiah. A few of them are not so obvious, but they are quoted by the inspired New Testament writers as messianic prophecies.

- He was to be of David's family (Matthew 22:44; Mark 12:36; Luke 1:69, 70; 20:42–44; John 7:42 / 2 Samuel 7:12–16; Psalms 89:3–4; 110:1; 132:11; Isaiah 9:6–7; 11:1).
- He would be born of a virgin (Matthew 1:23 / Isaiah 7:14).
- He would be born in Bethlehem (Matthew 2:6; John 7:42 / Micah 5:2).
- He would stay in Egypt for a while (Matthew 2:15 / Hosea 11:1).
- He would live in Galilee (Matthew 4:15 / Isaiah 9:1–2).
- He would live in Nazareth (Matthew 2:23 / Isaiah 11:1).
- His coming would be announced by an Elijah-like herald (Matthew 3:3; 11:10–14; Mark 1:2–3; Luke 3:4–6; 7:27; John 1:23 / Isaiah 40:3–5; Malachi 3:1; 4:5).
- His coming would lead to the murder of Bethlehem's children (Matthew 2:18 / Genesis 35:19–20; 48:7; Jeremiah 31:15).
- He would proclaim a jubilee to the world (Luke 4:18–19 / Isaiah 58:6; 61:1; for an explanation of Jubilee, see p.155).
- His mission would include Gentiles (Matthew 12:18–21 / Isaiah 42:1–4).
- His ministry would be one of healing (Matthew 8:17 / Isaiah 53:4).
- He would teach by means of parables (Matthew 13:14–15, 35 / Isaiah 6:9–10; Psalm 78:2).
- He would be disbelieved and rejected by the rulers (Matthew 15:8–9; 21:42; Mark 7:6–7; 12:10–11; Luke 20:17; John 12:38–40; 15:25 / Psalms 69:4; 118:22; Isaiah 6:10; 29:13; 53:1).
- He would make a triumphal entry into Jerusalem (Matthew 21:5; John 12:13–15 / Isaiah 62:11; Zechariah 9:9; Psalm 118:26).
- He would be like a shepherd who is struck down (Matthew 26:31; Mark 14:27 / Zechariah 13:7).
- He would be betrayed by a friend for 30 pieces of silver (Matthew 27:9–10; John 13:18 / Zechariah 11:12–13; Psalm 41:9).
- He would die with criminals (Luke 22:37 / Isaiah 53:9, 12).
- He would be buried by a rich man (Isaiah 53:9 / Matthew 27:57–60; fact stated, prophecy not quoted).
- He would be given vinegar and gall (Matthew 27:34; John 19:29 / Psalm 69:21).
- They would cast lots for His garments (John 19:24 / Psalm 22:18).
- Even His dying words were foretold (Matthew 27:46; Mark 15:34; Luke 23:46 / Psalms 22:1; 31:5).
- Not one of His bones would be broken (John 19:36 / Exodus 12:46; Numbers 9:12; Psalm 34:20).
- His side would be pierced (John 19:37 / Zechariah 12:10; Psalm 22:16).

child Messiah. But God planned differently and sent them back to their home in Galilee in a town called Nazareth. Luke tells us that this was the home of Mary and Joseph before Jesus' birth (Luke 2:4).

What Matthew points out especially is that it was in fulfillment of prophecy: "He will be called a Nazarene." These exact words are not found in the Old Testament but probably refer to Old Testament predictions that the prophet would be despised (Psalm 22:6; Isaiah 53:3). Another common opinion is that Matthew is referring to Jesus "the Nazarene," or Jesus the Branch, because the Hebrew word for "branch" is *neser.* The prophecy Matthew refers to here is thought to be Isaiah 11:1; Jeremiah 23:5; and Zechariah 3:8, where the Messiah is spoken of as the Branch.

Bethany beyond the Jordan. One of the reasons for the baptism of Jesus was His consecration into His rabbinic role.

Matt. 3 | THE BAPTISM OF JESUS

Told also in Mark 1:1–11 and Luke 3:1–22. (For note on John the Baptist, see Luke 3:1–20). In all three accounts, and in John 1:31–33, the two things specifically mentioned are the descent of the Holy Spirit and the voice from heaven. John 1:31–33 gives the impression that John did not know Jesus, but Matthew 3:14 implies that he did know Him. Undoubtedly Jesus and John had known each other as boys, for their families were related (Luke 1:36), and their mothers were together for three months just before their births (Luke 1:39, 56). It seems certain that the boys must have been told by their parents of the heavenly announcements concerning their respective missions.

But from the time when John withdrew to become a hermit of the desert (Luke 1:80), he may not have seen Jesus again until the day of His baptism. Then, with direct heavenly endorsement, Jesus was publicly anointed as the Son of God, the nation's Messiah, and the Savior of the world.

Jesus' baptism marked the beginning of His earthly ministry. There appear to be several important reasons for Jesus' baptism. The first reason was to "fulfill all righteousness." The baptism represented Jesus' being consecrated to God and publicly approved by Him (v. 17). All God's righteous requirements for the Messiah were fulfilled in Jesus. The second reason for the baptism was the public announcement by John the Baptist of the arrival of the Messiah that he had been preaching about. And finally, the baptism allowed Jesus to fully identify with man's sin and failure (even though Jesus had no sin), becoming our substitute (2 Corinthians 5:21).

In this scene we clearly see the manifestation of the holy Trinity. God the Father speaks from heaven (v. 17). The Holy Spirit descends like a dove and rests on Jesus, the Son of God (v. 16).

Matt. 4:1–10 | THE TEMPTATION OF JESUS

(Told also in Luke 4:1–13 and Mark 1:12–13.) The Holy Spirit, Satan (see pp. 594–95), and angels (see p. 539) all took a hand in the temptation of Jesus. The Holy Spirit guided Him, and angels helped Him, as Satan made attempt after attempt to turn Him aside from His mission. The whole universe was interested. The destiny of creation was at stake.

We wonder why the temptation of Jesus followed immediately after His baptism. The descent of the Holy Spirit upon Him at that time may have involved two things new in Jesus' human experience: the power to work miracles without limit, and a full restoration of His pre-incarnation knowledge.

Back in eternity, Jesus knew that He was coming into the world to suffer as the Lamb of God for human sin. But He came by way of the cradle. Are we to suppose that Jesus as a little baby knew all that He knew before He took upon Himself the limitations of human flesh? Is it not more natural to think that His pre-incarnation knowledge gradually came to Him as He grew up, along with His human education? Of course His mother had told Him of the circumstances of His birth. He knew He was the Son of God and the Messiah. He and His mother may even have talked about how He would do His work as the world's Messiah. But when the Holy Spirit came down upon Him without measure at His baptism, then there came to Him fully and clearly, for the first time since He became a human being, some of the things He had known before He became a man—among them the *cross* as the way by which He was to accomplish His mission.

What was the nature of His temptation? It may have included the ordinary temptations of men in their struggle for bread and their desire for fame and power. But there must have been more. Jesus was too great for us to think that such motives could weigh heavily with Him. We must believe that He already knew that it was His mission to save the world. The question was how to do it. By using the miraculous powers that had just been given Him—powers that no mortal man had ever known before, to give men bread without their having to work and to overcome the ordinary forces of nature, He could have become ruler of the world in short order. He could have made people do His will by force. That was Satan's suggestion. But Jesus' mission was to change the hearts of people, not to compel them to obey.

Although Jesus was the Son of God, He defeated Satan by using the weapon that all Christians have at their disposal—the "sword of the Spirit, which is the word of God" (Ephesians 6:17).

We are not told in what form the Devil appeared to Jesus. But Jesus unmistakably recognized the suggestions as coming from Satan, who was there, determined to thwart Jesus' mission. (See note on Satan under Luke 4:1–13.) The severe rebuke given to Satan in v. 10 mirrors another rebuke given later to Satan when he, through Peter, attempted to dissuade Jesus from going to the cross (Mark 8:33).

The place of Jesus' temptation is thought to have been in the barren heights of the mountain region overlooking Jericho (see map on p. 496).

Jesus fasted for 40 days (4:2). Moses had fasted for 40 days on Mount Sinai when the Ten Commandments were given (Exodus 34:28). Elijah had fasted for 40 days on the way to the same mountain (1 Kings 19:8). Moses represented the Law; Elijah, the Prophets. Jesus was the Messiah to whom the Law and the Prophets pointed. From the mountaintop where Jesus was fasting He could, looking eastward across the Jordan, see the mountain ranges of Nebo where, centuries before, Moses and Elijah had ascended to God.

Some three years after this encounter with Satan, these three men, Moses, Elijah, and Jesus, had a rendezvous, amid the glories of the Transfiguration on Mount Hermon, 100 miles to the north—first companions in suffering, then companions in glory.

After the temptation, Jesus went back to the Jordan, where John was baptizing. (See note on John 1:19–34.)

Matt. 4:11 | ANGELS *(See chart on facing page.)*

Matt. 4:12 | JESUS BEGINS THE GALILEAN MINISTRY

About a year elapsed between vv. 11 and 12, the year that included Jesus' early Judean ministry. (This period, omitted by Matthew, is covered in John 1:19–4:54 and Luke 4:16–30.)

Matthew goes directly to the period of Jesus' Galilean ministry and devotes 14 chapters, or one-half of his book, to it (4:12–19:1), as does Mark (eight chapters, 1:14–10:1), while Luke covers it in less than six chapters (4:14–9:51), and John omits it almost entirely.

Matt. 4:13–17 | RESIDENCE IN CAPERNAUM

This is one of the things foretold of the Messiah. *(See on Matthew 2:22–23.)*

Matt. 4:18–22 | CALL OF SIMON, ANDREW, JAMES, JOHN *(See on Mark 1:16–20; also on Matthew 10.)*

Matt. 4:23–25 | JOURNEYS, FAME, MULTITUDES, MIRACLES
(See on Mark 1:38–39.)

The Sermon on the Mount, Matthew 5 to 7

Matthew places the Sermon on the Mount in the forefront of his story of the Galilean ministry, although it seems to have come some months later, at the time of the choosing of the Twelve (Luke 6:12–20)—if indeed Luke is reporting the same sermon. It must have been that Matthew

Qarantal in the Jordan Valley, the traditional mount of temptation, from which Satan showed Jesus "all the kingdoms of the world."

Angels

Angels played an important role in the life of Jesus:

- An angel announced the birth of John (Luke 1:11–17).
- An angel named him (Luke 1:13).
- An angel foretold to Mary the birth of Jesus (Luke 1:26–37).
- An angel foretold to Joseph the birth of Jesus (Matthew 1:20–21).
- An angel named Him (Matthew 1:21).
- Angels announced to shepherds the birth of Jesus (Luke 2:8–15).
- They sang hallelujahs (Luke 2:13–14).
- An angel directed the child's flight to Egypt (Matthew 2:13, 20).
- Angels ministered to Jesus at His temptation (Matthew 4:11).
- An angel came to Jesus in Gethsemane (Luke 22:43).
- An angel rolled away the stone at His tomb (Matthew 28:2).
- An angel announced to the women His resurrection (Matthew 28:5–7).
- Two angels presented Him to Mary Magdalene (John 20:11–14).
- Jesus said a good deal about angels:

  - He saw angels ascending and descending upon Him (John 1:51).
  - He could have 12 legions of angels deliver Him (Matthew 26:53).
  - Angels will come with Him (Matthew 25:31; 16:27; Mark 8:38; Luke 9:26).
  - Angels will be the reapers (Matthew 13:39).
  - Angels will gather the elect (Matthew 24:31).
  - Angels will separate the wicked from the righteous (Matthew 13:41, 49).
  - Angels carried the beggar to Abraham's side (Luke 16:22).
  - Angels rejoice over the repentance of sinners (Luke 15:10).
  - Little children have guardian angels (Matthew 18:10).
  - Jesus will confess His people before the angels (Luke 12:8).
  - Angels have no gender and cannot die (Luke 20:35–36; Matthew 22:30).
  - The Devil has evil angels (Matthew 25:41).

Jesus Himself said these things. His statements about angels are so specific, so varied, and so abundant that to explain them on the theory that Jesus was merely accommodating Himself to current beliefs would undermine the validity of any of Jesus' words as truth.

For angels in the book of Revelation, see p. 836.

regarded the Sermon on the Mount as a summary of Jesus' teaching, of which His whole ministry was an illustration.

Since it contains the very heart of Jesus' teaching, we may think of the Sermon on the Mount as being to the New Testament what the Ten Commandments are to the Old Testament. Every Christian ought to read and be familiar with the Sermon on the Mount and strive earnestly to live according to its teachings. (For a comparison with Luke's record, see on Luke 6:20–49.)

Matt. 5:1–12 | THE BEATITUDES

Blessed, happy, are the spiritually humble, the sorrowful, the patient, the long-suffering, those spiritually hungry for righteousness, the merciful, the pure in heart, the peace makers and maintainers, and those who are persecuted for doing right and for Christ's sake. This is the exact opposite of the world's standards.

In these verses, Jesus reveals a model for how Christians are to live their lives and in so doing receive spiritual prosperity, filling their lives with joy and satisfaction in God's favor and salvation. This is all despite how the world interprets a Christian's outward conditions. Because of this worldly view, the Beatitudes are all too often misunderstood to suggest that Christ is advocating that Christians should live in unfortunate and depressed situations if they are to be blessed in heaven. On the contrary! Jesus goes on to say in the following verses that Christians are to be the salt of the earth and directs them to let their light shine before all men. In other words, Jesus is teaching that if we live as servants with humble and right hearts, we will be richly blessed here on earth as well as in heaven. Jesus wants to bless Christians so that unbelievers are drawn to them, and consequently the unbeliever can be led to salvation in Christ.

Matt. 5:13–16 | SALT AND LIGHT OF THE WORLD

That is, preserver and guide. Jesus Himself is the light of the world (John 8:12). His followers reflect His light and glory. The grandest motive a

The traditional site of the Sermon on the Mount, overlooking the Sea of Galilee.

The hillsides rising above the Sea of Galilee provided the setting for the Sermon on the Mount.

person can have is that his or her manner of life will lead others to glorify God.

Matt. 5:17–48 | JESUS AND THE LAW

Jesus came, not to destroy the Law, but to fulfill it. There is no contradiction here between Jesus' teaching and the teaching of Romans, Galatians, and Hebrews, all of which say that we are saved by faith in Christ rather than by works of the Law.

Jesus' meaning is that God's moral law is the expression of God's own holiness and is therefore an eternal obligation on God's people. In reality, Jesus came to give the Law a deeper meaning that did not call merely for outward acts but a change in the inner depths of the human heart (which, of course, had been the point of the Law all along). He then proceeds to illustrate this with five examples: murder, adultery, swearing, revenge, and hatred of enemy.

Murder (vv. 21–26). The law against murder was one of the Ten Commandments (Exodus 20:13; Deuteronomy 5:7; 16:18). Jesus forbids the nurturing of anger, which is equivalent to the act of murder.

Adultery (vv. 27–32). The law against adultery also was one of the Ten Commandments (Exodus 20:14; Deuteronomy 5:18). Jesus forbids our nurturing the lust that leads to the act. Notice that in connection with both anger and lust, Jesus warns of hell fire (vv. 22, 29, 30). He not only warns us to watch our inner feelings, but goes much further than Moses in restricting divorce (v. 32; Deuteronomy 24:1–4).

Swearing (vv. 33–37). Jesus here refers to judicial oaths and vows. The Law of Moses made it clear that a vow should not be broken and that an oath should be taken only in God's name ("Fear the LORD your God, serve him only and take your oaths in his name," Deuteronomy 6:13). But over the centuries a whole system of distinctions had developed in which a vow or oath was binding only to the degree to which it was related to God's name. Swearing by heaven and earth was not binding, nor was swearing by Jerusalem — but swearing *toward* Jerusalem *was* binding.

Jesus says that all things *are* related to God—there is no question of degree. And the integrity of our life should be such that oaths are superfluous.

Revenge (vv. 38–42). The eye-for-an-eye legislation was part of the civil law, administered by judges (Exodus 21:22–25; Leviticus 24:20). Jesus is not legislating here for courts of justice. Civil government is ordained of God (Romans 13:1–7), to save human society from its criminal elements. Jesus here teaches principles by which individuals should deal with other individuals. (See on Luke 6:27–38.)

Hatred of enemies (5:43–48) was not taught in the Old Testament. It may have been implied in some Old Testament dealings with Israel's enemies, but the Old Testament also teaches compassion toward enemies: "Do not gloat when your enemy falls; when he stumbles, do not let your heart rejoice" (Proverbs 24:17) and "If your enemy is hungry, give him food to eat; if he is thirsty, give him water to drink" (Proverbs 25:21). Jesus deepens the requirement of compassion to the deeper requirement of love. (See on Luke 6:27–38.) Jesus also suggests that praying for one's enemies is one of the ways in which we can express godly love (5:44).

Matt. 6–7 | HEAVENLY TEACHINGS

Secret motives of life (6:1–18). (See on Luke 12:1–12.) Here illustrated in three specific areas are the actions which lead to spiritual growth and maturity:

1. *Giving to the needy* (6:2–4). Give as if you give to God; do not make a show of it. (See on Matthew 23.)
2. *Prayer* (6:5–15). (See on Luke 11 and 18.)
3. *Fasting* (6:16–18). (See on Mark 2:18–22.)

Treasures in heaven (6:19–34). (See on Luke 12:13–34.)

Do not judge others (7:1–5). (See on Luke 6:39–45.)

Do not throw pearls before pigs (7:6). This means that we should use common sense and tact in talking about our religion—otherwise we may do our cause more harm than good.

Persistent prayer (7:7–11). (See on Luke 18:1–8.)

The Golden Rule (7:12). (See on Luke 6:27–38.)

The narrow road (7:13–14). Many will be lost, few saved—few, that is, in comparison to the number of the lost. But in the end, the saved will nevertheless be "a great multitude that no one can count" (Revelation 7:9).

False prophets (7:15–23). Jesus warned of false prophets and false teachers (Matthew 24:11, 24), as did the New Testament writers, again and again. The most devastating obstacle to the progress of Christianity has been its corruption at the hands of those who claim that they have been sent by God

"Ask and it will be given to you; seek and you will find; knock and the door will be opened to you. For everyone who asks receives; he who seeks finds; and to him who knocks, the door will be opened."

— Matthew 7:7–8

but who teach falsely. They can be recognized because they bear no good fruit.

Building on the rock (7:24–27). A very plain statement that it is useless to call ourselves Christians unless we practice the things Jesus taught in this Sermon on the Mount.

Matt. 8:1–4 **A LEPER HEALED** (*See on Mark 1:40–44.*)

Matt. 8:5–13 **THE CENTURION'S SERVANT**
(*See on Luke 7:1–10.*)

Matt. 8:14–15 **PETER'S MOTHER-IN-LAW**
(*See on Mark 1:29–31.*)

Matt. 8:16–17 **MANY ARE HEALED** (*See on Mark 1:32–34.*)

Matt. 8:18–22 **FOXES HAVE HOLES** (*See on Luke 9:57–62.*)

Matt. 8:23–27 **THE STILLING OF THE STORM**
(*See on Mark 4:36–41.*)

Matt. 8:28–34 **THE DEMON-POSSESSED GADARENES**
(*See on Mark 5:1–20.*)

Matt. 9:1–8 **A LAME MAN IS HEALED** (*See on Mark 2:1–12.*)

Matt. 9:9–13 **THE CALL OF MATTHEW** (*See on Mark 2:13–17.*)

Matt. 9:14–17 **A QUESTION ABOUT FASTING**
(*See on Mark 2:18–22.*)

Matt. 9:18–26 **JAIRUS'S DAUGHTER** (*See on Luke 8:40–56.*)

Matt. 9:27–31 **TWO BLIND MEN** (*See on Mark 8:22–26.*)

Matt. 9:32–34 **THE HEALING OF A MUTE DEMON-POSSESSED MAN** (*See on Mark 7:31–37.*)

Matt. 9:35–38 **TRAVELS** (*See on Mark 1:39.*)

Matt. 10 **THE TWELVE SENT OUT**

(Told also, more briefly, in Mark 6:7–13 and Luke 9:1–6.) It must have been shortly before Passover, because they returned at Passover time, just before the feeding of the 5000 (Luke 9:10–17; John 6:4).

These instructions of Jesus to the Twelve contain some wonderful advice for Christians: to be wise as serpents and harmless as doves; to expect hardship; to trust in God's unfailing care of His own; and to keep our eyes fixed on the eternal goal.

Some of Jesus' instructions were meant only for this occasion—for example, the command to take no money. With the power to heal, they would have no difficulty receiving lodging and meals. But later they were told to take money (Luke 22:35–38).

Matt. 11:1–19 | MESSENGERS FROM JOHN THE BAPTIST

This happened while John was in prison. Jesus was at the height of his popularity. John evidently was looking for a political Messiah (see on Luke 3:1–20); he could not understand why Jesus was not taking proper action toward that end.

Jesus' answer indicates that He considered His miracles as sufficient evidence of His Messiahship. Note that John's doubt did not lower him in Jesus' estimation: "There had not arisen a greater," said Jesus. Yet the lowliest in Christ's kingdom are greater than John, that is, in terms of privilege. What a comment on the privilege of being a Christian!

Has been forcefully advancing (v. 12). Another possible translation is, "The kingdom of heaven suffers violence, and violent men take it by force" (NASB), that is, the kingdom of heaven is considered a prize worth fighting for—a share in the heavenly kingdom pursued with ardent interest and passion. Jesus compares "this generation" to children who play the flute and want people to dance—but the people refuse. Then they sing a dirge, but the people refuse to mourn.

In other words, "this generation"—unbelievers—wanted God's messengers, John and Jesus, to behave in certain mutually exclusive ways. It is a double bind: John came "neither eating nor drinking," and the unbelievers say, "We wanted you to celebrate." Jesus came eating and drinking, and they say, "We wanted you to mourn."

Both Jesus and John refused to do what "this generation" wanted or expected them to do. John's actions and Jesus' actions were condemned because they did not fit the preconceived notions and expectations of the unbelieving Jews.

Matt. 11:20–24 | THE MIGHTY WORKS OF JESUS

Three cities at the north end of the Sea of Galilee are named as the main locations of Jesus' miracles (see map on p. 498). Capernaum (see p. 568), Bethsaida (see p. 625), and Korazin (or Chorazin; see below) were the most favored of all cities on earth. Jesus' pronouncement of their doom shows that Jesus considered His miracles to be proof that He was sent by God—proof that one ignored at one's peril.

Korazin. Jesus warned cities like Korazin, which saw His miracles but failed to turn to God.

Matt. 11:25–30 COME UNTO ME

The kindest words ever heard. Jesus seemed glad that it was the simple, common people who received Him. Paul said the same thing (see 1 Corinthians 1:26). It seems hard for intellectuals to humble themselves enough to acknowledge their need of a Savior. Mental pride is a great stumbling block.

Matt. 12:1–8 EATING ON THE SABBATH
(See on Mark 2:23–27.)

Matt. 12:9–14 HEALING ON THE SABBATH
(See on Mark 3:1–6.)

Matt. 12:15–21 MANY MIRACLES

Mark 3:7–12 states that the crowds came not only from Galilee but also from Judea, Jerusalem, and Idumea, from beyond the Jordan, and from the region of Tyre and Sidon. Thus, in days when travel was by foot, large numbers of people who had heard of His miracles came from 100 miles around, from the north, south, and east, bringing their sick, and Jesus healed them all (v. 15).

Korazin

Two miles to the northwest of Capernaum are the remains of the city of Korazin. Although it is only mentioned as being cursed by Jesus because of its failure to repent, it is implied that Jesus had visited the place, for miracles had been performed there (Matthew 11:20–24). The city is located in a basalt region, and all of the buildings were made out of the hard black rock. Excavations at Korazin have not yielded many finds from the time of Jesus, for many of the preserved remains were built in the 2nd to 4th centuries A.D. or later, including the black basalt synagogue.

Matt. 12:22–23 | A BLIND AND DUMB DEMONIAC HEALED

(Told also in Luke 11:14–15.) This was a great miracle. The people, who by now had become accustomed to miracles, were amazed.

Son of David (v. 23) was the commonly accepted title of the expected Messiah (Matthew 1:1; 9:27; 15:22; 20:30; 21:9; 22:42; John 7:42).

Matt. 12:24–37 | THE UNPARDONABLE SIN

(Told also in Mark 3:22–30; Luke 11:14–26; 12:8–10.) Note that the Pharisees, as heartily as they hated Jesus, did not deny His miracles, which were too numerous and too well known to deny. Although the miracles were all miracles of help and healing, the Pharisees attributed them to satanic origin. They had a simple choice—either they accepted the miracles as from God, in which case they had to accept Jesus, or the miracles had to be done in the power of Satan, since they were clearly superhuman in origin. Ironically, it was their own accusations rather than Jesus' miracles that were Satan-inspired. Their choice put them almost beyond redemption.

In Luke 12:10 the unpardonable sin is connected with the denial of Christ. Jesus seems to make a distinction between sin against Himself and sin against the Holy Spirit (v. 32). The unpardonable sin is often understood to mean that rejecting Christ, while He was on earth and His work was as yet unfinished, and when even His disciples did not understand Him, was forgivable. But after His work was completed and the Holy Spirit had come, then the deliberate, final rejection of the Holy Spirit's offer of Christ would constitute the eternal sin for which there is no forgiveness ever. Similar sin is spoken of in Hebrews 6:6; 10:26; and 1 John 5:16. (See notes on those passages.) Yet it is not always the vocal opponents of Christ who commit the unforgivable sin. Paul was as vocal and active against Christ as anyone, yet Jesus called him personally to be His apostle (see on Acts 9). The deliberate, final rejection of the Holy Spirit's offer of Christ is more likely to result in a total indifference rather than a vocal opposition to Christ.

Careless words (v. 36) are here mentioned in connection with the unpardonable sin. Our words show our character (v. 34). Our every word, as well as every secret act, is being recorded as evidence for the Day of Judgment.

Matt. 12:38–45 | THE SIGN OF JONAH

(Told also in Luke 11:29–32.) It was brazen impudence to ask Jesus for a sign just after they had been accusing Him of working signs by the aid of Beelzebub. Jesus promised them a sign even more astounding, which He called the sign of Jonah—His own resurrection from the dead, the greatest sign of all the ages.

The **homeless demon** (vv. 43–45). (See on Mark 5:1–20.)

Parables

The kingdom Jesus intended to establish was utterly different from what was commonly expected of the Messiah. The kingdom of God is grasped with the heart and the spirit. This is why Jesus used *stories* about ordinary, everyday events to illustrate the origin, development, present-day character, and future consummation of the kingdom. Stories can get truths across in a way logical explanations cannot. Understanding the meaning of the parables required a receptive heart rather than a logical mind — which is why the parables in fact *obscured* Jesus' message for those whose heart was unwilling to listen.

In interpreting the parables, the problem is to know which elements are significant and what are merely details included to make the story vivid and memorable. Ordinarily a parable was meant to show *one* point; we should not try to draw lessons from every detail of the story.

The number of Jesus' parables is variously put at anywhere from 27 to 50, since what some call parables others call metaphors. Most people agree that Jesus told about 30 parables. Some of them are quite similar. Jesus used different stories to illustrate the same point — and sometimes the same story to illustrate different points.

Matt. 12:46–50 | JESUS' MOTHER AND BROTHERS

(Told also in Mark 3:31–35 and Luke 8:19–21.) Jesus' reply teaches that spiritual ties are stronger than natural ties and implies that His mother was no closer to Him than anyone else who does the will of God.

Parables of the Kingdom, Matthew 13:1–53

Matt. 13:1–23 | THE PARABLE OF THE SOWER

Between Capernaum and Tabgha there is a small bay on the seashore in the shape of a natural theater that may have been the spot where Jesus "got into a boat and sat in it, while all the people stood on the shore. Then he told them many things in parables, saying . . ." (vv. 2–3).

(This parable is told also in Mark 4:1–25; Luke 8:4–16.) The seed is God's Word (Luke 8:11). Souls are born of God's Word (1-Peter 1:23). This parable is a prophecy of the Gospel's reception. Some people will not even listen. Some will accept it but soon fall away. Some will hold on longer but gradually lose interest. And some will hold on in varying degrees until their lives show in practice what the Gospel is all about.

Matt. 13:24–30; 36–43; 47–53 | THE PARABLES OF THE WEEDS AND THE NET

Two illustrations, with slightly different shades of emphasis, show that, even though the world shall be permeated by the Gospel, the bad shall persist along with the good until the end of the world, when there will be a final separation—the wicked will go to their unhappy destiny, the righteous into the kingdom of eternal glory. Jesus had no illusions about this world becoming a Utopia. He knew full well that until the end, His

Gospel would be rejected by a large part of the world. He recognized only two classes of people, the saved and the lost. Again and again He spoke of the miseries of the lost, their weeping and gnashing of teeth. He surely knew what He was talking about.

Matt. 13:31–33 | THE PARABLES OF THE MUSTARD SEED AND THE LEAVEN

(Told also in Mark 4:30–32; Luke 13:18–20.) Two similar parables, illustrating the small beginnings of Christ's kingdom, its gradual and imperceptible growth, both in the individual and in the world at large, and its final, majestic presence that will permeate all institutions, philosophies, and governments.

Matt. 13:44–46 | THE PARABLES OF THE HIDDEN TREASURE AND THE PEARL

A double illustration of the same thing: the priceless value of Christ to the human soul. What Christ offers is worth giving up everything for—even life itself.

Matt. 13:54–58 | VISIT TO NAZARETH *(See on Mark 6:1–6.)*

Matt. 14:1–12 | JOHN BEHEADED *(See on Luke 3:1–20.)*

Matt. 14:13–21 | THE 5000 FED *(See on John 6:1–15.)*

Matt. 14:22–33 | JESUS WALKS ON WATER
(See on John 6:16–21.)

Period from the Feeding of the 5000 to the Transfiguration, Matthew 14:34 to 16:12

Matt. 14:34–36 | CROWDS IN GENNESARET
(See on Mark 6:53.)

Matt. 15:1–20 | CLEAN AND UNCLEAN *(See on Mark 7:1–23.)*

Matt. 15:21–28 | THE CANAANITE WOMAN
(See on Mark 7:24–30.)

Matt. 15:29–39 | THE 4000 FED *(See on Mark 8:1–9.)*

The Kingdom

The word "kingdom" occurs more than 40 times in Matthew; it is found in every chapter except the first two and chapters 14, 15, and 17.

A political kingdom, in which the Jewish nation, under their Messiah, would rule the world, is what the people were expecting.

- Herod shared that notion and tried to destroy Jesus in childhood, because he thought that Messiah's kingdom would be a rival political kingdom that would pose a threat to his own.
- John the Baptist shared that notion, and when Jesus gave no indication of being that kind of king, John began to doubt whether Jesus was the Messiah after all (Matthew 11:3).
- The 12 apostles shared the notion until after Jesus' resurrection. The last question they asked Jesus was, "Lord, will you now restore the kingdom to Israel?" (Acts 1:6). Their minds were on political independence for their country rather than on personal eternal salvation.

What was the kingdom that Jesus came to found? Not a political kingdom, but God's reign in the hearts of people that will control and transform their lives. The human heart is the realm in which Jesus came to reign. He came for all mankind to love Him, so that He can change us into His own image. Out of an affection for Him, devotion to Him, and adoration of Him will grow all the beauty and comfort of life, the transformation of character, the regeneration of the soul.

The word "kingdom," as used in the New Testament, has a range of meanings. The basic idea of the word implies Jesus' dominion in the hearts of His people through all dispensations, onward into eternity. But sometimes it refers more specifically to one of the various aspects or stages of that dominion: sometimes it seems to mean the reign of God in the individual; sometimes, the general reign of righteousness among men; sometimes, the church; sometimes, Christendom; sometimes, the millennial reign; and sometimes, heaven.

Matt. 16:1–12 | **THE LEAVEN OF THE PHARISEES** *(See on Mark 8:10–21.)*

Matt. 16:13–20 | **PETER'S CONFESSION**

(Told also in Mark 8:27–29 and Luke 9:18–20.) It had been some three years since Peter had first accepted Jesus as the Messiah (John 1:41–42). A year later he had called Him Lord (Luke 5:8). Half a year after that he called Him the Holy One of God (John 6:68–69). Now, after two and a half years of traveling with Jesus, he expresses his conviction that Jesus is the Son of the living God.

On this rock (v. 18). The rock on which Christ would build His church is not Peter, but the truth to which Peter confessed, that Jesus is the Son of God. The deity of Jesus is the foundation on which the church

Caesarea Philippi

Situated in the northernmost part of Israel, at one of the headwaters of the Jordan River at the foot of Mount Hermon, 50 miles southwest of Damascus, was the city known in New Testament times as Caesarea Philippi — so called to distinguish it from the huge port city of Caesarea (also known as Caesarea Maritima), located on the shore of the Mediterranean Sea.

Built by Herod the Great and especially by his descendants, a huge pleasure palace has been discovered, as have sanctuaries dedicated to Caesar, Pan, Echo, goat deities, and others. The site is situated at the foot of a huge rock cliff, and it was here, in this area, that Peter confessed that Jesus is "the Christ, the Son of the living God" and where Jesus responded "and I tell you that you are Peter, and on this rock I will build my church."

Jesus and the disciples were looking at the rocky escarpment and cave which the Romans believed to be the entrance into Hades, when Jesus stated, "And I tell you that you are Peter [rock], and on this rock I will build my church, and the gates of Hades will not overcome it." (Matt 16:18)

rests, the fundamental creed of Christendom. This is the unmistakable meaning of the language.

The keys of the kingdom (v. 19). The ordinary interpretation of this verse is that Peter opened the door of salvation, on the Day of Pentecost, to the Jews (Acts 2) and later to the Gentiles (Acts 10). He was not given the power to forgive sins but to proclaim the terms of forgiveness. Whatever authority it gave to Peter was also given to the other apostles (Matthew 18:18; John 20:23) — and only in the sense that they could declare Christ's forgiveness.

Matt. 16:21–28 | PASSION FORETOLD *(See on Mark 9:30–32.)*

Matt. 17:1–13 | JESUS IS TRANSFIGURED *(See on Mark 9:2–13.)*

Matt. 17:14–20 | THE EPILEPTIC BOY *(See on Mark 9:14–29.)*

Matt. 17:22–23 | THE PASSION AGAIN FORETOLD
(See on Mark 9:30–32.)

Matt. 17:24–27 | THE TAX MONEY

This was a sort of poll tax for the sanctuary, required of every male over 20 (Exodus 30:11–15). A drachma was about a day's wages. Jesus, as Lord of the sanctuary, was exempt; yet He paid it, lest His attitude toward the temple be misunderstood.

Matt. 18:1–6 | WHO IS THE GREATEST? *(See on Luke 9:46–48.)*

Matt. 18:7–14 | OCCASIONS OF STUMBLING
(See Mark 9:41–50.)

FORGIVENESS

A talent (v. 24) was equal to 6000 drachmas (the Greek name) or denarii (the Roman name). Since the drachma was equal to about a day's wages, it would take an average laborer almost 20 years to earn one talent. Ten thousand talents was thus equal to the lifetime earnings of the population of several good-sized villages. The man was forgiven 60 million drachmas but was unwilling to forgive 100. That is how Jesus compares our own sins against God with the sins others commit against us. Notice Jesus' statement that there is no hope of forgiveness *unless* we forgive (v. 35).

The Perean Ministry, Matthew 19 and 20

Matt. 19:1–2 | **DEPARTURE FROM GALILEE** *(See on Luke 9:51.)*

Matt. 19:3–12 | **QUESTION ABOUT DIVORCE**

Jesus' teaching about divorce is recorded also in Matthew 5:31; Mark 10:2–12; and Luke 16:18. Paul discusses the subject in 1 Corinthians 7. One man and one woman married for life is God's will for the human race. Christ seems to allow only one cause for divorce (v. 9).

Matt. 19:13–15 | **LITTLE CHILDREN** *(See on Luke 18:15–17.)*

Matt. 19:16–30 | **THE RICH YOUNG RULER**
(See on Luke 18:18–30.)

Matt. 20:1–16 | **THE PARABLE OF THE WORKERS IN THE VINEYARD**

This parable does not teach that all will be treated alike in heaven, or that there will be no rewards. The parable of the talents (Matthew 25:14–30) seems to teach that there will be rewards, which Paul taught as well (1 Corinthians 3:14–15).

Jesus here meant to teach just one thing: that some who think they are first in this world are going to find themselves last in heaven. He

Perea

A region/district located to the south of the Sea of Galilee, but east of the Jordan River. According to Josephus (*War* 3.3.3 [46]), it was bounded on the north by Pella and stretched to the south of Machaerus, where Josephus says John the Baptist was beheaded. On the west the Jordan River was its boundary, and on the east it approached, but did not include, the Decapolis city of Philadelphia. The region was settled by Jews. Its capital was Gadora, and other prominent cities or forts included Ammathus, Abila, Beth-ramatha (Livias/Julias), Callirrhoe, and Machaerus. Herod Antipas was granted this territory after the death of his father and controlled both it and Galilee. Perea, Galilee, and Judea are called "the three Jewish provinces" in the Mishnah (a compilation of Jewish oral tradition, ca. A.D. 200).

said that a number of times (Matthew 19:30; 20:16; Mark 10:31; Luke 13:30). Heavenly standards and earthly standards are so utterly different that many of earth's humblest Christians, slaves and servants, will have the highest places in heaven, while many of the powerful and the great church dignitaries, if there at all, will be under those who were their servants here. (See further on Luke 16:19–31.)

Matt. 20:17–19   THE PASSION AGAIN FORETOLD
(See on Mark 9:30–32.)

Matt. 20:20–28   THE REQUEST OF JAMES AND JOHN

The pity of this request for prestige and power is that it was their reaction to Jesus' announcement that He was on His way to the cross. (See on Luke 9:46–48.) Jesus' reply reminded them of one of the central themes of His ministry — that the key to heavenly reward is the degree of our earthly service and love for others.

Matt. 20:29–34   THE BLIND MAN AT JERICHO
(See on Luke 18:35–43.)

Jesus' Last Week, Matthew 21 to 28

Matt. 21:1–11   THE TRIUMPHAL ENTRY

(Told also in Mark 11:1–10; Luke 19:29–38; John 12:12–19.) It was on the Sunday before His death. Jesus had come as the long-foretold Messiah. For three years He had proclaimed Himself to the nation by unceasing travel and miracles and through the journeys and miracles of the Twelve (see pp. 543–44) and of the Seventy-two (see p. 602). He knew that His death had been decided on by the rulers. He was ready for it. In a grand public demonstration that gave final notice to the Holy City, He entered amid the hallelujahs and hosannas of the expectant crowds. The people were jubilant. They thought the hour of deliverance was at hand. Jesus rode on a colt, because it was foretold that Messiah would come that way (Zechariah 9:9).

Matt. 21:12–17   JESUS CLEARS THE TEMPLE AREA

(Told also in Mark 11:15–18; Luke 19:45–47.) This was Monday. He had done the same thing three years before, at the beginning of His public ministry (see John 2:13–22). The enormous profits from the market stalls inside the temple area went in part to enrich the family of the high priest. Jesus burned with indignation at such a perversion of the uses of God's house.

A watchtower in Samaria, perhaps like the one mentioned in the parable of the vineyard.

Matt. 21:18–22 | JESUS AND THE FIG TREE

(Told also in Mark 11:12–14; 20–24.) This was Monday morning, as Jesus walked the two miles from Bethany, over the Mount of Olives, into Jerusalem. The disciples noticed it the next morning, as they came into the city. Evidently they had gone to Bethany Monday evening along the road around the foot of the Mount of Olives rather than *over* the Mount of Olives.

Matt. 21:23–27 | BY WHAT AUTHORITY?

(Told also in Mark 11:27–33; Luke 20:1–8.) The rulers were bitter, and they made every conceivable effort to trap Jesus. But He was a master debater, and He turned every question around so that they ended up embarrassing themselves.

Matt. 21:28–32 | THE PARABLE OF THE TWO SONS

This parable is aimed directly at religious leaders: chief priests, elders, scribes, and Pharisees. (For the meaning of these terms, see pp. 481–86.) They rejected Jesus. But the common people, whom the religious leaders considered sinful and unworthy of God's favor, accepted God's welcoming forgiveness and grace joyfully.

Matt. 21:33–46 | THE PARABLE OF THE VINEYARD

(Told also in Mark 12:1–12 and Luke 20:9–19.) The parable of the two sons was aimed primarily at the leaders of the Jewish nation. This parable is aimed at the nation itself.

Matt. 22:1–14 | THE PARABLE OF THE MARRIAGE FEAST

Another illustration of the same point: God's elect nation, the Jews, was now to be cast off for its shameful treatment of God's messengers, and other nations were being called in. This is a parable with a double message: it also includes a warning for the newcomers to be careful, lest they meet the same fate.

| Matt. 22:15–22 | **PAYING TAXES TO CAESAR** *(See on Mark 12:13–17.)*

| Matt. 22:23–33 | **THE RESURRECTION** *(See on Mark 12:18–27.)*

| Matt. 22:34–40 | **THE GREAT COMMANDMENT** *(See on Mark 12:28–34.)*

| Matt. 22:41–46 | **THE SON OF DAVID** *(See on Mark 12:35–37.)*

| Matt. 23 | **WOE TO THE TEACHERS OF THE LAW AND THE PHARISEES**

For the teachers of the Law and the Pharisees, see pp. 481, 484.

Great Discourse on the End, Matthew 24 and 25

(Told also in Mark 13 and Luke 21.) This discourse was delivered after Jesus had left the temple for the last time. It was about the destruction of Jerusalem, His coming, and the end of the world. Some of His words seem so mixed up that it is difficult to know to which event they refer. Perhaps it was intentional.

It seems plain that Jesus had in mind two distinct events, separated by an interval of time, indicated by "these" in 24:34 and "that day" in 24:36. Some would explain "this generation" (24:34) to mean "this nation," that is, the Jewish race shall not pass away until the Lord comes. The more common view is that He meant that Jerusalem would be destroyed within the lifetime of those then living.

The traditional cave on the Mount of Olives where Jesus discussed His second coming with the disciples.

When we look at two distant mountain peaks, one behind the other, they seem close together, though they may be far apart. So in Jesus' perspective these two events, the one in some respects typical of the other, stood in close proximity, although there is a long interval between them. What He said in a sentence may refer to an age, and what happened in the one event may be the beginning of the fulfillment of what will happen in the other.

His words concerning Jerusalem were fulfilled, literally, in less than 40 years. The magnificent buildings of marble and gold were so completely demolished by the Roman army in A.D. 70 that Josephus said it looked as if its site had never been inhabited. (See further on Hebrews 13.)

Matt. 24:45–51 | **FAITHFUL AND WISE SERVANTS**

From here on, Jesus' discourse is an exhortation to watchfulness. His second coming was uppermost in His thoughts. So it should be in ours.

Matt. 25:1–13 | THE PARABLE OF THE 10 VIRGINS

This parable means just one thing: that we should keep our minds on the Lord and be ready when He comes.

Matt. 25:14–30 | THE PARABLE OF THE TALENTS

This means that we are in training for a larger service in a realm yet to be, and that our place and standing there will depend on the faithfulness of our stewardship here.

Matt. 25:31–46 | THE FINAL JUDGMENT SCENE

One of the most magnificent passages in the Bible, a picture of how the degree of our love for God's people will affect our standing in the eternal world.

There are two common interpretations of this judgment. The first is that the judgment will occur at the beginning of Christ's earthly millennial kingdom (vv. 31, 34; Revelation 20). The purpose of the judgment will be to determine who will be allowed to enter the kingdom (v. 34) based on how they have treated the Jewish people ("these brothers of mine") during the tribulation period (vv. 35–40, 42–45). The second interpretation suggests that the judgment refers to that which takes place at the great white throne at the end of the millennial kingdom (Revelation 20:11–15). The purpose of this judgment is to determine who will enter eternal salvation in heaven and who will be consigned to eternal punishment in hell (vv. 34, 46).

Matt. 26:1–5 | THE PLOT TO KILL JESUS *(See on Mark 14:1–2.)*

Matt. 26:6–13 | THE ANOINTING AT BETHANY
(See on Mark 14:3–9.)

Matt. 26:14–16 | JUDAS AGREES TO BETRAY JESUS

(See on Mark 14:10–11.)

Matt. 26:17–29 | THE LAST SUPPER

(Told also in Mark 14:12–25; Luke 22:7–38; John 13–14.) This was the night before Jesus' death. There were two suppers: the Passover supper and the Lord's Supper. The Lord's Supper was instituted at the close of the Passover supper. Luke mentions two cups (22:17–20). Matthew, Mark, and Luke mention both suppers; John mentions only the Passover.

For 14 centuries the Passover had been pointing forward to the coming of Jesus, the Passover Lamb. Jesus ate the Passover, replaced it with His own supper, and then was Himself slain as the Passover Lamb. Jesus died on the cross on the very day on which the Passover lambs were being killed in the temple.

The Passover had served its purpose and had now made way for the new memorial Supper that was to be kept in loving remembrance of Jesus until He comes again (1-Corinthians 11:23–26).

As the Passover pointed back to Israel's deliverance from Egypt and forward to Jesus' coming in grace, so this memorial points back to His death and forward to His coming in glory.

Matt. 26:30–46 | THE AGONY IN GETHSEMANE

(See on Luke 22:39–46.)

Matt. 26:47–56 | BETRAYAL AND ARREST

(See on John 18:1–12.)

Matt. 26:57–68 | BEFORE THE HIGH PRIEST *(See on Mark 14:53.)*

Matt. 26:69–75 | PETER'S DENIAL *(See on John 18:15–27.)*

Matt. 27:1–2 | THE OFFICIAL VERDICT *(See on Mark 14:53.)*

Matt. 27:3–10 | JUDAS'S SUICIDE *(See on Mark 14:10–11.)*

Matt. 27:11–25 | THE TRIAL BEFORE PILATE

(For a note on the successive steps in the trial of Jesus, see p. 500.)

"Let his blood be on us and on our children" (v. 25). How fearfully this has been fulfilled!

Matt. 27:26 | JESUS IS FLOGGED

Flogging usually preceded capital punishment. In this case Pilate seems to have hoped that the crowd would consider it sufficient punishment. Flogging was done with a whip made of a number of leather strips weighted with pieces of lead or sharp metal. The victim was stripped to the waist, then bound to a post in a bent-over position and beaten on the bare back with the whip until the flesh was torn open. Sometimes death resulted.

Matt. 27:27–31 | JESUS IS MOCKED

The Jews, in their trial, had mocked him (Luke 22:63–65). Herod and his soldiers had mocked him (Luke 23:11). Now Pilate's soldiers mock him. And a little later, on the cross, priests, elders, and teachers of the Law mock him (27:29–43). To their brutal minds it was great sport to see one who claimed to be the Son of God having to submit to such humiliation and torture.

Matt. 27:32 | SIMON OF CYRENE

In John 19:17 it is said that Jesus went out bearing His own cross. Exhausted by His night of agony and the scourging, He had not gone far when He became too weak to carry it further. Then Simon was pressed

---

Pilate

Pontius Pilate was the Roman governor of Judea from A.D. 26 to 37. He assumed office about the time that Jesus began His public ministry. His official residence was at Caesarea (see pp. 683–85). He came to Jerusalem during major feast days to keep order. He was merciless and cruel, noted for his habitual brutality. Like the Roman emperors of his day, he rather enjoyed the spectacle of the torture and death of a man. At one time he had mingled the blood of Galileans with their sacrifices—that is, he had them killed while they were bringing sacrifices (Luke 13:1).

Remarkably, in 1961 a stone was found in the theater of Caesarea with a partial inscription that includes the words "[Pon]tius Pilatus." It was originally part of a building built in honor of or dedicated to Emperor Tiberius but had been reused in the construction of a landing between two flights of stairs in the theater. This is the first archaeological evidence pertaining to Pilate.

One of the strangest pictures in history is the impression that Jesus made on this hard-hearted Roman governor. Whether Jesus was erect and handsome, as one tradition has it, or stoop-shouldered and ugly, as another tradition says, there must have been something so commanding about His presence that although He was dressed in the robes of mock royalty, with the crown of thorns on His head and the blood streaming down His face, Pilate could not keep his eyes off Him.

Pilate's efforts to avoid having to crucify Jesus make a pitiful story. He did not want to do it. He appealed first to the Jewish rulers, then to Herod. And then again to the Jewish rulers. And then to the crowd. And when the crowd turned against Jesus, Pilate tried to appeal to their pity by having Jesus whipped, in hope that they would be satisfied with this limited punishment and not require Him to go all the way to crucifixion. Pilate's wife warned him to have nothing to do with this innocent man, based on a dream she had earlier that day.

When all of Pilate's attempts failed, he did not make up his mind to crucify Jesus until the Jews threatened to report him to Caesar. Not until it began to look as if it might cost him his position as governor of Judea did Pilate finally give his consent to the death of Jesus. Pilate is said to have committed suicide. Tradition says that Pilate's wife, Procula, became a Christian.

---

into service. Little is known of Simon. He was probably a Jew who was celebrating the Passover in Jerusalem. Cyrene was an important city in North Africa (in modern Libya) that had a large Jewish population; today all that is left of the city is a small settlement.

Kochim tombs. The body of Jesus was placed on the bench in front of the niches (*kochim*). The women planned to complete the burial preparation before His body would be placed in the niche.

Matt. 27:33–56 | JESUS IS CRUCIFIED

(See also on Mark 15:21–41; Luke 23:32–43; and John 19:17–30.)

The darkness. For three hours (v. 45), inanimate nature hid her face in shame at the unspeakable wickedness of men. God may have meant the darkness to be creation's symbolic mourning for Jesus while He was suffering the pains of the lost on our behalf.

The earthquake. The earthquake, the splitting rocks, and the opening of the tombs (vv. 51–55) were God's salute to the conquering Savior. The tearing of the curtain in the temple (v. 51) was God's own proclamation that in the death of Christ the barrier between God and man disappeared (Hebrews 9:1–14; 10:14–22). The risen saints (vv. 52–53) were God's evidence and guarantee that the power of death had been broken. Only Matthew's Gospel mentions this resurrection of saints. Note that even the centurion, the officer of the Roman soldiers who crucified Jesus, was convinced that Jesus was indeed the Son of God (v. 54).

ARCHAEOLOGICAL NOTE: Crucifixion Ossuary. From the literary sources it is evident that crucifixion was practiced by the Romans in Palestine, but now there is also archaeological confirmation. In a tomb from the 1st century A.D., discovered in the north Jerusalem neighborhood of Giv'at MaHivtar, the calcified heel bone of a man in his late twenties was discovered in an ossuary (see "Caiaphas Ossuary" on p. 582). A seven-inch iron nail was still embedded in his heal bone. He had been crucified! We even know his name: "Yehohanan, son of Hagakol."

Matt. 27:57–61 | THE BURIAL (See on John 19:38–42.)

The Third Day

"The third day" (v. 64) is here used as being identical with "after three days" (v. 63). In Hebrew usage, parts of days at the beginning and end of a period were counted as days (Esther 4:16; 5:1). "Three days and three nights" (Matthew 12:40; cf. 1 Samuel 30:12–13), "after three days" (Mark 8:31; 10:34; John 2:19), and "the third day" (Matthew 16:21; 17:23; 20:19; Luke 9:22; 24:7, 21, 46) are interchangeable phrases for the period Jesus was in the tomb, from Friday afternoon until Sunday morning.

Two locations lay claim to being the place where Jesus was crucified, buried, and resurrected. The first, the place where today the Church of the Holy Sepulchre stands, is the traditional (and more likely) one. The other one, less likely though in many ways more appealing, was discovered by General Charles George Gordon in 1882. He noticed a skull-like rock formation outside the walls of Jerusalem (top), as well as a nearby tomb, today known as the Garden Tomb (middle). Inside is a burial chamber with two burial places, one of which is unfinished (bottom).

Matt. 27:62–66 THE TOMB IS SEALED

(See on Matthew 28:11–15.)

Matt. 28:1–8 | THE WOMEN VISIT THE TOMB

This is told in all four Gospels (Mark 16:1–8; Luke 24:1–11; John 20:1–3). Mary Magdalene is named in all four; Mary, the mother of James and Joses, who is also called "the other Mary," is mentioned in Matthew, Mark, and Luke; Salome, the mother of James and John, in Mark; Joanna, the wife of Herod's steward, in Luke. Luke also mentions "other women." In all, there were half a dozen or possibly a dozen or more women. They had spices to complete the embalming of Jesus' body for permanent burial, with no thought whatever that He would rise.

The women arrived as it began to dawn (Matthew); very early, when the sun was risen (Mark); at early dawn (Luke); while it was yet dark (John). All these statements taken together evidently mean that they started while it was still dark and reached the tomb about sunrise. Some of their homes or the places where they stayed in Bethany or in Jerusalem were probably several miles from the tomb.

They saw an angel sitting on the stone (Matthew); a young man sitting in the tomb (Mark); two men who stood by them (Luke); two angels sitting in the tomb (John). These different expressions simply mean that the angels, in human form, were waiting outside the tomb to greet the women, then led them inside and explained that Jesus had risen. Part of the time two were visible, and part of the time only one. Probably there were myriad angels hovering over the tomb that morning, waiting to welcome the risen Savior, for it was a triumphant moment in the annals of heaven. Angels will have charge of the general resurrection (Matthew 24:31).

A great earthquake (v. 2). There had also been an earthquake when Jesus died on the cross (Matthew 27:51), and also many centuries before, at the giving of the Law on Mount. Sinai (Exodus 19:16, 18). It is one of God's ways of calling attention to momentous events.

Matt. 28:9–10 | JESUS APPEARS TO THE WOMEN

We gather from the Gospel records that between vv. 8 and 9 the women had told the disciples and were returning again to the tomb. In the meantime, Peter and John had run to the tomb and left again. Mary Magdalene, ahead of the others, was at the tomb alone, and Jesus appeared to her. A little later He appeared also to the other women. (See p. 502 for the order of events.) Thus, Jesus' first two appearances were to women.

Through woman, without the aid of man, came the Savior, and now to women first comes the glorious news of His resurrection.

Matt. 28:11–15 | THE GUARDS ARE BRIBED

The Roman soldiers had been put at the tomb at the request of the Sanhedrin, as a precaution against the possibility of Jesus' body being stolen. Terrified at the earthquake, the angel, and the absence of Jesus' body from the tomb, they fled to report to the Sanhedrin. The Sanhedrin bribed them to say that they had fallen asleep. Falling asleep while on duty could have meant summary execution for them; this is why the priests reassure the guards that they will set things right with the governor if Pilate should get wind of it. This inside knowledge of what took place at the tomb no doubt had something to do with the conversion of a large number of priests a little later (Acts 6:7).

Matt. 28:16–20 | JESUS APPEARS TO THE ELEVEN

Jesus appeared to the Eleven on a mountain in Galilee, where Jesus had told them to go (26:32; 28:7; this may have been the time when more than 500 were present; 1-Corinthians 15:6). The Great Commission (v. 20) is recorded, in substance, four times (see on Mark 16:14–18).

(For an overview of Jesus' appearances after His resurrection, see p. 542.)

Surely I am with you always (v. 20). This is our favorite verse in all the Bible. Jesus rose, nevermore to die. He is *alive* now and is with His people, with His guiding and protecting power, all the time.

Views of the model of Jerusalem in the time of Christ, displayed at the Holyland Hotel in Jerusalem.

The temple built by Herod, seen from the east, with East Gate in the foreground (top).

The temple platform had colonnades on all four sides. The moneychangers and vendors probably had their tables set up under these. This is the largest, the Royal Stoa at the south end (bottom).

He is not merely the Commander-in-Chief of some vast organization of angels and archangels. He is that. But He is more: the Commander-in-Chief of heaven's armies is personally interested in, and personally with, each one of His people all the time.

We cannot understand how one Person can be with millions and billions of persons at the same time. Yet Jesus said it in the plainest possible language: "I am with you all the time." Jesus said that, and He did not use idle words. He did not talk just to hear Himself talk. He meant something when He said it, and we believe that, in some real sense beyond our comprehension, mystic but real, He is with each one of us all the time.

No matter how weak, or humble, or unimportant we may be, Jesus is our friend, our companion. Invisible, but there. Now. Tonight while we are asleep. Tomorrow while we are at work. Next week. Next year. Walking by our side and watching with interest every detail of life's pitiful struggle, trying so patiently to lead us up to a place of immortal happiness in His Father's home. This all seems like just a beautiful dream. But it is the one fundamental fact of our existence.

Antonia Fortress, attached to the northwest corner of the temple platform (top).

View from the west (bottom). The four towers of the Antonia Fortress are on the left. Golgotha was approximately in the center of the picture, where today the Church of the Holy Sepulchre stands.

Approaching Jerusalem from the west. The section of wall just right of center is the Western Wall, or Wailing Wall. The Dome of the Rock is approximately where the temple was located. Beyond the temple platform are the Kidron Valley and the Mount of Olives. Just outside the corner of the temple platform on the far left once stood the Antonia Fortress.

Mark

Jesus the Wonderful

"If anyone would come after me, he must deny himself and take up his cross and follow me. For whoever wants to save his life will lose it, but whoever loses his life for me and for the gospel will save it. What good is it for a man to gain the whole world, yet forfeit his soul? Or what can a man give in exchange for his soul?" —MARK 8:34–37

- For a general introduction to all four Gospels, see p. 517.
- For an overview of the life of Jesus, see p. 493.

Mark's Emphasis: The Superhuman Power of Jesus

The special emphasis of Mark is the superhuman power of Jesus, demonstrating His deity by His miracles. Mark narrates the things Jesus *did* rather than the things Jesus *said*. That is why he omits most of Jesus' discourses. It appears that Mark wrote his Gospel for non-Jews.

Mark

From the beginning, and by unbroken tradition, this Gospel has been regarded as the work of Mark. John Mark was the son of a woman named Mary, whose home in Jerusalem was a meeting place for the disciples of Jesus (Acts 12:12). Since he was a cousin of Barnabas (Colossians 4:10), he may have been a Levite (Acts 4:36). It has been thought that he was the young man who fled naked on the night of Jesus' arrest (Mark 14:51–52). Mark's mother must have been quite an influential leader in the Jerusalem church. It was to her home that Peter went after the angel released him from prison (Acts 12:12).

Around A.D. 44, Mark went with Paul and Barnabas to Antioch (Acts 12:25) and started with them on their first missionary journey, but he soon left them and went back (Acts 13:13).

Later, around A.D. 50, Mark wanted to go with Paul on his second missionary journey, but Paul refused to take him. This caused the separation of Paul and Barnabas (Acts 15:36–39). Mark then went with Barnabas to Cyprus.

Some 12 years later, about A.D. 62, Mark appears in Rome with Paul (Colossians 4:10; Philemon 24), and four or five years after that, Paul is asking for Mark to come to him (2 Timothy 4:11). Thus it seems that Mark in his later years became one of Paul's close co-workers.

Mark and Peter

Mark may have been a convert of Peter (1 Peter 5:13), and early Christian tradition states that Mark was for most of his "career" a companion of Peter. He was with Peter in Babylon (Rome? See p. 798) when Peter wrote his first epistle (1 Peter 5:13). Mark's Gospel is believed to contain essentially the story of Jesus as told by Peter. It is thought to have been written in Rome between A.D. 60 and 70 and before the destruction of Jerusalem in A.D. 70.

Papias (A.D. 70–155) was a student of the apostle John and wrote in his *Explanation of the Lord's Discourses* that he had established the following after careful inquiry: Mark became the interpreter of Peter and wrote down accurately all that he remembered of the words and deeds of Christ. Peter would adapt his instruction to the need of the occasion, but he did not present a connected, chronological account of the Lord's acts and sayings. Thus Mark made no mistake when he wrote down some things as he remembered them. For he had one goal: to omit nothing that he had heard and to make no false statements.

Mark 1:1–8 **PREACHING OF JOHN THE BAPTIST**

This is told in all four Gospels (see note under Luke 3:1–20). Mark starts his book with a quotation from the Old Testament. He skips the story of Jesus' birth and launches at once into the crowded memoirs of Jesus' public life.

Mark 1:9–11 **JESUS IS BAPTIZED** *(See on Matthew 3:13–17.)*

Mark 1:12–13 **JESUS' TEMPTATION** *(See on Matthew 4:1–10.)*

The Galilean Ministry, Mark 1:14 to 10:1

Jesus' Galilean ministry occupies about one-half of Mark.

Mark 1:14–15 **JESUS BEGINS GALILEAN MINISTRY**

Mark skips about a year between vv. 13 and 14, that is, between Jesus' temptation and the beginning of His Galilean ministry. Some of the events of that year are described in John 1:19–4:54:

- The first disciples, after Jesus' baptism by John
- Water turned to wine at Cana
- Cleansing of the temple

Trammel boat used for fishing on the Sea of Galilee. Jesus called James and John to follow Him while they were in similar fishing boats.

- Conversation with Nicodemus
- Preaching in the lower Jordan region for about eight months
- Conversation with the Samaritan woman
- Healing of the son of the royal official from Cana
- Rejection at Nazareth (Luke 4:16–30)

Jesus had been preaching in the lower Jordan region (John 3:22–24; 4:1–3). But growing hostility of Pharisees (John 4:1–3) and Herod's imprisonment of John (Matthew 4:12) made it look dangerous. Having work to do before His death, He thought best to get farther away from Jerusalem.

Mark 1:16–20 | THE CALL OF SIMON, ANDREW, JAMES, JOHN

(Told also in Matthew 4:18–22; Luke 5:1–11.) Two of these men had been disciples of John the Baptist and had come to faith in Jesus a year before, after John baptized Jesus (John 1:35–42). They are now called to become Jesus' disciples and travel companions. (See further under Matthew 10 and Mark 3:13–19.)

Mark 1:21–28 | THE HEALING OF A DEMON-POSSESSED MAN

(Told also in Luke 4:31–37.) This is Jesus' first recorded miracle in Capernaum after making the town His headquarters. Shortly before, He had healed, while in Cana, the son of a royal official in Capernaum, 15 miles distant (John 4:46–54). (For note on demons, see under Mark 5:1–20.)

In this account we see that the evil spirit had the ability to possess the body of a man with the intent of tormenting and destroying him. The demon spoke through the man, recognizing Jesus' divinity and calling Him "Holy One." Jesus commanded the demon to be quiet and to come out of the man. The evil spirit, knowing Jesus' authority over Satan and all demonic spirits, immediately obeyed Jesus' commandment and left the man's body. Jesus would not let the demons speak of His deity. He wanted to demonstrate to the people through His teaching and actions that He was the long-awaited Messiah before declaring Himself the Son of God.

Capernaum: Synagogue and House of Peter

The site of Capernaum, the "home base" of Jesus during His earthly ministry (Matthew 4:13; Mark 2:1), is located on the northwestern shore of the Sea of Galilee. He performed many miracles there (Matthew 8:5 – 13; Mark 2:1 – 13; John 4:46 – 54). Three of the disciples were from Capernaum, and Peter and Andrew had evidently moved there from Bethsaida (Mark 1:29). Fishing was probably the major trade, although it is possible that basalt implements (such as olive presses and grain grinders) were produced there as well. The village sat astride the international trade route that ran from the Mediterranean Sea to Transjordan and Damascus, and it seems that a customs station was located there because of its proximity to the Jordan River and Philip the Tetrarch's territory (Matthew 9:9; Mark 2:14).

In spite of Jesus' remarkable works and teachings, the people did not repent, and He predicted that Capernaum would "go down to the depths" in judgment (Matthew 11:23 – 24; Luke 10:15).

Synagogue: The large, beautiful white limestone synagogue has been known for years and probably dates to the 4th century A.D. In recent years the Franciscan fathers who have excavated below this synagogue have found the black basalt, three-foot-high foundation walls of an even earlier synagogue – probably dating back to the 1st century A.D. This indeed may have been the very synagogue built by the centurion (Luke 7) and the one in which Jesus preached.

House of Peter: In their excavations of a residential area in the village of Capernaum, the Franciscan fathers have found a very special 1st-century building, in which there was a room that was venerated. On the plastered walls of this room were graffiti mentioning the "Lord Jesus Christ," "Christ," and crosses. Evidently Judeo-Christians of the 1st century A.D. venerated this room as the home of Peter, the disciple of Jesus, the place where Jesus must have stayed on many occasions. In the 4th century a church was built over the house, and in the 5th century an octagonal church was built in such a way that the "room" was at the center of the church.

Mark 1:29–31 | PETER'S MOTHER-IN-LAW HEALED

(Told also in Matthew 8:14 – 15; Luke 4:38 – 39.) This means that Peter was married. Jesus' first miracle was indirectly a blessing on marriage: He healed the mother-in-law of His leading apostle.

Mark 1:32–34 | JESUS HEALS MANY

(Told also in Matthew 8:16 – 17; Luke 4:40 – 41.) This was after sunset, because sunset marked the end of the Sabbath. The news about the demon-possessed man and Peter's mother-in-law had spread all over the city, and great crowds, with their sick, gathered around the house. And Jesus healed them. It was His miracles that attracted the crowds. The light of divine compassion for suffering humanity had begun to shine. It was a great day in Capernaum.

Mark 1:35–37 | PRAYING IN SOLITUDE

(Told also in Luke 4:42–43.) It had been a busy day. Jesus had healed many people, perhaps several hundred. He was now in the full swing of His public work. He often slipped away from the crowds, seeking solitude to keep in touch with God. If the Son of God needed solitude and time alone with God, away from the demands of daily life, how much more do we need to break away from the incessant noise and demands of our society to talk with and listen to God! (See note on Jesus' prayer life under Luke 11:1–13.)

Mark 1:38–39 | TRAVEL THROUGHOUT GALILEE

Jesus made many trips, always returning to Capernaum (Matthew 4:23–25; 9:35–38; Luke 4:44). Galilee was crossed by famous international highways on which merchants traveled between Egypt and the Euphrates. One of these highways passed through Capernaum. Later the Romans would pave some of the most important international highways that ran through Palestine, but in Jesus' day all roads were still unpaved and dusty in the summer and in places muddy in the rainy season.

Mark 1:40–45 | A LEPER CLEANSED

(Told also in Matthew 8:2–4; Luke 5:12–16.) The Greek word translated "leprosy" can refer to a number of diseases that affect the skin, including leprosy. Jesus told the leper to show himself to the priest to be officially declared healed, because that was a requirement of the Law (Leviticus 13–14). Jesus also told him not to talk about his being healed, to avoid having the popular movement that wanted to draft Jesus to make Him king get out of control. The point of the miracles was to show God's compassion, not to gain political power. Jesus looked for faith, not fame.

Mark 2:1–12 | A PARALYTIC HEALED

(Told also in Matthew 9:2–8 and Luke 5:18–26.) The paralyzed man was lying on a bed carried by four friends. Their faith in Jesus' power to heal and their determination to get to Him pleased Jesus. Notice that Jesus first met the paralyzed man's spiritual needs, "Son, your sins are forgiven," and then his physical needs by healing him with the words, "I tell you, get up, take your mat and go home."

Jesus' fame had spread so widely that Pharisees and teachers of the Law from Jerusalem and from all over the land (Luke 5:17) had come to investigate. Before their critical, hostile eyes, Jesus boldly asserted His deity by offering to forgive the man's sins—and He worked the miracle, as Jesus Himself said, to prove His deity. It had an amazing effect on the people, but it only further irritated the Pharisees and teachers of the Law, the religious custodians of the nation.

Mark 2:13–17 THE CALL OF LEVI (MATTHEW)

Jesus had recently chosen four fishermen to be His associates in the establishment of His kingdom. Now He adds a tax collector. (For a note on Matthew, see introduction to Matthew.)

Mark 2:18–22 A QUESTION ABOUT FASTING

(Told also in Matthew 9:14–17; Luke 5:33–38.) The question probably came up because of Jesus' participation in Matthew's feast, which greatly surprised John's disciples, the Pharisees, and probably even some of Jesus' own disciples. Feasting was so different from the way John the Baptist had lived. There may be times of crisis when fasting is a proper expression of humility and penitence and religious devotion. Also, there was special significance in it in the case of John the Baptist (see under Luke 3:1–20). But the religionists of Jesus' day greatly overdid it. Jesus did not attach a great deal of importance to fasting as generally practiced (Matthew 6:16–18), although Moses, Elijah, and Jesus Himself each fasted for 40 days (Exodus 34:28; 1 Kings 19:8; Matthew 4:1–2).

But this was in a period of great strain. The three metaphors—the bridegroom, the torn garment, the old wineskins (wine containers made from goat skins)—seem to mean that there are occasions, usually involving sorrow, when fasting is proper, but that it is out of place in most aspects of ordinary life.

In the metaphor of the bridegroom surrounded by guests, Jesus clearly identifies Himself as the bridegroom and His disciples as wedding guests. This analogy refers to Jewish wedding customs, which are always joyous celebrations. The guests at a wedding would never consider fasting during the wedding celebration. This account is one of many in which Jesus foretells to His disciples that there will be a future time when He will be taken away from them, and on that occasion they will be fasting in sorrow.

The second metaphor refers to a new, unshrunk patch being sewn onto an old garment. The likely result will be that the new patch will tear away from the old garment, making the original tear more significant after the garment is washed and the new patch shrinks. Jesus may be suggesting the need for the apostles, representing the new patch, to break away from the old Jewish religious practices, which had become religious traditions and more of an advertisement of one's holiness than true worship of God (Matthew 6:16–18).

The final metaphor, of the new wine poured into new wineskins, refers to the Word of God being taught to new believers. The new believer must become a new creation in Christ and leave the beliefs of the world behind in order to allow for spiritual growth (see note on Matthew 9:17). If new wine is poured into old wineskins, the skins will crack and break as the wine matures and expands.

Mark 2:23–27 | EATING GRAIN ON THE SABBATH

(Told also in Matthew 12:1–8; Luke 6:1–5.) The Old Testament had strict laws about Sabbath observance, but Jewish tradition had added so many restrictions to avoid breaking the Law that the Sabbath almost became a burden rather than a day of spiritual, mental, and physical rest—the people had to work at avoiding work on the Sabbath. Jesus' assertion that He was Lord of the Sabbath was equivalent to a claim of deity.

Mark 3:1–6 | A HEALING ON THE SABBATH

(Told also in Matthew 12:9–14; Luke 6:6–11.) The healing on the Sabbath of the man who had a shriveled hand so irritated the Pharisees and the Herodians (influential Jewish members of the political party that supported King Herod, with whom the Pharisees would normally have nothing to do) that they laid plans to kill Jesus. To these professional religionists, a common deed of kindness on the Sabbath was a terrible crime, let alone this very uncommon deed. There are seven recorded healings by Jesus on the Sabbath (see under John 5).

Mark 3:7–12 | MULTITUDES AND MIRACLES

The crowds that came to Jesus were motivated by two things: to have their sick healed and freed from demons, and the popular expectation that He was the Messiah.

Mark 3:13–19 | THE TWELVE CHOSEN *(See p. 513.)*

Mark 3:20–30 | THE UNPARDONABLE SIN
(See on Matthew 12:24–37.)

The healing of the demoniac occurred on the hills rising above the east shoreline of the Sea of Galilee.

Mark 3:31–35 | JESUS' MOTHER AND BROTHERS

(See on Matthew 12:46–50.)

Mark 4:1–20 | THE PARABLE OF THE SOWER

(See on Matthew 13:1–23.)

Mark 4:21–25 | A LAMP ON A STAND *(See Matthew 5:14–16.)*

Mark 4:26–29 | THE PARABLE OF THE GROWING SEED

It was generally expected that the messianic kingdom would be inaugurated in a display of glory and power that would shake the world. This parable means that it would, instead, be unspectacular: a very small beginning, and slow, long growth, moving quietly, imperceptibly, but irresistibly on to the day of harvest. (See Joel 3:13; Revelation 14:14–20.) It also signifies that the Gospel has a power of its own. Only Mark records this parable.

Mark 4:30–34 | THE MUSTARD SEED

(See on Matthew 13:31–32.)

Mark 4:35–41 | THE STORM STILLED

(Told also in Matthew 8:23–27; Luke 8:22–25.) In this account, Jesus clearly establishes His authority over all creation. The disciples were frightened in the tossing boat, but Jesus was calmly sleeping. How we would love to know the inner processes and powers by which His word stilled the raging waters! What a rebuke to the disciples: Why are you afraid? Where is your faith?

Mark 5:1–20 | THE DEMON-POSSESSED MAN IN THE REGION OF THE GERASENES

(Told also in Matthew 8:28–34; Luke 8:26–37.) The Decapolis was not an area frequently visited by Jesus, for He had said that His mission was primarily to the "lost sheep of Israel" (Matthew 15:24), but on one occasion He healed a demon-possessed man, who, after having been healed, went into the Decapolis to tell of all that Jesus had done for him (Mark 5:20). This event is recorded in all three of the Synoptic Gospels, but Mark and Luke seem to mention only the most prominent of the two men who were healed (Mark 5:2; Luke 8:27; cf. Matthew 8:28).

The demon called himself "Legion" (a legion was a Roman army unit of 6000 men). There were thus many demons in the two men, probably most of them in the more violent one. There were 2000 swine, and probably at least that many demons. They recognized the authority of Jesus immediately.

The Roman theater at Jerash (Gerasa, one of the cities of the Decapolis, some 30 miles north of Amman) shows the stage and the highly decorated wall behind the stage, which at one time reached the same height as the top row of seats. In many Roman theaters, a canvas roof could be extended over the seats (top).

Emperor Hadrian, who made Jerusalem a Roman military colony in A.D. 135 and prohibited Jews from entering the city under penalty of death, erected this triumphal arch in Gerasa (bottom). The Gerasenes asked Jesus to leave their region, but later numerous churches were built here; 13 have been found to date.

Notice that the demons would rather live in swine than be sent into eternal punishment, "into the Abyss" (Luke 8:31). But they soon went there anyway; they could control the men, but not the swine. They did not drive the swine into the sea. Neither the swine nor the demons wanted to go into the sea. The swine got panic-stricken with the demons inside and lost control of themselves on the precipitous hillside. Once on the move, they could not stop.

Notice, too, that the local population wanted Jesus to get out of their country. He had healed their insane neighbors but had, in the process, destroyed their swine. They thought more of their property than they did of their people. Their tribe is still around today!

Jesus had commanded the leper to say nothing about his cure (Matthew 8:4), but He told this man to go out and tell people about his (5:19). The reason for the difference was that in the region east of the Sea of Galilee, Jesus was not as yet widely known, whereas in Galilee His publicity was already out of hand with a grass-roots movement under way to proclaim Him a political king.

Mark 5:21–43 JAIRUS'S DAUGHTER RAISED (*See on Luke 8:40–56.*)

A view from the cave where, according to tradition, the man possessed of a legion of demons lived. The pigs went down the slope to drown in the Sea of Galilee, in the background.

Mark 6:1–6 | A VISIT TO NAZARETH

(Told also in Matthew 13:54–58.) This seems to have been Jesus' second visit to Nazareth after He began His public ministry, about a year after the visit recorded in Luke 4:16–30. Note that Jesus had four brothers as well as sisters (more than one). They did not at that time believe in Him (John 7:5). They did afterward, and according to common opinion, two of them, James and Jude, were authors of the two New Testament letters that bear their names. The other two brothers were Joseph and Simon.

Mark 6:7–13 | THE TWELVE SENT OUT *(See on Matthew 10.)*

Mark 6:14–29 | JOHN BEHEADED *(See on Luke 3:1–20.)*

Mark 6:30–44 | THE 5000 FED *(See on John 6:1–14.)*

Mark 6:45–52 | JESUS WALKS ON THE WATER *(See on John 6:15–21.)*

From the Feeding of the 5000 to the Transfiguration, Mark 6:53 to 8:26

(See also Matthew 14:34–16:12.) This was a period in Jesus' life of probably about eight months, from April to November, of which we have only slight knowledge. It is told only by Matthew and Mark. Luke goes directly from the feeding of the 5000 to the Transfiguration (Luke 9:17–18). John goes immediately from the feeding of the 5000 to Jesus' visit to Jerusalem for the Feast of Tabernacles, six months later (John 6:71; 7:1).

Part of these eight months was spent in the region of Tyre and Sidon (west and northwest of Galilee), Caesarea-Philippi (north of Galilee), and the Decapolis (lit., "Ten Cities," southeast of Galilee), areas with largely gentile populations. Herod was ruler over Galilee. He had recently murdered John the Baptist and was beginning to eye Jesus with suspicion, especially since some of the people had turned against Jesus after the feeding of the 5000, when Jesus in Capernaum had explained His mission in terms that many were not able to understand: "I am the bread of life. He who comes to me will never go hungry, and he who believes in me will never be thirsty" (John 6:35).

Mark 6:53–56 | CROWDS IN GENNESARET

(Told also in Matthew 14:34–36.) Gennesaret was the plain along the shore southwest of Capernaum. It appears that the day after Jesus fed the 5000, He explained to the crowd in Capernaum the nature of His mission. Many of His followers did not like what He said and left Him (John 6:66). Then He went southward to Gennesaret, where great crowds gathered, and He healed many.

Mark 9:2–13 | JESUS IS TRANSFIGURED

(Told also in Matthew 17:1–13; Luke 9:28–36.) This is thought to have taken place at Mount Hermon, shortly before Jesus' final departure from Galilee, about four months before His death. One of the purposes of the Transfiguration was to strengthen the faith of the disciples in the divine nature of Christ before they experienced the shock of the difficult days ahead. Peter never forgot it. It gave him a sense of certainty as he was facing his own martyrdom (2 Peter 1:14–18). Also, it was a sort of grand, climactic testimony direct from heaven that Jesus was the One in whom all Old Testament prophecies converged and found their fulfillment.

Mark 9:14–29 | THE EPILEPTIC BOY

(Told also in Matthew 17:14–19; Luke 9:37–42.) It was a bad case of demon possession that baffled the disciples. (See on Mark 5:1–20.)

Mark 9:30–32 | THE PASSION AGAIN FORETOLD

Up to this time Jesus had not talked much about His coming crucifixion. But from here on He wanted them to understand plainly what was going to happen to Him. Between Peter's confession and their arrival in Jerusalem, He told them at least five (recorded) times that He would be killed and would rise from the dead:

1. After Peter's confession (Matthew 16:21; Mark 8:31; Luke 9:22)
2. After the Transfiguration (Matthew 17:9, 12; Mark 9:9, 12)
3. After the healing of the epileptic (Luke 9:44)
4. While passing through Galilee (Matthew 17:22–23; Mark 9:31)
5. Near Jerusalem (Matthew 20:17–19; Mark 10:32–34; Luke 18:31–34)

Mark 9:33–37 | WHO IS THE GREATEST? *(See on Luke 9:46–48.)*

Mark 9:38–40 | THE UNKNOWN MIRACLE WORKER
(See on Luke 9:49–50.)

Mark 9:41–50 | CAUSING TO SIN

A supreme Christian motive is that we conduct ourselves in such a way that no one else may be lost on account of our example. Jesus said this a number of times, in different connections (Matthew 18:7–14; Luke 17:1–10).

The Perean Ministry, Mark 10:1–52

Mark 10:1 | THE DEPARTURE FROM GALILEE
(See on Luke 9:51.)

Mark 10:2–12 A QUESTION ABOUT DIVORCE *(See on Matthew 19:3–12.)*

Mark 10:13–16 LITTLE CHILDREN *(See on Luke 18:15–17.)*

Mark 10:17–31 THE RICH YOUNG RULER *(See on Luke 18:18–30.)*

Mark 10:32–34 THE PASSION AGAIN FORETOLD *(See on Mark 9:30–32.)*

Mark 10:35–45 THE REQUEST OF JAMES AND JOHN *(See on Matthew 20:20–28.)*

Mark 10:46–52 BLIND BARTIMAEUS *(See on Luke 18:35–43.)*

Jesus' Last Week, Mark 11 to 16

Mark 11:1–11 THE TRIUMPHAL ENTRY *(See on Matthew 21:1–11.)*

Mark 11:15–18 THE CLEARING OF THE TEMPLE AREA *(See on Matthew 21:12–17.)*

Mark 11:12–14; 19–25 THE FIG TREE *(See on Matthew 21:18–22.)*

Mark 11:27–33 BY WHAT AUTHORITY? *(See on Matthew 21:23–27.)*

Mark 12:1–12 THE PARABLE OF THE VINEYARD *(See on Matthew 21:33–46.)*

Mark 12:13–17 PAYING TAXES TO CAESAR

(Recorded also in Matthew 22:15–22; Luke 20:20–26.) This was an effort to trap Jesus into making a statement of some kind that could be used as evidence of disloyalty to the Roman government and thus give His opponents an excuse to hand Jesus over to Pilate. Jesus, with a master stroke, proclaimed the separation of church and state. Christians must be obedient to their government; but the government has no right to dictate the religion of its subjects.

Mark 12:18–27 | QUESTION ABOUT THE RESURRECTION

(Recorded also in Matthew 22:23–33; Luke 20:27–40.) The Sadducees were the materialists of that day. They were not numerous, but were educated, wealthy, and influential. They did not believe in the resurrection. The question with which they tried to baffle Jesus involved a case that would require polygamy in heaven. Jesus settled the matter instantly and simply: there will be no marrying in heaven.

Mark 12:28–34 | THE GREAT COMMANDMENT

(Recorded also in Matthew 22:34–40.) What Jesus gave as the first great commandment is found in Deuteronomy 6:4–5; the second, in Leviticus 19:18. Note that Jesus put God first, our neighbor second. The one most important thing in life is our attitude toward God. Everything depends on that. Jesus is God incarnate, and the one thing He wants is that we love Him more than we love even our own life. Later, after the resurrection, the one last thing that Jesus wanted to know of Peter—He asked Him three times over—was, "Do you love me?" (John 21:15, 16, 17).

Mark 12:35–37 | THE SON OF DAVID

(Recorded also in Matthew 22:41–46; Luke 20:41–44.) The point of the question is, How could a man call his own son "Lord"? Simple as the answer seems to us, it silenced Jesus' opponents (Matthew 22:46).

Mark 12:38–40 | TEACHERS OF THE LAW DENOUNCED
(See on Matthew 23.)

Mark 12:41–44 | THE WIDOW'S GIFT

(Told also in Luke 21:1–4.) This was just after Jesus' denunciation of the teachers of the Law and the Pharisees. It was His last act in the temple after a day of controversy. He took time to pay this glowing tribute to the widow who gave little (two mites, small copper coins that were worth almost nothing)—but it was the gift of all she had, which made it a gift of incomparable value to God. Then Jesus left the temple, never again to enter.

Mark 13 | DISCOURSE ON THE SECOND COMING *(See on Matthew 24.)*

Mark 14:1–2 | THE PLOT TO KILL JESUS

(Told also in Matthew 26:1–5; Luke 22:1–2.) This was on Tuesday evening. About a month before this, after Jesus had raised Lazarus from the dead, the Sanhedrin had definitely decided that Jesus must be put to death (John 11:53). But Jesus' popularity made it difficult (Luke 22:2). Even in

Jerusalem the crowds surrounded Him (Mark 12:37; Luke 19:48). Their opportunity came two nights after this, through the treachery of Judas, who delivered Jesus to them in the night, while the city was asleep. They hurried to get Him condemned before daybreak, and before nine o'clock that morning (the "third hour"), they had Him on the cross.

Mark 14:3–9 | THE ANOINTING AT BETHANY

(Told also in Matthew 26:6–13; John 12:1–8.) This seems to have occurred on the Saturday evening before the Triumphal Entry (John 12:2, 12). But Matthew and Mark tell it in connection with the plot of the priests, as providing a motivation for Judas's betrayal. (See further under John 12:1–8.)

Mark 14:10–11 | THE BARGAIN OF JUDAS

(Told also in Matthew 26:14–16; Luke 22:3–6.) Judas's part was to deliver Jesus to the leaders when there were no crowds around. They did not dare arrest Him openly, lest they be stoned by the people. Judas led them to Jesus after the city had gone to sleep.

Jesus knew from the beginning that Judas would betray Him. Why Judas was chosen is one of the mysteries of God's ways. Judas may have thought that Jesus would use His miraculous power to deliver Himself. Yet in God's eyes, His deed was evil, for Jesus said it would have been better for him if he had never been born (Matthew 26:24). The whole performance was amazingly prophesied (Zechariah 11:12–13; "Jeremiah" in Matthew 27:9–10 is either a copyist's error or may have been used because the whole group of prophetic books was sometimes called by Jeremiah's name.)

The ossuary and inscription of Joseph, son of Caiaphas.

Mark 14:12–25 THE LAST SUPPER *(See on Matthew 26:17–29.)*

Mark 14:26–31, 66–72 PETER'S DENIAL
(See on John 18:15–27.)

Mark 14:32–42 THE AGONY IN GETHSEMANE *(See on Luke 22:39–46.)*

Mark 14:43–52 BETRAYAL AND ARREST
(See on John 18:1–12.)

Mark 14:53–15:20 THE TRIAL OF JESUS

(Told also in Matthew 26:57–27:31; Luke 22:54–23:25; John 18:12–19:16.) There were two trials: the first before the Sanhedrin, at night, and the second before Pilate, the Roman governor. Judea was subject to Rome. The Sanhedrin could not carry out a death sentence without the Roman governor's consent. There were three stages in each trial, six in all. For a summary of Jesus' trial, see p. 500.

ARCHAEOLOGICAL NOTE: Caiaphas Ossuary. During the days of Jesus, in what is called the Second Temple Period, the Jews of Jerusalem and environs often buried their dead in long niches carved into bedrock. Although there are many variations, in a typical tomb there was a central room carved into the rock. In one wall were the steps that led down into it, and in each of the other three walls were long niches, called *kokhim*, into each of which a body could be placed. After decomposition

---

The Site of the Crucifixion

According to the Gospel accounts, Jesus was led outside the city and crucified at a place called "the Skull" (Matthew 27:33; Mark 15:22; Luke 23:33; John 19:17; "Calvary" is derived from the Latin, "Golgotha" from the Hebrew word for skull). He was buried in a nearby tomb belonging to Joseph of Arimathea.

In Jerusalem today there are two localities that lay claim to being the place of these events. The first of these is Gordon's Calvary, to the north of the present-day Damascus Gate, with the nearby Garden Tomb. Although this site lies outside the ancient as well as the present-day city walls and is quite amenable to certain types of piety, there is no compelling reason to think that this is either Calvary or the tomb. In fact, the Garden Tomb may date back to the Iron Age (1000 – 586 B.C.) and thus could not have been a tomb "in which no one had yet been laid" (Luke 23:53).

More compelling, although not certain, is the suggestion that the Church of the Holy Sepulchre marks the spot of these dramatic events. It is probable that this site was outside the walled city of Jesus' day and was in fact a burial ground. Very ancient Christian traditions, dating back to at least the days of Eusebius (4th century A.D.), suggest that the church marks the more probable of the two sites.

had taken place, perhaps a year later, the bones were removed and placed into small rectangular boxes called *ossuaries*. The niche could then be reused for another burial.

Hundreds of ossuaries from this period have been found in the Jerusalem area. In 1990 an Israeli archaeologist, Zvi Greenhut, excavated a Second Temple tomb on a hill to the south of Jerusalem. The tomb contained 12 ossuaries, and on two of them the name "Caiaphas" was scratched. On another the name "Joseph, son of Caiaphas" was scratched, who, according to the Jewish historian Josephus, was the very person who presided at Jesus' trial. The name Caiaphas (high priest from A.D. 18–36) appears some nine times in the Gospels and Acts.

Mark 15:21–41 **THE CRUCIFIXION** *(See on Matthew 27:32–60; Luke 23:26–49; and John 19:17–30.)*

Mark 15:42–47 **THE BURIAL OF JESUS** *(See on John 19:38–42.)*

Mark 16:1–8 **THE WOMEN VISIT THE TOMB**

(Told also in Matthew 28:1–8.) Peter, after his denial of the Lord, no doubt felt that he had been disowned and needed this special message (v. 7). How gracious of Jesus to send it to him! Later in the day Jesus Himself appeared to Peter (Luke 24:34). What took place at that meeting we can only imagine: hot tears, burning shame, loving forgiveness. It sealed a devotion that never again was broken, even in Peter's martyrdom. (See further on John 21:15–19.)

The women ran to tell the disciples. Peter and John ran to the tomb (John 20:3–10.)

(For a summary of the events on the resurrection morning, see p. 502.)

Mark 16:9–11 **JESUS APPEARS TO MARY MAGDALENE**

(Recorded also in John 20:11–18.) He also appeared to the other women (Matthew 28:9–10) and to the two disciples from Emmaus (Mark 16:12–13; see on Luke 24:13–32).

Mark 16:14–18 **JESUS APPEARS TO THE ELEVEN**

(Told also in Luke 24:33–43; John 20:19–25; see notes on these passages.) The final commission to go into all the world (vv. 15–16) seems to have been given at this appearance. It may, however, have been a summary of final instructions that Jesus repeated over and over during His 40 days of ministry after the resurrection.

The power to work miracles (vv. 17–18) was a divine attestation of the apostles' mission in founding the church. (See on Acts 3.)

A tomb from shortly after the time of Christ shows the rolling stone, which in this case rolls down to close the tomb. This is the tomb of Queen Helena at the Tomb of the Kings in Jerusalem (ca. A.D. 60).

Forty days elapsed between vv. 18 and 19, during which Jesus appeared to His disciples and others (see p. 502 for a summary of Jesus' appearances after His resurrection).

| **Mark 16:19–20** | **JESUS' ASCENSION** *(See on Luke 24:44–53.)* |

The Last 12 Verses of Mark (16:9 – 20)

The last 12 verses of Mark (often called "the long ending") are not in the Sinaitic and Vatican manuscripts (see p. 994), but were accepted early in the history of the church as a genuine part of Mark's Gospel. It is thought likely that the last page of the original copy was lost and added later. It does not seem that verse 8 could have been a proper ending for the book.

Luke

Jesus the Son of Man

But the angel said to them, "Do not be afraid. I bring you good news of great joy that will be for all the people. Today in the town of David a Savior has been born to you; he is Christ the Lord. This will be a sign to you: You will find a baby wrapped in cloths and lying in a manger." Suddenly a great company of the heavenly host appeared with the angel, praising God and saying, "Glory to God in the highest, and on earth peace to men on whom his favor rests."

—LUKE 2:10–14

- For a general introduction to all four Gospels, see p. 517.
- For an overview of the life of Jesus, see p. 493.

Luke's Emphasis: The Humanity of Jesus

The special emphasis of Luke is the humanity of Jesus. Representing Jesus as the Son of God, Luke shows His kindness toward the weak, the suffering, and the outcast.

While each of the Gospels was intended ultimately for all mankind, Matthew seems to have had in immediate view the Jews; Mark, the Romans; and Luke, the Greeks.

- Jewish culture had been built around their Scriptures — our Old Testament. Therefore **Matthew** appeals to their Scriptures.
- Roman civilization gloried in the idea of government and power. Therefore **Mark** calls particular attention to the miracles of Jesus as exhibiting His superhuman power.
- Greek civilization represented culture, philosophy, wisdom, reason, beauty, education. Therefore, to appeal to the thoughtful, cultured, philosophic Greek mind, **Luke,** in a complete, orderly, and classical story, depicts the glorious beauty and perfection of Jesus, the ideal, universal man. In addition, Luke includes more references to various classes of people and identifies women and children more than any of the other Gospel writers.
- Then **John** added his Gospel to these three, to make it clear and unmistakable that Jesus was God in human form.

Luke

Luke's name is mentioned only three times in the New Testament: Colossians 4:14, where he is called "our dear friend Luke, the doctor"; Philemon 24, where he is called Paul's fellow worker; and 2 Timothy 4:11, where Paul indicates that Luke was with him in the dark hours of approaching martyrdom. All three passages also mention Mark, which would appear to indicate that Mark and Luke worked together.

In the story of Paul's travels in the book of Acts, the varying use of the pronouns *they* and *we* indicate that Luke was with Paul during the early part of Paul's second missionary journey—from Troas to Philippi—and that about six years later he rejoined Paul in Philippi at the close of Paul's third missionary journey and was with him through his imprisonment in Caesarea and Rome, to the end (see further, p. 656).

Date

It is thought that Luke wrote his Gospel about the year A.D. 60, while Paul was in prison in Caesarea, and that he wrote the book of Acts in the next two years, during Paul's imprisonment in Rome. (The Gospel of Luke and the book of Acts are both addressed to the same person, Theophilus, and are in fact one work in two volumes.)

Luke's two-year stay in Caesarea (A.D. 58–60) afforded him abundant opportunity to get firsthand, accurate information concerning all details of the story of Jesus from the original companions of Jesus and the founders of the church—the apostles.

Caesarea was less than 60 miles from Jerusalem. Jesus' mother may have been still alive, living at John's home in Jerusalem. Luke may have spent many hours with her, listening to her reminiscences of her wondrous Son. And James, bishop of Jerusalem, Jesus' own brother, could have supplied Luke with full details of the whole story of Jesus' life.

Luke 1:1–4 | INTRODUCTION

Many accounts (v. 1) about Jesus were already in existence. Luke carefully and painstakingly examined the available records and interviewed all available eyewitnesses and original companions of Jesus in order to be able to write an orderly account based on the facts.

Theophilus (v. 3), to whom this Gospel and the book of Acts are addressed (or dedicated), was probably a Roman official of high rank, as indicated by the title "most excellent." His name means "lover of God." It is not known who he was. He may have been one of Luke's converts in Philippi or Antioch. It may also be that—as was often done by the person to whom a book was dedicated—he bore the expense of publication of Luke's two books by having copies made for many churches.

THE BIRTH OF JOHN THE BAPTIST

Luke is the only Gospel that provides the story of the birth of John the Baptist, and only Matthew and Luke tell of the birth and childhood of Jesus. Luke tells the story more fully than Matthew, and each narrates different incidents. (See below, on Luke 2:39.)

Luke 1:5–25 **THE ANNOUNCEMENT TO ZECHARIAH**

The event on which Old Testament prophecy converged was at hand: the arrival of the Messiah. Isaiah tells us that a voice of one calling in the desert will prepare the way for the Lord (Isaiah 40:3), and Malachi, in the final book of the Old Testament, prophesies, "See, I will send my messenger who will prepare the way before me" (Malachi 3:1). It was an Ancient Near Eastern custom that a royal representative would be sent ahead to prepare the way for the visit of a king. An angel now notifies Zechariah, the saintly old priest, that his child, yet to be born of his barren wife, Elizabeth, is the one to whom the prophecies pointed (v. 17).

Jesus validated that John the Baptist was the fulfillment of the Old Testament prophecies about the messenger who would prepare the people, bringing them to repentance before the Lord's coming (11:10). Jesus also tells us that John is the Elijah who was to come (11:14),

---

The Glow of the Supernatural

It was the evident intention of the writers to show that Christianity had a supernatural origin. Long foretold, the birth of Jesus did not take place without heavenly evidence that the event of the ages was at hand. He was born of a virgin. His forerunner was born of a barren woman who was past child-bearing age. Angels appeared to Zechariah, to Mary, to Joseph, and to the shepherds. They saved the child from being murdered. Wise Men were supernaturally guided from distant lands to pay their homage and to provide means for the child's flight from Herod.

The Virgin Birth

Luke is thought to have gotten his story of Jesus' birth directly from Mary herself. Matthew probably got his from Joseph. Both state plainly, explicitly, unmistakably, and unequivocally that Jesus was born of a virgin. From the beginning, in unbroken sequence, it has been held as a belief of the church — until, that is, the rise of modern criticism, which attempts to discredit this miracle of God. This viewpoint is abhorred.

If we believe in the deity of Jesus and His resurrection from the dead, what is gained by discrediting the Virgin Birth? God's plan of redemption required that Jesus be born of a virgin. Since the fall of Adam, all mankind has possessed from birth a sinful nature that separates man from God. Mortal man was therefore unable to reconcile all mankind to God. Redemption required a man of godly nature, like Adam before the Fall, to pay the penalty for mankind's sins. Thus it was essential that the seed of Jesus was divine and incorruptible. The Holy Spirit impregnated Mary with God's Son made flesh. This is a symbol, or type, of how the Holy Spirit indwells the hearts of born-again Christians. To call Jesus an illegitimate child is nothing less than blasphemy.

referring to Malachi's prophecy that Elijah would reappear before the day of the Lord. The people remembered this prophecy and asked John the Baptist whether he was Elijah. He told them that he was not Elijah, but it is understood that he was ministering in the spirit and power of Elijah the prophet.

| Luke 1:26–38 | **THE ANNOUNCEMENT TO MARY**

This event is also called the Annunciation. The Messiah was to be born into David's family. It had been 1000 years since the time of David, and there had come to be thousands of families of Davidic descent. God, in choosing the one family through whom His Son should come into the world, bypassed the ruling families around Jerusalem and instead went to a humble woman, from a lowly home, in an obscure village in the distant hills of Galilee. What a woman she must have been to be thus chosen of God to impart and mold the human nature of His Son! And how her heart must have thrilled at the angelic message that she was to be the mother of the divine King of the ages!

| Luke 1:39–56 | **MARY'S VISIT TO ELIZABETH**

Mary and Elizabeth were relatives (1:36). We are not told in which town or village Elizabeth's home was, except that it was in the hill country of Judah (v. 39). Since she was of the tribe of Levi (1:5), it may have been Hebron, which was a Levitical city (see Joshua 21:11).

Mary's song of thanksgiving (vv. 46–55), also called the Magnificat (the first word of the hymn in Latin, "Glorifies"), is similar to Hannah's song at the birth of Samuel (1-Samuel 2:1–10). In her meditations and

The angel announced to Mary that she would be the mother of the Messiah. This cave and altar beneath the Church of the Annunciation commemorate that event.

reflections Mary had probably uttered these thoughts over and over until they took on the beautiful poetic form in which they here appear as her personal liturgy. Mary was with Elizabeth for three months (v. 56), until the time of John's birth (v. 36). Then she returned to Nazareth. (See on Matthew 1:18–24.)

Luke 1:57–80 | THE BIRTH OF JOHN THE BAPTIST

The naming of the child, and his father's prophecy, filled the countryside with expectancy. (See below, on Luke 3:1–20.)

Luke 2:1–38 | THE BIRTH OF JESUS

What is told in the first two chapters of Luke is omitted in the other Gospels, except for the statement in Matthew 1:25–2:1 that Jesus was born in Bethlehem and the statement in Matthew 2:22–23 that the family returned to Galilee.

Bethlehem

The town is located six miles south of Jerusalem. Bethlehem was called Ephrath in Jacob's time and was the burial place of Rachel (Genesis 35:16, 19; 48:7). It was the home of Ibzan, the tenth Judge (Judges 12:8 – 10); of Elimelech, the father-in-law of Ruth (Ruth 1:1 – 2), as well as of Boaz, her husband (2:1, 4). David was anointed king by Samuel in Bethlehem (1 Samuel 16:13, 15), which is why it was also known as "the city of David" (Luke 2:4, 11).

Here the Messiah was born (Matthew 2:1; Luke 2:1 – 7), which is how this town, which was "small among the clans of Judah" (Micah 5:2), achieved its great fame. Its male children under two years of age were murdered in Herod's attempt to kill the King of the Jews (Matthew 2:16). Today the city focuses on the Church of the Nativity, essentially a structure built by the Byzantine emperor Justinian in the first part of the 6th century A.D. on an older church built during the reign of the first Christian emperor, Constantine, and dedicated in May of A.D. 339. Under the altar of this church is a grotto which, according to local tradition, is the cave where Jesus was born. In a nearby underground chamber, the Latin scholar Jerome spent 30 years making his Latin translation of the Bible (see p. 999).

The Amazing Providence of God

The Messiah is to be of the family of David and is to be born in Bethlehem (Micah 5:2 – 5). But the chosen parents live in Nazareth, 100 miles from Bethlehem. A decree of Rome requires them to go to Bethlehem just as the child is about to be born. Thus God makes the decree of a pagan empire the instrument for fulfilling His prophecies.

Luke 2:1–5 | THE CENSUS OF QUIRINIUS

This was a census of the Roman Empire. (The purpose of the census was taxation, as the KJV indicates.) Roman historical records place the census of Quirinius in A.D. 7, which was 10 to 13 years *after* Jesus was born. This historical discrepancy was for a long time troublesome to Bible students. But in recent years ancient papyri have been found that show that Quirinius was governor of Syria *twice*. Luke expressly says that this was the *first* census. It has also been discovered that people were indeed required to go to their ancestral homes for the census. Thus the spade of the archaeologist goes on, confirming one by one and in detail the historical accuracy of biblical statements.

Luke 2:6–7 | BORN IN A STABLE

The word translated *inn* may mean a public lodging place or the guest room built onto a private home. Here it is thought to have been the latter, probably the home of their Davidic kin, the same house where the Wise Men later came (Matthew 2:11). The 100-mile journey from Nazareth, by foot or on a donkey, must have been long and hard for a woman about to give birth to a child. Crowded out of the guest room, at least temporarily, by others who had arrived earlier, they had to stay in the stable. The sacred moment arrived, and the cradle of the Son of God was a feed-trough for animals. Luke does not say so, but it would not be surprising if, after the shepherds told their story to all who wanted to listen, the best the home afforded was open to Joseph and Mary.

Luke 2:8–20 | THE SHEPHERDS

The traditional shepherds' field, where the angelic choirs sang the birthday hallelujahs of earth's new King, is a few miles east of the ancient village of Bethlehem.

Luke 2:21–38 | JESUS' CIRCUMCISION AND PRESENTATION

The fact that they offered two pigeons instead of a lamb and a pigeon is an indication that Joseph and Mary were not wealthy. Levitical law required a woman, after the birth of a son, to purify herself for 40 days before going to the temple to offer a sacrifice for her purification. The law stated that she was to offer a lamb and a dove, but if she could not afford these, she could offer two pigeons or doves (Leviticus 12:2–8).

Luke 2:39 | RETURN TO NAZARETH

Luke here proceeds directly from the presentation in the temple to the return to Nazareth, omitting the events recorded in Matthew 2:1–21: the visit of Magi or Wise Men, the flight to Egypt, the killing of the infants in Bethlehem, and the return from Egypt.

Luke 2:40 | JESUS' CHILDHOOD

The Bible says little about Jesus' childhood: first a few months as a baby in Bethlehem, then a year or two in Egypt, and then to Nazareth. The only event that is mentioned from the entire period between the return to Nazareth and the beginning of His public ministry almost 30 years

The Roman emperor Augustus, during whose reign Jesus was born. Image was everything, even 2000 years ago. In Rome, Augustus's statue shows him as the victorious soldier (left). In the Greek city of Corinth, his statue shows him as the Greek sage in flowing robes.

Jesus' Birthday — December 25?

Jesus' birthday is now celebrated on December 25, but there is nothing in the Bible to support that date. It first appears as the date of Jesus' birthday in the 4th century, in the Western church. In the Eastern church the date is January 6th. (For more on the Eastern and Western churches, see pp. 902, 907.)

Gabriel

Gabriel was the name of the prince of angels sent from heaven to direct the arrangements for the arrival of the Son of God. He was the messenger to Zechariah to tell him the good news that he would have a son, John the Baptist (1:19). Gabriel was also the angel who appeared to Mary to tell her that she was to bear the Son of God (1:26). We presume that he was the angel who appeared to the shepherds (2:9, 13), the one sent to Joseph (Matthew 1:24), and the one who directed the flight to Egypt (Matthew 2:13, 19). He had given the prophecy of the 70 Weeks to Daniel (Daniel 9:21). How interested he was in the redemption of the human race — and how we will love to make his acquaintance when we get to heaven!

later is the incident in the temple when Jesus was 12 (see below, on Luke 2:41–50), which indicates that He was a remarkably precocious boy.

What little else we know we find elsewhere in the Gospels. Jesus was eldest of a family of seven children. They lived on a carpenter's income, which met the needs of their family and was probably considered an average family income. It is likely that Jesus, along with the other children in His family, learned responsibility early. How we wish we had a glimpse of His home life — how the Son of God as a growing boy handled Himself under the daily round of irritations usual in such a situation.

Later, stories about miracles and other — sometimes rather silly — feats Jesus performed as a boy came into circulation. Had these been true, Luke or the other Gospel writers could have verified and used these stories to support Jesus' claim to be the Son of God. But the very simplicity and sparseness of the Gospels when talking about Jesus' childhood lends credibility to the rest of what is recorded in the Gospels. It also indicates that there was little in Jesus' childhood that hinted at His future as the Savior of the world. The people of Nazareth rejected Him because they saw Him as a boy who had grown up among and with them (Luke 4:16–30).

Jesus was 12 years old. This is thought to have been His first trip to Jerusalem. He was so interested and utterly engrossed in what the teachers said that He failed to miss His parents for three days after they were gone. And they failed for a whole day to notice His absence from the group in which they traveled, until they stopped for the night. It must have been a rather large company, extending a long distance over the road. The parents felt sure that their self-reliant boy was somewhere along the line and that He was abundantly able to take care of Himself until evening. Besides, in those days friends and neighbors were virtually an extended family—they would keep an eye on Him.

Nazareth

Nazareth is situated in a basin on the south side of a hill, 1,150 feet above sea level. From the top of the hill, a 10-minute climb, one has a view unrivaled in Galilee. To the north is a beautiful panorama of fertile hills and valleys, dotted with prosperous cities and snow-capped Mount Hermon in the distance. Nearby, a mere three miles away, was Gath Hepher, the ancient home of the prophet Jonah. To the south is the Plain of Esdraelon (Jezreel Valley), extending from the Jordan to the Mediterranean. Ten miles to the west of Nazareth, in full view, rises Mount Carmel, where Elijah called down fire from heaven in his contest with Baal (1 Kings 18:16 – 46).

To the southwest, at about the same distance, is the pass of Armageddon, which is mentioned in Revelation 16:16 as the place of the great final battle of the ages in which Jesus Himself will lead His own to victory.

Eight miles south of Nazareth lies Shunem, where Elisha raised the son of the Shunammite widow to life (2 Kings 4:8 – 37). Nearby is the River Kishon, where Deborah and Barak subdued the Canaanites (Judges 4); the spring of Harod, where Gideon with his 300 routed the Midianites (Judges 7); Endor, where the witch summoned Samuel's spirit for Saul (1 Samuel 28:1 – 24); Mount Gilboa, where King Saul committed suicide (1 Samuel 31:1 – 6); and Jezreel, where the infamous Jezebel met her unhappy fate (2 Kings 9:30 – 37).

Jesus was raised in this small village of Nazareth, only 31/2 miles southeast of the capital Sepphoris. Although Nazareth itself was small and insignificant, its residents probably had numerous contacts with their more cosmopolitan neighbors. In all probability they came into contact with some of the caravans and Greek-speaking gentile traders who passed through Sepphoris on the north or the Esdraelon Valley on the south. Excavations near the modern Church of the Annunciation at Nazareth have revealed some 1st-century remains of silos, oil presses, storage areas, and houses.

Jesus' knowledge of the Old Testament (v. 47). At that time the Old Testament constituted the written Word of God. Jesus loved it. His familiarity with it at the age of 12 astounded the great theologians of the temple. He lived by the Word of God. He later used it to resist the Tempter (Matthew 4:4, 7, 10). He went to the cross to fulfill the Old Testament (Matthew 26:54). In His dying agony He quoted from it (Matthew 27:46).

To the Old Testament writings has been added another group of writings, the New Testament, centered around the life of Jesus Himself. If what Jesus had of our Bible was dear to Him, it would seem that what we have — both Testaments — ought to be 1000 times more so to us.

In my Father's house (v. 49), or "about my Father's business" (KJV, lit., "in the [things] of my Father"). This saying rather puzzled Jesus' mother. Probably she had not yet told Him of the nature of His birth.

Artistic rendition of Mary's purification at the temple in Jerusalem after the birth of Jesus.

She had just spoken of Joseph as His father (v. 48). His reply, His speaking of God as "my Father," possibly conveyed to her a hint that He knew her secret.

Luke 2:51–52 THE 18 YEARS' SILENCE

How we would love to know something of Jesus' life from 12 to 30! But God, in His wisdom, has drawn a veil over it.

Luke 3:1–20 JOHN THE BAPTIST

The preaching of John is told by all four Gospels (Matthew 3:1–12; Mark 1:1–8; John 1:6–8; 19–28). Luke's account is fullest.

The story of John's childhood and youth is passed over in one sentence (1:80). He lived in the solitude of the wild and bleak region west of the Dead Sea. He had known from childhood that the greatest event of the ages was at hand, and that he had been born to be the herald of its arrival.

Knowing he was to be the Elijah of prophecy (1:17; Matthew 11:14; 17:10–13; Malachi 4:5 — though not Elijah in person, John 1:21), he copied, perhaps intentionally, the habits and dress of Elijah. He lived on locusts and wild honey (Matthew 3:4). Locusts have been used as food from earliest times. They were roasted or sun-dried.

John's call came when he was 30 years old. The nation was electrified by the voice of this strange, rugged, fearless hermit of the desert crying on the banks of the Jordan that the long-foretold Deliverer was at hand.

The burden of his cry was, "Repent." His preaching was immensely popular and successful. The whole land was stirred up by his words alone, since he did not perform any miracles (John 10:41). Great multitudes came to be baptized by him (Matthew 3:5). Even Herod liked to listen to him (Mark 6:20). Josephus says that John had great influence over the people, who seemed ready to do anything he might tell them.

He required that those who professed repentance be baptized—which was a foreshadowing of the later ceremony of Christian baptism.

At the height of John's popularity, he baptized Jesus and proclaimed Him to be the Messiah. Then, his mission accomplished, he passed off the stage. He had roused the nation and had presented the Son of God. His work was done.

However, he continued preaching and baptizing for a few months, moving northward to Aenon (John 3:23; see map on p. 496).

About a year after he baptized Jesus, John was imprisoned by Herod to satisfy the whim of a wicked woman (Matthew 14:1–5). This was at the close of Jesus' early Judean ministry (Matthew 4:12; John 3:22; 4:35).

Satan

Is there really a Devil? Some chose to ignore the reality that there is a literal Devil who seeks to devour and destroy. The language of Jesus certainly indicates His own belief in the Devil's existence.

- He is the evil one (Matthew 13:38).
- He is the enemy (Matthew 13:39).
- He is the prince of this world (John 12:31; 14:30).
- He is a liar and the father of lies (John 8:44).
- He is a murderer (John 8:44).
- Jesus saw him fall from heaven (Luke 10:18).
- He has a kingdom (Matthew 12:26).
- Evil men are his sons (Matthew 13:38).
- He sows tares among the wheat (Matthew 13:38–39).
- He snatches the Word from hearers (Matthew 13:19; Mark 4:15; Luke 8:12).
- He bound a woman for 18 years (Luke 13:16).
- He desired to have Peter (Luke 22:31).
- He has angels (Matthew 25:41).
- Eternal fire is prepared for him (Matthew 25:41).

Jesus knew what He was talking about. If Jesus was merely accommodating Himself to popular error, His words are no revelation of truth at all, for who then can discern between the actual truth that He is aiming to teach and the error that He speaks of as if it were truth?

Not only Jesus, but both the Old and the New Testaments speak of the Devil as real:

- He is the seducer of Adam and Eve (Genesis 3:1–20).
- He moved David to sin (1 Chronicles 21:1).
- He caused Job's troubles (Job 1:7–2:10).

The place of his imprisonment is not named. It is thought to have been at Machaerus, east of the Dead Sea, or at Tiberias, on the western shore of the Sea of Galilee. Herod had a residence at both places. John was beheaded at about the time of the second Passover (Matthew 14:12–13; John 6:4).

We wonder about John's doubt (Matthew 11:3). He had been so confident and positive that Jesus was the Lamb of God and the Son of God (John 1:29–34). But now, as he mused behind dungeon walls, he was puzzled. Jesus was not doing what he thought the Messiah would do. John evidently shared the popular notion of a political messianic kingdom. God did not reveal to him everything about the nature of His kingdom. Even the Twelve were slow to grasp what the kingdom was all about. (See on Matthew 10.)

Assuming that John began his ministry shortly before he baptized Jesus, it lasted about a year and a half. Thirty years in seclusion, 1½ years of public preaching, a year and 4 months in prison — and then the final curtain. This is the resume of the man who ushered in the Savior of the world, and of whom Jesus said there had not been born anyone greater (Matthew 11:11).

- He was the adversary of Joshua (Zechariah 3:1 – 9).
- He is the tempter (Matthew 4:3).
- He perverts the Scripture (Matthew 4:4; Luke 4:10 – 11).
- He is the source of demon possession (Matthew 12:22 – 29; Luke 11:14 – 23).
- He is the prince of demons (Matthew 12:24; Mark 3:22; Luke 11:15).
- He put the betrayal into the heart of Judas (John 13:2, 27).
- He caused Ananias to lie (Acts 5:3).
- The Gentiles are under his power (Acts 26:18).
- He tries to outwit Christians (2 Corinthians 2:11).
- He is the god of this world (2 Corinthians 4:4).
- He blinds the minds of unbelievers (2 Corinthians 4:4).
- He fashions himself into an angel of light (2 Corinthians 11:14).
- He caused Paul's thorn in the flesh (2 Corinthians 12:7).
- He is the prince of the power of the air (Ephesians 2:2 kjv).
- He is the spirit that works in the disobedient (Ephesians 2:2).
- He is wily (Ephesians 6:11).
- He hindered Paul's missionary plans (1 Thessalonians 2:18).
- He is the moving spirit of the apostasy (2 Thessalonians 2:9).
- He can produce false miracles (2 Thessalonians 2:9).
- He will flee if resisted (James 4:7).
- Like a roaring lion he seeks to devour Christians (1 Peter 5:8).
- He is our adversary (1 Peter 5:8).
- He is overcome by faith (1 Peter 5:9).
- Evil men are his children (1 John 3:8, 10).
- False teachers are a "synagogue of Satan" (Revelation 2:9; 3:9).
- He is the deceiver of the whole world (Revelation 12:9; 20:3, 8, 10).
- He is "the great dragon, . . . the ancient serpent" (Revelation 12:9; 20:2).

Oh, how the realization of the reality of the Devil could transform people's lives if they would respond by turning to the great Protector and Savior, Jesus!

Luke 3:21–22 | **JESUS IS BAPTIZED** *(See on Matthew 3:13–17.)*

Luke 3:23–28 | **GENEALOGY OF JESUS**
(See on Matthew 1:1–17.)

Luke 4:1–13 | **THE 40 DAYS' TEMPTATION**

See note on Matthew 4:1–11. All three accounts—Matthew, Mark, and Luke—state that it was Satan who tempted Jesus.

The Galilean Ministry, Luke 4:14 to 9:51

Luke devotes much less space to the Galilean ministry than do Matthew and Mark. (See notes under Matthew 4:12 and Mark 1:14).

Luke 4:14–15 | **JESUS BEGINS HIS GALILEAN MINISTRY**

Luke, like Matthew and Mark, skips entirely the events of the year between Jesus' temptation and the beginning of His Galilean ministry, which are told in John 1:19–4:54. (See on Mark 1:14–15.)

Luke 4:16–30 | **REJECTION AT NAZARETH**

This seems to have been Jesus' first return to Nazareth since His baptism more than a year before. As far as we know, He spent the intervening time in the desert, in Cana, in Capernaum, and in Judea (John 2:1, 12; 4:46). The people marveled at His gracious, magnetic, and evidently powerful personality in speaking. They were amazed—they could hardly believe that this was the boy they had watched grow up. Even in that small town, Jesus had lived so quiet a life, and was from such a lowly family, that the people in the synagogue scarcely recognized Him (v. 22). The point of His reference to Elijah and Elisha is that they had been sent to Gentiles, not to Israelites—a hint of His own mission. This—as well as the miracles He performed in towns other than His own—so offended their narrow provincialism that they flew into a frenzy and attempted to kill Him.

Luke 4:31–37 | **THE HEALING OF A DEMON-POSSESSED MAN**
(See on Mark 1:21–28.)

Luke 4:38–39 | **PETER'S MOTHER-IN-LAW** *(See on Mark 1:29–31.)*

Luke 4:40–41 | **MANY ARE HEALED** *(See on Mark 1:32–34.)*

Luke 4:42 | **PRAYING IN SOLITUDE** *(See on Mark 1:35–37.)*

Some people who listened to Jesus speak in the Nazareth synagogue were so infuriated by certain statements that they took Him to the brow of the hill of the city to throw Him off of the precipice which was the cultural method of stoning.

Luke 4:43–44 | **TRAVEL THROUGHOUT GALILEE** *(See on Mark 1:38–39.)*

Luke 5:1–11 | **THE CALL OF PETER, JAMES, AND JOHN** *(See on Mark 1:16–20.)*

Luke 5:12–16 | **A LEPER HEALED** *(See on Mark 1:40–45.)*

Luke 5:17–26 | **A PARALYTIC HEALED** *(See on Mark 2:1–12.)*

Luke 5:27–32 | **THE CALL OF LEVI (MATTHEW)** *(See on Matthew 1:1.)*

Luke 5:33–39 | **A QUESTION ABOUT FASTING** *(See on Mark 2:18–22.)*

Luke 6:1–11 | **PICKING GRAIN AND HEALING ON THE SABBATH** *(See on Mark 2:23.)*

Luke 6:12–19 | **THE TWELVE CHOSEN**

To these men Jesus was entrusting the results of His life's work. He knew, of course, that He Himself, from heaven, through His Spirit, would guide and direct and help them. Nevertheless, their natural traits and talents had to be considered. And before making His final choice, Jesus spent all night in prayer to God.

After two years of training (see under Matthew 10), He sent them forth to be His witnesses to the farthest corners of the earth. The New Testament tells only a little of their work, in Palestine, Asia Minor, Greece, and Rome.

Perhaps the Twelve agreed among themselves to go in different directions. Or, each may have been guided to go wherever he thought best. They went, for a time, in pairs. No doubt each visited the work of others.

In about A.D. 62, Paul said that the Gospel had been preached in all creation under heaven (Colossians 1:23). Thus, within 30 years the story of Christ had been told all over the then-known world. Various—and not all equally reliable—traditions claim that most of the Twelve sealed their testimony to Christ with their martyrdom.

All in all, allowing for one traitor in the group, Jesus' choice and training of the Twelve was a grand success.

Luke 6:20–49 | THE SERMON ON THE MOUNT

This is commonly taken to be an abbreviated form of the same sermon that is recorded in Matthew 5–7. The two records are somewhat different. We cannot be sure whether they are different reports of the same sermon or substantially the same sermon delivered on different occasions. Jesus was teaching continually, and it is likely that He uttered some of these words, in varying forms, hundreds of times. This may be a collection of His representative sayings, a sort of summary of His main teachings. Their literary beauty, as well as their matchless teaching, is unexcelled in literature.

Luke 6:20–26 | THE BEATITUDES (See on Matthew 5:1–12.)

Luke 6:27–36 | THE GOLDEN RULE

Here is a kind of condensation of Matthew 5 and 7. Some of Jesus' teachings, such as "Love your neighbor as yourself," "Love your enemies," and "Do to others as you would have them do to you," are already found in the Old Testament—they have been the foundation of godly living all along. For example, "Do not seek revenge or bear a grudge against one of your people, but love your neighbor as yourself. I am the LORD" (Leviticus 19:18). Yet they seem to be so high above our selfish human nature that we are in the habit of excusing ourselves from even trying to live up to them by saying to ourselves that Jesus surely knew that He was setting impossible ideals before us.

However, Jesus Himself lived up to them and taught unequivocally that we must keep our hearts free from resentment, no matter how we may be mistreated. And not only that, but we should actually seek the welfare of those who seek to hurt us. Not possible? Yes, it is possible, in some measure, by the gracious help of God and the strictest self-discipline, to love those who hate us.

To practice the Golden Rule, even in small measure, makes us happy, helps us in our business and in every relationship. It is the most practical thing in this world. In serving others we serve ourselves. People like to deal with those who believe in and practice the Golden Rule. Try it and see!

The Golden Rule is not a sufficient basis for exemption from military service. Jesus was speaking to individuals, not governments. Governments are ordained of God (Romans 13:1–7; 1-Peter 2:13–17). Criminal elements have to be suppressed. Jesus expressly stated that His kingdom could exist within the kingdom of Caesar (Matthew 22:21). The first Gentile to be admitted into the church was a Roman soldier (Acts 10:1); he was not required to renounce military service. A judge, a police officer, or a military man may in his own heart and life practice the principles of the Golden Rule, so far as he can as an individual, while as an officer of the law or the government he must strictly follow the rules of justice.

Governments may, in some respects and in limited measure, follow the Golden Rule. But if force were abandoned altogether, the reality is that anarchy would result. Let us have clear thinking on this point. As much as we abhor war, a Christian is not to be commended for making the Golden Rule an *excuse* for letting others do the fighting to preserve his liberty. On the other hand, there are those who are conscientious objectors to military service out of deep *conviction*. Each one should be fully convinced in his own mind (Romans 14:5), without judging others.

Luke 6:37–42 | JUDGING OTHERS

In these passages Jesus encourages the disciples to consider their own actions first. We cannot judge or condemn if our own behavior is not righteous. Instead of being critical, we are to forgive and become givers. The yardstick we use to measure others will be used to measure our own behaviors. The blessings we bestow on others will be returned to us in "good measure, pressed down, shaken together and running over."

Luke 6:43–49 | BUILDING ON THE ROCK

Such words as these—and there are plenty of them—make it very plain that Jesus intends to be taken seriously. There is going to be a day of sad disillusionment for many who make glib profession of His name (Matthew 7:22–23). Hearing, believing, and *doing* the things Jesus taught, *practicing* them in our lives, is what will count on the last day.

Luke 7:1–10 | THE CENTURION'S SERVANT

This story is told also in Matthew 8:5–13. A centurion was a Roman officer in charge of 100 soldiers. At that time Palestine had been under Roman control for about 100 years. Roman officers, all too often, were brutal and despised men. But some of them, influenced perhaps by the Jewish religion, were good men. The first Gentile to be received into the church was a centurion named Cornelius (Acts 10).

Luke 7:11–17 | THE SON OF THE WIDOW OF NAIN RAISED

This is one of three recorded resurrections. The others are the daughter of Jairus (Mark 5:22) and Lazarus (John 11:1). Jesus may have raised others as well (Luke 7:22). He commissioned the Twelve to raise the dead (Matthew 10:8).

Luke 7:18–35 | MESSENGERS FROM JOHN *(See on Matthew 11:1–19.)*

Luke 7:36–50 | THE SINFUL WOMAN

There is not the slightest basis for identifying this woman with Mary Magdalene or Mary of Bethany. This anointing is not the same as the anointing at Bethany shortly before Jesus' crucifixion (John 12:1–8). An oriental banquet was a sort of public affair. As was customary, Jesus would be half reclining on a couch, His face toward the table, His knees bent back, so it was easy for the woman to approach. Weeping, kissing His feet, bathing them with the costly perfume, and wiping away the falling tears with her hair—how she puts us respectable people to shame in thus bowing low at the feet of her Lord in abject humility and devoted adoration.

Jesus was very tender in His attitude toward women who had made a misstep (John 4:18; 8:1–11)—yet no one ever attributed His attitude to questionable motives (John 4:27).

Luke 8:1–3 | THE WOMEN WHO SUPPORTED JESUS

Three are named, although there were many others. Nothing further is known of Susanna. Joanna was the wife of Herod's steward, from the king's palace. She belonged to the group of Jesus' closest friends. She was among those at the tomb (Luke 24:10).

Luke 8:4–18 | THE PARABLE OF THE SOWER *(See on Matthew 13:1–23.)*

Luke 8:19–21 | JESUS' MOTHER AND BROTHERS *(See on Matthew 12:46–50.)*

Luke 8:22–25 | THE STILLING OF THE STORM *(See on Mark 4:35–41.)*

Luke 8:26–39 | THE DEMON-POSSESSED GERASENE *(See on Mark 5:1–20.)*

Luke 8:40–56 | THE RAISING OF JAIRUS'S DAUGHTER

(Told also in Matthew 9:18–26; Mark 5:21–43.) Three times Jesus raised the dead. (See on Luke 7:11–17 and John 11.)

Luke 9:1–6 | THE TWELVE SENT OUT *(See on Matthew 10.)*

Luke 9:7–9 | HEROD'S PERPLEXITY *(See on Luke 3:1–20.)*

Luke 9:10–17 | THE FEEDING OF THE 5000

(See on John 6.) About eight months elapse between vv. 17 and 18.

Luke 9:18–20 | PETER'S CONFESSION *(See on Matthew 16:13–20.)*

Luke 9:21–27 | THE PASSION FORETOLD *(See on Mark 9:30–32.)*

Luke 9:28–36 | THE TRANSFIGURATION *(See on Mark 9:2–13.)*

Luke 9:37–43 | THE EPILEPTIC BOY *(See on Mark 9:14–29.)*

Luke 9:43–45 | THE PASSION AGAIN FORETOLD *(See on Mark 9:30–32.)*

Luke 9:46–48 | WHO IS THE GREATEST?

What is so sad about this incident is that it happened right after these disciples experienced the Transfiguration. Furthermore, it was in response to Jesus' announcement of His approaching crucifixion. And worse yet, they repeated the performance when they got to Capernaum (Matthew 18:1–5; Mark 9:33–37) and again as they neared His crucifixion (see on Matthew 20:20–28). What infinite patience Jesus must have had!

Luke 9:49–50 | THE UNKNOWN WONDER WORKER

(Told also in Mark 9:38–40.) Another rebuke of John, this time for wanting to monopolize the privilege of working miracles. And a third one immediately after that, for anger (9:52–56). Three rebukes in a row!

The Perean and Later Judean Ministry, Luke 9:51 to 19:28

The period between Jesus' final departure from Galilee and His last week is usually spoken of as the later Judean and Perean ministry; it took place partly in Perea and partly in Judea. Perea was east of the Jordan (see map on p. 497), in Herod's jurisdiction; Judea, west of Jordan, was under Pilate's jurisdiction.

Luke 9:51 THE FINAL DEPARTURE FROM GALILEE

(Mentioned also in Matthew 19:1 and Mark 10:1.) This is thought to be identical with Jesus' visit to Jerusalem at the Feast of Dedication (John 10:22). Thus the Perean and later Judean ministry covered a period of about four months.

Luke 9:52–56 SAMARITANS REJECT JESUS

The rejection of Jesus by the Samaritans infuriated James and John, who then and there gave an exhibition of why Jesus had nicknamed them "Sons of Thunder" (Mark 3:17). Jesus, without resentment, changed His route on His way toward Jerusalem.

Luke 9:57–62 FOXES HAVE HOLES

More than a year earlier, Jesus had said the same thing to a scribe who offered to follow Him across the lake (Matthew 8:19–22). Probably he had given that same answer many times to those who were looking for a kind of preferment that He did not have to offer. Jesus' reply to the second and third men does not, of course, mean that we should ignore

"Foxes have holes and birds of the air have nests, but the Son of Man has no place to lay his head." (Luke 9:58)

our day-to-day responsibilities toward people. The Bible teaches over and over that one of the truest marks of a Christian is to be thoughtful and considerate in all family relationships, especially in times of grief. It is likely that if the man's father had already died, the man would have been busy with burial preparations. Instead, Jesus knew that the man was suggesting that he would like to go home and care for his father until his death — to put off serving Jesus until there was a more convenient time in his busy life. Jesus means that sharing the Word of God with others is of infinitely greater importance than all our worldly responsibilities, and in case of conflict between the two, there should not be a moment's hesitation — God first always.

Luke 10:1–16 THE SEVENTY-TWO SENT OUT

This seems to have taken place when Jesus left Galilee for the last time. His purpose was to complete the proclamation to the nation that the Messiah was here. They were sent ahead of Him, down the Jordan valley, four or five months before His death.

Luke 10:17–24 THE RETURN OF THE SEVENTY-TWO

We are not told how far they traveled. Probably it was all the way down to the Jericho region, while Jesus followed more slowly. Their success, to Jesus, was a portent of Satan's overthrow. But notice that Jesus warned them not to base their joy on the knowledge that Satan and his spirits are under the authority of Jesus; rather, the real cause of joy is the assurance of our salvation in Christ and the promise of our eternal home in heaven (v. 20).

How Did Jesus Finance His Work?

Jesus did not appear to be a wealthy man by worldly standards. He did not own a place He could call His own (Luke 9:58), and He didn't occupy Himself with worldly concerns such as fancy clothes and possessions. For some three years He traveled about, much of the time with a considerable entourage; and at least twice He organized large preaching expeditions (Luke 9 – 10). In part, Jesus and His disciples lived on the hospitality of the people (Matthew 10:11). He received offerings from the well-to-do and from others (Luke 8:3). Jesus could have amassed a fortune and lived like a king from donations from the crowds that followed Him and from the sick He had healed — if He had so chosen. Jesus needed no accumulated wealth because He had complete and total faith that God would always provide for all His needs and the needs of his entourage. His every need and desire were fulfilled. What a testimony this is to us if we can only put our trust in the Lord!

Luke 10:25–37 THE GOOD SAMARITAN

This is one of the most superb illustrations of human kindness in all literature. Luke had just told about Jesus' being rejected by Samaritans (9:52). Here is Jesus' reaction: He makes a Samaritan the example of love for all future ages.

Luke 10:38–42 MARY AND MARTHA

This is thought to have happened at the end of Jesus' great publicity campaign down the Jordan valley, with the Seventy-two traveling ahead of Him to announce His coming. He was now approaching Jerusalem, perhaps for the Feast of Dedication (John 10:22). Mary and Martha lived in Bethany, on the eastern slope of the Mount of Olives, about two miles from Jerusalem. This incident is recorded to show that Jesus thought that focusing on the Word of the Lord and growing spiritually are far more important than all the busy work that we allow to get in the way of developing our relationship with God. Jesus wants us to put aside some of the things that fill our day so that we can rest quietly in His presence, abiding in Him and in His Word.

The road from Jerusalem down to Jericho goes through the Wadi Kelt, a narrow canyon with steep sides and many places for bandits to hide and attack travelers. St. George's Monastery shows the steepness and barrenness of the wadi.

Luke 11:1 | JESUS PRAYING

Jesus, although He was the Son of God and claimed to have been in some respects equal with God, nevertheless appears to have felt Himself utterly dependent on a Power higher than Himself during His life on earth; He prayed a great deal.

Luke 11:2–4 | THE LORD'S PRAYER

Given in a somewhat longer form in Matthew 6:9–13. It is likely that this prayer was meant to be a sort of norm to guide us in our approach to God and in the subject matter of our petitions.

Luke 11:5–13 | PERSISTENCE IN PRAYER *(See on Luke 18:1–8.)*

Jesus' Prayers

- At His baptism (Luke 3:21)
- In a solitary place (Mark 1:35)
- In the lonely places (Luke 5:16)
- All night, before choosing the Twelve (Luke 6:12)
- Before His invitation, "Come to me" (Matthew 11:25–27)
- At the feeding of the 5000 (John 6:11)
- After the feeding of the 5000 (Matthew 14:23)
- When He gave the Lord's Prayer (Luke 11:1–4)
- At Caesarea-Philippi (Luke 9:18)
- Before His Transfiguration (Luke 9:28–29)
- For little children (Matthew 19:13)
- Before the raising of Lazarus (John 11:41–42)
- In the temple (John 12:27–28)
- At the Last Supper (Matthew 26:26–27)
- For Peter (Luke 22:32)
- For the disciples (John 17)
- In Gethsemane (Matthew 26:36–44)
- On the cross (Luke 23:34)
- At Emmaus (Luke 24:30)

In every recorded prayer Jesus addressed God as "Father" (Matthew 6:9; 11:25; 26:39, 42; Luke 11:2; 23:34; John 11:41; 12:27, 28; 17:1, 5, 11, 21, 24, 25), so different from the bombastic, labored, lofty, and ponderous openings of many pastoral prayers.

Luke 11:14–26 | CASTING OUT DEMONS *(See on Matthew 12:22–37.)*

Luke 11:27–28 | THE WORD OF GOD

A woman called out to Jesus, "Blessed is the mother who gave you birth and nursed you." Jesus answered, "Blessed rather are those who hear the Word of God and obey it."

We are awash in a tidal wave of words. We are assaulted constantly by written and spoken words that drown out the "still, quiet voice" of the Word of God. It takes effort to sit still, to shut out all other noises and voices, and to read and listen to the Word of God. Not read books *about* the Word, or listen to Christian radio, or watch religious TV—but read and listen to the Word of God. Jesus did not think it something optional—if we claim to follow Him, reading and listening to His Word are as essential to life as breathing and eating.

- In Bethany, Mary sat at His feet and listened to His word. Jesus said that Mary had chosen "what is better" (Luke 10:42; KJV, the good part).
- When someone came and said, "Your mother and brothers are standing outside, wanting to see you," Jesus answered, "My mother and brothers are those who hear God's word and put it into practice" (Luke 8:19–21).
- Jesus also said, "The seed [of the kingdom] is the word of God" (Luke 8:11). A soul can be born into the kingdom of God *only* through the seed of the kingdom, the Word of God (1-Peter 1:23).
- "Man does not live on bread alone, but on every word that comes from the mouth of God" (Matthew 4:4).
- If a man does not believe the Scriptures, neither will he believe even if somebody were to rise from the dead (Luke 16:31).
- "Heaven and earth will pass away, but my words will never pass away" (Matthew 24:35).
- "In the beginning was the Word, and the Word was with God, and the Word was God" (John 1:1).
- "The Word became flesh and made his dwelling among us" (John 1:14).

Luke 11:29–32 SIGNS *(See on Matthew 12:39–42.)*

Luke 11:33–36 | THE LIGHTED LAMP *(See on Matthew 5:13–16.)*

Luke 11:37–54 | "WOE TO YOU PHARISEES" *(See on Matthew 23.)*

Luke 12:1–12 | THE SECRET MOTIVES OF LIFE

Jesus dealt a good deal with our motives—that is, that quality within us that makes us do what we do and guides our conduct. To Him, what motivates us is who and what we are. Our one grand motive should be the desire for God's approval and fear of God's disapproval.

The religious people of Jesus' day performed many of their religious practices for the sake of people's approval (Matthew 6:1–18). It is still a part of our nature with which we have a constant struggle. When we are with irreligious people, we are tempted to be ashamed of our religion. But when we are with religious people, we want to be considered religious or spiritual, and this desire sometimes leads us to pretend to be more spiritual than we really are—which is hypocrisy. The desire for people's approval, within proper bounds, is legitimate and laudable. But the most basic fact of existence is God. The one thing that really matters is our relation to Him. Let us always keep Him in mind, and let us be mindful of how our thoughts, motives, and deeds stack up in His sight.

Many of the things in this chapter are contained in the Sermon on the Mount (Matthew 5–7). Jesus had favorite sayings He repeated again and again. One of them was about God's unfailing care for and guidance of His people (vv. 6–12).

Notice especially Jesus' warning about Satan, who has the power to deceive us and ultimately lead us to an eternal existence in hell (v. 5). We must realize that our decision to either follow Christ or not will have eternal consequences. (See on Luke 16:19–31.)

Notice, too, His saying that one day every secret thing about our hypocritical selves shall be known (vv. 2–3). God records our every inner thought and secret act, to be played aloud one day before our startled selves and the assembled universe, when we shall be recognized for what we really are.

The unpardonable sin (v. 10). See on Matthew 12:24–37.

Luke 12:13–21 | PARABLE OF THE RICH FOOL

Notice that Jesus declined to enter into this man's selfish family dispute. Jesus did not attempt to run everybody else's business. Instead, he replied with a parable about the consequences of greed. The lesson of this story offered the man eternal riches if he allowed Jesus' words to change his life.

The rich fool had gotten his money honestly—through the productiveness of his land. Nevertheless, he was a fool in God's eyes (v. 20),

Indoor storage bins used in Israelite homes during the New Testament period are a reminder of the man in Jesus' parable who proclaimed, "I will tear down my barns and build bigger ones." (Luke 12:18)

because he had his heart set on this world and not on the world to come. Rich in this world, a pauper in the next. This world lasts only a little while, the other world lasts forever.

Luke 12:22–34 | TREASURES IN HEAVEN

This is also part of the Sermon on the Mount (Matthew 6:19–34). Jesus was right at home when He was talking about heaven. His language here is superb, and the words are among the most important He ever uttered.

Christians are citizens of heaven who live here temporarily. Jesus teaches not to be focused on earthly concerns but rather to give generously and to walk in faith that the Lord will provide. Jesus says, Seek His kingdom, and these *things* will be given to you as well. The Lord will provide for all needs and desires if we use the excess of what He has given us to minister to others. In this way we become a channel for God to do His work in the world.

Only that which we give to God is ours forever. Said one man to another, of an acquaintance who had just died, "How much did he leave?" Answered the other, "He left it all." Shortly we must, every one of us, leave our earthly tent and leave to others that which we called ours. What will matter is what we have sent ahead for a reservation in the eternal mansion of God.

Luke 12:35–48 | WATCHFULNESS

Jesus' thoughts pass from heaven to the glorious day of His second coming, and He warns that He may come back to a sleeping world in the dead of night (v. 38). Blessed are the faithful who are ready to welcome their returning Lord.

This parable (vv. 41–48) is meant for every Christian. But degrees in talent and position entail corresponding degrees in responsibility. Fearful is the warning here for faithless pastors.

It is a glorious picture of the heavenly Father and His angels welcoming home returning souls. When we grow discouraged over our sinfulness, this is a good chapter to read.

Jesus told these parables after the Pharisees and the teachers of the law complained about His welcoming sinners and eating with them. The account of the three parables ends with the complaint of the elder son, who betrayed a total lack of understanding of the loving heart of the father—like the Pharisees, who had no idea why Jesus would want to associate Himself with sinners.

Luke 16:1–13 | THE PARABLE OF THE SHREWD MANAGER

Jesus commends his foresight, not his dishonesty; his providing for his future, not his crooked method of doing it.

A measure of oil was about nine gallons; a measure of wheat, about 11 bushels.

As the steward made friends by the dishonest use of his master's goods, so we should make friends by the honest use of the gifts God has given us, financial and otherwise. It is a beautiful picture (v. 9): those whom we have befriended will be at the door to welcome us home to heaven.

Jesus said hard things about money, or rather about the love of money. Greed is one of the most pernicious sins since it focuses entirely on ourselves and our wants (rather than needs). We have to have money to supply our daily needs. But the struggle is in our hearts as to whom we really serve and depend on—the money itself or Him who gives the money.

Luke 16:14–18 | THE PHARISEES SCOFF

They ridiculed Jesus' teachings about money because they themselves loved money—they were worldly minded professional religionists.

It is difficult to see the connection in the verses about the Law and divorce. Perhaps Jesus meant that since the Gospel was influencing the people so profoundly, it was harder for Pharisees to justify their hypocritical teachings. While they professed to be guardians of the Law, they ignored the teachings of the Law about divorce, allowing divorce for any trivial cause.

Luke 16:19–31 | THE RICH MAN AND LAZARUS

Abraham's side (v. 22; KJV, Abraham's bosom) is Paradise, the intermediate state in which the souls of the just await resurrection, as Hades is the intermediate state of the lost who are awaiting judgment.

Jesus here presents a conversation between Abraham and Lazarus after death. To what extent it is imaginary we do not know, but its implications are rather plain. For one thing, angels are on hand at the death of saints to bear them away to glory. For another, the lost are in torment (v. 23). There is an impassable gulf between Paradise and Hades, implying that death ends our opportunity for salvation. The Scriptures are entirely sufficient to bring men to repentance (v. 31). And the standards of this world do not apply in heaven: many of those who are first here will be last there. Those who occupy high places here may be the lowliest there. And many of those who are ignored by church dignitaries here may be their masters there (Matthew 19:30; 20:1–16; Mark 10:31).

Luke 17:1–10 FORGIVENESS

Jesus seems to imply here that unwillingness to forgive is the cause of many people losing their souls.

In Matthew 18:21–35, Peter asked Jesus, How often must we forgive? Jesus answered, 77 times—meaning times without number.

Then the disciples cried out, "Lord, increase our faith!" If we have to be that forgiving, we cannot do it without more faith.

Then, to help their faith, Jesus speaks of the unlimited power of faith, and by the parable of the obedient servant He shows them that humility

Heaven and Hell

The story of the rich man and Lazarus is one of the many, many sidelights on the hereafter found in Jesus' teachings. He talked much about the future life. He appealed to the hope of heaven and the fear of hell. He spoke often of the unhappy fate of the lost as well as of the blessedness of the redeemed, setting them over against each other. Run through these passages and see:

- Matthew 5:12, 22, 29 – 30; 6:20; 7:21 – 27; 10:28; 13:39 – 43, 49 – 50; 18:8 – 9; 22:13; 23:33; 25:23, 30, 34, 41, 46
- Mark 9:43 – 48
- Luke 12:4 – 5; 16:22 – 28
- John 3:15 – 16, 36; 5:24, 28 – 29, 39; 6:27, 39 – 40, 44, 47, 49 – 51, 54; 17:2

Note how often the words "heaven," "hell," and "eternal life" occur.

It is a pity that the present-day pulpit so generally ignores and even looks down on the very motives that Jesus Himself appealed to. One of the most powerful stimulants to do good and most powerful deterrents from evil in this life is a profound conviction as to the reality of the future life — the fact that our place there will depend on our decisions and actions in this life. A heart firmly fixed on heaven will surely mean a more careful walk in this world. This world has an end. That one lasts forever.

is the foundation of faith. As we seek the Lord, our desire to serve Him and do His work will provide us with the power and faith we need to thrive as we serve others in His name.

Luke 17:11–19 THE 10 LEPERS

This seems to be told, not only as one of Jesus' miracles, but also to show that He gladly used His power to heal on behalf of those who would not even thank Him for it, illustrating the kind, unresentful heart He had just been talking about. Also, it shows the Samaritan in a good light, compared with those of Jesus' own race.

A widow pleading her case regarding harvest concerns. "There was a widow in that town who kept coming to a godless judge with a plea, 'Grant me justice against my adversary.'" (Luke 18:3)

Luke 17:20–37 | THE COMING KINGDOM

To the Pharisees, Jesus said, "The kingdom of God is within you" — it is a matter of the heart. Then His thoughts moved ahead to the future, and He talked to the disciples about the glorious day when He would come in power with the redeemed of all ages. (See on Matthew 24.)

Luke 18:1–8 | THE PERSISTENT WIDOW

This, like the story of the friend at midnight in Luke 11:5–13, was told for the one specific purpose of teaching that God will honor patient, persistent, persevering prayer. The widow in this parable repeatedly goes to an unjust judge with her petition and eventually wears him down so that he grants her request. Jesus contrasts this with what we can expect when we make our requests to God. He says that God will see that we get justice and get it quickly.

To learn how to pray successfully is a matter of lifetime study and self-discipline. For one thing, we must learn how to forgive (Mark 11:25). And in Matthew 7:12 prayer is directly connected with the practice of the Golden Rule. The single most important requirement, however, is faith. God's promises for those who have faith are simply amazing. Note below the emphasis on faith in the statements of Jesus. (See also James 1:5–7.)

But Jesus called the children to him and said, "Let the little children come to me, and do not hinder them, for the kingdom of God belongs to such as these. I tell you the truth, anyone who will not receive the kingdom of God like a little child will never enter it."
— Luke 18:16 – 17

Luke 18:9–14 | THE PHARISEE AND THE TAX COLLECTOR

Pharisees were generally so self-righteous and hypocritical in their haughty attitude toward others that the word "Pharisee" has almost become a synonym for sham. They had that same self-satisfied attitude toward God, as if they thought God would feel honored to have them pray to Him.

Jesus detested religious pretense from the depth of His soul. The bitterest words He ever uttered were against the hypocrisy of the Pharisees (Matthew 23). He did not condone the sins of tax collectors and

The Power of Faith and Prayer

Jesus prayed a great deal (see on Luke 11:1). And He talked much about prayer. Here are some of the things He said about faith as a part of the act of prayer:

- In Nazareth He did not do many mighty works because of their *unbelief* (Matthew 13:58).
- To the disciples, in the storm: "Why are you so afraid? Do you still have no *faith?*" (Mark 4:40; Luke 8:25).
- To Jairus: "Just *believe*, and she will be healed" (Luke 8:50).
- To the woman with a bleeding disorder: "Your *faith* has healed you" (Mark 5:34).
- The centurion to Jesus: "Just say the word, and my servant will be healed." Jesus' response: "I have not found anyone in Israel with such great *faith*." And the servant was healed (Matthew 8:8, 10, 13).
- To the blind men: "Do you *believe* that I am able to do this? . . . According to your faith will it be done to you" (Matthew 9:28 – 29).
- To the disciples: "If you have *faith* and do not doubt," you shall do what is done to this fig tree (Matthew 21:21).
- To the Canaanite woman, "Woman, you have great *faith*! Your request is granted" (Matthew 15:28).
- To Peter, sinking in the water, "You of little *faith*, . . . why did you doubt?" (Matthew 14:31).
- To the disciples: "O *faithless* generation, . . . how long shall I suffer you?" (Mark 9:19).
- The disciples to Jesus: "Why couldn't we drive it out?" Jesus' response: "Because you have so little *faith*" (Matthew 17:19 – 20).
- To the disciples: "If you have *faith* as small as a mustard seed, you can say to this mountain, 'Move from here to there' and it will move. Nothing will be impossible for you. . . . If you *believe*, you will receive whatever you ask for in prayer. . . . Everything is possible for him who *believes*" (Matthew 17:20; 21:22; Mark 9:23; also 11:22—-25).
- To Martha, at the grave of Lazarus: "Did I not tell you that if you *believed*, you would see the glory of God?" (John 11:40).
- To the multitudes in Capernaum: "The work of God is this: to *believe* in the one he has sent" (John 6:29).

The emphasis Jesus put on faith is simply astounding. When Jesus talked about prayer and faith, strange as some of His words may sound to us, He knew what He was talking about. He came out of the unseen world, and He was perfectly familiar with the forces and powers that are at work behind the scenes but about which we know nothing. We ought not to be too determined to explain everything that Jesus said about prayer so as to bring it within range of our finite understanding. It might be that, if only we would apply ourselves with enough patience and persistence and perseverance to the practice of prayer, we could achieve things that we do not ordinarily dream are possible.

Jesus certainly meant something by these words. He did not talk just to hear Himself talk. We think that He was aiming to teach some of the most fundamental lessons of human existence for all mankind of all generations. God holds in His hands the workings of the interrelated forces of the universe, and He is able to bring into play powers that we know nothing about to supplement and control those that we do know about. Jesus said that God may be induced to do this through our faith in Him.

prostitutes—He came to save them. But they knew they were sinners, and therefore it was easier for them to take the first step and confess it. This parable is aimed at showing that the only basis for approaching God is a realization of our sinfulness and the need of His mercy.

Luke 18:15–17 LITTLE CHILDREN

(Told also in Matthew 19:13 and Mark 10:13–16.) Jesus had just spoken of the tax collector being on his way to salvation because he was deeply perturbed by his sinfulness. Here Jesus indicates that heaven will be exclusively occupied by child-like people. No pompous fellows in heaven, strutting around as if they owned the universe. There are plenty of them in the church here—but not so up there. Jesus said flatly that unless we become like little children, we shall never enter the kingdom of heaven (Matthew 18:3). A little child is teachable, trustful, free from mental pride, unsophisticated, and loving. The disciples did not think children were important enough to bother with. That made Jesus indignant—He loved children (Mark 10:13–14).

Luke 18:18–30 THE RICH YOUNG RULER

(Told also in Matthew 19:16–30 and Mark 10:17–31.) Jesus told him to give all. Jesus did not mean that everybody should give up all their money to follow Him. Zacchaeus offered to give half, and Jesus was pleased with him (Luke 19:9). But this young ruler was too much in love with his riches to be of any use in the kingdom of Christ.

The eye of a needle (v. 25) is thought by some to be the small gate for pedestrians, in or near the large city gate, through which a camel might be able to pass, but only by kneeling and with great difficulty. More generally it is thought to be a literal needle. At any rate, Jesus meant an impossible thing (v. 27). Then He modified the idea by saying that what is impossible for human beings is possible for God.

Note the wonderful promise to those who give up all to follow Jesus (vv. 28–30). It is amplified in Mark 10:28–31. A hundred times as much in this life, and life eternal in the world to come.

Luke 18:31–43 A BLIND MAN AT JERICHO

(Told also in Matthew 20:29–34 and Mark 10:46–52.) Matthew says there were two blind men; Mark and Luke mention only one. Luke says Jesus was entering Jericho; Matthew and Mark say it was as He went out. Mark calls him Bartimaeus. Possibly one was healed as Jesus entered the city, and the other as He left. It is likely that as Jesus entered the city, they followed along, and after Jesus was finished at the house of Zacchaeus, they placed themselves by the road where they knew He would pass. Just before He healed the blind man, Jesus had told His disciples—for the fifth time—that he was on His way to be crucified (vv. 31–34). But they still did not understand what He was talking about (v. 34).

Luke 19:1–10 ZACCHAEUS

Zacchaeus was a chief tax collector, head of a large office of tax collectors. Tax collectors were considered to be on a par with prostitutes (v. 7; Matthew 21:31–32). They were generally hated, because the taxes went to a foreign power. Jericho was a city of priests. Jesus chose a tax collector rather than a priest to stay with. Zacchaeus was converted immediately and gave genuine evidence of it. Jesus had told the rich young ruler to give all (Luke 18:22). Zacchaeus gave half (v. 8), and Jesus pronounced him an heir of salvation.

Luke 19:11–28 PARABLE OF THE 10 MINAS

This differs in some points from the parable of the talents (Matthew 25:14–30), but it illustrates the same general truths: we are accountable to the Lord for the way we use our means and time; there will be rewards and punishments both in our earthly life and in heaven; we are in training here for life there. It is a parable of the Second Advent. "A distant country" (v. 12), in this parable and in the parable of the talents (Matthew 25:19), hints at a long interval between Jesus' first and second comings. (See further under 2-Thessalonians and 2-Peter 3.)

A sycamore tree in Jericho—an ideal place for Zacchaeus to watch Jesus unseen.

Jesus' Last Week, Luke 19:29 to 23:56

Luke 19:29–44 THE TRIUMPHAL ENTRY *(See on Matthew 21:1–11.)*

Luke 19:45–48 THE CLEARING OF THE TEMPLE AREA *(See on Matthew 21:12–17.)*

Luke 20:1–8 BY WHAT AUTHORITY? *(See on Matthew 21:23–27.)*

Luke 20:9–20 THE PARABLE OF THE VINEYARD *(See on Matthew 21:33–46.)*

Luke 20:21–26 PAYING TAXES TO CAESAR *(See on Mark 12:13–17.)*

Luke 20:27–40 THE RESURRECTION *(See on Mark 12:18–27.)*

Luke 20:41–44 DAVID'S SON *(See on Mark 12:35–37.)*

Luke 20:45–47 THE TEACHERS OF THE LAW DENOUNCED *(See on Matthew 23.)*

Luke 21:1–4 THE WIDOW'S OFFERING *(See on Mark 12:41–44.)*

Luke 21:5–36 DISCOURSE ON THE END *(See on Matthew 24.)*

Luke 21:37–22:2 THE PLOT TO KILL JESUS *(See on Mark 14:1–2.)*

Luke 22:3–6 JUDAS AGREES TO BETRAY JESUS *(See on Mark 14:10–11.)*

Luke 22:7–38 THE LAST SUPPER *(See on Matthew 26:17–29.)*

Luke 22:39–46 THE AGONY IN GETHSEMANE

(Told also in Matthew 26:36–46; Mark 14:32–42; and John 18:1.) The traditional site of this garden cannot be far from the actual site.

The human race started in a garden. Jesus suffered His agony in a garden. He was crucified near a garden and buried in a garden (John 19:41). Paradise will be a garden.

Jesus had come out of eternity knowing that the cross was at the end of the road, for He knew that He was coming as the Lamb of God to take away the sin of the world. As a man, He left Galilee and went to Jerusalem with determination, walking with steady tread, never wavering, never faltering.

But now He had come to the end of the road, and there stood that ghastly thing. Jesus knew that He not only was called to die a physical death, but more importantly, was also required to die a spiritual death. Spiritual death meant separation from God, the ultimate sacrifice for this divine man who had never known sin. Jesus knew that He was required to take on the sin of mankind, which required separation from His Father and a descent into the depths of hell. It made even Jesus the Son of God ask the question, "Lord, if there is any other way, take this cup from me." However, Jesus knew that there was no other way. He alone was the way, and His mission was clear. He was to conquer death and pay the penalty so that all of mankind could be reunited with God.

As the two or three or four hours of fervent prayer passed, His agony and resolve made Him sweat drops of blood, and He felt so weak that God sent an angel to strengthen Him.

Our human minds cannot comprehend the immensity of His task and His sacrifice. We simply know that it was to save us and that Jesus' suffering is the most blessed influence the world has ever known.

Luke 22:47–53 | JESUS IS ARRESTED *(See on John 18:1–12.)*

Luke 22:54–62 | PETER'S DENIAL *(See on John 18:15–18.)*

Luke 22:54–23:25 | THE TRIAL OF JESUS *(See on Mark 14:53.)*

Luke 23:26 | SIMON OF CYRENE *(See on Matthew 27:32.)*

Luke 23:27–31 | WEEPING AT THE FOOT OF THE CROSS

On the way to Calvary Jesus says, "Do not weep for me; weep for yourselves and for your children" (v. 28). Behind these words we hear the echo of the words the crowd had just spoken, "Let his blood be on us and

---

Gethsemane

A garden located at the foot of the western slope of the Mount of Olives, just east of the city of Jerusalem. Jesus and His disciples may not have been alone in the olive garden, for at Passover time (April), thousands of pilgrims streamed into Jerusalem, and it is probable that many of them were camping out on the Mount of Olives. It is noteworthy that Jesus could have merely taken a 15- minute walk eastward, over the top of the mountain, and vanished into the Judean desert. Yet He chose not to flee, but to stay and be captured, tried, tortured, humiliated, and crucified on our behalf.

This rock located inside of the Church of All Nations commemorates the location where Jesus suffered great agony in Gethsemane.

Crucifixion

Crucifixion was Rome's punishment for slaves, foreigners, and criminals who were not Roman citizens. It was the most agonizing and ignominious death a cruel age could devise. Nails were driven through the hands and feet, and the victim was left hanging there in agony, suffering starvation, insufferable thirst, and excruciating convulsions of pain. The cause of death was not loss of blood but heart failure. Death usually followed in two to six days. In Jesus' case it was over in six hours, when Jesus declared that "It is finished" and willfully gave up His spirit. (See under John 19:33–34.)

---

on our children!" (Matthew 27:25). How these words have been fulfilled through the centuries!

Luke 23:32–49 | **THE CRUCIFIXION** *(See also on Matthew 27:26–56; Mark 15:21–41; and John 19:17–37.)*

Luke 23:32–43 | **THE PENITENT CRIMINAL**

Both criminals at first joined in the mockery (Matthew 27:44). But one changed his mind. And in one respect, he put the disciples to shame. For two years or more Jesus had tried so hard to teach them that His kingdom was not to be a kingdom of this world. Now He was dying, and to the disciples this meant the end of His kingdom. They had no thought that He would come to life again to reign in glory (see p. 708). But not so this criminal. Perhaps, standing at the fringe of the crowds, he had heard Jesus talk of His kingdom. And though Jesus was now dying, the criminal still believed that He had a kingdom beyond the grave (v. 42). A criminal understood Jesus better than Jesus' own intimate friends! Jesus surely loved repentant sinners. And as He returned to God, He bore in His arms the soul of a criminal, the firstfruits of His mission to redeem the world.

Luke 23:50–56 | **BURIAL** *(See on John 19:38–42.)*

The Resurrection, Luke 24:1–53

Luke 24:1–10 | **THE WOMEN AT THE TOMB** *(See on Matthew 28:1–8.)*

Luke 24:11–12 | **PETER RUNS TO THE TOMB** *(See on John 20:3–10.)*

Luke 24:13–32 | **JESUS APPEARS TO THE TWO**

This encounter took place in the afternoon. In the early morning Jesus had already appeared to Mary Magdalene (Mark 16:9–11; John 20:11–18) and also to the other women (Matthew 28:9–10). But these two disciples had only heard the report that the tomb was empty and that angels had announced that Jesus was risen (vv. 22–24).

Luke 24:33–35 | JESUS APPEARS TO PETER

The time is not stated. It was probably just before or just after Jesus had appeared to the two disciples on the road to Emmaus in the afternoon. In the early morning He had sent a special message to Peter via the angels and the women (see on Mark 16:7).

Luke 24:36–43 | JESUS APPEARS TO THE ELEVEN

(See also on Mark 16:14–18 and John 20:19–23.) The group was referred to as "the Eleven" (v. 33). In this case there were only 10, for Thomas was absent (John 20:24). Note their joyous belief (v. 34) and yet also their disbelief (v. 41), even after Jesus had shown them His hands and feet. Faith and doubt alternate.

(See p. 502 for a list of Jesus' appearances after His resurrection.)

Luke 24:44–53 | THE FINAL APPEARANCE AND ASCENSION

(Told also in Mark 16:19 and Acts 1:3–12.) Verses 44–49 seem to belong to Jesus' final appearance rather than to the appearance just mentioned in vv. 36–43; for that evidently was on the first Sunday evening, and here He tells them to stay in Jerusalem (v. 49), which must have been after they had gone to Galilee and returned to Jerusalem. Then He led them out of Jerusalem to His beloved Bethany. His 40 days of post-resurrection ministry were finished, His earthly mission accomplished, and waiting angels bore the triumphant Savior away to the throne of God.

John

Jesus the Son of God

"For God so loved the world that he gave his one and only Son, that whoever believes in him shall not perish but have eternal life. For God did not send his Son into the world to condemn the world, but to save the world through him." —JOHN 3:16–17

Jesus answered, "I am the way and the truth and the life. No one comes to the Father except through me." —JOHN 14:6

- For a general introduction to all four Gospels, see p. 517.
- For an overview of the life of Jesus, see p. 493.

John's Emphasis: The Deity of Jesus

The special emphasis of John is the deity of Jesus. It begins with Jesus' pre-existence and focuses on the unity between Jesus and God, His Father. This Gospel consists mainly of Jesus' discourses and conversations—it presents what Jesus *said* rather than what He *did*.

Author

The author does not identify himself until the end of the book (21:20, 24), where he states that he is "the disciple whom Jesus loved" (13:23; 20:2), that is, John the Apostle, the most intimate earthly friend of Jesus.

Ancient tradition and unbroken subsequent opinion have recognized his authorship, until the rise of modern criticism. The same class of critics who deny the Virgin Birth of Jesus, His deity, and His bodily resurrection have concluded that the author was not John the Apostle but another John of Ephesus. They base their hypothesis on an ancient, vague mention of a certain John the presbyter (elder) of Ephesus. This theory, which would undermine the value of the book as a testimony to the deity of Jesus, is based on such flimsy evidence that it does not deserve serious consideration by Christian believers.

John

His father's name was Zebedee (Matthew 4:21). His mother seems to have been Salome (Matthew 27:56; Mark 15:40), who may have been a sister of Mary, the mother of Jesus (compare John 19:25). If this is true, then John was a cousin of Jesus and about the same age; they must have known each other from childhood.

John was a businessman of some means. He was one of five partners in a fishing business that employed hired servants (Mark 1:16–20).

Besides his fishing business in Capernaum, he had a house in Jerusalem (John 19:27), and he was a personal acquaintance of the high priest (John 18:15 – 16).

He was a disciple of John the Baptist (John 1:35, 40). If he was a cousin of Jesus, as seems implied in passages cited above, then he was also related to John the Baptist (Luke 1:36) and must have known of the angels' announcements about John and Jesus (Luke 1:17, 32). So when John the Baptist appeared, crying that the kingdom of heaven was at hand, John the son of Zebedee was ready to take his stand with him.

On the strength of the Baptist's testimony, he immediately became a disciple of Jesus (John 1:35 – 51) — one of the first five — and returned

9th-century illustration of the apostle John, "the disciple whom Jesus loved," writing the Gospel.

with Jesus to Galilee (John 2:2, 11). Then he went back, it seems, to his fishing business. Later, probably about a year later, Jesus called him to leave his business and travel around with Him. He was thereafter with Jesus continually and thus was an eyewitness of what is written in this Gospel.

Jesus nicknamed him "Son of Thunder" (Mark 3:17), which seems to imply that he had a vehement, violent temper. The incident of forbidding a stranger to use the name of Christ in casting out demons (Mark 9:38) and the desire to call down fire on the Samaritans (Luke 9:54) are interesting sidelights on his nature. But he appears to have brought his temper under control.

John was one of the three disciples of Jesus' inner circle, and he was recognized as the one closest to Jesus. Five times he is spoken of as "the disciple whom Jesus loved" (John 13:23; 19:26; 20:2; 21:7, 20). He must have been a man of rare qualities of character.

John and Peter became the recognized leaders of the Twelve and were generally together, although they had very different dispositions (John 20:2; Acts 3:1, 11; 4:13; 8:14).

John seems to have lived mainly in Jerusalem for a number of years. According to well-established tradition, his later years were spent at Ephesus, where he lived to a ripe old age. Nothing is known of his activities or whereabouts in the meantime. In Ephesus he wrote his Gospel, three letters, and possibly Revelation.

The date of John's Gospel is usually thought to be about A.D. 90.

| John 1:1–3 | ETERNITY AND DEITY OF JESUS |

These verses remind us of the opening words of Genesis. Jesus is called God and Creator. John is very positive that Jesus was a personality who existed from eternity, and that He had had a hand in the creation of the universe. Jesus is here called the Word. In Genesis we read again and again, "And God said." In John 17:5, Jesus is quoted as referring to the glory He had with the Father before the world existed. Thus Jesus is God's expression of Himself to humanity. He is God's Message to us.

Son of Man

This was Jesus' favorite name for Himself. It occurs about 70 times in the Gospels: 30 times in Matthew, 5 in Mark, 25 in Luke, and 10 times in John.

It was used in Daniel 7:13–14, 27 as a name of the coming Messiah. Jesus' use of it to refer to Himself may have amounted to a claim that He was the Messiah.

On the other hand, it suggests that Jesus rejoiced in His experience as God in human form, sharing the life of mankind. He carried the title with Him to heaven (Acts 7:56; Revelation 1:13; 14:14). Ezekiel was addressed about 90 times as "son of man" (Ezekiel 2:1, 3, 6, 8, etc), implying the lowliness of man compared with God.

John 1:4–13 | JESUS THE LIGHT OF THE WORLD

Jesus said this again and again (8:12; 9:5; 12:46). It is one of the keynotes in John's thought about Jesus (1-John 1:5–7). It means that Jesus, as Light of the World, is the One who makes clear the meaning and destiny of human existence.

Verse 6 introduces John the Baptist, who was sent from God, not as the Light, but as a witness to the Light. All references to John in this Gospel refer to John the Baptist and not the author.

John's Gospel emphasizes that membership in God's family is provided to all who receive Him and believe in His name (v. 12). Salvation is received through God's grace and never through human works.

John 1:14–18 | THE INCARNATION

God became a man in order to win humanity to Himself. God could have made human beings with an instinct to do His will, but He chose rather to give them the power to decide for themselves their attitude toward their Creator. But God is Spirit, and we are hedged in by the limitations of a material body and have little conception of what a spirit is. So the Creator came to His creatures in the form of one of them to give them an idea of the kind of Being He is. God is like Jesus. Jesus is like God.

John 1:19–34 | JOHN'S TESTIMONY

After brief statements about the deity of Jesus and his pre-existence and incarnation, John's Gospel, passing over Jesus' birth, childhood, baptism, and temptation, starts with the testimony to the deity of Jesus given by John the Baptist to the investigating committee from the Sanhedrin.

This was at the close of the 40 days of Jesus' temptation (Matthew 4:1–11). It is nowhere stated that Jesus returned from the temptation in the wilderness to the Jordan, where John was baptizing. The three Synoptic Gospels pass directly from the temptation to the Galilean ministry (Matthew 4:11–12; Mark 1:13–14; Luke 4:13–14). But the three successive phrases "the next day" (vv. 29, 35, 43), followed by "the third day" (2:1), on which he arrived in Galilee, make it evident that Jesus, before departing for Galilee, went back from the wilderness to the place where John was preaching.

The Prophet (v. 21) was a descriptive title of the Messiah and was generally understood as such by the people in Jesus' day (6:14).

Note John's profound humility in his devotion to Christ (v. 27)—he did not consider himself worthy even to untie His shoe—a servant's job. This is so noteworthy that it is recorded in all four Gospels (Matthew 3:11; Mark 1:7; Luke 3:16). What a powerful statement to the world if all Christians could exhibit the same humble adoration of the Lord!

Lamb of God (v. 29), a descriptive title of Jesus used only here and in v. 36. John is foretelling that Jesus will be the sacrifice that atones for the sins of the world.

| John 1:35–51 | THE FIRST DISCIPLES |

There were five of them: John, Andrew, Simon, Philip, and Nathanael. They had been prepared by the preaching of John the Baptist, and all five later became apostles. This was one of the contributions of the Baptist's ministry to the work of Christ. Temporarily, however, they went back to their regular occupations. About a year later they were called to follow Christ continuously. (See note under Matthew 10.)

John the Apostle is assumed to be the unnamed disciple (v. 40). If he was a cousin of Jesus (see introductory note above), he must already have known Jesus before this.

The tenth hour (v. 39) was 10 A.M. John uses Roman time, which was, like ours, counted from midnight or noon (4:6; 19:14).

Simon, being a business partner of John, may already have known Jesus personally. But he did not know that Jesus was the Messiah until John the Baptist's public proclamation. The fact that Jesus gave Simon a new name at this, their first recorded meeting, seems to indicate that Jesus already had him in mind for the apostleship.

Bethsaida

Only Jerusalem and Capernaum are mentioned more frequently in the Gospels than Bethsaida, which was the birthplace of Peter and Andrew (Matthew 1:44) and the home of the apostle Philip (Matthew 12:21). Some think that Zebedee and his sons, James and John, were from Bethsaida before moving to Capernaum, a few miles to the west.

In Bethsaida a blind man was healed (Mark 8:22–26), and in a deserted place nearby, probably along the northeast shore of the sea, the feeding of the 4000 took place. Like Korazin and Capernaum, the town was "cursed" by Jesus because of the unbelief of its inhabitants.

One possible location of Bethsaida is the mound called et-Tell, which is located east of the Jordan River, about 1 1/2 miles north of the Sea of Galilee. This city was built by Philip, the son of Herod the Great, early in his reign (4 B.C.–A.D. 34), probably as a way station on the international highway that led to the Mediterranean and as a port for himself on the Sea of Galilee (the ancient shoreline may have been further north than it is now). He named the city Julias, after Julia, the emperor's daughter. However, the archaeological profile does not completely agree with what we expect Bethsaida to be like on the basis of literary sources.

Recently, support has grown for the theory that there were in fact two Bethsaidas, one in Philip's territory (Bethsaida-Julias), the other "in Galilee" (John 12:21). The latter has been tentatively identified with the small site of Aradj (el-Araj), located very close to the shore of the Sea of Galilee. It is proposed that at the time of Jesus the Jordan followed a more easterly course than it does now, so that Aradj at that time was west of the river, that is, "in Galilee." Extensive excavations have not yet taken place there, however, to fully test these claims.

Nathanael was converted by the majesty of Jesus' person (vv. 46–49). Jesus' statement about angels (v. 51) marks Him as the connecting highway between earth and heaven (Genesis 28:12).

John 2:1–11 | WATER CHANGED INTO WINE

Nathanael was from Cana (21:2). He did not have a very high opinion of the neighboring town of Nazareth (1:46). The marriage, evidently, was in the home of some friend or relative of either Jesus or Nathanael.

"**Woman**" (v. 4), was a title of respect in the usage of that day. Jesus used it again, on the cross, at a time when there could have been no possible hint of disrespect (19:26). The point of His remark seems to be: "Suppose the wine is gone—what have I to do with it? It is not My affair. My time to work miracles has not yet come." Perhaps He had just told his mother of the new miraculous powers He had received by the descent of the Holy Spirit at His baptism. (See note on Jesus' temptation under Matthew 4:1–10). She saw in the situation an opportunity for Him. While He did this miracle at her suggestion, the time (v. 4) for the general use of His miraculous powers did not come until about four months later, at the official beginning of His public ministry in Jerusalem at the time of the Passover (v. 13).

Stone water jars (v. 6). The jars held about 20 or 30 gallons each. The six jars together would have held between 120 and 180 gallons, equivalent to somewhere between 550 and 840 of our wine bottles.

The significance of this miracle is that Jesus had just submitted Himself, for 40 days, to every suggestion Satan was capable of offering as to how He should use His miraculous powers, and He had steadfastly refused to use them for His own need. Then from the wilderness He went directly to a wedding. And although He did subsequent miracles largely to relieve suffering, this first miracle was done at a wedding feast, on a festive occasion. Jesus ministered to human joy, making people happy, as if He wanted to announce right at the beginning of His ministry that the religion which He was now introducing to the world was not a religion of asceticism, but a religion of natural joy. It was also Jesus' blessing on marriage.

Manifested his glory (v. 11), as Creator (1:3, 14). The miracle required actual creative power. (See note on Jesus' miracles under Mark 5:21–43.)

Cana of Galilee

Cana of Galilee, where Jesus performed His first and second miracles (John 2:1–11; 4:46–54) was also the home of Nathanael (21:2). It was located at the as yet unexcavated site of Khirbet Qana, eight miles north of Nazareth–rather than at the "traditional site" of Kefar Kana, which is conveniently located along a heavily traveled road.

John 2:12 | BRIEF STAY IN CAPERNAUM

This was a sort of family visit that included Jesus' mother and brothers, probably to the home of John or Peter, to make plans for His future work. About a year later, Capernaum became His main residence. He did no more miracles in Galilee until after His return from the Judean ministry (4:54).

The Early Judean Ministry, John 2:13 to 4:42

This is told only in John's Gospel. It lasted eight months, beginning in April, at Passover time (2:13), and ending in December, four months before the harvest (4:3, 35). It includes the clearing out of the temple area, the visit of Nicodemus, and Jesus' ministry by the Jordan.

John 2:13–25 | JESUS CLEARS THE TEMPLE AREA

Evidently there were two cleansings, three years apart: this one, at the beginning of his public ministry (note the word "after," 3:22), the other one at its close, during His last week (Matthew 21:12–16; Mark 11:15–18; Luke 19:45–46). In this cleansing He drove out the cattle; in the other, He drove out the traders. In this one He called the temple a market; in the other, a "den of robbers."

The formal opening act of Jesus' public work, which He intended as a sign to the nation that He was the Messiah (for so it was expected, Malachi 3:1–3), was in open and utter defiance of the religious leaders, whose antagonism was immediately aroused and which, it seems, Jesus never cared to pacify. Thus He began His ministry, and thus He closed it.

There must have been something very majestic in Jesus' personal appearance or in His presence, or, more likely, it may have been through His miraculous power that a lone stranger, with only a scourge in His hand, could have cleared and held control of the temple area, so that (the second time) not even a vessel could be carried through (Mark 11:16). Even the police were cowed into silence.

What was it that was so displeasing to Jesus in the temple? They were profiteering to such an extent that the whole service of God had been commercialized and trivialized—inside the sacred area that had been dedicated to other purposes. (See further under Matthew 21:12–17.)

The temple, built by Herod the Great of marble and gold, was magnificent. Surrounded by four courts, on lower successive levels: for priests, male Israelites, women, and Gentiles. The temple area was bordered by covered colonnades, with pillars of whitest marble, each 40 feet high and made of a single stone. The colonnade on the east was called Solomon's Portico, or Colonnade, which is where the traders were. The whole area was surrounded by a massive wall, about 1000 feet on each side, and was about the size of 25 football fields or four average city blocks.

Little remains of the Jerusalem of Jesus' day. The city walls and gates we see today (top) were built by the Turkish sultan Suleiman the Magnificent in A.D. 1542. One of the few visible remains of the temple built by Herod the Great is a portion of the Western Wall of the temple platform (also known as the Wailing Wall). The massive blocks of stone in the lower courses are Herodian (bottom).

Miracles (v. 23). Until now, Jesus had done only one miracle, in Galilee (2:11; 4:54). But now, along with the opening of His campaign by the spectacular demonstration in the temple, He performed so many miracles that many were ready to accept Him as the Messiah. But He knew all too well what they expected of the Messiah.

John 3:1–21 | NICODEMUS

The cleansing of the temple and the accompanying miracles had made a deep impression on the city. Nicodemus, an influential man—a Pharisee and a member of the Sanhedrin—cautiously sought a private interview with Jesus. He was interested, but he wanted to satisfy himself as to Jesus' claims. To what extent he believed we do not know. Two years later, he took Jesus' side in the Sanhedrin (7:50–52). Later still, he and Joseph of Arimathea, another member of the council, buried Jesus (19:39). He was a secret disciple in the formative days of his faith, but later he was willing to openly share with Jesus the shame of His cross. His coming out of the shadows in the hour of Jesus' humiliation, when even the Twelve had fled for cover, risking his own life on that final day, is one of the noblest incidents of Scripture. He surely made up for his original inclination to secrecy, especially considering that he was a member of the Sanhedrin, right in the very heart of the enemy camp.

The new birth Jesus talked about is not merely a metaphor, but an actual reality that results from the impregnation of the human heart by the Spirit of God (see on Romans 8:1–11). Nicodemus, no doubt, shared the common notion that the Messiah's kingdom was to be a political kingdom in which his nation would be freed from Roman domination. Jesus tried to tell him of its personal, spiritual nature. This was so different from what was in Nicodemus's mind that he did not understand what Jesus was talking about. He just could not see how he, a good man, a genuine Pharisee, one of the rulers of the messianic nation, would not be welcomed into the messianic kingdom with open arms. He just could not take it in that, instead, he himself, as well as his ideas, needed to be reconstructed from the ground up.

Must be lifted up (v. 14). This is an announcement at the beginning of Jesus' ministry that the cross would be His messianic throne. It is a reference to the brass serpent, to which those who had been bitten by the poisonous snakes in the wilderness looked up and lived (Numbers 21:9), meaning that the new birth into eternal life, of which He had just been speaking, would come by virtue of His death.

John 3:22–36 | JESUS' MINISTRY IN THE LOWER JORDAN REGION

This was the same region where He had been baptized. John, in the meantime, had moved farther north, to a place called Aenon. Both men were preaching the same thing: the long-foretold kingdom of heaven is at hand. Soon Jesus had a larger following than John, for several reasons: His miracles; and because John had pointed to Jesus as the Messiah. Some of John's disciples were evidently envious of Jesus' success. John reminds them that "He must become greater; I must become less" (v. 30). John was full of joy at hearing of Jesus' popularity and success.

Eight months later, John was put in prison (Matthew 4:12). The rulers in Jerusalem were taking notice (John 4:1), and it began to look as if it might be dangerous for Jesus to continue to work in that region.

So He withdrew to Galilee, lest He be silenced prematurely, before His work was completed.

This period began at about Passover time (April, v. 22; 2:13) and ended four months before harvest (December, 4:35), a total of eight months.

John 4:1–42 | THE SAMARITAN WOMAN

Jesus returned to Galilee through Samaria instead of taking the more common route up the Jordan valley, perhaps out of caution. Samaria was outside the jurisdiction of Herod, who had just imprisoned John. Jesus was merely passing through, and His conversation with the Samaritan woman was only incidental. Yet it is one of the most beautiful and revealing stories in the life of Jesus.

The Samaritans were a mixture of the few Israelites who stayed behind when the northern kingdom was deported by the Assyrians, and people from elsewhere whom the Assyrians, 700 years before the time of Jesus, had brought into what had been the northern kingdom (2 Kings 17:6, 24, 26, 29; Ezra 5:1, 9–10). The Samaritans accepted the Pentateuch (the five books of Moses: Genesis through Deuteronomy). They were expecting the Messiah to make Samaria, not Jerusalem, his seat of government.

Jesus was being eyed with suspicion by the rulers of His own nation, but here the despised Samaritans received Him gladly. One of the constantly recurring contrasts in the Gospels is the repudiation of Jesus by the religious leaders of His nation and His acceptance by the outcasts, sinners, and common people.

The sixth hour (v. 6) would probably have been about 4 P.M., reckoning Roman time. The woman did not expect to encounter a man at the well at that time, nor did she expect a Jew to talk to her.

Greek Orthodox priest at the church at Jacob's well. Jesus declared Himself to be the Messiah at Jacob's well while speaking to the Samaritan woman.

I . . . am He (v. 26). This is the only time prior to His trial that Jesus declared that He was the Messiah.

This visit of Jesus laid the groundwork for the hearty reception of the Gospel by Samaritans a few years later (Acts 8:4–8).

ARCHAEOLOGICAL NOTE: Jacob's Well. The well of Jacob, 100 feet deep and nine feet in diameter, is one of the few places in the life of Jesus that can be identified with certainty and precision. It lies at the foot of Mount Gerizim, which was (and still is, see p. 479) the center of Samaritan worship. Recent archaeological excavations at the summit of Mount Gerizim have begun to uncover the remains of an ancient Samaritan temple.

From Galilee to Judea to Perea, John 4:43 to 11:57

John 4:43–54 | THE ROYAL OFFICIAL'S SON

Jesus was welcomed when He returned to Galilee, but sadly, only for His miraculous works and not as the Messiah. Once in Galilee, He went to Cana, the home of Nathanael and the place where, a year earlier, Jesus had performed His first miracle (John 2:1–11). Cana was probably about eight miles north of Nazareth. Capernaum was 19 miles northeast of Cana (see map on p. 498). The official was one of Herod's representatives in Capernaum. This miracle was performed from a distance of almost 20 miles. Jesus did not need to physically see or touch the child to heal him. In this case it only required faith on the part of the official for Jesus' miraculous power to be manifested.

Second miraculous sign (v. 54) means the second time a sign was performed in Galilee. He had done miracles in the meantime in Jerusalem (2:23).

After this miracle, Jesus seems to have gone back to Nazareth for a time (Luke 4:16–30). The healing of the official's son in Capernaum was what the inhabitants of Nazareth had heard about, and they wanted Jesus to repeat it in His own city (Luke 4:23).

John 5 | A SABBATH HEALING AT THE POOL OF BETHESDA

This was during a feast (v. 1), although it is not stated which feast.

The feasts which the Jews observed in Jesus' day, and which Jesus no doubt attended regularly, were these:

- Passover (April) celebrated the Exodus 1,400 years before (see pp. 169–70).
- Pentecost (June), 50 days after Passover, celebrated the giving of the Law (see pp. 169–70).
- Tabernacles (October) celebrated the ingathering of the harvest (see pp. 169–70).

- Dedication (December) was started by Judas Maccabaeus (see p. 475).
- Purim (shortly before Passover) is not mentioned in the Gospels (see pp. 169–70).

Jesus had returned to Galilee in December, around the time of the Feast of Dedication. The next feast on the calendar would be Purim, followed by the Passover, which is quite generally accepted as the time of this visit.

A year earlier, Jesus had cleared the temple, an introductory sign that He was the Messiah. This time He performed a miracle on the Sabbath. His purpose, it would seem, was to get the attention of the rulers by violating their ideas of the Sabbath, thus giving His claims to deity the fullest possible publicity in the nation's capital. It gave Him a hearing for a detailed explanation of His claims—and resulted in the Sanhedrin's determination to kill him (v. 18), which it took them two years to implement.

The man Jesus spoke to did not see Jesus as the Healer but rather was focused on the healing pools (v. 13). Ordinarily, faith in Jesus was essential to miraculous healing; however, in contrast to the healing of the royal official's son, Jesus chose to heal this man who did not even know who He was. Jesus' power can transcend all human intervention, as evidenced here as He sought to make His point with the Sanhedrin.

Stop sinning (v. 14). The eternal consequences of sin are far worse than temporal physical infirmities.

A year and a half later, Jesus referred to this miracle and to the Sanhedrin's determination to kill him. It was one of the main contentions of His enemies (John 9:14; Luke 13:14). They planned to kill Him for healing a man with a withered hand on the Sabbath (Mark 3:6). Jesus called them inconsistent for circumcising on the Sabbath while objecting to healing on the Sabbath.

One of the few recorded instances of Jesus' anger comes when they object to His healing on the Sabbath (Mark 3:5); elsewhere, He was "indignant" when the disciples tried to keep children from Him (Mark 10:14). And we can assume He felt "righteous indignation" in cleansing the temple of money changers (Matthew 21:12; John 2:14).

John 6 | THE FEEDING OF THE 5000

This is the only one of Jesus' miracles that is told in all four Gospels (Matthew 14:13–33; Mark 6:32–52; Luke 9:10–17).

The Pools of Bethesda

The pools of Bethesda are located just to the north of the Temple Mount area. Portions of the double pools have been excavated (in places they are over 30 feet deep), and it is evident that they could have had five porticos: four around the outside, and the fifth on the broad retaining wall that separates the northern from the southern pool.

Healings on the Sabbath

Seven healings on the Sabbath are recorded:

- A demon-possessed man in Capernaum (Mark 1:21–27)
- Peter's mother-in-law in Capernaum (Mark 1:29–31)
- An invalid man, in Jerusalem (John 5:1–9)
- A man with a withered hand (Mark 3:1–6)
- A woman bent over (Luke 13:10–17)
- A man with dropsy (Luke 14:1–6)
- A man born blind (John 9:1–14)

The exact location of the feeding of the 5000 is not completely certain, but it may have been near the northern shore of the Sea of Galilee, possibly a mile or so west of where the Jordan River enters into the sea.

The time was Passover (v. 4), one year before Jesus' death, when the passing crowds were on their way to Jerusalem. Jesus Himself did not go to Jerusalem for this Passover, because on His previous visit they had formed a plot to kill him (John 5:1, 18). It was probably the first Passover for which He did not go to Jerusalem since He was 12 (Luke 2:42–52). He did one of His most marvelous miracles for the crowds going to Jerusalem for the Passover.

Notice Jesus' love of order: He made the people sit down in groups of 50 and 100 (Mark 6:39–40), probably arranged around Him in a circle or semi-circle. This is also reminiscent of the Mosaic camp in the desert (for example, Exodus 18:21). He commanded that the leftovers be collected (vv. 12–13). Bread was regarded by the Jews as a gift from God. It was customary that all scraps be gathered at the end of mealtime. This also served to demonstrate the magnitude of Jesus' miracle.

The miracle made a great impression. The people wanted to make Him king immediately (vv. 14–15).

John 6:16–21 | JESUS WALKS ON THE WATER

This was in the "fourth watch" (Mark 6:48), that is, after three in the morning. Jesus had spent most of the night alone on the mountainside (Mark 6:46).

After the feeding, the disciples got into a boat to head toward Bethsaida on the other side of the lake (Mark 6:45; see KJV). A strong "wind was against them" (Matthew 14:24; Mark 6:48), and it blew them off course so that they "landed at Gennesaret" (Matthew 14:34; Mark 6:53; John 6:17, 21) — they were probably blown off course by a strong east wind coming down from the Golan Heights.

When Jesus appeared, they were about three or four miles out, or halfway across. When Peter saw Jesus walking on the water, he wanted to do it, too (Matthew 14:28). Dear, impetuous Peter! But he began to sink. Then Jesus reprimanded him for his lack of faith. To us it seems that Peter had a good deal of faith to even try it — a good deal according to our way of looking at things, but in Jesus' eyes so little.

John 6:22–71 | JESUS' DISCOURSE ON THE BREAD OF LIFE

Jesus had worked this mighty miracle as a setting for a plain talk on His true mission in the world. While He had spent much time ministering to people's physical needs, the real purpose of His coming into the world was to save people's souls.

When He told them that, they began to lose interest. As long as He fed their bodies, they thought He was great. They wanted Him to be their king. It would have been just wonderful if they could have had a king who would feed them miraculously every day, as He had done the day before, and as Moses had done in the desert with the daily manna.

John 7 | JESUS AGAIN IN JERUSALEM

This was at the Feast of Tabernacles (October), a year and a half since Jesus had last been there, and six months before His death.

On His previous visit He had healed a man on the Sabbath and announced to the rulers that He was the Son of God (5:18), for which they planned to kill Him. He had stayed away during the intervening Passover (6:4).

But now His work was drawing to a close, and He again went to the capital of His nation to further present His claim that He was sent from God. But it was not time for Him to die quite yet. Knowing their plan to kill Him (for it was generally known, v. 25), He made the journey incognito until He appeared in the midst of the crowds in the temple. Then He began His speech by referring to their plot to kill Him (vv. 19–23).

When the rulers heard this, they sent officers to arrest Jesus. But the officers somehow were awed by His presence. And Jesus went ahead with His message from God.

John 8:1–11 | THE WOMAN TAKEN IN ADULTERY

There are three instances of Jesus' dealings with women who had made a misstep: this one; the sinful woman of Luke 7:36–50; and the

Jesus instructed the blind man to wash his eyes in the water reservoir known as the Pool of Siloam. This excavation reveals the ancient staircase that runs into the tree-lined depression where the Pool was.

Samaritan woman (John 4:18). In all three cases Jesus was exceedingly considerate. And He was always ready to welcome back the prodigal (see under Luke 15).

In this instance the Pharisees attempted to trap Jesus with His reply. Had Jesus said that she should be stoned, He would have been in conflict with Roman law, which did not allow the Jews to carry out death sentences. On the other hand, if He declared that she should be let go, He would be considered to be ignoring the Law given by Moses. The language of v. 7 may imply that Jesus knew that the men who were accusing the woman were themselves guilty of the very thing of which they accused her. In the end, everyone left because of their internal guilt or fear. Jesus did not condone her actions and told her to leave her life of sin (v. 11).

John 8:12–59 | JESUS CONTINUES THE DISCOURSE ON HIS DEITY

His categorical and amazing statements about Himself infuriated the rulers, and they attempted to stone him (v. 59). The discourses recorded here demonstrate that Jesus had no tolerance for disbelief, especially that of the religious leaders of His day. Their unbelief, including references to Jesus' birth as illegitimate (vv. 19, 41), were met with probably the harshest words of Jesus recorded in the Bible.

John 9 | JESUS HEALS A MAN BORN BLIND

On a previous visit to Jerusalem (5:9), Jesus had healed an invalid on the Sabbath, for which — in addition to His claim that He was the Son of God — they attempted to stone Him (John 8:52–59). He now proceeds to perform a still more notable Sabbath miracle (v. 14).

The Pool of Siloam

John 13:1–30 | THE LAST SUPPER

(See more fully on Matthew 26:17–29.)

Jesus washes the disciples' feet (vv. 1–20). This was occasioned by their arguing among themselves as to which of them were to have the most important jobs in the kingdom. That had been one of their ongoing problems (see on Luke 9:46–48). In spite of Jesus' repeated statements that He was going to be crucified (see on Mark 9:30–32)—which they somehow, even to the very last, took to be a parable or metaphor rather than a statement of fact—they seemed to think that the Triumphal Entry, five days before, indicated that it was about time for Him to erect the throne of a world empire in Jerusalem.

Jesus finally had to get down on His hands and knees and wash their feet, the menial service of a slave, to burn into their minds that He had called them to serve, not to rule. Oh, how the church has suffered through all the centuries because so many of its leaders have been consumed by the passion to be great! Powerful organizations and high offices have been created to satisfy men's worldly and selfish ambitions. Great churchmen, instead of humbly serving Christ, have used the name of Christ to serve themselves.

Jesus points out the betrayer (vv. 21–30). So shrewdly had Judas kept his secret that none of the disciples suspected him. (See on Mark 14:10–11.) Judas knew that Jesus knew his secret. But with a heart of steel he went forward with his cowardly crime.

John 13:31–17:26 | JESUS' FINAL FAREWELL TO THE ELEVEN

These four chapters are the tenderest words in the Bible. Chapter 14 was spoken while yet at the table, chapters 15–17 while on the way to Gethsemane.

He knew the end had come. He was ready for it. Instead of calling it "crucified," He called it "glorified" (13:31). He dreaded the pain, but He kept His eye on the joy beyond the pain.

The disciples were mystified at His statement that He was leaving them. What could He mean? But had He not told them over and over? We think His heart must have ached for them more than it did at the thought of His own suffering.

Peter, suspecting that Jesus meant He was going on a dangerous mission, offered to follow even at the cost of His own life. Jesus reminded Peter that he did not realize what he was saying.

The house of many rooms (chap. 14). This is one of the best-loved chapters in all the Bible, the one that goes with us as we near the "valley of the shadow of death" (Psalm 23). Jesus, as a master workman, is preparing the heavenly palace for the glorious day when He will receive His bride, the elect of all the ages, unto Himself. But the bride needs to be made ready. The church must be gathered, nurtured, and perfected to be fit for the mansion of God. The occupants as well as the place must be prepared.

As Jesus departs to make the eternal home ready, He promises to send the Holy Spirit to train, comfort, and lead the saints on the way homeward.

John 15–16   DISCOURSE ON THE WAY TO GETHSEMANE

The ideas that keep recurring in these chapters are that the disciples must love one another, that they must keep Christ's commandments, that they must abide in Him, that they must expect pruning and persecution, that it was necessary for Jesus to go away, that the Holy Spirit would take His place, that their sorrow would be turned to joy, and that in His absence wondrous answers to their prayers would be granted. The blessed Master going into the depths of His own sorrow and suffering was doing His best to comfort His bewildered disciples.

John 17   JESUS' INTERCESSORY PRAYER

He closes His tender farewell by commending them to God, praying both for Himself and for them. Remembering His pre-human existence and its glory (v. 5) gave Him courage. He prayed for His own (v. 9), not for the world. He came to save the world, but His special interest was in those who believed in Him. He drew a definite line between those who were His and those who were not; this runs all the way through John's writings.

John 18:1–12   JESUS IS ARRESTED

(Told also in Matthew 26:47–56; Mark 14:43–50; Luke 22:47–53.) It was about midnight. The Roman garrison, consisting of a cohort of soldiers (about 500 or 600) and its commander, with emissaries from the high priest evidently thinking they were on a dangerous mission, were guided by Judas to the place where Jesus was. As they streamed out of the East Gate, down the Kedron road, with lanterns, torches, and weapons, they were visible from the garden where Jesus was. As they approached, Jesus, by His unseen power, caused them to fall to the ground to make them understand that they could not take Him against His will. To make Jesus' identification certain, Judas pointed Him out by kissing Him.

John 18:12–19:16   TRIAL OF JESUS *(See on Mark 14:53.)*

John 18:15–27   PETER'S DENIAL

It happened in the court of the high priest as Jesus was being condemned. Peter had just a short while before been willing to fight the whole Roman garrison alone. He was not a coward by any means. He deserves some credit. We can never know the whirl of emotions that tore at Peter's soul that night. As Peter was vehemently denying that he knew Jesus, Jesus turned and looked at him. That look broke Peter's heart.

John 19:17–37 | JESUS IS CRUCIFIED

(See also notes on Matthew 27:33–56; Mark 15:21–41; and Luke 23:32–49.) The legs of the two criminals who were crucified with Jesus were broken (v. 32) to hasten death, which otherwise might not have occurred for four or five days.

An artistic representation of the crucifixion of Jesus.

The games are traditionally said to have been scratched into the pavement by the Roman soldiers guarding Jesus. They actually date from about a century later, although the soldiers with Jesus may well have played these same games.

BURIAL

Joseph of Arimathea and Nicodemus, both members of the Sanhedrin and secret disciples of Jesus in the hour of Jesus' popularity, now, in the hour of His humiliation, come out boldly to share with Jesus the shame of His cross.

John 19:41–42 **THE TOMB OF JESUS** (*See under Mark 15:21–41.*)

The Resurrection, John 20 and 21

John 20:1–2 **MARY MAGDALENE GOES TO THE TOMB**

Other women were with her. (See on Matthew 28:1–8 and p. 503.)

John 20:3–10 **PETER AND JOHN RUN TO THE TOMB**

(Told also in Luke 24:12.) They may have been staying at a place closer to the tomb than the other disciples, probably at John's home, where Jesus' mother also was staying (19:27).

John 20:11–18 **JESUS APPEARS TO MARY MAGDALENE**

This was His first appearance (Mark 16:9–11). The other women had gone. Peter and John had gone. Mary is there alone, weeping as if her heart would break. She had no thought that Jesus might have risen. She had not heard the angel's announcement that He was alive. Jesus Himself had repeatedly said that He would rise on the third day, but somehow she had not understood Him. But, oh, how she loved Him! And now He was dead. Even His body was gone. In that moment of grief, Jesus stood by her and called her name. She recognized His voice and cried out in ecstatic joy. Jesus not dead, but alive!

A little later, He appeared to the other women (Matthew 28:9–10). That afternoon He appeared to the two followers on the road to Emmaus (Luke 24:13–32). And then to Peter (Luke 24:33–35).

John 20:19–25 **JESUS APPEARS TO THE ELEVEN**

That evening, in Jerusalem, Thomas was absent (v. 24). This appearance is recorded three times: here, in Mark 16:14, and in Luke 24:33–43. (See notes on those passages.) Jesus was in the same body, with the wound marks in His hands, feet, and side; and He ate food. Yet He had power to pass through walls, to appear and disappear at will.

"If you forgive anyone his sins" (v. 23; see on Matthew 16:19).

John 20:26–29 **JESUS APPEARS AGAIN TO THE ELEVEN**

A week later, in Jerusalem, Thomas was present. No modern critic could possibly be more skeptical than Thomas, or more scientific in His demand for evidence.

John 20:30–31 | PURPOSE OF THE BOOK

Here is the author's unequivocal statement that his purpose was to demonstrate and illustrate the deity of Jesus—to show that Jesus is God.

John 21 | JESUS APPEARS TO THE SEVEN

The disciples had now returned to Galilee, as Jesus had told them to do (Matthew 28:7, 10; Mark 16:7). He had selected a certain mountain (Matthew 28:16) and probably had set the time. While waiting, they resumed their old business. It may have been at, or near, the same spot where two or three years before He had first called them to become fishers of men (Luke 5:1–11). This time He gave them a miraculous haul of fish, as He had also done the first time, several years before.

The Disciples' Slowness to Believe That Jesus Was Risen

They were not expecting Jesus to rise from the dead, even though Jesus had repeatedly and plainly told them that He would rise on the third day (Matthew 16:21; 17:9, 23; 20:19; 26:32; 27:63; Mark 8:31; 9:31; Luke 18:33; 24:7). They must have taken His words to be a parable or metaphor with some mysterious meaning.

When the women went to the tomb, it was not to see if Jesus had risen, but to prepare His body for permanent burial. John alone, of all the disciples, believed at the sight of the empty tomb (John 20:8).

Mary Magdalene had only one thought—that someone had removed the body (John 20:13, 15). The report of the women that Jesus was risen seemed nonsense to the disciples (Luke 24:11). When the Two from Emmaus told the Eleven that Jesus had appeared to them, they did not believe them (Mark 16:13). Peter reported that Jesus had appeared to him (Luke 24:34). But still they did not believe (Mark 16:14).

Jesus had repeatedly foretold it. Angels announced it. The tomb was empty. His body was gone. Mary Magdalene had seen Him. The other women had seen Him. Cleopas and his companion had seen Him. Peter had seen Him. Still the group as a whole did not believe. It just seemed incredible to them.

Then, when Jesus appeared to the Ten that night, He reproached them for their hard-hearted unwillingness to believe those who had seen Him (Mark 16:14). Still they thought He was only a ghost, and He invited them to look closely at His hands, side, and feet, and to touch Him. Then He asked for food and ate in front of them (Luke 24:38–43; John 20:20).

After all that, Thomas—gloomy, doubting Thomas—was sure that there was a mistake somewhere, and he did not believe until he personally saw Jesus a week later (John 20:24–29).

Thus, those who first proclaimed the story of Jesus' resurrection were themselves totally unprepared to believe it, determined not to believe it—and came to believe it in spite of themselves. This renders untenable any possibility that the story was born of an excited and expectant imagination. There is no conceivable way to account for the origin of the story except that it was actual fact. We, too, one day, by His grace, shall rise.

The third time (v. 14), that is, to the assembled disciples; the other two appearances were those of 20:19, 26. Counting the individuals to whom Jesus had appeared—Mary Magdalene, the women, the Two, Peter—it was His seventh appearance.

More than these (v. 15). These things? Or these men? The masculine and neuter forms of the Greek word for "these" are the same. There is no way to tell in which sense it is here used. Do you love Me more than these other disciples love Me? Or, do you love Me more than you love this fishing business? Was Jesus asking Peter these questions because of his threefold denial? Or was He gently chiding him for returning to the fishing business? We are inclined to think the latter.

Do you love me? (vv. 15, 16, 17). Jesus uses the verb *agapao*. Peter uses *phileo*. Two Greek words for love. *Agapao* expresses a higher type of devotion, the kind of love God has for His children. Peter refuses to use it. He uses instead a verb that means "love as a friend." The third time Jesus comes down to Peter's word: "Do you love me as a friend?" Peter was hurt because the third time Jesus questions what Peter had just affirmed twice. Jesus gently pushes Peter to acknowledge that he really did love Jesus—to the best of his ability, which was enough.

Feed my sheep (vv. 15, 16, 17), three times in different forms. The idea may be that Jesus calls Peter to His business—shepherding people—rather than Peter's fishing business. This is not the end of Peter's discipleship—it has only just begun, and it will take him where he would never choose to go himself.

Jesus' prophecy of Peter's martyrdom (vv. 18–19). It had actually taken place long before John wrote this. (See note on 1 Peter.)

The author's identification and endorsement (v. 24). A specific statement that John the Apostle was the author of this book. The endorsement, "We know that his testimony is true," may be that of John's secretary or of the church in Ephesus. In any case, it indicates that this Gospel was written for the second generation of believers, who could no longer very easily verify John's narrative.

The Five Most Important Chapters

The five most important chapters in the entire Bible may be Matthew 28, Mark 16, Luke 24, and John 20–21, because they tell of the most important event in human history, the resurrection of Christ from the dead, the capstone of the whole Bible.

Painting of Pentecost.

THE EARLY CHURCH

Acts – Jude

The Early Church and the Roman Empire

The history recorded in the Gospels and the book of Acts takes place in the context of the Roman Empire, the largest empire the Western world had yet known. In the Gospels we encounter several Romans, chiefly centurions and the soldiers who crucified Jesus and stood guard at Jesus' tomb.

In the book of Acts, as the church spreads beyond Jerusalem, Judea, and Samaria, the Roman Empire plays a more significant role. Acts ends with Paul under house arrest in the city of Rome, waiting for the emperor of Rome to hear his case.

A number of aspects of Roman culture have a bearing on the narrative of Acts, and several of the Roman emperors figure more or less directly in the story of 1st-century Judaism and of the early church.

Roman Emperors

Augustus (31 B.C.–A.D. 14) is the only Roman emperor mentioned directly in the Bible (Luke 2:1). He ushered in a period of peace throughout the empire (known as the *pax Romana* or *pax Augustana*), which was marked by stable government, economic prosperity, and improved communications—all of which were of great significance for the spread of the Gospel in the 1st century.

Tiberius (A.D. 14–37) was Augustus's stepson; he plays only an indirect role in the Gospels. Tiberius spent the second half of his reign in isolation on the island of Capri and left **Sejanus,** the commander of the praetorian guard (the elite of the army), in power. Sejanus was an anti-Semite who expelled the Jews from Rome. He also appointed Pontius Pilate governor of Judea (A.D. 26–36). But in A.D. 31 Tiberius had Sejanus killed because he had overstepped his authority. It is possible that the radical change in Pilate's attitude toward the Jews—from indifferent arrogance in the early years to an almost embarrassing effort at the trial of Jesus to stay in the Jews' good graces—was a direct result of Sejanus's fall from power, which left Pilate without a protector in Rome.

Caligula (Gaius Caligula; A.D. 37–41). The grandson of Tiberius's brother Drusus, "Caligula" ("little boots") was the nickname he was given by the soldiers among whom he grew up. He showed clear signs of mental derangement and was assassinated by the praetorian guards after he depleted the treasury and became fully convinced that he was a god.

Bust of Claudius Caesar. Although Claudius supported Jews in Alexandria, he had Jews exiled from Rome.

His reign was marked by conflict with the Jews, not so much with the Jews in Palestine as those elsewhere in the empire (see Diaspora, p. 479).

King Herod Agrippa I was a friend of Caligula, who made him king of Judea. On the way back from Rome, after receiving his appointment, Agrippa stopped in Alexandria in Egypt, which had a large Jewish population; this became the occasion for an anti-Jewish riot, in which statues of Caligula were set up in the synagogues and the Jewish sections of the city were burned and looted. (Later Herod Agrippa killed the apostle James, put the apostle Peter in jail, and subsequently died a horrible death; Acts 12:1–24.)

When in A.D. 40 the Jews in Jamnia (west of Jerusalem, near the Mediterranean coast) tore down an altar that had been erected to him, Caligula gave the order that a statue of himself be set up in the temple in Jerusalem — an order that was never executed, thanks to the intervention of the Roman governor in Syria.

Claudius (A.D. 41–54) was Caligula's uncle. King Herod Agrippa I played an active role in getting Claudius's rule on track, for which he received an enlarged kingdom throughout Palestine. Claudius supported the presence of the Jews in Alexandria, but he warned them not to seek further privileges.

Nero (A.D. 54–68) was the son of Claudius and his fourth wife, Agrippina, who according to ancient rumors had Claudius poisoned when he was of no further use to her in getting her son Nero on the throne. The first five years of Nero's reign were peaceful; Seneca, the brother of Gallio (Acts 18:12), was in charge of the affairs of state. Paul's description of the Roman state (Romans 13) was written during this period of stability. But Nero increasingly took the reigns of power into his own hands. He removed his mother from her position of influence and ordered her killed in A.D. 59. In A.D. 62 he had his wife killed so that he could marry Poppaea, who is described by Josephus as a "worshiper of God," perhaps a Jewish proselyte (a non-Jewish convert to Judaism). He ordered Seneca to commit suicide in A.D. 65.

Nero is best remembered for the great fire of Rome in A.D. 64, which he probably had set himself to speed up the process of urban renewal but

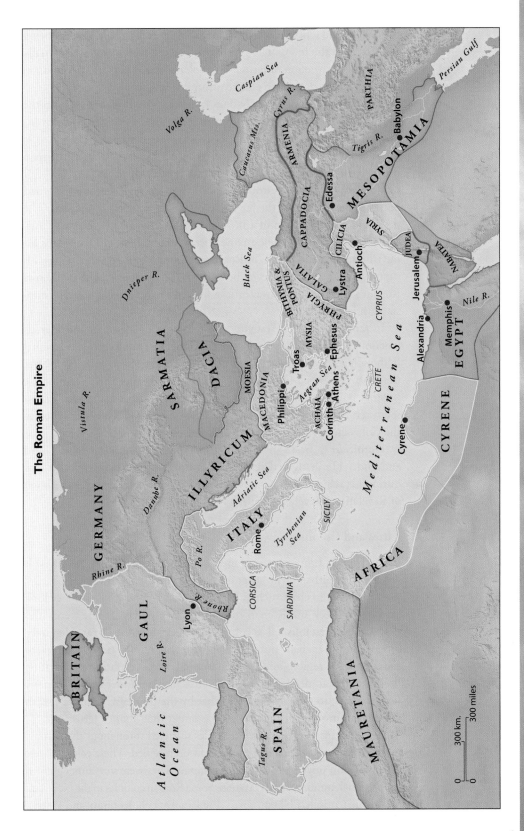

The Roman Empire

BRITAIN

GAUL

GERMANY

SPAIN

Tagus R.

Atlantic Ocean

Loire R.

Rhine R.

Rhone R.

Lyon

Po R.

ITALY

Rome

CORSICA

SARDINIA

Tyrrhenian Sea

SICILY

MAURETANIA

AFRICA

Adriatic Sea

ILLYRICUM

Danube R.

DACIA

SARMATIA

Vistula R.

Dnieper R.

Volga R.

Caspian Sea

Caucasus Mts.

ARMENIA

Cyrus R.

PARTHIA

Persian Gulf

Tigris R.

Babylon

MESOPOTAMIA

Edessa

CAPPADOCIA

CILICIA

SYRIA

Antioch

NABATEA

JUDEA

Jerusalem

Nile R.

Memphis

EGYPT

Alexandria

CYRENE

Cyrene

Mediterranean Sea

CYPRUS

CRETE

Aegean Sea

Ephesus

MYSIA

Troas

Philippi

MACEDONIA

MOESIA

Black Sea

BITHYNIA & PONTUS

GALATIA

PHRYGIA

Lystra

Athens

Corinth

ACHAIA

300 km.

300 miles

blamed on the Christians (who were now generally recognized as being distinct from the Jews). The great Jewish revolt, which would eventually lead to the destruction of Jerusalem, took place in A.D. 66, and Vespasian was the Roman general in charge of suppressing it.

The Jews were not the only ones to revolt. The Roman armies in the west revolted, and then the praetorian guard in Rome. Nero fled for his life and committed suicide in A.D. 68—at a mere 30 years of age.

Civil war (A.D. 68–69). Four rulers succeeded each other in the span of one year during this turbulent time, until **Vespasian** (A.D. 69–79) made great efforts to restore economic and cultural stability. He had become emperor before the Jewish revolt was completely suppressed. The destruction of Jerusalem in A.D. 70 was carried out by his general, Titus.

Titus (A.D. 79–81) is best remembered among Jews and Christians for the triumphal arch he built in Rome to celebrate, among other things, his suppression of the Jewish revolt before he became emperor. The arch shows Roman soldiers carrying away articles from the temple, including the lampstand (menorah).

In A.D. 79, Mount Vesuvius erupted, burying Pompeii and Herculaneum. During Titus's reign the magnificent Colosseum was opened (although it was not finished until later, under Emperor Domitian). Over the centuries, much of its marble and stones have been removed for use in other buildings in Rome, but even in its cannibalized state, the Colosseum remains impressive. In later persecutions, many Christians died in the Colosseum, killed either by gladiators or wild animals.

Domitian (A.D. 81–96) insisted on the title *dominus et deus,* "lord and god." He instigated severe persecutions of Christians, and it was during his reign that John was banished to Patmos and wrote the book of Revelation (Revelation 1:9).

Cities and Colonies

In the Roman Empire, power and government centered in the cities. It was the most urban civilization in the West until modern times.

In addition to cities such as Jerusalem that had been in existence long before the Greek and Roman empires came into being, there were cities that had been established as colonies by Alexander the Great. He established colonies such as Alexandria, in Egypt, as administrative centers for the conquered regions and as fountainheads of Greek culture by settling them with Macedonian and Greek citizens. Alexander induced many Jews to move to these colonies, so that by the time of Christ the Jewish population in some of these cities was larger than that of Jerusalem.

The Romans also established colonies scattered throughout the empire, mostly towns where military veterans had been settled. These colonies were given the most privileged status in the empire. They were sometimes granted full or partial immunity from taxation. Some Roman colonies in the New Testament are Corinth, Philippi, Troas, Pisidian Antioch, Iconium, and Lystra.

The ancient city of Tadmor (2 Chronicles 8:4) was renamed Palmyra (City of Palms) by the Romans. Most of the magnificent ruins date from the 2nd century A.D., but they give an idea of what many Roman cities in the time of Paul must have looked like. The colonnaded street was a feature of all Roman cities of any significance. In Palmyra this street stretched the length of about 6½ football fields (top left). Monumental arches, often in memory of an emperor or a military victory, were also a common feature (top right). And no city would be complete without a theater (bottom). Most cities also had a racetrack or hippodrome and several temples.

There were other cities with a more or less privileged status, and a few cities, such as Syrian Antioch, Ephesus, Smyrna, and Tarsus, still called themselves "free," which meant that they could govern their internal affairs on the basis of their own laws.

Client Kings

In the eastern part of the Roman Empire, Rome often left the government of areas that had not yet been fully Hellenized in the hands of native rulers. The rulers of these areas were "client kings" who held the title of king only by Rome's permission. Herod the Great and the later Herods (Matthew 2:1; Acts 12:1; 25:13) ruled Palestine as client kings. They were free to rule the internal affairs of their country as they saw fit, but they could not pursue any foreign policy. They were expected to maintain order and security on the frontiers, protect the trade routes, and pay taxes to Rome.

As time went by, the client kingdoms disappeared and were integrated into the provincial structure of the empire, as can be seen in Palestine in the course of the 1st century A.D.

A CHRONOLOGY OF THE LIFE OF THE APOSTLE PAUL

(All dates are A.D.)

5(?)	Birth		
35	Stoning of Stephen **Paul's Conversion**	Acts 7:57–50 Acts 9	
36			
37	Arabian trip	Acts 9:26–29; Gal. 1:17	
38	(*15 days in Jerusalem*)	Gal. 1:18	
39			
40	Ministry in Syria and Silicia	Acts 9:30; Gal. 1:21	
41			
42			
43	Arrival in Antioch	Acts 11:25–26	
44	Famine visit to Jerusalem	Acts 11:27–30; 12:25	
45			
46			
47	**First Missionary Journey**	Acts 13:2– 14:28	
48			
49	**Jerusalem Conference**	Acts 15:1–29	
50			
51	**Second Missionary Journey**	Acts 15:40– 18:23	**1 Thess.** from Corinth
52			**2 Thess.** from Corinth (51/52) **Gal.** (51/52 or 53) or (48/49?)
53			
54			
55	**Third Missionary Journey**	Acts 18:23– 21:17	**1 Cor.** from Ephesus **2 Cor.** from Macedonia
56			
57			**Rom.** from Cenchrea or Corinth

58	**Caesarean Imprisonment**	Acts 23:23–26:32	
59			
60	**First Roman Imprisonment**	Acts 28:16–31	**Eph.** from Rome; **Col. + Philem.** from Rome
61			**Phil.** from Rome
62			
63			
64	**Fourth Missionary Journey**	Titus 1:5	**I Tim. + Titus** from Macedonia (63-65)
65			
66			
67	**Second Roman Imprisonment**		
68	**Trial and Execution**		**2 Tim.** from prison in Rome (67/68)

Military

The Roman military was divided into **legions**, consisting ideally of 6000 soldiers. These were divided into 10 cohorts of six **centuries** each; a century consisted of 100 soldiers and was under the command of a **centurion**. The centurions were professional soldiers and were generally stationed in one area for some length of time. This is why we frequently meet centurions in the Gospels and in Acts (for example, Matthew 8:5; Mark 15:39; Acts 10:1; 21:32; 27:1).

Slaves

Slavery was common in nearly all ancient societies. A slave had the legal status of a "thing" ("The slave is a living tool and the tool is a lifeless slave," according to Aristotle) and as such had no legal rights. Some slaves worked under the harsh conditions we usually associate with slavery (slaves who worked in the mines, for example, whose life expectancy was limited), and the actual treatment of slaves depended on the goodwill (or lack thereof) of their master.

It is surprising to us that in the Roman Empire, slaves could hold virtually all occupations. Slaves of the state or of a city constituted the workforce that kept the bureaucracy functioning, including some of the highest administrative duties. Slaves were sometimes better educated than their masters, and many were used as teachers and secretaries. A slave could be the manager of a business and function as the official representative of his owner.

One incentive for slaves to give good service was the fact that they were paid "wages" — money retained by the owner but available to slaves for their own use. When sufficient money had accumulated, a slave could buy his or her freedom. A master could also give a slave freedom, either unconditionally or conditionally; in the latter case the former slave had continuing obligations to his former master, but as a free man.

The New Testament neither condemns nor endorses slavery. It gives guidelines for behavior within the existing social order (Colossians 3:22 – 4:1; 1 Timothy 6:1 – 2; Philemon 5 – 9; 1 Peter 2:16 – 21; but see 1 Corinthians 7:21 – 24).

The practical side of emperor worship. This headless statue from Caesarea represents the emperor. Rather than sculpting an entirely new statue when a new emperor came to power, a new head would be placed on the old torso.

What made Christianity a threat, nevertheless, was that it put master and slave on equal footing in the church, a condition which was perceived as dangerous to the social and economic stability of Rome.

Roman Citizenship

By the time of the New Testament, Roman citizenship had expanded from being the sole privilege of those who were born in or lived in the city of Rome. It was possible for people who were born elsewhere and lived in other parts of the empire (and most likely had never set foot in the city of Rome) to gain Roman citizenship, usually in addition to citizenship in their city or province. The Romans thus pioneered the concept of dual citizenship, which is why Paul could be a citizen of Tarsus (Acts 21:39) as well as a Roman citizen (Acts 22:26 – 27).

Paul was born a Roman citizen (Acts 22:28), which means that his parents or their families had acquired citizenship, most likely by providing special service to the empire, or possibly by his father or grandfather serving in the Roman military. Later, especially under Emperor Claudius (A.D. 41 – 54), it became rather easy to obtain Roman citizenship, especially if one had the funds to bribe a government official to add one's name to the list of candidates for citizenship. This is how Claudius Lysias, the commander who saved Paul's life in Jerusalem, had obtained his citizenship (Acts 22:25 – 28).

Roman citizenship had a number of privileges. It gave the right to vote (a rather harmless privilege from the Roman perspective, since one had to be in Rome to exercise this right), exemption from degrading forms of punishment such as flogging (Acts 16:22 – 40; 22:25), and the right to appeal to the emperor in Rome as the highest court (Acts 25:10 – 12).

Roman Law

Roman law evolved into a highly complex system that ultimately became the basis for modern Western law. There was no public prosecutor, and all cases had to be brought by private initiative, via a formal act of accusation. This explains the role of the Jewish Sanhedrin in the trial of Jesus: they had to formulate sustainable charges and take them before the Roman governor, who would hear and decide the case from the judge's seat (John 19:13; Acts 18:12). The accused had the right to meet his accuser(s) face to face (Acts 25:16).

The system had an effective safeguard against its abuse: a person bringing frivolous or false charges was subject to the same punishment he had sought against the accused (if the court found malicious intent).

Emperor Worship

In the Roman Empire, the early church was faced with the emperor cult, or emperor worship. The emperor was worshiped as "lord and god," or "lord and savior"—exactly the claims the Christians made for Jesus Christ.

In the Greek-Roman world, religion was closely interwoven with society; it was part of the civil order. Each city had its own deity or deities. The worship of these deities was less a matter of spiritual fervor than of patriotic and civic pride. The deity represented the city and its great (perhaps mythic) past, which the city supposedly owed to the deity. This blending of religion and patriotism became civil religion.

In a religious climate that was nonexclusive (one could worship more than one deity), it was easy to extend civic religion to include worship of the emperor, who personified the great empires. Rome had brought peace and prosperity to the world, and Emperor Augustus, who had inaugurated this era of peace, was unhesitatingly called "savior."

Emperor worship thus was a patriotic duty. It was one way of creating a common sense of civic pride as participants in the Roman Empire. The fact that some of the emperors (Caligula and Domitian among them) believed in their own divinity did not detract from the fact that the emperor cult was a powerful glue for holding the empire together.

In the conflict between the Gospel and the emperor cult, the issue was not the claims the church made for Jesus. These religious claims were acceptable to the Romans as long as they did not preempt the claims of the emperor. The problem was that these were exclusive claims: only Christ was Lord and Savior. The refusal to subscribe to the emperor cult was thus not so much a religious as a civic problem that in principle had the potential to undermine the cohesion of the empire.

Coin with the portait of Domitian. Domitian believed in his own divinity.

Acts

Formation and Spread of the Church
The Gospel Also for the Gentiles
Life and Work of Paul

"Salvation is found in no one else, for there is no other name under heaven given to men by which we must be saved."

—ACTS 4:12

"What must I do to be saved?" They replied, "Believe in the Lord Jesus, and you will be saved—you and your household."

—ACTS 16:30–31

The theme of the book of Acts is best summarized in 1:8, when the resurrected Jesus said to the apostles, "You will be my witnesses in Jerusalem and in all Judea and Samaria, and to the ends of the earth." And preach they did! Within the first apostolic generation of the church, the Gospel of Christ expanded in all directions until it reached every nation of the then known world (Colossians 1:23; see map on p. 689).The book of Acts specifically tells the story of this expansion of the Gospel throughout Palestine, northward to Antioch, and from there westward, through Asia Minor and Greece, to Rome—the region that constituted the backbone of the Roman Empire.

Although this book was given the title Acts of the Apostles, it tells mostly the story of the acts of two of the apostles, Peter and Paul, and mainly those of Paul. Acts provides us with an account of much of Paul's life, which helps us better understand his letters that are included in the New Testament. Paul was "the apostle to the Gentiles," that is, to the non-Jewish nations. One of the leading subjects of the book, then, is the spread of the Gospel to Gentiles.

The Old Testament is the story of God's agelong dealing with the Hebrew nation for the specific purpose of blessing all nations through them. The Hebrew Messiah, long foretold by the prophets, has come at last, and in this book of Acts the great and wonderful work of spreading the good news of Jesus, the Messiah, among the nations begins. From now on, the people of God are no longer defined by national or ethnic boundaries. In the book of Acts we see them become a worldwide family.

The book of Acts links the Gospels, which are primarily an account of Jesus' life and ministry, to the apostolic letters. The accounts in Acts also geographically link Jerusalem, where the church began, to Rome, the political center of the world. Acts gives us insight into how the apostles laid the foundation of the new Christian church. In this we clearly

Mary the mother of Jesus (v. 14): this is the last mention of her in the New Testament. She is the esteemed and honored mother of our Savior. Beyond this, not much is known of her life after Jesus' ascension, during the early years of the church.

Acts 1:15–26 | THE CHOICE OF JUDAS'S SUCCESSOR

When the day of Pentecost came, they were all together in one place. Suddenly a sound like the blowing of a violent wind came from heaven and filled the whole house where they were sitting. They saw what seemed to be tongues of fire that separated and came to rest on each of them. All of them were filled with the Holy Spirit and began to speak in other tongues as the Spirit enabled them.

—Acts 2:1–4

Judas, after betraying Jesus, hanged himself (Matthew 27:5). Then his body fell and "burst open" (Acts 1:18). This all happened in fulfillment of a prophecy written in the Psalms and quoted by Peter (Psalms 69:25; 109:8). The money Judas had received for betraying Jesus was used to buy "the potter's field as a burial place for foreigners," on the southern slope of the Hinnom Valley (Matthew 27:7).

Joseph (also known as Barsabbas and Justus) and Matthias were proposed as candidates to become the 12th apostle. The apostles began the selection process in prayer, asking for the Lord's guidance in the selection. Then they cast lots to allow God to have a hand in choosing the right man.

Matthias was chosen to take Judas's place, to keep the number of apostles at 12. Nothing further is known of Matthias. The number 12 appears to represent God's people. Israel consisted of 12 tribes, the church was built on 12 apostles, and the foundations of the New Jerusalem, which has 12 gates, bear the names of the 12 apostles (Revelation 21).

Acts 2:1–13 | PENTECOST

The birthday of the church, in the year of our Lord (*A*nno *D*omini, A.D.) 30, on the 50th day after Jesus' resurrection and the 10th day after His ascension to heaven. It was the beginning of the Gospel era.

Pentecost was also called Feast of Firstfruits and the Feast of Harvest (see pp. 169–70). How fitting then to have been chosen as the day for the firstfruits of the harvest of the Gospel for all nations!

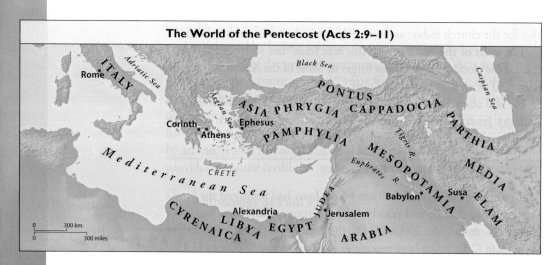

The World of the Pentecost (Acts 2:9–11)

Jesus, in John 16:7–14, had spoken of the coming of the era of the Holy Spirit. It is now inaugurated in a mighty, miraculous manifestation of the Holy Spirit, with a sound as of a roaring wind and with tongues as of fire that divided and came to rest on each of them. It was the initial public proclamation to the world of the resurrection of Jesus, to Jews and Jewish proselytes who had come to Jerusalem for Pentecost from all the countries of the then-known world — 15 nations are named (2:9–11). They heard the apostles, men from Galilee who had never left the vicinity of Palestine, speak to them in their own languages. This was a fulfillment of Jesus' last words to the apostles in 1:5, 8 and Luke 24:49. The apostles were completely under the control of the Holy Spirit, and the Spirit spoke through them in languages they had not learned before. For other accounts of speaking in tongues, see Acts 10:46; 19:6; and 1 Corinthians 12–14.

Some of the original steps to the southern entrance of the Temple Mount still remain and mark the most likely spot for Peter's powerful sermon on the day of Pentecost.

Acts 2:14–26 | PETER'S SERMON

Peter explains (vv. 15–21) that this amazing spectacle of the apostles speaking under tongues of fire, in the languages of all nations represented, is in fulfillment of the prophecy from Joel 2:28–32, where God tells us that He will pour out His Spirit on *all* people. Peter later emphasizes this point in Acts 2:38, where he proclaims, "Repent and be baptized every one of you, in the name of Jesus Christ for the forgiveness of your sins. And you will receive the gift of the Holy Spirit. The promise is for you and your children and for all that are a far off—and for all whom the Lord our God will call."

Fulfillment of prophecy. Note the repeated statement that what was happening had been foretold: the betrayal by Judas (1:16, 20), the crucifixion (3:18), the Resurrection (2:25–28), the ascension of Jesus (2:33–35), and the coming of the Holy Spirit (2:17).

All the prophets (3:18, 24): for an outline of messianic prophecy, see p. 453.

The resurrection of Jesus. Note, too, the unceasing emphasis on the Resurrection throughout this book. It was the pivotal point in Peter's sermon on Pentecost (2:24, 31–32), in his second sermon (3:15), and in his defense before the Sanhedrin (4:2, 10). It was the burden of the apostles' preaching (4:33). It was Peter's defense in his second arraignment (5:30). A vision of the risen Christ converted Paul (9:3–6). Peter preached the resurrection to Cornelius (10:40). Paul preached it in Antioch (13:30–37), Thessalonica (17:3), Athens (17:18, 31), and Jerusalem (22:6–11), to Felix (24:15, 21), and to Festus and Agrippa (26:8, 23).

Acts 2:37–47 | THE NEWBORN CHURCH

About three thousand (v. 41): a testimony to the unmistakable evidence of the resurrection of Jesus.

Baptized (vv. 38, 41).

They had everything in common (vv. 44–45). This communal life of the church was intended to be an extraordinary example of what the Spirit of Christ could do for humanity. This was the model of living that Jesus had taught and lived with His apostles and followers throughout His years of ministry. The disciples had come to understand that the Lord would provide for them if they lived as brothers and sisters in Christ, members of one body with Christ as the head. We see that while

Where Were the 3000 Baptized?

Although the location of the "baptism" of the 3000 converts is not mentioned in Acts, Professor Benjamin Mazar discovered more than 40 ritual baths in his excavations south of the Temple Mount area. They had been used by Jewish worshipers to ritually purify themselves before entering the temple precincts. In the same area, remnants of a monumental staircase were found that led into and out of the temple area—in all probability the one walked on by Jesus and His followers.

the members of the early church spent much of their time together in the temple, learning from the apostles' teaching, they also broke bread in their own homes (v. 46). For example, Philip, one of the seven who ministered at the tables (Acts 6:1–7), later lived in his own home in Caesarea (Acts 21:8).

The communal life allowed for individual family and vocational activities as well as significant time spent together in fellowship. The members of the early church shared voluntarily with their new brothers and sisters in Christ to provide for those who did not have enough for the basic necessities of life. There were many poor Christians in Jerusalem; years later, Paul took offerings from churches outside Palestine for the mother church in Jerusalem (Acts 11:29; 24:17).

Acts 3 | PETER'S SECOND SERMON

On the Day of Pentecost, the fiery tongues and the roaring as of a mighty wind brought together the astonished crowds. This gave Peter a large audience for his first public proclamation of the Gospel. Apparently some days had passed (2:46–47). The crowds that had come for the Feast of Pentecost had returned home, and the city had quieted down. The apostles kept busy instructing the believers and doing miraculous signs (2:42–47). And a lame man, a familiar sight to the whole city, who sat in the temple gate every day to beg, is healed by Peter and John—and the city is all astir once again. And in front of the amazed crowds, Peter attributes the healing to the power of the risen Christ. As Peter tells the Gospel story again, the number of believers increases to 5000 (4:4).

Acts 4:1–31 | PETER AND JOHN IMPRISONED

The rulers who had crucified Jesus are now alarmed at the spreading reports of His resurrection from the dead and the growing popularity of His name. They arrest Peter and John and order them to stop speaking in the name of Jesus. Note the boldness of Peter (vv. 9–12, 19–20)—the same Peter who a few weeks earlier, in the same place and before the same people, had cowed at the sneer of a girl and denied his Master (Matthew 26:69–75). Now, in utter fearlessness, he defies his Master's murderers.

Miracles in the Book of Acts

Miracles are a conspicuous part of the book of Acts.

- The book starts with the visible appearances of Jesus after His death, to His disciples (1:3).
- Then, before their eyes, He ascends to heaven (1:9).
- On Pentecost comes the first miraculous, visible manifestation of the Holy Spirit in tongues as of fire (2:3).
- Wonders and signs are performed by the apostles (2:43).
- The healing of the lame man, at the temple gate (3:7–11), makes a deep impression on the whole city (4:16–17).
- God answers prayer by an earthquake (4:31).
- Ananias and Sapphira die (5:5–10).
- Signs and wonders by the apostles continue (5:12).
- Many people from surrounding cities are healed by Peter's shadow (5:15–16)—it reads like the days of Jesus in Galilee.
- Prison doors are opened by an angel (5:19).
- Stephen performs great wonders and signs (6:8).
- In Samaria, Philip does great miracles and signs (8:6–7, 13), and many people believe.
- Saul is converted by a direct voice from heaven (9:3–9).
- At the word of Ananias, "something like scales" falls from Saul's eyes (9:17–18).
- In Lydda, Peter heals Aeneas, and the whole region is converted to Christ (9:32–35).
- In Joppa, Peter raises Dorcas from the dead, and many believe on the Lord (9:40–42).
- Cornelius is converted by the appearance of an angel and speaking in tongues (10:3, 46).
- A voice from God sends Peter to Cornelius (10:9–22) and convinces the Jews that Peter was right (11:15, 18).

After one night in prison (vv. 5, 21), Peter and John are released. And God shows His approval of their boldness by an earthquake (vv. 29, 31).

Acts 4:32–35 | CONTINUED GROWTH OF THE CHURCH

The threat of the rulers makes little impression on the church. The church continues in its spirit of brotherly love—and it keeps on growing by leaps and bounds. Three thousand on the first day (2:41), then 5000 men (4:4), then "more and more men and women" (5:14). The number of disciples kept increasing rapidly—including many priests (6:7).

All believers were one in heart and mind (v. 32). The perfect unity of the early church is directly associated with the great power the apostles had in performing miracles and reaching unbelievers with the message of the Gospel. Think of the powerful influence today's church members could have on their churches, cities, nation, and the entire world—if we could only come together as the early church members did and be of one heart and one mind, with Christ at the center of our unity!

Acts 4:36–37 | BARNABAS

Barnabas was a Levite from Cyprus, a cousin of John Mark (Colossians 4:10), whose mother's home was a meeting place for Christians (Acts 12:12). He must have been a man of commanding appearance, as implied in 14:12. He was a good man and full of the Holy Spirit (11:24). He persuaded the disciples in Jerusalem to receive Paul (9:27) and was sent to receive the Gentiles at Antioch (11:19–24). Barnabas brought Paul from Tarsus to Antioch (11:25–26) and accompanied Paul on his first missionary journey.

Acts 5:1–11 | ANANIAS AND SAPPHIRA

Their lie was pretending to have given all when in fact they had only given a part. Their death was an act of God, not of Peter, and was evidently intended to be an example for all time of God's displeasure at the sins of greed and religious hypocrisy. God does not strike us dead every time we are guilty of them. If He did, people would be falling down dead in the churches all the time. But the incident shows God's attitude toward a wrong heart; it is a warning, in the beginning days of the church, against using—or rather misusing—the church as a means of self-glorification. The incident, as a disciplinary example, did have an immediate salutary effect on the church (v. 11).

Acts 5:12–42 | THE SECOND IMPRISONMENT OF THE APOSTLES

When they were imprisoned the first time, after the healing of the lame man, Peter and John had been warned to speak no more in the name of Jesus (4:17–21). But they kept right on proclaiming the resurrection of Jesus, and God kept on doing mighty miracles (vv. 12–16). And the number of believers kept on growing (v. 14).

The rulers stood aghast at the expanding power of the Nazarene whom they had crucified. They arrested the apostles again, and had it not been for their fear of the people and the restraining influence of Gamaliel, the rulers would have stoned them.

Note Peter's continuing, undaunted defiance of the rulers (vv. 29–32). The apostles, though they were flogged (v. 40), kept proclaiming Jesus and rejoicing "because they had been counted worthy" of suffering for Him (vv. 41–42).

Gamaliel, who temporarily saved the day for the apostles (vv. 34–40), was the most famous rabbi of his day. It was he at whose feet Saul (later called by his Latin name, Paul) had been brought up (22:3). Young Saul may have been present in this meeting of the Sanhedrin, since he was a member (26:10), and not long after this, when the council stoned Stephen, Saul was a participant (7:58).

Acts 6:1–7 | THE APPOINTMENT OF THE SEVEN

It appears that up to this time the apostles took care of the business affairs of the church, which included the ministry of the Word of God and the care of the needy (4:37). In a few months, or at most a year or two, the church had grown enormously. Attending to the physical needs of the new church (e.g., waiting on tables) absorbed too much of the apostles' time.

When weighing the priority between ministering to the new church's spiritual needs and its physical needs, the apostles realized that they must devote the majority of their time to preaching the Word of God, which would have eternal results in saving souls. Their decision had nothing to do with the apostles considering themselves too important to wait on tables. The apostles were the ones who had firsthand knowledge of the marvelous story of Jesus. The only means of making that story known was by word of mouth. Their one business, from morning till night, in public and in private, to their last ounce of energy, was to keep on telling that story to the crowds who came and went. So these seven assistants were appointed. The arrangement worked well: it was followed by an enormous increase of believers (v. 7) as a result of the apostles' preaching.

Acts 6:8 – 15 | STEPHEN

Two of the seven were great preachers: Stephen and Philip. Stephen had the honor of being the church's first martyr. Philip carried the Gospel to Samaria and western Judea.

Stephen's particular sphere of labor seems to have been among the Greek Jews. At that time there were about 460 synagogues in Jerusalem, some of which were built by Jews from various countries for their own use. One of these synagogues included members from Cyrene, Alexandria, Cilicia, Asia, and Rome (v. 9). Since Tarsus was in Cilicia, Saul may have been in this very group. Some of these foreign-born Jews, who had been brought up in centers of Greek culture and had acquired a cosmopolitan outlook, felt themselves superior to the Jews of Palestine. But they met their match in Stephen. Unable to withstand him in argument, they hired false witnesses and brought him before the council. Stephen must have been a very brilliant man — and God was there, helping with miracles (v. 8).

Acts 7 | STEPHEN'S MARTYRDOM

Stephen stood before the same council that had crucified Jesus and that had just recently attempted to stop the apostles' speaking in the name of Jesus (4:18) — the same Annas and Caiaphas were there (4:6).

The rocky escarpment just north of Jerusalem's Old City wall is the traditional setting for the stoning of Stephen, the first Christian martyr.

Stephen's address before the council was mainly a recital of Old Testament history, climaxing in a stinging rebuke for their murder of Jesus (vv. 51–53). As he spoke, his face shone as the face of an angel (6:15). They rushed at him like wild beasts. As the stones began to fly, he looked steadfastly up into heaven and saw the glory of God, and Jesus standing at the right hand of God, as if heaven were reaching its hand across the divide to welcome him home. He died as Christ had died, without a trace of resentment toward his contemptible murderers, saying, "Lord, do not hold this sin against them" (v. 60).

A young man named Saul (v. 58). Here is one of the turning points of history. Saul, young as he was, appears already to have been a member of the Sanhedrin (26:10). He may have been present at one or both of the Sanhedrin meetings in which they tried to stop the apostles from preaching Christ (4:1–22; 5:17–40), and he may have witnessed Peter's bold, defiant refusal.

But in all his life he had never seen a death like that of Stephen. Though its immediate effect was to start Saul on his rampage of persecuting the disciples, it may well be that Stephen's dying words went straight to the mark and lodged deep in Saul's mind and heart, quietly working there to make him ready and receptive for the great vision on the road to Damascus (26:14). Through the power and grace of God, Saul of Tarsus was the one man who, more than any other, established Christianity in the main centers of the then-known world and altered the course of history.

Acts 8:1–4 | THE DISPERSION OF THE CHURCH

This was the first persecution of the church, which was by now perhaps a year or two old. The persecution lasted probably a few months. Saul (later to be called Paul) was a leader in the persecution. He had two relatives who were already Christians (Romans 16:7). But the persecution, triggered by the stoning of Stephen, was furious and severe. Saul, "breathing out murderous threats" (9:1), laid waste the church, dragging men and women into prison (8:3), beating those who believed (22:19–20), putting many to death (26:10–11), and wreaking havoc in the church (Galatians 1:13).

This persecution resulted in the dispersion of the church. In Jerusalem the church had become a formidable and irrepressible movement. Jesus' last command to the disciples was to proclaim the Gospel to all the world (Matthew 28:19; Acts 1:8). Now, in the providence of God, this persecution started the missionary work of the church. The people had listened to the apostles long enough to have learned the whole story of Jesus and His death and resurrection. Wherever they went, they carried the marvelous news. The apostles, however, who were at this point too popular and too powerful to be persecuted, remained temporarily in Jerusalem to care for the church. Later they would also travel about, preaching the Gospel.

GALILEE

Sea of Galilee

Mediterranean Sea

Caesarea Maritima

SAMARIA

Jordan R.

Sebaste

Sychar

Antipatris

Joppa

Lydda

JUDEA

Azotus

Jerusalem

Lachish

Gaza

IDUMEA

Dead Sea

0   10 km.
0   10 miles

Acts 8:4–40 | PHILIP IN SAMARIA AND JUDEA

God sent Philip to preach the Good News of the kingdom of God and the name of Jesus Christ, even into Samaria, whose people were despised by the Jews. The people of Samaria believed Philip and were baptized. Even Simon, a sorcerer who was famous for his magic and who claimed to be the personification of the divine power, himself believed and was baptized. The people of Samaria as well as Simon must have clearly seen a distinction between Philip's miracles by the power of the Holy Spirit and the false magic that Simon had practiced (vv. 6–7, 13).

As the people of Samaria came to believe the Gospel, Philip baptized them into the name of the Lord Jesus (vv. 12, 16). It is interesting to note, however, that they did not receive the Holy Spirit until Peter and John prayed and laid hands on them that they might receive the Spirit (v. 15). Could it be true for the church today, as it was for the people of Samaria, that while its members have been saved and baptized, they lack the power of God in their lives because they have not yet received the Holy Spirit? Remember Jesus' last words before His ascension: "Wait for the gift my Father promised, which you have heard me speak about. For John baptized with water, but in a few days you will be baptized with the Holy Spirit"(1:4–5) and then "you will receive power when the Holy Spirit comes on you" (1:8).

God directed Philip southward, to the treasurer of Ethiopia, to send the Gospel on its way into the heart of Africa.

Then Philip told the Gospel story in all the cities from Azotus (the Greco-Roman name for the ancient Philistine city of Ashdod) to Caesarea (his home; 21:8–9).

Baptism (vv. 36–39): the mention here of baptism is quite conspicuous. Jesus commanded that His followers be baptized as an outward sign of their new belief in the Gospel of Christ (Matthew 28:19). On the Day of Pentecost 3000 people were baptized (2:38). The Samaritans are baptized (8:12), as are Saul (9:18; 22:16), Cornelius (10:47–48), Lydia (16:15), the Philippian jailer (16:33), believers in Corinth (18:8) and in Ephesus (19:5; see also Romans 6:4; Colossians 2:12).

Acts 9:1–30 | THE CONVERSION OF SAUL

Saul was of the tribe of Benjamin (Philippians 3:5). He was a native of Tarsus, the third most important center of learning in the world, surpassed at that time only by Athens and Alexandria. He was born a Roman citizen (Acts 22:28) of an influential family. His background thus was Jewish, Greek, and Roman. He belonged to the party of the Pharisees, which meant that while he knew Greek and Roman culture, he was wholeheartedly devoted to serving the God of Israel by strict adherence to the Law. It was this devotion that made him see Jesus as a

Paul's hometown, Tarsus. The gate (left) is known as Cleopatra's Gate, since it is claimed that she met Mark Anthony here, a half-century before the apostle Paul was born.

Little did young Saul know that one day as a world traveler he would several times cross the Taurus Mountains he could see from Tarsus (below).

blasphemer who claimed to be the Son of God, and the church as a serious threat to the Law of Moses and thus to the future of the Jewish people.

He evidently had determined to destroy the church. Having crushed and scattered the church in Jerusalem, he set out for Damascus to ferret out Christians who had fled there.

On the way, the Lord appeared to him. His conversion is told three times: Luke's historical account here, and Paul's two accounts in 22:5–16 and 26:12–18, which stress aspects of his conversion relevant to the immediate situation. It was a real vision, not just a dream. He was actually blinded (vv. 8–9, 18). His traveling companions heard the voice (v. 7). From that moment on, he served the Christ he had sought to destroy, with a devotion unmatched in history.

Paul spent many days in Damascus preaching Christ (v. 23). Then the Jews tried to kill him. He went away and spent three years in Arabia and Damascus before returning to Jerusalem (Galatians 1:18), where he stayed 15 days. The Jews in Jerusalem also tried to kill him (Acts 9:29), so he returned to Tarsus (v. 30). Some years later, Barnabas brought him to Antioch (11:25).

Acts 9:31–43   PETER IN JOPPA

In Lydda, Peter healed Aeneas, and in Joppa he raised Dorcas from the dead—miracles that led many to believe (vv. 35, 42).

The eastern end of Straight Street in Damascus, the street where Ananias went to find Saul at the house of Judas.

Peter stayed in Joppa for some time (v. 43). Thus, in the providence of God, Peter was nearby when God was ready for the Gospel door to be opened to the Gentiles, in Caesarea, 30 miles to the north.

Acts 10 | THE GOSPEL ALSO FOR THE GENTILES

Cornelius was the first gentile Christian. Until now the Gospel had been preached only to Jews, Jewish proselytes, and Samaritans, all of whom observed the Law of Moses.

The apostles must have understood from Jesus' Great Commission (Matthew 28:19) that they were to preach the Gospel to all nations. But it had not yet been revealed to them that Gentiles were to be received *as Gentiles*. They seem to have thought that before Gentiles could be accepted into the household of God as Christians, they first had to become Jewish proselytes by being circumcised and by keeping the Law of Moses.

Looking northwest over the excavations of Caesarea Maritima. The Lord instructed Peter to travel from Joppa to Caesarea to bring the Good News to the house of the gentile commander, Cornelius.

There were Jews scattered among all nations, and the apostles may have thought their mission was to these Jews in the Diaspora. For a while they preached only to Jews (11:19). But then God showed them otherwise. Judea, Samaria, and Galilee had been evangelized, and the time had come to offer the Gospel to Gentiles.

Cornelius was an officer of the Roman army in Caesarea, the Roman capital of Palestine, the residence of the Roman governor, and the military headquarters of the province (see pp. 683–85). Cornelius was the officer in charge of what appears to have been an elite regiment known as the Italian Regiment. It may have been the governor's bodyguard. Thus Cornelius must have been one of the most important and best-known men in the whole region.

Cornelius was a good and devout man. He must have known something of the God of the Jews and of the Christians, possibly because Caesarea was Philip's home. But though Cornelius prayed to the God of the Jews, he was still a Gentile.

It was God who chose Cornelius to be the first Gentile to whom the Gospel door was opened. God Himself directed the sequence of events. He told Cornelius to send for Peter (v. 5).

It took a special vision from God to induce Peter to go, but he went (vv. 9–23).

And God put His own seal of approval on the reception of Cornelius into the church (vv. 44–48) — the firstfruits of the gentile world! After this, Peter baptized Cornelius and the other Gentiles in the group.

This probably happened about five to 10 years after the founding of the church in Jerusalem, perhaps around A.D. 40. Knowledge of what had happened in Caesarea no doubt gave impetus to the founding of the gentile church in Antioch (11:20). But it was hard for some Jews to accept (see 11:1–18; 15:1–35).

It was from Joppa (v. 5) that God sent Jewish Peter to gentile Cornelius. In this same Joppa, 800 years before, God had to use a little extra persuasion on Jewish Jonah to get him to go to gentile Nineveh (Jonah 1:3).

(It is interesting to note that, as far as we know, the question did not arise as to whether Cornelius should quit his career in the army.)

Acts 11:1–18   APOSTLES' APPROVAL

Peter's acceptance of Cornelius, the Gentile, into the church, without first requiring circumcision, was approved by the rest of the apostles only after Peter explained that it was God's doing: God told Cornelius to send for Peter; God told Peter to go to Cornelius; and God sealed the transaction by sending the Holy Spirit (vv. 12–15). But a group of Jewish Christians who belonged to the party of the Pharisees refused to accept this (15:5).

The church at Antioch was founded, soon after the stoning of Stephen, by those who were scattered abroad in the persecution that followed, probably about A.D. 32. At first this church consisted only of Jewish Christians (v. 19).

Some years later, probably about A.D. 42, some Christians from Cyprus and Cyrene in North Africa (modern Libya), who may have heard of the reception of Cornelius into the church, came to Antioch and began to preach to the Gentiles that they could be Christians without becoming Jewish proselytes first; and that God Himself, in some way, showed His approval (v. 21).

The church in Jerusalem heard of it. Convinced by Peter's story of Cornelius that the work was of God, they sent Barnabas to Antioch to convey the blessing of the mother church. And many Gentiles joined the church (v. 24).

Then Barnabas went to Tarsus, about 130 miles northwest of Antioch, found Saul, and brought him to Antioch. This seems to have been some eight years after Saul's conversion, three years of which he had spent in Damascus and Arabia, and the rest, as far as we know, in Tarsus. God had called Saul to carry the Gospel to the Gentiles (22:21). No doubt he had spent the time since his conversion, wherever he may have been, unceasingly telling the story of Jesus and reflecting with new understanding on the Law of Moses and the rest of the Hebrew Bible, our Old Testament. Now he becomes an active leader in this newborn center of gentile Christianity.

The cave church of St. Peter in Antioch in Syria (modern Antakya, Turkey). The city holds a special place in the early history of the church. One of the original seven deacons, Nicolas, was a gentile convert from Antioch (Acts 6:5). During the persecution after Stephen's stoning, some disciples went as far north as Antioch and preached to the Jews (Acts 11:9). The disciples were first called "Christians" there, and the church there sent generous support to the church in Jerusalem during a famine (Acts 11:26–30).

Acts 11:27–30 ANTIOCH SENDS RELIEF TO JERUSALEM

Barnabas and Saul took gifts to the church in Jerusalem, which was under great pressure. This seems to have been Saul's second return to Jerusalem after his conversion (Galatians 2:1). On his first visit the Jews had attempted to kill him (Acts 9:26–30). Saul's arrival in Jerusalem (11:30) would seem to have taken place in A.D. 44, since it is mentioned just before Herod's killing of James and his imprisonment of Peter (12:1–4), while his return to Antioch (12:25) is mentioned just after the death of Herod (12:23), which occurred in A.D. 44.

Acts 12 JAMES KILLED. PETER IMPRISONED

This James, the brother of John, one of the three disciples who constituted Jesus' inner circle, was the first of the Twelve to die (A.D. 44). Another James, the brother of Jesus, came to be recognized as the leading bishop of Jerusalem.

When Herod imprisoned Peter, the church earnestly prayed to God for him. God Himself took a hand: He delivered Peter (v. 7) and struck down Herod (v. 23). This Herod was not the Herod who had killed John the Baptist and mocked Christ (see p. 1019).

Acts 13–14 PAUL'S FIRST MISSIONARY JOURNEY (TO GALATIA; CA. A.D. 45–48)

Antioch rapidly became the leading center of gentile Christianity. One of the teachers in the church in Antioch had been brought up with Herod

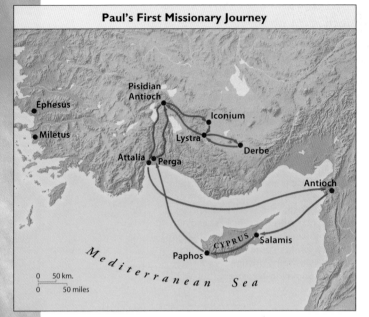

Paul's First Missionary Journey

Ephesus

Miletus

Pisidian Antioch

Iconium

Lystra

Derbe

Attalia

Perga

Antioch

CYPRUS

Salamis

Paphos

Mediterranean Sea

0   50 km.

0   50 miles

(13:1), from which we can infer that the church had considerable prestige. It became Paul's headquarters for his missionary work. From Antioch he started on his three missionary journeys, and to Antioch he returned at the end of the first two to bring a report.

Paul had been a Christian now for some 12 or 14 years. He had become a leader in the church in Antioch. The time had come for him to move out to do the work of taking the name of Christ to the far reaches of the gentile world (22:21).

The region of Galatia to which he went was in central Asia Minor (modern Turkey), about 300 miles northwest from Antioch—a long, and to our mind, daunting journey, since it could only be made on foot, on the back of a donkey or camel, or by boat. The trip was made somewhat easier by the fact that the Romans had built a system of paved roads throughout the empire that made travel easier and more predictable than it had ever been.

The route would have been more direct by land, going through Tarsus, the southeastern gateway to Asia Minor. But Paul had already been in Tarsus for some seven or eight years. So he and his entourage went via the island of Cyprus, and from the western end of Cyprus they went north into central Asia Minor.

View of the modern city of Antioch with mountains to the north.

The remains of Perga (Acts 13:13). The twin towers (top) stood at the beginning of the typical Roman colonnaded street, which here shows the ruts made by centuries of cart traffic (bottom).

In **Cyprus**, the Roman governor became a convert. A miracle convinced him (vv. 11–12). The blinding of the sorcerer was an act of God, not of Paul. From here on out, as if to signal that he is officially on his mission to the Roman Empire at large, the apostle is no longer called by his Hebrew name, Saul, but rather by his Roman name, Paul (v. 9), possibly marking the beginning of his ministry to the Gentiles.

Up to this point in the book, Barnabas is mentioned first, Paul second. From here on, Paul takes the lead ("Paul and Barnabas").

In **Pisidian Antioch** (some 300 miles northwest of Syrian Antioch as the crow flies), Paul, as was his custom, started his work in the Jewish synagogue. Some Jews in the region believed, as did many Gentiles (13:43, 48–49). But the unbelieving Jews stirred up a persecution and drove Paul and Barnabas out of the city.

In **Iconium**, about 100 miles east of Pisidian Antioch, they stayed a "considerable time" (14:3). They performed miraculous signs and wonders, and a large number of people believed (14:1). But again, a coalition of Gentiles and Jews drove them out of the city.

In **Lystra**, about 20 miles south of Iconium, Paul healed a cripple—and the crowds thought he was a god. Later, they stoned him and left him for dead. Lystra was the home of Timothy (16:1). It is possible that Timothy witnessed the stoning (2 Timothy 3:11).

In **Derbe**, about 30 miles southeast of Lystra, they made many disciples. And then they returned via Lystra, Iconium, and Antioch.

Paul received his "thorn in the flesh" (2 Corinthians 12:2, 7) apparently 14 years before he wrote 2 Corinthians, which was about the time he entered Galatia (Galatians 4:13; see further p. 718).

Acts 15:1–35 | THE COUNCIL OF JERUSALEM

In about A.D. 50, some 20 years after the founding of the church and probably about 10 years after Gentiles were first received into the church, a key question needed to be settled once and for all.

Although God had expressly revealed to Peter that Gentiles should be received without circumcision (chap. 10), and the apostles and elders were convinced (11:18), yet a sect of believers who belonged to the party of the Pharisees persisted in teaching that circumcision was necessary. And the church was torn by disagreement on the issue.

At the Council of Jerusalem, God led the apostles to make a unanimous and formal decision: circumcision is *not* necessary for gentile believers. They sent a low-key letter to that effect to Antioch, insisting that gentile Christians must abstain from idolatry and from immorality, which was so commonly practiced among Gentiles. They also required abstention from eating blood, a regulation that preceded the Law of Moses (Genesis 9:4). This reference may be to drinking blood apart from meat, which was associated with certain pagan religious rituals.

This is the last mention of Peter in the book of Acts (v. 7). Up to chapter 12, Peter had been the leading figure; now the focus is on Paul. (For Peter's earlier life, see p. 513; for his later life, see p. 797.)

Acts 15:36–18:22 | PAUL'S SECOND MISSIONARY JOURNEY (TO GREECE; CA. A.D. 50–53)

Silas was Paul's companion on this journey (15:40). Little is known of Silas, who is also called Sylvanus. He first appears as one of the leaders of the church in Judea (15:22, 27, 32). Like Paul, he was a Jew and a Roman citizen (16:21, 37). He was sent with the letter from the Jerusalem Council to verbally confirm and authenticate the contents of the letter (15:27). Later, he joined in Paul's letters to the Thessalonians (1 Thessalonians 1:1; 2 Thessalonians 1:1). And he carried 1 Peter to its first readers (1 Peter 5:12).

Mark, also called John Mark, quit partway into Paul's first journey and went back (13:13), perhaps due to timidity or fear, or maybe because he was not fully convinced of the validity of evangelizing Gentiles. Now he did want to go on this second journey, but Paul thought it best for him not to. (For a note on Mark, see p. 565.)

Paul and Barnabas went their separate ways after disagreeing over whether John Mark should join them on the second journey. But later they worked together again (1 Corinthians 9:6; Colossians 4:10; for Barnabas, see p. 662).

Paul's Second Missionary Journey

At Lystra, Paul found Timothy and took him along (16:1). From then on, Timothy was Paul's unfailing companion (see p. 759).

It seems that Paul was making his way west, toward Ephesus ("Asia," v. 6), but God stopped him. Then he started northeastward into Bithynia, and again God stopped him (v. 7). Then he turned northwest and came to Troas. Even Paul, intimate as he was with the Spirit of God, was in some cases a little slow in finding out the will of God for himself.

Troas lies about 20 miles from the location of the ancient city of Troy, immortalized by Homer in *The Iliad* and rediscovered by Heinrich Schliemann in 1870. Luke joined the travelers (note the change from "they" in v. 8 to "we" in v. 10). He went with them to Philippi and remained there after Paul left (Luke changes back to "they" in 17:1). He rejoined Paul six years later (20:6).

God, who had steered Paul away from Ephesus and Bithynia (16:6–7), now beckoned him to **Philippi** (v. 10). In prison, Paul and Silas sang hymns, and God sent an earthquake (vv. 25–26). The church they founded here turned out to be one of the best in all of the New Testament.

Philippi, in the northeastern corner of Greece, was the site of Paul's first European church. Thessalonica, about 120 miles west of Philippi, was the largest city of Macedonia. They were there only a short time, but

In Paul's day, the city of Athens lived on its past glory, having once been known as "the birthplace of Western civilization." The Acropolis ("High City") contained a spectacular collection of 5th-century B.C. buildings, the remains of which are still impressive. This view is from the Areopagus (Mars Hill), where Paul spoke (top); closer view (middle) gives an idea of the scale of the Acropolis and its buildings.

On the Acropolis was the Parthenon (bottom), a temple dedicated to the Greek goddess of wisdom, Athena Parthenos. It survived intact until the 5th century A.D., when it was remodeled to become a church, dedicated ironically to St. Sophia, the Christian saint of wisdom.

In 1546, the Turks captured Athens and the Parthenon became a mosque. Later, the Turks used the temple as a powder magazine; it was shelled and the middle part destroyed.

The great sculptures and friezes from the temple were removed by Lord Elgin and taken to the British Museum in 1816.

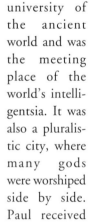

they made a large number of converts (17:1–9). (For a description of Philippi, see p. 736.)

In **Berea** (17:10–14), they made many believers.

Athens (17:15–34) was the home of the great philosophers of the golden age of Greece — Pericles, Socrates, Demosthenes, Plato — and remained a center of philosophy, literature, science, and art. It boasted the greatest university of the ancient world and was the meeting place of the world's intelligentsia. It was also a pluralistic city, where many gods were worshiped side by side. Paul received his poorest reception here — but it was also his most challenging task yet. It was not a failure, as some, misreading the first letter to the Corinthians, have maintained, but rather a brilliant translation of his message into Hellenic thought and language. Nor was his speech without notable results. It revealed how truly at home Paul was with Greek thought.

Corinth, in Greece, was one of the great cities of the Roman Empire (see pp. 702–3). Here Paul stayed a year and a half and established a great church (vv. 10–11).

He then returned to Jerusalem and Antioch, stopping on the way in Ephesus, a visit on which his mind had so long been set. (He may have been headed toward Ephesus on his first journey when, at Pisidian Antioch, on the western border of Galatia, he was forced to go back eastward by his "thorn in the flesh"; Galatians 4:13; 2 Corinthians 12:2, 7). On his second journey he was definitely headed toward Ephesus when God turned him northward and sent him to Troas and Greece instead (16:6–7). And now at last, he reached Ephesus, where he would return on his third missionary journey.

Aquila and Priscilla. Paul stayed with Aquila and Priscilla in Corinth (18:2–3), and they went with him as far as Ephesus (18:18–19). There are inscriptions in the catacombs in Rome that hint that Priscilla was of a distinguished family of high standing in Rome. She is usually mentioned first and must have been a woman of unusual talent. A church met in their house in Ephesus (1 Corinthians 16:19), and later also in their house in Rome (Romans 16:3–5). Some years later, they were again in Ephesus (2 Timothy 4:19).

| Acts 18:23–20:38 | **PAUL'S THIRD MISSIONARY JOURNEY** |

(TO EPHESUS; ca. A.D. 54–57)

Here Paul did the most marvelous work of all his marvelous life. Ephesus, a magnificent city with a population of almost a quarter of a million people, was located at the center of the Imperial Highway from Rome to the East, the backbone of the Roman Empire. (For a description of this great city, see pp. 678–79, 728.)

Interior of a 1st–3rd century house in Ephesus. Paul spoke publicly for three years In Ephesus, moving from house to house.

Ephesus was Paul's home for two years on his third missionary journey (Acts 19:8, 10), and it later became the home of the apostle John. A 35-foot-wide road led from the harbor to the theater (bottom); there was once a wall behind the stage that blocked the view of the seats from the road.

The marketplace (agora) had shops on either side under arches (top).

The great temple of Artemis (Diana) was a major source of revenue, which, when threatened by Paul's preaching, was defended in a riot (Acts 19) (above left).

Everyday life in Ephesus was not uncomfortable, although concepts of privacy have changed. Most people made use of public latrines, which were kept flushed with running water in the channel underneath. This facility boasted a pool in the middle and mosaic floors (above right).

Large numbers of worshipers of the most important deity in Ephesus, the goddess Diana (Artemis), became Christians. Churches were founded for 100 miles around (19:10, 26). Ephesus rapidly became the leading center of the Christian world.

Apollos (18:24–28) was an eloquent Jew who became a powerful leader in the Corinthian church (1-Corinthians 3:6) and in Ephesus (1 Corinthians 16:12). Some years later, he was still helping Paul (Titus 3:13).

Special miracles in Ephesus (19:11). With a lecture hall as his headquarters (19:9), Paul spoke publicly, and from house to house (20:20), day and night, for three years (20:31). He supported himself by working at his own trade (20:34). With the occasional aid of special miracles (19:11–12), Paul shook the mighty city of Ephesus to its foundations. Magicians, who pretended to work miracles, were so awed that they made a great bonfire of their books (19:19).

It appears that Paul was able to work miracles in certain places or situations. He performed miracles in Cyprus, Iconium, Lystra, Philippi, Ephesus, and Malta, and apparently in Corinth (1 Corinthians 2:4) and in

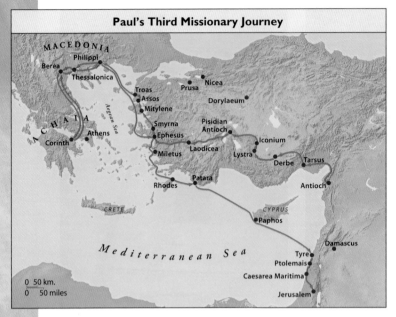

Paul's Third Missionary Journey

Thessalonica (1 Thessalonians 1:5). But none are mentioned while Paul is in Damascus, Jerusalem, Tarsus, Syrian Antioch, Pisidian Antioch, Derbe, Athens, or Rome. Nor could Paul heal his own fellow worker Trophimus (2 Timothy 4:20).

Paul's plan to go to Rome (19:21). Having begun his work at Antioch in Syria at the eastern end of the Roman Empire, and having just done his greatest work at Ephesus in the center of the empire, Paul now plans to travel to the western end of the empire.

Paul visits Greece again (20:1–5). Paul left Ephesus in June A.D. 57 (1 Corinthians 16:18). He spent the summer and fall in Macedonia (1 Corinthians 16:5–8) and the three winter months in Corinth (1 Corinthians 16:6). He then returned through Macedonia (Acts 20:3) and sailed away from Philippi in April A.D. 58 (20:6). Altogether he spent nearly a year in Greece. This may also have been the time when he went to Illyricum, north of Macedonia (Romans 15:19).

Paul's four greatest letters were written during this period: 1 Corinthians, from Ephesus; 2 Corinthians and Galatians, probably at about the same time, from Macedonia; and Romans, from Corinth.

Farewell to the Ephesian elders (20:17–38). They were tender words. Paul expected to never see them again (v. 25). (It is possible that Paul saw them again on his fourth missionary journey.)

This was the end of the three missionary journeys, which together covered about 12 years, from A.D. 45 to 57. The result was a number of powerful Christian centers, planted in almost every city of Asia Minor and Greece, in the very heart of the then-known world. (Paul may have made a fourth missionary journey, after the events recorded in Acts; see p. 688.)

| Acts 21:1–16 | PAUL'S JOURNEY TO JERUSALEM |

One purpose of Paul's journey to Jerusalem was to deliver the money he had collected from the gentile churches in Greece and Asia Minor for the poor saints in Jerusalem (Acts 24:17; Romans 15:25–26; 1 Corinthians 16:1–4; 2 Corinthians 8:10; 9:1–15). It was a great offering, which had taken more than a year to collect. It was a demonstration of the spirit of brotherly love and kindness between Jews and Gentiles.

It has been suggested that Paul went to Jerusalem against the direction of the Spirit. But Paul proceeded to Jerusalem with resolve because of the guidance of the Spirit (20:22). Those who knew and loved Paul pleaded with him not to go (21:4, 12) because the Spirit had revealed to them that Paul would be captured there (21:11–12) and they anticipated that Paul would be killed there. Paul trusted in the Lord's plan for his life, and this gave him the resolve to put aside the warnings of his friends and to focus on the call of the Lord.

Acts 21:17–23:30 | PAUL IN JERUSALEM

Paul arrived in Jerusalem about June A.D. 58 (20:16). It was his fifth recorded visit to Jerusalem after his conversion. In intervening years he had won large numbers of Gentiles to the Christian faith, for which unbelieving Jews hated him.

Rumors circulating in Jerusalem had it that Paul tried to turn Jews away from the Law of Moses. Paul was at risk, and the most prudent thing he could do was to demonstrate publicly that he did not try to undermine the Law of Moses.

At the end of the second journey Paul had made a vow, and when a vow came to an end it was marked, in Jewish custom, by certain rites of purification (sometimes with sacrifices) and the shaving of the hair

The island of Rhodes, off the coast of Turkey, had been in decline for some time when Paul was there. It was for a short time home to one of the Seven Wonders of the Ancient World: a 100-foot bronze statue of the sun god Helios at the harbor entrance, known as the Colossus of Rhodes. Historians at one time claimed that it stood astride the harbor, its feet planted where the statues stand, but this would have required greater bronze-casting skills than existed then. The Colossus was toppled in 225 B.C., some 55 years after it was built, by an earthquake that caused the statue to break at the knees.

(18:18). Now Paul endorses the vows made by a group of four men by paying the expenses involved in buying the sacrificial animals, by going through the purification rites with them, and by being the one to give formal notice to the priests of the date when the offering would be made for the four men. But it was not enough.

After he had been there nearly a week, certain Jews recognized him in the temple. They began to yell, and in no time, a mob was on him like a pack of wild dogs. Roman soldiers appeared on the scene just in time to save him from being beaten to death.

On the stairway to the Roman fortress, the Antonia (see illustration on pp. 482–83), the same place where Pilate had condemned Jesus to death 28 years before, Paul, with the consent of the soldiers, made a speech to the mob, in which he told the story of Christ's appearance to him on the way to Damascus. They listened until he mentioned the word "Gentiles," at which the mob broke loose again.

The next day the Roman commander brought Paul before the Sanhedrin to try to figure out why Paul was being accused by the Jewish crowds — a question that as a non-Jew must have genuinely perplexed him. It was the same Sanhedrin that had crucified Jesus; the same Sanhedrin of which Paul had once been a member; the same Sanhedrin that had stoned Stephen and had made repeated efforts to crush the church. Paul instigated "a great uproar" (23:9), the cause of which was undoubtedly incomprehensible to the Roman commander, who ordered the soldiers to take Paul back to the barracks.

That night, in the fortress, the Lord stood by Paul and assured him that Paul would testify about Jesus in Rome (23:11). Paul had often hoped to get to Rome (Romans 1:13). In Ephesus, the plan to go to Rome after visiting Jerusalem took definite shape (19:21), although he was not sure that he would get out of Jerusalem alive (Romans 15:31–32). But from now on, Paul was sure he would get to Rome.

Paul found trouble with the temple leaders, accused of bringing Gentiles past the warning barrier that held this inscription which prohibited Gentiles from entering the temple courts upon penalty of death.

The next day the Jews formed a conspiracy to kill Paul and vowed not to eat or drink until Paul was dead. But Paul's nephew got wind of the ambush and warned Paul. It took 70 horsemen, 200 soldiers, and 200 spearmen to get him out of the city, and that under cover of darkness. It is doubtful that the conspirators died of starvation, however.

ARCHAEOLOGICAL NOTE: Caesarea. Caesarea was located 31 miles north of Joppa on the Mediterranean coast. (It is also called Caesarea Maritima to distinguish it from Caesarea Philippi, which was located some 25 miles north of the Sea of Galilee.)

The Mediterranean coast of Palestine has no natural harbors. Herod the Great built Caesarea between 25 and 13 B.C. at an immense cost, complete with a splendid, 25-acre artificial harbor, remains of which can still be seen. The breakwaters were constructed of large blocks of stone and a Roman invention, hydraulic concrete. Herod named the city in honor of his patron, Caesar Augustus.

Unlike many archaeological sites, the site of Caesarea was abandoned for many centuries, which gives excavators easy access to the remains of the city. Recent, ongoing excavations have revealed, from the New Testament era, the structure and outline of the harbor, a huge seashore, a 10,000-seat amphitheater, and remnants of the temple platform that supported the temple dedicated to Roma and Augustus. The Jewish war that ended in the destruction of Jerusalem began with a riot in Caesarea. By the Byzantine era, the city encompassed some 437 acres and was home to at least 100,000 people. It served as the capital of Palestine for about 600 years—until the time of the Arab conquest in A.D. 639 (see p. 943).

The Herodian city was home to at least 40,000 people and served as the military headquarters for the Roman forces and the residence of the procurators in Palestine. It was the home of Cornelius (Acts 10) and the place of residence of Philip the evangelist (8:40; 21:8–9). Paul was a prisoner there for two years and preached before King Agrippa (23:31–26:32), possibly in the recently discovered "Promontory Palace," which is located just to the northwest of the theater. It may have been in this theater that Herod Agrippa I met his untimely death (Acts 12:19–23).

One surprising find has been the name of Pontius Pilate in a fragmentary inscription in a block of stone in the theater. The garrison town, of course, was his headquarters as procurator, and it was the scene of a famous contest between Pilate and a Jewish deputation from Jerusalem. Obstinate and overbearing, Pilate brought army standards with busts of the emperor attached to them into Jerusalem, in direct violation of Jewish law, which forbade the making of images. The Jews sent a deputation to Caesarea to complain. They won their point by being willing to be killed by Pilate's soldiers rather than giving in. Pilate's symbols of his clumsy loyalty were transferred to Rome's shrine in Caesarea.

For years the ancient accounts of the construction of Caesarea and its harbor met with skepticism because of the high standard of engineering required to build them. But the accounts have been proven true. The massive breakwaters (almost 1,800 feet and 900 feet in length) were a remarkable feat of underwater engineering (top). Herod built an aqueduct along the coast to bring water to the city from Mount Carmel, 12 miles away. During the Byzantine period, a second aqueduct was added (middle, bottom). (For map, see p. 666.)

During the Crusader period, Caesarea was turned into a European fortress, with massive walls (top) and a moat (bottom).

Acts 23:31–26:32 | PAUL IN CAESAREA

Paul spent two years in Caesarea, from the summer of A.D. 58 until the fall of 60.

Caesarea was the Roman capital of Judea, where the first Gentile had been received into the church some 20 years before — Cornelius, an officer of the Roman army.

Here, in this most important Roman city of Palestine, Paul spent two years as a prisoner in the palace of the Roman governor (23:35), with the privilege of receiving visitors. What an opportunity to make Christ known!

Paul before Felix (24:1–27). Felix had been Roman governor of Palestine for a number of years. He knew something about Christians, since there were many of them under his jurisdiction. Now he was to sit in judgment on the most noted of all Christian teachers. Paul made a deep impression on Felix, who sent for Paul often. But his greed kept him from accepting Christ or releasing Paul (v. 26). Drusilla was a sister of King Agrippa (25:13).

Paul before Festus (25:1–12). Festus succeeded Felix as governor in A.D. 60. The Jews were still plotting to murder Paul. Festus, though convinced of Paul's innocence, was inclined to turn him over to the Jews—which Paul knew would mean death. So Paul appealed to Caesar (v. 11), which, as a Roman citizen, he had a right to do. And Festus had the legal obligation to honor the appeal.

Paul's Roman citizenship, probably conferred on his father for some service to the state, saved his life more than once.

Paul before Agrippa (25:13–26:32). This was Herod Agrippa II, the son of Herod Agrippa I, who 16 years earlier had killed James (12:2). He was also the grandson of Herod Antipas, who had killed John the Baptist and mocked Christ. And he was the great-grandson of Herod the Great, who had murdered the children of Bethlehem. This scion of the murderous Herodian family is king over the province on the northeast border of Palestine, and he is now asked to help Festus. (See p. 1019 for the family tree of the Herodian family.)

Bernice was Agrippa's sister, who lived with him as his wife. A woman of rare beauty, she had already been married to two kings (one of which had been her uncle, Herod of Chalcis) and had come back to be her own brother's wife. Later she became mistress to Emperor Vespasian and Emperor Titus.

Herod and Bernice—quite a pair for Paul to make his defense in front of!

Surprisingly, Agrippa was profoundly impressed (26:28). But Festus thought that the idea of a resurrection from the dead was so absurd that he cried out that Paul must be crazy (26:24). They all agreed, however, that Paul was innocent of any wrongdoing (26:31).

Luke, though not in prison, was with Paul in Caesarea (note the "we" in 21:17–18; 27:1). It is thought that this was when Luke wrote his Gospel (Luke 1:1–3). His two years' stay in Caesarea would have given him opportunity to spend time in Jerusalem, and perhaps in Galilee, talking with the apostles and original companions of Jesus, gathering firsthand information. Mary, the mother of Jesus, may still have been alive; from her lips Luke could have learned her own story of Jesus' birth and childhood and of many incidents of His life.

Acts 27:1–28:15 | PAUL'S VOYAGE TO ROME

The trip to Rome began in the early fall of A.D. 60. The three winter months were spent in Malta. They arrived in Rome in the early spring of A.D. 61.

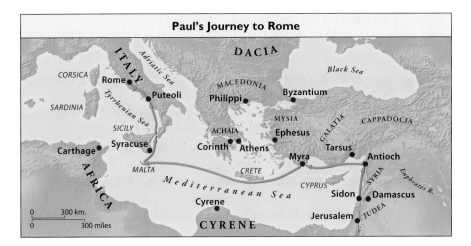

Paul's Journey to Rome

The voyage was made in three different ships: one from Caesarea to Myra; another from Myra to Malta; and the third from Malta to Puteoli.

Soon after leaving Myra, they ran into fierce adverse winds and were driven off course, and after many days all hope was gone. But God, who two years before in Jerusalem had told Paul that He would testify in Rome (23:11), now again appeared to Paul to assure him that He would make good on His word (27:24). And He did.

Acts 28:16–31 | PAUL IN ROME

Paul was in Rome at least two years (28:30). Though a prisoner, he was allowed to live in his own rented house, with his guard (28:16), and with the freedom to receive visitors and to teach Christ. There were already many Christians in Rome (see Paul's greetings in Romans 16, written three years earlier). Paul's two years in Rome were very fruitful, reaching even into the imperial palace (Philippians 4:23). While in Rome he wrote the letters to the Ephesians, Philippians, Colossians, and Philemon. (For more on the city of Rome, see p. 692.)

The Maritime prison is the traditional location of Paul's detention in Rome.

Paul's Later Life

It is generally accepted that Paul was acquitted in about A.D. 61 or 62. We know that he had planned to go on to Spain (Romans 15:28). Based on tradition, it is possible that Paul made a fourth missionary journey to Spain, Greece, and Asia Minor in about A.D. 63 to 67, during which time he wrote the letters to Timothy and Titus. He was then arrested again, taken back to Rome, and beheaded around A.D. 67.

Paul's ministry lasted about 30 years. In those years he won vast numbers to Christ. At times God helped him with miracles. In almost every city he was persecuted. Again and again they mobbed him and tried to kill him. He was beaten, flogged, imprisoned, stoned, driven from city to city. On top of all this, he had to contend with his "thorn in the flesh" (2 Corinthians 12). His sufferings are almost unbelievable. We believe that it was the Holy Spirit who gave him the supernatural power to live against all odds and in the midst of his suffering to bring thousands of people to Christ.

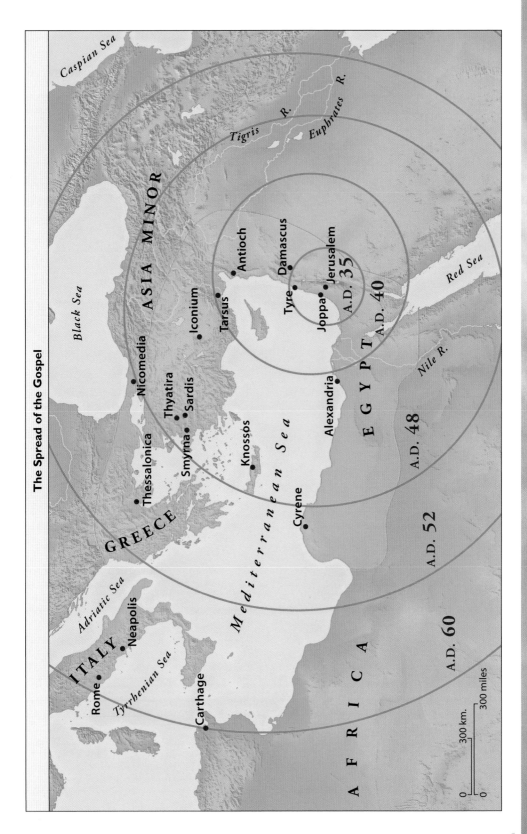

The Spread of the Gospel

A.D. 35
A.D. 40
A.D. 48
A.D. 52
A.D. 60

Caspian Sea
Black Sea
Tigris R.
Euphrates R.
ASIA MINOR
Antioch
Damascus
Jerusalem
Tyre
Joppa
Tarsus
Iconium
Nicomedia
Thyatira
Sardis
Smyrna
Thessalonica
Knossos
GREECE
Mediterranean Sea
Cyrene
Alexandria
EGYPT
Nile R.
Red Sea
AFRICA
Adriatic Sea
Neapolis
ITALY
Rome
Tyrrhenian Sea
Carthage

0   300 km.
0   300 miles

Romans

The Nature of Christ's Work
Justification by Faith

I am not ashamed of the gospel, because it is the power of God for the salvation of everyone who believes: first for the Jew, then for the Gentile. —ROMANS 1:16

For I am convinced that neither death nor life, neither angels nor demons, neither the present nor the future, nor any powers, neither height nor depth, nor anything else in all creation, will be able to separate us from the love of God that is in Christ Jesus our Lord. —ROMANS 8:38–39

Paul was chosen by God to be the chief explainer of the Gospel to the world, and his letter to the Romans is Paul's most complete explanation of his understanding of the Gospel.

Date and Occasion of the Epistle

In the spring of A.D. 57 (or perhaps in the winter of A.D. 57–58), Paul was in Corinth, at the end of his third missionary journey. He was about to leave for Jerusalem with the offering of money for the poor saints there (15:22–27). A woman named Phoebe, of Cenchreae, a suburb of Corinth, was going to Rome (16:1–2), and Paul made use of the opportunity to send this letter with her. There was no postal service in the Roman Empire except for official business. Personal letters had to be carried by friends or travelers.

Purpose of the Epistle

Paul wrote to the Roman Christians to let them know that he was on his way to Rome. This was before God had told Paul that he would be His witness in Rome (Acts 23:11), and Paul did not yet feel sure that he would get out of Jerusalem alive (Romans 15:31). It seemed proper that he, the apostle to Gentiles, should leave on file, in the capital of the world, a written explanation of the nature of the Gospel of Christ, in case he was killed before he could reach Rome.

The Church in Rome

Paul had not yet been to Rome. He finally arrived there three years after he wrote this letter. The nucleus of the church in Rome was probably formed by the Jews from Rome who had been in Jerusalem on the Day of Pentecost (Acts 2:10).

In the 28 years since then, many Christians from various parts of the East had for one reason or another migrated to the capital city, including some of Paul's own converts and intimate friends (see chapter 16).

Paul's martyrdom, and probably Peter's, occurred in Rome, about eight years after this letter was written.

The Background of the Epistle

The Jews believed in the finality of the Mosaic Law as the universally binding expression of the will of God. Therefore many Jewish Christians insisted that Gentiles who wanted to become Christians first had to be circumcised and keep the Law of Moses. Thus the question whether a Gentile could be a Christian without becoming a Jewish proselyte first was one of the great problems of the time. Christianity started as a Jewish religion, and certain powerful Jewish leaders were determined that it should remain so. Circumcision was a physical rite that stood as the initial ceremony in the process of Gentiles becoming Jewish proselytes.

Paul's Main Point

Paul's main point in Romans is that an individual's justification before God rests fundamentally on the mercy of Christ and *not* on the Law of

The administrative center of 1st century Rome (bottom to top): Circus Maximus, Palatine hill, Forum and Colosseum. Paul had longed to come to Rome. (Romans 1:9–15)

Moses. It is not a matter of law at all, because no person can ever fully live up to God's Law, which is an expression of God's holiness.

We are justified solely because Christ, out of the profound goodness of His heart, forgives people's sins. In the final analysis, a person's standing before God depends not on what that person has done or can do; rather, it is based completely on what Christ has done for him or her and each person's acceptance of His gift of salvation by grace. And therefore Christ is entitled to the absolute and wholehearted allegiance, loyalty, devotion, and obedience of every human being.

Rom. 1–2 | THE UNIVERSAL NEED FOR THE GOSPEL

The universal sinfulness of mankind (1:1–32). The first sentence is a long one that covers four verses (1:1–4). It is a summary of Paul's life: Jesus, as foretold in prophecy, rose from the dead and commissioned Paul to preach Him to all nations.

Paul's long-time desire to come to Rome (1:9–15). Paul was kept from coming by the call to preach to people elsewhere who had never heard the Gospel (15:20).

Not ashamed of the Gospel (1:16). This would be true even in Rome, the gilded and arrogant cesspool of every foul thing. The terrible depravity, described in vv. 18–32, had reached its depths in Rome.

The Jews are also guilty (2:1–29). Paul's frightful picture of man's sinfulness is equally true of the Jews—even though they are God's own nation—for they also practice the sins that are common to humanity.

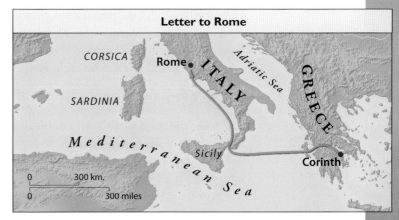

Letter to Rome

CORSICA
Rome
ITALY
Adriatic Sea
GREECE
SARDINIA
Mediterranean Sea
Sicily
Corinth

0   300 km.
0   300 miles

You have no excuse (2:1) includes every one of us. Not that everyone does all the things mentioned in 1:29–31; it is a picture of the human race as a whole. But each one of us is guilty of some of the things mentioned there.

The day when God will judge men's secrets (2:16). In that day the test will not be race, not whether one is a Jew or a Gentile, but the inner state of the heart and its attitude toward God and people in everyday life.

| Rom. 3 | **CHRIST IS THE PROPITIATION FOR SIN** |

Why the Jews? (vv. 1–20). If Jews, in the matter of sinfulness, have the same standing before God as other nations, why then had there been the need for the Jewish nation at all?

The answer is that the Jewish nation had come into being to be entrusted with the revelation of God and to pave the way for the coming of Christ. Under God, the Hebrew nation was founded to serve a special purpose in the working out of God's plan for human redemption. But that does not mean that the Jews are intrinsically any better in God's sight than other nations. One of the purposes of the Law was to make people understand that they are sinners (v. 20) in need of a Savior.

Christ our propitiation (vv. 21–31). In the eternal nature of things, sin is sin, right is right, and God is just—therefore there can be no mercy apart from justice. Sin must be punished. So God Himself, in the person of Christ, took upon Himself the punishment for mankind's sin. Therefore He can forgive people's sin and regard those who gratefully accept the Savior's sacrifice as having the Savior's own righteousness.

| Rom. 4 | **THE CASE OF ABRAHAM** |

Paul takes up the case of Abraham because those who were teaching that Gentiles must become Jewish proselytes in order to be Christians based their claims on God's promises to Abraham, which were linked to the sign of circumcision: if one was not of the seed of Abraham by nature, he would have to become so by circumcision.

Paul explains that the promise was *given on the basis of Abraham's faith, while he was still uncircumcised.* Thus, Abraham's heirs are those who have the same *faith*, rather than those who are *circumcised*. The grand thing in Abraham's life was his faith, not his circumcision.

| Rom. 5 | **CHRIST AND ADAM** |

Paul bases the efficacy of Christ's death as an atonement for human sin on the unity of the race in Adam.

How could one individual die for many? One person might die as a substitute for another one—there is some justice in that. But how can one person die for millions?

Paul's answer is that human beings are not to blame for being sinners. They are born that way, brought into life without being asked if they wanted existence. They woke up in this world to find themselves in a body with a sinful nature. But, says Paul, the founder of our race, Adam, did not have a sinful nature from the beginning.

Adam was the natural head of the human race and was perfectly made in God's own likeness. Christ is the spiritual head and the only man since Adam to be of a godly, sinless nature. What one head did, the other undid. One man's sin brought death to our race. Therefore one man's death is sufficient to bring life to those who will accept it.

Rom. 6 | WHAT, THEN, IS THE MOTIVE FOR RIGHT LIVING?

If we are no longer under the Law, and Christ forgives our sins, then why not keep on sinning — and Christ will keep on forgiving?

Paul answers that such a thing is unthinkable. Christ died to save us from our sins. His forgiveness is for the purpose of making us hate our sins.

We cannot be servants of sin and servants of Christ at the same time. We must choose one or the other. It is not possible to please Christ *and* continue to live in sin at the same time.

This does not mean that we can entirely overcome all our sins and place ourselves beyond the need of His mercy. But it does mean that there are two essentially different ways of life: the way of Christ and the way of sin. In our heart we belong to one or the other, but not to both.

> For the wages of sin is death, but the gift of God is eternal life in Christ Jesus our Lord.
> —Romans 6:23

Christ, the perfect embodiment of the Law of God, furnishes us with the motive and supplies us with the power to struggle on toward that perfect holiness which, by His grace, ultimately shall be ours.

Rom. 7 | WHY THE LAW?

If we are no longer under the Law, why then was the Law given? It was not given as a way to attain salvation, but rather as a means to prepare humanity to see its need of a Savior. The Law makes us aware of the difference between right and wrong and demonstrates to us that man, born with a sinful nature, will always fall short of complete obedience to the Law. Not until we realize our helplessness is there a desire for, and an appreciation of, a Savior.

The struggle between our sinful nature and our inner being (7:14–25). Here Paul presents the great human dilemma: the struggle between our sinful nature, which wants to follow its own desires, and our spiritual nature, which longs to obey God. The other law that Paul refers to in v. 23 is our God-given free will, which is too often influenced and controlled by our sinful nature instead of our godly spiritual nature. Our struggle is that, knowing what is right, we yet let our sinful nature persuade us to do something else that we find more pleasant. Paul expresses gratitude to Christ for deliverance from the sinful nature against which he felt himself powerless.

In this chapter we are reminded of Martin Luther's unbounded joy when he realized all at once that Christ could do for him what he had vainly struggled to do for himself! It is an illustration of the hold the Law can have on an earnest soul depressed by his or her inability to live up to it, and the relief that is found in Christ.

Rom. 8 | THE LAW OF THE SPIRIT

This is one of the best-loved chapters in the Bible.

The indwelling Spirit (vv. 1–11). In Christ we not only have our sins forgiven, but we also receive a new life. A new birth. Our natural life is, so to speak, impregnated by the Spirit of God, and a baby spirit, a divine nature, is born within us, in a manner somewhat similar to that in which our physical life, our Adam nature, was started by our parents.

Our natural life from Adam, and a new, divine life from Christ. This is a reality within us. We may not feel it or be conscious of it, but it is there. We accept it as a matter of faith. There is within ourselves, beyond the realm of our conscious knowledge, a divine life, born of God's Spirit, that is, under His loving care, working in stillness, untiring, to gain control of our whole being and to transform us into the image of God. This is the life that will blossom into immortal glory in the day of resurrection.

Our obligation to the Spirit (vv. 12–17). Living in accordance with the Spirit means that, while we depend wholly and implicitly on Christ for our salvation, we still struggle to the utmost to obey His Word. Paul is very explicit that the grace of Christ does *not* release us from the obligation to do everything in our power to live right.

On the other hand, "living according to the sinful nature" means giving in to the gratification of the desires of our sinful nature. Some desires are perfectly natural and necessary, such as the desire for food. Some are wrong. Those that are wrong we must abstain from altogether. The others we may enjoy, but we must always be careful to keep our true affections focused on Christ.

The suffering of the whole creation (vv. 18–25). The whole natural creation, including us, is groaning for a better order of existence that will be revealed in the day of God's completed redemption, when "this body of death" (7:24) shall receive the ultimate freedom of heaven's glory. It is a grand conception of the work of Christ.

Intercession of the Spirit (vv. 26–30). Not only is the indwelling Spirit our pledge of resurrection and future glory, but through His prayers in our behalf we are assured that God will make everything that has happened, and may yet happen, to us work together for our good. We may forget to pray—the Spirit never does. God will see us through. Let us never forget to trust Him.

Nothing can separate us from the love of Christ (vv. 31–39). He died for us. He has forgiven us. He has given Himself to us in the person of His Spirit. If we are His, no power on earth or in heaven or in hell can prevent His bringing us to Himself in the eternal presence of God. This is one of the most magnificent passages in all the Bible.

| Rom. 9–11 | THE PROBLEM OF JEWISH UNBELIEF |

One of the greatest stumbling blocks to the general acceptance of the Gospel of Christ was Jewish unbelief. While considerable numbers of Jews, especially in Judea, had become Christians, the nation as a whole was not only unbelieving but bitterly antagonistic.

The Jewish rulers had crucified Christ. They had persecuted the church at every opportunity. It was Jewish unbelievers who made trouble for Paul in almost every city he went.

If Jesus was really the Messiah promised in the prophetic writings of their own Scriptures, how did it happen that God's own nation rejected Him? These three chapters contain Paul's answer.

Paul's sorrow for Israel (9:1–5). A very expressive statement of his feelings for Israel: he would be willing to give his own soul if it meant that Israel would be saved. After all he endured from his fellow Jews, there is no anger or resentment, only profound sadness.

The sovereignty of God (9:6–24). In this passage Paul is not discussing the predestination of individuals to salvation or condemnation. Rather, he asserts God's absolute sovereignty in the choice and management of the nations of the world so as to bring all at last in subjection to Him. The strong statement in verse 16 places all responsibility for the outcome on God's mercy. (This verse speaks of a nation, but it may also refer to individuals; other, similar passages certainly do: Acts 2:23; 4:28; 13:48; Romans 8:28–30.)

> *If you confess with your mouth, "Jesus is Lord," and believe in your heart that God raised him from the dead, you will be saved.*
> —Romans 10:9

How to reconcile the sovereignty of God and the freedom of the human will we do not know. Both doctrines are plainly taught in the Bible. We believe them both. But to explain how both can be true we shall have to leave to others for now. Some things we now see are but a poor reflection, as in a mirror — but some day we shall know, even as we are known (1 Corinthians 13:12).

Foretold in the Scriptures (9:25–33). Israel's rejection and the adoption of gentile peoples by God were both foretold. So, instead of stumbling at it, we should have expected it.

The Jews have themselves to blame (10:1–21). God did not make the Jews reject Christ; they did it of their own accord. It was simply a matter of hearing (vv. 8–17). The Jews heard and were willfully disobedient (vv. 18–21). How to reconcile this with 9:16 we do not know; one day we will fully understand, although the questions that now perplex us will undoubtedly fade into insignificance in the radiance of His presence.

Israel's future salvation (11:1–36). Israel's rejection of Christ is temporary. The day will come when all Israel shall be saved (v. 26). When or how that will be is not stated. Nor is it stated whether it will be in connection with their return to Palestine—merely the bare fact that it will come about. One of the darkest spots in the panorama of human history is the agelong suffering of God's chosen people. But one day it will end. Israel shall turn in penitence to the Lord. And all creation shall give thanks to God for the wisdom of His providence.

Rom. 12	THE TRANSFORMED LIFE

A magnificent chapter. In tone it reminds us of Jesus' Sermon on the Mount. Paul invariably closed any theological discussion with an earnest exhortation to a Christian way of life. And so here. In previous chapters he has been insisting that our standing before God depends wholly on the mercy of Christ, and not on our own good works. Here he is equally insistent that that mercy, which so graciously forgives, is the very thing that supplies us with a powerful and irresistible urge to do good works and that transforms our whole outlook on life.

Humility of spirit (vv. 3–8). This is addressed to all Christians but is of special importance for church leaders. So often a position of leadership, which should make us humble, puffs us up. And so often a person with a certain talent is inclined to disparage the value of different talents possessed by others. (See more fully on 1-Corinthians 12–14.)

God gives each Christian a "measure of faith" to fulfill certain ministries in the body of Christ, the church. The power for these gifts comes from God. As a result, there is no place for pride in thinking oneself more important than others on account of the gifts freely given to us.

Paul uses the human body as a picture of the church. There must be unity and integration—but each member of the body has a different purpose and function. The unity of the church is centered in Christ. God freely gives gifts to the individual members for the purpose of meeting the needs of the overall church body. These gifts, given for ministry, include prophecy, servicing, teaching, encouraging, contributing to the needs of others, leadership, and showing mercy (12:5–8). Church members must use these gifts if the church is to function as God intends.

Heavenly qualities (vv. 9–21). If ever we become convinced that we are pretty good Christians, this list of exhortations will serve as a mirror to show us how far we still have to go and how much we need Christ's help and mercy!

Rom. 13	OBEDIENCE TO CIVIL LAW

Civil governments are established by God (v. 1) to restrain the criminal elements of human society—even though these offices are often filled and run by evil people. We must divorce our feelings about the people that hold these offices from the authority of the office itself. Christians

The Caesars lived in Rome at Palatine Hill. In the midst of Roman persecution against Jews and Christians, Paul instructed believers in his letter to the Romans to submit to the governing authorities.

should be law-abiding citizens, obedient to the government under which they live, governing themselves in all their attitudes and relations of life by the principles of the Golden Rule (vv. 8–10) and making special efforts continuously to be honorable in all things and considerate of others.

The approaching dawn (vv. 11–14). "The night is nearly over; the day is almost here." This refers to individuals who have been Christians for some time, or to the Christian era moving on toward its consummation, or to both the Lord's coming in glory and our going to Him through death.

Rom. 14 | JUDGING ONE ANOTHER

We should not judge one another in such things as the eating or not eating of certain foods and the observing of special days. The food referred to may be meat that had been offered in sacrifice to idols (see on 1 Corinthians 8). The "sacred" days may refer to the Jewish insistence that Gentiles observe the Sabbath and other Jewish feast days. The Lord's day, the first day of the week, was the Christian's day. If Jewish or gentile Christians wanted to observe, in addition, the Jewish Sabbath, that was their privilege. But they must not insist that others do the same thing.

Rom. 15:1–14 | BROTHERLY UNITY

Paul urges stronger Christians, those who are more mature in their faith, to patiently support newer, "weaker" Christians with the purpose of building up their faith. Christ exemplified this with His focus being entirely on building the church with little regard for His own interests. Paul understood that unity in the church was critical to building a glorious church.

Rom. 15:15–33 | PAUL'S PLAN TO COME TO ROME

If Paul had been like some people, he would, as soon as he received his commission from Christ as special apostle to the Gentiles, have immediately set out for Rome, capital of the gentile world, and made it his headquarters for the evangelization of the Roman Empire. One reason he did not was probably that ever since the Day of Pentecost (Acts 2:10) there had been a church in Rome. And Paul's mission was to carry the name of Christ to regions where Christ was not yet known. His plan was to preach wherever he went, working his way gradually westward. And now, after 25 years, after firmly planting the Gospel in Asia Minor and Greece, he is ready to go on to Spain with a stopover in Rome on the way (v. 24). Paul arrived in Rome about three years after he wrote this letter. (For the question whether he made it to Spain, see on Acts 28.)

Rom. 16 | PERSONAL MATTERS

This is a chapter of personal greetings to 26 church leaders who were Paul's personal friends.

- Phoebe (vv. 1–2) carried the letter; she was probably on a business errand to Rome. Cenchrea was the eastern port of Corinth (see map on p. 675).
- Priscilla and Aquila (vv. 3–5) had formerly lived in Rome (Acts 18:2) and had been with Paul in Corinth and Ephesus. They had returned to Rome, and a church met in their house.
- Epenetus (v. 5), the first convert in Asia, who now lived in Rome.
- Mary (v. 6); note how many of the people whom Paul greets are women.
- Andronicus and Junias (v. 7) were Paul's relatives. They were now old men, for they had been Christians longer than Paul and had been in prison with him.
- Ampliatus, Urbanus, Stachys, and Apelles (vv. 8–10), Paul's friends.
- The households of Aristobulus (v. 10) and of Narcissus (v. 11); they probably had churches meet in their homes.
- Herodion, another of Paul's relatives.
- Tryphena, Tryphosa, Persis (v. 12), three women.
- Rufus (v. 13) may have been the son of Simon who bore Jesus' cross (Mark 15:21), whose mother had taken a motherly interest in Paul.
- The last nine individuals Paul mentions (vv. 14–15) cannot be identified beyond the fact that they belonged to the church in Rome.

Then there are greetings from the people who were with Paul:

- Tertius (v. 22) was Paul's amanuensis who wrote down what Paul dictated.
- Gaius (v. 23) was the Christian brother in whose home Paul was living at the time and whose home was a general meeting place for Corinthian Christians.
- Erastus (v. 23), the director of public works of the city of Corinth, must have been a man of considerable influence.

1 Corinthians

Church Disorders
Spiritual Gifts
The Love Chapter
The Importance of the Resurrection

Jews demand miraculous signs and Greeks look for wisdom, but we preach Christ crucified: a stumbling block to Jews and foolishness to Gentiles. —1 CORINTHIANS 1:22

And if Christ has not been raised, our preaching is useless and so is your faith.
—1 CORINTHIANS 15:14

Date and Occasion of the Letter

First Corinthians was probably written around A.D. 55, toward the end of Paul's three-year stay in Ephesus (16:5–9; Acts 20:31). Paul was planning to spend the following winter in Corinth (16:5–8), which he in fact did (Acts 20:2–3).

About three years after he left Corinth, Paul was in Ephesus, some 275 miles to the east, across the Aegean Sea, doing the most marvelous work of all his marvelous life. Corinth and Ephesus were both on a busy trade route, with ships plying between them constantly. (See map, p. 675.) A delegation of leaders of the Corinthian church was sent to Ephesus to consult Paul about some very serious problems and disorders that had arisen in the church. In response, Paul wrote this letter. He had written at least one previous letter, which is now lost (5:9).

In this letter Paul responds to several issues brought to his attention by the delegation. These include division among the church members (1:10–24), immorality (5; 6:12–20), legal issues with each other (6:1–8), and inappropriate practice of the Lord's Supper (11:17–34). Paul also addresses false teaching about the resurrection of the body (chap. 15) and encourages the church of Corinth to provide offerings for the poor believing Jews in Jerusalem (16:1–4).

1 Cor. 1 | FACTIONS IN THE CHURCH

In Corinth, as everywhere else at that time, Christians did not have one central meeting place. (The one exception was Jerusalem, where Christians could meet in the temple courts.) Church buildings did not begin to be erected until 200 years later, when the persecutions began to let up (see p. 901).

The City of Corinth

Corinth lies 56 miles west of Athens, on the narrow strip of land (isthmus) between the Peloponnesus and the Greek mainland. Ever since the Golden Age of Greece, Athens had been the leading cultural center (see pp. 676–77), but under Roman rule, Corinth had been made the capital of the Roman province called Achaia (which also included Athens) and was the most important city in the country. Land traffic between the north and south had to pass the city, and much of the commerce between Rome and the East was brought to its harbors.

In Roman times Corinth was a city of wealth, luxury, and immorality–with a growing population that reached more than 300,000 free citizens and 460,000 slaves in the 2nd century A.D. The theater in Paul's day seated 14,000 spectators. In the past, more than 1,000 *hierodouloi*—temple prostitutes—had been active in pagan worship rites, but these practices probably had ceased by Paul's time, although the memory of that era was still fresh. "To live like a Corinthian" meant to live a life of sexual immortality and drunkenness. The Isthmian games, held every two years, made Corinth a great center of Hellenic life. (The Olympian Games were held every four years at Olympia, some 100 miles west of Corinth.)

Paul visited Corinth for the first time on his second missionary journey (Acts 18). He became acquainted with Aquila and Priscilla, fellow Christians and, like himself, tentmakers. During his stay of 1½ years he lived at their home. Paul later wrote two New Testament letters to that church and at least one other letter, now lost (1 Corinthians 5:9). Paul also wrote the letter to the Romans while in Corinth (Romans 16:23).

They met in homes or halls or wherever they could. There were multitudes of Christians in Corinth, not in one great congregation but in many small congregations, each with its own leadership. These congregations, it seems, were developing into rival, competing groups rather than cooperating in the general cause of Christ in this wicked city.

Some of the Greeks, with their fondness for intellectual speculation and pride in their knowledge, were very boastful about their philosophic interpretations of Christianity. And in addition to grouping themselves around one doctrine or another, they were rallying as partisans around one leader or another. Thus the church was split into factions, each trying to stamp Christ with its own little trademark—a practice that still prevails today on a frightful scale.

I Cor. 2 | THE WISDOM OF GOD

The "knowledge party" came in for the brunt of Paul's scathing rebuke. Corinth was close to Athens, where the atmosphere was dominated by egoists who paraded themselves as philosophers. The spirit of Athens had penetrated the church in Corinth.

Paul was a university man, an outstanding scholar of his generation. But Paul despised any pedantic show of learning. True learning and true scholarship should make us humble and more broadminded toward the

On the Acrocorinth, a steep, flat-topped rock that dominates the city, once stood the temple of Aphrodite, the goddess of love, whose service was connected with immorality, although by the time of the New Testament the licentiousness had been abandoned.

The remains of the *bema,* or judgment seat (NIV, court), of Acts 18:12 – 16, where Paul was brought before Gallio, the proconsul.

"ignorant"—who may not have our knowledge but who may be our superiors in wisdom and spiritual understanding.

Paul contrasts the wisdom of God with the wisdom of the unbelieving world. The world's wisdom fails to recognize God by means of its own philosophy. So God sent Christ, who is the wisdom of God (1:24), to reveal to us a knowledge of the divine plan of salvation that had until then been a mystery. Now God's wisdom is revealed to believers through the Holy Spirit.

I Cor. 3 | THE CHURCH IS GOD'S

The philosophic arrogance and pretentiousness of some people in the church was a sign of their spiritual infancy. It produced factions, tended to destroy the church (v. 17), and resulted in nothing of permanent value (vv. 12–15). The church is God's creation and workmanship. It is eternal in nature and too big to become the exclusive province of one group of partisans (vv. 21–23). Why not be big and wise enough to see this?

I Cor. 4 | PAUL'S SELF-VINDICATION

There must have been a considerable group of church leaders, Paul's own converts, who in Paul's absence had become influential and self-important and were trying to run away with the church. They had become haughty, overbearing, and boastful in their attitude toward Paul. Hence Paul's vindication of himself.

Paul cautions the leaders of the church not to teach beyond what is written, lest they become arrogant in their leadership and forget who gave them their spiritual wisdom. Paul directs them to follow his example, as their spiritual father in Christ, which he set for them in his manner of teaching, course of conduct, and overall way of life in Christ.

I Cor. 5 | THE CASE OF INCEST

One of the members of the church was openly living in sin with his father's wife. And the church, instead of administering discipline, was proud of their broadmindedness in harboring such a person. Paul directed that this man be delivered to Satan (v. 5)—that is, formally excommunicated from the church—to serve as an example that would keep practices such as this (as well as the dangerous open-mindedness) from spreading, and also in hope of bringing the guilty party to repentance. This case is referred to again in 2 Corinthians 2.

I Cor. 6:1–8 | LAWSUITS

It is clearly very inappropriate for followers of a religion of brotherly love to air their difficulties in heathen courts. Christians will eventually rule and reign with Christ over the universe and will be involved in settling ultimate questions of right and wrong, of eternal life and death (6:2; Matthew 19:28; Luke 22:30). Why, then, are they unable to settle their own quarrels? Paul asks if there isn't one man of integrity and piety among them that is wise and competent enough to decide, based on the wisdom of God, the private grievances and disputes between members of the brotherhood. The fact that the members had disputes among themselves was bad enough, but to bring these suits to the pagan courts so that they could be ruled over by unrighteous judges was senseless. Paul suggests that it would be better for the church members to suffer the wrong inflicted by the fellow brother in Christ and be deprived of one's fair due than to air such disputes and to be judged by unrighteous judges.

I Cor. 6:9–20 | IMMORALITY

Aphrodite, the goddess of love, had been one of the main deities at Corinth. Prior to Paul's day, her temple on the Acrocorinth (acropolis) had over 1,000 temple priestesses/prostitutes available for "worship" and immoral indulgence.

Some of the Corinthian Christians, having been used to a religion that encouraged immoral living, were finding it a little hard to adapt themselves to their new religion, which prohibited immoral living. In earlier discussions, Paul had said that all things are lawful (v. 12). Some of them evidently were quoting this to justify their promiscuous sexual indulgence. Paul emphatically states that they are wrong. He categorically, in unmistakable language, prohibits Christians from such indulgences.

Paul reminds the church that their bodies are members of the united body of Christ. When they engage in immoral behavior, they sin against their own bodies. In Genesis 2:24 it is written that man and woman shall become one flesh. Paul points out that this spiritual law applies to whoever has sexual relations. Those who have relations with prostitutes become one body with the unrighteous (v. 16). The person who is united to the Lord becomes one spirit with Him (v. 17).

I Cor. 7 | MARRIAGE

They had written Paul, asking him if it was legitimate for Christians to marry. Strangely, they were on the one hand puffed up over the case of incest (5:2), yet they had scruples when it came to lawful marriage. Paul advises marriage for those who desire it. Paul himself was not married (v. 8). Some think that he may have been a widower and lost his wife while still young, for two reasons: he voted in the Sanhedrin (Acts 26:10), for which marriage was a prerequisite; and this chapter seems to have been written by one who knew something of the intimacies of married life.

Paul instructs the church members to marry if they are tempted by sexual desires so that they are not drawn into immoral behavior. He suggests, as a matter of permission — not as a command — that married couples should not deprive themselves and each other of the marriage bed lest they allow Satan to tempt them to sin through their own lack of restraint of sexual desire. Paul urges the single church members and widows to remain single and celibate.

Paul also addresses the church members who are married to unbelievers. He urges them to not divorce lest the children be raised outside of Christian influence and teaching. In these situations Paul encourages the believing spouses to conduct their lives in Christ's love and serve their spouses and others so as to lead the unbelieving spouses to the Lord. However, if the unbelieving spouses leave the home, Paul instructs the church member to let them leave. In such cases, the believer and unbeliever were not morally bound to each other (1 Peter 3).

I Cor. 8 | MEAT SACRIFICED TO IDOLS

There were many gods in Greece, and much of the meat offered for sale in public marketplaces had first been offered as a sacrifice to some idol. (Sacrificing an animal did not necessarily mean that the entire animal was burnt on an altar. In the Old Testament, some offerings involved only the burning of certain parts of the animal, while the rest served as food for priests. Similarly, the Passover lamb was taken to the temple to be killed but was eaten that night by the family during the Passover celebration.) At issue was not only the eating of the meat, but also the matter of participating in social functions with their heathen friends, functions that were often accompanied by shameful licentiousness. (See below on 10:14–33.)

Paul points out that stronger Christians who participate in unrighteous activities may hinder the spiritual growth of new Christians or even cause those who observe this unrighteous behavior to fall away from Christ. Paul reminds the stronger Christians that when they engage in unrighteous behavior, they are not only sinning before the Lord but also sinning against their brothers and sisters in Christ.

I Cor. 9 | SALARIED MINISTRY?

One of the objections of Paul's critics against him was that he had taken no pay for his work in Corinth (2 Corinthians 12:13). The church leaders in Corinth wanted Paul to confirm that those who preach the Gospel should be able to live by the Gospel. Paul explains that he had every right to be supported by the church (vv. 4–7). The Lord had definitely ordained that the ministry should be supported by those who were ministered to (v. 14). But as far as we can determine from the record, Paul took pay from no church except the church in Philippi. In Corinth, Ephesus, and Thessalonica he supported himself by working at his trade. It was his life principle to preach without pay insofar as possible (vv. 16–18). It gave Paul great personal satisfaction to think that he was doing more than he had been commanded to do. Furthermore, he did not want to set an example that could be abused by false teachers whose main concern was their salary (2 Corinthians 11:9–13).

I Cor. 10:1–13 | THE DANGER OF FALLING

Paul had just spoken of exerting himself to the utmost lest he should be disqualified (KJV, a castaway). He reminds the Corinthians that they are faced with the same danger. They had better take their religion seriously. He uses the Israelites as an example. Most of those who were delivered out of Egypt never got to the Promised Land. The temptations that caused them to fall by the wayside were very much the same ones the Corinthians were facing (vv. 7–8): lustful indulgence. If they would strive wholeheartedly, with resolute determination, to overcome temptation, as he was doing (9:25–27), they would find that God's promise of protection against any temptation is sure (v. 13).

I Cor. 10:14–33 | MEAT SACRIFICED TO IDOLS

This is a continuation of chapter 8. There Paul had stated the general principle that our conduct in such matters should be governed by the law of brotherly love: there are things that are more important than meat. Here Paul forbids Christians to participate in heathen temple festivals. But he explains that when they buy meat in the markets, or are served meat at a feast in a private home (v. 27), it is not necessary to ask whether it had been sacrificed to an idol (v. 25). On the other hand, if someone informs them that the meat has been sacrificed to idols, they should refrain from eating it.

I Cor. 11:1–16 | WOMAN'S PART IN CHURCH

It was customary in Greek and Near Eastern cities for women to cover their heads in public—except women of immoral character. Within recent memory, Corinth had been full of temple prostitutes. Some of the Christian women, taking advantage of their newfound liberty in Christ, decided to lay aside their head covering in church meetings, which horrified the more modest types. Paul tells these women not to defy public opinion as to what is considered proper in society at large.

Men and women are of equal value in God's sight. But there are certain natural distinctions between women and men without which human society could not exist. Christian women living in a heathen society should be cautious in their innovations lest they bring reproach on their religion. Angels (v. 10) are onlookers in Christian worship.

I Cor. 11:17–34 | THE LORD'S SUPPER

Immediately after Pentecost, the Christians in Jerusalem had all their possessions in common (Acts 2:44–45). It seems that later, after this community of goods ceased to be the norm, the wealthier members of a church would bring food to certain services for a love feast (Jude 12), to be held after the Communion, in which rich and poor came together in fellowship.

In Corinth this love feast seems to have overshadowed the Lord's Supper. Those who brought the food ate it in their own clique without waiting for the whole congregation to assemble.

Imitating the drunken revels of heathen peoples in their idol temples, Christians were thus making their love feasts occasions for gluttony, losing sight entirely of the true significance of the Lord's Supper.

Illustration of the Last Supper at a triclinium table. Paul summarized the Passover/Last Supper of Jesus in order to redirect the Corinthian church to a proper handling of the Lord's Supper.

Paul reminds them of Jesus' words at the Last Supper and encourages them to examine themselves before they eat the bread and drink of the cup in remembrance of the Lord.

1 Cor. 12 | SPIRITUAL GIFTS

Throughout the Old Testament and during Jesus' ministry, God gave special miraculous manifestations of the Holy Spirit in certain places and at certain times to help the community of believers guide themselves in the truth. John the Baptist prophesied that the Messiah, Jesus, would baptize Christians with the Holy Spirit. In Jesus' final days with the disciples, He promised them that when He left them, His Father would send them (and all New Testament Christians) another Counselor to be with them forever — the Spirit of truth (John 14:16). This promise was fulfilled for the disciples at Pentecost, when all of them were filled with the Holy Spirit. The outward sign of the indwelling of the Spirit manifested itself in the speaking of tongues, one of the many spiritual gifts (1 Corinthians 14; Acts 2:4).

The various gifts of the Spirit, some natural, some supernatural, are enumerated in verses 8–10 and include

- Wisdom
- Knowledge
- Faith
- Healings
- Miracles
- Prophecy
- Tongues
- Interpretation of tongues

The great love chapter that follows is part of the discussion of the relative value of these various gifts.

Paul uses the human body as a metaphor for the unity and diversity of the spiritual gifts given to Christians who are individual members of the one body of Christ. He emphasizes that we are all baptized by one Spirit into one body. In the church of Christ there are no social distinctions. Paul specifically addresses the church members who feel that their spiritual gifts are inferior to those received by others. He exalts them and suggests that those Christians with gifts and functions that may seem insignificant should be given special honor (12:24).

Paul stresses the importance of unity in the body and encourages the believers to have concern for each other. If one church member suffers, then the whole church suffers with that person. If one church member is honored, then the whole church body should rejoice with him or her. Paul encourages the church to eagerly desire these spiritual gifts, not for one's own selfish pride, but because they are God's way — *the more excellent way*. They are the way of love, which is a fruit of the Spirit.

Apparently there had recently been a brilliant display of gifts of the Holy Spirit in Corinth. While Paul had undoubtedly prayed that these gifts would bring only joy and peace, he heard that envy had been developing over those in the church who had received the spiritual gift of tongues. Paul reminds the church that every member of the body of Christ has been given some spiritual gift that is evidence of the Spirit working in his or her life. God intends these gifts to build up the church body. The spiritual gifts are not to be used selfishly, to build up one's position in the church, as apparently some in the Corinthian community were doing.

I Cor. 13 | LOVE

This chapter contains the premier teaching of Christianity. It is an undying expression of Jesus' doctrine of heavenly love. This chapter is more potent for the building of the church than any, or all, of the various manifestations of God's power.

Love is the church's most effective weapon. Love is the essence of God's nature. Love is the perfection of human character. Love is the most powerful, ultimate force in the universe. Without love, all the various gifts of the Spirit are of no avail.

"If I give all I possess to the poor and surrender my body to the flames, but have not love, I gain nothing" (v. 3). The gift of speaking like an angel, of prophesying, of having all knowledge, of faith that moves mountains, of giving the last dollar to charity, even martyrdom—all are of no use *unless* we have the spirit of Christian love. What a call to self-examination!

I Cor. 14 | TONGUES AND PROPHESYING

This chapter is a discussion of the relative value of tongues and prophesying, which seem to have been the two gifts most valued.

Tongues is a supernatural way to talk with God and is intended for spiritual edification of God's children (vv. 2–4). Paul encourages the church of Corinth to continue the practice of speaking in tongues as a means of spiritual edification. Through tongues, God has given the church a supernatural way of communicating with Him.

Prophesying refers to the predicting of future events and teaching with the special aid of the Spirit, with special God-given insight. Ordinarily prophesying was more valuable than speaking in tongues, because everybody could understand it. However, speaking in tongues could also be enlightening to the church if the speaker also had the gift of interpretation or if someone else in the church could interpret what was being spoken in tongues.

The discussion of the role of women in the church (vv. 33–40) is a continuation of 11:2–16. Paul here forbids (vv. 34–35) what he seems to allow in 11:5. There must have been some local circumstance, unknown

Now we see but a poor reflection as in a mirror; then we shall see face to face. Now I know in part; then I shall know fully, even as I am fully known. And now these three remain: faith, hope and love. But the greatest of these is love.

—I Corinthians 13:12–13

to us, that gave point to these instructions—possibly some bold women unbecomingly putting themselves forward.

I Cor. 15 | THE RESURRECTION

The fact that some of the Corinthian church leaders were already denying the Resurrection (v. 12) is an indication of the extent to which false teaching of the very worst kind had crept into the church.

Paul insists, in the strongest language of which he is capable, that apart from the hope of resurrection there is no excuse for the existence of Christianity (vv. 13–19).

The resurrection of Jesus from the dead was the one unvarying refrain of the apostles. This chapter is the fullest discussion of it in the New Testament. It is one of the most significant and grandest chapters in the Bible because of the meaning it gives to human life.

The resurrection of Jesus from the dead was a fact attested by actual witnesses who had seen Jesus alive after His resurrection (see p. 502). Paul himself had seen Him. There is no other explanation for the phenomenon of Paul's radically changed life. What happened to him on the road to Damascus (Acts 9:1–30) was no hallucination: Jesus Himself was actually there.

> *For what I received I passed on to you as of first importance: that Christ died for our sins according to the Scriptures, that he was buried, that he was raised on the third day according to the Scriptures.*
>
> *—1 Corinthians 15:3–4*

Besides a number of appearances to the apostles, individually or in groups, Jesus had appeared to a crowd of 500 people at one time. That was 27 years earlier, and more than half of these 500 were still living (v. 6). It must have been real—a crowd of people could not just imagine the same thing or suffer from identical hallucinations all at the same time.

The disciples at first were slow to believe that Jesus had indeed risen from the dead (see p. 642). But when they were finally convinced that it was a fact, that Jesus had actually broken the chains of death and had come out of the grave alive, it put such a new meaning into life that nothing else seemed worthwhile. They knew the resurrection of Jesus to be a fact—a fact they believed with such certainty that they were willing to die for it. And they went up and down the highways of the Roman Empire, telling the story of it with such earnestness and sincerity that unnumbered thousands believed it also, even unto death.

The resurrection of Jesus from the dead is the one most important and best established fact in all history. And the story of it has come down to us through the centuries, beautifying human life with the halo of immortality; making us feel sure that because He lived again we too shall live; making our hearts thrill with the thought that we are immortal, that we have begun an existence that shall never end; that nothing can harm us; that death is merely an incident in passing from one phase of existence to another; that whether here or there we are His, doing the thing He has for us to do; that millions of ages after the sun has grown cold we ourselves shall still be young in the eternities of God.

The one most exhilarating thing in the whole range of human experience is the thought that we are immortal, eternal beings. That we cannot die. Whatever may happen to the body, we ourselves shall live on and on and on and on. Those of us who call Jesus our Lord and Savior will live on for an eternity with Christ. Those who turn their backs on the truth of Christ's word, His death and resurrection, will live on for an eternity in hell, separated from God. If this story of Jesus is true, life is beautiful, life is glorious, looking down an infinite and infinitely beautiful vista.

But if this story of Jesus should turn out to be a myth, then the mystery of existence is an unsolved riddle, and for humanity there is nothing left but the blankness and blackness of eternal despair.

By all the laws of historic evidence, it is a true story. Christ was. Christ is. He is a living person. He is with His people, with guiding and protecting power, leading them on to the day of their own glorious resurrection.

The end of Christ's work (vv. 23–28). Here is a glimpse, through successive future ages, into the endless end of things, when Christ's work shall have been finished and God's created universe shall have entered its final stage.

Baptized for the dead (v. 29). This seems to mean vicarious baptism, that is, baptism for a dead friend or relative. But there is no other biblical

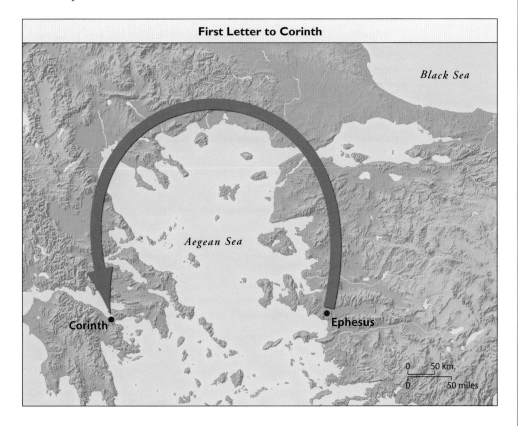

First Letter to Corinth

Black Sea

Aegean Sea

Corinth

Ephesus

0   50 km.

0   50 miles

reference to such a practice and no evidence that it existed in the apostolic church. Perhaps a better translation would be "baptized in hope of resurrection."

Resurrection of the body (vv. 35–58). Our hope is not merely immortality of the spirit, but the actual resurrection of the body. The teaching of the New Testament is very plain on this (Romans 8:23; 1 Thessalonians 5:23; 2 Corinthians 5:4). It will not be the same corrupt earthly body, but a spiritual body partaking of the nature of God's own heavenly glory.

| I Cor. 16 | **PERSONAL MATTERS** |

The collection (vv. 1–4). This was a collection for poor saints in Jerusalem (2 Corinthians 8:10).

Paul's instruction to the churches in Galatia (v. 1) is not mentioned in the Galatian epistle. Paul must have written them another letter that has not been preserved.

The first day of the week (v. 2) was the established day for Christian worship (Acts 20:7).

Paul's plans (vv. 5–9). This was the spring of A.D. 57, before Pentecost (v. 8). He spent the summer in Macedonia, from where he wrote 2 Corinthians. He arrived in Corinth in the fall and stayed there for the winter. He wrote the epistle to the Romans that winter and set out for Jerusalem the following spring.

Apollos (v. 12). They probably had asked Apollos to come to Corinth, but he refused to go at the time, no doubt because certain Corinthians were determined to make him a party leader.

My own hand (v. 21). Sosthenes, a Corinthian who had gone to Ephesus, probably wrote down this epistle from Paul's dictation (1:1; Acts 18:17). Then Paul signed it with his own hand (v. 21) and added the Aramaic words *Marana tha* (v. 22), which mean "Come, O Lord."

2 Corinthians

**Paul's Vindication of His Apostleship
The Glory of His Ministry**

For Christ's love compels us, because we are convinced that one died for all, and therefore all died. And he died for all, that those who live should no longer live for themselves but for him who died for them and was raised again.

— 2 Corinthians 5:14–15

Therefore, if anyone is in Christ, he is a new creation; the old has gone, the new has come!

— 2 Corinthians 5:17

Date and Occasion of Writing

During the latter part of his second missionary journey, around A.D. 52–53, Paul had spent 1½ years in Corinth and had made a large number of disciples (Acts 18:10–11). Then, on his third missionary journey, he spent three years at Ephesus (A.D. 54–57). In the spring of A.D. 55, while still at Ephesus, Paul wrote 1 Corinthians (1 Corinthians 16:8). Soon afterward, a great riot took place, in which Paul nearly lost his life (Acts 19).

Leaving Ephesus, Paul went into Macedonia on his way to Corinth (see map, p. 680). While in Macedonia, in the summer and fall of A.D. 55, Paul visited churches in the region of Philippi and Thessalonica, in the midst of many anxieties and sufferings. After waiting long to hear from the church in Corinth, Paul met Titus, who came from Corinth with word that Paul's letter had accomplished much good (2 Corinthians 7:6) but that some of the leaders in the Corinthian church still denied that Paul was a genuine apostle of Christ.

That is when Paul wrote this letter and sent it ahead with Titus (8:6, 17), expecting to reach Corinth soon himself.

The purpose of the letter appears mainly to have been Paul's vindication of himself as an apostle of Christ and to remind them that, inasmuch as he himself had founded the church in Corinth, he did have a right to have a say in its management.

Looking northwest over the ancient site of Corinth. It was to the church at Corinth that Paul wrote a second letter in order to defend his apostleship.

A little later, Paul reached Corinth and spent the winter there (Acts 20:2–3), as he had planned (1 Corinthians 16:5–6). While in Corinth, he wrote his great epistle to the Romans.

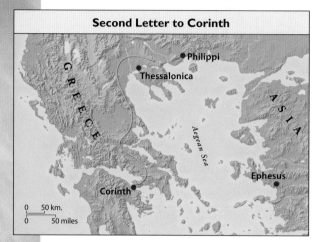

Second Letter to Corinth

GREECE

Philippi

Thessalonica

Aegean Sea

ASIA

Ephesus

Corinth

0   50 km.
0   50 miles

2 Cor. 1 | PAUL'S COMFORT IN HIS SUFFERING

After the initial greeting, Paul begins by writing about "the God of all comfort" (vv. 3–4) because he had met Titus (7:6–7), who had brought him the good news of the Corinthians' loyalty. This, together with his thankfulness for escape from death in Ephesus (vv. 8–9; Acts 19:23–41), accounts for Paul's note of joy in the midst of his sufferings.

Ephesus and Corinth were only about 275 miles apart, with ships plying between the two cities constantly. It seems that Paul had paid an earlier, "painful" visit to Corinth from Ephesus (2:1; 12:14; 13:1–2); the reason for that difficult visit was a very grave crisis that had arisen in Paul's relationship with the Corinthian church, probably shortly after he had written 1 Corinthians to them. This may, in part, account for Paul's anxiety to meet Titus.

2 Cor. 2 | A CASE OF DISCIPLINE

This seems to be the same incestuous person whom Paul, in his first letter, had ordered to be delivered to Satan (1 Corinthians 5:3–5); as a result, a revolt of considerable proportions against Paul had spread in the church.

It was so serious that Paul went personally from Ephesus to Corinth (v. 1), but he was rebuffed to such an extent that he speaks of it here as a "painful" visit.

It is thought that between the two letters we have, Paul wrote another letter to the Corinthians, which is now lost; this may be concluded from 2:3, 9; 7:8, 12; and 10:10, which imply things not found in 1 Corinthians. It must have been quite a stern letter, for it changed the tide in Corinth to such an extent that those who had been upholding the disciplined person turned against him (7:11). But Paul did not know this until he saw Titus (7:6–7).

The **distress, anguish of heart,** and **many tears** (v. 4), were caused not only by the terrible experience he had just gone through in Ephesus (1:8–9), but by his bitter anxiety over the situation in Corinth. He was so distressed about not meeting Titus in Troas as planned (2:12–13) that he passed up a grand opportunity for the Gospel in Troas in order to hurry on to Macedonia, hoping to find Titus there, who he knew was on his way with the news from Corinth.

Smell of death, fragrance of life (vv. 14–16): this imagery is of a Roman triumph in which the victorious general leads his army and the prisoners of war in a festive procession. Such a parade was often accompanied by the burning of sweet spices in the streets. For the victorious army, it was a celebration—they had survived the battles and returned home in glory. But for the prisoners in the procession, it was a reminder that they faced death—perhaps in a battle with wild animals or gladiators, staged for the amusement of the people of Rome—or at best slavery. To them, the smell of incense was the smell of death.

Similarly, Christians are led by the victorious Savior, Christ. It is through Christ, and ultimately through the church, that God spreads the "fragrance" of knowledge of Christ. As the Gospel is spread into the world, it is always received as sweet smelling by believers, as a celebration of life. However, to those who reject Christ, the Gospel message becomes the smell of death. In rejecting Christ, unbelievers choose death for themselves.

2 Cor. 3 | THE GLORY OF HIS MINISTRY

Letters of recommendation (v. 1). This expression was probably suggested by the fact that the Judaizing teachers carried letters of introduction from Jerusalem. They were always encroaching on Paul's work and were among his chief troublemakers, who availed themselves of every possible excuse or opportunity to fight him. They were now asking, Who is Paul? Can he show letters from anybody of standing in Jerusalem? That, on the face of it, was absurd. Letters commending Paul to a church which Paul himself had founded? The church itself was Paul's letter!

This led to the contrast between their ministry and his: the Law as opposed to the Gospel. One written on stone, the other on hearts. One of the letter, the other of the Spirit. One unto death, the other unto life. One veiled, the other unveiled. One unto condemnation, the other unto righteousness. One passes, the other remains. Reflecting Christ, we are changed, from glory to glory, into His image.

2 Cor. 4 | PAUL'S LIVING MARTYRDOM

In this letter Paul speaks much of his sufferings, especially in chapters 4, 6, and 11. At his conversion the Lord had said, "I will show him how much he must suffer for my name" (Acts 9:16). The sufferings began immediately and continued in unbroken succession for over 30 years:

- They plotted to kill him in Damascus (Acts 9:24) and again in Jerusalem (Acts 9:29).
- They drove him out of Antioch (Acts 13:50).
- They attempted to stone him in Iconium (Acts 14:5).
- They did stone him and left him for dead in Lystra (Acts 14:19).
- In Philippi they beat him with rods and put him in stocks (Acts 16:23–24).
- In Thessalonica the Jews and the rabble tried to mob him (Acts 17:5).

> *He has made us competent as ministers of a new covenant—not of the letter but of the Spirit; for the letter kills, but the Spirit gives life.*
> —2 Corinthians 3:6

- They drove him out of Berea (Acts 17:13–14).
- They plotted against him in Corinth (Acts 18:12).
- In Ephesus they almost killed him (Acts 19:29; 2 Corinthians 1:8–9).
- In Corinth, shortly after he had written this epistle, they again plotted his death (Acts 20:3).
- In Jerusalem they again would have made a quick end of him if he had not been rescued by the Roman soldiers (Acts 22).
- He was imprisoned in Caesarea for two years, and for two more years in Rome.
- Besides all this, there were unrecorded beatings, imprisonments, shipwrecks, and endless deprivations of every kind (2 Corinthians 11:23–27).
- Finally, he was taken to Rome to be executed as a criminal (2 Timothy 2:9).

Paul must have had amazing endurance, for he sang as he suffered (Acts 16:25). Nothing but an iron constitution could have lived through it all—and even that would not have been sufficient apart from the marvelous grace of God. By the Lord's help, Paul must have felt himself immortal until his work was done.

2 Cor. 5 | AFTER DEATH—WHAT?

This chapter is a continuation of the reason for his joy in the midst of sufferings. He has just said that the greater the suffering for Christ's sake in this present world, the greater will be the glory in eternity. Paul's mind was on the future world.

What is the teaching here? Is the new body put on at the moment of death? Death is spoken of, not as an unclothing, but as a being clothed (v. 4). To be absent from the body is to be at home with the Lord (v. 8). In Philippians 1:23 death is regarded as a departure to be with Christ.

But in 1 Corinthians 15 and 1 Thessalonians 4 the resurrection body is connected with the second coming of Christ. Evidently the teaching is that those who die before the Lord's coming enter immediately into a state of conscious blessedness with the Lord, which is far better than life in the flesh but still short of the glorious existence following the Resurrection.

2 Cor. 6 | PAUL'S SUFFERINGS AGAIN

Paul continues to vindicate his own ministry. The negative feelings against him in the Corinthian church must have been considerable (v. 12); otherwise he surely would not have devoted so much of this letter to a defense of himself. In vv. 14–18 he seems to blame the trouble, at least in part, on the heathen atmosphere in which they lived. The people of Corinth were very lax in their morals.

2 Cor. 7 | THE REPORT OF TITUS

Earlier, Paul had sent Timothy to Corinth (1 Corinthians 4:17; 16:10). Timothy was timid by nature and not exactly suited for the stern disciplinary measures required by the Corinthian situation.

Then Paul sent Titus (2 Corinthians 2:13; 7:6, 13; 12:18), who for such situations was probably the most capable helper Paul had. He probably went after Paul's second visit, carrying the letter referred to in 2:3. Titus's mission was successful.

The person over whom the trouble had arisen (1 Corinthians 5:1–5) was probably very influential. It seems that he persisted in his sin and led an open revolt against Paul, carrying some of the leaders with him. But the impact of Paul's second letter and the presence of Titus brought the church as a whole back into line, which resulted in the humiliation of the offender. This was the good news that Titus reported (vv. 7–16).

2 Cor. 8–9 | THE OFFERING FOR THE MOTHER CHURCH

These two chapters contain instructions about the collection Paul took up at the close of his third missionary journey for the poor saints in Jerusalem. It was probably gathered in all the churches of Asia Minor and Greece, although only those of Macedonia, Achaia, and Galatia are named. It had been started a year before (8:10). The Macedonian churches had entered into it wholeheartedly. Even the very poor were giving generously. Paul was there at the time he wrote this.

Philippi, the leading Macedonian church, was the only church from which Paul had accepted pay for his work, and then only after he had left there.

In these two chapters we have the most complete instructions in the New Testament about church giving. Though Paul talks about an offering for charity, we assume that the principles stated here should be the guide for churches in the taking of all their offerings, those for self-support as well as those for missionary and benevolent enterprises: any gift or offering

For our light and momentary troubles are achieving for us an eternal glory that far outweighs them all. So we fix our eyes not on what is seen, but on what is unseen. For what is seen is temporary, but what is unseen is eternal.

—2 Corinthians 4:17–18

should be (1) voluntary, (2) proportionate, and (3) systematic; those handling the offerings should be people of integrity who are capable of administering the funds (8:19–21). Paul emphasizes especially that God will abundantly reward those who give liberally. The spirit of brotherly kindness that is thus manifested is called the "indescribable gift" (9:15).

2 Cor. 10 PAUL'S PERSONAL APPEARANCE

Some things in this chapter seem to have been suggested by the charge of his enemies that Paul was weak in personal appearance (vv. 1, 10). There is no hint in the New Testament as to what Paul looked like. There are indications in the New Testament that he may have had eye trouble which at times made him repulsive in appearance (see p. 719). But the charge of his enemies that he was a weak personality (v. 10) certainly was unfounded. It is just not possible to think that a man who turned city after city upside down, as Paul did, was weak. Unquestionably, Paul was a powerful and dominating personality. In reply to the charge that he was weak, Paul tells them that he at least founded his own churches instead of going around troubling churches founded by others, as his opponents were doing!

2 Cor. 11 PAUL'S APOLOGY FOR BOASTING

In parts of this letter Paul addresses the loyal majority, in other parts the disloyal minority in the church. The latter seem to be on his mind in the last four chapters. He realizes the unseemliness of boasting about himself, but they have forced him to it.

His opponents had been making capital out of the fact that he had refused to accept pay for his work in Corinth (vv. 7–9). He explains that, though as an apostle of Christ he had the right to accept pay (1 Corinthians 9), he nevertheless had purposely refused it lest his example be abused by false teachers who were seeking to make money off the church. From the beginning of his work in Corinth, Paul must have noticed tendencies toward greedy leadership in some of his converts, and so he acted accordingly. Now one of the things of which Paul could boast was that they could not accuse him of greed.

Then, in a passage of dramatic power (vv. 22–33), he challenges his critics to compare themselves with him by every standard—both as a loyal Hebrew and as an effective worker for Christ, he had done more than all of them put together. And as for suffering for Christ—his whole career as a Christian apostle had been an unbroken story of living martyrdom.

2 Cor. 12 PAUL'S THORN IN THE FLESH

Paul's vision of paradise (vv. 1–7). He was "caught up to the third heaven" (v. 2) and "to paradise" (v. 4); the term "the third heaven" is generally considered synonymous with paradise. It is the place where believers who have died are even now "at home with the Lord" (v. 5:8; Philippians 1:23). Jesus went into paradise immediately at death (Luke 23:43). There are several references which imply that the "third heaven" is a place beyond the immediate heaven of the earth's atmosphere and beyond the further heaven of outer space and its constellations into the presence of God Himself. These references to "heavens" include Hebrews 4:14, which speaks of the risen Lord who is said to have passed through the "heavens" (see also Hebrews 7:26 and Ephesians 4:10).

Paul speaks as if paradise and the third heaven are two separate parts of the future world. The Greek text says "*up to* the third heaven" and "*into* paradise." It is possible that "the third heaven" is a reference to a celestial body of sorts called heaven and paradise is a more specific location on that celestial body. This would be similar to the planet earth with the Garden of Eden being a specific location on the earth.

What Paul saw and heard in his vision of paradise, it was not lawful for him to utter (v. 4). This may mean that God gave Paul a special vision of future glory to strengthen him for his special mission and the exceptional suffering he was to endure. He could not communicate what he saw, both because he was not permitted to tell and because it could not be put into words ("inexpressible")—there is no human language adequate to describe the glory of heaven, just as the idea of color could not be conveyed to a person born blind.

Paul's thorn in the flesh (v. 7). There are various opinions as to what this was. The view generally held, and which seems most likely to be correct, is that it was chronic ophthalmia, a disease of the eyes that was not extremely painful but at times made him repulsive in appearance.

This seems to be borne out by the language of the epistles.

- The "thorn" struck Paul 14 years before he wrote this epistle (vv. 2, 7), which was about the time when he entered Galatia on his first missionary journey.
- His entrance into Galatia was accompanied by some sort of physical infirmity (Galatians 4:13), and Paul was so offensive in appearance that it constituted a sore trial to anyone in his presence (Galatians 4:14).
- They would have given him their own eyes (Galatians 4:15)—why eyes, unless that was his particular need?
- Paul's customary "large" handwriting (Galatians 6:11) may have been due to poor eyesight. This may have been the reason Paul dictated his letters to his helpers.

2 Cor. 13 | PAUL'S INTENDED VISIT TO CORINTH

Paul wrote this epistle in the summer of A.D. 57. He arrived in Corinth in the fall and spent the winter there. The following spring he left for Jerusalem.

The region of Galatia. In the letter to the Galatians, Paul instructs all believers in Jesus to avoid using the Law as a means to eternal life.

Some think that Galatians was probably written from Antioch about A.D. 49, soon after Paul's first return from Galatia and before the Jerusalem council of A.D. 49/50. That council wrote a letter to the churches in Antioch, Syria, and Cilicia, stating clearly that circumcision was not necessary (Acts 15:1–16:4). If Paul had written this letter after that, we might expect him to mention the decision of the Jerusalem council. On the other hand, "I *first* preached the gospel to you" (4:13) implies that Paul had been in Galatia at least a second time, which would favor a later date for the letter, after his second missionary journey—perhaps A.D. 51/52 or 53.

The Judaizers

The Judaizers were a sect of Jewish Christians who, not willing to accept the teaching of the apostles on the question of circumcision (Acts 15), continued to insist that Christians must come to God through Judaism, and that therefore a Gentile, in order to be a Christian, must first become a Jewish proselyte, be circumcised, and keep the Jewish Law.

Galatia

In New Testament times, *Galatia* could refer to a region in north-central Asia Minor (modern Turkey) or to a Roman province in central Asia Minor (1 Corinthians 16:1; Galatians 1:2; 2 Timothy 4:10; 1 Peter 1:1). Pisidian Antioch, Iconium, Lystra, and Derbe were cities in the province of Galatia, all of which Paul visited on his first missionary journey (Acts 13–14). Both Peter and Paul appear to use the term to refer to the province as a whole (1 Peter 1:1; Galatians 1:1; 1 Corinthians 16:1).

The Galatians were Gauls, originally from north of the Black Sea. They split off from the main migration westward that ended up in what today is France (in Paul's day called Gallia or Gaul) and settled in Asia Minor in the third century B.C.

The Judaizers made it their business to visit and unsettle and trouble gentile churches. They were simply determined to stamp Christ with the Jewish trademark.

Against this Paul stood adamant. If the observance of the Law were imposed on gentile converts, Paul's whole life's work would have been wrecked and the Gospel of grace would have been subverted.

The expansion of Christianity from a Jewish sect into a world religion was Paul's consuming passion, in pursuit of which he broke every hindering tie and strained every faculty of mind and body for more than 30 years.

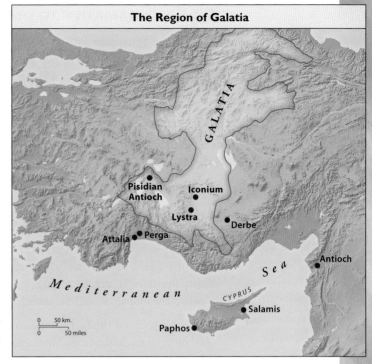

The Region of Galatia

The effort to Judaize the gentile churches was brought to an end by the fall of Jerusalem in A.D. 70, which severed all connections between Judaism and Christianity. Up to this time, Christianity was regarded as a sect or branch of Judaism. But from then on, Jews and Christians were separate. A small sect of Jewish Christians, the Ebionites, remained in dwindling numbers for two more centuries, hardly recognized by the church and regarded as apostates by the Jews.

Gal. 1 | PAUL'S GOSPEL DIRECT FROM GOD

It seems that the Judaizers, to discredit Paul in the eyes of the Galatians, were saying that Paul was not an original apostle, that he had not been taught by Jesus but by the Twelve. This may supply the background for his passionate vindication of himself as an independent, true apostle. He received his Gospel directly from God—and there is no other gospel.

Arabia (v. 17). There is no mention of this in the account in Acts. The three years (v. 18) includes the time he was in Damascus and in Arabia (Acts 9:23). According to the Jewish custom of reckoning partial years at the beginning and end of a period as full years, the three years may have been only one full year and parts of two years. Arabia is the desert country southeast of Palestine, consisting today of Saudi Arabia and Yemen. Paul was so stunned by the stroke from heaven, and the instant realization that his whole life had been wrong, that he felt he had better think things through. He sought solitude to get himself reoriented, and it was in Arabia that some of his revelations came (v. 16).

Gal. 2 | PAUL'S RELATION TO THE OTHER APOSTLES

The visit to Jerusalem (vv. 1–10). Paul waited three years after his conversion before he returned to Jerusalem, where he had once tried to destroy the church. He was there for only 15 days, talking things over with Peter (v. 18). (Compare the account in Acts 9:26–30.) Then, after 14 years, he went again to Jerusalem. This must have been the visit recorded in Acts 11:27–30, which was in A.D. 44, for the context, along with the statement "I went up again to Jerusalem" in verse 1, indicates that this was his second visit to Jerusalem after his conversion. He took Titus, one of his gentile converts, along as a test case in the question of the need for gentile circumcision. Paul stood his ground and won the complete endorsement of the other apostles (v. 9).

Peter's hypocrisy at Antioch (vv. 11–21). It is not stated when this visit took place. Probably it was soon after Paul's return to Antioch from the visit referred to in verse 1, but before Paul set out on his first missionary journey. To get the setting and significance of the incident, our tentative chronology would be something like this:

> *Know that a man is not justified by observing the law, but by faith in Jesus Christ.*
> —Galatians 2:16

- Peter received the first gentile convert, Cornelius (Acts 10), without circumcision, probably around A.D. 40.
- This action was approved by the other apostles (Acts 11).
- Some two years later, around A.D. 42, the gentile church in Antioch was founded, with the approval of Barnabas as emissary from Jerusalem (Acts 11:22–24).
- Paul's trip to Jerusalem with Titus took place in A.D. 44, and Peter joined in the endorsement of Paul's reception of Gentiles without circumcision.
- Very soon thereafter, in A.D. 44 or 45, Peter took this trip to Antioch, during which he separated himself from the uncircumcised Gentiles out of fear of the Judaizers. This drew the scathing rebuke from Paul (v. 11). However, five or six years later, at the Jerusalem council in A.D. 50, Peter was the first to speak out in favor of Paul's work (Acts 15:7–11).

What does this vacillation on the part of Peter, and this disagreement between the two leading apostles over so fundamental a teaching, mean? In this particular incident, either Peter or Paul was wrong. How can we know which of the two it was? If either of them was mistaken in one thing, how do we know that he was not mistaken in other things? Doesn't this incident undermine the doctrine that the apostles were inspired of God?

Not at all. The simple fact is that God did not reveal the full, complete truth about His kingdom to the apostles all at once. Jesus had told them that He still had many things to teach them, more than they could then bear (John 16:12). Jesus dealt very patiently with human prejudice. He allowed them to hold on to their old notions of the messianic kingdom until, as the need arose, He led them step by step into a new and deeper understanding of the kingdom. He did not bother them with the gentile problem until the problem arose. Then, after the Gospel had been fully proclaimed among the Jews in their Palestinian homeland, God, by direct and special revelation, instructed Peter on the question of including Gentiles in the church (Acts 10), which was probably about 10 years after the Pentecostal birthday of the church.

It took a few years for the apostles to adjust their thinking and attitudes to the new teaching. Paul was able to discard the old notion more readily than Peter was. The Galatian incident happened after Paul had fully embraced the new revelation, while Peter was still struggling with it. Yet Peter came to a full acceptance of the new revelation before any of the New Testament books were written, and there is not an iota of difference between the teachings of Paul and Peter in the New Testament.

Gal. 3–4 | BONDAGE UNDER THE LAW

These gentile Galatians had swallowed the Judaizers' message so completely that they had instituted Jewish festival days and ceremonies in the church (4:8–11), evidently trying to combine the Gospel with the Mosaic Law. But Paul tells them that the two systems are not compatible and cannot be combined. Did the Judaizers work any miracles among them, as he had done? (3:5). Did not that mean anything to them? Abraham looms large in these two chapters, because the Jewish message they had accepted was based largely on the promise to Abraham. They were misinterpreting the promise, as the narrative about Abraham itself clearly shows (4:21–31). The Galatians' early love for Paul was in sad contrast to their present coolness (4:12–20). (For a note on the illness mentioned in 4:13, see under 2-Corinthians 12.)

Gal. 5–6 | FREEDOM IN CHRIST

Paul could not understand how any human being would deliberately choose to risk his salvation by basing it on his or her own works rather than on the gracious mercy of Christ. Christ saves us—we do not save ourselves. It is the difference between freedom and slavery. But freedom in Christ does not mean license to continue in sin. Paul never fails to lay special stress on that. Those who follow the desires of the sinful nature cannot be saved (5:19–21), but those who seek the Lord will receive the fruits of the Spirit, which are love, joy, peace, patience, kindness, goodness, faithfulness, gentleness, and self control (5:22–23). One of the spiritual laws of the natural world is that a man shall reap what he sows (6:7); it is an inexorable law, whether the seed be wheat or weeds.

Carry each other's burdens, and in this way you will fulfill the law of Christ.

—Galatians 6:2

Large letters (6:11): evidence of the genuineness of Paul's own handwriting (see the note on his "thorn in my flesh" under 2 Corinthians 12).

The marks of Jesus (6:17). His enemies claimed that Paul was not a genuine apostle of Christ. His battered, bruised, and scarred body was his testimony (see 2 Corinthians 4, 6, 11).

Ephesians

**The Unity of the Church
Jews and Gentiles Are One in Christ**

Now to him who is able to do immeasurably more than all we ask or imagine, according to his power that is at work within us, to him be glory in the church and in Christ Jesus throughout all generations, for ever and ever! Amen. —Ephesians 3:20–21

Paul's Letters from Prison

This is one of the four letters Paul wrote during his imprisonment in Rome (A.D. 59–61/62); the others are Philippians, Colossians, and Philemon. With the exception of Philippians, they were written at the same time and carried by the same messengers (6:21; Colossians 4:7–9; Philemon 10–12). We know of one other letter Paul wrote from prison that is now lost (Colossians 4:16). These letters are often called the "prison epistles."

The Purpose of the Letter

Paul spent his life teaching Gentiles that they could be Christians without becoming Jewish proselytes (converts). This was very displeasing to Jews generally, for they thought of the Mosaic Law as binding for all people, and they were bitterly prejudiced against any uncircumcised Gentiles who presumed to call themselves disciples of the Jewish Messiah.

While Paul taught gentile Christians to stand like a rock for their liberty in Christ, as he did in the letters to the Galatians and the Romans, he did not want them to be prejudiced against their Jewish fellow Christians but to regard them as brothers in Christ.

Paul did not want to see two churches, a Jewish church and a gentile church, but *one* church: Jews and Gentiles one in Christ. Paul's gesture on behalf of unity made to the *Jewish* elements in the church was the great offering of money from gentile churches, which he took at the close of his third missionary journey to the poor in the mother church at Jerusalem (Acts 21). His hope was that this demonstration of Christian love might make Jewish Christians feel more kindly toward their gentile brothers and sisters.

Paul's gesture on behalf of unity to the *gentile* elements in the church was this letter, written to the leading center of his own gentile converts, exalting the *oneness, universality,* and *unspeakable grandeur* of the body of Christ.

To Paul, Christ was so marvelously great that in Him there is room for people of all different races, viewpoints, and prejudices. He is One who has power to solve all the problems of mankind and to bring all earthly social and family life (even the myriads of beings in the infinite, unseen universe; 3:10) into unity and harmony with God (5:22 – 6:9).

Eph. 1 | SPIRITUAL BLESSINGS

"In Ephesus" (v. 1) is not in some of the most ancient manuscripts. It is thought that this was probably intended as a circular letter to the churches in Asia Minor. In this case Tychicus would have carried a number of copies, with space for each city to insert its own name. This would also account for the lack of personal greetings in this letter, which is unlike most of Paul's letters.

Paul had spent three years in Ephesus and had many devoted friends there; yet this letter is rather formal in tone. This would not be surprising if this was indeed a circular letter for Ephesus and its neighboring cities.

God's eternal purpose (vv. 3 – 14). A magnificent summary of God's plan: the redemption, adoption, forgiveness, and sealing of a people for God's own possession, determined from eternity, now being brought about by God Himself.

"Heavenly realms" (v. 3) is a key phrase of this book (1:10, 20; 2:6; 3:10; 6:12). It means the unseen sphere beyond this world of the senses, which is the Christian's ultimate home and with which we now, in a measure, have communication.

Ephesus

Ephesus was a proud, rich, busy port at the end of the caravan route from Asia. From Ephesus goods were shipped to other Mediterranean ports. This huge city contained a theater (seating about 25,000; Acts 19:29), an agora ("town square" that also served as the marketplace of goods and ideas), public baths, a library, and a number of temples. (See photos on pp. 678–79.)

Ephesus was built near the shrine of an old Anatolian fertility goddess and became the center of her cult; this deity was known to the Greeks as Artemis and to the Romans as Diana. The temple of Diana was discovered by J. T. Wood in 1870; it may have been the largest building in the Greek world. Grotesquely represented with turreted head and many breasts, the goddess and her cult found expression in the famous temple, served, like that of Aphrodite at Corinth, by a host of priestess courtesans.

The Diana cult generated much trade. Ephesus became a place of pilgrimage for worshipers, all eager to carry away talismans and souvenirs—hence the prosperous guild of the silversmiths, whose livelihood was the manufacture of silver shrines and images of the meteoric stone that was said to be Diana's image "fallen from heaven." This trade became increasingly important as the harbor of Ephesus silted up and commerce declined. In A.D. 65 an attempt was made to improve the seaway, but the task proved too great. Ephesus in the 1st century was a dying city.

It is probable that during Paul's two-year stay the Gospel spread to other cities in the province of Asia (e.g., to Colosse). Later, the apostle John lived in Ephesus, and it is the first of the churches addressed in Revelation (2:1–7).

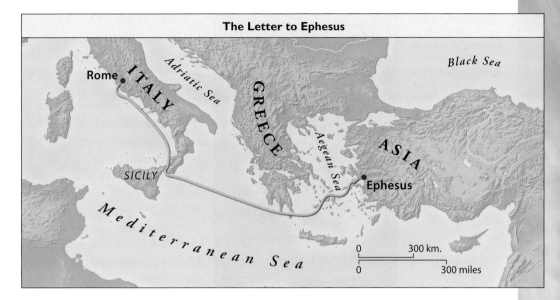

The Letter to Ephesus

Divine election (v. 11) is a common theme in Paul's letters. He emphasizes this in phrases such as "he chose us," "he predestined us," "we were also chosen," and "having been predestined" before the creation of the world.

Paul's prayer for them (vv. 15–23). This is the way Paul usually begins his letters. Four such prayers are especially beautiful: this prayer and those in 3:14–19; Philippians 1:9–11; and Colossians 1:9–12.

Eph. 2–3 THE CHURCH, ONE IN CHRIST

In the first chapter Paul lays out God's ultimate goal—universal unity between Himself, the Creator, and all of His creation. This unity existed before Adam and Eve sinned. God has a plan for reestablishing this unity. In the second chapter Paul reveals the steps that God is taking to reestablish universal unity.

Paul's proclamation of Jesus as Messiah impacted not only Ephesus but the surrounding regions as well.

A statue of Sophia, the goddess of wisdom, in the wall of the library at Ephesus. Paul mentions wisdom three times in this letter (1:8; 1:17; 3:10).

ΣΟΦΙΑ
ΚΕΛΣΟΥ

Saved by grace (2:1–10). First God reconciles individuals to Himself as an act of grace. The body of Christ is being built up out of unworthy, sinful people, to be an everlasting demonstration of the kindness of God. When God's work in us is completed, we will be creatures of unutterable bliss in a state of heavenly glory beyond anything we can now imagine. It will be God's work, not ours, and through the ages heaven will never cease to resound with the glad hallelujahs from the grateful hearts of the redeemed.

Once only one nation, now all nations (2:11–22). The next step in God's ultimate plan of universal unity is to reconcile Christians to each other and into one unified church body. The term "the circumcision" came to be used as a name of the Jews, as distinct from other nations which were spoken of as "the uncircumcised" (v. 11). For a while the Jews constituted the body of God's people, of which circumcision was the physical sign and from which other nations were excluded. But now the call from God rings out clear and strong to all, from every tribe and nation, to come and join His household.

The mystery of Christ (3:1–13), which for ages past was kept hidden in God (v. 9), in this passage plainly means that the nations are heirs to the promises that God gave to the Jews, which the Jews until now had thought belonged to them exclusively. That phase of God's plan had been hidden until the coming of Christ, though He had purposed it from the beginning (1:5); but now it is fully revealed, namely, that God's future world of glory will be built, not only out of the Jewish nation, but from all mankind.

The united church will be the primary means by which God will display His "manifold wisdom" to the rulers and authorities in the heavenly realms. God's eternal purpose is that Christ, the head of the church, will ultimately assume headship over the universe. The eternal destiny of the church is to rule and reign with Christ on the earth (2 Timothy 2:12; Revelation 20:2) and across the universe (Revelation 22:5). These verses put our Christian lives here on earth into an awesome perspective. We might consider our earthly experiences as God's "training camp" through which He is gathering and preparing believers for their eternal rulership with Christ.

Paul's prayer (3:14–21). Paul does not pray for knowledge—not even knowledge of the Bible—but for that which far surpasses all knowledge: the love of Christ. That love illumines and brings to life the pages of the Scriptures.

Eph. 4 | THE ONENESS OF THE CHURCH

One body (vv. 1–16). A complex organism, with many parts, each in its own place and with its own function, working together in harmony. Its basic principle is love (v. 16), while Christ Himself is its head and directive force.

The fundamental requisite for the proper functioning of the body of Christ, which is composed of many members of diverse talents and tempers, is a spirit of humility, gentleness, and mutual support on the part of the members (v. 2).

The purpose of the body is to nurture each of its members into the perfect image of Christ (vv. 12–15). The idea of growth, as expressed in these verses, seems to apply both to individuals and to the church as

> *"In your anger do not sin": Do not let the sun go down while you are still angry, and do not give the devil a foothold.*
> —Ephesians 4:26–27

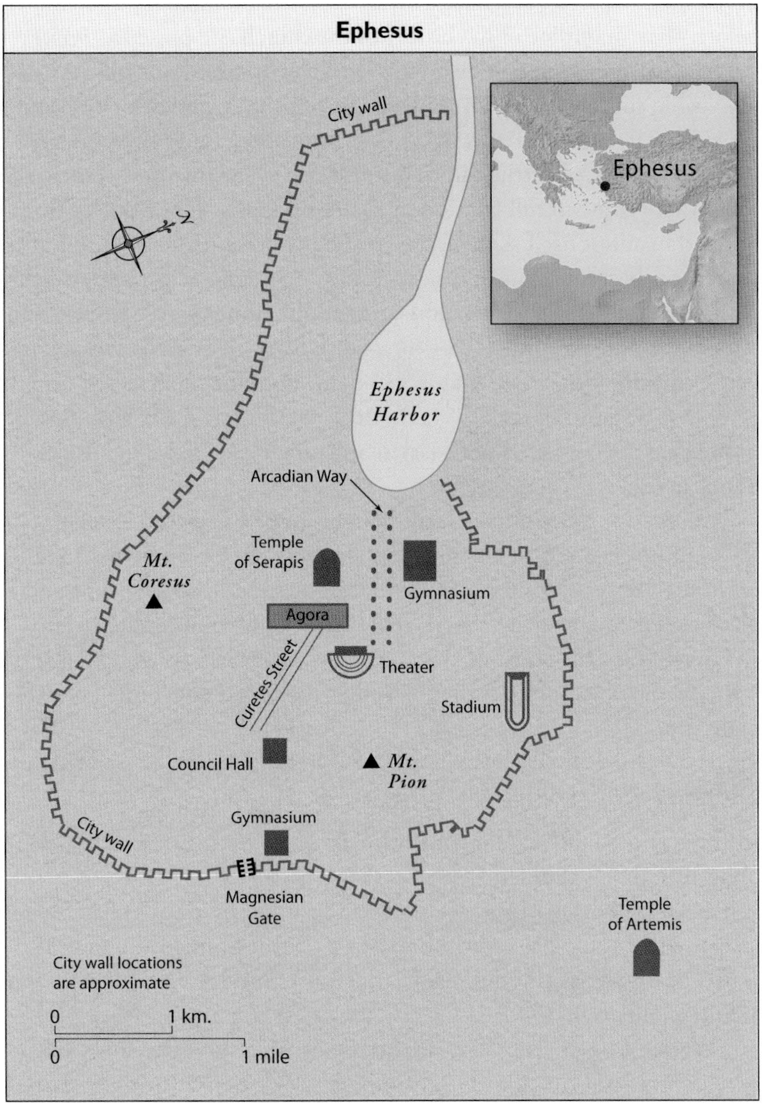

Ephesus

City wall

Ephesus

Ephesus Harbor

Arcadian Way

Temple of Serapis

Mt. Coresus ▲

Agora

Gymnasium

Curetes Street

Theater

Stadium

Council Hall

▲ *Mt. Pion*

Gymnasium

City wall

Magnesian Gate

Temple of Artemis

City wall locations are approximate

0   1 km.

0   1 mile

a whole. The childhood of the church will pass. Its maturity will come. (Compare the companion passage, 1 Corinthians 12–13.)

The church is now nearly 2,000 years old. Yet it is still in its childhood state—it has not yet known unity in its full, visible manifestation. Paul's unceasing fight was against factions in local churches and against the divisions between Jews and Gentiles. Later came the bitter controversies of the 2nd, 3rd, and 4th centuries. This was followed by the imperial church, with its outward *semblance* of unity under state authority, and the major split of the church into the Western (Roman Catholic) church and the Eastern (Orthodox) church.

Then, almost 500 years ago, came the Reformation, which taught people to read the Bible for themselves and to think for themselves. This almost inevitably led to a division of the Protestant church into many denominations and groups. We still have a divided Christendom, more so than ever before. (For an outline of the history of the church, see pp. 893–935.)

Whether there will ever be, in this world, an outward, organic unity of the visible church, we do not know. The selfishness and pride of people are against it. But there always has been, and still is, a unity in the invisible church of God's true saints, a unity that will somehow, sometime, somewhere come to full fruition in answer to Christ's own prayer (John 17) and manifest itself as the full-grown body of Christ. It is a unity that sometimes becomes evident, unexpectedly, on a small scale when we talk with Christians from a tradition or denomination very different from ours in theology or form of worship and suddenly realize that we are one in our love for Christ and that in His light our differences fade.

A new way of life (vv. 17–32). Since the church is a community of brothers and sisters, it is necessary that its members be very considerate of one another.

"Anger" (v. 26). Perhaps Paul thought it was a little too much to tell them not to get angry at all, so he cautions them to be careful not to hold on to their anger. Or he may have understood that there is a time and a place for legitimate anger that, if repressed, can do much damage later.

"Steal" (v. 28). Some of them evidently had been tough characters, but now they must respect the rights of others. (See note on 2 Thessalonians 3:6–15.)

Eph. 5–6 NEW OBLIGATIONS

In these two chapters Paul continues the topic he began in 4:17: their obligation to live differently.

Sexual immorality (5:3–14). It was a very common sin in Paul's day; in many places temple prostitution was a part of heathen worship. Paul warns against it again and again. (See notes on 1 Corinthians 7 and 1 Thessalonians 4:1–8.)

Singing (5:18–21). The joyful praise of Christian meetings is here contrasted with the riotous indulgence of noisy, drunken parties

(vv. 18–19). Hymn singing is by far the most natural, simplest, best loved, and by all odds the most spiritually stimulating part of religious meetings.

Husbands and wives (5:22–33). If we are Christians, we must show it in all areas of life—business, social, and domestic. The relationship between husband and wife is here represented as being a counterpart of the relation between Christ and the church (vv. 25, 32). Paul exhorts to mutual love and devotion—he in no way suggests that a man has a right to make a slave of his wife. Each is dependent on the other because of the different functions that each has in human society. Each serves him- or herself best by serving the other (v. 28). He that loves his wife loves himself: husbands, take note.

Parents and children (6:1–4). One of the Ten Commandments (Exodus 20) states that we must honor those who gave us life. Doing so would prolong that life. This was the promise of God and is a fact of nature. Fathers are cautioned against being too severe with their children, both here and in Colossians 3:21. Parental authority was generally too austere then, as it is now generally too lax. Fathers are named because mothers tend to be more lenient. We suspect that back then, when change was slower and there were far fewer continuous external influences on the children, it was easier for parents to raise children as they themselves had been raised.

Servants and masters (6:5–9). Half the population of Rome, and a large percentage of the population of the empire, were slaves. Many of the Christians were slaves. They are told here that faithful service to their master is what Christ expects of them. It is a remarkable teaching: in the performance of our earthly tasks, however menial, we are always under the watchful eye of Christ, for His approval or disapproval, as we may deserve. But the same applies to masters in their treatment of slaves. Today we would apply this primarily to the attitude of employees toward their employers and of employers toward employees.

The Christian's armor (6:10–20). This passage certainly means that the Christian's warfare is

Paul instructs the church at Ephesus to put on the whole armor of God and take up the shield of faith. (Ephesians 6:16)

against more than the natural temptations of the sinful nature. There are powers in the unseen world against which we alone are powerless, powers we can resist only with the aid of Christ. Truth, righteousness, peace, faith, salvation, the Word, prayer—these are the weapons that will "extinguish all the flaming arrows" of the unseen enemy and allow us to stand against the deception of Satan.

Philippians

A Letter of Joy

But one thing I do: Forgetting what is behind and straining toward what is ahead, I press on toward the goal to win the prize for which God has called me heavenward in Christ Jesus.

—PHILIPPIANS 3:13–14

I can do everything through him who gives me strength.

—PHILIPPIANS 4:13

It is not easy to state the subject of this letter. It is, like most letters, about a number of things. But since it was occasioned by the reception of an offering of money from one of Paul's churches to help support him in his foreign missionary work, it is not inappropriate to call it a missionary letter.

As a rule, Paul would not take pay for preaching. He supported himself by working at his trade as a tentmaker (1 Corinthians 9:12; Acts 18:3). His reason was that there were many false teachers who would use his example wrongly to enrich themselves by preaching. There might also be people who would misinterpret Paul's motivation for accepting money. However, he did accept offerings from the church in Philippi while he was in Thessalonica (4:16) and also while he was in Corinth (2 Corinthians 11:9).

The Church in Philippi

This was the first church Paul established in Europe, early in his second missionary journey, around A.D. 51 (Acts 16). Lydia and the jailer of Philippi were among the converts. Luke the physician, author of one of the Gospels and the book of Acts, was its pastor for the first six years.

Philippi may have been Luke's home, where he practiced medicine. Luke must have had a hand in the development of the character of the Philippian church, which, as far as we know, was one of the purest of the New Testament churches.

The Occasion of the Letter

In A.D. 61–63, Paul was in prison in Rome, about 10 years after he had founded the church in Philippi and about three or four years after he had last visited there. Apparently he had begun to wonder if they had forgotten him (4:10). Then Epaphroditus arrived from faraway Philippi with an offering of money. Paul was deeply touched. Epaphroditus had nearly lost his life on the journey. When he recovered (2:25–30; 4:18), Paul sent him to Philippi with this beautiful letter.

Philippi

A city of Macedonia (north of Greece), located about 10 miles inland from Neapolis on the Aegean Sea. The original settlement was called Krenides, but in 356 B.C. the name was changed by Philip, king of Macedonia (359–336 B.C.; the father of Alexander the Great), when he enlarged the city with many new inhabitants and considerable construction.

The first emperor of Rome, Augustus, made Philippi a Roman colony, which gave the city many advantages over most other cities in the Roman Empire: its citizens had an autonomous government, were immune from tribute, and were treated the same as if they actually lived in Italy. The Philippians' pride in their city may be seen in Acts 16:20–21 as well as in some of Paul's terminology (Philippians 1:27; 3:20).

The Via Egnatia, the main highway from Asia to the west, passed through Philippi and ran alongside the forum of the city. Paul's choice of Philippi as the location of ministry throws light on the strategy of his evangelism.

The church at Philippi was founded in the course of Paul's second missionary journey (Acts 16), as Philippi became the first European city in which he preached. Near the city was the river Gangites (modern Angitis), where apparently the small Jewish population in Philippi congregated for prayer. The new church did not forget its founder, however, for gifts were sent to Paul on several occasions (Philippians 4:15–16).

Paul made a second, and possibly third, visit to Philippi on his third missionary journey (Acts 20:1–6).

Phil. 1 | THE GOSPEL IN ROME

Timothy (v. 1) probably wrote the letter at Paul's dictation. He had helped Paul found the Philippian church, so Paul had him join in the salutation. Timothy had also helped in the writing of other letters: 1 Corinthians, Colossians, 1 and 2 Thessalonians, and Philemon.

Paul's prayer for them (vv. 3–11). This is the way Paul nearly always starts his letters. Compare the beautiful prayers in Ephesians 1:16:23; 3:14–19; Colossians 1:9–12.

Partnership in the gospel (v. 5) refers to the gift of money they had sent him. This made them participants in his work. (See further under 4:17.)

The Gospel in Rome (vv. 12–18). His coming to Rome as a prisoner had turned out to be a help rather than a hindrance in making Christ known in the imperial city. It had given him access to official circles, so that he had some converts at Nero's court (4:22). As he had rejoiced that night in the Philippian jail (Acts 16:25), so now he was rejoicing in his Roman chains (v. 18).

Paul's desire for death (vv. 19–26). No doubt there were ever-present pains in his scarred and broken body from repeated stonings and beatings. He was by now an old man. He knew that the churches needed him, but he longed to go home to be with Christ. Still, it was no great matter. Whether he was in prison or in paradise, Christ was his life and joy. Whether he was to depart or remain was in God's hands. And in

The Via Egnatia once passed near the modern Church of Lydia near the ruins of Philippi. Paul used the Via Egnatia (Egnatian Way) as he traveled through Philippi on his way to Thessalonica.

spite of his desire to be with Christ, he was still hoping to return to Philippi (v. 26; 2:24).

The sufferings of the Philippians (vv. 27 – 30). The church in Philippi had been in existence for 10 years, and they were still being persecuted. Paul kept his eye on the day of vindication, when the tables would be turned and their persecutors would reap what they had sown (v. 28; 2 Thessalonians 1:5 – 10).

Phil. 2 | THE HUMILITY OF CHRIST

An example of humility (vv. 1 – 11). There is less rebuke in this letter than in most of the other New Testament letters. But we wonder, judging from the context of this charming exhortation to humility, whether perhaps Epaphroditus had brought Paul hints that there were seeds of divisiveness in the pride of certain Philippian leaders, perhaps specifically Euodia and Syntyche (4:2).

Something to be grasped (v. 6), to be held on to. The humility and suffering of Christ are often set over against His exaltation and glory, as in vv. 8 – 11. (See Hebrews 2:9 – 10; 1 Peter 1:11.)

Paul's joy in the day of Christ (vv. 12 – 18). Paul conceived of earthly friendships as continuing on into eternity. He expected his happiness to come to a rapturous climax when he would greet his beloved friends in the kingdom, at the feet of Jesus, and they would be his own offering to the Lord, saved forever, because he himself had brought them to Jesus (v. 16).

His plan to return to Philippi (vv. 19–30). This reads as if he were expecting his trial to come to a speedy end, especially in v. 24. There is no hint here of going on to Spain, as he had planned originally (Romans 15:24). His long imprisonment seems to have changed his plans. The commonly held view is that he was acquitted and did revisit Philippi and other churches in the East (1 Timothy 1:3), but was arrested again some five years later, brought back to Rome, and executed.

Phil. 3 | THE HEAVENLY GOAL

The background of the picture in this chapter seems to have been the appearance in Philippi of the Judaizers. They apparently had not made much headway with their emphasis on the observance of the Law and their quarreling over unessential matters, like dogs worrying a bone (v. 2). Paul himself had possessed the righteousness of the Law, which the Judaizers were preaching, to a marked degree (vv. 4–6). But he now counts it as refuse or rubbish (v. 8). His whole dependence was on Christ. His one aim was to know Him.

Paul pictures himself as in a race, straining every nerve and muscle and exerting every ounce of strength, like a runner, with bulging veins, lest he fall short of the goal. That goal was that he might attain unto the resurrection from the dead (v. 11). This was the secret of Paul's life. He had had a glimpse of the glory of heaven (2 Corinthians 12:4) and was determined that he would, by the grace of Christ, get there, with as many others as he could possibly persuade to come along. This chapter is one of the fullest statements of Paul's own, personal hope of heaven, where our citizenship is (v. 20). We are strangers here; our homeland is there. Our walk is here; our hearts are there.

Phil. 4 | JOY

Euodia and Syntyche (vv. 2–3). Two women leaders; they may have been deaconesses or socially prominent women whose homes were used as churches. They were allowing their personal differences to become an annoyance to the church.

Rejoice! Rejoice! (vv. 4–7). Joy is the predominant note of this letter, written by a man in prison who during 30 years had been mobbed, beaten, stoned, and manhandled — enough to make the angels gasp. Yet he is overflowing with joy. The very things that would naturally tend to make him sour only added to his happiness. It is simply amazing what Christ can do in one's life.

"The Lord is near" (v. 5): Paul had said, 10 years earlier, in 2 Thessalonians 2, that the Lord would not come until after the revolution

According to tradition, this is what remains of the prison where Paul and Silas were praying and singing in the night. (Acts 16)

(falling away, apostasy); but that apostasy was working fast in some of Paul's churches, and he never got his mind completely off the approaching and nearness of the Lord's coming. This was one of the secrets of his perennial joy. Another was his unceasing prayer with thanksgiving (v. 6). Gratitude to God for what He does give us will surely incline Him to grant that which we do not have.

The coming of Epaphroditus (vv. 10–20). He had brought the gift of money from the church to Paul (v. 18). Paul was profoundly grateful, for as a prisoner he had no means of sustenance except what the prison allowed. The most beautiful and exquisitely delicate touch in this entire letter is in v. 17, where, in thanking them for the money, he tells them that he appreciated it, not so much because he needed it (though he did need it badly, 2:25), but because it gave them a share in the rewards for his work that would be credited to their account. Because they supported him, his work was theirs. In the final day they would be rewarded for the multitudes of souls they had helped him to save.

The lesson applies to our missionary offerings today. Each offering, by itself, does

> *Do not be anxious about anything, but in everything, by prayer and petition, with thanksgiving, present your requests to God. And the peace of God, which transcends all understanding, will guard your hearts and your minds in Christ Jesus.*
> —Philippians 4:6–7

The lion of Amphipolis, a 4th-century B.C. funerary statue guarding a bridge over the Strimon River. Paul and Silas would have seen this statue on their way from Berea to Athens. (Acts 17:14–15)

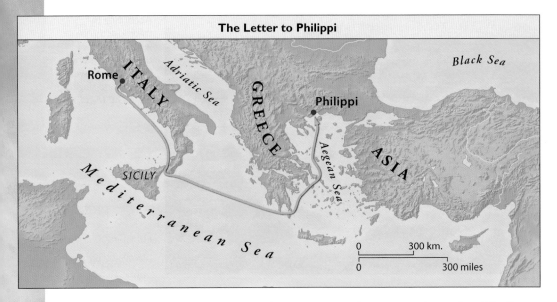

The Letter to Philippi

not amount to much. But even as the tiny raindrops that fall all over the central part of the North American continent make possible the torrent that rolls over Niagara Falls, so these offerings from hundreds of thousands of Christians all over the land together constitute the stream of funds that is supporting the noblest army of men and women the sun ever shone on, the vast army of foreign missionaries out on the far-flung battle lines of the Cross, enduring hardships for Christ we would not think of enduring here at home. Those who, by their offerings to missions, make themselves a part of this mightiest movement of all the ages will, in the day of final reckoning, be entitled to share in its rewards.

Social standing of New Testament Christians (v. 22). Most of the early Christians were of the humbler classes. Many of them were slaves. Some of the converts belonged to the emperor's household, whether as slaves or as freedmen, or even as persons of importance. They may have been members of the palace guard (1:13). Other people of high social standing include the treasurer of Ethiopia (Acts 8:27), Cornelius the centurion (Acts 10:1), a foster-brother of Herod (Acts 13:1), the proconsul of Cyprus (Acts 13:12), prominent women of Thessalonica (Acts 17:4), Greek women of honorable estate in Berea (Acts 17:12), the city treasurer of Corinth (Romans 16:23), and Joanna, the wife of Herod's steward (Luke 8:3).

Colossians

The Deity and
All-Sufficiency of Christ

Christ in you, the hope of glory.

—Colossians 1:27

Let the peace of Christ rule in your hearts, since as members of one body you were called to peace. And be thankful.

—Colossians 3:15

The Church at Colosse

The church at Colosse was established on Paul's third missionary journey, during his three years in Ephesus, not by Paul himself (Colossians 2:1), but by Epaphras (1:7; 4:12–13). Archippus also exercised a fruitful ministry there (4:17; Philemon 2). Philemon was an active member of this church, as was Onesimus (Colossians 4:9).

Occasion and Date of the Epistle

Paul was in prison in Rome, in A.D. 59–61/62. He spent at least two years under house arrest (Acts 28:16–31). He had written a previous letter with instructions about Mark (4:10). In the meantime, Epaphras, a member of the church in Colosse, had come to Rome with word that a dangerous heresy was making headway in the church. It seems that Epaphras then was also imprisoned in Rome (Philemon 23). Paul then wrote this letter and sent it with Tychicus and Onesimus (4:7–9), who also carried Paul's letter to the Ephesians and the one to Philemon (Ephesians 6:21).

The Colossian Heresy

The heresy seems to have been a mixture of Greek, Jewish, and Oriental religions, a sort of higher-thought cult that presented itself as a philosophy (2:8). It called for the worship of angels as intermediaries between God and man (2:18) and insisted on the strict observance of certain Jewish requirements, almost to the point of asceticism (2:16, 21). It was proclaimed in high-sounding phrases and with an air of superiority—as part of the Gospel of Christ.

The Similarity to the Letter to the Ephesians

Colossians and Ephesians were written at the same time. Both are carefully developed statements of the great doctrines of the Gospel, to be read aloud in the churches, and are very similar in many of their passages. But their main themes are entirely different:

Colosse

An ancient city in Phrygia (in modern Turkey), situated about 110 miles inland of Ephesus and about 10 miles up the Lycus valley from Laodicea. Colosse stood on the most important trade route from Ephesus to the Euphrates and was a place of great importance from early times.

But when Laodicea was founded a short distance away, traffic was rerouted through the new city, leaving Colosse to decline in social and commercial importance. In Paul's day it was only an insignificant market town, and the site is now uninhabited.

- Ephesians focuses on the unity and grandeur of the church;
- Colossians emphasizes the deity and all-sufficiency of Christ as contrasted with the emptiness of mere human philosophy.

Col. 1 | THE DEITY OF CHRIST

Paul's thanksgiving for the Colossians (1:3–8). **We always thank God** (v. 3). Paul often starts his letters this way (Romans 1:8; 1 Corinthians 1:4; Ephesians 1:16; Philippians 1:3; 1 Thessalonians 1:2; 2 Thessalonians 1:3; 2 Timothy 1:3; Philemon 4). Good news from the scattered churches filled his soul with joyful gratitude.

Faith, love, hope (vv. 4–5) are his favorite words: faith in Christ, love toward the saints, hope of heaven. Note that their hope is the motive that produces their love (v. 5; see 1 Corinthians 13; 1 Thessalonians 1:3).

"Heard of" (v. 4) does not necessarily mean he had not been to Colosse, for he uses the same phrase in Ephesians 1:15, and we know he had been in Ephesus, although he had not been there for some years.

All over the world (v. 6) and **every creature under heaven** (v. 23) mean that by the time Paul wrote this, some 32 years after the death and resurrection of Jesus, the Gospel had been preached to the whole then-known world. Within the first generation, the church became established worldwide.

Now in ruins and covered by vegetation, the ancient city of Colosse was located on an important trade route in the Lycus Valley.

Paul's prayer for them (1:9–12). One of the four most beautiful of Paul's prayers for his churches; the other three are Ephesians 1:16–19; 3:14–19; and Philippians 1:9–11.

Spiritual wisdom (v. 9) means knowing how to live a Christlike life.

Strengthened with all power (v. 11), so as to be joyfully patient under all circumstances.

The Deity of Christ (vv. 13–20). Statements Paul makes about Christ in this letter are

- Image of the invisible God
- Firstborn over all creation
- All things were created by Him
- He is before all things
- In Him all things hold together
- Head of the church
- The beginning
- The firstborn from among the dead
- In Him all fullness dwells
- Through Him all things are reconciled
- Christ in you is the hope of glory
- In Him are all the treasures of wisdom and knowledge
- In Him all the fullness of the Deity lives in bodily form
- In Him you have been given fullness (brought to perfection)
- The head over every power and authority

Firstborn over all creation (v. 15) does not mean that He was created, but rather that He is heir to the created universe, even as the firstborn in the Old Testament was heir to the family land.

Thrones, powers, rulers, authorities (v. 16). This, and passages such as Ephesians 6:12, are a biblical hint that in the unseen world there are numerous varieties of persons and governments of which our visible world is a tiny counterpart, and that Christ's death not only made possible humanity's redemption, but became the means of restoring the broken harmony of the whole, vast universe.

Suffering for the church (vv. 24–29). **"What is still lacking in regard to Christ's afflictions"** (v. 24) does not mean that the suffering of Christ is insufficient for our salvation, but rather that the church as a whole cannot arrive at perfection until it has gone through suffering. Paul was anxious to bear his share. (See 1-Peter 4.)

The mystery (vv. 26–27): see note on Ephesians 3:3.

Christ in you, the hope of glory (v. 27). The essence of Paul's message in this letter is this: Christ is the Head of the Universe. We approach Him directly, not through intermediaries, not even through angels. Christ Himself, not this or that philosophy or this or that set of rules, is our Wisdom, our Life, our Hope of glory. Being a Christian, essentially, is loving *Him* and living *in Him,* a Person, a glorious, divine Person,

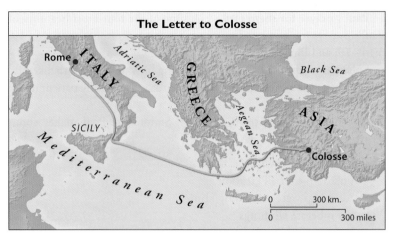

The Letter to Colosse

Rome • ITALY

Adriatic Sea

GREECE

Black Sea

SICILY

Aegean Sea

ASIA

• Colosse

Mediterranean Sea

0   300 km.

0   300 miles

through whom the universe was created and in whom is full sufficiency for mankind's redemption and eternal perfection.

Col. 2 | **CHRIST IS ALL-SUFFICIENT**

All who have not met me personally (v. 1) is taken by some to mean that Paul had not been in Colosse. But there is no way of knowing whether it includes, or is in addition to, the "you" that precedes this phrase. The personal greetings of 4:7–18 certainly indicate that Paul was well acquainted with the church in Colosse. He was hoping to come there soon (Philemon 22; Philemon was a member of the church in Colosse).

Laodicea (v. 1) was a nearby city, about 10 miles away. Paul had written them a letter also, along with this one to the Colossians (4:16). Some think that the letter sent to Laodicea may have been a copy of the letter to the Ephesians.

The mystery (v. 2). This may have been one of the pet words of the philosophers of Colosse. It is used four times in this letter (1:26, 27; 2:2; 4:3) and six times in Ephesians with reference to certain aspects of God's purpose that had not been revealed earlier. (See note on Ephesians 3:3–9.)

The philosophers of Colosse (vv. 4, 8). A philosopher is a man who spends his life trying to understand what he knows before he begins to realize that he cannot understand. Christ is the center of a whole realm of truth, some of it very easy to understand and some not so easy, that stretches out to things beyond the reaches of our souls. A philosopher sees in Christian teaching certain things that fit in with his philosophy. He accepts Christ and calls himself a Christian. But in his thinking, certain of his *philosophic abstractions remain central*, and Christ Himself is just a sort of shadow in the background. We all know people like that: militant proponents of some pet theory or doctrine—but you would never suspect them of having much love or admiration for Christ as a Person.

The legalists of Colosse (vv. 16; 20–22). Unlike the philosopher, a man with a more practical turn of mind does not bother much about things he cannot understand; rather, he wants to know what to *do* to be a Christian. He sees certain plain commandments—or what appear to him to be plain commandments—and he obeys them. And *to him those commandments are central,* while Christ Himself is just a sort of shadow in the background. We know people like that, too.

Worship of angels (v. 18). Some were teaching that human beings are too unworthy to approach Christ directly, that they need the mediation of angels. And they were proud of their humility, which was in fact directly contrary to the Gospel Paul had preached: Christ is the *only* mediator between God and humanity (Hebrews 9:15).

Asceticism (vv. 20–23). Paul is not specific about the practices he refers to. But self-imposed austerities and self-chosen humiliations in certain areas of life are of no value in offsetting unrestrained indulgence in other areas. Self-denial is of no value if it replaces our love for Christ and thus makes us rather than Him our focus.

| Col. 3 | LIFE IN CHRIST |

The person-to-person relationship with Christ is the emphasis of this letter: "Christ in you, the hope of glory" (1:27). Live in Him, rooted in Him, built up in Him (2:6–7). You have been given fullness in Him (2:10), you died with Him (2:20), you have been raised with Him (3:1), your life is now hidden with Him in God (3:3).

The **Word and singing** (v. 16) are mentioned together. This refers to Christian gatherings where the teaching of the Word and the singing of hymns are the main means of promoting the growth of Christian life. O for more of both in our churches!

> *For in Christ all the fullness of the Deity lives in bodily form, and you have been given fullness in Christ, who is the head over every power and authority.*
> —Colossians 2:9–10

What Is a Legalist?

Legalists are those people who base their salvation on themselves and what they do — especially their religious behavior — rather than on Christ. Of course, we want to believe all the doctrines correctly and obey all the commandments to our utmost. But if in our own thinking we put too much stress on what we believe or what we do, are we not perilously close to basing our salvation on ourselves? Christ — not a doctrine, not a commandment — is our Savior. He — not I myself — is the basis of my hope. We must not minimize the necessity of believing right doctrines. But after all is said and done, being a Christian is essentially loving Christ, a Person, rather than believing this or that doctrine or obeying this or that commandment or having a particular experience.

We believe doctrines and obey commandments because of Christ. We must not love them more than we love Him. If we love a doctrine overmuch, we are apt to grow cross and hard and sour toward those who do not agree with our doctrine. If we love a Person, Christ the Person, we grow like Him. In this letter, Paul wants to correct the false doctrines of the Judaizers on the one hand and of the Greek philosophers on the other, and also the resultant compromise doctrines. But even if our beliefs are scripturally sound, there is such a thing as exalting some truth about Christ above Christ Himself. And when we thus tip the balance of our partnership with Christ toward our own side, we are legalists. It is possible to be a legalist over a doctrine of grace!

Col. 4 | PERSONAL MATTERS

In the early years of the church, local churches had to meet where they could. Usually they met in the home of a church member, several of whom are mentioned: Nymphas in Laodicea (Colossians 4:15), Philemon in Colosse (Philemon 2), Gaius in Corinth (Romans 16:23), and Aquila and Priscilla in Ephesus (1 Corinthians 16:19) and later in Rome (Romans 16:5). It was not until the 3rd century that church buildings came into general use. Yet the church grew marvelously. Many small congregations are better than a few large ones!

1 Thessalonians

The Lord's Second Coming

May the Lord make your love increase and overflow for each other and for everyone else, just as ours does for you. May he strengthen your hearts so that you will be blameless and holy in the presence of our God and Father when our Lord Jesus comes with all his holy ones.

—1 THESSALONIANS 3:12–13

Be joyful always; pray continually; give thanks in all circumstances, for this is God's will for you in Christ Jesus. Do not put out the Spirit's fire; do not treat prophecies with contempt. Test everything. Hold on to the good. Avoid every kind of evil.

—1 THESSALONIANS 5:16–22

The first letter to the Thessalonian church is probably Paul's earliest surviving letter and is generally dated around 51 A.D. The letter was intended to encourage the Christian growth of new believers in the Thessalonian church and to settle questions they had, primarily about the Lord's second coming.

The Church in Thessalonica

Paul founded the church in Thessalonica on his second missionary journey in about A.D. 51 (Acts 17:1–9). Acts 17:2 gives the impression that Paul spent only three weeks there, but Philippians 4:16; 1 Thessalonians 2:9; and 2 Thessalonians 3:8 seem to imply that he was there longer. It may be that he preached in the synagogue three Sabbaths in a row and then later in some other place. In any case, he wasn't there long enough to fully instruct the church.

The church likely included some Jews, since Paul began his ministry in the synagogue. However, 1:9–10 and Acts 17:4 suggest that church membership was predominantly gentile.

Why Paul Wrote This Letter

Although he was there only a short time, Paul created a great stir in Thessalonica. His enemies accused him of turning "the world upside down" (Acts 17:6 KJV). A large number of Greeks and prominent women believed (Acts 17:4). It was talked about all over Greece (1 Thessalonians 1:8–9).

Driven out of Thessalonica, Paul went to Berea, about 50 miles to the west. But soon he was also driven from Berea, leaving Silas and Timothy there. When he got to Athens, 300 miles to the south, he was lonesome and sent word back to Berea for Silas and Timothy to come to him with all possible speed (Acts 17:14–15). When they reached Athens, Paul, filled with anxiety about the young church in Thessalonica, immediately sent Timothy back. By the time Timothy returned from Thessalonica, Paul had gone from Athens to Corinth.

Timothy brought word that the Thessalonian Christians were enduring their persecutions courageously (1:6; 2:14; and Acts 17:5–14). But some Christians had died, and the others were puzzled as to how those who had died would benefit from the Lord's coming, a doctrine that Paul evidently had especially stressed in Thessalonica. Then Paul wrote this letter, mainly to tell them that those who had died would not be at any disadvantage when the Lord comes. He also instructed them regarding godly living (4:1–8) and urged them not to neglect their daily work (4:11–12).

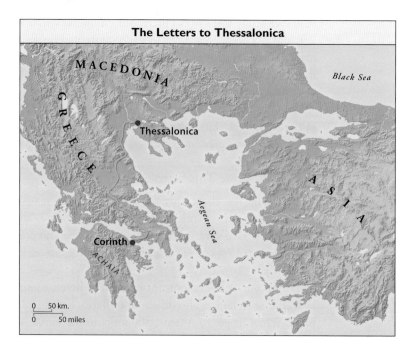

The Letters to Thessalonica

Modern Saloniki and its harbor.
During the days of Paul, the city and its harbor were the largest in Macedonia.

I Thess. I | THE REPUTATION OF THE CHURCH

Silas and Timothy helped Paul found the Thessalonian church (Acts 17: 1 – 14) and are included here in the salutation of his first letter. Paul recognizes the church's faithfulness and how they have become a model church even while suffering severe persecution.

With power (v. 5) must refer to miracles that accompanied and attested Paul's preaching, though none are mentioned in Acts.

A model (v. 7). The Thessalonian church was an example to all of Greece, of perseverance under persecution and of a genuinely Christian manner of life.

Wait for his Son (v. 10). Paul closes every chapter with a reference to the Lord's coming (2:19; 3:13; 4:16 – 18; 5:23).

I Thess. 2 | PAUL'S CONDUCT AMONG THEM

This chapter is mainly Paul's vindication of his conduct in Thessalonica. The language gives the impression that the enemies who were so bitterly persecuting the Thessalonian Christians were also militantly engaged in a campaign to destroy Paul's character.

He reminds them that he had taken no pay from them, which was in itself evidence that he could not have been motivated by greed, as some traveling philosophers were. And he reminds them of his unselfish and tender devotion to them, and how he was in every way an example to them of the things he preached.

Chapter 2 presents a profile for effective ministry (both from the pulpit and in our daily lives):

- Preach the good news of the Gospel courageously, even in the face of persecution (v. 2)
- Avoid impure motives and trickery (v. 3) and preaching to please people (v. 4)
- Our motive should be to please God (v. 4) and not to receive praise from men (v. 6)

- Avoid using flattery, and do not be greedy (v. 5)
- Do not be a burden, and be gentle (v. 7)
- Minister with great love (v. 8), hard work (v. 9), and holiness (v. 10)
- Encourage, comfort, and urge (v. 12)

Their suffering (vv. 13–16). It seems that the unbelieving Jews and the "bad characters" (Acts 17:5) who had driven Paul out of Thessalonica were still venting their anger against the rest of the Christians in the city with relentless fury. Paul tries to comfort them by reminding them that the mother churches in Judea had been persecuted in the same way. So had Christ. So had he himself. But the wrath of God will come on those who killed the Lord and persecute the church (v. 16). Unrepentant, sinful humanity from all of history will face their eternal doom in the Day of Judgment.

Paul's plan to return to Thessalonica (vv. 17–20). "Again and again" (v. 18) means that at least twice he had made an effort to get back to Thessalonica, but Satan had hindered him. In the early part of this same missionary journey Paul had made certain plans that the Holy Spirit had hindered him from carrying out (Acts 16:6–7). Then it was God who was interfering with his plans; now it is Satan. Paul knew that it was the archenemy of the church who was keeping him away from his beloved Thessalonian church. He was still praying night and day (3:10–11) that he might return to them. He felt that one of the brightest stars in his crown in the day of the Lord's coming would be the Thessalonian church—his hope, joy, crown, and glory (vv. 19–20).

I Thess. 3 | TIMOTHY'S REPORT

Paul, in deepest anxiety for the newborn Thessalonian church, had sent Timothy back to encourage them in their time of bitter persecution. (See above and Acts 17:15; 18:1, 5; 1 Thessalonian 3:1–2, 6.) Timothy's return with the news of their steadfastness and devotion filled Paul with unbounded joy.

I Thess. 4 | IMMORALITY. LOVE. THE LORD'S COMING

Chapter 4 contains a wealth of exhortations to the church concerning how to live a godly life in preparation for the second coming of Christ.

Sexual immorality (vv. 1–8) was common among heathen peoples. It may be that Timothy had mentioned some cases of moral laxness in his otherwise glowing report of the general steadfastness of the Thessalonian Christians, which then was the reason for this exhortation.

Sanctification (v. 3), as here used, means sexual purity.

Body (v. 4): the word literally means "vessel" (KJV, NASB). It seems to mean body here, although some people think that it means "wife," in which case Paul refers to fidelity to the marriage vow or to the fact that in order to avoid immorality, each should have his own wife.

Wrong his brother (v. 6). Sexual immorality harms more than those directly engaged. Spouses are always wronged. Children are tragically affected. This also refers to premarital sex, which robs the future spouse of the virginity that should be brought to the marriage.

Brotherly love (vv. 9–12). It seems that those who were well off—of whom there were many (Acts 17:4)—took the doctrine of Christian charity seriously and were distributing their assets to the poorer brothers and sisters in all the Macedonian churches. Unfortunately, this was an opportunity for those who were inclined to be lazy, and they were making the most of it. Perhaps it was because they expected the imminent return of Christ. Whatever the motivation, Paul commends the charitable, but he rebukes the idle: their willingness to live off their neighbors' charity runs contrary to every principle of brotherly love. Paul exhorts them to earn their own wages, living a good and respectable life, so that they may win the respect of unbelievers and not be dependent on anyone.

The Lord's second coming (vv. 13–18). Here we come to the main topic of the letter. Paul must have given it particular emphasis in his preaching at Thessalonica, since it is mentioned in every chapter.

Though it is commonly spoken of as the Lord's coming or appearing, it is specifically called the Second Coming in Hebrews 9:28. And Jesus' word "again" in John 14:3 means "a second time." So it is perfectly proper and scriptural to speak of the Lord's coming as the Second Coming. It is mentioned or referred to in almost every New Testament book. The chapters in which it is explained most fully are Matthew 24–25; Luke 21; 1 Thessalonians 4–5; and 2-Peter 3.

Christ's return is the great event that Christians hope for, as mentioned in 5:10; 2 Corinthians 5:8; Philippians 1:23; Colossians 3:4; and John 14:3. The second coming of Christ is viewed as the climax and culmination of His redemptive work. It is considered by most to be a literal, bodily return of Christ as He gathers His church.

"Fallen asleep" (v. 14) is a scriptural expression for the Christian's death (Matthew 27:52; John 11:11; Acts 7:60; 13:36; 1 Corinthians 15:6, 18, 20, 51; 2 Peter 3:4). It is found often on Christian epitaphs in the catacombs of Rome. Jesus taught it. It must be true. Only asleep—and one day we shall awake. Glorious morning! This does not mean that we lapse into a state of unconsciousness until the day of the resurrection—rather, we will experience the presence of Christ immediately (Philippians 1:23).

With a loud command, with the voice of the archangel and with the trumpet call of God (v. 16). This is similar to Jesus' words in Matthew 24:30–31. It is at this point that the dead in Christ shall rise (v. 17). This may be a literal resurrection of the body, in an imperishable, glorious state as described at 1 Corinthians 15:42–43.

We who are still alive will be caught up together with them (v. 17). This may be the only place in the New Testament where a "rapture" is clearly referred to. (For "we will be caught up," the Latin Vulgate uses

2 Thessalonians

Further Teaching about the Lord's Coming

We ought always to thank God for you, brothers, and rightly so, because your faith is growing more and more, and the love every one of you has for each other is increasing.

— 2 THESSALONIANS 1:3

Don't let anyone deceive you in any way, for that day will not come until the rebellion occurs and the man of lawlessness is revealed, the man doomed to destruction. He will oppose and will exalt himself over everything that is called God or is worshiped, so that he sets himself up in God's temple, proclaiming himself to be God. — 2 THESSALONIANS 2:3–4

This letter was probably written only a few weeks or months after 1 Thessalonians, in about A.D. 52. In his first letter Paul had spoken of the Lord's coming as being sudden and unexpected. In this letter he explains that it will not be until after the apostasy (the falling away from or renouncing of the Christian faith). (For a note on the city of Thessalonica, see 1 Thessalonians.)

2 Thess. 1 | THE DAY OF THE LORD

The particular feature of the Lord's coming that is emphasized in this chapter is that it will be a day of terror for the disobedient — those who have rejected God and the Gospel of Jesus Christ.

In 1 Thessalonians 4 Paul had said that Christ will descend from heaven and that at the shout of the archangel, the church will be taken up to be forever with the Lord.

Here Paul adds that the Lord will be accompanied by His powerful angels, in blazing fire (v. 7), to punish the disobedient. Jesus had spoken of eternal fire (Matthew 25:41) and unquenchable fire (Mark 9:43). In Revelation 20 and Hebrews 10:27, devouring fire is connected with the Day of Judgment. In 2 Peter 3:7, 10, the destiny of the earth is to be burned with fire (see note on that passage).

2 Thess. 2 | THE REBELLION

The express purpose of this letter was to caution the Thessalonians that the Lord's coming was not immediately at hand — it would not be until after the "rebellion" (KJV, falling away; NASB, apostasy).

What is the rebellion, or apostasy? It is the "falling away," in which a person called the "man of lawlessness" will, sitting in the temple of

God, proclaim that he is God and will exalt himself "over everything that is called God" (vv. 3–4). A false church headed by an impostor!

This "man of lawlessness" is better known to us as the Antichrist (1 John 2:18). The early fathers unanimously looked for a personal Antichrist, who would be manifested after the fall of the Roman Empire. The Protestant Reformers, seeing the corruption of the church in the Middle Ages, believed that the papacy embodied the Antichrist.

In our own day, after 2000 years of church history, there is still wide difference of opinion as to the identity of the "man of lawlessness" and the form the apostasy will take. There are many who think that the Antichrist will reveal himself in the last days in conjunction with the Great Tribulation period and the Lord's second coming (Daniel 12:2; Matthew 24:21; Revelation 7:14).

The spirit of the apostasy was already at work in Paul's day (v. 7) and in many ways has continued even to this day.

"What is holding him back" (v. 6) was generally interpreted by the early fathers to have been the Roman Empire. Today most scholars believe it to mean the Holy Spirit or the restraining ministry of the Holy Spirit through the Christian church.

Paul's ideas on the Second Coming. It is quite common among a certain class of critics to say that Paul had to revise his ideas about the Lord's second coming, that his earlier and cruder view contradicts his later view. This is absolutely not true. Paul's earlier view was his only view — first, last, and always.

Paul specifically states in the earliest writings we have of him — the Thessalonian epistles — that he did *not* expect the immediate appearance of the Lord, and that it would not be until *after* the rebellion, apostasy, or falling away, which in his day was only beginning to work. It may not have been revealed to Paul specifically what the apostasy would be. But whatever his understanding of it, it did not preclude the possibility that the Lord would come in his own lifetime, as evidenced by the expression "we who are still alive, who are left till the coming of the Lord" (1 Thessalonians 4:15; compare also 1 Corinthians 15:52).

First and last, Paul looked for the Lord's coming as a glorious consummation, but at the same time he also anticipated the possibility that he would die before it happened ("to depart and be with Christ," Philippians 1:23). It did not matter a great deal to him whether he was alive or "asleep" (1 Thessalonians 4:15) at the time of Christ's coming. In his last written word (2 Timothy 4:6, 8), close before his death, his mind was on the appearing of the Lord.

---

2 Thess. 3 | **THE IDLE**

Pray for us (vv. 1–2), that we may be delivered from "wicked and evil men." At that very time Paul was in trouble in Corinth, and their prayers on Paul's behalf were answered (Acts 18:9–10).

Shops and storerooms of ancient Thessalonica. Some believed the Second Coming to be so imminent that they laid down their work to await the Lord's arrival.

The idle (vv. 6–15; KJV, disorderly) were lazy people who took advantage of the charitable disposition of the church (see 1 Thessalonians 4:9–10) and used the expectation of the immediate appearance of the Lord as an excuse for abandoning their ordinary occupations. They claimed the right to be supported by the members in the church who were well off.

Paul was an ardent advocate of charity toward those who were really in need, and he spent a good deal of time collecting gifts of money for the poor. But he spared no words in condemning the able-bodied who could work but would not. In these verses he positively forbids the church to support such people—he even commands the church not to associate with them.

There is nothing in the teaching of Paul, or of Christ, or anywhere in the Bible, to encourage charity to able-bodied, lazy people who make begging their profession.

1 Timothy

Care of the Church at Ephesus

*For everything God created is good, and nothing is to be rejected if it is received with
thanksgiving, because it is consecrated by the word of God and prayer.*   —1 TIMOTHY 4:4–5

*But godliness with contentment is great gain. For we brought nothing into the world, and we
can take nothing out of it. But if we have food and clothing, we will be content with that.*
                                                                      —1 TIMOTHY 6:6–7

The Pastoral Letters

Three letters, 1 and 2 Timothy and Titus, are commonly called "the
pastoral letters." First Timothy and Titus were probably written between
Paul's first and second imprisonments, that is, between A.D. 61/62 and
67. Second Timothy was written during his second imprisonment in A.D.
67/68, shortly before his execution for his faith.

Some modern critics have advanced the theory that these letters are
the work of some unknown author who, 30 to 50 years after Paul's death,
wrote in Paul's name to promote certain doctrines. There is no historical
basis for this opinion. These letters have, from the very beginning, been
regarded as genuine writings of Paul.

Timothy

Timothy was a native of Lystra (Acts 16:1). His mother was Jewish,
his father Greek. We know that his mother's name was Eunice and
his grandmother's name Lois (2 Timothy 1:5). He was Paul's convert
(1 Timothy 1:2), and he joined Paul on his second journey, about A.D. 51
(Acts 16:3). Timothy was a chosen servant of God (1 Timothy 1:18). He
was set apart by the elders and Paul (1 Timothy 4:14; 2 Timothy 1:6).
As outlined below, Timothy was with Paul on many of his journeys and
was named by Paul as the co-sender of six of his letters (2 Corinthians,
Philippians, Colossians, 1 and 2 Thessalonians, and Philemon).

Timothy accompanied Paul to Troas, Philippi, Thessalonica, and Berea,
where he stayed until Paul sent for him to come to Athens (Acts 17:14–15).
Then Paul sent him back to Thessalonica (1 Thessalonians 3:1–2). By the
time he returned from Thessalonica, Paul had gone to Corinth (Acts 18:5;
1 Thessalonians 3:6). He joined Paul in Corinth in the writing of the
Thessalonian letters (1 Thessalonians 1:1; 2 Thessalonians 1:1).

Later, on the third missionary journey, Paul sent Timothy from Ephesus to Corinth (1 Corinthians 4:17). Paul joined him in Macedonia, and
Timothy joined in the writing of 2 Corinthians (Acts 19:22; 2 Corinthians
1:1). He went part of the way with Paul to Jerusalem (Acts 20:4). Whether

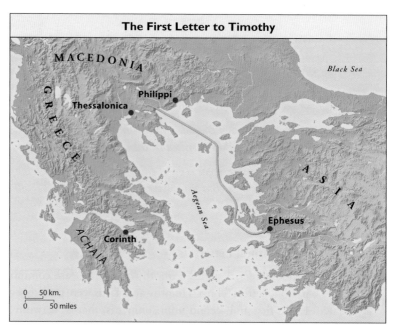

he accompanied Paul all the way to Jerusalem and Rome is not stated, but he appears with Paul in Rome (Philippians 1:1; 2:19–22; Colossians 1:1; Philemon 1). Later he is in Ephesus, where this letter is addressed to him. He is urged to come to Rome (2 Timothy 4:9). Whether he reached Rome before Paul's death in A.D. 67 or 68 is not known. Timothy is mentioned in Hebrews 13:23 as having been released from prison.

Timothy appears to have been timid and retiring by nature, and not as well suited as Titus for handling troublemakers, and he was not in the best of health (1 Timothy 5:23). He and Luke were Paul's two most constant companions. Paul loved him dearly and was lonesome without him.

Tradition says that after Paul's death, Timothy's work was the care of the Ephesian church, and that he suffered martyrdom under Emperor Nerva or Emperor Domitian. This would make him a co-worker with the apostle John.

Ephesus

This is the city where Paul had done his greatest work, around A.D. 54–57 (Acts 19). Some four years after he had left Ephesus, Paul had written the letter to the church at Ephesus, around A.D. 62. Now, a little later, probably about A.D. 65, he addressed this letter to Timothy about the work in Ephesus. Ephesus later became the home of the apostle John, where he wrote his Gospel, his letters, and possibly the book of Revelation (see p. 827; for a description of Ephesus, see p. 728).

The Occasion of the Epistle

When Paul said farewell to the Ephesian elders, he told them that they would not see him again (Acts 20:25). But it seems that his long

The main street (*cardo*) of Ephesus. Paul wrote this letter to Timothy, who was serving the church at Ephesus.

imprisonment changed his plans and that he did visit Ephesus again some six or seven later, after his release from prison in Rome. Paul went on to Macedonia, leaving Timothy behind at Ephesus, expecting himself to return soon (1 Timothy 1:3; 3:14). But Paul was detained in Macedonia longer than he had planned (3:15), and he wrote this letter of instruction about the work that Timothy was to do.

The Church at Ephesus

From the narrative in Acts 19, it appears that Paul had made a large number of Christian converts in Ephesus. In the years since his first visit, the number of converts had continued to grow, and in the next 50 years Christians became so numerous in Asia Minor that the pagan temples were almost abandoned. Within the first generation of the church, Ephesus became the numerical as well as the geographical center of Christendom, the region where Christianity won its quickest laurels.

The Church Situation

Houses for Christian worship did not begin to be built until 200 years after the days of Paul, and church buildings did not come into general use until Constantine put an end to the persecutions of Christians. In Paul's day there were no church buildings. Churches met mostly in the homes of the Christians. The thousands of Christians in and around Ephesus met, therefore, not as one megachurch, or even in a few larger congregations, but in hundreds of small groups in various homes, each congregation under its own pastoral leadership.

The Pastors

There must have been hundreds of pastors in Ephesus. In Acts 20:17 they are called elders; in this letter they are called bishops (meaning "overseers"; 3:1). These are simply different names for the office held by leaders of congregations.

Timothy's work was primarily with these congregational leaders. There were no seminaries to supply Paul with trained pastors; he had to develop his pastors out of his converts. Sometimes he got brilliant men, but most of his pastors were probably from the ordinary walks of life. He had to do the best he could with available material. Yet, without seminaries, without church buildings, and in spite of persecution, the church made more rapid progress than anytime since, because it had to keep its mind on the essentials of Christianity rather than on peripheral issues.

I Tim. I | FALSE TEACHERS

The false teachers (vv. 3–11). When Paul left Ephesus seven years before, he had warned that savage wolves would ravage the Ephesian church (Acts 20:29–30). Now they had appeared in full force and constituted Timothy's main problem. They appear to have been the same brand of false teachers as those whom Titus had to deal with in Crete, who based strange teachings on apocryphal Jewish legends connected with Old Testament genealogies.

Paul's sinfulness (vv. 12–17). The man who had perhaps done more for Christ than all others combined, bowed to the depths with feelings of unworthiness. The closer the walk with Christ, the deeper the sense of humility. Paul thought of his conversion as intended by God to be an everlasting example of God's patience with sinners.

Hymenaeus and Alexander (vv. 19–20) were two ringleaders of the false teachers from whom, in his apostolic authority, Paul had withdrawn church membership ("handed over to Satan," v. 20). This is probably the same Alexander who later went to Rome to testify against Paul, and possibly the one who earlier had been Paul's devoted friend (2 Timothy 4:14).

I Tim. 2 | PRAYER. THE PLACE OF WOMEN

Prayer for rulers (vv. 1–8). At the time Paul wrote this letter, Nero was ruler of the Roman Empire. Under him, Paul had been imprisoned and was soon to be executed. This shows that prayers and intercessions should be made for bad as well as for good rulers.

The place of women in church (vv. 9–15; see comments on 1 Corinthians 11:5–15; 14:34–35). The caution here is against wearing apparel that is immodest or deliberately draws attention to the wearer, especially in Christian worship, and also against becoming too much like men. In heaven there will be no gender (after the Resurrection, people will be like the angels in heaven; Matthew 22:30), but in this world there is a natural difference between the sexes, which it is best not to override. "Saved through childbearing" (v. 15) probably refers to the birth of Jesus, who was born of a woman without the agency of man. Even if sin did come into the world through woman (v. 14), so did the Savior.

I Tim. 3 | OVERSEERS AND DEACONS

Their qualifications (vv. 1–16). "One wife" (v. 2) probably is meant to exclude, not single men, but polygamists. Paul was a single man (1 Corinthians 7:8). "Pillar of the truth" (v. 15): without the church,

Christ's name would disappear. Verse 16 is thought to have been a fragment of a Christian hymn.

I Tim. 4 | THE COMING APOSTASY. A MINISTER'S WORK

Apostasy (vv. 1–5). This passage states that, although the church is the pillar of the truth, within the church gross systems of error will appear, of demonic origin, resulting in the teaching of unbiblical doctrines such as forbidding people to marry and ordering abstinence from certain foods rather than teaching the Gospel of grace. This was one of the forms of Gnosticism that was then developing and that later grew to vast proportions.

A good minister (vv. 6–16). The best way to combat incipient or prevailing error is by constantly restating the simple Gospel truth: reading, exhortation, teaching (v. 13). The Bible itself will do the job, if only given a chance—studying it in private, reading and expounding it in public. If ministers today would only give heed to Paul's advice, the church would take on new life and grow by leaps and bounds. Why, O why cannot ministers understand that the simple exposition of God's Word is more desired by the people, and more powerful by far, than their finely worked out sermonic platitudes?

I Tim. 5 | WIDOWS. ELDERS

Widows (vv. 1–16). The church in Ephesus was about 10 years old, and its charitable work was well developed and carefully administered. A Christian who refuses to support his own dependents is worse than an unbeliever (v. 8).

Elders (vv. 17–25). They are called overseers in 3:1–7 (KJV, bishops), where their qualifications were discussed. Here Paul writes about their treatment. Then—as now—busybodies were whispering against their church leaders (v. 19). "A little wine" (v. 23): note that it was little, and that it was for medicinal purposes.

I Tim. 6 | SLAVES. RICHES

Slaves (vv. 1–2; compare 1 Corinthians 7:20–24). It is of no great importance whether one is slave or free. Become free if you can, but if you cannot, be a good slave. Paul says this on several occasions (Ephesians 6:5–9; Colossians 3:22–25; Titus 2:9–10). Christianity abolished slavery, not by denouncing it, but by teaching the doctrine of human brotherhood.

The love of money (vv. 3–21) was the motive behind much false teaching (v. 5). Through the ages, church doctrines have been corrupted to produce income for the church. "A root of all kinds of evils" (v. 10 NASB, NIV) is more accurate than "the root of all evil" (KJV). O man of God, flee from all this (v. 11) and turn away from the godless, empty chatter of what is incorrectly called knowledge (v. 20).

2 Timothy

Paul's Final Word

All Scripture is God-breathed and is useful for teaching, rebuking, correcting and training in righteousness, so that the man of God may be thoroughly equipped for every good work.
—2 Timothy 3:16–17

I have fought the good fight, I have finished the race, I have kept the faith. Now there is in store for me the crown of righteousness, which the Lord, the righteous Judge, will award to me on that day—and not only to me, but also to all who have longed for his appearing.
—2 Timothy 4:7–8

The book of Acts closes with Paul in prison in Rome, around A.D. 63. The common belief is that he was acquitted and released, returned to Greece and Asia Minor, was later arrested again, taken back to Rome, and executed in about A.D. 67 or 68. This letter was written while he was awaiting martyrdom.

Background of the Epistle

In A.D. 64, a great fire destroyed much of the city of Rome. The people suspected that Emperor Nero himself had set fire to the city. Though an inhuman brute, he was a great builder, and the purpose behind setting the city on fire was urban renewal: he wanted to build a new and grander Rome. While the city was ablaze, Nero, according to tradition, played the fiddle. Historians have commonly regarded it as a fact that Nero was the perpetrator of the crime, and that in order to divert suspicion from himself he accused the Christians of burning Rome and began to persecute them.

The Bible makes no mention of Nero's persecution of Christians, though it happened in New Testament times and is the direct background of at least two New Testament books, 1 Peter and 2 Timothy. It was this persecution that led to Paul's martyrdom and, according to some traditions, to Peter's also. Our source of information is the Roman historian Tacitus. He knew that the Christians did not burn Rome. But somebody had to be made the scapegoat for the emperor's crime. Here was a new and despised sect of people, mostly from the humbler walks of life, without prestige or influence, many of them slaves. Nero accused them of burning Rome and ordered their punishment.

In and around Rome, multitudes of Christians were arrested and put to death in the most cruel ways. They were crucified; or tied in skins of animals and thrown into the arena, to be badgered to death by dogs, for the entertainment of the people; or thrown to the wild beasts; or tied to stakes in Nero's gardens, pitch poured over their bodies, and their burning bodies used as torches to light Nero's gardens at night.

It was in the wake of this persecution that Paul was rearrested, in Greece or Asia Minor, possibly at Troas (2 Timothy 4:13), and brought back to Rome. This time by the government of Rome rather than by his own choice, by appealing to Caesar; this time as an alleged criminal (2:9), not on some technical violation of Jewish law, as had been the case the first time he was taken to Rome. For all we know, it may have been in connection with the burning of Rome. For was not Paul the world leader of the people who were being punished for that crime? And had not Paul been in Rome for two years just preceding the fire? It would have been very easy to lay this crime at Paul's door, although we do not know whether that was indeed the charge. Paul, at any rate, was indicted. His trial had proceeded far enough that he knew there was no hope of escape.

While waiting in the Roman dungeon for the time of his departure, he wrote this last letter to Timothy, his bosom friend and trusted co-worker, begging him to be faithful, in spite of everything, to his calling as a minister of Christ, and to hurry to Rome before winter (4:21).

Paul's Note of Triumphant Faith

Out of that dark hour came one of the noblest passages of Scripture. He would soon be executed for a crime he did not commit, and his friends left him to suffer alone. The cause for which he had given his life was being wiped out in the West from the outside, by persecution, and in the East from the inside, through false teachings. Yet there is no hint of regret that he had given his life to the service of Christ and the church. No hint of doubt but that the church, though now apparently being defeated, would eventually be triumphant. And no hint of doubt but that the moment his head was cut from his body, he would go straight to the arms of Him whom he had loved and served so devotedly. This letter is the exultant cry of a dying conqueror.

2 Tim. 1   "I KNOW WHOM I HAVE BELIEVED"

His prayers for Timothy (vv. 3–5). Paul opens almost every one of his letters with prayers and thanksgiving (Romans 1:9–10; 1 Corinthians 1:4–8; 2 Corinthians 1:3–4; Ephesians 1:3; Philippians 1:3, 9–11; Colossians 1:3–10; 1 Thessalonians 1:2–3; 2 Thessalonians 1:3). "Your tears" (v. 4): probably at their separation at Troas (4:13). When Paul wrote 1 Timothy, he was in Macedonia and Timothy was in Ephesus. They may have met later at Troas, and possibly it was here that Roman soldiers seized Paul and took him to Rome on the humiliating charge of setting fire to the city.

Paul's certainty (vv. 6–14). He had seen Christ. He had suffered for Him. Christ, though unseen, was the one unquestioned reality of Paul's life.

He was Paul's intimate companion, and Paul knew Him (v. 12) as one knows his best friend. "Herald, . . . apostle, . . . teacher" (v. 11): herald—a proclaimer of the Gospel to those who never heard it, a "foreign missionary"; apostle—with direct personal authority from Christ; teacher—an instructor of settled Christian communities, our pastor.

The disaffection at Ephesus (vv. 5–18). This was one of the saddest things in Paul's life. In Ephesus, where Paul had done his greatest work, and where almost the whole city turned to Christ, the false teachers had so gotten the upper hand that they were able to make capital out of Paul's arrest and turn the church against him at the time when he needed their love and sympathy more than ever.

2 Tim. 2 | ADVICE TO TIMOTHY

Avoid business entanglements (vv. 1–7). Paul advises Timothy to take pay for his work as a minister, the very thing Paul had for the most part refused to do before the churches had become established. Perhaps Timothy had been of a well-to-do family but had by now lost his money in persecutions. Being reticent about the matter, he may have needed this advice.

Endure suffering (vv. 8–12). Paul at that time was enduring the cruelest of all suffering for a good man: the false charge of being a criminal (v. 9). But note that his mind is on eternal glory (v. 10). The quotation in vv. 11–13 may have been from a hymn.

Handle the Word correctly (vv. 14–21). Do not distort its natural meaning to bolster pet doctrines. The church will depart from the teachings of the Word, but within the historical, visible church God will always have a remnant of true believers (v. 19).

Be gentle (vv. 22–26). God's Word, in the hands of a ministry possessed of true Christian gentleness and grace, will break down opposition and keep the church on its true course.

2 Tim. 3 | TERRIBLE TIMES

The coming apostasy (vv. 1–14). The determined effort of mankind to corrupt the Gospel and thwart the work of Christ is one of the themes of the New Testament. It is spoken of again and again (Matthew 7:15–23; 2 Thessalonians 2; 2-Timothy 4; 2 Peter 2; Jude; Revelation 17). The terrible picture in vv. 2–5 is, with the exception of temporary periods of reform, a fairly correct picture of the visible church as a whole until this present time.

Jannes and Jambres (v. 8) are, according to tradition, the names of the magicians of Pharaoh (see Exodus 7:11–22). Lystra (v. 11) is where Paul was stoned. It was also the home of Timothy, who may have witnessed the stoning of Paul. "Everyone . . . will be persecuted" (v. 12): we are told this over and over (Matthew 5:10–12; John 15:20; Acts 14:22; 1 Thessalonians 3:4), so that we may be prepared for it when it comes.

The Bible (vv. 14–17) is the one antidote against apostasy and corruption in and of the church. The church pushed the Bible aside and brought on the Dark Ages. The Protestant Reformation rediscovered the Bible, but now it is again neglected. Many prominent church leaders not only neglect the Bible, but with great intellectual pride resort, in the name of modern scholarship, to every conceivable means to undermine its divine origin and toss it aside as a patchwork of Hebrew thought.

| I Tim. 4 | **PAUL'S LAST WORDS**

Paul's solemn farewell charge (vv. 1–5). Paul knew that the day of his execution was approaching, and he was not sure that he would ever see Timothy again or even have the opportunity to write him another letter. He begs Timothy to keep his mind on the day of the Lord's appearing and to preach Jesus with unceasing diligence. Again Paul mentions false teachers (vv. 3–4): O how the perverse determination of people to corrupt the Gospel of Christ bothered Paul!

Paul's triumphant future (vv. 6–8). This is the grandest utterance of the grandest mortal man who ever lived. The battle-scarred old warrior of the Cross, looking back over a long and hard and bitter fight, cries out in exultation, "I have won!" Not long afterward, the executioner's ax released Paul's soul from his worn and broken body, to be borne away by flights of angels to his beloved Lord. We imagine that his welcome in heaven surpassed any triumphal procession of returning conquerors he had ever witnessed in Rome. Our guess is that when he got to heaven, his very first act, after a rendezvous with the Lord, was to hunt up Stephen to beg his forgiveness.

Personal matters (vv. 9–22). Whether Timothy got to Rome before Paul's martyrdom (v. 9) we do not know. The first stage of Paul's trial had already passed (v. 16). Things looked so bad for him that even three of his four travel companions had fled, so that Luke alone remained (vv. 10–11). Whether Titus went to Dalmatia (v. 10) of his own accord or was sent by Paul, as he and Paul may have planned in Nicopolis (Titus 3:12), is not stated.

Those were dark days in Rome. Many Christians had been murdered. Now the great Christian leader himself was on trial. It was dangerous to be seen with him.

The Stadium of Aphrodisias. Paul compared the close of his proclaiming the Gospel with the training and completion of the athletic competition.

Mark (v. 11): Paul wanted him. They had separated years before (Acts 15:36–41), but Mark had been with Paul during his first Roman imprisonment (Colossians 4:10). Mark and Peter worked together, and if Mark got to Rome,

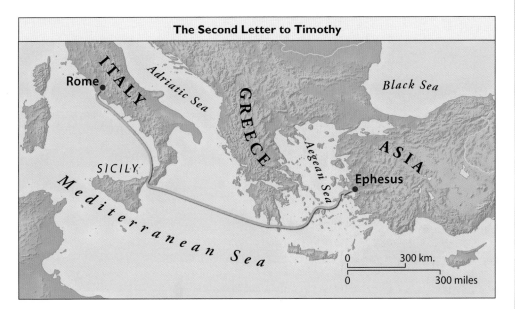

The Second Letter to Timothy

perhaps Peter did also. One of the traditions is that Peter was martyred in Rome at about the same time as Paul or soon thereafter. The "cloak" (v. 13): winter was coming (v. 21), and Paul needed it. The "scrolls" or books (v. 13) were probably parts of the Scripture. Alexander (v. 14) was no doubt the same Alexander whom Paul had delivered to Satan (1-Timothy 1:20), who now had his opportunity to get even. And he did. He had traveled all the way from Ephesus to Rome to testify against Paul, which he did with considerable success. The "lion" (17) may be a veiled reference to Nero, or it may refer to Satan (1-Peter 5:8).

Trophimus (v. 20): this is a very interesting sidelight on Paul's power to work miracles. Paul had healed many people in various places, but here was one of his own beloved friends he could not heal.

Titus

Concerning the Churches of Crete

For the grace of God that brings salvation has appeared to all men. It teaches us to say "No" to ungodliness and worldly passions, and to live self-controlled, upright and godly lives in this present age, while we wait for the blessed hope—the glorious appearing of our great God and Savior, Jesus Christ, who gave himself for us to redeem us from all wickedness and to purify for himself a people that are his very own, eager to do what is good.

—TITUS 2:11–14

Titus

Titus was a Greek, one of Paul's converts (Titus 1:4), who accompanied Paul to Jerusalem. Paul steadfastly resisted having Titus circumcised (Galatians 2:3–5).

Some years later, Titus appears with Paul in Ephesus and is sent to Corinth to look into certain disorders in the church, and to initiate the offering for the poor saints in Jerusalem (2 Corinthians 8:6, 10). Returning from Corinth, he meets Paul in Macedonia. After explaining the situation in Corinth to Paul, Titus is sent back to Corinth ahead of Paul, with what we know as the second letter to the Corinthians, to pave the way for Paul's coming and to complete the offering (2 Corinthians 2:3, 12–13; 7:5–6, 13–14; 8:16–18, 23; 12:14, 18). The fact that Titus was chosen to look after the troubled situation in Corinth indicates that Paul must have considered him a very capable, wise, and tactful Christian leader.

We hear of Titus again some seven or eight years later, in this letter written to him by Paul, in about A.D. 65. Titus is in Crete; the phrase "left you in Crete" (Titus 1:5) shows that Paul had been there with him. Paul's ship, on his voyage to Rome (Acts 27), touched on the south shore of Crete, but it is hardly likely that that could have been the time when he left Titus there. The prevailing opinion is that, after Paul's release from his first imprisonment in Rome, about A.D. 63, he went east and included Crete in his itinerary. After setting the Cretan churches in order, Titus will be replaced by Artemas or Tychicus, and he is asked to rejoin Paul in Nicopolis, in western Greece (Titus 3:12).

The last time we hear of Titus is in 2 Timothy 4:10, where it is said that he had gone from Rome to Dalmatia. Evidently he had rejoined Paul and was with him when Paul was arrested and then accompanied him to Rome. Whether he left Paul in that dark and lonely hour because of threatening dangers or Paul sent him to finish the evangelization of the coast northwest of Greece, we do not know. Let us hope the latter, for he

Crete

An island in the Mediterranean Sea, 160 miles long and ranging from 7 to 35 miles in width. It is mountainous, with fertile valleys, and well populated.

In Greek mythology, Mount Ida (3,195 feet) was the birthplace of Zeus, the head of the Greek gods. King Minos, a half-historical and half-mythological figure (alleged to be a son of Zeus), was an early ruler of Crete. The most important of the ancient cities of Crete is the royal city of Knossos, where extensive ruins of the great palace have been found.

Around 140 B.C., the Jews established a large enough colony on this island to be able to appeal successfully for the protection of Rome.

In the Old Testament, the Kerethites (1 Samuel 30:14; Ezekiel 25:16), believed to have been a group of Philistines, are identified as Cretans. In the New Testament, a number of Cretans are represented as being present on the Day of Pentecost (Acts 2:11). The ship on which Paul, as a prisoner, was traveling to Rome stopped in Fair Havens, on the south shore of Crete, before the ill-fated attempt to winter at Phoenix (Acts 27:12). Paul probably later visited Crete, after his first Roman imprisonment, and he left his assistant Titus in charge.

Paul had a low view of Cretans' moral character: "Even one of their own prophets has said, 'Cretans are always liars, evil brutes, lazy gluttons'" (Titus 1:12). This description is a quote from the Cretan poet, prophet, and religious reformer Epimenides (6th–5th century B.C.). The particular lie of which the Cretans were always guilty was that they said the tomb of Zeus, a nonexistent personage, was located on their island.

was a good and great man. Tradition says that Titus became bishop of Crete and died peaceably at an advanced age.

Similarity to 1 Timothy

Titus and 1 Timothy are thought to have been written at about the same time, around a.d. 65. They deal with the same general subject, the

The ruins of Knossus on the island of Crete. According to tradition, Titus was bishop of Crete.

The Letter to Titus

appointment of proper leaders—Titus in Crete, Timothy in Ephesus. The problem in both places was very much the same.

Titus 1 | ELDERS

The hope of eternal life (v. 2). As he neared the end of his life, Paul, like Peter (1 Peter 1:3–5), kept his eyes steadfastly fixed on heaven. It had been the unceasing burden of his preaching and the one grand motivation of his life:

- The glories of existence when the body shall have been redeemed (Romans 8:18, 23); the ecstasy of the day when "the perishable has been clothed with the imperishable, and the mortal with immortality" (1 Corinthians 15:51–55);
- His longing for the house "not built by human hands" (2 Corinthians 5:1–2);
- His citizenship in heaven, which will be complete when he has received a body like the Savior's (Philippians 3:20–21);
- His joy at the thought of being caught up to be forever with the Lord (1 Thessalonians 4:13–18);
- The crown of righteousness which he would receive in that day (2 Timothy 4:6–8).

Qualifications of an elder (vv. 5–9). "Elder" (v. 5), and "overseer" (v. 7; KJV, bishop) are here used as identical terms for the same office. The qualifications listed here are practically the same as those Paul gave to Timothy (see comments on 1 Timothy 3:1–7).

The false teachers (vv. 10–16). The Cretan churches were beset with false teachers who, like those spoken of in 2 Peter 2 and in Jude, while professing to be Christian teachers, were in fact "detestable" and "unfit for doing anything good" (v. 16). The false teachers had to be silenced, not by force but by vigorous proclamation of the truth (v. 11). "Whole households" probably means whole congregations, for churches then met in family homes. The Cretan "prophet" (v. 12) is the poet Epimenides, who lived around 600 B.C.

Titus 2–3 | GOOD WORKS

The grand emphasis of this letter is good works. We are saved, not by good works, but by God's mercy (3:5), and we are justified by His grace (3:7). But because of this we are under strict obligation to

- Be eager to do what is good (2:14)
- Be an example by doing what is good (2:7)
- Be ready to do whatever is good (3:1)
- Be careful to devote ourselves to what is good (3:8)
- Do good in order to live productive lives (3:14)

One of the indictments of the false teachers is that they are "unfit for doing anything good" (1:16).

The power of beautiful lives (2:1–14). Aged men, aged women, young women, mothers, young men, and slaves are exhorted to be so faithful to the natural obligations of their station in life that critics of their religion will be silenced (2:8).

Slaves, of whom there were many in the early church, are exhorted to be so obedient, diligent, and faithful that their lives would support their profession of faith (2:10), and their heathen masters will be constrained to think, if that is what the Christian religion does for slaves, there must be something to it.

The blessed hope (2:11–14). The Lord is coming again; this supplies the motive for godly living in this present world. It is mentioned in almost every one of the New Testament books.

Obedience to civil authorities (3:1–2) is a prime Christian virtue. Citizens of heaven should be good citizens of the earthly government under which they live (Romans 13:1–7; 1 Peter 2:13–17).

Genealogies (3:9), referred to here and in 1 Timothy 1:4, seem to have figured quite prominently in the doctrine of the false teachers who were at that time infesting the churches of Crete and Ephesus. They may have based their claims on Davidic ancestry and kinship to Jesus, with inside information on the Gospel. Or their strange doctrines may have been grounded on abstruse interpretations of passages in the genealogies, such as those in 1 Chronicles 1–9.

Divisive persons (3:10; KJV, heretics). After a reasonable effort to set a false teacher right, avoid him. Artemas (3:12) is nowhere else mentioned. Tradition says he became bishop of Lystra. Tychicus (v. 12) was from Asia (Acts 20:4). Either he or Artemas was to take Titus's position in Crete. Nicopolis (v. 12) is a city in Greece, about 100 miles northwest of Corinth. (See note on Paul's Later Life under Acts 28:31, p. 688.) Zenas (v. 13) is mentioned nowhere else; he may have been a Jewish scribe or a Greek civil lawyer. It appears that Zenas and Apollos (v. 13; see on Acts 18), on a journey to some unknown destination, delivered this letter to Titus.

Philemon

Concerning a Runaway Slave

Grace to you and peace from God our Father and the Lord Jesus Christ. . . . The grace of the Lord Jesus Christ be with your spirit.
—Philemon 3, 25

Welcome him as you would welcome me.
—Philemon 17

Date

Paul wrote this letter and his letter to the Colossians while in prison in Rome (A.D. 60).

Philemon

Philemon was a Christian of Colosse, a convert of Paul's, a very well-to-do man. A church met in his house, and it seems that he and Paul were intimate friends. It is likely, though not recorded, that Paul visited Colosse during his three-year stay at Ephesus (Acts 19).

Onesimus

Onesimus was a slave who belonged to Philemon. He may have been a very talented young man. The Roman army, on its campaigns, often took the brightest and best young men and women from the conquered peoples and brought them home to be sold into slavery.

The Occasion of the Letter

Some four or five years after Paul had left the region of Colosse, Onesimus, it seems, stole some money from his master, Philemon, and ran away to Rome, where by that time Paul was in prison. While in Rome, perhaps after the stolen money had run out, Onesimus managed to find Paul. Possibly he had learned to love him in his master's home years before. It is not likely that he could have just met him by accident in a city of more than a million people. During his visit with Paul, Onesimus became a Christian, and Paul sent him back to his master, bearing this beautiful little letter.

Purpose of the Letter

Paul wanted to intercede with Philemon on Onesimus's behalf and asked him to forgive the runaway slave. Under Roman law, stealing was punishable by death. Paul appealed to Philemon to receive him as a Chris-

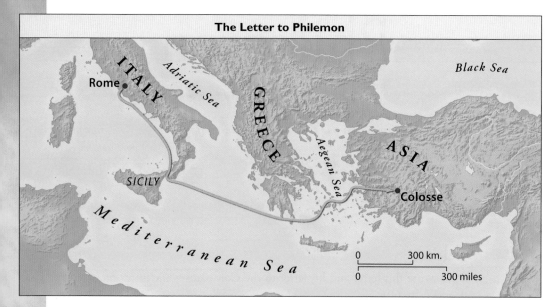

Black Sea

ITALY

Adriatic Sea

Rome

GREECE

Aegean Sea

ASIA

SICILY

Colosse

Mediterranean Sea

0   300 km.

0   300 miles

tian brother and even offered to repay the stolen money himself. The letter is a perfect gem for its courtesy, tact, delicacy, and generosity. The high point is the tender appeal to Philemon to receive Onesimus "as you would welcome me" (v. 17).

The Slave's Reception

The Bible gives no hint as to how the master received his returning slave. But there is a tradition that says that his master did welcome him back and took Paul's veiled hint and gave Onesimus his liberty.

That is the way the Gospel works. Christ in the heart of the slave made the slave recognize the social institutions of his day and made him go back to his master, determined to be a good slave and live out his natural life as a slave. Christ in the heart of the master made the master recognize the slave as a Christian brother and give him his liberty. There is a tradition that says that Onesimus afterward became a bishop in Berea.

Apphia (v. 2) was probably Philemon's wife.

Archippus (v. 2) was probably the pastor of the congregation.

Onesimus (v. 10) means "profitable." Note the play on the word.

"For good" (v. 15) is a hint of the persistence into eternity of earthly friendships.

Epaphras (v. 23) was a Colossian imprisoned in Rome.

Mark, Aristarchus, Demas, and Luke (v. 24) were colleagues of Paul and personal friends of Philemon.

Hebrews

Christ the Mediator of a New Covenant

For the word of God is living and active. Sharper than any double-edged sword, it penetrates even to dividing soul and spirit, joints and marrow; it judges the thoughts and attitudes of the heart. Nothing in all creation is hidden from God's sight. Everything is uncovered and laid bare before the eyes of him to whom we must give account. —Hebrews 4:12–13

Now faith is being sure of what we hope for and certain of what we do not see. —Hebrews 11:1

Who Wrote Hebrews?

In the King James Version it is called "The Epistle of Paul to the Hebrews." Later Bible translations simply call it "The Epistle to the Hebrews," because in the oldest manuscripts, found since the King James translation was made, its author is not named.

The Eastern church (see p. 907) accepted from the beginning that this letter was written by Paul. Not until the 4th century did the Western church accept it as the work of Paul. The church fathers (see p. 902) were not unanimous in their opinion. Eusebius and Origen considered Paul the author, Tertullian called it the Epistle of Barnabas, and Clement of Alexandria thought that Paul wrote it in Hebrew and that Luke translated it into Greek (it is written in most excellent Greek). Later, Martin Luther guessed it was Apollos, an opinion for which there is no ancient evidence but some indirect support (see Acts 18:24; 1-Corinthians 1:12; 3:4–6, 22). Other possible authors include Priscilla and Aquila, as well as Clement of Rome, one of the early church fathers.

We do know that the author was well known in the early church and that Timothy was with the writer (13:23). "Those from Italy send you their greetings" (13:24) may indicate that the letter was written from Italy, although this is not a necessary conclusion. But whoever the author was, as a literary work Hebrews is superb: orderly and logical, "in balanced and resonant sentences of remarkable precision, rising to wonderful heights of eloquence."

To Whom Addressed

This letter does not name the person or persons to whom it is addressed. It has an unmistakable Jewish flavor, since it is a discussion of the relationship of Christ to the Levitical priesthood and the temple sacrifices. The letter continually quotes the Old Testament to support the statements it makes. The traditional and commonly accepted view is that it was addressed to the Jewish Christians of Palestine, especially those in Jerusalem.

Date

The content of the letter makes it clear that it was written before A.D. 70, when the destruction of Jerusalem and the temple put an end to the Jewish sacrificial system. The author consistently uses the present tense ("is," "are") when speaking of the temple and the priestly activities connected with it.

Purpose

One of the reasons for this letter was to prepare Jewish Christians for the approaching destruction of Jerusalem. After accepting Jesus as their Messiah, the Jewish Christians continued to be zealous for the temple rites and sacrifices, thinking that their beloved city was about to become the capital of the world under their Messiah's reign. Instead, they were to receive the shock of their lives. By one stroke of the Roman army, the Holy City would be wiped out and the temple rites would cease.

This letter was written to explain to the Jewish Christians that animal sacrifices, to which they were so attached, were no longer of any use, that the killing of a bull or a lamb could never take away sin. Those sacrifices had never been intended to be forever; they had been planned to be a sort of picture ("type") of the coming sacrifice of Christ, and now that Christ had come, they had served their purpose. God's people must look only to Christ for redemption and salvation.

Hebrews and the Letter to the Romans

Romans was addressed to the capital of the gentile world; Hebrews, to the capital of the Jewish nation. God had founded the Jewish nation and cared for it through long centuries, for the purpose of bringing, through this one nation, blessing to all nations. A great king would come out of this one nation and rule over all nations. But now the King had come.

- Romans deals with the relationship of the King to his universal kingdom.
- Hebrews focuses on the relationship of the King to the one nation out of which he came.

Heb. 1:1–4 | THE DEITY OF JESUS

This opening sentence is one of the most magnificent passages in the Bible, comparable in grandeur to the opening sentences of Genesis and John's Gospel. Jesus, in His deity and His inexpressible glory, is the Creator, Preserver, and Heir of the universe. By an eternal act of God, Jesus made purification for the sin of humanity, once and for all, and brought eternal salvation.

Heb. 1:1–14 | JESUS COMPARED WITH THE ANGELS

The main argument of the letter is that Christ is the fulfillment of the Mosaic system rather than its administrator. Christ is compared with

- The **angels,** through whom the Law was given (chap. 1; see Acts 7:53)
- **Moses,** the Lawgiver (chap. 3)
- **The Levitical priesthood,** through whom the Law was administered (4:14–10:18)

The writer goes to great lengths to ensure that the reader understands that Christ is clearly superior to the angels, to Moses, and to the Levitical priesthood. The language also seems to indicate that human beings are a higher order of creation than angels. Human spirits and angels are not the same. We do not become angels when we die. Angels are, and in heaven will be, our servants (v. 14). Angels worship Christ, as we do (v. 6).

Heb. 2:1–8 | HUMANITY, NOT ANGELS, WILL RULE

In v. 7, man is spoken of as "a little lower than the angels," but in 1:14, angels are "sent to serve those who will inherit salvation." In 2 Peter 2:11, angels are spoken of as stronger and more powerful. According to Hebrews 2:9, Jesus was made a little lower than the angels. ("Little" in vv. 7 and 9 may also mean "for a little while.") Whatever the nature of angels relative to the nature of human beings, this passage points to the ultimate grandeur of God's redeemed human creation.

Note the fearful warning, in vv. 2–3, that if disobeying the word of God spoken by angels was dangerous, how much more dangerous to neglect the words spoken by Jesus!

Heb. 2:9–18 | CHRIST'S UNITY WITH HUMANITY

God created humanity to have lordship over all things (2:6–8). But not yet. Christ has become one with man, sharing with man his temptations, sufferings, even death itself, that He might enable humanity to become one with Him, to share with Him His nature and His rule. And because of this, Christ has been crowned with glory and honor.

And now mankind has the assurance that Christ is gracious, kind, and understanding, and will help those who love Him to become one with Him and thus qualify for His glorious inheritance (vv. 17–18).

Heb. 3:1–6 | CHRIST COMPARED WITH MOSES

Many Jewish Christians in their immaturity (5:11–13) had not yet fully grasped the relationship between Christ and Moses. It seems that they still thought of Moses as the Lawgiver and of Christ as the One who would impose the Law of Moses on all other nations: Moses first, Christ under him. But they had it backward. Christ is as far above Moses as the heir of a house is above the servants in that house.

Heb. 3:7–19 | WARNING AGAINST UNBELIEF

We share in Christ if we hold firmly until the end and guard ourselves against falling into unbelief and disobedience. This warning is one of the keynotes of the letter, repeated with increasing earnestness in 6:4–6 and 10:26–29.

The author cites the example of the Israelites who, after having been delivered out of Egypt with mighty signs and wonders, nevertheless perished in the wilderness and never reached the Promised Land because of unbelief and disobedience (vv. 16–19). If they failed because they were disobedient to the word of Moses, what hope can there be for those who are disobedient to Christ, who is far greater?

The danger of apostasy among the Jewish Christians must have been immediate and serious. The writer may have had in mind the approaching destruction of Jerusalem, the most awful calamity in Jewish history, which would tempt Jews to lose faith in Jesus because they had not yet understood that Christ had made the temple and its rituals unnecessary.

Heb. 4:1–11 | A SABBATH-REST FOR GOD'S PEOPLE

Those who entered the Promised Land under Joshua found an earthly haven, a land of liberty and plenty. An earthly picture of the heavenly homeland in the eternal beyond. (This kind of picture is also called a "type.") However, this rest cannot ultimately refer to the rest in Canaan given to the Israelites. This temporary, earthly rest, given to Joshua and the Israelites, was symbolic of the eternal spiritual rest we have through salvation in Christ Jesus. Those who believe in Christ enter salvation-rest by their faith in the person and work of Jesus. The rest that God invites us to enjoy is His rest. His work has been done since the seventh day of creation (see v. 4; Genesis 2:2). When a person is born again into the salvation of Christ, he no longer needs to work to gain his salvation through his own efforts but can rest in the finished work of Christ on the cross. Christians must make every effort to enter into this salvation-rest lest they cause others to follow their disobedience (see Numbers 13–14).

Heb. 4:12–13 | THE POWER OF GOD'S WORD

We ourselves scarcely know our own motives and desires. But God's Word, living and active, has the power to penetrate into the innermost depths of the human heart and to distinguish, separate, and view every motive and desire and purpose, and assess them at their true value. The Israelites in the wilderness missed the Promised Land because they disregarded God's Word (3:17; 4:11). Our best hope of reaching our Promised

> For we do not have a high priest who is unable to sympathize with our weaknesses, but we have one who has been tempted in every way, just as we are—yet was without sin. Let us then approach the throne of grace with confidence, so that we may receive mercy and find grace to help us in our time of need.
>
> —Hebrews 4:15–16

Reconstruction of the breastplate of the high priest. The book of Hebrews points to Jesus as our great High Priest.

Land lies in obedience to God's Word. If only our churches could realize what power they would gain by giving God's Word its proper place in the services!

Heb. 4:14–16 | CHRIST OUR HIGH PRIEST

Here begins the main theme of the letter: a comparison of Christ and the Levitical priesthood, which continues into chapter 10.

Heb. 5:1–10 | CHRIST COMPARED WITH LEVITICAL PRIESTS

The priests were of the tribe of Levi, Christ was of the tribe of Judah. There were many Levites; Christ is one. They offered animal sacrifices; He offered Himself. They died; He lives.

Heb. 5:11–14 | DULL OF HEARING

Here is a personal message to the original recipients of this letter. At one time they had been notably zealous in helping God's people (6:10) — but now they have forgotten even the first principles of the Gospel (5:12).

If the traditional view that this letter was addressed to the Judean church is correct, then this passage evidently refers to the decline of the spiritual and brotherly qualities in the church in Jerusalem described in Acts 4:32–35. The letter of James, written shortly before, implies a worldly, selfish church.

As time passed, many thousands of Jews had accepted Jesus as their Messiah (Acts 21:20) while still holding to the old, materialistic idea of the messianic kingdom: it would be a political kingdom in which the Jewish nation, under their Messiah, would rule the world. Their Christian faith was largely in the nature of a political slogan.

After the death of James, this idea seems to have so dominated the church in Jerusalem that the writer tells them that, instead of being teachers of the Christian world, as the mother church should have been, they, like little children, needed to be instructed all over again in the first principles of the Gospel of Christ (v. 12).

Heb. 6 | WARNING AGAINST APOSTASY

The language seems to imply that the Jerusalem church had largely fallen from the high standards of Christian living that had once characterized it, and that they were headed away from the goals toward which they should be earnestly struggling.

The fall of a Christian, spoken of in v. 6, may be partial or total, as a person may fall from the top of a building partway down to a projecting ledge, or all the way to the bottom. As long as the apostasy is partial, there may be hope. When it becomes total, recovery may be impossible.

The sin spoken of here may be similar to the unpardonable sin mentioned by Jesus (Matthew 12:31–32; Mark 3:28–30), where the implication is that that sin consisted in attributing the miracles of Jesus to Satan, and which, in Luke 12:9–10, is connected with denying Jesus; it could be committed by a person outside the church. The sin referred to in Hebrews 6:6 is the fall of a Christian. The essence of the fatal sin, whether by a Christian or by a non-Christian, is the deliberate and final rejection of Christ. It is as if a person at the bottom of a well, to whom a rope is let down, slashes the rope above his reach, thus cutting off his only hope of escape. For those who reject Christ, there will never be another sacrifice for sin (10:26–31). They will have to suffer for their own sin.

Over against this fearful warning against falling away from Christ, the writer is very positive that for those who remain faithful and true to Christ, the hope of eternal salvation is absolutely sure and steadfast, based on the immutability of God's promises to those who trust Him (vv. 9–20).

Heb. 7:1–10 | MELCHIZEDEK

Christ is a priest "in the order of Melchizedek" (7:17). That is, Jesus was not a Levitical priest, but His priesthood was similar to that of Melchizedek, a person from the dim past, who lived some 600 years before the Levitical priesthood was instituted. He was a priest far greater than the Levitical priests, greater even than Abraham: Abraham, and the as yet unborn Levitical priests who would descend from Abraham, paid tithes to Melchizedek.

The account of Melchizedek is found in Genesis 14:18–20. He was king of Salem and priest of God Most High: a king and a priest.

Before the time of Moses, sacrifices were offered by the heads of families. The oldest living man in the paternal line — the great-grandfather, grandfather, or father — was the priest of the family. As the family grew to be a tribe, the head came to be king of the tribe as well as its priest; and thus he was a king-priest, or priest-king.

In the days of Moses, when God's chosen people had grown into a nation, the nation was organized, a specific place was set apart for sacrifice, a ritual was prescribed, and a special hereditary order of priests was created from the family of Levi, the Levites.

Later, another family was set apart to give the nation its kings: the family of David. A king ruled the people. A priest, as mediator between God and man, offered sacrifices. One family supplied the kings; another, the priests. But Christ was both king and priest, like Melchizedek.

What is the meaning of "Without father or mother, without genealogy, without beginning of days or end of life" (v. 3)? This was not actually true of Melchizedek—but it appeared to be so in the Old Testament records. Levitical priests were priests because of their genealogy. But Melchizedek, without genealogy, was the recognized priest of the human race at that time. Hebrew tradition claims that Melchizedek was the same as Shem, who was still alive in the days of Abraham (see p. 100) and, as far as is known, the oldest living man at the time. A mysterious, solitary picture ("type"), in the dim past, of the coming eternal priest-king.

Heb. 7:11–12 THE LEVITICAL PRIESTHOOD WAS TEMPORARY

The Levitical priesthood and the system of sacrifices were imperfect, because those sacrifices were insufficient to take away sin (10:4). It was on the basis of a regulation as to ancestry (v. 16)—that is, they were priests solely because they were of a certain family, without regard to spiritual qualifications. And the covenant under which they operated has been superseded by another covenant (8:8).

Heb. 7:13–28 CHRIST'S PRIESTHOOD IS ETERNAL

Levitical priests offered sacrifices year in, year out. Christ died once and for all. Theirs were unavailing. His removed sin forever. Christ lives on, Mediator of an eternal covenant and an endless life.

Eternal is one of the favorite words of the letter.

- Eternal salvation (5:9)
- Eternal judgment (6:2)
- Eternal redemption (9:12)
- Eternal Spirit (9:14)
- Eternal inheritance (9:15)
- Eternal covenant (13:20)

"Eternal" is also a favorite word in John's Gospel.

Heb. 8 THE NEW COVENANT

Christ brought humanity a new covenant. The first covenant, which centered around the tabernacle services and the Ten Commandments, had served its purpose (9:1–5). Its laws had been written on tablets of stone (9:4). Christ's laws would be written on our hearts (8:10). The first covenant was temporal. Christ's covenant would be everlasting (13:20). The first covenant was sealed with the blood of animals. Christ's covenant was sealed with His own blood (10:29). It was a better covenant, with better promises, based on the unchangeableness of God's Word (6:18).

Better is also one of this letter's favorite words.

- Better hope (7:19)
- Better covenant (8:6 KJV; NIV, superior)
- Better promises (8:6)
- Better possessions in heaven (10:34)
- Better country: heaven, not Canaan (11:16)
- Better resurrection: never to die again (11:35)
- Blood that speaks a better word than that of Abel (12:24)

Heb. 9:1–14   CHRIST AND THE TABERNACLE

Throughout the Old Testament, God instructed the Jewish nation to follow laws that would eventually prepare them to understand His spiritual laws, revealed in Christ. In this chapter, the writer highlights how some of the central elements of the Old Testament Law, including those relating to the high priest, to the tabernacle, and to the sacrifices, were symbolic ("types") of Christ and His eternal, spiritual laws. Christ and the Gospel are the true central elements of the New Testament (new covenant), which superseded the Law of the Old Testament and became our spiritual law for the rest of eternity.

- The tabernacle was a sanctuary of this world; the true tabernacle, not made with hands, is the dwelling place of God in heaven (vv. 1, 11, 24).
- The high priest entered the tabernacle once a year; Christ entered the heavenly tabernacle and reigns on the throne once for all (vv. 7, 12).
- The high priest obtained annual redemption; Christ obtained eternal redemption (v. 12; 10:3).
- The high priest offered the blood of animals as sacrifice for a specific sin; Christ became the sacrificial lamb and offered His own blood as redemption for all mankind's sins (v. 12).
- The high priest's sacrifices made mankind outwardly clean; Christ's sacrifice makes mankind spiritually clean and presents us righteous before God (vv. 13–14).

Heb. 9:15–28   THE NEW TESTAMENT

In this section the writer of the letter makes use of the fact that the Greek word for "covenant" can also mean "testament."

A covenant is a formal agreement between two parties, and the new covenant is God's agreement with humanity; this is how the author of Hebrews generally uses the word.

This is where we get the names of the two divisions of the Bible: Old Testament and New Testament. The Old Testament is the covenant of the Law. The New Testament is the covenant of Christ. The abundant use of blood in the rites of the old covenant prefigured the urgent necessity of some great sacrifice for human sin (vv. 19–22).

A testament, by contrast, is a last will that takes effect only after the death of the maker. The new covenant (or new testament) is the will Christ made for His heirs, a will that could not take effect until after His death, by which He atoned for their sins (vv. 15–16).

Another major emphasis in Hebrews is "once for all" (vv. 26–28):

- Christ offered Himself once for all (7:27).
- Once for all He entered the Holy Place (9:12).
- He has appeared once for all at the end of the ages to put away sin (9:26).
- Men are appointed once [for all] to die (9:27).
- Christians are sanctified once for all by the offering of Christ (10:10).
- Christ, once [for all] offered, shall appear a second time for His waiting heirs (9:28).

Heb. 10:1–25 SIN REMOVED FOREVER

There is no need for further sacrifice. Christ's death is entirely sufficient to take care of all previous sins and those sins we may in weakness commit in daily life. God can now forgive, and will forgive, those who place their trust in Christ.

Let us therefore hold to Christ (v. 23). He, and He alone, is our Hope and our Savior.

Heb. 10:26–39 THE REJECTION OF CHRIST

Another fearful warning against falling away from Christ, similar to that in 6:1–8. Addressed to Christians who had once been "publicly exposed to insult and persecution" in their sufferings for the name of Christ, and who had given their all in their compassion for their fellow sufferers (vv. 32–34). But some of these very same people were now losing interest in the things of Christ (v. 25).

The point is that there has been one sacrifice for sin. There will never be another. Those who will not avail themselves of what Christ has done for them on the cross may as well make up their minds to say good-bye to God forever, and go their own way, and suffer for their own sin (vv. 27–31).

Heb. 11 THE HEROES OF FAITH

In this chapter the writer defines faith as the assurance or confirmation of the things that the believer hopes for, as proof of things that the believer

> Let us fix our eyes on Jesus, the author and perfecter of our faith, who for the joy set before him endured the cross, scorning its shame, and sat down at the right hand of the throne of God.
>
> —Hebrews 12:2

Late medieval carving depicting the beheading of James. Hebrews 11 encourages us to remember those who held on to the hope in Jesus even amidst great persecution.

has not yet seen. Believers, living by faith, can rest confidently that God's promises will be fulfilled — that their fulfillment is in fact a reality in their lives before it becomes manifest to the believer's senses. The writer mentions the following Old Testament men and women, whose faith is legendary, as being worthy of recognition as heroes of faith:

Abel's faith: he offered the first sacrifice for sin made by faith and not works (v. 4; Genesis 4:1 – 15).

Enoch's faith: he walked with God, pleased Him, and was taken away by Him (vv. 5 – 6; Genesis 5:22, 24).

Noah's faith: he kept on building the ark when nobody thought there would be any use for it (v. 7; Genesis 6:14 – 22).

Abraham's faith: he set out to find the city of God without knowing where it was; he was willing to offer his son as a sacrifice, in confidence that God would bring him back to life (vv. 8 – 12, 17 – 19; Genesis 12:1 – 7; 22).

Sarah's faith: she came to believe what she at first had laughed at as impossible (vv. 11 – 12; Genesis 17:19; 18:11 – 14).

Isaac's faith: he foretold the future by faith (v. 20; Genesis 27:27 – 29).

Jacob's faith: he believed that God would fulfill His promises (v. 21; Genesis 49).

Joseph's faith: he believed that his bones would rest in Canaan (v. 22; Genesis 50:25).

Moses' faith: he chose to suffer with Israel and turned his back on Egypt; he kept the Passover; he crossed the Red Sea; he saw Him who is invisible (vv. 23 – 29; Exodus 2:2 – 11; 12:21, 50; 14:22 – 29).

Joshua's faith: it made the walls of Jericho fall (v. 30; Joshua 6:20).

Rahab's faith: she cast her lot with Israel (v. 31; Joshua 2:9; 6:23).

Gideon's faith: he became mighty in war (v. 32; Judges 7:21).

Barak's faith: he subdued kingdoms (v. 32; Judges 4).

Samson's faith: his weakness was turned into strength (vv. 32, 34; Judges 16:28).

Jepthah's faith: he defeated armies (v. 32, 34; Judges 11).

David's faith: he obtained promises (vv. 32–33; 2 Samuel 7:11–13).

Daniel's faith: he stopped the mouths of lions (vv. 32–33; Daniel 6:22).

Jeremiah's faith: he was tortured for his faith (vv. 32, 35; Jeremiah 20:2).

Elijah's faith: he raised the dead (vv. 32, 35; 1 Kings 17:17–24).

Elisha's faith: he raised the dead (vv. 32, 35; 2 Kings 4:8–37).

Zechariah's faith: he was stoned for his faith (vv. 32, 37; 2 Chronicles 24:20–21).

Isaiah's faith: he was sawed in two for his faith, according to tradition (vv. 32, 37).

| Heb. 12 | **KEEP YOUR EYES ON JESUS** |

Surrounded by a vast crowd of those who, in former ages, had run their race for God victoriously and who were now gazing with breathless interest at the initial struggles of the newborn church, the runners are urged to keep their eyes on the goal and to strain every nerve and muscle to win (vv. 1–2).

The author exhorts them not to be discouraged by their sufferings, for discipline is one of the means by which God's saints are perfected (vv. 3–13). He also urges them to be very careful to guard against defiling themselves in any way lest they sell their birthright (vv. 14–17).

Sinai and Zion (vv. 18–29). The terrifying experiences that accompanied the inauguration of the old covenant at Sinai are contrasted with the heavenly fellowship of the church: one vast brotherhood, in which the saints on earth, the spirits of the redeemed, and infinite hosts of angels are in sweet and mystic communion around the throne of God, forever and ever and ever (vv. 22–24).

| Heb. 13 | **GRACIOUS EXHORTATIONS** |

This letter, though argumentative in nature, closes with gentle appeals to its readers to be loyal to Christ and to follow Him in all aspects of everyday life—especially in brotherly love and kindness and purity and goodness, and with unceasing prayer and unwavering faith in God.

Even as Malachi was the Old Testament's final message to the nation that had been founded to bring the Messiah into the world, so Hebrews is the New Testament's final message to the nation after the Messiah had come. These final words were written shortly before Jerusalem was destroyed and the Jewish state was swept away. (See p. 939.)

James

Christian Wisdom, Good Works, Pure Religion

If any of you lacks wisdom, he should ask God, who gives generously to all without finding fault, and it will be given to him. But when he asks, he must believe and not doubt.

—JAMES 1:5–6

The prayer of a righteous man is powerful and effective.   —JAMES 5:16

James

Two apostles were named James: one was the brother of John; the other, the son of Alphaeus (Matthew 10:2–3; see p. 515).

The oldest brother of Jesus was named James (Matthew 13:55). At first, James did not believe that Jesus was the Messiah (John 7:2–5). He later believed, became prominent, and was recognized as the leading overseer of the Judean church (Acts 12:17; Galatians 1:19). He is commonly regarded as the writer of this letter.

He was known as an unusually good man and was surnamed "the Just" by his countrymen. It is said that he spent so much time on his knees in prayer that they became hard and callused like a camel's knees. He is thought to have been married (1-Corinthians 9:5). He was very influential both among the Jews and in the church. Peter reported to James upon his release from prison (Acts 12:17). Paul acted on his advice (Acts 21:18–26). James was a very strict Jew himself, but he was also the author of the tolerant letter to gentile Christians in Acts 15:13–29. He endorsed Paul's work among the Gentiles but was himself mainly concerned with Jews. His life work was to win Jews and to "smooth their passage to Christianity."

The Story of His Martyrdom

According to the Jewish historian Josephus and Hegesippus, a Christian historian of the 2nd century, whose narrative Eusebius (p. 902) accepts, James ended his life a martyr for Jesus, his brother and his Lord.

Shortly before Jerusalem was destroyed by the Roman army (A.D. 70; see p. 939), Jews were embracing Christianity in large numbers. Ananias, the high priest, and the scribes and Pharisees assembled the Sanhedrin, around the year A.D. 62 (possibly A.D. 66), and commanded James, "the brother of Jesus who was called Christ," to proclaim from one of the galleries of the temple that Jesus was not the Messiah. Instead, James cried out that Jesus was the Son of God and the Judge of the World.

Then his enraged enemies hurled him to the ground and stoned him until a charitable bystander ended his sufferings with a club, while James was on his knees praying, "Father, forgive them, they know not what they do."

The Letter

Addressed to Christian Jews (2:1), scattered among the nations (1:1), this seems like a book of Christian proverbs that cover a number of subjects, all bearing on the practical aspects of the Christian life. (It resembles Hebrew wisdom literature; see p. 286.)

The letter was probably written around A.D. 60, near the end of James's life, after he had pastored the Judean church for 30 years. However, some date this letter prior to A.D. 50, primarily because of its distinctively Jewish character, which suggests that it was written when the church was primarily composed of Jews. If this is correct, it would make this letter the earliest of the New Testament writings, with the probable exception of Galatians.

James 1:1–8 | TRIALS. PERSEVERANCE. WISDOM. FAITH

If anyone considers himself religious and yet does not keep a tight rein on his tongue, he deceives himself and his religion is worthless.

—James 1:26

Consider it pure joy whenever you face trials (v. 2), whether they be persecution, sickness, or suffering of one kind or another. Perseverance proves our faith and helps build us into the kind of person that Christ came to make us. Peter says that trials strengthen faith (1 Peter 1:7).

Trials teach perseverance (vv. 3–4). Perseverance in time of suffering is the ability to go on, waiting calmly and in joy for that glad day when God shall wipe away all tears (Revelation 21:4).

Perseverance brings maturity and completeness (v. 4). We are just poor sinners saved by grace. But spiritual maturity is our ultimate goal. Some day we shall be perfect, as He is (1 John 3:2).

Wisdom (v. 5). Sound judgment about the practical things of daily life, in all its phases, so that we live, in all things, as Christians should.

Prayer (v. 5) will help attain such wisdom. The letter begins and ends with an exhortation to prayer (5:13–18).

Faith (vv. 6–8). Unwavering faith that stands sure and undisturbed in all the storms of life is the condition of effective prayer. All things are possible to them who believe (Mark 9:23).

James 1:9–18 | RICHES. TEMPTATION. THE NEW BIRTH

Riches (vv. 9–11). A solemn reminder that not our status here but our status in eternity should be our main concern. Even the poor may rejoice in their glorious destiny. (See further on 2:1–13.)

Trials (v. 12). This is the same word as in v. 2. There it seems to mean "being proved by suffering." Here it means "enticement to sin." And sin, born in lust, gives birth to death.

Tempted (vv. 13–15). This refers to temptations that test an individual's moral strength. God cannot be tempted because His very nature is holy and there is nothing in Him to which sin could appeal. Satan tempts us (1 Corinthians 7:5) in order to make us fall. God tests us (Genesis 22:1; Exodus 20:20) in order to confirm our faith and to prove our commitment.

The Christian's newborn soul (vv. 16–18). As desire brings forth sin, and sin gives birth to death, so God, through His Word and in the name of Christ, gives birth to the newborn souls in those who are destined to constitute His inheritance through the endless ages of eternity. Peter also speaks of the Word of God as being the imperishable seed that brings forth the newborn soul of a Christian (1 Peter 1:23).

James 1:19–27 THE TONGUE. THE WORD. PURE RELIGION

Watch your tongue (vv. 19–21). Control your temper. Be a good listener. Abstain from filthy talk.

Be doers of the word (vv. 21–25). In v. 18 the word is called the instrument of the soul's birth. In v. 21 it is the agent of the soul's salvation. In v. 23 it is represented as a mirror, showing us ourselves in our true light. If we act on what we are taught in the Word—if we do what it says, we will be blessed!

Pure religion (vv. 26–27). A magnificent passage. The tongue is involved again. An uncontrolled tongue in a religious person indicates that his or her religion is useless. A life of charity and kindness, free from too much attachment to earthly things, is religion's glory. (Compare what Jesus said on the simplicity and importance of kindness; Matthew 25:31–46.)

James 2:1–13 FAVORITISM

There must have been a decidedly worldly element in the Judean church to call forth such words as these. This is so different from the way the church had started (Acts 2:45; 4:34).

Christ taught that the glory of His church would be its kindness to the poor. But evidently some of the congregations were developing into social cliques in which the poor were given to understand that they were not wanted or at best tolerated. But God loves the poor—and the rich ought to love them, too.

James 2:14–26 FAITH AND WORKS

Paul's doctrine of justification by faith and James's doctrine of justification by works are supplementary, not contradictory. Neither was opposing the teaching of the other. Paul and James were devoted friends and co-workers. James fully endorsed Paul's work (Acts 15:13–29; 21:17–26).

Paul preached faith as the basis of justification before God but insisted that it must issue in the right kind of life. Faith that saves produces deeds. James was writing to those who had accepted the doctrine of justification by faith but were not living right, telling them that such faith was no faith at all. Again, righteous action is evidence of genuine faith.

James 3:1–12 | THE TONGUE

Sins of the tongue are not only harsh and angry words, but also false and foolish doctrines. From the general tone of this chapter we suspect that there must have been many presumptuous, quarrelsome, worldly minded people of uncontrolled temper who put themselves forward as leaders and teachers.

Babylonian design of a horse with bit and bridle. "When we put bits into the mouths of horses to make them obey us, we can turn the whole animal." (James 3:3)

Power of the tongue. The tongue is the main expression of our personality and usually calls forth an immediate reaction, of one kind or another, in others. Mean words have wrecked many a home, divided many a church, and sent unnumbered millions to despair and ruin. Yet we know many very religious people who seem never to make even the slightest effort to control their tongues. James compares the tongue to the rudder on a ship or the bit in a horse's mouth. Both are relatively small parts that have significant influence on the steering of the whole in one direction or another. Our words steer our lives and direct our destiny.

James 3:13–18 | WISDOM

This passage seems to be aimed at certain teachers who, hung up on some pet doctrine and ambitious to be considered brilliant in argument, but with little personal affection for Christ, were producing only jealousy and faction. James calls such wisdom "of the devil" and suggests that the best way to show real wisdom is by a good and fruitful life. What you sow throughout your life, you will reap in harvest.

James 4:1–17 | WORLDLY MINDEDNESS

Covetousness (v. 1–2). Covetousness, the desire to get that which belongs to others, has been the cause of most wars.

Unanswered prayer (v. 3). Some prayers go unanswered because they are nothing but requests for the gratification of our worldly desires.

Double-mindedness (vv. 4–10). An expansion of Jesus' statement that a person cannot serve God and mammon (Matthew 6:24), and similar to John's warning against love of the world (1 John 2:15–17). Such passages suggest the need of unceasing self-examination. We have to live in the world, and worldly things are necessary for our daily subsistence, but it requires great watchfulness to keep our affections and our hearts focused on the things that are above. We need constantly to draw near to God, to cleanse our hands, to purify our hearts, and to humble ourselves.

The tongue again (vv. 11–12). This time James shows the utter absurdity of one sinner setting himself up as judge over another sinner.

If it is the Lord's will (vv. 13–17). One of the most amazing doctrines of Scripture is that God, with the infinite universe on His hands, yet has a definite plan for each of His people (Acts 18:21; Romans 1:10; 15:32; 1 Corinthians 4:19; 1 Peter 3:17).

James 5:1–19 RICHES. PATIENCE. THE TONGUE. PRAYER

The rich (vv. 1–6). This is James's fourth and strongest blast at the rich (the others are in 1:9–11; 2:1–13; 4:1–10). There must have been a good many rich people in the Judean church who were thoroughly unchristian in their deeds, who were bent on worldly pleasure instead of caring about the things of God. James's warning of coming retribution is frightful to those who hoard wealth in these last days

Patience under suffering (vv. 7–11). One day the Lord will come, and all suffering will be over. Keep your eyes and your heart fixed on that glad day.

The tongue once again (v. 12). Our sinful tongue, which is the cause of so much trouble. This time James addresses the problem of swearing an oath: "I swear that such and such is true." If we bring God into our casual oath, it is a serious sin that is very displeasing to God — it is a profaning of God's name. Even a pious phrase such as "The Lord told me . . . ," if used casually and without thought simply to reinforce something we say, can fall under this warning by James. Yet how many professed Christians, in their ordinary conversation, profane God's name by using it lightly, as a formula, and without a sense of awe before the majesty of God? A better use of the tongue is to sing (v. 13).

Prayer, again (vv. 13–18). Believing prayer will surely be answered. Elijah's closing and opening of the heavens was a rare and mighty miracle (1 Kings 18) — yet it is quoted to us as an incentive to pray!

Anointing with oil (v. 14). The word for "anointing" James uses may be used here as an outward sign of the healing to be brought about by God in response to prayer offered in faith. Oil is often used as a symbol of the Holy Spirit (see Mark 6:13). Others believe that James may be using the application of oil as a recognized medical treatment (Isaiah 1:6; Luke 10:34). The application of oil was to be reinforced by prayer, not to be used for magical purposes.

Winning a soul for Christ (vv. 19–20) pleases God immensely. For this He loves us and overlooks our weaknesses. For this we shall shine as the stars forever (Daniel 12:3).

1 Peter

A Letter of Hope in the Midst of Suffering

In this you greatly rejoice, though now for a little while you may have had to suffer grief in all kinds of trials. These have come so that your faith—of greater worth than gold, which perishes even though refined by fire—may be proved genuine and may result in praise, glory and honor when Jesus Christ is revealed. Though you have not seen him, you love him; and even though you do not see him now, you believe in him and are filled with an inexpressible and glorious joy, for you are receiving the goal of your faith, the salvation of your souls.

—1 Peter 1:6–9

Peter

For Peter's early life, see page 513. Other than his two letters, there are no scriptural records of his later life. As the leader of the Twelve it seems likely that he visited the leading church centers of the Roman world. From Jesus' words in John 21:18 we judge that he must have died a martyr's death.

Some church historians think that there is not sufficient evidence that Peter was ever in Rome. Most of them, however, agree that it is probable that in or about the last year of his life, Peter did go to Rome, either by order of Nero or of his own accord, to help steady the Christians under the terrific blows of Nero's persecutions.

There is a tradition that says that Peter, giving in to the urging of friends to save himself, was fleeing from Rome when, in the night on the Appian Way, he met Jesus in a vision and said, "Where are you going, Lord?" *(Quo vadis, Domine?)*. Jesus answered, "I am going to Rome to be

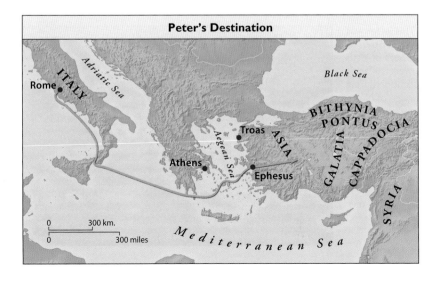

Peter's Destination

crucified again." Peter, utterly ashamed and humiliated, returned to the city and was crucified upside down at his own request, feeling not worthy to be crucified as his Lord had been. This is only a tradition, and we do not know how much historical fact it may contain.

To Whom?

This letter was written to the churches in Asia Minor (1:1; modern-day Turkey, see map p. 63). Many or most of these churches had been founded by Paul. We assume that Peter had at one time or another visited these churches, though this is not stated. Paul had written letters to these churches, of which we still have several: Galatians, Ephesians, and Colossians. (First Peter has some striking similarities to Ephesians.) Later, John addressed the book of Revelation to some of the same churches to which Peter wrote this letter.

From Where?

Peter wrote from "Babylon" (5:13). Some take this to be the literal Babylon on the Euphrates, in modern Iraq. (See map p. 63.) But generally it is thought to refer to the city of Rome, figuratively called Babylon. (The same is usually thought to be the case in Revelation 17:5, 18.) In those times of persecution, Christians had to be careful how they spoke of the ruling powers, and they had a code name for it that they among themselves would understand, though an outsider would not.

Mark was with Peter at the time (5:13), and 2 Timothy 4:11 seems to indicate that Mark may have been in Rome about the time this letter was written.

The Occasion

Nero's persecution of Christians in A.D. 64–67 was very severe in and around Rome, but not in the rest of the Roman Empire, although the

This letter was initially written to followers of Jesus who were suffering persecution during the reign of Nero. Caesars like Nero were "entertained" by watching persecutions that occurred in the elongated oval depression which once held the Circus Maximus.

example of the emperor encouraged the enemies of Christians everywhere to take advantage of the slightest pretext to persecute Christians. It was a trying time. The church as a whole was about 35 years old. It had suffered persecutions in various places at the hands of local authorities. But now imperial Rome, which had thus far been indifferent—and even in some cases friendly—had accused the church of a terrible crime and was taking steps to punish it (see p. 898).

The church worldwide was undergoing a time of trial (5:9). It seemed as if the end had come. It was in the most literal sense a "fiery trial" (4:12 KJV). Christians were being burned nightly in Nero's gardens. It did look as if the devil was about to devour the church as a "roaring lion" (5:8).

It is thought that Peter may have written this letter immediately after Paul's martyrdom, about A.D. 67/68, and sent it with Silas (5:12), who had been one of Paul's helpers, to these churches, which Paul had founded, to encourage them to bear up under their suffering. Silas thus would have personally carried the news of Paul's martyrdom to Paul's churches.

Therefore the letter was born in the atmosphere of suffering, shortly before Peter's own martyrdom, and exhorted Christians not to think it strange that they had to suffer, reminding them that Christ did His work by suffering.

| I Peter I | THE CHRISTIAN'S GLORIOUS INHERITANCE

This is a magnificent chapter in which almost every word has profound meaning.

Strangers (v. 1) seems to refer to scattered Jewish Christians. But 2:10 indicates that they were mainly Gentiles. Peter addresses them as "resident aliens," pilgrims, citizens of another world, living for a little while in this world, away from home, journeying along toward their homeland.

Suffering and glory (v. 7). Those who are one in Christ will suffer for His name's sake but will also enter into His glory. The believer will benefit in the earthly suffering from Christ's already having entered glory. Trials here and now, glory at the coming of the Lord. Again and again, suffering and glory are paired.

- "The sufferings of Christ and the glories that would follow" (1:11)
- "Rejoice that you participate in the sufferings of Christ, so that you may be overjoyed when his glory is revealed" (4:13)
- Peter, "a witness of Christ's sufferings . . . who also will share in the glory to be revealed" (5:1)
- "After you have suffered a little while," you will see "his eternal glory" (5:10)

We are brothers and sisters in a common, glorious hope; let us be brothers and sisters to one another in time of suffering!

The painful trial (4:12–19). Nero's persecution of Christians was the direct work of the devil (5:8). Nevertheless, in the mysterious providence of God, it would turn out for the good of the church: the faith of those who suffer will "result in praise, glory and honor when Jesus Christ is revealed" (1:7). There have been many persecutions since, many of them more brutal and widespread than Nero's, in which unnumbered millions of Christians have endured every conceivable kind of torture. When we think of this, we ought to be ashamed of ourselves for our fretfulness over our petty troubles. Peter's humility (5:1–7) is discernible in this section, all the more remarkable because humility was not Peter's most notable trait in the Gospels.

Mark (5:13) was with Peter at the time. He is thought to have written his Gospel under Peter's direction, possibly about the time Peter wrote this letter.

2 Peter

Prediction of Apostasy

For this very reason, make every effort to add to your faith goodness; and to goodness, knowledge; and to knowledge, self-control; and to self-control, perseverance; and to perseverance, godliness; and to godliness, brotherly kindness; and to brotherly kindness, love. . . . Therefore, my brothers, be all the more eager to make your calling and election sure. For if you do these things, you will never fall.   —2 PETER 1:5–7, 10

The Author

The letter specifically claims to be the work of Simon Peter (1:1). The writer represents himself as having been present at the transfiguration of Christ (1:16–18) and as having been warned by Christ of his impending death (1:14). This means that the letter is either a genuine writing of Peter or the work of someone who claimed to be Peter.

Although it was slow in being accepted as part of the New Testament canon (see p. 988), the early church recognized it as a genuine letter of Peter, and it has through the centuries been revered as a part of Holy Scripture.

Some modern critics regard it as a pseudonymous work from the end of the 2nd century, written 100 years after Peter's death by some unknown person who assumed Peter's identity. To the average mind, this would be just plain common forgery, an offense against civil and moral law and ordinary decency. The critics, however, insist over and over that there is nothing at all unethical in thus counterfeiting another's name.

To Whom?

Unlike most of the New Testament letters, this one does not mention any locality. It was, however, Peter's "second letter" to people to whom he had written before (3:1). While Peter may have written many letters that have not been preserved, the assumption is that the first letter was the one we know as 1 Peter, which was addressed to churches of Asia Minor (1 Peter 1:1), churches to whom Paul also had written (2 Peter 3:15).

When?

If 1 Peter was written during Nero's persecution (see p. 898), and if Peter was martyred in that persecution (see p. 797), then this letter must have been written shortly before Peter's death, probably around A.D. 67.

Facsimile of early manuscript of 2 Peter where Peter encourages believers to stay true in the face of coming apostasy.

2 Peter and Jude

Some passages in 2 Peter and Jude are so similar that some scholars think that one of the two must have copied from the other. But this is not a necessary conclusion. The apostles had constantly heard one another talk, and certain expressions and scriptural illustrations became part of the common Christian vocabulary—especially in a culture that relied heavily on hearing and remembering.

---

2 Peter 1:1–11 | MAKING SURE OF SALVATION

Knowledge of Christ, which is the foundation of our faith, is here emphasized as the medium of grace and peace (v. 2), of all things that pertain to life and godliness (v. 3), and one of the means by which we may make our calling and election sure (v. 10) and by which the corruption by the world is overcome (2:20). "Grow in the grace and knowledge of our Lord and Savior Jesus Christ" is the closing exhortation of the letter (3:18). Original, authentic knowledge about Christ is contained in God's Word, so Peter's farewell warning was, Don't neglect God's Word!

The precious promises (v. 4) include not only the external glories of the eternal kingdom (v. 11), but also a changed, divine nature within ourselves—a nature that God will, of His own grace, give us and that we, for our part, must do our best to develop (vv. 5–11).

Seven divine qualities (vv. 5–11). Goodness, knowledge, self-control, perseverance, godliness, brotherly kindness, love. These are the fruits (v. 8) of our precious faith (v. 1), which we are to add (v. 5) to the blessings that God has already given to us. These qualities should be evidence of increased spiritual knowledge. While one might interpret Peter's message to imply that the believer is to develop each quality in succession, each one building on the preceding one, it is more probable to assume that we develop theses qualities simultaneously. The more a Christian grows and matures in the knowledge of Christ, the more we expect to see a corresponding increase in these qualities in one's life.

| 2 Peter 1:12–15 | PETER'S MARTYRDOM IS NEAR |

This seems to be a reference to what Jesus had told Peter some 37 years before (John 21:18–19). Or Jesus may have recently appeared to Peter. (If the tradition of Jesus' appearing to Peter on the Appian Way [see p. 797] is true, it could refer to that encounter.) At any rate, he had a premonition that martyrdom was at hand (v. 14). These verses remind us of Paul's dying shout of triumph (2 Timothy 4:6–8). Putting aside "the tent of this body" (vv. 13–14; KJV, this tabernacle) is a beautiful scriptural image for death.

| 2 Peter 1:16–21 | THE GOSPEL TESTIMONY IS SURE |

It seems that already in Peter's day there were forerunners of our modern critics who were calling the story of Jesus and His mighty works a set of cleverly invented stories (v. 16). But Peter had seen with his own eyes, and he *knew* that what he told about Jesus was *true*. Over a period of three years he had seen Jesus heal multitudes of sick people with simply a word. He had seen Him walk on water and still the storm. He had seen Him transfigured. Three times he saw Him raise the dead. He saw Jesus alive after the crucifixion. And, after Pentecost, Peter himself, in Jesus' name, did many mighty miracles (Acts 5:15) and even raised Dorcas from the dead (Acts 9:40).

All this, confirmed in marvelous detail in Old Testament prophecies of the coming Messiah (vv. 19–21; see also pp. 453–68), gave Peter full assurance and made him ready for his approaching martyrdom. He knew that, for him, the door of glory was about to open and he would enter into the immediate presence of his beloved Lord, nevermore to leave.

| 2 Peter 2 | APOSTASY |

The coming of false teachers is spoken of again and again in the New Testament. Jesus warned of ferocious wolves who would come into the church in sheep's clothing (Matthew 7:15) and lead many astray (Matthew 24:11). Paul warned of wolves who would arise in the church, distorting the truth (Acts 20:29–30). Again Paul predicted that, before the second coming of the Lord, there would be a falling away of appalling magnitude and satanic nature in the church (2 Thessalonians 2:1–12). Again Paul foretold the rise to church leadership of ungodly men, traitors and hypocrites who, with outward godliness, would fill the church with doctrines of demons (1 Timothy 4: 1–3; 2 Timothy 3:19). Jude seems to have been written mainly to warn of an ominous and deadly trend toward apostasy which he saw surfacing in the church in his own day (Jude 4–19).

Peter, in his first letter, wrote to encourage the church to bear up under persecution from without. Here, in this second letter, he cautions the church to guard against corruption from within.

He warns of coming apostasy, when leaders in the church would, for financial gain, permit licentiousness and general wrongdoing. He speaks of it as being in the future (v. 1). Yet some of the language implies that false teachers were already at work within the church.

Peter speaks of their destructive heresies (v. 1), their shameful ways (v. 2), their greed (v. 3), their following the corrupt desire of the sinful nature (v. 10), their being like brute beasts (v. 12) with eyes full of adultery (v. 14), slaves of depravity (19). Note that these expressions are used as referring, not to the world, but to *leaders within the church*.

It is a sorry picture. Even within the apostolic generation, the world and the devil had succeeded in making heavy onslaughts on the purity of the church. Then followed the long centuries of corruption. And even now, in our own enlightened age, in many sections of the church the Gospel of Christ in its original beauty and simplicity and purity is still buried and hid from view by the rubbish of forms and doctrines heaped upon the church, through the ages, by the world and the devil.

It is a terrible sin to corrupt the church. All the ungodly shall be destroyed: this is an unceasing note of Scripture. But one of the worst of sins is to foist, in the name of Christ, lies upon the church that replace Christian truth. Let those who do it take warning from what happened to the fallen angels (v. 4), to the world of Noah's time (v. 5), and to Sodom and Gomorrah (v. 6).

2 Peter 3 | THE DELAY OF THE LORD'S COMING

Jesus had said things that could have been construed to imply His return in that first generation of the church (Matthew 16:28; 24:34). The apostles used expressions that indicated His near appearance (Romans 13:12; Hebrews 10:25; James 5:8; Revelation 1:3).

Yet Jesus hinted that His return might come after a long time (Matthew 25:19) and suggested that it would be wise to prepare for a delay (Matthew 25:4). Paul expressly stated that it would not be until *after* the apostasy (2 Thessalonians 2:2–3). Peter, in this chapter, makes it clear that with God 1000 years are like a day (v. 8; Psalm 90:4). He will keep His promise according to His own chronology. These passages when put together seem to indicate that God designed that each successive generation should live in constant expectation of the Lord's coming.

What bearing should all this, after 2000 years of delay, have on our thinking about the Lord's coming? The Lord is not slow in keeping His promise; rather, He is patiently waiting for His people to come to repentance. He desires that no one should perish. Praise God for His loving mercy and grace! His coming is now 2000 years nearer than it was then. The night is far spent. Day may be nearer than we think. Who knows but what the Lord's train, at long last, may even now be whistling for the Grand Central Station, with the angels ready to shout, "All aboard!"

One of the subjects ridiculed by the false teachers mentioned in chapter 2 is the Lord's second coming (3:3–4). But the Lord will come (v. 10). And it will be a day of destruction for the ungodly (v. 7), like the Flood in the days of Noah. Next time it will be by fire, as is very plainly stated (v. 10). Whether by explosion or by collision with another heavenly body or by some other means, we do not know. But from it all, God's people will be delivered, and for them there will be a new heaven and a new earth (vv. 13–14; Revelation 21–22).

In closing, Peter mentions letters of Paul (v. 15) and calls them Scripture (v. 16). And, as in his first letter Peter spoke of the Word of God as being the source of the new birth (1 Peter 1:23) and the means of growth (1 Peter 2:2) for the Christian, so he does here. In this letter that foretells apostasy in the church, Peter insists that knowledge of Christ through His word will help us make our calling and election sure (1:2, 4, 10). The way for the church to combat apostasy and to keep itself pure and free from worldly corruption is to hold fast to the Word of God as given by the Prophets and Apostles (1:19; 3:2).

1 John

Jesus Is the Son of God
If We Belong to Him, We Will Love One Another

You, dear children, are from God and have overcome them, because the one who is in you is greater than the one who is in the world. —1 JOHN 4:5

Dear friends, since God so loved us, we also ought to love one another. —1 JOHN 4:11

This letter, like the letter to the Hebrews, mentions neither its author nor the people to whom it was addressed, even though it is very personal, as the frequent use of *I* and *you* shows. It has always been recognized as a circular letter of the apostle John to the churches around Ephesus, in which he emphasizes the main essentials of the Gospel and warns against heresies that are beginning to creep in and that, unchecked, would produce a corrupt and paganized form of Christianity.

This letter is one of the latest writings in the New Testament. It was most likely written after John's Gospel, some time between between A.D. 85 and A.D. 95.

John

According to a very ancient tradition, John made Jerusalem his headquarters. There he cared for Jesus' mother, Mary, until her death, and after the destruction of Jerusalem, he moved to Ephesus (see map p. 680), which by the end of the apostolic generation had become the geographic and numerical center of the Christian church. Here John lived to a very old age, and here he wrote his Gospel and his three letters. John is also the author of the book of Revelation (he received the vision recorded in Revelation while on Patmos). Among his pupils were Polycarp, Papias, and Ignatius, who became bishops of Smyrna, Hierapolis, and Antioch, respectively. We still have writings from all three; they are among the earliest of the so-called church fathers (see p. 902).

The Background of the Letter

When John wrote this letter, Christianity had been in existence some 60 or 70 years, and in many parts of the Roman Empire it had become an important religion and a powerful influence. Naturally, all sorts of efforts were made to combine the Gospel with prevailing philosophies and systems of thought.

One such effort was the blending of Christianity and the philosophy known as Gnosticism. The form of Gnosticism that was disrupting the churches in John's day taught that human nature consists of two separate, irreconcilable entities: body and spirit. Sin resides in the body (or "flesh") only. The human spirit occupied itself with the things of God, while at the same time the body could do as it pleased. One could transcend from the mundane to a spiritual realm by acquiring knowledge, or "gnosis." Thus a lofty mental, mystical piety was entirely consistent with a voluptuous, sensual lifestyle!

The Gnostics also denied the Incarnation: God had in Christ *not* actually become flesh—Christ was a phantom, a man in appearance only. This theory was called Docetism. Another gnostic theory was Cerinthianism, which suggested that the divine Christ joined the man Jesus at baptism and left him before he died. A man named Cerinthus was the leader of this cult in Ephesus. He claimed for himself inner mystic experiences and an exalted knowledge of God, but his life centered around the gratification of sensual appetites. Throughout this letter John appears to have had these heretics in mind: he insists that Jesus was the actual, material, authentic manifestation of God in the flesh who died on the cross for our sins and was resurrected, and that genuine knowledge of God must result in moral transformation.

I John 1:1–4 | THE INCARNATION

God became flesh, in human form. John calls Jesus "the Son of God" 21 times in this letter, and he speaks of God as the Father 12 times. Thus the deity of Jesus and the Father-Son relationship between God and Jesus are a special emphasis of this letter.

John was Jesus' most intimate earthly friend. For three years John accompanied Jesus on His journeys through Palestine, ministering to Him day and night as Jesus performed His mighty miracles. At the Last Supper, John "was reclining next to him" as Jesus talked of His approaching crucifixion (John 13:23). To John, Jesus was no phantom or dream or mere vision. He was a real person, the embodiment of Life—eternal life (v. 2).

And John wrote this letter so that others might share his feeling of fellowship, companionship, and joy, in Christ and in the Father and with one another (vv. 3–4).

I John 1:5–10 | GOD IS LIGHT

That is the way John's Gospel also starts: the Word of God is the light of men (John 1:1, 4). Jesus Himself said, "I am the light of the world" (John 8:12).

Light stands for God's realm of truth, righteousness, purity, joy, ineffable glory. Darkness stands for this world of error, evil, ignorance, and wickedness—the realm of the lost.

In a more real and literal sense, light may be an attribute of God beyond the understanding of human eyes.

- God "wraps Himself in light" (Psalm 104:2).

- God "lives in unapproachable light" (1 Timothy 6:16).
- "Father of the heavenly lights" is one of God's names (James 1:17).
- Jesus' clothes, at His transfiguration, became dazzling white (Mark 9:3).
- The angel at Jesus' resurrection was dressed "white as snow" (Matthew 28:3).
- The two who stood beside Jesus at His ascension were in white (Acts 1:10).

  - In the vision in Revelation 1:14–16, Jesus' head and hair were "white as snow." (See further on Revelation 3:4.)

I John 2:1–17 | WALKING IN THE LIGHT

Walking with God does not mean that we are without sin. We have sinned in the past, and we still have sin in our nature. It is not by virtue of our sinlessness that we have fellowship, a relationship, with God, but because of Christ's death for our sin. If the moment we are conscious of any sinful act we confess it in genuine penitence and humility, our fellowship with God may remain unbroken. The saintliest of men invariably have been most deeply conscious of their own sinfulness.

One of the conditions of having our sins forgiven is that we keep God's commandments (vv. 1–6). Yet sin is itself the failure to keep His commandments! This is one of John's paradoxes. (See further on 3:1–12.)

I John 2:18–29 | ANTICHRIST

The word "Antichrist" is mentioned in 2:18, 22; 4:3; and in 2 John 7. It occurs nowhere else in the Bible, not even in the book of Revelation. It is commonly identified with the "man of lawlessness" of 2 Thessalonians 2 and the beast of Revelation 13. But the Bible itself does not make that identification.

John's language implies that his readers had been taught to expect an anti-Christ in connection with the closing days of the Christian Era (2:18). John, however, applies the word, not to one person, but to a whole group of anti-Christian teachers (2:18; 4:3). The New Testament idea seems to be that the *spirit* of Antichrist would arise in Christendom, manifesting itself in many ways, both in and outside the church, culminating finally in one person, or in an institution, or both. (See also p. 860.)

I John 3:1–12 | RIGHTEOUSNESS

John makes some very strong statements about sin:

- "No one who continues to sin has either seen [God] or known him" (v. 6).

- "He who does what is sinful is of the devil" (v. 8).
- "No one who is born of God will continue to sin" (v. 9).

Yet, John had just said what seems to be the opposite:

- "If we claim to be without sin, we deceive ourselves" (1:8).
- "If we claim we have not sinned, we make [God] out to be a liar" (1:10).

How can we explain these paradoxical statements? There is a difference between sins of weakness and willful, habitual sin. An eagle may dip its wings in the mud, but it is still an eagle. A righteous man may have sins of weakness and yet be a righteous man. John may have had in mind certain heretical teachers (such as Jezebel, Revelation 2:20) who, while claiming special, superior fellowship with God, were at the same time wallowing in the filth of immorality.

I John 3:13–24 | LOVE

The dominant note of this letter is love.

- "We should love one another" (v. 11).
- "Anyone who does not love his brother" is not a child of God (v. 10).
- "We know that we have passed from death to life, because we love our brothers" (v. 14).
- "Anyone who does not love remains in death" (v. 14).
- "Anyone who hates his brother is a murderer" (v. 15).
- "Let us love one another" (4:7).
- "Everyone who loves has been born of God and knows God" (4:7).
- "Love comes from God" (4:7).
- "We . . . ought to love one another" (4:11).
- "God is love" (4:16).
- "Whoever lives in love lives in God" (4:16).
- "If we love one another, God lives in us" (4:12).
- "Perfect love drives out fear" (4:18).
- "We love because he first loved us" (4:19).
- "If anyone says, 'I love God,' yet hates his brother, he is a liar" (4:20).
- "For anyone who does not love his brother, whom he has seen, cannot love God, whom he has not seen" (4:20).

I John 4:1–6 | FALSE PROPHETS

Apparently many churches were the target of false teachers who claimed special inspiration from the Holy Spirit for their doctrines. Generally, John says, their trustworthiness can be tested by their loyalty to the deity of Jesus (v. 2).

Persian sun god Mithras slaying a bull. John warned against following after individuals who led people into false religions such as the cult of Mithras.

I John 4:7–21 | LOVE

John returns to the keynote of the letter, his favorite theme: love. He is very insistent that being saved by the grace of Christ does not release us from the necessity of obeying Christ's commandments. And Christ's main commandment is love.

- We have come to know Christ "if we obey his commands" (2:3).
- "The man who says, 'I know him,' but does not do what he commands is a liar" (2:4).
- We "receive from him anything we ask, because we obey his commands" (3:22).
- "This is his command: . . . to love one another" (3:23).
- "Those who obey his commands live in him" (3:24).
- "He has given us this command: Whoever loves God must also love his brother" (4:21).
- "This is love for God: to obey his commands" (5:3).

It is told of John that when he was old and too feeble to walk, he would be carried into the church, and when he spoke he would always say, "Little children, love one another. It is the Lord's commandment."

I John 5 | THE ASSURANCE OF ETERNAL LIFE

"Know" is one of the key words of this letter.

- "We know that we have come to know" God (2:3).

- "We know we are in him" (2:5).
- "We know that when he appears, we shall be like him" (3:2).
- "We know that we have passed from death to life, because we love our brothers" (3:14).
- "We know that we belong to the truth" (3:19).
- "We know that [God] lives in us" (3:24).
- "We know that we live in" God (4:13).
- "I write these things to you . . . so that you may know that you have eternal life" (5:13).
- "We know that [God] hears us" (5:15).
- "We know that we are children of God" (5:19).

Many Christians are discouraged because they do not feel sure that they are saved. Sometimes we hear it said that if we do not *know* that we are saved, it is a sign that we are not saved. But it is a mistake to identify assurance with salvation. A newborn babe scarcely knows it has been born, but it has. Assurance comes with growth. We believe it is possible for a Christian's faith to get stronger and stronger, until it reaches the full assurance of knowledge.

Eternal life (v. 13) begins when a person becomes a Christian, and it never ends. It is a life of divine quality and endless duration. Assurance of this eternal life is the object of this letter.

The sin that leads to death (5:16) probably refers to the unpardonable sin spoken of by Jesus — blasphemy against the Holy Spirit (Matthew 12:31 – 32; see note on Hebrews 6:46).

2 John

Caution Against False Teachers

I ask that we love one another. And this is love: that we walk in obedience to his commands. As you have heard from the beginning, his command is that you walk in love. —2 JOHN 5–6

This letter and 3 John are personal notes to friends whom John expected to visit soon. He wrote other letters (see 1 John 2:14; 3 John 9), perhaps many of them. Personal letters such as these would, because of their brevity and private nature, be less generally read in Christian assemblies than letters addressed to churches and would consequently be less widely known. These two short letters were, under the guidance of God's Spirit, rescued from oblivion and preserved for the church, possibly by being attached to a copy of 1 John in the particular church or churches where they had been received.

The Elder (v. 1)

The other apostles had all died years before. John alone was left, the last surviving companion of Jesus, the leader of all Christendom. How appropriate this title, "The Elder."

The Chosen Lady (v. 1)

She may have been an individual, a well-known and prominent woman, somewhere near Ephesus, in whose home a church met. Or John may be

Interior of a 1st-century Roman house in Ephesus. "If anyone comes to you and does not bring this teaching, do not take him into your house or welcome him." (2 John 10)

referring to a local church, symbolically called a lady (just as the church as a whole is called "the Bride of Christ"). Her "chosen sister" (v. 13) is then either another prominent Christian woman leader in the congregation in which John was resident, or the congregation itself.

Truth (vv. 1–4)

The word "truth" is used five times in the first four verses.

- Love in truth (v. 1)
- "Know the truth" (v. 1)
- Truth lives in us (v. 2)
- "Grace, mercy and peace . . . will be with us in truth and love" (v. 3)
- "Walking in the truth" (v. 4)

Furthermore, the true doctrine of Christ is truth (v. 9), as is the fact that He is the Son of God and that following Him means walking in His commandments (v. 6). And His chief commandment is that we love one another (v. 5).

False Teachers (vv. 7–11)

These are the teachers John already referred to in 1 John 2:18–29: they go from church to church, teaching in the name of Christ doctrines that are utterly subversive of the Christian faith. This letter seems to have been written to caution the "chosen lady" to be on her guard and to refuse hospitality to such teachers. Note that the warning is prefaced by an exhortation to love (vv. 5–6), as if to indicate that the practice of Christian love does not mean that we should give encouragement to enemies of the truth.

3 John

The Rejection of John's Helpers

I pray that you may enjoy good health and that all may go well with you, even as your soul is getting along well. . . . I have no greater joy than to hear that my children are walking in the truth.

—3 JOHN 2, 4

Dear friend, do not imitate what is evil but what is good.

—3 JOHN 11

Gaius (v. 1)

There was a Gaius in Corinth, a convert of Paul's (1 Corinthians 1:14; Romans 16:23), in whose home a church met in Paul's day. A tradition says that this Gaius later became John's amanuensis (assistant/secretary). But v. 4 calls Gaius one of John's "children," that is, converts. Whoever Gaius was, he was a greatly beloved Christian leader. John loved him and four times calls him "dear friend" (vv. 1, 2, 5, 11).

That All May Go Well with You (v. 2)

Here is a prayer, from one who was very close to Christ, that a Christian might have temporal as well as spiritual blessings: an indication that it is not wrong, in the sight of Christ, for one to possess this world's goods and benefits. John himself, in early life, had been a man of means. But this same John warns against loving the things of this world (1 John 2:15–17).

Truth (v. 1)

A favorite word of John's. He uses it more than 20 times in his Gospel, nine times in 1 John, five times in 2-John, and five times in this very short letter: love in the truth (v. 1), walk in the truth (vv. 2–3), work for the truth (v. 8), the witness of the truth (v. 12).

John's Helpers (vv. 5–8)

Paul, some 40 years earlier, had established churches in and around Ephesus. With no seminaries to train pastors, he had to develop his pastors from among his converts. Later, John assumed the pastoral oversight of these churches, and it appears that he trained a great number of teachers and preachers to aid him and sent them out among the churches.

Diotrephes (v. 9)

Diotrephes was one of the domineering false teachers who would have nothing to do with John. It seems that Diotrephes and Gaius were pastors of different congregations in the same city. Apparently some of John's evangelists, on one of their recent tours, had been refused admission to the

Remains of a Byzantine church structure in Ephesus sits atop the traditional burial of the apostle John. John's burial place in Ephesus is a reminder of his service to the church in Ephesus. While there, John wrote this letter of concern (3 John) to address the false teaching of Diotrephes.

congregation over which Diotrephes presided, but Gaius had taken them in. On returning to Ephesus, they told the story in John's home church. John was now sending another delegation to the same city with this short letter addressed to Gaius. Demetrius (v. 12) may have been the bearer of the letter.

Jude

Warning Against Apostasy

To him who is able to keep you from falling and to present you before his glorious presence without fault and with great joy—to the only God our Savior be glory, majesty, power and authority, through Jesus Christ our Lord, before all ages, now and forevermore! Amen.

—JUDE 24–25

Jude

The author identifies himself as Jude, which is also another form of the Hebrew word Judah (Greek *Judas*). Of those so named in the New Testament, the author of this letter is most likely either Judas, one of the 12 apostles (not Judas Iscariot; Luke 6:16; see p. 514), or Judas, the brother of Jesus (Matthew 13:55). The latter is commonly regarded as the writer of this letter.

When and Where?

The similarity of the situation in Jude and that mentioned in 2 Peter suggests the possibility that this letter may have been addressed to the same churches as those to which Peter addressed his first and second letters: churches in Asia Minor (1 Peter 1:1; 2 Peter 3:1). It was probably written around A.D. 67.

Why?

Evidently Jude had been planning to write a more general statement about the doctrine of salvation to this group of churches when news of the appearance of a devastating heresy prompted him to send this stern warning (vv. 3–4).

The False Teachers (vv. 4–19)

Jude does not mince words as to their nature. The frightful epithets which he uses refer to certain *leaders within the church*.

- "Godless men" (v. 4)
- They "change the grace of our God into a license for immorality" (v. 4)
- They "deny Jesus Christ" (v. 4)
- Like Sodom, they are given to sexual immorality (v. 7)
- They are "dreamers" who "pollute their own bodies" (v. 8)
- "Like unreasoning animals" they destroy themselves (v. 10)

- "Blemishes at your love feasts" (v.12)
- "Shepherds who feed only themselves" (v. 12)
- "Clouds without rain" (v. 12)
- "Trees, without fruit" (v. 12)
- "Wild waves of the sea, foaming up their shame" (v. 13)
- "Wandering stars, for whom blackest darkness has been reserved" (v. 13)
- "Grumblers" (v. 16)
- "Faultfinders" (v. 16)
- Boasting about themselves (v. 16)
- "Scoffers who . . . follow their own ungodly desires" (v. 18)
- They "do not have the Spirit" (v. 19)
- They "flatter others for their own advantage" (v. 16)
- They are people "who divide you" (v. 19)

Foaming waves coming into the ancient harbor at Selucea Perea. "They [false teachers] are wild waves of the sea, foaming up their shame." (Jude 13)

These false teachers had already crept in (v. 4), yet they were spoken of as appearing in "the last time." While primarily referring to some particular class of men that belonged to Jude's day, this may possibly be a general characterization of the whole body of false teachers who would, through the centuries, corrupt the church from within and thus attempt to thwart the redemptive work of Christ. Those who are acquainted with church history know well how the church has suffered from such men.

The Fallen Angels (v. 6)

This verse and 2 Peter 2:4 are the only direct Scripture references to the fall of the angels (Revelation 12:9 seems to refer to their later defeat). Some think this is an allusion to Genesis 6:1–5, where the "sons of God" intermarried with the "daughters of men." More probably it refers to an earlier event, when Satan led certain of the angels in rebellion against

God (Isaiah 14:12–15). This occurred prior to Adam and Eve's encounter with Satan which led to their sin in the Garden of Eden.

Michael Disputes with the Devil (v. 9)

Michael is mentioned in Daniel 10:13, 21 as a "chief prince," and in Revelation 12:7 as a leader of angels, but only in this passage is he called "the archangel." Moses' burial is told in Deuteronomy 34:5–7, but Michael's dispute with Satan about Moses' body is not mentioned. Origen, an early church father, says that Jude's statement is a reference to a passage in the apocryphal book *The Assumption of Moses,* which was written about the time of the birth of Christ. Only a part of this book survives, and the part we have does not contain such a passage. Jude may have had knowledge of the incident from other sources. Josephus says that God hid Moses' body lest it be made an idol. Possibly Satan wanted it in order to tempt Israel into idolatry. Jude's use of the incident seems to sanction its historicity. This section also serves as an example against the sin of bringing slanderous accusations against people: even the archangel, highest of creatures, did not do this when faced with the devil, the most degraded of creatures.

The Prophecy of Enoch (vv. 14–15)

This is the only scriptural allusion to the prophecy of Enoch. The brief story of his life is told in Genesis 5:18–24, but there is no mention of any of his words. Jude's quotation is from the apocryphal book of Enoch, which claims to have been written by the Enoch of Genesis 5 but actually did not appear until about 100 B.C. He evidently regards this comment as a genuine word of Enoch. Thus, while Adam, founder of the race, was yet alive, Enoch (contemporary with Adam for 300 years) prophesied of the eventual second coming of the Lord to execute judgment upon the disobedient race. Accompanying Christ will be "thousands upon thousands of his holy ones," referring to angels (2 Thessalonians 1:7) or possibly the raptured saints (Christians) who are returning with the Lord (1 Thessalonians 3:13), or both.

Jude's sanction of one passage in the book of Enoch does not sanction the whole book, however.

Judean hills.

THE AGE TO COME

Revelation

The book of Revelation is also known as the Apocalypse. Both words mean the same: an uncovering (*Revelation* comes from Latin, *Apocalypse* from Greek). The book is an "uncovering" of the age to come, of the final victory of God and the Lamb, Jesus.

Apocalyptic Literature

The book of Revelation seems stranger to us than it did to John's first (Jewish) readers. In the period from about 200 B.C. to A.D. 100, many writings like the book of Revelation were written. They are known as "apocalyptic literature" or simply "apocalyptic."

The period in which apocalyptic literature flourished was a difficult time in Jewish history. After the return from the Babylonian exile, the Jews expected that at last the golden age would arrive, in which the throne of David would be restored and all God's promises would be fulfilled. The apocalyptic writings claimed to be the prophetic promise that, despite appearances, God's kingdom was still coming.

Many of these writings followed a pattern:

- They claimed to be a revelation made through an angel or heavenly messenger to some great person from the past, such as Abraham, Moses, or Ezra.
- In the Old Testament, God was always seen as working in this world. The apocalypticists, on the other hand, made a radical distinction between this world and the heavenly world. This world was seen as heading for disaster and ruin, while the heavenly world would replace it.
- The visions and revelations and dreams of the apocalyptic writers were full of strange creatures and symbolic numbers.
- These revelations described the past as prophecies given *before* the events to the presumed author of the book — prophecies that were then fulfilled in marvelous detail. But prophecies that were still to be fulfilled when the book was written were generally very vague.
- They are generally full of Old Testament images and references.

An example of an apocalyptic book is the apocryphal book of 2 Esdras (see pp. 1005–1007).

Differences Between Apocalyptic and Revelation

Although the book of Revelation fits in many ways in the general category of apocalyptic, there are two essential differences that also make it a prophetic book:

- John does not use a pseudonym—he makes it quite clear who he is.
- The book of Revelation does not derive its authority from an angel or heavenly messenger who spoke long ago. It is authoritative because it is the living Christ who speaks to John—in the present.

Revelation

Grand Finale of the Bible Story
The Ultimate Triumph of Christ
The New Heaven and the New Earth

Blessed is the one who reads the words of this prophecy, and blessed are those who hear it and take to heart what is written in it because the time is near. —REVELATION 1:3

Then I saw a new heaven and a new earth. . . . And I heard a loud voice from the throne saying, "Now the dwelling of God is with men, and he will live with them. They will be his people, and God himself will be with them and be their God. He will wipe every tear from their eyes. There will be no more death or mourning or crying or pain, for the old order of things has passed away." —REVELATION 21:1, 3–4

The book of Revelation is the only book of the New Testament that is prophetic in nature. The book is an explanation of Christ's discourse on things to come (Matthew 24; Mark 13; and Luke 21). It is full of expressions used by Jesus and direct and indirect references to the prophetic writings of the Old Testament. Revelation is a book that offers the reader a unique blessing.

Revelation Is a Book with Jesus Christ at the Center

The very first words of the book declare that it is "the revelation of Jesus Christ." Jesus dominates the scene from the beginning to the end of the book. Jesus, the Son of God who has provided the way for the church to be redeemed and reunited with its Creator, is further revealed in this writing. His second coming, His millennial reign on earth, and His judgment of the earth are foretold. And it describes His final victory over our enemy, Satan.

Jesus will establish His everlasting kingdom, and the redeemed saints will rule with Him eternally. What a glorious, hope-giving, and comforting message this book is during a time when it often appears that God and His church are being overpowered by this world!

Revelation Is a Book of Prophecy

The book of Revelation belongs to the class of apocalyptic literature in which the divine message is conveyed by visions and dreams (for more on apocalyptic literature, see p. 823). The first two verses of the book state that it is a "revelation" from God, to Jesus, to the apostle John of things to come—a revealing, unveiling, explaining, making known, of things that are in the future (1:1, 19; 4:1). That is what it was written for: to unfold the future, to chart the course and destiny of the Jews, the Gentiles, and the church of the Lord Jesus Christ.

Revelation Is a Very Practical Book

Even though it is a book that contains sometimes strange images and many things we do not fully understand, it also has many things we *do* understand.

Embedded in its imagery are some of the most salutary warnings and most precious promises of all of Scripture.

Very likely, John himself did not understand some of the things he saw and wrote. The imagery in John's writing undoubtedly stemmed from the challenge of describing visions of future events — events that must have both terrified him and thrilled his soul. No doubt, God had a meaning in some of the visions that were to be revealed only as the story of the passing ages unfolded. Alternating simplest truth with mystical symbolism, Revelation is a book of undiluted *optimism* for God's people, assuring us again and again that, come what may, we are under God's protection, with a life of everlasting blessedness ahead.

It is also a book of the "wrath of God," in which scenes alternating between earth and heaven contrast the joys of the redeemed with the agonies of the lost. And oh how we need to be reminded of that in this careless and godless generation!

Revelation Is a Book That Asks for Reverent Humility

A thing that strikes one who browses around in the vast literature about the book of Revelation is the *utter dogmatism* with which so many put forth their opinions — not as opinions but as categorical statements about the meaning of even the most obscure passages, as if they know all about it and their say-so settles the matter. We think a spirit of reverent humility and openness of mind would be more becoming in those seeking to interpret a book like this.

Revelation Is a Book That Requires Balance

The book of Revelation should neither be neglected nor overly exalted above other Bible books. But it most certainly is entitled to, and will greatly reward, a reasonable share of a Christian's study and devotion. Other books of the Bible, such as Genesis, Daniel, Isaiah, 1 Corinthians, and 1 and 2 Thessalonians, to name a few, add significant insight into the interpretation of imagery in Revelation. Conversely, God has given the book of Revelation to provide insight into other passages throughout the Bible.

If we insist on understanding and explaining every detail, we may lose sight of the powerful message of the book as a whole: God is in charge of

John saw the vision recorded in the book of Revelation while banished to the island of Patmos.

history, and Jesus has won the victory that will one day be manifested in a new heaven and a new earth, where God lives with His people.

Who Wrote Revelation?

God himself wrote Revelation, according to the book's first statement. God dictated it, through Christ, by an angel, to John, who wrote it down and sent the completed book to the seven churches (1:1, 4). Modern critics see no inspired prophecy at all in the book, but only the "unbridled play of religious fantasy, clothing itself in unreal visual form." We abhor such a view.

We believe absolutely

- That the book is exactly what it itself says it is;
- That it bears the stamp of its author;
- That some of its passages are among the most superb and most precious in all the Bible;
- That its climactic grandeur makes it a fitting close to the Bible story; and
- That its glorious visions of the completed work of Christ make it a veritable roadway of God into the human soul.

The *human author,* by well-established tradition from the days of the Apostolic Fathers, and in the judgment of the great body of Christian believers, was the apostle John, the "Beloved Disciple," the most intimate earthly friend of Jesus and writer of the Gospel of John (1:1, 4, 9; 22:8; John 21:20, 24).

When Was It Written?

John had been banished to the island of Patmos (1:9; see on 1:9 and map on p. 938). This happened, according to apostolic tradition, during the persecution of Christians under Emperor Domitian, around A.D. 95. The next year John was released and permitted to return to Ephesus. The use of the past tense ("[I] was on the island of Patmos") may indicate that he saw the visions on Patmos but wrote the book after his release and his return to Ephesus, around A.D. 96. Others believe that John transcribed the visions immediately while on Patmos, in response to Jesus' command to "write" (9:11, 19).

The Historical Background of Revelation

These visions were given, and the book was written, in the lurid light of burning martyrs. The church was 66 years old. It had grown enormously. It had suffered, and was suffering, terrific persecutions.

The first imperial persecution of Christians, 30 years before this book was written, was instigated by Emperor Nero in A.D. 64–67. In that persecution many Christians were crucified, or thrown to wild beasts, or wrapped in combustible garments and burned to death while Nero laughed at the pitiful shrieks of burning men and women. Paul and Peter suffered martyrdom in Nero's persecution.

The second imperial persecution was under Emperor Domitian (A.D. 95). It was short but extremely severe. More than 40,000 Christians were tortured and killed. It was during this period of persecution in which John was banished to the island of Patmos.

The third imperial persecution, that of Trajan, was soon to begin (A.D. 98). John had lived through the first two and was now about to enter the third of Rome's efforts to blot out the Christian faith. Those were dark days for the church. And still darker days were coming (see pp. 898–900).

But persecution from without was not the only problem. The church itself, from within, was beginning to show signs of corruption and apostasy.

God gave these visions, evidently, to help prepare and steady the church for the awful days ahead, and to comfort the church with the certainty that He stands at the beginning as well as at the end of history.

We believe that this book is every bit as relevant for the modern-day church as it was for the churches of John's day. "He who has an ear, let him hear what the Spirit says to the churches. To him who overcomes, I will give the right to eat from the tree of life, which is in the paradise of God" (2:7).

Interpreting the Book of Revelation

In interpreting the book of Revelation, several things must be kept in mind:

- Revelation is full of references and allusions to the Old Testament, especially to the books of Ezekiel, Daniel, and Zechariah. We cannot read the book apart from its Old Testament background.
- It is a book of visions. As with the parables of Jesus, we must be careful not to miss the main point of John's visions by trying

to explain every last detail. We must also recognize that John is attempting to describe images from the future — images of events, places, and things that he had absolutely no frame of reference to.

- Bible prophecy, to the Western mind, has a disconcerting way of telescoping events so that one prophecy can apply to several instances that are separated in time. It is also true that many of the prophecies that have already been fulfilled — for example, prophecies concerning Christ — are clear in retrospect but were not clear ahead of time, not even to the prophets themselves (see 1 Peter 1:10). This should make us cautious.

The Main Interpretations of Revelation

There are many interpretations of the book of Revelation. The four most common are usually called the *preterist, historical, futurist,* and *idealist* interpretations. Each one has many variations, and each has its difficulties. Whatever interpretation one accepts, some details in the book require straining to fit.

The **idealist** (or **symbolic** or **spiritualizing**) interpretation separates the book entirely from any reference to historical events — whether those of John's day, or those at the time of the end, or those at any time in between. It is seen as a pictorial representation, in highly figurative language, of the great principles of divine government and of good overcoming evil, which are applicable to all times.

The **preterist** interpretation regards the book as referring entirely to its own day: Christianity's struggle with the Roman Empire. It assumes that everything was fulfilled during the period it was written and that the story was told with imagery and symbolism to hide its meaning from the late-1st-century pagans.

The **historical** interpretation sees in Revelation a prediction of the whole period of church history, from John's time to the end of the world — a sort of panorama, a series of pictures, delineating the successive steps and outstanding features of the church's struggle to final victory.

The **futurist** interpretation centers the book largely around the time of the Lord's coming and end of the world. This interpretation holds that most of the book (chaps. 4–22) reveals events that are yet to be fulfilled.

The futurist view is the view most widely held in American evangelical churches and is the primary basis for the remainder of this study on Revelation.

The Book Is in Three Parts

In Revelation 1:19 God commands John to write about three distinct time periods.

Chapter 1: "Write, therefore, what you have seen," that is, things that were in John's day (that had already taken place), including his vision of Christ.

Chapters 2–3: "What is now," represented by the seven letters to seven churches in Asia Minor. These letters outline the condition of the churches in John's day, but they can also be viewed as prefiguring the modern-day church as well as the individual believer throughout the church age. The first three chapters are, in a sense, introductory to the main body of the book that follows.

Chapters 4–22: "And what will take place thereafter" covers events yet to be revealed, from the end of the church age (4:1) to the establishment of a new heaven and new earth (21:1–27).

| Rev. 1:1–3 | THE REVELATION OF JESUS CHRIST |

The revelation of Jesus Christ . . . what must soon take place (v. 1). (See above.)

Blessed is the one who reads the words of this prophecy (v. 3). And those who hear and take to heart the words of this book. Thus the book opens. And thus it closes (22:7). Revelation is the only Bible book that pronounces this specific blessing! It is also interesting to note that John writes of a curse to those who might add or take away from the words of this book of prophecy (22:18–19).

Reading includes both reading it for ourselves and "hearing" it being read in church. "He who has an ear, let him hear what the Spirit says to the churches" is a common instruction throughout the book of Revelation. In John's day, books had to be written by hand and were scarce and expensive. People had to depend in large measure on the reading and teaching in church for their knowledge of Scripture. The invention of printing in modern times has made Bibles readily available to all—but this does not in any way eliminate the need for, and value of, the regular reading and exposition of God's Word in church services.

The Seven Beatitudes of Revelation

There are seven *blesseds* in the book:

- Blessed is the one who reads the words of this prophecy, and blessed are those who hear it and take to heart what is written in it (1:3; the Greek uses "blessed" only once in this verse).
- Blessed are the dead who die in the Lord from now on (14:13).
- Blessed is he who stays awake (for the Lord's coming) (16:15).
- Blessed are those who are invited to the wedding supper of the Lamb (19:9).
- Blessed and holy are those who have part in the first resurrection (20:6).
- Blessed is he who keeps the words of the prophecy in this book (22:7).
- Blessed are those who wash their robes (22:14).

The Number Seven in Revelation

The book of Revelation is built around the number seven.

- Seven letters to seven churches (chaps. 1 – 3)
- Seven seals and seven trumpets (chaps. 4 – 11)
- Seven bowls (chaps. 15, 16)
- Seven lampstands (1:12, 20)
- Seven stars (1:16, 20)
- Seven angels (1:20)
- Seven spirits (1:4)
- A lamb with seven horns and seven eyes (5:6)
- Seven lamps (4:5)
- Seven thunders (10:3 – 4)
- A red dragon with seven heads and seven crowns (12:1)
- A leopard-like beast with seven heads (13:1)
- A scarlet-colored beast with seven heads (17:3, 7)
- Seven hills (17:9)
- Seven kings (17:10)
- Seven beatitudes (see above)

The Number Seven in the Bible

The Bible begins with seven days of creation; it ends with a book built on sevens that tells of the ultimate destiny of that creation.

The Sabbath was the seventh day. The Levitical system of the Old Testament was built on a cycle of sevens (see p. 156).

Jericho fell after seven priests with seven trumpets marched around its walls for seven days and blew their trumpets seven times on the seventh day. Naaman dipped himself in the Jordan seven times.

Seven is a favorite number of God's. There are seven days in a week. Seven notes in Western music. Seven colors in the rainbow.

Used as often as it is, in the way it is, it must have some significance over and above its mere numerical value. Symbolically, it is thought to stand for completeness, fullness, totality, a whole — both negative and positive: the beast of Revelation 13 has seven heads, and we can be assured that it does not stand for holiness!

The Significance of Some Other Numbers

Certain other numbers are used in such a way that they are thought to be in themselves a sort of language, with meanings beyond their numerical value. Here are some of them:

- 3 — the numerical signature of God
- 4 — the numerical signature of nature, creation
- 6 — the number of incompleteness (1 less than 7); the number 666 is the number of the beast
- 7 (3 + 4) — the signature of totality
- 12 (3 x 4) — the signature of God's people
- 10 — the signature of worldly power

God's Word was intended to have the central place in church services
—then, and now, and always. It is the one thing designed by God to
hold the church true to its mission. Not talking *about* the Word, but simply reading and hearing God's Word, which is sometimes rightly called
"the Ministry of the Word."

| Rev. 1:4–8 | THE GREETING TO THE SEVEN CHURCHES |

The **seven** churches to which John has to write letters—located in
Ephesus, Smyrna, Pergamum, Thyatira, Sardis, Philadelphia, and Laodicea—were connected by a great triangular highway. They are named
in chapters 2 and 3 in clockwise geographical order, beginning with
Ephesus in the southwest, via Pergamum about 100 miles to the north,
to Laodicea, about 100 miles east of Ephesus. (See map on p. 838.)

Patmos is a small island in the Aegean, off the coast of modern Turkey, that was
used by the Romans as a place to send exiles. When John was on Patmos, it
probably looked much as some of the island still does (top). Here as elsewhere
the Crusaders left their mark: a monastery that doubled as a fort (bottom).

Apparently, each church received a complete copy of Revelation, including all seven letters (1:11).

Asia (v. 4) was a Roman province in the western part of what was then known as Asia Minor and is now Turkey. Ephesus was its main city, Pergamum its political capital.

There were many churches in Asia in John's day. These, called *the* seven churches, must have been the main centers in their respective districts. According to tradition, John lived in Ephesus, and these seven churches may have been the key churches under John's pastoral care.

Of these seven cities, only Ephesus plays a significant role elsewhere in New Testament history (Acts 18:18–19:41). Thyatira is mentioned as the home of Lydia (Acts 16:14), and we know that Paul wrote at least one letter (now lost) to Laodicea (Colossians 4:13–16). The other four cities are not mentioned elsewhere in the New Testament, but their churches were probably offshoots from Paul's work in Ephesus.

The Main Emphases of the Book

The general greeting to the seven churches contains some of the main emphases of the book as a whole.

He Who Is, and Who Was, and Who Is to Come (1:4)

One of the emphases is the eternity of God's nature.

- Him who lives for ever and ever (4:10).
- Lord God, who was, and is, and is to come (4:8).
- I am the Alpha and the Omega, the First and the Last, the Beginning and the End (21:6; 22:13).
- "I am the Alpha and the Omega," says the Lord God, "who is, and who was, and who is to come, the Almighty" (1:8).
- "I am the First and the Last. I am the Living One; I was dead, and behold I am alive for ever and ever! And I hold the keys of death and Hades" (1:17–18).

In a world where empires rise and fall, where all things die and pass away, we are reminded that God is changeless, timeless, and eternal. And we are promised by Him that His nature may be imparted to us, and that we, like Him, and by His grace, unhurt by death, may live on and on. Alive for ever and ever! Immortal youth! What a meaning it gives to life! And what a comfort to saints facing martyrdom then and now!

Christ the Ruler of the Kings of the Earth (1:5)

This affirms His unconditional supremacy over the world. It does not always seem to be so. Kings and rulers have defied and continue to defy Christ with blatant, brazen boldness. Even today monsters from hell walk the earth as rulers of men. But their doom is certain.

Christ will rule the kingdom that Satan once offered and Christ refused (Matthew 4:8–10)—but he will have it in His way, not in Satan's way. The redeemed of all ages, souls in Paradise and saints now living, are longing for that happy day. It will come, as sure as the morning. Christ is on the throne, even when things look darkest. Let us never forget this.

He Who Has Freed Us from Our Sins by His Blood (1:5)

Another emphasis of this book is that we are saved by the blood of Christ.

- "With your [Christ's] blood you purchased men for God" (5:9).
- "They overcame him [Satan] by the blood of the Lamb" (12:11).
- "These are they who . . . have washed their robes and made them white in the blood of the Lamb" (7:14).
- "Blessed are those who wash their robes, that they may have the right to the tree of life" (22:14).

There are fastidious intellectuals who rebel at the thought of salvation that involves blood. But it is an unbroken biblical teaching, emphasized again and again in the New Testament. And how it touches our hearts! How we love and adore Him for it, now and through the endless ages of eternity!

To Him Be Glory and Power for Ever and Ever (1:6)

Revelation is filled with doxologies of praise to God.

- "You are worthy, our Lord and God, to receive glory and honor and power" (4:11).
- "Worthy is the Lamb . . . to receive . . . glory and praise!" (5:12).
- "To him who sits on the throne and to the Lamb be praise and honor and glory and power, for ever and ever!" (5:13; 7:10, 12).
- "Great and marvelous are your deeds. . . . Just and true are your ways, King of the ages" (15:2–3).
- "Hallelujah! Salvation and glory and power belong to our God. . . . Hallelujah! . . . Hallelujah! . . . Hallelujah! For our Lord God Almighty reigns. Let us rejoice and be glad and give him glory!" (19:1–7).

The 24 elders and the four living creatures (see 4:4–11), 100 million angels, and vast multitudes of redeemed people from all nations, in voices like the ocean's roar, make heaven resound with praise to God. Why not have it in our churches—singing, not out of habit or for entertainment, but to His praise and His glory!

He Is Coming with the Clouds (1:7)

Another keynote of the book is the Lord's coming.

- Every eye will see him, even those who pierced him (1:7).
- "Hold on . . . until I come" (2:25).
- "I will come like a thief" (3:3).
- "I am coming soon. Hold on to what you have" (3:11).
- "Behold, I come like a thief!" Blessed is he who stays awake" (16:15).
- "Behold, I am coming soon!" (22:7).
- "Behold, I am coming soon! My reward is with me" (22:12).
- "Yes, I am coming soon" (22:20).
- Amen. Come, Lord Jesus (22:20).

One of the first statements in the book is "He is coming." The Lord's last words in the book are "Yes, I am coming soon."

Christ is coming again in the grand consummation of human history. He will come "with the clouds," in power and glory, visible to all the world. A day of distress and terror for those who have rejected him. A day of unspeakable joy for those who are His.

Jesus Himself said these same things over and over (Matthew 13:42, 50; 24:30, 51; 25:30; 26:64; Luke 21:25–28). And in the book of Acts we read, after Jesus ascended in a cloud, the angel's promise was heard, "he will come back in the same way" (1:9, 11).

Nearly 2000 years have passed, and He has yet to come. But against the background of eternity, 1000 years is as a day. Jesus came into the world at the appointed time. He will come again at the time of the Father's choosing. One day He will come, with catastrophic suddenness.

"The time is near." So the book opens (1:3). And so it closes (22:10). It may be nearer than we think. And with John we say, "Amen. Come, Lord Jesus" (22:20).

Rev. 1:9–20 CHRIST IN THE MIDST OF THE CHURCHES

Patmos (v. 9), the island to which John was banished in the persecution of Domitian and where he received these visions, is in the Aegean Sea, about 60 miles southwest of Ephesus and about 150 miles east of Athens. (See map on p. 838.) It is 10 miles long and six miles wide, volcanic, rocky, and mostly treeless. It was one of many places to which the Romans banished exiles.

The Lord's Day (v. 10) evidently was the "first day of the week" (Acts 20:7; 1 Corinthians 16:2), the day on which Christians met for worship in commemoration of the Lord's resurrection. The seventh day, the Sabbath, had been kept in commemoration of God's creative work; the first day, the Lord's Day, was set aside to keep forever fresh in people's minds the story of the most momentous day of all history, the one event that gives meaning to human life: Jesus' resurrection from the dead.

Angels in the Book of Revelation

Angels play a large part in directing the panorama and scenery of the visions, and in the writing of the book. Altogether we find 27 references to the activities of angels in Revelation.

- An angel dictated the book to John (1:2; 22:16).
- Each of the seven churches had an angel (1:20; 2:1, etc.).
- An angel called out about the sealed book (5:2).
- 100 million angels sang praise to the Lamb (5:11).
- Four angels were given power to hurt the earth.
- An angel sealed the elect (7:1–4).
- The angels fell down on their faces before God (7:11).
- An angel was used in answering prayers of the saints (8:3–5).
- Seven angels sounded the seven trumpets (8:6–7, etc.).
- An angel of the abyss was king of the locust army (9:1–11).
- Four angels loosed 200 million Euphratean horsemen (9:15–16).
- An angel had the open book, announcing the end (10:1–2, 6).
- Michael and his angels warred with the dragon and his angels (12:7).
- A flying angel proclaimed the Gospel to the nations (14:6).
- Another flying angel proclaimed the fall of Babylon (14:8).
- An angel pronounced doom on the beast's followers (14:9–10).
- An angel announced the harvest of the earth (14:15).
- An angel announced the vintage of the earth (14:18–19).
- Seven angels had the seven last plagues (15:1).
- An angel announced judgment on Babylon (17:1, 5).
- An angel again announced the fall of Babylon (18:2).
- An angel had a part in dealing Babylon its death-blow (18:21).
- An angel presided over the destruction of the beast (19:17).
- An angel bound Satan (20:12).
- An angel showed John the new Jerusalem (21:9).
- 12 angels guarded the 12 gates of the new Jerusalem (21:19).
- An angel told John not to worship him (22:9).

The word "angel" literally means "messenger." As used in the Bible, it applies mostly to supernatural beings of the unseen world, used as messengers in the service of God or Satan. Angels also played an important role in the life of Jesus (see p. 539).

The "angels" of the seven churches (2:1, etc.) are thought by some to have been messengers sent by the churches to visit John on Patmos. Others think they are the pastors of the churches, or the guardian angels of the churches, or heavenly representatives of the churches.

In the Spirit (v. 10; 4:2; 17:3; 21:10) seems to mean that his faculties were wholly taken over by the Spirit of God.

Write (v. 11). John is clearly commanded to write.

- Write on a scroll what you see (1:11).
- Write therefore what you have seen, what is now and what will take place later (1:19).
- To Ephesus . . . write. To Smyrna . . . write. To Pergamum . . . write. To Thyatira . . . write. To Sardis . . . write. To Philadelphia . . . write. To Laodicea . . . write. (2:1, 8, 12, 18; 3:1, 7, 14).
- Write, "Blessed are the dead who die in the Lord" (14:13).
- Write, "Blessed are those who are invited to the wedding supper" (19:9).

Thus it is emphasized, again and again, in the strongest possible manner, that God Himself commanded that the book be written, and that He Himself told John exactly what to write.

The Vision of Christ (1:13–18)

John sees Jesus, his friend and his Lord, in a breathtaking vision.

- His robe and sash are the garments worn by the high priests of the Old Testament. Christ is risen and is in heaven where He performs His ministry of intercession on our behalf (Hebrews 4:14; 7:25).
- He holds the angels of the churches in His hand.
- His hair is white as snow, his eyes are like a blazing fire.
- His face is like the sun shining in all its brilliance, His feet are like bronze glowing in a furnace, and His voice is like the sound of rushing waters.
- Out of His mouth comes a sharp, double-edged sword (the Word).

This is how the gentle Savior of the Gospels now presents Himself to His church: girded for battle, a warrior, a conqueror, with desperate and powerful enemies to encounter. It is a bid to His church for confidence in His leadership. It is also a stern and earnest warning to His church, with its growing signs of corruption and apostasy, that He will not tolerate half-heartedness or disloyalty.

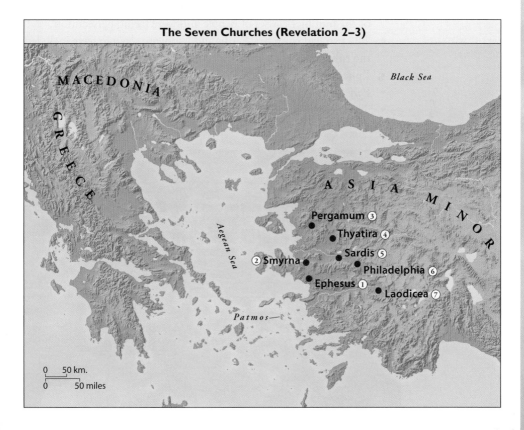

The Seven Churches (Revelation 2–3)

Letters to the Seven Churches, Revelation 2 to 3

In the seven letters to the churches of Asia, John, under Jesus' direction, gives heavenly appraisals of earthly churches.

Each letter consisted of the whole book of Revelation, with a brief special message to each church by way of introduction. We may assume that seven copies of the book were made, and one sent to each city. Each church could thus read the Lord's estimate, not only of itself, but also of the other churches.

In addition to being real letters to real churches in John's day, the letters also have current application. Today's churches should evaluate themselves with the help of these seven letters. This internal review should also extend to us as individuals. How we should all pray that, under close and honest examination, we more resemble Smyrna and Philadelphia! There is nothing hidden from God—He knows where we stand probably more accurately than we do. God's promises to the seven churches can be received by each of us if we recognize our shortcomings and become right with Him!

The Character of the Churches

Two were very good: Smyrna and Philadelphia.
Two were very bad: Sardis and Laodicea.
Three were partly good, partly bad: Ephesus, Pergamum, Thyatira.

- The two good churches, Smyrna and Philadelphia, were composed of the humbler classes of people and were facing persecution.
- The two bad churches, Sardis and Laodicea, seem to have included the ruling classes, nominally Christian, but pagan in lifestyle.
- Ephesus was orthodox in teaching but losing its first love.
- Pergamum was faithful to the name of Christ but did permit heresy.
- Thyatira was growing in zeal but tolerated the heresy of Jezebel.

Roman forum at Smyrna. In John's vision the challenges of martyrdom and poverty faced by the church at Smyrna are addressed.

The seven letters all follow the same pattern, consisting of seven elements. This pattern can be clearly seen in the letter to Ephesus, a great and powerful church but one that was losing its zeal for Christ and one another:

The Seven Elements in Each of the Seven Letters		
I.	Opening instruction to John that occurs in all seven letters.	"To the angel of the church in Ephesus write: ..."
2.	The title or aspect of Christ that is relevant for each particular church's situation.	"These are the words of him who holds the seven stars in his right hand."
3.	Christ's commendation of each church. (Sardis and Laodicea received none.)	"I know your deeds, your hard work and your perseverance."
4.	Christ's condemnation or criticism of each church. (Smyrna and Philadelphia received none.)	"Yet I hold this against you...."
5.	Christ's correction or instructions to each church.	"Remember ... and repent...."
6.	Christ's admonition. Identical for all seven churches.	"He who has an ear, let him hear what the Spirit says to the churches."
7.	Christ's promise to each church.	"To him who overcomes I will give the right to eat from the tree of life."

The elements of the letters to the other churches can be summarized as follows—excluding the opening instruction (1) and the admonition (6 or 7):

To **Smyrna**, a poor, suffering church facing martyrdom:

2. "These are the words of him who is the First and the Last, who died and came to life again."
3. "I know your afflictions and your poverty—yet you are rich."
4. Smyrna received no condemnation or correction.
5. "Do not be afraid of what you are about to suffer. . . . Be faithful, even unto the point of death, and I will give you the crown of life."
7. "He who overcomes will not be hurt at all by the second death."

To **Pergamum**, a church that tolerated teachers of immorality:

2. "These are the words of him who has the sharp, double-edged sword."
3. "I know where you live—where Satan has his throne. Yet you remain true to my name."
4. "Nevertheless, I have a few things against you. You have people there who hold to the teaching of Balaam. Likewise, you also have those who hold to the teaching of the Nicolaitans."
5. "Repent therefore! Otherwise I will soon come to you and will fight against them with the sword of my mouth."
7. "To him who overcomes, I will give some of the hidden manna [and] a white stone with a new name written on it. . . ."

To **Thyatira**, a church growing in zeal but tolerating Jezebel:

2. "These are the words of the Son of God, whose eyes are like blazing fire. . . ."
3. "I know your deeds, your love and faith, your service and perseverance. . . ."
4. "Nevertheless . . . you tolerate that woman Jezebel, who calls herself a prophetess."
5. "To you who do not hold to her teaching . . . hold on to what you have until I come."
6. "To him who overcomes, I will give authority over the nations . . . [and] also . . . the morning star."

To **Sardis**, a church that had a reputation of being alive but was dead:

2. "These are the words of him who holds the seven spirits of God and the seven stars."
3. Sardis received no commendation or correction.
4. "I know your deeds; you have a reputation of being alive, but you are dead."
5. "Wake up! Strengthen what remains and is about to die. . . ."
6. "He who overcomes will . . . be dressed in white. I will never blot out his name from the book of life."

To **Philadelphia**, a humble and faithful church:

2. "These are the words of him who is holy and true, who holds the key of David. What he opens no one can shut, and what he shuts no one can open."
3. "I know your deeds. . . . you have kept my word and have not denied my name."
4. Philadelphia received no condemnation.
5. "I am coming soon. Hold on to what you have, so that no one will take your crown."
6. "Him who overcomes I will make a pillar in the temple of my God."

To **Laodicea**, the lukewarm "rich" church:

2. "These are the words of the Amen, the faithful and true witness, the ruler of God's creation."
3. Laodicea received no commendation.
4. "I know your deeds, that you are neither cold nor hot. I wish that you were either one or the other."
5. "So be earnest and repent."
6. "To him who overcomes, I will give the right to sit with me on my throne. . . ."

"He who has an ear, let him hear what the Spirit says to the churches." Thus closes each letter with an admonition from the Lord, warning the churches that they had better take seriously what He is saying to them.

We all need to listen.

(For more on the city of Ephesus, see p. 728.)

Ephesus had a population of almost a quarter million people. It was a true metropolis and the commercial center of Asia Minor. The temple of Artemis in Ephesus was one of the Seven Wonders of the Ancient World.

There, 40 years before, Paul had done his most successful work (A.D. 54–57). So many people became converts to Christ that almost overnight the church became one of the most powerful influences in the city and soon one of the most famous churches in the world. It became the mother church of Asia Minor.

It is said that Timothy, after the death of Paul, spent most of his time in Ephesus and suffered martyrdom there under Domitian, in the same persecution that sent John to Patmos.

John spent his old age in Ephesus, and if he was no longer an active pastor due to his age, as the last surviving apostle of Christ he must have been a dominating influence among pastors. While in Ephesus, John wrote his Gospel, three letters, and possibly the book of Revelation (after his return from Patmos).

Three of Paul's letters relate to Ephesus: Ephesians and 1 and 2 Timothy. And it is thought that possibly the two letters of Peter and that of Jude originated in that region.

Ephesus, about halfway between Jerusalem and Rome, was the approximate geographic center of the Roman Empire. And in John's lifetime it had become the approximate geographic and numerical center of the Christian population of the world.

About 10 years after the death of John, the Emperor Trajan sent Pliny into the Asia Minor region to investigate whether to persecute Christians. Pliny wrote back to Trajan that Christians had become so numerous that pagan temples were almost deserted.

In many cities of the region, the Christian churches included large and influential elements of the population, and Ephesus was the queen church of them all.

It had been some 65 years since Pentecost, the birthday of the church in Jerusalem. The church everywhere had seen phenomenal growth. But signs of corruption were beginning to appear—and that, we think, is one of the things that called forth the book of Revelation.

The church in Ephesus (v. 1). It was before the days of church buildings. They had to meet in halls, or homes, or wherever they could. Not one great, central First Church of Ephesus, but many, perhaps hundreds, of small congregations, each under its own pastoral leadership. Yet the letter is addressed to "the church in Ephesus." Hundreds of congregations, yet one church.

Him who holds the seven stars in his right hand (v. 1). The seven stars are the emblem of His power. Perhaps this image is intended as a suggestive warning that the church was becoming too proud of its prestige and was glorying in what was of little use to its real mission.

The **"false apostles"** (v. 2). These, evidently, were men who claimed to have known Christ and to have received authority from Him for their teaching, in their effort to harmonize the immoral indulgences of idol worship with the Christian faith.

Forsaken your first love (vv. 4–5). This was their failing. Their zeal for Christ was cooling off. They no longer loved Him as they once did. They were becoming indifferent, half-hearted—not yet lukewarm, like the Laodicean church (see 3:16), but headed in that direction. This hurt Christ. They receive a stinging rebuke and are warned to repent (v. 5), else their "lampstand will be removed." It has indeed. The site of Ephesus is deserted today.

The **"Nicolaitans"** (v. 6) are thought to have been a sect who advocated licentiousness as the proper way of life.

These false teachers had caused great trouble in the church. The Ephesian pastors, it seems, had as a body stood patiently and solidly against their teaching, for which they were commended (vv. 2–3).

The tree of life (v. 7). Those who overcome the allurements of false teaching and natural temptations to fleshly indulgence and worldly ease are promised access to the Tree of Life.

While the Ephesian church, as a church, has perished, the promise of the Tree of Life still holds for individuals in any church who overcome.

The Tree of Life is first mentioned as a special tree in the Garden of Eden (Genesis 2:2, 22, 25). This tree appears again in Revelation 22:2 as a tree which bears everlasting, health-producing fruit.

Rev. 2:8–11 | THE LETTER TO SMYRNA

For Smyrna, a suffering church, Christ gives John no words of fault, but only loving comfort.

The church in Smyrna was composed of poor people, with nothing like either the numbers or the prestige of the church in Ephesus. They were "poor, but rich" (v. 9). In other words, their faithful preaching of the Gospel brought them great persecution and tribulation. With this came material poverty. Jesus assures them that they have great riches in heavenly storage.

Surprisingly, the church in Smyrna grew and flourished during this period of horrific persecution. This "good fruit" is clear evidence that God was at the center of their works.

Who died and came to life again (v. 8). This Christ says to those facing martyrdom. He reminds them that He had already suffered what they are about to suffer—and that they too, shortly, like Him, will be *alive forevermore!*

I know the slander of those who say they are Jews and are not (v. 9). The church of Smyrna experienced persecution from internal as well as external sources. External persecution came from people who openly rejected the Gospel, including governing officials and common

Smyrna

Smyrna (modern Izmir, Turkey) was an important port on the west coast of Asia Minor, with a well-protected harbor, and the natural terminal of a great inland trade route up the Hermus River valley. It was a rival of Ephesus, with the proud tradition that it had been the birthplace of the great Greek poet Homer, the author of *The Iliad* and *The Odyssey*.

Smyrna was destroyed by the Lydians in 627 B.C. and for three centuries was little more than a village. It was refounded in the middle of the 4th century B.C. and rapidly became the chief city of Asia.

A common danger, the aggression of Antiochus the Great of Syria, had united Rome and Smyrna at the end of the 3rd century B.C. In A.D. 26, Smyrna appealed to this treaty when it petitioned Tiberius to allow the community to build a temple to his deity. Permission was granted, and Smyrna built the second Asian temple to the emperor (the first one having been built in Pergamum).

Smyrna was famous for science, medicine, and the majesty of its buildings. Apollonius of Tyana refers to her "crown of porticoes," a circle of beautiful public buildings that ringed the summit of Mount Pagos like a diadem; hence John's reference (Revelation 2:10). Polycarp, Smyrna's bishop who was martyred in A.D. 155, had been a disciple of John.

citizens. Internal persecution came from Jews who superficially accepted the Gospel and became church members but had not really accepted Christ and the New Testament teachings in their hearts. These false teachers caused confusion and strife within the church body because they wanted to hold onto many of the Old Testament traditions — including the requirement that new believers become physically circumcised. Romans 2:29 says, "A man is a Jew [or Christian] if he is one inwardly; and circumcision is circumcision of the heart, by the Spirit." Physical circumcision does not make one a Christian. Jesus designates these false Christians as being of the "synagogue of Satan."

Persecution for ten days (v. 10). This may mean a persecution of brief duration. Or it may refer to the persecution of Trajan that was about to begin, in which the famous Bishop Ignatius was martyred, and that may have hit Smyrna extra hard. Or the "ten days" may prefigure the 10 imperial persecutions (see p. 898).

The crown of life (v. 10). The promise to Ephesus was "the tree of life" (v. 7). Here, to Smyrna, it is the "crown of life" (v. 10), and the promise that they will not be "hurt by the second death" (v. 11; 21:8).

While these promises were intended for individuals who "overcome," in another sense Smyrna, as a city, has been given a crown of life: it has survived through all the centuries. It is now the largest city in what once was Asia Minor, with a population of more than 1.7 million.

| Rev. 2:12–17 | **THE LETTER TO PERGAMUM** |

The church in Pergamum was faithful to the name of Christ, even to the point of martyrdom (v. 13), but it was tolerant of false teachers — probably the same type of false teachers as those in Ephesus. Yet it seems that while in Ephesus the pastors as a body stood solidly against the false teachers, here in Pergamum the pastors, though not themselves holding to the false teaching, tolerated within their ranks those who did. The false teaching proclaimed the right of Christians to indulge in pagan immoralities. The Lord, while commending the church for its faithfulness to His name, nevertheless presents Himself as "Him who has the sharp, double-edged sword." They had better beware—the Lord is not pleased with His church when it tolerates sinful indulgence.

Where Satan has his throne (v. 13). Pergamum was a seat of emperor worship, where incense was offered before the statue of the "divine emperor." Often, Christians who refused to offer incense were put to death. There were also the temples of Zeus and of Asclepius, who was worshiped in the form of a serpent, a symbol of Satan. Beside these, it was also a stronghold

Remains of the altar of Zeus at Pergamum.

of Balaamite and Nicolaitan teachers. Thus, as a notorious center of heathenism and wickedness, the city was called "Satan's throne."

And Satan, who was about to persecute Christians in Smyrna (2:10), had already begun in Pergamum (v. 13).

The teaching of Balaam (v. 14). In Numbers 25 we read how the Israelites indulged in sexual immorality with Moabite women, and in Numbers 31:16 it is said that they did this on the advice of Balaam. So, in Pergamum, devotees of heathen practices, who had infiltrated the ranks of Christians and were advising them to participate in the sexual vices of pagan worship, were nicknamed Balaamites. Evidently they had quite a following.

The hidden manna (v. 17). The promise to those who overcome (true believers in Christ Jesus) is "hidden manna" and a "white stone" with a "new name" known only to its owner. The hidden manna may be the fruit of the Tree of Life (22:2). White stones were often used in ancient legal courts to signify a judgment of acquittal. Praise God that through Christ's death on the cross, He has presented the white stones with our names on them. (For the presence of white in the book of Revelation, see p. 847.)

| Rev. 2:18–29 | **THE LETTER TO THYATIRA** |

The church at Thyatira is a church of compromise. The people have some good qualities. They are noted for their "love and faith, . . . service and perseverance." They are growing in zeal, "their last works are more than their first" (v. 19)—just the opposite of Ephesus, which has "forsaken its first love" (2:4).

But, like Pergamum, they were tolerant of false teachers, only worse—they tolerated Jezebel in their midst.

Who Was Jezebel?

Thyatira was famous for its magnificent temple of Artemis (another name for the goddess Diana). It is thought that Jezebel may have been

---

Thyatira

Thyatira was perhaps the least illustrious of the seven cities of Revelation. Its history was uneventful, and it is scarcely mentioned by ancient writers. Coinage suggests that, lying as it did on a great highway linking two river valleys, Thyatira was a garrison town for many centuries.

The city was a center of commerce, and the records preserve references to more trade guilds than those listed for any other Asian city. Lydia, whom Paul met in Philippi, was a Thyatiran seller of "turkey red," a purple dye for which Thyatira was famous (Acts 16:14).

Necessity for guild membership in a trading community must have strengthened the temptation to compromise. Thus it is appropriate to find a woman, named (or nicknamed?) after Jezebel, the princess who by marrying Ahab sealed his trading partnership with the Phoenicians, leading a party of compromise in the Thyatiran church (Revelation 2:20–21). Thyatira played no significant part in the later history of the church.

a prominent woman devotee of Diana, with a gift for leadership, who had a following of influential people in the city and who, attracted to the growing cause of Christianity, attached herself to the church, militantly insisting, however, on the right to teach and practice licentious indulgence and claiming inspiration for her teaching.

She was called "Jezebel" because, like Jezebel the devilish wife of Ahab, who had introduced the abominations of Astarte worship into Israel (1 Kings 16), she was introducing the same vile practices into the Christian church.

Not all of the pastors in Thyatira accepted her teaching. But in an attempt to be tolerant, and thinking that she might be a help in winning the whole city to the name of Christ, they accepted her as a fellow pastor.

With that the Lord was greatly displeased. And, in a stinging rebuke He presented Himself "with eyes like fire and feet like brass" (v. 18). No trifling with such a church!

Satan's so-called deep secrets (v. 24). This is the third mention of Satan in the seven letters. In Smyrna, Satan directed the casting of Christians into prison (2:9–10). In Pergamum, "Satan's throne," he was persecuting the church and corrupting it from within by false teachings (2:13–14). Here in Thyatira, Jezebel's teachings were known as "Satan's so-called deep secrets" (v. 24). Later he is mentioned as the enemy of the church in Philadelphia (3:9).

God in all His great mercy has given those people who follow Jezebel's teaching "time to repent." But they are unwilling. Their punishment will be suffering and the death of their children.

The morning star (v. 28). Those who "overcome" are promised the "morning star." Jesus Himself is the Morning Star (22:16). One of the earliest prophecies concerning the Messiah calls Him a "Star" (Numbers 24:17). Those who resist Satan will have no other burdens. These faithful believers are instructed to hold on until Christ returns. By faithfulness, not by compromise, will the church attain true leadership.

Rev. 3:1–6 | THE LETTER TO SARDIS

Sardis was a "dead" church that was alive in name only—although there were a few who "have not soiled their clothes" (v. 4). To such a church, Christ presented Himself as the Empowered One, who has the "seven Spirits of God" (v. 1) and can remove them from heaven's roll.

There are people in all types of churches today who call themselves Christians but who do not know what it means to become a new creature in Christ Jesus (2 Corinthians 5:17). This may be the reason that thousands of people are leaving "dead" churches today and returning to Bible-based, Gospel-preaching churches which are alive with the Spirit of Christ.

I will never blot out his name from the book of life (v. 5). True believers can rest assured that their name will remain in the Book of Life and that Christ will be their advocate before God and all the host of heaven. The Book of Life records that our citizenship in heaven is confirmed.

Sardis

Sardis, near the junction of the roads from central Asia Minor, Ephesus, Smyrna, and Pergamum, was the capital of Lydia under its last king, Croesus, and the seat of the governor after the Persian conquest.

Sardis was famous for arts and crafts and was the first center to mint gold and silver coinage. So wealthy were the Lydian kings that Croesus became a byword for wealth. Unfortunately, Croesus also became a legend for pride and presumptuous arrogance, when his attack on Persia led to the fall of Sardis and the eclipse of his kingdom. Cyrus and the Persians captured the citadel in a surprise attack in 549 B.C., as did the Romans three centuries later, which may have provided the imagery for John's warning in Revelation 3:3 ("I will come like a thief"). The great earthquake of A.D. 17 ruined Sardis physically and financially. The Romans contributed 10 million sesterces in relief, an indication of the damage done, but the city never recovered.

The Seven Spirits (Revelation 3:1)

- Seven spirits shared in the greeting to the churches (1:4).
- Christ Himself dictated the seven letters (1:19), yet each letter was what the Spirit said (2:7).
- Later we see that seven spirits were before the throne (4:5), and that the Lamb's seven eyes were the seven spirits (5:6).
- The seven spirits seem to represent the sevenfold, or complete, operation of the Holy Spirit, the Spirit of Christ, the Spirit of God, all one and the same Spirit, in the fullness of His power—the form in which Christ works in and with His churches in the age between His first coming and His second coming.

The Presence of White in Revelation

- Jesus' head was "white" as snow (1:14).
- "I will give him a white stone with a new name written on it" (2:17).
- "They will walk with me, dressed in white" (3:4).
- He who overcomes will be dressed in "white" (3:5).
- Heaven's citizens will be clothed in "white" (3:18).
- The 24 elders were dressed in "white" (4:4).
- The martyrs wore "white" robes (6:11).
- Redeemed multitudes were arrayed in "white" robes (7:9).
- Robes made "white" in the blood of the lamb (7:14).
- The Lord will come on a "white" horse (19:11).
- His armies, clothed in "white," will be on "white" horses (19:14).

White is the color of dazzling light, in opposition to darkness and night. It may reflect purity and innocence, but more often joy and triumph. God dwells in light unapproachable (1 Timothy 6:16). Jesus' garments in the Transfiguration were white (Mark 9:3).

Rev. 3:7–13 | THE LETTER TO PHILADELPHIA

The church in Philadelphia was a humble but faithful church, content to exemplify the life of Jesus in the midst of a pagan and corrupt society. The name "Philadelphia" means "brotherly love." They were lovers of

God's Word and intent on keeping it. They were greatly beloved of the Lord—He speaks not a word of reproof to them.

An open door that no one can shut (v. 8). God had warned the churches of Ephesus and Sardis against being proud of their influential standing. Here He cautions the church in Philadelphia not to be discouraged because they "have little strength" (perhaps referring to a small church membership), for God is not dependent on worldly prestige.

Kept from trial (v. 10). The church in Smyrna had been told that they were to suffer persecution (2:10). The church in Philadelphia is given the promise that they will be kept from suffering. Both were faithful churches. However, God does not deal with all in the same way, but with each as He Himself knows best, beyond our understanding until we reach the other shore.

The new name (v. 12). In 2:17, a "new name" seemed to refer to unimaginable joys to be realized in heaven. Here, he that overcomes will receive God's own name. It is a sign of ownership and a mark of citizen-

Byzantine church remains at Philadelphia. The church at Philadelphia was commended for its humility and faithfulness.

ship. In the same way, followers of the beast receive the mark of their master (13:16–17). Each of us belongs either to the Lord or to the beast.

Rev. 3:14–22 | THE LETTER TO LAODICEA

The church of Laodicea was a lukewarm church. Its members were materially prosperous, but God tells them that He sees them as spiritually wretched, miserable, poor, blind, and naked.

Spit you out of my mouth (v. 16). A pretty strong expression of indignant disapproval of the lukewarm church. From this statement one would think that Christ prefers outright opposition to lukewarmness. Laodicea has been spewed out of his mouth.

I stand at the door and knock (v. 20). This is a strange picture: Christ Himself on the outside, asking to be let in to one of His own churches. In measure, it is true of many churches of today, operating in the name of Christ but with Christ Himself little in evidence.

Sit with me on my throne (v. 21). That is, share with Christ the glory of His kingdom. The unfailing repetition in every letter that final

---

Laodicea

Laodicea was a wealthy city in Asia Minor founded by Antiochus II (261–246 B.C.). It lay on one of the great Asian trade routes, which ensured its great commercial prosperity (gained, in part, at the expense of Colosse, when traffic was rerouted from that city and through Laodicea instead). Laodicea was a leading banking center. In 51 B.C., Cicero, en route for his Cilician province, cashed drafts there.

It was no doubt the rich banking firms that financed the reconstruction of the city after the great earthquake of A.D. 60 virtually destroyed it. Laodicea refused the Roman Senate's earthquake relief. She was "rich and increased with goods" and had "need of nothing" (Revelation 3:17).

The Lycus Valley produced a glossy black wool, the source of black cloaks and carpets for which the city was famous. Laodicea was also the home of a medical school and the manufacture of collyrium, a famous eye-salve (3:17–18). The scornful imagery of the apocalyptic letter to Laodicea is obviously based on these activities. It also has reference to the emetic qualities of the soda-laden warm water from nearby Hierapolis, whose thermal springs ran into the Maeander River. Laodicea's water supply came from Hierapolis and most likely arrived lukewarm.

blessedness is only for those who overcome seems to imply that many who had started in the Christian way were, one way or another, falling by the wayside.

Smyrna and Philadelphia, the two cities with good churches, are still flourishing cities today (Izmir and Alasehir in Turkey). Sardis and Laodicea, the two cities with bad churches, are now deserted and uninhabited sites.

The Typical Significance of the Seven Churches

The seven churches may have been chosen as representing a fair cross-section of churches of that generation. They may also be typical, in varying degrees, of churches in all generations, in varying stages of maturity and apostasy, infiltrated to varying degrees by worldly traditions, each church largely the product of its leadership, with varying proportions of faithful leaders and faithful saints, and many congregations a pitiful mixture of church and world, of true and false.

The seven churches may also be symbolic references to the individual believer, who is a temple of the Holy Spirit (1-Corinthians 6:19). Perhaps the conditions of the seven churches could also apply to the "Christian" or "not so Christian" walk of each individual church member—for we are many parts that form one body (1-Corinthians 12:12). It is the individual member within these churches ("He who has an ear") to whom Jesus is speaking. It is the individual church member who must "overcome." Jesus says, "To him who overcomes":

- "I will give the right to eat from the tree of life which is in the paradise of God" (2:7).
- I "will not be hurt at all by the second death" (2:11).
- "I will give some of the hidden manna. I will also give a white stone with a new name written on it, known only to Him who receives it" (2:17).
- "I will give authority over the nations—'He will rule them with an iron scepter; he will dash them to pieces like pottery'—just as I have received authority from my Father. I will also give him the morning star" (2: 26–28).
- I "will, like them [the worthy believers of Sardis] be dressed in white. I will never blot out his name from the book of life, but will acknowledge his name before my Father and his angels" (3:5–6).
- "I will make a pillar in the temple of my God. Never again will he leave it. I will write on him the name of my God and the name of the city of my God, the new Jerusalem, which is coming down out of heaven from my God; and I will also write on him my new name" (3:12).
- "I [Jesus] will give the right to sit with me on my throne, just as I overcame and sat down with my Father on his throne" (3:21).

Glory to God! May we all be worthy!

There is an abrupt shift in setting between chapters 3 and 4, from the seven churches in Asia Minor to God's throne in heaven.

At the beginning of the vision of the horrible disasters to come, God reassures His church through John that He is on the throne, in control, regardless of what may happen (chap. 4) and that the terrible things that are about to happen are the final stage of the redemptive work of Jesus, who is the only one worthy to complete what He has begun (chap. 5).

Preterist interpreters see in chapters 4 and 5 an interlude before the appearance of the first rider (on the white horse) in chapter 6, which is the victorious Roman army on its way to Jerusalem in A.D. 67. The remainder of the book then tells in cryptic form the rest of what had happened in John's own lifetime.

Historical interpreters also see an interlude in these chapters, before the history of the church after John's time begins in chapter 6.

Futurist interpreters believe that at the end of chapter 3, the rapture of the church takes place: "Come up here" (4:1). The church is mentioned 16 times in chapters 1–3 but not at all beyond this point in the rest of the book. The period that follows, beginning with chapter 4 and ending with the Battle of Armageddon (19:19) and the 1000-year reign of Christ on earth (the Millennium; chap. 20), covers a terrible seven-year period at the time of the end referred to as the Great Tribulation (7:14; also Matthew 24:21 and Revelation 2:22 KJV). These seven years are the same as the 70th set of seven years the prophet Daniel spoke about (see under Daniel 9:27).

The Rapture is a term that refers to the visible and audible coming of Jesus Christ to call bodily out of this world every born-again believer (first the believing dead, then the living believers). The Rapture is expected to occur in an instant, "in the twinkling of an eye" (see also 1 Corinthians 15:51–54, 1 Thessalonians 4:16–17).

Chapters 4 and 5 seem to detail the events that occur in *heaven* after the church is raptured, and chapters 6–18 the events that occur on the *earth* after the church is raptured. It is the same event told from two different vantage points.

The Throne of the Creator, vv. 2–3

The Holy Spirit takes complete control of John and presents him with a vision of events taking place in heaven. The first thing John sees in heaven is God Himself on His throne. His form is not described, except that He had the appearance of jasper and carnelian. In 21:11 jasper is called a stone "clear as crystal," perhaps a diamond. Carnelian is red, the color of fire—perhaps the fire of His righteous wrath. Thus God appears as clear, dazzling white, shaded with red, under a rainbow of emerald green—an attempt to describe the indescribable, the God who "lives in unapproachable light" (1 Timothy 6:16).

The **flashes of lightning, rumblings and peals of thunder** (v. 5) denote the majesty and power of God. The **seven lamps** are a visual representation of the Holy Spirit in His complete working. The **sea of glass, clear as crystal** (v. 6) is in contrast to the usual biblical image of the sea as representing the tumultuous, rebellious nations opposed to God (see 21:1: there will no longer be any "sea" on the new earth); the sea of glass, which reflects His light and splendor, in this interpretation represents the calmness and peace of God's rule.

The 24 Elders, v. 4

Most interpreters consider the 24 elders to represent all of God's people glorified: 12 patriarchs and 12 apostles, signifying the union of God's people in the Old Testament and New Testament. John observes the 24 elders as having their crowns in this scene. We know from Luke 14:14 that the believers "will be repaid [crowned] at the resurrection of the righteous," and when the Chief Shepherd appears, they will receive the crown of glory that will never fade away (1 Peter 5:4). The elders lay their crowns at Christ's feet (vv. 10–11).

Others see the elders as heavenly counterparts of the earthly church. Still other Bible students regard them, like the living creatures in the following verses, as a distinct class of heavenly beings rather than redeemed human beings, because in the doxologies that follow they seem to be separate from, rather than a part of, the multitudes of redeemed saints. This latter view is thought to be least likely, as elders always represent humans everywhere else in the Bible.

The Four Living Creatures, vv. 6–11

"Beasts" in the KJV is a mistranslation; the word here is a different word than that translated "beast" in chapter 13. In these verses the Greek word for beast is *zoon* and means "a living creature." God identifies them as both living creatures and symbolic entities with the use of "like a" and "as a." These creatures are commonly understood to be cherubim, actual beings of an angelic order. They seem to be identical with those spoken of in Ezekiel 1 and 10, where Ezekiel says, "I knew they were cherubim."

Cherubim were present at the fall of humanity (Genesis 3) and afterward guarded the Tree of Life. Here they join in the celebration of humanity's redemption. We will see them worshiping God again in 19:4.

There are, however, many varieties of opinion about these living creatures. Whatever their specific identity, they, along with all of heaven, worship the One on the throne, in a crescendo of praise to God the Creator of all.

The theme of chapter 4 is the creative power of God; of chapter 5, the redemptive power of Christ. John continues to describe the scene in heaven.

The sealed scroll. The scroll contains the secrets of the future, the final stage of Christ's redemptive work. All creation wants to know the outcome, but the only way to open the book is to break the seven seals. And only one Person in all of creation can do this, not because He is strong, but because He is worthy—that person, of course, is Jesus.

As the seven seals are broken by Jesus, one by one, there comes into John's vision a panorama of the future, rolling on to the end. The opening of each of the seven seals results in terrible happenings on earth. It is not until all the seals have been broken that the ultimate future becomes clear: the new heaven and the new earth—God living with His redeemed and restored creation.

The last seal was the most terrible of the seven. When it was opened, it turned out to contain seven trumpets, each of which heralded more disasters. And some interpreters see the seventh trumpet as containing the seven bowls filled with plagues that are poured on the earth before the final end. Thus we see seven seals (6:1–8:1), seven trumpets (8:2–11:19), and seven bowls (15–16).

Many interpreters, however, see the seven seals and the seven trumpets in chapters 6–11 as the complete sequence of judgments. In this interpretation, it is assumed that the seven bowl judgments occur concurrently with the seven trumpet judgments. (However, the bowl judgments are not shown to John until the visions in chapters 15 and 16.) The same event takes place at both the sounding of the seventh trumpet (11:15–19) and after an angel pours out the seventh bowl (16:17–18): all heaven reverberates with the glad hallelujahs of final victory (11:15) as God's wrath is showered on the earth in the form of lightning, thunder, an earthquake, and a great hailstorm. Chapters 12–20 are, then, a retelling of the events of the preceding chapters.

The seven seals and the seven trumpets together form the main framework of Revelation and carry the story swiftly forward to the end. Then the writer, following a common literary method of Scripture, returns to the beginning and, starting with chapter 12, begins over again with additional or explanatory details.

The Lion of Judah Is the Lamb, vv. 5–6

At the beginning of the book of Revelation, Christ appeared as a warrior in relation to His church. Here he is called a Lion—but when the Lion appears, He is a Lamb. Throughout the remaining chapters Christ is generally called the Lamb. The Lion represents power; the Lamb, sacrifice and ultimate victory. The Lamb has come to power through His death. The secret of Christ's power is His suffering, paradoxical as it may seem.

Seven eyes represents all knowledge; the seven horns, all-conquering might. Christ not only knows the future, but He has the power to control it.

The Doxologies, vv. 8–14

In 4:8–11 the songs of praise, or doxologies, were sung to the Creator. Here, the first two are to the Redeemer, and the third one to both the Creator and the Redeemer. A **new song** (v. 9): the song of redemption is new relative to the song of Creation. It is a scene of transcendent grandeur: the living creatures, the elders, 100 million angels, and the whole created universe, in ecstasy over the redemption of the human race: "Heaven is the homeland of music." The **prayers of the saints** (v. 8) are part of this grand doxology! It is at this point that Philippians 2:9–11 will be fulfilled: "Therefore God exalted him to the highest place and gave him the name that is above every name, that at the name of Jesus every knee should bow, in heaven and on earth and under the earth, and every tongue confess that Jesus Christ is Lord, to the glory of God the Father."

Rev. 6 | THE FIRST SIX SEALS

With chapter 6 begins the account of the events that take place on the earth during the seven years of tribulation. Futurist interpreters believe that these events begin immediately after the rapture of the church (4:1).

The sequence of seals marks a progression during the tribulation period. It is interesting to note that these signs follow in the exact same order as the signs that Jesus speaks of in Matthew 24, where He

---

"Lamb" is Revelation's favorite name for Christ:

- The Lamb took the sealed book and opened it (5:6–7; 6:1).
- The living creatures and elders worship the Lamb (5:8, 14).
- 100,000,000 angels worship the Lamb (5:11–13).
- The great day of the Lamb's wrath is come (6:16–17).
- Multitudes from all nations worship the Lamb (7:9–10).
- Their robes were washed in the blood of the Lamb (7:14).
- The Lamb leads them to fountains of living waters (7:17).
- They overcame Satan by the blood of the Lamb (12:11).
- The 144,000 follow the Lamb (14:1, 4).
- They sing the song of Moses and the Lamb (15:3).
- The Lamb is Lord of Lords and King of Kings (17:14).
- Marriage of the Lamb to His bride has come (19:7, 9; 21:9).
- The 12 foundations of the city are named for the 12 apostles of the Lamb (21:14).
- The Lamb is the temple and light of the city (21:22, 23).
- Only those in the Lamb's Book of Life shall enter (21:27).
- Water of life from the throne of the Lamb (22:1, 3).

is responding to His disciples' questions regarding the signs that will foretell His return and the end of the age. (These parallel verses from Matthew 24 are included in the sections below.)

The First Seal, vv. 1–2

The white horse and rider represent, according to some, Christ setting out on His triumphant career, because later (in 19:11), Christ appears on a white horse. But to others, the rider on the white horse is the Antichrist who inaugurates the seven years of the Great Tribulation. But this is not open war yet—war does not begin until the second seal. Rather, just as Satan presents himself as an angel of light, so the Antichrist presents himself first as the picture of goodness.

Matthew 24:3–5: "As Jesus was sitting on the Mount of Olives, the disciples came to him privately. 'Tell us,' they said, 'when will this happen, and what will be the sign of your coming and of the end of the age?' Jesus answered: 'Watch out that no one deceives you. For many will come in my name, claiming, "I am the Christ" and will deceive many.'"

The Second Seal, vv. 3–4

The fiery red horse and its rider represent open warfare; the false peace under the white horse and its rider is removed and civil war ensues.

Matthew 24:6: "You will hear of wars and rumors of wars, but see to it that you are not alarmed. Such things must happen, but the end is still to come."

The Third Seal, vv. 5–6

The black horse and its rider represent famine. The scales are used to weigh food, which will become scarce and be sold by weight. A quart of wheat is one-eighth of the normal amount of wheat a day's wages would buy. "Do not damage the oil and the wine!" may allude to God setting limits on the degree of destruction. The olive tree and the vine have roots that go deep and would not be immediately affected by a drought.

Matthew 24:7: "Nation will rise against nation, and kingdom against kingdom. There will be famines. . . ."

The Fourth Seal, vv. 7–8

The pale horse represents death, the natural result of war and famine. When civilization collapses, the wild beasts of the earth will once again regain their dominance and add to the suffering and death already experienced.

Matthew 24:7–8: "Nation will rise against nation, and kingdom against kingdom. There will be famines and earthquakes in various places. All these are the beginning of birth pains."

The Fifth Seal, vv. 9–11

A vision of the souls of the martyrs. Historians record 10 persecutions of the church in the first 300 years of its existence. One was already past (Nero, A.D. 64), the second was just coming to an end (Domitian, A.D. 96), and the third was soon to follow (Trajan, A.D. 98–117). The image of martyrs was not alien to the first readers of Revelation. Nor is it unfamiliar in our own time, when Christians are killed in other countries. Some think that this seal refers to Christians converted after the Rapture and martyred during the reign of Antichrist at the time of the end. Their question is the question of all suffering Christians: How much longer?—which is another way of asking, Why? The answer is, Be patient; God's plan will be accomplished.

Matthew 24: 9–13: "Then you will be handed over to be persecuted and put to death, and you will be hated by all nations because of me. At that time many will turn away from the faith and will betray and hate each other, and many false prophets will appear and deceive many people. Because of the increase of wickedness, the love of most will grow cold, but he who stands firm to the end will be saved."

The Sixth Seal, vv. 12–17

The sixth seal contains terrible convulsions that will shake the earth and affect the sun, moon, and stars. A meteor shower will bring destruction, and the earth's crust will shift. This is not a localized natural disaster but worldwide terror. It will be so terrible that everyone—including the mighty—will realize that these events are "acts of God" in the most horrifyingly real sense of the term. They realize that this is judgment, and that the end cannot be far off. In some respects this is similar to the description of the Battle of Armageddon (16:12–21), of which it may be a preliminary hint.

Jesus used similar language when He spoke of the time of His coming again (Matthew 24:29–30; Luke 21:26). So had Isaiah, in predicting the fall of Babylon (Isaiah 13:10) and Ezekiel in predicting the fall of Egypt (Ezekiel 32:7). Similar language appears also in Isaiah 34:4; Joel 2:30–31; Acts 2:20, where it appears to refer to God's judgments on the nations, or the final Day of Judgment.

Matthew 24:29: "The sun will be darkened, and the moon will not give its light; the stars will fall from the sky, and the heavenly bodies will be shaken."

Chapter 7 is an interlude between the sixth and seventh seals, though some see it as part of the sixth seal. It is divided into two sections, each dealing with a different group, one group on earth, the other in heaven. Similar to chapters 4–6, Jesus again provides John with visions of what is occurring on earth and in heaven simultaneously through the seven years of tribulation. Verses 1–8 are John's vision of the 144,000 elect of Israel on earth, and vv. 9–17 describe his vision of "the great multitude that no one could count, from every nation, tribe, people and language, standing before the throne and in front of the Lamb."

The 144,000, vv. 1–8

The terrible judgment just described in 6:15–17 would seem to be so severe that no one could survive. Yet there is mercy even in the midst of judgment. After the immense turmoil, there is a sudden stillness in which the winds of destruction are held back. The angels are commanded to hold back the four winds of the earth (they will blow again when the seven trumpets sound in chapters 8 and 9) until the 144,000 of God's servants from all the tribes of Israel are sealed on the forehead with God's seal (the sign of God's ownership). It is no surprise that later this seal is imitated by the Antichrist in 13:17–18, when people receive the "666" seal, the "mark of the beast."

There are many interpretations of the number 144,000. The futurist interpretation is that this is a literal number of Jews, 12,000 from each of the 12 tribes of Israel (vv. 4–8), who become believers during the tribulation period. Others interpret the 144,000 not numerically but symbolically, as representing the totality of the elect of Israel (although some see this as the totality of Christians, or of all believers, Jews and Christians).

The Great Multitude in Heaven, vv. 9–17

The 144,000 were the elect of Israel, while the multitude is from all nations. The scene in vv. 1–8 was on earth — the 144,000 were sealed by God before the worst of the tribulation years began (7:3). Beginning with v. 9, John sees a great multitude of people in heaven *after* the seven years of "great tribulation" are complete. John is told by one of the elders in heaven the identity of the multitudes and how they came to be in heaven: "These are they who have come out of the great tribulation [we were told in chapter 6 that many would be martyred during the tribulation]; they have washed their robes and made them white in the blood of the Lamb" (v. 14). The great multitude, safe at last in the Father's house, is the answer to the cry of the martyrs under the fifth seal.

There is difference of opinion among Bible students as to whether the 144,000 and the great multitude are two separate groups, or one and the same group under different aspects. It does seem that "Israel" in v. 4 is in contrast with "every nation" in v. 9, and that the former means Jewish Christians while the latter means Christians of "every nation, tribe, people and language." Many believe that the 144,000 who were sealed by God and protected through the Tribulation were God's evangelists during the tribulation period. Through their efforts, great multitudes of peoples accepted Christ and died as martyrs during the Tribulation. "These are they" that John sees in heaven.

Rev. 8 | THE FIRST FOUR TRUMPETS

The seventh seal contains the terrible plagues of the seven trumpets, which are even more horrible than those of the first six seals. And the last three trumpets bring such disaster on the earth that they are called "woes" (v. 13). When the seventh seal was opened, there was a "silence in heaven for about half an hour," as if something momentous were going to happen at any moment. Then the trumpet blasts.

The Prayers of the Saints, vv. 3–6

In Revelation 6:10 we hear the saints crying out in a loud voice under the altar in heaven, "How long, Sovereign Lord, holy and true, until you judge the inhabitants of the earth and avenge our blood?" Here we see an angel (Jesus) offering incense and acting as a mediator between God and man. The smoke of the incense rises up before God from the hand of Jesus—the prayers of the saints are answered and judgment is prepared. Jesus takes fire from the heavenly altar and casts it to the earth, and "there came peals of thunder, rumblings, flashes of lightning and an earthquake" (v. 5).

Some believe that the angel in this vision is Jesus Christ. They quote the apostle Paul—who tells us that "there is one God and one mediator between God and men, the man Christ Jesus, who gave himself as a ransom for all men—the testimony given in its proper time" (1 Timothy 2:5–6)—as their evidence.

The First Four Trumpets, vv. 7–12

These appear to be a fuller representation of the "four winds" of the "wrath of the Lamb" (6:16–7:3), held back until the servants of God were sealed but now ready to be unleashed:

- A third of the earth and its vegetation are burned
- A third of the sea becomes incapable of sustaining life and shipping
- A third of the world's fresh water supply becomes poisonous
- The sun, moon, and stars are struck, and the regular cycle of day and night is changed: a day will be only 16 hours

Some take the trumpets to be symbolic, but most futurist interpreters understand these trumpets to represent literal convulsions of nature that occur during the reign of the Antichrist.

"Woe, Woe, Woe," v. 13

John hears an angel flying through heaven saying, "Woe, woe, woe, to the inhabitants of the earth, because of the trumpet blasts about to be sounded by the other three angels!" It's a warning that the worst is yet to come.

This is in alignment with what we know about the tribulation period from Daniel 9, where he describes the 70th week. Here we learn that the first three-and-one-half years of the tribulation ("the beginning of birth pains," Matthew 24:8) will not be as horrible as the final three-and-one-half years ("for then there will be great distress unequaled from the beginning of time until now," Matthew 24:21).

Rev. 9 | **THE FIFTH AND SIXTH TRUMPETS**

The Fifth Trumpet (The First Woe), vv. 1–11

The plague of demon locusts, loosed from the Abyss by a fallen star. Satan is the "star that had fallen to the earth from the sky" due to a prideful heart (see Isaiah 14:12). Satan is given, by God, the key to the bottomless pit — the Abyss. The demon locusts are terrifying. Shaped like war horses, they have humanlike faces, with women's hair and lions' teeth. Their breastplates are like iron and their crowns like gold. Their wings sound like an army of chariots and horses rushing to war. They have the power to sting like scorpions. They feed, not on vegetation like regular locusts (in fact, they are forbidden to do so), but on terror. The locusts are given strict orders to torment only those who do not have the seal of God on their foreheads. The locusts are also prohibited from killing people. They can only torment people for five months, like the normal period for locusts (May to September).

The futurist interpreter holds that demon locusts will literally infest the earth in the days of the Tribulation after being unloosed by Satan.

There are parallels in the prophecies in the book of Joel, which also predicts a locust plague as part of the events leading to the coming Day of Judgment. A locust plague is also described in Exodus 10:1–20.

The Sixth Trumpet (The Second Woe), vv. 12–21

The second woe will bring more than just torment — it will kill one-third of humanity. Instead of demon locusts, four fallen angels are now unleashed from the ties that bind them at the Euphrates River. (The Euphrates River is in the Middle East in the present-day location of Iraq and Syria.) An army of 200 million horsemen accompanies them. They were loosed for "the" hour, day, month, and year, which appears to mean the exact appointed time. Under the fourth seal, one-fourth of all people had been killed (6:4); now one-third of those left are killed, leaving only half of the world's population.

But incredibly, all this has no effect on the survivors. They persist in their rejection of God by refusing to repent of worshiping idols, murder, magic arts, fornication, and stealing. To the futurist, the army of 200 million is the literal army of the Antichrist, aided by the superhuman activity of demons.

| Rev. 10 | THE LITTLE SCROLL IS OPEN |

Chapter 10 and the beginning of chapter 11 are again a brief interlude—or a "behind the scenes" look at events that occur between the sixth and seventh trumpets (similar to the interlude between the sixth and seventh seals in chapter 7).

Here we are presented with two scenes: the angel with the little scroll (chap. 10) and the two witnesses (chap. 11).

The angel is likely Christ. First, we note that Christ is often depicted as being surrounded by clouds (see Exodus 19:9, 16; 40:34; Matthew 17:5; Luke 21:27; and Acts 1:9). In chapter 5 John saw God holding a sealed scroll; here he describes an angel with an open scroll. It is referred to as the "little scroll," which seems to distinguish it from the sealed scroll. Also, the sealed scroll in chapter 5 was to be opened, whereas the little scroll here is to be eaten.

The angel plants his right foot on the sea and his left foot on the land and gives "a shout like the roar of a lion" (v. 3). The cry seems to be a warning, in a setting of awful majesty, that the end is near, but that there is yet another prophetic period to cover before the end actually comes.

With utter finality—he swears by God Himself—the angel announces, "There will be no more delay!" The forces of evil will no

---

The Antichrist

The word "antichrist" may mean either "against Christ" or "in the place of Christ," that is, either an enemy or a usurper. Surprisingly, the word is found only four times in the Bible, in the letters of John (1 John 2:18, 22; 4:3; 2 John 7). But the concept is found throughout Scripture, and apparently it was well known. Paul speaks of "the man of lawlessness" in a way that appears to assume that his readers know what he writes about (2 Thessalonians 2:3−6), and John similarly does not think it necessary to explain the term.

In the Old Testament, see Psalm 2; Ezekiel 38−39; Zechariah 12−14. The book of Daniel in particular gives vivid descriptions of the Antichrist (compare Daniel 11:36−37 and 2 Thessalonians 2:4; also Daniel 7:8, 20−21; 8:24; 11:28−30; and Revelation 13:8).

Jesus Himself warned against false Christs and false prophets (Matthew 24:24), and He referred to "the abomination that causes desolation" mentioned by Daniel (Matthew 24:15).

The beast of Revelation 13:1−8 and 17:8 recalls the horned beast of Daniel 7−8. He claims divine honor for himself and receives it, and he makes war on God's people. He is finally destroyed by the Lord in a great battle (Revelation 19:19−20).

Reconstruction of Jerusalem's Second Temple altar. "I was given a reed like a measuring rod and was told, 'Go and measure the temple of God and the altar, and count the worshipers there.'" (Rev 11:1)

longer delay the final and inevitable outcome. The great day of God has come, and the hour of doom has struck for those who oppose God. Futurist interpreters understand this announcement to be that the reign of the Antichrist is at hand. The seventh angel will sound in Revelation 11:15.

At this point, John is told to take and eat the little book which is open in the hand of the angel. This book seems to be all or a portion of the Book of Judgments. As Christ forewarned, the Word of God was both "sweet" and "bitter." This may mean that, while it was gratifying to know the glorious future that awaits the believer, yet the frightfulness of the coming judgments on those who refuse to repent filled John with grief. John is then instructed to go tell the many peoples and nations and tongues and kings. Faithfully, he tells the good news and the bad through the remaining chapters of Revelation.

Rev. 11 | THE TWO WITNESSES

The Temple Measured, vv. 1–2

A continuation of the interlude between the sixth and seventh trumpets. John is instructed to measure the temple of God, the altar, and the worshipers in the temple. He is told not to measure the outer court, which was the court for the Gentiles. We are told that the Holy City will be left to be trampled by the Gentiles for 42 months (3½ years—half of the seven years of tribulation). Some think this refers to the destruction of Jerusalem in A.D. 70. Others understand it to be, not the material temple, but "spiritual Israel," the church. Some futurist interpreters believe that a new temple will literally be built, leading up to and during the first 3½ years of the tribulation period.

The image seems to draw a distinction between the worshipers in the temple and the "Gentiles" outside. Futurist interpreters, many of whom believe that the church will be raptured at the beginning of the tribulation period, see the worshipers referred to here as the faithful, believing Jews or as all people who have accepted Christ during the Great Tribulation.

The Two Witnesses, vv. 3–13

The two witnesses are said to prophesy in sackcloth during the same period that the Holy City will be trampled by the nations (a thousand, two hundred, and three score days = 1,260 days or 42 weeks or 3½ years). They are identified as the "two olive trees and two lampstands." This is a reference to Zechariah 4:1–14, where it is explained that the lampstand is the temple of God and the olive trees the Spirit, through whom Zerubbabel, of the messianic family, would complete the temple of God that had for years lain in ruins (see p. 443).

Who are the two witnesses? Many are the answers, but none of them is without difficulties. Some would say Paul and Peter, whose bodies at that time lay in the city of Rome. Others see them as the true church, which will bear witness to Christ throughout the whole Christian age. The futurist interpreter generally believes that the witnesses are two literal people, returned to earth and testifying with supernatural power in the days of the Antichrist. There is a great deal of speculation regarding the identity of these witnesses. The most common theories are that the witnesses are Elijah and Enoch or Elijah and Moses. In Malachi 3:1 and 4:5 we see a specific prophecy that suggests that Elijah will be sent "before the coming of the great and dreadful day of the Lord." In one sense this was fulfilled in John the Baptist (Matthew 11:13–14), but it may be that there is another fulfillment in the future. It is also interesting to note that Elijah did not die a physical death but was taken up into heaven in a fiery chariot (2 Kings 9–11). Elijah was a prophet to Israel. Many believe Moses to be the other witness along with Elijah. He appeared with Elijah during the Transfiguration (Matthew 17:1–8), and his body was protected by God (Jude 9). Enoch is a candidate for being one of the two witnesses because, like Elijah, he did not die but was taken up by God.

While the identity of the witnesses is a matter that is unclear at present, in time it will become clear. The heart of the matter is that God will provide witnesses—prophets who speak on His behalf, even during the most terrible time the earth has seen.

God will provide divine protection for the witnesses during the 1,260 days (3½ years) during which they will prophesy. There will be many who will hate them and reject their warning messages. Those who try to harm them will be devoured by fire that comes from the witnesses' mouths. The witnesses will also have power to create a drought (like Elijah), turn water to blood, and start any kind of plague (like Moses).

After the 3½ years, "the beast" from the Abyss will attack and kill them in the same city where Christ was crucified. This is the first time that the beast is mentioned in Revelation, and clearly he is a demonic being.

The bodies of the witnesses will lie in the streets for 3½ days, and "men from every people, tribe, language and nation will gaze on their bodies and refuse them burial." Today's global communications could easily make it possible for every person around the world to see the witnesses' dead bodies. People will actually be celebrating their death. What a wretched situation!

After 3½ days (notice the similarity to Christ's time in the tomb), God will breath life into them. Their resurrection will bring terror to the earth. Shortly after they come to life, they will be called up to heaven and ascend in a cloud while the world watches (note the similarity with 4:1). Their rapture will be followed by a violent earthquake that kills 7000 people.

This is the end of the sixth trumpet and the second woe (see 9:12). The third woe is about to begin (v. 14).

The Seventh Trumpet, vv. 15–19

The end has come. The long conflict is over. We are transported beyond the Day of Judgment. The whole has reached its glorious consummation. Some believe that the rest of the book is a continuation of the first part. However, there are so many similarities that connect the following chapters to the earlier chapters that it seems more likely that the writer returns to proceed anew on a different line. In other words, chapters 6–11 run parallel or concurrently with chapters 12–19:15. The worship service John witnesses in chapter 11 is the same worship of the returning King that we are told about in chapter 19.

Rev. 12 | THE WOMAN, CHILD, AND DRAGON

Up to this point, the seals and trumpets carried the story forward to the final judgment, dealing largely with the fate of the world. In chapter 12 the writer returns to the starting place and in another series of visions portrays things previously omitted, relating largely to the fate of those who refuse to repent.

The Woman

The woman is commonly thought to represent Israel. The imagery is similar to the sun, moon, and 12 stars that bowed down to Joseph in his dream (Genesis 37:9–11). In v. 2 we see Isaiah's prediction (Isaiah 66:7–8) of a woman (Israel) bringing forth a man child fulfilled.

it is easy to image that its physical appearance is strange and animal-like. However, the resemblance to the leopard, bear, and lion may very well be in nonphysical characteristics, such as being a cunning hunter, someone who camouflages himself well in his setting.

Like the dragon, to whom it was subservient, the beast had seven heads and 10 horns (see chap. 17). The "seven heads" loaded with blasphemy are explained further in chapter 17. They symbolize seven empires and seven kings that are, or were, under the control of the beast, who receives his power from Satan. John tells us that five (empires/kings) are fallen, one is, and one is yet to come (17:10). There is much speculation on the identity of the five that are fallen. Some believe them to be the significant empires that ruled through the ages, including the Egyptian, Assyrian, Babylonian, Medo-Persian, and Grecian empires (see also p. 397). The one that "is" is generally thought to be the Roman Empire. The Roman Empire was never conquered; it rotted from within and eventually lost its position of world power.

Others believe that the seven heads represent the five kings who reigned up to John's day, the sixth king that was in power during John's life, and a seventh king that is yet to come, which is generally thought to be the Antichrist.

The "ten horns with ten crowns on his horns" seem to be identical to the 10 toes of the fourth beast in Nebuchadnezzar's dream (Daniel 2:33, 40–43) and the 10 horns of the fourth beast in Daniel's dream (Daniel 7:7, 24). An angel tells Daniel what the 10 horns represent: "the ten horns are ten kings who will come from this kingdom [the final kingdom]. After them another king will arise, different from the earlier ones; he will subdue three kings. He will speak against the Most High and oppress his saints and try to change the set times and the laws" (Daniel 7:24).

"One of the heads of the beast *seemed* to have had a fatal wound, but the fatal wound had been healed" (13:3). It comes as no surprise that Satan, the great imitator, orchestrates the "death and resurrection" of the Antichrist. A cheap imitation, indeed, but the "whole world was astonished and followed the beast." How easily people are deceived if they don't know the truth found in God's Word!

To the preterist interpreter, this first beast is the old Roman Empire, whose mission was to persecute the church. The futurist interpreter believes that this beast (the Antichrist) is a literal man who will rise to political power in a revived Roman Empire and will continue as a world power for 42 months. He will blaspheme the name of God and will be given power by Satan to make war on the saints (God's true believers)—but the rest of the world (those whose names are not written in the Book of Life) will worship the demon-possessed politician. It will be a time of trouble the like of which the world has never known. At the end of this 3½ years of terror, Christ will return to reclaim His dominion of the earth from Satan.

The Second Beast, vv. 11–18

This beast looked like a lamb and will hold a place of religious authority. The first beast looked like a leopard, bear, and lion and possessed political power. Both received power from Satan and appear to be allies. It appears that we have the making of an impostor trinity!

The second beast was able to influence *the earth itself* and its inhabitants to worship the first beast. Can you imagine that even the rocks were influenced by this man? Satan's power to deceive is truly frightening.

John previously mentioned that the first beast seemed to have a fatal wound but had been healed (v. 3). Here we learn that it was the lamb beast that brought him (the first beast) to life again. The lamb beast is afterward called the "false prophet" (16:13; 19:20; 20:10), that is, the pretender-lamb.

To the preterist interpreter, the lamb beast is the priestly system of the Roman Empire, organized to enforce emperor worship. To the futurist interpreter, the lamb beast is the ecclesiastical head of the world's last empire, of which the political head will be the leopard beast, the Antichrist himself.

The Number 666

This number represents the name of a man, or possibly a group of men, or an institution headed by a man or group of men. Neither Hebrew nor Greek has separate symbols for numbers; rather, letters were also used as

Emperor Nero (AD 54-68). Some believe that the number 666 directly relates to the Roman emperor Nero since the Hebrew script for Caesar Nero (qsr nrwn) = 100 + 60 + 200 + 50 + 200 + 6 + 50 = 666.

numerals. Thus, in Greek, A=1, B=2, etc. The letters of the name, when added together, total 666.

Few things in the Bible have given rise to such speculation as the meaning of "the number of the beast." Each era in history has discovered the name of a leader who is seen as impersonating the ultimate evil of the Antichrist, from the head of the Roman Empire of Paul's day, to Napoleon, to Adolf Hitler.

In our time it has been claimed that the object is a number rather than a name, and that this number is incorporated in the barcodes on consumer products.

Others understand the number symbolically: 6 is man's number, just short of 7, which is God's number; 666 is a "trinity" of sixes. The square of 6 is 36; when we add up all numbers from 1 through 36, the total is 666. The significance, then, is that the beast, powerful as he is — and no matter how powerful he may become — is still not as powerful as God.

At the close of chapter 13, John tells us that the false prophet, who receives his power from the great imitator, Satan, requires everyone to receive a mark on his right hand or his forehead. Without this mark, people could not buy or sell anything (vv. 16–17). Remember the seal God placed on the forehead of all the servants of God at the beginning of the Great Tribulation (7:3).

Rev. 14 | THE LAMB AND HIS FOLLOWERS

John describes seven visions in this chapter. These visions seem to be given here to provide us with "the big picture," and the following chapters provide us with more of the details. As the details unfold in later chapters, we see that the visions presented here do not necessarily appear in chronological order.

The 144,000, vv. 1–5

The Lamb and His faithful followers are set over against the beast and his followers of the preceding chapter.

- The Lamb's followers have His name on their foreheads (v. 1; 7:3–4), even as the beast's followers are marked with his name (13:16–17).
- They do not speak lies (v. 5), in contrast to the lying wonders of the beast (13:14).
- They have "kept themselves pure" (v. 4; KJV, virgins), in contrast to the prostitution of the beast (17:5). We are not to understand that they were literal celibates, for the New Testament never regards the married state as sinful — on the contrary, it exalts it as a symbol of the relation between Christ and His bride (see 2 Corinthians 11:2). Their celibacy was spiritual. They have kept themselves from spiritual idolatry and remain pure to the one true God.

- They were faithful to Christ in contrast to the adultery of Babylon, which includes the apostate church.

The *new* song (vv. 2–3), breaking on the ear like the ocean's roar, was one that only the redeemed tribulation saints could know. Although probably similar to the praise songs sung earlier by the saints (see 5:9), it is differentiated as a new song. Perhaps the redeemed of each dispensation will have something uniquely joyous to sing about as they join others in worship and praise in heaven. An unsaved person cannot know the joys of the redeemed, and the redeemed themselves, when they reach heaven, will experience rapture exquisite beyond anything they could imagine. In heaven everybody will sing, and sing, and sing.

Who are the 144,000? They are probably the same as the 144,000 of 7:4. As discussed earlier, most believe that the 144,000 are the elect of Israel (most likely Jews) sealed by God halfway through the seven-year tribulation period (see p. 857 for additional information on the 144,000 Israelites). They are the "firstfruits" (v. 4), in contrast to the general "harvest" (vv. 15–16). They may be referred to as *firstfruits* because they were the first to be saved during the tribulation period. Others believe that this confirms that the 144,000 were Jews, God's bride, His firstfruits, much as the church is the bride of Christ.

At the beginning of this chapter we see the Lamb (Christ) standing on Mount Zion. He is with the 144,000 on the earth. Mount Zion is another name for Jerusalem. There are many passages in the Bible, especially in Psalms, which tell us that Zion is God's chosen place on the earth: "For the LORD has chosen Zion, he has desired it for his dwelling: 'This is my resting place for ever and ever . . .'" (Psalm 132:13–14). Although this is the only reference to Zion in Revelation, it seems to confirm several Old Testament passages that suggest that Jerusalem will be the center of Christ's earthly kingdom when He returns (see Isaiah 2:3–4; Psalm 48:2).

The Angel with the Everlasting Gospel, vv. 6–7

The 144,000 were the firstfruits. Here the picture symbolizes the general evangelization of the whole world. The Lamb's weapon in leading His army against the beast is the preaching of the simple Gospel. To some, this image represents the carrying of the Gospel to the Gentiles after it had been preached to Israel. To others, it typifies the era of modern worldwide missions, preceding the fall of "Babylon," which is announced in the next verse. To others it is an announcement that the millennial reign of Christ is at hand.

In any case, the angel is giving a warning to the people of the world, a sort of "last call" for those have yet to repent, that Christ is coming soon.

The Fall of Babylon, v. 8

The second angel announces the fall of Babylon. This is the first mention of Babylon in the book of Revelation. Babylon's fall is mentioned again in 16:19. The fall of Babylon is thus mentioned twice before there is any further statement about Babylon, which is fully described in chapters 17–18. Babylon was so horrible that the writer wanted to assure his readers, before telling them about it in more detail, that it would have only a temporary existence. Babylon was the name given to the working alliance of the revived political beast and the religious pretender-lamb of chapter 13. The satanic trinity is able to make "all the nations drink of the maddening wine of her [spiritual] adulteries." This seems to allude to the formation of a one-world religion and a single, worldwide political system. This is hardly a stretch for our imagination as we see the news of our world unfold in current events. Perhaps this angel's warning is relevant to us—be warned of a movement to create an ecumenical religion based more on the premise of "brotherly love and tolerance" than on one's relationship with Jesus Christ.

The Doom of the Beast's Worshipers, vv. 9–12

The book of Revelation recognizes only two classes of people: those who belong to God, and those who belong to the beast. Here the unhappy lot of those who have the mark of the beast is in sad contrast to the unspeakable joy of those who have the mark of the Lamb (v. 3). Their doom is more fully described in chapters 19–20. The contrasting of the fate of the redeemed and the lost, which is so prominent in this book, was also a characteristic of Jesus' teaching in the Gospels. It is interesting to note that "the smoke of their torment rises *for ever and ever*" (v. 11). This is a confirmation of the comparison made between the "life eternal" for God's people and "everlasting punishment" for the doomed in Matthew 25:46 (see also 19:20 and 20:10).

The Blessed Dead, v. 13

This is, again, in contrast to the torment of the wicked mentioned in v. 11. The suffering of the martyrs, at long last, is over. The time prayed for in 6:9–11 has come at last.

The Harvest of the Earth, vv. 14–16

This chapter began with a vision of the "firstfruits" (v. 4) and closes with visions of the final harvest, with an era of Gospel preaching in between. The seals and trumpets had carried the panorama to the final end in chapter 11. Chapters 12–14, returning to the start, contain another series that runs to the end: the development of the beast, ending in his defeat at the hands of the Lamb. This vision is another representation of the parable of the weeds (Matthew 13:37–43); both picture the final ingathering of the elect.

The harvest of the earth is ripe (v. 15) has a bearing on the reason the Lord delays His coming: He is waiting for the harvest to ripen. The harvest of the human race had been spoken of long before in the Old Testament, in Joel 3:9–14: "Swing the sickle, for the harvest is ripe. Come, trample the grapes, for the winepress is full and the vats overflow — so great is their wickedness! . . . For the day of the LORD is near in the valley of decision." It is an ancient picture of John's flying angel herald, followed later by the angels of the harvest.

The Grapes from the Earth's Vine, vv. 17–20

This vision refers to the wicked, for the winepress is the "great winepress of God's wrath" (v. 19). It is another representation of the doom of the wicked, as Jesus said: "They [the angels] will weed out of his kingdom everything that causes sin and all who do evil. They will throw them into the fiery furnace, where there will be weeping and gnashing of teeth" (Matthew 13:42) and "they will go away to eternal punishment" (Matthew 25:46).

1,600 stadia (v. 20) is about 180 miles, which is approximately the length of Palestine (Israel) from north to south. The blood of those fallen covered this area and reached as high as the bridles on the horses. It is thought to mean the complete destruction of the Holy Land or perhaps of the whole world. Joel prophesies about this war (Joel 3:2, 10–14), and the comparison is striking. It is likely a description of the Battle of Armageddon (16:16). Also see Zechariah 14:2, which refers to the gathering of all the nations to fight against Jerusalem.

Outside the city (v. 20) probably refers to the valley (perhaps the Kidron Valley/Valley of Jehoshaphat) just outside Jerusalem, the City of God. In Zechariah 14:2 we learn that "the city will be captured, the houses ransacked, and the women raped. Half of the city will go into exile, but the rest of the people will not be taken from the city." Those who go into exile likely signify God's people who will be kept safe from the wrath that comes on the wicked.

Rev. 15–16 **SEVEN BOWLS OF GOD'S WRATH**

Chapter 15 is an introductory chapter that sets the stage for the seven bowls containing plagues, which are the judgments of God by which the power of Babylon is broken (16:19). Up to this point there has been no mention of Babylon, except the announcement of its fall (14:8). Babylon is explained in chapters 17–18 as a coalition of a political beast and the false prophet.

The Song of the Victors, 15:2–4

John describes the scene in heaven. Seven angels hold seven bowls of God's wrath and prepare to pour out these final plagues on the earth. The tribulation saints, those who died but overcame the beast during the tribulation period, are standing on "the sea of glass" with the harps of God. The "sea of glass" is perhaps symbolic for the calm and peaceful rest of God's people in heaven. They are praising God with the song called the song of Moses and the song of the Lamb. As God's people, after going through the Red Sea (Exodus 15; Deuteronomy 32), were safe from Pharaoh and the armies of Egypt, so here they have reached heaven's shore and are safe from harm forever. It is similar to the "new song" of 5:9–14: it is the outburst of unutterable joy in the presence of God.

Perhaps one of the objects of this preliminary vision was to assure the saints of their safety from the terrifying disasters about to come, and to contrast the glorious destiny of the saved with the fearful doom of the lost. The judgments are directed against Babylon, an institution or organization, and also against individuals who bear the mark of the institution. The book portrays the course of governments, world powers, and empires on their way to ruin, but it never loses sight of the destiny of individuals, of whom there are only two classes: those who have the mark of the beast, and those who wear the name of the Lamb.

The Wrath of God, 15:1–8

The bowls are called the bowls of the wrath of God: "with them God's wrath is complete." It is His wrath at the wickedness of Babylon. God is a God of love and mercy, but those who spurn His mercy once too often will one day learn, to their regret, that the greater His mercy has been, the greater will be His wrath.

No one could enter the temple (v. 8) may mean that none can enter His presence to intercede to avert the judgments. The day for intercession is past. The temple is filled with smoke from the glory of God and from His power—perhaps no created being could survive being in the presence of such extreme glory and power.

The First Four Bowls, 16:2–9

Like the first four trumpets, the judgment of the bowls is poured successively out on the earth, sea, rivers, and sun. God Himself is directing the angels to carry out these judgments.

The first bowl judgment is poured out on the earth and causes those who have the mark of the beast to be covered with ulcerated sores. This plague is similar to the plague on Egypt in Moses' day (Exodus 9:8–11).

The second bowl judgment was poured out upon the sea. This, too, is similar to the account where Moses and Aaron turned the waters of Egypt to blood (Exodus 7:17–21). In addition, you may recall that the second seal (6:3–4) was an account of the red horse which caused a great war with much bloodshed, and the second trumpet caused one-third of the sea to become blood.

The rivers and fountains of water on which the third bowl was poured became blood also. It was blood that could have saved these people, and now it is blood that will kill all living creatures in the sea and probably many people, for there is no more water to drink.

The fourth bowl, unlike the fourth trumpet which darkened the sun, intensified the sun's heat. Perhaps God's darkening of the sun was to

An aerial view looking west at the site of ancient Megiddo. Some believe that Armageddon will be the site of a literal battle associated with the ancient city of Megiddo.

keep the intensity of the sun's heat from getting so extreme that all would perish. There is also an interesting passage in Matthew where Jesus, while describing the end of the age, says, "If those days had not been cut short, no one would survive, but for the sake of the elect [those with God's seal in their foreheads] those days will be shortened" (Matthew 24:22). Even through the worst of days, God makes provision for His people.

Even as God pours out these final warnings to mankind, the people refuse to repent and continue to blaspheme Him.

The Fifth Bowl, 16:10–11

The fifth bowl is poured onto the throne of the political beast, whose realm had suffered terrifically from the first four bowls. Darkness—probably literal darkness—fills his kingdom. Perhaps this is like the darkness that fell over the land of Egypt (Exodus 10:21–23). Humanity continues to blaspheme.

The Sixth Bowl, 16:12–16

This bowl, like the sixth trumpet, affects the River Euphrates. Under the sixth trumpet, the demon army of 200 million horsemen was released from the Euphrates. Here the Euphrates is dried up to make way for "the kings of the east" and their vast army. This is in the area of present-day Iran, Iraq, and Syria. In years past, an army of 200 million men seemed inconceivable, but with current populations in China, Russia, and other eastern countries today, it is entirely feasible.

The spirits of the dragon, the beast, and the false prophet assemble the kings of the whole earth at Armageddon for the battle of the great day of God. This war is predicted in Psalm 2:2–4: "The kings of the earth take their stand and the rulers gather together against the LORD."

Note the parenthetical warning (v. 15) that with the approach of this battle, the Lord's coming is near. A thief gives no notice of his approach. So the Lord's coming will not "close on you unexpectedly like a trap" (Luke 21:34).

The Seventh Bowl, 16:17–21

The stage is set for the great Battle of Armageddon, but God preempts the actual battle with this seventh bowl poured out on the air. With the pounding of 100-pound hailstones and the greatest earthquake in all of history, Babylon falls.

Futurist interpreters see the bowls as representing literal convulsions of nature and calamities that will befall the confederated empire of the Antichrist, climaxing in a literal battle at Megiddo, the historic battlefield of Palestine. The earthquake will be a literal earthquake, and the 100-pound hailstones, actual hailstones. Can you imagine what such a hailstorm would do to some of our fancy, sophisticated modern-day war machines? Isn't it interesting that God uses hail as the final judgment? Stoning was the Old Testament punishment for one who committed blasphemy! (Leviticus 24:16).

Rev. 17 | BABYLON, THE GREAT PROSTITUTE

Chapters 17 and 18 are again somewhat of an interlude or parenthetical section and give us more information about the fall of Babylon. Chapter 17 provides greater insight into and more detail regarding the demise of the religious system called Mystery Babylon the Great (v. 5; 14:8). Chapter 18 provides us with more information about the destruction of the political/military/economic system represented by the city of Babylon (16:19). These two systems are run by the false prophet (lamb beast) and the Antichrist (leopard beast) respectively.

The Plain of Megiddo, stretching out peacefully on a sunny day. Here, one day, will be fought the great, final battle between God and the forces of evil—the Battle of Armageddon (Har Megiddo).

The **great prostitute** (v. 1) who sits on many waters is the worldwide ecumenical religious system that develops during the tribulation period and is led by the false prophet (who receives his power from Satan). Her name is Mystery Babylon the Great (v. 5). The many waters are the multitude of people on the earth who are deceived and led into *spiritual* adultery through this worldly religion, which requires worshiping the Antichrist instead of the one true Christ. The angel makes this clear in v. 15: "the waters you saw, where the prostitute sits, are peoples, multitudes, nations and languages." (Keep in mind that the futurist interpreters believe that the true church, those who accepted Christ as their Lord and Savior, were taken out of the earth before the tribulation; 4:1.)

She (the false prophet and the entire ungodly religious system) is seated on a scarlet beast (the Antichrist), with seven heads and 10 horns, covered with blasphemous names (v. 3). Remember that Satan is the power behind these two beasts and that they are working in partnership. John explained his vision of the lamb beast "who exercised all the authority of the first beast on his behalf, and made the earth and its inhabitants worship the first beast" (13:12).

The false prophet, and her idolatrous religious system — Mystery Babylon — is dressed in purple and scarlet and fine jewels, the pay received for her prostitution (v. 4). Purple and scarlet are often the colors worn by rulers and religious leaders, and the fine jewels likely represent the wealth the false religion collects and lavishes selfishly on the false prophet. She is holding a golden cup filled with abominations and filthiness. She is the mother of all abominations, and is drunk with the blood of the saints (vv. 5–6). Here again we see Satan, the great imitator, at work trying to make his lamb beast look and act like Jesus (Luke 22:17–22).

John later describes another woman — the New Jerusalem, God's Holy City with all its inhabitants — as the "bride, beautifully dressed for her husband" (Christ), who is the true Lamb. Two broadly contrasted women are identified with two broadly contrasted cities. One woman belongs to the beast, the other to the Lamb. One is foul, the other is pure. One is clothed in scarlet, the other in fine linen. One is headed for doom, the other is headed for eternal glory.

Verses 8–17 give us more information about the political beast, the Antichrist, and are similar to some of the visions regarding the beast that John described in chapter 13. Here the angel unfolds the mystery of the woman and the beast she rides (v. 7). First we hear again that the beast "once was, now is not, and will come up out of the Abyss and go to his destruction." This is similar to the previous account, which explained that the beast lived, was fatally wounded, and then brought back to life by the false prophet (13:3, 12) — a mockery of Christ's death and resurrection.

The seven heads are seven kings or kingdoms, five of whom have fallen (v. 10). These are thought to be the world empires; the five fallen kingdoms are the Egyptian, Assyrian, Babylonian, Persian, and Greek empires. The sixth and seventh empires refer to the old Roman Empire, which lost its place of world power long ago but was never conquered, and finally the new revived Roman Empire. It is interesting to note that Rome sits on seven hills: Aventine, Caelian, Capitoline, Esquiline, Palatine, Quirinal, and Viminal. "The beast who once was, and now is not, is the eighth king" (v. 11). He was originally the seventh king, but he died and was brought back to life as the eighth king.

The 10 horns are 10 kings who have not yet received their kingdom (v. 12). These 10 kings, with the Antichrist beast at the helm, will receive their power and authority from Satan during the "final hour," which we understand from previous chapters to be the last 3½ years (42 months) of the seven-year tribulation period. As discussed earlier, the first half of the seven-year tribulation period will be "the beginning of sorrows" and less horrible than the latter 3½ years, which are referred to as the period of Great Tribulation. In Daniel 7:8, 24 we learn that the Antichrist will "uproot" three of the original kings and replace them. Perhaps the original three were unwilling to yield their power and wealth to him, for John tells us that the resultant 10 kings have one mind and give *all* their power (wealth) and authority to the Antichrist (v. 11). We are also told that God "put it in their [the kings'] hearts to accomplish his purpose by agreeing to give the beast their power to rule until God's words are fulfilled" (v. 17). Isn't it interesting that it took an act of God for these selfish men to submit their power and authority to the beast? Even Satan's influence was not strong enough to ensure that this sleazy coalition would remain faithful to the Antichrist. The solidarity of this demonic leadership team must have been important to the fulfillment of God's final plan of judgment.

In the end, the religious Babylon will fall because the Antichrist and his committee of 10 kings will turn their backs and betray the false prophet by usurping all power and authority from the world religion. The false prophet himself will not be destroyed until later (chap. 19), but the religious system is dismantled and left powerless. The kings prepare to make war against the Lamb (Christ), and the Lamb will overcome them — "and with him will be his called, chosen and faithful followers" (v. 14). We see this prediction fulfilled in Revelation 19:14.

Other New Testament passages, such as 2 Thessalonians 2:3 – 10; 1 Timothy 4:1 – 3; 2 Peter 2; and Jude 18, also predict the rise and temporary ascendancy of an apostate power.

To the futurist interpreter, Babylon, among other things, is a literal city of the future, where the Antichrist will set up his headquarters. Perhaps this will be the ancient city of Babylon rebuilt or an existing city in that area, such as Baghdad. Some think this city will be the capital city of a revived Roman Empire, a confederacy of 10 Western countries or world powers that will conspire together to rule and control the world in the end times. It is thought that this city will be the headquarters for the Antichrist's political system as well as the worship center for the worldwide religious system established by the false prophet, who convinces the world's people to worship the Antichrist.

We see many signs today that suggest that the governance of our world is becoming more and more global. Financial systems are essentially global today, commerce with the introduction of the internet and expanding free-trade agreements is global, and we are even seeing a convergence in the world's political governance, such as the European Economic Community and the increasing power and jurisdiction of the United Nations. We are also sadly seeing many signs of growing spiritual idolatry in our world. The New Age movement that encourages "spiritualism" of the kind that teaches that we are all our own gods. The many churches that leave Christ out of the center of their teaching and assure their congregations that living a good life is all it takes to get to heaven. The growing mandate for "tolerance" of immoral behavior while there is an equal growth of intolerance for Christian values like abstinence from sex before marriage, the sanctity of traditional marriage and family, and overall sexual purity. We are surely near the appointed time!

Rev. 18 | THE FALL OF BABYLON

Babylon, the city on the Euphrates, whose Hanging Gardens were one of the Seven Wonders of the Ancient World, was the city that had taken God's Old Testament people captive. So God uses it as the name of the world power that would take most of the earth's inhabitants captive. John names the "Euphrates," under both the sixth trumpet and the sixth bowl, as the land from which the enemies of God will come.

Chapter 18 describes the destruction of the city of Babylon, which is the seat of Antichrist's political and economic power (also referred to as Babylon the Great). In chapter 17 John described the destruction of the one-world, idolatrous religious system. John begins chapter 18 with "after this," meaning after the religious Babylon is destroyed. He saw a vision of the fall of the city of Babylon the Great. The city, which represents the political and economic systems of the world, had "become a home for demons" (v. 2). The kings of the earth had committed (spiritual) adultery with her and the merchants grew rich from her excessive luxuries (v. 3). For the love of money is the root of all kinds of evil (1-Timothy 6:10).

Then John hears a voice from heaven, presumably God's voice, saying, "Come out of her, my people, so you will not share in her sins, so that you will not receive any of her plagues" (v. 4). Similarly, John told us in chapter 12 that "the woman [representing the tribulation saints of Israel] fled into the desert to a place prepared for her by God, where she might be taken care of for 1,260 days [during the Great Tribulation]" (v. 6).

Mystery Babylon Versus Babylon the Great

This table summarizes some key differences between Mystery Babylon, the adulterous religious system, and Babylon the Great, the corrupt political and commercial system, both of which rise to power during the Great Tribulation.

Title	Mystery Babylon	Babylon the Great
Represents	Worldwide religious system	Worldwide political and commercial system
Leader	Lamb beast; false prophet; head of worldwide religion	Leopard beast; Antichrist; world's political ruler
Likened to	An adulterous woman; a mother	A great city
Mission	Deceive all the people into worshiping and giving power and wealth to the Antichrist	Rally all earth's resources together under satanic leadership for one final war with God so as not to lose dominion of the earth
Position	Sitting on seven hills	Visible from the sea
Destruction	Ruined by the kings of the earth	Utterly destroyed by the wrath of God
Reaction to its destruction	Not known for sure, but likely the kings celebrate	Kings, merchants, and seamen weep and mourn the loss of their power and wealth

Three groups mourn as they see the city of Babylon burn and be utterly destroyed, and with it the heart of the political and commercial system: the kings, the merchants, and the seamen (perhaps a figurative term referring to someone who makes or collects money from the "sea" of mankind). Here John seems to describe a corrupt form of capitalism that eventually brings destruction to the world.

At the turn of the millennium there were fears that the world's computer systems would crash. Imagine what would happen if all computers and telecommunications were totally dependent on one city—and that city was destroyed.

The city of Babylon is destroyed as an angel casts **a stone, like a great millstone**, into the sea (v. 21). This event is foretold in Daniel 2:34–35: "While you were watching, a rock was cut out, but not by human hands. It struck the statue on its feet of iron and clay and smashed them. Then the iron, the clay, the bronze, the silver and the gold were broken to pieces at the same time and became like chaff on a threshing floor in the summer. The wind swept them away without leaving a trace. But the rock that struck the statue became a huge mountain and filled the whole earth" (also see 2:44–45). Most people believe that the stone is Christ. Note the similarities to Jeremiah's dirge over the destruction of the Old Testament city of Babylon in Jeremiah 50–51 (especially the incident of casting the stone into the sea; compare v. 21 and Jeremiah 51:63–64).

The marriage of leopard beast and lamb beast, this adultery of church and world, called "Babylon," is doomed. As it goes down, all heaven will resound with Hallelujahs! (19:1–5). Then follows the glad strains of the wedding procession, as the Lamb espouses to Himself His true bride.

Rev. 19 | THE DESTRUCTION OF THE BEAST AND THE FALSE PROPHET

Shouts of "Hallelujah!" meaning "Praise the Lord" fill the air as John hears the roar of a great multitude in heaven shouting and lifting up their God in glory and praises. Nowhere else in the New Testament is *Hallelujah* used, but it occurs four times in the first six verses of chapter 19. Great is the celebration in heaven as the saints, the 24 elders, the four cherubim and seraphim beasts (chap. 4) and all the other hosts of heaven recognize that Babylon — both the apostate religious system, Mystery Babylon, and the corrupt political system, called the city of Babylon — is fallen and completely destroyed.

The Wedding Supper of the Lamb, v. 9.

The heavens sing, "Let us rejoice for the wedding supper of the Lamb has come, and her bride has made herself ready." The futurist interpreters believe that the church was taken up to heaven at the beginning of the seven-year tribulation period (4.1). During these seven years they have been preparing themselves for the wedding. In 2 Corinthians 5:10 we read, "For we must all appear before the judgment seat of Christ, that each one may receive what is due him for the things done while in the body, whether good or bad." This judgment has no effect on one's salvation — one's salvation is sure (see 1 Corinthians 3:14–15). Instead, this judgment considers how well we lived for Christ, starting at the point of our Christian conversion. Those who have worked diligently for God in their Christian walk will be greatly rewarded — how we long to hear our Master Jesus say to us, "Well done, good and faithful servant! You have been faithful with a few things; I will put you in charge of many things.

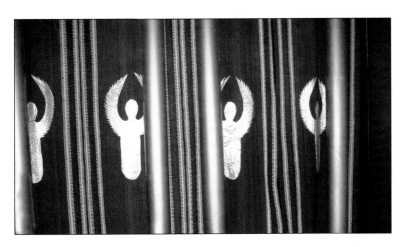

Reconstruction of the tabernacle curtain with embroidered cherubim. The cherubim shout their praise at the victory of the Lamb.

Come and share your master's happiness" (Matthew 25:21). After the judgment, God's people are arrayed in fine linen, clean and white because Christ's shed blood has washed away their sins. They are presented righteous and pure to their bridegroom, Christ. At the marriage supper, individual believers are guests, but collectively they are the bride.

Christ Returns, Riding a White Horse, with the Armies of Heaven, vv. 11–16

At this moment, John sees the heavens open and Christ return to the earth, riding a white horse, followed by all the armies of heaven also riding white horses. What a glorious sight! This event is called "the Revelation," for this is the moment when Christ reveals Himself to all the world. This is the second time in the book of Revelation that heaven's door is opened. The first event is when the doors of heaven are opened for the Rapture of the church into heaven (4:1). The second event is the Revelation, when the doors of heaven open as Christ and all the armies of heaven return to earth (v. 11). All the redeemed saints in heaven — including Old Testament saints, the church-age saints, and tribulation saints — return to fight with Christ at the Battle of Armageddon — but in the end Christ alone "treads the winepress of the fury of the wrath of God" in execution of judgment on the people of the earth. Christ's weapon is His Word, the sword from His mouth (v. 15). In chapter 14, the result of this battle is told in detail: bloodshed for a distance of almost 200 miles and as deep as a horse's bridle. The great supper for the birds of prey is in contrast to the marriage supper of the Lamb.

The Final Doom of Beast and False Prophet, vv. 17–21

Next we see God deal out His judgment on the satanic trinity. First, the Antichrist (leopard beast) and the false prophet (lamb beast) are destroyed. Later (in chap. 20), the dragon, Satan himself, goes to his final doom.

After the fall of Babylon, which was the working alliance of the beast and the false prophet, the beast and the false prophet continued for a while, each in his own field. Now their turn has come. The two of them are thrown alive into the fiery lake of burning sulfur, where they will suffer eternally (v. 20).

Rev. 20 | THE 1000 YEARS ("MILLENNIUM")

The only actual mention of the "thousand-year" reign of Jesus Christ as King of Kings and Lord of Lords in the Bible is in this chapter. However, there are passages throughout the Bible that allude to this time of peace when Christ will dwell on earth — for example, Isaiah 11:6: "The wolf will live with the lamb, the leopard will lie down with the goat, . . . and a little child will lead them."

Some believers understand the 1000 years to refer to one of the ages of eternity, after the physical order of existence has passed. Other believers think that the Millennium will be an age of blessedness in this world, either exactly 1000 years or a long period of time. This most certainly must be true, or hundreds of the Bible's prophecies cannot be fulfilled—consider the Old Testament prophecies regarding the future glorious state of Israel (see Genesis 49 and Deuteronomy 33).

An argument to be made for the validity of an earthly millennial reign of Christ is something Jesus Himself said: "I tell you the truth, at the *renewal* of all things, when the Son of Man sits on his glorious throne, you who have followed me will also sit on twelve thrones, judging the twelve tribes of Israel" (Matthew 19:28). Also, Peter said, "Repent, then, and turn to God, so that your sins may be wiped out, that times of refreshing may come from the Lord, and that he may send the Christ, who has been appointed for you—even Jesus. He must remain in heaven

Three Approaches to the Subject of the Millennium

Amillennialism

This approach suggests that the millennium represents the current reign of the redeemed saints with Christ in heaven. It is thought that the present-day form of God's kingdom will be followed by Christ's return, a general resurrection, and the final White Throne Judgment. After this, Christ will continue to reign over the perfect new heaven and new earth for an eternity. In this approach, the 1000 years is figurative and represents an eternal amount of time.

Premillennialism

This approach (which is the main approach used in this commentary) suggests that the present form of God's kingdom is rapidly approaching the glorious return of Christ, which will occur after a seven-year period of tribulation. With Christ's return, Satan will be bound in the Abyss, and the first resurrection will occur. All the redeemed saints in heaven will return to the earth with Christ to reign with Him for a literal 1000 years. This millennial period will be characterized predominately by peace—at least initially. As the millennial period progresses, the earth will become repopulated with people who have free will. Over time, people's self-confidence and pride will harden their hearts. God will loose Satan for a short time at the end of the 1000 years. Satan will make one last effort to war with God. God will strike Satan and all who have joined to fight Him with a fire that devours them. God will throw Satan into the lake of burning sulfur to be tormented eternally. This is followed by the White Throne Judgment and a second resurrection of the millennial-age saints. Finally, God will establish a new heaven and new earth, where He will dwell with His people forever.

Postmillennialism

This approach assumes that eventually the world will be Christianized—in other words, all the world's people will accept Christ as their Lord and Savior. This will result in a long period of world peace called the Millennium. This glorious period of time will be followed by Christ's second coming, the resurrection of the dead, the White Throne Judgment and the establishment of an eternal new heaven and new earth.

until the time comes for God to *restore everything,* as he promised long ago through his holy prophets" (Acts 3:19–21). Both of these passages refer to renewing something, to bringing it back to its former state. It's unlikely that they refer to heaven—for heaven needs no restoration. It seems more likely that they allude to the restoration of the earth to its former godly state, prior to man's sin, when God reigned and walked the earth with His creation (Genesis 2).

In addition, there are many verses in Psalms, Isaiah, and Zechariah that point to Jerusalem as being the center of millennial activity.

- "And the Redeemer will come to Zion" (Isaiah 59:20);
- "The LORD will roar from Zion and thunder from Jerusalem;. . . then you will know that I, the LORD your God, dwell in Zion, my holy hill. Jerusalem will be holy" (Joel 3:16–17);
- "This is what the LORD says: 'I will return to Zion and dwell in Jerusalem. Then Jerusalem will be called the City of Truth, and the mountains of the LORD Almighty will be called the Holy Mountain. . . . Once again men and women of ripe old age will sit in the streets of Jerusalem, each with cane in hand because of his age. The city streets will be filled with boys and girls playing there'" (Zechariah 8:3–4).

These are covenant verses that God has made with His people. One could hardly make a case that these covenant promises have already been fulfilled. God never breaks His promises, so one would assume that these promises will be fulfilled during the 1000 years.

Regardless of what each of us believes about the 1000 years, that which unites us all as Christians is the living hope, the return of Jesus Christ. Our various understandings of the future and the Millennium will, without exception, pale in the radiant light of God's presence with His people (21:22–23).

Satan Bound, vv. 1–3

Satan's expulsion from heaven in chapter 12 was connected with the start of the Great Tribulation (the final 3½ years of Satan's dominion of the earth); here Satan's binding is connected with the second advent of Christ. Some think the two passages refer to the same event, but in chapter 12 Satan made trouble for the earth, while here he is kept from making trouble. The Abyss (bottomless pit; v. 1) was the home of demons (Luke 8:31). Satan's domain, presided over by one of his archangels (9:11), now becomes his prison. He had been the ruler of this world, but will not be during the Millennium. The Abyss is not the lake of burning sulfur (v. 10), which will be the final destination of the Devil.

The Millennial Reign, vv. 4–6

It will last 1000 years. This is understood by some to be a literal 1000 years, the final 1000 years or "Sabbath rest." Some take it to mean an indefinitely long time. If the expression in 2-Peter 3:8—"One day is with the Lord as a thousand years, and a thousand years as one day"—were applied here, it might mean, in God's chronology, anywhere from one day to 360,000 years.

All persons entering the 1000 years have been redeemed, according to Isaiah 60:21 and Joel 2:28.

Thrones occupied for judgment (v. 4). Who were on these thrones? It seems that the thrones were occupied by Old Testament saints, New Testament saints, and tribulation saints (those who died during the Tribulation with the seal of God on their foreheads). We assume that the resurrection of the tribulation saints occurred at Christ's second coming (see Titus 2:13 and Revelation 6:9–11). The thrones are filled with people possessing resurrected bodies.

The first resurrection (v. 5). Many believe that the second sentence of v. 5 really refers to v. 4—meaning that the first resurrection occurs at the beginning of the millennial reign. A second resurrection is not mentioned, but the expression "the rest of the dead did not come to life until the thousand years were ended" indicates that there will be two resurrections, one before and one after the Millennium. The rest of the unsaved dead will remain in their graves until the end of the Millennium and will be raised for the Great White Throne Judgment (v. 11).

Satan's Final Doom, vv. 7–10

Babylon, the beast, and the false prophet—the agencies through which Satan had done his destructive work—have been destroyed (chaps. 17–19), and Satan's own time has come at last. He makes a furious but brief and futile effort to regain his hold on the earth.

Magog (v. 8) is the general name of the northern nations of Japheth's posterity (Genesis 10:2). Gog is their prince. In Ezekiel 38–39 they attack God's people from the north. Here they are from the "four corners of the earth." Probably these names are used to refer to the enemies of God from among all nations.

How could Satan muster such a vast following, when he had been bound for 1000 years and there had been a reign of righteousness? The answer lies in the fact that, like now, the people living during the Millennium will have free will, just as God created them from the beginning.

Procreation of the earth (v. 6). As mentioned before, those resurrected at the start of the 1000 years will have resurrected or glorified bodies and will not bear children. However, there are potentially two other groups of people who enter the Millennium: (1) those who had been sealed by God and protected so that they survived the tribulation period and entered into the 1000 years (including but perhaps not limited to the 144,000 who were sealed; chap. 7); and (2) perhaps others who survived through the Tribulation but neither accepted Christ nor took the mark of the beast during this time. It is assumed that these two groups of people will enter the 1000 years and will have children who, like us, will be born with a sinful nature. With Christ living in their midst and Satan bound in the Abyss, it is likely that most people living during the 1000 years will accept Christ as their Savior. However, it is likely that the inherent sin nature of man over time will also result in many who choose to ignore the salvation message. "Thus the Millennium will prove . . . that a perfect earthly environment and even universal knowledge of the Lord will not change men's hearts" (Charles Ryrie).

Satan is released for a short time (v. 7). When evil is not real to an individual, there seems to be no compelling reason to need a Savior. This is a very real problem in today's generation, because it is not "politically correct" to talk about evil or about Satan — even in many of today's churches! For this reason, perhaps, God releases the Devil at the end of the 1000 years so that he becomes real to people and hopefully they are compelled to accept Christ as their Savior. Nevertheless, there will be countless multitudes of people at the end of the 1000 years who reject Christ and team with Satan in his one last attempt to make war with God. Once again, God's enemies surround His Holy City, Jerusalem. In an instant God devours them with fire.

The lake of burning sulfur (v. 10) is the final destination of Satan, the beast, the false prophet, and the lost. It may surprise some that Satan does not reach his final destination in hell until after the Millennium. Many people grow up thinking that Satan is a little red guy with horns and a pitchfork who wanders around hell waiting for lost souls. Nothing could be further from the truth. Satan is "prince of the power of the air" (Ephesians 2:2 KJV), he is "the god of this age" (2 Corinthians 4:4). He and his demonic army are free to roam the heavens and the earth until he is cast out of heaven (Revelation 12:7–9), half way through the seven years of tribulation. After this, he is restricted to roaming only the earth for 3½ years during the Great Tribulation. With Christ's return, he is bound and chained in the Abyss for the 1000 years and then released at the end for just a short time. Finally, he is cast into the lake of burning sulfur where he, along with all lost souls, will live on and on in torment, "day and night forever and ever" (v. 10).

The Final Judgment, vv. 11–15

This passage contains one of the Bible's most personal messages. We ought to read it often. It will help us to be ready to answer the roll call.

The flight of the earth and sky from the presence of Him who sat upon the "great white throne" (v. 11) may have been by fire (2 Peter 3:10–12). Those who had already been judged have their judgment confirmed here, in the presence of the assembled universe.

The judgment is complete. Every person from every era and every region will be there. Every deed and motive will have been recorded. It

Scene of the final judgment from the Church of Annunciation in Nazareth is a reminder of the close of the book of Revelation.

is the day spoken of by Paul in Romans 2:16: "the day when God will judge men's secrets." The more we know ourselves, the more it will make us serious and thoughtful to think of this.

There will be only two classes: the saved and the lost. The "books" contain the records of people's works. The Book of Life is a separate book that contains the names of all the redeemed. This includes people saved during the 1000 years and all those people who were part of the first resurrection: "Blessed and holy are those who have part in the first resurrection. The second death has no power over them" (20:6). The Great White Throne Judgment only applies to those people whose names are not written in the Book of Life.

The "second death" is the final doom at the end, as distinguished from physical death, which is the lot of all humanity. It is here called the "lake of fire," the same thing Jesus talked about in the Gospels: the place where "the fire is not quenched" (Mark 9:48) — "the eternal fire prepared for the devil and his angels" (Matthew 25:41). Literal fire? Who knows? It may well be that a literal fire would be preferable over eternal torments of the soul, which would be more painful to the soul than fire is to the body.

Rev. 21 | HEAVEN

This chapter does not refer to a new social order in this present world, but to the eternal home of the redeemed, the "Father's house with many rooms" (John 14:2). It is one of the most beautiful, comforting, and precious chapters in the whole Bible, a chapter we will never tire of reading.

The **new heaven and new earth** (v. 1). The first heaven and earth have passed away, as Peter had said (2 Peter 3:10), the heaven with a great noise (an explosion?) and the earth and its works simply burned up. What amount of change in the physical universe is involved, we do not know. Nor do we know whether it will be this earth made over and renewed by fire, or an entirely different earth. Nor to what extent, with our glorified, incorruptible, spiritual bodies, we may be confined to any material planet or star, or be free to roam in the limitless spheres of space and eternity. How we would love to know! Someday we shall.

There is **no longer any sea** (v. 1), but there is a river (22:1). So we wonder if it is to be taken literally. Perhaps the "fire" by which the earth was consumed left no sea. Perhaps the "river of the water of life" is not real water. Some think that the "sea" is a symbol of perpetual unrest and wickedness, and its absence indicates the unruffled peace prevailing in heaven. Or, since the sea was viewed as a barrier between nations, its absence may mean universal brotherhood.

The **New Jerusalem** (vv. 9–10), the Holy City. The Bible presents two Jerusalems. The first is on earth and becomes the earthly home of Christ during the Millennium. The other is in heaven, a celestial city that is a mirror image of the earthly Jerusalem (see Galatians 4:25–26; Hebrews 12:22; and Psalm 122). It is this heavenly city which Abraham left his home in Ur of the Chaldees to find (Hebrews 11:10). This city, "whose architect and builder is God," is now brought to completion, with Abraham and the rest of the redeemed saints reveling in its glories.

The tabernacle of God (v. 5). The tabernacle or dwelling place of God has been in heaven. Now, in the person of Jesus, God dwells among His people (v. 3). God's dwelling place—"the Father's house with many rooms." In Eden, humanity—Adam and Eve—was driven from the actual, immediate, conscious presence of God. Here God's presence is restored. We shall actually see His face and will be with Him throughout the ceaseless cycles of never-ending ages. No more death, no tears, no pain, no heartaches, no sorrow, for the old order of things has passed away. Christ says, "I am making everything new!" and then commands John to write what is trustworthy and true: "It is done. I am the Alpha and Omega, the Beginning and the End. To him who is thirsty I will give to drink without cost from the spring of the water of life. He who overcomes will inherit all this, and I will be his God and he will be my son" (vv. 6–7).

Those who live without God will be on the outside, in the fiery lake of burning sulfur (v. 8; 22:15). To God there are only two classes: those who are His, and those who are not.

The City of Gold, 21:9–22:5

The bride of Christ, a city, is shown to John by the same angel who had shown him the adulterous church (chap. 17), which was also a city: Babylon. The ancient city of Babylon was a "city of gold" (see "Babylon," p. 396). Now the real city of gold appears in its infinite splendor and magnificence. The city is, of course, filled with God's people.

The measurements of the city (21:15–17). Twelve thousand stadia (about 1,400 miles). This may be the length of each side or the entire distance around, which would make each side 3000 stadia and the 12 gates 1000 stadia apart. The wall was 144 cubits (about 200 feet) thick. The measurements are in multiples of 12. Twelve is the signature of God's people. There are 12 gates, inscribed with the names of the 12 tribes of Israel, and 12 foundations, with the names of the 12 apostles. The city was a perfect cube, as was its prototype, the Holy of Holies in the tabernacle. Placed over the United States of America, it would extend from the northernmost tip of Maine to the southernmost tip of Florida and from the east coast westward to the state of Colorado — and it also extends 1,400-plus miles into the sky. Twelve thousand, then, is the symbol of God's people, multiplied by 1000; it represents the completed, perfected, and glorious state of redeemed creation.

The names of the 12 tribes inscribed on the gates, and the 12 apostles on the foundations, may be meant to indicate that the founders of the city would never be forgotten but would be held in loving remembrance by the city's inhabitants throughout the endless ages of eternity.

The precious stones (21:18–21). The breastplate of the high priest, bearing 12 stones inscribed with the names of the 12 tribes (Exodus 28:15–30) must have been a sort of dim foreshadowing, given in the distant past, of what God was working toward. The stones are similar to those of the New Jerusalem. There is difficulty in identifying some of these stones. They may not have been the same as those which now bear their names.

The colors the stones are thought to represent: jasper, clear; sapphire, blue; chalcedony, sky-blue; emerald, green; sardonyx, red and white; sardius, fiery red; chrysolite, golden; beryl, sea-green; topaz, transparent green; chrysoprase, purple; jacinth, red; and amethyst, violet.

The foundations sparkle with the colors of the rainbow. Each gate is a pearl, and the whole is composed of the most valuable and beautiful material things known to man, constructed together in a spectacle resplendent beyond imagination — a spectacle of eternal beauty, glory, peace, security.

Rev. 22 | FINAL WORDS

The Tree of Life, vv. 1–5

The Garden of Eden is restored in the midst of the city of gold. Paradise and immortality. After Adam and Eve sinned in the Garden of Eden, God posted an angel at the Tree of Life to prevent them from eating of its fruit and consequently be condemned to live eternally in their sinful state. Hallelujah! A new era has arrived, and God's redeemed people can eat all they want from the Tree of Life. The tree will promote our eternal health and well-being.

What will we do in heaven? Sing? Most assuredly. Would it be heaven without music? But more. There will, no doubt, be every opportunity to develop our unsatisfied aspirations of earth. Life, growing, advancing, ever onward, ever upward, taking our place in God's administration of the universe, incorruptible bodies, in incorruptible surroundings.

The Importance of the Book, vv. 6–16

At the end of the book is a reaffirmation that it *is the Word of God* (1:2). The book began by pronouncing blessing on those who read and keep its words (1:3), and so it closes (v. 7). **Do not seal up the words of the prophecy of this book** (v. 10) is a grave warning not to neglect it, but to study it. Daniel was told to seal up his prophecy "until the time of the end" (Daniel 12:4); the end has now come.

Let him who does wrong continue to do wrong; . . . let him who is holy continue to be holy (v. 11) is a solemn resignation of the lost to their fate, and of the saved to theirs. In this world, character may become better or worse while the era of grace lasts. But the time comes when it is fixed for eternity. Eternal punishment and eternal life are not arbitrary decrees of God but an inevitable result, as the fruit comes from the bud. The punishment of sin is sin. The reward of holiness is holiness.

Notice again (vv. 14–15) the absolute separation of the tares and wheat. Over and over and over it is stated that there are only two classes of people and only two destinies.

Genesis and Revelation	
The Bible is all one story. The last part of the last book in the Bible reads like the close of the story begun in the first part of the first book.	
The first word in Genesis: "In the beginning God created the heavens and the earth" (1:1).	Almost the last word in Revelation: "I saw a new heaven and a new earth" (21:1).
Genesis: "The gathered waters he called seas" (1:10).	Revelation: "And there was no longer any sea" (21:1).
Genesis: "The darkness he called night" (1:5).	Revelation: "There will be no night there" (21:25).
Genesis: "God made two great lights [sun and moon]" (1:16).	Revelation: "The city does not need the sun or moon to shine on it, for the glory of God gives it light" (21:23).
Genesis: "When you eat of it you will surely die" (2:17).	Revelation: "There will be no more death" (21:4).
Genesis: "I will greatly increase your pain" (3:16).	Revelation: "There will be no more pain" (21:4).
Genesis: "Cursed is the ground because of you" (3:17).	Revelation: "No longer will there be any curse" (22:3).
Genesis: Satan appears as the deceiver of mankind (3:1, 4).	Revelation: Satan disappears forever (20:10).
Genesis: Adam and Eve were driven from the Tree of Life (3:22–24).	Revelation: The Tree of Life reappears; all are invited to eat from it (22:2).
Genesis: Adam and Eve were driven from God's presence (3:24).	Revelation: "They will see His face" (22:4).
Genesis: Man's primeval home was in a garden by a river (2:20).	Revelation: Redeemed man's eternal home will be beside a river flowing forever from the throne of God (22:1).

"I am the Root and the Offspring of David, and the bright Morning Star" (v. 16; see Numbers 24:17). Jesus says, "I am the *One* toward whom all prophecy pointed. There is no other."

The Final Invitation, v. 17

Jesus had just said, "I am coming soon!" (v. 12). The Spirit, the bride, and whoever hears, join in the chorus and prayer, "Come." Jesus answers, "Yes, I am coming soon" (v. 20). It is His last recorded word, the parting message to His waiting bride as He passes out of sight. The passage contains an invitation to sinners to come to Him, that they may be ready when He comes. As a result, some will ask Christ to save them and others will harden their hearts further. It is for each individual to decide — choose life or choose death. This decision has eternal consequences. If you have not accepted Christ as your Savior yet — don't delay. Ask Jesus to be your Lord and Savior and receive His free gift of eternal life! (2 Corinthians 5:17; 6:2; John 14:6; Romans 5:8; Mark 1:15; see p. 977 for a simple prayer of salvation).

A Final Warning Against the Mutilation of God's Word, vv. 18–19

Rationalistic critics do not like this passage and would limit its meaning to this one book, because it condemns them for assuming to themselves the liberty to eliminate whatever portions of Scripture they do not like. This warning is also found in Deuteronomy 4:2 and 12:32. Here it does refer particularly to Revelation, but it is also a serious warning against treating lightly any part of God's Word.

Masada.

After the New Testament

Chapel of the Ascension on the Mount of Olives, built in the 12th century.

A Brief History of the Western Church

Contents

Introduction

It is impossible to squeeze the history of the church into a few pages. What follows is merely a brief summary of the history of the Western church (that is, the church in Europe and North America). The last section, "The Twentieth Century," is even more narrowly focused: it is specifically about the history of the church in the United States.

It is tempting to view the history of the church as mostly a matter of struggles over the purity of doctrine and of the church. But the church is intertwined with the cultures in which it exists, and from its very beginning at Pentecost, the church had to deal with questions raised by Judaism and the Roman Empire. It was not just a matter of keeping the faith pure; it was also a never-ending struggle to understand how the Christian faith should be defined and expressed in each era.

Social and cultural trends never bypass the church entirely. The Reformation is a good example. While it is correct to say that it was the result of the spiritual bankruptcy of the medieval Roman Catholic Church and led to a revitalization of the church, this is not the whole picture. There were numerous contributing factors—such as the invention of the printing press, the weakening of the feudal system, and the general movement in the direction of individualism—that played a significant role. Without these contributing factors it is difficult to imagine the Reformation taking place at all.

This does not mean that God is not in charge of His church. On the contrary, as the existence of the Roman Empire made the rapid spread of the church in the first centuries possible, so the confluence of religious, social, and cultural trends led to the renewal of the church in the Reformation.

(If you are interested in reading more about church history, a more detailed but readable book is *Christianity Through the Centuries* by Earle E. Cairns [3rd edition, Zondervan, 1996].)

The First Centuries: From Pentecost to A.D. 313

The Spread of the Church

The church began on the Day of Pentecost (Acts 1–2) and spread rather quickly throughout the Roman Empire. The apostle Peter and many others worked to spread the Gospel mostly to the approximately four million Jews who were scattered throughout the empire. The apostle Paul and others worked mainly among gentile converts in Jewish synagogues as well as among Gentiles who did not know Judaism, mostly in the major cities. From there the Gospel spread to the countryside.

Persecution often followed, but in the early days it was instigated by Jews rather than by the Roman Empire. The Romans had granted freedom to existing religions such as Judaism, and they regarded Christianity as a branch of Judaism, as is shown by Felix, the Roman governor, when he discussed Paul's case with King Herod Agrippa: "They had some

The Colosseum, begun by Emperor Vespasian in A.D. 72 and completed by Titus in A.D. 80. The largest monument of Roman antiquity (617 × 512 feet), it consists of three tiers of arched galleries and a fourth floor with square windows that supported a retractable canvas awning against the summer sun. It could seat 50,000 spectators, who watched trained gladiators fight one another to the death and then, later on, watched Christians being killed by lions. The Colosseum fell into disuse after A.D. 404 and suffered neglect. Pope Benedict XIV (1740–58) declared it a sacred monument in honor of the Christian martyrs who died there.

- *The Shepherd of Hermas* is an allegory, written about A.D. 150, that is full of symbolism and visions. It is modeled after the book of Revelation and could be called the *Pilgrim's Progress* of the early church. It was also included in the Codex Sinaiticus, at the end of the New Testament.

These and the other writings of the Apostolic Fathers are not to be confused with the many apocryphal books that began appearing in the 2nd century and consist mostly of spurious Gospels (such as the Gospel of Nicodemus and the Gospel of Peter), Acts (such as the Acts of John and the Acts of Andrew), and letters (such as the Letters of Paul to Seneca and the Letter of Peter to James). All these are later fabrications and range from the well-intentioned to the patently absurd.

External Problems: Persecutions

In its early days, as throughout most of its history, the church faced both external and internal problems. The external problems mostly took the form of persecutions. Before A.D. 250, persecutions were local, sporadic, and often the result of mob action rather than of civil policy.

One reason for the persecutions was political. Christianity grew very fast, and it made exclusive claims. One could not be a Christian and worship local deities or participate in the emperor cult (see p. 652). This eventually began to be considered disloyalty to the state, and after A.D. 250 Christianity was classed as an illegal secret society and a threat to the safety of the empire.

Another reason was social. Christianity had great appeal to the lower

Colosseum of Rome (ca. A.D. 80). Built after the martyrdom of Peter and Paul, this Colosseum witnessed the persecution of Christians for over two centuries.

classes, which caused the aristocracy to fear it, especially since it taught that in Christ all are equal—even slaves and masters.

Christians were hated for economic reasons. Those who made a living from idol worship and various occult practices saw Christianity as a threat to their livelihood (Acts 16:16–19; 19:24–27), and Christians were blamed for plagues and famines.

Finally, Christianity was considered by many to be atheism, since it had no images and worship was spiritual and internal rather than focused on rituals and sacrifices.

After the Jews, Emperor Nero was the first persecutor of the church. In A.D. 64 he needed a scapegoat to take the blame for the burning of Rome (a fire that from the very beginning was generally believed to have been set by Nero himself), so he had Christians accused of arson and had them killed in cruel ways. Peter and Paul died in this persecution.

In A.D. 95, the Jews had refused to pay a tax levied to support one of the Roman deities. Since Christians were still associated with the Jews, they also suffered the consequences under Emperor Domitian. During this persecution John was exiled to the island of Patmos, where he received the visions recorded in the book of Revelation.

Christianity then was officially under a state ban that was only loosely enforced until about A.D. 250. In A.D. 112 a governor, Pliny, wrote to Emperor Trajan asking for clarification of policy toward Christians. Pliny's approach, when someone informed on a Christian, was to have the Christian brought before a tribunal and asked three times if he or she were a Christian. If the answer was yes, the Christian was sentenced to death. Trajan wrote that this was indeed correct procedure: Christians were not to be sought out, but they were to be killed if someone informed on them and they confessed.

The Empire of Constantine

However, in A.D. 250, Emperor Decius issued an edict that demanded an annual offering of sacrifices to the gods and the emperor. After offering a sacrifice, one received a certificate of compliance. Christians generally refused to do this, and Christianity now became illegal.

Decius was followed by Emperor Diocletian, who faced a deteriorating empire. He believed that a strong monarchy supported by a strong military could save the empire, and he saw the refusal of the Christians to support the state religion as a threat to what remained of the empire's stability. In A.D. 303, he issued the first edicts for the active persecution of Christians, who by now numbered 50–75 million, or as much as 15 percent of the total population of the empire. They were now to be sought out and imprisoned if they persisted in loyalty to Christ and killed if they refused to sacrifice to the emperor. Scriptures were confiscated and burned. Prisons became so crowded with Christians that there was no room for criminals, so Christians were exiled, stripped of property, killed by sword or wild beasts, or sent to labor camps where they were worked to death.

Internal Problems: Controversies and Heresies

But the church also faced internal problems, which began at least as early as A.D. 49 with the Council of Jerusalem (Acts 15). Here the leaders of the church met to decide the question whether or not gentile Christians had to be circumcised (a religious act practiced by the Jews as evidence of becoming a Jew). Peter argued yes, but Paul's no carried the day. There were, however, many Christians who did not regard this decision as final and continued to insist on circumcision because they believed Jewish law to be the highest expression of God's will and therefore applicable to Christians.

Other early controversies had to do with philosophical heresies such as Gnosticism, which taught that the spirit was good but matter was evil and that if Jesus had a material body He had to be evil. Thus they insisted that Jesus was only spirit and denied that His crucifixion and bodily resurrection could have occurred. For them, salvation was only for the soul, not for the body. Gnostics also believed that the God of the Old Testament was evil and only the New Testament God was good. This made it easy for Christians deceived by Gnosticism to hate Jews. Interestingly, there were two opposite forms of Gnosticism: some Gnostics believed in strict asceticism to avoid contamination by the desires of the body, while others taught unbridled licentiousness, since what one did in the body had no effect on the soul. Paul, John, and other leaders of the church spent a great deal of time and energy trying to counter this heresy.

Problems also arose when new converts brought some of their old ideas with them into the church, or when Christians tried to make Christianity acceptable to upper-class Roman intellectuals. The persecutions created issues that had to be settled—for example, how to treat Christians who had offered sacrifices or given up Scriptures to be burned.

The burning of Scriptures forced the church to decide what was indeed inspired Scripture, and this led to the formal adoption of the canon of the New Testament (see p. 991). Questions regarding the nature of human beings (are we born sinful or do we learn sinful behavior; do we have free will to choose between good and evil?) and concerning how we are saved from our sins developed and were "settled" by church councils, but they persist today and have caused many bitter disputes through the centuries.

From the Edict of Milan (A.D. 313) to Charlemagne (A.D. 800)

The Edict of Milan (a.d. 313)

The persecutions ended in 313 with the Edict of Milan, issued by Emperor Constantine. Unlike Diocletian, Constantine saw Christianity as an ally to help save the empire and Greco-Roman culture. When he and his army had been almost crushed by enemies, Constantine reportedly had a vision of a cross with the words *In hoc signo vinces* ("In this sign conquer") on it. He took this as a favorable omen, defeated his enemies, and took control of the state.

After the Edict of Milan, the Roman Empire favored the church. There was freedom of worship, confiscated property was returned to Christians, and clergy were exempted from public service. Eventually the church was subsidized by the state, and Sunday was made the official day of rest and worship.

Looking from the Colosseum (see pp. 898–99) down on the Arch of Constantine, erected by Emperor Constantine after his victory in A.D. 312, which came after he saw a cross in the sky and the words *In hoc signo vinces* ("In this sign conquer").

Constantine had continued to be chief priest of the pagan state and was not baptized until just before his death. But with the exception of one setback, under Emperor Julian, Constantine's successor, Christianity continued on its way to becoming the official state religion. This meant that the state would be involved in attempting to settle the internal problems faced by the church.

The Church Fathers

For more than a century after the Edict of Milan, a group of scholars invested great energy and brilliance in the careful study of the Scriptures to find their theological meaning. They are known as the post-Nicene church fathers, because they lived and worked after the First Council of Nicea, held in 325 (see below; the earlier church fathers are known as the apostolic fathers—see p. 897—and the ante-Nicene church fathers). Six of these post-Nicene church fathers stand out, three in the eastern half of the empire, and three in the west.

In the east, **Chrysostom** from Antioch (347–407) taught that the Cross and ethics are inseparable; **Theodore**, bishop of Mopsuestia (350–428), wrote biblical commentaries, insisting on a thorough understanding of grammar and the historical background of the text; and **Eusebius** (265–339) wrote, at the request of Constantine, a church history using and carefully evaluating primary sources. Most of our knowledge of the first centuries of the church comes from Eusebius's work.

While the Eastern fathers wanted to discover the meaning of Scriptures by looking at grammar and history, the Western fathers translated Scriptures and wrote theological treatises. **Jerome** from Venice (347–420) went into retreat at Bethlehem to create the *Vulgate,* a translation from Hebrew into Latin, which was until recently the official Bible of the Roman Catholic Church. **Ambrose** (340–397) was an administrator and preacher who was not afraid to oppose the emperor and who made the state respect the church and refrain from entering into the spiritual realm.

The best-known and most influential of the fathers was **Augustine** of Hippo (354–430). His mother had prayed for his conversion to Christianity from the loose life he lived, and one day he was in a garden where he heard a voice telling him to read the Bible, which he had opened to Romans 13:13–14. He became a priest and later bishop of Hippo. Augustine wrote more than 100 books, 500 sermons, 200 letters, and one of the great autobiographies of all time, the *Confessions*. He created a Christian philosophy of history with his *City of God,* which he saw as a spiritual civilization that could replace the dying Roman classical civilization. Today both Catholics and Protestants look to him as an authority. Catholics like his emphasis on the church as a visible institution, his doctrine of purgatory, and emphasis on the sacraments (baptism, communion). Protestants like his emphasis on salvation from sin as a result of the grace of God, who gave His Son so that we all could be saved from sin and reconciled to God.

The Seven Church Councils

Several of these church fathers participated in a series of seven church councils (also called ecumenical councils because they involved the whole church) held between A.D. 325 and 787 to define basic Christian doctrines. They were attended by bishops and convened by emperors, which meant that after the fall of the Western Roman Empire in A.D. 476 most of the participants were from the Eastern church. The statements issued by the first four councils are still unanimously accepted by Christian churches even today.

Augustine was the primary figure at the Council of Ephesus (431). It was convened to deal with the so-called Pelagian controversy, which revolved around the question as to how human beings are saved. Pelagius, a British theologian, held that each person is created free and has the power

The Hagia Sophia (Church of Holy Wisdom), a Byzantine structure in Constantinople (Istanbul), was built by Emperor Constantine (A.D. 360), burned (404), and was rebuilt by Emperor Justinian (537). The dome is 100 feet across and nearly 200 feet high. The minarets were added when the Muslims conquered Constantinople in 1453 and turned the church into a mosque. It is now a museum.

to choose good or evil because he or she is a separate creation and therefore uncontaminated by Adam's sin. Thus individuals can attain salvation by choice and effort. Pelagius's opponent was Augustine, who argued that all persons are born sinful by nature and therefore cannot choose freely between good and evil, so salvation must come by grace on God's part. The Council of Ephesus adopted Augustine's view, and although the question has continued to come up many times since, the decision stands as orthodox Christian doctrine.

The other important councils were Nicaea I (325), which declared Jesus Christ to be deity along with the Father; Constantinople I (381) which upheld the deity of the Holy Spirit; and Chalcedon (451), which affirmed the two natures of Christ (divine and human) in one person.

Monasticism

The barbarian tribes had increasingly encroached on the western part of the Roman Empire from the end of the 1st century until it finally fell apart in 476. After the church was free from persecutions, it turned its energy toward evangelizing these peoples who were migrating around Western Europe. The spread of Christianity helped to preserve elements of the Greco-Roman culture, but the mass conversions of barbarians affected the church in that they brought many pagan practices into the church that had tried to Christianize them. Christians began celebrating Christmas after A.D. 350 on the date of an old pagan winter solstice celebration; the pagan elements were eliminated and replaced with the commemoration of Christ's birth. Some would say that this weakened the church, but others argue that this is an example of the way Christianity has adapted itself to and transformed cultural practices as it continued to spread through the following two centuries.

Many barbarians had only partially converted to Christianity and church discipline became lax, so the church accommodated these barbarians who had been used to worshiping images by materializing the

The monastery of St. Catherine at the base of Mt. Sinai (Jebel Musa). The monastic movement sought to isolate itself from the decadence of society.

liturgy with the veneration of saints through relics, pictures, and statues. A more colorful liturgy developed along with a sharp distinction between clergy and laity. The number of holy days and festivals expanded as did the number of ceremonies that were ranked as sacraments. In the early church the sacraments were baptism and communion, but marriage, penance (doing something physical to atone for sins), ordination (ceremony to ordain bishops and other church officials), confirmation (ceremony to confirm one's faith in Christ when one is old enough to have a clear understanding of the Gospel), and extreme unction (ceremony done when one is dying) were added as sacraments.

During the period when the Roman Empire was weakening, many Christians felt that society was becoming decadent and that the church had lost its spiritual focus. They responded by retreating into solitude to try to achieve personal holiness through contemplation and asceticism. The monastic movement had its origins in the 4th century, grew considerably during the 6th, was widely popular during the 10th and 11th centuries and again in the 16th, and is still practiced today by comparatively few.

The psychological need to escape from the world of harsh realities and civil disorder was, these men (and women) believed, supported by some Scriptures; for example, they took 1 Corinthians 7:1 to mean that Paul advocated celibacy. Monasteries also offered a more individual approach to God and salvation than the formal corporate worship of the times, and the pure monastic lifestyle was a living social criticism. Geographic factors, such as the warm, dry caves along the Nile (where monasticism began), along with the ability to raise food easily along the river, fostered its spread, and the nearness to the desert stimulated meditation. Indeed, when it spread to the West, the colder climate made communal organization necessary to provide food and warm buildings for winter.

Benedict was the best-known organizer of the movement in Europe. He founded Monte Cassino (in Italy) in about 529; it survived until World War II, when it was destroyed by bombs. Benedict organized and controlled several monasteries. His program of work and worship with dietary rules, vows of poverty, chastity, and obedience—along with divisions of the day into periods for reading, worship, and work, as laid down in the still widely used Rule of St. Benedict—was almost universal by 800.

The monasteries served as the medieval equivalent of experimental farms as the monks cleared forests, drained marshes, built roads, and improved seeds and livestock breeds. They kept scholarship alive during the period A.D. 500–1000, when urban life was disrupted as the barbarians took over. The monasteries ran schools and copied manuscripts, collected and translated literature, and recorded history. Monks became missionaries and won whole tribes to Christianity, provided a refuge for social outcasts who needed help, ran hospitals, and provided food and shelter for travelers. However, when many of the best men and women of the Roman Empire went into monasteries, the world lost out on their leadership.

Eventually some monasteries became wealthy due to their community thrift, so laziness, greed, and gluttony crept in. Monasteries aided in the development of a hierarchical, centralized church organization as monks were bound by obedience to superiors who in turn had superiors.

Church and State

Between A.D. 313 and 590, the catholic (universal) church in the West became the Roman Catholic Church that in structure and canon law reflected imperial Rome. The bishops had all been equal until 313, when the bishop of Rome became known as *primus inter pares*, "first among equals"; but beginning with Leo I in 440, the Roman bishop began to claim supremacy over other bishops. The need for efficiency and coordination led to the centralization of power. The Roman bishop was considered the guarantor of orthodox doctrine mostly because people had looked to him for temporal as well as spiritual leadership during times of crisis. For example, when the emperor was in Constantinople in 410, Rome was sacked by the Visigoths and the bishop with clever diplomacy saved the city from fire. Thus, when the western half of the empire fell in A.D. 476, people looked to the Roman bishop for political leadership.

The bishop of Constantinople was considered next in prominence to the bishop of Rome, and both political and ecclesiastical leaders acknowledged this hierarchy. Gregory I (the Great) in 590 claimed that Leo had been the first pope because he saved the city from destruction, defined orthodoxy by writing against heresies, and developed a central court of appeals to make final decisions after cases had gone through bishops.

Rulers had to submit to the pope because spiritual authority was more important than temporal. Gregory himself rejected the title "pope" (which literally means "papa"), but he had all the power of later popes and indeed fought the bishop (or patriarch) of Constantinople, who claimed the title of universal bishop.

When others wanted to make Gregory the supreme head of the church, he declined the title but would not allow anyone else to take it. Yet no one dared to go against Gregory's will, and he made the bishopric of Rome one of the wealthiest, due to his talents as an administrator, and brought the English and the Spanish under Roman control. Along with his other talents, Gregory was a good preacher, writer, theologian, and musician; it was he who developed the Gregorian chant, which gained great importance in worship.

The Roman Catholic Church continued as the primary institution in the West, but not without threat. The emperors in the east (Constantinople) tried to get the church to be subordinate to the state, and followers of various heresies fought with the Roman bishop. Thus, by the 8th century the papacy was looking for a powerful ally who would acknowledge its claims to spiritual power as well as to physical possessions, since a developing system of taxation had enriched the papacy by requiring people to pay various kinds of taxes to the church. The pope found this ally in Charlemagne.

The Middle Ages: ca. 800–1300

Charlemagne and the Holy Roman Empire

A family known as the Carolingians had consolidated power in what is now much of Western Europe, including most of France and the Low Countries as well as what are now German-speaking countries, and eventually Italy.

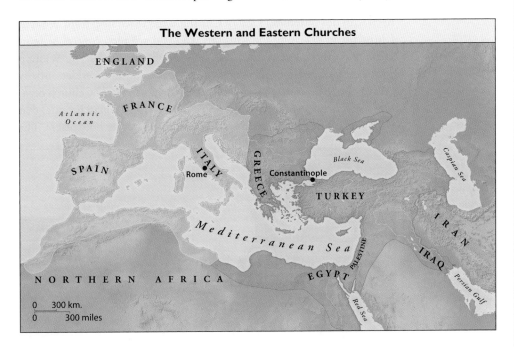

The Western and Eastern Churches

Through the reigns of the Carolingians Charles Martel (who defeated the Muslims at Tours and thus halted the advance of Islam in Europe) and Pepin, relationships between the church and political rulers were nurtured, so that by 800, when Pepin's son Charlemagne was to be crowned emperor, he asked the pope to perform the coronation. Thus, the German barbarian Charlemagne revived the Roman Empire as a Christian empire, with the pope, responsible for people's spiritual well-being, and the emperor, responsible for their physical well-being, working closely together.

The Split Between East and West

By this time the Eastern Roman Empire and the Western Roman Empire were clearly two separate entities, and church in each of the two had also developed in different directions. The church in the Western Empire became the Roman Catholic Church, the church in the Eastern Empire the Eastern Orthodox Church (today consisting mostly of the Greek Orthodox and Russian Orthodox churches). The Western church concentrated more on polity, the Eastern on theology. During the 9th and 10th centuries the two clashed bitterly in a series of controversies, until by 1054 the Western pope and the Eastern patriarch (the Eastern equivalent of the pope) excommunicated each other over, of all things, whether communion bread should be leavened or unleavened. This split has never been healed, although in recent years the Roman Catholic Church and the Eastern Orthodox Church have taken cautious first steps toward a possible reconciliation.

The Crusades and Their Effects

Even with this bitterness, Eastern Christians requested help from Western Christians in defeating the Muslims who had assumed control of Jerusalem and other places regarded as holy by all Christians. The Western church responded by organizing the Crusades, which were essentially military operations that took place from 1095 to 1291. The church organized large armies (funded by the nobles in the Holy Roman Empire) that went to the Middle East to liberate Jerusalem and other holy places. The

The Crac des Chevaliers (Castle of the Knights) was built by the Crusaders in a break in the mountain range between Antakya, Turkey (ancient Antioch), and Beirut, Lebanon. Controlling this break meant controlling inland Syria. The fortress was built ca. 1150–1250 and could house 4000 soldiers. Unlike Belvoir Castle (see p. 946), the fortress was not destroyed after its capture by the Turks, but was put to good use, and towers were added.

Kingdom of Jerusalem was established and lasted for less than a century (1100–1187). Today the legacy of the Crusaders consists mostly of the remains of massive, European-style fortifications and castles left behind when the Muslims pushed the Crusaders out of the Middle East again.

The motive behind the Crusades was certainly not purely religious. The economic issue of opening the East for trade with the West, and the political issue of who would control the Middle East, enhanced the religious motivation and led to massive support for the Crusades. Popes and Christian leaders promoted the Crusades, while kings and other political rulers led them. (An exception was the tragic Children's Crusade in 1212, where the average age of the participants was 12.) The Crusades ended in 1291 with the fall of Acre to the Muslims.

The Crusades changed Western society in several ways. The power of the papacy grew during the wars, but the developing nationalism of the participants ultimately weakened the power of the popes. Cities became stronger, as nobles either did not return from the east or sold their property to townsmen to finance the Crusades. The zeal that had fed the Crusades was turned to building beautiful gothic cathedrals, which told Bible stories to an illiterate population in glass and stone, as well as to new forms of spirituality and new monastic orders.

Scholasticism

This era also saw the rise of scholasticism. For centuries, Arabian scholarship and classical Greek learning had been lost to the West. They enjoyed a resurgence, due in part to the efforts of the Sephardic Jews of Spain (see p. 947). Efforts were made to synthesize Greek science and literature with Christian theology.

This led to a systematic application of reason to theology in what is known as scholasticism. The decisions of the various church councils had been responses to specific issues, and they had never been integrated into a systematic whole. This is what scholasticism now did.

Two of the most influential scholastics were **Anselm of Canterbury** (ca. 1033–1109) and **Thomas Aquinas** (ca. 1225–1274). Aquinas was a nobleman who decided to become a monk. He wrote the brilliant *Summa Theologiae,* which is still a foundational work for many Roman Catholics and other Christians today. The methodology of the scholastics was later adopted by Reformed theologians in the 16th through 18th centuries.

Renaissance and Reformation: ca. 1300–1648

Paving the Way for the Reformation

Changes in Europe

Beginning in the 14th century, Western Europe underwent profound changes that ended in restructuring of society, politics, economics, art, thought, and Christian practice. Individualism replaced the structures of feudal society. In Southern Europe this found expression mostly in humanism, with man becoming the measure of all things instead of God; this is broadly referred to as the **Renaissance**. In Northern Europe the expression was more religious in nature, with growing protest against the Roman Catholic Church that resulted in the **Reformation**.

The changes began with the Black Death, the plague that entered Europe in 1347 on a merchant ship and killed half the population of the continent in the next 20 years. Since half the workforce had been killed, the remaining workers flexed newfound muscle in political insurrections. This general weakening of authority structures also made religious protests possible.

Forerunners of the Reformation

In Italy, the Franciscan order, founded by Francis of Assisi (1182–1226), preached a new, individual form of salvation and built churches wide, simple, and with no aisles so that the congregation would have a better view of the pulpit. In England, John Wycliffe (or Wyclyf; ca. 1325–84) challenged church teaching and set forth new views. He taught against transubstantiation, the doctrine that the elements actually change into Christ's body and blood during the communion service; he said that Christ is the head of the church, not the pope; he insisted that the Bible is the sole authority for a believer, not the church; and asserted that the church had use and possession of property but not ownership. Wycliffe also translated the New Testament into English so that people could have it available to read in the language they spoke. Students carried Wycliffe's views to Bohemia, where John Hus took them up. Hus and his followers sparked a civil war, and he was burned at the stake.

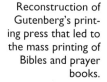

Reconstruction of Gutenberg's printing press that led to the mass printing of Bibles and prayer books.

The Invention of Printing

The event most responsible for focusing and spreading the profound changes in Europe, and ultimately the world, was the invention of the printing press in Johannes Gutenberg's metalworking shop in southern Germany around 1450. Before Gutenberg, the church was the main source of information. News of the world, both ecclesiastic and civil, came from the pulpit or the town crier. Most transactions were done orally because the majority of the population—often including local priests—were illiterate.

Bibles and prayer books were among the first books printed, and people demanded to learn to read them. When print superseded copying by hand, the accuracy of biblical texts was easier to ascertain.

It was now easier for church and state to impose controls on what could be printed or read—but it was also easier for dissidents to get their message out to all people.

The print revolution contributed so greatly to the spread of the Protestant Reformation that Martin Luther called printing the best of God's inventions. Indeed, from the beginning of his protest against the Roman Catholic Church, Luther's views were spread in printed form, so that within three years 300,000 copies of his works were on the market (making him a highly successful author even by modern standards), and he won a propaganda war with the Roman Catholic Church.

Religious Causes of the Reformation

In the 14th and 15th centuries the clergy reached new moral lows. Some clergy lived luxuriously, and many had illegitimate children. Few were as interested in church affairs as they were in secular pursuits. The Great Schism occurred when in 1305 the weak pope Clement V, influenced by the French king, moved the papacy from Rome to Avignon, France. It stayed there until 1377, when a godly mystic, Catherine of Siena, convinced Pope Gregory XI to move back to Rome. But when Gregory died, the resulting squabble led to the election of two popes, one in Rome and one in France. During the next century there were even three popes for a short time.

Supporting two papal courts was a tax burden for the people of Europe. Society had so many other financial obligations to the church that there was a substantial money transfer from national treasuries to the papal treasury. As nation-states became stronger, their resentment of this taxation grew.

Dogmas of the church were accepted and worship was practiced, but there was a divorce between religious life and daily life. There were attempts at reform. On a personal level, mysticism grew because many people desired to have personal contact with God. On the institutional level, the church called several councils to solve the problem of the two popes and eliminate corrupt leaders as well as solve other problems. The councils were to end the schism, deal with heresy, and continue to meet every decade.

Other Causes of the Reformation

Other factors set the stage for protest.

- Politically, the increasingly centralized nation-states were ready to support the Reformation. Leaders of these nation-states were opposed to the power of the church and its courts as well as to the church's ownership of vast tracts of land that generated no taxes for the independent countries in which they were located. They saw the Reformation as a way to create national churches that could be more easily controlled.

- Economically, by 1500 there were many new markets and increasing trade. The middle-class merchants who conducted the booming trade chafed under Roman Catholic economic restrictions, such as the prohibition of usury (lending money at interest) and guild regulations (guilds were a form of trade union), as well as at the lack of prestige it allowed businessmen.
- Socially, the new spirit of individualism demanded changes in the tight, hierarchical social order.
- Intellectually, Christian humanists such as Erasmus of Rotterdam studied the Bible in the original languages and became critics of the medieval Roman Catholic Church when they saw the differences between the New Testament church and the church of their time. They convinced people that salvation was a personal matter for individuals to settle with God, without a priest as mediator between themselves and God. They believed that individuals should study the Bible for themselves, and this helped create a general skepticism toward the Roman Catholic Church.

The Reformation

The First Reformer: Martin Luther (Germany)

The first man to break with the church was Martin Luther. Born in 1483, Luther from childhood began a long struggle of searching for salvation for his soul. His father wanted him to study law, but he became frightened in a thunderstorm and promised God he would become a monk if God spared his life.

He began teaching theology at the University of Wittenberg, then traveled as a church agent to Rome, where he saw the corruption first-hand. He then transferred back to Wittenberg, earned a doctorate of theology, and continued to lecture in biblical theology until his death. He lectured in the vernacular (the common spoken language, as opposed to the Latin most used in theological settings), and to do that intelligently he began to study the Bible in the original languages. He concluded that only in the Bible could truth be found *(sola scriptura)*. In 1516, when reading Romans 1:17, he became convinced that only through faith in Christ could he be justified before God *(sola fide)*.

Indulgences

One of the church practices that Luther considered corrupt was the sale of indulgences. Indulgences were documents that were given to the faithful in return for prayer, penitence, pilgrimage to a shrine, a good deed, or — especially — payment of money to the church. An indulgence could be purchased to free one from the penalty of sin. The theory behind it was that Christ and the saints had achieved so much merit in their lives that the excess merit was placed in a heavenly bank on which the pope could draw for people on earth or in purgatory (the halfway habitat between earth and heaven). The money paid for indulgences could then be used by the church to pay for expensive artists like Michelangelo to embellish Rome.

It was in Germany that the abuse of indulgences upset people most. Church law forbade one man to hold more than one church office, but Archbishop Albert controlled two provinces of the church and wanted to add a third that was vacant in 1514. At the time, Pope Leo X was building St. Peter's cathedral in Rome, so he needed money and promised Albert the extra offices for an exhorbitant sum. A papal bull (a solemn papal

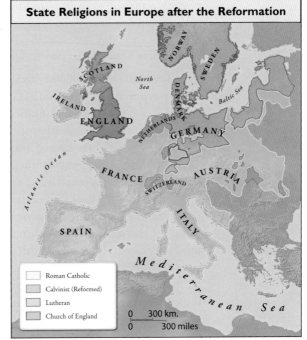

State Religions in Europe after the Reformation

Roman Catholic
Calvinist (Reformed)
Lutheran
Church of England

0   300 km.
0   300 miles

letter or decree sealed with a round, usually lead, seal called a *bulla*) granted Albert the right to sell indulgences to raise the necessary money. Albert's agent was a monk named Johannes Tetzel, whose flamboyant marketing techniques created a huge demand for the indulgences.

In 1517 Luther nailed a document to the door of the castle church in Wittenberg that contained Ninety-five Theses (position statements) that criticized abuses of the indulgence system. In 1518 he appeared at the Diet (deliberative assembly) of Augsburg, where he asserted that Scripture was the final authority, not the pope. In 1520 he published a series of pamphlets on the same theme, adding that princes should reform the church when necessary and that it was unnecessary to have priests dispense sacraments because individual believers were priests.

Leo responded with the bull *Exsurge Domine* ("Rise up, O Lord"), which eventually resulted in Luther's excommunication. Luther's books were burned at Cologne, so he publicly burned Leo's bull. In 1521 Luther was summoned to the Diet of Worms to answer for his views, but he received protection from the German princes. He refused to recant his views. His friends kidnapped him and hid him at Wartburg Castle, where he did much writing, worked to set up the German school system, and translated the New Testament into German. Luther said nuns and priests could marry, and he himself married Katherine von Bora in 1525.

In 1525 Luther also opposed the Peasants' Revolt after some radical reformers joined it, because he thought it would endanger the Reformation and subvert orderly government. The aftermath was that southern German peasants remained in the Roman Catholic Church. But Luther continued to develop a new liturgy and organize the Lutheran church.

John Calvin (France and Switzerland)

John Calvin (1509–64), the other primary figure in the Protestant movement, was only a small child when Luther posted his theses at Wittenberg, yet by mid-century he had numerous followers in the Netherlands, Switzerland, Scotland, and France. While Luther was the prophet of Protestantism, Calvin organized it. Luther emphasized preaching whereas Calvin developed a systematic theology. Luther focused on justification by faith while Calvin emphasized the sovereignty and centrality of God.

While living in Basel, Switzerland, Calvin (who was French) wrote the *Institutes of the Christian Religion* to try to get King Francis of France to accept the ideas of the Reformation. He wrote that all people are totally depraved (sinful) from birth due to Adam's sin, and that salvation from that original sin is a matter of unconditional election apart from human merit. The Holy Spirit irresistibly draws people to Christ, but those elected to salvation must persevere in the faith.

Calvin was a member of the professional class and studied philosophy, theology, law, and liberal arts. He encouraged education for all believers and set up an education system in Geneva. He believed that church and state were both created by God for the good of humans and the two institutions should work together amicably to further Christianity. He taught representative government for both church and state and so influenced the development of democratic movements in the centuries after him. And his emphasis on a divine call to a vocation and on thrift and hard work stimulated the growth of capitalism.

An attempt to modify Calvinism occurred in the Netherlands in 1618–19 at the Synod of Dort. Jacobus Arminius believed that people could resist the grace of God, whereas Calvin had believed God's grace to be irresistible and that believers could not fall away from salvation. The Calvinists won, asserting that once one is saved from sin, one is always secure with God; they began to persecute Arminians. However, Arminius's views would endure and have an influence on the large Methodist movement that emerged in the 18th century.

The Reformation in England

The Anglican Church (Church of England)

England slid into the Reformation through politics. King Henry VIII (1509–47) needed an heir to his throne, which his wife was unable to produce. He sent Cardinal Woolsey to the pope to try to obtain a divorce, but the pope said no. So Henry decided to get his divorce by getting the British parliament to accept him as head of the church in England. He then appropriated the property of the church and made the church submit to the crown.

Henry's daughter, Mary Tudor, was a staunch Catholic who persecuted Protestants when she became queen. Her reign was not long, and Henry's second daughter, Elizabeth, took the throne. She reinstituted Protestantism, but in a moderate form so as not to anger the pope too much. When her English Armada defeated the Spanish fleet of Philip II in 1588, Catholicism was permanently replaced by Anglicanism in England. The only country in the British Isles to remain Roman Catholic was Ireland, which would prove to be an ongoing problem for the British.

The Puritans

One group in England believed that Elizabeth had not gone far enough with reforms and that the Anglican church was too much like the Catholic church. They were called Puritans because they wanted to purify the English church and structure it on the biblical model. They preached keeping Sunday as a day of rest, modesty in dress and behavior, and maintaining a consciousness of sin.

Some Puritans wanted to separate church and state because their loyalty was to Christ and not the state church. They formed covenant communities that were supposed to have Christ as the head, and it was these groups who left England to found Plymouth and Boston in the New World. The Puritans in England briefly controlled government during the 17th century; their defeat led to the development of the British Constitution, on which much of the United States Constitution would be based.

The Radical Reformers

Zwingli (Switzerland)

Another group of reformers is generally called the "radical reformers." They were mostly linked to the early reform movement led by Huldreich Zwingli (1484–1531). Zwingli, from the German section of Switzerland, was trained as a clergyman and became a follower of Erasmus's teachings and a serious Bible scholar while pastoring.

In 1519 he had a conversion experience after reading Luther's views. His first public act was opposition to the compulsory taxes that went to the church. He then married secretly, but made it publicly legitimate in 1524. The authorities of Zurich then decided to have Zwingli debate all comers so they could decide what faith to follow. Both Zurich and Bern became Protestant as a result of these debates.

In 1529 Zwingli and Luther met in the Marburg Colloquy, agreed on 14 points but opposed each other on whether Christ was physically present in communion. As several Swiss cantons (states) became Protestant, a Roman Catholic league of cantons was formed, and the two groups went to war. Zwingli served as a chaplain and died in the fighting.

Anabaptists

Zwingli's emphasis on the Bible as the basis for Christian belief encouraged another Swiss movement, known as Anabaptists because of their emphasis on rebaptizing Christians in the "believer's baptism." They worked closely with Zwingli until 1525, when Zwingli decided that the view that Scripture does not teach infant baptism kept too many people out of the Reformation faith. Zwingli tried debate to persuade them to change, but they also opposed state control of the church, and the city council of Zurich expelled them. These Christians fled to other countries, and many of them eventually came to America as the Amish and the Mennonites led by Menno Simons of the Netherlands. They influenced Baptists and Quakers as well as Separatist Puritans, many of whom would later settle in North America.

French Protestantism: Huguenots

Another Reformation group that would be scattered due to persecution and then settle in North America were the Huguenots, whose religious practice began in France as a fusion of Luther's and Calvin's teachings. In spite of the fact that Calvin wrote his *Institutes* in 1536 to convince the French king to convert to Protestantism, by 1572, after eight wars, the rulers were still Roman Catholic.

In Paris on August 24, 1572, on the eve of the Feast of St. Bartholomew, as many as 3000 Huguenots were massacred, with as many as 8000 killed in the provinces. But in 1598 the Edict of Nantes granted religious toleration to the Huguenots. Later, when Louis XIV wanted to have a state with a single church, the edict was revoked (1685) and the Huguenots were forced to flee to other countries. Many historians believe that with this expulsion, France lost many of the people who would have been most valuable to the state because they were skilled craftsmen, merchants, and entrepreneurs.

The Counter-Reformation

The Roman Catholic Church responded to the Protestant Reformation by reforming and renewing itself. The Counter-Reformation was led by the upper-class clergy and the papacy. They developed new monastic orders, such as the Jesuits, who would spread Christianity to the Americas and even the Far East. They created a morals commission to clean up clerical excesses, reaffirmed their theology at the Council of Trent, pushed the Muslims out of Spain completely, created some gorgeous baroque churches, developed new musical forms such as polyphony, and also formed the Inquisition to persecute Protestants.

Effects of the Reformation

All of Western Europe spent about a century sorting itself out religiously. The most bitter conflict occurred during the Thirty Years' War (which was actually much longer; in the Low Countries it was the Eighty

Years' War). The creative spirit of the 16th century was replaced by bitter contention over what areas would be Catholic or Protestant. The conflict ended formally in 1648 with the Peace of Westphalia.

By 1648 most of the main denominations and associations of Christianity were in existence and Russia had become the center of Eastern Orthodox Christianity. All of these forms were European, but almost immediately there would be a push to establish the same denominations in all parts of the globe through Christian missions, which went along with the developing European colonialism.

Some of the effects of the Reformation were far-reaching. There was a new emphasis on religious individualism which led to other forms of individualism. Authority shifted from the priests of the church to the priesthood of the believer, and from tradition to the Bible. A demand developed for universal education so everyone could read the Bible; an educated electorate and workforce would be critical to future democratic governments and industry. The insistence on the spiritual equality of all believers led to insistence on political equality, at least for all men. Lay leadership and democratic church government would ultimately translate into political democracy. Protestantism stimulated capitalism because usury was not forbidden and there was an emphasis on thrift, hard work, and on not indulging excessively in worldly amusements. The early stages of the welfare state began as the states had to assume responsibility for those who had lost property in the Reformation. There was also a revival of preaching, which led to revival of political oratory, and the use of printed tracts by reformers to spread their views would evolve into widespread use of political pamphlets.

Martin Luther. The writings of Martin Luther played a critical role in restoring the authority of the Bible in the church.

Christianity in North America

Roman Catholics had been the first European settlers in North America. They established St. Augustine, Florida, in 1565, and native Americans became Catholic as a result of Jesuit missions. English Protestants followed within 40 years, settling in Jamestown and then Massachusetts. Later, various Reformation groups settled in the Northeast, driven by a desire to worship freely in the new ways they believed were ordained by God.

By the end of the 17th century, Anglicanism was dominant in Virginia, Congregational Puritanism dominated New England, Dutch Reformed groups were strongest in New York, Baptists were predominant in Rhode Island, Lutherans in Delaware, Quakers and minority groups (known as nonconformists in England) in Pennsylvania, and Roman Catholics in Maryland, while most of the South became Baptist or Presbyterian.

This pluralism characterized the colonies that later became the United States—and still is very much in evidence today.

When the United States Constitution was written, religion was "privatized," that is, the government could not have a role in it. This separation of church and state gave individuals freedom to worship as they desired and protected religious groups from coercion or taxation by the state.

Orthodoxy and Revival (1648–1750)

During the Reformation period, the Protestant churches knew why they existed, and there was a religious fervor (albeit sometimes mixed with political and other concerns) that kept the churches alive. But after this initial period, the Protestant churches by and large experienced what happens in most movements: after the generations that fought the battles and understood what was at stake pass away, those who come after them allow the movement to slip into a dead formalism or orthodoxy. Thus the movement of the Spirit that had fueled the Reformation was replaced by an intellectual acceptance of certain doctrines and reliance on certain forms and practices.

Ironically, the theologians of the Reformation churches followed in the footsteps of Thomas Aquinas and created a Reformed kind of scholasticism that resembled the Catholic scholasticism (see p. 909). They applied reason to theology, creating brilliantly coherent, detailed systems that had little bearing or impact on the everyday life of the people. Once again there was a great need for a work of God's Spirit.

On the European continent, one of the responses to this dead orthodoxy was a movement whose impact continues even today: Pietism. It began as a movement within German Lutheranism that focused less on abstract theology than on a personal relationship with God. Some Pietist groups migrated to North America—for example, the Moravian Brethren, led by the German Count Nikolaus von Zinzendorf (1700–1760), who set up a model community based on Christian principles in Bethlehem, Pennsylvania, which gained a reputation for thrift, hard work, and strict living, and whose inhabitants are now known as the Pennsylvania Dutch.

The First Great Awakening

As stated, many of the early settlers found it difficult to sustain through succeeding generations the religious fervor that had led them to form their colonies. Their children and grandchildren had little memory of why they left Europe, concentrated on economic endeavors, moved to the frontier, or simply lost interest in Christianity. The First Great Awakening (1725–75) was a revival that swept the North American colonies. It was dominated by Jonathan Edwards, an energetic genius whose books and sermons were used by God to spark a revival.

John Wesley and Methodism

Another who fostered the First Great Awakening in the North American colonies was John Wesley (1703–91). Wesley was ordained in the Church of England (Anglican). He came to North America to minister in the new colony of Georgia, which had been settled by prisoners forcibly transported from England. In 1737 he felt his faith evaporating after his ministry was a failure. Wesley was attracted to the views of Pietism, and in 1738 he experienced conversion when his "heart was strangely warmed" during the reading of Luther's Preface to the Epistle to the Romans at Aldersgate, London.

For more than 50 years Wesley worked to share his discovery, preaching throughout the British Isles in churches, in the fields, at the pitheads of coal mines, and in jails. His brother, Charles, composed more than 6,500 hymns, and in America his talented associates George Whitefield and Francis Asbury did circuit preaching in the back country and trained many others to do the same.

When Wesley died, he still considered himself an Anglican, but his movement separated from the Anglican Church and began to be called Methodism because of its methodical devotion to piety and plain living. At Wesley's death the movement was about 100,000 strong and continued to grow quickly, especially among the lower and middle classes.

The Methodists worked to improve the conditions in society through private charity rather than public reform. They agitated against drunkenness, slavery, and mistreatment of prisoners and of the physically and mentally ill. Methodism is credited by many historians with helping to keep England from the revolutionary movements that swept Europe and erupted in the French Revolution in 1789, because it was a religion that appealed to average people. Historians call Methodism a "frontier religion" because it was so successful in the United States. It still flourishes in the United States and played a role in the emergence of movements such as the Holiness churches and Pentecostalism (see p. 931).

The Church in the Modern World (1750–1914)

The history of the church after the Reformation period is a complex mosaic of people, movements, and events that is difficult if not impossible to fit into a simple outline. Historians call the period from roughly 1750 until the present "the modern era," which is characterized by a combination of two things: rationalism and industrialism.

Rationalism is the belief that the world and all of reality are structured logically and coherently and can therefore be understood and controlled by human reason. Traditional social, religious, and political ideas must be rejected because they are based on nonrational beliefs (or myths). For many people, this includes God and faith. The philosophical movement that made rationalism the dominant worldview in the last 2½ centuries is known as the Enlightenment, which emerged in the 18th century.

Industrialism is the practical relative of rationalism. Until the mid-18th century, the production of goods was in the hands of craftsmen and guilds. The Industrial Revolution, which began at about the same time as the Enlightenment, set aside tradition, craftsmanship, and the focus on the individual, and made production a "rational" process in which workers were simply a means of production rather than human beings—they were "human capital" in the developing system of capitalism and could be (and were) replaced by machines as technology progressed.

Thus, the trend toward individualism that had begun well before the Reformation now applied mostly to the middle and upper classes, while the lower, working classes faced dehumanizing conditions that reduced them from individuals to numbers in a system.

In this modern world, the church faced enormous challenges and problems. The brief overview that follows shows that many of the key issues the church faced in the 18th and 19th centuries are still very much with us.

The Challenge of the Scientific Revolution

The Reformation was not the only challenge the Roman Catholic Church faced in the 16th century. The work and writings of Copernicus (1473–1543) and Galileo (1564–1642) reduced the earth from being the center of the universe, around which the sun, moon, and stars revolved (the geocentric view), to being one of several planets revolving around the sun, which in turn was just one of many stars (the heliocentric view). Copernicus's ideas, published a year before his death in his book *On the Revolutions of Heavenly Bodies,* was rejected by some of the Protestant Reformers but found remarkably little opposition in the Roman Catholic Church. (In fact, the church used some of his findings to make necessary changes to the calendar!)

But this was not true for Galileo Galilei, who became convinced that Copernicus had been correct. He wrote and published in defense of the heliocentric view, until in 1616 the church declared this view to be heretical. (Galileo essentially ignored the church's order to cease and desist and was later placed under house arrest but continued to write until his death in 1642.)

The heliocentric view made it difficult to maintain the idea that the universe existed for the sake of humanity, which thus literally and figuratively ceased to be the center of the universe. To make matters worse, in 1687 Isaac Newton (a lifelong Calvinist) published his *Principia Mathematica,* which outlined his theory of universal gravity. This destroyed the image of the world as a structure moved by the unseen hand of God. Now the earth was just a small planet in a vast universe that behaved according to scientific laws. God's providential involvement in the affairs of humankind seemed to be no longer necessary. The net result was that humanity, though it was no longer the center of the universe, became "the measure of all things" in the absence of God. Scientific rationalism would be a major challenge to Christianity.

Not only would this scientific revolution reorient Western thought so that the universe was seen as a giant machine functioning according to universal laws; it also led directly to the (optimistic) assumption that humans could "rationalize" society—to bring about change and progress by human effort. This resulted in the Industrial Revolution and the Enlightenment (see above).

The Second Great Awakening (1800–1861)

In America, the Second Great Awakening (1800–1861) occurred in response to rationalism and industrialization. Revivalist preaching and personal piety swept back and forth across the new country. Nearly all the denominations used the camp meetings to effect the conversions to Christ of tens of thousands of people. The camp meetings evolved into permanent campgrounds and then into Bible conference centers, some of which are still thriving today. Charles Finney was the most prominent evangelist of that era, changing the way evangelism was done and adapting it to city ministry. Later in the century, Dwight L. Moody would use Finney's revivalist techniques, adding colportage (door-to-door literature distribution) and the founding of several educational institutions, of which the best-known is the Moody Bible Institute in Chicago.

Dwight L. Moody founded several educational institutions, including the Moody Bible Institute.

The Rise of Modern Missions

The spirit of the Second Great Awakening moved in England (and to some extent in Northern Europe) as well as in North America. Revivalism linked up with 19th–century imperialism to foster great enthusiasm for Protestant missions. The missionary emphasis began in England, just before 1800. The first missionary to go out was William Carey (1761–1834), who is considered "the father of modern missions." He founded the Baptist Missionary Society in England in 1792, and in 1793 he left for India, where he had a remarkable ministry. Soon the London Missionary Society and many others sent people all over the globe to spread the Gospel of Christ to millions of people who had not heard it. From about 1860 to 1920 Americans "took missions to their hearts" so that even presidents and others in high places supported them.

Among the best-known names in missions are Hudson Taylor (1832–1905), who founded the interdenominational China Inland Mission and ministered in China; David Livingstone (1813–73), who went to Africa with the London Missionary Society and, in addition to his missionary work, explored the continent; and Amy Carmichael

(1867–1951), who went to India and was one of many single women who served God in missions. In God's books there are many more names, long forgotten on earth, of those who gave their lives to God and to the people they went to serve out of love for their Savior.

The call was for "World evangelization in this generation," a slogan used by Moody and many others. The sense of mission that led Americans to settle their large continent also stimulated foreign missions. Many of the mission organizations that began in the 19th century, both denominational and interdenominational, are alive and well today.

Unfortunately, since in many areas missions were linked with colonial governments, the Gospel was often perceived as part of a cultural imperialism rather than as the liberating truth of God's love in Jesus. Even in American missions the term "evangelization" meant both evangelism and civilizing functions.

The Challenge of Higher Criticism

The scientific revolution had only been the beginning of a general attempt to study and understand the universe and the way it works. One result of this sort of inquiry was questioning the validity of the Bible. Many intellectuals left the Christian faith since they were unable to reconcile the Gospel and reason. They thought there were too many contradictions in the Bible to make it historically credible, and its scientific credibility seemed impossible to establish. In 1835, David Friederich Strauss published *A Life of Jesus*, in which he questioned whether the biblical record was based on historical evidence. He concluded that the story of Jesus was a myth that arose from social and intellectual conditions in 1st-century Palestine. Jesus' life and character represented what people wanted rather than what actually happened.

Authors such as Julius Wellhausen followed with the contention that the books of the Bible were written by human authors with the problems of Jewish society and politics in mind. They thought that the books of the Bible were not inspired and that many of them were somewhat clumsily pieced together from earlier writings. In fact, it seemed that many of the stories of the Bible were immoral, with a cruel, unpredictable God who sacrificed the only perfect being to walk the earth—Jesus. Biblical Christianity did not fit well with the progressive, tolerant, rational values of the Enlightenment, and some clergymen found it difficult to preach doctrines they felt were unbelievable or even immoral.

From Europe, this critical attitude toward the Bible (known as "higher criticism" to distinguish it from "textual" or "lower criticism"; see p. 997) soon infiltrated North America and created major problems for the church (see p. 924).

The Challenge of Darwinism

Another major challenge the church faced centered around the theories of Charles Darwin (1809–82). Darwin's father was a wealthy doctor, and his mother was the daughter of Josiah Wedgewood, a leading china manufacturer in England. Darwin failed in studying medicine and then theology because of a passionate interest in studying the natural world. He sailed as an unpaid naturalist on the HMS *Beagle* in 1831 and did research in the Galapagos and Falkland Islands for five years. The book he published in 1859, The *Origin of Species,* combined his research with the idea (originally proposed by Thomas Malthus, one of whose books Darwin had with him during his voyage) that survival was a matter of constant competition for limited resources. Only those species best able to commandeer the food supply could survive and increase. The rest would die off or become a minority.

Many evangelical Christians could accept this theory of Darwin's, but his next book, *The Descent of Man,* published in 1871, caused a major stir. In it, Darwin attempted to show that the human race evolved from an ape-like ancestor. The controversy between creationism and evolution has persisted through our own time, especially in the United States. In 1925, the Scopes Trial, which was held to decide whether creation or evolution should be taught in schools, would split not only Christianity but also American culture.

Social Darwinism

Darwin's theory was appropriated by academics and industrialists and applied to contemporary society. This "social Darwinism" held to the view that the evolutionary process is at work in society and that in the end unrestrained capitalism will lead to a better world.

This appealed to the upper middle classes in industrial society; the lower classes, however, would need to find help from their misery caused by harsh working conditions and low wages. The Salvation Army (founded in 1878) and the rescue mission movements were formed to minister to the poorer classes by giving them the Gospel as well as seeing to their physical needs; they are still very active today.

The Roman Catholic Church also sided with the workers. In 1895 Pope Leo XIII issued an encyclical (a letter to all bishops), *Rerum Novarum,* which sanctioned action by the workers against owners when necessary.

The Social Gospel

Another movement, known as the Social Gospel, emerged with a view to helping the poor in order to Christianize America. Washington Gladden and Walter Rauschenbusch, the movement's early leaders, believed that the political and social institutions of American culture could be made Christian and remade to biblical standards. Many Christians worked to reform society in the late 19th and early 20th centuries as part of the social gospel movement. Charles Sheldon wrote *In His Steps,* which raised the question, once again current today, "What would Jesus do?" The book sold 25 million copies.

The social gospel, however, appealed most to liberal Protestants (who, because of their ties to industry and business, were also called "modern") who had questioned the validity of the Bible and found more substance in social action than in the personal work of God through Jesus Christ and the Holy Spirit in their lives. This liberal Protestant movement became the dominant social institution, not only in North America, but also in many Protestant European countries. Most of its members were middle- and upper-class urban business and professional people and industrialists.

Responses to Modernism

Most Christians during the 19th century embraced the basic values of modernism: optimism and faith in progress. But many also realized that this optimism was misplaced if it ignored the most basic truths of the Gospel, such as humanity's need for redemption from sin. Some Protestant churches thus responded to this creeping "modernism" with **revivalism** (see above).

Other Christians, mostly Protestant, tried to synthesize some of these trends into a Christian socialism that led to experiments with **utopian** (perfectly egalitarian) communities, such as Oneida in New York (originally in Vermont), the Amana Colonies in Iowa, and New Harmony in Indiana; these worked best in the United States but not terribly well anywhere else.

The Roman Catholic Church's response was very different from Protestant revivalism. It tried to counter modern rationalism with an essentially conservative reaction. The Vatican church council, held in 1870 (now known as Vatican I), reasserted the infallibility of the pope and restricted certain types of biblical scholarship.

Many Protestants believed that liberal Christianity had essentially stripped the church of the true Gospel and turned Christ into a good social teacher and role model rather than the Savior. They aligned themselves with **evangelicalism,** a movement that emphasizes the basic Christian doctrines of salvation, personal experience of God's grace, and inspiration of the Bible; it has been strongest in England, the United States, and Canada since 1800 and is estimated to have at least 50 million adherents in North America. Others would later join the new **fundamentalist** movement (see below).

The 20th Century in the United States (1914–2000)

The End of Optimism

The modern era had begun with faith in reason and in the stability and predictability of the universe. It looked with almost unbounded optimism to the future, and marvels of invention and technology that came into being or became available to the masses in the decades around the turn of the century—the automobile, airplane, telephone, radio, and electric light, among others—certainly seemed to justify the general optimism.

But while optimism was at its height, the seeds were sown for its destruction. The accepted social structures would be undermined by, among other things, the writings of Karl Marx (1818–83; the first volume of his main work, *Das Kapital*, was published in 1867; the second and third volumes were completed after Marx's death by Friedrich Engels). The understanding of man as rational and autonomous would be challenged by Sigmund Freud (1856–1939), and Newton's universe began to wobble when Albert Einstein published his special theory of relativity (1905) and his general law of relativity (1915).

The death blow came in 1914, with World War I. About 10 million men were sacrificed by stubborn generals operating with premodern principles of warfare. The world would never be the same, especially after crippling conditions were imposed on Germany by the victorious Allies. Thus victory became the incubator for the Second World War. In America, the quiet optimism of the turn of the century was replaced with the frantic Roaring 20s, which were silenced in the Crash of 1929 and the Great Depression.

Churches and Denominations in the 20th Century

The focus of this brief survey is on the 20th century church in the United States. Developments in Canada, Europe, and elsewhere were different.

The label "denomination" is no longer as useful as is once was, especially when we speak of large, historic denominations such as Presbyterians, Lutherans, and Methodists. (Baptists, Plymouth Brethren, and other groups consider themselves *associations* rather than denominations, since they lack centralized authority structures, but the same problem is found there.) In the past, each denomination was characterized by a specific theology, so that one could more or less determine an individual's theological perspective by the denomination he or she belonged to. Today, by contrast, the most important theological differences are not so much between denominations as between, on the one hand, conservative groupings and, on the other hand, those who would once have been labeled "liberal" but are now perhaps best described as "nonevangelical," largely because that appears to be the clearest common denominator. Within all denominations and associations there are evangelical and nonevangelical groupings. Thus it is possible, for example, for evangelical Presbyterians to have more in common with evangelical Baptists or Catholics than with nonevangelical Presbyterians.

For convenience' sake we will use the following four groupings:

- Mainline churches (nonevangelical)
- Roman Catholic

- Evangelical and Fundamentalist
- Pentecostal/Charismatic/Third Wave

The Mainline Churches

Until the latter part of the 19th century, the historic, nonevangelical denominations were the unquestioned guardians and messengers of the Gospel. The historical reasons for the distinctions between them were still relatively clear (generally differing on core doctrinal statements); denominational loyalty was the norm, and institutions of higher education were mostly church related.

The problems began when higher-critical views from Europe infiltrated the American universities and seminaries (see above, p. 922). For a while the issues remained within the academic ivory towers, although schools such as the University of Chicago (Baptist) embraced the modern views wholeheartedly. The crisis came when large numbers of clergy who had been trained in these institutions came into pulpits from the 1880s on; these men were able to dominate denominational or associational meetings and to direct funds to projects that more conservative people viewed as ungodly.

Some institutions reacted against the modern approach, foremost among them Princeton Seminary (Presbyterian), where theologians such as B. B. Warfield and Charles Hodge presented a consistent and academically respectable defense of the Bible as traditionally understood. The defense revolved around five main points: (1) the inerrancy of the Bible; (2) the virgin birth; (3) Christ's atonement for sin; (4) Jesus' resurrection from the dead; and (5) the reality of miracles.

Later, however, Princeton also turned toward modernism, so the conservative faculty members founded Westminster Seminary in Philadelphia (1929). J. Gresham Machen was their foremost spokesman and became, not altogether willingly, involved in the modernist-fundamentalist controversy (see below).

As a broad generalization it can be said that during the 20th century the mainline churches gradually declined in membership as their conservative members withdrew to found new churches, associations, and denominations.

The Roman Catholic Church

The Roman Catholic Church in America gained high visibility immediately after World War II through Bishop J. Fulton Sheen, who used his consummate preaching and teaching skills in regular programs on national television and in many books that were understandable to the average person. His ministry helped pave the way for an event that would have been unthinkable a few decades earlier: the election of a Catholic president, John Fitzgerald Kennedy.

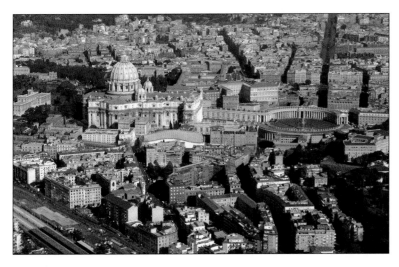

St. Peter's and
Vatican City.

But the most significant response to the cultural trends of the 20th century came from Pope John XXIII, who convened a church council, Vatican II (1962–65), that brought about drastic changes in the church.

One of the reasons Vatican II was called was to encourage Christian unity. After WWII, as the ecumenical movement was developing among mainline Protestants, Catholics began to engage in serious dialogue with Lutherans and other Protestant groups, who after Vatican II were called "separated brethren" instead of "schismatics."

Other reasons for Vatican II were to promote world peace and social justice, to revitalize the believers' individual life in Christ, to change ecclesiastical practice, and to help the Catholic church cope with modern life. The laity became more important; they were now allowed to participate in the Mass, which was no longer done in Latin but in the vernacular, the language of the people. Individuals were encouraged to read the Bible, and freedom of worship style was encouraged.

The popes and the church have held to positions such as forbidding clerical marriage and birth control, purgatory, veneration of Mary, papal infallibility, and transubstantiation. Still, the Roman Catholic Church has worked toward ecumenism during the latter half of the 20th century and has engaged in cooperative ventures with evangelicals and fundamentalists on common issues such as opposing abortion and homosexual practice.

Like the mainline denominations, the Roman Catholic Church also faces the internal conflict between conservative and more liberal interpretations of the Bible and tradition. There are Catholics whose theology is virtually indistinguishable from evangelical theology. Furthermore, in the mid-1960s the charismatic movement (see below) crossed over theological dividing lines as the Holy Spirit began to work in the Catholic church, creating a unity with other believers that could not have been achieved with theological debates.

The Evangelical and Fundamentalist Churches

Strictly speaking, there was no fundamentalism before 1915. Informal reaction to modernism began in the 19th century, but the true polarization did not harden into more or less fixed positions until about 1915. (Note that it is extremely difficult to give exact definitions of the terms "fundamentalism" and "evangelicalism." The differences between the two are often more matters of emphasis, attitude, and ethos than of doctrine.)

The Rise of Premillennialism and Dispensationalism

In the emergence of fundamentalism, premillennialism played a significant role in uniting otherwise often very divergent people. The church has always believed in the return of Jesus (the Second Coming); the problems lie in the specifics. Revelation 20:2 says that Satan will be bound for 1000 years. Most churches through the ages have held to an amillennial view—there will be no literal 1000-year period; rather, Satan has been bound and God will work through the church to bring about the kingdom of peace on earth.

Premillennialism, by contrast, is the belief that Jesus will return and institute a literal reign on earth of 1000 years. Most premillennialists believe that this kingdom will be preceded by a general apostasy, wars, famine, earthquakes, the appearance of the Antichrist, and a period of tribulation. Although Christ will rule during the millennium, there will at the end be a battle, the Battle of Armageddon, between Christ and His saints and those who have rebelled against Him.

From the mid-1870s on, evangelicals organized Bible conferences to study the Bible and especially prophecy. These prophetic conferences, as well as the writings of the speakers at these conferences, were premillennial in outlook; they were eminently successful and helped make premillennialism a core belief. At the 1898 Niagara (N.Y.) Conference, a statement of faith was adopted that was essentially identical to the five points adopted by the Presbyterian Assembly (see above, "Mainline Churches"), except that the last point (the reality of miracles) was replaced by the millennial return of Christ.

But further refinements were adopted by some in the form of dispensationalism. This is a theological system that divides time into seven periods or dispensations, which are stages in God's progressive revelation. The key point in dispensationalism is that in the church age God's plan for the Jews is different from His plan for the church. Thus the Jews will go through the Great Tribulation and will turn to Christ during that period, while the church is taken away (raptured) before the Tribulation. In the end, of course, both Jews and Gentiles will stand before God together.

This dispensational system was developed by John Darby, an Englishman who was a leader of the Plymouth Brethren. Darby's views on the pretribulational rapture split the Plymouth Brethren but migrated to America in the 1870s and spread via Bible and prophetic conferences. Dispensationalism became entrenched after C. I. Scofield published the Scofield Reference Bible in 1909. This Bible shows in detail how the dispensationalist system works. It had wide appeal and still sells well today. In 1924, Dallas Theological Seminary was founded with the specific goal to train men in dispensational theology.

The Emergence of Fundamentalism

Informal networks had thus been developing through Bible conferences, through books and pamphlets from publishers such as Fleming H. Revell (Moody's brother-in-law, who founded his publishing house in 1870), and through the many Bible schools that were established. At one point there were several hundred, many of which disappeared without a trace, but others still exist today—for example, Moody Bible Institute (1886) and the Bible Institute of Los Angeles (1908; now Biola University). The core of the curriculum at these schools consisted of Bible and theology, with an emphasis on the inerrancy of the Bible and premillennialism.

Then, between 1910 and 1915, a group of men published a set of 12 small volumes called *The Fundamentals,* to which "old-school" Calvinists such as B. B. Warfield as well as Dispensationalists such as C. I. Scofield contributed. These pamphlets articulated the basic truths and values of the Christian faith and were mailed out free of charge to more than 300,000 people. Various groups and denominations in turn drew up their own lists of the essentials of the faith; all of them contained the inspiration of the Bible and the substitutionary atonement of Christ and His bodily resurrection.

The term "fundamentalist" was coined in 1920 as a name for those who were willing "to do battle royal for the fundamentals of the faith" in the face of theological modernism. It became a badge of honor for those inside the movement and a derogatory term to others, especially after the 1925 Scopes Trial, which dealt with the teaching of evolution in public schools. Until 1925 the Fundamentalist movement had made strides toward being a force in American religious life and culture, but the Scopes Trial effectively dashed any hopes the fundamentalists had of achieving the dominance that the modernists now held.

Eventually fundamentalism sorted itself into two camps: "closed" or "separatist" fundamentalism, which emphasized separation, not only from non-Christians, but also from other Christians who did not agree with them in every detail, and "open" fundamentalism, which had a more positive orientation and broader vision of winning the world for Christ. The first group made separation (even from orthodox fellow Christians with whom they were not in full agreement on all points) an absolute requirement for church membership; the second was more inclusivist, choosing to work with groups espousing basic orthodoxy to achieve the larger evangelistic goals. This second camp went on to become the evangelicals of today.

The Emergence of Contemporary Evangelicalism

In Great Britain, evangelicalism had not gone through the same historical developments; it was more open and academic than its American cousin. But during the 1940s and '50s a movement took hold in the United States that also pushed for a more open and intellectually grounded evangelicalism. (Many separatist fundamentalists were distinctly anti-intellectual and saw any kind of academic training as at best a waste of time and at worst a tool of the Devil to lead the church astray.) This movement is often referred to as "neo-evangelicalism" to distinguish it from the earlier and less open and academically inclined evangelicalism. Men such as Harold Ockenga, Carl F. H. Henry, and Francis Schaeffer; schools such as Fuller Seminary (founded 1947); and periodicals such as *Christianity Today* (1956) moved toward open and direct engagement with the issues of society and the contemporary world. A landmark book was *The Uneasy Conscience of Modern Fundamentalism* (1947) by Carl Henry, which was a call for evangelicals to participate in social reform.

In the past decades, evangelicalism has created its own support structures: evangelical publishing houses, bookstores, recording companies, concert and lecture circuits, and its own Bible versions, such as the Living Bible, the New American Standard Bible, and the New International Version.

Black and White Churches

Throughout the late 19th and the 20th centuries, we observe a rich history of black churches emerging primarily in the southern United States. As black Africans were forcibly brought to the States and sold as slaves, it is surprising that they would have anything to do with their oppressors' religion. But upon arrival, the slaves were immediately taught Christianity (especially and repeatedly Paul's exhortation "Slaves, obey your earthly masters with respect and fear"—Ephesians 6:5), and slaves were deliberately kept illiterate. The part of the Bible that spoke most directly to them was the Gospels. And thus, over the years, a black Christianity developed.

While white churches tended to be theological and focus on issues such as justification and atonement, the black churches drew their strength from the Jesus who came to liberate, heal, and restore. For most white churches the New Testament letters, especially those of Paul, were important. For the black churches the Gospels were their lifeline to God, who in Jesus had come to stand beside them, who alone "knew the trouble they were in," and who would bring them to the other shore, to life everlasting. After the Civil War, the white and black churches never successfully integrated, and when around the turn of the century the Supreme Court articulated the doctrine of "separate but equal" for schools, the

"Jim Crow" laws seemed to carry over so that churches were also separate. In the 19th and early 20th centuries, white denominations would found new black churches with the understanding that they would be separate, and eventually the black churches founded their own denominations.

Over time, white and black evangelicals have begun listening seriously to their fellow Christians and have discovered that these two different emphases are in effect two necessary aspects of the Gospel. We need each other's strengths and must help each other in our weakness.

Pentecostal — Charismatic — Third Wave Churches

Pentecostalism

The beginning of the Pentecostal movement is usually traced to January 1, 1901, when Agnes Ozman, a student at Charles Parham's Bethel Bible College in Topeka, Kansas, began to speak in tongues. Parham moved to Houston, and one of his students, William Seymour, a black man, later became the leader of a mission at 312 Azusa Street in Los Angeles in 1906, which is where the Pentecostal movement exploded. From Azusa Street the Pentecostal message, which included speaking in tongues as the sign of the baptism with the Holy Spirit, spread to the rest of America and throughout the world. (There had, in fact, been similar experiences of the baptism with the Holy Spirit in the late 1800s, both in the United States and overseas, in places as far apart as India and Finland, although they remained isolated incidents.)

The Pentecostal churches formed denominations such as Charles H. Mason's Church of God in Christ, which has grown to be the largest Pentecostal body in America, with more than 6½ million members. The Assemblies of God has become the largest Pentecostal body worldwide, with 2.2 million members in the United States and a total of 22 million worldwide. Another major, though smaller, group is the United Pentecostal Church; its doctrine is non-Trinitarian and is therefore also referred to as Oneness or Jesus Only Pentecostalism.

The Pentecostal churches have generally kept themselves separate from other churches (and vice versa). They did not play a significant role in the development of evangelicalism, and it has only been within the last generation that serious scholarship has emerged and been encouraged in Pentecostalism.

The Charismatic Movement

In the 1960s, the mainline churches were surprised by the charismatic movement, as were the Pentecostal churches. Some members and pastors of these denominations began to speak in tongues, and charismatic groups soon became a more or less accepted phenomenon in most denominations. Some of its leaders were Dennis Bennett, an Episcopalian clergyman; Larry Christenson, a Lutheran; Harald Bredesen, the Dutch Reformed Church; James Brown, Presbyterian; and Michael Harper, Church of England.

In the Roman Catholic Church the first manifestations of the charismatic renewal occurred at Duquesne University, and it later reached Notre Dame University, from where it spread throughout the church. Pope Paul gave cautious approval to the movement, and its strongest supporter in the hierarchy became Leo Cardinal Suenens of Belgium.

There is agreement on the key doctrines of the faith in the charismatic churches, with an added emphasis on healing. The charismatic Word of Faith/positive confession movement adds emphasis on personal and material well-being and prosperity.

The Third Wave

In the late 1970s and early '80s there emerged what is called the Third Wave; this large movement includes those who do not care to link up with the Pentecostal charismatics. The Third Wave emphasizes the work of the Holy Spirit in healing, casting out demons, prophecy, and "signs and wonders." Its best-known representative is the late John Wimber, founder of the Vineyard Christian Fellowship.

Although the three groups—Pentecostal, charismatic, and Third Wave—differ demographically and doctrinally, there is an underlying agreement on the place and work of the Holy Spirit, even though there are different understandings of how the Spirit manifests Himself in the church.

Recent Phenomena

Parachurch Groups

After World War I, nondenominational church organizations were formed, especially in the United States, to work on missions and social reform. These multiplied and proliferated after World War II, which also saw the rise of the ecumenical movement. The majority of these so-called parachurch organizations were evangelical, due to the fact that evangelicals and fundamentalists saw the ecumenical movement as dominated by modernists who had given up the basic tenets of the Christian faith.

The first of these groups, InterVarsity Christian Fellowship (IVCF), had been started in England in 1877 (as the Christian Union) but spread to Canada in the 1920s and to the United States in the 1930s and '40s. Its Student Foreign Missions Fellowship still sponsors missionary conventions at the University of Illinois at Urbana every third year. These conventions have inspired thousands of students and others to go to the mission field. IVCF has its own publishing house, InterVarsity Press.

Another early group was the Gideons (1898), who have distributed millions of Bibles in hotels, motels, and schools.

Campus Crusade for Christ was organized by Bill Bright in 1951 at UCLA. It is perhaps most widely known for its "Four Spiritual Laws" booklet that is used to explain the Gospel to nonbelievers.

Other parachurch organizations include Youth for Christ, which was founded in 1945, with Billy Graham as its first traveling representative (it has since changed it name to Campus Life); Young Life (1941), aimed at high-school students; the Navigators (founded during World War II), aimed at reaching sailors and discipling them but broadening after the war to reach college students and working adults (their publishing house is NavPress); Focus on the Family (1977), which helps families live godly lives in modern society; Promise Keepers (1990), which helps men achieve spiritual leadership in their families; and many others.

Some parachurch organizations focus on social issues, for example, Ron Sider's Evangelicals for Social Action and Jim Wallis's Sojourners.

All of these are independent, maintain a sense of their mission, attract adherents from Protestant, Catholic, and even Eastern Orthodox and minority Christian backgrounds. Their ministries cross racial, national, and denominational lines, and many have publishing arms, radio or television programs, or use the internet to attract new members and teach and encourage current ones.

Megachurches

The parachurch groups are probably partly responsible for the development of another 20th-century phenomenon, the megachurch. These are churches with more than 2000 members that may or may not be affiliated with a denomination. The megachurches originated in the United States but are popular in the Pacific Rim, East Asia, Africa, and Latin America as well. In fact, the world's largest church—with more than 800,000 members and 55,000 deacons and deaconesses—is the Yoido Full Gospel Church in Seoul, Korea.

Megachurches have a large staff with a number of pastors, each of whom is responsible for the needs of a particular segment of the membership, such as youth or the infirm. Generally the spiritual life of the church depends on small groups that function to minister in the daily lives of members. Examples in the United States are Willow Creek Community Church near Chicago; Living Work Christian Center in Minneapolis; and Calvary Chapel and the Crystal Cathedral in California.

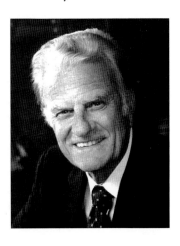

For over sixty years, Billy Graham has proclaimed the Good News of Jesus to mass audiences from around the world.

Mass Evangelism

Evangelists such as George Whitefield preached in the American colonies to surprisingly large crowds, but it was not until the invention of microphones, amplifiers, and loudspeakers that evangelistic mass meetings became possible. The name still most identified with mass evangelism is Billy Graham, who in 1949 held a crusade in Los Angeles that gave him national attention, due in part to the unlikely support of William Randolph Hearst, who told his newspapers to give Billy Graham coverage: "Puff Graham." Graham appears at or near the top of every list of most influential or respected people; he remains one of the towering figures of the latter half of the 20th century, due to his complete integrity and unflinching, unapologetic commitment to the simple message of the Cross.

Graham had a dramatic call to preaching on a golf course in 1938. He then attended Wheaton College, where he met his wife Ruth, the daughter of Presbyterian missionaries. He became an evangelist for Youth for Christ in 1944, but within a short time was making trips to England for evangelistic tours. After his Los Angeles crusade, he founded the Billy Graham Evangelistic Association (BGEA) in 1950, which has held crusades all around the world, bringing multitudes to Christ. He, like so many others, also has made use of radio, television, and printed materials to convey his message. Graham's son, Franklin Graham, is now actively involved in the ministry of BGEA and also founded a missions outreach called Samaritan's Purse. (In 1964, the BGEA distributed some 750,000 copies of *Halley's Bible Handbook* free of charge.)

Mass Media

Evangelicals have successfully used the mass media, especially radio and television. The first regular, licensed radio broadcast took place in 1920 from station KDKA in Pittsburgh, Pennsylvania. Two years later, Paul Rader began a regular evangelistic radio broadcast in Chicago, and in 1923 R. R. Brown of the Omaha Gospel Tabernacle began regular broadcasts. Over the years, a number of programs have had a major impact, among them Charles E. Fuller's *Old Fashioned Revival Hour* and Walter Maier's *Lutheran Hour*. Billy Graham's *Hour of Decision* began on radio and later moved to television. Other programs are *The Back to God Hour* and *Radio Bible Class.*

The potential of television attracted evangelicals, fundamentalists, Pentecostals, and charismatics. Names such as Rex Humbard, Oral Roberts, Pat Robertson, Jerry Falwell, Paul and Jan Crouch, Jim and Tammy Bakker, and Kathryn Kuhlman became household words.

Although undoubtedly God has touched many through the mass media, they are, sadly, not an unmixed blessing. In the 1930s, Father Francis Coughlin's radio program from Detroit preached racial hatred, fascism, and anti-Semitism to a population suffering through the Great Depression. In the 1980s, scandals erupted that involved some well-known television evangelists.

Contemporary Issues

In each generation the church faces specific issues. In the 1970s, the question of biblical inerrancy was the focus of much controversy in evangelicalism. In the 1980s, the question of the role and place of women, especially in the church, became a burning issue that continues to be of critical importance. The last several decades have witnessed increased direct political involvement on the part of Christians. In 1976, Jimmy Carter was the first "born-again" Christian to be elected U.S. president.

One of the key issues facing the church in the coming decades may well be that of racism. As the white majority is rapidly moving toward becoming a minority in the United States in the 21st century, the church, which preaches a Gospel of reconciliation with God, must be in the forefront of racial reconciliation. In recent years, individual denominations and parachurch groups—both black and white—are taking steps toward racial reconciliation and have made it a priority for the near future.

Another issue facing Christianity today is the growing societal demand for "tolerance"—tolerance for people living "alternative" lifestyles, tolerance for abortion, tolerance for New Age and cultic spiritual practices. This "politically correct" cry for tolerance seems to be accompanied by an overall cultural decline in the importance of moral values. Some view this growing anti-Christian environment as being just a phase in history similar to the days of the early church. Others see this as a sign that Christ may be returning soon.

The Single Most Important Issue

In the early years of the new millennium, we can do no better than to go back to the beginning of this book (see pp. 15–20) and point once again to the single most important issue that faces the church today and tomorrow and in the days and years to come. A church that does not enthrone the Bible in the lives of its people is false to its mission. The church and the Bible go together. The church exists to proclaim and exalt the Christ of the Bible, and for no other reason.

Every Christian ought to be a Bible reader. It is the one habit, which, if done in the right spirit, more than any other one habit, will make a Christian what he or she ought to be in every way.

- If the church could get its people as a whole to be devoted readers of God's Word, it would revolutionize the church.

- If the churches of any community, as a whole, could get their people, as a whole, to be regular readers of the Bible, not only would it revolutionize the churches, but it would also purge and purify the community as nothing else could.

Arch of Titus built in A.D. 81 to celebrate the Romans' destruction of Judea.

A Brief History of the Holy Land and the Jews Since the Time of Christ

Why Is This Important?

Two of God's promises to Abraham were that his descendants would become a large nation and that they would live in the land that God promised him (see pp. 107–8). The Jewish people and the Promised Land play key roles in the biblical narratives. But there is generally a gap of almost 2000 years in our awareness of the story of the Promised Land and the Jews, God's covenant people—a gap from the end of the book of Acts, where clear delineation occurs between Judaism and Christianity, to the founding of the State of Israel in 1948, which marks the fulfillment of many prophecies regarding the regathering of Jews in Israel (see Ezekiel 37:3, 7–11, 21–23; Matthew 24:32–34).

During this significant historical gap, Christianity grew from a small Jewish sect into a world religion; Islam was founded and became a major religious and political force. The histories of the three major monotheistic world religions—Judaism, Christianity, and Islam—became intertwined. The Promised Land was under Islamic control for almost 1,300 years. The Jews have been persecuted for many centuries, sadly mostly in countries that considered themselves to be Christian.

The story of the land and the Jewish people from the end of Acts to the present shows how incredible it is that the Jews have survived and once again live in the land, albeit seemingly somewhat precariously at times. It is difficult not to see God's hand at work through all of this. The history of God's dealings with His people Israel did not end with the Bible but has continued and continues today. This should not surprise us, for God promised that He would regather and restore the Jews in the end times.

The Jews and Palestine in the First Two Centuries A.D.

During most of the last 2,500 years, from the Babylonian exile through the New Testament era to the present, the majority of Jews have lived outside the land that God had given them. It was not until 1948 that Jews were able to return to Israel in large numbers and take political, economic, and social control of at least part of the land.

During these 2½ millennia, the Jews have achieved the impossible: they have kept their religious and ethnic identity and culture alive, in spite of (and often because of) persecutions and attempts to eradicate them. What enabled them to do this is, in part, that they have celebrated and retold their biblical history and heritage on each Sabbath, especially on feasts such as the Passover, and on holy days such as Yom Kippur, the Day of Atonement. (See also "The Development of Judaism," p. 940.)

The Early Diaspora (Dispersion or Scattering)

In 586 B.C., Nebuchadnezzar destroyed Jerusalem and took most of the Jewish population to Babylonia. The Babylonian exile officially came to an end 50 years later, when King Darius of Persia allowed the Jews to return to Jerusalem and to rebuild the temple under Ezra and Zerubbabel.

Many Jews chose to remain in Babylonia, however, where Jewish communities flourished. Later, during the Greek period that followed the conquests of Alexander the Great (around 330 B.C.), many Jews voluntarily settled elsewhere outside Palestine. By the time of Christ, some 4 million Jews lived in the Roman Empire and constituted about 7 percent of the empire's total population. Of these 4 million, less than 20 percent lived in Palestine (about 700,000). There were, in fact, more Jews in

The remains of this 1st-century Jerusalem house is evidence that Rome's response to the first Jewish revolt led to the destruction of the temple and precipitated major Jewish Diaspora.

Alexandria, Egypt, than in Jerusalem, and in some parts of Palestine, Gentiles outnumbered Jews.

When the church began on the Day of Pentecost, Jews from all over the Roman Empire were in Jerusalem. They spoke a variety of languages, and it is likely that many did not speak Aramaic (then the common language in the Near East) at all. On his missionary travels Paul found a synagogue in nearly every city he visited. An exception was Philippi, where there was merely a "place of prayer" by the river, where a group of women gathered.

The First Revolt

During the life of Jesus, Palestine had been uncharacteristically quiet. The Roman historian Tacitus, speaking of Palestine under Emperor Tiberius (A.D. 14–37), says, almost with a sigh of relief, "Peace under Tiberius!" But it was not to last.

The rebuilding and beautifying of the temple in Jerusalem, begun by Herod the Great in 20 B.C., was finally completed in A.D. 64—sixty years after Herod's death. A mere two years later, the Zealots, a fanatical Jewish sect, instigated a violent insurrection against Rome. In A.D. 70 the revolt was crushed, and Jerusalem and the temple were destroyed.

The last fortress of the revolutionaries was Masada, a massive, flat-topped rock near the Dead Sea. Herod had built palaces on Masada, choosing the location in large part because it was easy to defend, with steep slopes on all sides. The Roman army laid siege to Masada in A.D. 70. They built a camp—the remains of which are still visible—and spent several frustrating years attacking the mountain with catapults and other war machines. Finally, the Romans decided on the only strategy left: they constructed a massive earthen ramp up the side of the mountain until they were able to walk to the top. (See photos on pp. 941–42.)

The Second Revolt

After this, Judea was once again relatively peaceful for about 60 years. But then Emperor Hadrian (A.D. 117–138) decided to rebuild Jerusalem as a pagan city, to be named Aelia Capitolina, in honor of Jupiter, the chief god of the Romans. He also banned circumcision, which for two millennia had been the indelible mark of Jewishness.

These two insults caused a second major revolt against Rome in A.D. 132, led by Simon Bar Kochba (or Cocheba). The Jews were able to hold off the Romans for three years, but by A.D. 135 the Romans had crushed the rebellion, and their punitive measures were severe. The province was no longer to be called Judea, but Syria Palestine. Jerusalem was rebuilt as a pagan city, and any Jew who entered the city was summarily executed.

The arch of Titus was erected by Emperor Domitian and the Roman senate to honor Emperor Titus. One of Titus's achievements was the destruction of Jerusalem in A.D. 70. The relief on the inside of the arch (top right) shows the menorah (the seven-armed candelabrum from the temple) being carried away by Roman soldiers.

More important, the fall of Judea led to persecutions of the Jews throughout the Roman Empire. It also widened the rift between Jews and Christians, since the Christians saw all this as proof that God had transferred His favor from the Jews to the Christian church. The Diaspora, or scattering of the Jews, which, with the exception of the period of the Babylonian exile, had been a matter of choice for most Jews, now became a matter of necessity.

The Development of Judaism

When the temple was destroyed in A.D. 70, the Jews lost their religious center. It had happened once before, when the Babylonians destroyed Jerusalem and the temple in 586 B.C. At that time the response had been the development of the synagogue and a focus on the Scriptures, especially the Torah (the first five books of the Old Testament).

Few ancient sites speak to the imagination as Masada does. An almost 500-foot-high rock with a flat top approximately 750 feet long and 325 feet wide. Herod built a palace on top and a three-level palace on the northern edge (the three levels are visible on the top right). Looking up from the lower palace (bottom).

Now both the synagogue and the Torah became even more important. The center of Jewish learning moved from Jerusalem to Jabneh (or Jamnia; modern Yavne, 15 miles south of Tel Aviv on the Mediterranean coast). There, and in other centers, especially Babylonia, the Jewish religion changed from being centered around, and dependent on, Jerusalem and the temple to what is known today as Judaism — a religion centered around the synagogue and the religious school, unified by a common language and literary heritage, a community knit together by social and religious values and traditions and a messianic hope. This change ensured the survival of the Jews as a distinct ethnic group with a religion adapted to the realities of life in the Diaspora after A.D. 70.

During the first revolt, which ended with the destruction of Jerusalem in A.D. 70, some rebels killed the Roman soldiers stationed on Masada. The surviving rebels (about 1000 men, women, and children) fled to Masada. For three years, the Romans laid siege to Masada. In the end they built a massive earthen ramp up the west side of the rock to gain entrance (top). Looking down the ramp from the top, we can only imagine those on top watching it being built, knowing that the end was inexorably approaching. When the Romans finally broke through, only two women and five children were still alive, the rest having committed suicide rather than surrender. Like the ramp, the pile of rocks on top of Masada, shot up by Roman catapults (bottom), are also mute witnesses to the drama of the siege.

During the century before Jesus' birth, the rabbis (teachers of the law) were already becoming important in Jewish life and worship. When the temple was gone, there were no more sacrifices or elaborate rituals, so there was no longer a need for priests. Jews who wanted to continue their tradition had to do it through study of the Torah, which made the rabbis the key to the survival of the Jewish religion. One of the greatest rabbis ever was Hillel, who lived just before Jesus' time. He was elected patriarch of Palestine, and his successors continued through the 5th century A.D. Hillel was a model of humility, who taught that every man should have the right to study the Torah because study is a way to worship God.

Due to the growing importance of study among Jews, Jewish scholars, especially in Jabneh and Babylonia but also elsewhere, set themselves the task of writing down the great body of oral law and religious interpretation that had been formed over the centuries. This body of laws

After the second, or Bar Kochba, revolt, Emperor Hadrian turned Jerusalem into a Roman city, off-limits to Jews. The Damascus Gate dates from the time of Hadrian. Like most remains from the first two centuries A.D., it is now well below street level.

and interpretations is known as the Talmud. The scholars in Palestine completed the Palestinian Talmud (also called the Jerusalem Talmud) in the 5th century A.D. The Babylonian scholars completed the more extensive Babylonian Talmud a cen-

Silver shekels of the second Jewish revolt. Simon Bar Kochba began a second major revolt against Roman occupation in A.D. 132

tury later. Well into the Middle Ages, the Babylonian Talmudic scholars served as the final authority on religious questions, sent to them from all parts of the world.

The Jewish calendar became of primary importance since there was no longer a physical focal point for worship. The yearly calendar determines the rhythm of the year and begins with the New Year, Rosh Hashanah. It is designed to reiterate their biblical history for Jews. The rituals are intended to create inner meaning and relationship with God. The Sabbath is the focus of the week, beginning on Friday at sundown, when the woman of the house lights the candles and says a prayer, and ending on Saturday at sundown. It includes the Sabbath meal as well as collective worship in the synagogue or other meeting place.

Palestine from A.D. 324 to 1918

The Byzantine Period (324–640)

The land of Palestine remained under Roman control until A.D. 324, when the capital of the empire was transferred from Rome in the west to Constantinople in the east. In A.D. 313 the emperor Constantine, who had converted to Christianity, legalized Christianity and encouraged its growth, but by edict made conversion to Judaism punishable by death. The major motivation behind this edict was probably the important role Jews played in trade: the Christian church banned usury (lending money at interest), and Jews were prohibited from many other activities that would earn them a living, so they financed commerce. Another effect of Constantine's edict was that many sites in Palestine that were associated with Jesus' life were consecrated as shrines and thus were visited by large numbers of Christian pilgrims. This resulted in the building of many monasteries and churches in the Holy Land.

The Early Arab Period (640–1099)

The next event that would have a major impact on the country of Palestine and the Jews was the founding of Islam by Mohammed in A.D. 622. Not only was Islam to be the third major monotheistic world religion (after Judaism and Christianity), it also marked the beginning of Arab territorial expansion. In 637 Muslim armies conquered Mesopotamia,

The Dome of the Rock, also known as the Mosque of Omar, was built in 688–91. It stands about where the temple once stood and where, it is claimed, Mohammed ascended to heaven. A more cynical suggestion has been that it was built to overshadow the Christian churches in the area, which were attracting Arab converts, who saw these church buildings as images of power.

and Islam became the state religion. Jerusalem was captured in 638 and became a center for Muslim as well as Christian pilgrims.

The Dome of the Rock, which still stands where the Jewish temple stood until A.D. 70, was built during this relatively peaceful period. Although Caliph Omar I had issued a decree restricting Jewish life, including the required wearing of yellow patches on their sleeves and a prohibition on the building and repairing of synagogues, the caliphs of Baghdad did not consider themselves bound by these decrees and allowed the Jews there to live without restrictions.

The Crusader Period (1099–1291)

This relatively peaceful period came to an end in 1009 when Caliph Hakim began to persecute Christians and destroy churches. The Turks, who captured Jerusalem in 1071, then closed the places in Palestine viewed as holy by Christians. The papacy responded by initiating the Crusades in 1095 to take back control.

The Crusaders were essentially armies sent under the auspices of the church. They were determined to rid the Holy Land of Islam and took Jerusalem in 1099, massacring all Muslim inhabitants. They established the Kingdom of Jerusalem and built massive fortresses on the medieval European feudal model (see below and pp. 832, 908, 946).

But after their initial successes, the tide turned against the Crusaders and they ultimately failed in less than two centuries. Their last bastion fell in 1291.

The Mameluke Period (1250–1517)

The Mamelukes (armies of slaves that won political control of several Muslim states during the Middle Ages) took control of the region around 1250. Palestine became a region of little importance because the Mamelukes were preoccupied elsewhere. Reminders of their presence are

Crusader armies established massive fortresses throughout the Middle East in their attempts to obtain control of the Holy Land. This one borders the Mediterranean Sea.

The Crusaders left behind massive structures in various places, built like medieval European castles or fortresses. An outstanding example is Belvoir Castle, built in the Jordan Valley some 10 miles south of the Sea of Galilee. It consisted of three concentric squares with heavy walls and a moat. After defeating the Crusaders, the Turks destroyed Belvoir. The ruins still impress us with the massive scale on which Belvoir was built. (See also pp. 832, 908.)

the Citadel in Jerusalem and the Haram es-Sharif, or Temple Mount, on which the Dome of the Rock stands. (Today observant Jews do not visit the Haram es-Sharif because no one except the high priest was allowed to enter the Most Holy Place in the temple; since no one knows the exact location of the Most Holy Place, the Chief Rabbinate has ruled the entire Temple Mount off-limits.)

The Ottoman Period (1517–1918)

The Ottoman Turks captured Constantinople in 1453, and in 1517 the Ottoman Turks gained control of Palestine. (In that same year, Martin Luther nailed his Ninety-five Theses to the door of the church in Wittenberg, which marked the beginning of the Reformation; see p. 913). The second sultan to rule in Palestine was Suleiman the Magnificent, who rebuilt the walls of Jerusalem, which still stand today (see p. 947).

The present walls and gates of Jerusalem date back less than 500 years. They were built by Suleiman the Magnificent in 1537–42 and have since been renovated. This is the Damascus Gate.

After Suleiman, Palestine was again relegated to a status of lesser importance. Its rulers were violent and corrupt. Nevertheless, the end of the 17th century saw an increase in Jewish immigration, the result of persecutions in the Diaspora. This continued in the 18th century, and Jews from Eastern Europe established communities in Safed and Tiberias.

The Jews in Europe Before the Reformation

Spain

There were many disadvantages to being Jewish in Christian countries, but in Muslim countries Jews had a reasonably secure place. In Spain, for example, the Jews had suffered persecutions for several centuries while it was a Christian country. But with the Muslim conquest of Spain in 711, the persecutions ceased. Not only that, but the center of Jewish learning shifted from Babylonia to Spain. The Jews in Spain came to occupy prominent positions and contributed to the 12th-century Renaissance by translating the Greek classics, to which they had access through Arabic connections, for the first time in Western Europe since the fall of the Roman Empire.

When the Muslim domination of Spain came to an end in the 13th century, the Spanish Jews, known as **Sephardic Jews,** came under the same kind of harsh treatment that Jews received elsewhere in Europe.

Northern Europe

In the northern European countries the Jews were persecuted and condemned because they were viewed as being guilty of the suffering and death of Jesus. Especially during the period of the Crusades (1095–1291), which was marked by Christian religious fervor, thousands of Jews were massacred. In 1215 the church formally adopted restrictions on Jewish life similar to those that had been decreed by Caliph Omar I, including

Maimonides (1135–1204) was a major Jewish scholar and commentator in the field of Jewish law. This document is a response by Maimonides to a dispute related to a circumstance involving circumcision.

the requirement to wear a badge to indicate that one was a Jew. In the cities Jews were forced to live in special areas (ghettos), and eventually they were expelled from a number of countries, such as England (1290), France (1394), Spain (1492), and Portugal (1497). The Jews were even accused of causing the Black Death (the plague), which decimated the population of Europe in the 14th century.

Eastern Europe

The Jews who were expelled moved eastward. In the 16th century, Constantinople (now Istanbul, Turkey) had the largest Jewish community in Europe. Most of the Jews expelled from the northern European countries moved to Poland and Russia. The Jews of Eastern Europe are called

Ashkenazi or **Ashkenazic Jews**. By the mid-17th century there were half a million Jews in Poland. But a decade of major persecutions (1648–58) destroyed many Jewish communities there. Laws kept Jews from all professions and skilled occupations, forcing them to live by means of small-scale buying and selling and money-lending (banking), but they still were allowed to keep the Sabbath and the feasts in the prescribed way.

Maimonides

The most famous Jewish scholar in Spain was Maimonides (1135–1204). A religious thinker but also important in law, philosophy, medicine, astronomy, and logic, he was considered the leader of Jewry. Born in Spain, he was forced to flee with his family to Morocco at age 13 because a radical Muslim family came into power. There he became a physician, but his activities in encouraging Jews to secretly follow the Jewish commandments caused him to flee again to Palestine, then to Egypt. He wrote the *Mishneh Torah*, a commentary on the entire field of Jewish law contained in 14 books, and the *Guide for the Perplexed* and *Thirteen Articles*, or principles of belief, which influenced Christians and Muslims as well as Jews.

The Jews after the Reformation

Western Europe

The increased social and political freedom resulting from the Reformation included the reestablishment of tolerance for Jews in Western Europe. For example, England, which had expelled the Jews in 1290, now encouraged their immigration under Cromwell, as did the American colonies.

Many Jews became leading intellectuals, artists, scientists, and politicians.

- As Jews gained a fuller participation in the larger culture, philosophers emerged to mediate between European culture and Judaism. One of these was **Baruch Spinoza** (1632–77). Excommunicated from the Jewish community, he did not convert to another faith, but wrote about freedom as a humanist and engaged in biblical criticism from the historical angle. Thus he was the first of many Jews to hold onto his Jewishness without the religion.
- **Moses Mendelssohn** (1729–86), a deist, became a founder of the Jewish Enlightenment. He espoused being German in culture and Jewish in personal life. He also taught that there should be separation of church and state. Mendelssohn's son had himself and his family baptized as Lutherans to spare them the social stigma of being Jewish; his grandson, Felix, was the great composer who, among his many great works, wrote the oratorios *Elijah* and *Moses*.
- By the mid-19th century, **Karl Marx** (1818–83), a German Jew who had been baptized a Christian at age six and who avoided participation in Jewish life, effected profound changes in the

larger culture. In collaboration with Fredrich Engels, Marx wrote *The Communist Manifesto* in 1848, which called workers to engage in violent revolution against their capitalist oppressors. Exiled from France and Germany, Marx settled in London and there published *Das Kapital (Capital)*, which deplored capitalism as exploitative.

- In England, **Benjamin Disraeli** (1804–81) was an example of the increased political participation of Jews. His ancestors had been driven out of Spain, and his father had him baptized due to social and political discrimination practiced against Jews and nonconformist Protestants. Yet, when British reforms in the 1830s allowed nonconformists to participate in politics, he served in several offices, twice as prime minister. He enlarged and strengthened the British Empire while working to allow Jews and others to vote and participate fully in political life.

- Many intellectual Jews in Europe at the turn of the 20th century were ambivalent about their Jewish heritage. One such was **Sigmund Freud** (1856–1939), the founder of psychoanalysis. Exploring the mysteries of the human personality and the unconscious, he was the first to acknowledge the importance of early childhood experiences in human development, as well as the importance of sexual drive. He fled to England in 1938 after the Nazi invasion of Austria. He once advised a friend that letting his son grow up as a Jew would force him to struggle, whereas not to do so would "deprive him of those sources of energy which cannot be replaced by anything else."

- While Freud revolutionized, for better or worse, the way we look at people, **Albert Einstein** (1879–1955) revolutionized our understanding of the physical world. His general and special theories of relativity paved the way for the demise of the Newtonian worldview and eventually led to the development of nuclear fission and nuclear energy.

Eastern Europe

While in Western Europe tolerance toward the Jews had increased, the reverse happened in Eastern Europe. Until the mid-17th century there had been a policy of tolerance toward the Jews, but then the Jews became objects of official persecution. Eastern Poland, where most of the Polish Jews lived, became part of the Russian Empire at the end of the 18th century. Life was made extremely hard for these Jews. They could only live in specific areas and had very few educational and occupational possibilities. But making life especially insecure were the periodic *pogroms*—unprovoked, violent attacks on Jews, sanctioned and sometimes even financed by the government. These persecutions lasted until the Bolshevik Revolution in 1917. Between 1890 and 1917, about 2 million Jews emigrated to the United States from areas under Russian control. Others emigrated to

Canada, South America, South Africa, and Palestine, where they established communities that lived and worshiped together.

One visible reminder of this migration is the typical garb still worn by many Orthodox Jews—wide-brimmed hat or fur hat and long black coat—which originated in Eastern Europe. Another reminder, now disappearing, is the language of the Eastern European or Ashkenazi Jews—Yiddish, a form of low German incorporating many Hebrew words. Yiddish literature flourished for a period, with such well-known writers as Sholem Aleichem and Isaac Bashevis Singer.

North America

Many Jews settled in North America because of its religious freedom and pluralism. (Today the largest Jewish populations are in the United States and Israel.) In fact, most of the current forms of Judaism either developed in or were created in the United States. As waves of immigrants came, the three major modern forms of Judaism developed.

- **Reform Judaism.** In 1869 a group of rabbis, mostly of German background, produced a statement which rejected the idea of a personal Messiah and the literal restoration of Zion. They saw Judaism as part of a universal religion in which God's kingdom would be established to unite all human beings. This developed into Reform Judaism, which roughly corresponded to 19th-century liberal American Protestantism. Reform Jews called their places of worship temples instead of synagogues and founded Hebrew Union College in Cincinnati as their foremost training center. Their theology was modernist and combined literary and historical criticism with traditional Jewish interpretation.
- **Orthodox Judaism.** Immigrants from Eastern Europe tended to hold to Orthodox Judaism; many of them were Hasidim, or Hasidic Jews. Hasidism originated around 1750 in Poland with the charismatic Baal Shem Tov; it was a reaction against a religious orthodoxy that had become rigid and unrelated to the life of the common people. Hasidism is characterized by a combination of Torah study and expressive, often ecstatic, forms of worship. (Today thriving Hasidic communities are found in Jerusalem and, among other places, the Williamsburg and Crown Heights areas of Brooklyn, New York). Orthodox Jews created Yeshiva University to train rabbis. While living in the social and economic institutions of the United States, Orthodox Jews have been able to keep to the revealed Torah and follow the traditional laws. Orthodox Jews see Reform Jews as having abandoned the substance of the faith.
- **Conservative Judaism.** Between Reform and Orthodox Judaism is the third major category, Conservative Judaism, which combines modern scholarship with religious practice that follows traditional Law.

Many American Jews fit none of these three categories and are known as nonobservant or secular Jews, who have moved entirely away from traditional religious belief and practice but acknowledge their Jewish ancestry and parentage.

Anti-Semitism in Western Europe

While the Jews in Western Europe were no longer officially discriminated against or persecuted, there were undercurrents of anti-Semitism.

The Dreyfus Affair

The French Revolution had led to a formal acceptance of the Jews in France. They were granted full citizenship in 1791, and Napoleon made a point of opening ghettos and securing Jews' rights as he marched across Europe. After Napoleon was defeated, however, many of the states where he had emancipated the Jews reverted to their old policies for a few decades. In 1894 the trial of Alfred Dreyfus became one of the most famous cases in legal history and illustrated the fact that anti-Semitism persisted in European society in spite of political reforms. Dreyfus, the only Jewish officer on the French General Staff, was charged with treason and convicted. Two years later, the French government suppressed evidence that proved Dreyfus was not guilty of spying and that in fact another General Staff member was the real culprit. Dreyfus's innocence became public knowledge, and another trial was held. It was generally assumed that Dreyfus would be acquitted, but since an openly anti-Semitic government had been elected in 1898, he was deemed "guilty with extenuating circumstances" and sentenced to 10 years' imprisonment. Even though he was pardoned by the president of France, people lobbied for his exoneration, which occurred in 1906; he was then reinstated in the army. Dreyfus's attorney was Emile Zola, the well-known French Jewish writer and novelist.

The Holocaust

With their claims that there are superior and inferior individuals and races, late-19th-century movements such as Social Darwinism and Monism contributed to anti-Semitism. Thus, at the end of World War I there was resentment against Jews and other ethnic groups who were viewed as inferior, especially in Germany and Eastern Europe. When economic depression and hyperinflation in Germany became severe in the 1930s, many people blamed the Jews because of their history of success in banking and business. This made it easy for Adolf Hitler and his Nazi regime to devise the "final solution," an attempt to exterminate the Jews by mass killings. They first used the techniques of the medieval Caliph Omar I (see p. 945): they required all Jews to wear a yellow Star of David and instituted restrictions, such as curfews and exclusion from conducting certain types of business or social activity. They succeeded in killing more than 6 million Jews, thus significantly reducing the Jewish population of Europe.

The Holocaust raised questions for many Jews (and Christians as well). The main question was, How could a good God have allowed such an atrocity? Some Jews left the faith; some argued that the Holocaust was so monstrous that it released Jews from the covenant and its obligations to keep the Law; some believed that it was God's plan and that the Jews were used as sacrificial victims to create a new society. Many continue to struggle with these questions. Central in post-Holocaust thought is the idea that Judaism has come through darkness that has injured them, but the Jews still are living testimony to God's light.

Palestine: The British Mandate (1919–1948)

A concrete result of the Holocaust was the establishment of the State of Israel in 1948, when the British gave over the land for Jewish settlement.

The Ottoman Empire had been weakening in the 19th century, and Great Britain and other nations became interested in the region, especially after the opening of the Suez Canal in 1869 made it strategically important. During World War I, Britain and the Allies sought support from Arabs and Jews to overthrow the Ottoman Empire. The politics and diplomacy of the period were rather muddy. It appeared that promises for an independent state in Palestine were made to both Arabs and Jews. The infamous Balfour Declaration (1917), which "viewed with favour the establishment of a national home for the Jewish people," is so ambiguous that both Jews and Arabs have used it to back their claims.

After World War I, Palestine was placed under the tutelage of a "more advanced nation," Britain. This began the so-called British Mandate (1919–48). It turned out to be a period in which Jewish and Arab interests clashed—often violently. It was also a period of increased Jewish immigration into Palestine, due in large measure to Zionism (from Zion, the traditional name for Jerusalem and Palestine).

Zionism

Zionism was a Jewish nationalist movement whose goal was to create and support a Jewish national state in Palestine. Toward the end of the 19th century, Theodore Herzl, after seeing anti-Semitism at work in the Dreyfus Affair in France in 1893–94, realized the need for a Jewish national state. He became the founder of political Zionism, which half a century later, in 1948, realized its goal with the founding of the State of Israel.

The concept of the return to Zion is part of Jewish Law. Reform Jews stated in 1885 that they consider themselves to be a religious community rather than a nation; however, that view was replaced in the 20th century with enthusiastic Zionism. Other Jews believe that mankind will be redeemed in "the days of the Messiah," in Zion, with the rebuilding of lost institutions of national and religious life. Many Orthodox Jews did not question the need to return to Zion, but they believed that political Zionists were trying to preempt God's action. Most of these Jews died in the Holocaust, and Orthodox Jews are enthusiastically settling in Israel today.

The State of Israel (Since 1948)

The situation in Palestine became increasingly complex and unmanageable, so in 1947 the British decided to end their mandate and turn the solution over to the United Nations General Assembly. The U.N. proposed a division of Palestine into an Arab state and a Jewish state; Jerusalem would be an international zone. The Jews accepted, the Arabs rejected the plan.

On May 14, 1948, the day before the official end of the British Mandate, when the last of the British troops left the country, David Ben Gurion proclaimed Israel an independent state and became the Jewish nation's first prime minister. Both the United States and Russia recognized the new nation, which was, after great debate, accepted as a member of the United Nations by a vote of 37 to 12. This led to a war with its Arab neighbors that ended a year later with Israel holding more territory than the partition plan would have allotted them.

The State of Israel is governed by elected leaders who meet at the Knesset.

Ever since its inception, the State of Israel has lived in tension with its Arab neighbors. The issues are complex, and emotions run deep on both sides. After four wars—the Sinai (Suez) War in 1956; the Six-Day War in 1967; the War of Attrition in 1969–70; and the Yom Kippur War in 1973—the peace efforts have intensified, but they have also shown the depth of the political and religious conflicts, both in rhetoric and in terrorist activities.

> Pray for the peace of Jerusalem:
>   "May those who love you be secure.
> May there be peace within your walls
>   and security within your citadels."
> For the sake of my brothers and friends,
>   I will say, "Peace be within you."
> For the sake of the house of the LORD our God,
>   I will seek your prosperity.
>   —Psalm 122:6–9

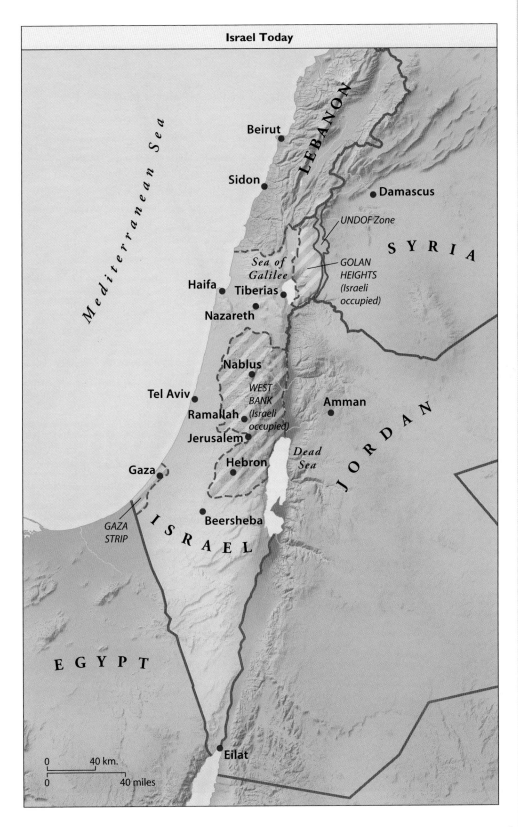

Israel Today

Mediterranean Sea

LEBANON

Beirut

Sidon

Damascus

UNDOF Zone

SYRIA

Sea of Galilee

GOLAN HEIGHTS (Israeli occupied)

Haifa   Tiberias

Nazareth

Nablus

WEST BANK (Israeli occupied)

Amman

Tel Aviv

Ramallah

Jerusalem

JORDAN

Dead Sea

Gaza   Hebron

GAZA STRIP

ISRAEL

Beersheba

EGYPT

0   40 km.

0   40 miles

Eilat

Reading and Studying the Bible

Reading Through the Bible

Plans of Bible Reading

There are many plans for reading the Bible. One plan will appeal to one person, another plan may be more suited to another. In fact, the same person may like and need different plans at different times. The particular plan does not greatly matter. The essential thing is that we read the Bible with some degree of regularity. (See "The Habit of Bible Reading," pp. 14ff.)

Begin with One of the Gospels

If you have never read the Bible or are unfamiliar with it, a good place to start is to read one of the first three Gospels: Matthew, Mark, or Luke. The Gospels present Jesus, who stands at the center of the Bible. The Old Testament looks forward to His coming, and the New Testament shows us the importance of His life, death, and resurrection.

Selected Readings: The Plan and Story of the Bible

On the following pages is a plan that will help you read through major, selected portions of the Bible, mostly historical, to help you get a grasp on how the Bible fits together and what its overall story is. It will be helpful to have the section on pp. 33–42, "What the Bible Is About," alongside as you read the Bible.

We suggest that you read in the books of Psalms and Proverbs on a regular basis as you go through the plan below.

1. In the Beginning (Genesis 1–11)

Creation, Adam & Eve, Fall, Cain & Abel, Noah and the Flood, Babel

Read:

- Introduction to this section on p. 81.
- Genesis 1–11

2. The Patriarchs (Genesis 12–50)

Abraham, Isaac, Jacob, Joseph

Read:

- Introduction to this section on p. 103.
- Genesis 12–50

A Plan of Weekly Readings

A simple plan involves reading one or more books per week (depending on their length), rather than specific chapters each day. The plan on the following page takes you through the Old Testament once and the New Testament twice over the course of a year.

Deciding on Your Bible Reading Plan

- Decide which plan is best for you. Set up a schedule and **_write on a calendar_** which section or chapters you will read each day.
- It is better to faithfully read a small section each day than to occasionally read large sections.
- Most importantly, if for some reason you miss a day or even a few days, **_don't abandon the plan and quit reading the Bible._** Either catch up or adjust the rest of the plan. But don't quit.

In the Middle of a Busy Day

Bible reading is not something that stands outside of daily life. It should be part of our daily living, like food and water.

Why not, in the middle of a busy day, when you feel stretched to the breaking point, take a few minutes and read a Psalm or a few Proverbs? Or read a few verses from other books of the Bible that have spoken to you. Keep a small Bible or New Testament with Psalms on your desk, in your locker, or in your lunch box, with a list of special verses. If you do this, you will be amazed how often the Psalm, Proverbs, or other Bible selection will make a difference in your day.

1st Week	Genesis	2nd Week	Matthew
3rd Week	Exodus	4th Week	Mark
5th Week	Leviticus	6th Week	Luke
7th Week	Numbers	8th Week	Luke
9th Week	Deuteronomy	10th Week	John
11th Week	Joshua, Judges	12th Week	Acts
13th Week	Ruth, 1 Samuel	14th Week	Romans
15th Week	2 Samuel	16th Week	1 & 2 Corinthians
17th Week	1 Kings	18th Week	Galatians, Ephesians, Philippians, Colossians
19th Week	2 Kings	20th Week	1 & 2 Thessalonians, 1 & 2 Timothy, Titus, Philemon
21st Week	1 Chronicles	22nd Week	Hebrews, James
23rd Week	2 Chronicles	24th Week	1 & 2 Peter, 1 & 2 & 3 John, Jude
25th Week	Ezra, Nehemiah, Esther	26th Week	Revelation
27th Week	Job	28th Week	Matthew
29th Week	Psalms	30th Week	Matthew or John
31st Week	Psalms	32nd Week	Mark
33rd Week	Psalms	34th Week	Luke
35th Week	Proverbs, Ecclesiastes, Song	36th Week	John
37th Week	Isaiah	38th Week	Acts
39th Week	Isaiah	40th Week	Romans
41st Week	Jeremiah	42nd Week	1 & 2 Corinthians
43rd Week	Jeremiah, Lamentations	44th Week	Galatians, Ephesians, Philippians, Colossians
45th Week	Ezekiel	46th Week	1 & 2 Thessalonians, 1 & 2 Timothy, Titus, Philemon
47th Week	Daniel	48th Week	Hebrews, James
49th Week	Hosea, Joel, Amos, Obadiah,	50th Week	1 & 2 Peter, 1 & 2 & 3 John, Jude, Jonah, Micah
51st Week	Nahum, Habakkuk, Zephaniah,	52nd Week	Revelation, Haggai, Zechariah, Malachi

Basic Bible Study Tools

When you read the Bible, you will find yourself asking questions about the meaning of words, or the meaning of verses or sections, and you will want to find other, perhaps half-remembered, verses that are related to what you are reading. There are many tools available to help you. But always keep in mind that the best reference library in the world and the most intense study can never be a substitute for simply reading the Bible, listening to it, and reflecting on it, allowing the Holy Spirit to illuminate your understanding.

Why Study the Bible?

The main purpose of Bible study is to help us deepen our relationship with the Lord and to be more and more transformed into the likeness of Christ (2 Corinthians 3:18). The Scriptures can be used to lead us to salvation, train us for righteousness, and equip us to do good works (2 Timothy 3:15–17). But while it is appropriate to spend time and effort to continually deepen our understanding of the Scriptures, we always run the risk of drowning our love for Jesus in a sea of factual knowledge, measuring our spirituality by how much we know, or making Bible study an end in itself.

Jesus' harshest words were reserved for Bible scholars and religious leaders. He told the Pharisees, "You have never heard his [God the Father's] voice . . . , nor does his word dwell in you. . . . You diligently study the Scriptures because you think that by them you possess eternal life. These are the Scriptures that testify about me, yet you refuse to come to me to have life" (John 5:38–40). So how can we avoid this pitfall? The Bible itself tells us how:

1. Be humble. God gives wisdom and grace to the humble (Proverbs 3:34; 11:2). Be willing to have your old opinions and assumptions challenged, and to be shown sins that you need to repent and be forgiven of.
2. Cry out for supernatural help! Ask God to give you His "Spirit of wisdom and revelation, so that you may know him better" (Ephesians 1:17) and to open your eyes so you may see wonderful things in His Law (Psalm 119:18). God is happy to give us His Holy Spirit (Luke 11:13).
3. Be ready to obey. Jesus said, "If anyone loves me, he will obey my teaching. My Father will love him, and we will come to him and

make our home with him" (John 14:23). We don't want to be like the person who studies his face in the mirror and then goes away and forgets what he looks like; instead we want to do what the Word says and so be blessed (James 1:22–25).

4. Balance Bible study with prayer, worship, meeting with other believers, and serving Jesus.

How to Approach Studying the Bible

God has taken the trouble to have His truth written down and preserved for us over the centuries. We should not be casual or loose about the way we read and understand the Bible. It is important to interpret the Bible honestly, carefully, and consistently, rather than simply picking out verses that support what we would like the truth to be. Bible reference tools can help us handle God's Word correctly (2 Timothy 2:15) and study it with the reverence and care it deserves.

Serious Bible study is work. People often like the idea of doing Bible study better than the actual work. There are no magic books that will give you all the answers without effort on your part.

So, keep your expectations realistic. You will never master the Bible—no one has done so yet, even though some people may sound like it. The point is not to become a master of the Bible but to be a servant to the Word.

On the other hand, don't underestimate yourself. The Bible is not a complex database that requires highly skilled technicians to unlock—there are no passwords or special codes to be learned. The spirit in which we approach the Bible and read and study it is far more important than our ability to use even the most sophisticated Bible study tools.

Three general books that provide useful approaches to Bible study are *Understanding the Bible* by John R. W. Stott, *Applying the Bible* by Jack Kuhatschek, and *How to Read the Bible for All Its Worth* by Gordon Fee and Douglas Stuart.

The Basic Tools

When you walk into a bookstore with a wide selection of Bible reference tools (or begin an online search), the sheer number and variety can be overwhelming—especially when you're not sure how to even start deciding which ones you need.

But don't be intimidated—when you buy tools to help you study the Bible, you're not making a lifetime decision. All you need to do is find which tools meet your needs now. Furthermore, there are indeed a lot of choices, but it becomes much simpler when you realize that most of them fall into just a few categories.

- Tools that give you an *overview* of the Bible and help you *read* the Bible with understanding:
  1. Bible Handbook
  2. Study Bible

- Tools that help you *find* verses and passages in the Bible:
  1. Concordance
  2. Topical Bible
- Tools that help you *understand* things in the Bible:
  1. Bible Dictionary
  2. Commentary

Here is what each of these does:

1. A **Bible Handbook**, such as this one, is a companion to Bible reading. It is arranged in the order of the books of the Bible and provides background before you read through a Bible book, explanation and illustrations as you read, and topical and historical notes to expand your understanding.

   Incidentally, *Halley's Bible Handbook* was the first Bible handbook ever published. It was a revolutionary concept that came out of Dr. Halley's desire to get people to read the Bible with more understanding. It remains a perennial best-seller to this day.

2. A **Study Bible** is the foundation of any Bible reference library. It is the complete Bible with notes and other helpful materials added, such as maps, introductions to each book of the Bible, and cross-references to other Scriptures.

3. A **Concordance** lists common words found in the Bible and shows the places where they occur. For example, under the entry "Faith" you would find the locations in the Bible where the word "faith" is used. A concordance enables you to do word studies as well as locate verses you vaguely remember.

4. A **Topical Bible** is a guide to different subjects or topics addressed in the Bible. Under "Faith," it will list not only the most important verses where the word "faith" is found, but also verses that talk about faith without using the word — for example Genesis 15:6, "Abraham believed the LORD."

5. A **Bible Dictionary** gives more detailed information about people, places, words, and events in the Bible. You could use it to learn more about what the Bible says about children, for example, or about Peter, or Egypt, or miracles.

NIV Study Bible

6. A **Commentary** is a single or multivolume work that explains the meaning of Bible passages.

How to Choose and Use the Tools You Need

Study Bible

First you must decide which Bible translation (Bible version) you will use for Bible study. (See pp. 1000–1004.)

Second, Study Bibles can have different emphases and purposes. For example, the *NIV Life Application Study Bible* focuses more on practical questions, the *NIV Study Bible* on understanding the text. Look up a few passages in both and compare the notes. You will see very quickly how — and how much! — they differ. You may even want to consider buying both, since the two complement each other. Buying one in a different Bible translation will give you the added benefit of having two translations to work with.

But keep in mind that *not all Bibles with added materials are Study Bibles.* Devotional Bibles contain a number of devotions in addition to the text of the Bible but are designed for daily reading rather than for study of the text.

Choosing a Study Bible

Because you'll use your Study Bible more than the other books in your reference library, it's worth taking time to compare the various ones that are available. Pick a few sample sections (perhaps short books such as Jonah, 1 John, or 2 Peter) and compare the notes on them. Then look at the other materials provided.

Ask yourself:

- Do the notes that explain the text address the kinds of things I want to know?
- How clear, detailed, and helpful are the introductions and outlines to each book of the Bible?
- How many cross-references to other Scripture are there? Are they easy to read?
- How extensive is the dictionary? Are the definitions clear and helpful?
- What kind of things are in the index? Are the topics in the topical Scripture index helpful for today's reader?
- How long is the concordance? Does it list words I would want to look up?
- How many maps are there, and of what quality? Is the index to them easy to use? Does the book have charts, and do they contain relevant information? Does the book have illustrations, and are they helpful or simply "filler"?
- Does the book have a harmony of the Gospels (a single, chronological summary of the four Gospels)?

- Do I prefer a "red-letter edition" (with words of Jesus printed in red)?

Concordance

A concordance is an index to the words found in the Bible. It lists the references of the verses where they occur, and a piece of each sentence where the word occurs. For example, under "Love" in the *Zondervan NIV Exhaustive Concordance* you will find:

Lev	19:18	but L your neighbor as yourself.	170
	19:34	L him as yourself,	170
Nu	14:18	in L and forgiving sin and rebellion.	2876
	14:19	In accordance with your great L,	2876
Dt	5:10	but showing L to a thousand [generations]	2876
	5:10	*those who* L me and keep my commandments	170
	6: 5	L the LORD your God with all your heart	170
	7: 9	the faithful God, keeping his covenant of L	2876
	7: 9	a thousand generations of *those who* L him	170
	7:12	will keep his covenant of L with you,	2876

Unlike most Bible reference books, **a concordance is based on a specific Bible translation** (NIV, KJV, NASB, etc.) **and should be used only with that translation**. For example, the word "charity" in the KJV is usually translated "love" in the NIV. Similarly, the Hebrew word that is usually translated "unfailing love" in the NIV is translated as "mercy," "goodness," "kindness," or "lovingkindness" in the KJV. Similarly, the word "peace" is found around 400 times in the KJV, but only just over 200 times in the NIV.

If you were raised on the KJV but now use a modern translation, you may want a concordance for each version so that you can also find verses you remember from your KJV days.

Choosing a Concordance

Concordances come in different sizes, ranging from brief, abridged concordances (found in the back of most Study Bibles) to Exhaustive Concordances of almost 2,000 pages. There are four basic types:

- **Handy, Concise,** or **Compact Concordances** are in some way abridged. Only the most important words found in the Bible are included, and only the most important references for those words are listed. This type may be adequate if you only use a concordance occasionally to find a Bible verse.
- A **Complete Concordance** is still abridged, but in a different way. Not all words found in the Bible are included, but the list of references for each of the words that is included is complete. If you want to do English word studies, a Complete Concordance is a necessity, and an Exhaustive Concordance is even better.
- An **Unabridged Concordance** indexes every word and lists every reference.

- An **Exhaustive Concordance** indexes every word and lists every reference, and it also shows for every occurrence of every word in the English Bible version which Hebrew or Greek word it translates. If you want to do in-depth word studies based on the occurrences of Greek and Hebrew words, an Exhaustive Concordance is indispensable.

The best-known Exhaustive Concordance is *The New Strong's Exhaustive Concordance,* which is based on the King James Version. It has cross-references to some of the words translated differently in other Bible translations but is somewhat more difficult to use with Bible translations such as the NIV or NASB.

A very useful feature of Exhaustive Concordances is a numbering system that assigns a specific number to each of the Greek and Hebrew words that are found in the Bible. The *Zondervan NIV Exhaustive Concordance* uses the Goodrick/Kohlenberger numbering system, which reflects modern linguistic standards and is increasingly used in newer reference works.

Using a Concordance

Read the introduction to your concordance so you know its features and limitations.

If you can't locate a word, look for its dictionary form. (For example, if you can't find "went," look for "go.")

Many concordances direct you to the various inflected forms of words (e.g., come, comes, coming, came) or even to words of the same "root" (e.g., heart, fainthearted, halfhearted). By looking up the other forms or spellings you can do a more thorough word or concept study.

When doing a word study, use an English thesaurus to find synonyms and related words. For example, under "faith" a thesaurus will list words such as belief, hope, confidence, assurance, dependence, and trust.

Do not study in the concordance alone — use your Bible. Always read the context in which a verse is found, not just the verse or piece of a verse. For example, Psalm 14:1 says, "There is no God" — but the context tells you that that's what the fool says.

When you do a word study, read the verses you find, in their context, in several translations. It is also useful to find several places in the Bible where the same word is used. Most study Bibles will have cross-reference systems which assist you in finding other occurrences of the word or the concept that you are studying so that you can gain greater insight to the meaning of the text. Very few words — especially abstract words — have only one, clear-cut meaning.

Topical Bible

Choosing a Topical Bible

You can use a Topical Bible *with any translation of the Bible,* even if it quotes from a particular translation.

Some Topical Bibles list only biblical and theological topics, while others focus more on practical topics.

The size of a Topical Bible doesn't necessarily reflect the number of topics or references it contains. A small one that gives only verse references may actually be more complete than a big one that prints out the full text of many verses.

Since a concordance and a Topical Bible complement each other, they should be used together rather than only one or the other.

Ask yourself:

- Which one best addresses the subjects I want to study?
- How much information does each Topical Bible contain?
- Does the editor's choice of topics and their relative length seem balanced?
- Are the topics well subdivided and indexed?
- Are the Bible verses printed out in full? How important is this feature to me?
- When was it originally published and last revised?
- Which one seems most user-friendly to me?

Using a Topical Bible

If you want to study a topic such as "baptism," a concordance will only give you a list of all the verses in which the word "baptism" occurs.

A Topical Bible, by contrast, will help you also find verses and passages in the Bible that talk about the subject of baptism without using the word as such.

Bible Dictionary

A Bible Dictionary is more like an encyclopedia than like a regular English dictionary. It gives definitions and pronunciations, but it also provides biblical, historical, and theological information on people, places, words, and events in the Bible, all in alphabetical order. (A Bible Encyclopedia is simply a multivolume Bible Dictionary.)

Bible Dictionaries and Encyclopedias, such as the *New International Bible Dictionary* and the *Zondervan Pictorial Encyclopedia of the Bible,* don't define every word of the Bible. They focus mostly on nouns—people, places, and things—although some also have articles on theological terms that are not in the Bible, such as "Trinity."

Choosing a Bible Dictionary

It is helpful to have a Bible Dictionary that matches the version(s) of the Bible you use. The spelling of some people and place names may be different from one translation to another, and sometimes words are translated differently altogether. For example, there is a Hebrew word that the KJV, NIV, NASB, and NRSV translate as cormorant, desert owl, pelican, and hedgehog respectively.

When comparing dictionaries, pick a few words — for example, a place name like Shiloh; a person, perhaps Mary; an abstract biblical word such as grace; and a theological word like Trinity — and read the entries for these words in several dictionaries.

It can be very helpful to have more than one Bible Dictionary, especially if they are somewhat different in focus or orientation.

Look for thorough cross-referencing. If you don't know the exact word to look up, a good cross-reference system will anticipate many of your guesses and help direct you to the topic you're looking for. For example, if you look up "perfume" in the *NIV Compact Dictionary of the Bible,* it tells you, "See OINTMENTS AND PERFUMES."

Ask yourself:

- What kind of information will I most likely want to look up?
- How many articles does the Bible Dictionary have? Do I prefer many shorter articles, or fewer but longer ones?
- Does it have good cross-references?
- What size Dictionary is best for me? What type size and page layout do I like?
- Do I want a Dictionary that uses everyday English or a more scholarly one?
- When was this Dictionary originally published and last revised? (Historical, archaeological, and linguistic knowledge has grown dramatically over the past few decades.)

Using a Bible Dictionary

Cross-references or cross-indexing can help you find articles of related interest. An article about Jesus might end with "See also ATONEMENT, MESSIAH, MIRACLES, PARABLES, SECOND COMING," to name just a few.

A good **English Dictionary** is an indispensable tool for use with your Bible Dictionary. There may be unfamiliar words in the Bible that you won't find in a Bible Dictionary. Take, for example, Isaiah 14:23 in the *New English Bible:* "I will make her a haunt of the bustard, a waste of fen, and sweep her with the besom of destruction." Your Bible Dictionary probably won't help you here, but your English dictionary will.

An **English Thesaurus** is another valuable tool. For example, if you can't find an article on "Gentiles" in your Bible Dictionary, a thesaurus may suggest "heathen" as a synonym, and that may be the right heading in the Bible Dictionary.

Commentary

Choosing a Commentary

The choice of commentaries is, more than the choice of other Bible reference books, a personal matter. The key issue is, *Which commentary answers the kinds of questions I am likely to ask?*

Take time to look at what is available and compare before you buy. One consideration is what theological perspective the author is writing from.

Another consideration is the date of publication—some historical and cultural information in older Bible commentaries may be outdated or incorrect, although the devotional material in them would be timeless.

Commentaries come in many different sizes—from a single commentary on the whole Bible to a set of commentaries on each individual book of the Bible.

There are three basic types:

- **Devotional Commentaries**, such as *Matthew Henry's Commentary*, focus on the spiritual significance of the text for our lives.
- **Expository Commentaries** focus on explaining the text. Most Expository Commentaries, such as the *Expositor's Bible Commentary*, use historical, geographical, and cultural information as well as discussions of the original languages to explain the text. Others—for example, the *NIV Application Commentary*—concentrate on bridging the cultural gap between Bible times and today.
- **Exegetical or Critical Commentaries** focus primarily on technical issues related to the Greek or Hebrew text and its interpretation, and are written primarily for specialists (for example, the *Word Biblical Commentary*).

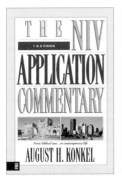  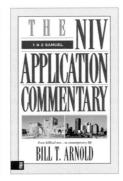

NIV Application Commentary

Using a Commentary

Commentaries give the commentator's perspective on passages in the Bible. They should never be the first books you check when doing a Bible study—if you do that, you start with somebody else's conclusions rather than finding your own. There is no substitute for firsthand study, using the tools of the core library and relying on the illuminating presence of the Holy Spirit.

On the other hand, commentaries can be helpful in supplementing your own study by giving you other perspectives and additional insights.

Ask yourself:

- Is the Bible text included? Is it the author's own translation?
- Is there an explanation of the text?

- Is historical, geographical, and cultural information included?
- Are there word studies and grammatical explanations?
- Are there critical notes dealing with textual criticism — form, literary, and other "higher" criticisms; history and comparison of different interpretations?
- Are footnotes, bibliography, and indexes included?

Bible Atlas

A Bible Atlas can be very helpful for understanding the historical and geographical context in which the Bible stories take place. An atlas such as the *Zondervan NIV Atlas of the Bible* contains

- Maps that show the location of places, groups of people, and nations in the Bible as well as maps that illustrate specific historical events.
- Geographical information about the various regions of Israel and Jordan, as well as Egypt, Syria and Lebanon, and Mesopotamia.
- Information about climate and weather, travel and roads.
- Historical geography — a historical survey of the Bible that shows where and how geography played a role in the history of Bible times.
- A gazetteer or index of biblical places.

Software for Bible Study

The invention of the personal computer revolutionized the art of Bible study. Whole libraries of Bible study books are available on CD-ROMs for a fraction of their cost in print form. Bible software allows you to locate information instantaneously and helps you to study the Bible more thoroughly and faster than in any other manner.

There are many things to consider when selecting Bible software. Will the software run on your computer? How easy is it to use? Are the reference works of value? Is the Bible translation you use included in the software? Three basic things set apart good Bible software:

- The "**search engine**": how easy, flexible, and powerful are the program's searching capabilities?
- The **core library:** does the program have the book you want to include in your study?
- **Interactivity:** can you easily display related topics and passages in many books at once?

Some Bible software is designed for both entertainment and Bible study. Be careful when selecting interactive software, as many have "bells and whistles" — that is, attractive features — but minimal study value.

Prayers

Prayers

A Prayer for Salvation

God in heaven,
I come to You in the name of Jesus.
I confess I have not lived my life for You. But I am glad to know I can change that.
I have decided to accept that Jesus is Your Son, and that He died on the cross and rose again from the dead, so I might have eternal life and the blessings of life now.
Jesus, come into my heart, be my Savior, be my Lord.
From this day forward, and to the best of my ability, I will live my life for You.
In Jesus' name I pray.
Amen.

A Blessing

The Lord bless you and keep you;
The Lord make His face shine upon you
    and be gracious to you;
The Lord turn His face toward you
    and give you peace.
Amen.

—Numbers 6:24–26

A Blessing

May the Lord answer you when you are in distress;
    may the name of the God of Jacob protect you.
May He send you help and grant you support.
May he give you the desire of your heart
    and make all your plans succeed.
May the Lord grant all your requests.
Amen.

—From Psalm 20

A Prayer for Our Nation

Lord,
Grant us peace, your most precious gift.
O eternal Source of peace, bless our country, that it may ever be a stronghold of peace and the advocate of peace in the councils of nations.
May contentment reign within its borders, health and happiness within its homes.

Strengthen the bonds of friendship and fellowship between all the inhabitants of our land.

Plant virtue in every soul; and may the love of your name hallow every home and every heart.

May You be praised, O Lord, Giver of peace.

Amen.

—Adapted from
The Methodist Hymnal

A Morning Prayer

O Lord,
Give ear to my words;
 consider my sighing.
Listen to my cry for help, my King and my God,
 for to you I pray.
In the morning, O Lord, you hear my voice;
 in the morning I lay my requests before you
 and wait in expectation.
Amen.

—From Psalm 5

A Prayer in Distress

O Lord,
Do not rebuke me in your anger
 or discipline me in your wrath.
Be merciful to me, Lord, for I am faint;
 O Lord, heal me, for my bones are in agony.
My soul is in anguish.
 How long, O Lord, how long?
Turn, O Lord, and deliver me;
 save me because of your unfailing love.
The Lord has heard my cry for mercy;
 the Lord accepts my prayer.
Amen.

—From Psalm 6

A Prayer of Trust

O Lord,
You are my shepherd, I shall not be in want.
 You make me lie down in green pastures,
you lead me beside quiet waters,
 you restore my soul.
You guide me in paths of righteousness
 for your name's sake.

Even though I walk through the valley
  of the shadow of death,
I will fear no evil,
  for you are with me;
your rod and your staff,
  they comfort me.
You prepare a table before me
  in the presence of my enemies.
You anoint my head with oil;
  my cup overflows.
Surely goodness and love will follow me
  all the days of my life,
and I will dwell in your house forever.
Amen.

—From Psalm 23

A Prayer for Direction

O Lord,
To you I lift up my soul;
  in you I trust, O my God.
Do not let me be put to shame.
Show me your ways, O Lord,
  teach me your paths;
guide me in your truth and teach me,
    for you are God my Savior,
    and my hope is in you all day long.
Remember, O Lord, your great mercy and love,
  for they are from of old.
Remember not the sins of my youth
  and my rebellious ways.
According to your love remember me,
  for you are good, O Lord.
Amen.

—From Psalm 25

A Prayer of Thanksgiving for Healing

O Lord,
I will exalt you,
    for you lifted me out of the depths
    and did not let my enemies gloat over me.
O Lord my God, I called to you for help
  and you healed me.
O Lord, you brought me up from the grave;
  you spared me from going down into the pit.

To you, O Lord, I called;
  to the Lord I cried for mercy:
What gain is there in my destruction,
  in my going down into the pit?
Will the dust praise you?
    Will it proclaim your faithfulness?
Hear, O Lord, and be merciful to me;
  O Lord, be my help.
You turned my wailing into dancing;
    you removed my sackcloth and clothed me with joy,
that my heart may sing to you and not be silent.
    O Lord my God, I will give you thanks forever.
Amen.

—From Psalm 30

A Prayer of Confession

O God,
Have mercy on me,
    according to your unfailing love;
according to your great compassion
    blot out my transgressions.
Wash away all my iniquity
    and cleanse me from my sin.
For I know my transgressions,
    and my sin is always before me.
Against you, you only, have I sinned
    and done what is evil in your sight,
so that you are proved right when you speak
    and justified when you judge.
Cleanse me, and I will be clean;
    wash me, and I will be whiter than snow.
Create in me a pure heart, O God,
    and renew a steadfast spirit within me.
Restore to me the joy of your salvation
    and grant me a willing spirit, to sustain me.
Then I will teach transgressors your ways,
    and sinners will turn back to you.
O Lord, open my lips,
    and my mouth will declare your praise.
The sacrifices of God are a broken spirit;
    a broken and contrite heart,
    O God, you will not despise.
Amen.

—From Psalm 51

A Prayer for the Awareness of God's Presence

O God,
You are my God,
    earnestly I seek you;
my soul thirsts for you,
    my body longs for you,
in a dry and weary land
    where there is no water.
I have seen you in the sanctuary
    and beheld your power and your glory.
Because your love is better than life,
    my lips will glorify you.
I will praise you as long as I live,
    and in your name I will lift up my hands.
Because you are my help,
    I sing in the shadow of your wings.
My soul clings to you;
    your right hand upholds me.
Amen.

—From Psalm 63

A Prayer of Praise

O God,
My heart is steadfast;
    I will sing and make music with all my soul.
Awake, harp and lyre!
    I will awaken the dawn.
I will praise you, O Lord, among the nations;
    I will sing of you among the peoples.
For great is your love, higher than the heavens;
    your faithfulness reaches to the skies.
Be exalted, O God, above the heavens,
    and let your glory be over all the earth.
Amen.

—From Psalm 108

A Prayer of Repentance

O Lord,
Out of the depths I cry to you;
    O Lord, hear my voice.
Let your ears be attentive
    to my cry for mercy.

If you, O Lord, kept a record of sins,
  O Lord, who could stand?
But with you there is forgiveness;
  therefore you are feared.
I wait for you, my soul waits,
  and in your word I put my hope.
My soul waits for you
    more than watchmen wait for the morning,
    more than watchmen wait for the morning.
I put my hope in you,
  for with you is unfailing love
  and with you is full redemption.
You yourself have redeemed us from all our sin.
Amen.

—From Psalm 130

A Prayer of Awe at God's Greatness

O Lord,
you have searched me
  and you know me.
You know when I sit and when I rise;
  you perceive my thoughts from afar.
You discern my going out and my lying down;
  you are familiar with all my ways.
Before a word is on my tongue
  you know it completely, O Lord.
You hem me in — behind and before;
  you have laid your hand upon me.
Such knowledge is too wonderful for me,
  too lofty for me to attain.
Where can I go from your Spirit?
  Where can I flee from your presence?
If I go up to the heavens, you are there;
  if I make my bed in the depths, you are there.
If I rise on the wings of the dawn,
  if I settle on the far side of the sea,
even there your hand will guide me,
  your right hand will hold me fast.
If I say, "Surely the darkness will hide me
  and the light become night around me,"
even the darkness will not be dark to you;
  the night will shine like the day,
  for darkness is as light to you.
How precious to me are your thoughts, O God!
  How vast is the sum of them!

Were I to count them,
    they would outnumber the grains of sand.
When I awake,
    I am still with you.
Search me, O God, and know my heart;
    test me and know my anxious thoughts.
See if there is any offensive way in me,
    and lead me in the way everlasting.
Amen.

                       —From Psalm 139

Petra.

Supplemental Materials

How We Got the Bible

1. How the Bible Books Came Together

The Two Testaments

The word "testament," as used in "Old Testament" and "New Testament," means "covenant" (solemn agreement or contract).

The **Old Testament** (the name the Christian church has given to the **Hebrew Bible**) is about the covenant God made with Abraham (Genesis 15). God promised Abraham that

- He would become a great nation
- The land of Canaan would belong to his descendants (Israel)
- Through the nation of Israel the world would be blessed

The **New Testament** is about the new covenant God made with all people through the life, death, and resurrection of Jesus, Abraham's greatest descendant. The new covenant is the fulfillment of God's promise to Abraham that he would be a blessing to the whole world.

Since the New Testament had not yet been written, the Hebrew Bible was the Bible of Jesus and the apostles. Thus, when Jesus and the apostles refer to Scripture, they have in mind the Hebrew Bible. Similarly, "It is written in the Law" has the same force as our "the Bible says."

How Did We End Up with the 66 Books in the Bible?

How did the Bible as we have it—66 books, written over a period of more than 1,500 years—come together?

The 66 books that are included in all Bibles are called the **canon** of the Bible (the books are therefore referred to as the **canonical** books). "Canon" means "rule or standard," and the canonical books are those that have been formally accepted by the church as part of the inspired Word of God.

Most Protestant Bibles contain only the 66 canonical books, but some Protestant Bibles as well as Roman Catholic and Eastern Orthodox Bibles also include books that are not part of the canon but are considered "good to read." These are the **Apocrypha**, or **apocryphal books** (from a Greek word meaning "obscure, secret"). For more on the Apocrypha, see p. 1003.

The Old Testament Canon

It is not clear exactly when it was decided that the Hebrew Bible (our Old Testament) should be limited to the 39 books it contains now, which are considered the Old Testament canon. It is likely that the Old Testament canon achieved its final form in the centuries immediately before Christ. In Jesus' day this book was referred to as "the Scriptures" and was taught regularly and read publicly in synagogues. It was regarded among the people as the "Word of God." Jesus Himself repeatedly called it the "Word of God."

The books in the Hebrew Bible were (and are) arranged differently, however. There are three divisions:

- **The Law** (or the five books of Moses): Genesis, Exodus, Leviticus, Numbers, and Deuteronomy
- **The Prophets**: Joshua, Judges, 1–2 Samuel, 1–2 Kings (the Former Prophets) and Isaiah, Jeremiah, Ezekiel, and the 12 Minor Prophets (the Latter Prophets)
- **The Writings**: Ruth, Psalms, Job, Proverbs, Ecclesiastes, Song of Songs, Lamentations, Esther, Daniel, Ezra-Nehemiah, and 1–2 Chronicles

The Hebrew names for these divisions are *Torah, Nebiim, Ketubim.* The first letters of these — T, N, K — are used to form the name for the whole Hebrew Bible: the **Tanakh.**

In the Septuagint, the Greek translation of the Hebrew Bible that was made in about 250 B.C., the order of the books was changed to the order we now have in our Bible: historical (Genesis – Deuteronomy), poetic (Job – Song of Songs), and prophetic (Isaiah – Malachi) books.

The Septuagint became the basis for the Old Testament of the Latin Bible, the Vulgate. After the Reformation in the 16th century, the Protestant churches decided to use the Hebrew Bible rather than the Septuagint for the translation of the Old Testament (since it had become clear that the Septuagint was in many places a rather poor translation of the Hebrew original), but they kept the order of the books found in the Septuagint rather than the order of the Tanakh.

The New Testament Canon

New Testament Beginnings of the Canon

We know a great deal more about how the canon of the New Testament was formed. There are hints in the New Testament itself that, while the apostles were yet living, and under their own supervision, collections of their writings began to be made for the churches and placed with the Old Testament as the Word of God.

- Paul claimed for his teaching the inspiration of God (1 Corinthians 2:7 – 13; 14:37; 1 Thessalonians 2:13).
- So did John for the book of Revelation (Revelation 1:2).
- Paul intended that his epistles should be read in the churches (Colossians 4:16; 1 Thessalonians 5:27; 2 Thessalonians 2:15).
- Peter wrote that "these things" might remain in the churches "after my departure" (2 Peter 1:15; 3:1 – 2).
- Paul quoted as Scripture "The laborer is worthy of his reward" (1 Timothy 5:18 KJV). This sentence is found nowhere in the Bible except Matthew 10:10 and Luke 10:7 — evidence that Matthew or Luke was then in existence and was regarded as Scripture.
- Peter classified Paul's epistles with "other Scriptures" (2 Peter 3:15 – 16).

The apostles, it seems, wrote many letters with the immediate needs of the churches in mind. As to which of those letters were to be preserved for future ages, we believe that God Himself watched over the matter and made His own choice.

Where the Various New Testament Books First Appeared

Palestine, Asia Minor, Greece, and Rome were far apart. The books of the Old Testament had originated mostly within one small country, but the New Testament books were written in widely separated countries.

- **Palestine**: Matthew, James, and Hebrews (uncertain)
- **Asia Minor**: John, Galatians, Ephesians, Colossians, 1 and 2 Timothy, Philemon, 1 and 2 Peter, 1, 2, and 3 John, Jude, and Revelation
- **Greece**: 1 and 2 Corinthians, Philippians, 1 and 2 Thessalonians, Luke (uncertain)
- **Crete**: Titus
- **Rome**: Mark, Acts, and Romans

The Earliest Collections

The New Testament books were written in a world in which communication had become easier than ever before. Yet, by our standards, communication was still slow and travel could be dangerous. What is now a trip of a few hours would then have required weeks or months. Printing was unknown, and books and letters had to be copied by hand — a slow and laborious process.

Moreover, beginning with Emperor Nero in A.D. 64, it was an age of persecution, when precious Christian writings had to be kept hidden. And there were as yet no church councils or conferences, where Christians from distant parts could come together and compare notes on what writings they had, until the days of Emperor Constantine (A.D. 306–37). So, naturally, the earliest collections of New Testament books would vary in different regions; and the process of reaching unanimity as to what books properly belonged in the New Testament was slow.

Besides the books that would ultimately be accepted as canonical New Testament books, there were many others that ranged from good to silly to fraudulent. Some of these were so fine and valuable that they were for a while, in some areas, regarded as Scripture. Ultimately, the one criterion by which a book was judged before acceptance into the canon was whether it was of genuine apostolic origin, written either by an apostle (e.g., John's Gospel) or under the auspices of an apostle (e.g., Mark's Gospel, which is based on the preaching of the apostle Peter). It was not always easy to determine this, especially in the case of lesser-known books from a distant region.

Early Testimony to New Testament Books

Because of the perishable nature of the writing material and because it was a period of persecution in which Christian writings were destroyed, we have few writings of Christians whose lives overlapped the lives of the apostles. But though few in number, they bear unimpeachable testimony to the existence, in their day, of a group of authoritative writings which Christians regarded as Scripture, either by direct statement or, more often, by quoting from or referring to specific Christian writings as "Scripture"—writings that would later become part of the official New Testament canon. For example,

Clement of Rome, in his Epistle to the Corinthians (A.D. 95), quotes from, or refers to, Matthew, Luke, Romans, Corinthians, Hebrews, 1 Timothy, 1 Peter.

Polycarp, in his Letter to the Philippians (about A.D. 110), quotes Philippians and reproduces phrases from nine other of Paul's epistles and 1-Peter.

Ignatius, in his seven letters written about A.D. 110 during his journey from Antioch to Rome for his martyrdom, quotes from Matthew, 1-Peter, and 1-John and cites nine of Paul's epistles; his letters also bear the imprint of the other three Gospels.

Papias (A.D. 70–155), a pupil of the apostle John, wrote *An Explanation of the Lord's Discourses,* in which he quotes from John and records traditions about the origin of Matthew and Mark.

The Didache, written between A.D. 80 and 120, contains 22 quotations from Matthew, has references to Luke, John, Acts, Romans, Thessalonians, and 1 Peter, and speaks of "the Gospel" as a written document.

The Epistle of Barnabas, written between A.D. 90 and 120, quotes from Matthew, John, Acts, and 2 Peter and uses the expression "it is written," a formula commonly applied only to Scripture.

There are many more, similar examples. Together they cover all books of the New Testament, although a number of books remained "doubtful" in some areas until the 4th century, when Emperor Constantine issued his Edict of Toleration.

Eusebius's List of New Testament Books

Eusebius (A.D. 264–340) was bishop of Caesarea. He was the first great church historian, and we owe to him much of our knowledge of what happened during the first centuries of the Christian church. Eusebius lived through, and was imprisoned during, Diocletian's persecution of Christians, which was Rome's final effort to blot out Christianity. One of Diocletian's special objects was the destruction of all Christian Scriptures. For 10 years, Bibles were hunted by the agents of Rome and burned in public marketplaces. To Christians, the question of just what books composed their Scriptures was no idle matter!

Eusebius lived into the reign of Emperor Constantine, who accepted Christianity. Eusebius became Constantine's chief religious adviser. One of Constantine's first acts upon ascending the throne was to order 50 Bibles for the churches of Constantinople, to be prepared by skillful copyists under the direction of Eusebius, on the finest of vellum, and to be delivered by royal carriages from Caesarea to Constantinople.

What books constituted the New Testament of Eusebius? Exactly the same ones that we have now in our New Testament. Eusebius, by extensive research, informed himself as to what books had been generally accepted by the churches. In his *Church History* he speaks of four classes of books:

1. The universally accepted books
2. The "disputed" books: James, 2 Peter, 2 and 3 John, and Jude, which, though included in his own Bibles, were doubted by some
3. The "spurious" books, among which he mentions the Acts of Paul, the Shepherd of Hermas, the Apocalypse of Peter, the Epistle of Barnabas, and the Didache
4. The "forgeries of heretics": the Gospel of Peter, the Gospel of Thomas, the Gospel of Matthias, the Acts of Andrew, and the Acts of John

The Canon Adopted by the Council of Carthage (A.D. 397)

In A.D. 397, the Council of Carthage formally established the New Testament canon by ratifying the 27 books of the New Testament as we know them, expressing what had already become the unanimous judgment of the churches, and accepted the Book that was destined to become humanity's most precious heritage.

2. How the Text of the Bible Was Preserved

The Text of the Old Testament

The Old Testament was written primarily in **Hebrew**, the language of the Israelites. But in the millennium before Christ, **Aramaic**, a language related to Hebrew, became the language of international commerce and communication throughout the Ancient Near East; it even became the official language of the Persian Empire (ca. 600–540 B.C.).

Thus it is interesting that three sections of the Old Testament are written in Aramaic. Official correspondence between local officials and the Persian kings Artaxerxes and Darius concerning the rebuilding of Jerusalem and the temple (Ezra 4:8–6:18) as well as a letter of authorization from King Artaxerxes to Ezra (Ezra 7:12–26) are included in their original Aramaic form rather than in a Hebrew translation. A major portion of the book of Daniel is also in Aramaic (2:4b–7:28), which was the language in use in Babylonia.

All copies had to be made by hand, and not all copyists were equally careful. Sometimes notes or comments written in the margins of the text were erroneously incorporated in the text as it was being copied. Already well before the time of Christ, a concerted effort was made to standardize the Hebrew text and to arrive at the most reliable text possible. This was complicated by the fact that the Hebrew script in which the Old Testament was written was different from the Aramaic script that was adopted later (the square letters still used in modern written Hebrew). Also, only consonants were written, while vowels were omitted (although later on, letters were used to indicate long vowels). And finally, by the 8th century B.C., the habit of separating words by putting small dots or strokes between them disappeared, so that all letters were simply run together. An English parallel might be CMPTRNTWRK, which could be read either as "Computer network" or as "Came Peter in to work?"

The "Masoretic Text"

The Hebrew text, without vowels or accents, was more or less fixed by the end of the 1st century A.D., although exactly how this was accomplished is not clear. By the 6th century A.D., the so-called Masoretes (from the Hebrew for "tradition") had added a system of small dots and lines below and above the consonants, which ensured that the text would be read correctly. (There were originally three separate systems — the Babylonian, Palestinian, and Tiberian; the Tiberian system of "vowel pointing" is the one still in use.)

There were also instances in which the written text was difficult to understand. In those cases the Masoretes would mark the word(s) in the written text, indicating that this is how the text is to be written, and add another word or form in the margin, indicating that this is what was to be read. This minimized the possibility that a copyist would look at the text that did not make complete sense and would make his own corrections, either intentionally or without thinking.

The Masoretes had such respect for the text that they left in all the peculiarities of the various books of the Bible, including archaic words, idiomatic expressions, and differences in dialect and spelling. In a number of instances a more modern name is added to explain a name that was no longer recognized—for example, in Genesis 14:2, where it is explained that Bela is the same city they know as Zoar (see also Genesis 14:3, 7; 15:15, 52, 60; etc.).

The Text of the New Testament

The New Testament was written in Greek, the language of the majority of the earliest Christians. The original manuscripts of all the New Testament books, as far as we know, have been lost. From the very first, copies of these precious writings began to be made for distribution to other churches, and then copies of copies, and copies of copies of copies, generation after generation, as the older ones wore out.

Writing Materials

From Papyrus to Vellum

The writing material in common use was papyrus, made of slices of the papyrus reed, a water plant that grew in Egypt. Horizontal and vertical slices were pressed together and polished. Ink was made of charcoal, gum, and water.

Papyrus had a problem: it was not very durable. It became brittle with age, or rotted with dampness, and soon wore out—except in Egypt, where the dry climate and shifting sands have preserved for discovery in modern times an amazing collection of ancient documents.

Papyrus reeds like these were sliced and dried to create "paper" which could then be used by scribes to write down the Scriptures.

In the 4th century A.D., papyrus was replaced by vellum as the main writing material. Vellum is prepared from fine-grained calfskin or lambskin and is much more durable.

Until the recent discovery of the Egyptian papyri (see below), all known manuscripts of the Bible in existence were on vellum.

From Scroll to Codex

For short compositions such as letters, single sheets of papyrus were used. For longer letters and books, sheets were glued side to side to form rolls, usually called scrolls. A scroll was usually about 30 feet long and 9 or 10 inches high.

The drawback of the scroll was that it was not practical to make it longer than about 30 feet, since it then became too large to handle easily. Thus, in the 2nd century A.D., the scroll began to be replaced by what was called the codex, which has essentially the same form as our modern book—all pages are glued on one side. Many more pages could be put into a codex than could practically be glued together in a scroll, and thus the entire New Testament could be put into a single codex.

Besides, the codex made it possible to use vellum instead of papyrus, since vellum scrolls would have been impossible to work with.

The making of manuscript Bibles ceased with the invention of printing in the 15th century.

The Manuscripts of the Bible

There are now about 4000 known manuscripts of the Bible or parts of the Bible, made between the 2nd and 15th centuries A.D. This seems few to us, but it is far more than we have of any other ancient writings. For example, there is no complete known copy of Homer earlier than A.D. 1300, nor of Herodotus earlier than A.D. 1000.

The manuscripts of the New Testament are divided into two groups, based on the type of Greek letters they use: *uncials* and *cursives*. The uncials were written in large, capital letters. There are about 160 of them, made between the 4th and 10th centuries. The cursives were written in small, running letters, often linked together, and were made between the 10th and 15th centuries. The uncials are far more valuable, since they are much older.

The three oldest, most complete, best-known, and most valuable manuscripts of the New Testament are the Codex Sinaiticus, the Codex Vaticanus, and the Codex Alexandrinus, which were originally complete Bibles.

The Codex Sinaiticus

The discovery of the Codex Sinaiticus, or Sinaitic codex, is one of the more interesting stories in archaeology. It was found in 1844 by a German scholar named L. F. K. von Tischendorf, in the Monastery of St. Catherine at the foot of Mount Sinai. During a visit to the monastery in 1844 he noticed, in a wastebasket of leaves set aside to be burned, vellum pages with Greek writing. On closer examination they proved to be parts of an ancient manuscript of the Septuagint Old Testament. There were 43 leaves. He searched and searched, but could find no more.

In 1853 he returned to the monastery to continue the search, but found nothing. He returned again in 1859. As he talked with the steward about the Septuagint, the steward remarked that he had an ancient copy of it and brought it to Tischendorf wrapped in a paper napkin. It was the rest of the manuscript of which Tischendorf had seen the 43 leaves 15 years before. As he looked through its pages, he realized that he held in his hand the most precious writing in existence. It contained 199 leaves of the Old Testament, the entire New Testament, plus the noncanonical Epistle of Barnabas and part of the Shepherd of Hermas, on 148 leaves, making 347 leaves in all. They were written in a beautiful hand, on the finest of vellum leaves measuring 15 by 13½ inches. It was made in the first half of the 4th century. It is the only ancient manuscript that contains the entire New Testament.

The 43 leaves which Tischendorf secured on his first visit are in the University Library at Leipzig. The rest of the manuscript was secured, after long international negotiations, for the Imperial Library in St. Petersburg, where it remained until 1933, when it was sold to the British Museum for half a million dollars.

The Codex Vaticanus

The Vatican codex was made in the 4th century and has been in the Vatican Library since 1481, hence its name. Some fragments of the New Testament are missing.

The Codex Alexandrinus

The Alexandrian codex was made in the 5th century in Alexandria, Egypt. It contains the entire Bible, with some fragments missing, as well as the noncanonical Epistles of Clement and the Psalms of Solomon. It has been in the British Museum since 1627.

The Papyri

Sir Flinders Petrie, a renowned Egyptologist, noticed during excavations in central Egypt old sheets of papyrus appearing in rubbish heaps that had been buried beneath the sand, and he suggested that they might be valuable. In 1895, two of his students, Grenfell and Hunt, began a systematic search for these papyri.

In the following 10 years, they found 10,000 manuscripts and parts of manuscripts at Oxyrhynchus and nearby places. Other excavators also found great quantities of similar manuscripts in sand-covered rubbish

The monastery of St. Catherine, at the foot of Mount Sinai. Here Friedrich von Tischendorf found and rescued what is known as the Codex Sinaiticus, one of the oldest and most important manuscripts of the Bible.

heaps, in stuffings in mummy cases, and in embalmed crocodile bodies. They consisted mostly of letters, bills, receipts, diaries, certificates, almanacs, and such. Some of them were valuable historical documents dating as far back as 2000 B.C. Most of them, however, dated from 300 B.C. to A.D. 300. Among them were some early Christian writings, which is what makes them of interest to the Bible student.

One of the papyri, a tiny scrap measuring a mere 3½ by 2½ inches, contains fragments of John's Gospel: on one side John 18:31–33, and on the other side John 18:37–38. It is a part of one leaf of a manuscript that had been originally 130 pages, measuring 8¼ by 8 inches. Comparing the shape of the letters and the style of writing with manuscripts whose date had been established with certainty, scholars assign it to the first part of the 2nd century. It is thus the oldest known Bible manuscript, and it is evidence that the Gospel of John was in existence and in circulation in Egypt in the years immediately following the death of John. The papyrus was found in 1920 and is now in the Rylands Library, Manchester, England.

Many other papyri have been found from somewhat later dates, containing parts of the rest of the New Testament (and Old Testament).

Besides the many fragments of papyrus leaves containing parts of Bible books, there are some that contained sayings of Jesus that are not found in the Gospels but that were apparently current in the 3rd century.

The Language of the Papyri

Adolf Deissmann, a German scholar, in the late 19th century noticed that the Greek of the papyri was the same as the Greek used in the New Testament, called *koine,* and not the classical Greek of earlier ages. There are 500 words in the Greek New Testament not found in classical Greek at all. This discovery that the New Testament was apparently written in the everyday language of the common people gave impulse to the modern-language translations of the New Testament that have appeared in this century.

3. Do We Have the "Original" Text of the Bible?

The Old Testament

The text of the Old Testament was fixed shortly after the end of the 1st century A.D. (see p. 987). The oldest manuscripts we have, the Dead Sea Scrolls from Qumran (which date back to at least the 1st century A.D.), show essential agreement (with minor variations) with the Hebrew text we have today. Unless we find manuscripts from an even earlier date (which is not very likely), we must assume that the Hebrew text of the Old Testament is indeed an accurate copy of the original text.

The New Testament

The oldest manuscripts of the New Testament that we have were also copied several centuries after the books or letters were written, so how do we know that in the process of copying the books (sometimes many times) no errors or intentional changes were made?

To begin with, we have several thousand manuscripts of all or portions of the New Testament. Although these manuscripts differ in details, none of these details involve matters that would in any way cause us to question the truths of the Christian faith.

Nevertheless, it is important to make every effort to determine which of these variations (called *variants* or *variant readings*) among the manuscripts are most likely the correct ones. A special field of study, called *textual criticism,* is devoted to this.

The Importance of Textual Criticism

The word *criticism* does not necessarily mean "being critical of" or "criticizing" in a negative sense. Rather, it can mean "careful investigation"—which means looking at something for the purpose of determining what is true. This is how the word *criticism* is used in the term "textual criticism."

Qumran fragment. Some of the earliest evidence of biblical texts comes from small manuscript fragments.

Textual criticism involves the comparison of the various manuscripts or editions to determine as exactly as possible the original text. Thus, a "critical edition" of Shakespeare's plays is not an edition that tries to discredit Shakespeare, but rather an edition that is based on careful scrutiny of all available manuscripts and printed editions and tries to determine, in the case of differences among those editions, which "variant reading" is most likely the original one that Shakespeare wrote.

We have several thousand manuscripts of Scripture, some dating back to the 2nd century A.D. The variants in the manuscripts are usually the result of mistakes (and — very rarely — of intentional changes, deletions, or additions) made by copyists. Since every single copy of a manuscript had to be made by hand until the invention of printing with movable type in the 15th century, copying errors were unavoidable — especially since in the Greek of the uncials (capital letters; see below), all letters were written together, without any space between words, with the result that it was easy to skip words.

John 1:1–2 looked like this:

ENARCHHNOLOGOS

KAIOLOGOSHNPROSTON

QEONKAIQEOSHNOLOGOS

OUTOSHNENARCHPROS

TONQEON

What could happen, for example, was that the copyist would read the first line (which ends with LOGOS [*logos*, word]), copy that line, and then go back to the original, looking for the last word he copied: LOGOS. But his eye might inadvertently go to the LOGOS at the end of the third line, so that he would start copying the *fourth* line, skipping the second and third lines. This is one of the several kinds of mistakes that happened so often that they have special names; this type of error is called *homoioteleuton* ("similar ending").

Manuscript Families

When all available manuscripts are put side by side, it appears that they can be divided into several "families" — groups of manuscripts that contain many of the same variants. This makes sense when we think of what happened when the manuscripts were copied.

Let's say that copyist A makes a very accurate copy of the original manuscript but with one mistake: he writes the same word twice. But copyist B, who also makes a copy of the same original manuscript, makes a different mistake — he leaves out a line because his eye skipped down too far.

Copyist C now makes an accurate copy of the copy made by B — *including* the mistake B made. Any further copies of B's work will all have the same mistake B made — they will all miss the line B skipped.

But any further copies made of copyist A's copy will have the same double word. Thus there are two "families" of manuscripts—one with A's mistake, the other with B's mistake.

The Oldest Manuscripts or the Majority of Manuscripts?

Most textual critics assume that the *oldest manuscripts* should be considered more reliable, since they are closest in time to the original manuscript—there was less time for errors to creep into the Greek text. This means that for each variant in the text we must determine which variant reading is found in the oldest manuscripts, and also which variant readings can be most easily explained on the basis of copyists' errors, such as skipping a line. This results in what is called the "critical text."

Others assume that any text variants that are found in the *majority of the manuscripts* we have of the New Testament are closest to the original. This results in the "majority text."

The King James Version is based on a Greek manuscript that represents the majority text, while most modern versions, such as the New International Version (NIV), are based on the critical text.

One thing to keep in mind is that debate between proponents of the majority text and of the critical text is *not* a debate between a godly and an ungodly approach to the Scriptures. Nor is it a debate in which one side is intellectually dishonest or deficient. Most Bible-believing scholars accept, with full integrity, the critical text, while other scholars, equally with full integrity, support the majority text.

Ancient Translations

Ancient translations are another piece in the puzzle of textual criticism.

The New Testament was written in Greek, the common language of the Roman Empire. The Old Testament had been translated into Greek several centuries B.C., so that the early church had the whole Bible, both Old and New Testament, in Greek.

But as the church spread, it reached countries where Greek was not the common language, so translations were needed from the Greek. Some of the ancient translations of the New Testament of which we have copies were made in the 2nd, 3rd, and 4th century A.D., and were thus based on very early copies of the New Testament writings. In the case of specific variants, the translations *may* give us some indication which of the variants was likely used by the translator.

The **Old Syriac** translation was made in the 2nd century A.D. for use among the Syrians. Interestingly, another, simpler translation was needed, which accounts for the **Peshito,** a 4th-century simplified version ("Peshito" means "simple").

The **Old Latin** translation was also made in the 2nd century. Its Old Testament was translated, not from the Hebrew, but from the Septuagint. The great Bible scholar Jerome (A.D. 382–404) realized that the Old Latin version was inadequate, so he made the **Vulgate,** a revision of the Old Latin but with the Old Testament (except the Psalms) translated directly from the Hebrew. The Vulgate became the Bible of the West for 1000 years.

Other early translations include the Coptic (the vernacular language of Egypt; 2nd century A.D.); Ethiopic and Gothic (4th century); Armenian (5th century); Arabic and Slavic (9th century).

4. English Translations of the Bible

The Earliest Translations

The first translations into Anglo-Saxon (an early form of English) of portions of the Bible were made around A.D. 700 — some 900 years before the King James Version was published.

Bishop Aldhelm of Sherborne (who died in 709) translated the Psalms, which were then put into verse form by traveling bards so that they were easy to remember. They were sung by the people and taught to the children.

The first true English Bible is **Wycliffe's** (or Wyclif's) translation, published in 1382. He based his translation on the Vulgate. Wycliffe's Bible existed only in manuscript form, since the printing press was not invented until 70 years later by John Gutenberg. This means that not many copies were in circulation, but these copies were used by traveling preachers who reached many people in all parts of England. The Roman Catholic Church condemned Wycliffe's work; he was excommunicated, and many of the copies of his Bible were burned. About 150 survive, but only one of those is complete.

Tyndale's Bible, published in 1525, was more accurate than Wycliffe's, since it was translated from the original Greek and Hebrew. When church authorities tried to stop the publication of his Bible, he fled from England to Hamburg, then to Cologne and Worms, where his New Testament was printed and then smuggled into England in bales of merchandise. On October 6, 1536, Tyndale was burned at the stake for translating the Bible into the language of the people.

Other early English translations were the **Coverdale** Bible (1535; from Dutch and Latin sources); **Rogers'** Bible (1537; almost wholly copied from Tyndale's); and the "Great Bible" (1539; a compilation of Tyndale, Rogers, and Coverdale).

The **Geneva** Bible (1560; translated by a group of scholars who had fled England for Geneva, the city of John Calvin) had the distinction of being the first Bible that divided the text into verses. The division into verses was done by Robert Estienne of Paris, a printer of Greek New Testaments.

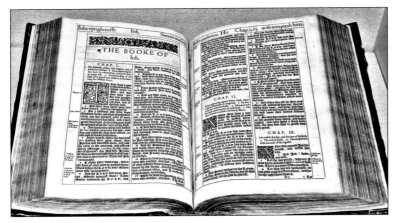

A first edition of the King James Version (1611), authorized by King James of England.

The King James Version

King James VI of Scotland was crowned as King James I of England. One of the measures he took to create some sense of unity among the religious parties and factions in his kingdom was the creation of a new Bible translation, to be used by all churches.

He appointed 54 scholars, who used for the New Testament the Greek text published by Erasmus of Rotterdam and a Greek-Latin text from the 6th century. This Greek text is a representative of what we now call the majority text (see p. 999).

The King James Version (KJV) — which is also called the Authorized Version (AV), since it was authorized by the king — was published in 1611 and revised in 1615, 1629, 1638, and 1762. (The KJV currently in use is the 1762 revision.) The translators adopted the chapter divisions created by Stephen Langton in 1551 as well as Robert Estienne's verse divisions.

The KJV was a marvel, not only of scholarship, but also of language. It set a standard for all future translations of the Bible by using the common language of its day, while at the same time endowing it with the cadences of poetry and with a dignity that has not diminished over time.

Modern Translations

Over the centuries, the English language, like any language, has changed. What sounded natural to and was easily understood by the original readers of the KJV has become more difficult to understand for readers almost four centuries later. For example, "Wherefore lay apart all filthiness and superfluity of naughtiness" (KJV) is no longer common English. The same phrase from James 1:21 is more easily understood when translated "Therefore putting aside all filthiness and all that remains of wickedness" (NASB) or "Therefore, get rid of all moral filth and the evil that is so prevalent" (NIV).

This condition led to the publication of a number of modern translations during the past century, some of the whole Bible, others of the New Testament only. Many of these translations were in use for a time but have all but disappeared (for example, the *American Standard Version* [ASV, 1901], Weymouth's New Testament [1903], Moffat's Translation [1926], Smith and Goodspeed [1923], the *Berkeley Version of the Bible* [1959], and many others). It was not until the publication of the complete *New International Version* (NIV) in 1978 that a single modern translation came into general use. (It has outsold the KJV since 1993.)

Approaches to Translation

There are two basic approaches to translating from one language into another.

1. A **word-for-word** translation stays as close as possible to the words and sentence structure of the original. (This is also called the "formal equivalency" approach.) But a strict word-for-word translation would often end up being incomprehensible to the intended readers.

   a. One reason this happens is cultural. For example, a literal translation of the English expression "going to bat for someone" into German or Swahili would not make sense to readers who are not familiar with baseball.

   b. Another reason why word-for-word translations don't always work has to do with the way language works. A word in one language may not have an exact equivalent in another language. For example, English has two words, *faith* and *belief*, to express what most languages achieve in only one (for example, *Glaube* in German). The distinction between faith (an attitude of trust) and belief (that which we accept as true) can therefore not be expressed by a simple word-for-word translation.

   Conversely, the Hebrew word *shalom* has no true English equivalent. One meaning is "peace," but *shalom* is much broader than that; it includes wholeness, wellness, well-being. In Genesis 29:6, for example, Jacob asks literally, "Is *shalom* unto him?" The KJV and all other versions translate this "Is he well?"

   Examples of word-for-word Bible translations are the KJV, NKJV (New King James Version), and NASB (New American Standard Bible). The main drawback of the word-for-word approach is that it is often not very readable.

2. The second approach to translating is the **thought-for-thought** approach (also called the "dynamic equivalency" approach). Here the intent is to translate in such a way that the readers of the translation get the equivalent *meaning* as the original readers. The example above,

"Is he well?" illustrates a thought-for-thought translation. Examples of thought-for-thought Bible translations are the NIV, NIrV (New International Reader's Version), NVC (New Century Version), NLT (New Living Translation). They are generally much more readable than word-for-word translations.

3. A thought-for-thought translation should stay as close as possible to the original. When it moves too far away from the original, it becomes a **paraphrase**. An example of a paraphrase is the *Living Bible.*

For Bible *reading,* a thought-for-thought translation is best. For Bible *study,* a more literal (word-for-word) translation may be better.

A Comparison of Modern Translations

The chart on the next page shows how one verse of Scripture—Job 36:33—is rendered in the King James Version of 1611 and various translations developed during the latter half of the 20th century.

5. The Apocrypha

The Apocrypha (lit., "obscure, hidden [books]") comprises 14 books that are found in some Bibles between the Old and New Testaments. They originated in the 3rd to 1st centuries B.C. and are mostly of uncertain authorship.

These books are not in the Hebrew Bible (our Old Testament). They were written after Old Testament prophecy, oracles, and direct revelation had ceased. At some point, however, these books were added to the Septuagint, a Greek translation of the Hebrew Bible that was made during that period.

The Apocrypha was never recognized by the Jews as part of the Hebrew Scriptures. Josephus rejected them as a whole. They were never quoted by Jesus, nor anywhere in the New Testament. They were not recognized by the early church as either canonical or divinely inspired. Then how did they end up in many Bibles?

When the Bible was translated into Latin in the 2nd century A.D., its Old Testament was not translated from the Hebrew Old Testament but from the Greek (Septuagint) version of the Old Testament. Thus the apocryphal books were included in the early Latin translation of the Bible. From this early Latin version came the Latin **Vulgate,** which became the common version in western Europe until the time of the Reformation.

The apocryphal books are not recognized as canonical by Protestants but are included in some Protestant Bibles between the Old and New Testaments as "books that are good to read." In Roman Catholic Bibles the Apocrypha (with the exception of 1 and 2 Esdras and the Prayer of Manasseh) are interspersed with the canonical Old Testament books and are called **deuterocanonical books.**

Version	Abbrev.	Job 36:33
New International Version	NIV	His thunder announces the coming storm; even the cattle make known its approach.*
New International Reader's Version	NIrV	His thunder announces that a storm is coming. Even the cattle let us know it's approaching.
King James Version	KJV	The noise thereof sheweth concerning it; the cattle also concerning the vapour.
New King James Version	NKJV	His thunder declares it, the cattle also, concerning the rising storm.
New Century Version	NCV	His thunder announces that a storm is coming. Even the cattle show that a storm is coming.
International Children's Version	ICB	Same as NCV
Living Bible	LB	We feel his presence in the thunder. May all sinners be warned.
New Living Translation	NLT	His thunder announces his presence; the storm announces his indignant anger.
New American Standard Bible	NASB	Its noise declares His presence; The cattle also, concerning what is coming up.
Revised Standard Version	RSV	Its crashing declares concerning him, who is jealous with anger against iniquity.
New Revised Standard Version	NRSV	Its crashing tells about him: he is jealous with anger against iniquity.†
Amplified Bible	AB	His thunderings speak [awesomely] concerning Him; the cattle are told of His coming storm.
Contemporary English Version	CEV	The thunder tells of his anger against sin.‡

*The NIV has this note: Or announces his coming——the One zealous against evil.
†The NRSV adds a note that the meaning of the Hebrew words translated crashing and jealous is uncertain.
‡The CEV has this note: sin: one possible meaning for the difficult Hebrew text of verse 33.

To complicate matters, the Roman Catholic Church uses the term **apocrypha** for another group of books, such as the Testament of Adam and 3 and 4 Maccabees, that are not usually included in Roman Catholic or Protestant Bibles. The Protestant term for this group is **pseudepigrapha**.

	Protestant Bibles	Roman Catholic Bibles
THE APOCRYPHA, DEUTEROCANONICAL BOOKS, AND PSEUDEPIGRAPHA		
• Tobit • Judith • Wisdom (of Solomon) • Ecclesiasticus • 1 Maccabees • 2 Maccabees • Baruch	**Apocrypha** (between Old and New Testaments)	**Deuterocanonical books** (interspersed with canonical books)
• Additions to Esther • Letter of Jeremiah • Additions to Daniel (Prayer of Azariah, Susanna, Bel and the Dragon)		[included in Esther] [included in Baruch] [included in Daniel]
• 1 Esdras • 2 Esdras • Prayer of Manasseh		[not included]
• The Testament of Adam • 1 and 2 Enoch • Testament of Job • 3 and 4 Maccabees • and many others	**Pseudepigrapha**	**Apocrypha**

A Brief Overview of the Apocrypha

Historical Books

First Esdras. Esdras is the Greek form of Ezra. This book is a compilation of passages from Ezra, 2-Chronicles, and Nehemiah, with added legends about Zerubbabel. Its object was to picture the generosity of Cyrus and Darius toward the Jews as a pattern for the Ptolemies of Egypt to emulate.

First Maccabees. A historical work of great value on the Maccabean period, relating the events of the Jews' heroic struggle for liberty (175–135 b.c.). It was written about 100 b.c. by a Palestinian Jew.

Second Maccabees. This is also an account of the Maccabean struggle, confining itself to the period of 175–161 B.C. It professes to be an abridgment of a work written by a certain Jason of Cyrene, of whom nothing is known. It supplements 1 Maccabees, but is inferior to it.

Religious Fiction

Tobit. A romance, entirely devoid of historical value, of a rich young Israelite captive in Nineveh who was led by an angel to wed a "virgin-widow" who had lost seven husbands.

Judith. A historical romance of a rich, beautiful, and devout Jewish widow who, in the days of the Babylonian invasion of Judah, adroitly went to the tent of the Babylonian general and, under guise of offering herself to him, cut off his head and thus saved her city.

Additions to the Book of Esther. Interpolated passages in the Septuagint version of the Old Testament book of Esther, mainly to show the hand of God in the story. These fragments were gathered and grouped together by Jerome.

Three additions to the book of Daniel:

Prayer of Azariah and the Song of the Three Jews. An inauthentic addition to the book of Daniel, inserted after 3:23, purporting to give their prayer while in the fiery furnace, and their triumphal song of praise for deliverance.

Susanna. Another inauthentic amplification of the book of Daniel, relating how the godly wife of a wealthy Jew in Babylon, falsely accused of adultery, was cleared by the wisdom of Daniel.

Bel and the Dragon. Another inauthentic addition to the book of Daniel. It consists of two stories, in both of which Daniel proves that the

The Apocrypha consists of fourteen inter-testamental books not found in the Protestant Bible. This is a version of the second book of Maccabees dating to A.D. 1715.

idols Bel and the Dragon are not gods; one of these is based on the story of the lions' den.

Wisdom Literature

Wisdom of Solomon, or simply **Wisdom.** Very similar to parts of Job, Proverbs, and Ecclesiastes. It is a kind of fusion of Hebrew thought and Greek philosophy and was written by an Alexandrian Jew who presents himself as Solomon.

Ecclesiasticus. Also called the **Wisdom of Jesus, the Son of Sirach,** or simply **Sirach.** It resembles the book of Proverbs and was written by a widely traveled Jewish philosopher. It gives rules for conduct in all details of civil, religious, and domestic life and extols a long list of Old Testament heroes.

Baruch. A book that purportedly comes from Baruch, the scribe of Jeremiah (see Jeremiah 32:12–13; 45:1), who is represented as spending the last portion of his life in Babylon. It is addressed to the exiles. It consists mostly of paraphrases from Jeremiah, Daniel, and other prophets.

The Letter of Jeremiah. An appendix to Baruch.

Prayer of Manasseh. A book that purports to be the prayer of Manasseh, king of Judah, when he was held captive in Babylon (see 2 Chronicles 33:12–13). The author is unknown, but the book probably comes from the 1st century B.C.

Apocalyptic Literature

Second Esdras. Sometimes called 4 Ezra. It purports to contain visions given to Ezra, dealing with God's government of the world, a coming new age, and the restoration of certain lost Scriptures.

simply made up, unless there was archaeological evidence to back up the Bible. For example, it was assumed that, since the only place the Hittites were mentioned was the Bible, they were simply a figment of the biblical author's imagination. But then, near the village of Bogazkoy in Turkey, thousands of ancient documents were found from the capital city of the Hittites, whose empire once extended as far south as Palestine.

Then there was the popular assumption that writing was not known in Moses' day, so that Moses and Joshua could not have written any part of the Bible and would not have had access to ancient documents. But archaeology has uncovered documents written in ancient Canaanite long before Moses' time.

Another instance is King Belshazzar, who was, according to Daniel, the last king of Babylonia before the Medes and Persians conquered Babylonia in 539 B.C. But Belshazzar was not mentioned in any other documents and was therefore assumed to have been created by the biblical author. Then inscriptions were found that *did* mention Belshazzar — but not as the last king of Babylonia. That dubious honor went, according to the inscriptions, to Belshazzar's father, Nabonidus. But more recent finds have shown that Nabonidus fled Babylon in the last years of his reign, leaving his son to rule the city.

On the other hand, it is important to realize that the purpose of the Bible is *not* to present simply a historical chronicle. Rather, it is to show how God has been at work in and through history — which is why the

On some occasions, artifacts are discovered that mention names of people in the Bible such as this seal with the name Gemaryahu ben Shaphan, referred to in Jeremiah 36:9 – 12.

historical books often provide details where we would not expect them and leave out facts that to us seem important. There is, for example, a gap of several hundred years between the last verse of Genesis and the beginning of the book of Exodus. And the kings of Israel and Judah are presented, not in terms of their political power, but according to their role in the spiritual life of the nation.

For example, the entire reign of King Omri of the northern kingdom, Israel (885–874 B.C.), is covered in a few verses in 1 Kings (16:16–28). But we know from extrabiblical sources that Omri was one of the most powerful and influential kings of the northern kingdom. An inscription of the Assyrian king Adad-nirari III (810–782 B.C.) refers to the land of Israel as "Omri"—long after Omri's death. Yet Omri was insignificant in the unfolding of God's plan of redemption.

Rediscovering the Past

It is relatively easy to find remains of ancient cities. There are many "tells" (see p. 1016) in the Middle East, and each one contains what is left of an ancient town or city. One part of rediscovering the past is digging it up, which is what we usually think of when we talk about archaeology.

The more difficult problem often is, however, discovering which town or city lies buried in a particular tell. It is the task of biblical geographers to identify biblical place-names and other geographical references with existing cities, towns, villages, antiquity sites, regions, and so on.

Identifying Ancient Sites (Biblical Geography)

The Bible contains a surprisingly large number of documents that are of geographical and archaeological interest. There are also ancient inscriptions that have been found in the Near East that help in the search.

The Biblical Documents

The Bible contains three kinds of documents of geographical interest.

1. The first of these, the **historical-geographical descriptions**, appear to have been written primarily for geographical purposes. Among them are the Table of Nations (Genesis 10), the list of conquered Canaanite kings (Joshua 12), and possibly the descriptions of "the land that remains" (Joshua 13:1–6; Judges 3:1–4), as well as the wilderness itinerary of the Israelites (Numbers 33).

2. The second kind of useful documents is **territorial descriptions**. In some instances the area belonging to a state or tribe is defined by means of a boundary description. Some of these boundary descriptions are very brief—for example, the description of the land of Israel as stretching "from Dan [in the north] to Beersheba [in the south]" (e.g., 2 Samuel 24:2) and the description of the Promised Land (Exodus 23:31) as stretching "from the Red Sea to the Sea of the Philistines and from the desert to the River."

There are also boundary descriptions that list a number of points along the border, for example, the description of the boundaries of the land of Canaan in Numbers 34:1–19 and several of the tribal boundary descriptions in Joshua, such as those of Judah (15:2–12). Some of these are quite detailed indeed, such as the description of the border between Judah and Benjamin in the Jerusalem area (Joshua 15:7–9; 18:15–17).

The more detailed boundary descriptions can be very useful. They can be plotted on a map, and because the names usually follow a logical geographical sequence, the location of unknown places can be guessed at. For example, the exact location of Ekron, a Philistine town, was disputed for many years, but its general location was known because the biblical text placed it on the western portion of the northern boundary of Judah—specifically, to the west of Beth Shemesh but to the east of Jabneel (Joshua 15:10–11), two towns whose identifications were generally agreed upon.

In addition, territories were described by drawing up a list of the names of the towns assigned to a given tribe or district, such as the town lists of Judah (Joshua 15:21–63; more than 100 towns are mentioned!).

3. Finally, there are **records of military expeditions and conquests**. The routes of military expeditions, such as those of Abijah (2 Chronicles 13:19), Ben-Hadad (1 Kings 15:20), and Tiglath-pileser (2 Kings 15:29), can be traced with some certainty. Given the reasonable assumption that these expeditions followed a more or less sensible geographical progression and that the texts faithfully record these invasions, the identification of certain biblical towns can be confirmed, while in the case of unknown towns at least their general location can be surmised. For example, although the exact location of Janoah is disputed, it is reasonable, on the basis of 2 Kings 15:29, to place it in the vicinity of Abel Beth Maacah, Kedesh, and Hazor.

Modern Place-Names (Toponymy)

Another way to locate a specific ancient city or town is, surprisingly, by checking to see whether its name has somehow been preserved through the centuries. At first glance this may seem somewhat futile, given the thousands of years that separate us from the time of the Bible. But it is not as unlikely as it seems. Many cities in western Europe, for example, still bear the names of Roman military camps that were established almost 2,000 years ago—such as London, which was called Londinium in Roman times. Although more than half of the biblical place names have left no trace, an astoundingly large number of place-names have survived in modern place-names.

The well-watered areas of the land of Israel/Palestine have been inhabited by a rather continuous chain of indigenous peoples who could have, and in many cases in fact have, handed down the name of a given place—usually orally, but sometimes in written form—from generation to generation. Thus names like Jerusalem, Hebron, Acco, and Tiberias have been preserved for thousands of years.

The preservation of ancient place-names has been helped by the fact that, through the ages, the languages of the indigenous population groups have all been Semitic: Canaanite was related to Hebrew, Hebrew in turn to Aramaic, and Aramaic to Arabic (recognizing, of course, that there were also many linguistic differences among these languages). Therefore identifications such as Micmash with the Arab village of Mukhmas are fairly certain. In more remote areas, such as the Sinai peninsula, there seem to have been significant gaps in the chain of indigenous inhabitants, and thus the ancient geographical names have not been well preserved through the centuries.

A problem is that while modern place-names may preserve the name of an ancient settlement, those names may not always be attached to the exact place where the biblical settlement was located. For example, the ancient site of biblical Jericho has been located at Tell es-Sultan, but the name was preserved at the nearby village of er-Rahia. (While "er-Rahia" may not look like "Jericho," experts who are familiar with the sounds, scripts, and phonetic laws of Hebrew, Aramaic, and Arabic are able to make such identifications with confidence.)

Forms of the Greek and Latin names of cities that were *established* during the Roman period have often been preserved by the local Semitic populace: Tiberias is preserved as Tabariyeh, and Caesarea as Qeisarieh. In a few rare instances, old Semitic names have been replaced by a Greco-Roman name; for example, biblical Shechem was renamed Neapolis during the Greco-Roman period, and it is that name which is preserved in the name of the modern city of Nablus.

Digging Up the Past (Archaeology)

Once a site has been chosen, two major methods are used to excavate a tell.

The first method of excavation opens up large areas of the tell, which will give a clear picture of overall building designs, town planning, and such for a given level or layer (stratum). This method is quite time-consuming and costly, and once a given layer has been completely removed from the mound, it can never be reexcavated. In fact, some of the great controversies of modern archaeology have little chance of resolution because past excavators have completely removed a particular stratum or layer from a mound, and their excavation records do not contain the data necessary to answer questions that are being asked today.

Beth Shan was one of the Canaanite cities the Israelites failed to capture (Judges 1:27). After Saul committed suicide, his body and those of his sons were "fastened to the wall" of Beth Shan (1 Samuel 31). David finally captured the city, but it remained insignificant until it was refounded in the Hellenistic era as Scythopolis.

The new city was built next to the tell—more than 250 feet high—of the Old Testament city (photos on previous page). An aerial view shows the excavations on the top of the tell (top). The city became a Roman city, with a *cardo,* or colonnaded street, running the length of the city (bottom).

The second method can be called the "trench method": the archaeologists select an area of the mound (tell), usually somewhere near its edge, where they dig a "trench" that resembles a thin slice taken from a layer cake. This "trench" is actually a series of five-by-five-meter square holes, dug in a straight line and sometimes arranged in pairs, that are separated by one-meter-wide dividers (baulks) of undisturbed soil. The sides of the five-meter square holes are kept perfectly vertical.

The hope is that this trench will in fact cut through all the occupation levels (strata) that are represented in the mound, and also that it will cut through any fortifications (walls, etc.) that may be preserved along the outer edge. As the excavation progresses, scrupulous records are kept, and drawings, photographs, and measurements are made. The exact place where each artifact—be it a pot, a piece of jewelry, or something else—is found is recorded, and thus each artifact can later be studied in relation to the context in which it was found. In addition, the architectural remains (walls, buildings, floors, fortifications, etc.) are plotted in an effort to reconstruct the layout and defenses of the ancient settlement. Some tells, such as Megiddo or Hazor, may have more than 20 strata, while others, such as the lower city at Arad, may have four or even fewer.

A problem, of course, is that the levels or strata are not always neat layers. For example, the earliest occupants would have left behind a relatively "neat" layer of debris. After the city was destroyed by earthquake or war, the new occupants built on top of the remains left behind by the first occupants. This happened again, but this time the new occupants did two things: they reused building materials salvaged from the second city, and they also dug a hole that cut through the first two layers, in which they stored jars. Thus in a few places, materials from the second city ended up in the remains of the third one, while remains of the third city ended up in those of the first one.

This is what makes interpretation far more difficult than the uncovering.

The question is, how can a more or less exact date be assigned to each of the strata? Written evidence, found in a given stratum, that mentions a known historical figure or event can be very useful here, but unfortunately not much written material from the biblical period is found in the tells of Israel/Palestine, with the exception of coins from the Hellenistic and Roman periods. In some cases modern technology can help, such as the use of the carbon-14 method for the dating of organic remains, but these techniques are not as precise as archaeologists would wish—at least not for the historical periods in question.

Often more useful is the fact that fashions change over time. Just as a Victorian teacup looks different from a modern coffee mug, so did oil lamps, cooking pots, gates, palaces, temple designs, and so on differ from period to period. Over the past 50 years the various types of design—particularly pottery types with their various forms, decorations, and textures—have been correlated with particular periods. Thus today, in spite of the lack of written clues, a given stratum can usually be dated on the basis of the type of pottery (usually pottery fragments) it contains.

The advantage of the trench method of excavation is that it allows the archaeologist to get an overview of the total history of the tell with relatively little outlay of time and money. Besides, this method leaves large areas of the tell untouched, so that future generations of archaeologists, with better techniques and equipment, can return to reexcavate the site to check and improve upon earlier conclusions.

A disadvantage of this method is that a given stratum may not be represented in the area where a trench is dug. Thus an entire period in the history of the tell is missed, which will result in an erroneous view of the history of a site.

Why Archaeology Is Important

Many of the archaeological discoveries made in recent years by those who have been digging in the ruins of biblical cities coincide exactly with the biblical narratives. Piece by piece, the Old Testament is being confirmed, supplemented, and illustrated. Even things that once seemed most like a myth are being shown to have been factual.

Does that not enhance the trustworthiness of the Bible as a whole, and make it easier for us to rely on all that the Bible says—even its wondrous promises, both for this life and for the life to come?

The most important single statement in the Bible is that Christ rose from the dead. This is the thing for which the whole Bible was written, apart from which it would mean nothing. It is what gives meaning to life, apart from which life would mean nothing. It is the basis of our hope of resurrection and eternal life.

It is comforting to know that the book that is built around this event is being proved to be a consistently historical book, making it all the more certain that this most important event of the ages is an actual fact.

Jewish Calendar

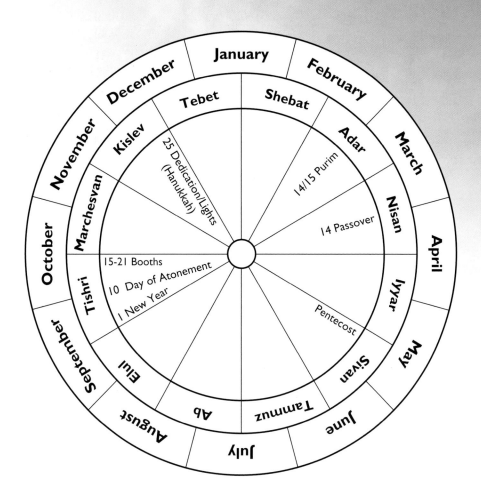

The religious year begins with Nisan.

The civil year begins with Tishri.

Ancient Roman road.

Distance Charts

I. Old Testament Cities

	Babylon	Beersheba	Bethel	Damascus	Dan	Haran	Hazor	Hebron	Jericho	Jerusalem	Joppa	Megiddo	Nineveh	Samaria	Shechem	Sidon	Susa	Thebes	Tyre	Ur
Babylon																				
Beersheba	930																			
Bethel	869	58																		
Damascus	724	206	145																	
Dan	764	166	105	45																
Haran	422	549	488	343	383															
Hazor	783	147	86	59	19	402														
Hebron	901	28	31	177	137	520	118													
Jericho	869	61	12	134	105	488	86	36												
Jerusalem	880	47	11	149	116	500	97	21	15											
Joppa	868	62	32	133	104	396	85	45	43	36										
Megiddo	824	116	50	98	59	443	41	80	54	61	53									
Nineveh	264	752	691	546	586	215	605	723	691	702	548	646								
Samaria	845	80	26	121	80	464	62	51	32	37	31	25	667							
Shechem	847	78	22	123	82	466	64	53	26	33	36	29	669	8						
Sidon	779	190	129	55	29	398	43	161	129	140	112	75	601	105	107					
Susa	218	1148	1087	942	982	660	1001	1119	1087	1098	1086	1042	453	1063	1065	997				
Thebes	1504	591	635	773	740	1123	721	629	639	624	633	680	1326	661	657	755	1722			
Tyre	792	176	115	68	28	411	29	147	115	126	89	53	614	77	80	25	1110	733		
Ur	170	1100	1039	894	934	612	953	1071	1039	1050	1038	994	434	1015	1017	949	145	1674	962	

Note: These distances are meant to give rough estimates. They do not take terrain obstacles into account, although they do generally follow ancient routes (e.g., around the Fertile Crescent rather than across the desert). Adapted from John Walton, *Chronological and Background Charts of the Old Testament* (Grand Rapids: Zondervan, 1978), 116. Used by permission.

2. New Testament Cities (The Gospels)

	Bethlehem	Bethsaida	Caesarea by the Sea	Caesarea Philippi	Cana	Capernaum	Chorazin	Damascus	Emmaus/Qolonia	Jericho	Jerusalem	Joppa	Magdala/Dalmanutha	Mount Hermon	Nazareth	Ptolemais	Samaria	Sychar/Mt. Gerizim	Tiberias
Bethsaida	97																		
Caesarea by the Sea	68	84																	
Caesarea Philippi	122	25	109																
Cana	89	21	40	47															
Capernaum	94	3	81	28	19														
Chorazin	96	5	83	26	21	2													
Damascus	191	66	151	52	97	69	71												
Emmaus/Qolonia	10	95	60	120	87	92	94	189											
Jericho	19	80	65	105	96	77	79	172	17										
Jerusalem	6	91	62	116	83	88	90	185	4	13									
Joppa	38	115	31	140	71	112	114	217	28	45	32								
Magdala/Dalmanutha	87	9	75	34	14	6	8	75	86	71	82	106							
Mount Hermon	128	31	115	6	53	34	32	126	27	111	122	146	40						
Nazareth	80	28	31	53	9	25	27	98	78	87	74	62	19	59					
Ptolemais	106	40	38	48	19	37	38	107	96	113	100	69	31	54	22				
Samaria	47	62	25	87	42	59	61	129	45	40	41	31	53	93	33	53			
Sychar/Mt. Gerizim	38	57	34	82	51	54	56	170	36	31	32	39	50	88	42	62	9		
Tiberias	85	12	72	37	18	9	11	79	83	68	79	103	3	43	19	31	50	47	
Tyre	134	43	66	31	47	40	38	83	124	141	128	97	34	36	50	28	81	90	31

3. New Testament Cities (Acts)

This chart is a triangular distance table. Each city listed reads across to give its distance from the cities named above it in the list.

From \ To	Alexandria (Egypt)	Antioch (Pisidian)	Antioch (Syrian)	Athens (Greece)	Caesarea (Palestine)	Colosse (Turkey)	Corinth (Greece)	Ephesus (Turkey)	Iconium (Turkey)	Jerusalem (Judea)	Patmos (Greece)	Perga (Turkey)	Philadelphia (Turkey)	Philippi (Greece)	Rome (Italy)	Salamis (Cyprus)	Tarsus (Turkey)	Thessalonica (Greece)
Antioch (Pisidian)	562																	
Antioch (Syrian)	500	429																
Athens (Greece)	485	627	1413															
Caesarea (Palestine)	315	547	270	745														
Colosse (Turkey)	560	125	555	331	545													
Corinth (Greece)	620	1040	1469	56	770	387												
Ephesus (Turkey)	485	235	665	220	670	111	275											
Iconium (Turkey)	595	111	318	1095	485	62	607	347										
Jerusalem (Judea)	377	761	332	807	65	600	832	521	548									
Patmos (Greece)	460	473	475	165	412	176	220	65	271	662								
Perga (Turkey)	400	162	307	385	160	176	521	138	273	447	310							
Philadelphia (Turkey)	635	200	630	808	75	429	486	304	311	682	203	235						
Philippi (Greece)	755	555	983	430	895	1241	578	559	262	512	286	590	355					
Rome (Italy)	1270	1412	1480	895	1500	1241	1130	1523	1315	1562	1250	990	1268	1130				
Salamis (Cyprus)	360	137	384	200	446	440	578	304	280	512	262	500	260	792	1440			
Tarsus (Turkey)	517	297	132	300	1281	533	186	362	1435	313	623	474	497	1460	120	150		
Thessalonica (Greece)	765	674	1103	310	915	1337	341	366	185	1435	195	623	474	1130	825	1070	730	
Troas (Turkey)	665	411	840	573	780	286	629	185	522	1172	446	211	143	1070	708	708	143	263

Italic type indicates basically a route of Paul, intimated in the book of Acts; on occasion, more direct routes are possible.
Normal type signifies travel by land; land routes have been chosen over sea routes in some instances where it is probable that Paul traveled by land.
An underline indicates combined travel by land and sea in an attempt to follow Pauline routes where possible.
Boldface type indicates travel mainly by sea.
Copyright © Carl Rasmussen

The House of Herod

1st Generation	2nd Generation	3rd Generation	4th Generation
	Herod Philip II* (Mother: Cleopatra) Tetrarch of Iturea and Traconitis (4 B.C.–A.D. 34) (Luke 3:1)		
	Archelaus* (Mother: Malthace) Governor of Judea, Idumea, and Samaria (4 B.C.–A.D. 6) When Joseph and Mary left Egypt, they avoided Judea and settled in Nazareth (Mt. 2:19–23)	**Herod of Chalcis**	
Herod the Great King of Judea, Galilee, Iturea, Traconitis (37–4 B.C.) Birth of Jesus (Mt. 2:1–19; Luke 1:5)	**Aristobulus** (Mother: Mariamne) (d. 10 B.C.) Not mentioned in the Bible	**Herod Agrippa I** King of Judea (A.D. 37–44) Killed James, put Peter into prison, was struck down by an angel (Acts 12:1–24)	Felix Governor of Judea **Drusilla** Married Felix, governor of Judea (A.D. 52–59) Tried Paul (Acts 24:24)
	Herod Antipas* (Mother: Malthace) Tetrarch of Galilee and Perea (4 B.C.– A.D. 39) (Luke 3:1) Second husband of Herodias. Put John the Baptist to death (Mt. 14:1–2; Mark 6:14–29). Pilate sent Jesus to him (Luke 23:7–12)		**Herod Agrippa II** King of Judea Paul made a legal defense before him (Acts 25:13–26:32) **Bernice** With her brother at the time of Paul's defense (Acts 25:13)
	Herod Philip I (Mother: Mariamne) Did not rule. First husband of Herodias (Mt. 14:3; Mark 6:17) (d. ca. A.D. 34)	**Herodias** Married her uncle, Herod Philip I, and then a second uncle, Herod Antipas (Mt. 14:3; Mark 6:17)	**Salome** Daughter of Herodias and Herod Philip I. Danced for the head of John the Baptist (Mt. 14:1–12; Mark 6:14–29)
	Antipater (Mother: Doris)		

*Tetrarch: ruler over a 4th part of a kingdom or province in the Roman Empire

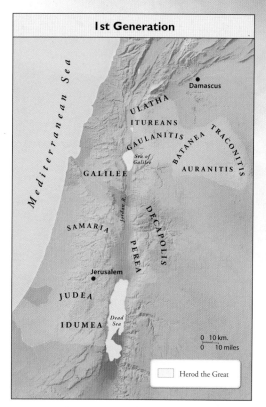

1st Generation

Mediterranean Sea

Damascus

ULATHA

ITUREANS

GAULANITIS

BATANEA

TRACONITIS

Sea of
Galilee

GALILEE

AURANITIS

SAMARIA

DECAPOLIS

PEREA

Jerusalem

JUDEA

IDUMEA

Dead
Sea

0   10 km.
0   10 miles

Herod the Great

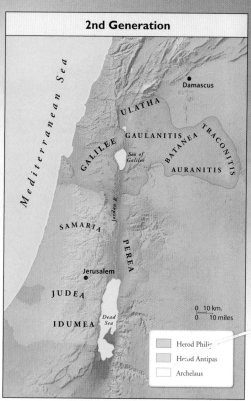

2nd Generation

Mediterranean Sea

Damascus

ULATHA

GALILEE

GAULANITIS

BATANEA

TRACONITIS

Sea of
Galilee

AURANITIS

SAMARIA

PEREA

Jerusalem

JUDEA

IDUMEA

Dead
Sea

0   10 km.
0   10 miles

Herod Philip

Herod Antipas

Archelaus

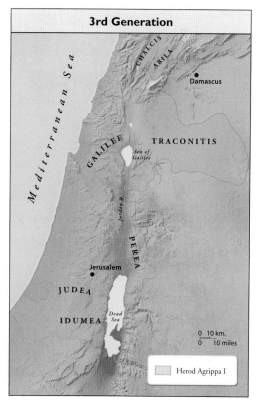

3rd Generation

Mediterranean Sea

CHALCIS

ABILA

Damascus

GALILEE

TRACONITIS

Sea of
Galilee

PEREA

Jerusalem

JUDEA

IDUMEA

Dead
Sea

0   10 km.
0   10 miles

Herod Agrippa I

4th Generation

Mediterranean Sea

ABILA

Damascus

Sea of
Galilee

TIBERIAS

BATANEA

TRACONITIS

AURANITIS

Controlled
by Roman
procurators

ABILA

Jerusalem

JUDEA

IDUMEA

Dead
Sea

0   10 km.
0   10 miles

Controlled by Roman procurators

Herod Agrippa II

1025

Spring in the Judean hills.

Henry H. Halley—
A Memoir

Henry H. Halley— A Memoir

Henry H. Halley, in a photograph taken in 1960, holds a copy of the original 16-page booklet published in 1924 and a copy of the 22nd edition, published in 1959, by which time there were just under a million copies in print.

Henry Hampton Halley lived from 1874 to 1965. I remember him as a tall, quiet man who always had a smile on his face and a twinkle in his eye. Our family called him Papa Daddy. He was my great-grandfather, and while I knew him for only a short time, the many stories shared by my parents and grandparents about his life and ministry have created a long-lasting memory. He was a loving and devoted husband, father, grandfather, and great-grandfather—but more importantly, he was a great man of God. His calling was simple—God put it on his heart to help people read, understand, and love God's Word.

Henry Halley was born on a Kentucky bluegrass farm and grew up in the environment of a Christian home. His father had been a Confederate soldier who was one of "Morgan's Men." The public school system in White Sulpher, Kentucky, was poor, so Henry's parents joined with other farmers in conducting a private school for their children. At age 16, the young Henry enrolled at Kentucky University in Lexington (now Transylvania College), getting his A.D. and B.D. degrees in five years. He taught at his alma mater for a year, followed by another year on the faculty of the Women's Missionary College in Hazel Green, Kentucky.

His first pastorate in the Disciples of Christ Church began in 1897 in Kalkaska, Michigan, a lumber camp region. He duly called on all the people, including the Canadian-born, lady principal of the high school. Papa Daddy would often tell the story with a smile: "It was my pastoral duty to call on the principal, Madge Gillis—but could I help it when my heart started thumping as we talked about schools and souls?" It wasn't long before duty calls became pleasure calls—and then, to the delight of the Kalkaskans, courtship, love, and a marriage that lasted 65 years!

The young clergyman now had what it took—a fine faith and a fine wife. The Kalamazoo (Mich.) Christian Church heard of the up-and-coming minister and called him. Upon arrival, the Halleys found a congregation worshiping in a hall. They led the people in building first a chapel, then an impressive sanctuary. For eight years Henry and Madge worked like beavers in their new parish. Their 1900–1908 pastorate ended when the doctor gave Henry an ultimatum.

"You'll have to get outdoors and do physical labor—or else," he said. Henry obeyed. He resigned his pulpit, but remained an active member of the congregation. This seemed to Henry to be the end of his pastoral career—but God had other plans for his life.

Henry started building houses—doing the rough labor while craftsmen he hired took on the skilled work—and selling them when finished. One year sped past and then another as Henry, an ambitious young contractor and Realtor, found it impossible to break away from his business. In 1912, a friend interested him in real estate speculation in the orange groves of California. Moving there for one year, he got the groves under way, then returned to Kalamazoo.

He made seven round trips to the Pacific Coast the next year to look after the orange trees. Each journey was a monotonous four-day ride. Henry, being rather shy, was not inclined to make acquaintances on the train, and time hung heavy. One day as he gazed out of the car window at the endless prairies, the idea struck him to improve the hours by memorizing Bible passages. He first tackled the Sermon on the Mount, next the Epistle of James. Although he was then 39, he found that by intensive application he could retain in his mind whole passages even though, as he said, "I had not only an untrained but also a very ordinary memory." He was soon to prove he could make it extraordinary by constant drills.

Although his work as a building contractor boomed, Henry was so fascinated by his Scripture memorizing experiment that he started devoting several hours a day to it — mostly in the evenings. One day his telephone rang.

"Come over and preach for us Sunday," a deacon from a church outside Kalamazoo asked him. He agreed to go. When it came time for the sermon, he stepped into the pulpit only to discover he had no notes and had forgotten his outline. The Lord directed him to deliver his message to the people literally in Bible language — reciting to them in a quiet but deeply moving manner, verbatim, the Sermon on the Mount and other Scripture selections. So great was the response that the church service eventually was to prove a turning point in Henry's career. Many calls came from other churches, and in each he recited whole passages from memory.

Henry moved his growing family to Chicago in 1914. By then, he and Madge were the parents of four children: two sons and two daughters. He entered the real estate business there, but it was at this time that the idea came to memorize the *entire* Bible in abridged form, covering the heart of every book in it. Up to this point he had been memorizing various selections, but the "big idea," which at first almost overwhelmed him, would not fade from his thoughts.

He tackled the job — between sales and after hours — in a double-barreled manner. One task was to select the passages to be committed to memory and arrange them in connected form; the other was to intensify the memorization process. At night he would pore over an American Standard (Revised) Version of the Bible, thumbing the pages, marking sections, and underscoring verses in his effort to condense it into the one-third he finally learned by heart. This volume, which was worn to tatters, is now a sacred family keepsake.

Henry found, in going to and returning from his office, in riding streetcars and in walking to make business calls, in odd moments between office duties and even at meals, that he had much time available for memory work. Sometimes in the middle of the night he would awaken to find his subconscious mind actively imprinting passages on his brain.

Thus, over a period of 10 years, the preacher-builder spent at least 10,000 hours in achieving probably one of the greatest feats of memorization of Scripture known to man. He could recite a total of 25 hours of nothing but Scripture, including narratives of every book from the longest to the shortest. Job, for example, took only 15 minutes for giving the whole theme of the story, while Genesis took a whole evening's lecture of some 45 minutes.

The Gospels he treated differently, dividing them up into eight readings — four on the life of Christ, compiled from a harmony of the Gospels, and four on the sayings of Jesus. In his reading of the life of Christ he gave predominate emphasis to the Resurrection, for, he said, "that is the most important part of the New Testament."

As Henry's fame spread, calls came not only for individual Scripture "sermons," but for a series running a week or more, from individual congregations to groups of interfaith churches assembled from different towns and cities. He found himself gradually getting away from the business world and into "business for the King."

From coast to coast, in 35 states, Henry delivered his Bible lectures. He always opened his recitals with a brief background sketch of the Bible or passages he was to present. Although there were many instances of conversions to Christ through his ministry, his main purpose was always to teach the Bible and encourage the reading of it.

Because of the religious interest of the day, the lectures were more popular in the earlier years than in the hectic days of the late 1920s and early '30s. People liked best the Crucifixion and Resurrection accounts, the Creation story from Genesis, the book of Job, Paul's missionary journeys, the story of Ruth, and the book of Revelation.

Henry was often asked if his memory ever failed him. He would tell the story of one embarrassing incident that occurred while he was reciting the list of the 20 kings of Israel. He got down to the second Jeroboam, but couldn't remember which king followed. So he automatically started with the names following the first Jeroboam, the son of Nebat. When he got down to the second Jeroboam, he was again stumped. So he apologized for his lapse of memory and took up the story . . . omitting the kings.

The other question people often asked was, "Did you always have such an amazing memory?" Henry responded, "As a boy I could stuff my mind easily with my school lessons, and hold the facts long enough to get through tests." He would grin as he continued, "Then it would all evaporate. As for memorizing permanently, that seemed an impossibility. Through college I had much the same experience. Intensive application is the key to victory. If an ordinary person like me can commit to memory one-third of the Bible after he's well along into middle age, why can't millions of others learn the golden passages of God's Word by heart? Of course they can—and they'll get the thrill of a lifetime in doing it!

"What you memorize of the Bible is a constant spur to memorize more," he added. "As you learn a passage word for word, new meanings constantly pour into your mind. You may have read a passage a hundred times, yet hidden truths come out crystal clear as memorization spotlights every sentence into importance."

In 1922, while lecturing in New Albany, Indiana, an incident occurred which was to open up a new phase of his life and later to carve for him a niche in literature's hall of fame.

Every night that week as he was lecturing, an ambitious woman stenographer in the front row noisily shuffled her paper, recording the brief resume of the background of the book with which he opened his lecture. This irritating distraction upset him for the entire lecture. She meant well, not knowing that her turning of the pages annoyed the speaker. Henry made no criticism, but the incident caused a momentous decision—as revealed by succeeding years.

"I'll get out a leaflet containing this information," he told his wife afterward. He printed 20,000 copies of a 16-page leaflet titled "Suggestions Concerning Bible Study." Free for the asking, they went quickly. Then Henry doubled the size, added a heavier paper cover, and gave away another edition of 10,000. This booklet listed the dates of all the books of the Bible and gave the main idea and a brief summary of each.

Each year saw an elaboration of the booklet, but it was not until the seventh edition of 144 pages that the name *Halley's Pocket Bible Handbook* arrived and stuck. The *Handbook* soon had a summary of church history, brief outlines, and interesting sidelight facts on the Bible books.

Late in the 1930s another significant addition was made. Henry became passionately interested in archaeology and voraciously read everything he could find on the topic. He wrote to places such as the British Museum, the Louvre, and the Oriental Institute of Chicago for information and pictures. Roughly 90 selected pictures of archaeological discoveries that illuminated Bible characters and times and a mine of facts that formed a convincing apologetic for the scriptural stories were added to the *Handbook*.

Soon after the second edition came out, Henry could no longer afford to give away the books, so great was the demand for and increasingly expensive the cost of the books. Not wishing to even appear commercial in his ministry, he hit upon the idea of lending books to interested persons. Then if they wished to keep them, they could remit the price. This system was followed for many years, his only distribution outlet being his lectures.

For 20 years, from 1921 to 1941, Henry continued his Bible Recital ministry, supported by freewill offerings. He spoke before an estimated 2 million people. In the meantime, the *Pocket Bible Handbook* had now become a volume of several hundred pages and the circulation between the 13th edition in 1939 and the 14th edition in 1941 doubled.

The coming of World War II brought another major change to Henry's career. Travel conditions became almost impossible, significantly impacting his recital ministry. He accepted it as the will of God and felt led to turn his energies full-time to the *Handbook*.

In 1941, Madge Halley, who in 1923 had resumed her career as a teacher in the Chicago public schools, retired and united efforts with her husband in further developing the *Handbook* and in compiling a new book called *Best Bible Verses*. Together they spent 10 to 15 hours daily handling worldwide correspondence, revising and enlarging the publications, and answering Bible queries.

Mr. and Mrs. Halley loved the busy, bustling city. They had their office in the heart of Chicago's famous "Loop," and their home in a lofty apartment just a few blocks away, adjoining State Street. By this time their children had been scattered — their sons both became doctors, one daughter a homemaker, and the other a recognized artist and business-woman. The number of grandchildren was increasing, as evidenced by home and office walls adorned with their pictures.

Apart from the *Handbook*, Henry had no real hobbies. That is, no hobbies unless you consider his pet theme of Sunday morning churchgoing a hobby. Perhaps an interest picked up from his many years on the road, he would visit a different congregation each Sunday morning to observe its worship service. From this study, he formulated definite ideas of what the Sunday morning service should include.

Henry became increasingly concerned with what he considered "a lack of leadership in the pulpit" in guiding and leading church members in reading the Bible. He felt that churches were growing cold and people were losing their love of the faith. The recipe for revival, in his opinion, was following the admonition: "The most important thing in this book is this simple suggestion: that each church have a congregational plan of Bible reading and that the pastor's sermon be from the part of the Bible read the past week." Henry believed that this suggestion, if followed, would produce a revitalized church and bring about a grand revival, provided the minister himself thoroughly believes that the Bible is God's Word.

Henry's second pet peeve about the average church service was the preaching. He was heard to say, "There is almost no Bible preaching in the average church—too much allegorizing and metaphorizing. People can sit for a lifetime even in the modern fundamental church and not know anything about the Bible. Preaching should be plain simple Bible teaching."

In the 1950s, the Halleys began work with foreign missionaries who translated the *Handbook* into other languages. The initial translations were in Japanese and Korean. In 1956, as many as 20,000 copies of the Japanese edition of the *Handbook* had been sold. That year word came from a prominent missionary: "*Halley's Bible Handbook* is the undisputed Christian best-seller in Japan; only the Bible stands before it. In fact, in the history of Christian literature in Japan, nothing comparable can be cited." The list of foreign-language editions printed over time includes Spanish, Chinese, French, Greek, Italian, Portuguese, Thai, Russian, Swahili, and many more.

The early editions of the *Pocket Bible Handbook* were printed by Rand McNally & Company in Indiana. In May 1960, Andrew McNally III, president of Rand McNally, presented Henry and Madge Halley with a specially bound millionth copy. At this point, it was in its 22nd edition, ran to 968 pages, and sold for $3.75. It had been selling more than 60,000 copies a year.

On June 17, 1960, Henry granted Zondervan Publishing House the rights to *Halley's Bible Handbook*. It became one of the most important books that Zondervan has ever published and for many years was one of the top-selling volumes on Zondervan's list. Today there are more than 5 million copies in print. The *Handbook* was last revised—its 24th edition—in 1964 just before Henry Halley's death in 1965 at the age of 91. Mr. and Mrs. Halley are laid to rest near their family roots in Lexington, Kentucky.

Henry Halley's daughter, Julia Halley Berry, and her husband, Henry S. Berry, became active in the development of the 24th edition of the *Handbook*. They also assumed management responsibilities for Halley's Bible Handbook, Inc., after Henry Halley's death. Mrs. Berry designed all of the maps included in the 24th edition. The maps on the endpapers of this new edition were among those she designed; they have been included as a tribute to her tireless efforts over many years to preserve the spirit and continuing impact of her father's life work.

In 1997, Mrs. Henry Berry, my grandmother, entrusted the ongoing management of the *Handbook* to my husband and me. We are greatly blessed to have the opportunity to lead the ongoing ministry of *Halley's Bible Handbook* into the new millennium. We pray that this 25th edition of *Halley's Bible Handbook* will continue the God-directed, global ministry that Henry H. Halley began with the heartfelt desire that every person who reads this *Handbook* will gain a greater understanding and love for God's Word.

— PATRICIA WICKER
January 10, 2000
Minneapolis, Minnesota

Index

Index

Italic type indicates photographs and illustrations. **Boldface** indicates maps and charts.

What the Bible is about, 33–40
Wilderness wandering, 145, 177, 217, 385
Wisdom literature, 286–87
Wise Men, the, 532–33
  star of, 532
World of the Bible today, **50**
World powers of biblical times, 47–48
  See also Assyria; Babylonia; Egypt; Greece; Persia; Rome
Writing
  ancient libraries, 68–70
  Bible and, 73–77
  development of, 70–73
  hieroglyphics, 66–67, *72*

in Egypt, 66–67
in Mesopotamia, 67–68
invention of alphabet, 72–73

Y

Year of Jubilee, 155

Z

Zealots, 484
Zechariah, Malachi, Haggai, 437
Zechariah, prophecies of, 446
Zerubbabel, 268, 274
Zionism, 953–54
Zwingli, 915